Handbook of Cost Management

Second Edition

This book is printed on acid-free paper. ♾

Published by John Wiley & Sons, Inc., Hoboken, New Jersey
Published simultaneously in Canada

For general information on our other products and services, or technical support, please contact our Customer Care Department within the United States at 800-762-2974, outside the United States at 317-572-3993 or fax 317-572-4002.

Wiley also publishes its books in a variety of electronic formats. Some content that appears in print may not be availab in electronic books.

Library of Congress Cataloging-in-Publication Data

Handbook of cost management / [edited by] Roman L. Weil, Michael W. Maher.--
2nd ed.
p. cm.
Rev. ed. of: Handbook of cost management. c1978.
Includes index.
ISBN-13 978-0-471-67814-4
ISBN-10 0-471-67814-7 (cloth)
1. Cost accounting--Handbooks, manuals, etc. 2. Managerial accounting--Handbooks, manuals, etc. I. Weil, Roman L. II. Maher, Michael, 1946- III. Handbook of cost management.
HF5686.C8H237 2005
657'.42--dc22

Printed in the United States of America

Handbook of Cost Management

Second Edition

Roman L. Weil
Michael W. Maher

WILEY
John Wiley & Sons, Inc.

Update Service

BECOME A SUBSCRIBER!

Did you purchase this product from a bookstore?

If you did, it's important for you to become a subscriber. John Wiley & Sons, Inc. may publish, o a periodic basis, supplements and new editions to reflect the latest changes in the subject matte that you ***need to know*** in order to stay competitive in this ever-changing industry. By contacting the Wiley office nearest you, you'll receive any current update at no additional charge. In additio you'll receive future updates and revised or related volumes on a 30-day examination review.

If you purchased this product directly from John Wiley & Sons, Inc., we have already recorded you subscription for this update service.

To become a subscriber, please call **1-800-225-5945** or send your name, company name (if applicable), address, and the title of the product to:

mailing address: **Supplement Department**
John Wiley & Sons, Inc.
One Wiley Drive
Somerset, NJ 08875

e-mail: **subscriber@wiley.com**
fax: **1-732-302-2300**
online: **www.wiley.com**

For customers outside the United States, please contact the Wiley office nearest you:

Professional & Reference Division
John Wiley & Sons Canada, Ltd.
22 Worcester Road
Rexdale, Ontario M9W 1L1
CANADA
(416) 675-3580
Phone: 1-800-567-4797
Fax: 1-800-565-6802
Email: canada@jwiley.com

John Wiley & Sons, Ltd.
Baffins Lane
Chichester
West Sussex, PO19 1UD
ENGLAND
Phone: (44) 1243 779777
Fax: (44) 1243 770638
Email: cs-books@wiley.co.uk

Jacaranda, Wiley Ltd.
PRT Division
P.O. Box 174
North Ryde, NSW 2113
AUSTRALIA
Phone: (02) 805-1100
Fax: (02) 805-1597
Email: headoffice@jacwiley.com.au

John Wiley & Sons (SEA) Pte., Ltd.
2 Clementi Loop #02-01
SINGAPORE 129809
Phone: 65 463 2400
Fax: 65 463 4605; 65 463 4604
Email: wiley@singnet.com.sg

CONTENTS

Preface xi

About the Editors xiii

Contributors xv

1 Glossary of Cost Management Concepts *(Roman L. Weil)* 1

This glossary contains hundreds of accounting and management-related terms, including a summary of financial statement ratios and a chart that explains the distinction between cost terms.

2 Economic Concepts of Cost in Managerial Accounting *(Gordon Shillinglaw* and *Roman L. Weil)* 157

This chapter defines basic economic terms and explains their application to and interface with management accounting.

3 Different Costs for Different Purposes *(Russell A. Taussig* and *Roman L. Weil)* 175

This chapter explains how the purpose of costs affects their definition and measurement. The chapter discusses cost classification, including costs for internal decision making and costs for responsibility accounting.

4 Accounting Magic *(Roman L. Weil)* 187

This chapter shows how alternative accounting treatments of identical events can lead to reported income figures that differ from each other.

5 Mathematical Concepts in Cost Accounting *(Joel S. Demski)* 197

This chapter discusses the role of mathematics in management, including probability as a model of uncertainty and decision theory as a model of choice behavior.

Because of the rapidly changing nature of information in this field, this product may be updated with annual supplements or with future editions. Please call 1-877-762-2974 or email us at *subscriber@wiley.com* to receive any current update at no additional charge. We will send on approval any future supplements or new editions when they become available. If you purchased this product directly from John Wiley & Sons, Inc., we have already recorded your subscription for this update service.

6 Activity-Based Costing and Management *(Michael W. Maher)* 217

This chapter explains the mechanics of activity-based costing and the value that this tool offers to management, including analysis of unused resources and analysis of activities that add value versus those that do not.

7 Target Costing for New Product Development *(Robin Cooper* and *Regine Slagmulder)* 243

This chapter shows how companies can use target costing in the design stage of a product. It considers market-driven costing, product-level costing, and component-level costing.

8 Kaizen Costing for Existing Products *(Robin Cooper* and *Regine Slagmulder)* 271

This chapter discusses the mechanics of kaizen costing and how companies can use this process for continuous improvement toward manufacturing efficiency and quality.

9 Interorganizational Costing *(Robin Cooper* and *Regine Slagmulder)* 289

This chapter explains how companies can use interorganizational cost management to manage costs through the cooperative actions of firms in a supplier network.

10 Costs and Benefits of Quality Improvement *(Christopher D. Ittner* and *David F. Larcker)* 313

This chapter discusses some methods to assess the quality improvement projects that offer the highest returns and shows how firms can quantify the financial payback from these investments.

11 Logistics and Marketing Costs *(James M. Reeve)* 329

This chapter discusses the logistics of supply chain activities, which include marketing and selling activities. It discusses expense planning and control through activity-based costing and how to calculate the total cost of delivering a product.

12 Estimating Cost Behavior *(Michael W. Maher* and *M. Laurentius Marais)* 351

This chapter explains the distinction among costs, expenses, and expenditures. It also examines the function and methods of cost estimation, from simple costs with a single cost driver to costs with several cost drivers.

13 Spoilage, Waste, and Scrap, Including Green Accounting *(William N. Lanen)* 367

This chapter explains the mechanics of cost accounting for spoilage, waste, and scrap. It also considers the implications for management in controlling the generation, handling, and disposal of such material.

14 Job, Process, and Operations Costing *(Michael W. Maher)* 389

This chapter provides an overview of the basic cost flow model. It also discusses four production systems—just-in-time, job, process, and operation—and their implications for cost measurement and management.

15 Standard Costing Systems *(James A. Largay III)* 425

This chapter shows the mechanics of variance analysis for costs, including raw material, variable and fixed overhead, and direct labor expenses. It then discusses different methods to investigate such variances.

16 Allocations of Cost and Revenue *(Roman L. Weil)* 465

This chapter examines more advanced topics related to allocation: that of joint products, byproducts, and common—other than joint—products. It also discusses allocation of revenue. The chapter appendix explains the mechanics of step-down and reciprocal allocation methods.

17 Cost-Volume-Profit Analyses *(Nicholas Dopuch* and *Michael W. Maher)* 483

This chapter discusses breakeven analysis that considers changes in prices, costs, and output volume. It also considers the implications for management decisions, such as whether to add or drop a product, and whether to make or buy a unit.

18 Forecasting Pro Forma Financial Statements *(James M. Wahlen)* 503

This chapter shows the mechanics and uses of pro forma financial statements.

19 Operating Budgets and Budgeting—Benefits and Costs *(Michael D. Shields)* 539

This chapter discusses management issues related to budgeting: participation, motivation, and evaluation. It considers several budgeting methods and management implications of each.

20 Theory of Constraints *(Eric Noreen)* 573

This chapter explains how firms can identify, exploit, and focus on a constraint, then relax the constraint. It discusses the implications for efficiency, process reengineering, and pricing.

21 Capital Budgeting: Concepts and Methods *(Roman L. Weil)* 587

This chapter discusses and evaluates various methods used to compare investment opportunities for companies. It also considers issues related to leasing.

22 Capital Budgeting: Implementation *(Roman L. Weil)* 611

This chapter offers guidance for investment management, which includes relating investment decisions to strategic plans, evaluating investments by financial and nonfinancial criteria, and assessing risk of investments.

23 Compound Interest: Concepts and Applications *(Roman L. Weil)* 627

This chapter explains simple and compound interest and how to perform future value calculations. It also discusses annuities and perpetuities and shows calculations for these financial instruments under different scenarios.

24 Performance Evaluation in Decentralized Organizations *(Michael W. Maher)* 645

This chapter discusses why firms should adopt a decentralized structure, the organizational options for a decentralized structure, and performance measurement in such organizations.

25 The Balanced Scorecard and Nonfinancial Performance Measures *(Michael W. Maher)* 657

This chapter considers the value of nonfinancial performance measures, different perspectives related to the balanced scorecard, and how firms can measure and improve performance related to nonfinancial goals.

26 Economic Value Added (EVA®) *(James J. Wallace)* 669

This chapter discusses EVA®, a shareholder value and management concept derived from residual income. It also discusses evidence of EVA®'s success and problems, as well as implementation issues.

27 Transfer Pricing *(Michael W. Maher)* 683

This chapter explains how transfer pricing affects performance measurements. It also discusses transfer pricing calculations and issues under four scenarios and shows how the buying and selling divisions can negotiate a price or decide to transact with entities outside the firm.

28 A Managerial Accounting Guide for Nonprofit Managers *(Leslie G. Eldenburg* and *Naomi Soderstrom)* 697

This chapter discusses cost accounting practices in nonprofit organizations, including hospital and government entities. It also discusses issues related to environmental accounting reports.

29 Introduction to Costs in Litigation *(Elizabeth A. Evans)* 721

This chapter explains concepts of costs that litigation questions frequently employ. It shows how cost accounting issues apply to questions of both liability and damages.

30 The Historical Development of Management Accounting *(Richard Vangermeersch* and *Henry R. Schwarzbach)* 731

This chapter recounts the history and progress of the accounting profession from the first book of accounting (printed in the 1200s) to current writings.

31 Corporate Scandals: The Accounting Underpinnings *(Kathleen Fitzgerald* and *Roman L. Weil)* 759

This chapter surveys the current financial reporting environment, discusses management incentives to report fraudulent earnings, and explains specific methods used to manipulate financial reports.

Appendix: Compound Interest, Present Value, and Annuity Tables 809

Index 819

PREFACE

As the structure and size of companies have changed, so, too, have the practice of and implications for cost management. Global competition forces firms to study the cost management methods of others. Companies have adopted organizational structures that can move cash flow and resources across divisions, partnerships, and oceans. Moreover, as technology changes the type and amount of data, managers have more flexibility and capability to control resource use, measure performance, and make timely decisions. These changes, and others, prompted us to revise the first edition of *Handbook of Cost Accounting*, which included many timeless concepts, but needed an update to reflect the last 30 years of changes in the business world.

We target this book (renamed to *Handbook of Cost Management*) to a readership of consultants, financial managers who want an update on cost management, and nonfinancial managers who want to learn about the management implications of cost measurement and control. We hope that readers will use this as a reference to answer questions, explain concepts, and give guidance.

We cannot allow the readers to progress another paragraph into this book without acknowledging Debbie Asakawa, who made it all possible. She single-handedly brought this book to fruition when the Herculean task of producing this book lay before us and we had already committed our time to other endeavors. She chased down the missing exhibits, the errant passive verbs, and the home addresses of retired professors. She kept us all on task with unfailing good humor from the deck of her home through the summer heat as well as the dark and cold of night. We could *never* thank you enough, Debbie, so we will just stop here. We thank Judy Howarth, Rose T. Sullivan and John DeRemigis, our liaisons at John Wiley & Sons. Finally, Sidney Davidson. What can we say? The first edition of this book, 30 years ago, originated with him. He has taught us and guided us for more than three decades. Thank you.

Roman L. Weil
Michael W. Maher
March 2005

ABOUT THE EDITORS

ROMAN L. WEIL, PhD, CMA, CPA, is V. Duane Rath Professor of Accounting at the Graduate School of Business of the University of Chicago. He is co-director of the Chicago/Wharton/Stanford Law School Directors' Consortium.

He received his BA in Economics and Mathematics from Yale University in 1962. He received his MS in Industrial Administration in 1965 and PhD in Economics in 1966, both from Carnegie-Mellon University. He joined the faculty at the University of Chicago in 1965, where he has held positions in Mathematical Economics, Management and Information Sciences, Accounting, and in the Law School. He directs the University's Directors' College, which trains corporate board members to do their jobs better; his own specialty in that training focuses on financial literacy. He co-founded The Directors' Consortium, a joint venture of Chicago, Stanford Law School, and The Wharton School.

He has been a CPA in Illinois since 1973 and a CMA since 1974. He has served on the faculties of the Georgia Institute of Technology, New York University Law School, and Stanford University in its Graduate School of Business, Economics Department, and Law School. At Stanford, he has, since its inception, organized the sessions at Directors' College on Audit Committee duties. He has served on the Board of Academic Advisors of the U.S. Business School in Prague and has taught there. He has served on the accrediting committee of the American Association of Collegiate Schools of Business. He has designed and implemented continuing education programs for partners at the accounting firms of Andersen and PriceWaterhouseCoopers, as well as for employees at Goldman Sachs, Montgomery Ward, Merck, and William Blair, and for business executives in Great Britain and Singapore.

He has served as editor or associate editor of *The Accounting Review, Communications of the Association for Computing Machinery, Management Science, Journal of Accounting and Economics,* and the *Financial Analysts Journal.*

He has co-edited four professional reference books for McGraw-Hill, Simon Schuster, Prentice-Hall, and John Wiley & Sons. He has co-authored more than a dozen textbooks for Holt, Rinehart, and Winston, The Dryden Press, Harcourt, Brace & Jovanovich, and Thomson Learning. He is the senior editor of, and contributor to, the *Litigation Services Handbook,* now in its third edition. His articles have appeared in *Barron's* and *The Wall Street Journal.* He has published more than 80 articles in academic and professional journals. He has served as the principal investigator on various research projects of the National Science Foundation.

He served on the Securities and Exchange Commission Advisory Committee on Replacement Cost Accounting. At the Financial Accounting Standards Board, he has served on two task forces—one on consolidations and the other on interest methods—and on the Financial Accounting Standards Advisory Council.

He is a member of the American Accounting Association, the American Economics Association, the American Institute of Certified Public Accountants, the American Law and Economics Association, the Illinois Society of Certified Public Accountants, and the Institute of Management Sciences.

He has consulted to governmental agencies, including the U.S. Treasury Department and the Securities and Exchange Commission. He has consulted for a variety of private clients.

He serves on the board of directors of mutual funds affiliated with New York Life Insurance Company and chairs the Audit Committee. He serves on the Independent Directors Council of the Investment Company Institute, an advisory group for independent directors of mutual funds.

MICHAEL W. MAHER, PhD, is Professor of Management and Accounting at the Graduate School of Management, University of California, Davis, where he has taught since 1987. Prior to that, he taught at the University of Michigan for nine years and the University of Chicago for three years. He was interim dean at the University of California, Davis, from 1988 to 1989 and associate dean from 1996 to 1999. Prior to beginning his teaching career, Maher received a BBA (magna cum laude) from Gonzaga University in 1969, worked for Arthur Andersen & Co. for one year, then returned to school at the University of Washington, where he received his MBA in 1972 and his PhD in 1975.

Maher has co-authored or co-edited 11 books and more than 50 other academic and professional publications. He won the AAA Competitive Manuscript Award and the AICPA/AAA Notable Contribution to the Literature Award for his research on the effects of anti-bribery regulation on internal controls in U.S. corporations. He also won a national award for research in taxation, and five awards for teaching and service from students of the Graduate School of Management at UC Davis. His current research programs are (1) corporate accountability and (2) cost-effectiveness. He teaches cost management, incentives and controls, and business ethics.

Maher has two children, Krista and Andrea.

CONTRIBUTORS

ROBIN COOPER, DBA *Goizueta Business School, Emory University* (co-author Chapters 7, 8, and 9)

JOEL S. DEMSKI, PhD *Fisher School of Accounting, University of Florida* (Chapter 5)

NICHOLAS DOPUCH, PhD, CPA *Olin School of Business, Washington University* (co-author Chapter 17)

LESLIE G. ELDENBURG, PhD *Eller School of Management, University of Arizona* (co-author Chapter 28)

ELIZABETH A. EVANS, MBA, JD, CPA, CMA, CFA *Analysis Group* (Chapter 29)

KATHLEEN FITZGERALD, MBA, CPA *University of Chicago* (co-author Chapter 31)

CHRISTOPHER D. ITTNER, DBA *Wharton School of Business, University of Pennsylvania* (co-author Chapter 10)

WILLIAM N. LANEN, PhD *Stephen M. Ross School of Business, University of Michigan* (Chapter 13)

DAVID F. LARCKER, PhD *Wharton School of Business, University of Pennsylvania* (co-author Chapter 10)

JAMES A. LARGAY III, PhD, CPA *College of Business and Economics, Lehigh University* (Chapter 15)

MICHAEL W. MAHER, PhD *Graduate School of Management, University of California, Davis* (author Chapters 6, 14, 24, 25, 27; co-author Chapters 12 and 17)

M. LAURENTIUS MARAIS, MS, PhD *William E. Wecker Associates, Inc* (co-author Chapter 12)

ERIC W. NOREEN, PhD, CMA, CPA, *Professor Emeritus, University of Washington* (Chapter 20)

JAMES M. REEVE, PhD, CPA *College of Business Administration, University of Tennessee, Knoxville* (Chapter 11)

HENRY R. SCHWARZBACH, PhD, CPA *College of Business Administration, University of Rhode Island* (co-author Chapter 30)

MICHAEL D. SHIELDS, PhD *Eli Broad Graduate School of Management, Michigan State University* (Chapter 19)

GORDON SHILLINGLAW, PhD *Professor Emeritus, Graduate School of Business, Columbia University* (co-author Chapter 2)

REGINE SLAGMULDER, PhD *INSEAD* (co-author Chapters 7, 8, and 9)

NAOMI SODERSTROM, PhD *School of Business Administration, University of Colorado, Boulder* (co-author Chapter 28)

RUSSELL A. TAUSSIG, PhD *Professor Emeritus, College of Business Administration, University of Hawaii* (co-author Chapter 3)

RICHARD VANGERMEERSCH, PhD, CPA, CMA *Professor Emeritus, College of Business Administration, University of Rhode Island* (co-author Chapter 30)

JAMES M. WAHLEN, PhD *Kelley School of Business, Indiana University* (Chapter 18)

JAMES J. WALLACE, PhD *Claremont Graduate University* (Chapter 26)

ROMAN L. WEIL, PhD, CPA, CMA *Graduate School of Business, University of Chicago* (author Chapters 1, 4, 16, 21, 22, 23; co-author Chapters 2, 3, 31)

CHAPTER 1

GLOSSARY OF COST MANAGEMENT CONCEPTS*

ROMAN L. WEIL, PHD, CPA, CMA, EDITOR
University of Chicago

The definitions of many words and phrases in the glossary use other glossary terms. In a given definition, we *italicize* terms that themselves (or variants thereof) appear elsewhere under their own listings. The cross-references generally take one of two forms:

1. absorption costing. See *full absorption costing.*

2. ABC. *Activity-based costing.*

Form (1) refers you to another term for discussion of this bold-faced term. Form (2) tells you that this bold-faced term is synonymous with the *italicized* term, which you can consult for discussion if necessary.

A

AAA. *American Accounting Association.*

Abacus. A scholarly journal containing articles on theoretical aspects of accounting, published by Basil Blackwell for the Accounting Foundation of the University of Sydney.

abatement. A complete or partial cancellation of a levy imposed by a government unit.

ABC. *Activity-based costing.*

abnormal spoilage. Actual spoilage exceeding that expected when operations are normally efficient. Usual practice treats this cost as an *expense* of the period rather than as a *product cost.* Contrast with *normal spoilage.*

aboriginal cost. In public utility accounting, the *acquisition cost* of an *asset* incurred by the first *entity* devoting that asset to public use; the cost basis for most public utility regulation. If regulators used a different cost basis, then public utilities could exchange assets among themselves at ever-increasing prices in order to raise the rate base and, then, prices based on them.

---

* I have developed this glossary over the last 30 years with the help of named co-authors Sidney Davidson, Michael Maher, Patricia O'Brien, James Schindler, and Clyde Stickney. In addition, Katherine Schipper and Steven Zeff have provided much helpful input. My thanks to all of you. RLW

absorbed overhead. *Overhead costs* allocated to individual products at some *overhead rate;* also called *applied overhead.*

absorption costing. See *full absorption costing.*

Abstracts of the EITF. See *Emerging Issues Task Force.*

accelerated cost recovery System (ACRS). A form of accelerated depreciation that Congress enacted in 1981 and amended in 1986, so that now most writers refer to it as *MACRS*, or *Modified Accelerated Cost Recovery System.* The system provides percentages of the asset's cost that a firm depreciates each year for tax purposes. The percentages derive, roughly, from 150-percent *declining-balance depreciation* methods. ACRS ignores salvage value. We do not generally use these amounts for *financial accounting.*

accelerated depreciation. In calculating *depreciation* charges, any method in which the charges become progressively smaller each period. Examples are *double declining-balance depreciation* and *sum-of-the-years'-digits depreciation* methods.

acceptance. A written promise to pay; equivalent to a *promissory note.*

account. A device for representing the amount (*balance*) for any line (or a part of a line) in the *balance sheet* or *income statement.* Because income statement accounts explain the changes in the balance sheet account Retained Earnings, the definition does not require the last three words of the preceding sentence. An account is any device for accumulating additions and subtractions relating to a single *asset*, *liability,* or *owners' equity* item, including *revenues* and *expenses.*

account analysis method. A method of separating *fixed costs* from *variable costs* based on the analyst's judgment of whether the cost is fixed or variable. Based on their names alone, the analyst might classify *direct labor (materials) costs* as variable and *depreciation* on a factory building as fixed. In our experience, this method results in too many fixed costs and not enough variable costs—that is, analysts have insufficient information to judge management's ability to reduce costs that appear to be fixed.

account form. The form of *balance sheet* in which *assets* appear on the left and *equities* appear on the right. Contrast with *report form.* See *T-account.*

accountability center. *Responsibility center.*

accountancy. The British word for *accounting.* In the United States, it means the theory and practice of accounting.

accountant's comments. Canada: a written communication issued by a public accountant at the conclusion of a review engagement. It consists of a description of the work performed and a statement that, under the terms of the engagement, the accountant has not performed an audit and consequently expresses no opinion. (Compare *auditor's report; denial of opinion.*)

accountant's opinion. *Auditor's report.*

accountant's report. *Auditor's report.*

accounting. A system conveying information about a specific *entity.* The information is in financial terms and will appear in accounting statements only if the accountant can measure it with reasonable precision. The *AICPA* defines accounting as a service activity whose "function is to provide quantitative information, primarily financial in nature, about economic entities that is intended to be useful in making economic decisions."

accounting adjustments. *Prior-period adjustments*, changes in accounting principles accounted for on a cumulative basis, and corrections of errors. See *accounting changes.* The *FASB* indicates that it will tend to call these items "accounting adjustments," not "accounting changes," when it requires the reporting of *comprehensive income*.

Accounting and Tax Index. A publication that indexes, in detail, the accounting literature of the period. Published by UMI, a subsidiary of Bell & Howell.

accounting changes. As defined by *APB Opinion No. 20*, a change in (1) an *accounting principle* (such as a switch from *FIFO* to *LIFO* or from *sum-of-the-years'-digits depreciation* to *straight-line depreciation*), (2) an accounting estimate (such as estimated useful lives or salvage value of depreciable assets and estimates of *warranty* costs or *uncollectible accounts*), or (3) the reporting *entity*. The firm should disclose changes of type (1). It should include in reported earnings for the period of change the cumulative effect of the change on *retained earnings* at the start of the period during which it made the change. The firm should treat changes of type (2) as affecting only the period of change and, if necessary, future periods. The firm should disclose reasons for changes of type (3) in statements reporting on operations of the period of the change, and it should show the effect of the change on all other periods, for comparative purposes. In some cases (such as a change from *LIFO* to other inventory *flow assumptions* or a change in the method of accounting for long-term construction contracts), *GAAP* treat changes of type (1) like changes of type (3). That is, for these changes the firm should restate all statements shown for prior periods to show the effect of adopting the change for those periods as well. See *all-inclusive (income) concept* and *accounting errors*.

accounting conventions. Methods or procedures used in accounting. Writers tend to use this term when the method or procedure has not yet received official authoritative sanction by a pronouncement of a group such as the *APB, EITF, FASB*, or *SEC*. Contrast with *accounting principles*.

accounting cycle. The sequence of accounting procedures starting with *journal entries* for various transactions and events and ending with the *financial statements* or, perhaps, the *post-closing trial balance*.

accounting deficiency. Canada: a failure to adhere to generally accepted *accounting principles* or to disclose essential information in *financial statements*.

accounting entity. See *entity*.

accounting equation. *Assets = Equities; Assets = Liabilities + Owners' equity.*

accounting errors. Arithmetic errors and misapplications of *accounting principles* in previously published financial statements. The firm corrects these during the current period with direct *debits* or *credits* to *retained earnings*. In this regard, the firm treats them like *prior-period adjustments*, but technically *APB Opinion No. 9* does not classify them as prior-period adjustments. See *accounting changes*, and contrast with changes in accounting estimates as described there.

accounting event. Any occurrence that is recorded in the accounting records.

Accounting Horizons. A quarterly journal of the *American Accounting Association*.

accounting methods. *Accounting principles;* procedures for carrying out accounting principles.

accounting period. The time period between consecutive *balance sheets;* the time period for which the firm prepares *financial statements* that measure *flows*, such as the *income statement* and the *statement of cash flows*. See *interim statements*.

accounting policies. *Accounting principles* adopted by a specific *entity*.

accounting principles. The methods or procedures used in accounting for events reported in the *financial statements*. We tend to use this term when the method or procedure has received official authoritative sanction from a pronouncement of a group such as the *APB, EITF, FASB,* or *SEC.* Contrast with *accounting conventions* and *conceptual framework.*

Accounting Principles Board. See *APB.*

accounting procedures. See *accounting principles.* However, this term usually refers to the methods for implementing accounting principles.

accounting rate of return. Income for a period divided by average investment during the period; based on income, rather than discounted cash flows, and hence a poor decision-making aid or tool. See *ratio.*

Accounting Research Bulletin (ARB). The name of the official pronouncements of the former *Committee on Accounting Procedure (CAP)* of the *AICPA.* The committee issued 51 bulletins between 1939 and 1959. *ARB No. 43* restated and codified the parts of the first 42 bulletins not dealing solely with definitions.

Accounting Research Study (ARS). One of a series of studies published by the Director of Accounting Research of the *AICPA* and "designed to provide professional accountants and others interested in the development of accounting with a discussion and documentation of accounting problems." The AICPA published 15 such studies in the period 1961–1973.

Accounting Review. A journal of the *American Accounting Association.*

Accounting Series Release (ASR). See *SEC.*

accounting standards. *Accounting principles.*

Accounting Standards Executive Committee (AcSEC). The senior technical committee of the *AICPA* authorized to speak for the AICPA in the areas of *financial accounting* and reporting as well as *cost accounting.*

accounting system. The procedures for collecting and summarizing financial data in a firm.

Accounting Terminology Bulletin (ATB). One of four releases of the Committee on Terminology of the *AICPA* issued in the period 1953–57.

Accounting Trends and Techniques. An annual *AICPA* publication that surveys the reporting practices of 600 large corporations. It presents tabulations of specific practices, terminology, and disclosures along with illustrations taken from individual annual reports.

accounts payable. A *liability* representing an amount owed to a *creditor;* usually arising from the purchase of *merchandise* or materials and supplies, not necessarily due or past due; normally, a *current liability.*

accounts receivable. Claims against a *debtor;* usually arising from sales or services rendered, not necessarily due or past due; normally, a *current asset.*

accounts receivable turnover. Net sales on account divided by average accounts receivable. See *ratio.*

accretion. Occurs when a *book value* grows over time, such as a *bond* originally issued at a *discount;* the correct technical term is "accretion," not "amortization." This term also refers to an increase in economic worth through physical change caused by natural growth, usually said of a natural resource such as timber. Contrast with *appreciation.* See *amortization.*

accrual. Recognition of an *expense* (or *revenue*) and the related *liability* (or *asset*) resulting from an *accounting event,* frequently from the passage of time but not signaled by an explicit cash transaction; for example, the recognition of interest expense or revenue (or wages, salaries, or rent) at the end of a period even though the firm makes no explicit cash transaction at that time. Cash flow follows accounting recognition; contrast with *deferral.*

accrual basis of accounting. The method of recognizing *revenues* as a firm sells *goods* (or delivers them) and as it renders *services*, independent of the time when it receives cash. This system recognizes *expenses* in the period when it recognizes the related revenue, independent of the time when it pays cash. *SFAC No. 1* says,

> Accrual accounting attempts to record the financial effects on an enterprise of transactions and other events and circumstances that have cash consequences for the enterprise in the periods in which those transactions, events, and circumstances occur rather than only in the periods in which cash is received or paid by the enterprise.

Contrast with the *cash basis of accounting*. See *accrual* and *deferral*. We could more correctly call this "accrual/deferral" accounting.

accrue. See *accrued,* and contrast with *incur*.

accrued. Said of a *revenue (expense)* that the firm has earned (recognized) even though the related *receivable (payable)* has a future due date. We prefer not to use this adjective as part of an account title. Thus, we prefer to use Interest Receivable (Payable) as the account title rather than Accrued Interest Receivable (Payable). See *matching convention* and *accrual*. Contrast with *incur*.

accrued depreciation. An incorrect term for *accumulated depreciation*. Acquiring an asset with cash, capitalizing it, and then amortizing its cost over periods of use is a process of *deferral* and allocation, not of *accrual*.

accrued payable. A *payable* usually resulting from the passage of time. For example, *salaries* and *interest* accrue as time passes. See *accrued*.

accrued receivable. A *receivable* usually resulting from the passage of time. See *accrued*.

accumulated benefit obligation. See *projected benefit obligation* for definition and contrast.

accumulated depreciation. A preferred title for the asset *contra account* that shows the sum of *depreciation* charges on an asset since the time the firm acquired it. Other account titles are *allowance* for *depreciation* (acceptable term) and *reserve* for *depreciation* (unacceptable term).

accumulated other comprehensive income. *Balance sheet* amount in *owners' equity* showing the total of all *other comprehensive income* amounts from all prior periods.

accurate presentation. The qualitative accounting objective suggesting that information reported in financial statements should correspond as precisely as possible with the economic effects underlying transactions and events. See *fair presentation* and *full disclosure*.

acid test ratio. *Quick ratio*.

acquisition cost. Of an *asset*, the net *invoice* price plus all *expenditures* to place and ready the asset for its intended use. The other expenditures might include legal fees, transportation charges, and installation costs.

ACRS. *Accelerated Cost Recovery System.*

AcSEC. *Accounting Standards Executive Committee* of the *AICPA*.

activity accounting. *Responsibility accounting.*

activity-based costing (ABC). Method of assigning *indirect costs*, including nonmanufacturing *overhead costs,* to products and services. ABC assumes that almost all overhead costs associate with activities within the firm and vary with respect to the *drivers* of those activities. Some practitioners suggest that ABC attempts to find the drivers for all indirect costs; these people note that in the long run, all costs are *variable*, so *fixed* indirect costs do not occur. This method first assigns costs to activities and then to products based on the products' usage of the activities.

activity-based depreciation. *Production method (depreciation).*

activity-based management (ABM). Analysis and management of activities required to make a product or to produce a service. ABM focuses attention to enhance activities that add value to the customer and to reduce activities that do not. Its goal is to satisfy customer needs while making smaller demands on costly resources. Some refer to this as "activity management."

activity basis. *Costs* are *variable* or *fixed* (*incremental* or *unavoidable*) with respect to some activity, such as production of units (or the undertaking of some new project). Usage calls this activity the "activity basis."

activity center. Unit of the organization that performs a set of tasks.

activity variance. *Sales volume variance.*

actual cost (basis). *Acquisition* or *historical cost.* Also contrast with *standard cost.*

actual costing (system). Method of allocating costs to products using actual *direct materials*, actual *direct labor*, and actual *factory overhead.* Contrast with *normal costing* and *standard costing.*

actuarial. An adjective describing computations or analyses that involve both *compound interest* and probabilities, such as the computation of the *present value* of a life-contingent *annuity.* Some writers use the word even for computations involving only one of the two.

actuarial accrued liability. A 1981 report of the Joint Committee on Pension Terminology (of various actuarial societies) agreed to use this term rather than *prior service cost.*

ad valorem. A method of levying a tax or duty on goods by using their estimated value as the tax base.

additional paid-in capital. An alternative acceptable title for the *capital contributed in excess of par (or stated) value account.*

additional processing cost. *Costs* incurred in processing *joint products* after the *split-off point.*

adequate disclosure. An auditing standard that, to achieve *fair presentation* of *financial statements,* requires *disclosure* of *material* items. This *auditing standard* does not, however, require publicizing all information detrimental to a company. For example, the company may face a lawsuit, and disclosure might require a *debit* to a *loss* account and a *credit* to an *estimated liability.* But the court might view the making of this entry as an admission of liability, which could adversely affect the outcome of the suit. The firm should debit expense or loss for the expected loss, as required by *SFAS No. 5*, but need not use such accurate account titles that the court can spot an admission of liability.

adjunct account. An *account* that accumulates additions to another account. For example, Premium on Bonds Payable is adjunct to the liability Bonds Payable; the effective liability is the sum of the two account balances at a given date. Contrast with *contra account.*

adjusted acquisition (historical) cost. Sometimes said of the *book value* of a *plant asset,* that is, *acquisition cost* less *accumulated depreciation.* Also, cost adjusted to a *constant-dollar* amount to reflect *general price-level changes.*

adjusted bank balance of cash. The *balance* shown on the statement from the bank plus or minus amounts, such as for unrecorded deposits or outstanding checks, to reconcile the bank's balance with the correct cash balance. See *adjusted book balance of cash.*

adjusted basis. The *basis* used to compute gain or loss on the disposition of an *asset* for tax purposes. See also *book value.*

adjusted book balance of cash. The *balance* shown in the firm's account for cash in bank plus or minus amounts, such as for *notes* collected by the bank or bank service charges, to reconcile the account balance with the correct cash balance. See *adjusted bank balance of cash.*

adjusted trial balance. *Trial balance* taken after *adjusting entries* but before *closing entries.* Contrast with *pre-* and *post-closing trial balances.* See *unadjusted trial balance* and *post-closing trial balance.* See also *work sheet.*

adjusting entry. An entry made at the end of an *accounting period* to record a *transaction* or other *accounting event* that the firm has not yet recorded or has improperly recorded during the accounting period; an entry to update the accounts. See *work sheet.*

adjustment. An *account* change produced by an *adjusting entry.* Sometimes accountants use the term to refer to the process of restating *financial statement* amounts to *constant dollars.*

administrative costs (expenses). *Costs (expenses)* incurred for the firm as a whole, in contrast with specific functions such as manufacturing or selling; includes items such as salaries of top executives, general office rent, legal fees, and auditing fees.

admission of partner. Occurs when a new partner joins a *partnership.* Legally, the old partnership dissolves, and a new one comes into being. In practice, however, the firm may keep the old accounting records in use, and the accounting entries reflect the manner in which the new partner joined the firm. If the new partner merely purchases the interest of another partner, the accounting changes the name for one capital account. If the new partner contributes *assets* and *liabilities* to the partnership, then the firm must recognize them. See *bonus method.*

ADR. See *asset depreciation range.*

advances from (by) customers. A preferred title for the *liability* account representing *receipts* of *cash* in advance of delivering the *goods* or rendering the *service.* After the firm delivers the goods or services, it will recognize *revenue.* Some refer to this as "deferred revenue" or "deferred income," terms likely to confuse the unwary because the item is not yet *revenue* or *income.*

advances to affiliates. *Loans* by a parent company to a *subsidiary;* frequently combined with "investment in subsidiary" as "investments and advances to subsidiary" and shown as a *noncurrent asset* on the parent's *balance sheet.* The consolidation process eliminates these advances in *consolidated financial statements.*

advances to suppliers. A preferred term for the *asset* account representing *disbursements* of cash in advance of receiving *assets* or *services.*

adverse opinion. An *auditor's report* stating that the financial statements are not fair or are not in accord with *GAAP.*

affiliated company. A company controlling or controlled by another company.

after closing. Post-closing; a *trial balance* at the end of the period.

after cost. *Expenditures* to be made after *revenue* recognition. For example, *expenditures* for *repairs* under warranty are after cost. Proper recognition of after cost involves a debit to expense at the time of the sale and a credit to an *estimated liability.* When the firm discharges the liability, it debits the estimated liability and credits the assets consumed.

AG (Aktiengesellschaft). Germany: the form of a German company whose shares can trade on the stock exchange.

agency cost. The *cost* to the *principal* caused by *agents* pursuing their own interests instead of the principal's interests. Includes both the costs incurred by principals to control agents' actions and the cost to the principals if agents pursue their own interests that are not in the interest of the principals.

agency fund. An account for *assets* received by governmental units in the capacity of trustee or agent.

agency theory. A branch of economics relating the behavior of *principals* (such as owner nonmanagers or bosses) and that of their *agents* (such as nonowner managers or subordinates). The principal assigns responsibility and authority to the agent, but the agent's own risks and preferences differ from those of the principal. The principal cannot observe all activities of the agent. Both the principal and the agent must consider the differing risks and preferences in designing incentive contracts.

agent. One authorized to transact business, including executing contracts, for another.

aging accounts receivable. The process of classifying *accounts receivable* by the time elapsed since the claim came into existence for the purpose of estimating the amount of uncollectible accounts receivable as of a given date. See *sales contra, estimated uncollectibles,* and *allowance for uncollectibles.*

aging schedule. A listing of *accounts receivable*, classified by age, used in *aging accounts receivable.*

AICPA (American Institute of Certified Public Accountants). The national organization that represents *CPA*s. See *AcSEC.* It oversees the writing and grading of the Uniform CPA Examination. Each state sets its own requirements for becoming a CPA in that state. See *certified public accountant.* Web Site: http://www.aicpa.org. Although the AICPA sets many auditing and professional standards for public accountants, the *PCAOB* regulates auditing of public companies and the profession.

all-capital earnings rate. *Rate of return on assets.*

all-current method. *Foreign currency translation* in which all *financial statement* items are translated at the *current exchange rate.*

all-inclusive (income) concept. A concept that does not distinguish between *operating* and *nonoperating revenues* and *expenses.* Thus, the only entries to retained earnings are for *net income* and *dividends.* Under this concept, the *income statement* reports all *income*, *gains*, and *losses*; thus, net income includes events usually reported as *prior-period adjustments* and as *corrections of errors. GAAP* do not include this concept in its pure form, but *APB Opinions No. 9* and *No. 30* move far in this direction. They do permit retained earnings entries for prior-period adjustments and correction of errors.

allocate. To divide or spread a *cost* from one *account* into several accounts, to several products or activities, or to several periods.

allocation base. The systematic method that assigns *joint costs* to *cost objectives.* For example, a firm might assign the cost of a truck to periods based on miles driven during the period; the allocation base is miles. Or the firm might assign the cost of a factory supervisor to a product based on *direct labor* hours; the allocation base is direct labor hours.

allocation of income taxes. See *deferred income tax.*

allowance. A balance sheet *contra account* generally used for *receivables* and depreciable assets. See *sales* (or *purchase*) *allowance* for another use of this term.

allowance for funds used during construction. In accounting for public utilities, a *revenue* account *credited* for *implicit interest* earnings on *shareholders' equity* balances. One principle of public utility regulation and rate setting requires that customers should pay the full costs of producing the services (e.g., electricity) that they use, nothing more and nothing less. Thus, an electric utility must capitalize into an *asset* account the full costs, but no more, of producing a new electric power-generating plant. One of the costs of building a new plant is the *interest* cost on cash tied up during construction. If *funds* are explicitly borrowed by an ordinary business, the journal entry for interest of $1,000 is typically:

Interest Expense	1,000	
Interest Payable		1,000
Interest expense for the period.		

If the firm is constructing a new plant, then another entry would be made, capitalizing interest into the plant-under-construction account:

Construction Work-in-Progress . .	750	
Interest Expense.		750
Capitalize relevant portion of interest relating to construction work in progress into the asset account.		

The cost of the *plant asset* increases; when the firm uses the plant, it charges *depreciation*. The interest will become an expense through the depreciation process in the later periods of use, not currently as the firm pays for interest. Thus, the firm reports the full cost of the electricity generated during a given period as expense in that period. But suppose, as is common, that the electric utility does not explicitly borrow the funds but uses some of its own funds, including funds raised from equity issues as well as from debt. Even though the firm incurs no explicit interest expense or other explicit expense for capital, the funds have an *opportunity cost*. Put another way, the plant under construction will not have lower economic cost just because the firm used its own cash rather than borrowing. The public utility using its own funds, on which it would have to pay $750 of interest if it had explicitly borrowed the funds, will make the following entry:

Construction Work-in-Progress . . .	750	
Allowance for Funds Used during Construction		750
Recognition of interest, an opportunity cost, on own funds used.		

The allowance account is a form of *revenue*, to appear on the income statement, and the firm will close it to Retained Earnings, increasing it. On the *statement of cash flows* it is an income or revenue item not producing funds, and so the firm must subtract it from net income in deriving *cash provided by operations*. *SFAS No. 34* specifically prohibits nonutility companies from capitalizing, into plant under construction, the opportunity cost (interest) on their own funds used.

allowance for uncollectibles (accounts receivable). A *contra account* that shows the estimated *accounts receivable* amount that the firm expects not to collect. When the firm uses such an allowance, the actual write-off of specific accounts receivable (*debit* allowance, *credit* specific customer's account) does not affect *revenue* or *expense* at the time of the write-off. The firm reduces revenue when it debits *bad debt expense* (or, our preference, a revenue contra account) and credits the allowance; the firm can base the amount of the credit to the allowance on a percentage of sales on account for a period of time or compute it from *aging accounts receivable*. This contra account enables the firm to show an estimated receivables amount that it expects to collect without identifying specific uncollectible accounts. See *allowance method*.

allowance method. A method of attempting to match all *expenses* of a transaction with their associated *revenues;* usually involves a debit to expense and a credit to an *estimated liability*, such as for estimated warranty expenditures, or a debit to a revenue (*contra*) account and a credit to an asset (*contra*) account, such as in some firms' accounting for uncollectible accounts. See *allowance for uncollectibles* for further explanation. When the firm uses the allowance method for *sales discounts*, the firm records sales at gross invoice prices (not reduced by the amounts of discounts made available). The firm *debits* an estimate of the amount of discounts to be taken to a revenue contra account and *credits* an allowance account, shown contra to *accounts receivable*.

American Accounting Association (AAA). An organization primarily for academic accountants but open to all interested in accounting. It publishes the *Accounting Review* and several other journals.

American Institute of Certified Public Accountants. See *AICPA*.

American Stock Exchange (AMEX) (ASE). A public market where various corporate *securities* are traded.

AMEX. *American Stock Exchange*.

amortization. Strictly speaking, the process of liquidating or extinguishing ("bringing to death") a *debt* with a series of payments to the *creditor* (or to a *sinking fund*). From that usage has evolved a related use involving the accounting for the payments themselves: "amortization schedule" for a mortgage, which is a table showing the allocation between *interest* and *principal*. The term has come to mean writing off ("liquidating") the cost of an asset. In this context it means the general process of *allocating* the *acquisition cost* of an asset either to the periods of benefit as an *expense* or to *inventory* accounts as a *product cost*. This is called *depreciation* for *plant assets, depletion* for *wasting assets* (natural resources), and "amortization" for *intangibles*. *SFAC No. 6* refers to amortization as "the accounting process of reducing an amount by periodic payments or write-downs." The expressions "unamortized debt discount or premium" and "to amortize debt discount or premium" relate to *accruals*, not to *deferrals*. The expressions "amortization of long-term assets" and "to amortize long-term assets" refer to deferrals, not accruals. Contrast with *accretion*.

amortized cost. A measure required by *SFAS No. 115* for *held-to-maturity securities*. This amount results from applying the method described at *effective interest method*. The firm records the security at its initial cost and computes the *effective interest rate* for the security. Whenever the firm receives cash from the issuer of the security or whenever the firm reaches the end of one of its own *accounting periods* (that is, reaches the time for its own *adjusting entries*), it takes the following steps. It multiplies the amount currently recorded on the books by the effective interest rate (which remains constant over the time the firm holds the security). It debits that amount to the Debt Security account and credits the amount to Interest Revenue. If the firm receives cash, it debits Cash and credits the debt security account. The firm recomputes the book value of the Debt Security as the book value before these entries plus the increase for the interest revenue less the decrease for the cash received. The resulting amount is the amortized cost for the end of that period.

analysis of variances. See *variance analysis*.

annual report. A report prepared once a year for shareholders and other interested parties. It includes a *balance sheet*, an *income statement*, a *statement of cash flows*, a reconciliation of changes in *owners' equity* accounts, a *summary of significant accounting principles*, other explanatory *notes*, the *auditor's report*, and comments from management about the year's events. See *10-K* and *financial statements*.

annuitant. One who receives an *annuity*.

annuity. A series of payments of equal amount, usually made at equally spaced time intervals.

annuity certain. An *annuity* payable for a definite number of periods. Contrast with *contingent annuity*.

annuity due. An *annuity* whose first payment occurs at the start of period 1 (or at the end of period 0). Contrast with *annuity in arrears*.

annuity in advance. An *annuity due*.

annuity in arrears. An *ordinary annuity* whose first payment occurs at the end of the first period.

annuity method of depreciation. See *compound interest depreciation*.

antidilutive. Said of a *potentially dilutive* security that will increase *earnings per share* if its holder *exercises* it or *converts* it into common stock. In computing *primary* and *fully diluted earnings per share*, the firm must assume that holders of antidilutive securities will not exercise their options or convert securities into common shares. The opposite assumption would lead to increased reported earnings per share in a given period.

APB. Accounting Principles Board of the *AICPA*. It set *accounting principles* from 1959 through 1973, issuing 31 *APB Opinions* and 4 *APB Statements*. The *FASB* superseded it.

APB Opinion. The name for the APB pronouncements that compose much of *generally accepted accounting principles*; the APB issued 31 *APB Opinions* from 1962 through 1973.

APB Statement. The *APB* issued four *APB Statements* between 1962 and 1970. The *Statements* were approved by at least two-thirds of the board, but they state recommendations, not requirements. For example, *Statement No. 3* (1969) suggested the publication of *constant-dollar* financial statements but did not require them.

APBs. An abbreviation used for *APB Opinions*.

applied cost. A *cost* that a firm has *allocated* to a department, product, or activity; not necessarily based on actual costs incurred.

applied overhead. *Overhead costs* charged to departments, products, or activities. Also called *absorbed overhead*.

appraisal. In valuing an *asset* or *liability*, a process that involves expert opinion rather than evaluation of explicit market transactions.

appraisal costs. *Costs* incurred to detect individual units of products that do not conform to specifications, including end-process sampling and field-testing. Also called "detection costs."

appraisal method of depreciation. The periodic *depreciation* charge that equals the difference between the beginning-of-period and the end-of-period appraised values of the *asset* if that difference is positive. If negative, there is no charge. Not based on *historical cost*, this method is thus not generally accepted.

appreciation. An increase in economic value caused by rising market prices for an *asset*. Contrast with *accretion*.

appropriated retained earnings. See *retained earnings, appropriated*.

appropriation. In governmental accounting, an *expenditure* authorized for a specified amount, purpose, and time.

appropriation account. In governmental accounting, an account set up to record specific authorizations to spend. The governmental unit credits this account with appropriation amounts. At the end of the period, the unit closes to (debits) this account all *expenditures* during the period and all *encumbrances* outstanding at the end of the period.

approximate net realizable value method. A method of assigning joint costs to *joint products* based on revenues minus *additional processing costs* of the end products.

ARB. *Accounting Research Bulletin.*

arbitrage. Strictly speaking, the simultaneous purchase in one market and sale in another of a *security* or commodity in hope of making a *profit* on price differences in the different markets. Often, writers use this term loosely when a trader sells an item that is somewhat different from the item purchased; for example, the sale of shares of common stock and the simultaneous purchase of a *convertible bond* that is convertible into identical common shares. The trader hopes that the market will soon see that the similarities of the items should make them have equal market values. When the market values converge, the trader closes the positions and profits from the original difference in prices, less trading costs.

arbitrary. Having no causation basis. Accounting theorists and practitioners often, properly, say, "Some cost allocations are arbitrary." In that sense, the accountant does not mean that the allocations are capricious or haphazard but does mean that theory suggests no unique solution to the allocation problem at hand. Accountants require that arbitrary allocations be systematic, rational, and consistently followed over time.

arm's length. A transaction negotiated by unrelated parties, both acting in their own self-interests; the basis for a *fair market value* estimation or computation.

arrears. *Cumulative dividends* that the firm has not yet declared. See *annuity in arrears* for another context.

ARS. *Accounting Research Study.*

articles of incorporation. Document filed with state authorities by persons forming a corporation. When the state returns the document with a certificate of incorporation, the document becomes the corporation's *charter.*

articulate. The relation between any operating statement (for example, *income statement* or *statement of cash flows*) and comparative balance sheets, where the operating statement explains (or reconciles) the change in some major balance sheet category (for example, *retained earnings* or *working capital*).

ASE. *American Stock Exchange.*

ASR. *Accounting Series Release.*

assess. To value property for the purpose of property taxation; to levy a charge on the owner of property for improvements thereto, such as for sewers or sidewalks. The taxing authority computes the assessment.

assessed valuation. For real estate or other property, a dollar amount that a government uses as a basis for levying taxes. The amount need not have some relation to *market value.*

asset. *SFAC No. 6* defines assets as "probable future economic benefits obtained or controlled by a particular entity as a result of past transactions. . . . An asset has three essential characteristics: (a) it embodies a probable future benefit that involves a capacity, singly or in combination with other assets, to contribute directly or indirectly to future net cash inflows, (b) a particular entity can obtain the benefit and control others' access to it, and (c) the transaction or other event giving rise to the entity's right to or control of the benefit has already occurred." A footnote points out that "probable" means that which we can reasonably expect or believe but that is not certain or proved. You may understand condition (c) better if you think of it as requiring that a future benefit cannot be an asset if it arises from an *executory contract,* a mere exchange of promises. Receiving a purchase order from a customer provides a future benefit, but it is an executory contract, so the order cannot be an asset. An asset may be *tangible* or *intangible*, short-term (current) or long-term (noncurrent).

asset depreciation range (ADR). The range of *depreciable lives* allowed by the *Internal*

Revenue Service for a specific depreciable *asset*.

asset securitization. *Securitization.*

asset turnover. Net sales divided by average assets. See *ratio*.

assignment of accounts receivable. Transfer of the legal ownership of an account receivable through its sale. Contrast with *pledging* accounts receivable, where the receivables serve as *collateral* for a *loan*.

ATB. *Accounting Terminology Bulletin.*

at par. A *bond* or *preferred shares* issued (or selling) at *face amount*.

attachment. The laying claim to the *assets* of a borrower (or debtor) by a lender (or creditor) when the borrower has failed to pay debts on time.

attest. An auditor's rendering of an *opinion* that the *financial statements* are fair. Common usage calls this procedure the "attest function" of the CPA. See *fair presentation*.

attestor. Typically independent *CPA*s, who *audit financial statements* prepared by management for the benefit of users. The *FASB* describes accounting's constituency as comprising preparers, attestors, and users.

attribute measured. The particular *cost* reported in the balance sheet. When making physical measurements, such as of a person, one needs to decide the units with which to measure, such as inches or centimeters or pounds or grams. One chooses the attribute height or weight independently of the measuring unit, English or metric. Conventional accounting uses *historical cost* as the attribute measured and *nominal dollars* as the measuring unit. Some theorists argue that accounting would better serve readers if it used *current cost* as the attribute measured. Others argue that accounting would better serve readers if it used *constant dollars* as the measuring unit. Some, including us, think accounting should change both the measuring unit and the attribute measured. One can measure the attribute historical cost in nominal dollars or in constant dollars. One can also measure the attribute current cost in nominal dollars or constant dollars. Choosing between the two attributes and the two measuring units implies four different accounting systems. Each of these four has its uses.

attribute(s) sampling. The use of sampling technique in which the observer assesses each item selected on the basis of whether it has a particular qualitative characteristic in order to ascertain the rate of occurrence of this characteristic in the population. See also *estimation sampling*. Compare *variables sampling*. Example of attributes sampling: take a sample population of people, note the fraction that is male (say, 40 percent), and then infer that the entire population contains 40 percent males. Example of variables sampling: take a sample population of people, observe the weight of each sample point, compute the mean of those sampled people's weights (say, 160 pounds), and then infer that the mean weight of the entire population equals 160 pounds.

audit. Systematic inspection of accounting records involving analyses, tests, and *confirmations*. See *internal audit*.

audit committee. A committee of the board of directors of a *corporation*, usually comprising outside directors, who nominate the independent auditors and discuss the auditors' work with them. If the auditors believe the shareholders should know about certain matters, the auditors, in principle, first bring these matters to the attention of the audit committee; in practice, the auditors may notify management before they notify the audit committee.

Audit Guides. See *Industry Audit Guides*.

audit program. The procedures followed by the *auditor* in carrying out the *audit*.

audit trail. A reference accompanying an entry, or *post,* to an underlying source record or document. Efficiently checking the accuracy of accounting entries requires an audit trail. See *cross-reference.*

Auditing Research Monograph. Publication series of the *AICPA.*

auditing standards. Standards promulgated by the *PCAOB* for auditors to follow in carrying out their *attest* functions. The PCAOB began operations in earnest in 2003, and initially has said that is would use the standards originally promulgated by the *AICPA*, including general standards, standards of field work, and standards of reporting. According to the AICPA, these standards "deal with the measures of the quality of the performance and the objectives to be attained" rather than with specific auditing procedures. As time passes, the PCAOB will substitute its rules for those of the AICPA.

Auditing Standards Board. *AICPA* operating committee that promulgates auditing rules. The new operations of the PCAOB, after 2003, render uncertain what this Board will do.

auditor. Without a modifying adjective, usually refers to an external auditor—one who checks the accuracy, fairness, and general acceptability of accounting records and statements and then *attests* to them. See *internal auditor.*

auditor's opinion. *Auditor's report.*

auditor's report. The auditor's statement of the work done and an opinion of the *financial statements.* The auditor usually gives unqualified ("clean") opinions but may qualify them, or the auditor may disclaim an opinion in the report. Often called the "accountant's report." See *adverse opinion.*

AudSEC. The former Auditing Standards Executive Committee of the *AICPA*, now functioning as the *Auditing Standards Board.*

authorized capital stock. The number of *shares* of stock that a corporation can issue; specified by the *articles of incorporation.*

available for sale, securities. *Marketable securities* a firm holds that are classified as neither *trading securities* nor *held-to-maturity (debt) securities.* This classification is important in *SFAS No. 115*, which requires the owner to carry marketable equity securities on the balance sheet at market value, not at cost. Under *SFAS No. 115*, the income statement reports *holding gains and losses* on trading securities but not on securities available for sale. The required accounting *credits (debits)* holding gains (losses) on securities available for sale directly to an *owners' equity* account. On sale, the firm reports realized gain or loss as the difference between the selling price and the original cost, for trading securities, and as the difference between the selling price and the book value at the beginning of the period of sale, for securities available for sale and for debt securities held to maturity. By their nature, however, the firm will only rarely sell debt securities "held to maturity."

average. The arithmetic mean of a set of numbers; obtained by summing the items and dividing by the number of items.

average collection period of receivables. See *ratio.*

average-cost flow assumption. An inventory *flow assumption* in which the cost of units equals the *weighted average* cost of the *beginning inventory* and purchases. See *inventory equation.*

average tax rate. The rate found by dividing *income tax* expense by *net income* before taxes. Contrast with *marginal tax rate* and *statutory tax rate.*

avoidable cost. A *cost* that ceases if a firm discontinues an activity; an *incremental* or *variable cost.* See *programmed cost.*

B

backflush costing. A method of *allocating indirect costs* and *overhead;* used by companies that hope to have zero or small *work-in-process inventory* at the end of the period. The method *debits* all *product costs* to *cost of goods sold* (or *finished goods inventory*) during the period. To the extent that work in process actually exists at the end of the period, the method then debits work-in-process and *credits* cost of goods sold (or finished goods inventory). This method is "backflush" in the sense that costing systems ordinarily, but not in this case, allocate first to work-in-process and then forward to cost of goods sold or to finished goods. Here, the process allocates first to cost of goods sold (or finished goods) and then, later if necessary, to work-in-process.

backlog. Orders for which a firm has insufficient *inventory* on hand for current delivery and will fill in a later period.

backlog depreciation. In *current cost accounting*, a problem arising for the *accumulated depreciation* on *plant assets*. Consider an *asset* costing $10,000 with a 10-year life depreciated with the straight-line method. Assume that a similar asset has a current cost of $10,000 at the end of the first year but $12,000 at the end of the second year. Assume that the firm bases the depreciation charge on the average current cost during the year, $10,000 for the first year and $11,000 for the second. The depreciation charge for the first year is $1,000 and for the second is $1,100 (= .10 × $11,000), so the *accumulated depreciation account* is $2,100 after two years. Note that at the end of the second year, the firm has used 20 percent of the asset's future benefits, so the accounting records based on current costs must show a *net book value* of $9,600 (= .80 × $12,000), which results only if accumulated depreciation equals $2,400, so that book value equals $9,600 (= $12,000 – $2,400). But the sum of the depreciation charges equals only $2,100 (= $1,000 + $1,100). The *journal entry* to increase the accumulated depreciation account requires a *credit* to that account of $300. The backlog depreciation question arises: What account do we debit? Some theorists would *debit* an *income* account, and others would *debit* a *balance sheet owners' equity* account without reducing current-period earnings. The answer to the question of what to debit interrelates with how the firm records the *holding gains* on the asset. When the firm debits the asset account for $2,000 to increase the recorded amount from $10,000 to $12,000, it records a holding gain of $2,000 with a credit. Many theorists believe that whatever account the firm credits for the holding gain is the same account that the firm should debit for backlog depreciation. This is sometimes called "catch-up depreciation."

bad debt. An *uncollectible account;* see *bad debt expense* and *sales contra, estimated uncollectibles*.

bad debt expense. The name for an *account debited* in both the *allowance method* for *uncollectible accounts* and the *direct write-off method*. Under the allowance method, some prefer to treat the account as a revenue contra, not as an expense, and give it an account title such as Uncollectible Accounts Adjustment.

bad debt recovery. Collection, perhaps partial, of a specific account receivable previously written off as uncollectible. If a firm uses the *allowance method*, it will usually *credit* the *allowance* account, assuming that it has correctly assessed the amount of bad debts but has merely misjudged the identity of one of the nonpaying customers. If the firm decides that its charges for bad debts have been too large, it will credit the Bad Debt Expense account. If the firm uses the *direct write-off* method, it will credit a *revenue account*.

bailout period. In a *capital budgeting* context, the total time that elapses before accumulated cash inflows from a project, including the potential *salvage value* of assets at various times, equal or exceed the accumulated cash outflows. Contrast with *payback period*, which assumes completion of the project and uses terminal salvage value. Bailout, in contrast with payback, takes into account, at least to some degree, the *present value* of the cash flows after the termination date that the analyst is considering. The potential salvage value at any time includes some estimate of the flows that can occur after that time.

balance. As a noun, the opening balance in an *account* plus the amounts of increases less the amounts of decreases. (In the absence of a modifying adjective, the term means closing balance, in contrast to opening balance. The closing balance for a period becomes the opening balance for the next period.) As a verb, "balance" means to find the value of the arithmetic expression described above.

balance sheet. Statement of financial position that shows Total *assets* = Total *liabilities* + *Owners' equity*. The *balance sheet* usually classifies Total Assets as (1) *current assets*, (2) *investments*, (3) *property, plant, and equipment*, or (4) *intangible assets*. The balance sheet accounts composing Total Liabilities usually appear under the headings Current Liabilities and Long-term Liabilities.

balance sheet account. An account that can appear on a balance sheet; a *permanent account*. Contrast with *temporary account*.

balanced scorecard. A set of performance targets, not all expressed in dollar amounts, for setting an organization's goals for its individual employees or groups or divisions. A community relations employee might, for example, set targets in terms of number of employee hours devoted to local charitable purposes.

balloon. Most *mortgage* and *installment loans* require relatively equal periodic payments. Sometimes the loan requires relatively equal periodic payments with a large final payment. Usage calls the large final payment a "balloon" payment and the loan, a "balloon" loan. Although a coupon bond meets this definition, usage seldom, if ever, applies this term to bond loans.

bank balance. The amount of the balance in a checking account shown on the *bank statement*. Compare with *adjusted bank balance of cash*, and see *bank reconciliation schedule*.

bank prime rate. See *prime rate*.

bank reconciliation schedule. A schedule that explains the difference between the book balance of the cash in a bank account and the bank's statement of that amount; takes into account the amount of items such as checks that have not cleared or deposits that have not been recorded by the bank, as well as errors made by the bank or the firm.

bank statement. A statement sent by the bank to a checking account customer showing deposits, checks cleared, and service charges for a period, usually one month.

bankrupt. Occurs when a company's *liabilities* exceed its *assets* and the firm or one of its creditors has filed a legal petition that the bankruptcy court has accepted under the bankruptcy law. A bankrupt firm is usually, but need not be, *insolvent*.

base stock method. A method of inventory valuation that assumes that a firm must keep on hand at all times a minimum normal, or base stock, of goods for effective continuity of operations. The firm values this base quantity at *acquisition cost* of the inventory on hand in the earliest period when inventory was on hand. Firms may not use this method, either for financial reporting or for tax reporting, but most theorists consider it to be the forerunner of the *LIFO* cost flow assumption.

basic accounting equation. *Accounting equation.*

basic cost-flow equation. *Cost-flow equation.*

basic earnings per share (BEPS). *Net income* to *common shareholders*, divided by the weighted average number of common shares *outstanding* during the period. Required by *SFAS No. 128* and by *IASB*. See *primary earnings per share (PEPS)* for contrast. Because BEPS does not deal with *common-stock equivalents,* it will almost always give a larger earnings-per-share figure than PEPS.

basis. *Acquisition cost*, or some substitute therefor, of an *asset* or *liability* used in computing gain or loss on disposition or retirement; *attribute measured*. This term appears in both *financial* and *tax reporting*, but the basis of a given item need not be the same for both purposes.

basis point. One one-hundredth (=1/100). Terminology usually quotes *interest rates* in percentage terms, such as "5.60 percent" or "5.67 percent." The difference between those two interest rates is described as "7 basis points" or seven one-hundredths of one percent. Financial writers often extend this usage to other contexts involving decimals. For example, if the mean grade point average in the class is 3.25 and a given student scores 3.30, we might say that the student scored "5 basis points" above the class average.

basket purchase. Purchase of a group of *assets* (and *liabilities*) for a single price; the acquiring firm must assign *costs* to each item so that it can record the individual items with their separate amounts in the *accounts*.

batch-level activities. Work required to ready equipment or people for a production run.

bear. One who believes that security prices will fall. A "bear market" refers to a time when stock prices are generally declining. Contrast with *bull*.

bearer bond. See *registered bond* for contrast and definition.

beginning inventory. Valuation of *inventory* on hand at the beginning of the *accounting period*, equals *ending inventory* from the preceding period.

behavioral congruence. *Goal congruence.*

benchmarking. Process of measuring a firm's performance, products, and services against standards based on best levels of performance achievable or, sometimes, achieved by other firms.

BEPS. *Basic earnings per share.*

betterment. An *improvement*, usually *capitalized*, not *expensed*.

bid. An offer to purchase, or the amount of the offer.

big bath. A *write-off* of a substantial amount of costs previously treated as *assets;* usually occurs when a corporation drops a business line that earlier required a large investment but that proved to be unprofitable. The term is sometimes used to describe a situation in which a corporation takes a large write-off in one period in order to free later periods of gradual write-offs of those amounts. In this sense it frequently occurs when the top management of the firm changes.

Big 4, Final 4. The four largest U.S. *public accounting* partnerships; in alphabetical order: Deloitte & Touche; Ernst & Young; KPMG Peat Marwick; and PricewaterhouseCoopers. See *Big N.*

Big N. The largest U.S. *public accounting* partnerships. When we first prepared this glossary, there were eight such partnerships, referred to as the "Big 8." See *Big 4.* The term "Big N" came into use when various of the *Big 8* proposed to merge with each other and the ultimate number of large partnerships was in doubt, which it still is, although we don't expect the number to change before 2010.

bill. An *invoice* of charges and *terms of sale* for *goods* and *services;* also, a piece of currency.

bill of materials. A specification of the quantities of *direct materials* that a firm expects to use to produce a given job or quantity of output.

blocked currency. Currency that the holder, by law, cannot withdraw from the issuing country or exchange for the currency of another country.

board. *Board of directors.*`

board of directors. The governing body of a corporation; elected by the shareholders.

bond. A certificate to show evidence of debt. The *par value* is the *principal* or face amount of the bond payable at maturity. The *coupon rate* is the amount of the yearly payments divided by the principal amount. Coupon bonds have attached coupons that the holder can redeem at stated dates. Increasingly, firms issue not coupon bonds but registered bonds; the firm or its agent keeps track of the owners of registered bonds. Normally, bonds call for semiannual payments.

bond conversion. The act of exchanging *convertible bonds* for *preferred* or *common shares.*

bond discount. From the standpoint of the issuer of a *bond* at the issue date, the excess of the *par value* of a bond over its initial sales price and, at later dates, the excess of par over the sum of the following two amounts: initial issue price and the portion of discount already *amortized;* from the standpoint of a bondholder, the difference between par value and selling price when the bond sells below par.

bond indenture. The contract between an issuer of *bonds* and the bondholders.

bond premium. Exactly parallel to *bond discount* except that the issue price (or current selling price) exceeds *par value.*

bond ratings. Corporate and *municipal bond* issue ratings, based on the issuer's existing *debt* level, its previous record of payment, the *coupon rate* on the bonds, and the safety of the *assets* or *revenues* that are committed to paying off *principal* and *interest.* Moody's Investors Service and Standard & Poor's Corporation publish bond ratings: Moody's top rating is Aaa; Standard & Poor's is AAA.

bond redemption. Retirement of *bonds.*

bond refunding. To incur *debt,* usually through the issue of new *bonds,* intending to use the proceeds to retire an *outstanding* bond issue.

bond sinking fund. See *sinking fund.*

bond table. A table showing the current price of a *bond* as a function of the *coupon rate,* current (remaining) term *maturity,* and effective *yield to maturity* (or *effective rate*).

bonus. Premium over normal *wage* or *salary,* paid usually for meritorious performance.

bonus method. One of two methods to recognize an excess, say $10,000, when a *partnership* admits a new partner and when the new partner's capital account is to show an amount larger than the amount of *tangible* assets that he or she contributes. First, the old partners may transfer $10,000 from themselves to the new partner. This is the bonus method. Second, the partnership may recognize goodwill in the amount of $10,000, with the credit to the new partner's capital account. This is the *goodwill method.* (Notice that the new partner's percentage of total ownership differs under the two methods.) If the new partner's capital account is to show an amount smaller than the tangible assets that he or she contributed, then the old partners will receive bonus or goodwill, depending on the method.

book. As a verb, to record a transaction; as a noun, usually plural, the *journals* and *ledgers*; as an adjective, see *book value*.

book cost. *Book value.*

book inventory. An *inventory* amount that results not from physical count but from the amount of beginning inventory plus *invoice* amounts of net purchases less invoice amounts of *requisitions* or withdrawals; implies a *perpetual inventory* method.

book of original entry. *Journal.*

book value. The amount shown in the books or in the *accounts* for an *asset, liability*, or *owners' equity* item. The term is generally used to refer to the *net* amount of an *asset* or group of assets shown in the account that records the asset and reductions, such as for *amortization*, in its cost. Of a firm, it refers to the excess of total assets over total liabilities; *net assets*.

book value per share of common stock. Common *shareholders' equity* divided by the number of shares of common stock outstanding. See *ratio*.

bookkeeping. The process of analyzing and recording transactions in the accounting records.

boot. The additional cash paid (or received) along with a used item in a trade-in or exchange transaction for another item. See *trade-in*.

borrower. See *loan*.

bottleneck. An operation in which the work to be performed equals or exceeds the available capacity, thus holding up further operations.

branch. A sales office or other unit of an enterprise physically separated from the home office of the enterprise but not organized as a legally separate *subsidiary*. Writers seldom use this term to refer to manufacturing units.

branch accounting. An accounting procedure that enables the firm to report the financial position and operations of each *branch* separately but later combine them for published statements.

brand, brand name. See *trademark* and *trademark right.*

breakeven analysis. See *breakeven chart*.

breakeven chart. Two kinds of breakeven charts appear here. The charts use the following information for one month. Revenue is $30 per unit.

Cost Classification	Variable Cost, Per Unit	Fixed Cost, Per Month
Manufacturing Costs		
Direct Material	$ 4	
Direct Labor	9	
Overhead.	4	$ 3,060
Total Manufacturing Costs	$ 17	$ 3,060
Selling, general, and administrative costs.	5	1,740
Total costs.	$ 22	$ 4,800

The cost-volume-profit graph presents the relation between changes in volume to the amount of *profit*, or *income*. Such a graph shows total *revenue* and total *costs* for each volume level, and the user reads profit or loss at any volume directly from the chart. The profit-volume graph does not show revenues and costs but more readily indicates profit (or loss) at various output levels. Keep in mind two caveats about these graphs:

1. Although the curve depicting *variable cost* and total cost appears as a straight line for its entire length, at low or high levels of output, variable cost will probably differ from $22 per unit. The variable cost figure usually results from studies of operations at some broad central area of production, called the *relevant range*. The chart will not usually provide accurate results for low (or high) levels of activity. For this reason, the total cost and the profit-loss curves sometimes

appear as dotted lines at lower (or higher) volume levels.
2. This chart, simplistically, assumes a single-product firm. For a multiproduct firm, the horizontal axis would have to be stated in dollars rather than in physical units of output. Breakeven charts for multiproduct firms necessarily assume that the firm sells constant proportions of the several products, so that changes in this mixture, as well as in costs or selling prices, invalidate such a chart.

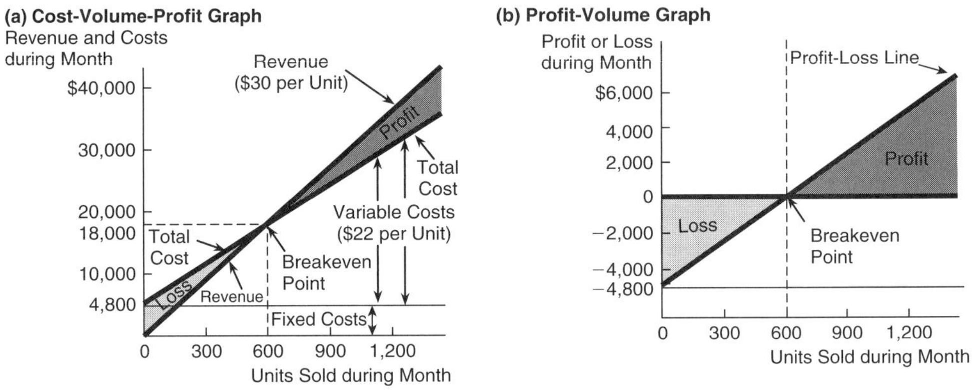

breakeven point. The volume of sales required so that total *revenues* equals total *costs;* may be expressed in units (*Fixed costs ÷ Contribution per unit*) or in sales dollars [Selling price per unit × (Fixed costs ÷ Contribution per unit)].

break-even time. Time required before the firm recovers the amounts it invested in developing a new product.

budget. A financial plan that a firm uses to estimate the results of future operations; frequently used to help control future operations. In governmental operations, budgets often become the law. See *standard costs* for further elaboration and contrast.

budgetary accounts. In governmental accounting, the accounts that reflect estimated operations and financial condition, as affected by estimated *revenues, appropriations*, and *encumbrances*. Contrast with *proprietary accounts,* which record the transactions.

budgetary control. Management of governmental (nongovernmental) unit in accordance with an official (approved) *budget* in order to keep total expenditures within authorized (planned) limits.

budgeted cost. See *standard costs* for definition and contrast.

budgeted statements. *Pro forma statements* prepared before the event or period occurs.

bull. One who believes that security prices will rise. A "bull market" refers to a time when stock prices are generally rising. Contrast with *bear.*

burden. See *overhead costs.*

burn rate. A new business usually begins life with cash-absorbing operating losses but with a limited amount of cash. The "burn rate" measures how long the new business can survive before operating losses must stop or the firm must receive a new infusion of cash. Writers usually express the burn rate in months.

business combination. As defined in *APB Opinion No. 16*, the bringing together into a single accounting *entity* of two or more incorporated or unincorporated businesses. The new entity will account for the *merger* either with the *purchase method* or, outside the United States, with the *pooling-of-interests method.* See *conglomerate.*

business entity. *Entity; accounting entity.*

BV *(besloten vennootschap).* Netherlands: a private limited-liability company.

bylaws. The rules adopted by the shareholders of a corporation; specify the general methods for carrying out the functions of the corporation.

byproduct. A *joint product* whose sales value is so small relative to the sales value of the other joint product(s) that it does not receive normal accounting treatment. The costs assigned to byproducts reduce the costs of the main product(s). Accounting allocates byproducts a share of joint costs such that the expected gain or loss at their sale is zero. Thus, byproducts appear in the *accounts* at *net realizable value.*

C

C corporation. In tax terminology, a corporation paying its own income taxes. Contrast with *S corporation.*

CA. *Chartered accountant.*

call. An option to buy *shares* of a publicly traded corporation at a fixed price during a fixed time span. Contrast with *put.*

call premium. See *callable bond.*

call price. See *callable bond.*

callable bond. A *bond* for which the issuer reserves the right to pay a specific amount, the call price, to retire the obligation before its *maturity* date. If the issuer agrees to pay more than the *face amount* of the bond when called, the excess of the payment over the face amount is the "call premium."

called-up share capital. United Kingdom: *common stock* at *par value.*

Canadian Institute of Chartered Accountants The national organization that represents *chartered accountants* in Canada. Web Site: www.cica.ca.

cancelable lease. See *lease.*

CAP. *Committee on Accounting Procedure.*

capacity. Stated in units of product, the amount that a firm can produce per unit of time; stated in units of input, such as *direct labor-hours,* the amount of input that a firm can use in production per unit of time. A firm uses this measure of output or input in allocating *fixed costs* if the amounts producible are normal, rather than maximum, amounts.

capacity cost. A *fixed cost* incurred to provide a firm with the capacity to produce or to sell. Consists of *standby costs* and *enabling costs.* Contrast with *programmed costs.*

capacity variance. *Production volume variance.*

capital. *Owners' equity* in a business; often used, equally correctly, to mean the total assets of a business; sometimes used to mean *long-term assets.* Sometimes used to mean *funds* raised or all assets or long-term financing. This word causes confusion in accounting and finance. Uninformed users mix up the funds (and their uses) with the sources of the funds. Consider the following transactions. A firm raises $100 cash by issuing shares and uses the $100 to acquire *inventory* and *plant assets.* Did the investor "invest capital" of $100 or did the firm "invest capital" of $100 or both? You will hear "invest capital" used for both sides of that transaction. Now focus on the firm that issued the shares and received the cash. Some would say the first transaction, the issue of shares, "raised capital." (If you ask of a person who answers this way, "What is the *capital,* the increase in owners' equity or the increased cash?" you will not get a clear answer, consistent across all such people.) Others would say only the second transaction, spending the cash, raised capital and only then for the plant assets, not the inventory. When a regulator focuses on a bank's capital ratios, it looks to the right-hand side of the balance sheet, not to how the firm has invested its funds. Sometimes bank regulators will take the owners' equity total and subtract from that amount the amount of intangible assets, resulting in a total with no clear conception, which they call "tangible capital." See *cost of capital* for further discussion of the confusion between the cost of raising funds and the return to, or *opportunity cost* of, investing funds. The confusion is so prevalent that we tend to avoid using the word, except to mean *shareholders' equity.*

capital asset. Properly used, a designation, for income tax purposes, that describes property held by a taxpayer except *cash*, inventoriable *assets*, goods held primarily for sale, most depreciable property, *real estate, receivables*, certain *intangibles*, and a few other items. Sometimes writers use this term imprecisely to describe *plant* and *equipment*, which are clearly not capital assets under the income-tax definition. Writers often use the term to refer to an *investment* in *securities*.

capital budget. Plan of proposed outlays for acquiring long-term *assets* and the means of *financing* the acquisition.

capital budgeting. The process of choosing *investment* projects for an enterprise by considering the *present value* of cash flows and deciding how to raise the funds the investment requires.

capital consumption allowance. The term used for *depreciation expense* in national income accounting and the reporting of funds in the economy.

capital contributed in excess of par (or stated) value. A preferred title for the account that shows the amount received by the issuer for *capital stock* in excess of *par (or stated) value*.

capital expenditure (outlay). An *expenditure* to acquire long-term *assets*.

capital gain. The excess of proceeds over *cost*, or other *basis*, from the sale of a *capital asset* as defined by the Internal Revenue Code. If the taxpayer has held the capital asset for a sufficiently long time before sale, then the gain is taxed at a rate lower than that used for other gains and ordinary income.

capital lease. A *lease* treated by the *lessee* as both the borrowing of funds and the acquisition of an *asset* to be *amortized*. The lessee (tenant) recognizes both the *liability* and the asset on its balance sheet. Expenses consist of *interest* on the *debt* and *amortization* of the asset. The *lessor* (landlord) treats the lease as the sale of the asset in return for a series of future cash receipts. Contrast with *operating lease*.

capital loss. A negative capital gain; see *capital gain.*

capital rationing. In a *capital budgeting* context, the imposition of constraints on the amounts of total capital expenditures in each period.

capital stock. The ownership shares of a corporation. Consists of all classes of *common* and *preferred shares.*

capital structure. The composition of a corporation's equities; the relative proportions of short-term debt, long-term debt, and *owners' equity*.

capital surplus. An inferior term for *capital contributed in excess of par (or stated) value*.

capitalization of a corporation. A term used by investment analysts to indicate *shareholders' equity* plus bonds outstanding.

capitalization of earnings. The process of estimating the *fair value* of a firm by computing the *net present value* of the predicted *net income* (not *cash flows*) of the firm for the future.

capitalization rate. An *interest rate* used to convert a series of payments or receipts or earnings into a single *present value.*

capitalize. To record an *expenditure* that may benefit a future period as an *asset* rather than to treat the expenditure as an *expense* of the period of its occurrence. Whether expenditures for advertising or for research and development should be capitalized is controversial, but *SFAS No. 2* forbids capitalizing *R&D* costs. We believe GAAP should allow firms to capitalize expenditures when they lead to future benefits and thus meet the criterion to be an asset.

carryback, carryforward, carryover. The use of losses or tax credits in one period to reduce income taxes payable in other periods. Two common kinds of carrybacks exist: for net operating losses and for *capital losses.* They apply against taxable income. In general, carrybacks are for three years, with the earliest year first. The taxpayer can carry forward operating losses for fifteen years. Corporate capital loss carryforwards are for five years. Individuals can carry forward capital losses indefinitely.

carrying cost. Costs (such as property taxes and insurance) of holding, or storing, *inventory* from the time of purchase until the time of sale or use.

carrying value (amount). *Book value.*

CASB (Cost Accounting Standards Board). A board authorized by the U.S. Congress to "promulgate cost-accounting standards designed to achieve uniformity and consistency in the cost-accounting principles followed by defense contractors and subcontractors under federal contracts." The *principles* the CASB promulgated since 1970 have considerable weight in practice wherever the *FASB* has not established a standard. Congress allowed the CASB to go out of existence in 1980 but reinstated it in 1990.

cash. Currency and coins, negotiable checks, and balances in bank accounts. For the *statement of cash flows,* "cash" also includes *marketable securities* held as *current assets.*

cash basis of accounting. In contrast to the *accrual basis of accounting,* a system of accounting in which a firm recognizes *revenues* when it receives *cash* and recognizes *expenses* as it makes *disbursements.* The firm makes no attempt to match *revenues* and *expenses* in measuring *income.* See *modified cash basis.*

cash budget. A schedule of expected cash *receipts* and *disbursements.*

cash change equation. For any *period,* the change in *cash* equals the change in *liabilities* plus the change in *owners' equity* minus the change in noncash *assets.*

cash collection basis. The *installment method* for recognizing *revenue.* Do not confuse with the *cash basis of accounting.*

cash conversion cycle. *Cash cycle.*

cash cycle. The period of time during which a firm converts *cash* into *inventories,* inventories into *accounts receivable,* and *receivables* back into cash. Sometimes called *earnings cycle.*

cash disbursements journal. A specialized *journal* used to record *expenditures* by *cash* and by *check.* If a *check register* is also used, a cash disbursements journal records only expenditures of currency and coins.

cash discount. A sales or purchase price reduction allowed for prompt payment.

cash dividend. See *dividend.*

cash equivalent. According to *SFAS No. 95,* "short-term, highly liquid investments that are both readily convertible to known amounts of cash [and] so near their maturity that they present insignificant risk of changes in value because of changes in interest rates. . . . Examples of items commonly considered to be cash equivalents are Treasury bills, commercial paper, [and] money market funds."

cash equivalent value. A term used to describe the amount for which an *asset* could be sold. Sometimes called *market value* or *fair market price (value).*

cash flow. Cash *receipts* minus *disbursements* from a given *asset*, or group of assets, for a given period. Financial analysts sometimes use this term to mean *net income + depreciation + depletion + amortization*. See also *operating cash flow* and *free cash flow*.

cash flow from operations. Receipts from customers and from investments less expenditures for inventory, labor, and services used in the usual activities of the firm, less interest expenditures. See *statement of cash flows* and *operations*. Same as *cash provided by operations*.

cash-flow hedge. A hedge of an exposure to variability in the cash flows of a recognized *asset* or *liability* or of a forecasted transaction, such as expected future foreign sales. The cash flows hedged do not themselves appear on the *balance sheet.* The hedging instrument itself is a *marketable security* and appears on the balance sheet at market value. If the firm uses hedge accounting and the hedging instrument is highly effective, then it will be able to report in *other comprehensive income* the *gains* and *losses*, so these amounts will not appear in periodic net income.

cash flow statement. *Statement of cash flows*.

cash provided by operations. An important subtotal in the *statement of cash flows*. This amount equals the total of revenues producing *cash* less *expenses* requiring cash. Often, the amount appears as *net income* plus expenses not requiring cash (such as depreciation charges) minus revenues not producing cash (such as revenues recognized under the *equity method* of accounting for a long-term investment). The statement of cash flows maintains the same distinctions between *continuing operations, discontinued operations*, and *income* or *loss* from *extraordinary items* as does the *income statement.*

cash receipts journal. A specialized *journal* used to record all *receipts* of *cash.*

cash (surrender) value of life insurance. An amount equal not to the face value of the policy to be paid in the event of death but to the amount that the owner could realize by immediately canceling the policy and returning it to the insurance company for cash. A firm owning a life insurance policy reports it as an asset at an amount equal to this value.

cash yield. See *yield.*

cashier's check. A bank's own *check* drawn on itself and signed by the cashier or other authorized official. It is a direct obligation of the bank. Compare with *certified check.*

catch-up depreciation. *Backlog depreciation.*

cause-and-effect analysis. An identification of potential causes of defects and taking actions to cure the problem found. To use this analysis, first define the effect and then identify the causes of the problem. The potential causes fall into four categories: human factors, methods and design factors, machine-related factors, and materials or components factors. As management identifies the prevailing causes, it develops and implements corrective measures.

CCA. *Current cost accounting; current value accounting.*

central corporate expenses. General *overhead expenses* incurred in running the corporate headquarters and related supporting activities of a corporation. Accounting treats these expenses as *period expenses*. Contrast with *manufacturing overhead. Line of business reporting* must decide how to treat these expenses—whether to allocate them to the individual segments and, if so, how to allocate them.

central processing unit (CPU). The computer system component that carries out the arithmetic, logic, and data transfer.

certificate. The document that is the physical embodiment of a *bond* or a *share of stock;* a term sometimes used for the *auditor's report*.

certificate of deposit. A form of *deposit* in a bank or thrift institution. Federal law constrains the rate of interest that banks can pay to their depositors. Current law allows banks to pay a rate higher than the one allowed on a *time deposit* if the depositor promises to leave funds on deposit for several months or more. When the bank receives such funds, it issues a certificate of deposit. The depositor can withdraw the funds before maturity by paying a penalty.

certified check. The *check* of a depositor drawn on a bank. The bank inserts the words "accepted" or "certified" on the face of the check, with the date and a signature of a bank official. The check then becomes an obligation of the bank. Compare with *cashier's check*.

certified financial statement. A financial statement attested to by an independent *auditor* who is a *CPA*.

certified internal auditor. See *CIA*.

certified management accountant. *CMA*.

certified public accountant (CPA). An accountant who has satisfied the statutory and administrative requirements of his or her jurisdiction to be registered or licensed as a public accountant. In addition to passing the Uniform CPA Examination administered by the *AICPA*, the CPA must meet certain educational, experience, and moral requirements that differ from jurisdiction to jurisdiction. The jurisdictions are the 50 states, the District of Columbia, Guam, Puerto Rico, and the Virgin Islands.

CFA. *Chartered Financial Analyst.*

CGA (Certified General Accountant). Canada: an accountant who has satisfied the experience, education, and examination requirements of the Certified General Accountants' Association.

chain discount. A series of *discount* percentages. For example, if a chain discount of 10 and 5 percent is quoted, then the actual, or *invoice*, price is the nominal, or list, price times .90 times .95, or 85.5, percent of invoice price.

change fund. Coins and currency issued to cashiers, delivery drivers, and so on.

changes, accounting. See *accounting changes*.

changes in financial position. See *statement of cash flows*.

channel stuffing. Assume a company's ordinary practices record *revenue* when it ships to customers goods previously ordered. A company engaging in channel-stuffing will ship goods not yet ordered but record them as *sales,* as though a real customer had ordered them. It might even get permission from the customer to ship, saying it will not bill the customer until next period and that the customer will get its usual grace period to pay the bill starting from that later date, next period. Often, sales staff eager to boost their own sales commissions will send a letter to the customer laying out the agreement: the customer will accept the shipment and if asked, confirm that it ordered the goods, but the seller will not send an invoice until later, and the customer need not pay until later or can return the goods. Such a letter is called a "side letter" and even honest managements have a hard time locating these. All a management can do is to be diligent and deal severely with employees found issuing side letters.

charge. As a noun, a *debit* to an account; as a verb, to debit.

charge off. To treat as a *loss* or *expense* an amount originally recorded as an *asset*; use of this term implies that the charge is not in accord with original expectations.

chart of accounts. A list of names and numbers, systematically organized, of *accounts*.

charter. Document issued by a state government authorizing the creation of a corporation.

chartered accountant(s) (CA). The title used in British Commonwealth countries, such as Australia, Canada, India, Scotland and New Zealand, for an accountant who has satisfied the requirements of the institute of his or her jurisdiction to be qualified to serve as a *public accountant*. In the United Kingdom other than Scotland, members use the initials ACA or FCA: *A* means Associate and *F* means Fellow; the Associate has less experience than does the Fellow. A partnership of chartered accountants signs its firm name with the letters *CA*. In Canada, each provincial institute or order has the right to administer the examination and set the standards of performance and ethics for Chartered Accountants in its province. For a number of years, however, the provincial organizations have pooled their rights to qualify new members through the Inter-provincial Education Committee, and the result is that there are nationally set and graded examinations given in English and French. Deviation from the pass/fail grade awarded by the Board of Examiners (a subcommittee of the Inter-provincial Education Committee) is rare.

Chartered Financial Analyst (CFA). A person who has passed three examinations, over at least an 18-month period, covering topics in accounting, economics, financial economics, portfolio management, and security analysis. The Association for Investment Management and Research (AIMR) administers the program though its Institute of Chartered Financial Analysts. Beyond passing examinations, the person needs to have approved working experience and satisfy standards of professional conduct.

check. The Federal Reserve Board defines a check as "a *draft* or order upon a bank or banking house purporting to be drawn upon a deposit of funds for the payment at all events of a certain sum of money to a certain person therein named or to him or his order or to bearer and payable instantly on demand." It must contain the phrase "pay to the order of." The amount shown on the check must be clearly readable, and the check must have the signature of the drawer. The drawer need not date the check. In the accounts, the drawer usually reduces the *balance* in the *cash account* when it issues the check, not later when the check clears the bank. See *remittance advice*.

check register. A *journal* to record *checks* issued.

CIA (Certified Internal Auditor). One who has satisfied certain requirements of the *Institute of Internal Auditors* including experience, ethics, education, and passing examinations.

CICA. *Canadian Institute of Chartered Accountants.*

CIF (cost, insurance, and freight). In contracts, a term used along with the name of a given port, such as New Orleans, to indicate that the quoted price includes insurance, handling, and freight charges up to delivery by the seller at the given port.

circulating capital. *Working capital.*

clean opinion. See *auditor's report*.

clean surplus concept. The notion that all entries to the *retained earnings* account must record *net income* and *dividends*. See *comprehensive income*. Contrast with *current operating performance concept*. This concept, with minor exceptions, now controls *GAAP*. (See *APB Opinions No. 9* and *No. 30*.)

clearing account. An account containing amounts to be transferred to another account(s) before the end of the *accounting period*. Examples are the *income summary* account (whose balance transfers to *retained earnings*) and the purchases account (whose balance transfers to *inventory* or to *cost of goods sold*).

close. As a verb, to transfer the *balance* of a *temporary* or *contra* or *adjunct account* to the main account to which it relates; for example, to transfer *revenue* and *expense* accounts directly, or through the *income summary* account, to an *owners' equity* account or to transfer *purchase discounts* to purchases.

closed account. An *account* with equal *debits* and *credits*, usually as a result of a *closing entry*.

closing entries. The *entries* that accomplish the transfer of balances in *temporary accounts* to the related *balance sheet accounts*. See *work sheet*.

closing inventory. *Ending inventory*.

CMA (Certified Management Accountant) certificate. Awarded by the *Institute of Certified Management Accountants* of the *Institute of Management Accountants* to those who pass a set of examinations and meet certain experience and continuing-education requirements.

CoCoA. *Continuously Contemporary Accounting*.

coding of accounts. The numbering of *accounts*, as for a *chart of accounts*, that is necessary for computerized accounting.

coinsurance. Common condition of insurance policies that protect against hazards such as fire or water damage. These often specify that the owner of the property may not collect the full amount of insurance for a loss unless the insurance policy covers at least some specified "coinsurance" percentage, usually about 80 percent, of the *replacement cost* of the property. Coinsurance clauses induce the owner to carry full, or nearly full, coverage.

COLA. Cost-of-living adjustment. See *indexation*.

collateral. *Assets* pledged by a *borrower* who will surrender those assets if he or she fails to repay a *loan*.

collectible. Capable of being converted into *cash*—now if due, later otherwise.

collusion. Cooperative effort by employees to commit fraud or another unethical act.

combination. See *business combination*.

comfort letter. A letter in which an auditor conveys negative assurances as to unaudited financial statements in a prospectus or draft financial statements included in a preliminary prospectus.

commercial paper. Short-term notes issued by corporate borrowers.

commission. Employee remuneration, usually expressed as a percentage, based on an activity rate, such as sales.

committed costs. *Capacity costs*.

Committee on Accounting Procedure (CAP). Predecessor of the *APB*. The *AICPA*'s principles-promulgating body from 1939 through 1959. Its 51 pronouncements are *Accounting Research Bulletins*.

common cost. *Cost* resulting from the use of *raw materials*, a facility (e.g., plant or machines), or a service (e.g., fire insurance) that benefits several products or departments. A firm must allocate this cost to those products or departments. Common costs result when two or more departments produce multiple products together even though the departments could produce them separately; *joint costs* occur when two or more departments must produce multiple products together. Many writers use "common costs" and "joint costs" synonymously. See *joint cost, indirect costs, overhead;* and *sterilized allocation.*

common-dollar accounting. *Constant-dollar accounting.*

common monetary measuring unit. For U.S. corporations, the dollar. See also *stable monetary unit assumption* and *constant-dollar accounting.*

common shares. *Shares* representing the class of owners who have residual claims on the *assets* and *earnings* of a *corporation* after the firm meets all *debt* and *preferred shareholders'* claims.

common-size statement. A *percentage statement* usually based on total *assets* or *net sales* or *revenues.*

common-stock equivalent. A *security* whose primary value arises from its holder's ability to exchange it for *common shares*; includes *stock options*, *warrants*, and also *convertible bonds* or *convertible preferred stock* whose *effective interest rate* at the time of issue is less than two-thirds the average Aa corporate bond yield. See *bond ratings.*

company-wide control. See *control system.*

comparative (financial) statements. *Financial statements* showing information for the same company for different times, usually two successive years for balance sheets and three for *income* and *cash flow statements.* Nearly all published financial statements are in this form. Contrast with *historical summary.*

compensating balance. The amount required to be left on deposit for a loan. When a bank lends funds to customers, it often requires that the customers keep on deposit in their checking accounts an amount equal to some percentage—say, 20 percent—of the loan. Such amounts effectively increase the *interest rate.* The borrower must disclose the amounts of such balances in *notes* to the *financial statements.*

completed contract method. Recognizing *revenues* and *expenses* for a job or order only when the firm finishes it, except that when the firm expects a loss on the contract, the firm must recognize all revenues and expenses in the period when the firm first foresees a loss. Accountants generally use this term only for long-term contracts. This method is otherwise equivalent to the *sales basis of revenue recognition.*

completed sales basis. See *sales basis of revenue recognition.*

compliance audit. Objectively obtaining and evaluating evidence regarding assertions, actions, and events to ascertain the degree of correspondence between them and established performance criteria.

compliance procedure. An *audit* procedure used to gain evidence as to whether the prescribed internal controls are operating effectively.

composite cost of capital. See *cost of capital.*

composite depreciation or composite life method. *Group depreciation* when the items are of unlike kind. The term also applies when the firm depreciates as a whole a single item (e.g., a crane, which consists of separate units with differing service lives, such as the chassis, the motor, the lifting mechanism, and so on), rather than treating each of its components separately.

compound entry. A *journal entry* with more than one *debit* or more than one *credit* or both. See *trade-in transaction* for an example.

compound interest. *Interest* calculated on *principal* plus previously undistributed interest.

compound interest depreciation. A method designed to hold the *rate of return* on an asset constant. First find the *internal rate of return* on the cash inflows and outflows of the asset. The periodic depreciation charge equals the cash flow for the period less the internal rate of return multiplied by the asset's book value at the beginning of the period. When the cash flows from the asset are constant over time, usage sometimes refers to the method as the "annuity method" of depreciation.

compounding period. The time period, usually a year or a portion of a year, for which a firm calculates *interest*. At the end of the period, the borrower may pay interest to the lender or may add the interest (that is, convert it) to the principal for the next interest-earning period.

comprehensive budget. *Master budget*.

comprehensive income. Defined in *SFAC No. 3* as "the change in equity (net assets) of an entity during a period from transactions and other events and circumstances from nonowner sources. It includes all changes in equity during a period except those resulting from investments by owners and distributions to owners." In this definition, "equity" means *owners' equity* or *shareholders' equity*. *SFAS No. 130* requires firms to report comprehensive income as part of a statement showing *earnings* (primarily from realized transactions), comprehensive income (with additions for all other changes in owners' equity, primarily *holding gains and losses* and *foreign exchange gains and losses*), and comprehensive income plus *accounting adjustments*. The *FASB* encourages the discontinuation of the term "net income." The terms "earnings" and "comprehensive income" denote different concepts, with totals different from that of the old "net income." *SFAS No. 130* requires that the firm report comprehensive income in a format having the same prominence as other *financial statements*. We cannot predict which "income total"—earnings or comprehensive income—users of financial statements will focus on. See Exhibit 1.1 for two formats the FASB suggests firms use. General Electric uses a different one, harder to follow.

ONE-STATEMENT APPROACH	
Statement of Net Income and Comprehensive Income	
Revenues	$100,000
Expenses	(25,000)
Gain on Sale of Securities	2,000
Other Gains and Losses	8,000
Earnings from Continuing Operations before Income Tax	$ 85,000
Income Tax Expense	(21,250)
Earnings before Discontinued Operations and Extraordinary Items	$ 63,750
Discontinued Operations, Net of Tax	30,000
Extraordinary Items, Net of Tax	(28,000)
Income before Cumulative Effect of Accounting Change	$ 65,750
Cumulative Effect of Accounting Change, Net of Tax	(2,500)
Net Income (or, as preferred by the FASB, Earnings)	**$ 63,250**

EXHIBIT 1.1 REPORTING COMPREHENSIVE INCOME, TWO ALLOWED FORMATS

ONE-STATEMENT APPROACH (continued)		
Other Comprehensive Income, Net of Tax:		
Foreign Currency Translation Adjustments		$ 7,000
Unrealized Gains and Losses on Securities:		
Unrealized Holding Gains Arising during Period	$13,000	
Less: Reclassification Adjustment for Gain Included in Net Income (Earnings)	(1,500)	11,500
Minimum Pension Liability Adjustment		(2,500)
Other Comprehensive Income (Loss)		**$ 16,000**
Comprehensive Income (Loss)		**$ 79,250**

TWO-STATEMENT APPROACH

Statement of Net Income	
Revenues	$100,000
Expenses	(25,000)
Gain on Sale of Securities	2,000
Other Gains and Losses	8,000
Earnings from Continuing Operations before Income Tax	$ 85,000
Income Tax Expense	(21,250)
Earnings before Discontinued Operations and Extraordinary Items	$ 63,750
Discontinued Operations, Net of Tax	30,000
Extraordinary Items, Net of Tax	(28,000)
Income before Cumulative Effect of Accounting Change	$ 65,750
Cumulative Effect of Accounting Change, Net of Tax	(2,500)
Net Income (or, as preferred by the FASB, Earnings)	**$ 63,250**

Statement of Comprehensive Income		
Net Income (or, as preferred by the FASB, Earnings)		**$ 63,250**
Other Comprehensive Income, Net of Tax:		
Foreign Currency Translation Adjustments		$ 7,000
Unrealized Gains and Losses on Securities:		
Unrealized Holding Gains Arising during Period	$13,000	
Less: Reclassification Adjustment for Gain Included in Net Income (Earnings)	(1,500)	11,500
Minimum Pension Liability Adjustment		(2,500)
Other Comprehensive Income (Loss)		**$ 16,000**
Comprehensive Income (Loss)		**$ 79,250**

EXHIBIT 1.1 REPORTING COMPREHENSIVE INCOME, TWO ALLOWED FORMATS *(CONTINUED)*

comptroller. Same meaning and pronunciation as *controller*. Modern users, however, tend to use this form for government and not-for-profit entities and *controller* for profit-seeking ones.

conceptual framework. A coherent system of interrelated objectives and fundamentals, promulgated by the *FASB* primarily through its *SFAC* publications, expected to lead to consistent standards for *financial accounting* and reporting.

confidence level. The measure of probability that the actual characteristics of the population lie within the stated precision of the estimate derived from a sampling process. A sample estimate may be expressed in the following terms: "Based on the sample, we are 95 percent sure [confidence level] that the true population value is within the range of X to Y [precision]." See *precision*.

confirmation. A formal memorandum delivered by the customers or suppliers of a company to its independent *auditor* verifying the amounts shown as receivable or payable. The auditor originally sends the confirmation document to the customer. If the auditor asks that the customer return the document whether the *balance* is correct or incorrect, usage calls it a "positive confirmation." If the auditor asks that the customer return the document only if it contains an error, usage calls it a "negative confirmation."

conglomerate. *Holding company*. This term implies that the owned companies operate in dissimilar lines of business.

conservatism. A *reporting objective* that calls for anticipation of all *losses* and *expenses* but defers recognition of *gains* or *profits* until they are *realized* in *arm's-length* transactions. In the absence of certainty, report events to minimize cumulative income. Conservatism does not mean reporting low income in every *accounting period*. Over long-enough time spans, income is cash-in less cash-out. If a (conservative) reporting method shows low income in early periods, it must show higher income in some later period.

consignee. See *on consignment*.

consignment. See *on consignment*.

consignor. See *on consignment*.

consistency. Treatment of like *transactions* in the same way in consecutive periods so that financial statements will be more comparable than otherwise; the reporting policy implying that a reporting *entity*, once it adopts specified procedures, should follow them from period to period. See *accounting changes* for the treatment of inconsistencies.

consol. A *bond* that never matures; a *perpetuity* in the form of a bond; originally issued by Great Britain after the Napoleonic wars to consolidate debt issues of that period. The term arose as an abbreviation for "consolidated annuities."

consolidated financial statements. Statements that are issued by legally separate companies and that show financial position and income as they would appear if the companies were one economic *entity*.

constant dollar. A hypothetical unit of *general purchasing power*, denoted "C$" by the *FASB*.

constant-dollar accounting. Accounting that measures items in *constant dollars*. See *historical cost/constant-dollar accounting* and *current cost/nominal-dollar accounting*. Sometimes called "general price level–adjusted accounting" or "general purchasing-power accounting."

constant-dollar date. The time at which the *general purchasing power* of one *constant dollar* exactly equals the *general purchasing power* of one *nominal dollar*; that is, the date when C$1 = $1. When the constant-dollar date is midperiod, the nominal amounts of *revenues* and *expenses* spread evenly throughout the period equal their constant-dollar amounts but end-of-period *balance sheet* amounts measured in constant midperiod dollars differ from their nominal-dollar amounts. When the constant-dollar date is at the end of the period, the constant-dollar amounts equal the nominal-dollar amounts on a balance sheet for that date.

constrained share company. Canada: a public company whose *charter* specifies that people who are Canadian citizens or who are corporations resident in Canada must own a prescribed percentage of the shares.

constructive liability. *FASB's* term for an item recorded as an accounting *liability*, which the firm has no obligation to pay but intends to pay. An example is the liability with related *expense* that management establishes for future cash payments for severance payments for employees it intends to discharge in a restructuring.

constructive receipt. An item included in taxable income when the taxpayer can control funds whether or not it has received cash. For example, *interest* added to *principal* in a savings account is constructively received.

Consumer Price Index (CPI). A *price index* computed and issued monthly by the Bureau of Labor Statistics of the U.S. Department of Labor. The index attempts to track the price level of a group of goods and services purchased by the average consumer. The CPI is used in *constant-dollar accounting*.

contingency. A potential *liability*. If a specified event occurs, such as a firm's losing a lawsuit, it would recognize a liability. The notes disclose the contingency, but so long as it remains contingent, it does not appear in the balance sheet. *SFAS No. 5* requires treatment as a contingency until the outcome is "probable" and the amount of payment can be reasonably estimated, perhaps within a range. When the outcome becomes probable (the future event is "likely" to occur) and the firm can reasonably estimate the amount (using the lower end of a range if it can estimate only a range), then the firm recognizes a liability in the accounts, rather than just disclosing it. A *material* contingency may lead to a qualified, "*subject to*" auditor's opinion. Firms do not record *gain* contingencies in the accounts but merely disclose them in notes.

contingent annuity. An *annuity* whose number of payments depends on the outcome of an event whose timing is uncertain at the time the annuity begins; for example, an annuity payable until death of the *annuitant*. Contrast with *annuity certain*.

contingent issue (securities). Securities issuable to specific individuals at the occurrence of some event, such as the firm's attaining a specified level of earnings.

contingent liability. *Contingency*. Avoid this term because it refers to something not (yet) a *liability* on the *balance sheet*.

continuing appropriation. A governmental *appropriation* automatically renewed without further legislative action until altered or revoked or expended.

continuing operations. See *income from continuing operations*.

continuity of operations. The assumption in accounting that the business *entity* will continue to operate long enough to carry out its current plans. The *going-concern assumption*.

continuous budget. A *budget* that adds a future period as the current period ends. This budget, then, always reports on the same number of periods.

continuous compounding. *Compound interest* in which the *compounding period* is every instant of time. See *e* for the computation of the equivalent annual or periodic rate.

continuous flow processing. Mass production of homogeneous products in a continuous flow. Companies manufacturing with continuous flow processes use *process costing* to account for product costs.

continuous improvement. Modern *total quality management (TQM)* practitioners believe that the process of seeking quality is never complete. This attitude reflects that assumption, seeking always to improve activities.

continuous inventory method. The *perpetual inventory* method.

Continuously Contemporary Accounting (CoCoA). A name coined by the Australian theorist Raymond J. Chambers to indicate a combination of *current value accounting* in which the *measuring unit* is *constant dollars* and the *attribute measured* is *exit value*.

contra account. An *account*, such as *accumulated depreciation*, that accumulates subtractions from another account, such as machinery. Contrast with *adjunct account*.

contributed capital. Name for the *owners' equity* account that represents amounts paid in, usually in *cash*, by owners; the sum of the balances in *capital stock* accounts plus *capital* *contributed in excess of par (or stated) value* accounts. Contrast with *donated capital.*

contributed surplus. An inferior term for *capital contributed in excess of par value.*

contribution approach. *Income statement* preparation method that reports *contribution margin*, by separating *variable costs* from *fixed costs*, in order to emphasize the importance of cost-behavior patterns for purposes of planning and control.

contribution margin. *Revenue* from *sales* less all variable *expenses*. Contrast with *gross margin.*

contribution margin ratio. *Contribution margin* divided by *net sales*; usually measured from the price and cost of a single unit; sometimes measured in total for companies with multiple products.

contribution per unit. Selling price less *variable costs* per unit.

contributory. Said of a *pension plan* in which employees, as well as employers, make payments to a pension *fund.* Note that the provisions for *vesting* apply only to the employer's payments. Whatever the degree of vesting of the employer's payments, employees typically gets back all their payments, with interest, in case of death or other cessation of employment before retirement.

control (controlling) account. A summary *account* with totals equal to those of entries and balances that appear in individual accounts in a *subsidiary ledger*. Accounts Receivable is a control account backed up with an account for each customer. Do not change the balance in a control account unless you make a corresponding change in one of the subsidiary accounts.

control charts. Presentations of warning signals that help management distinguish between random or routine variations in quality and variations that it should investigate. The presentations show the results of statistical process-control measures for a sample, batch or some other unit. These presentations depict variation in a process and its behavior over time. Management specifies an acceptable level of variation and plans to investigate the causes of deviations beyond that level.

control system. A device used by top management to ensure that lower-level management carries out its plans or to safeguard assets. Control designed for a single function within the firm is "operational control"; control designed for autonomous segments that generally have responsibility for both revenues and costs is "divisional control"; control designed for activities of the firm as a whole is "companywide control." Systems designed for safeguarding *assets* are "internal control" systems.

controllable cost. A *cost* influenced by the way a firm carries out operations. For example, marketing executives control advertising costs. These costs can be *fixed* or *variable.* See *programmed costs* and managed costs.

controlled company. A company in which an individual or corporation holds a majority of the voting shares. An owner can sometimes exercise effective control even though it owns less than 50 percent of the shares.

controller. A title for the chief accountant of an organization; often spelled *comptroller* when used to identify that person in a government or not-for-profit entity.

conversion. The act of exchanging a convertible security for another security.

conversion audit. An examination of changeover procedures, and new accounting procedures and files, that takes place when a significant change in the accounting system (e.g., a change from a manual to a computerized system or a change of computers) occurs.

conversion cost. *Direct labor* costs plus factory *overhead* costs incurred in producing a product; that is, the cost to convert raw materials to finished products. *Manufacturing cost.*

conversion period. *Compounding period;* also, period during which the holder of a *convertible bond* or *convertible preferred stock* can convert it into *common shares.*

convertible bond. A *bond* whose owner may convert it into a specified number of shares of *capital stock* during the *conversion period.*

convertible preferred stock. *Preferred shares* whose owner may convert them into a specified number of *common shares.*

cookie-jar accounting. A name, most prominently used by a chairman of the *SEC,* to indicate the practice of reporting lower *income* in an early period, so that management, at its discretion, can report higher income in a later period. Consider, for example, the entry to estimate *warranty costs* for products sold. The *journal entry debits* an *expense account,* reducing income, and *credits* a *liability* account. In some later period, the firm can debit a warranty cost to the liability account, not to an expense account, relieving that later period of the income reduction that an expense would have caused. See *quality of earnings.* Often, users refer to the excess liability amount, the amount in the cookie jar, later available for income enhancement, as a "reserve." See *reserve* for our warnings about using that word in any context.

cooperative. An incorporated organization formed for the benefit of its members (owners), who are either producers or consumers, in order to acquire for them profits or savings that otherwise accrue to middlemen. Members exercise control on the basis of one vote per member.

coproduct. A product that shares production facilities with another product. For example, if an apparel manufacturer produces shirts and jeans on the same line, these are coproducts. Distinguish coproducts from *joint products* and *byproducts* that, by their very nature, a firm must produce together, such as the various grades of wood a lumber factory produces.

copyright. Exclusive right granted by the government to an individual author, composer, playwright, or the like for the life of the individual plus 50 years. If a firm receives the copyright, then the right extends 75 years after the original publication. The *economic life* of a copyright can be less than the legal life, such as, for example, the copyright of this book.

core deposit intangible. A bank borrows funds from its customers, called "depositors," who open checking and savings accounts. Those depositors can take out their funds at any time, but usually don't. The amount that depositors leave on deposit for long periods of time are called "core deposits." The bank lends those funds to other customers, called "borrowers," at *interest rates* larger than the amount it pays the depositors for the funds. (For checking accounts, the rate the bank pays depositors is often zero.) The fact that the depositors can remove their funds at any time, but, on average, leave amounts on deposit relatively permanently means that the bank can lend those funds for relatively long periods of time, usually at higher interest rates, than it can charge for shorter-term loans. (See *yield curve.*) The bank's ability to borrow from some customers at a low rate and lend to other customers at a high rate creates wealth for the bank. Bankers and banking analysts call this wealth the "core deposit intangible." It represents an *asset* not recognized in the financial statements by the bank that created with wealth, although some *SEC* commissioners have expressed the thought that accounting should recognize such items as assets. When one bank buys another in a *purchase*, however, it will pay for this asset and will record it as an asset. Usually, the acquiring bank does not use the specific account title "Core Deposit Intangible," but instead uses the account title *Goodwill.*

corner. The control, of a quantity of shares or a commodity, sufficiently large that the holder can control the market price.

corporation. A legal entity authorized by a state to operate under the rules of the entity's *charter.*

correcting entry. An *adjusting entry* that properly records a previously, improperly recorded *transaction.* Do not confuse with entries that correct *accounting errors.*

correction of errors. See *accounting errors.*

cost. The sacrifice, measured by the *price* paid or to be paid, to acquire *goods* or *services.* See *acquisition cost* and *replacement cost.* Terminology often uses "cost" when referring to the valuation of a good or service acquired. When writers use the word in this sense, a cost is an *asset.* When the benefits of the acquisition (the goods or services acquired) expire, the cost becomes an *expense* or *loss.* Some writers, however, use "cost" and "expense" as synonyms. Contrast with *expense.* The word "cost" appears in more than 50 accounting terms, each with sometimes subtle distinctions in meaning. See *cost terminology* for elaboration. Clarity requires that the user include with the word "cost" an adjective or phrase to be clear about intended meaning.

cost accounting. Classifying, summarizing, recording, reporting, and allocating current or predicted *costs;* a subset of *managerial accounting.*

Cost Accounting Standards Board. See *CASB.*

cost accumulation. Bringing together, usually in a single *account,* all *costs* of a specified activity. Contrast with *cost allocation.*

cost allocation. Assigning *costs* to individual products or time periods. Contrast with *cost accumulation.*

cost-based transfer price. A *transfer price* based on *historical costs.*

cost behavior. The functional relation between changes in activity and changes in *cost;* for example: *fixed* versus *variable costs*; *linear* versus *curvilinear cost.*

cost–benefit criterion. Some measure of *costs* compared with some measure of *benefits* for a proposed undertaking. If the costs exceed the benefits, then the analyst judges the undertaking not worthwhile. This criterion will not yield good decisions unless the analyst estimates all costs and benefits flowing from the undertaking.

cost center. A unit of activity for which a firm accumulates *expenditures* and *expenses.*

cost driver. A factor that causes an activity's costs. See *driver* and *activity basis.*

cost driver rate. Rate at which the *cost driver* causes *costs.*

cost-effective. Among alternatives, the one whose benefit, or payoff, per unit of cost is highest; sometimes said of an action whose expected benefits exceed expected costs whether or not other alternatives exist with larger cost–benefit ratios.

cost estimation. The process of measuring the functional relation between changes in activity levels and changes in cost.

cost flow assumption. See *flow assumption.*

cost-flow equation. Beginning balance + Transfers in = Transfers out + Ending balance

$$BB + TI = TO + EB.$$

cost flows. Costs passing through various classifications within an entity. See *flow of costs* for a diagram.

cost hierarchy. Categorizes costs according to whether they are *capacity, product, customer, batch* or *unit costs.*

cost method (for investments). In accounting for an investment in the *capital stock* or *bonds* of another company, method in which the firm shows the investment at *acquisition cost* and treats only *dividends* declared or *interest receivable* as *revenue;* not allowed by *GAAP*.

cost method (for treasury stock). The method of showing *treasury stock* in a *contra account* to all other items of *shareholders' equity* in an amount equal to that paid to reacquire the stock.

cost object(ive). Any activity for which management desires a separate measurement of *costs*. Examples include departments, products, and territories.

cost of capital. *Opportunity cost* of funds invested in a business; the rate of return that rational owners require an asset to earn before they will devote that asset to a particular purpose; sometimes measured as the average annual rate that a company must pay for its *equities*. In *efficient capital markets*, this cost is the *discount rate* that equates the expected *present value* of all future cash flows to common shareholders with the market value of common stock at a given time. Analysts often measure the cost of capital by taking a *weighted average* of the firm's *debt* and various *equity securities*. We sometimes call the measurement so derived the "composite cost of capital," and some analysts confuse this measurement of the cost of capital with the cost of capital itself. For example, if the equities of a firm include substantial amounts for the *deferred income tax liability*, the composite cost of capital will underestimate the true cost of capital, the required rate of return on a firm's assets, because the deferred income tax liability has no explicit cost.

cost of goods manufactured. The sum of all costs allocated to products completed during a period, including materials, labor, and *overhead*.

cost of goods purchased. Net purchase price of goods acquired plus costs of storage and delivery to the place where the owner can productively use the items.

cost of goods sold. Inventoriable *costs* that firms *expense* because they sold the units; equals *beginning inventory* plus *cost of goods purchased* or *manufactured* minus *ending inventory*.

cost of sales. Generally refers to *cost of goods sold,* occasionally to *selling expenses*.

cost or market, whichever is lower. See *lower of cost or market*.

cost percentage. One less *markup percentage; cost* of *goods available for sale* divided by selling prices of goods available for sale (when FIFO is used); *cost* of *purchases* divided by selling prices of purchases (when LIFO is used). See *markup* for further detail on inclusions in the calculation of cost percentage.

cost-plus transfer pricing. *Transfer price* equal to the *cost* of the transferred product plus a *markup*.

cost pool. *Indirect cost pool;* groupings or aggregations of costs, usually for subsequent analysis.

cost principle. The *principle* that requires reporting *assets* at *historical* or *acquisition cost*, less accumulated *amortization*. This principle relies on the assumption that cost equals *fair market value* at the date of acquisition and that subsequent changes are not likely to be significant.

cost-recovery-first method. A method of *revenue* recognition that *credits inventory* as the firm receives cash collections and continues until the firm has collected cash equal to the sum of all costs. Only after the firm has collected cash equal to costs does it recognize *income*. A firm may not use this method in financial reporting unless the total amount of collections is highly uncertain. It is never allowed for income tax reporting. Contrast with the *installment method*, allowed for both book and tax, in which the firm credits *constant* proportions of each cash collection both to cost and to income.

cost sheet. Statement that shows all the elements composing the total cost of an item.

cost structure. For a given set of total costs, the percentages of fixed and variable costs, typically two percentages adding to 100 percent.

cost terminology. The word "cost" appears in many accounting terms. Exhibit 1-2 classifies some of these terms according to the distinctions between the terms in accounting usage. Joel Dean was, to our knowledge, the first to attempt such distinctions; we have used some of his ideas here. We discuss some of the terms in more detail under their own listings.

TERMS (SYNONYMS GIVEN IN PARENTHESES)			DISTINCTIONS AND COMMENTS
1. The following pairs of terms distinguish the basis measured in accounting.			
Historical Cost (Acquisition Cost)	vs.	Current Cost	A distinction used in financial accounting. Current cost can be used more specifically to mean replacement cost, net realizable value, or present value of cash flows. "Current cost" is often used narrowly to mean replacement cost.
Historical Cost (Actual Cost)	vs.	Standard Cost	The distinction between historical and standard costs arises in product costing for inventory valuation. Some systems record actual costs while others record the standard costs.
2. The following pairs of terms denote various distinctions among historical costs. For each pair of terms, the sum of the two kinds of costs equals total historical cost used in financial reporting.			
Variable Cost	vs.	Fixed Cost (Constant Cost)	Distinction used in breakeven analysis and in designing cost accounting systems, particularly for product costing. See (4), below, for a further subdivision of fixed costs and (5), below, for the economic distinction between marginal and average cost closely paralleling this one.
Traceable Cost	vs.	Common Cost (Joint Cost)	Distinction arises in allocating manufacturing costs to product. Common costs are allocated to product, but the allocations are more-or-less arbitrary. The distinction also arises in segment reporting and in separating manufacturing from nonmanufacturing costs.
Direct Cost	vs.	Indirect Cost	Distinction arises in designing cost accounting systems and in product costing. Direct costs can be traced directly to a cost object (e.g., a product, a responsibility center), whereas indirect costs cannot.
Out-of-Pocket Cost (Outlay Cost; Cash Cost)	vs.	Book Cost	Virtually all costs recorded in financial statements require a cash outlay at one time or another. The distinction here separates expenditures to occur in the future from those already made and is used in making decisions. Book costs, such as for depreciation, reduce income without requiring a future outlay of cash. The cash has already been spent. See future v. past costs in (5), below.

EXHIBIT 1.2 COST TERMINOLOGY: DISTINCTIONS AMONG TERMS CONTAINING THE WORD "COST"

TERMS (SYNONYMS GIVEN IN PARENTHESES)			DISTINCTIONS AND COMMENTS
Incremental Cost (Marginal Cost; Differential Cost)	vs.	Unavoidable Cost (Inescapable Cost; Sunk Cost)	Distinction used in making decisions. Incremental costs will be incurred (or saved) if a decision is made to go ahead (or to stop) some activity, but not otherwise. Unavoidable costs will be reported in financial statements whether the decision is made to go ahead or not, because cash has already been spent or committed. Not all unavoidable costs are book costs, as, for example, a salary promised but not yet earned, that will be paid even if a no-go decision is made. The economist restricts the term *marginal cost* to the cost of producing one more unit. Thus the next unit has a marginal cost; the next week's output has an incremental cost. If a firm produces and sells a new product, the related new costs would properly be called incremental, not marginal. If a factory is closed, the costs saved are incremental, not marginal.
Escapable Cost	vs.	Inescapable Cost (Unavoidable Cost)	Same distinction as incremental v. sunk costs, but this pair is used only when the decision maker is considering stopping something-ceasing to produce a product, closing a factory, or the like. See next pair.
Avoidable Cost	vs.	Unavoidable Cost	A distinction sometimes used in discussing the merits of variable and absorption costing. Avoidable costs are treated as product cost and unavoidable costs are treated as period expenses under variable costing.
Controllable Cost	vs.	Uncontrollable Cost	The distinction here is used in assigning responsibility and in setting bonus or incentive plans. All costs can be affected by someone in the entity; those who design incentive schemes attempt to hold a person responsible for a cost only if that person can influence the amount of the cost.
3. In each of the following pairs, used in historical cost accounting, the word "cost" appears in one of the terms where "expense" is meant.			
Expired Cost	vs.	Unexpired Cost	The distinction is between *expense* and *asset*.
Product Cost	vs.	Period Cost	The terms distinguish product cost from period expense. When a given asset is used, is its cost converted into work in process and then finished goods on the balance sheet until the goods are sold or is it an expense shown on this period's income statement? Product costs appear on the income statement as part of cost of goods sold in the period when the goods are sold. Period expenses appear on the income statement with an appropriate caption for the item in the period when the cost is incurred or recognized.

EXHIBIT 1.2 COST TERMINOLOGY: DISTINCTIONS AMONG TERMS CONTAINING THE WORD "COST" *(CONTINUED)*

TERMS (SYNONYMS GIVEN IN PARENTHESES)			DISTINCTIONS AND COMMENTS

4. The following subdivisions of fixed (historical) costs are used in analyzing operations. The relation between the components of fixed costs is:

Fixed Costs = Capacity Costs + Programmed Costs

Fixed Costs = Semifixed Costs + Fixed Portions of Semi-variable Costs + "Pure" Fixed Costs

Capacity Costs = Standby Costs + Enabling Costs

Capacity Cost (Committed Cost)	vs.	Programmed Cost (Managed Cost; Discretionary Cost)	Capacity costs give a firm the capability to produce or to sell. Programmed costs, such as for advertising or research and development, may not be essential, but once a decision to incur them is made, they become fixed costs.
Standby Cost	vs.	Enabling Cost	Standby costs will be incurred whether capacity, once acquired, is used or not, such as property taxes and depreciation on a factory. Enabling costs, such as for a security force, can be avoided if the capacity is unused.
Semifixed Cost	vs.	Semivariable Cost	A cost fixed over a wide range but that can change at various levels is a semifixed cost or "step cost." An example is the cost of rail lines from the factory to the main rail line where fixed cost depends on whether there are one or two parallel lines, but are independent of the number of trains run per day. Semivariable costs combine a strictly fixed component cost plus a variable component. Telephone charges usually have a fixed monthly component plus a charge related to usage.

5. The following pairs of terms distinguish among economic uses or decision-making uses or regulatory uses of cost terms.

Fully Absorbed Cost	vs.	Variable Cost (Direct Cost)	Fully absorbed costs refer to costs where fixed costs have been allocated to units or departments as required by generally accepted accounting principles. Variable costs, in contrast, may be more relevant for making decisions, such as in setting prices.
Fully Absorbed Cost	vs.	Full Cost	In full costing, all costs, manufacturing costs as well as central corporate expenses (including financing expenses) are allocated to product or divisions. In full absorption costing, only manufacturing costs are allocated to product. Only in full costing will revenues, expenses, and income summed over all products or divisions equal corporate revenues, expenses, and income.

Exhibit 1.2 Cost Terminology: Distinctions among Terms Containing the Word "Cost" *(Continued)*

TERMS (SYNONYMS GIVEN IN PARENTHESES)			DISTINCTIONS AND COMMENTS
Opportunity Cost	vs.	Outlay Cost (Out-of-Pocket Cost)	Opportunity cost refers to the economic benefit foregone by using a resource for one purpose instead of for another. The outlay cost of the resource will be recorded in financial records. The distinction arises because a resource is already in the possession of the entity with a recorded historical cost. Its economic value to the firm, opportunity cost, generally differs from the historical cost; it can be either larger or smaller.
Future Cost	vs.	Past Cost	Effective decision making analyzes only present and future outlay costs, or out-of-pocket costs. Opportunity costs are relevant for profit maximizing; past costs are used in financial reporting.
Short-Run Cost	vs.	Long-Run Cost	Short-run costs vary as output is varied for a given configuration of plant and equipment. Long-run costs can be incurred to change that configuration. This pair of terms is the economic analog of the accounting pair, see (2) above, variable and fixed costs. The analogy is not perfect because some short-run costs are fixed, such as property taxes on the factory, from the point of view of breakeven analysis.
Imputed Cost	vs.	Book Cost	In a regulatory setting some costs, for example the cost of owners' equity capital, are calculated and used for various purposes; these are imputed costs. Imputed costs are not recorded in the historical costs accounting records for financial reporting. Book costs are recorded.
Average Cost	vs.	Marginal Cost	The economic distinction equivalent to fully absorbed cost of product and variable cost of product. Average cost is total cost divided by number of units. Marginal cost is the cost to produce the next unit (or the last unit).
Differential Cost (Incremental Cost)	vs.	Variable Cost	Whether a cost changes or remains fixed depends on the activity basis being considered. Typically, but not invariably, costs are said to be variable or fixed with respect to an activity basis such as changes in production levels. Typically, but not invariably, costs are said to be incremental or not with respect to an activity basis such as the undertaking of some new venture. For example, consider the decision to undertake the production of food processors, rather than food blenders, which the manufacturer has been making. To produce processors requires the acquisition of a new machine tool. The cost of the new machine tool is incremental with respect to a decision to produce food processors instead of food blenders, but, once acquired, becomes a fixed cost of producing food processors. If costs of direct labor hours are going

Exhibit 1.2 Cost Terminology: Distinctions among Terms Containing the Word "Cost" *(Continued)*

TERMS (SYNONYMS GIVEN IN PARENTHESES)	DISTINCTIONS AND COMMENTS
	to be incurred for the production of food processors or food blenders, whichever is produced (in a scenario when not both are to be produced), such costs are variable with respect to production measured in units, but not incremental with respect to the decision to produce processors rather than blenders. This distinction is often blurred in practice, so a careful understanding of the activity basis being considered is necessary for understanding of the concepts being used in a particular application.

EXHIBIT 1.2 COST TERMINOLOGY: DISTINCTIONS AMONG TERMS CONTAINING THE WORD "COST" *(CONTINUED)*

cost-to-cost. The *percentage-of-completion method* in which the firm estimates the fraction of completion as the ratio of costs incurred to date divided by the total costs the firm expects to incur for the entire project.

cost-volume-profit analysis. A study of the sensitivity of *profits* to changes in units sold (or produced) or costs or prices.

cost-volume-profit graph (chart). A graph that shows the relation between *fixed costs, contribution per unit, breakeven point*, and *sales*. See *breakeven chart*.

costing. The process of calculating the cost of activities, products, or services; the British word for *cost accounting*.

counterparty. The term refers to the opposite party in a legal contract. In accounting and finance, a frequent usage arises when an entity purchases (or sells) a *derivative* financial contract, such as an *option, forward contract,* and *futures contract.*

coupon. That portion of a *bond* document redeemable at a specified date for payments. Its physical form resembles a series of tickets; each coupon has a date, and the holder either deposits it at a bank, just like a check, for collection or mails it to the issuer's agent for collection.

coupon rate. Of a *bond,* the total dollar amount of coupons paid in any one year divided by par value. Contrast with *effective rate*.

covenant. A promise with legal validity. A loan covenant specifies the terms under which the lender can force the borrower to repay funds otherwise not yet due. For example, a *bond* covenant might say that the *principal* of a bond issue falls due on December 31, 2010, unless the firm's *debt-equity ratio* falls below 40 percent, in which case the amount becomes due immediately.

CPA. See *certified public accountant.* The *AICPA* suggests that no periods appear in the abbreviation.

CPI. *Consumer price index.*

CPP. Current purchasing power; usually used, primarily in the United Kingdom, as an adjective modifying the word "accounting" to mean the accounting that produces *constant-dollar financial statements*.

Cr. Abbreviation for *credit,* always with initial capital letter. Quiz: What do you suppose *Cr.* stands for? For the answer, see *Dr.*

creative accounting. Selection of *accounting principles* and interpretation of transactions or events designed to manipulate, typically to increase but sometimes merely to smooth, reported *income from continuing operations;* one form of *fraudulent financial reporting*. Many attempts at creative accounting involve premature *revenue recognition*.

credit. As a noun, an entry on the right-hand side of an *account;* as a verb, to make an entry on the right-hand side of an account; records increases in *liabilities, owners' equity, revenues*, and *gains*; records decreases in *assets* and *expenses*. See *debit and credit conventions*. This term also refers to the ability or right to buy or borrow in return for a promise to pay later.

credit bureau. An organization that gathers and evaluates data on the ability of a person to meet financial obligations and sells this information to its clients.

credit loss. The amount of accounts receivable that the firm finds, or expects to find, *uncollectible*.

credit memorandum. A document used by a seller to inform a buyer that the seller is crediting (reducing) the buyer's account receivable because of *errors, returns*, or *allowances;* also, the document provided by a bank to a depositor to indicate that the bank is increasing the depositor's balance because of some event other than a deposit, such as the collection by the bank of the depositor's *note receivable*.

creditor. One who lends. In the United Kingdom, *accounts payables. See Dr.*

critical accounting judgments. All numbers on a *balance sheet,* except the date, require some judgment or estimate. (The previous sentence passes for a joke in accounting.) The SEC requires that management in its annual report to shareholders identify the accounting issues whose judgments and estimates have potential for significant effect on *earnings* and *financial position.* Examples include *inventory valuation, measurement of goodwill impairment,* accounting for *hedges,* and *revenue recognition*.

critical path method (CPM). A method of *network analysis* in which the analyst estimates normal duration time for each activity within a project. The critical path identifies the shortest completion period based on the most time-consuming sequence of activities from the beginning to the end of the network. Compare *PERT.*

critical success factors. The important things a company must do to be successful; may vary from one company to another.

cross-reference (index). A number placed beside each *account* in a *journal entry* indicating the *ledger* account to which the record keeper posted the entry and placing in the ledger the page number of the journal where the record keeper first recorded the journal entry; used to link the *debit* and *credit* parts of an entry in the ledger accounts back to the original entry in the journal. See *audit trail.*

cross-section analysis. Analysis of *financial statements* of various firms for a single period of time; contrast with *time-series analysis,* in which analysts examine statements of a given firm for several periods of time.

Crown corporation. Canada and United Kingdom: a corporation that is ultimately accountable, through a minister of the Crown, to Parliament or a legislature for the conduct of its affairs.

cum div, (dividend). The condition of shares whose quoted market price includes a declared but unpaid dividend. This condition pertains between the declaration date of the dividend and the record date. Compare *ex div. (dividend).*

cum rights. The condition of securities whose quoted market price includes the right to purchase new securities. Compare *ex rights.*

cumulative dividend. Preferred stock *dividends* that, if not paid, accrue as a commitment that the firm must pay before it can declare dividends to common shareholders.

cumulative preferred shares. *Preferred* shares with *cumulative dividend* rights.

current assets. *Cash* and other *assets* that a firm expects to turn into cash, sell, or exchange within the normal operating cycle of the firm or one year, whichever is longer. One year is the usual period for classifying asset balances on the balance sheet. Current assets include *cash, marketable securities, receivables, inventory,* and *current prepayments.*

current cost. *Cost* stated in terms of current values (of *productive capacity*) rather than in terms of *acquisition cost.* See *net realizable value* and *current selling price.*

current cost accounting. The *FASB's* term for *financial statements* in which the *attribute measured* is *current cost.*

current cost/nominal-dollar accounting. Accounting based on *current cost* valuations measured in *nominal dollars.* Components of *income* include an *operating margin* and *holding gains and losses.*

current exchange rate. The rate at which the holder of one unit of currency can convert it into another at the end of the *accounting period* being reported on or, for *revenues, expenses, gains,* and *losses,* the date of recognition of the transaction.

current exit value. *Exit value.*

current fund. In governmental accounting, a synonym for *general fund.*

current funds. *Cash* and other assets readily convertible into cash; in governmental accounting, funds spent for operating purposes during the current period; includes *general,* special revenue, *debt service,* and *enterprise funds.*

current (gross) margin. See *operating margin based on current costs.*

current liability. A debt or other obligation that a firm must discharge within a short time, usually the *earnings cycle* or one year, normally by expending *current assets.*

current operating performance concept. The notion that reported *income* for a period ought to reflect only ordinary, normal, and recurring operations of that period. A consequence is that *extraordinary* and nonrecurring items are entered directly in the Retained Earnings account. Contrast with *clean surplus concept.* This concept is no longer acceptable. (See *APB Opinion No. 9* and *No. 30.*)

current ratio. Sum of *current assets* divided by sum of *current liabilities.* See *ratio.*

current realizable value. *Realizable value.*

current replacement cost. Of an *asset,* the amount currently required to acquire an identical asset (in the same condition and with the same service potential) or an asset capable of rendering the same service at a current *fair market price.* If these two amounts differ, use the lower. Contrast with *reproduction cost.*

current selling price. The amount for which an *asset* could be sold as of a given time in an *arm's-length* transaction rather than in a forced sale.

current service costs. *Service costs* of a *pension plan.*

current value accounting. The form of accounting in which all assets appear at *current replacement cost (entry value)* or *current selling price* or *net realizable value (exit value)* and all *liabilities* appear at *present value.* Entry and exit values may differ from each other, so theorists have not agreed on the precise meaning of "current value accounting."

current yield. Of a *bond,* the annual amount of *coupons* divided by the current market price of the bond. Contrast with *yield to maturity.*

currently attainable standard cost. *Normal standard cost.*

curvilinear (variable) cost. A continuous, but not necessarily linear (straight-line), functional relation between activity levels and *costs.*

customer-level activities. Work performed to meet the needs of a specific customer, aggregated over all customers.

customer response time. Period that elapses from the moment a customer places an order for a product or requests service to the moment the firm delivers the product or service to the customer.

customers' ledger. The *ledger* that shows *accounts receivable* of individual customers. It is the *subsidiary ledger* for the *control account* Accounts Receivable.

cutoff rate. *Hurdle rate.*

D

data bank. An organized file of information, such as a customer name and address file, used in and kept up-to-date by a processing system.

database. A comprehensive collection of interrelated information stored together in computerized form to serve several applications.

database management system. Generalized software programs used to handle physical storage and manipulation of databases.

days of average inventory on hand. See *ratio.*

days of grace. The days allowed by law or contract for payment of a debt after its due date.

DCF. *Discounted cash flow.*

DDB. *Double declining-balance depreciation.*

debenture bond. A *bond* not secured with *collateral.*

debit. As a noun, an entry on the left-hand side of an *account;* as a verb, to make an entry on the left-hand side of an account; records increases in *assets* and *expenses*; records decreases in *liabilities, owners' equity*, and *revenues*. See *debit and credit conventions*.

debit and credit conventions. The conventional use of the *T-account* form and the rules for debit and credit in *balance sheet accounts* (see below). The equality of the two sides of the *accounting equation* results from recording equal amounts of *debits* and *credits* for each *transaction.*

Typical Asset Account

Opening Balance	
Increase	Decrease
+	–
Dr.	Cr.
Ending Balance	

Typical Liability Account

	Opening Balance
Decrease	Increase
–	+
Dr.	Cr.
	Ending Balance

Typical Owners' Equity Account

	Opening Balance
Decrease	Increase
–	+
Dr.	Cr.
	Ending Balance

Revenue and expense accounts belong to the owners' equity group. The relation and the rules for debit and credit in these accounts take the following form:

Owners' Equity

Decrease	Increase
–	+
Dr.	Cr.

Expenses

Dr.	Cr.
+	–
*	

Revenues

Dr.	Cr.
–	+
	*

*Normal balance before closing

debit memorandum. A document used by a seller to inform a buyer that the seller is debiting (increasing) the amount of the buyer's *accounts receivable*. Also, the document provided by a bank to a depositor to indicate that the bank is decreasing the depositor's *balance* because of some event other than payment for a *check*, such as monthly service charges or the printing of checks.

debt. An amount owed. The general name for *notes, bonds, mortgages*, and the like that provide evidence of amounts owed and have definite payment dates.

debt capital. *Noncurrent liabilities.* See *debt financing,* and contrast with *equity financing*.

debt-equity ratio. Total *liabilities* divided by total equities. See *ratio*. Some analysts put only total shareholders' equity in the denominator. Some analysts restrict the numerator to *long-term debt*.

debt financing. *Leverage.* Raising *funds* by issuing *bonds, mortgages*, or *notes*. Contrast with *equity financing*.

debt guarantee. See *guarantee*.

debt ratio. *Debt-equity ratio.*

debt service fund. In governmental accounting, a *fund* established to account for payment of *interest* and *principal* on all general-obligation *debt* other than that payable from special *assessments*.

debt service payment. The payment required by a lending agreement, such as periodic coupon payment on a bond or installment payment on a loan or a lease payment. It is sometimes called "interest payment," but this term will mislead the unwary. Only rarely will the amount of a debt service payment equal the interest expense for the period preceding the payment. A debt service payment will always include some amount for interest, but the payment will usually differ from the interest expense.

debt service requirement. The amount of cash required for payments of *interest*, current maturities of *principal* on outstanding *debt*, and payments to *sinking funds* (corporations) or to the debt service fund (governmental).

debtor. One who borrows; in the United Kingdom, *accounts receivable.*

decentralized decision making. Management practice in which a firm gives a manager of a business unit responsibility for that unit's *revenues* and *costs*, freeing the manager to make decisions about prices, sources of supply, and the like, as though the unit were a separate business that the manager owns. See *responsibility accounting* and *transfer price.*

declaration date. Time when the *board of directors* declares a *dividend.*

declining-balance depreciation. The method of calculating the periodic *depreciation* charge by multiplying the *book value* at the start of the period by a constant percentage. In pure declining-balance depreciation, the constant percentage is $1 - \sqrt[n]{s/c}$, where *n* is the *depreciable life*, *s* is *salvage value*, and *c* is *acquisition cost.* See *double declining-balance depreciation*.

deep discount bonds. Said of *bonds* selling much below (exactly how much is not clear) *par value*.

defalcation. Embezzlement.

default. Failure to pay *interest* or *principal* on a *debt* when due.

defeasance. Transaction with the economic effect of *debt retirement* that does not retire the debt. When *interest rates* increase, many firms find that the *market value* of their outstanding *debt* has dropped substantially below its *book value*. In *historical cost accounting* for debt retirements, retiring debt with a *cash* payment less than the book value of the debt results in a gain (generally, an *extraordinary item*). Many firms would like to retire the outstanding debt issues and report the gain. Two factors impede doing so: (1) the gain can be a taxable event generating adverse *income tax* consequences; and (2) the transaction costs in retiring all the debt can be large, in part because the firm cannot easily locate all the debt holders or persuade them to sell back their bonds to the issuer. The process of "defeasance" serves as the economic equivalent to retiring a debt issue while it saves the issuer from experiencing adverse tax consequences and from actually having to locate and retire the bonds. The process works as follows. The debt-issuing firm turns over to an independent trustee, such as a bank, amounts of cash or low-risk government bonds sufficient to make all debt service payments on the outstanding debt, including bond retirements, in return for the trustee's commitment to make all debt service payments. The debt issuer effectively retires the outstanding debt. It debits the liability account, credits Cash or Marketable Securities as appropriate, and credits Extraordinary Gain on Debt Retirement. The trustee can retire debt or make debt service payments, whichever it chooses. For income tax purposes, however, the firm's debt remains outstanding. The firm will have taxable interest *deductions* for its still-outstanding debt and taxable interest *revenue* on the investments held by the trustee for debt service. In law, the term "defeasance" means "a rendering null and void." This process renders the outstanding debt economically null and void, without causing a taxable event.

defensive interval. A financial *ratio* equal to the number of days of normal cash *expenditures* covered by *quick assets*. It is defined as follows:

$$\frac{\text{Quick Assets}}{\text{(All Expenses Except Amortization and Others Not Using Funds} \div 365)}$$

The denominator of the ratio is the cash expenditure per day. Analysts have found this ratio useful in predicting *bankruptcy*.

deferral. The accounting process concerned with past *cash receipts* and *payments*; in contrast to *accrual;* recognizing a liability resulting from a current cash receipt (as for magazines to be delivered) or recognizing an asset from a current cash payment (as for prepaid insurance or a long-term depreciable asset).

deferral method. See *flow-through method* (of accounting for the *investment credit*) for definition and contrast.

deferred annuity. An *annuity* whose first payment occurs sometime after the end of the first period.

deferred asset. *Deferred charge.*

deferred charge. *Expenditure* not recognized as an *expense* of the period when made but carried forward as an *asset* to be *written off* in future periods, such as for advance rent payments or insurance premiums. See *deferral.*

deferred cost. *Deferred charge.*

deferred credit. Sometimes used to indicate *advances from customers.*

deferred debit. *Deferred charge.*

deferred expense. *Deferred charge.*

deferred gross margin. *Unrealized gross margin.*

deferred income. *Advances from customers.*

deferred income tax (liability). An *indeterminate-term liability* that arises when the pretax income shown on the tax return is less than what it would have been had the firm used the same *accounting principles* and *cost basis* for *assets* and *liabilities* in tax returns as it used for financial reporting. *SFAS No. 109* requires that the firm debit income tax *expense* and credit deferred income tax with the amount of the taxes delayed by using accounting principles in tax returns different from those used in financial reports. See *temporary difference*, *timing difference*, *permanent difference,* and *installment sales.* If, as a result of temporary differences, cumulative taxable income exceeds cumulative reported income before taxes, the deferred income tax account will have a *debit* balance, which the firm will report as a *deferred charge.*

deferred revenue. Sometimes used to indicate *advances from customers.*

deferred tax. See *deferred income tax.*

deficit. A *debit balance* in the Retained Earnings account; presented on the balance sheet in a *contra account* to *shareholders' equity*; sometimes used to mean negative *net income* for a period.

defined-benefit plan. A *pension plan* in which the employer promises specific dollar amounts to each eligible employee; the amounts usually depend on a formula that takes into account such things as the employee's earnings, years of employment, and age. The employer adjusts its cash contributions and pension expense to *actuarial* experience in the eligible employee group and investment performance of the pension *fund.* This is sometimes called a "fixed-benefit" pension plan. Contrast with *money purchase plan.*

defined-contribution plan. A *money purchase (pension) plan* or other arrangement, based on formula or discretion, in which the employer makes cash contributions to eligible individual employee *accounts* under the terms of a written plan document. The trustee of the funds in the account manages the funds, and the employee-beneficiary receives at retirement (or at some other agreed time) the amount in the fund. The employer makes no promise about that amount. Profit-sharing pension plans are of this type.

deflation. A period of declining *general price-level changes.*

Delphi technique. Forecasting method in which members of the forecasting group prepare individual forecasts, share them anonymously with the rest of the group, and only then compare forecasts and resolve differences.

demand deposit. *Funds* in a *checking account* at a bank.

demand loan. See *term loan* for definition and contrast.

denial of opinion. Canada: the statement that an *auditor*, for reasons arising in the *audit*, is unable to express an opinion on whether the *financial statements* provide *fair presentation.*

denominator volume. Capacity measured in the number of units the firm expects to produce this period; when divided into *budgeted fixed costs*, results in fixed costs applied per unit of product.

department(al) allocation. Obtained by first accumulating *costs* in *cost pools* for each department and then, using separate rates, or sets of rates, for each department, allocating from each cost pool to products produced in that department.

dependent variable. See *regression analysis.*

depletion. Exhaustion or *amortization* of a *wasting asset* or *natural resource.* Also see *percentage depletion.*

depletion allowance. See *percentage depletion.*

deposit intangible. See *core deposit intangible.*

deposit, sinking fund. Payments made to a *sinking fund.*

deposit method (of revenue recognition). A method of *revenue* recognition that is the same as the *completed sale* or *completed contract method.* In some contexts, such as when the customer has the right to return goods for a full refund or in retail land sales, the customer must make substantial payments while still having the right to back out of the deal and receive a refund. When the seller cannot predict with reasonable precision the amount of cash it will ultimately collect and when it will receive cash, the seller must *credit* Deposits, a *liability account*, rather than *revenue*. (In this regard, the accounting differs from that in the completed contract method, in which the account credited offsets the *Work-in-Process* inventory account.) When the *sale* becomes complete, the firm credits a revenue account and *debits* the Deposits account.

deposits (by customers). A *liability* that the firm *credits* when receiving *cash* (as in a bank, or in a grocery store when the customer pays for soda-pop bottles with cash to be repaid when the customer returns the bottles) and when the firm intends to discharge the liability by returning the cash. Contrast with the liability account *Advances from Customers*, which the firm credits on receipt of cash, expecting later to discharge the liability by delivering goods or services. When the firm delivers the goods or services, it credits a *revenue* account.

deposits in transit. Deposits made by a firm but not yet reflected on the *bank statement*.

depreciable cost. That part of the *cost* of an asset, usually *acquisition cost* less *salvage value*, that the firm will charge off over the life of the asset through the process of *depreciation*.

depreciable life. For an *asset*, the time period or units of activity (such as miles driven for a truck) over which the firm allocates the *depreciable cost*. For tax returns, depreciable life may be shorter than estimated *service life*.

depreciation. *Amortization of plant assets*; the process of allocating the cost of an asset to the periods of benefit—the *depreciable life;* classified as a *production cost* or a *period expense*, depending on the asset and whether the firm uses *full absorption* or *variable costing*. Depreciation methods described in this glossary include the *annuity method, appraisal method, composite method, compound interest method, declining-balance method, production method, replacement method, retirement method, straight-line method, sinking fund method*, and *sum-of-the-years'-digits method.*

depreciation reserve. An inferior term for *accumulated depreciation*. See *reserve*. Do not confuse with a replacement *fund.*

derivative (financial instrument). A financial instrument, such as an option to purchase a share of stock, created from another, such as a share of stock; an instrument, such as a *swap,* whose value depends on the value of another asset called the "underlying"—for example, the right to receive the difference between the interest payments on a fixed-rate five-year loan for \$1 million and the interest payments on a floating-rate five-year loan for \$1 million. To qualify as a derivative under *FASB* rules, *SFAS No. 133,* the instrument has one or more underlyings, and one or more notional amounts or payment provisions or both, it either does not require an initial net investment or it requires one smaller than would be required for other types of contracts expected to have a similar response to changes in market factors, and its terms permit settlement for cash in lieu of physical delivery or the instrument itself trades on an exchange. See also *forward contract* and *futures contract.*

Descartes' rule of signs. In a *capital budgeting* context, a rule that says a series of cash flows will have a nonnegative number of *internal rates of return*. The number equals the number of variations in the sign of the cash flow series or is less than that number by an even integer. Consider the following series of cash flows, the first occurring now and the others at subsequent yearly intervals: –100, –100, +50, +175, –50, +100. The internal rates of return are the numbers for r that satisfy the following equation:

$$-100 - \frac{100}{(1+r)} + \frac{50}{(1+r)^2} + \frac{175}{(1+r)^3} - \frac{50}{(1+r)^4} + \frac{100}{(1+r)^5} = 0.$$

The series of cash flows has three variations in sign: a change from minus to plus, a change from plus to minus, and a change from minus to plus. The rule says that this series must have either one or three internal rates of return; in fact, it has only one, about 12 percent. But also see *reinvestment rate*.

detection costs. See *appraisal costs*.

detective controls. *Internal controls* designed to detect, or maximize the chance of detection of, errors and other irregularities.

determination. See *determine*.

determine. A term often used (in our opinion, overused) by accountants and those who describe the accounting process. A leading dictionary associates the following meanings with the verb "determine": settle, decide, conclude, ascertain, cause, affect, control, impel, terminate, and decide upon. In addition, accounting writers can mean any one of the following: measure, allocate, report, calculate, compute, observe, choose, and legislate. In accounting, there are two distinct sets of meanings: those encompassed by the synonym "cause or legislate" and those encompassed by the synonym "measure." The first set of uses conveys the active notion of causing something to happen, and the second set of uses conveys the more passive notion of observing something that someone else has caused to happen. An accountant who speaks of cost or income "determination" generally means measurement or observation, not causation; management and economic conditions cause costs and income to be what they are. One who speaks of accounting principles "determination" can mean choosing or applying (as in "determining depreciation charges" from an allowable set) or causing to be acceptable (as in the *FASB*'s "determining" the accounting for *leases*). In the long run, income is cash-in less cash-out, so management and economic conditions "determine" (cause) income to be what it is. In the short run, reported income is a function of accounting principles chosen and applied, so the accountant "determines" (measures) income. A question such as "Who determines income?" has, therefore, no unambiguous answer. The meaning of "an accountant determining acceptable accounting principles" is also vague. Does the clause mean merely choosing one principle from the set of generally acceptable principles, or does it mean using professional judgment to decide that some of the generally accepted principles are not correct under the current circumstances? We try never to use "determine" unless we mean "cause." Otherwise we use "measure," "report," "calculate," "compute," or whatever specific verb seems appropriate. We suggest that careful writers will always "determine" to use the most specific verb to convey meaning. "Determine" seldom best describes a process in which those who make decisions often differ from those who apply technique. The term *predetermined (factory) overhead rate* contains an appropriate use of the word.

development stage enterprise. As defined in *SFAS No. 7*, a firm whose planned principal *operations* have not commenced or, having commenced, have not generated significant *revenue*. The financial statements should identify such enterprises, but no special *accounting principles* apply to them.

diagnostic signal. See *warning signal* for definition and contrast.

differentiable cost. The cost increments associated with infinitesimal changes in volume. If a total cost curve is smooth (in mathematical terms, differentiable), then we say that the curve graphing the derivative of the total cost curve shows differentiable costs.

differential. An adjective used to describe the change (increase or decrease) in a *cost, expense, investment, cash flow, revenue, profit,* and the like as the firm produces or sells one or more additional (or fewer) units or undertakes (or ceases) an activity. This term has virtually the same meaning as *incremental*, but if the item declines, "decremental" better describes the change. Contrast with *marginal*, which means the change in cost or other item for a small (one unit or even less) change in number of units produced or sold.

differential analysis. Analysis of *differential costs, revenues, profits, investment, cash flow*, and the like.

differential cost. See *differential.*

differential cost analysis. See *relevant cost analysis.*

dilution. A potential reduction in *earnings per share* or *book value* per share by the potential *conversion* of securities or by the potential exercise of *warrants* or *options.*

dilutive. Said of a *security* that will reduce *earnings per share* if it is exchanged for *common shares.*

dip(ping) into LIFO layers. See *LIFO inventory layer.*

direct access. Access to computer storage where information can be located directly, regardless of its position in the storage file. Compare *sequential access.*

direct cost. Cost of *direct material* and *direct labor* incurred in producing a product. See *prime cost.* In some accounting literature, writers use this term to mean the same thing as *variable cost.*

direct costing. Another, less-preferred, term for *variable costing.*

direct-financing (capital) lease. See *sales-type (capital) lease* for definition and contrast.

direct labor (material) cost. Cost of labor (material) applied and assigned directly to a product; contrast with *indirect labor (material).*

direct labor variance. Difference between actual and *standard direct labor* allowed.

direct method. See *statement of cash flows.*

direct posting. A method of bookkeeping in which the firm makes *entries* directly in *ledger accounts*, without using a *journal.*

direct write-off method. See *write-off method.*

disbursement. Payment by *cash* or by *check.* See *expenditure.*

DISC (domestic international sales corporation). A U.S. *corporation*, usually a *subsidiary*, whose *income* results primarily from exports. The parent firm usually defers paying *income tax* on 50 percent of a DISC's income for a long period. Generally, this results in a lower overall corporate tax for the *parent* than would otherwise be incurred.

disclaimer of opinion. An *auditor's report* stating that the auditor cannot give an opinion on the *financial statements.* Usually results from *material* restrictions on the scope of the audit or from material uncertainties, which the firm has been unable to resolve by the time of the audit, about the accounts.

disclosure. The showing of facts in *financial statements, notes* thereto, or the *auditor's report.*

discontinued operations. See *income from discontinued operations.*

discount. In the context of *compound interest, bonds* and *notes*, the difference between *face amount* (or *future value*) and *present value* of a payment; in the context of *sales* and *purchases*, a reduction in price granted for prompt payment. See also *chain discount, quantity discount*, and *trade discount.*

discount factor. The reciprocal of one plus the *discount rate*. If the discount rate is 10 percent per period, the discount factor for three periods is $1/(1.10)^3 = (1.10)^{-3} = 0.75131$.

discount rate. *Interest rate* used to convert future payments to *present values*.

discounted bailout period. In a *capital budgeting* context, the total time that must elapse before discounted value of net accumulated cash flows from a project, including potential *salvage value* at various times of assets, equals or exceeds the *present value* of net accumulated cash outflows. Contrast with *discounted payback period.*

discounted cash flow (DCF). Using either the *net present value* or the *internal rate of return* in an analysis to measure the value of future expected cash *expenditures* and *receipts* at a common date. In discounted cash flow analysis, choosing the alternative with the largest *internal rate of return* may yield wrong answers given *mutually exclusive projects* with differing amounts of initial investment for two of the projects. Consider, to take an unrealistic example, a project involving an initial investment of $1, with an *IRR* of 60 percent, and another project involving an initial investment of $1 million, with an IRR of 40 percent. Under most conditions, most firms will prefer the second project to the first, but choosing the project with the larger IRR will lead to undertaking the first, not the second. Usage calls this shortcoming of choosing between alternatives based on the magnitude of the internal rate of return, rather than based on the magnitude of the *net present value* of the cash flows, the "scale effect."

discounted payback period. The shortest amount of time that must elapse before the discounted *present value* of cash inflows from a project, excluding potential *salvage value,* equals the discounted present value of the cash outflows.

discounting a note. See *note receivable discounted* and *factoring*.

discounts lapsed (lost). The sum of *discounts* offered for prompt payment that the purchaser did not take because the discount period expired. See *terms of sale*.

discovery sampling. Acceptance sampling in which the analyst accepts an entire population if and only if the sample contains no disparities.

discovery value accounting. See *reserve recognition accounting*.

discretionary cost center. See *engineered cost center* for definition and contrast.

discretionary costs. *Programmed costs.*

***Discussion Memorandum*.** A neutral discussion of all the issues concerning an accounting problem of current concern to the *FASB*. The publication of such a document usually signals that the FASB will consider issuing an *SFAS* or *SFAC* on this particular problem. The discussion memorandum brings together material about the particular problem to facilitate interaction and comment by those interested in the matter. A public hearing follows before the FASB will issue an *Exposure Draft*.

dishonored note. A *promissory note* whose maker does not repay the loan at *maturity,* for a *term loan*, or on demand, for a *demand loan*.

disintermediation. Moving funds from one interest-earning account to another, typically one promising a higher rate. Federal law regulates the maximum *interest rate* that both banks and savings-and-loan associations can pay for *time deposits*. When free-market interest rates exceed the regulated interest ceiling for such time deposits, some depositors withdraw their funds and invest them elsewhere at a higher interest rate. This process is known as "disintermediation."

distributable income. The portion of conventional accounting net income that the firm can distribute to owners (usually in the form of *dividends*) without impairing the physical capacity of the firm to continue operations at current levels. Pretax distributable income is conventional pretax income less the excess of *current cost* of goods sold and *depreciation* charges based on the replacement cost of *productive capacity* over cost of goods sold and depreciation on an *acquisition cost basis*. Contrast with *sustainable income.* See *inventory profit.*

distributable surplus. Canada and United Kingdom: the statutory designation to describe the portion of the proceeds of the issue of shares without *par value* not allocated to share capital.

distributed processing. Processing in a computer information network in which an individual location processes data relevant to it while the operating system transmits information required elsewhere, either to the central computer or to another local computer for further processing.

distribution expense. *Expense* of selling, advertising, and delivery activities.

dividend. A distribution of assets generated from *earnings* to owners of a corporation. The firm may distribute cash (cash dividend), stock (stock dividend), property, or other securities (dividend in kind). Dividends, except stock dividends, become a legal liability of the corporation when the corporation's board declares them. Hence, the owner of stock ordinarily recognizes *revenue* when the board of the corporation declares the dividend, except for stock dividends. See also *liquidating dividend* and *stock dividend.*

dividend yield. *Dividends* declared for the year divided by market price of the stock as of the time for which the analyst computes the yield.

dividends in arrears. Dividends on *cumulative preferred stock* that the corporation's board has not yet declared in accordance with the preferred stock contract. The corporation must usually clear such arrearages before it can declare dividends on *common shares.*

dividends in kind. See *dividend.*

division. A more or less self-contained business unit that is part of a larger family of business units under common control.

divisional control. See *control system.*

divisional reporting. See *segment reporting.*

division return on investment (ROI). Equals the *division profit* divided by the investment in the division.

dollar sign rules. In accounting statements or schedules, place a dollar sign beside the first figure in each column and beside any figure below a horizontal line drawn under the preceding figure.

dollar-value LIFO method. A form of *LIFO* inventory accounting with inventory quantities (*layers*) measured in dollar, rather than physical, terms. The method adjusts for changing prices by using specific price indexes appropriate for the kinds of items in the inventory.

domestic international sales corporation. See *DISC.*

donated capital. A *shareholders' equity* account credited when the company receives gifts, such as land or buildings, without issuing shares or other owners' equity interest in return. A city might donate a plant site hoping the firm will build a factory and employ local residents. Do not confuse with *contributed capital.*

double declining-balance depreciation (DDB). *Declining-balance depreciation* in which the constant percentage used to multiply by book value in computing the depreciation charge for the year is $2/n$, where n is the *depreciable life* in periods. Omit *salvage value* from the depreciable amount. Thus, if the asset cost \$100 and has a depreciable life of five years, the depreciation in the first year would be \$40 = 2/5 × \$100, in the second year would be \$24 = 2/5 × (\$100 – \$40), and in the third year would be \$14.40 = 2/5 × (\$100 – \$40 – \$24). By the fourth year, the remaining undepreciated cost could be depreciated under the straight-line method at \$10.80 = ½ × (\$100 – \$40 – \$24 – \$14.40) per year for tax purposes. Note that salvage value does not affect these computations except that the method will not depreciate the book value below salvage value.

double entry. In recording transactions, a system that maintains the equality of the accounting equation or the balance sheet. Each entry results in recording equal amounts of *debits* and *credits*.

double taxation. Occurs when the taxing authority (U.S. or state) taxes corporate income as earned (first tax) and then the same taxing authority taxes the after-tax income, distributed to owners as dividends, again as personal income tax (second tax).

doubtful accounts. *Accounts receivable* that the firm estimates to be *uncollectible*.

Dr. The abbreviation for *debit*, always with the initial capital letter. *Dr.* is a shortened from of the word *debitor*, and *Cr.* comes from the word *creditor*. In the early days of double-entry record-keeping in the United Kingdom, the major asset was accounts receivable, called *creditors*, and the major liability was accounts payable, called *debitors*. Thus the *r* in *Cr.* does not refer to the *r* in *credit* but to the second *r* in *creditor*.

draft. A written order by the first party, called the drawer, instructing a second party, called the drawee (such as a bank) to pay a third party, called the payee. See also *check, cashier's check, certified check, NOW account, sight draft*, and *trade acceptance*.

drawee. See *draft*.

drawer. See *draft*.

drawing account. A *temporary account* used in *sole proprietorships* and *partnerships* to record payments to owners or partners during a period. At the end of the period, the firm closes the drawing account by crediting it and debiting the owner's or partner's share of income or, perhaps, his or her capital account.

drawings. Payments made to a *sole proprietor* or to a *partner* during a period. See *drawing account*.

driver, cost driver. A cause of costs incurred. Examples include processing orders, issuing an engineering change order, changing the production schedule, and stopping production to change machine settings. The notion arises primarily in product costing, particularly *activity-based costing*.

drop ship(ment). Occurs when a distributor asks a manufacturer to send an order directly to the customer (ordinarily a manufacturer sends goods to a distributor, who sends the goods to its customer). Usage calls the shipment a "drop shipment" and refers to the goods as "drop shipped."

dry-hole accounting. See *reserve recognition accounting* for definition and contrast.

dual-transactions assumption (fiction). Occurs when an analyst, in understanding cash flows, views transactions not involving *cash* as though the firm first generated cash and then used it. For example, the analyst might view the issue of *capital stock* in return for the *asset* land as though the firm issued stock for *cash* and then used cash to acquire the land. Other examples of transactions that could involve the dual-transaction assumption are the issue of a *mortgage* in return for a noncurrent asset and the issue of stock to bondholders on *conversion* of their *convertible bonds*.

dual transfer prices. Occurs when the *transfer price charged* to the buying *division* differs from that *credited* to the selling division. Such prices make sense when the selling division has excess capacity and, as usual, the *fair market value* exceeds the *incremental cost* to produce the goods or services being transferred.

duality. The *double-entry* record-keeping axiom that every *transaction* must result in equal *debit* and *credit* amounts.

dumping. A foreign firm's selling a good or service in the United States at a price below market price at home or, in some contexts, below some measure of cost (which concept is not clearly defined). The practice is illegal in the United States if it harms (or threatens to harm) a U.S. industry.

E

e. The base of natural logarithms; 2.71828. . . . If *interest* compounds continuously during a period at stated rate of r per period, then the effective *interest rate* is equivalent to interest compounded once per period at rate i where $i = e^r - 1$. Tables of e^r are widely available. If 12 percent annual interest compounds continuously, the effective annual rate is $e^{.12} - 1 =$ 12.75 percent. Interest compounded continuously at rate r for d days is $e^{rd/365} - 1$. For example, interest compounded for 92 days at 12 percent is $e^{.12 \times 92/365} - 1 = 3.07$ percent.

earn-out. For two merging firms, an agreement in which the amount paid by the acquiring firm to the acquired firm's shareholders depends on the future earnings of the acquired firm or, perhaps, of the *consolidated entity*.

earned surplus. A term that writers once used, but no longer use, for *retained earnings*.

earnings. A term with no precise meaning but used to mean *income* or sometimes *profit*. The *FASB,* in requiring that firms report *comprehensive income,* encouraged firms to use the term "earnings" for the total formerly reported as *net income*. Firms will likely only slowly change from using the term "net income" to the term "earnings."

earnings, retained. See *retained earnings*.

earnings cycle. The period of time, or the series of transactions, during which a given firm converts *cash* into *goods* and *services*, then sells goods and services to customers, and finally collects cash from customers. *Cash cycle*.

earnings per share (of common stock). *Net income* to common shareholders (net income minus *preferred dividends)* divided by the average number of *common shares* outstanding; see also *primary earnings per share* and *fully diluted earnings per share*. See *ratio*.

earnings per share (of preferred stock). *Net income* divided by the average number of *preferred shares* outstanding during the period. This ratio indicates how well income covers (or protects) the preferred dividends; it does not indicate a legal share of *earnings*. See *ratio*.

earnings statement. *Income statement*.

easement. The acquired right or privilege of one person to use, or have access to, certain property of another. For example, a public utility's right to lay pipes or lines under the property of another and to service those facilities.

EBIT. *Earnings* before *interest and (income) taxes;* acronym used by analysts.

EBITDA. *Earnings* before *interest, (income) taxes, depreciation,* and *amortization;* acronym used by analysts to focus on a particular measure of *cash flow* used in valuation. This is not the same as, but is similar in concept to, *cash flow from operations.* Some analysts exclude *nonrecurring* items from this total.

economic consequences. The *FASB* says that in setting *accounting principles,* it should take into account the real effects on various participants in the business world. It calls these effects "economic consequences."

economic depreciation. Decline in *current cost* (or *fair value*) of an *asset* during a period.

economic entity. See *entity.*

economic life. The time span over which the firm expects to receive the benefits of an *asset.* The economic life of a *patent, copyright,* or *franchise* may be less than the legal life. *Service life.*

economic order quantity (EOQ). In mathematical *inventory* analysis, the optimal amount of stock to order when demand reduces inventory to a level called the "reorder point." If A represents the *incremental cost* of placing a single order, D represents the total demand for a period of time in units, and H represents the incremental holding cost during the period per unit of inventory, then the economic order quantity is:

$$EOQ = \sqrt{2AD/H}$$

Usage sometimes calls *EOQ* the "optimal lot size."

economic transfer pricing rule. Transfer at the *differential outlay cost* to the selling division (typically *variable costs*), plus the *opportunity cost* to the company of making the internal transfers ($0 if the seller has idle capacity, or selling price minus variable costs if the seller is operating at capacity).

economic value added (EVA®). The amount of earnings generated above the cost of funds invested to generate those earnings. To calculate economic value added, find the difference between (the net after-tax operating profit) and (the product of the weighted-average cost of capital multiplied by the investment in the economic unit).

ED. *Exposure Draft.*

EDGAR. Electronic Data, Gathering, Analysis, and Retrieval system; rules and systems adopted by the *SEC* in 1993 to ensure that all the paperwork involved in the filings submitted by more than 15,000 public companies are electronically submitted.

EDP. *Electronic data processing.*

effective interest method. In computing *interest expense* (or *revenue*), a systematic method that makes the interest expense (revenue) for each period divided by the amount of the net *liability (asset)* at the beginning of the period equal to the *yield rate* on the liability (asset) at the time of issue (acquisition). Interest for a period is the yield rate (at time of issue) multiplied by the net liability (asset) at the start of the period. The *amortization* of discount or premium is the *plug* to give equal *debits* and *credits.* (Interest expense is a debit, and the amount of debt service payment is a credit.)

effective (interest) rate. Of a liability such as a bond, the *internal rate of return* or *yield to maturity* at the time of issue. Contrast with *coupon rate.* If the borrower issues the bond for a price below *par,* the effective rate is higher than the coupon rate; if it issues the bond for a price greater than par, the effective rate is lower than the coupon rate. In the context of *compound interest,* the effective rate occurs when the *compounding period* on a *loan* differs from one year, such as a nominal interest rate of 12 percent compounded monthly. The effective interest is the single rate that one could use at the end of the year to multiply the *principal* at the beginning of the year and give the same amount as results from compounding interest each period during the year. For example, if 12 percent per year compounds monthly, the effective annual interest rate is 12.683 percent. That is, if you compound $100 each month at 1 percent per month, the $100 will grow to $112.68 at the end of the year. In general, if the nominal rate of r percent per year compounds m times per year, then the effective rate is $(1 + r/m)^m - 1$.

efficiency variance. A term used for the *quantity variance* for materials or labor or *variable overhead* in a *standard costing system.*

efficient capital market. A market in which security prices reflect all available information and react nearly instantaneously and in an unbiased fashion to new information.

efficient market hypothesis. The finance supposition that security prices trade in *efficient capital markets.*

EITF. *Emerging Issues Task Force.*

electronic data processing. Performing computations and other data-organizing steps in a computer, in contrast to doing these steps by hand or with mechanical calculators.

eligible. Under income tax legislation, a term that restricts or otherwise alters the meaning of another tax or accounting term, generally to signify that the related assets or operations may receive a specified tax treatment.

eliminations. In preparing *consolidated statements, work sheet* entries made to avoid duplicating the amounts of *assets, liabilities, owners' equity, revenues,* and *expenses* of the consolidated *entity* when the firm sums the accounts of the *parent* and *subsidiaries.*

Emerging Issues Task Force (EITF). A group convened by the *FASB* to deal more rapidly with accounting issues than the FASB's due-process procedures can allow. The task force comprises about 20 members from public accounting, industry, and several trade associations. It meets every six weeks. Several FASB board members usually attend and participate. The chief accountant of the *SEC* has indicated that the SEC will require that published financial statements follow guidelines set by a consensus of the EITF. The EITF requires that nearly all its members agree on a position before that position receives the label of "consensus." Such positions appear in *Abstracts of the EITF*, published by the FASB. Since 1984, the EITF has become one of the promulgators of *GAAP.*

employee stock option. See *stock option.*

Employee Stock Ownership Trust (or Plan). See *ESOT.*

employer, employee payroll taxes. See *payroll taxes.*

enabling costs. A type of *capacity cost* that a firm will stop incurring if it shuts down operations completely but will incur in full if it carries out operations at any level. Examples include costs of a security force or of a quality-control inspector for an assembly line. Contrast with *standby costs.*

encumbrance. In governmental accounting, an anticipated *expenditure* or *funds* restricted for an anticipated expenditure, such as for outstanding purchase orders. *Appropriations* less expenditures less outstanding encumbrances yields unencumbered balance.

ending inventory. The *cost* of *inventory* on hand at the end of the *accounting period;* often called "closing inventory." Ending inventory from the end of one period becomes the *beginning inventory* for the next period.

endorsee. See *endorser.*

endorsement. See *draft.* The *payee* signs the draft and transfers it to a fourth party, such as the payee's bank.

endorser. A *note* or *draft payee,* who signs the note after writing "Pay to the order of X," transfers the note to person X, and presumably receives some benefit, such as cash, in return. Usage refers to person X as the "endorsee." The endorsee then has the rights of the payee and may in turn become an endorser by endorsing the note to another endorsee.

engineered cost center. Responsibility center with sufficiently well-established relations between inputs and outputs that the analyst, given data on inputs, can predict the outputs or, conversely, given the outputs, can estimate the amounts of inputs that the process should have used. Consider the relation between pounds of flour (input) and loaves of bread (output). Contrast discretionary cost center, where such relations are so imprecise that analysts have no reliable way to relate inputs to outputs. Consider the relation between advertising the corporate logo or trademark (input) and future revenues (output).

engineering method (of cost estimation). To estimate unit cost of product from study of the materials, labor, and *overhead* components of the production process.

enterprise. Any business organization, usually defining the accounting *entity.*

enterprise fund. A *fund* that a governmental unit establishes to account for acquisition, operation, and maintenance of governmental services that the government intends to be self-supporting from user charges, such as for water or airports and some toll roads.

entity. A person, *partnership, corporation,* or other organization. The *accounting entity* that issues accounting statements may not be the same as the entity defined by law. For example, a *sole proprietorship* is an accounting entity, but the individual's combined business and personal assets are the legal entity in most jurisdictions. Several affiliated corporations may be separate legal entities but issue *consolidated financial statements* for the group of companies operating as a single economic entity.

entity theory. The corporation view that emphasizes the form of the *accounting equation* that says *assets = equities.* Contrast with *proprietorship theory.* The entity theory focuses less on the distinction between *liabilities* and *shareholders' equity* than does the proprietorship theory. The entity theory views all equities as coming to the corporation from outsiders who have claims of differing legal standings. The entity theory implies using a *multiple-step* income statement.

entry value. The *current cost* of acquiring an asset or service at a *fair market price. Replacement cost.*

EOQ. *Economic order quantity.*

EPS. *Earnings per share.*

EPVI. *Excess present value index.*

equalization reserve. An inferior title for the allowance or *estimated liability* account when the firm uses the *allowance method* for such things as maintenance expenses. Periodically, the accountant will debit maintenance *expense* and credit the allowance. As the firm makes *expenditures* for maintenance, it will debit the allowance and credit cash or the other asset used in maintenance.

equities. *Liabilities* plus *owners' equity.* See *equity.*

equity. A claim to *assets*; a source of assets. *SFAC No. 3* defines equity as "the residual interest in the assets of an entity that remains after deducting its liabilities." Thus, many knowledgeable people use "equity" to exclude liabilities and count only owners' equities. We prefer to use the term to mean all liabilities plus all owners' equity because there is no other single word that serves this useful purpose. We fight a losing battle.

equity financing. Raising *funds* by issuing *capital stock.* Contrast with *debt financing.*

equity method. In accounting for an *investment* in the stock of another company, a method that debits the proportionate share of the earnings of the other company to the investment account and credits that amount to a *revenue* account as earned. When the investor receives *dividends*, it debits *cash* and credits the investment account. An investor who owns sufficient shares of stock of an unconsolidated company to exercise significant control over the actions of that company must use the equity method. It is one of the few instances in which the firm recognizes revenue without an increase in *working capital.*

equity ratio. *Shareholders' equity* divided by total *assets*. See *ratio.*

equivalent production. *Equivalent units.*

equivalent units (of work). The number of units of completed output that would require the same costs that a firm would actually incur for the production of completed and partially completed units during a period. For example, if at the beginning of a period the firm starts 100 units and by the end of the period has incurred costs for each of these equal to 75 percent of total costs to complete the units, then the equivalent units of work for the period would be 75. This is used primarily in *process costing* calculations to measure in uniform terms the output of a continuous process.

ERISA (Employee Retirement Income Security Act of 1974). The federal law that sets most *pension plan* requirements.

error accounting. See *accounting errors.*

escalator clause. Inserted in a purchase or rental contract, a clause that permits, under specified conditions, upward adjustments of price.

escapable cost. *Avoidable cost.*

ESOP (Employee Stock Ownership Plan). See *ESOT.*

ESOT (Employee Stock Ownership Trust). A trust *fund* that is created by a corporate employer and that can provide certain tax benefits to the corporation while providing for employee stock ownership. The corporate employer can contribute up to 25 percent of its payroll per year to the trust. The corporation may deduct the amount of the contribution from otherwise taxable income for federal *income tax* purposes. The trustee of the assets must use them for the benefit of employees—for example, to fund death or retirement benefits. The assets of the trust are usually the *common shares,* sometimes nonvoting, of the corporate employer. For an example of the potential *tax shelter*, consider the case of a corporation with $1 million of *debt* outstanding, which it wants to retire, and an annual payroll of $2 million. The corporation sells $1 million of common stock to the ESOT. The ESOT borrows $1 million with the loan guaranteed by, and therefore a *contingency* of, the corporation. The corporation uses the $1 million proceeds of the stock issue to retire its outstanding debt. (The debt of the corporation has been replaced with the debt of the ESOT.) The corporation can contribute $500,000 (= .25 × $2 million payroll) to the ESOT each year and treat the contribution as a deduction for tax purposes. After a little more than two years, the ESOT has received sufficient funds to retire its loan. The corporation has effectively repaid its original $1 million debt with pretax dollars. Assuming an income tax rate of 40 percent, it has saved $400,000 (= .40 × $1 million) of after-tax dollars *if* the $500,000 expense for the contribution to the ESOT for the pension benefits of employees would have been made, in one form or another, anyway. Observe that the corporation could use the proceeds ($1 million in the example) of the stock issued to the ESOT for any of several different purposes: financing expansion, replacing plant assets, or acquiring another company. Basically this same form of pretax-dollar financing through pensions is available with almost any corporate pension plan, with one important exception. The trustees of an ordinary pension trust must invest the assets prudently, and if they do not, they are personally liable to the employees. Current judgment about prudent investment requires diversification—trustees should invest pension trust assets in a wide variety of investment opportunities. (The trustee may not ordinarily invest more than 10 percent of a pension trust's assets in the parent's common stock.) Thus, the ordinary pension trust cannot, in practice, invest all, or even most, of its assets in the parent corporation's stock. This constraint does not apply to the investments of an ESOT. The trustee may invest all ESOT assets in the parent company's stock. The ESOT also provides a means for closely held corporations to achieve wider ownership of shares without *going public*. The laws enabling ESOTs provide for the independent professional appraisal of shares not traded in public markets and for transactions between the corporation and the ESOT or between the ESOT and the employees to be based on the appraised values of the shares.

estate planning. The arrangement of an individual's affairs to facilitate the passage of assets to beneficiaries and to minimize taxes at death.

estimated expenses. See *after cost*.

estimated liability. The preferred terminology for estimated costs the firm will incur for such uncertain things as repairs under *warranty*. An estimated liability appears on the *balance sheet*. Contrast with *contingency*.

estimated revenue. A term used in governmental accounting to designate revenue expected to accrue during a period independent of whether the government will collect it during the period. The governmental unit usually establishes a *budgetary account* at the beginning of the budget period.

estimated salvage value. Synonymous with *salvage value* of an *asset* before its retirement.

estimates, changes in. See *accounting changes*.

estimation sampling. The use of sampling technique in which the sampler infers a qualitative (e.g., fraction female) or quantitative (e.g., mean weight) characteristic of the population from the occurrence of that characteristic in the sample drawn. See *attribute(s) sampling*; *variables sampling*.

EURL (entreprise unipersonnelle à responsabilité limitée). France: similar to *SARL* but having only one shareholder.

ex div (dividend). Said of *shares* whose market price quoted in the market has been reduced by a *dividend* already declared but not yet paid. The *corporation* will send the dividend to the person who owned the share on the *record date*. One who buys the share ex dividend will not receive the dividend even though the corporation has not yet paid it.

ex rights. The condition of securities whose quoted market price no longer includes the right to purchase new securities, such rights having expired or been retained by the seller. Compare *cum rights*.

except for. Qualification in *auditor's report*, usually caused by a change, approved by the auditor, from one acceptable accounting principle or procedure to another.

excess present value. In a *capital budgeting* context, *present value* (of anticipated net cash inflows minus cash outflows including initial cash outflow) for a project. The analyst uses the *cost of capital* as the *discount rate*.

excess present value index. *Present value* of future *cash* inflows divided by initial cash outlay.

exchange. The generic term for a transaction (or, more technically, a reciprocal transfer) between one entity and another; in another context, the name for a market, such as the New York Stock Exchange.

exchange gain or loss. The phrase used by the *FASB* for *foreign exchange gain or loss.*

exchange rate. The *price* of one country's currency in terms of another country's currency. For example, the British pound sterling might be worth U.S.$1.60 at a given time. The exchange rate would be stated as "one pound is worth one dollar and sixty cents" or "one dollar is worth £.625" (= £1/$1.60).

excise tax. Tax on the manufacture, sale, or consumption of a commodity.

executory contract. A mere exchange of promises; an agreement providing for payment by a payor to a payee on the performance of an act or service by the payee, such as a labor contract. Accounting does not recognize benefits arising from executory contracts as *assets,* nor does it recognize obligations arising from such contracts as *liabilities*. See *partially executory contract.*

exemption. A term used for various amounts subtracted from gross income in computing taxable income. Usage does not call all such subtractions "exemptions." See *tax deduction.*

exercise. Occurs when owners of an *option* or *warrant* purchase the security that the option entitles them to purchase.

exercise price. See *option.*

exit value. The proceeds that would be received if assets were disposed of in an *arm's-length transaction. Current selling price; net realizable value.*

expectancy theory. The notion that people act in ways to obtain rewards and prevent penalties.

expected value. The mean or arithmetic *average* of a statistical distribution or series of numbers.

expected value of (perfect) information. Expected *net benefits* from an undertaking with (perfect) information minus expected net benefits of the undertaking without (perfect) information.

expendable fund. In governmental accounting, a *fund* whose resources, *principal*, and earnings the governmental unit may distribute.

expenditure. Payment of *cash* for goods or services received. Payment may occur at the time the purchaser receives the goods or services or at a later time. Virtually synonymous with *disbursement* except that disbursement is a broader term and includes all payments for goods or services. Contrast with *expense.*

expense. As a noun, a decrease in *owners' equity* accompanying the decrease in *net assets* caused by selling goods or rendering services or by the passage of time; a "gone" (net) asset; an expired cost. Measure expense as the *cost* of the (net) assets used. Do not confuse with *expenditure* or *disbursement*, which may occur before, when, or after the firm recognizes the related expense. Use the word "cost" to refer to an item that still has service potential and is an asset. Use the word "expense" after the firm has used the asset's service potential. As a verb, "expense" means to designate an expenditure—past, current, or future—as a current expense.

expense account. An *account* to accumulate *expenses*; *closed* to *retained earnings* at the end of the accounting period; a *temporary owners' equity* account; also used to describe a listing of expenses that an employee submits to the employer for reimbursement.

experience rating. A term used in insurance, particularly unemployment insurance, to denote changes from ordinary rates to reflect extraordinarily large or small amounts of claims over time by the insured.

expired cost. An *expense* or a *loss.*

***Exposure Draft (ED)*.** A preliminary statement of the *FASB* (or the *APB* between 1962 and 1973) showing the contents of a pronouncement being considered for enactment by the board.

external failure costs. *Costs* that a firm *incurs* when it detects nonconforming products and services after delivering them to customers, including warranty repairs, product liability, marketing costs, and *sales allowances*.

external reporting. Reporting to shareholders and the public, as opposed to internal reporting for management's benefit. See *financial accounting,* and contrast with *managerial accounting*.

extraordinary item. A *material expense* or *revenue* item characterized both by its unusual nature and by its infrequency of occurrence; appears along with its income tax effects separately from ordinary income and *income from discontinued operations* on the *income statement*. Accountants would probably classify a *loss* from an earthquake as an extraordinary item. Accountants treat gain (or loss) on the retirement of *bonds* as an extraordinary item under the terms of *SFAS No. 4*.

extrinsic rewards. Rewards that come from outside the individual, such as rewards from a teacher, a parent, an organization, and a spouse; they include grades, money, praise, and prizes. Contrast with *intrinsic rewards*.

F

face amount (value). The nominal amount due at *maturity* from a *bond* or *note* not including the contractual periodic payment that may also come due on the same date. Good usage calls the corresponding amount of a stock certificate the *par* or *stated value*, whichever applies.

facility-level activities. Work that supports the entire organization. Examples include top management, human resources, and research and development.

factoring. The process of buying *notes* or *accounts receivable* at a *discount* from the holder owed the debt; from the holder's point of view, the selling of such notes or accounts. When the transaction involves a single note, usage calls the process "discounting a note."

factory. Used synonymously with *manufacturing* as an adjective.

factory burden. *Manufacturing overhead*.

factory cost. *Manufacturing cost*.

factory expense. *Manufacturing overhead. Expense* is a poor term in this context because the item is a *product cost*.

factory overhead. Usually an item of *manufacturing cost* other than *direct labor* or *direct materials*.

fair market price (value). See *fair value*.

fair presentation (fairness). One of the qualitative standards of financial reporting. When the *auditor's report* says that the *financial statements* "present fairly . . . ," the auditor means that the accounting alternatives used by the entity all comply with *GAAP*. In recent years, however, courts have ruled that conformity with *generally accepted accounting principles* may be insufficient grounds for an opinion that the statements are fair. *SAS No. 5* requires that the auditor judge the accounting principles used in the statements to be "appropriate in the circumstances" before attesting to fair presentation.

fair value, fair market price (value). Price (value) negotiated at *arm's length* between a willing buyer and a willing seller, each acting rationally in his or her own self-interest. The accountant may estimate this amount in the absence of a monetary transaction. This is sometimes measured as the present value of expected cash flows.

fair-value hedge. A hedge of an exposure to changes in the *fair value* of a recognized *asset* or *liability* or of an unrecognized firm commitment. If the firm uses *hedge accounting,* it will report both the hedged item and the hedging instrument at fair value, with *gains* and *losses* reported in *net income.* If the hedge is effective, the gains and losses on these items will offset each other, although both will appear in net income.

FASAC. ***Financial Accounting Standards Advisory Council.*** **FASB (Financial Accounting Standards Board).** An independent board responsible, since 1973, for establishing *generally accepted accounting principles.* Its official pronouncements are *Statements of Financial Accounting Concepts (SFAC), Statements of Financial Accounting Standards (SFAS),* and *FASB Interpretations.* See also *Discussion Memorandum* and *Technical Bulletin.* Web site: www.fasb.org.

FASB Interpretation FIN. An official *FASB* statement interpreting the meaning of *Accounting Research Bulletins, APB Opinions,* and *Statements of Financial Accounting Standards. FIN 46,* for example, has curtailed the use of *off-balance-sheet financings.*

FASB Technical Bulletin. See *Technical Bulletin.*

favorable variance. An excess of actual *revenues* over expected revenues; an excess of *standard cost* over actual cost.

federal income tax. *Income tax* levied by the U.S. government on individuals and corporations.

Federal Insurance Contributions Act. See *FICA.*

Federal Unemployment Tax Act. See *FUTA.*

feedback. The process of informing employees about how their actual performance compares with the expected or desired level of performance, in the hope that the information will reinforce desired behavior and reduce unproductive behavior.

FEI. *Financial Executives Institute.*

FICA (Federal Insurance Contributions Act). The law that sets *Social Security taxes* and benefits.

fiduciary. Someone responsible for the custody or administration of property belonging to another; for example, an executor (of an estate), agent, receiver (in *bankruptcy*), or trustee (of a trust).

FIFO (first-in, first-out). The *inventory flow assumption* that firms use to compute *ending inventory* cost from most recent purchases and *cost of goods sold* from oldest purchases including beginning inventory. FIFO describes cost flow from the viewpoint of the income statement. From the balance sheet perspective, *LISH* (last-in, still-here) describes this same cost flow. Contrast with *LIFO.*

finance. As a verb, to supply with *funds* through the *issue* of stocks, bonds, notes, or mortgages or through the retention of earnings.

financial accounting. The accounting for *assets, equities, revenues,* and *expenses* of a business; primarily concerned with the historical reporting, to external users, of the *financial position* and operations of an *entity* on a regular, periodic basis. Contrast with *managerial accounting.*

Financial Accounting Foundation. The independent foundation (committee), governed by a board of trustees, that raises funds to support the *FASB* and *GASB.*

Financial Accounting Standards Advisory Council (FASAC). A committee of academics, preparers, attestors, and users giving advice to the *FASB* on matters of strategy and emerging issues. The council spends much of each meeting learning about current developments in standard-setting from the FASB staff.

Financial Accounting Standards Board. *FASB.*

Financial Executives Institute (FEI). An organization of financial executives, such as chief accountants, *controllers*, and treasurers, of large businesses. In recent years, the FEI has been a critic of the FASB because it views many of the FASB requirements as burdensome while not *cost-effective*.

financial expense. An *expense* incurred in raising or managing *funds*.

financial flexibility. As defined by *SFAC No. 5*, "the ability of an entity to take effective actions to alter amounts and timing of cash flows so it can respond to unexpected needs and opportunities."

financial forecast. See *financial projection* for definition and contrast.

financial instrument. The *FASB* defines this term as follows.

> Cash, evidence of an ownership interest in an entity, or a contract that both:
>
> [a] imposes on one entity a contractual obligation (1) to deliver cash or another financial instrument to a second entity or (2) to exchange financial instruments on potentially unfavorable terms with the second entity, and
>
> [b] conveys to that second entity a contractual right (1) to receive cash or another financial instrument from the first entity or (2) to exchange other financial instruments on potentially favorable terms with the first entity.

financial leverage. See *leverage*.

financial literacy. The *NYSE* and the *NASDAQ* have required that companies who list their shares with these groups have an audit committee comprising at least three independent board members who are financially literate. The organizations mention the ability to understand the *financial statements,* but leave the definition of financial literacy to the individual boards to define. We think financial literacy in this sense requires the ability to understand the transactions requiring critical accounting judgments or estimates; the accounting issues and choices for those judgments; what management chose, and why; and what opportunities management's choices provide for earnings management. See *critical accounting judgments.*

financial model. Model, typically expressed with arithmetic relations, that allows an organization to test the interaction of economic variables in a variety of settings.

financial position (condition). Statement of the *assets* and *equities* of a firm; displayed as a *balance sheet.*

financial projection. An estimate of *financial position*, results of *operations*, and changes in cash flows for one or more future periods based on a set of assumptions. If the assumptions do not represent the most likely outcomes, then auditors call the estimate a "projection." If the assumptions represent the most probable outcomes, then auditors call the estimate a "forecast." "Most probable" means that management has evaluated the assumptions and that they are management's judgment of the most likely set of conditions and most likely outcomes.

financial ratio. See *ratio*.

financial reporting objectives. Broad objectives that are intended to guide the development of specific *accounting standards;* set out by *FASB SFAC No. 1.*

Financial Reporting Release. Series of releases, issued by the SEC since 1982; replaces the *Accounting Series Release.* See *SEC.*

financial statements. The *balance sheet, income statement, statement of retained earnings, statement of cash flows*, statement of changes in *owners' equity accounts*, statement of *comprehensive income,* and *notes* thereto.

financial structure. *Capital structure.*

financial vice-president. Person in charge of the entire accounting and finance function; typically one of the three most influential people in the company.

financial year. Australia and United Kingdom: term for *fiscal year.*

financing activities. Obtaining resources from (a) owners and providing them with a return on and a return of their *investment* and (b) *creditors* and repaying amounts borrowed (or otherwise settling the obligation). See *statement of cash flows.*

financing lease. *Capital lease.*

finished goods (inventory account). Manufactured product ready for sale; a *current asset* (inventory) account.

firm. Informally, any business entity. (Strictly speaking, a firm is a *partnership.*)

firm commitment. The *FASB,* in *SFAS No. 133,* defines this as "an agreement with an unrelated party, binding on both parties and usually legally enforceable," which requires that the firm promise to pay a specified amount of a currency and that the firm has sufficient disincentives for nonpayment that the firm will probably make the payment. A firm commitment resembles a *liability,* but it is an *executory contract,* so is not a liability. *SFAS No. 133* allows the firm to recognize certain financial *hedges* in the balance sheet if they hedge firm commitments. The *FASB* first used the term in *SFAS No. 52* and *No. 80* but made the term more definite and more important in *SFAS No. 133.* This is an early, perhaps the first, step in changing the recognition criteria for assets and liabilities to exclude the test that the future benefit (asset) or obligation (liability) not arise from an executory contract.

first-in, first-out. See *FIFO.*

fiscal year. A period of 12 consecutive months chosen by a business as the *accounting period* for *annual reports,* not necessarily a *natural business year* or a calendar year.

FISH. An acronym, conceived by George H. Sorter, for *f*irst-*i*n, *s*till-*h*ere. FISH is the same cost flow assumption as *LIFO.* Many readers of accounting statements find it easier to think about inventory questions in terms of items still on hand. Think of LIFO in connection with *cost of goods sold* but of FISH in connection with *ending inventory.* See *LISH.*

fixed assets. *Plant assets.*

fixed assets turnover. *Sales* divided by average total *fixed assets.*

fixed benefit plan. A *defined-benefit plan.*

fixed budget. A plan that provides for specified amounts of *expenditures* and *receipts* that do not vary with activity levels; sometimes called a "static budget." Contrast with *flexible budget.*

fixed charges earned (coverage) ratio. *Income* before *interest expense* and *income tax expense* divided by interest expense.

fixed cost (expense). An *expenditure* or *expense* that does not vary with volume of activity, at least in the short run. See *capacity costs,* which include *enabling costs* and *standby costs,* and *programmed costs* for various subdivisions of fixed costs. See *cost terminology.*

fixed cost price variance (spending variance). The difference between actual and *budgeted fixed costs.*

fixed interval sampling. A method of choosing a sample: the analyst selects the first item from the population randomly, drawing the remaining sample items at equally spaced intervals.

fixed liability. *Long-term* liability.

fixed manufacturing overhead applied. The portion of *fixed manufacturing overhead cost* allocated to units produced during a period.

fixed overhead variance. Difference between *actual fixed manufacturing costs* and fixed manufacturing costs applied to production in a *standard costing system.*

flexible budget. *Budget* that projects receipts and expenditures as a function of activity levels. Contrast with *fixed budget.*

flexible budget allowance. With respect to manufacturing overhead, the total cost that a firm should have incurred at the level of activity actually experienced during the period.

float. *Checks* whose amounts the bank has *added* to the depositor's bank account but whose amounts the bank has not yet reduced from the *drawer's* bank account.

flow. The change in the amount of an item over time. Contrast with *stock.*

flow assumption. An assumption used when the firm makes a *withdrawal* from *inventory.* The firm must compute the cost of the withdrawal by a flow assumption if the firm does not use the *specific identification* method. The usual flow assumptions are *FIFO, LIFO,* and *weighted average.*

flow of costs. *Costs* passing through various classifications within an *entity* engaging, at least in part, in manufacturing activities. See the accompanying diagram for a summary of *product* and *period cost* flows.

Flow of Costs (and Sales Revenue)

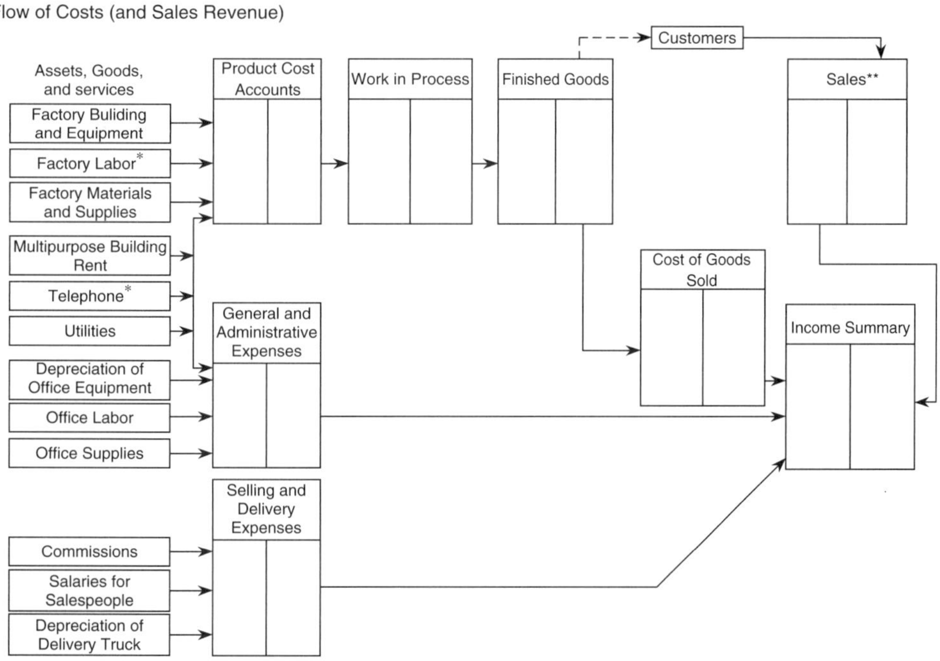

* The credit in the entry to record these items is usually to a payable; for all others, the credit is usually to an asset, or to an asset contra account.

** When the film records sales to customers, it credits the Sales account. The debit is usually to Cash or Accounts Receivable.

flow-through method. Accounting for the *investment credit* to show all income statement benefits of the credit in the year of acquisition rather than spreading them over the life of the asset acquired (called the "deferral method"). The *APB* preferred the deferral method in *Opinion No. 2* (1962) but accepted the flow-through method in *Opinion No. 4* (1964). The term also applies to *depreciation* accounting in which the firm uses the *straight-line method* for financial reporting and an *accelerated depreciation* method for tax reporting. Followers of the flow-through method would not recognize a *deferred tax liability*. *APB Opinion No. 11* prohibits the use of the flow-through approach in financial reporting, although some regulatory commissions have used it.

FOB. Free on board some location (for example, FOB shipping point, FOB destination). The *invoice* price includes delivery at seller's expense to that location. Title to goods usually passes from seller to buyer at the FOB location.

folio. A page number or other identifying reference used in posting to indicate the source of entry.

footing. Adding a column of figures.

footnotes. More detailed information than that provided in the *income statement, balance sheet, statement of retained earnings*, and *statement of cash flows*. These are an integral part of the statements, and the *auditor's report* covers them. They are sometimes called "notes."

forecast. See *financial projection* for definition and contrast.

foreclosure. Occurs when a lender takes possession of property for his or her own use or sale after the borrower fails to make a required payment on a *mortgage*. Assume that the lender sells the property but that the proceeds of the sale are too small to cover the outstanding balance on the loan at the time of foreclosure. Under the terms of most mortgages, the lender becomes an unsecured creditor of the borrower for the still-unrecovered balance of the loan.

foreign currency. For *financial statements* prepared in a given currency, any other currency.

foreign currency translation. Reporting in the currency used in financial statements the amounts denominated or measured in a different currency.

foreign exchange gain or loss. Gain or loss from holding *net* foreign *monetary items* during a period when the *exchange rate* changes.

foreign sales corporation. See *FSC*.

forfeited share. A share to which a subscriber has lost title because of nonpayment of a *call*.

Form 10-K. See *10-K*.

Form 20-F. See *20-F*.

forward contract. An agreement to purchase or sell a specific commodity or financial instrument for a specified price, the *forward price*, at a specified date. Contrast with *futures contract*. Typically, forward contracts are not traded on organized exchanges (unlike *futures contract*), so the parties to the agreement sacrifice liquidity but gain flexibility in setting contract quantities, qualities, and settlement dates.

forward-exchange contract. An agreement to exchange at a specified future date currencies of different countries at a specified rate called the "forward rate."

forward price. The price of a commodity for delivery at a specified future date; in contrast to the "spot price," the price of that commodity on the day of the price quotation.

franchise. A privilege granted or sold, such as to use a name or to sell products or services.

fraudulent conveyance. A transfer of goods or cash that a court finds illegal. *Creditors* of a *bankrupt* firm usually receive less than the firm owed them. For example, a creditor of a bankrupt firm might collect from the trustee of the bankrupt firm only $.60 for every dollar the bankrupt firm owed. Creditors, anticipating bankruptcy, sometimes attempt to persuade the firm to pay the debt in full before the firm declares bankruptcy, reducing the net assets available to other creditors. Bankruptcy laws have rules forbidding such transfers from a near-bankrupt firm to some of its creditors. Such a transfer is called a "fraudulent conveyance." Courts sometimes ask accountants to judge whether a firm had liabilities exceeding assets even before the firm went into bankruptcy. When the court can find that economic bankruptcy occurred before legal bankruptcy, it will declare transfers of assets to creditors after economic bankruptcy to be fraudulent conveyances and have the assets returned to the trustees (or to a legal entity called the "bankrupt's estate") for redistribution to all creditors.

fraudulent financial reporting. Intentional or reckless conduct that results in materially misleading *financial statements*. See *creative accounting*.

free cash flow. This term has no standard meaning. Some financial statement analysts use it to mean *Cash flow from operations* + *Interest expense* + *Income tax expense*. Others mean the excess of cash flow from operations over cash flow for investing. Usage varies so much that you should ascertain the meaning intended in context by this phrase.

free on board. *FOB*.

freight-in. The *cost* of freight or shipping incurred in acquiring *inventory*, preferably treated as a part of the cost of *inventory;* often shown temporarily in an *adjunct account* that the acquirer closes at the end of the period with other purchase accounts to the inventory account.

freight-out. The *cost* of freight or shipping incurred in selling *inventory*, treated by the seller as a selling *expense* in the period of sale.

FSC (foreign sales corporation). A foreign *corporation* engaging in certain export activities, some of whose *income* the United States exempts from federal *income tax*. A U.S. corporation need pay no income taxes on *dividends* distributed by an FSC out of *earnings* attributable to certain foreign income.

full absorption costing. The *costing* method that assigns all types of manufacturing costs (*direct material, direct labor, fixed* and *variable overhead*) to units produced; required by *GAAP;* also called "absorption costing." Contrast with *variable costing*.

full costing, full costs. The total cost of producing and selling a unit; often used in *long-term* profitability and pricing decisions. Full cost per unit equals *full absorption cost* per unit plus *marketing, administrative, interest*, and other *central corporate expenses*, per unit. The sum of full costs for all units equals total costs of the firm.

full disclosure. The reporting policy requiring that all significant or *material* information appear in the financial statements. See *fair presentation*.

fully diluted earnings per share. For *common stock*, smallest *earnings per share* figure that one can obtain by computing an earnings per share for all possible combinations of assumed *exercise* or *conversion* of *potentially dilutive securities*. This figure must appear on the *income statement* if it is less than 97 percent of earnings available to common shareholders divided by the average number of common shares outstanding during the period.

fully vested. Said of a *pension plan* when an employee (or his or her estate) has rights to all the benefits purchased with the employer's contributions to the plan even if the employee does not work for this employer at the time of death or retirement.

function. In governmental accounting, said of a group of related activities for accomplishing a service or regulatory program for which the governmental unit has responsibility; in mathematics, a rule for associating a number, called the dependent variable, with another number (or numbers), called independent variable(s).

functional classification. *Income statement* reporting form that classifies *expenses* by function, that is, cost of goods sold, administrative expenses, financing expenses, selling expenses. Contrast with *natural classification.*

functional currency. Currency in which an entity carries out its principal economic activity.

fund. An *asset* or group of assets set aside for a specific purpose. See also *fund accounting*.

fund accounting. The accounting for resources, obligations, and *capital* balances, usually of a not-for-profit or governmental *entity*, which the entity has segregated into *accounts* representing logical groupings based on legal, donor, or administrative restrictions or requirements. The groupings are "funds." The accounts of each fund are *self-balancing*, and from them one can prepare a *balance sheet* and an operating statement for each fund. See *fund* and *fund balance.*

fund balance. In governmental accounting, the excess of assets of a *fund* over its liabilities and reserves; the not-for-profit equivalent of *owners' equity.*

funded. Said of a *pension plan* or other obligation when the firm has set aside *funds* for meeting the obligation when it comes due. The federal law for pension plans requires that the firm fund all *normal costs* when it recognizes them as expenses. In addition, the firm must fund *prior service cost* of pension plans over 30 or over 40 years, depending on the circumstances.

funding. Replacing *short-term* liabilities with *long-term* debt.

funds. Generally *working capital*; current assets less current liabilities; sometimes used to refer to *cash* or to cash and *marketable securities.*

funds provided by operations. See *cash provided by operations.*

funds statement. An informal name often used for the *statement of cash flows.*

funny money. Said of securities, such as *convertible preferred stock, convertible bonds, options*, and *warrants,* that have aspects of *common shares* but that did not reduce reported *earnings per share* before the issuance of *APB Opinion No. 9* in 1966 and *No. 15* in 1969.

FUTA (Federal Unemployment Tax Act). Provides for taxes to be collected at the federal level, to help subsidize the individual states' administration of their unemployment compensation programs.

future value. Value at a specified future date of a sum increased at a specified *interest rate.*

futures contract. An agreement to purchase or sell a specific commodity or financial instrument for a specified price, at a specific future time or during a specified future period. Contrast with *forward contract.* When traded on an organized exchange, the exchange sets the minimum contract size and expiration date(s). The exchange requires that the holder of the contract settle in cash each day the fluctuations in the value of the contract. That is, each day, the exchange marks the contract to market value, called the "(daily) settlement price." A contract holder who has lost during the day must put up more cash, and a holder who has gained receives cash.

G

GAAP. *Generally accepted accounting principles;* a plural noun. In the United Kingdom and elsewhere, this means "generally accepted accounting practices."

GAAS. *Generally accepted auditing standards;* a plural noun. Do not confuse with *GAS*.

gain. In *financial accounting* contexts, the increase in *owners' equity* caused by a transaction that is not part of a firm's typical, day-to-day operations and not part of owners' *investment* or *withdrawals*. Accounting distinguishes the meaning of the term "gain" (or *loss*) from that of related terms. First, gains (and losses) generally refer to nonoperating, incidental, peripheral, or nonroutine transactions: gain on sale of land in contrast to *gross margin* on *sale* of *inventory*. Second, gains and losses are *net* concepts, not gross concepts: gain or loss results from subtracting some measure of *cost* from the measure of inflow. *Revenues* and *expenses*, on the other hand, are gross concepts; their difference is a net concept. Gain is nonroutine and net, *profit* or *margin* is routine and net; revenue from *continuing operations* is routine and gross; revenue from *discontinued operations* is nonroutine and gross. Loss is net but can be either routine ("loss on sale of inventory") or not ("loss on disposal of segment of business").

In *managerial accounting* and lay contexts, the difference between some measure of *revenue* or *receipts* or *proceeds* and some measure of costs, such as direct costs or variable costs or fully absorbed costs or full costs (see *cost terminology*). Because the word can have so many different meanings, careful writers should be explicit to designate one.

gain contingency. See *contingency*.

GAS. *Goods available for sale*. Do not confuse with *GAAS*.

GASB (Governmental Accounting Standards Board). An independent body responsible, since 1984, for establishing accounting standards for state and local government units. It is part of the *Financial Accounting Foundation*, parallel to the *FASB*, and currently consists of five members.

GbR (Gesellschaft des bürgerlichen Rechtes). Germany: a *partnership* whose members agree to share in specific aspects of their own separate business pursuits, such as an office. This partnership has no legal form and is not a separate accounting *entity*.

GDP Implicit Price Deflator (index). A *price index* issued quarterly by the Office of Business Economics of the U.S. Department of Commerce. This index attempts to trace the price level of all *goods and services* composing the *gross domestic product*. Contrast with *Consumer Price Index*.

gearing. United Kingdom: *financial leverage*.

gearing adjustment. A *revenue* representing part of a *holding gain*. Consider a firm that has part of its assets financed by *noncurrent liabilities* and that has experienced *holding gains* on its *assets* during a period. All the increase in wealth caused by the holding gains belongs to the owners; none typically belongs to the lenders. Some British accounting authorities believe that published *income statements* should show part of the holding gain in *income* for the period. The part they would report in income is the fraction of the gain equal to the fraction that debt composes of total financing; for example, if debt equals 40 percent of total equities and the holding gain equals $100 for the period, the amount to appear in income for the period would be $40. Usage calls that part the "gearing adjustment."

general debt. A governmental unit's debt legally payable from general revenues and backed by the full faith and credit of the governmental unit.

general expenses. *Operating expenses* other than those specifically identified as cost of goods sold, selling, and administration.

general fixed asset (group of accounts). Accounts showing a governmental unit's long-term assets that are not accounted for in *enterprise, trust,* or intragovernmental service funds.

general fund. A nonprofit entity's assets and liabilities not specifically earmarked for other purposes; the primary operating fund of a governmental unit.

general journal. The formal record in which the firm records transactions, or summaries of similar transactions, in *journal entry* form as they occur. Use of the adjective "general" usually implies that the journal has only two columns for cash amounts or that the firm also uses various *special journals*, such as a *check register* or *sales journal*.

general ledger. The name for the formal *ledger* containing all the financial statement accounts. It has equal debits and credits, as evidenced by the *trial balance*. Some of the accounts in the general ledger may be *control accounts*, supported by details contained in *subsidiary ledgers*.

general partner. *Partnership* member who is personally liable for all debts of the partnership; contrast with *limited partner*.

general price index. A measure of the aggregate prices of a wide range of goods and services in the economy at one time relative to the prices during a base period. See *Consumer Price Index* and *GDP Implicit Price Deflator*. Contrast with *specific price index*.

general price level–adjusted statements. See *constant-dollar accounting*

general price-level changes. Changes in the aggregate prices of a wide range of goods and services in the economy. These price measurements result from using a *general price index*. Contrast with *specific price changes*.

general purchasing power. The command of the dollar over a wide range of goods and services in the economy. The general purchasing power of the dollar is inversely related to changes in a general price index. See *general price index*.

general purchasing-power accounting. See *constant-dollar accounting*.

generally accepted accounting principles (GAAP). As previously defined by the *CAP, APB,* and now the *FASB*, the conventions, rules, and procedures necessary to define accepted accounting practice at a particular time; includes both broad guidelines and relatively detailed practices and procedures. In the United States, the FASB defines GAAP to include accounting pronouncements of the *SEC* and other government agencies as well as a variety of authoritative sources, such as this book.

generally accepted auditing standards (GAAS). The *PCAOB* has explicitly stated that it began compiling its auditing promulgations with GAAS, as issued by the AICPA, but "a reference to generally accepted auditing standards in auditors' reports is no longer appropriate or necessary." The phrase has referred to the standards, as opposed to particular procedures, that the *AICPA* promulgated (in *Statements on Auditing Standards*) and that concern "the auditor's professional quantities" and "the judgment exercised by him in the performance of his examination and in his report." Currently, there have been 10 such standards: 3 general ones (concerned with proficiency, independence, and degree of care to be exercised), 3 standards of field work, and 4 standards of reporting. The first standard of reporting requires that the *auditor's report* state whether the firm prepared the *financial statements* in accordance with *generally accepted accounting principles*. Thus, before the PCAOB became the auditing rulemaker, the typical auditor's report says that the auditor conducted the examination in accordance with generally accepted auditing standards and that the firm prepared the statements in accordance with generally accepted accounting principles. The report will not refer to the standards of the Public Company Accounting Oversight Board (United States). See *auditor's report.*

geographic segment. A single operation or a group of operations that are located in a particular geographic area and that generate revenue, incur costs, and have assets used in or associated with generating such revenue.

GIE (groupement d'intérêt économique). France: a joint venture, normally used for exports and research-and-development pooling.

GmbH (Gesellschaft mit beschränkter Haftung). Germany: a private company with an unlimited number of shareholders. Transfer of ownership can take place only with the consent of other shareholders. Contrast with *AG.*

goal congruence. The idea that all members of an organization have incentives to perform for a common interest, such as *shareholder* wealth maximization for a *corporation.*

going-concern assumption. For accounting purposes, accountants' assumption that a business will remain in operation long enough to carry out all its current plans. This assumption partially justifies the *acquisition cost* basis, rather than a *liquidation* or *exit value* basis, of accounting.

going public. Said of a business when its *shares* become widely traded rather than being closely held by relatively few shareholders; issuing shares to the general investing public.

goods. Items of merchandise, supplies, raw materials, or finished goods. Sometimes the meaning of "goods" is extended to include all *tangible* items, as in the phrase "goods and services."

goods available for sale. The sum of *beginning inventory* plus all acquisitions of merchandise or finished goods during an *accounting period.*

goods-in-process. *Work-in-process.*

goodwill. The excess of cost of an acquired firm (or operating unit) over the current *fair market value* of the separately identifiable *net assets* of the acquired unit. Before the acquiring firm can recognize goodwill, it must assign a *fair market value* to all identifiable assets, even when not recorded on the books of the acquired unit. For example, if a firm has developed a *patent* that does not appear on its books because of *SFAS No. 2,* if another company acquires the firm, the acquirer will recognize the patent at an amount equal to its estimated fair market value. The acquirer will compute the amount of goodwill only after assigning values to all assets it can identify. Informally, the term indicates the value of good customer relations, high employee morale, a well-respected business name, and so on, all of which the firm or analyst expects to result in greater-than-normal earning power.

goodwill method. A method of accounting for the *admission* of a new partner to a *partnership* when the new partner will receive a portion of capital different from the value of the *tangible* assets contributed as a fraction of tangible assets of the partnership. See *bonus method* for a description and contrast.

Governmental Accounting Standards Advisory Council. A group that consults with the *GASB* on agenda, technical issues, and the assignment of priorities to projects. It comprises more than a dozen members representing various areas of expertise.

Governmental Accounting Standards Board *GASB.*

GPL (general price level). Usually used as an adjective modifying the word "accounting" to mean *constant-dollar accounting.*

GPLA (general price level–adjusted accounting). *Constant-dollar accounting.*

GPP (general purchasing power). Usually used as an adjective modifying the word "accounting" to mean *constant-dollar accounting*.

graded vesting. Said of a *pension plan* in which not all employees currently have fully *vested* benefits. By law, the benefits must vest according to one of several formulas as time passes.

grandfather clause. An exemption in new accounting *pronouncements* exempting transactions that occurred before a given date from the new accounting treatment. For example, *APB Opinion No. 17*, adopted in 1970, exempted *goodwill* acquired before 1970 from required *amortization*. The term "grandfather" appears in the title to *SFAS No. 10*.

gross. Not adjusted or reduced by deductions or subtractions. Contrast with *net,* and see *gain* for a description of how the difference between net and gross affects usage of the terms *revenue*, *gain, expense*, and *loss*.

gross domestic product (GDP). The market value of all goods and services produced by capital or labor within a country, regardless of who owns the capital or of the nationality of the labor; most widely used measure of production within a country. Contrast with gross national product (GNP), which measures the market value of all goods and services produced with capital owned by, and labor services supplied by, the residents of that country regardless of where they work or where they own capital. In the United States in recent years, the difference between GDP and GNP equals about two-tenths of 1 percent of GDP.

gross margin. *Net sales* minus *Cost of goods sold*.

gross margin percent. 100 × (1 – *Cost of goods sold/net sales)* = 100 × *(Gross margin/Net sales)*.

gross national product (GNP). See *gross domestic product* for definition and contrast.

gross price method (of recording purchase or sales discounts). The firm records the *purchase* (or *sale*) at the *invoice price*, not deducting the amounts of *discounts* available. Later, it uses a *contra* account to purchases (or sales) to record the amounts of discounts taken. Since information on discounts lapsed will not emerge from this system, most firms should prefer the *net price method* of recording purchase discounts.

gross profit. *Gross margin.*

gross profit method. A method of estimating *ending inventory* amounts. First, the firm measures *cost of goods sold* as some fraction of sales; then, it uses the *inventory equation* to value *ending inventory*.

gross profit ratio. *Gross margin* divided by *net sales*.

gross sales. All *sales* at *invoice* prices, not reduced by *discounts*, *allowances*, *returns*, or other adjustments.

group depreciation. In calculating *depreciation* charges, a method that combines similar assets rather than depreciating them separately. It does not recognize gain or loss on retirement of items from the group until the firm sells or retires the last item in the group. See *composite life method*.

guarantee. A promise to answer for payment of debt or performance of some obligation if the person liable for the debt or obligation fails to perform. A guarantee is a *contingency* of the *entity* making the promise. Often, writers use the words "guarantee" and "warranty" to mean the same thing. In precise usage, however, "guarantee" means some person's promise to perform a contractual obligation such as to pay a sum of cash, whereas "warranty" refers to promises about pieces of machinery or other products. See *warranty*.

H

half-year convention. In *tax accounting* under *ACRS*, and sometimes in *financial accounting*, an assumption that the firm acquired *depreciable assets* at midyear of the year of acquisition. When the firm uses this convention, it computes the *depreciation charge* for the year as one-half the charge that it would have used if it had acquired the assets at the beginning of the year.

hardware. The physical equipment or devices forming a computer and peripheral equipment.

hash total. Used to establish accuracy of data processing; a control that takes the sum of data items not normally added together (e.g., the sum of a list of part numbers) and subsequently compares that sum with a computer-generated total of the same values. If the two sums are identical, then the analyst takes some comfort that the two lists are identical.

Hasselback. An annual directory of accounting faculty at colleges and universities; gives information about the faculty's training and fields of specialization. James R. Hasselback, of Florida State University, has compiled the directory since the 1970s; Prentice-Hall distributes it. On-line, you can find it at the Rutgers University accounting Web site: *http://www.rutgers.edu/Accounting/*.

health-care benefits obligation. At any time, the present value of the nonpension benefits promised by an employer to employees during their retirement years.

hedge. To reduce, perhaps cancel altogether, one risk the entity already bears, by purchasing a security or other financial instrument. For example, a farmer growing corn runs the risk that corn prices may decline before the corn matures and can be brought to market. Such a farmer can arrange to sell the corn now for future delivery, hedging the risk of corn price changes. A firm may have a *receivable* denominated in euros due in six months. It runs the risk that the exchange rate between the dollar and the euro will change and the firm will receive a smaller number of dollars in the future than it would receive from the same number of marks received today. Such a firm may hedge its exposure to risk of changes in the exchange rate between dollars and euros in a variety of ways. See *cash-flow hedge* and *fair-value hedge*. Do not confuse with *hedge accounting*.

hedge accounting. Firms may, but need not, use hedge accounting. If the firm elects hedge accounting and if its hedging instrument is highly effective, it will report *gains* and *losses* on hedging instruments for *cash-flow hedges* in *other comprehensive income*, rather than in *net income*. For *fair-value hedges*, the firm using hedge accounting will report the hedged *asset* or *liability* at *fair value;* it reports the hedging instrument at fair value in any event.

held-to-maturity securities. *Marketable debt securities* that a firm expects to, and has the ability to, hold to *maturity*; a classification important in *SFAS No. 115*, which generally requires the owner to carry marketable securities on the balance sheet at market value, not at cost. Under *SFAS No. 115*, the firm may show held-to-maturity debt securities at *amortized cost*. If the firm lacks either the expectation or the intent to hold the debt security to its maturity, then the firm will show that security at market value as a security *available for sale*.

hidden reserve. An amount by which a firm has understated *owners' equity*, perhaps deliberately. The understatement arises from an undervaluation of *assets* or overvaluation of *liabilities*. By undervaluing assets on this period's *balance sheet*, the firm can overstate *net income* in some future period by disposing of the asset: actual *revenues* less artificially low cost of assets sold yields artificially high net income. No *account* in the *ledger* has this title.

hire-purchase agreement (contract). United Kingdom: a *lease* containing a purchase *option.*

historical cost. *Acquisition cost; original cost;* a *sunk cost.*

historical cost/constant-dollar accounting. Accounting based on *historical cost* valuations measured in *constant dollars.* The method restates *nonmonetary items* to reflect changes in the *general purchasing power* of the dollar since the time the firm acquired specific *assets* or incurred specific *liabilities.* The method recognizes a *gain* or *loss* on *monetary items* as the firm holds them over time periods when the general purchasing power of the dollar changes.

historical exchange rate. The rate at which one currency converts into another at the date a transaction took place. Contrast with *current exchange rate.*

historical summary. A part of the *annual report* that shows items, such as *net income, revenues, expenses, asset* and *equity* totals, *earnings per share*, and the like, for 5 or 10 periods including the current one. Usually not as much detail appears in the historical summary as in *comparative statements*, which typically report as much detail for the two preceding years as for the current year. Annual reports may contain both comparative statements and a historical summary.

holdback. Under the terms of a contract, a portion of the progress payments that the customer need not pay until the contractor has fulfilled the contract or satisfied financial obligations to subcontractors.

holding company. A company that confines its activities to owning *stock* in, and supervising management of, other companies. A holding company usually owns a controlling interest in—that is, more than 50 percent of the voting stock of—the companies whose stock it holds. Contrast with *mutual fund.* See *conglomerate.* In British usage, the term refers to any company with controlling interest in another company.

holding gain or loss. Difference between end-of-period price and beginning-of-period price of an asset held during the period. The financial statements ordinarily do not separately report realized holding gains and losses. Income does not usually report unrealized gains at all, except on *trading securities.* See *lower of cost or market.* See *inventory profit* for further refinement, including *gains* on *assets* sold during the period.

holding gain or loss net of inflation. Increase or decrease in the *current cost* of an asset while it is held; measured in units of *constant dollars.*

horizontal analysis. *Time-series analysis.*

horizontal integration. An organization's extension of activity in the same general line of business or its expansion into supplementary, complementary, or compatible products. Compare *vertical integration.*

house account. An account with a customer who does not pay sales commissions.

human resource accounting. A term used to describe a variety of proposals that seek to report the importance of human resources—knowledgeable, trained, and loyal employees—in a company's earning process and total assets.

hurdle rate. Required rate of return in a *discounted cash flow* analysis.

hybrid security. *Security*, such as a *convertible bond*, containing elements of both *debt* and *owners' equity.*

hypothecation. The *pledging* of property, without transfer of title or possession, to secure a loan.

I

IAA. *Interamerican Accounting Association.*

IASB. *International Accounting Standards Board.*

ICMA (Institute of Certified Management Accountants). See *CMA* and *Institute of Management Accountants.*

ideal standard costs. *Standard costs* set equal to those that a firm would incur under the best-possible conditions.

IFRS. International Financial Reporting Standard(s). Refers broadly to all the pronouncements of the *IASB* and, with numbers after the letters, to specific reporting standards issued by the IASB.

IIA. *Institute of Internal Auditors.*

IMA. *Institute of Management Accountants.*

impairment. Reduction in *market value* of an *asset.* When the firm has information indicating that its long-lived *assets*, such as *plant*, identifiable *intangibles*, and *goodwill,* have declined in *market value* or will provide a smaller future benefit than originally anticipated, it tests to see if the decline in value is so drastic that the expected future cash flows from the asset have declined below *book value*. If then-current book value exceeds the sum of expected cash flows, an asset impairment has occurred. At the time the firm judges that an impairment has occurred, the firm writes down the book value of the asset to its then-current *fair value*, which is the market value of the asset or, if the firm cannot assess the market value, the expected *net present value* of the future cash flows.

implicit interest. *Interest* not paid or received. See *interest, imputed.* All transactions involving the deferred payment or receipt of cash involve interest, whether explicitly stated or not. The implicit interest on a single-payment *note* equals the difference between the amount collected at maturity and the amount lent at the start of the loan. One can compute the implicit *interest rate* per year for loans with a single cash inflow and a single cash outflow from the following equation:

$$\left[\frac{\text{Cash Received at Maturity}}{\text{Cash Lent}}\right]^{(1/t)} - 1$$

where t is the term of the loan in years; t need not be an integer.

imprest fund. *Petty cash fund.*

improvement. An *expenditure* to extend the useful life of an *asset* or to improve its performance (rate of output, cost) over that of the original asset; sometimes called "betterment." The firm capitalizes such expenditures as part of the asset's cost. Contrast with *maintenance* and *repair.*

imputed cost. A cost that does not appear in accounting records, such as the *interest* that a firm could earn on cash spent to acquire inventories rather than, say, government bonds. Or, consider a firm that owns the buildings it occupies. This firm has an imputed cost for rent in an amount equal to what it would have to pay to use similar buildings owned by another or equal to the amount it could collect from someone renting the premises from the firm. *Opportunity cost.*

imputed interest. See *interest, imputed.*

in the black (red). Operating at a profit (loss).

in-process R&D. When one firm acquires another, the acquired firm will often have *research and development* activities under way that, following *GAAP,* it has *expensed.* The acquiring firm will pay for these activities to the extent they have value and will then, following GAAP, write off the activities. For each dollar of in-process R&D that the acquiring firm identifies and immediately *expenses,* it will have one less dollar of *goodwill* or other assets to *amortize.* Some acquirers have overstated the valuations of acquired in-process R&D in order to increase immediate *write-offs* and subsequent, recurring *income.*

incentive compatible compensation. Said of a compensation plan that induces managers to act for the interests of owners while acting also in their own interests. For example, consider that a time of rising prices and increasing inventories when using a *LIFO* cost flow assumption implies paying lower *income taxes* than using *FIFO.* A bonus scheme for managers based on accounting *net income* is not incentive-compatible because owners likely benefit more under LIFO, whereas managers benefit more if they report using FIFO. See *LIFO conformity rule* and *goal congruence.*

income. *Excess of revenues* and *gains* over *expenses* and *losses* for a period; *net income.* The term is sometimes used with an appropriate modifier to refer to the various intermediate amounts shown in a *multiple-step income statement* or to refer to revenues, as in "rental income." See *comprehensive income.*

income accounts. *Revenue* and *expense accounts.*

income before taxes. On the *income statement,* the difference between all *revenues* and *expenses* except *income tax* expense. Contrast with *net income.*

income determination. See *determine.*

income distribution account. *Temporary account* sometimes debited when the firm declares *dividends*; closed to *retained earnings.*

income from continuing operations. As defined by *APB Opinion No. 30,* all *revenues* less all *expenses* except for the following: results of operations (including *income tax* effects) that a firm has discontinued or will discontinue; *gains* or *losses,* including income tax effects, on disposal of segments of the business; gains or losses, including income tax effects, from *extraordinary items*; and the cumulative effect of *accounting changes.*

income from discontinued operations. *Income,* net of tax effects, from parts of the business that the firm has discontinued during the period or will discontinue in the near future. Accountants report such items on separate lines of the *income statement,* after *income from continuing operations* but before *extraordinary items.*

income (revenue) bond. See *special revenue debt.*

income smoothing. A method of timing business *transactions* or choosing *accounting principles* so that the firm reports smaller variations in *income* from year to year than it otherwise would. Although some managements set income smoothing as an objective, no standard-setter does.

income statement. The statement of *revenues, expenses, gains,* and *losses* for the period, ending with *net income* for the period. Accountants usually show the *earnings-per-share* amount on the income statement; the *reconciliation* of beginning and ending balances of *retained earnings* may also appear in a combined statement of income and retained earnings. See *income from continuing operations, income from discontinued operations, extraordinary items, multiple-step,* and *single-step.*

income summary. In problem solving, an *account* that serves as a surrogate for the *income statement.* In using an income summary, close all *revenue* accounts to the Income Summary as *credits* and all *expense* accounts as *debits.* The *balance* in the account, after you make all these *closing entries,* represents income or loss for the period. Then, close the income summary balance to retained earnings.

income tax. An annual tax levied by the federal and other governments on the income of an entity.

income tax allocation. See *deferred income tax (liability)* and *tax allocation: intra-statement.*

incremental. An adjective used to describe the increase in *cost, expense, investment, cash flow, revenue, profit*, and the like if the firm produces or sells one or more units or if it undertakes an activity. See *differential.*

incremental cost. See *incremental.*

incur. Said of an obligation of a firm, whether or not that obligation is *accrued.* For example, a firm incurs interest expense on a loan as time passes but accrues that interest only on payment dates or when it makes an *adjusting entry.*

indenture. See *bond indenture.*

independence. The mental attitude required of the *CPA* in performing the *attest* function. It implies that the CPA is impartial and that the members of the auditing CPA firm own no stock in the corporation being audited.

independent accountant. The *CPA* who performs the *attest* function for a firm.

independent variable. See *regression analysis.*

indeterminate-term liability. A *liability* lacking the criterion of being due at a definite time. This term is our own coinage to encompass the *minority interest.*

indexation. An attempt by lawmakers or parties to a contract to cope with the effects of *inflation.* Amounts fixed in law or contracts are "indexed" when these amounts change as a given measure of price changes. For example, a so-called escalator clause (COLA—cost of living allowance or adjustment) in a labor contract might provide that hourly wages will be increased as the *Consumer Price Index* increases. Many economists have suggested the indexation of numbers be fixed in the *income tax* laws. If, for example, the personal *exemption* is $2,500 at the start of the period, if prices rise by 10 percent during the period, and if the personal exemption is indexed, then the personal exemption would automatically rise to $2,750 (= $2,500 + .10 × $2,500) at the end of the period.

indirect cost pool. Any grouping of individual costs that a firm does not identify with a *cost objective.*

indirect costs. Production costs not easily associated with the production of specific goods and services; *overhead costs.* Accountants may *allocate* them on some *arbitrary* basis to specific products or departments.

indirect labor (material) cost. An *indirect cost* for labor (material), such as for supervisors (supplies).

indirect method. See *statement of cash flows.*

individual proprietorship. *Sole proprietorship.*

***Industry Audit Guides*.** A series of *AICPA* publications providing specific accounting and *auditing principles* for specialized situations. Audit guides have been issued covering government contractors, state and local government units, investment companies, finance companies, brokers and dealers in securities, and many other subjects.

inescapable cost. A *cost* that the firm or manager cannot avoid (see *avoidable*) because of an action. For example, if management shuts down two operating rooms in a hospital but still must employ security guards in unreduced numbers, the security costs are "inescapable" with respect to the decision to close the operating rooms.

inflation. A time of generally rising prices.

inflation accounting. Strictly speaking, *constant-dollar accounting.* Some writers incorrectly use the term to mean *current cost accounting.*

information circular. Canada: a document, accompanying the notice of a shareholders' meeting, prepared in connection with the solicitation of proxies by or on behalf of the management of the corporation. It contains information concerning the people making the solicitation, election of directors, appointment of auditors, and other matters to be acted on at the meeting.

information system. A system, sometimes formal and sometimes informal, for collecting, processing, and communicating data that are useful for the managerial functions of decision making, planning, and control and for financial reporting under the *attest* requirement.

inherent interest rate. *Implicit interest* rate.

initial cash flows. *Cash flows* associated with the beginning of an investment project. Often include *asset* cost, freight and installation costs, reduced by cash proceeds from disposing of existing assets made redundant or unnecessary by the new project, and *income tax* effect of *gain (loss)* on disposal of existing assets.

insolvent. Unable to pay debts when due; said of a company even though *assets* exceed *liabilities.*

installment. Partial payment of a debt or partial collection of a receivable, usually according to a contract.

installment contracts receivable. The name used for *accounts receivable* when the firm uses the *installment method* of recognizing revenue. Its *contra account, unrealized gross margin*, appears on the balance sheet as a subtraction from the amount receivable.

installment sales. Sales on account when the buyer promises to pay in several separate payments, called *installments.* The seller may, but need not, account for such sales using the *installment method.* If the seller accounts for installment sales with the sales *basis of revenue recognition* for financial reporting but with the installment method for income tax returns, then it will have *deferred income tax (liability).*

installment (sales) method. Recognizing *revenue* and *expense* (or *gross margin*) from a sales transaction in proportion to the fraction of the selling price collected during a period; allowed by the *IRS* for income tax reporting but acceptable in *GAAP* (*APB Opinion No. 10*) only when the firm cannot estimate cash collections with reasonable precision. See *realized* (and *unrealized*) *gross margin.*

Institute of Certified Management Accountants (ICMA). See *CMA* and *Institute of Management Accountants.*

Institute of Internal Auditors (IIA). The national association of accountants who are engaged in internal auditing and are employed by business firms; administers a comprehensive professional examination. Those who pass the exam qualify to be designated *CIA* (Certified Internal Auditor).

Institute of Management Accountants (IMA). Formerly, the National Association of Accountants, NAA; a society open to those engaged in management accounting; parent organization of the *ICMA*, which oversees the *CMA* program.

insurance. A contract for reimbursement of specific losses; purchased with insurance premiums. "Self-insurance" is not insurance but is merely the noninsured's willingness to assume the risk of incurring losses while saving the premium.

intangible asset. A nonphysical right that gives a firm an exclusive or preferred position in the marketplace. Examples are *copyright, patent, trademark, goodwill, organization costs, capitalized* advertising cost, computer programs, licenses for any of the preceding, government licenses (e.g., broadcasting or the right to sell liquor), *leases*, franchises, mailing lists, exploration permits, import and export permits, construction permits, and marketing quotas. Invariably, accountants define "intangible" using a "for example" list, as we have just done, because accounting has been unable to devise a definition of "intangible" that will include items such as those listed above but exclude stock and bond certificates. Accountants classify these items as tangibles, even though they give their holders a preferred position in receiving dividends and interest payments.

Interamerican Accounting Association (IAA). An organization, headquartered in Miami, devoted to facilitating interaction between accounting practitioners in the Americas. intercompany elimination. See *eliminations.*

intercompany profit. Profit within an organization. If one *affiliated company* sells to another, and the goods remain in the second company's *inventory* at the end of the period, then the first company has not yet realized a *profit* by a sale to an outsider. The profit is "intercompany profit," and the accountant eliminates it from net *income* when preparing *consolidated income statements* or when the firm uses the *equity method.*

intercompany transaction. *Transaction* between a *parent company* and a *subsidiary* or between subsidiaries in a *consolidated entity;* the accountant must eliminate the effects of such a transaction when preparing *consolidated financial statements.* See *intercompany profit.*

intercorporate investment. Occurs when a given *corporation* owns *shares* or *debt* issued by another.

interdepartment monitoring. An *internal control* device. The advantage of allocating *service department costs* to *production departments* stems from the incentives that this gives those charged with the costs to control the costs incurred in the service department. That process of having one group monitor the performance of another is interdepartment monitoring.

interest. The charge or cost for using cash, usually borrowed funds. Interest on one's own cash used is an *opportunity cost, imputed interest.* The amount of interest for a loan is the total amount paid by a borrower to a lender less the amount paid by the lender to the borrower. Accounting seeks to allocate that interest over the time of the loan so that the interest rate (= interest charge/amount borrowed) stays constant each period. See *interest rate* for discussion of the quoted amount. See *effective interest rate* and *nominal interest rate.*

interest, imputed. The difference between the face amount and the present value of a promise. If a borrower merely promises to pay a single amount, sometime later than the present, then the face amount the borrower will repay at *maturity* will exceed the present value (computed at a *fair market* interest rate, called the "imputed interest rate") of the promise. See also *imputed cost.*

interest factor. One plus the *interest* rate.

interest method. See *effective interest method.*

interest rate. A basis used for computing the cost of borrowing funds; usually expressed as a ratio between the number of currency units (e.g., dollars) charged for a period of time and the number of currency units borrowed for that same period of time. When the writers and speakers do not state a period, they almost always mean a period of one year. See *interest, simple interest, compound interest, effective (interest) rate,* and *nominal interest rate.*

interest rate swap. See *swap.*

interfund accounts. In governmental accounting, the accounts that show transactions between funds, especially interfund receivables and payables.

interim statements. Statements issued for periods less than the regular, annual *accounting period.* The *SEC* requires most corporations to issue interim statements on a quarterly basis. In preparing interim reports, a problem arises that the accountant can resolve only by understanding whether interim reports should report on the interim period (1) as a self-contained accounting period or (2) as an integral part of the year so that analysts can make forecasts of annual performance. For example, assume that at the end of the first quarter, a retailer has dipped into old LIFO layers, depleting its *inventory*, so that it computes *LIFO cost of goods sold* artificially low and *net income* artificially high, relative to the amounts the firm would have computed if it had made the "normal" purchases, equal to or greater than sales. The retailer expects to purchase inventory sufficiently large so that when it computes cost of goods sold for the year, there will be no *dips into old LIFO layers* and income will not be artificially high. The first approach will compute the quarterly income from low cost of goods sold using data for the dips that have actually occurred by the end of the quarter. The second approach will compute quarterly income from cost of goods sold, assuming that purchases were equal to "normal" amounts and that the firm did not dip into old LIFO layers. *APB Opinion No. 28* and the *SEC* require that interim reports be constructed largely to satisfy the second purpose.

internal audit, internal auditor. An *audit* conducted by the firm's own employees, called "internal auditors," to ascertain whether the firm's *internal control* procedures work as planned. Contrast with an external audit conducted by a *CPA.*

internal controls. Policies and procedures designed to provide management with reasonable assurances that employees behave in a way that enables the firm to meet its organizational goals. See *control system.*

internal failure costs. *Costs incurred* when a firm detects nonconforming products and services before delivering them to customers; these include scrap, rework, and retesting.

internal rate of return (IRR). The discount rate that equates the net *present value* of a stream of cash outflows and inflows to zero.

internal reporting. Reporting for management's use in planning and control. Contrast with *external reporting* for financial statement users.

Internal Revenue Service (IRS). Agency of the U.S. Treasury Department responsible for administering the Internal Revenue Code and collecting income and certain other taxes.

International Accounting Standards Board (IASB). An organization that promotes the international convergence of accounting standards. Web site: http://*www.iasb.org*. Successor to the International Accounting Standards Committee, IASC, which it superceded in 2001. A good site for tracing developments in international accounting is http.//*www.iasplus.com*, maintained by the worldwide Deloitte Touche Tohmatsu firm, and recommended by the renowned expert on international accounting, Professor Stephen A. Zeff of Rice University.

International Organization of Securities Commissions. *IOSCO.*

interperiod tax allocation. See *deferred income tax (liability).*

interpolation. The estimation of an unknown number intermediate between two (or more) known numbers.

Interpretations. See *FASB Interpretation.*

intrastatement tax allocation. See *tax allocation: intrastatement.*

intrinsic rewards. Rewards that come from within the individual, such as the satisfaction from studying hard, providing help to someone in need, or doing a good job. Contrast with *extrinsic rewards.*

inventoriable costs. *Costs* incurred that the firm adds to the cost of manufactured products; *product costs* (*assets*) as opposed to *period expenses.*

inventory. As a noun, the *balance* in an asset *account,* such as raw materials, supplies, work-in-process, and finished goods; as a verb, to calculate the *cost* of goods on hand at a given time or to count items on hand physically.

inventory equation. *Beginning inventory* + Net additions – Withdrawals = *Ending inventory.* Ordinarily, additions are net purchases, and withdrawals are *cost of goods sold.* Notice that ending inventory, appearing on the balance sheet, and cost of goods sold, appearing on the income statement, must add to a fixed sum. The larger is one; the smaller must be the other. In valuing inventories, the firm usually knows beginning inventory and net purchases. Some inventory methods (for example, some applications of the *retail inventory method*) measure costs of goods sold and use the equation to find the cost of ending inventory. Most methods measure cost of ending inventory and use the equation to find the cost of goods sold (withdrawals). In *current cost* (in contrast to *historical cost*) *accounting,* additions (in the equation) include holding gains, whether realized or not. Thus the current cost inventory equation is as follows: Beginning inventory (at Current cost) + Purchases (where Current cost is Historical cost) + Holding gains (whether realized or not) – Ending inventory (at Current cost) = Cost of goods sold (Current cost).

inventory holding gains. See *inventory profit.*

inventory layer. See *LIFO inventory layer.*

inventory profit. A term with several possible meanings. Consider the data in the accompanying illustration. The firm uses a *FIFO cost flow assumption* and derives its *historical cost* data. The assumed *current cost* data resemble those that the FASB suggested in *SFAS No. 89.* The term *income from continuing operations* refers to revenues less expenses based on current, rather than historical, costs. To that subtotal, add realized holding gains to arrive at realized (conventional) income. To that, add unrealized holding gains to arrive at economic income. The term "inventory profit" often refers (for example in some *SEC* releases) to the realized holding gain, $110 in the illustration. The amount of inventory profit will usually be material when the firm uses FIFO and when prices rise. Other analysts, including us, prefer to use the term "inventory profit" to refer to the total *holding gain,* $300 (= $110 + $190, both realized and unrealized), but writers use this meaning less often. In periods of rising prices and increasing inventories, the realized holding gains under a FIFO cost flow assumption will exceed those under LIFO. In the illustration, for example, assume under LIFO that the historical cost of goods sold is $4,800, that historical LIFO cost of beginning inventory is $600, and that historical LIFO cost of ending inventory is $800. Then income from continuing operations, based on current costs, remains $350 (= $5,200 – $4,850), realized holding gains are $50 (= $4,850 – $4,800), realized income is $400 (= $350 + $50), the unrealized holding gain for the year is $250 [= ($1,550 – $800) – ($1,100 – $600)], and economic income is $650 (= $350 + $50 + $250). The cost flow assumption has only one real effect on this series of calculations: the split of the total holding gain into realized and unrealized portions. Thus, economic income does not depend on the cost flow assumption. Holding gains total $300 in the illustration. The choice of cost flow assumption determines the portion reported as realized.

Inventory Profit Illustration

	(Historical) Acquisition Cost Assuming FIFO	Current Cost
ASSUMED DATA		
Inventory, 1/1	$ 900	$1,100
Inventory, 12/31	1,160	1,550
Cost of Goods Sold for the Year	4,740	4,850
Sales for the Year	$5,200	$5,200
INCOME STATEMENT FOR THE YEAR		
Sales..................	$5,200	$5,200
Cost of Goods Sold	4,740	4,850
(1) Income from Continuing Operations.		$ 350
Realized Holding Gains ...		110[a]
(2) Realized Income = Conventional Net Income (under FIFO)...	$ 460	$ 460
Unrealized Holding Gain ..		190[b]
(3) Economic Income		$ 650

[a]Realized holding gain during a period is current cost of goods sold less historical cost of goods sold; for the year the realized holding gain under FIFO is $110 – $4,850 – $4,740. Some refer to this as "Inventory profit."

[b]The total unrealized holding gain at any time is current cost of Inventory on hand at that time less historical cost of that inventory. The unrealized holding gain during a period is unrealized holding gain at the end of the period less the unrealized holding gain prior to this year is: $200 = $1,100 – $900.

inventory turnover. Number of times the firm sells the average *inventory* during a period; *cost of goods sold* for a period divided by average inventory for the period. See *ratio.*

invested capital. *Contributed capital.*

investee. A company in which another entity, the "investor," owns stock.

investing activities. Acquiring and selling *securities* or productive *assets* expected to produce *revenue* over several *periods.*

investment. An *expenditure* to acquire property or other *assets* in order to produce *revenue*; the asset so acquired; hence a *current* expenditure made in anticipation of future income; said of other companies' *securities* held for the long term and appearing in a separate section of the *balance sheet*; in this context, contrast with *marketable securities.*

investment center. A *responsibility center*, with control over *revenues, costs*, and *assets.*

investment credit. A reduction in income tax liability sometimes granted by the federal government to firms that buy new equipment. This item is a credit in that the taxpayer deducts it from the tax bill, not from pretax income. The tax credit has been a given percentage of the purchase price of the assets purchased. The government has changed the actual rules and rates over the years. As of 1999, there is no investment credit. See *flow-through method* and *carryforward.*

investment decision. The decision whether to undertake an action involving production of goods or services; contrast with financing decision.

investment tax credit. *Investment credit.*

investment turnover ratio. A term that means the same thing as *total assets turnover ratio.*

investments. A balance sheet heading for tangible assets held for periods longer than the operating cycle and not used in revenue production (assets not meeting the definitions of *current assets* or *property, plant, and equipment*).

invoice. A document showing the details of a sale or purchase *transaction.*

IOSCO (International Organization of Securities Commissions). The name, since 1983, of a confederation of regulators of securities and futures markets. Members come from over 80 countries. The IOSCO encourages the *IASB* to eliminate accounting alternatives and to ensure that accounting standards are detailed and complete, with adequate disclosure requirements, and that financial statements are user-friendly.

I.O.U. An informal document acknowledging a debt, setting out the amount of the debt and signed by the debtor.

IRR. *Internal rate of return.*

IRS. *Internal Revenue Service.*

isoprofit line. On a graph showing feasible production possibilities of two products that require the use of the same, limited resources, a line showing all feasible production possibility combinations with the same *profit* or, perhaps, *contribution margin.*

issue. A corporation exchange of its stock (or *bonds*) for cash or other *assets*. Terminology says the corporation "issues," not "sells," that stock (or bonds). Also used in the context of withdrawing supplies or materials from inventory for use in operations and of drawing a *check*.

issued shares. Those shares of *authorized capital stock* that a *corporation* has distributed to the shareholders. See *issue.* Shares of *treasury stock* are legally issued but are not *outstanding* for the purpose of voting, *dividend declarations,* and *earnings-per-share* calculations.

J

JIT. See *just-in-time inventory.*

job cost sheet. A schedule showing actual or budgeted inputs for a special order.

job development credit. The name used for the *investment credit* in the 1971 tax law, since repealed, on this subject.

job (-order) costing. Accumulation of *costs* for a particular identifiable batch of product, known as a job, as it moves through production.

jobs. Customized products.

joint cost. Cost of simultaneously producing or otherwise acquiring two or more products, called joint products, that a firm must, by the nature of the process, produce or acquire together, such as the cost of beef and hides of cattle. Generally, accounting allocates the joint costs of production to the individual products in proportion to their respective sales value (or, sometimes and usually not preferred, their respective physical quantities) at the *split-off* point. Other examples include *central corporate expenses* and *overhead* of a department when it manufactures several products. See *common cost* and *sterilized allocation.*

joint cost allocation. See *joint cost.*

joint process. A process that converts a common input into several outputs.

joint product. One of two or more outputs with significant value that a firm must produce or acquire simultaneously. See *byproduct* and *joint cost.*

journal. The place where the firm records transactions as they occur; the book of original entry.

journal entry. A dated *journal* recording, showing the accounts affected, of equal *debits* and *credits*, with an explanation of the *transaction*, if necessary.

Journal of Accountancy. A monthly publication of the *AICPA*.

Journal of Accounting and Economics. Scholarly journal published by the William E. Simon Graduate School of Business Administration of the University of Rochester.

Journal of Accounting Research. Scholarly journal containing articles on theoretical and empirical aspects of accounting; published by the Graduate School of Business of the University of Chicago.

journal voucher. A *voucher* documenting (and sometimes authorizing) a *transaction*, leading to an entry in the *journal*.

journalize. To make an entry in a *journal*.

judgment(al) sampling. A method of choosing a sample in which the analyst subjectively selects items for examination, in contrast to selecting them by statistical methods. Compare *random sampling*.

junk bond. A low-rated *bond* that lacks the merit and characteristics of an investment-grade bond. It offers high yields, typically in excess of 15 percent per year, but also possesses high risk of default. Sometimes writers, less pejoratively, call these "high-yield bonds." No clear line separates junk from nonjunk bonds.

just-in-time inventory (production) (JIT). In managing *inventory* for manufacturing, system in which a firm purchases or manufactures each component just before the firm uses it. Contrast with systems in which firms acquire or manufacture many parts in advance of needs. JIT systems have much smaller carrying costs for inventory, ideally none, but run higher risks of incurring *stockout* costs.

K

k. Two to the tenth power (2^{10} or 1,024), when referring to computer storage capacity. The one-letter abbreviation derives from the first letter of the prefix "kilo-" (which means 1,000 in decimal notation).

Kaizen costing. A management concept that seeks continuous improvements, likely occurring in small incremental amounts, by refinements of all components of a production process.

KG (Kommanditgesellschaft). Germany: similar to a general partnership (*OHG*) except that some of its members may limit their liability. One of the partners must be a *general partner* with unlimited liability.

kiting. A term with slightly different meanings in banking and auditing contexts. In both, however, it refers to the wrongful practice of taking advantage of the *float*, the time that elapses between the deposit of a *check* in one bank and its collection at another. In the banking context, an individual deposits in Bank A a check written on Bank B. He (or she) then writes checks against the deposit created in Bank A. Several days later, he deposits in Bank B a check written on Bank A, to cover the original check written on Bank B. Still later, he deposits in Bank A a check written on Bank B. The process of covering the deposit in Bank A with a check written on Bank B and vice versa continues until the person can arrange an actual deposit of cash. In the auditing context, kiting refers to a form of *window dressing* in which the firm makes the amount of the account Cash in Bank appear larger than it actually is by depositing in Bank A a check written on Bank B without recording the check written on Bank B in the *check register* until after the close of the *accounting period*.

know-how. Technical or business information that is of the type defined under *trade secret* but that a firm does not maintain as a secret. The rules of accounting for this *asset* are the same as for other *intangibles*.

L

labor efficiency variance. Measures labor productivity by multiplying the *standard* labor price times the difference between the standard labor hours and the actual labor hours.

labor price (or wage) variance. Measures the difference between the actual and *standard* labor prices (wage rates).

labor variances. The *price* (or *rate*) and *quantity* (or *usage*) *variances* for *direct labor* inputs in a *standard costing system.*

laid-down cost. Canada and UK: the sum of all direct costs incurred for procurement of goods up to the time of physical receipt, such as invoice cost plus customs and excise duties, freight and cartage.

land. An *asset* shown at *acquisition cost* plus the *cost* of any nondepreciable *improvements*; in accounting, implies use as a plant or office site rather than as a *natural resource*, such as timberland or farmland.

lapping (accounts receivable). The theft, by an employee, of cash sent in by a customer to discharge the latter's *payable*. The employee conceals the theft from the first customer by using cash received from a second customer. The employee conceals the theft from the second customer by using cash received from a third customer, and so on. The process continues until the thief returns the funds or can make the theft permanent by creating a fictitious *expense* or receivable write-off or until someone discovers the fraud.

lapse. To expire; said of, for example, an insurance policy or discounts that are made available for prompt payment and that the purchaser does not take.

last-in, first-out. See *LIFO*.

layer. See *LIFO inventory layer.*

lead time. The time that elapses between placing an order and receiving the *goods* or *services* ordered.

learning curve. A mathematical expression of the phenomenon that incremental unit costs to produce decrease as managers and labor gain experience from practice.

lease. A contract calling for the lessee (user) to pay the lessor (owner) for the use of an asset. A cancelable lease allows the lessee to cancel at any time. A noncancelable lease requires payments from the lessee for the life of the lease and usually shares many of the economic characteristics of *debt financing.* Most long-term noncancelable leases meet the usual criteria for classifying them as *liabilities,* and GAAP require the firm to show them as liabilities. *SFAS No. 13* and the *SEC* require disclosure, in notes to the financial statements, of the commitments for long-term noncancelable leases. See *capital lease* and *operating lease.*

leasehold. The *asset* representing the right of the lessee to use leased property. See *lease* and *leasehold improvement.*

leasehold improvement. An *improvement* to leased property. The firm should *amortize* it over the *service life* or the life of the lease, whichever is shorter.

least and latest rule. Paying the least amount of taxes as late as possible within the law to minimize the *present value* of tax payments for a given set of operations. Sensible taxpayers will follow this rule. When a taxpayer knows that tax rates will increase later, the taxpayer may reduce the present value of the tax burden by paying smaller taxes sooner. Each set of circumstances requires its own computations.

ledger. A book of accounts; book of final entry. See *general ledger* and *subsidiary ledger.* Contrast with *journal.*

legal capital. The amount of *contributed capital* that, according to state law, the firm must keep permanently in the firm as protection for creditors.

legal entity. See *entity.*

lender. See *loan.*

lessee. See *lease.*

lessor. See *lease.*

letter stock. Privately placed *common shares*; so called because the *SEC* requires the purchaser to sign a letter of intent not to resell the shares.

leverage. More than proportional result from extra effort or financing. Some measure of output increases faster than the measure of input. "Operating leverage" refers to the tendency of *net income* to rise at a faster rate than sales in the presence of *fixed costs.* A doubling of sales, for example, usually implies a more than doubling of net income. "Financial leverage" (or "capital leverage") refers to an increase in rate of return larger than the increase in explicit financing costs—the increased rate of return on *owners' equity* (see *ratio*) when an *investment* earns a return larger than the after-tax *interest rate* paid for *debt* financing. Because the interest charges on debt usually do not change, any *incremental* income benefits owners and none benefits debtors. When writers use the term "leverage" without a qualifying adjective, the term usually refers to financial leverage, the use of *long-term* debt in securing *funds* for the *entity.*

leveraged lease. A special form of lease involving three parties: a *lender*, a *lessor*, and a *lessee*. The lender, such as a bank or insurance company, lends a portion, say 80 percent, of the cash required for acquiring the *asset.* The lessor puts up the remainder, 20 percent, of the cash required. The lessor acquires the asset with the cash, using the asset as security for the loan, and leases it to the lessee on a *noncancelable* basis. The lessee makes periodic lease payments to the lessor, who in turn makes payments on the loan to the lender. Typically, the lessor has no obligation for the debt to the lender other than transferring a portion of the receipts from the lessee. If the lessee should default on the required lease payments, then the lender can repossess the leased asset. The lessor usually has the right to benefit from the tax deductions for *depreciation* on the asset, for *interest expense* on the loan from the lender, and for any *investment credit.* The lease is leveraged in the sense that the lessor, who takes most of the risks and enjoys most of the rewards of ownership, usually borrows most of the funds needed to acquire the asset. See *leverage.*

liability. An obligation to pay a definite (or reasonably definite) amount at a definite (or reasonably definite) time in return for a past or current benefit (that is, the obligation arises from a transaction that is not an *executory contract*); a probable future sacrifice of economic benefits arising from present obligations of a particular *entity* to *transfer assets* or to provide services to other entities in the future as a result of past *transactions* or events. *SFAC No. 6* says that "probable" refers to that which we can reasonably expect or believe but that is neither certain nor proved. A liability has three essential characteristics: (1) the obligation to transfer assets or services has a specified or knowable date, (2) the entity has little or no discretion to avoid the transfer, and (3) the event causing the obligation has already happened, that is, it is not executory.

lien. The right of person A to satisfy a claim against person B by holding B's property as security or by seizing B's property.

life annuity. A *contingent annuity* in which payments cease at the death of a specified person(s), usually the *annuitant(s).*

LIFO (last-in, first-out). An *inventory* flow assumption in which the *cost of goods sold* equals the cost of the most recently acquired units and a firm computes the *ending inventory cost* from the costs of the oldest units. In periods of rising prices and increasing inventories, LIFO leads to higher reported expenses and therefore lower reported income and lower balance sheet inventories than does FIFO. Contrast with *FIFO*. See *FISH* and *inventory profit.*

LIFO conformity rule. The *IRS* rule requiring that companies that use a *LIFO cost flow assumption* for *income taxes* must also use LIFO in computing *income* reported in *financial statements* and forbidding the disclosure of *pro forma* results from using any other cost flow assumption.

LIFO, dollar-value method. See *dollar-value LIFO method.*

LIFO inventory layer. A portion of LIFO inventory cost on the *balance sheet.* The *ending inventory* in physical quantity will usually exceed the *beginning inventory.* The *LIFO cost flow assumption* assigns to this increase in physical quantities a cost computed from the prices of the earliest purchases during the year. The LIFO inventory then consists of layers, sometimes called "slices," which typically consist of relatively small amounts of physical quantities from each of the past years when purchases in physical units exceeded sales in units. Each layer carries the prices from near the beginning of the period when the firm acquired it. The earliest layers will typically (in periods of rising prices) have prices much less than current prices. If inventory quantities should decline in a subsequent period—a "dip into old LIFO layers"—the latest layers enter cost of goods sold first.

LIFO reserve. *Unrealized holding gain* in *ending inventory*: current or *FIFO historical* cost of ending inventory less LIFO *historical cost.* A better term for this concept is "excess of current cost over LIFO historical cost." See *reserve.*

limited liability. The legal concept that shareholders of corporations are not personally liable for debts of the company.

limited partner. A *partnership* member who is not personally liable for debts of the partnership. Every partnership must have at least one *general partner,* who is fully liable.

line-of-business reporting. See *segment reporting.*

line of credit. An agreement with a bank or set of banks for short-term borrowings on demand.

linear programming. A mathematical tool for finding profit-maximizing (or cost-minimizing) combinations of products to produce when a firm has several products that it can produce but faces linear constraints on the resources available in the production processes or on maximum and minimum production requirements.

liquid. Said of a business with a substantial amount (the amount is unspecified) of *working capital*, especially *quick assets.*

liquid assets. *Cash, current marketable securities*, and sometimes, *current receivables.*

liquidating dividend. A *dividend* that a firm declares in the winding up of a business to distribute its assets to the shareholders. Usually the recipient treats this as a return of *investment*, not as *revenue.*

liquidation. Payment of a debt; sale of assets in closing down a business or a segment thereof.

liquidation value per share. The amount each *share* of stock will receive if the *board* dissolves a corporation; for *preferred stock* with a liquidation preference, a stated amount per share.

liquidity. Refers to the availability of *cash*, or near-cash resources, for meeting a firm's obligations.

LISH. An acronym, conceived by George H. Sorter, for *l*ast-*i*n, *s*till-*h*ere. LISH is the same cost flow assumption as *FIFO*. Many readers of accounting statements find it easier to think about inventory questions in terms of items still on hand. Think of FIFO in connection with *cost of goods sold* but of LISH in connection with *ending inventory*. See *FISH*.

list price. The published or nominally quoted price for goods.

list price method. See *trade-in transaction*.

loan. An arrangement in which the owner of property, called the lender, allows someone else, called the borrower, the use of the property for a period of time, which the agreement setting up the loan usually specifies. The borrower promises to return the property to the lender and, often, to make a payment for the use of the property. This term is generally used when the property is *cash* and the payment for its use is *interest*.

LOCOM. *Lower of cost or market*.

long-lived (term) asset. An asset whose benefits the firm expects to receive over several years; a *noncurrent* asset, usually includes *investments*, *plant assets*, and *intangibles*.

long run, long term. A term denoting a time or time periods in the future. How far in the future depends on context. For some securities traders, "long-term" can mean anything beyond the next hour or two. For most managers, it means the period of time long enough to allow change in total productive capacity. For government policymakers, it can mean anything beyond the next decade or two. For geologists, it can mean millions of years. In contrast to the *short run*. Use a hyphen when the phrase is an adjective, but no hyphen when it is a noun.

long-term (construction) contract accounting. The *percentage-of-completion method* of *revenue* recognition; sometimes used to mean the *completed contract method*.

long-term debt ratio. *Noncurrent liabilities* divided by total *assets*.

long-term liability (debt). *Noncurrent liability*.

long term. See *long run*.

long-term solvency risk. The risk that a firm will not have sufficient *cash* to pay its *debts* sometime in the *long run*.

loophole. Imprecise term meaning a technicality allowing a taxpayer (or *financial statements*) to circumvent the intent, without violating the letter, of the law (or *GAAP*).

loss. Excess of *cost* over net proceeds for a single transaction; negative *income* for a period; a cost expiration that produced no *revenue*. See *gain* for a discussion of related and contrasting terms and how to distinguish loss from *expense*.

loss contingency. See *contingency*.

lower of cost or market (LOCOM). A basis for valuation of *inventory* and, formerly in the United States, of *marketable securities*. This basis sets inventory value at the lower of *acquisition cost* or *current replacement cost* (market), subject to the following constraints. First, the market value of an item used in the computation cannot exceed its *net realizable value*—an amount equal to selling price less reasonable costs to complete production and to sell the item. Second, the market value of an item used in the computation cannot be less than the net realizable value minus the normal *profit* ordinarily realized on disposition of completed items of this type. The basis chooses the lower-of-cost-or-market valuation as the lower of acquisition *cost* or replacement cost *(market)* subject to the upper and lower bounds on replacement cost established in the first two steps. Thus,

Market Value = Midvalue of (Replacement Cost, Net Realizable Value, Net Realizable Value Less Normal Profit Margin)

Lower of Cost or Market Valuation = Minimum (Acquisition Cost, Market Value)

The accompanying exhibit illustrates the calculation of the lower-of-cost-or-market valuation for four inventory items. Notice that each of the four possible outcomes occurs once in measuring lower of cost or market. Item 1 uses acquisition cost; item 2 uses net realizable value; item 3 uses replacement cost; and item 4 uses net realizable value less normal profit margin.

	Item			
	1	2	3	4
Calculation of Market Value				
(a) Replacement Cost . . .	$92	$96	$92	$96
(b) Net Realizable Value . .	95	95	95	95
(c) Net Realizable Value Less Normal Profit Margin [= (b) – $9]	86	86	86	86
(d) Market = Midvalue [(a), (b), (c)]	92	95	92	95
Calculation of Lower of Cost or Market				
(e) Acquisition Cost	$90	$97	$96	$90
(f) Market [= (d)].	92	95	92	95
(g) Lower of Cost or Market = Minimum [(e), (f)]	90	95	92	90

A taxpayer may not use the lower-of-cost-or-market basis for inventory on tax returns in combination with a *LIFO cost flow assumption*. In the context of inventory, once the firm writes down the asset, it establishes a new "original cost" basis and ignores subsequent increases in market value in the accounts.

The firm may apply lower of cost or market to individual items of inventory or to groups (usually called *pools*) of items. The smaller the group, the more *conservative* the resulting valuation.

Omit hyphens when you use the term as a noun, but use them when you use the term as an adjectival phrase.

Ltd, Limited. United Kingdom: a private limited corporation. The name of a private limited company must include the word "Limited" or its abbreviation "Ltd."

lump-sum acquisition. *Basket purchase.*

M

MACRS. *Modified Accelerated Cost Recovery System.* See *Accelerated Cost Recovery System.* Since 1986, MACRS has been the accelerated depreciation method required for U.S. income tax purposes.

maintenance. *Expenditures* undertaken to preserve an *asset's* service potential for its originally intended life. These expenditures are *period expenses* or *product costs*. Contrast with *improvement,* and see *repair.*

make money, making money. Users of these words can mean any of the following: earn *income*; earn *other comprehensive income*; save *opportunity costs*; earn *revenues;* earn *gross margin;* sell for *cash;* and maybe others, as well. You can see that you should avoid these words in clear communications. See *money.*

make-or-buy decision. A managerial decision about whether the firm should produce a product internally or purchase it from others. Proper make-or-buy decisions in the short run result only when a firm considers *incremental costs* in the analysis.

maker (of note) (of check). One who signs a *note* to borrow; one who signs a *check*; in the latter context, synonymous with "drawer." See *draft*.

management. Executive authority that operates a business.

management accounting. See *managerial accounting*.

Management Accounting. Monthly publication of the *IMA*.

management audit. An audit conducted to ascertain whether a firm or one of its operating units properly carries out its objectives, policies, and procedures; generally applies only to activities for which accountants can specify qualitative standards. See *audit* and *internal audit*.

management by exception. A principle of management in which managers focus attention on performance only if it differs significantly from that expected.

management by objective (MBO). A management approach designed to focus on the definition and attainment of overall and individual objectives with the participation of all levels of management.

management information system (MIS). A system designed to provide all levels of management with timely and reliable information required for planning, control, and evaluation of performance.

management's discussion and analysis (MD&A). A discussion of management's views of the company's performance; required by the *SEC* to be included in the *10-K* and in the *annual report* to shareholders. The information typically contains discussion of such items as liquidity, results of *operations*, *segments*, and the effects of *inflation*.

managerial (management) accounting. Reporting designed to enhance the ability of management to do its job of decision making, planning, and control. Contrast with *financial accounting*.

manufacturing cost. Cost of producing goods, usually in a factory.

manufacturing expense. An imprecise, and generally incorrect, alternative title for *manufacturing overhead*. The term is generally incorrect because these costs are usually *product costs*, not expenses.

manufacturing overhead. General manufacturing *costs* that are not directly associated with identifiable units of product and that the firm incurs in providing a capacity to carry on productive activities. Accounting treats *fixed* manufacturing overhead cost as a *product cost* under *full absorption costing* but as an *expense* of the period under *variable costing*.

margin. *Revenue* less specified expenses. See *contribution margin*, *gross margin*, and *current margin*.

margin of safety. Excess of actual, or budgeted, sales over *breakeven* sales; usually expressed in dollars but may be expressed in units of product.

marginal cost. The *incremental cost* or *differential cost* of the last unit added to production or the first unit subtracted from production. See *cost terminology* and *differential* for contrast.

marginal costing. *Variable costing*.

marginal revenue. The increment in *revenue* from the sale of one additional unit of product.

marginal tax rate. The amount, expressed as a percentage, by which income taxes increase when taxable income increases by one dollar. Contrast with *average tax rate*.

markdown. See *markup* for definition and contrast.

markdown cancellation. See *markup* for definition and contrast.

market-based transfer price. A *transfer price* based on external market data rather than internal company data.

market price. See *fair value.*

market rate. The rate of *interest* a company must pay to borrow *funds* currently. See *effective rate.*

market value. *Fair market value.*

marketable equity securities. *Marketable securities* representing *owners' equity* interest in other companies, rather than *loans* to them.

marketable securities. Other companies' *stocks* and *bonds* held that can be readily sold on stock exchanges or over-the-counter markets and that the company plans to sell as cash is needed; classified as *current assets* and as part of "cash" in preparing the *statement of cash flows.* If the firm holds these same securities for *long-term* purposes, it will classify them as *noncurrent assets. SFAS No. 115* requires that all marketable equity and all debt securities (except those debt securities the holder has the ability and intent to hold to maturity) appear at market value on the balance sheet. The firm reports changes in market value in income for *trading securities* but debits holding losses (or credits holding gains) directly to owners' equity accounts for *securities available for sale.*

marketing costs. Costs incurred to sell; includes locating customers, persuading them to buy, delivering the goods or services, and collecting the sales proceeds.

mark to market. As a verb, to record an item in the books at *current fair market value.* When used as an adjective, hyphenate the phrase.

markon. See *markup* for definition and contrast.

markup. The difference between the original selling price of items acquired for *inventory* and the cost. Precise usage calls this "markon," although many businesspeople use the term "markup." Because of confusion of this use of "markup" with its precise definition (see below), terminology sometimes uses "original markup." If the originally established retail price increases, the precise term for the amount of price increase is "markup," although terminology sometimes uses "additional markup." If a firm reduces selling price, terminology uses the terms "markdown" and "markup cancellation." "Markup cancellation" refers to reduction in price following "additional markups" and can, by definition, be no more than the amount of the additional markup; "cancellation of additional markup," although not used, is descriptive. "Markdown" refers to price reductions from the original retail price. A price increase after a markdown is a "markdown cancellation." If original cost is $12 and original selling price is $20, then markon (original markup) is $8; if the firm later increases the price to $24, the $4 increase is markup (additional markup); if the firm later lowers the price to $21, the $3 reduction is markup cancellation; if the firm further lowers the price to $17, the $4 reduction comprises $1 markup cancellation and $3 markdown; if the firm later increases the price to $22, the $5 increase comprises $3 of markdown cancellation and $2 of markup (additional markup). Accountants track markup cancellations and markdowns separately because they deduct the former (but not the latter) in computing the selling prices of goods available for sale for the denominator of the *cost percentage* used in the conventional *retail inventory method.*

markup cancellation. See *markup* for definition and contrast.

markup percentage. *Markup* divided by (acquisition cost plus *markup*).

master budget. A *budget* projecting all *financial statements* and their components.

matching convention. The concept of recognizing cost expirations *(expenses)* in the same accounting period during which the firm recognizes related *revenues;* combining or simultaneously recognizing the revenues and expenses that jointly result from the same *transactions* or other events.

material. As an adjective, it means relatively important, capable of influencing a decision (see *materiality*); as a noun, *raw material.*

materiality. The concept that accounting should disclose separately only those events that are relatively important (no operable definition yet exists) for the business or for understanding its statements. *SFAC No. 2* suggests that accounting information is material if "the judgment of a reasonable person relying on the information would have been changed or influenced by the omission or misstatement."

materials efficiency variance. Measures materials waste by multiplying the *standard* materials price times the difference between the standard materials quantity used and the actual materials quantity used.

materials price variance. Measures the difference between the actual and *standard* materials prices.

materials variances. *Price* and *quantity variances* for *direct materials* in *standard costing systems;* difference between actual cost and standard cost.

matrix. A rectangular array of numbers or mathematical symbols.

matrix inverse. For a given square *matrix* A, the matrix, A^{-1} such that $AA^{-1} = A^{-1}A = I$, the identity matrix. Not all square matrices have inverses. Those that do not are "singular"; those that do are "nonsingular."

maturity. The date at which an obligation, such as the *principal* of a *bond* or a *note*, becomes due.

maturity value. The amount expected to be collected when a loan reaches *maturity*. Depending on the context, the amount may be *principal* or principal and *interest*.

MBO. *Management by objective.*

MD&A. *Management's discussion and analysis* section of the *annual report.*

measuring unit. See *attribute measured* for definition and contrast.

merchandise. *Finished goods* bought by a retailer or wholesaler for resale; contrast with finished goods of a manufacturing business.

merchandise costs. Costs incurred to sell a product, such as commissions and advertising.

merchandise turnover. *Inventory turnover* for merchandise. See *ratio*. .

merchandising business. As opposed to a manufacturing or service business, one that purchases (rather than manufactures) *finished goods* for resale.

merger. The joining of two or more businesses into a single *economic entity*. See *holding company*.

minority interest. A *balance sheet account* on *consolidated statements* showing the *equity* in a less-than-100-percent-owned *subsidiary* company; equity allocable to those who are not part of the controlling (majority) interest; may be classified either as shareholders' equity or as a liability of *indeterminate term* on the consolidated balance sheet. The *income statement* must subtract the minority interest in the current period's income of the less-than-100-percent-owned subsidiary to arrive at consolidated *net income* for the period.

minority investment. A holding of less than 50 percent of the *voting stock* in another corporation; accounted for with the *equity method* when the investor owns sufficient shares that it can exercise "significant influence" and as *marketable securities* otherwise. See *mutual fund*.

minutes book. A record of all actions authorized at corporate *board of directors* or shareholders' meetings.

MIS. *Management information system.*

mix variance. One of the *manufacturing variances*. Many *standard cost* systems specify combinations of inputs—for example, labor of a certain skill and materials of a certain quality grade. Sometimes combinations of inputs used differ from those contemplated by the standard. The mix variance attempts to report the cost difference caused by those changes in the combination of inputs.

mixed cost. A *semi-fixed* or a *semi-variable* cost.

Modified Accelerated Cost Recovery System (MACRS). Name used for the *Accelerated Cost Recovery System,* originally passed by Congress in 1981 and amended by Congress in 1986.

modified cash basis. The *cash basis of accounting* with long-term assets accounted for using the *accrual basis of accounting*. Most users of the term "cash basis of accounting" actually mean "modified cash basis."

monetary assets and liabilities. See *monetary items*.

monetary gain or loss. The firm's *gain* or *loss* in *general purchasing power* as a result of its holding *monetary assets* or liabilities during a period when the *general purchasing power of the dollar* changes; explicitly reported in *constant-dollar accounting*. During periods of *inflation*, holders of net monetary assets lose, and holders of net monetary liabilities gain, general purchasing power. During periods of *deflation*, holders of net monetary assets gain, and holders of net monetary liabilities lose, general purchasing power.

monetary items. Amounts fixed in terms of dollars by statute or contract; *cash, accounts receivable, accounts payable*, and *debt*. The distinction between monetary and nonmonetary items is important for *constant-dollar accounting* and for *foreign exchange gain or loss* computations. In the foreign exchange context, account amounts denominated in dollars are not monetary items, whereas amounts denominated in any other currency are monetary.

monetary-nonmonetary method. *Foreign currency translation* that translates all *monetary items* at the *current exchange rate* and translates all *nonmonetary items* at the *historical rate*.

money. A word seldom used with precision in accounting, at least in part because economists have not yet agreed on its definition. Economists use the term to refer to both a medium of exchange and a store of value. See *cash* and *monetary items*. Consider a different set of issues concerning the phrase, "making money." Lay terminology uses this to mean "earning *income*" whether, as a result, the firm increased its *cash* balances or other *net assets*. The user does not typically mean that the firm has increased cash equal to the amount of net income, although the unaware listeners often think the phrase means this. Given that usage equates "making money" with "earning income," in this sense "money" has a credit balance not a debit balance. Since cash typically has a debit balance, the phrase "making money" is even more troublesome. Consider the following language from the U.S. statutes on forfeitures required of some who commit illegal acts: "… the amount of money acquired through illegal transactions …." Does the law mean the cash left over after the lawbreaker has completed the illegal transactions, the income earned from the transactions, or something else?

Focus on the following four sets of questions and see how much difficulty you have in answering the questions associated with 3 and 4.

1. I took a cab and it cost $10; I spent money. Did the cabbie earn money? If so, how much?
2. I asked Jerry to give me a ride and he did, so I didn't spend $10. Did I earn money? If so, how much?
3. I decided to walk, so I didn't spend $10. Did I earn money? If so, how much?
4. I canceled the trip, so I didn't spend $10. Did I earn money? If so, how much?

Now, you can better appreciate why careful writers avoid using the word.

Consider a different set of issues concerning the phrase, "making money." Lay terminology uses this to mean "earning *income*" whether, as a result, the firm increased its *cash* balances or other *net assets.* The user does not typically mean that the firm has increased cash equal to the amount of net income, although the unaware listeners often think the phrase means this. Given that usage equates "making money" with "earning income," in this sense "money" has a credit balance not a debit balance. Since cash typically has a debit balance, the phrase "making money" is even more troublesome. Consider the following language from the U.S. statutes on forfeitures required of some who commit illegal acts: "... the amount of money acquired through illegal transactions ...." Does the law mean the cash left over after the lawbreaker has completed the illegal transactions, the income earned from the transactions, or something else? Sometimes "making money" means avoiding a cost that financial accounting does not recognize.

Consider the following sets of questions and see how you have to think to decide whether, in a given question, "money" refers to a debit or a credit. Assume I start with $10 in cash.

1. I took a cab and it cost $10; I spent money. Did the cabbie make money? Does the cabbie have money?
2. I decided to walk, so I didn't spend $10. Did I make money?
3. I canceled the trip. Did I make money?

"Money" sometimes refers to debits and sometimes to credits; "making money" sometimes means earning accounting income and sometimes avoiding a cost, not reported in accounting, so careful writing about accounting avoids the word.

money purchase plan. A *pension plan* in which the employer contributes a specified amount of cash each year to each employee's pension fund; sometimes called a *defined-contribution plan;* contrast with *defined-benefit plan.* The plan does not specify the benefits ultimately received by the employee, since these benefits depend on the rate of return on the cash invested. As of the mid-1990s, most corporate pension plans were defined-benefit plans because both the law and *generally accepted accounting principles* for pensions made defined-benefit plans more attractive than money purchase plans. *ERISA* makes money purchase plans relatively more attractive than they had been. We expect the relative number of money purchase plans to continue to increase.

mortality table. Data of life expectancies or probabilities of death for persons of specified age and sex.

mortgage. A claim given by the borrower (mortgagor) to the lender (mortgagee) against the borrower's property in return for a loan.

moving average. An *average* computed on observations over time. As a new observation becomes available, analysts drop the oldest one so that they always compute the average for the same number of observations and use only the most recent ones.

moving average method. *Weighted-average inventory method.*

multiple-step. Said of an *income statement* that shows various subtotals of *expenses* and *losses* subtracted from *revenues* to show intermediate items such as *operating income*, income of the enterprise (operating income plus *interest* income), income to investors (income of the enterprise less *income taxes*), net income to shareholders (income to investors less interest charges), and income retained (net income to shareholders less dividends). See *entity theory*.

municipal bond. A *bond* issued by a village, town, or city. *Interest* on such bonds is generally exempt from federal *income taxes* and from some state income taxes. Because bonds issued by state and county governments often have these characteristics, terminology often calls such bonds "municipals" as well. These are also sometimes called "tax-exempts."

mutual fund. An investment company that issues its own stock to the public and uses the proceeds to invest in securities of other companies. A mutual fund usually owns less than 5 or 10 percent of the stock of any one company and accounts for its investments using current *market values*. Contrast with *holding company*.

mutually exclusive (investment) projects. Competing investment projects in which accepting one project eliminates the possibility of undertaking the remaining projects.

N

NAARS. *National Automated Accounting Research System.*

NASDAQ (National Association of Securities Dealers Automated Quotation System). A computerized system to provide brokers and dealers with price quotations for securities traded *over the counter* as well as for some *NYSE* securities.

National Association of Accountants (NAA). Former name for the *Institute of Management Accountants (IMA)*.

National Automated Accounting Research System (NAARS). A computer-based information-retrieval system containing, among other things, the complete text of most public corporate annual reports and *Forms 10-K*. Users may access the system through the *AICPA*.

natural business year. A 12-month period chosen as the reporting period so that the end of the period coincides with a low point in activity or inventories. See *ratio* for a discussion of analyses of financial statements of companies using a natural business year.

natural classification. *Income statement* reporting form that classifies *expenses* by nature of items acquired, such as materials, wages, salaries, insurance, and taxes, as well as depreciation. Contrast with *functional classification*.

natural resources. Timber, oil and gas, ore deposits, and other products of nature that have economic value. Terminology uses the term *depletion* to refer to the process of *amortizing* the cost of natural resources. Natural resources are "nonrenewable" (for example, oil, coal, gas, ore deposits) or "renewable" (timber, sod fields); terminology often calls the former "wasting assets." See also *reserve recognition accounting* and *percentage depletion*.

negative confirmation. See *confirmation*.

negative goodwill. See *goodwill*. When a firm acquires another company, and the *fair market value* of the *net assets* acquired exceeds the purchase price, *APB Opinion No. 16* requires that the acquiring company reduce the valuation of noncurrent assets (except *investments* in *marketable securities*) until the purchase price equals the adjusted valuation of the fair market value of net assets acquired. If, after the acquiring company reduces the valuation of noncurrent assets to zero, the valuation of the remaining net assets acquired still exceeds the purchase price, then the difference appears as a credit balance on the balance sheet as negative goodwill. For negative goodwill to exist, someone must be willing to sell a company for less than the fair market value of net current assets and marketable securities. Because such bargain purchases are rare, one seldom sees negative goodwill in the financial statements. When it does appear, it generally signals unrecorded obligations, such as a contingency related to a pending lawsuit.

negotiable. Legally capable of being transferred by *endorsement.* Usually said of *checks* and *notes* and sometimes of *stocks* and *bearer bonds.*

negotiated transfer price. A *transfer price* set jointly by the buying and the selling divisions.

net. Reduced by all relevant deductions.

net assets. Total *assets* minus total *liabilities;* equals the amount of *owners' equity*. Often, we find it useful to split the balance sheet into two parts: owners' equity and all the rest. The "rest" is total assets less total liabilities. To take an example, consider one definition of *revenue*: the increase in owners' equity accompanying the net assets increase caused by selling goods or rendering services. An alternative, more cumbersome way to say the same thing is: the increase in owners' equity accompanying the assets increase or the liabilities decrease, or both, caused by selling goods or rendering services. Consider the definition of *goodwill*: the excess of purchase price over the fair market value of identifiable net assets acquired in a purchase transaction. Without the phrase "net assets," the definition might be as follows: the excess of purchase price over the fair market value of identifiable assets reduced by the fair market value of identifiable liabilities acquired in a purchase transaction.

net bank position. From a firm's point of view, *cash* in a specific bank less *loans* payable to that bank.

net book value. *Book value.*

net current asset value (per share). *Working capital* divided by the number of common shares outstanding. Some analysts think that when a common share trades in the market for an amount less than net current asset value, the shares are undervalued and investors should purchase them. We find this view naive because it ignores, generally, the efficiency of capital markets and, specifically, unrecorded obligations, such as for executory contracts and contingencies, not currently reported as *liabilities* in the *balance sheet* under *GAAP*.

net current assets.

Working capital = *Current assets* – *Current liabilities*.

net income. The excess of all *revenues* and *gains* for a period over all *expenses* and *losses* of the period. The FASB is proposing to discontinue use of this term and substitute *earnings*. See *comprehensive income.*

net loss. The excess of all *expenses* and *losses* for a period over all *revenues* and *gains* of the period; negative *net income*.

net markup. In the context of *retail inventory methods, markups* less markup cancellations; a figure that usually ignores *markdowns* and markdown cancellations.

net of tax method. A nonsanctioned method for dealing with the problem of *income tax allocation*; described in *APB Opinion No. 11*. The method subtracts deferred tax items from specific *asset* amounts rather than showing them as a deferred credit or *liability*.

net of tax reporting. Reporting, such as for *income from discontinued operations, extraordinary items*, and *prior-period adjustments*, in which the firm adjusts the amounts presented in the *financial statements* for all income tax effects. For example, if an extraordinary loss amounted to $10,000, and the marginal tax rate was 40 percent, then the extraordinary item would appear "net of taxes" as a $6,000 loss. Hence, not all a firm's income taxes necessarily appear on one line of the income statement. The reporting allocates the total taxes among *income from continuing operations, income from discontinued operations, extraordinary items*, cumulative effects of *accounting changes*, and *prior-period adjustments*.

net operating profit. *Income from continuing operations*.

net present value. Discounted or *present value* of all cash inflows and outflows of a project or of an *investment* at a given *discount rate*.

net price method (of recording purchase or sales discounts). Method that records a *purchase* (or *sale*) at its *invoice* price less all *discounts* made available, under the assumption that the firm will take nearly all discounts offered. The purchaser debits, to an *expense* account, discounts lapsed through failure to pay promptly. For purchases, management usually prefers to know about the amount of discounts lost because of inefficient operations, not the amounts taken, so that most managers prefer the net price method to the *gross price method*.

net realizable (sales) value. Current selling price less reasonable costs to complete production and to sell the item. Also, a method for *allocating joint costs* in proportion to *realizable values* of the joint products. For example, joint products A and B together cost $100; A sells for $60, whereas B sells for $90. Then a firm would allocate to A ($60/$150) × $100 = .40 x $100 = $40 of cost while it would allocate to B ($90/$150) × $100 = $60 of cost.

net sales. Sales (at gross invoice amount) less *returns, allowances*, freight paid for customers, and *discounts* taken.

net working capital. *Working capital;* the term "net" is redundant in accounting. Financial analysts sometimes mean *current assets* when they speak of working capital, so for them the "net" is not redundant.

net worth. A misleading term with the same meaning as *owners' equity*. Avoid using this term; accounting valuations at historical cost do not show economic worth.

network analysis. A project planning and scheduling method, usually displayed in a diagram, that enables management to identify the interrelated sequences that it must accomplish to complete the project.

new product development time. The period between a firm's first consideration of a product and delivery of it to the customer.

New York Stock Exchange (NYSE). A public market in which those who own seats (a seat is the right to participate) trade various corporate *securities*.

next-in, first-out. See *NIFO*.

NIFO (next-in, first-out). A *cost flow assumption,* one not allowed by GAAP. In making decisions, many managers consider *replacement costs* (rather than *historical costs*) and refer to them as NIFO costs.

no par. Said of *stock* without a *par value*.

nominal accounts. *Temporary accounts*, such as *revenue* and *expense* accounts; contrast with *balance sheet accounts*. The firm *closes* all nominal accounts at the end of each *accounting period*.

nominal amount (value). An amount stated in dollars, in contrast to an amount stated in *constant dollars*. Contrast with *real amount (value)*.

nominal dollars. The measuring unit giving no consideration to differences in the *general purchasing power of the dollar* over time. The face amount of currency or coin, a *bond*, an *invoice*, or a *receivable* is a nominal-dollar amount. When the analyst adjusts that amount for changes in *general purchasing power*, it becomes a *constant-dollar* amount.

nominal interest rate. A rate specified on a *debt* instrument; usually differs from the market or *effective rate;* also, a rate of *interest* quoted for a year. If the interest compounds more often than annually, then the *effective interest rate* exceeds the nominal rate.

noncancelable. See *lease*.

nonconsolidated subsidiary. An *intercorporate investment* in which the parent owns more than 50 percent of the shares of the *subsidiary* but accounts for the investment with the *cost method*.

noncontributory. Said of a *pension plan* in which only the employer makes payments to a pension *fund*. Contrast with *contributory*.

noncontrollable cost. A cost that a particular manager cannot *control*.

noncurrent. Of a *liability*, due in more than one year (or more than one *operating cycle*); of an *asset*, the firm will enjoy the future benefit in more than one year (or more than one operating cycle).

nonexpendable fund. A governmental fund whose *principal*, and sometimes earnings, the entity may not spend.

noninterest-bearing note. A *note* that does not specify explicit interest. The *face value* of such a note will exceed its *present value* at any time before *maturity* value so long as *interest rates* are positive. *APB Opinion No. 21* requires that firms report the present value, not face value, of long-term noninterest-bearing notes as the *asset* or *liability* amount in financial statements. For this purpose, the firm uses the *historical interest rate*. See *interest, imputed*.

nonmanufacturing costs. All *costs* incurred other than those necessary to produce goods. Typically, only manufacturing firms use this designation.

nonmonetary items. All items that are not monetary. See *monetary items*.

nonoperating. In the *income statement* context, said of *revenues* and *expenses* arising from *transactions* incidental to the company's main line(s) of business; in the *statement of cash flows* context, said of all financing and investing sources or uses of cash in contrast to cash provided by operations. See *operations*.

nonprofit corporation. An incorporated *entity*, such as a hospital, with owners who do not share in the earnings. It usually emphasizes providing services rather than maximizing income.

nonrecurring. Said of an event that is not expected to happen often for a given firm. *APB Opinion No. 30* requires firms to disclose separately the effects of such events as part of *ordinary* items unless the event is also unusual. See *extraordinary* item.

non-value-added activity. An activity that causes costs without increasing a product's or service's value to the customer.

normal cost. Former name for *service cost* in accounting for pensions and other postemployment benefits.

normal costing. Method of charging costs to products using actual *direct materials*, actual *direct labor*, and predetermined *factory overhead* rates.

normal costing system. *Costing* based on *actual material* and *labor* costs but using *predetermined overhead* rates per unit of some *activity* basis (such as *direct labor-hours* or machine-hours) to apply overhead to production. Management decides the rate to charge to production for overhead at the start of the period. At the end of the period the accounting multiplies this rate by the actual number of units of the base activity (such as actual direct labor-hours worked or actual machine-hours used during the period) to apply overhead to production.

normal spoilage. Costs incurred because of ordinary amounts of spoilage. Accounting prorates such costs to units produced as *product costs*. Contrast with *abnormal spoilage*.

normal standard cost, normal standards. The *cost* a firm expects to incur under reasonably efficient operating conditions with adequate provision for an average amount of rework, spoilage, and the like.

normal volume. The level of production that will, over a time span, usually one year, satisfy purchasers' demands and provide for reasonable *inventory* levels.

note. An unconditional written promise by the maker (borrower) to pay a certain amount on demand or at a certain future time.

note receivable discounted. A *note* assigned by the holder to another. The new holder of the note typically pays the old holder an amount less than the *face value* of the note, hence the word "discounted." If the old holder assigns the note to the new holder with recourse, the old holder has a *contingent liability* until the maker of the note pays the debt. See *factoring*.

notes. Some use this word instead of *footnotes* when referring to the detailed information included by management as an integral part of the *financial statements* and covered by the *auditor's report*.

NOW (negotiable order of withdrawal) account. Negotiable order of withdrawal. A *savings account* whose owner can draw an order to pay, much like a *check* but technically not a check, and give it to others, who can redeem the order at the savings institution.

number of days sales in inventory (or receivables). Days of average inventory on hand (or average collection period for receivables). See *ratio*.

NV (naamloze vennootschap). Netherlands: a public limited liability company.

NYSE. *New York Stock Exchange*.

O

OASDHI. *Old Age, Survivors, Disability, and Health Insurance*.

objective. See *reporting objectives* and *objectivity*.

objective function. In *linear programming*, the name of the profit (or cost) criterion the analyst wants to maximize (or minimize).

objectivity. The reporting policy implying that the firm will not give formal recognition to an event in financial statements until the firm can measure the magnitude of the events with reasonable accuracy and check that amount with independent verification.

obsolescence. An asset's *market value* decline caused by improved alternatives becoming available that will be more *cost-effective*. The decline in market value does not relate to physical changes in the asset itself. For example, computers become obsolete long before they wear out. See *partial obsolescence*.

Occupational Safety and Health Act. *OSHA*.

off-balance-sheet financing. A description often used for an obligation that meets all the tests to be classified a liability except that the obligation arises from an *executory contract* and, hence, is not a *liability*. Consider the following example. Miller Corporation desires to acquire land costing $25 million, on which it will build a shopping center. It could borrow the $25 million from its bank, paying interest at 12 percent, and buy the land outright from the seller. If so, both an asset and a liability will appear on the balance sheet. Instead, it borrows $5 million and purchases for $5 million from the seller an *option* to buy the land from the seller at any time within the next six years for a price of $20 million. The option costs Miller Corporation $5 million immediately and provides for continuing "option" payments of $2.4 million per year, which precisely equal Miller Corporation's borrowing rate multiplied by the remaining purchase price of the land: $2.4 million = .12 × $20 million. Although Miller Corporation need not continue payments and can let the option lapse at any time, it also has an obligation to begin developing on the site immediately. Because Miller Corporation has invested a substantial sum in the option, will invest more, and will begin immediately developing the land, Miller Corporation will almost certainly exercise its option before expiration. The seller of the land can take the option contract to the bank and borrow $20 million, paying interest at Miller Corporation's borrowing rate, 12 percent per year. The continuing option payments from Miller Corporation will be sufficient to enable the seller to make its payments to the bank. *Generally accepted accounting principles* view Miller Corporation as having acquired an option for $5 million rather than having acquired land costing $25 million in return for $25 million of debt. The firm will likely be able to structure this transaction so that it need not recognize debt on the balance sheet until it borrows more funds to exercise the option.

The *FASB* has curtailed the use of such financings with *FIN 46*. See also *variable interest entity*.

off-balance-sheet risk. A contract that exposes an entity to the possibility of loss but that does not appear in the financial statements. For example, a *forward-exchange contract* generally does not appear on the balance sheet because it is an *executory contract*. The contract may reduce or increase the entity's exposure to foreign-exchange risk (the chance of loss due to unfavorable changes in the foreign-exchange rate). It may also expose the entity to credit risk (the chance of loss that occurs when the *counterparty* to the contract cannot fulfill the contract terms). *SFAS No. 105* requires entities to describe contracts with off-balance-sheet risk.

OHG (Offene Handelsgesellschaft). Germany: a general *partnership*. The partners have unlimited *liability*.

Old Age, Survivors, Disability, and Health Insurance, or OASDHI. The technical name for Social Security under the Federal Insurance Contributions Act (*FICA*).

on consignment. Said of goods delivered by the owner (the consignor) to another (the consignee) to be sold by the consignee. On delivery of the goods from the consignor to the consignee, the consignor can, but need not, make an entry transferring the goods at cost from Finished Goods Inventory to another inventory account, such as Goods out on Consignment. The consignor recognizes revenue only when the consignee has sold the goods to customers. Under such an arrangement, the owner of the goods bears the inventory holding costs until the ultimate seller (consignee) sells them. The owner also bears the risk that the items will never sell to final customers, but manufacturers or distributors who provide generous return options to their customers can achieve this aspect of consignment sales in an outright sale. The consignment protects the consignor from the consignee's bankruptcy, as the arrangement entitles the owner either to the return of the property or to payment of a specified amount. The goods are assets of the consignor. Such arrangements provide the consignor with better protection than an outright sale on account to the consignee in bankruptcy. In event of bankruptcy, the ordinary seller, holding an account receivable, has no special claim to the return of the goods, whereas a consignor can reclaim the goods without going through bankruptcy proceedings, from which the consignor might recover only a fraction of the amounts owed to it.

on (open) account. Said of a *purchase* (or *sale*) when the seller expects payment sometime after delivery and the purchaser does not give a *note* evidencing the *debt*. The purchaser has generally signed an agreement sometime in the past promising to pay for such purchases according to an agreed time schedule. When the firm sells (purchases) on open account, it *debits* (*credits*) *Accounts Receivable (Payable)*.

one-line consolidation. Said of an *intercorporate investment* accounted for with the *equity method*. With this method, the *income* and *balance sheet* total *assets* and *equities* amounts are identical to those that would appear if the parent consolidated the investee firm, even though the income from the investment appears on a single line of the income statement and the net investment appears on a single line in the Assets section of the balance sheet.

one-write system. A system of bookkeeping that produces several records, including original documents, in one operation by the use of reproductive paper and equipment that provides for the proper alignment of the documents.

on-time performance. The firm delivers the product or service at the time scheduled for delivery.

open account. Any *account* with a nonzero *debit* or *credit balance*. See *on (open) account*.

operating. An adjective used to refer to *revenue* and *expense* items relating to the company's main line(s) of business. See *operations*.

operating accounts. *Revenue, expense*, and *production cost accounts*. Contrast with *balance sheet accounts*.

operating activities. For purposes of the *statement of cash flows*, all *transactions* and *events* that are neither *financing activities* nor *investing activities*. See *operations*.

operating budget. A formal *budget* for the *operating cycle* or for a year.

operating cash flow. *Cash flow from operations*. Financial statement analysts sometimes use this term to mean

Cash flow from operations –
Capital expenditures – dividends.

This usage leads to such ambiguity that the reader should always confirm the definition that the writer uses before drawing inferences from the reported data.

operating cycle. *Earnings cycle*.

operating expenses. *Expenses* incurred in the course of *ordinary* activities of an *entity;* frequently, a classification including only *selling, general*, and *administrative expenses*, thereby excluding *cost of goods sold, interest*, and *income tax* expenses. See *operations*.

operating lease. A *lease* accounted for by the *lessee* without showing an *asset* for the lease rights (*leasehold*) or a *liability* for the lease payment obligations. The lessee reports only rental payments during the period, as *expenses* of the period. The asset remains on the lessor's *books,* where rental collections appear as *revenues.* Contrast with *capital lease*.

operating leverage. Usually said of a firm with a large proportion of *fixed costs* in its *total costs*. Consider a book publisher or a railroad:

such a firm has large costs to produce the first unit of service; then, the *incremental costs* of producing another book or transporting another freight car are much less than the *average cost*, so the *gross margin* on the sale of the subsequent units is relatively large. Contrast this situation with that, for example, of a grocery store, where the *contribution margin* equals less than 5 percent of the selling price. For firms with equal profitability, however defined, we say that the one with the larger percentage increase in income from a given percentage increase in dollar sales has the larger operating leverage. See *leverage* for contrast of this term with "financial leverage." See *cost terminology* for definitions of terms involving the word "cost."

operating margin. *Revenues* from *sales* minus *cost of goods sold* and *operating expenses.*

operating margin based on current costs. *Revenues* from *sales* minus *current cost* of goods sold; a measure of operating efficiency that does not depend on the *cost flow assumption* for *inventory;* sometimes called "current (gross) margin." See *inventory profit* for illustrative computations.

operating ratio. See *ratio.*

operational control. See *control system.*

operational measures of time. Indicators of the speed and reliability with which organizations supply products and services to customer. Companies generally use two operational measures of time: *customer response time* and *on-time performance.*

operations. A word not precisely defined in *accounting*. Generally, analysts distinguish operating activities (producing and selling *goods* or *services*) from financing activities (raising funds) and *investing activities*. Acquiring goods on account and then paying for them one month later, though generally classified as an operating activity, has the characteristics of a financing activity. Or consider the transaction of selling plant assets for a price in excess of book value. On the *income statement*, the gain appears as part of income from operations ("continuing operations" or "discontinued" operations, depending on the circumstances), but the *statement of cash flows* reports all the funds received below the Cash from Operations section, as a nonoperating source of cash, "disposition of noncurrent assets." In income tax accounting, an "operating loss" results whenever deductions exceed taxable revenues.

opinion. The *auditor's report* containing an attestation or lack thereof; also, *APB Opinion.*

opinion paragraph. Section of *auditor's report*, generally following the *scope paragraph* and giving the auditor's conclusion that the *financial statements* are (rarely, are not) in accordance with *GAAP* and present fairly the *financial position*, changes in financial position, and the results of *operations.*

opportunity cost. The *present value* of the *income* (or *costs)* that a firm could earn (or save) from using an *asset* in its best alternative use to the one under consideration.

opportunity cost of capital. *Cost of capital.*

option. The legal right to buy or sell something during a specified period at a specified price, called the *exercise* price. If the right exists during a specified time interval, it is known as an "American option." If it exists for only one specific day, it is known as a "European option." Do not confuse employee *stock options* with *put* and *call* options, traded in various public markets.

ordinary annuity. An *annuity in arrears.*

ordinary income. For income tax purposes, reportable *income* not qualifying as *capital gains.*

organization costs. The *costs* incurred in planning and establishing an *entity*; example of an *intangible* asset. The firm must treat these costs as *expenses* of the period, even though the *expenditures* clearly provide future benefits and meet the test to be *assets*.

organization goals. Broad objectives for an organization established by management.

original cost. *Acquisition cost;* in public utility accounting, the acquisition cost of the *entity* first devoting the *asset* to public use. See *aboriginal cost*.

original entry. Entry in a *journal*.

OSHA (Occupational Safety and Health Act). The federal law that governs working conditions in commerce and industry.

other comprehensive income. According to the FASB, *comprehensive income* items that are not themselves part of earnings. See *comprehensive income*. To define comprehensive income does not convey its essence. To understand comprehensive income, you need to understand how it differs from *earnings* (or *net income*), the concept measured in the *earnings (income) statement*. The term *earnings* (or *net income*) refers to the sum of all components of comprehensive income *minus* the components of other comprehensive income.

outlay. The amount of an *expenditure*.

outlier. Said of an observation (or data point) that appears to differ significantly in some regard from other observations (or data points) of supposedly the same phenomenon; in a *regression analysis,* often used to describe an observation that falls far from the fitted regression equation (in two dimensions, line).

out-of-pocket. Said of an *expenditure* usually paid for with cash; an *incremental* cost.

out-of-stock cost. The estimated decrease in future *profit* as a result of losing customers because a firm has insufficient quantities of *inventory* currently on hand to meet customers' demands.

output. Physical quantity or monetary measurement of *goods* and *services* produced.

outside director. A corporate board of directors member who is not a company officer and does not participate in the corporation's day-to-day management.

outstanding. Unpaid or uncollected; when said of *stock*, refers to the shares issued less *treasury stock;* when said of *checks*, refers to a check issued that did not clear the *drawer's* bank prior to the *bank statement* date.

over-and-short. Title for an *expense account* used to account for small differences between book balances of cash and actual cash and vouchers or receipts in *petty cash* or *change funds*.

overapplied (overabsorbed) overhead. Costs applied, or *charged*, to product and exceeding actual *overhead costs* during the period; a *credit balance* in an overhead account after overhead is assigned to product.

overdraft. A *check* written on a checking account that contains funds less than the amount of the check.

overhead costs. Any *cost* not directly associated with the production or sale of identifiable goods and services; sometimes called "burden" or "indirect costs" and, in the United Kingdom, "oncosts"; frequently limited to manufacturing overhead. See *central corporate expenses* and *manufacturing overhead*.

overhead rate. Standard, or other predetermined rate, at which a firm applies *overhead costs* to products or to services.

over-the-counter. Said of a *security* traded in a negotiated transaction, as on *NASDAQ*, rather than in an auctioned one on an organized stock exchange, such as the *New York Stock Exchange*.

owners' equity. *Proprietorship; assets* minus *liabilities; paid-in capital* plus *retained earnings* of a corporation; partners' capital accounts in a *partnership*; owner's capital account in a *sole proprietorship.*

P

paid-in capital. Sum of balances in *capital stock* and *capital contributed in excess of par (or stated) value* accounts; same as *contributed capital* (minus *donated capital).* Some use the term to mean only *capital contributed in excess of par (or stated value).*

paid-in surplus. See *surplus.*

P&L. Profit-and-loss statement; *income statement.*

paper profit. A *gain* not yet realized through a *transaction;* an *unrealized holding gain.*

par. See *at par* and *face amount.*

par value. *Face amount* of a *security.*

par value method. In accounting for *treasury stock,* method that *debits* a common stock account with the *par value* of the shares required and allocates the remaining debits between the *Additional Paid-in Capital* and *Retained Earnings* accounts. Contrast with *cost method.*

parent company. Company owning more than 50 percent of the voting shares of another company, called the *subsidiary.*

Pareto chart. A graph of a skewed statistical distribution. In many business settings, a relatively small percentage of the potential population causes a relatively large percentage of the business activity. For example, some businesses find that the top 20 percent of the customers buy 80 percent of the goods sold. Or, the top 10 percent of products account for 60 percent of the revenues or 70 percent of the profits. The statistical distribution known as the Pareto distribution has this property of skewness, so a graph of a phenomenon with such skewness has come to be known as a Pareto chart, even if the underlying data do not actually well fit the Pareto distribution. Practitioners of *total quality management* find that in many businesses, a small number of processes account for a large fraction of the quality problems, so they advocate charting potential problems and actual occurrences of problems to identify the relatively small number of sources of trouble. They call such a chart a "Pareto chart."

partial obsolescence. One cause of decline in *market value* of an *asset.* As technology improves, the economic value of existing *assets* declines. In many cases, however, it will not pay a firm to replace the existing asset with a new one, even though it would acquire the new type rather than the old if it did make a new acquisition currently. In these cases, the accountant should theoretically recognize a loss from partial obsolescence from the firm's owning an old, out-of-date asset, but *GAAP* do not permit recognition of partial obsolescence until the sum of future cash flows from the asset total less than book value; see *impairment.* The firm will carry the old asset at *cost* less *accumulated depreciation* until the firm retires it from service so long as the *undiscounted* future *cash flows* from the asset exceed its book value. Thus management that uses an asset subject to partial obsolescence reports results inferior to those reported by a similar management that uses a new asset. See *obsolescence.*

partially executory contract. *Executory contract* in which one or both parties have done something other than merely promise.

partially funded. Said of a *pension plan* in which the firm has not funded all earned benefits. See *funded* for funding requirements.

partially vested. Said of a *pension plan* in which not all employee benefits have *vested.* See *graded vesting.*

participating dividend. *Dividend* paid to preferred shareholders in addition to the minimum preferred dividends when the *preferred stock* contract provides for such sharing in earnings. Usually the contract specifies that dividends on *common shares* must reach a specified level before the preferred shares receive the participating dividend.

participating preferred stock. *Preferred stock* with rights to *participating dividends.*

participative budgeting. Using input from lower- and middle-management employees in setting goals.

partner's drawing. A payment made to a partner and debited against his or her share of income or capital. The name of a *temporary account,* closed to the partner's capital account, to record the debits when the partner receives such payments.

partnership. Contractual arrangement between individuals to share resources and operations in a jointly run business. See *general* and *limited partner* and *Uniform Partnership Act.*

patent. A right granted for up to 20 years by the federal government to exclude others from manufacturing, using, or selling a claimed design, product, or plant (e.g., a new breed of rose) or from using a claimed process or method of manufacture; an *asset* if the firm acquires it by purchase. If the firm develops it internally, current *GAAP* require the firm to *expense* the development costs when incurred.

payable. Unpaid but not necessarily due or past due.

pay-as-you-go. Said of an *income tax* scheme in which the taxpayer makes periodic payments of income taxes during the period when it earns the income to be taxed; in contrast to a scheme in which the taxpayer owes no payments until the end of, or after, the period when it earned the income being taxed (called PAYE—pay-as-you-earn—in the United Kingdom). The phrase is sometimes used to describe an *unfunded pension plan,* or retirement benefit plan, in which the firm makes payments to pension plan beneficiaries from general corporate funds, not from cash previously contributed to a fund. Under this method, the firm debits expense as it makes payments, not as it incurs the obligations. This is not acceptable as a method of accounting for pension plans, under *SFAS No. 87,* or as a method of *funding,* under *ERISA.*

payback period. Amount of time that must elapse before the cash inflows from a project equal the cash outflows.

payback reciprocal. One divided by the *payback period.* This number approximates the *internal rate of return* on a project when the project life exceeds twice the payback period and the cash inflows are identical in every period after the initial period.

PAYE (pay-as-you-earn). See *pay-as-you-go* for contrast.

payee. The person or entity who receives a cash payment or who will receive the stated amount of cash on a *check.* See *draft.*

payout ratio. *Common stock dividends* declared for a year divided by net *income* to common stock for the year; a term used by financial analysts. Contrast with *dividend yield.*

payroll taxes. Taxes levied because the taxpayer pays salaries or wages; for example, *FICA* and unemployment compensation insurance taxes. Typically, the employer pays a portion and withholds part of the employee's wages.

PCAOB. *Public Company Accounting Oversight Board.*

P/E ratio. *Price–earnings ratio.*

Pension Benefit Guarantee Corporation (PBGC). A federal corporation established under *ERISA* to guarantee basic pension benefits in covered pension plans by administering terminated pension plans and placing *liens* on corporate assets for certain unfunded pension liabilities.

pension fund. *Fund*, the assets of which the trustee will pay to retired ex-employees, usually as a *life annuity;* generally held by an independent trustee and thus not an *asset* of the employer.

pension plan. Details or provisions of employer's contract with employees for paying retirement *annuities* or other benefits. See *funded, vested, service cost, prior service cost, money purchase plan*, and *defined-benefit plan*.

per books. An expression used to refer to the *book value* of an item at a specific time.

percent. Any number, expressed as a decimal, multiplied by 100.

percentage depletion (allowance). Deductible *expense* allowed in some cases by the federal *income tax* regulations; computed as a percentage of gross income from a *natural resource* independent of the unamortized cost of the *asset*. Because the amount of the total deductions for tax purposes usually exceeds the cost of the asset being *depleted*, many people think the deduction is an unfair tax advantage or *loophole*.

percentage-of-completion method. Recognizing *revenues* and *expenses* on a job, order, or contract (1) in proportion to the *costs* incurred for the period divided by total costs expected to be incurred for the job or order ("cost to cost") or (2) in proportion to engineers' or architects' estimates of the incremental degree of completion of the job, order, or contract during the period. Contrast with *completed contract method*.

percentage statement. A statement containing, in addition to (or instead of) dollar amounts, ratios of dollar amounts to some base. In a percentage *income statement*, the base is usually either *net sales* or total *revenues,* and in a percentage *balance sheet*, the base is usually total *assets*.

period. *Accounting period.*

period cost. An inferior term for *period expense*.

period expense (charge). *Expenditure*, usually based on the passage of time, charged to operations of the accounting period rather than *capitalized* as an asset. Contrast with *product cost*.

periodic cash flows. *Cash flows* that occur during the life of an investment project. Often include *receipts* from *sales, expenditures* for *fixed* and *variable production costs,* and savings of *fixed* and *variable* production costs, to name a few. They do not include noncash items, such as *financial accounting depreciation charges* or *allocated* items of *overhead* not requiring *differential* cash expenditures.

periodic inventory. In recording *inventory,* a method that uses data on beginning inventory, additions to inventories, and ending inventory to find the cost of withdrawals from inventory. Contrast with *perpetual inventory*.

periodic procedures. The process of making *adjusting entries* and *closing entries* and preparing the *financial statements*, usually by use of *trial balances* and *work sheets*.

permanent account. An account that appears on the *balance sheet*. Contrast with *temporary account*.

permanent difference. Difference between reported income and taxable income that will never reverse and, hence, requires no entry in the *deferred income tax (liability)* account; for example, nontaxable state and municipal *bond* interest that will appear on the financial statements. Contrast with *temporary difference.* See *deferred income tax liability*.

permanent file. The file of working papers that are prepared by a public accountant and that contain the information required for reference in successive professional engagements for a particular organization, as distinguished from working papers applicable only to a particular engagement.

perpetual annuity. *Perpetuity.*

perpetual inventory. *Inventory* quantity and amount records that the firm changes and makes current with each physical addition to or withdrawal from the stock of goods; an inventory so recorded. The records will show the physical quantities and, frequently, the dollar valuations that should be on hand at any time. Because the firm explicitly computes *cost of goods sold*, it can use the *inventory equation* to compute an amount for what *ending inventory* should be. It can then compare the computed amount of ending inventory with the actual amount of ending inventory as a *control* device to measure the amount of *shrinkages*. Contrast with *periodic inventory*.

perpetuity. An *annuity* whose payments continue forever. The *present value* of a perpetuity in *arrears* is p/r where p is the periodic payment and r is the *interest rate* per period. If a perpetuity promises $100 each year, in arrears, forever, and the interest rate is 8 percent per year, then the perpetuity has a value of $1,250 = $100/.08.

perpetuity growth model. See *perpetuity*. A *perpetuity* whose cash flows grow at the rate g per period and thus has *present value* of $1/(r - g)$. Some call this the "Gordon Growth Model" because Myron Gordon wrote about applications of this formula and its variants in the 1950s. John Burr Williams wrote about them in the 1930s.

personal account. *Drawing account.*

PERT (Program Evaluation and Review Technique). A method of *network analysis* in which the analyst makes three time estimates for each activity—the optimistic time, the most likely time, and the pessimistic time—and gives an expected completion date for the project within a probability range.

petty cash fund. Currency and coins maintained for expenditures that the firm makes with cash on hand.

physical units method. A method of allocating a *joint cost* to the *joint products* based on a physical measure of the joint products; for example, allocating the cost of a cow to sirloin steak and to hamburger, based on the weight of the meat. This method usually provides nonsensical (see *sterilized allocation)* results unless the physical units of the joint products tend to have the same value.

physical verification. *Verification*, by an *auditor*, performed by actually inspecting items in *inventory, plant assets*, and the like, in contrast to merely checking the written records. The auditor may use statistical sampling procedures.

planning and control process. General name for the management techniques comprising the setting of organizational goals and *strategic plans, capital budgeting, operations* budgeting, comparison of plans with actual results, performance evaluation and corrective action, and revisions of goals, plans, and budgets.

plant. *Plant assets.*

plant asset turnover. Number of dollars of *sales* generated per dollar of *plant assets;* equal to sales divided by average *plant assets.*

plant assets. *Assets* used in the revenue-production process. Plant assets include buildings, machinery, equipment, land, and natural resources. The phrase "property, plant, and equipment" (though often appearing on balance sheets) is therefore a redundancy. In this context, "plant" used alone means buildings.

plantwide allocation method. A method for *allocating overhead costs* to product. First, use one *cost pool* for the entire plant. Then, allocate all costs from that pool to products using a single overhead *allocation* rate, or one set of rates, for all the products of the plant, independent of the number of departments in the plant.

PLC (public limited company). United Kingdom: a publicly held *corporation*. Contrast with *Ltd.*

pledging. The borrower assigns *assets* as security or *collateral* for repayment of a loan.

pledging of receivables. The process of using expected collections on *accounts receivable* as *collateral* for a loan. The borrower remains responsible for collecting the receivable but promises to use the proceeds for repaying the debt.

plow back. To retain *assets* generated by earnings for continued investment in the business.

plug. Process for finding an unknown amount. For any *account*, Beginning balance + Additions – Deductions = Ending balance; if you know any three of the four items, you can find the fourth with simple arithmetic, called "plugging." In making a *journal entry*, often you know all *debits* and all but one of the *credits* (or vice versa). Because *double-entry* bookkeeping requires equal debits and credits, you can compute the unknown quantity by subtracting the sum of the known credits from the sum of all the debits (or vice versa), also called "plugging." Accountants often call the unknown the "plug." For example, in amortizing a *discount* on *bonds payable* with the *straight-line depreciation* method, *interest expense* is a plug: Interest expense = Interest payable + *Discount amortization.* See *trade-in transaction* for an example. The term sometimes has a bad connotation for accountants because plugging can occur in a slightly different context. During the process of preparing a *preclosing trial balance* (or *balance sheet*), often the sum of the debits does not equal the sum of the credits. Rather than find the error, some accountants are tempted to force equality by changing one of the amounts, with a plugged debit or credit to an account such as Other Expenses. No harm results from this procedure if the amount of the error is small compared with asset totals, since spending tens or hundreds of dollars in a bookkeeper's or accountant's time to find an error of a few dollars will not be *cost-effective.* Still, most accounting teachers rightly disallow this use of plugging because exercises and problems set for students provide enough information not to require it.

point of sale. The time, not the location, at which a *sale* occurs.

pooling-of-interests method. Accounting for a *business combination* by adding together the *book value* of the *assets* and *equities* of the combined firms; generally leads to a higher reported *net income* for the combined firms than results when the firm accounts for the business combination as a purchase because the *market values* of the merged assets generally exceed their book values. US GAAP do not allow this method, although it previously did, so financial statements still reflect the effects of pooling accounting. Contrast with *purchase method.* Called *uniting-of-interests method* by the *IASB.*

population. The entire set of numbers or items from which the analyst samples or performs some other analysis.

positive confirmation. See *confirmation.*

post. To record entries in an *account* to a *ledger,* usually as transfers from a *journal.*

post-closing trial balance. *Trial balance* taken after the accountant has *closed* all *temporary accounts*.

post-statement events. Events that have *material* impact and that occur between the end of the *accounting period* and the formal publi cation of the *financial statements*. Even though the events occur after the end of the period being reported on, the firm must disclose such events in notes if the auditor is to give a *clean opinion*.

potentially dilutive security. A *security* that its holder may convert into, or exchange for, common stock and thereby reduce reported *earnings per share; options, warrants, convertible bonds*, and *convertible preferred stock*.

PPB. *Program budgeting*. The second "P" stands for "plan."

practical capacity. Maximum level at which a plant or department can operate efficiently.

precision. The degree of accuracy for an estimate derived from a sampling process, usually expressed as a range of values around the estimate. The analyst might express a sample estimate in the following terms: "Based on the sample, we are 95 percent sure [confidence level] that the true population value is within the range of X to Y [precision]." See *confidence level*.

preclosing trial balance. *Trial balance* taken at the end of the period before *closing entries;* in this sense, an *adjusted trial balance;* sometimes taken before *adjusting entries* and then synonymous with *unadjusted trial balance*.

predatory prices. Setting prices below some measure of cost in an effort to drive out competitors with the hope of recouping losses later by charging monopoly prices. Illegal in the United States if the prices set are below long-run variable costs. We know of no empirical evidence that firms are successful at recoupment.

predetermined (factory) overhead rate. Rate used in applying *overhead costs* to products or departments developed at the start of a period. Compute the rate as estimated overhead cost divided by the estimated number of units of the overhead allocation base (or *denominator volume*) activity. See *normal costing*.

preemptive right. The privilege of a *shareholder* to maintain a proportionate share of ownership by purchasing a proportionate share of any new stock issues. Most state corporation laws allow corporations to pay shareholders to waive their preemptive rights or state that preemptive rights exist only if the *corporation charter* explicitly grants them. In practice, then, preemptive rights are the exception rather than the rule.

preference as to assets. The rights of *preferred shareholders* to receive certain payments before common shareholders receive payments in case the board dissolves the corporation.

preferred shares. *Capital stock* with a claim to *income* or *assets* after *bondholders* but before *common shares*. *Dividends* on preferred shares are *income distributions*, not *expenses*. See *cumulative preferred stock*.

premium. The excess of issue (or market) price over *par value*. For a different context, see *insurance*.

premium on capital stock. Alternative but inferior title for *capital contributed in excess of par (or stated) value*.

prepaid expense. An *expenditure* that leads to a *deferred charge* or *prepayment*. Strictly speaking, this is a contradiction in terms because an *expense* is a gone asset, and this title refers to past *expenditures*, such as for rent or insurance premiums, that still have future benefits and thus are *assets*. We try to avoid this term and use "prepayment" instead.

prepaid income. An inferior alternative title for *advances from customers*. Do not call an item *revenue* or *income* until the firm earns it by delivering goods or rendering services.

prepayments. *Deferred charges*; *assets* representing *expenditures* for future benefits. Rent and insurance premiums paid in advance are usually current prepayments.

present value. Value today (or at some specific date) of an amount or amounts to be paid or received later (or at other, different dates), discounted at some *interest* or *discount rate*; an amount that, if invested today at the specified rate, will grow to the amount to be paid or received in the future.

prevention costs. *Costs incurred* to prevent defects in the products or services they produce, including procurement inspection, processing control (inspection), design, quality training and machine inspection.

price. The quantity of one *good* or *service*, usually *cash*, asked in return for a unit of another good or service. See *fair value*.

price–earnings (P/E) ratio. At a given time, the market value of a company's *common share*, per share, divided by the *earnings per* common *share* for the past year. The analyst usually bases the denominator on *income from continuing operations* or, if the analyst thinks the current figure for that amount does not represent a usual situation—such as when the number is negative or, if positive, close to zero—on some estimate of the number. See *ratio*.

price index. A series of numbers, one for each period, that purports to represent some *average* of prices for a series of periods, relative to a base period.

price level. The number from a *price index* series for a given period or date.

price level–adjusted statements. *Financial statements* expressed in terms of dollars of uniform purchasing power. The statements restate *nonmonetary* items to reflect changes in general *price levels* since the time the firm acquired specific *assets* and incurred *liabilities*. The statements recognize a *gain* or *loss* on *monetary items* as the firm holds them over time periods when the general *price level changes*. Conventional financial statements show *historical costs* and ignore differences in purchasing power in different periods.

price variance. In accounting for *standard costs*, an amount equal to (Actual cost per unit – Standard cost per unit) × Actual quantity.

primary earnings per share (PEPS). Net *income* to common shareholders plus *interest* (net of tax effects) or *dividends* paid on *common-stock equivalents* divided by (weighted average of common shares outstanding plus the net increase in the number of common shares that would become *outstanding* if the holders of all common stock equivalents were to exchange them for common shares with cash proceeds, if any, used to retire common shares). As of 1997 and *SFAS No. 128*, replaced with *basic earnings per share*.

prime cost. Sum of *direct materials* plus *direct labor* costs assigned to product.

prime rate. The loan rate charged by commercial banks to their creditworthy customers. Some customers pay even less than the prime rate and others, more. The *Federal Reserve Bulletin* is the authoritative source of information about historical prime rates.

principal. An amount on which *interest* accrues, either as *expense* (for the borrower) or as *revenue* (for the lender); the *face amount* of a *loan;* also, the absent owner (principal) who hires the manager (agent) in a "principal-agent" relation.

principle. See *generally accepted accounting principles*.

prior-period adjustment. A *debit* or *credit* that is made directly to *retained earnings* (and that does not affect *income* for the period) to adjust earnings as calculated for prior periods. Such adjustments are now rare. Theory suggests that accounting should correct for errors in accounting estimates (such as the *depreciable life* or *salvage value* of an asset) by adjusting retained earnings so that statements for future periods will show correct amounts. But *GAAP* require that corrections of such estimates flow through current, and perhaps future, *income statements*. See *accounting changes* and *accounting errors*.

prior service cost. *Present value* at a given time of a *pension plan's* retroactive *benefits*. "Unrecognized prior service cost" refers to that portion of prior service cost not yet *debited* to *expense*. See *actuarial accrued liability* and *funded*. Contrast with *normal cost*.

pro forma income. See *pro forma statements*.

pro forma statements. Hypothetical statements; financial statements as they would appear if some event, such as a *merger* or increased production and sales, had occurred or were to occur; sometimes spelled as one word, "proforma." The phrase "pro forma income" has come to disrepute, as some companies have published pro forma income statements showing their good news, their recurring income, and omitting the bad news, as nonrecurring. They have attempted to focus the investment community on their own presentation of this good news, de-emphasizing GAAP net income. The *SEC* and others have attempted to make these disclosures less misleading.

probable. In many of its definitions, the *FASB* uses the term "probable." See, for example, *asset, firm commitment, liability*. A survey of practicing accountants revealed that the average of the probabilities that those surveyed had in mind when they used the term "probable" was 85 percent. Some accountants think that any event whose outcome is greater than 50 percent should be called "probable." The FASB uses the phrase "more likely than not" when it means greater than 50 percent.

proceeds. The *funds* received from the disposition of assets or from the issue of securities.

process costing. A method of *cost accounting* based on average costs (total cost divided by the *equivalent units* of work done in a period); typically used for assembly lines or for products that the firm produces in a series of steps that are more continuous than discrete.

product. *Goods* or *services* produced.

product cost. Any *manufacturing cost* that the firm can—or, in some contexts, should—debit to an *inventory* account. See *flow of costs*, for example. Contrast with *period expenses*.

product life cycle. Time span between initial concept (typically starting with research and development) of a good or service and the time when the firm ceases to support customers who have purchased the good or service.

production cost. *Manufacturing cost*.

production cost account. A *temporary account* for accumulating *manufacturing costs* during a period.

production department. A department producing salable *goods* or *services*; contrast with *service department*.

production method (depreciation). One form of *straight-line depreciation*. The firm assigns to the depreciable asset (e.g., a truck) a *depreciable life* measured not in elapsed time but in units of output (e.g., miles) or perhaps in units of time of expected use. Then the *depreciation* charge for a period is a portion of depreciable cost equal to a fraction computed as the actual output produced during the period divided by the expected total output to be produced over the life of the asset. This method is sometimes called the "units-of-production (or output) method."

production method (revenue recognition). *Percentage-of-completion method* for recognizing *revenue*.

production volume variance. Standard fixed *overhead* rate per unit of normal *capacity* (or base activity) times (units of base activity budgeted or planned for a period minus actual units of base activity worked or assigned to product during the period); often called a "volume variance."

productive capacity. One *attribute measured* for *assets*. The *current cost* of *long-term assets* means the cost of reproducing the productive capacity (e.g., the ability to manufacture one million units a year), not the cost of reproducing the actual physical assets currently used (see *reproduction cost*). *Replacement cost* of productive capacity will be the same as reproduction cost of assets only in the unusual case when no technological improvement in production processes has occurred and the relative prices of goods and services used in production have remained approximately the same as when the firm acquired the currently used goods and services.

product-level activities. Work that supports a particular product or service line. Examples include design work, supervision, and advertising that are specific to each type of product or service.

production cycle efficiency. Measures the efficiency of the production cycle by computing the ratio of the time spent processing a unit divided by the *production cycle time*. The higher the percentage, the less the time and costs spent on *non-value-added activities*, such as moving and storage.

production cycle time. The total time to produce a unit. Includes processing, moving, storing, and inspecting.

profit. Excess of *revenues* over *expenses* for a *transaction*; sometimes used synonymously with *net income* for the period.

profit-and-loss account. United Kingdom: *retained earnings*.

profit-and-loss sharing ratio. The fraction of *net income* or loss allocable to a partner in a *partnership*. Need not be the same fraction as the partner's share of capital.

profit-and-loss statement. *Income statement*.

profit center. A *responsibility center* for which a firm accumulates both *revenues* and *expenses*. Contrast with *cost center*.

profit margin. *Sales* minus all *expenses*.

profit margin percentage. *Profit margin* divided by *net sales*.

profit maximization. The doctrine that the firm should account for a given set of operations so as to make reported *net income* as large as possible; contrast with *conservatism*. This concept in accounting differs from the profit-maximizing concept in economics, which states that the firm should manage operations to maximize the present value of the firm's wealth, generally by equating *marginal costs* and *marginal revenues*.

profit plan. The *income statement* portion of a *master budget*.

profit-sharing plan. A *defined-contribution plan* in which the employer contributes amounts based on *net income*.

profit variance analysis. Analysis of the causes of the difference between budgeted profit in the *master budget* and the profits earned.

profit-volume analysis (equation). Analysis of effects, on *profits*, caused by changes in volume or *contribution margin* per unit or *fixed costs*. See *breakeven chart*.

profit-volume graph. See *breakeven chart*.

profit-volume ratio. *Net income* divided by net sales in dollars.

profitability accounting. *Responsibility accounting*.

program budgeting (PPB). Specification and analysis of inputs, outputs, costs, and alternatives that link plans to *budgets*.

programmed cost. A *fixed cost* not essential for carrying out operations. For example, a firm can control costs for research and development and advertising designed to generate new business, but once it commits to incur them, they become fixed costs. These costs are sometimes called managed costs or *discretionary costs*. Contrast with *capacity costs*.

progressive tax. Tax for which the rate increases as the taxed base, such as income, increases. Contrast with *regressive tax*.

project financing arrangement. As defined by *SFAS No. 47*, the financing of an investment project in which the lender looks principally to the *cash flows* and *earnings* of the project as the source of funds for repayment and to the *assets* of the project as *collateral* for the loan. The general *credit* of the project entity usually does not affect the terms of the financing either because the borrowing entity is a *corporation* without other assets or because the financing provides that the lender has no direct *recourse* to the entity's owners.

projected benefit obligation. The *actuarial present value* at a given date of all pension benefits attributed by a *defined-benefit pension* formula to employee service rendered before that date. The analyst measures the obligation using assumptions as to future compensation levels if the formula incorporates future compensation, as happens, for example, when the plan bases the eventual pension benefit on wages of the last several years of employees' work lives. Contrast to "accumulated benefit obligation," where the analyst measures the obligation using employee compensation levels at the time of the measurement date.

projected financial statement. *Pro forma* financial statement.

projection. See *financial projection* for definition and contrast.

promissory note. An unconditional written promise to pay a specified sum of cash on demand or at a specified date.

proof of journal. The process of checking the arithmetic accuracy of *journal entries* by testing for the equality of all *debits* and all *credits* since the last previous proof.

property dividend. A *dividend in kind*.

property, plant, and equipment. See *plant assets*.

proportionate consolidation. Canada: a presentation of the *financial statements* of any investor-investment relationship, whereby the investor's pro rata share of each *asset, liability, income* item, and *expense* item appears in the *financial statements* of the investor under the various *balance sheet* and *income statement* headings.

proprietary accounts. See *budgetary accounts* for definition and contrast in the context of governmental accounting.

proprietorship. *Assets* minus *liabilities* of an *entity*; equals *contributed capital* plus *retained earnings*.

proprietorship theory. The corporation view that emphasizes the form of the *accounting equation* that says *assets – liabilities = owners' equity*; contrast with *entity theory*. The major implication of a choice between these theories deals with the treatment of *subsidiaries*. For example, the proprietorship theory views *minority interest* as an *indeterminate-term liability*. The proprietorship theory implies using a *single-step income statement*.

prorate. To *allocate* in proportion to some base; for example, to allocate *service department* costs in proportion to hours of service used by the benefited department or to allocate *manufacturing variances* to product sold and to product added to *ending inventory*.

prorating variances. See *prorate.*

prospectus. Formal written document describing *securities* a firm will issue. See *proxy.*

protest fee. Fee charged by banks or other financial agencies when the bank cannot collect items (such as *checks*) presented for collection.

provision. Part of an *account* title. Often the firm must recognize an *expense* even though it cannot be sure of the exact amount. The entry for the estimated expense, such as for *income taxes* or expected costs under *warranty*, is as follows:

Retained Earnings (Estimated)	X	
Liability Increase (Estimated)		X

American terminology often uses "provision" in the expense account title of the above entry. Thus, Provision for Income Taxes means the estimate of income tax expense. (British terminology uses "provision" in the title for the estimated liability of the above entry, so that Provision for Income Taxes is a balance sheet account.)

proxy. Written authorization given by one person to another so that the second person can act for the first, such as to vote shares of stock; of particular significance to accountants because the *SEC* presumes that management distributes financial information along with its proxy solicitations.

public accountant. Generally, this term is synonymous with *certified public accountant.* Some jurisdictions, however, license individuals who are not CPAs as public accountants.

public accounting. That portion of accounting primarily involving the *attest* function, culminating in the *auditor's report.*

Public Company Accounting Oversight Board, PCAOB. A board established by the Sarbanes-Oxley Act of 2002 which regulates the auditing profession and sets standards for audits of public companies. The *SEC* appoints its members.

PuPU. Acronym for *pu*rchasing *p*ower *u*nit; conceived by John C. Burton, former chief accountant of the *SEC*. Those who think that *constant-dollar accounting* is not particularly useful poke fun at it by calling it "PuPU accounting."

purchase allowance. A reduction in sales *invoice price* usually granted because the purchaser received *goods* not exactly as ordered. The purchaser does not return the goods but agrees to keep them for a price lower than originally agreed upon.

purchase discount. A reduction in purchase *invoice price* granted for prompt payment. See *sales discount* and *terms of sale.*

purchase investigation. An investigation of the financial affairs of a company for the purpose of disclosing matters that may influence the terms or conclusion of a potential acquisition.

purchase method. Accounting for a *business combination* by adding the acquired company's assets at the price paid for them to the acquiring company's assets. Contrast with *pooling-of-interests method.* The firm adds the acquired assets to the books at current values rather than original costs; the subsequent *amortization expenses* usually exceed those (and reported income is smaller than that) for the same business combination accounted for as a pooling of interests. US *GAAP* now require that the acquirer use the purchase method, but other countries still allow poolings.

purchase order. Document issued by a buyer authorizing a seller to deliver goods, with the buyer to make payment later.

purchasing power gain or loss. *Monetary gain or loss.*

push-down accounting. An accounting method used in some *purchase transactions.* Assume that Company A purchases substantially all the *common shares* of Company B but that Company B must still issue its own *financial statements.* The question arises, shall Company B change the *basis* for its *assets* and *equities* on its own books to the same updated amounts at which they appear on Company A's *consolidated financial statements*? Company B uses "push-down accounting" when it shows the new asset and equity bases reflecting Company A's purchase, because the method "pushes down" the new bases from Company A (where *GAAP* require them) to Company B (where the new bases would not appear in *historical cost accounting*). Since 1983, the *SEC* has required push-down accounting under some circumstances.

put. An option to sell *shares* of a publicly traded corporation at a fixed price during a fixed time span. Contrast with *call.*

Q

qualified report (opinion). *Auditor's report* containing a statement that the auditor was unable to complete a satisfactory examination of all things considered relevant or that the auditor has doubts about the financial impact of some *material* item reported in the financial statements. See *except for* and *subject to.*

quality. In modern usage, a product or service has quality to the extent it conforms to specifications or provides customers the characteristics promised them.

quality of earnings. A phrase with no single, agreed-upon meaning. Some who use the phrase use it with different meanings on different occasions. "Quality of earnings" has an accounting aspect and a business cycle aspect.

In its accounting aspect, managers have choices in measuring and reporting *earnings.* This discretion can involve any of the following: selecting *accounting principles* or standards when *GAAP* allow a choice; making estimates in the application of accounting principles; and timing transactions to allow recognizing *nonrecurring* items in earnings. In some instances the range of choices has a large impact on reported earnings and in others, small. (1) Some use the phrase "quality of earnings" to mean the degree to which management can affect reported income by its choices of accounting estimates even though the choices recur every period. These users judge, for example, insurance companies to have low-quality earnings. Insurance company management must reestimate its liabilities for future payments to the insured each period, thereby having an opportunity to report periodic earnings within a wide range. (2) Others use the phrase to mean the degree to which management actually takes advantage of its flexibility. For them, an insurance company that does not vary its methods and estimating techniques, even though it has the opportunity to do so, has high-quality earnings. (3) Some have in mind the proximity in time between *revenue* recognition and cash collection. For them, the smaller the time delay, the higher will be the quality. (4) Still others use the phrase to mean the degree to which managers who have a choice among the items with large influence on earnings choose the ones that result in income measures that are more likely to recur. For them, the more likely an item of earnings is to recur, the higher will be its quality. Often these last two groups trade off with each other. Consider a dealer leasing a car on a long-term *lease,* receiving monthly collections. The dealer who uses *sales-type lease* accounting scores low on proximity of revenue recognition (all at the time of signing the lease) to cash collection but highlights the nonrepetitive nature of the transaction. The leasing dealer who uses *operating lease* accounting has perfectly matching revenue recognition and cash collection, but the *recurring* nature of the revenue gives a misleading picture of a repetitive transaction. The phrase "item of earnings" in (4) is ambiguous. The writer could mean the underlying economic event (which occurs when the lease for the car is signed) or the revenue recognition (which occurs every time the dealer using operating lease accounting receives cash). Hence, you should try to understand what other speakers and writers mean by "quality of earnings" when you interpret what they say and write. Some who refer to "earnings quality" suspect that managers will usually make choices that enhance current earnings and present the firm in the best light, independent of the ability of the firm to generate similar earnings in the future.

In the business cycle aspect, management's action often has no impact on the stability and recurrence of earnings. Compare a company that sells consumer products and likely has sales repeating every week with a construction company that builds to order. Companies in noncyclical businesses, such as some public utilities, likely have more stable earnings than ones in cyclical businesses, such as steel. Some use "quality of earnings" to refer to the stability and recurrence of basic revenue-generating activities. Those who use the phrase this way rarely associate earnings quality with accounting issues.

quality of financial position. Because of the *articulation* of the *income statement* with the *balance sheet,* the factors that imply a high (or low) *quality of earnings* also affect the balance sheet. Users of this phrase have in mind the same accounting issues as they have in mind when they use the phrase "quality of earnings."

quantitative performance measure. A measure of output based on an objectively observable quantity, such as units produced or *direct costs* incurred, rather than on an unobservable quantity or a quantity observable only nonobjectively, like quality of service provided.

quantity discount. A reduction in purchase price as quantity purchased increases. The Robinson-Patman Act constrains the amount of the discount. Do not confuse with *purchase discount*.

quantity variance. *Efficiency variance;* in *standard cost* systems, the standard price per unit times (actual quantity used minus standard quantity that should be used).

quasi-reorganization. A *reorganization* in which no new company emerges or no court has intervened, as would happen in *bankruptcy*. The primary purpose is to rid the balance sheet of a *deficit* (negative *retained earnings*) and give the firm a "fresh start."

quick assets. *Assets* readily convertible into *cash*; includes cash, current marketable securities, and current receivables.

quick ratio. Sum of (cash, current marketable securities, and current receivables) divided by *current liabilities;* often called the "acid test ratio." The analyst may exclude some nonliquid receivables from the numerator. See *ratio*.

R

R^2. The proportion of the statistical variance of a *dependent variable* explained by the equation fit to *independent variable(s)* in a *regression analysis*.

Railroad Accounting Principles Board (RAPB). A board brought into existence by the Staggers Rail Act of 1980 to advise the Interstate Commerce Commission on accounting matters affecting railroads. The RAPB was the only cost-accounting body authorized by the government during the decade of the 1980s (because Congress ceased funding the CASB during the 1980s). The RAPB incorporated the pronouncements of the CASB and became the government's authority on cost accounting principles.

R&D. See *research and development.*

random number sampling. For choosing a sample, a method in which the analyst selects items from the *population* by using a random number table or generator.

random sampling. For choosing a sample, a method in which all items in the population have an equal chance of being selected. Compare *judgment(al) sampling.*

RAPB. *Railroad Accounting Principles Board.*

rate of return on assets. *Return on assets.*

rate of return on common stock equity. See *ratio.*

rate of return on shareholders' (owners') equity. See *ratio.*

rate of return (on total capital). See *ratio* and *return on assets.*

rate variance. *Price variance*, usually for *direct labor costs.*

ratio. The number resulting when one number divides another. Analysts generally use ratios to assess aspects of profitability, solvency, and liquidity. The commonly used financial ratios fall into three categories: (1) those that summarize some aspect of *operations* for a period, usually a year, (2) those that summarize some aspect of *financial position* at a given moment—the moment for which a balance sheet reports, and (3) those that relate some aspect of operations to some aspect of financial position. Exhibit 1-3 lists common financial ratios and shows separately both the numerator and the denominator for each ratio.

Ratio	Numerator	Denominator
Profitability Ratios		
Rate of return on assets	Net income + Interest expense (net of tax effects)[a]	Average total assets during the period
Profit margin for ROA (before interest effects)	Net income + Interest expense (net of tax effects)[a]	Sales
Various expense ratios	Various expenses	Sales
Total assets turnover ratio	Sales	Average total assets during the period
Accounts receivable turnover ratio	Sales	Average accounts receivable during the period
Inventory turnover ratio	Cost of goods sold	Average inventory during the period

EXHIBIT 1.3 SUMMARY OF FINANCIAL STATEMENT RATIOS

Ratio	Numerator	Denominator
Fixed asset turnover ratio	Sales	Average fixed assets during the period
Rate of return on common shareholders' equity	Net income – Preferred stock dividends	Average common shareholders' equity during the period
Profit margin for ROCE (after interest expense and preferred dividends)	Net income – Preferred stock Dividends	Sales
Capital structure leverage ratio	Average total assets during the period	Average common shareholders' equity during the period
Earnings per share of common stock[b]	Net income – Preferred stock dividends	Weighted-average number of common shares outstanding
Short-term Liquidity Ratios		
Current ratio	Current assets	Current liabilities
Quick or acid test ratio	Highly liquid assets (cash, marketable securities, and receivables)[c]	Current liabilities
Cash flow from operations to current liabilities ratio	Cash flow from operations	Average current liabilities during the period
Accounts payable turnover ratio	Purchases[d]	Average accounts payable during the period
Days accounts receivable outstanding	365 days	Accounts receivable turnover ratio
Days inventories held	365 days	Inventory turnover ratio
Days accounts payable outstanding	365 days	Accounts payable turnover ratio
Long-term Liquidity Ratios		
Long-term debt ratio	Total long-term debt	Total long-term debt plus shareholders' equity
Debt–equity ratio	Total liabilities	Total equities (total liabilities + shareholders' equity = total assets)
Cash flow from operations to total liabilities ratio	Cash flow from operations	Average total liabilities during the period
Interest coverage ratio	Income before Interest and income taxes	Interest expense

[a] If the parent company does not own all of a consolidated subsidiary, the calculation also adds back to net income the minority interest share of earnings. See Chapter 11 for discussion of minority interest.

[b] This calculation is more complicated when there are convertible securities, options, or warrants outstanding.

[c] The calculation could conceivably exclude receivables for some firms and include inventories for others.

[d] Purchases = Cost of goods sold + Ending inventories – Beginning inventories

EXHIBIT 1.3 SUMMARY OF FINANCIAL STATEMENT RATIOS *(CONTINUED)*

For all ratios that require an average balance during the period, the analyst often derives the average as one half the sum of the beginning and the ending balances. Sophisticated analysts recognize, however, that particularly when companies use a fiscal year different from the calendar year, this averaging of beginning and ending balances may mislead. Consider, for example, the rate of *return on assets* of Sears Company, whose fiscal year ends on January 31. Sears chooses a January 31 closing date at least in part because inventories are at a low level and are therefore easy to count—it has sold the Christmas merchandise, and the Easter merchandise has not yet all arrived. Furthermore, by January 31, Sears has collected for most Christmas sales, so receivable amounts are not unusually large. Thus at January 31, the amount of total assets is lower than at many other times during the year. Consequently, the denominator of the rate of return on assets, total assets, for Sears more likely represents the smallest amount of total assets on hand during the year rather than the average amount. The return on assets rate for Sears and other companies that choose a fiscal year-end to coincide with low points in the inventory cycle is likely to exceed the ratio measured with a more accurate estimate of the average amounts of total assets.

raw material. Goods purchased for use in manufacturing a product.

reacquired stock. *Treasury shares.*

real accounts. *Balance sheet accounts,* as opposed to *nominal accounts.* See *permanent accounts.*

real amount (value). An amount stated in *constant dollars.* For example, if the firm sells an investment costing $100 for $130 after a period of 10 percent general *inflation,* the *nominal amount* of *gain* is $30 (= $130 − $100) but the real amount of gain is C$20 (= $130 − 1.10 × $100), where "C$" denotes constant dollars of purchasing power on the date of sale.

real estate. *Land* and its *improvements,* such as landscaping and roads, but not buildings.

real interest rate. Interest rate reflecting the productivity of capital, not including a premium for inflation anticipated over the life of the loan.

realizable value. *Fair value* or, sometimes, *net realizable (sales) value.*

realization convention. The accounting practice of delaying the recognition of *gains* and *losses* from changes in the market price of *assets* until the firm sells the assets. However, the firm recognizes unrealized losses on *inventory* (or *marketable securities* classified as *trading securities*) prior to sale when the firm uses the *lower-of-cost-or-market* valuation basis for inventory (or the *fair value* basis for marketable securities).

realize. To convert into *funds;* when applied to a *gain* or *loss,* implies that an *arm's-length transaction* has taken place. Contrast with *recognize*; the firm may recognize a loss (as, for example, on *marketable equity securities*) in the financial statements even though it has not yet realized the loss via a transaction.

realized gain (or loss) on marketable equity securities. An income statement account title for the difference between the proceeds of disposition and the *original cost* of *marketable equity securities.*

realized holding gain. See *inventory profit* for definition and an example.

rearrangement costs. Costs of reinstalling assets, perhaps in a different location. The firm may, but need not, *capitalize* them as part of the assets cost, just as is done with original installation cost. The firm will *expense* these costs if they merely maintain the asset's future benefits at their originally intended level before the relocation.

recapitalization. *Reorganization.*

recapture. Name for one kind of tax payment. Various provisions of the *income tax* rules require a refund by the taxpayer (recapture by the government) of various tax advantages under certain conditions. For example, the taxpayer must repay tax savings provided by *accelerated depreciation* if the taxpayer prematurely retires the item providing the tax savings.

receipt. Acquisition of *cash*.

receivable. Any *collectible*, whether or not it is currently due.

receivable turnover. See *ratio*.

reciprocal holdings. Company A owns stock of Company B, and Company B owns stock of Company A; or Company B owns stock of Company C, which owns stock of Company A.

recognize. To enter a transaction in the accounts; not synonymous with *realize*.

reconciliation. A calculation that shows how one balance or figure derives from another, such as a reconciliation of retained earnings or a *bank reconciliation schedule*. See *articulate*.

record date. The date at which the firm pays *dividends* on payment date to those who own the stock.

recourse. The rights of the lender if a borrower does not repay as promised. A recourse loan gives the lender the right to take any of the borrower's assets not exempted from such taking by the contract. See also *note receivable discounted*.

recovery of unrealized loss on trading securities. An *income statement account title* for the *gain* during the current period on *trading securities*.

recurring. Occurring again; occurring repetitively; in accounting, an adjective often used in describing *revenue* or *earnings*. In some contexts, the term "recurring revenue" is ambiguous. Consider a construction contractor who accounts for a single long-term project with the *installment method*, with revenue recognized at the time of each cash collection from the customer. The recognized revenue is recurring, but the transaction leading to the revenue is not. See *quality of earnings*.

redemption. Retirement by the issuer, usually by a purchase or *call*, of *stocks* or *bonds*.

redemption premium. *Call premium*.

redemption value. The price a corporation will pay to retire *bonds* or *preferred stock* if it calls them before *maturity*.

refinancing. An adjustment in the *capital structure* of a *corporation*, involving changes in the nature and amounts of the various classes of *debt* and, in some cases, *capital* as well as other components of *shareholders' equity*. *Asset* carrying values in the accounts remain unchanged.

refunding bond issue. Said of a *bond* issue whose proceeds the firm uses to retire bonds that are already *outstanding*.

register. A collection of consecutive entries, or other information, in chronological order, such as a check register or an insurance register that lists all insurance policies owned. If the firm records entries in the register, it can serve as a *journal*.

registered bond. A bond for which the issuer will pay the *principal* and *interest*, if registered as to interest, to the owner listed on the books of the issuer; as opposed to a bearer bond, in which the issuer must pay the possessor of the bond.

registrar. An *agent*, usually a bank or trust company, appointed by a corporation to keep track of the names of shareholders and distributions to them.

registration statement. Required by the Securities Act of 1933, statement of most companies that want to have owners of their securities trade the securities in public markets. The statement discloses financial data and other items of interest to potential investors.

regression analysis. A method of *cost estimation* based on statistical techniques for fitting a line (or its equivalent in higher mathematical dimensions) to an observed series of data points, usually by minimizing the sum of squared deviations of the observed data from the fitted line. Common usage calls the cost that the analysis explains the "dependent variable"; it calls the variable(s) we use to estimate cost behavior "independent variable(s)." If we use more than one independent variable, the term for the analysis is "multiple regression analysis." See R^2, *standard error*, and *t-value*.

regressive tax. Tax for which the rate decreases as the taxed base, such as income, increases. Contrast with *progressive tax*.

Regulation S-K. The *SEC*'s standardization of nonfinancial statement disclosure requirements for documents filed with the SEC.

Regulation S-T. The *SEC*'s regulations specifying formats for electronic filing and the *EDGAR* system.

Regulation S-X. The *SEC*'s principal accounting regulation, which specifies the form and content of financial reports to the SEC.

rehabilitation. The improving of a used *asset* via an extensive repair. Ordinary *repairs* and *maintenance* restore or maintain expected *service potential* of an asset, and the firm treats them as *expenses*. A rehabilitation improves the asset beyond its current service potential, enhancing the service potential to a significantly higher level than before the rehabilitation. Once rehabilitated, the asset may be better, but need not be, than it was when new. The firm will *capitalize expenditures* for rehabilitation, like those for *betterments* and *improvements*.

reinvestment rate. In a *capital budgeting* context, the rate at which the firm invests cash inflows from a project occurring before the project's completion. Once the analyst assumes such a rate, no project can ever have multiple *internal rates of return*. See *Descartes' rule of signs*.

relative performance evaluation. Setting performance targets and, sometimes, compensation in relation to the performance of others, perhaps in different firms or divisions, who face a similar environment.

relative sales value method. See *net realizable (sales) value*.

relevant cost. Cost used by an analyst in making a decision. *Incremental cost; opportunity cost.*

relevant cost analysis. Identifies the *costs* (or *revenues*) relevant to the decision to be made. A cost or revenue is relevant only if an amount differs between alternatives. Also called *differential cost analysis*

relevant range. Activity levels over which costs are linear or for which *flexible budget* estimates and *breakeven charts* will remain valid.

remit earnings. An expression likely to confuse a reader without a firm understanding of accounting basics. A firm generates *net assets* by earning *income* and retains net assets if it does not declare *dividends* in the amount of net income. When a firm declares dividends and pays the cash (or other net assets), some writers would say the firm "remits earnings." We think the student learns better by conceiving earnings as a *credit balance*. When a firm pays dividends it sends net assets, things with debit balances, not something with a credit balance, to the recipient. When writers say firms "remit earnings," they mean the firms send assets (or net assets) that previous earnings have generated and reduce *retained earnings*.

remittance advice. Information on a *check stub*, or on a document attached to a check by the *drawer*, that tells the *payee* why a payment is being made.

rent. A charge for use of land, buildings, or other assets.

reorganization. In the *capital structure* of a corporation, a major change that leads to changes in the rights, interests, and implied ownership of the various security owners; usually results from a *merger* or an agreement by senior security holders to take action to forestall *bankruptcy*.

repair. An *expenditure* to restore an *asset's* service potential after damage or after prolonged use. In the second sense, after prolonged use, the difference between repairs and maintenance is one of degree and not of kind. A repair is treated as an *expense* of the period when incurred. Because the firm treats repairs and maintenance similarly in this regard, the distinction is not important. A repair helps to maintain capacity at the levels planned when the firm acquired the *asset*. Contrast with *improvement*.

replacement cost. For an asset, the current fair market price to purchase another, similar asset (with the same future benefit or service potential). *Current cost*. See *reproduction cost* and *productive capacity*. See also *distributable income* and *inventory profit*.

replacement cost method of depreciation. Method in which the analyst augments the original-cost *depreciation* charge with an amount based on a portion of the difference between the *current replacement cost* of the asset and its *original cost*.

replacement system of depreciation. See *retirement method of depreciation* for definition and contrast.

report. *Financial statement; auditor's report*.

report form. *Balance sheet* form that typically shows *assets* minus *liabilities* as one total. Then, below that total appears the components of *owners' equity* summing to the same total. Often, the top section shows *current* assets less current liabilities before *noncurrent assets* less noncurrent liabilities. Contrast with *account form*.

reporting objectives (policies). The general purposes for which the firm prepares *financial statements*. The *FASB* has discussed these in *SFAC No. 1*.

representative item sampling. Sampling in which the analyst believes the sample selected is typical of the entire population from which it comes. Compare *specific item sampling*.

reproduction cost. The *cost* necessary to acquire an *asset* similar in all physical respects to another asset for which the analyst requires a *current value*. See *replacement cost* and *productive capacity* for contrast.

required rate of return (RRR). *Cost of capital*.

requisition. A formal written order or request, such as for withdrawal of supplies from the storeroom.

resale value. *Exit value; net realizable value*.

research and development (R&D). A form of economic activity with special accounting rules. Firms engage in research in hopes of discovering new knowledge that will create a new product, process, or service or of improving a present product, process, or service. Development translates research findings or other knowledge into a new or improved product, process, or service. *SFAS No. 2* requires that firms expense costs of such activities as incurred on the grounds that the future benefits are too uncertain to warrant *capitalization* as an asset. This treatment seems questionable to us because we wonder why firms would continue to undertake R&D if there was no expectation of future benefit; if future benefits exist, then R&D *costs* should be assets that appear, like other assets, at *historical cost*.

reserve. The worst word in accounting because almost everyone not trained in accounting, and some who are, misunderstand it. The common confusion is that "reserves" represent a pool of *cash* or other *assets* available when the firm needs them. Wrong. Cash always has a *debit balance*. Reserves always have a *credit* balance. When properly used in accounting, "reserves" refer to an account that appropriates *retained earnings* and restricts dividend declarations. Appropriating retained earnings is itself a poor and vanishing practice, so the word should seldom appear in accounting. In addition, "reserve" was used in the past to indicate an asset *contra account* (e.g., "reserve for depreciation") or an *estimated liability* (e.g., "reserve for warranty costs"). In any case, reserve accounts have *credit* balances and are not pools of *funds*, as the unwary reader might infer. If a company has set aside a pool of *cash* (or *marketable securities*) to serve some specific purpose such as paying for a new factory, then it will call that cash a *fund*. No other word in accounting causes so much misunderstanding by nonexperts—as well as by "experts" —who should know better. A leading unabridged dictionary defines "reserve" as "cash, or assets readily convertible into cash, held aside, as by a corporation, bank, state or national government, etc. to meet expected or unexpected demands." This definition is absolutely wrong in accounting. Reserves are not funds. For example, the firm creates a contingency fund of $10,000 by depositing cash in a fund and makes the following entry:

Contingency Fund	10,000	
Cash		10,000

The following entry may accompany the previous entry, if the firm wants to appropriate retained earnings:

Retained Earnings	10,000	
Reserve for Contingencies		10,000

The transaction leading to the first entry has economic significance. The second entry has little economic impact for most firms. The problem with the word "reserve" arises because the firm can make the second entry without the first—a company can create a reserve, that is, appropriate retained earnings, without creating a fund. The problem results, at least in part, from the fact that in common usage, "reserve" means a pool of assets, as in the phrase "oil reserves." The *Internal Revenue Service* does not help in dispelling confusion about the term "reserves." The federal *income tax* return for corporations uses the title "Reserve for Bad Debts" to mean "Allowance for Uncollectible Accounts" and speaks of the "Reserve Method" in referring to the *allowance method* for estimating *revenue* or *income* reductions from estimated *uncollectibles*.

reserve recognition accounting (RRA). One form of *accounting* for natural resources. In exploration for natural resources, the problem arises of how to treat the expenditures for exploration, both before the firm knows the outcome of the efforts and after it knows the outcome. Suppose that the firm spends $10 million to drill 10 holes ($1 million each) and that nine of them are dry whereas one is a gusher containing oil with a *net realizable value* of $40 million. Dry hole, or *successful efforts*, accounting would expense $9 million and *capitalize* $1 million, which the firm will *deplete* as it lifts the oil from the ground. *SFAS No. 19*, now suspended, required *successful efforts costing*. Full costing would expense nothing but would capitalize the $10 million of drilling costs that the firm will deplete as it lifts the oil from the single productive well. Reserve recognition accounting would capitalize $40 million, which the firm will deplete as it lifts the oil, with a $30 million *credit* to *income* or *contributed capital*. The *balance sheet* shows the *net realizable value* of proven oil and gas reserves. The *income statement* has three sorts of items: (1) current income resulting from production or "lifting profit," which is the *revenue* from sales of oil and gas less the expense based on the current valuation amount at which these items have appeared on the balance sheet, (2) profit or loss from exploration efforts in which the current value of new discoveries is revenue and all the exploration cost is expense, and (3) gain or loss on changes in current value during the year, which accountants in other contexts call a *holding gain or loss*.

reset bond. A bond, typically a *junk bond*, that specifies that periodically the issuer will reset the coupon rate so that the bond sells at *par* in the market. Investment bankers created this type of instrument to help ensure the purchasers of such bonds of getting a fair rate of return, given the riskiness of the issuer. If the issuer gets into financial trouble, its bonds will trade for less than par in the market. The issuer of a reset bond promises to raise the interest rate and preserve the value of the bond. Ironically, the reset feature has often had just the opposite effect. The default risk of many issuers of reset bonds has deteriorated so much that the bonds have dropped to less than 50 percent of par. To raise the value to par, the issuer would have to raise the interest rate to more than 25 percent per year. That rate is so large that issuers have declared bankruptcy rather than attempt to make the new large interest payments; this then reduces the market value of the bonds rather than increases them.

residual income. In an external reporting context, a term that refers to *net income* to *common shares* (= net income less *preferred stock dividends*). In *managerial accounting*, this term refers to the excess of income for a *division* or *segment* of a company over the product of the *cost of capital* for the company multiplied by the average amount of capital invested in the division during the period over which the division earned the income.

residual security. A *potentially dilutive security*. *Options, warrants, convertible bonds*, and *convertible preferred stock*.

residual value. At any time, the estimated or actual *net realizable value* (that is, proceeds less removal costs) of an *asset*, usually a depreciable *plant asset*. In the context of depreciation accounting, this term is equivalent to *salvage value* and is preferred to *scrap value* because the firm need not scrap the asset. It is sometimes used to mean net *book value*. In the context of a *noncancelable* lease, it is the estimated value of the leased asset at the end of the lease period. See *lease*.

resources supplied. *Expenditures* made for an activity.

resources used. *Cost driver* rate times cost driver volume.

responsibility accounting. Accounting for a business by considering various units as separate entities, or *profit centers*, giving management of each unit responsibility for the unit's *revenues* and *expenses*. See *transfer price*.

responsibility center. An organization part or *segment* that top management holds accountable for a specified set of activities. Also called "accountability center." See *cost center, investment center, profit center*, and *revenue center*.

restricted assets. Governmental resources restricted by legal or contractual requirements for specific purpose.

restricted retained earnings. That part of *retained earnings* not legally available for *dividends*. See *retained earnings, appropriated*. Bond indentures and other loan contracts can curtail the legal ability of the corporation to declare dividends without formally requiring a retained earnings appropriation, but the firm must disclose such restrictions.

retail inventory method. Ascertaining cost amounts of *ending inventory* as follows (assuming *FIFO*): cost of ending inventory = (selling price of *goods available for sale* – sales) × *cost percentage.* The analyst then computes cost of goods sold from the inventory equation; costs of beginning inventory, purchases, and ending inventory are all known. (When the firm uses *LIFO*, the method resembles the *dollar-value LIFO method.*) See *markup*.

retail terminology. See *markup*.

retained earnings. Net *income* over the life of a corporation less all *dividends* (including capitalization through *stock dividends*); *owners' equity* less *contributed capital.*

retained earnings, appropriated. An *account* set up by crediting it and debiting *retained earnings;* used to indicate that a portion of retained earnings is not available for dividends. The practice of appropriating retained earnings is misleading unless the firm marks all capital with its use, which is not practicable, nor sensible, since capital is fungible—all the *equities* jointly fund all the *assets*. The use of formal retained earnings appropriations is declining.

retained earnings statement. A *reconciliation* of the beginning and the ending balances in the *retained earnings account;* required by *generally accepted accounting principles* whenever the firm presents *comparative balance sheets* and an *income statement.* This reconciliation can appear in a separate statement, in a combined statement of income and retained earnings, or in the balance sheet.

retirement method of depreciation. A method in which the firm records no entry for *depreciation expense* until it retires an *asset* from service. Then, it makes an entry *debiting* depreciation expense and *crediting* the asset account for the cost of the asset retired. If the retired asset has a *salvage value*, the firm reduces the amount of the debit to depreciation expense by the amount of salvage value with a corresponding debit to cash, receivables, or salvaged materials. The "replacement system of depreciation" is similar, except that the debit to depreciation expense equals the cost of the new asset less the salvage value, if any, of the old asset. Some public utilities used these methods. For example, if the firm acquired 10 telephone poles in Year 1 for $60 each and replaces them in Year 10 for $100 each when the salvage value of the old poles is $5 each, the accounting would be as follows:

Retirement Method		
Plant Assets	600	
Cash		600
To acquire assets in Year 1.		
Depreciation Expense	550	
Salvage Receivable.	50	
Plant Assets		600
To record retirement and depreciation in Year 10.		
Plant Assets	1,000	
Cash		1,000
To record acquisition of new assets in Year 10.		
Replacement Method		
Plant Assets	600	
Cash		600
To acquire assets in Year 1.		
Depreciation Expense	950	
Salvage Receivable.	50	
Cash		1,000
To record depreciation on old asset in amount quantified by net cost of replacement asset in Year 10.		

The retirement method is like *FIFO* in that it records the cost of the first assets as depreciation and puts the cost of the second assets on the balance sheet. The replacement method is like *LIFO* in that it records the cost of the second assets as depreciation expense and leaves the cost of the first assets on the balance sheet.

retirement plan. *Pension plan.*

retroactive benefits. In initiating or amending a *defined-benefit pension plan,* benefits that the benefit formula attributes to employee services rendered in periods prior to the initiation or amendment. See *prior service costs.*

return. A schedule of information required by governmental bodies, such as the tax return required by the *Internal Revenue Service;* also the physical return of merchandise. See also *return on investment.*

return on assets (ROA). *Net income* plus after-tax *interest charges* plus *minority interest* in income divided by average total *assets;* perhaps the single most useful ratio for assessing management's overall operating performance. Most financial economists would subtract average noninterest-bearing *liabilities* from the denominator. Economists realize that when liabilities do not provide for explicit interest charges, the creditor adjusts the terms of contract, such as setting a higher selling price or lower discount, to those who do not pay cash immediately. (To take an extreme example, consider how much higher salary a worker who receives a salary once per year, rather than once per month, would demand.) This ratio requires in the numerator the income amount before the firm accrues any charges to suppliers of funds. We cannot measure the interest charges implicit in the noninterest-bearing liabilities because they cause items such as cost of goods sold and salary expense to be somewhat larger, since the interest is implicit. Subtracting their amounts from the denominator adjusts for their implicit cost. Such subtraction assumes that assets financed with noninterest-bearing liabilities have the same rate of return as all the other assets.

return on investment (ROI), return on capital. *Income* (before distributions to suppliers of capital) for a period; as a rate, this amount divided by average total assets. The analyst should add back *interest,* net of tax effects, to *net income* for the numerator. See *ratio.*

revenue. The *owners' equity* increase accompanying the *net assets* increase caused by selling goods or rendering services; in short, a service rendered; *sales* of products, merchandise, and services and earnings from *interest, dividends, rents,* and the like. Measure revenue as the expected *net present value* of the net assets the firm will receive. Do not confuse with *receipt* of *funds,* which may occur before, when, or after revenue is recognized. Contrast with *gain* and *income.* See also *holding gain.* Some writers use the term *gross income* synonymously with *revenue;* avoid such usage.

revenue center. Within a firm, a *responsibility center* that has control only over revenues generated. Contrast with *cost center.* See *profit center.*

revenue expenditure. A term sometimes used to mean an *expense,* in contrast to a capital *expenditure* to acquire an *asset* or to discharge a *liability.* Avoid using this term; use *period expense* instead.

revenue received in advance. An inferior term for *advances from customers.*

reversal (reversing) entry. An *entry* in which all *debits* and *credits* are the credits and debits, respectively, of another entry, and in the same amounts. The accountant usually records a reversal entry on the first day of an *accounting period* to reverse a previous *adjusting entry,* usually an *accrual.* The purpose of such entries is to make the bookkeeper's tasks easier. Suppose that the firm pays salaries every other Friday, with paychecks compensating employees for the two weeks just ended. Total salaries accrue at the rate of $5,000 per five-day workweek. The bookkeeper is accustomed to making the following entry every other Friday:

(1) Salary Expense	10,000	
Cash		10,000
To record salary expense and salary payments.		

If the firm delivers paychecks to employees on Friday, November 25, then the *adjusting entry* made on November 30 (or perhaps later) to record accrued salaries for November 28, 29, and 30 would be as follows:

(2) Salary Expense	3,000	
Salaries Payable		3,000
To charge November operations with all salaries earned in November.		

The firm would close the Salary Expense account as part of the November 30 closing entries. On the next payday, December 9, the salary entry would be as follows:

(3) Salary Expense	7,000	
Salaries Payable	3,000	
Cash		10,000
To record salary payments split between expense for December (seven days) and liability carried over from November.		

To make entry (3), the bookkeeper must look back into the records to see how much of the debit is to Salaries Payable accrued from the previous month in order to split the total debits between December expense and the liability carried over from November. Notice that this entry forces the bookkeeper both (a) to refer to balances in old accounts and (b) to make an entry different from the one customarily made, entry (1). The reversing entry, made just after the books have been closed for the second quarter, makes the salary entry for December 9 the same as that made on all other Friday paydays. The reversing entry merely *reverses* the adjusting entry (2):

(4) Salaries Payable	3,000	
Salary Expense		3,000
To reverse the adjusting entry.		

This entry results in a zero balance in the Salaries Payable account and a credit balance in the Salary Expense account. If the firm makes entry (4) just after it closes the books for November, then the entry on December 9 will be the customary entry (1). Entries (4) and (1) together have exactly the same effect as entry (3).

The procedure for using reversal entries is as follows: the firm makes the required adjustment to record an accrual (*payable* or *receivable*) at the end of an *accounting period*; it makes the closing entry as usual; as of the first day of the following period, it makes an entry reversing the adjusting entry; when the firm makes (or receives) a payment, it records the entry as though it had not recorded an adjusting entry at the end of the preceding period. Whether a firm uses reversal entries affects the record-keeping procedures but not the financial statements.

This term is also used to describe the entry reversing an incorrect entry before recording the correct entry.

reverse stock split. A stock split in which the firm decreases the number of shares *outstanding*. See *stock split*.

revolving fund. A fund whose amounts the firm continually spends and replenishes; for example, a *petty cash fund.*

revolving loan. A *loan* that both the borrower and the lender expect to renew at *maturity.*

right. The privilege to subscribe to new *stock* issues or to purchase stock. Usually, securities called *warrants* contain the rights, and the owner of the warrants may sell them. See also *preemptive right.*

risk. A measure of the variability of the *return on investment.* For a given expected amount of return, most people prefer less risk to more risk. Therefore, in rational markets, investments with more risk usually promise, or investors expect to receive, a higher rate of return than investments with lower risk. Most people use "risk" and "uncertainty" as synonyms. In technical language, however, these terms have different meanings. We use "risk" when we know the probabilities attached to the various outcomes, such as the probabilities of heads or tails in the flip of a fair coin. "Uncertainty" refers to an event for which we can only estimate the probabilities of the outcomes, such as winning or losing a lawsuit.

risk-adjusted discount rate. Rate used in discounting cash flows for projects more or less risky than the firm's average. In a *capital budgeting* context, a decision analyst compares projects by comparing their net *present values* for a given *interest* rate, usually the cost of capital. If the analyst considers a given project's outcome to be much more or much less risky than the normal undertakings of the company, then the analyst will use a larger interest rate (if the project is riskier) or a smaller interest rate (if less risky) in discounting, and the rate used is "risk-adjusted."

risk-free rate. An interest rate reflecting only the pure interest rate plus an amount to compensate for inflation anticipated over the life of a loan, excluding a premium for the risk of default by the borrower. Financial economists usually measure the risk-free rate in the United States from U.S. government securities, such as Treasury bills and notes.

risk premium. Extra compensation paid to employees or extra *interest* paid to lenders, over amounts usually considered normal, in return for their undertaking to engage in activities riskier than normal.

ROA. *Return on assets.*

ROI. *Return on investment*; usually used to refer to a single project and expressed as a ratio: *income* divided by average *cost* of *assets* devoted to the project.

royalty. Compensation for the use of property, usually a patent, copyrighted material, or natural resources. The amount is often expressed as a percentage of receipts from using the property or as an amount per unit produced.

RRA. *Reserve recognition accounting.*

RRR. Required rate of return. See *cost of capital.*

rule of 69. Rule stating that an amount of cash invested at r percent per period will double in $69/r + .35$ periods. This approximation is accurate to one-tenth of a period for interest rates between 1/4 and 100 percent per period. For example, at 10 percent per period, the rule says that a given sum will double in $69/10 + .35 = 7.25$ periods. At 10 percent per period, a given sum actually doubles in 7.27+ periods.

rule of 72. Rule stating that an amount of cash invested at r percent per period will double in $72/r$ periods. A reasonable approximation for interest rates between 4 and 10 percent but not nearly as accurate as the *rule of 69* for interest rates outside that range. For example, at 10 percent per period, the rule says that a given sum will double in 72/10 = 7.2 periods.

rule of 78. The rule followed by many finance companies for allocating earnings on *loans* among the months of a year on the sum-of-the-months'-digits basis when the borrower makes equal monthly payments to the lender. The sum of the digits from 1 through 12 is 78, so the rule allocates 12/78 of the year's earnings to the first month, 11/78 to the second month, and so on. This approximation allocates more of the early payments to interest and less to principal than does the correct, compound-interest method. Hence, lenders still use this method even though present-day computers can make the compound-interest computation as easily as they can carry out the approximation. See *sum-of- the-years'-digits depreciation*.

ruling (and balancing) an account. The process of summarizing a series of entries in an *account* by computing a new *balance* and drawing double lines to indicate that the new balance summarizes the information above the double lines. An illustration appears below. The steps are as follows: (1) Compute the sum of all *debit* entries including opening debit balance, if any—$1,464.16. (2) Compute the sum of all credit entries including opening credit balance, if any—$413.57. (3) If the amount in (1) exceeds the amount in (2), then write the excess as a credit with a checkmark—$1,464.16 – $413.57 = $1,050.59. (4) Add both debit and credit columns, which should both now sum to the same amount, and show that identical total at the foot of both columns. (5) Draw double lines under those numbers and write the excess of debits over credits as the new debit balance with a checkmark. (6) If the amount in (2) exceeds the amount in (1), then write the excess as a debit with a checkmark. (7) Do steps (4) and (5) except that the excess becomes the new credit balance. (8) If the amount in (1) equals the amount in (2), then the balance is zero, and only the totals with the double lines beneath them need appear.

Rutgers Accounting Web Site. See *http://www.rutgers.edu/Accounting/* for a useful compendium of accounting information.

An Open Account, Ruled and Balanced

(Steps Indicated in Parentheses Correspond to Steps Described in "Ruling an Account.")

	Date 2004	Explanation	Ref.	Debit (1)	Date 2004	Explanation	Ref.	Credit (2)	
	Jan. 2	Balance	√	100.00					
	Jan. 13		VR	121.37	Sept. 15		J	.42	
	Mar. 20		VR	56.42	Nov. 12		J	413.15	
	June 5		J	1,138.09	Dec. 31	Balance	√	1,050.59	(3)
	Aug. 18		J	1.21					
	Nov. 20		VR	38.43					
	Dec. 7		VR	8.64					
(4)	2005			1,464.16	2005			1,464.16	(4)
(5)	Jan. 1	Balance	√	1,050.59					

S

S corporation. A corporation taxed like a *partnership*. Corporation (or partnership) agreements allocate the periodic *income* to the individual shareholders (or partners) who report these amounts on their individual *income tax* returns. Contrast with *C corporation*.

SA (société anonyme). France: A *corporation*.

***SAB*.** *Staff Accounting Bulletin* of the *SEC*.

safe-harbor lease. A form of *tax-transfer lease*.

safety stock. Extra items of *inventory* kept on hand to protect against running out.

salary. Compensation earned by managers, administrators, and professionals, not based on an hourly rate. Contrast with *wage*.

sale. A *revenue* transaction in which the firm delivers *goods* or *services* to a customer in return for cash or a contractual obligation to pay.

sale and leaseback. A *financing* transaction in which the firm sells improved property but takes it back for use on a long-term *lease*. Such transactions often have advantageous income-tax effects but usually have no effect on *financial statement income*.

sales activity variance. *Sales volume variance*.

sales allowance. A sales *invoice* price reduction that a seller grants to a buyer because the seller delivered *goods* different from, perhaps because of damage, those the buyer ordered. The seller often accumulates amounts of such adjustments in a temporary *revenue contra account* having this, or a similar, title. See *sales discount*.

sales basis of revenue recognition. Recognition of *revenue* not when a firm produces goods or when it receives orders but only when it has completed the sale by delivering the goods or services and has received cash or a claim to cash. Most firms recognize revenue on this basis. Compare with the *percentage-of-completion method* and the *installment method*. This is identical with the *completed contract method*, but the latter term ordinarily applies only to *long-term* construction projects.

sales contra, estimated uncollectibles. A title for the contra-revenue account to recognize estimated reductions in income caused by *accounts receivable* that will not be collected. See *bad debt expense*, *allowance for uncollectibles*, and *allowance method*.

sales discount. A sales *invoice* price reduction usually offered for prompt payment. See *terms of sale* and *2/10, n/30*.

sales return. The physical return of merchandise. The seller often accumulates amounts of such returns in a temporary revenue contra account.

sales-type (capital) lease. A form of *lease*. See *capital lease*. When a manufacturer (or other firm) that ordinarily sells goods enters a capital lease as *lessor*, the lease is a "sales-type lease." When a financial firm, such as a bank or insurance company or leasing company, acquires the asset from the manufacturer and then enters a capital lease as lessor, the lease is a "direct-financing-type lease." The manufacturer recognizes its ordinary profit (sales price less *cost of goods sold*, where sales price is the *present value* of the contractual lease payments plus any down payment) on executing the sales-type capital lease, but the financial firm does not recognize profit on executing a capital lease of the direct-financing type.

sales value method. *Relative sales value method*. See *net realizable value method*.

sales volume variance. Budgeted *contribution margin* per unit times (planned sales volume minus actual sales volume).

salvage value. Actual or estimated selling price, net of removal or disposal costs, of a used *plant asset* that the firm expects to sell or otherwise retire. See *residual value.*

SAR. *Summary annual report.*

Sarbanes-Oxley Act. The law, passed in 2002 in the wake of the Enron and related scandals, to stiffen the requirements for corporate governance, including accounting issues. It speaks, among other things, to the regulation of the accounting profession, the standards for audit committees of public companies, the certifications managements must sign, and standards of internal control that companies must meet.

SARL (société à responsabilité limitée). France: a *corporation* with limited liability and a life of no more than 99 years; must have at least two and no more than 50 *shareholders.*

SAS. Statement on Auditing Standards of the *AICPA.*

scale effect. See *discounted cash flow.*

scatter diagram. A graphic representation of the relation between two or more variables within a population.

schedule. A supporting set of calculations, with explanations, that show how to derive figures in a *financial statement* or tax return.

scientific method. *Effective interest method* of *amortizing bond discount* or *premium.*

scrap value. *Salvage value* assuming the owner intends to junk the item. A *net realizable value. Residual value.*

SEC (Securities and Exchange Commission). An agency authorized by the U.S. Congress to regulate, among other things, the financial reporting practices of most public corporations. The SEC has indicated that it will usually allow the *FASB* to set accounting principles, but it often requires more disclosure than the FASB requires. The SEC states its accounting requirements in its *Accounting Series Releases (ASR*—replaced in 1982 by the following two*), Financial Reporting Releases, Accounting and Auditing Enforcement Releases, Staff Accounting Bulletins* (these are, strictly speaking, interpretations by the accounting staff, not rules of the commissioners themselves), and *Regulation S-X and Regulation S-K.* See also *registration statement, 10-K,* and *20-F.*

secret reserve. *Hidden reserve.*

Securities and Exchange Commission. *SEC.*

securitization. The process of bundling together a group of like *assets,* for example *accounts receivable,* into a single portfolio, then selling that portfolio or partial ownership shares in it. This has roughly the same economic effect as using the assets as *collateral* for a borrowing, but the securitization transaction removes the assets from the *balance sheet.*

security. Document that indicates ownership, such as a *share* of *stock,* or indebtedness, such as a *bond,* or potential ownership, such as an *option* or *warrant.*

security available for sale. According to *SFAS No. 115* (1993), a *debt* or *equity security* that is not a *trading security,* or a debt security that is not a *security held to maturity.*

security held to maturity. According to *SFAS No. 115* (1993), a *debt security* that the holder has both the ability and the intent to hold to *maturity;* valued in the *balance sheet* at amortized acquisition cost: the book value of the security at the end of each period is the book value at the beginning of the period multiplied by the historical *yield* on the security (measured as of the time of purchase) less any cash the holder receives at the end of this period from the security.

segment (of a business). As defined by *APB Opinion No. 30,* "a component of an *entity* whose activities represent a separate major line of business or class of customer. . . . [It may be] a *subsidiary*, a division, or a department, . . . provided that its *assets*, results of *operations*, and activities can be clearly distinguished, physically and operationally for financial reporting purposes, from the other assets, results of operations, and activities of the entity." In *SFAS No. 14,* a segment is defined as a "component of an enterprise engaged in promoting a product or service or a group of related products and services primarily to unaffiliated customers . . . for a profit." *SFAS No. 131* defines operating segments using the "management approach" as components of the enterprise engaging in revenue- and expense-generating business activities "whose operating results are regularly reviewed by the enterprise's chief operating decision maker to make decisions about resources . . . and asset performance."

segment reporting. Reporting of *sales, income,* and *assets* by *segments of a business*, usually classified by nature of products sold but sometimes by geographical area where the firm produces or sells goods or by type of customers; sometimes called "line of business reporting." The accounting for segment income does not allocate *central corporate expenses* to the segments.

self-balancing. A set of records with equal *debits* and *credits* such as the *ledger* (but not individual accounts), the *balance sheet*, and a *fund* in nonprofit accounting.

self-check(ing) digit. A digit forming part of an account or code number, normally the last digit of the number, which is mathematically derived from the other numbers of the code and is used to detect errors in transcribing the code number. For example, assume the last digit of the account number is the remainder after summing the preceding digits and dividing that sum by nine. Suppose the computer encounters the account numbers 7027261-7 and 9445229-7. The program can tell that something has gone wrong with the encoding of the second account number because the sum of the first seven digits is 35, whose remainder on division by 9 is 8, not 7. The first account number does not show such an error because the sum of the first seven digits is 25, whose remainder on division by 9 is, indeed, 7. The first account number may be in error, but the second surely is.

self-insurance. See *insurance*.

self-sustaining foreign operation. A foreign operation both financially and operationally independent of the reporting enterprise (owner) so that the owner's exposure to exchange-rate changes results only from the owner's net investment in the foreign entity.

selling and administrative expenses. *Expenses* not specifically identifiable with, or assigned to, production.

semifixed costs. *Costs* that increase with activity as a step function.

semivariable costs. *Costs* that increase strictly linearly with activity but that are positive at zero activity level. Royalty fees of 2 percent of sales are variable; royalty fees of $1,000 per year plus 2 percent of sales are semivariable.

senior securities. *Bonds* as opposed to *preferred stock; preferred stock* as opposed to *common stock*. The firm must meet the senior security claim against *earnings* or *assets* before meeting the claims of less-senior securities.

sensitivity analysis. A study of how the outcome of a decision-making process changes as one or more of the assumptions change.

sequential access. Computer-storage access in which the analyst can locate information only by a sequential search of the storage file. Compare *direct access*.

serial bonds. An *issue* of *bonds* that mature in part at one date, another part on another date, and so on. The various maturity dates usually occur at equally spaced intervals. Contrast with *term bonds*.

service basis of depreciation. *Production method*.

service bureau. A commercial data-processing center providing service to various customers.

service cost, (current) service cost. *Pension plan expenses incurred* during an *accounting period* for employment services performed during that period. Contrast with *prior service cost*. See *funded*.

service department. A department, such as the personnel or computer department, that provides services to other departments rather than direct work on a salable product. Contrast with *production department*. A firm must allocate costs of service departments whose services benefit manufacturing operations to *product costs* under *full absorption costing*.

service department cost allocation. A procedure in which firms *allocate* the *costs* of operating service departments to other departments.

service life. Period of expected usefulness of an asset; may differ from *depreciable life* for income tax purposes.

service potential. The future benefits that cause an item to be classified as an *asset*. Without service potential, an item has no future benefits, and accounting will not classify the item as an asset. *SFAC No. 6* suggests that the primary characteristic of service potential is the ability to generate future net cash inflows.

services. Useful work done by a person, a machine, or an organization. See *goods*.

setup. The time or costs required to prepare production equipment for doing a job.

SFAC. *Statement of Financial Accounting Concepts* of the *FASB*.

SFAS. *Statement of Financial Accounting Standards*. See *FASB*.

shadow price. An opportunity cost. A *linear programming* analysis provides as one of its outputs the potential value of having available more of the scarce resources that con strain the production process, for example, the value of having more time available on a machine tool critical to the production of two products. Common terminology refers to this value as the "shadow price" or the "dual value" of the scarce resource.

share. A unit of *stock* representing ownership in a corporation.

share premium. United Kingdom: *additional paid-in capital* or *capital contributed in excess of par value*.

shareholders' equity. *Proprietorship* or *owners' equity* of a corporation. Because *stock* means inventory in Australia, the United Kingdom, and Canada, their writers use the term "shareholders' equity" rather than the term "stockholders' equity."

short run. short term. Contrast with *long run*. Managers mean a period of time long enough to allow change the level of production or other activity within the constraints of current total productive capacity. In a *balance sheet* context, it means *current*, ordinarily due within one year. Use a hyphen when the phrase is an adjective, but no hyphen when it is a noun.

short-term liquidity risk. The risk that an *entity* will not have enough *cash* in the *short run* to pay its *debts*.

short-term operating budget. Management's quantitative action plan for the coming year.

shrinkage. An excess of *inventory* shown on the *books* over actual physical quantities on hand; can result from theft or shoplifting as well as from evaporation or general wear and tear. Some accountants, in an attempt to downplay their own errors, use the term to mean record-keeping mistakes that they later must correct, with some embarrassment, and that result in material changes in reported income. One should not use the term "shrinkage" for the correction of mistakes because adequate terminology exists for describing mistakes.

shutdown cost. Those fixed costs that the firm continues to incur after it has ceased production; the costs of closing down a particular production facility.

side letter. See *channel stuffing.*

sight draft. A demand for payment drawn by Person A to whom Person B owes cash. Person A presents the *draft* to Person B's (the debtor's) bank in expectation that Person B will authorize his or her bank to disburse the funds. Sellers often use such drafts when selling goods to a new customer in a different city. The seller is uncertain whether the buyer will pay the bill. The seller sends the *bill* of lading, or other evidence of ownership of the goods, along with a sight draft to the buyer's bank. Before the warehouse holding the goods can release them to the buyer, the buyer must instruct its bank to honor the sight draft by withdrawing funds from the buyer's account. Once the bank honors the sight draft, it hands to the buyer the bill of lading or other document evidencing ownership, and the goods become the property of the buyer.

simple interest. *Interest* calculated on *principal* where interest earned during periods before maturity of the loan does not increase the principal amount earning interest for the subsequent periods and the lender cannot withdraw the funds before maturity. Interest = principal × interest rate × time, where the rate is a rate per period (typically a year) and time is expressed in units of that period. For example, if the *rate* is annual and the time is two months, then in the formula, use 2/12 for *time*. Simple interest is seldom used in economic calculations except for periods of less than one year and then only for computational convenience. Contrast with *compound interest.*

single-entry accounting. Accounting that is neither *self-balancing* nor *articulated.* That is, it does not rely on equal *debits* and *credits.* The firm makes no *journal entries* and must *plug* to derive *owners' equity* for the *balance sheet.*

single proprietorship. *Sole proprietorship.*

single-step. Said of an *income statement* in which *ordinary revenue* and *gain* items appear first, with their total. Then come all ordinary *expenses* and *losses,* with their total. The difference between these two totals, plus the effect of *income from discontinued operations* and *extraordinary items,* appears as *net income.* Contrast with *multiple-step* and see *proprietorship theory.*

sinking fund. *Assets* and their earnings earmarked for the retirement of bonds or other long-term obligations. Earnings of sinking fund investments become taxable income of the company.

sinking fund method of depreciation. Method in which the periodic charge is an equal amount each period so that the *future value* of the charges, considered as an *annuity,* will accumulate at the end of the depreciable life to an amount equal to the *acquisition cost* of the asset. The firm does not necessarily, or even usually, accumulate a *fund* of cash. Firms rarely use this method.

skeleton account. *T-account.*

slide. The name of the error made by a bookkeeper in recording the digits of a number correctly with the decimal point misplaced; for example, recording $123.40 as $1,234.00 or as $12.34. If the only errors in a *trial balance* result from one or more slides, then the difference between the sum of the *debits* and the sum of the *credits* will be divisible by nine. Not all such differences divisible by nine result from slides. See *transposition error*.

SMAC (Society of Management Accountants of Canada). The national association of accountants whose provincial associations engage in industrial and governmental accounting. The association undertakes research and administers an educational program and comprehensive examinations; those who pass qualify to be designated CMA (Certified Management Accountants), formerly called RIA (Registered Industrial Accountant).

SNC (société en nom collectif). France: a *partnership*.

soak-up method. The *equity method*.

Social Security taxes. Taxes levied by the federal government on both employers and employees to provide *funds* to pay retired persons (or their survivors) who are entitled to receive such payments, either because they paid Social Security taxes themselves or because Congress has declared them eligible. Unlike a *pension plan*, the Social Security system does not collect funds and invest them for many years. The tax collections in a given year pay primarily for benefits distributed that year. At any given time the system has a multitrillion-dollar unfunded obligation to current workers for their eventual retirement benefits. See *Old Age, Survivors, Disability, and Health Insurance*.

software. The programming aids—such as compilers—sort and report programs, and generators, that extend the capabilities of and simplify the use of the computer, as well as certain operating systems and other control programs. Compare *hardware*.

sole proprietorship. A firm in which all *owners' equity* belongs to one person.

solvent. Able to meet debts when due.

SOP. *Statement of Position* (of the *AcSEC* of the *AICPA*).

sound value. A phrase used mainly in appraisals of *fixed assets* to mean *fair market price (value)* or *replacement cost* in present condition.

source of funds. Any *transaction* that increases *cash* and *marketable securities* held as *current assets*.

sources and uses statement. *Statement of cash flows*.

SOYD. *Sum-of-the-years'-digits depreciation*.

SP (société en participation). France: a silent *partnership* in which the managing partner acts for the partnership as an individual in transacting with others who need not know that the person represents a partnership.

special assessment. A compulsory levy made by a governmental unit on property to pay the costs of a specific improvement or service presumed not to benefit the general public but only the owners of the property so assessed; accounted for in a special assessment fund.

special journal. A *journal*, such as a sales journal or cash disbursements journal, to record *transactions* of a similar nature that occur frequently.

special purpose entity. The name for a business now known as a *variable interest entity*. *GAAP* never defined this name, but brought it into existence with an *EITF* consensus in 1990. The Enron financial manipulations depended in part on use of these entities to achieve *off-balance-sheet financing*.

special revenue debt. A governmental unit's debt backed only by revenues from specific sources, such as tolls from a bridge.

specific identification method. Method for valuing *ending inventory* and *cost of goods sold* by identifying actual units sold and remaining in inventory and summing the actual costs of those individual units; usually used for items with large unit values, such as precious jewelry, automobiles, and fur coats.

specific item sampling. Sampling in which the analyst selects particular items because of their nature, value, or method of recording. Compare *representative item sampling.*

specific price changes. Changes in the market prices of specific *goods* and *services*. Contrast with *general price-level changes*.

specific price index. A measure of the price of a specific good or service, or a small group of similar goods or services, at one time relative to the price during a base period. Contrast with *general price index*. See *dollar-value LIFO method.*

spending variance. In *standard cost systems*, the *rate* or *price variance* for *overhead costs*.

split. *Stock split*. Sometimes called "split-up."

split-off point. In accumulating and allocating costs for *joint products*, the point at which all costs are no longer *joint costs* but at which an analyst can identify costs associated with individual products or perhaps with a smaller number of *joint products*.

spoilage. See *abnormal spoilage* and *normal spoilage*.

spot price. The price of a commodity for delivery on the day of the price quotation. See *forward price* for contrast.

spreadsheet. For many years, a term that referred specifically to a *work sheet* organized like a *matrix* that provides a two-way classification of accounting data. The rows and columns both have labels, which are *account* titles. An entry in a row represents a *debit,* whereas an entry in a column represents a *credit*. Thus, the number "100" in the "cash" row and the "accounts receivable" column records an entry debiting cash and crediting accounts receivable for $100. A given row total indicates all debit entries to the account represented by that row, and a given column total indicates the sum of all credit entries to the account represented by the column. Since personal-computer software has become widespread, this term has come to refer to any file created by programs such as Lotus 1-2-3® and Microsoft Excel®. Such files have rows and columns, but they need not represent debits and credits. Moreover, they can have more than two dimensions.

squeeze. A term sometimes used for *plug*.

SSARS. *Statement on Standards for Accounting and Review Services.*

stabilized accounting. *Constant-dollar accounting*.

stable monetary unit assumption. In spite of *inflation,* which appears to be a way of life, the assumption that underlies historical cost/nominal-dollar accounting—namely that one can meaningfully add together current dollars and dollars of previous years. The assumption gives no specific recognition to changing values of the dollar in the usual *financial statements*. See *constant-dollar accounting*.

***Staff Accounting Bulletin*.** An interpretation issued by the staff of the Chief Accountant of the *SEC* "suggesting" how the accountants should apply various *Accounting Series Releases* in practice. The suggestions are part of *GAAP*.

stakeholder. An individual or group, such as employees, suppliers, customers, and shareholders, who have an interest in the corporation's activities and outcomes.

standard cost. Anticipated *cost* of producing a unit of output; a predetermined cost to be assigned to products produced. Standard cost implies a norm—what costs should be. Budgeted cost implies a forecast—something likely, but not necessarily, a "should," as implied by a norm. Firms use standard costs as the benchmark for gauging good and bad performance. Although a firm may similarly use a budget, it need not. A budget may be a planning document, subject to changes whenever plans change, whereas standard costs usually change annually or when technology significantly changes or when costs of labor and materials significantly change.

standard costing. *Costing* based on *standard costs*.

standard costing system. *Product costing* using *standard costs* rather than actual costs. The firm may use either *full absorption* or *variable costing* principles.

standard error (of regression coefficients). A measure of the uncertainty about the magnitude of the estimated parameters of an equation fit with a *regression analysis*.

standard manufacturing overhead. *Overhead costs* expected to be incurred per unit of time and per unit produced.

standard price (rate). Unit price established for materials or labor used in *standard cost systems*.

standard quantity allowed. The direct material or direct labor (inputs) quantity that production should have used if it had produced the units of output in accordance with preset *standards*.

standby costs. A type of *capacity cost*, such as property taxes, incurred even if a firm shuts down operations completely. Contrast with *enabling costs*.

stated capital. Amount of capital contributed by shareholders; sometimes used to mean *legal capital*.

stated value. A term sometimes used for the *face amount of capital stock*, when the *board* has not designated a *par value*. Where there is stated value per share, capital *contributed in excess of stated value* may come into being.

statement of affairs. A *balance sheet* showing immediate *liquidation* amounts rather than *historical costs*, usually prepared when *insolvency* or *bankruptcy* is imminent. Such a statement specifically does not use the *going-concern assumption*.

statement of cash flows. A schedule of *cash receipts* and *payments*, classified by *investing*, *financing*, and *operating activities;* required by the *FASB* for all for-profit companies. Companies may report operating activities with either the direct method (which shows only receipts and payments of cash) or the indirect method (which starts with *net income* and shows adjustments for *revenues* not currently producing cash and for *expenses* not currently using cash). "Cash" includes cash equivalents such as Treasury bills, commercial paper, and *marketable securities* held as *current assets*. This is sometimes called the "funds statement." Before 1987, the FASB required the presentation of a similar statement called the *statement of changes in financial position*, which tended to emphasize *working capital*, not cash.

statement of changes in financial position. As defined by *APB Opinion No. 19*, a statement that explains the changes in *working capital* (or cash) balances during a period and shows the changes in the working capital (or cash) accounts themselves. The *statement of cash flows* has replaced this statement.

statement of charge and discharge. A financial statement, showing *net assets* or *income*, drawn up by an executor or administrator, to account for receipts and dispositions of cash or other assets in an estate or trust.

Statement of Financial Accounting Concepts (SFAC). One of a series of *FASB* publications in its *conceptual framework* for *financial accounting* and reporting. Such statements set forth objectives and fundamentals to be the basis for specific financial accounting and reporting standards.

Statement of Financial Accounting Standards (SFAS). See *FASB*.

statement of financial position. *Balance sheet.*

Statement of Position (SOP). A recommendation, on an emerging accounting problem, issued by the *AcSEC* of the *AICPA*. The AICPA's Code of Professional Ethics specifically states that *CPAs* need not treat *SOPs* as they do rules from the *FASB*, but a CPA would be wary of departing from the recommendations of an *SOP*.

statement of retained earnings (income). A statement that reconciles the beginning-of-period and the end-of-period balances in the *retained earnings* account. It shows the effects of *earnings, dividend declarations*, and *prior-period adjustments*.

statement of significant accounting policies (principles). A summary of the significant *accounting principles* used in compiling an *annual report;* required by *APB Opinion No. 22*. This summary may be a separate exhibit or the first *note* to the financial statements.

Statement on Auditing Standards (SAS). A series addressing specific auditing standards and procedures. *No. 1* (1973) of this series codifies all statements on auditing standards previously promulgated by the *AICPA*.

Statement on Standards for Accounting and Review Services (SSARS). Pronouncements issued by the *AICPA* on unaudited *financial statements* and unaudited financial information of nonpublic entities.

static budget. *Fixed budget.* Budget developed for a set level of the driving variable, such as production or sales, which the analyst does not change if the actual level deviates from the level set at the outset of the analysis.

status quo. Events or cost incurrences that will happen or that a firm expects to happen in the absence of taking some contemplated action.

statutory tax rate. The tax rate specified in the *income tax* law for each type of income (e.g., *ordinary income, capital gain or loss).*

step allocation method. *Step-down method.*

step cost. *Semifixed cost.*

step-down method. In *allocating service department* costs, a method that starts by allocating one service department's costs to *production departments* and to all other service departments. Then the firm allocates a second service department's costs, including costs allocated from the first, to production departments and to all other service departments except the first one. In this fashion, a firm may allocate all service departments' costs, including previous allocations, to production departments and to those service departments whose costs it has not yet allocated.

step method. *Step-down method.*

step(ped) cost. *Semifixed cost.*

sterilized allocation. Desirable characteristics of cost allocation methods. Optimal decisions result from considering *incremental costs* only. Optimal decisions never require *allocations* of *joint* or *common costs*. A "sterilized allocation" causes the optimal decision choice not to differ from the one that occurs when the accountant does not allocate joint or common costs "sterilized" with respect to that decision. Arthur L. Thomas first used the term in this context. Because *absorption costing* requires that product costs absorb all manufacturing costs and because some allocations can lead to bad decisions, Thomas (and we) advocate that the analyst choose a sterilized allocation scheme that will not alter the otherwise optimal decision. No single allocation scheme is always sterilized with respect to all decisions. Thus, Thomas (and we) advocate that decisions be made on the basis of incremental costs before any allocations.

stewardship. Principle by which management is accountable for an *entity's* resources, for their efficient use, and for protecting them from adverse impact. Some theorists believe that a primary goal of accounting is to aid users of *financial statements* in their assessment of management's performance in stewardship.

stock. A measure of the amount of something on hand at a specific time. In this sense, contrast with *flow*. See *inventory* and *capital stock*.

stock appreciation rights. An employer's promise to pay to the employee an amount of *cash* on a certain future date, with the amount of cash being the difference between the *market value* of a specified number of *shares* of *stock* in the employer's company on the given future date and some base price set on the date the rights are granted. Firms sometimes use this form of compensation because changes in tax laws in recent years have made *stock options* relatively less attractive. *GAAP* compute compensation based on the difference between the market value of the shares and the base price set at the time of the grant.

stock dividend. A so-called *dividend* in which the firm distributes additional *shares* of *capital stock* without cash payments to existing shareholders. It results in a *debit* to *retained earnings* in the amount of the market value of the shares issued and a *credit* to *capital stock* accounts. Firms ordinarily use stock dividends to indicate that they have permanently reinvested earnings in the business. Contrast with a *stock split*, which requires no entry in the capital stock accounts other than a notation that the *par* or *stated value* per share has changed.

stock option. The right to purchase or sell a specified number of shares of *stock* for a specified price at specified times. Employee stock options are purchase rights granted by a corporation to employees, a form of compensation. Traded stock options are *derivative* securities, rights created and traded by investors, independent of the corporation whose stock is optioned. Contrast with *warrant*.

stock right. See *right*.

stock split(-up). Increase in the number of common shares outstanding resulting from the issuance of additional shares to existing shareholders without additional capital contributions by them. Does not increase the total *value* (or *stated value*) of *common shares* outstanding because the *board* reduces the par (or stated) value per share in inverse proportion. A three-for-one stock split reduces par (or stated) value per share to one-third of its former amount. A stock split usually implies a distribution that increases the number of shares outstanding by 20 percent or more. Compare with *stock dividend*.

stock subscriptions. See *subscription* and *subscribed stock*.

stock warrant. See *warrant*.

stockholders' equity. See *shareholders' equity*.

stockout. Occurs when a firm needs a unit of *inventory* to use in production or to sell to a customer but has none available.

stockout costs. *Contribution margin* or other measure of *profits* not earned because a seller has run out of *inventory* and cannot fill a customer's order. A firm may incur an extra cost because of delay in filling an order.

stores. *Raw materials*, parts, and supplies.

straight-debt value. An estimate of the *market value* of a *convertible bond* if the bond did not contain a conversion privilege.

straight-line depreciation. Method in which, if the *depreciable life* is n periods, the periodic *depreciation* charge is $1/n$ of the *depreciable cost;* results in equal periodic charges. Accountants sometimes call it "straight-time depreciation."

strategic plan. A statement of the method for achieving an organization's goals.

stratified sampling. In choosing a *sample,* a method in which the investigator first divides the entire *population* into relatively homogeneous subgroups (strata) and then selects random samples from these subgroups.

street security. A stock certificate in immediately transferable form, most commonly because the issuing firm has registered it in the name of the broker, who has endorsed it with "payee" left blank.

Subchapter S corporation. A firm legally organized as a *corporation* but taxed as if it were a *partnership*. Tax terminology calls the corporations paying their own income taxes *C corporations*.

subject to. In an *auditor's report,* qualifications usually caused by a *material* uncertainty in the valuation of an item, such as future promised payments from a foreign government or outcome of pending litigation.

subordinated. *Debt* whose claim on income or assets has lower priority than claims of other debt.

subscribed stock. A *shareholders' equity* account showing the capital that the firm will receive as soon as the share-purchaser pays the subscription price. A subscription is a legal contract, so once the share-purchaser signs it, the firm makes an entry *debiting* an *owners' equity contra account* and *crediting* subscribed stock.

subscription. Agreement to buy a *security* or to purchase periodicals, such as magazines.

subsequent events. *Poststatement events.*

subsidiary. A company in which another company owns more than 50 percent of the voting shares.

subsidiary ledger. The *ledger* that contains the detailed accounts whose total appears in a *controlling account* of the *general ledger*.

subsidiary (ledger) accounts. The *accounts* in a *subsidiary ledger*.

successful efforts costing. In petroleum accounting, the *capitalization* of the drilling costs of only those wells that contain gas or oil. See *reserve recognition accounting* for an example.

summary annual report (SAR). Condensed financial statements distributed in lieu of the usual *annual report*. Since 1987, the *SEC* has allowed firms to include such statements in the annual report to shareholders as long as the firm includes full, detailed statements in SEC filings and in *proxy* materials sent to shareholders.

summary of significant accounting principles *Statement of significant accounting policies (principles).*

sum-of-the-years'-digits depreciation (SYD, SOYD). An *accelerated depreciation* method for an asset with *depreciable life* of n years where the charge in period i ($i = 1, \ldots, n$) is the fraction $(n + 1 - i)/[n(n + 1)/2]$ of the *depreciable cost*. If an asset has a depreciable cost of \$15,000 and a five-year depreciable life, for example, the depreciation charges would be \$5,000 (= 5/15 × \$15,000) in the first year, \$4,000 in the second, \$3,000 in the third, \$2,000 in the fourth, and \$1,000 in the fifth. The name derives from the fact that the denominator in the fraction is the sum of the digits 1 through n.

sunk cost. Past *costs* that current and future decisions cannot affect and, hence, that are irrelevant for decision making aside from *income tax* effects. Contrast with *incremental costs* and *imputed costs*. For example, the *acquisition cost* of machinery is irrelevant to a decision of whether to scrap the machinery. The current *exit value* of the machinery is the *opportunity cost* of continuing to own it, and the cost of, say, the electricity to run the machinery is an incremental cost of its operation. Sunk costs become relevant for decision making when the analysis requires taking *income taxes* (*gain* or *loss* on disposal of asset) into account, since the cash payment for income taxes depends on the tax basis of the asset.

Avoid this term in careful writing because it is ambiguous. Consider, for example, a machine costing $100,000 with current *salvage* value of $20,000. Some (including us) would say that $100,000 (the *gross* amount) is "sunk"; others would say that only $80,000 (the *net* amount) is "sunk."

supplementary statements (schedules). Statements (schedules) in addition to the four basic *financial statements* (*balance sheet*, *income statement*, *statement of cash flows*, and the *statement of retained earnings*).

surplus. A word once used but now considered poor terminology; prefaced by "earned" to mean *retained earnings* and prefaced by "capital" to mean *capital contributed in excess of par* (*or stated*) *value*.

surplus reserves. *Appropriated retained earnings*. A phrase with nothing to recommend it: of all the words in accounting, *reserve* is the most objectionable, and *surplus* is the second-most objectionable.

suspense account. A *temporary account* used to record part of a transaction before final analysis of that transaction. For example, if a business regularly classifies all sales into a dozen or more different categories but wants to deposit the proceeds of cash sales every day, it may credit a sales suspense account pending detailed classification of all sales into Durable Goods Sales, Women's Clothing Sales, Men's Clothing Sales, Housewares Sales, and so on.

sustainable income. The part of *distributable income* (computed from *current cost* data) that the firm can expect to earn in the next accounting period if it continues operations at the same levels as were maintained during the current period. *Income from discontinued operations*, for example, may be distributable but not sustainable.

swap. A currency swap is a financial instrument in which the holder promises to pay to (or receive from) the *counterparty* the difference between *debt* denominated in one currency (such as U.S. dollars) and the payments on debt denominated in another currency (such as euros). An interest-rate swap typically obligates the party and counterparty to exchange the difference between fixed- and floating-rate interest payments on otherwise similar loans.

S-X. See *Regulation S-X.*

SYD. *Sum-of-the-years'-digits depreciation.*

T

T-account. Account form shaped like the letter T with the title above the horizontal line. *Debits* appear on the left of the vertical line, *credits* on the right.

take-home pay. The amount of a paycheck; earned wages or *salary* reduced by deductions for *income taxes, Social Security taxes*, contributions to fringe-benefit plans, union dues, and so on. Take-home pay might be as little as half of earned compensation.

take-or-pay contract. As defined by *SFAS No. 47*, a purchaser-seller agreement that provides for the purchaser to pay specified amounts periodically in return for products or services. The purchaser must make specified minimum payments even if it does not take delivery of the contracted products or services.

taking a bath. To incur a large loss. See *big bath*.

tangible. Having physical form. Accounting has never satisfactorily defined the distinction between tangible and intangible assets. Typically, accountants define intangibles by giving an exhaustive list, and everything not on the list is defined as tangible. See *intangible asset* for such a list.

target cost. *Standard cost.* Sometimes, target price less expected profit margin.

target price. Selling price based on customers' value in use of a good or service, constrained by competitors' prices of similar items.

tax. A nonpenal, but compulsory, charge levied by a government on income, consumption, wealth, or other basis, for the benefit of all those governed. The term does not include fines or specific charges for benefits accruing only to those paying the charges, such as licenses, permits, special assessments, admission fees, and tolls.

tax allocation: interperiod. See *deferred income tax liability.*

tax allocation: intrastatement. The showing of income tax effects on *extraordinary items, income from discontinued operations*, and *prior-period adjustments,* along with these items, separately from income taxes on other income. See *net-of-tax reporting*.

tax avoidance. See *tax shelter* and *loophole*.

tax basis of assets and liabilities. A concept important for applying *SFAS No. 109* on *deferred income taxes.* Two *assets* will generally have different *book values* if the firm paid different amounts for them, *amortizes* them on a different schedule, or both. Similarly, a single asset will generally have a book value different from what it will have for tax purposes if the firm recorded different *acquisition* amounts for the asset for book and for tax purposes, amortizes it differently for book and for tax purposes, or both. The difference between financial book value and income tax basis becomes important in computing deferred income tax amounts. The adjusted cost in the financial records is the "book basis," and the adjusted amount in the tax records is the "tax basis." Differences between book and tax basis can arise for *liabilities* as well as for assets.

tax credit. A subtraction from taxes otherwise payable. Contrast with *tax deduction*.

tax deduction. A subtraction from *revenues* and *gains* to arrive at taxable income. Tax deductions differ technically from tax *exemptions*, but both reduce gross income in computing taxable income. Both differ from *tax credits*, which reduce the computed tax itself in computing taxes payable. If the tax rate is the fraction t of pretax income, then a *tax credit* of \$1 is worth \$$1/t$ of *tax deductions*.

tax evasion. The fraudulent understatement of taxable revenues or overstatement of deductions and expenses or both. Contrast with *tax shelter* and *loophole*.

tax-exempts. See *municipal bonds*.

tax shelter. The legal avoidance of, or reduction in, *income taxes* resulting from a careful reading of the complex income-tax regulations and the subsequent rearrangement of financial affairs to take advantage of the regulations. Often writers use the term pejoratively, but the courts have long held that a taxpayer has no obligation to pay taxes any larger than the legal minimum. If the public concludes that a given tax shelter is "unfair," then Congress can, and has, changed the laws and regulations. The term is sometimes used to refer to the investment that permits tax avoidance. See *loophole*.

tax shield. The amount of an *expense*, such as *depreciation,* that reduces taxable income but does not require *working capital*. Sometimes this term includes expenses that reduce taxable income and use working capital. A depreciation deduction (or *R&D expense* in the expanded sense) of \$10,000 provides a tax shield of \$3,700 when the marginal tax rate is 37 percent.

taxable income. *Income* computed according to *IRS* regulations and subject to *income* *taxes*. Contrast with income, net income, income before taxes (in the *income statement*), and *comprehensive income* (a *financial reporting* concept). Use the term "pretax income" to refer to income before taxes on the income statement in financial reports.

tax-transfer lease. One form of *capital lease.* Congress has in the past provided business with an incentive to invest in qualifying *plant and equipment* by granting an *investment credit*, which, though it occurs as a reduction in *income taxes* otherwise payable, effectively reduces the purchase price of the assets. Similarly, Congress continues to grant an incentive to acquire such assets by allowing the *Modified Accelerated Cost Recovery System* (*MACRS*, form of unusually *accelerated depreciation*). Accelerated depreciation for tax purposes allows a reduction of taxes paid in the early years of an asset's life, providing the firm with an increased *net present value* of *cash flows*. The *IRS* administers both of these incentives through the income tax laws, rather than paying an outright cash payment. A business with no taxable income in many cases had difficulty reaping the benefits of the investment credit or of accelerated depreciation because Congress had not provided for tax refunds to those who acquire qualifying assets but who have no taxable income. In principle, a company without taxable income could lease from another firm with taxable income an asset that it would otherwise purchase. The second firm acquires the asset, gets the tax-reduction benefits from the acquisition, and becomes a lessor, leasing the asset (presumably at a lower price reflecting its own costs lowered by the tax reductions) to the unprofitable company. Before 1981, tax laws discouraged such leases. That is, although firms could enter into such leases, they could not legally transfer the tax benefits. Under certain restrictive conditions, the tax law now allows a profitable firm to earn tax credits and take deductions while leasing to the firm without tax liability in such leases. These are sometimes called "safe-harbor leases."

Technical Bulletin. The *FASB* has authorized its staff to issue bulletins to provide guidance on financial accounting and reporting problems. Although the FASB does not formally approve the contents of the bulletins, their contents are part of *GAAP*.

technology. The sum of a firm's technical *trade secrets* and *know-how*, as distinct from its *patents*.

temporary account. *Account* that does not appear on the *balance sheet; revenue* and *expense* accounts, their *adjuncts* and *contras, production cost accounts, dividend distribution accounts*, and purchases-related accounts (which close to the various inventories); sometimes called a "nominal account."

temporary difference. According to the *SFAS No. 109* (1992) definition: "A difference between the tax basis of an asset or liability and its reported amount in the financial statements that will result in taxable or deductible amounts in future years." Temporary differences include *timing differences* and differences between *taxable income* and pretax income caused by different cost bases for assets. For example, a plant asset might have a cost of $10,000 for financial reporting but a basis of $7,000 for income tax purposes. This temporary difference might arise because the firm has used an accelerated depreciation method for tax but straight-line for book, or the firm may have purchased the asset in a transaction in which the fair value of the asset exceeded its tax basis. Both situations create a temporary difference.

temporary investments. Investments in *marketable securities* that the owner intends to sell within a short time, usually one year, and hence classifies as *current assets*.

10-K. The name of the annual report that the *SEC* requires of nearly all publicly held corporations.

term bonds. A *bond issue* whose component bonds all mature at the same time. Contrast with *serial bonds*.

terminal cash flows. *Cash flows* that occur at the end of an *investment* project. Often include proceeds of *salvage* of equipment and tax on *gain (loss)* on disposal.

term loan. A loan with a *maturity* date, as opposed to a demand loan, which is due whenever the lender requests payment. In practice, bankers and auditors use this phrase only for loans for a year or more.

term structure. A phrase with different meanings in *accounting* and *financial economics*. In accounting, it refers to the pattern of times that must elapse before *assets* turn into, or produce, *cash* and the pattern of times that must elapse before *liabilities* require cash. In financial economics, the phrase refers to the pattern of interest rates as a function of the time that elapses for loans to come due. For example, if six-month loans cost 6 percent per year and 10-year loans cost 9 percent per year, this is called a "normal" term structure because the longer-term loan carries a higher rate. If the six-month loan costs 9 percent per year and the 10-year loan costs 6 percent per year, the term structure is said to be "inverted." See *yield curve*.

terms of sale. The conditions governing payment for a sale. For example, the terms *2/10, n(et)/30* mean that if the purchaser makes payment within 10 days of the invoice date, it can take a *discount* of 2 percent from *invoice* price; the purchaser must pay the invoice amount, in any event, within 30 days, or it becomes overdue.

theory of constraints (TOC). Concept of improving operations by identifying and reducing bottlenecks in process flows.

thin capitalization. A state of having a high *debt-equity ratio*. Under income tax legislation, the term has a special meaning.

throughput contract. As defined by *SFAS No. 47*, an agreement that is signed by a shipper (processor) and by the owner of a transportation facility (such as an oil or natural gas pipeline or a ship) or a manufacturing facility and that provides for the shipper (processor) to pay specified amounts periodically in return for the transportation (processing) of a product. The shipper (processor) must make cash payments even if it does not ship (process) the contracted quantities.

throughput contribution. Sales dollars minus the sum of all short-run variable costs.

tickler file. A collection of *vouchers* or other memoranda arranged chronologically to remind the person in charge of certain duties to make payments (or to do other tasks) as scheduled.

time-adjusted rate of return. *Internal rate of return*.

time cost. *Period cost*.

time deposit. Cash in bank earning interest. Contrast with *demand deposit*.

time-series analysis. See *cross-section analysis* for definition and contrast.

times-interest (charges) earned. Ratio of pretax *income* plus *interest* charges to interest charges. See *ratio*.

timing difference. The major type of *temporary difference* between taxable income and pretax income reported to shareholders; reverses in a subsequent period and requires an entry in the *deferred income tax* account; for example, the use of *accelerated depreciation* for tax returns and *straight-line depreciation* for financial reporting. Contrast with *permanent difference*.

Toronto Stock Exchange (TSX). A public market where various corporate securities trade.

total assets turnover. *Sales* divided by average total *assets*.

total quality management (TQM). Concept of organizing a company to excel in all its activities in order to increase the quality of products and services.

traceable cost. A *cost* that a firm can identify with or assign to a specific product. Contrast with a *joint cost*.

trade acceptance. A *draft* that a seller presents for signature (acceptance) to the buyer at the time it sells goods. The draft then becomes the equivalent of a *note receivable* of the seller and a *note payable* of the buyer.

trade credit. Occurs when one business allows another to buy from it in return for a promise to pay later. Contrast with "consumer credit," which occurs when a business extends a retail customer the privilege of paying later.

trade discount. A *list price discount* offered to all customers of a given type. Contrast with a *discount* offered for prompt payment and with *quantity discount*.

trade-in. Acquiring a new *asset* in exchange for a used one and perhaps additional cash. See *boot* and *trade-in transaction*.

trade-in transaction. The accounting for a trade-in; depends on whether the firm receives an asset "similar" to (and used in the same line of business as) the asset traded in and whether the accounting is for *financial statements* or for *income tax* returns. Assume that an old asset cost $5,000, has $3,000 of *accumulated depreciation* (after recording depreciation to the date of the trade-in), and hence has a *book value* of $2,000. The old asset appears to have a market value of $1,500, according to price quotations in used asset markets. The firm trades in the old asset on a new asset with a list price of $10,000. The firm gives up the old asset and $5,500 cash *(boot)* for the new asset. The generic entry for the trade-in transaction is as follows:

New Asset	A		
Accumulated Depreciation (Old Asset)	3,000		
Adjustment on Exchange of Asset	B	or	B
Old Asset			5,000
Cash			5,500

1. The *list price* method of accounting for trade-ins rests on the assumption that the list price of the new asset closely approximates its market value. The firm records the new asset at its list price (A = $10,000 in the example); B is a *plug* (= $2,500 credit in the example). If B requires a *debit* plug, the Adjustment on Exchange of Asset is a *loss*; if B requires a *credit* plug (as in the example), the adjustment is a *gain*.
2. Another theoretically sound method of accounting for trade-ins rests on the assumption that the price quotation from used-asset markets gives a market value of the old asset that is a more reliable measure than the market value of the new asset determined by list price. This method uses the *fair market price (value)* of the old asset, $1,500 in the example, to determine B (= $2,000 book value – $1,500 assumed proceeds on disposition = $500 debit or loss). The exchange results in a loss if the book value of the old asset exceeds its market value and in a gain if the market value exceeds the book value. The firm records the new asset on the books by plugging for A (= $7,000 in the example).
3. For income tax reporting, the taxpayer must recognize neither gain nor loss on the trade-in. Thus the taxpayer records the new asset for tax purposes by assuming B is zero and plugging for A (= $7,500 in the example). In practice, firms that want to recognize the loss currently will sell the old asset directly, rather than trading it in, and acquire the new asset entirely for cash.

4. *Generally accepted accounting principles (APB Opinion No. 29)* require a variant of these methods. The basic method is (1) or (2), depending on whether the list price of the new asset (1) or the quotation of the old asset's market value (2) provides the more reliable indication of market value. If the basic method requires a debit entry, or loss, for the Adjustment on Exchange of Asset, then the firm records the trade-in as in (1) or (2) and recognizes the full amount of the loss currently. If, however, the basic method requires a credit entry, or gain, for the Adjustment on Exchange of Asset, then the firm recognizes the gain currently if the old asset and the new asset are not "similar." If the assets are similar and the party trading in receives no cash, then it recognizes no gain and the treatment resembles that in (3); that is B = 0, plug for A. If the assets are similar and the firm trading in receives cash—a rare case—then it recognizes a portion of the gain currently. The portion of the gain recognized currently is the fraction cash received/fair market value of total consideration received. (When the firm uses the list price method, (1), it assumes that the market value of the old asset is the list price of the new asset plus the amount of cash received by the party trading in.)

A summary of the results of applying *GAAP* to the example follows.

More Reliable Information as to Fair Market Value	Old Asset Compared with New Asset	
	Similar	Not Similar
New Asset List	A = $7,500	A = $10,000
Price	B = 0	B = 2,500 gain
Old Asset Market	A = $7,000	A = $ 7,000
Price	B = 500 loss	B = 500 loss

trade payables (receivables). *Payables (receivables)* arising in the ordinary course of business transactions. Most *accounts payable (receivable)* are of this kind.

trade secret. Technical or business information such as formulas, recipes, computer programs, and marketing data not generally known by competitors and maintained by the firm as a secret; theoretically capable of having an indefinite, finite life. A famous example is the secret process for Coca-Cola® (a registered *trademark* of the company). Compare with *know-how.* The firm will capitalize this intangible asset only if purchased. If this *intangible* has a finite, expected useful life, *GAAP* require amortization over that estimate of its life. If the right has indefinite life, then *GAAP* require no amortization, but annual tests for *impairment.* If the firm develops the intangible internally, the firm will *expense* the costs as incurred and show no asset.

trademark. A distinctive word or symbol that is affixed to a product, its package, or its dispenser and that uniquely identifies the firm's products and services. See *trademark right.*

trademark right. The right to exclude competitors in sales or advertising from using words or symbols that are so similar to the firm's *trademarks* as possibly to confuse consumers. Trademark rights last as long as the firm continues to use the trademarks in question. In the United States, trademark rights arise from use and not from government registration. They therefore have a legal life independent of the life of a registration. Registrations last 20 years, and the holder may renew them as long as the holder uses the trademark. If this *intangible* has a finite, expected useful life, *GAAP* require amortization over that estimate of its life. If the right has indefinite life, then *GAAP* require no amortization, but annual tests for *impairment.* Under *SFAS No. 2,* the firm must *expense* internally developed trademark rights.

trading on the equity. Said of a firm engaging in *debt financing*; frequently said of a firm doing so to a degree considered abnormal for a firm of its kind. *Leverage.*

trading securities. *Marketable securities* that a firm holds and expects to sell within a relatively short time; a classification important in *SFAS No. 115*, which requires the owner to carry marketable equity securities on the balance sheet at market value, not at cost. Contrast with *available for sale, securities* and *held-to-maturity securities*. Under *SFAS No. 115*, the balance sheet reports trading securities at market value on the balance sheet date, and the income statement reports *holding gains and losses* on trading securities. When the firm sells the securities, it reports realized gain or loss as the difference between the selling price and the market value at the last balance sheet date.

transaction. A *transfer* (of more than promises—see *executory contract*) between the accounting *entity* and another party or parties.

transfer. Under *SFAC No. 6,* consists of two types: "reciprocal" and "nonreciprocal." In a reciprocal transfer, or "exchange," the entity both receives and sacrifices. In a nonreciprocal transfer, the entity sacrifices but does not receive (examples include gifts, distributions to owners) or receives but does not sacrifice (investment by owner in entity). *SFAC No. 6* suggests that the term "internal transfer" is self-contradictory and that writers should use the term "internal event" instead.

transfer agent. Usually a bank or trust company designated by a corporation to make legal transfers of *stock (bonds)* and, perhaps, to pay *dividends (coupons).*

transfer price. A substitute for a *market*, or *arm's-length, price* used in *profit*, or *responsibility center, accounting* when one segment of the business "sells" to another segment. Incentives of profit center managers will not coincide with the best interests of the entire business unless a firm sets transfer prices properly.

transfer-pricing problem. The problem of setting *transfer prices* so that both buyer and seller have *goal congruence* with respect to the parent organization's goals.

translation adjustment. The effect of *exchange-rate* changes caused by converting the value of a net investment denominated in a *foreign currency* to the entity's reporting currency. *SFAS No. 52* requires firms to translate their net investment in relatively self-contained foreign operations at the *balance sheet* date. Year-to-year changes in value caused by exchange-rate changes accumulate in an *owners' equity* account, sometimes called the "cumulative translation adjustment."

translation gain (or loss). *Foreign exchange gain (or loss).*

transportation-in. *Freight-in.*

transposition error. An error in recordkeeping resulting from reversing the order of digits in a number, such as recording "32" for "23." If the only errors in a *trial balance* result from one or more transposition errors, then the difference between the sum of the *debits* and the sum of the *credits* will be divisible by nine. Not all such differences result from transposition errors. See *slide.*

treasurer. The financial officer responsible for managing cash and raising funds.

treasury bond. A bond issued by a corporation and then reacquired. Such bonds are treated as retired when reacquired, and an *extraordinary gain or loss* on reacquisition is recognized. This term also refers to a *bond* issued by the U.S. Treasury Department.

treasury shares. *Capital stock* issued and then reacquired by the corporation. Such reacquisitions result in a reduction of *shareholders' equity* and usually appear on the balance sheet as contra to shareholders' equity. Accounting recognizes neither *gain* nor *loss* on transactions involving treasury stock. The accounting debits (if positive) or credits (if negative) any difference between the amounts paid and received for treasury stock transactions to *additional paid-in capital*. See *cost method* and *par value method.*

treasury stock. *Treasury shares.*

trend analysis. Investigation of sales or other economic trends. Can range from a simple visual extrapolation of points on a graph to a sophisticated computerized time series analysis.

trial balance. A two-column listing of *account balances*. The left-hand column shows all accounts with *debit* balances and their total. The right-hand column shows all accounts with *credit* balances and their total. The two totals should be equal. Accountants compute trial balances as a partial check of the arithmetic accuracy of the entries previously made. See *adjusted, preclosing, post-closing, unadjusted trial balance*, *plug*, *slide*, and *transposition error*.

troubled debt restructuring. As defined in *SFAS No. 15*, a concession (changing of the terms of a *debt*) that is granted by a *creditor* for economic or legal reasons related to the *debtor's* financial difficulty and that the creditor would not otherwise consider.

TSE. *Toronto Stock Exchange.*

t-statistic. For an estimated *regression* coefficient, the estimated coefficient divided by the *standard error* of the estimate.

turnover. The number of times that *assets*, such as *inventory* or *accounts receivable*, are replaced on average during the period. Accounts receivable turnover, for example, is total sales on account for a period divided by the average accounts receivable balance for the period. See *ratio*. In the United Kingdom, "turnover" means *sales*.

turnover of plant and equipment. See *ratio*.

t-value. In *regression analysis*, the ratio of an estimated regression coefficient divided by its *standard error*.

20-F. Form required by the *SEC* for foreign companies issuing or trading their securities in the United States. This form reconciles the foreign accounting amounts resulting from using foreign *GAAP* to amounts resulting from using U.S. GAAP.

two T-account method. A method for computing either (1) *foreign-exchange gains and losses* or (2) *monetary gains* or *losses* for *constant-dollar accounting statements*. The left-hand *T-account* shows actual net balances of *monetary items*, and the right-hand T-account shows implied (common) dollar amounts.

2/10, n(et)/30. See *terms of sale*.

U

unadjusted trial balance. *Trial balance* taken before the accountant makes *adjusting* and *closing entries* at the end of the period.

unappropriated retained earnings. *Retained earnings* not appropriated and therefore against which the *board* can declare *dividends* in the absence of retained earnings restrictions. See *restricted retained earnings*.

unavoidable cost. A *cost* that is not an *avoidable cost*.

uncertainty. See *risk* for definition and contrast.

uncollectible account. An *account receivable* that the *debtor* will not pay. If the firm uses the preferable *allowance method*, the entry on judging a specific account to be uncollectible *debits* the allowance for uncollectible accounts and *credits* the specific account receivable. See *bad debt expense* and *sales contra, estimated uncollectibles*.

unconsolidated subsidiary. A *subsidiary* not consolidated and, hence, not accounted for in the *equity method*.

uncontrollable cost. The opposite of *controllable cost*.

underapplied (underabsorbed) overhead. An excess of actual *overhead costs* for a period over costs applied, or charged, to products produced during the period; a *debit balance* remaining in an overhead account after the accounting assigns overhead to product.

underlying document. The record, memorandum, *voucher*, or other signal that is the authority for making an *entry* into a *journal*.

underwriter. One who agrees to purchase an entire *security issue* for a specified price, usually for resale to others.

undistributed earnings. *Retained earnings*. Typically, this term refers to that amount retained for a given year.

unearned income (revenue). *Advances from customers*; strictly speaking, a contradiction in terms because the terms "income" and "revenue" mean earned.

unemployment tax. See *FUTA*.

unencumbered appropriation. In governmental accounting, portion of an *appropriation* not yet spent or encumbered.

unexpired cost. An *asset*.

unfavorable variance. In *standard cost* accounting, an excess of expected revenue over actual revenue or an excess of actual cost over standard cost.

unfunded. Not *funded*. An obligation or *liability*, usually for *pension costs*, exists, but no *funds* have been set aside to discharge the obligation or liability.

Uniform Partnership Act. A model law, enacted by many states, to govern the relations between partners when the *partnership* agreement fails to specify the agreed-upon treatment.

unissued capital stock. *Stock* authorized but not yet issued.

uniting-of-interests method. The IASB's term for the *pooling-of-interests method*. The IASB allows uniting of interests only when the merging firms are roughly equal in size and the shareholders retain substantially the same, relative to each other, voting rights and interests in the combined entity after the combination as before.

unit-level activities. Work that converts resources into individual products. Examples include *direct materials, direct labor,* and energy to run the machines.

units-of-production method. The *production method of depreciation*.

unlimited liability. The legal obligation of *general partners* or the sole proprietor for all debts of the *partnership* or *sole proprietorship*.

unqualified opinion. See *auditor's report*.

unrealized appreciation. An *unrealized holding gain*; frequently used in the context of *marketable securities*.

unrealized gain (loss) on marketable securities. An *income statement account* title for the amount of *gain (loss)* during the current period on the portfolio of *marketable securities* held as *trading securities*. *SFAS No. 115* requires the firm to recognize, in the income statement, gains and losses caused by changes in market values, even though the firm has not yet *realized* them.

unrealized gross margin (profit). A *contra account* to *installment accounts receivable* used with the *installment method* of revenue recognition; shows the amount of profit that the firm will eventually realize when it collects the receivable. Some accountants show this account as a *liability*.

unrealized holding gain. See *inventory profit* for the definition and an example.

unrecovered cost. *Book value* of an *asset*.

unused capacity. The difference between resources supplied and resources used.

usage variance. *Efficiency variance*.

use of funds. Any transaction that reduces funds (however "funds" is defined).

useful life. *Service life*.

V

valuation account. A *contra account* or *adjunct account*. When the firm reports *accounts receivable* at expected collectible amounts, it will credit any expected uncollectible amounts to the *allowance for uncollectibles*, a valuation account. In this way, the firm can show both the gross receivables amount and the amount it expects to collect. *SFAC No. 6* says a valuation account is "a separate item that reduces and increases the carrying amount" of an asset (or liability). The accounts are part of the related assets (or liabilities) and are not assets (or liabilities) in their own right.

value. Monetary worth. This term is usually so vague that you should not use it without a modifying adjective unless most people would agree on the amount. Do not confuse with cost. See *fair market price (value), entry value*, and *exit value*.

value added. *Cost* of a product or *work-in-process* minus the cost of the material purchased for the product or work-in-process.

value-added activity. Any activity that increases the usefulness to a customer of a product or service.

value chain. The set of business functions that increase the usefulness to the customer of a product or service; typically including research and development, design of products and services, production, marketing, distribution, and customer service.

value engineering. An evaluation of the activities in the value chain to reduce costs.

value variance. *Price variance*.

variable annuity. An *annuity* whose periodic payments depend on some uncertain outcome, such as stock market prices.

variable budget. *Flexible budget*.

variable costing. In allocating costs, a method that assigns only *variable manufacturing costs* to products and treats *fixed manufacturing costs* as *period expenses*. Contrast with *full absorption costing*.

variable costs. *Costs* that change as activity levels change. Strictly speaking, variable costs are zero when the activity level is zero. See *semi-variable costs*. In accounting, this term most often means the sum of *direct costs* and variable *overhead*.

VIE (variable interest entity). An entity arranged so that one cannot analyze controlling financial interest by analyzing voting interest, because the entity has insufficient *owners' equity* at risk, which means it cannot finance its operations without additional financial support, such as the promises of another entity. The entity's owners' equity lacks attributes associated with equity: the ability to absorb losses, the right to receive residual returns, and the ability, conveyed by voting rights, to make decisions. The entity may, but need not, have a "primary beneficiary," which absorbs (or receives) a majority of the variability of outcomes of the entity. If there is a primary beneficiary, that business will consolidate the VIE, regardless of ownership.

variable overhead efficiency variance. The difference between the *actual* and *standard cost driver* volume times the standard cost driver rate.

variable overhead price variance. The difference between the *actual* and *standard cost driver* rate times the actual cost driver volume.

variable overhead variance. Difference between actual and *standard variable overhead costs*.

variable rate debt. *Debt* whose interest rate results from the periodic application of a formula, such as "three-month LIBOR [London Interbank Offered Rate] plus 1 percent [one hundred basis points] set on the 8th day of each February, May, August, and November."

variables sampling. The use of a sampling technique in which the sampler infers a particular quantitative characteristic of an entire population from a sample (e.g., mean amount of accounts receivable). See also *estimation sampling*. See *attribute(s) sampling* for contrast and further examples.

variance. Difference between actual and *standard costs* or between *budgeted* and actual *expenditures* or, sometimes, *expenses*. The word has completely different meanings in accounting and in statistics, where it means a measure of dispersion of a distribution.

variance analysis. *Variance investigation.* This term's meaning differs in statistics.

variance investigation. A step in managerial control processes. *Standard costing systems* produce *variance* numbers of various sorts. These numbers seldom exactly equal to zero. Management must decide when a variance differs sufficiently from zero to study its cause. This term refers both to the decision about when to study the cause and to the study itself.

variation analysis. Analysis of the causes of changes in financial statement items of interest such as *net income* or *gross margin.*

VAT (value-added tax). A tax levied on the market value of a firm's outputs less the market value of its purchased inputs.

vendor. A seller; sometimes spelled "vender."

verifiable. A qualitative *objective* of financial reporting specifying that accountants can trace items in *financial statements* back to *underlying documents*—supporting *invoices*, canceled *checks*, and other physical pieces of evidence.

verification. The auditor's act of reviewing or checking items in *financial statements* by tracing back to *underlying documents*—supporting *invoices*, canceled *checks*, and other business documents—or sending out *confirmations* to be returned. Compare with *physical verification*.

vertical analysis. Analysis of the financial statements of a single firm or across several firms for a particular time, as opposed to *horizontal* or *time-series analysis,* in which the analyst compares items over time for a single firm or across firms.

vertical integration. The extension of activity by an organization into business directly related to the production or distribution of the organization's end products. Although a firm may sell products to others at various stages, a vertically integrated firm devotes the substantial portion of the output at each stage to the production of the next stage or to end products. Compare *horizontal integration.*

vested. An employee's *pension plan* benefits that are not contingent on the employee's continuing to work for the employer.

VIE. *Variable interest entity.*

visual curve fitting method. One crude form of cost *estimation.* Sometimes, when a firm needs only rough approximations of the amounts of *fixed* and *variable costs*, management need not perform a formal *regression analysis* but can plot the data and draw a line that seems to fit the data. Then it can use the parameters of that line for the rough approximations.

volume variance. *Production volume variance*; less often, used to mean *sales volume variance*.

voucher. A document that signals recognition of a *liability* and authorizes the disbursement of cash; sometimes used to refer to the written evidence documenting an *accounting entry*, as in the term *journal voucher*.

voucher system. In controlling *cash*, a method that requires someone in the firm to authorize each *check* with an approved *voucher*. The firm makes no *disbursements* of currency or coins except from *petty cash funds*.

vouching. The function performed by an *auditor* to ascertain that underlying data or documents support a *journal entry*.

W

wage. Compensation of employees based on time worked or output of product for manual labor. But see *take-home pay*.

warning signal. Tool used to identify quality-control problems; only signals a problem. Contrast with *diagnostic signal*, which both signals a problem and suggests its cause

warrant. A certificate entitling the owner to buy a specified number of shares at a specified time(s) for a specified price; differs from a *stock option* only in that the firm grants options to employees and issues warrants to the public. See *right*.

warranty. A promise by a seller to correct deficiencies in products sold. When the seller gives warranties, proper accounting practice recognizes an estimate of warranty *expense* and an *estimated liability* at the time of sale. See *guarantee* for contrast in proper usage.

wash sale. The sale and purchase of the same or similar *asset* within a short time period. For *income tax* purposes, the taxpayer may not recognize *losses* on a sale of stock if the taxpayer purchases equivalent stock within 30 days before or after the date of sale.

waste. Material that is a residue from manufacturing operations and that has no sale value. Frequently, this has negative value because a firm must incur additional costs for disposal.

wasting asset. A *natural resource* that has a limited *useful life* and, hence, is subject to *amortization*, called *depletion*. Examples are timber, oil and gas, and ore deposits.

watered stock. Shares issued for *assets* with *fair market price (value)* less than *par* or *stated value*. The firm records the assets on the books at the overstated values. In the law, for shares to be considered watered, the *board of directors* must have acted in bad faith or fraudulently in issuing the shares under these circumstances. The term originated from a former practice of cattle owners who fed cattle ("stock") large quantities of salt to make them thirsty. The cattle then drank much water before their owner took them to market. The owners did this to make the cattle appear heavier and more valuable than otherwise.

weighted average. An average computed by counting each occurrence of each value, not merely a single occurrence of each value. For example, if a firm purchases one unit for $1 and two units for $2 each, then the simple average of the purchase prices is $1.50, but the weighted average price per unit is $5/3 = $1.67. Contrast with *moving average.*

weighted-average cost of capital. Measured as the *weighted-average* of the *after-tax cost* of *long-term debt* and the cost of *equity.*

weighted-average inventory method. Valuing either *withdrawals* or *ending inventory* at the *weighted-average* purchase price of all units on hand at the time of withdrawal or of computation of ending inventory. The firm uses the *inventory equation* to calculate the other quantity. If a firm uses the *perpetual inventory* method, accountants often call it the *moving average method.*

where-got, where-gone statement. A term allegedly used in the 1920s by W. M. Cole for a statement much like the *statement of cash flows.* Noted accounting historian S. Zeff reports that Cole actually used the term "where-got-gone" statement.

wind up. To bring to an end, such as the life of a corporation. The *board* winds up the life of a corporation by following the winding-up provisions of applicable statutes, by surrendering the charter, or by following *bankruptcy* proceedings. See also *liquidation.*

window dressing. The attempt to make financial statements show *operating* results, or a *financial position,* more favorable than they would otherwise show.

with recourse. See *note receivable discounted.*

withdrawals. *Assets* distributed to an owner. *Partner's drawings.* See *inventory equation* for another context.

withholding. Deductions that are taken from *salaries* or *wages,* usually for *income taxes,* and that the employer remits, in the employee's name, to the taxing authority.

without recourse. See *note receivable discounted.*

work sheet (program). (1) A computer program designed to combine explanations and calculations. This type of program helps in preparing *financial statements* and *schedules.* (2) A tabular schedule for convenient summary of *adjusting* and *closing entries.* The work sheet usually begins with an *unadjusted trial balance.* Adjusting entries appear in the next two columns, one for *debits* and one for *credits.* The work sheet carries the horizontal sum of each line to the right into either the *income statement* or the *balance sheet* column, as appropriate. The *plug* to equate the income statement column totals is, if a debit, the income or, if a credit, a loss for the period. That income will close retained earnings on the balance sheet. The income statement credit columns are the revenues for the period, and the debit columns are the expenses (and revenue contras) that appear on the income statement. "Work sheet" also refers to *schedules* for ascertaining other items that appear on the *financial statements* and that require adjustment or compilation.

working capital. *Current assets* minus *current liabilities;* sometimes called "net working capital" or "net current assets."

work(ing) papers. The schedules and analyses prepared by the *auditor* in carrying out investigations before issuing an *opinion* on *financial statements.*

work-in-process (inventory account). Partially completed product; appears on the balance sheet as *inventory.*

worth, *Value.* See *net worth.*

worth-debt ratio. Reciprocal of the *debt-equity ratio.* See *ratio.*

write down. To *write off,* except that the firm does not charge all the *asset*'s cost to *expense* or *loss;* generally used for nonrecurring items.

write off. To *charge* an *asset* to *expense* or *loss*; that is, to *debit* expense (or loss) and *credit* the asset.

write-off method. For treating *uncollectible accounts,* a method that *debits bad debt expense* and *credits* accounts receivable of specific customers as the firm identifies specific accounts as uncollectible. The firm cannot use this method when it can estimate uncollectible amounts and they are significant. See *bad debt expense, sales contra, estimated uncollectibles,* and the *allowance method* for contrast.

write up. To increase the recorded *cost* of an *asset* with no corresponding *disbursement* of *funds*; that is, to *debit* asset and *credit revenue* or, perhaps, *owners' equity;* seldom done in the United States because currently accepted accounting principles await actual transactions before recording asset increases. An exception occurs in accounting for *marketable equity securities.*

Y

yield. *Internal rate of return* of a stream of cash flows. Cash yield is cash flow divided by book value. See also *dividend yield.*

yield curve. The relation between *interest rates* and the term to maturity of loans. Ordinarily, longer-term loans have higher interest rates than shorter-term loans. This is called a "normal" yield curve. Sometimes long-term and short-term rates are approximately the same—a "flat" yield curve. Sometimes short-term loans have a higher rate than long-term ones—an "inverted" yield curve. *Term structure* of interest rates.

yield to maturity. At a given time, the *internal rate of return* of a series of cash flows; usually said of a *bond;* sometimes called the "effective rate."

yield variance. Measures the input-output relation while holding the standard mix of inputs constant: (Standard price × Actual amount of input used in the standard mix) – (Standard price × Standard quantity allowed for the actual output). It is the part of the *efficiency variance* not called the *mix variance.*

Z

zero-base(d) budgeting (ZBB). One philosophy for setting budgets. In preparing an ordinary *budget* for the next period, a manager starts with the budget for the current period and makes adjustments as seem necessary because of changed conditions for the next period. Since most managers like to increase the scope of the activities managed and since most prices increase most of the time, amounts in budgets prepared in the ordinary, incremental way seem to increase period after period. The authority approving the budget assumes that managers will carry out operations in the same way as in the past and that next period's expenditures will have to be at least as large as those of the current period. Thus, this authority tends to study only the increments to the current period's budget. In ZBB, the authority questions the process for carrying out a program and the entire budget for the next period. The authority studies every dollar in the budget, not just the dollars incremental to the previous period's amounts. The advocates of ZBB claim that in this way, (1) management will more likely delete programs or divisions of marginal benefit to the business or governmental unit, rather than continuing with costs at least as large as the present ones, and (2) management may discover and implement alternative, more cost-effective ways of carrying out programs. ZBB implies questioning the existence of programs and the fundamental nature of the way that firms carry them out, not merely the amounts used to fund them. Experts appear to divide evenly as to whether the middle word should be "base" or "based."

CHAPTER 2

ECONOMIC CONCEPTS OF COST IN MANAGERIAL ACCOUNTING*

GORDON SHILLINGLAW, PHD
Columbia University

UPDATED BY

ROMAN L. WEIL, CPA, CMA, PHD, EDITOR
University of Chicago

CONTENTS

2.1 INTRODUCTION 157

2.2 INTERFACES BETWEEN ECONOMICS AND MANAGEMENT ACCOUNTING 158

2.3 MEASUREMENT CONCEPTS 159
- (a) Short Run and Long Run 159
- (b) Variable Cost 160
- (c) Fixed Cost 161
- (d) Short-Run Marginal Cost 162
- (e) Marginal Contribution 164
- (f) Incremental Cost 166
- (g) Opportunity Cost 167
- (h) Long-Run Average Cost 167
- (i) Current Cost 169
- (j) Present Value 169

2.4 SITUATIONAL CONCEPTS 169
- (a) Common Cost 169
- (b) Joint Cost 170

2.5 APPLICATIONS IN MANAGEMENT ACCOUNTING 170
- (a) Fixed and Variable Costs 170
- (b) Incremental Cost and Opportunity Cost 171
- (c) Short-Run Marginal Cost 171
- (d) Marginal Contribution 171
- (e) Long-Run Average Cost 172
- (f) Current Cost 173
- (g) Present Value 173

2.6 SUMMARY 173

BIBLIOGRAPHY 174

2.1 INTRODUCTION

Management accounting springs from the needs of managers and others to make decisions affecting the allocation of economic resources. It does not, however, draw on a well-defined set of concepts drawn from economic theory. It uses some economic concepts

* Gordon Shillinglaw, then of the Columbia University Graduate School of Business, wrote the original version of this chapter for the first edition of *The Handbook of Cost Accounting*. I have preserved most of his ideas and words. RLW.

directly, particularly in cost estimation, but often the accountant can only approximate the economic concept.

This chapter discusses economic concepts, not economic principles. A *concept* describes a presumed phenomenon or relation. Economic *principles* serve as a basis for action. They include economic decision rules (e.g., maximization of present value) and analytical techniques (e.g., mathematical optimization), as well as presumed laws of economic behavior (e.g., raise a price and customers do not buy more; demand curves slope downward).

2.2 INTERFACES BETWEEN ECONOMICS AND MANAGEMENT ACCOUNTING

Although economics and management accounting deal with the same phenomena, they typically approach these differently. Often, economists prescribe and management accountants measure. At least four groups of economists have had some effect on management accounting or use some of its output:

1. *Microeconomists* focus on the forces that affect the allocation of resources within the economy.
2. *Managerial economists* make economic theory a useful tool in managerial planning and decision making.
3. *Industrial organization economists* apply microeconomic theory to public policy, particularly in antitrust analysis and issues involving intellectual property rights.
4. *Macroeconomists* study, and sometimes attempt to alter, relations among aggregative economic variables for regions, or nations, or the world.

The economic concepts embodied in most aspects of management accounting come mainly from microeconomics and managerial economics. Where management accounting stops and managerial economics begins is neither clear nor important. The microeconomist develops theoretical models to predict the behavior of individual firms and the markets in which they operate. The cost relations in these models rely on logical reasoning, although some economists attempt to identify them empirically.[1] Abstractions are both inevitable and necessary for this purpose. Rarely do we ask whether one can measure any of the variables in a theory—the theory stands or falls on its internal logic and the consistency of its predictions with observable conditions.

The management accountant's interest in cost is more mundane: management wants to know what things cost. Management wants this information partly to help it set prices on its products, partly to decide whether new products are worth introducing or old products are worth keeping, and partly to find out whether costs exceed expectations or budgets. Management wants numbers, not abstractions. Sometimes, the data that managers request will not help them make decisions, and the accountant must show the manager why other data are more pertinent than the cost data the manager requested.

Management accountants have found that they cannot provide numbers useful to managers without some theory underlying the measurements, and so they, too, have built up a theoretical structure.[2] This structure does not try to answer any major questions; instead, it helps the practicing accountant define costs in each of a number of situations.

1. J. Johnston, *Statistical Cost Analysis* (New York: McGraw-Hill, 1960), chapters 4 and 5. This is the classic text.
2. An early theoretical structure appeared in the American Accounting Association Committee on Concepts and Standards, "Tentative Statement of Cost Concepts Underlying Reports for Management Purposes," *Accounting Review*, XXXI, 2 (April 1956), pp. 182–193.

These definitions in effect paraphrase the questions that the measures of cost intend to answer. The question, "What would happen to cost if we were to use our current facilities to fill customer order 4276 for delivery to customer A in location B at time C?" calls for a different answer from the question, "What would happen to cost if we were to acquire, equip, and staff new facilities to make repeated deliveries to a number of customers in different locations over a period of years?" The theoretical structure of management accounting consists of guides to generating data that will provide answers to questions like these.

The management accountant must resolve the measurement problems that the microeconomist can assume away. The economist can, if the model's objective permits, ignore multiproduct situations and other complicating elements; management accountants must deal with costs as they find them, in all their complexity. The management accountant can accept any kind of cost behavior, unrestricted by any *a priori* assumptions as to the kinds of cost behavior that are consistent with a specific model. In practice, we observe that management accountants use linear (straight-line) cost relations more often than do economists.

The industrial organization economist, interested in such questions as the desirability of antitrust action or the need for government regulation, starts with the same models the microeconomist uses. The industrial organization economist, unlike the microeconomist, however, needs data drawn from actual experience, and, given power to intervene, can specify how to construct these data. In some situations, these economists must rely on accounting data supplied by the firms.

The macroeconomist has both less interest in the work of the management accountant and less power to influence it. The input-output models of macroeconomics will likely call for data on physical quantities that emerge from other parts of business information systems. National income statistics use data on business income and inventories, but so many others want to know these same quantities that the macroeconomist cannot prescribe the accounting methods to use.

2.3 MEASUREMENT CONCEPTS

This section presents ten measurement concepts that can guide management accountants by describing quantities that they might expect to measure or how they should measure them:

- **a.** Short run versus long run
- **b.** Variable cost
- **c.** Fixed cost
- **d.** Short-run marginal cost
- **e.** Marginal contribution
- **f.** Incremental cost
- **g.** Opportunity cost
- **h.** Long-run average cost
- **i.** Current cost
- **j.** Present value

(a) SHORT RUN AND LONG RUN. The capacity of any organization to carry out its activities can change only slowly. It takes time to recognize the need for new facilities, arrange for financing, complete facilities construction or acquisition, provide the necessary staff and personnel, and put all of these resources to work. Capacity reductions also take time. This means that during any short period of time, the firm must operate with a relatively constant stock of productive resources.

This fact provides the basis for the distinction the economist makes between the short run and the long run. The short run is a period long enough to permit management to change the volume of production of goods or services but too short to enable management to increase or decrease the amount of productive capacity. The long run is a period long enough to permit management to increase or decrease the organization's operating capacity so that total cost of production will be the lowest permitted by the available technology for that volume of activity. Short-run capacity may consist of a mixture of facilities of varying age, condition, and efficiency; in the long run, all facilities can be brand new, of the latest design, and operated smoothly by well-trained, efficient personnel.

(b) VARIABLE COST. Costs that change as a necessary response to small changes in the rate of use of existing capacity are known as *variable costs.* Variable cost is a short-run concept. In the long run all costs are variable, so accountants need to clarify the time horizon envisioned in identifying a cost as variable.

Exhibit 2.1 shows two of the many possible patterns of cost variation. The straight line in Exhibit 2.1 represents a cost that changes in direct proportion to changes in volume—for example, a royalty charge computed at a constant amount per unit sold. In contrast, the curved line shows costs rising sharply at first, then more gradually as volume achieves normal operating levels, and then sharply again as operations began to approach capacity limits.

Exhibit 2.1 illustrates two possible relations between total volume and total variable cost in a specified period of time. Exhibit 2.2 shows two possible relations between total volume and average variable cost per unit of activity. The horizontal line in this exhibit corresponds to the straight line in Exhibit 2.1. If total variable cost always increases in proportion to changes in volume, then average variable cost must remain constant as volume changes. For a variable cost described by the curved line in Exhibit 2.1, however,

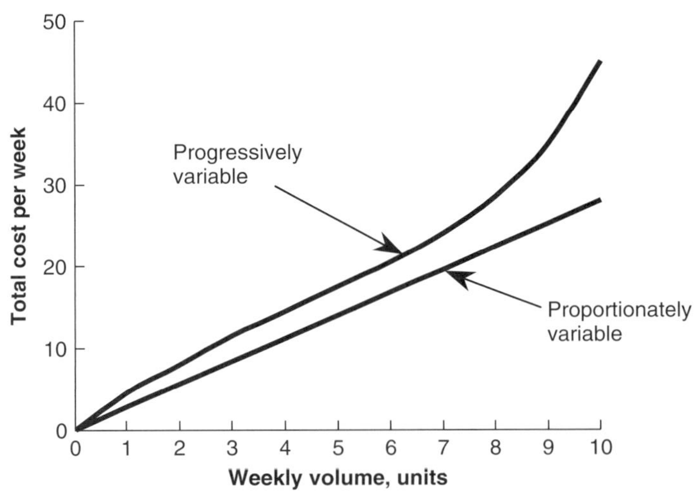

EXHIBIT 2.1 VARIABLE COSTS

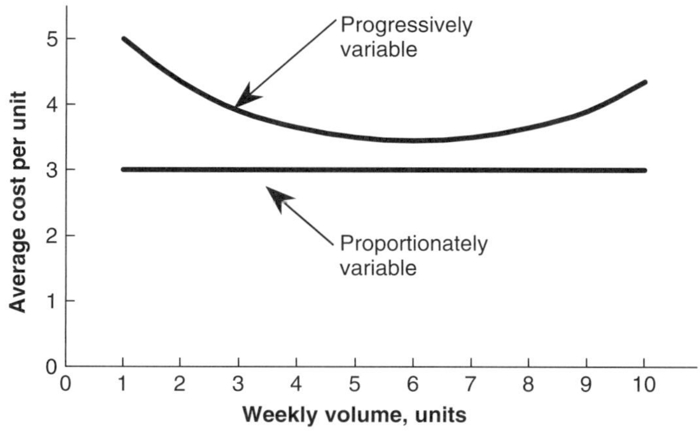

EXHIBIT 2.2 AVERAGE VARIABLE COST

average variable cost will vary, as illustrated in column (3) of Exhibit 2.3. The variable cost of the first 1,000 units produced is high, $5.00. As the total variable cost curve levels off, the increase in cost is less than proportional to the increase in volume, and average variable cost decreases. Total variable cost begins to climb more rapidly again at a volume of 7,000 units per week, and average variable cost starts to increase.

This illustration does not give the specific nature of the units of measurement for the volume. The most obvious choice is the number of units of goods or services produced, which we can use for operations that produce only a single product or service. When output involves multiple kinds of products or services, to measure volume requires some other units. Usually, the measure is some form of input, such as direct labor hours or pounds of materials used.

(c) FIXED COST. Fixed cost, like variable cost, is a short-run concept. The economist defines fixed cost as any cost that will remain the same amount whether the firm fully

(1) Weekly Volume (units)	(2) Weekly Variable Cost	(3) Average Variable Cost (2)/(1)
1,000	$ 5,000	$5.00
2,000	9,000	4.50
3,000	12,000	4.00
4,000	15,000	3.75
5,000	18,000	3.60
6,000	21,000	3.50
7,000	24,500	3.50
8,000	29,200	3.65
9,000	36,000	4.00
10,000	46,000	4.60

EXHIBIT 2.3 AVERAGE VARIABLE COST

uses existing capacity or leaves it idle. This ignores two phenomena: (1) indivisibilities in the short-run cost structure, such as step-function costs; and (2) activities where the current volume of activity does not technologically determine the scope of activity—typically capacity costs and programmed costs, discussed next. As a result, the accountant is likely to define as *fixed* any cost that does not change as a necessary response to small changes in the rate of use of existing capacity. Economists initially recognized only capacity costs, but the distinction between them and programmed costs warrants a separate discussion of each.

(i) Capacity Costs. Resources consumed in a period to provide or maintain the organization's capacity to produce or sell are known as *capacity costs* or *supportive overheads.*

Capacity costs further divide into *standby costs* and *enabling costs.* Standby costs will continue if the firm shuts down operations or facilities temporarily. Examples are depreciation, property taxes, and some executive salaries. The firm will not incur enabling costs if operations shut down, but will incur them if operations take place at all. Some of these will likely be constant over the entire output range; others will likely vary in steps. For example, a single-shift operation might require only one departmental supervisor, but operation of a second shift will require a second supervisor.

Economists classify step-variable capacity costs as variable costs, but managers and accountants classify them as fixed within the capacity range they support.

(ii) Programmed Costs. Some discussions of fixed costs focus on the relations between volume and total capacity costs, or, on a per-unit basis, between volume and average capacity costs. Fixed costs also include a second category fundamentally different from the first. These are costs designed neither to maintain current operating capacity nor to meet the demands placed on the system for the production and delivery of goods and services. Instead, management establishes them with separate decisions to meet objectives other than fulfilling service demands.

Costs of this sort have a variety of names, including *programmed costs, discretionary costs,* and *managed costs.* Some programmed costs generate and retain sales orders—this cost causes volume increase, rather than the other way around. Some programmed costs help achieve other kinds of results unrelated to current operating volume—generating ideas for new products, for example. Still others yield services to management, such as financial reporting systems.

Management budgets programmed costs at specified levels for individual time periods. The calculation of per-unit-of-output costs for these items has no business purpose.

(d) SHORT-RUN MARGINAL COST. The fourth economic concept underlying management accounting is short-run marginal cost, defined as the change in cost that results from increasing the rate of output by one unit per period of time. This nonmathematical definition is adequate for the purposes of this chapter, but for those who desire a precise definition, it is the rate of change in cost for an infinitely small change in the volume of activity, the derivative dc/dv of the relation between total cost (c) and volume (v).

A key factor in economic theories of how firms behave is whether marginal cost remains constant as output varies, or whether it will increase or decrease as volume increases. The behavior of marginal costs depends on the shape of the relation between volume and total cost. If total cost increases strictly proportionally to volume, it will appear as a straight line on a cost-volume chart, like the one illustrated earlier in Exhibit 2.1. A straight line indicates that each unit change in volume produces exactly the same change in total cost as every other unit change in volume. Only if cost traces a straight line on a cost-volume chart will marginal cost remain fixed as volume varies.

The curve in Exhibit 2.4 traces a different marginal cost curve, one that is familiar to most students of economics. This shows marginal cost decreasing at first due to economies achieved by production in larger quantities. This corresponds to the steep portion at the left-hand side of the total variable cost curve in Exhibit 2.1. The slope of the total cost curve at any volume represents the marginal cost at that volume.

As volume increases, the total cost curve flattens out and marginal cost remains constant for a while. In practice, this seems likely to cover a larger portion of the total output range than in this simple illustration. Finally, diseconomies begin as the organization approaches the limits of its capacity, meaning that additional output becomes increasingly costly to achieve. When this happens, the total cost curve begins to climb more and more sharply, and marginal cost goes up.

The marginal cost curve always crosses the average total cost curve at the lowest point on the average cost curve, as in Exhibit 2.4. Adding an amount smaller than an

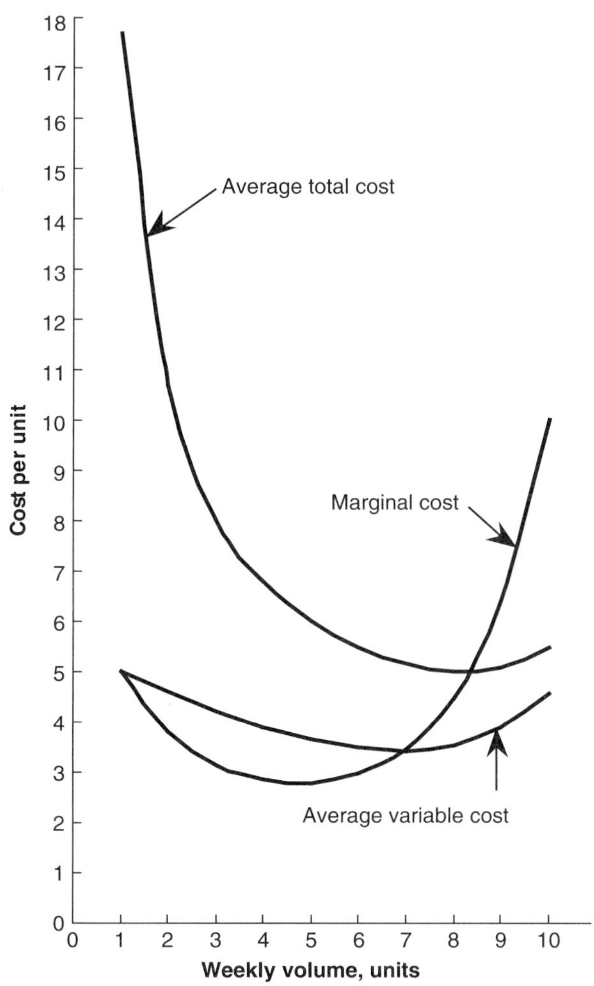

EXHIBIT 2.4 MARGINAL COST AND AVERAGE COST

existing average to any total will decrease the new average. If the added increment exceeds the previous average, then the average will rise.

The concept of marginal cost has no meaning in connection with programmed fixed costs. Marginal costs measure the effects of increasing volume; programmed costs do not change as a result of changes in volume and therefore cannot be marginal with respect to those changes. Accountants distinguish marginal costs from incremental costs, discussed in Section 2.3(f).

(e) MARGINAL CONTRIBUTION. Managerial economists seldom have interest in cost behavior alone. In studying possible ways of allocating any scarce resource, they look instead at the marginal contribution the resource can make in each use. Marginal contribution measures the spread between the amount of revenue to be received from one additional unit of the scarce resource and the amount of incremental cost necessary to produce that revenue. The cost of the scarce resource itself does not enter into this calculation because the way the firm uses the resource does not change the cost.

Some economic models reflect the assumption that marginal contribution declines as capacity usage increases. Exhibit 2.5 illustrates a relation of this kind. Marginal contribution is the spread between marginal revenue and marginal cost at any volume. In this case, as volume increases, marginal cost rises and marginal revenue falls. When the lines cross, marginal contribution is zero.

The microeconomist's definition of marginal contribution is a byproduct of the definitions of fixed and variable cost that exclude programmed fixed costs.[3] The managerial economist may use this definition or combine it with an estimated relation between programmed cost and sales volume. Exhibit 2.6 illustrates a relation of this sort. This case assumes a constant marginal contribution, which means assuming that the total contribution is proportional to volume. The total amount of programmed fixed cost necessary to

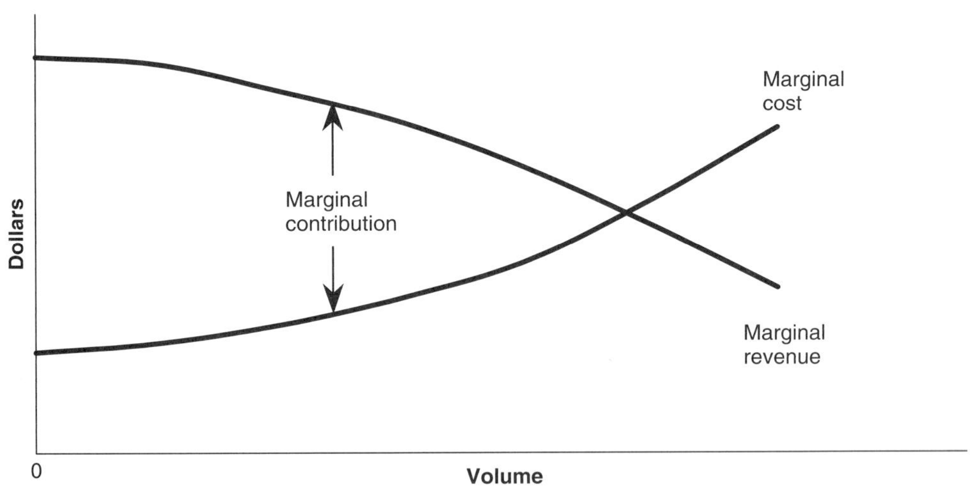

EXHIBIT 2.5 DECLINING MARGINAL CONTRIBUTION

3. The notion of programmed costs dates from the 1950s, or before. See Edward H. Chamberlin, *The Theory of Monopolistic Competition,* 7th ed. (Cambridge, Mass.: Harvard University Press, 1956), chaps. 6 and 7.

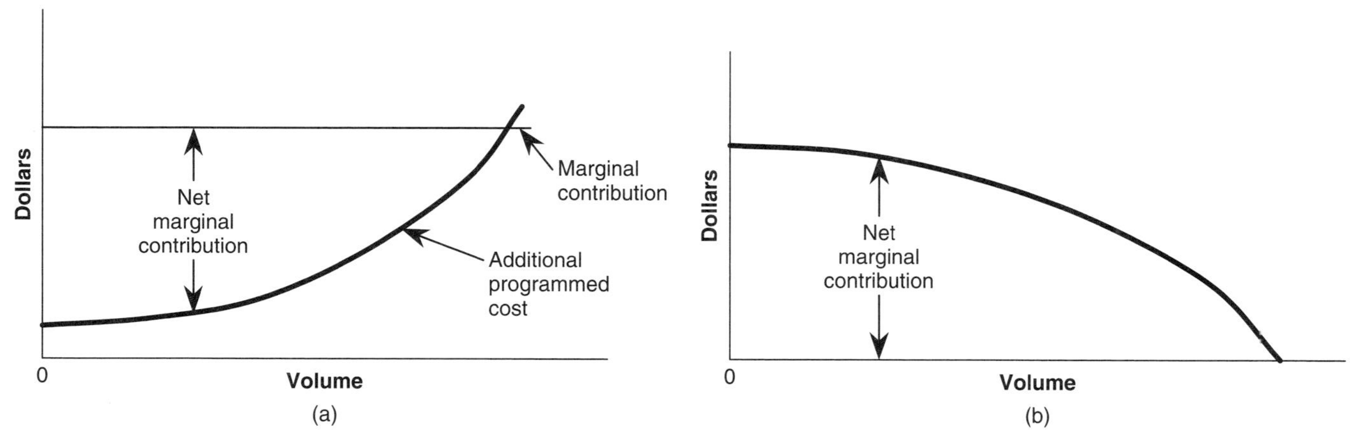

EXHIBIT 2.6 MARGINAL CONTRIBUTION

obtain additional volume is not, however, linear. As management adds more of the programmed cost, additional volume becomes more difficult to obtain. This makes the additional programmed cost curve rise more and more steeply as volume increases, as in Exhibit 2.6(a). (Additional programmed cost is the cost of obtaining one more unit of volume.) Exhibit 2.6(b) combines these two curves into one.

(f) INCREMENTAL COST. Incremental cost, or differential cost, is the difference in total net cash outlays that will result from choosing one alternative course of action instead of another. Accountants distinguish incremental costs from marginal costs, discussed in Section 2.3(d). Economists tend to think of incremental costs as synonymous with marginal costs, but when pressed will concede the difference.

For example, consider a shopping center proprietor studying the profitability of reopening a billiards hall in the rear of the mall. The billiard tables, although not used for several years, are in usable condition. The following table lists monthly cost estimates.

	Operate the Billiard Hall	Do Not Operate the Billiard Hall
Food and beverages	$45,000	$40,000
Salaries and wages	16,000	12,000
Supplies	1,500	1,000
Utilities and heat	600	500
Rent	5,000	5,000
Insurance	800	800
Miscellaneous	1,100	700
Total	$70,000	$60,000

The incremental cost in this case equals $70,000 minus $60,000, or $10,000 a month. The proprietor needs to consider this cost, and to compare it to the incremental cash inflows that opening for billiards will provide.

The term *incremental cost* often refers to the elements of cost that will change as a result of the decision. For example, in this illustration the only costs affected by the decision are the costs of food and beverages, salaries and wages, supplies, utilities and heat, and miscellaneous resources consumed. The analysis will be slightly simpler in this case, significantly so in others, by eliminating the unaffected items. The simplified comparison would be as follows:

	Operate the Billiard Room	Do Not Operate the Billiard Room
Food and beverages	$45,000	$40,000
Salaries and wages	16,000	12,000
Supplies	1,500	1,000
Utilities and heat	600	500
Miscellaneous	1,100	700
Total	$64,200	$54,200

(i) Sunk Cost. Any cost element that is unaffected by management's choice between alternatives is a *sunk cost.* In the first table above, two of the elements were sunk: rent \$5,000 and insurance \$800. Reopening the billiards hall would leave these costs unchanged, and they become, therefore, irrelevant to the decision.[4]

(ii) Negative Increments. The cost differences in the preceding example were additions to cost. Incremental cost can be negative; that is, a management decision may reduce costs. This reduction may be called a *cost saving,* but the analytical method is still incremental.

(g) OPPORTUNITY COST. Management's decisions often affect the use of resources that the organization already controls. The firm need make no cash outlay to obtain them. They have an incremental cost, however, measured by the net cash inflow that the firm will lose if the firm diverts these resources from their best alternative use. This differential cost is known as the *opportunity cost* of these resources. It measures the benefit that the firm would get from the opportunity foregone.

For example, a variety chain paid \$1,500,000 ten years ago for a plot of land as a site for a shopping center. Uncertainty as to state highway relocation plans forced management to postpone the project, and the land remains idle. The company now knows the route of the new highway, and is again considering using the land as a shopping center site.

The original purchase price of the land is a sunk cost, irrelevant to the decision. The shopping center proposal must be charged for the land, however, because building the shopping center would prevent the company from using it to generate cash in other ways. If the company can sell the land for a net price of \$800,000 after deducting all commissions, fees, and taxes, and if the chain has no other use for the land, then \$800,000 is its opportunity cost and the calculations in deciding on the shopping center proposal should include this amount.[5]

We would not need the opportunity cost concept if we always listed all the alternatives available to the decision maker. In the illustration, we could simply have labeled one alternative "build shopping center" and another "sell land" and compare the two. We cannot always do this, however. The owned resources to be incorporated into a particular project are often a small part of the total project, and there may be several such resources. A full set of alternatives would include one for each possible combination of resource uses, and the number could become unwieldy. The better procedure ordinarily is to compute an opportunity cost for each resource.

(h) LONG-RUN AVERAGE COST. All of the cost curves in the preceding diagrams reflected short-run conditions. A comparable set of cost curves represents long-run cost behavior. For example, each of the small U-shaped curves in Exhibit 2.7 represents the average total cost (ATC) for one possible size of the firm, operating at all possible volumes

---

4. Careful writers avoid the term *sunk cost* because it is ambiguous. Consider, for example, a machine costing \$100,000 with current *salvage* value of \$20,000. Some (including us) would say that \$100,000 (the *gross* amount) is "sunk"; others would say that only \$80,000 (the *net* amount) is "sunk." Nevertheless economists use the term often ("Ignore sunk costs") and the accountant will need to deal with it.
5. Refer to the preceding note. Some would say that only \$700,000 (= \$1,500,000 – \$800,000) is sunk. Management needs to take account of the \$800,000 in its decision making, and whether it says \$700,000 or \$1,500,000 is sunk will not affect the correct analysis.

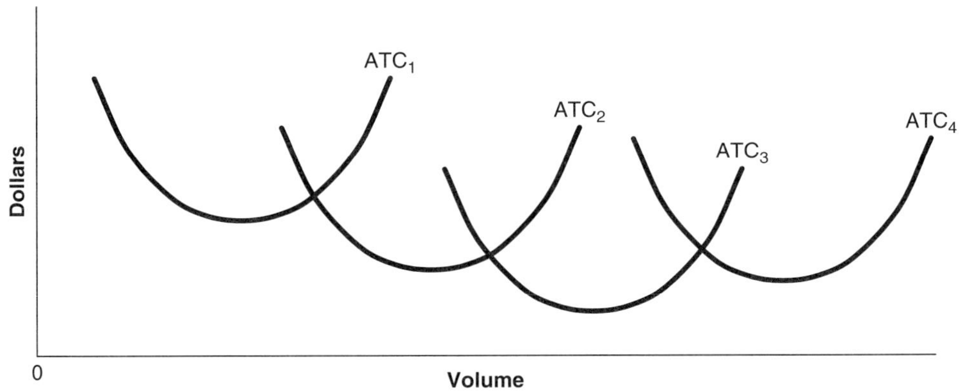

EXHIBIT 2.7 AVERAGE TOTAL COST FOR FIRMS OF DIFFERENT SIZES

for a firm of that size. In this case, the diagram pictures a situation in which average total cost decreases as capacity increases from size 1 to size 2 and from size 2 to size 3, then rises again as the firm expands to size 4. The downward-sloping section of the diagram represents a phenomenon known to economists as *increasing returns to scale,* meaning that larger plants or firms are more efficient than smaller plants or firms. When the costs of operating larger plants or firms exceed those of smaller plants or firms, as in the right-hand portion of the exhibit, the organization is subject to *diminishing returns to scale.* If the low point on the average total cost curve does not change as plant size or firm size changes, then the situation is one of *constant returns to scale.*

If enough short-run cost curves appear on a single diagram, a line tracing the lowest cost of operating at each possible level of activity might be a smooth curve like the one in Exhibit 2.8. Long-run marginal cost is the cost of increasing volume by one unit, including the costs of providing production capacity. Once again, average cost falls as long as marginal cost is lower than the average and rises after marginal cost rises above the average. When long-run marginal cost declines, the firm has an incentive to take actions that will expand its markets. In other words, an efficient large firm will have

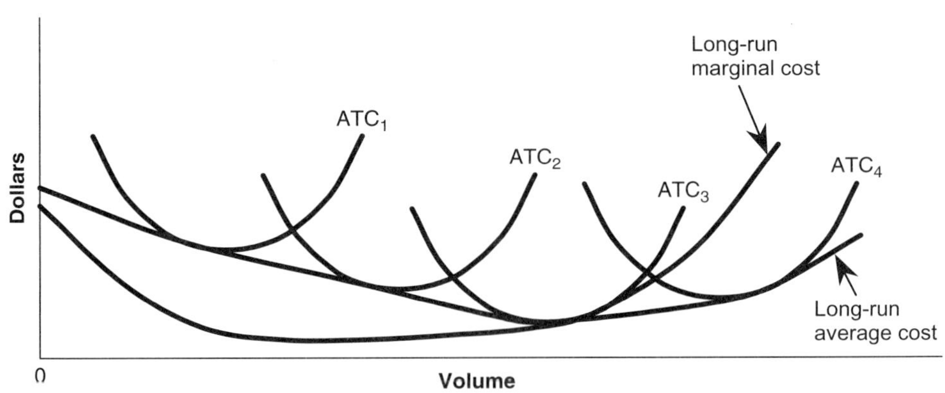

EXHIBIT 2.8 LONG-RUN AVERAGE COST

lower costs and a competitive advantage over efficient smaller firms. When this situation prevails over a large portion of the possible output range, one, or a few, large firms will likely dominate the industry.

(i) CURRENT COST. An economic concept of an entirely different order is current cost. Economists tabulating actual data usually attempt to adjust these data for changes in prices that have occurred. Analysts can do this in different ways, one of which is to measure the resources consumed in any period at their current cost—in other words, the amount that the firm would have to pay at the moment of consumption to obtain a quantity identical to the quantity consumed. Accountants often refer to *adjustments for inflation,* but careful analysis distinguishes changes in the general price level, as measured by the GDP deflator or consumers' price index, from changes in prices of specific goods or services. Strictly speaking, one should attribute only the former price changes to *inflation.*

The accountant can sometimes measure current cost directly, but sometimes must approximate it by applying index numbers to historical cost data. Current cost is more relevant than historical cost for decisions about use of an existing resource if use of the resource will require immediate replacement. For example, a company bought 50,000 pounds of material last year at $0.50 a pound. The company uses this material as a raw material for several products. If it uses 20,000 pounds to fill an order for a special product, the company will have to buy 20,000 pounds at the current price of $0.60 a pound to rebuild its inventories to the desired level. In this case, the cash outlay required by the special order would be 20,000 pounds × $0.60 = $12,000. The historical cost figure of $0.50 a pound has no relevance because it does not measure the current cash outlay that accepting the order would entail.

Current cost is not always the same as opportunity cost, however, because of transaction costs—the bid–ask spread. A firm cannot sell items for the same as their contemporaneous replacement cost. Whether to use replacement cost or opportunity cost for an item will depend on whether the firm plans to replace the items.

(j) PRESENT VALUE. The economic sacrifices (costs) made to reach specific cost objectives do not always occur immediately. When a cash outlay occurs later, the economic sacrifice is smaller than if the firm must make a payment of the same amount immediately. The reason is that the organization can invest the amount of the outlay to earn a return until it has to make the payment.

The economic concept that allows the accountant to deal with this phenomenon is *present value.* The present value of an anticipated future cash sum at a specified future date is the amount that, if invested at a specified rate of return, will grow to an amount equal to the anticipated cash sum at the specified future date. Chapter 21 discusses the mechanics of present value calculations.

2.4 SITUATIONAL CONCEPTS

Two other economic concepts the management accountant uses describe problems to be solved rather than quantities to measure. These are *common cost* and *joint cost.*

(a) COMMON COST. A common cost is a cost incurred to support two or more cost objectives, not traceable to any one of them. Accountants refer to these as indirect costs or, more clearly, as nontraceable costs. As this may suggest, a cost becomes a common cost only when considering specific cost objects. For example, if the cost object is the operation of factory department X, then the salary of the department's supervisor is not a common cost because it results from operating only that department. With respect to one of the several products the department makes, however, then the supervisor's salary becomes a common cost. The supervisor supports and oversees everything the department does; the accountant cannot trace any part of the supervisor's salary to any one product.

(b) JOINT COST. One class of common costs poses special analytical problems. These costs are the cost of joint products, otherwise known as *joint costs*. Joint products are any two or more products emerging simultaneously from a single set of inputs. Think of the beef and hides produced from a single cow. Joint costs are the costs of all the inputs that are necessary for the manufacture of all the joint products as a group. Costs incurred for the production of an individual joint product are known as *separable costs* or *specific costs*. Livestock purchasing and slaughtering costs are true joint costs of all the products that a meat packer markets, but tanning costs are specific costs of the tanned hides produced.

Firms tab joint costs for special attention because analysts can never trace them directly to individual products. This poses difficult analytical problems both for the economist and for the accountant. See Chapter 16.

2.5 APPLICATIONS IN MANAGEMENT ACCOUNTING

Merely describing the concepts in this short list does not indicate how management accountants use each one, nor to what extent. In general, the remaining chapters of this book must supply this information, but a thumbnail description here introduces concepts in the chapters that follow. We indicate how the management accountant relies on each measurement concept, both in measuring the costs of things that the organization has done and in estimating the costs of things it may or will do in the future. For convenience, we shall refer to the first of these as *cost assignment* and to the second as *cost estimation*.

(a) FIXED AND VARIABLE COSTS. Management accountants use the concepts of fixed and variable costs extensively in cost estimation. For periodic financial planning and flexible budgeting, for example, management needs estimates of the absolute levels of costs that will prevail at specified volumes during the next short-term operating period. The accountant cannot prepare these estimates in the absence of information of some sort on short-run cost behavior.

For specific decision choices, by contrast, management needs estimates of differential or incremental costs. Despite this difference, knowledge of cost variability has value here, too, to the extent that the available alternatives lead to different levels of activity. The management accountant also uses estimates of cost variability in analyzing differences between actual profit performance and the profit plan.

The distinction between fixed and variable costs affects cost assignments by manufacturing firms that develop product costs on a variable costing or direct costing basis. We lack statistical data on the incidence of the direct costing approach to product costing, but the amount of attention devoted to it in practitioners' publications indicates widespread use. Direct costing is not an acceptable procedure, however, for external financial reporting, nor for taxation, nor in most contract costing situations.

(b) INCREMENTAL COST AND OPPORTUNITY COST. Incremental cost and opportunity cost are decision concepts, reflecting comparisons between specified future courses of action. As such, they are an indispensable part of the management accountant's working vocabulary and form an integral part of the management accountant's method for cost estimation to support managerial decisions. If the manager has only two alternatives to consider, the incremental cost of one activity compared to another will be the opportunity cost. If more than two alternatives exist, then comparing any two of them generates an incremental cost, but not necessarily an opportunity cost, because opportunity cost measures assume a comparison with the next best alternative.

(c) SHORT-RUN MARGINAL COST. The uneasy and ambiguous relation between management accounting and economics becomes most apparent in the application of the concept of short-run marginal cost. One problem is that marginal cost in its purest sense refers to the cost increment accompanying an infinitesimal change in volume, whereas management's volume-determining decisions always relate to significant volume differences. If marginal cost is not constant throughout the entire range affected by the change, then management cannot use point values of marginal cost to estimate incremental cost.

An economist would solve this problem by integrating, or adding, all the marginal costs for the volume units affected by the decision. The management accountant would accept this, but would first have to make sure that steps in fixed costs were included in the marginal cost function. Economists define fixed costs as those that are fixed for all possible levels of activity, including zero. Most macroeconomic models also postulate nonfluctuating marginal cost curves, thereby leaving out steps in fixed costs entirely. The management accountant encounters more complex cost functions in practice because the conditions postulated by the economist do not exist. This leads to the recognition of steps in fixed costs within the limits of existing capacity. Estimates of incremental cost must include them when volume differentials are sufficient to move volume from one segment of the range to another with a different level of fixed costs.

The presence of programmed fixed costs (defined in Section 2.3(c)(ii)) raises a similar problem. Because these were rare in the firms familiar to the early microeconomists, they did not consider classifying programmed costs into fixed and variable categories. To the extent that they relate to volume at all, they produce volume rather than result from it. Because this excludes them from the marginal cost function, increments in these cost elements will not be part of the sum of marginal costs.

The lack of tools sensitive enough to trace a marginal cost function with precision presents another serious barrier to the direct adoption of the marginal cost concept by the management accountant. Few attempts to find close correlations by analytical means between marginal cost and volume have succeeded. The result of these measurement difficulties is that management accountants usually assume a constant marginal cost over wide portions of the operating range. Partly for this reason, the marginal cost concept does not enter into historical cost assignment systems.

(d) MARGINAL CONTRIBUTION. Marginal contribution has the same difficulties as marginal cost. Management accountants approximate it with the contribution margin. The inversion of the word order represents more than a trivial difference. *Contribution margin* is always a total or an average, whereas *marginal contribution* always refers to an incremental response to a change in volume. Nonlinearities in marginal cost and marginal revenue create disparities between marginal contribution and the average contribution margin.

Some management accountants have tried to identify something similar to marginal contribution by relating period-to-period changes in contribution margin to period-to-period changes in other factors, such as advertising expenditures. Changes in economic conditions or competitors' actions make these comparisons difficult to interpret, but management may find them useful.

Aside from calculations of this sort, the marginal contribution concept comes into play only in profit estimation, in which management accountants and others attempt to estimate the response of costs and profits to changes in various variables. Most such cases use the contribution margin to approximate marginal contribution. Linear programming decision models provide examples of this practice.

(e) LONG-RUN AVERAGE COST. Much management accounting reflects a full costing approach. Tax and financial reporting, for example, require the management accountant to state inventories at their average full cost of production up to the time of revenue recognition. Contract costing typically takes the same approach, and in the case of government contract costing in the United States, goes even further by including the average cost of nonmanufacturing administrative and supportive activities in contract cost. Cost figures given management for use in catalog pricing likely reflect a full costing approach.

Even though short-run decisions do not require long-run average cost data, which some call *full costs,* they prove useful for discussion of the long run. Full cost data, some argue, represent long-run average cost, and perhaps long-run marginal cost as well. If this is true, they show (1) the average cost of keeping the product or service in the line on a continuing basis; or (2) the costs that competing organizations will likely face if they enter the market; or (3) the long-run incremental cost of expanding capacity and increasing the volume of operations.

This chapter will not state whether decision makers should use long-run average cost for any particular decision. Instead, we describe the economic concepts the management accountant tries to implement and indicate how closely management accounting practice can approximate them. In this case, three influences may keep accounting average cost from having the long-run meanings attributed to it. First, average cost may vary with the size of the firm (as in Exhibit 2.7), meaning that expanding or contracting capacity would either increase or decrease average cost. Second, production takes place under conditions leading to common costs, and the allocations of these costs may not correspond to their long-run response to changes in capacity. Third, the average costs produced by management accounting systems reflect the organization's existing facilities, location, and personnel. These are the cumulative result of many past decisions or historical accidents. Even in the absence of any economies or diseconomies of scale, such happenstance will not likely produce average costs identical to those for new facilities of equal capacity. Only if none of these three influences seems particularly strong can management interpret the accountant's average cost as equivalent to long-run average cost.

To implement the concept of long-run average cost, the management accountant has developed a related concept. Most management accounting texts suggest that factory overhead costing rates represent the costs necessary to run the plant at "normal volume" rather than at full capacity or at estimated actual volume.

This approach argues that because total capacity costs vary with the size of the plant, management will build plants that will minimize the average cost of serving customers not in one year, but over the life of the plant. No one can expect average cost to be as low as it would be at full-capacity operation, because no plant can operate at that level all the time. If anticipated volume had been equal to full capacity, management would have built a larger plant to accommodate volume fluctuations. Similarly, the higher cost of lower-than-normal usage does not measure what management wants cost to represent, because if anticipated volume had been that low, management would have built a smaller plant and average costs would have been lower.

Not all management accounting systems implement the normal volume concept. In fact, government contractors even calculate their burden rates on the basis of the volume actually achieved, mainly because contracts specify that basis. Systems that use normal volume, however, do so because it likely gives management a better measure of long-run average cost than do other volume bases.

(f) CURRENT COST. Management accounting systems in the United States seldom use current cost. External financial statements reflect historical costs, and management designs accounting systems to provide the data for these statements. Consequently, macroeconomists attempt to adjust reported inventory and depreciation figures to allow for differences between historical cost and current cost.

Cost figures available to management often approximate current cost, however. Although some of the systems for producing such figures are highly informal, most of them are standard costing systems. Standard costs revised annually, or more often, will likely reasonably approximate current cost. If management wants greater accuracy than this, it must go to the records of current purchases.

(g) PRESENT VALUE. The concept of present value plays no role in the historical-cost assignment side of management accounting. Whether the management accountant uses it in preparing cost estimates likely depends on the issue. If management asks the accountant to evaluate a capital expenditure proposal and the company uses present value in screening such proposals, present values will enter into the calculations. But asked to estimate the annual cost of manufacturing and marketing a new product, the management accountant will likely not use the present value concept. Capital carrying charges, or interest, typically do not appear in the management accounting records, and management accounting estimates of annual operating costs are consistent with this. They will include depreciation as an undiscounted average annual cost, with no provision for interest.

2.6 SUMMARY

Management accounting uses a number of economic concepts. More of these enter into *ex ante* cost estimation than into *ex post* cost assignment, but they appear in both.

The relation between management accounting and economics is closer for some branches of economics than for others. The industrial organization economist and the macroeconomist will likely play a relatively passive role in management accounting, with little power to prescribe what the management accountant does. Managerial economists have the greatest influence on management accounting. In cost estimation, the management accountant and managerial economist build on the same concepts, and the work of one leads directly into the work of the other. The microeconomist, by contrast, deals with abstract models and therefore can adopt more stylized versions of certain concepts than the management accountant or managerial economist, who must work with real data.

By far the most pervasive economic concepts in management accounting are incremental and opportunity cost, present value, and long-run average cost. The first three of these enter into cost estimation; the latter is behind both *ex ante* and *ex post* measurements. The concepts of variable cost and fixed cost also have importance, but the management accountant will likely apply these in ways that the microeconomist would regard as unacceptable.

One problem occurs because neither the management accountant nor anyone else has tools sharp enough to measure the relations that the microeconomist knows exist. Another difficulty is that the management accountant, in adopting the terminology of microeconomics, has redefined some of the terms to reflect practical complexities.

But the main source of the difference probably lies in the differing orientation of the two disciplines. Management accounting deals with a specific organization and centers on the needs of that organization's management. Microeconomics deals with abstractions relating to the behavior of prices, output, and the sizes of the firms in markets. The management accountant must overcome measurement difficulties, even at the sacrifice of some theoretical elegance; the microeconomist can assume these measurement difficulties away. In the end, however, effective management accounting systems depend on a substantial underpinning of economic concepts.

BIBLIOGRAPHY

American Accounting Association Committee on Cost Concepts and Standards. "Tentative Statement of Cost Concepts Underlying Reports for Management Purposes." *Accounting Review,* XXXI, 2 (April 1956): 182–193.

Baumol, William J. *Economic Theory and Operations Analysis,* 3rd ed. Englewood Cliffs, N.J.: Prentice-Hall, 1972.

Chamberlin, Edward H. *The Theory of Monopolistic Competition,* 7th ed. Cambridge, Mass.: Harvard University Press, 1956.

Clark, John Maurice. *Studies in the Economics of Overhead Costs.* Chicago: University of Chicago Press, 1923.

Dean, Joel. *Managerial Economics.* Englewood Cliffs, N.J.: Prentice-Hall, 1951, especially chapter 5.

Horngren, Charles T. *Cost Accounting: A Managerial Emphasis,* 4th ed. Englewood Cliffs, N.J.: Prentice-Hall, 1977.

Johnston, J. *Statistical Cost Analysis.* New York: McGraw Hill Book Company, 1960.

Shillinglaw, Gordon. *Managerial Cost Accounting,* 4th ed. Homewood, Ill.: Richard D. Irwin, 1977.

Staubus, George J. *Activity Costing and Input-Output Accounting.* Homewood, Ill.: Richard D. Irwin, 1971, chapters 6 and 10.

CHAPTER 3

DIFFERENT COSTS FOR DIFFERENT PURPOSES*

RUSSELL A. TAUSSIG, PHD
(formerly of University of Hawaii)

UPDATED BY

ROMAN L. WEIL, CPA, CMA, PHD, EDITOR
University of Chicago

CONTENTS

3.1 NATURE OF COST 176
- (a) Cost Varies with Purpose 176
- (b) Alternative Definitions of Cost 176

3.2 COST ACCOUNT CLASSIFICATIONS 177
- (a) Classification by Object of Expenditure 177
- (b) Cost Objective versus Cost Object 177
- (c) Classification by Program 178
- (d) Classification by Responsibility Center 178
- (e) Master Coding System 178
- (f) Process and Service Industries 179

3.3 SUBDIVISION OF COST CLASSIFICATION BY OBJECT OF EXPENDITURES 179
- (a) Distinction Between Cost and Expense 180
- (b) Interest as a Manufacturing Cost 181
- (c) Extensions of the Object Classification 181

3.4 COST–VOLUME CLASSIFICATION 182
- (a) Subdivision of Fixed Costs 182
- (b) Alternative Terminology 182
- (c) Nature of Fixed Costs 183
- (d) Measuring the Cost-Volume Relation 183

3.5 RESPONSIBILITY ACCOUNTING AND CONTROLLABLE COSTS 183
- (a) Responsibility Accounting 184
- (b) Controllable and Uncontrollable Costs 184
- (c) Controllable, Variable, and Direct Costs 184

3.6 COSTS FOR DECISION MAKING 185
- (a) Incremental versus Sunk Cost 185
- (b) Opportunity versus Monetary Cost 186

3.7 SUMMARY 186

BIBLIOGRAPHY 186

* Russell A. Taussig, then of the University of Hawaii, wrote the original version of this chapter for the first edition of *The Handbook of Cost Accounting*. I have preserved most of his ideas and words. RLW.

3.1 NATURE OF COST

This chapter discusses the different meanings of cost and the various classifications of costs that have proven useful to management. The financial executive, whether accountant or manager, should understand that different questions about costs require different concepts for answers.

(a) COST VARIES WITH PURPOSE. Since at least 1923, writers have recognized that different purposes require different cost concepts. J. M. Clark wrote:[1]

> The general idea of cost covers a number of different meanings. . . . A great deal of controversy [exists] as to whether certain items are properly costs at all. Most of this controversy will disappear if we carry our study far enough to recognize that there are different kinds of problems for which we need information about costs, and the particular information we need differs from one problem to another.

Simon, Guetzkow, Kozmetsky, and Tyndall, in their classic research[2] on the control function, found that business uses cost data for various purposes: (1) as a *score-card* for the appraisal of an operating unit; (2) to *direct attention* to problems; and (3) to aid in the *solution of problems.*

They found that different purposes require different costs; moreover, they argued that different management levels require the same cost data in different forms. Information systems store and analyze data on multiple dimensions, but increased dimensionality has higher data accumulation, processing, and storage costs. Accordingly, the manager of the information system can make decisions about cost classifications only by balancing benefits against the price paid for them.

(b) ALTERNATIVE DEFINITIONS OF COST. Cost has many meanings, differing among accounting, economics, and engineering. We have prepared a chart showing more than 50 terms involving the word cost, each with meanings different from other terms with the word cost. See the Cost Terminology Chart, alphabetized under "Cost" in Chapter 1's glossary.

A charge to a cost account under traditional accounting theory debits an asset, whereas the expiration of a cost is an expense. For example, a purchase of raw materials is a cost, a number on the balance sheet, but the payment of current advertising is an expense. Think of *cost* with no further modification as an asset, or the amount of the sacrifice required to acquire the asset. Contrast with *expense,* an expired asset—one that has given up its future benefits.

Davidson, Schindler, and Weil express this dichotomy:[3]

> An expense is an expired asset. A firm acquires assets to obtain the services of future benefits that the assets provide. All acquisitions are acquisitions of assets, that is, of future benefits. As the services are used up, as the future benefits disappear, assets become expenses. Expenses may thus be described as "gone assets," that is, as benefits or resources used up in the process of securing revenue. To decide when an asset (or its synonym, a cost) loses its power to provide future benefits and, hence, has become an expense is one of the most difficult problems in accounting.

---

1. J. Maurice Clark, *Studies in the Economics of Overhead Costs* (Chicago: University of Chicago Press, 1923), p. 35.
2. Herbert A. Simon, Harold Guetzkow, George Kozmetsky, and Gordon Tyndall, *Centralization vs. Decentralization in Organizing the Controller's Department* (New York: Controllership Foundation, 1954), p. 3.
3. Sidney Davidson, James S. Schindler, and Roman L. Weil, *Fundamentals of Accounting,* 5th ed. (Hinsdale, Ill.: Dryden Press, 1975).

Thus, a traditional accounting definition of *cost* means the amount expended to acquire an asset. A more general concept equates cost with any sacrifice, past or future. It is the price paid for the selection of one alternative over another. Or, as Shillinglaw states this broader economic/accounting definition:[4] "A cost represents the resources that have been or must be sacrificed to attain a particular objective."

The concept of cost is multifaceted. A useful approach for understanding the various aspects of costs consists of examining alternative cost classification schemes, starting with the usual general ledger classification of costs for a typical manufacturing concern.

3.2 COST ACCOUNT CLASSIFICATIONS

David Solomons[5] points out that the Industrial Revolution created a need for more advanced methods of cost determination and control, particularly for manufacturing concerns. Generally, a data accumulation system can classify costs incurred by manufacturers into one of three taxonomies:

1. By *object* of expenditure (machinists' labor, setup labor, maintenance, etc.)
2. By *program* (such as cost of job No. 1, No. 2, etc.)
3. By *responsibility center* (machining, packing, distribution, etc.)

When accountants first established these taxonomies, direct labor and materials were 80 percent of total costs, with the remainder being overhead. The current manufacturing and service firm likely has less than 50 percent direct labor and materials costs. Still, these taxonomies prove useful in providing answers to a variety of questions.

(a) CLASSIFICATION BY OBJECT OF EXPENDITURE. The most primitive taxonomy classifies costs by object of expenditure—that is, descriptive charges such as direct labor, raw materials, manufacturing overhead, and subdivisions of these categories. External reporting generally uses this classification by natural elements (in contrast to functional elements, such as cost of goods sold, depreciation, general expenses). This classification is simple to implement and often is the only taxonomy available for uniform classification of expired costs in larger multiproduct organizations.

Classification by object of expenditure provides data in a convenient form for establishing trends, which helps with planning. The cost elements in a given set should respond to volume changes in the same way. If payroll tax varies with output while property tax varies with the value of equipment, then combining them in a single tax objective will confuse their relation to the amount of goods produced. Accordingly, a single account for taxes would not be appropriate.

(b) COST OBJECTIVE VERSUS COST OBJECT. In some applications, cost accountants define a *cost object* as any alternative, activity, or part of an organization for which management wants a separate cost measurement or aggregation. Thus, the "classification of cost by costing objective" differs from the "classification of cost objects of expenditure." Managers classify costs by different objects, depending on the problem they want to solve. They need the cost of an activity, such as filling an order, for pricing. They need

4. Gordon Shillinglaw, *Cost Accounting: Analysis and Control*, 3rd ed. (Homewood, Ill.: Richard D. Irwin, 1972), p. 11.
5. David Solomons, "The Historical Development of Costing," in *Studies in Cost Analysis*, 2nd ed., David Solomons, ed. (Homewood, Ill.: Richard D. Irwin, 1968).

the cost of holding inventories for ascertaining the economic lot size of those inventories. Classification of costs by object disaggregates costs into small building blocks that a manager can later reassemble in various ways. It is an approach for constructing a data base according to the specific needs of management. Aggregating and storing costs by *cost object* differs from the simple classification of costs by *object of expenditure.* See Chapter 6, which discusses activity based costing, for examples of the classification of costs by cost object.

(c) CLASSIFICATION BY PROGRAM. Cost classification by program, or project, plays a role in planning. A builder of custom homes, for example, accumulates costs for each job, aggregating costs by stages of construction from initial excavation to final painting. These figures assist the builder in planning future construction activities. They help signal cost overruns and builders use them for short-run pricing.

Job costs also show what work is in process at any time; thus, they enable the accountant to prepare financial reports without physical inventories. They simplify reporting income and financial position.

(d) CLASSIFICATION BY RESPONSIBILITY CENTER. Classification by responsibility center aids in internal control.

Managers control direct labor and raw material at the departmental level as work proceeds through a factory, but control indirect charges at a higher level. Managers implement control through departmental cost reports. These are attention-getting devices that signal the need for immediate corrective action, and they provide the facts for long-term decisions such as changes in methods and equipment.

(e) MASTER CODING SYSTEM. A master coding system facilitates the cross-classification of costs by object, project, and department. Modern account codes for use with data processing facilities generally are numbering plans with sections of digits reserved for object, project, and department.

The diagram in Exhibit 3.1 provides an example of a master coding system for Construction Corporation, which uses a 15-digit identification code for its costs comprising four elements: general ledger, cost center, project, and detail expense. The system assigns the 15 digits as follows:

The general ledger code, by expenditure objective, comes from the corporate level. All reports submitted for consolidation by the centralized information system use codes from

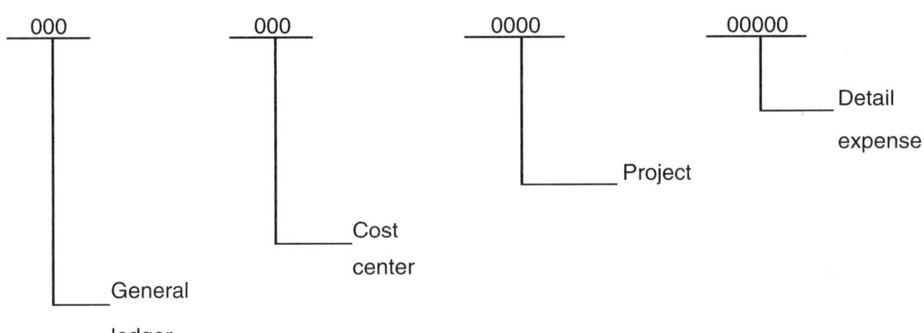

EXHIBIT 3.1 MASTER CODING SYSTEM

the standard chart of general ledger accounts. At an intermediate management level, the coding shows programs and services. At the operating level, the project code and the detail expense codes result from needs of lower levels of management. Detailed data processing is available for construction reporting, including estimating, progress reporting, payroll, equipment programs, and accounting. The last five digits provide further detail of expense accounts included in the general ledger code according to the dictates of the particular division. For example, one such list analyzes costs by specific kinds of materials, labor, and other costs, such as resins, hose assemblies, and so on. A list, prepared by another division, shows costs classified by excavation, labor, framing lumber, and so on, to meet the perceived needs of the managers in that division.

(f) PROCESS AND SERVICE INDUSTRIES. The foregoing classification illustrated the chart of accounts for a job-order firm, one manufacturing a heterogeneous mix of products, such as a construction company or a print shop. A similar threefold classification by object of expenditure, by project, and by responsibility center also applies to process firms such as oil refiners or fruit canners.

Process firms, characterized by long runs and repetitive production, can use to good effect the departmental performance indicators. The reports identify costs with aggregate output for a specific period, such as a week or month. Management focuses on average costs for control and pricing. The cost system might charge manufacturing supplies to overhead in a job shop, but directly to the product in a process plant.

The same costing techniques apply in a wide variety of nonmanufacturing situations, such as department stores, banks, and hotels where accountants classify costs by expenditure objective, project, and responsibility.

3.3 SUBDIVISION OF COST CLASSIFICATION BY OBJECT OF EXPENDITURES

Manufacturing classified by object of expenditure fall into the three categories: (1) direct materials, (2) direct labor, and (3) manufacturing overhead.

Direct materials are those materials, parts, and subassemblies whose cost conveniently can be identified with a particular job or process. Minor items are treated as indirect materials—manufacturing overhead. The distinction between direct and indirect materials is pragmatic, based on whether the savings can justify the expense of controlling the expenditure by job. Classify materials as direct because of their importance rather than physical inclusion in the end product. For instance, a catalyst used to effect the chemical reaction between caustic soda and animal fat in the making of soap is a direct cost, although the catalyst does not remain in the final bar of soap. By contrast, the system might reasonably charge the cost of nails used in building one of several houses to overhead rather than to the job. Classify materials as direct when their cost warrants identification with a job, or process, for managerial control and planning.

The cost of materials includes all charges necessary to acquire and prepare them for use, such as freight, taxes, and other acquisition charges. Theory suggests that firms should include carrying costs, such as storage and insurance, when the firm ages its inventories or normally keeps them on hand for a time before putting them into production. When such incidental charges are small, most systems classify them as overhead. *Cost* means spot cash price. Interest charged is a financial expense, not part of the cost of materials. Cash discounts represent a reduction in the invoice price, whether the firm takes them or not. Discounts lost represent a nonmanufacturing expense.[6]

Charge the job's cost with cost of scrap and defective materials unless they result from an abnormal cause, such as a power outage, in which case these costs are a loss of the period. Credit proceeds from scrap against the job, although when identifying recovery by job is difficult, deduct these proceeds from overhead.

Direct labor identifies costs of workers whose time readily associates with specific jobs: The pay of a cutter in a garment factory constitutes direct labor; the salary of a sweeper is indirect labor. Direct labor costs include supplementary payments such as payroll taxes, pension payments, and other fringe benefits of the workers whose wages are direct labor.

The outlay for overtime premium pay is overhead unless it results from a specific job. When a job worked on during overtime hours did not uniquely cause extra work, the overtime premium is attributable to all jobs, because aggregate demand caused the extra cost. Charging the overtime premium to manufacturing overhead isolates the cost for managerial attention.

Time spent on correcting defective production should be singled out as rework, often a critical cost. Charge the cost of rework to the job if product related, and to manufacturing overhead if process related.

Separate setup cost from other labor charges. The cost of a setup remains the same regardless of the size of a production run, and including it as direct labor would destroy the proportionality between direct labor and the number of units produced, a useful relation for cost analysis. Charge setup labor to jobs with a coding that permits segregation for cost analysis. The modern manufacturing firm will usually find that setup activities constitute a useful cost object.

Manufacturing overhead comprises all manufacturing costs other than direct materials and direct labor. Manufacturing overhead costs include items such as depreciation of factory buildings, property taxes, and machinery repairs that are not readily identifiable with any one contract or product. They are costs incurred jointly for all jobs during the fiscal period. Manufacturing overhead is also known as *burden*, *on-cost,* and, imprecisely, *manufacturing expense.* As indirect costs—such as those for setup or quality control become more pervasive, the term *indirect costs* becomes more prevalent than *manufacturing overhead* for all indirect costs.

(a) DISTINCTION BETWEEN COST AND EXPENSE. Manufacturing costs differ from selling and administrative expenses for financial reporting. Manufacturing overhead is a product cost (an asset, until the firm sells the manufactured item). Selling and administrative overheads are expenses (current period deductions from revenues).

Manufacturing costs are product costs, or assets, because the goods produced require the benefits the costs provide. Thus, the charge for depreciation of factory machinery constitutes an increase in an asset (work-in-process inventories). Contrast this with selling and administrative overhead expenses, deductible from revenues when incurred.

Depreciation of a factory building is a product cost; however, depreciation of a corporate office building generally is treated as an expense; although, arguably, production

6. Not taking discounts such as 2/10, net 30 (take off 2 percent if paid within 10 days; otherwise pay in 30 days) is an expensive way to borrow. Chapter 23 of this Handbook, which discusses compound interest, shows that not taking such a discount is equivalent to borrowing at an annual equivalent rate of about 45 percent.

would not be possible without corporate resources. This dichotomy between manufacturing cost and nonmanufacturing expense, though simple in concept, entails problems in application. For instance, the salary of a divisional controller who is responsible for the plant is part of manufacturing overhead and, hence, product cost. The cost of the same type of financial executive who works at corporate headquarters is also a product cost. Estimating and design costs incurred in bidding a job clearly are manufacturing costs. The accounting system holds these cost in suspense until the firm learns whether it won the job. If it loses, the costs become expense. Theory suggests treating promotional expenditures incident to the securing of a specific contract the same way.

Some of the language of accounting confuses *cost* and *expense*, and imprecise usage is widespread. "Cost of goods sold," for example, is an operating expense title in the income statement. The cost designates the expired cost of products sold. Also, in practice, the word *cost* sometimes attaches loosely to an expense item. Managers refer to the "cost of advertising," an expense of the current period. The common language reflects the logic that advertising costs are conceptually assets, providing future benefits. Generally accepted accounting principles (GAAP) treat such cost incurrences as expenses, with no future benefit.

(b) INTEREST AS A MANUFACTURING COST. Should manufacturing costs include interest? Not all agree.

Those who argue in favor of inclusion point out that capital is as important as labor for production so production costs should include both the cost of capital and the cost of labor. They also maintain that aging may be an essential part of manufacturing, as in the production of fine wines. When included, it logically should be a weighted average of the cost of debt and equity funds, not just the cost of borrowed funds, so the measurement of capital costs presents issues that make recognition unattractive to some. Reports for internal reporting and decision making, however, should include capital cost estimates.

Those who oppose inclusion note that GAAP have customarily distinguished financial expenses from manufacturing costs. They further point out the difficulty of measuring imputed interest with precision.

Firms generally do not capitalize interest except when aging is significant. Regardless of the disposition of interest for financial reporting, it should be included as a cost for economic analyses such as inventory planning and make-or-buy decisions.

(c) EXTENSIONS OF THE OBJECT CLASSIFICATION. The classification of costs into the threefold categories of materials, labor, and overhead can expand to suit circumstances. For example, a category *buyouts* or *outsourcing* accumulates data on purchases of services from subcontractors. Cost Accounting Standards Board standards for government contractors sometimes require separate classifications, such as one for test equipment without salvage value.[7]

Materials, labor, and overhead combine in various ways. The sum of direct labor and manufacturing overhead, called *conversion cost,* aids process costing because conversion cost generally varies with the number of units finished during a period, whereas material cost varies with the number of units started. The sum of materials and labor is called

7. Cost Accounting Standards Board, "Standards, Rules and Regulations as of June 30, 1975" (Washington, D.C.: U.S. Government Printing Office, 1975).

prime cost. Prime cost is charged directly to jobs, whereas manufacturing cost systems allocate overhead indirectly on the basis of some index of activity. Prime cost plus an appropriate markup covering other expenses and profits provide data frequently used for short-term pricing decisions.

Although the classification of costs by object of expenditure is simple and applies in a wide variety of industries, other classifications often prove more useful for cost control and managerial planning. Modern costing systems generally classify costs at the outset according to the way in which they vary with changes in output.

3.4 COST–VOLUME CLASSIFICATION

Costs are classified according to how they change with output for a variety of planning decisions, including the setting of prices and negotiation of budgets.

Fixed costs remain the same in total dollar amount for various levels of output. Typical fixed costs are property taxes, superintendence, and depreciation. *Variable costs* increase in total dollar amount as output increases. Examples include the costs of materials and power. The distinction between fixed and variable depends on the time window. Given long enough time periods, all costs become variable. Most cost analysis requires a time horizon long enough for firms to carry out current plans with respect to long-term assets.

Chapter 2 of this Handbook (Economic Concepts of Costs in Managerial Accounting) explores the relation between economic notions and accounting notions of the fixed-variable dichotomy.

(a) SUBDIVISION OF FIXED COSTS. Subdivide fixed costs further for planning and decision making. *Committed costs* are fixed costs that result from decisions of prior periods. They are the costs of basic operating capacity that continue at zero output. Examples include depreciation, insurance, property taxes, and the salaries of general managers. *Discretionary costs* are fixed costs that result from decisions in the current period. Examples include promotional expenditures, legal expenses, and research and development. The firm can eliminate discretionary costs during temporary plant closings, caused, say, by a strike, but not committed costs. Discretionary costs sometimes vary with volume, simply because management budgets them that way. They do not perforce increase with output.

The committed/discretionary dichotomy aids managerial control because management sets discretionary costs annually, but sets committed costs when it approves a project. The distinction is also pertinent for output reduction decisions. Management can use the data to decide, in the face of reduced demand, whether to retain skilled workers or to dismiss them and retrain new ones when demand resumes.

(b) ALTERNATIVE TERMINOLOGY. Programmed costs are those planned costs that the firm will incur for some particular period as a result of a management policy decision, so they are a type of discretionary costs. Standby costs are synonymous with committed costs; an example of these costs is the compensation for key supervisory personnel whom management would retain when it shuts down a plant.

The costs of providing capacity also are known as *capacity costs,* that is, costs that do not increase with volume. These are fixed costs planned at a specific amount for a period, sometimes called *period costs.*

(c) NATURE OF FIXED COSTS. What makes a cost fixed? This depends on organization policy and the time span being considered. Most costs are not inherently fixed or variable in nature. If management cuts the work force because of a drop in demand, labor cost is variable; otherwise it is fixed.

However, the argument that costs acquire the characteristics of being fixed or variable through operating decisions by management differs from the contention that costs become fixed or variable depending on management's choice of accounting method. The managerial significance of a cost does not change with the reporting of it. Some accountants would say, mistakenly in our view, that depreciation calculated by the straight-line method is fixed, but when calculated by the unit-of-production method is variable. Management does control how reported depreciation varies with volume, but the economic cost results from expiration of an asset's utility. As Keynes has noted,[8] one component of economic depreciation relates to physical wear and tear, and is a variable cost. A second component results from obsolescence and inadequacy, and is a fixed cost, unrelated to the use of the asset. Economic depreciation, the periodic change in some measure of value of the asset, differs from accounting depreciation, an allocation of original cost.

(d) MEASURING THE COST-VOLUME RELATION. Accountants use at least four methods, summarized by the following, for measuring the functional relation between costs and output.

1. Under the *engineering introspection approach*, the cost analyst decides how costs should increase with workload by examining time and motion studies or generalized productivity data, or both. An engineering estimate of fixed and variable costs emerges.
2. Using the *high-low approximation*, the analyst plots a representative number of weekly or monthly costs against output, then sketches a line through the high and low points.
3. The *visual scatter plot* resembles the high-low approximation, except the analyst fits the line by sight to an average of the points.
4. *Regression analysis* is a mathematical method for fitting a line to the data so as to minimize the squared differences of the points from the line of best fit. The function may be linear or nonlinear and can have several independent variables. (See Chapter 12 which discusses cost estimation.)

3.5 RESPONSIBILITY ACCOUNTING AND CONTROLLABLE COSTS

Reports for division managers have best use when they set out the costs that these managers can control. Departmental statements in the past often included both controllable and uncontrollable expenses without separation. A busy manager then had to sort out controllable variances from a confused list, which included some outside the manager's sphere of influence. For example, managers who had no voice in the acquisition of machines have often viewed the related depreciation charges in their budgets as unfair.

8. John Maynard Keynes, *The General Theory of Employment Interest and Money* (New York: Harcourt, Brace and Company, 1935), pp. 53–55.

(a) RESPONSIBILITY ACCOUNTING. Responsibility accounting focuses a manager's attention on costs that the manager can control. Practice differs among accountants in the reporting of uncontrollable costs. Some omit them entirely from reports to lower-echelon executives, which reduces confusion about uncontrollable variances. Others include them in a separate section to show an executive that the enterprise incurs costs beyond those directly controllable.

(b) CONTROLLABLE AND UNCONTROLLABLE COSTS. The success of responsibility accounting depends on the ability of a company to identify correctly which costs each level of management can control. Fundamentally, a manager controls a cost when the manager exerts spending authority over it. That is, *controllable costs* are those that the manager can curtail. The manager of a machining department controls indirect labor and manufacturing supplies used in that department. Such a manager does not control his or her own salary or the salary of higher-level managers. These salaries, allocated as a charge against departments under traditional methods, are separate from them under responsibility accounting.

Locus of control is relatively clear for some costs. Control of some costs resides with several managers. The control of maintenance costs depends both on the ability of a production manager to prevent abuse of equipment and on the proficiency of a maintenance manager to supervise repairs.

Service organizations also have jointly controllable costs. Branch managers of a bank might have little to say about the hiring of their employees; nonetheless, they control scheduling and assignment of work. Accordingly, a responsibility cost system might reasonably include the expense for branch salaries as controllable on branch statements. Cost classification is a practical art.

Cost controllability has a time dimension. Costs resulting from decisions of prior periods are not controllable in the short run by anyone. The control over a fixed-asset acquisition, for example, occurs when management approves its purchase. The subsequent depreciation expense is not controllable.

All costs are controllable by someone, at least to some extent, at some time. Occasionally, several executives jointly manage costs and the responsibility system reports to each of them. As a general management rule, not an accounting rule, one person should have responsibility for each expenditure. The existence of jointly managed costs may signal to management the need for a restructuring of its organization. The installation of responsibility accounting system frequently forces management to define its lines of authority more sharply.

(c) CONTROLLABLE, VARIABLE, AND DIRECT COSTS. Not all controllable costs are variable. Some fixed costs, such as the cost of lighting during a production shift, are also controllable. A watchful manager may generate cost savings even though costs do not directly relate to output.

Conversely, variable costs are not necessarily controllable costs. A cost is controllable by one who monitors it. A cost is variable when it is a function of output. The two are not the same. For example, a brewery found that the cost of cans varied with beer packaged; but with little wastage of cans, the cost of containers was not controllable by the manager of the container department. The cost of the cans varied mostly with the price of aluminum rather than with production.

Also, direct costs may not be controllable. Responsibility statements include controllable costs and exclude (or show separately) direct costs that are not controllable. "Direct costs" are generally costs incurred in a department, as opposed to indirect costs, or overhead, which accounting systems allocate to departments. (The term *direct costs* is also a synonym for *prime costs,* with context suggesting the meaning.) The direct costs of a machining department include the salary of the manager and depreciation of machinery, as opposed to joint departmental costs, such as building occupancy and corporate overheads. Depreciation of machinery is a direct cost but not controllable. Likewise, the manager's salary is direct but not controllable, because a higher authority approves it. Direct costs need not be controllable at the departmental level. Conventional accounting reports mingle controllable and uncontrollable direct costs, but responsibility accounting separates them.

3.6 COSTS FOR DECISION MAKING

Costs for decision making differ from those for managerial control. Costs for decisions are expected sacrifices that will result from specific actions. Costs for control are past expenditures from general operations.

The essence of decision making is the sorting out of options and the attaching of payoffs to them. The decision maker takes action based on an evaluation of the payoffs. The information specialist measures the expected costs and benefits that determine the payoffs.

(a) INCREMENTAL VERSUS SUNK COST. Costs relevant for decision making are those that change as a consequence of selecting one option as opposed to another. When a manufacturer with unused capacity in the short run decides whether to make or buy a component, the pertinent costs relate to the additional materials, labor, and direct supervision required to fabricate the component. The costs for rent, taxes, and insurance, which continue whether the company manufactures the component or not, have no relevance. The difference in total cost from selecting one option over another is called *incremental cost,* or *differential cost.*

Marginal cost is the increase in total cost for one additional unit of output, a special kind of incremental cost. It is the rate of incremental cost per unit of output at any given level of activity. Marginal cost is used for expansion and pricing decisions. Generally, a firm expands until marginal cost equals marginal revenue. That is, a firm expands so long as the increase in cost is less than the increase in revenue.

A *sunk cost* is one that a particular decision will not affect. It will never be an incremental cost. Amounts that have already been spent on research and development are sunk costs for a firm deciding whether to go ahead with a product's manufacture and marketing. The expenditures of prior years are sunk costs. They do not change with the decision to produce, and thus have no relevance for that decision. When the firm decides whether to undertake a project requiring R & D, but has not yet done it, the cost of contemplated R & D is an incremental cost with respect to the go/no go decision of whether to undertake a project.

Fixed costs need not be sunk costs. The firm can change future salaries of supervisors, though fixed over a broad range of output at current levels. Hence, these fixed costs are not sunk costs for capital budgeting. Also, sunk costs need not be fixed costs. For example, when a company decides whether to lease or buy a plant, the variable cost of power will not likely be affected; hence it lacks relevance and may be termed a sunk cost for this decision.

In the context of an abandonment decision, an *avoidable cost* is one that the firm will not incur when it discontinues part of the activities of an organization. Firms cannot avoid sunk costs. Avoidable costs from elimination of activities may be less than the incremental costs from their addition because of union agreements and other contractual obligations that preclude the reduction of some costs, at least in the short run.

(b) OPPORTUNITY VERSUS MONETARY COST. *Opportunity cost* is the net benefit that the firm would have received from an asset had it put the asset to its next best use. The concept of opportunity cost is implicit in any comparison of alternatives. The merit of any course of action is its relative merit, the difference between one action and another. Chapter 2 (Economic Concepts of Costs in Managerial Accounting) explores opportunity cost in more depth.

Opportunity cost becomes pertinent when the firm already owns some of the resources required for a proposed project. For example, when management decides to replace machinery with a book value of $60,000 and a resale value of $100,000, it should treat the resale value as the cost of using the machine. Although the firm receives no cash from selling the machinery, the cash foregone from resale (net of tax effects) is a cost—an opportunity cost.

3.7 SUMMARY

This chapter has summarized several different meanings of cost and the various cost classifications that have proven useful to management. Cost analysts have developed a number of different cost constructs to guide them in the classification of costs for a variety of managerial applications. Different purposes require different cost constructs.

BIBLIOGRAPHY

Clark, J. Maurice. *Studies in the Economics of Overhead Costs.* Chicago: University of Chicago Press, 1923.

Cost Accounting Standards Board. "Standards, Rules and Regulations as of June 30, 1975." Washington, D.C.: U.S. Government Printing Office, 1975.

Davidson, Sidney, James S. Schindler, and Roman L. Weil. *Fundamentals of Accounting,* 5th ed. Hinsdale, Ill.: Dryden Press, 1975.

Dean, Joel. *Statistical Determination of Costs, with Special Reference to Marginal Costs.* Chicago: University of Chicago Press, 1936.

Shillinglaw, Gordon. *Cost Accounting: Analysis and Control,* 3rd ed. Homewood, Ill.: Richard D. Irwin, 1972.

Simon, Herbert A., Harold Guetzkow, George Kozmetsky, and Gordon Tyndall. *Centralization vs. Decentralization in Organizing the Controller's Department.* New York: Controllership Foundation (now Financial Executives Institute), 1954.

CHAPTER 4

ACCOUNTING MAGIC

ROMAN L. WEIL, PHD, CPA, CMA, EDITOR
University of Chicago

CONTENTS

4.1 INTRODUCTION 187

4.2 THE SCENARIO 187

4.3 ACCOUNTING ALTERNATIVES 188
- (a) Inventory Cost Flow Assumption 188
- (b) Depreciation 188
- (c) Officers' Bonuses 189

4.4 PUBLISHED INCOME STATEMENTS AND INCOME TAX CALCULATION 189

4.5 COMPARISON OF CASH FLOWS 191

4.6 MANAGING REPORTED EARNINGS 191
- (a) Selection of Accounting Principles 191
- (b) Application of Accounting Principles 191
- (c) Timing of Asset Acquisitions and Dispositions 192

4.7 ARGUMENTS ABOUT MANAGING EARNINGS 192
- (a) Strategic Choices 192
- (b) Capital Market Efficiency 193
- (c) Management Incentives and Survival 194

4.1 INTRODUCTION

Generally accepted accounting principles (GAAP) permit alternative treatments for certain accounting events. The treatment a company chooses affects the financial statements that the company issues. This chapter shows how alternative accounting treatments of identical events can lead to reported income figures that are surprisingly different from each other.

4.2 THE SCENARIO[1]

On January 1, two companies start in business. The two companies engage in identical activities but account for them differently. Conservative Company chooses the accounting alternatives that will minimize its reported income while High Flyer Company chooses the alternatives that will maximize its reported income. Both companies choose, where permitted, accounting methods that will minimize income taxes. The following events occur during the year.

---

1. The idea for the chapter's title and scenario comes from an article by Leonard Spacek, "Business Success Requires an Understanding of Unsolved Problems of Accounting and Financial Reporting," Arthur Andersen Pamphlet (September 25, 1959), pp. 19–28. Since the time Spacek prepared his illustration, generally accepted accounting principles have changed, but several of the alternatives we illustrate he illustrated, too.

- Both companies issue common stock to raise funds necessary to commence a merchandising business.
- Both companies purchase $6,000,000 of equipment that they assume will have zero salvage value and useful life of 8 years.
- Both companies make the following purchases of merchandise inventory:

Date	Units Purchased	Unit Price		Cost of Purchase
January 1	85,000	@ $60	=	$ 5,100,000
May 1	95,000	@ $63	=	5,985,000
September 1	100,000	@ $68	=	6,800,000
Total	280,000			$17,885,000

- During the year, both companies sell 210,000 units at an average price of $100 each so that each realizes sales revenues of $21,000,000.
- During the year, both companies have selling, general, and administrative expenses, excluding officers' salaries, of $3,350,000.
- At the end of the year, both companies award officers options to purchase shares of common stock, as bonuses for jobs well done. These supplement the $350,000 paid to them during the year in salaries. Comparable options have market value of $150,000.

4.3 ACCOUNTING ALTERNATIVES

At the end of the year, both companies prepare financial statements. Both must decide how to report the various events that occurred during the year. The companies made the following decisions, all generally acceptable.

(a) INVENTORY COST FLOW ASSUMPTION. During the year, both companies purchased more goods than they sold. Each company must make an assumption about the cost of goods sold it will show on the income statement and, simultaneously, about the cost of ending inventory it will show on the balance sheet. Conservative Company makes a last-in, first-out (LIFO) cost flow assumption, while High Flyer Company makes a first-in, first-out (FIFO) assumption.

Because the beginning inventory is zero, the cost of goods available for sale by each company equals the purchases of $17,885,000 during the year. Both companies have 70,000 units in ending inventory. Conservative Company, using LIFO, reports a cost of goods sold of $13,685,000 (= $17,885,000 – 70,000 × $60) while High Flyer Company reports a cost of goods sold of $13,125,000 (= $17,885,000 – 70,000 × $68).

Income tax regulations require a company to use LIFO in its financial statements if it uses LIFO for its tax return. High Flyer wants to report high income, so does not use LIFO in its financial statements and, therefore, forgoes the savings in taxes from using LIFO on its tax returns.

(b) DEPRECIATION. Conservative Company depreciates its equipment using the double-declining-balance method on its financial statements while High Flyer Company uses the straight-line method. Conservative Company takes a full year of depreciation in the year it acquires equipment, while High Flyer Company uses a half-year convention under which it takes only one-half year of depreciation in the first year. (The modified accelerated cost recovery system, MACRS, used by both companies for income tax reporting, effectively requires that both take one-half year of depreciation on their tax returns.) Conservative Company therefore reports depreciation expense of \$1,500,000 (= 2 × 1/8 × \$6,000,000), while High Flyer Company reports depreciation expense of \$375,000 (= 1/8 × \$6,000,000 × 1/2).

(c) OFFICERS' BONUSES. Conservative Company reports expense of \$150,000 for the stock options awarded to officers, while High Flyer Company reports no expense for its officers' stock options. Generally accepted accounting principles recommend, but do not require, that the firm show the fair market value of qualified stock options granted to employees as an expense.[2] If the officers later exercise the options, both companies will record the cash received (i.e., the options' exercise price times the number of shares issued) as paid-in capital, but High Flyer will never record compensation expense for the options. The IRS allows no deduction on the firm's tax return when the employee earns the options, but allows a compensation expense tax deduction when the employees exercise the options. The deductible amount is the difference between the exercise price of the options and the market value of the shares issued.

4.4 PUBLISHED INCOME STATEMENTS AND INCOME TAX CALCULATION

We assume a combined federal and state income tax rate of 40 percent. Both companies show deductions for MACRS depreciation of equipment on the income tax return different from the depreciation expense reported to shareholders. Conservative Company also shows an expense for stock option compensation that does not appear on its tax return. Both are *temporary differences*. In other words, in subsequent years, the companies may report on their tax returns amounts different in opposite directions from the amounts they report to shareholders. Consequently, each company reports deferred income taxes on its income statement and deferred tax assets or liabilities on its balance sheet.

High Flyer Company reports smaller depreciation on the income statement than the amount of depreciation claimed on the tax return and will have deferred tax credits on its balance sheet. (Most published annual reports reflect this situation for depreciation.) Conservative Company reports larger depreciation and larger compensation expense on the income statement than the amounts it claims on the tax return and will have deferred tax assets on its balance sheet. (This phenomenon arises for Conservative's depreciation because the company depreciates only one item of equipment and because the first-year conventions for tax reporting and financial reporting differ.) The following equation holds for both companies (dollar amounts are in thousands):

$$\text{Income Tax Expense} = \text{Income Tax Payable} + \text{Deferred Tax Credits} - \text{Deferred Tax Debits}$$

Conservative Company:

$$\$786 = \$966 + \$0 - \$180$$

2. *SFAS No. 123: Accounting for Stock-Based Compensation* has been the most-debated issue ever on the FASB's agenda.

High Flyer Company:

$$\$1{,}520 = \$1{,}190 + \$330 - \$0$$

Deferred tax credits either increase a deferred tax liability or decrease a deferred tax asset, and the reverse is true of deferred tax debits. In this case, Conservative Company shows a deferred tax asset of $180,000, and High Flyer Company shows a deferred tax liability of $330,000.

The income statements for both companies appear in Exhibit 4.1. As a result of its conservative treatment of accounting alternatives, Conservative Company reports net

For the Year Ending December 31
(Amounts in Thousands Except Per Share Amounts)

	Conservative Company		High Flyer Company	
	Financial Statement	Tax Return	Financial Statement	Tax Return
Sales Revenues	$21,000	$21,000	$21,000	$21,000
Expenses				
Cost of Goods Sold	$13,685	$13,685	$13,125	$13,125
Depreciation on Equipment	1,500	1,200[a]	375	1,200[a]
Officers' Compensation:				
Salaries	350	350	350	350
Stock Options	150	0	0	0
Other Selling, General and Administrative Expenses	3,350	3,350	3,350	3,350
Expenses Before Income Taxes	$19,035	$18,585	$17,200	$18,025
Income Before Taxes	$ 1,965	$ 2,415	$ 3,800	$ 2,975
Income Tax Expense[b]	786		1,520	
Net Income	$ 1,179		$ 2,280	
Earnings Per Share in Dollars (500,000 Shares Outstanding)	$ 2.36		$ 4.56	

[a]Amounts based on MACRS, 5-year class; 20 percent of cost is deducted in the first year: .20 x $6,000 = $1,200.

[b]Computation of Income Tax Expense:

Income Before Taxes	$ 1,965	$ 2,415	$ 3,800	$ 2,975
Income Tax Expense on Current Income (at 40 percent)	$ 786		$ 1,520	
Income Tax Currently Payable		$ 966		$ 1,190
Income Taxes Deferred by the Timing Difference from Depreciation:				
Dr. = .40 × ($1,200 – $1,500)	$ (120)			
Cr. = .40 × ($1,200 – $375)		$ 330		
Income Taxes Deferred by the Timing Difference from Stock Options:				
Dr. = .40 × ($0 – $150)	$ (60)			

Exhibit 4.1 Accounting Magic Comparative Income Statements

income and earnings per share about half of High Flyer Company's. Both companies used generally accepted accounting principles and each would receive a clean opinion from its auditor.

4.5 COMPARISON OF CASH FLOWS

Until the two companies paid their income taxes, they were alike in all economically significant respects. Because High Flyer Company wished to report higher net income, it paid $224,000 (= $1,190,000 – $966,000) more in income taxes than did Conservative Company. Thus, after tax payments, Conservative Company, in a real sense, is wealthier than is High Flyer. Conservative Company ends the year with $224,000 more cash (or other net assets), than does High Flyer.

You might find it instructive to construct statements of cash flows for each of the two companies. You will find that Conservative Company generates $224,000 (= tax savings) more cash from operations than does High Flyer.

4.6 MANAGING REPORTED EARNINGS

The simple illustration for Conservative Company and High Flyer Company does not exhaust the set of choices available to a firm to manage its earnings. Managing earnings refers to a process of taking deliberate steps within the constraints of generally accepted accounting principles to bring about a desired level of reported earnings. This section describes some of the techniques for managing earnings and offers arguments for and against an earnings-management policy.

Techniques for managing earnings divide into three categories:

- Selection of accounting principles
- Application of accounting principles
- Timing of asset acquisitions and dispositions

Next, we give some examples of actions in each of these categories.

(a) SELECTION OF ACCOUNTING PRINCIPLES

- Revenue recognition: percentage of completion, completed contract, time of sale, installment
- Inventory cost-flow assumption: FIFO, LIFO, weighted average
- Depreciation method: straight-line, declining-balance, sum-of-the-years'-digits
- Leases: operating, capital
- Corporate acquisitions: purchase, pooling of interests
- Mineral resource activities: successful-efforts costing, full costing

(b) APPLICATION OF ACCOUNTING PRINCIPLES

- Estimates of degree of completion of contracts on which the percentage-of-completion method is used
- Estimates of service lives and salvage values of depreciable assets
- Estimates of uncollectible rate on accounts receivable
- Estimate of cost of warranty plans
- Treatment of indirect costs as product costs versus period expenses

- Classification of common stock investments as trading securities or as available-for-sale securities
- Selection of actuarial cost basis for pension plan
- Selection of interest rates for capitalized leases and for pension accounting

(c) TIMING OF ASSET ACQUISITIONS AND DISPOSITIONS

- Timing of discretionary expenditures for research and development, advertising, and maintenance costs, which become expenses in the period when the firm incurs costs.
- Timing of the sale of property, plant, and equipment or of investments to accelerate or delay the recognition of a gain or loss.
- Accelerating or delaying shipments of merchandise to customers at the end of a period.

These lists, although not exhaustive, indicate the variety of avenues available to management to manage earnings.

4.7 ARGUMENTS ABOUT MANAGING EARNINGS

Whether accounting magic matters to the reader of financial statements depends on the answers to two questions. First, do managers select accounting techniques strategically? Second, do managers or their firms gain anything by making strategic choices? Arguments on both sides of these questions, particularly the latter, vary, both as to their underlying logic and to the evidence cited to support the position. We present the arguments here in as unbiased a manner as possible so that readers can decide for themselves.

(a) STRATEGIC CHOICES. Even if managers could make all accounting decisions with the sole objective of reporting economic reality faithfully, they would face complex choices. Managers face conflicting goals and objectives when they make financial reporting decisions. For example, in choosing between LIFO and FIFO, a manager must decide what aspect of economic reality matters most. Nearly all firms manage their inventories internally using FIFO, and FIFO typically creates a more realistic balance sheet because the FIFO ending inventory amount reflects current costs. On one hand, managers cannot manipulate FIFO income with end-of-year purchases as they can LIFO, which may reassure investors. On the other hand, LIFO creates a more realistic income statement, because the LIFO cost of goods sold number reflects current costs. LIFO gives a tax savings[3] to firms facing increasing input prices, as our example illustrates, which leaves investors with more wealth. Last but not at all least, LIFO results in lower net income when used by firms with increasing inventory costs, as our example illustrates.

The LIFO/FIFO decision is the only accounting choice that affects both the firm's current tax bill and reported earnings. Many anecdotes and some academic studies, however, support the argument that managers make accounting decisions with the intent or hope of reporting higher earnings. Aside from changes to LIFO, most firms' voluntary (i.e., not mandated by changes in GAAP) changes of accounting procedure result in

---

3. More precisely, LIFO defers income taxes, sometimes for long periods of time. Because taxes paid later have smaller economic cost that taxes paid sooner, LIFO does save taxes measured in present value of cash flows.

higher earnings. Firms that make these changes have lower sales and earnings growth than other firms, on average, prior to making a change. When a change in GAAP mandates an accounting change, firms whose earnings increase most as a result of the new GAAP are most likely to adopt the new method before the rules require them to do so.[4] Although this evidence does not prove that managers make accounting choices for strategic reasons, it suggests such a conclusion.

(b) CAPITAL MARKET EFFICIENCY. One widely accepted view holds that earnings management is futile because capital markets are efficient. When market prices adjust quickly, fully, and in an unbiased manner to publicly available information, one cannot construct trading strategies based on observable data that consistently make money, and earnings management merely wastes valuable managerial time. Early theoretical and empirical studies provided support for the efficiency of capital markets.[5] For example, several studies examined the effects of changes in accounting methods on stock prices, and found that changes in accounting methods with no real or economic effects (i.e., those that do not affect cash flows) appear to have little effect on stock prices.[6] Using information from the financial statements and notes, investors can distinguish changes with real effects from those without, and react accordingly.

Proponents of the contrary view, namely that capital markets are not fully efficient, acknowledge this work but counter with two observations. First, the empirical work on market efficiency looks at average results for large numbers of firms. Because stock returns vary around these averages, in many cases the market has not priced securities efficiently for particular firms at particular times. Proponents of nonefficiency point to examples where the market prices of particular firms' shares decreased dramatically after analyses of the firms' (previously disclosed) accounting procedures appeared in the financial press.[7] Proponents of efficient capital markets counter that examples selected

---

4. See Morton Pincus and Charles Wasley, "The Incidence of Accounting Changes and Characteristics of Firms Making Accounting Changes," *Accounting Horizons* (June 1994): 1–24, and the references listed therein.
5. See Eugene F. Fama, "Efficient Capital Markets: A Review of Theory and Empirical Work," *Journal of Finance* (May 1970): 383–417; Nicholas J. Gonedes and Nicholas Dopuch, "Capital Market Equilibrium, Information-Production and Selecting Accounting Techniques: Theoretical Framework and Review of Empirical Work," *Studies on Financial Accounting Objectives: 1974*, Supplement to Vol. 12, *Journal of Accounting Research*: 48–129; and Robert S. Kaplan, "Information Content of Financial Accounting Numbers: A Survey of Empirical Evidence," in: *Symposium of Impact of Accounting Research in Financial Accounting and Disclosure on Accounting Practice*, ed. by T. Keller and R. Abdel-khalik (Durham: Duke University Press, 1978). See also Thomas R. Dyckman and Dale Morse, *Efficient Capital Markets and Accounting: A Critical Analysis*, 2nd ed. (Englewood Cliffs, N.J.: Prentice-Hall, 1986).
6. See, for example, Ray Ball, "Changes in Accounting Techniques and Stock Prices," *Empirical Research in Accounting: Selected Studies, 1972*, Supplement to Vol. 10, *Journal of Accounting Research*: 1–38; Robert S. Kaplan and Richard Roll, "Investor Evaluation of Accounting Information: Some Empirical Evidence," *Journal of Business* (April 1972): 225–257; Shyam Sunder, "Relationship Between Accounting Changes and Stock Prices: Problems of Measurement and Some Empirical Evidence," *Empirical Research in Accounting: Selected Studies, 1973*, Supplement to Vol. 11, *Journal of Accounting Research*: 1–45. A more recent study on the same topic is Bala G. Dharan and Baruch Lev, "The Valuation Consequences of Accounting Changes: A Multi-year Examination" *Journal of Accounting, Auditing and Finance* (Fall 1993): 475–494.
7. For several examples, see Abraham J. Briloff, *More Debits Than Credits* (New York: Harper & Row, 1976). For an analysis of these examples see George Foster, "Briloff and the Capital Market," *Journal of Accounting Research* (Spring 1979): 262–274.

after the fact cannot disprove market efficiency, because trading opportunities require one to predict *future* stock prices.

The second observation of the nonefficient-market proponents is that later studies provide evidence that capital markets do not adjust fully to available information, even in aggregate. Several recent studies document successful trading strategies for large portfolios of firms based on financial statement data, and suggest that stock prices reflect a naïve understanding of accounting information.[8]

If capital markets are fully efficient, then earnings management cannot produce a capital market advantage. However, if capital markets are not efficient in all cases, then by managing earnings, firms may take advantage of inefficiencies and obtain capital at a lower cost than if they do not practice earnings management. In this case, investors do not necessarily allocate the economy's capital resources in a socially optimal way.

(c) MANAGEMENT INCENTIVES AND SURVIVAL. Over sufficiently long time periods, net income equals cash-in minus cash-out, other than transactions with owners. Some corporate managers acknowledge that, because of this eventual reckoning, earnings management will not benefit the firm in the long run. They point out, however, that the long run comprises a series of short-run periods during which shareholders, creditors, and boards of directors make decisions based, in part, on accounting data. (See *agency theory*, page 8 of Chapter 1's Glossary.)

Financial contracts—such as bond indenture agreements and executive compensation contracts—often use accounting earnings as triggers for transactions and, thereby, provide managers with incentives to manage the reported numbers in the short run. For example, bond covenants frequently contain financial ratio constraints (see the Glossary at *bond indenture*, page 18 and *ratio*, page 117), which use reported accounting numbers. If an accounting change prevents violation of one of these constraints, the firm may avoid costly renegotiation with its creditors.[9] Likewise, corporate boards often link managers' bonus provisions to earnings performance. If managers can manipulate earnings numbers, they may be able to affect their own compensation.[10]

Managers sometimes prefer lower earnings for strategic reasons. For example, firms facing political or regulatory scrutiny, labor contract negotiations, or substantial legal

---

8. See the papers published in *Current Studies on The Information Content of Accounting Earnings*, Supplement to Vol. 27, *Journal of Accounting Research*, especially Victor L. Bernard and Jacob K. Thomas, "Post-earnings-announcement Drift: Delayed Price Response or Risk Premium?" (1989): 1–36; Robert N. Freeman and Senyo Tse, "The Multiperiod Information Content of Accounting Earnings: Confirmations and Contradictions of Previous Earnings Reports," (1989): 49–79; and Jane A. Ou and Stephen H. Penman, "Accounting Measurement, Price-Earnings Ratio, and the Information Content of Security Prices," (1989): 111–144. See also Jeffery S. Abarbanell and Brian J. Bushée, "Abnormal Returns to a Fundamental Analysis Strategy," *The Accounting Review* (January 1998): 19–46.

9. See Messod D. Beneish and Eric Press, "Costs of Technical Violation of Accounting-Based Debt Covenants," *The Accounting Review* (April 1993): 233–257; and Amy Patricia Sweeney, "Debt-covenant Violations and Managers' Accounting Responses," *Journal of Accounting and Economics* (May 1994): 281–308.

10. See Paul M. Healy, "The Effect of Bonus Schemes on Accounting Decisions," *Journal of Accounting and Economics* (April 1985): 85–107; and Paul M. Healy, Sok-Hyon Kang and Krishna Palepu, "The Effect of Accounting Procedure Changes on CEOs' Cash Salary and Bonus Compensation," *Journal of Accounting and Economics* (April 1987): 7–34. Interestingly, the latter paper finds that boards of directors appear not to adjust compensation formulas for accounting method changes.

damage awards may benefit if they can appear less profitable.[11] If managers propose a management buyout (a transaction in which managers buy the company from shareholders), they may be able to negotiate a lower buy-out price if the company appears unprofitable. Several studies suggest that managers use discretion in applying accounting procedures to reduce earnings when faced with strategic concerns like these.[12]

Corporate managers observe that, since other firms practice earnings management, their survival dictates that they do so as well. Shareholders, they argue, do not want to see wide, unexpected fluctuations in earnings from year to year. To smooth out these fluctuations and create the impression that management has operations under control, they claim, requires earnings management. In saying this, managers espouse the view that investors and creditors use accounting data naïvely, ignoring differences in accounting choices. Regardless of whether investors and creditors are naïve in using accounting numbers, if managers *believe* that it is true, then such managers have an incentive to manage earnings, and financial statement readers will find the managers' accounting choices to be informative.

---

11. See Jennifer J. Jones, "Earnings Management During Import Relief Investigations," *Journal of Accounting Research* (Autumn 1991): 193–228; Steven C. Hall and William W. Stammerjohan, "Damage Awards and Earnings Management in the Oil Industry," *The Accounting Review* (January 1997): 47–65; and Kimberly Galligan Key, "Political Cost Incentives for Earnings Management in the Cable Television Industry," *Journal of Accounting and Economics* (November 1997): 309–337;

12. See Linda Elizabeth DeAngelo, "Accounting Numbers as Market Valuation Substitutes: A Study of Management Buyouts of Public Stockholders," *The Accounting Review* (July 1986): 400–420; and Woody Y. Wu, "Management Buyouts and Earnings Management," *Journal of Accounting, Auditing and Finance* (Fall 1997): 373–389.

CHAPTER 5

MATHEMATICAL CONCEPTS IN COST ACCOUNTING

JOEL S. DEMSKI, PHD
University of Florida

CONTENTS

5.1 INTRODUCTION 197

5.2 MATHEMATICS AND COST ACCOUNTING 198
(a) Model Building 199
(b) Example of Model Specification 200

5.3 PROBABILITY AS A MODEL OF UNCERTAINTY 201
(a) Probability Example 201
(b) Definition of Probability 202
(c) Objective and Subjective Probabilities 203
(d) Uncertainty Representation and Summary Measures 203
(e) Use of Probability Theory 205

5.4 DECISION THEORY AS A MODEL OF CHOICE BEHAVIOR 206
(a) A Model of a Choice Problem 206
(b) Example of a Choice Problem 207
(c) Representation of Choice Behavior 207
(d) Information 210

5.5 GAME THEORY AS A MODEL OF STRATEGIC CHOICE BEHAVIOR 212

5.6 SUMMARY 215

BIBLIOGRAPHY 215

5.1 INTRODUCTION

The theory and practice of cost accounting extensively uses mathematics. A single chapter in a handbook cannot capture the various aspects of mathematics used, let alone the purposes for and manners in which accountants use mathematics. In addressing the topic of mathematical concepts, this chapter adopts a less ambitious goal than that of a coherent treatment or general survey.

This chapter concentrates on a central use of mathematics in cost accounting, that of building models and using the models to analyze issues in cost accounting. I provide references for the reader interested in more specific techniques or uses. As such, the chapter does not deal with the techniques of, say, statistics, matrix algebra, and the relation of linear programming to cost accounting. Rather, we concentrate on some conceptual underpinnings that apply to a host of cost accounting issues.

Section 5.2 explores the importance of mathematics in model building. Section 5.3 explores probability as a model of uncertainty. This provides an opportunity to explore a useful concept as well as to illustrate the model-building theme. Section 5.4 explores single-person decision theory as a model of choice behavior under uncertainty. Finally, Section 5.5 explores game theory as a model of choice behavior in a strategic setting.

5.2 MATHEMATICS AND COST ACCOUNTING

Mathematics is an integral part of cost accounting. Combining, relating, and allocating costs rests on the theory of numbers. In fact, if we view mathematics in a broad sense of "systematic treatment of relations among symbolic expressions," it becomes clear that cost accounting is a part of mathematics. One shouldn't find it surprising, then, that a large body of literature exists that employs mathematics to analyze cost accounting practices.

Mathematics has, for example, been used to *analyze various cost accounting procedures.* Discounting techniques, an application of time series, have been used to compare various depreciation patterns with conventional capital budgeting procedures.[1] Calculus has been used to analyze cost behavior patterns when significant learning patterns are present.[2] Algebra illuminates standard cost variance analysis procedures[3] and helps in comparing, say, direct with full costing procedures, depending on whether the firm uses LIFO or FIFO inventory cost flow assumptions.[4] Linear algebra has been used to explore allocation procedures,[5] and the basic double-entry framework has been analyzed as a network[6] as well as a functionally represented information structure.[7]

Similarly, analysts use various mathematical techniques to *examine the use of cost accounting data,* most commonly the application of algebra and probability in breakeven analysis.[8] In addition, some have used calculus and classical optimization techniques to examine various transfer pricing schemes[9] as well as allocation procedures in a single-entity

---

1. W. Beaver, *Financial Reporting: An Accounting Revolution,* 2nd ed. (Englewood Cliffs, N.J.: Prentice-Hall, 1998); G. Feltham and J. Ohlson. "Uncertainty Resolution and the Theory of Depreciation Measurement," *Journal of Accounting Research*, Autumn, 1996.
2. A. Corcoran, *Mathematical Applications in Accounting* (New York: Harcourt, Brace and World, 1968); J. Demski, *Managerial Uses of Accounting Information* (Boston: Kluwer Academic Publishers, 1996).
3. See Chapter 15 of this Handbook for a discussion of standard cost systems.
4. Y. Ijiri, R. Jaedicke, and J. Livingstone, "The Effect of Inventory Costing Methods on Full and Direct Costing," *Journal of Accounting Research* (Spring 1965); S. Sunder, "Properties of Accounting Numbers under Full Costing and Successful-Efforts Costing in the Petroleum Industry," *Accounting Review* (January, 1976).
5. Corcoran, *Mathematical Applications;* R. Kaplan, "Variable and Self-service Costs in Reciprocal Allocation Models," *Accounting Review* (October 1973); and J. Shank, *Matrix Methods in Accounting* (Reading, Mass.: Addison-Wesley, 1972).
6. A. Charnes, W. Cooper, and Y. Ijiri, "Breakeven Budgeting and Programming to Goals," *Journal of Accounting Research* (Spring 1963); and Y. Ijiri, *Management Goals and Accounting for Control* (Amsterdam, North Holland Publishing Co., 1965).
7. J. Demski and G. Feltham, *Cost Determination: A Conceptual Approach* (Ames, Iowa: Iowa State University Press, 1976); A. Arya *et al.*, "Inferring Transactions and Financial Statements," *Contemporary Accounting Research* (Fall, 2000).
8. R. Jaedicke and A. Robichek, "Cost-Volume-Profit Analysis Under Uncertainty," *Accounting Review,* October 1964; G. Johnson and S. Simik, "Multiproduct C.V.P. Analysis Under Uncertainty," *Journal of Accounting Research,* Autumn 1971; Demski, *Managerial Uses of Accounting Information.*
9. J. Hirshleifer, "On the Economics of Transfer Pricing," *Journal of Business,* July 1956; Demski, *Managerial Uses of Accounting Information*; I. Vaysman, "A Model of Negotiated Transfer Pricing," *Journal of Accounting & Economics*, (June 1998); R. Sansing, "Relationship-Specific Investments and the Transfer Pricing Paradox," *Review of Accounting Studies* (June 1999).

setting, where an emphasis on marginal cost estimation is essential.[10] Mathematical techniques have been used to analyze whether standard cost variances warrant investigation;[11] and probability theory has been used to determine consistent manners of revising cost expectations when internal or external changes occur for a firm.[12]

Most common, however, is the use of mathematical techniques to examine formal decision models that represent or describe management's resource allocation decisions, in order to identify which costing procedures to use. For example, firms often examine capital budgeting, cost-volume-profit analyses, and inventory control procedures in this light. Strategic considerations also enter at this point. The classic study of cost accounting, J. M. Clark's *Economics of Overhead Costs* (published in 1923 by the University of Chicago Press), employed this notion of letting uses of data determine which data the cost system accumulates, and it provides the structure of present-day textbooks as well as this *Handbook.*

Finally, mathematics is also used to *characterize the process of selecting among cost accounting alternatives.* Firms often must decide between the costliness of costing procedures and the quality of the resulting data. (We assess quality in terms of the decisions that firms make on the basis of the data provided.) For example, the questions of whether to adopt a full-fledged activity-based costing (ABC) system, how many cost elements to aggregate in a common overhead pool, or how detailed a recording of scrap to employ, force a firm to trade off costliness and quality of the data. Analysts have used mathematics to analyze such choices, employing the same techniques used to analyze management's allocation decisions.[13]

(a) MODEL BUILDING. These various applications have a central theme of *modeling* the process and using the model to analyze specific issues. In particular, we model various data generating, data use, and choice processes in cost accounting. In other words, we construct symbolic representations of the processes in question. (And in this sense, any cost accounting system, because it purports to represent some economic phenomenon, is a model.)

The essential idea here is deceptively simple. We merely detail the relation between some independent and dependent variables. We might depict this as follows:

$$z = f(c, u) \tag{1}$$

where z is the dependent variable or variables of interest, c and u are the independent variables, and f is the detailed functional relation in question. Often we distinguish the independent variables in terms of whether they are controllable, c, or uncontrollable, u.

Of course, specifying the variables and their relation provides the key to successful representation. We seek to study, say, the relation between alternative costing procedures but find experimentally controlled actual use of the competing procedures impractical.

---

10. R. Weil, Jr., "Allocating Joint Costs," *American Economic Review,* December 1968; J. Christensen and J. Demski, "Product Costing in the Presence of Endogenous Subcost Functions," *Review of Accounting Studies* (November, 1997).
11. R. Kaplan, "The Significance and Investigation of Cost Variances: Survey and Synthesis," *Journal of Accounting Research* (Autumn 1975), S. Baiman and J. Demski, "Economically Optimal Performance Evaluation and Control Systems," *Journal of Accounting Research,* 1980, supp; J. Christensen and J. Demski, *Accounting Theory: An Information Content Perspective* (Boston: McGraw-Hill/Irwin, 2003).
12. Demski and Feltham, *Cost Determination.*
13. Demski and Feltham, *Cost Determination*; H. Itami, *Evaluation of Adaptive Behavior and Information Timing in Management Control* (New York: American Accounting Association, 1977).

Alternatively, one could construct a model and use it to gain some insight into how the procedures differ. In specifying the model, however, it must remain adequately simple to address the question of interest, but rich enough to capture sufficient reality so that we retain confidence that results bear some relation to the real phenomena in question. Otherwise, the model's complexity will make it unmanageable (either in terms of data required or ability to take advantage of existing mathematical techniques of analysis) or so nonrepresentative that it is useless. The key, in other words, lies in balancing tractability with representational faithfulness in specifying the variables and their relation.[14]

(b) EXAMPLE OF MODEL SPECIFICATION. A simple inventory model illustrates this philosophy. Suppose we face a problem of assessing how much of a raw material to keep in stock. Two classes of assumptions will provide for a particularly straightforward analysis of such a question. First, we presume a known constant rate of usage for the material and do not allow any stock-outs (i.e., demand cannot exceed available inventory). Let D denote the known annual usage. Second, we presume a known linear cost structure consisting of ordering and storage cost components. The ordering cost increases directly with the number of units acquired during the year and with the number of orders placed during the year. The storage cost increases directly with the average level of inventory during the year.

Suppose the firm orders q units of the raw material with each order, and that the company times the orders to arrive just as the inventory on hand is fully depleted. The firm will then need to place D/q orders each year, and with the inventory on hand varying uniformly between zero and q, the average inventory throughout the year equals $q/2$. Hence, the presumed cost structure is linear in D, D/q, and $q/2$.

Now let F denote the fixed component of the total cost, P the variable cost per unit of material (e.g., price and shipping cost), C_p the variable cost per order placed and received (e.g., order and payment processing cost), and C_s the variable cost per unit of average inventory on hand (e.g., capital cost and insurance). We then have the following total cost structure:

$$\text{Total Cost} = TC = F + PD + C_p\,(D/q) + C_s\,(q/2) \qquad (2)$$

Relating to our basic description of a model, we now have total cost as the dependent variable, D, F, P, C_p, and C_s, as the independent, uncontrollable variables, and q as the independent, controllable variable. Relation (2) above specifies the functional relation.

Moreover, one can use calculus to analyze the presumed structure. In particular, we seek an order policy, q, that will minimize the total cost of acquiring D units of raw material per year. Differentiating total cost with respect to q, setting the result equal to zero, and solving for q produces the familiar economic order quantity or EOQ model:[15]

$$q^* = \sqrt{2DC_p / C_s} \qquad (3)$$

---

14. R. L. Ackoff, *Scientific Method: Optimizing Applied Research Decisions* (New York: John Wiley & Sons, 1962); C. Sims, "Macroeconomics and Methodology," *Journal of Economic Perspectives* (Winter 1996); Christensen and Demski, *Accounting Theory: An Information Content Perspective*. I use the term *representational faithfulness* to mean the same as in *Statement of Financial Accounting Concepts No. 2,* "Qualitative Characteristics of Accounting Information," FASB: May 1980.

15. Notice $dTC / dq = 0 = - C_pD / q^2 + C_s / 2$ and second-order conditions ensure a minimizing solution, as $d^2TC / dq^2 = 2C_pD / q^3 > 0$.

Several comments warrant mention. First, we term q^* an *optimal controllable variable* in that it produces the most desirable value of the dependent variable. Whether q^* represents a good or optimal solution to a specific problem depends on how well the model in (2) represents that problem. We have chosen a structure that, in this case, accommodates straightforward analysis. In other words, by endowing the model with requisite properties, we can appeal to mathematical techniques to perform the desired analysis. More specifically, the precise cost structure assumed provides for a straightforward, easy determination of the optimal controllable variable. Of course, one could make alternative assumptions (e.g., allow for stock-outs, recognize an uncertain or time varying demand, recognize quantity discounts, or engineer the cost of placing an order to the point that justifies a just-in-time system). But the basic point of trading off tractability and representativeness remains.

Second, even when a firm must make a decision, we do not always formulate the model to identify an optimal solution. Required complexity may be such that simulation is used to locate the optimal solution approximately, or extensive search procedures may be only partially implemented. Also, interactive models may be employed, in which the model is used to predict implications of various configurations of the controllable variables, but a decision maker directly intervenes and selects the controllable variables to be analyzed and ultimately implemented. For example, rather than directly express the benefits and costs of various stock-out admitting policies in some summary profit or utility measure, we might use a model to predict the pattern of costs and stock-outs associated with the various policies and then allow the manager to decide the most desirable (or least undesirable) of the possible trade-offs.[16]

Third, we see that the motivation for some types of cost measurements may arise in contexts much broader than that of traditionally construed cost analysis. Here, for example, an ability to analyze the inventory model has an impact on the basic form of cost function that is sought. Indeed, some of the cost elements, such as capital charges imbedded in the C_s term, are not measured in conventional costing systems. In a larger sense, an ABC system illustrates this point.

5.3 PROBABILITY AS A MODEL OF UNCERTAINTY

This section discusses the notion of probability. The cost accountant deals with this important element in many models.[17] And probability itself is an example of a model. We begin with a simple example.

(a) PROBABILITY EXAMPLE. Consider a situation in which someone tosses a fair die. We assume the die will come to rest on one of the six sides, and thus the possible outcomes are the first six positive integers: 1, 2, 3, 4, 5, 6. Before we toss the die, we do not know which of the six outcomes will obtain. Because the die is fair, however, we regard each outcome as equally likely. In other words, no outcome is more likely to occur than any other outcome. We then say in this case with six equally likely outcomes that the probability of observing "die face up = 1" is 1/6, the probability of observing "die face

16. More broadly, we are entering the domain of management science and operations management here. See R. Chase et al., *Operations Management for Competitive Advantage* (Boston: McGraw-Hill/Irwin, 2003) or F. Hiller and M. Hillier, *Introduction to Management Science* (Boston: McGraw-Hill/Irwin, 2002).

17. Probability is used, for example, in the formulation and interpretation of production standards, in the calculation of overhead budgets, in estimation of warranty and pension related costs, and so on.

up = 2" is 1/6, and so on. Alternatively, if you prefer the language of betting odds, we say that the odds of observing "die face up = 1" are 1 to 5, or 5 to 1 against. Similarly, in tossing a fair coin that we assume will always come to rest on one of its faces, we would say that the probability of observing a "head" is one-half.

One could consider probability, then, as a familiar concept with a straightforward interpretation. This interpretation is not, however, unique.[18] (In fact, three different interpretations of probability exist: the *classical* view expressed in the previous paragraph, a *relative frequency* view based on repeated trials of an experiment, and a *subjective view* that emphasizes information aspects of probability.) A mathematical point of view considers probability as a special type of model.

(b) DEFINITION OF PROBABILITY. To explore the meaning of probability, we envision some primitive experiment or uncertain event that will eventually result in some *outcome.* Note that one and only one of the outcomes will eventually obtain. For example, throwing a die in the previous illustration will result in one and only one of the first six positive integers being observed. Let $X = \{x_1, x_2, \ldots, x_N\}$represent a mutually exclusive and collectively exhaustive collection of possible outcomes from some experiment. One and only one member of X will obtain (and N is positive and finite).

A probability measure merely represents a rule that assigns—in a manner prescribed below—numbers to these outcomes and their various combinations. Let $\phi(x_j)$ denote the assigned probability of observing outcome x_j, $j = 1, \ldots, N$. We may also want to know various groupings of these possible outcomes and the probability that any outcome in a particular grouping will obtain. We refer to any such grouping of outcomes as an *event.* (Alternatively, an event is a subset of X.) For example, observing "die face up = 1" or "die face up = 2" is an event in our die tossing experiment. Denote this event by E_1, = {1, 2}. Other examples of events in the die-tossing experiment are $E_2 = \{4, 5\}$, $E_3 = \{5, 6\}$, and $E_4 = \{1\}$, where E_1 and E_2 are mutually exclusive events in the sense that if the actual outcome is a member of E_1 it is not a member of E_2, and vice versa.

In somewhat formal terms, now, a probability measure is a rule that assigns a number $\phi(x_j)$ to each possible outcome x_j, $j = 1, \ldots, N$ such that

- Each number is nonnegative, $\phi(x_j) \geq 0$;
- Their sum is unity, $\sum_{j=1}^{N} \phi(x_j) = 1$; and
- The assignments are additive across mutually exclusive events, such as $\phi(x_i \text{ or } x_j) = \phi(x_i) + \phi(x_j)$ where $i \neq j$.

In a strict sense, then, probability is a model, expressing a relation between numbers (the dependent variable) and outcomes (the independent variables). The probability model has only three requirements: nonnegativity, a total of unity, and additivity across mutually exclusive events. But the attachments have no meaning, as will become clearer in the next paragraph. Hence, one would correctly label all of the assignments for our die-tossing experiment in Exhibit 5.1 as probabilities. Of course, we may have strong feelings about which make more sense than others, an issue that we discuss next.

18. B. de Finetti, "Probability: Interpretations," in *International Encyclopedia of the Social Sciences* (New York: The Macmillan Company, 1968); and L. J. Savage, *The Foundations of Statistics* (New York: John Wiley, 1954).

Outcome	Probabilities			
	Case 1	Case 2	Case 3	Case 4
1.........	1/4	1/16	0	1/6
2.........	1/4	1/16	0	1/6
3.........	1/8	1/2	0	1/6
4.........	1/8	1/16	0	1/6
5.........	1/8	1/16	0	1/6
6.........	1/8	1/4	1	1/6

EXHIBIT 5.1 POSSIBLE PROBABILITY ASSIGNMENTS FOR DIE-TOSSING EXPERIMENT

(c) OBJECTIVE AND SUBJECTIVE PROBABILITIES. The pure theory of probability, in other words, does not address the related questions of how one should assign probabilities (e.g., which of the probability assignments in Exhibit 5.1 is best, or what *best* means in this context) and how one should interpret them. One answer to these questions lies in the assignment and interpretation that arise from a simple counting operation that, presumably, independent observers would agree upon. That is, if one tossed a die a large number of times, we would assign the relative frequencies as equal to the probability assignments. This is an *objective* assignment and interpretation of probability. It relies on the properties of the experiment for its justification.

Of course, we do not limit the concept of probability to situations in which one has counting operations available or one can make a large number of repeated trials of the experiment. Conceptually, for example, one can speak of the probability of an undiscovered element, the probability that changes in the money supply systematically relate to inflationary forces in the economy, or the probability that division Z will experience a cost overrun next year. These *subjective* probabilities serve as examples of another answer to the assignment and interpretation questions. We do not necessarily expect different individuals to agree here. And we interpret such an assignment as a "degree of belief" that the respective events will obtain.

To illustrate, suppose someone offers you a choice of two bets. Either way, winning provides you a $10,000 gain, whereas losing gives you nothing. The first requires betting on heads on the flip of a fair coin. The second requires betting on the Democratic candidate defeating the Republican candidate to win a particular election. If you feel indifferent between which bet you take, one could reasonably presume that you assign subjective probability 1/2 to the Democratic candidate's winning. Alternatively, if you strictly prefer the latter, then you assign subjective probability in excess of 1/2 to the Democratic candidate's winning. (We assume here that your personal wishes for who wins do not influence your thinking about who will likely win, or that you bet on a particular football team because you think it will more likely win and not because you want it to win.)

(d) UNCERTAINTY REPRESENTATION AND SUMMARY MEASURES. Consider a situation in which management wants to know the cost of two alternative product-redesign plans. No one knows for certain the cost of each alternative. Rather, analysts have identified the possible cost outcomes and encoded the beliefs as to the various likelihoods in an assignment of (subjective) probabilities to the various possible cost outcomes. Exhibit 5.2 shows an example of such probability assignments. Thus, the probability of a cost of

ASSIGNMENTS FOR PRODUCT-REDESIGN EXAMPLE

	Probability Assignments	
Possible Cost	Plan a_1	Plan a_2
$ 20,000......	.05	.00
30,000......	.10	.10
40,000......	.10	.10
50,000......	.15	.20
60,000......	.20	.20
70,000......	.15	.20
80,000......	.10	.20
90,000......	.10	.00
100,000......	.05	.00
	1.00	1.00

EXHIBIT 5.2 POSSIBLE OUTCOMES AND PROBABILITY

$90,000 for alternative a_1 equals .10; the probability of a cost of $60,000 for alternative a_2 equals .20; and so on.

At this point, analysts may want to summarize the distribution of outcome possibilities with some summary measures.[19] A common measure of central tendency is the mean or expected value, which we denote μ. For a discrete set of outcomes, we define it as

$$\mu = \sum_{j=1}^{N} x_j \phi(x_j) \tag{4}$$

For the two alternatives in Exhibit 5.2, we have

$$\begin{aligned} \mu_1 &= \$20{,}000(.05) + \$30{,}000(.10) + \cdots + \$100{,}000(.05) \\ &= \$60{,}000 \\ \mu_2 &= \$20{,}000(.00) + \$30{,}000(.10) + \cdots + \$100{,}000(.00) \\ &= \$59{,}000 \end{aligned}$$

Observe that computation of this measure requires summation over all possible outcomes, weighting each by its respective probability. The mean, in other words, is a weighted average of the outcomes.[20]

Further note that summarizing the two distributions in Exhibit 5.2 with their respective means tells only part of the story. One should also ask how disperse each is about its mean or measure of central tendency. Analysts commonly use the *variance* to measure

19. Numerous summary measures applicable to either probability distributions or summarizations of large numbers of data, are discussed in statistics textbooks. See D. Anderson, et al., *Essentials of Statistics for Business and Economics* (Cincinnati, Ohio: South-Western, 2002) and J. McClave et al., *Statistics for Business and Economics* (Englewood Cliffs, N.J.: Prentice-Hall, 2004).

20. Such a procedure requires that the outcomes be represented numerically. (The technical term here is that the outcome be a random variable.) We do not compute the expected value of flipping a coin; but we do compute the expected value of a dollar bet based on the outcome of flipping a coin.

dispersion. It is denoted σ^2 and is computed as the expected value of the square of the difference between the possible outcomes and their mean:

$$\sigma^2 = \sum_{j=1}^{N} (x_j - \mu)^2 \phi(x_j)$$

And for each of the distributions in Exhibit 5.2, we have

$$\begin{aligned}\sigma_1^2 &= (\$20{,}000 - \$60{,}000)^2(.05) + (\$30{,}000 - \$60{,}000)^2(.10) + \cdots \\ &\quad + (\$100{,}000 - \$60{,}000)^2(.05) \\ &= \$450{,}000{,}000\end{aligned}$$

$$\begin{aligned}\sigma_2^2 &= (\$20{,}000 - \$59{,}000)^2(.00) + (\$30{,}000 - \$59{,}000)^2(.10) + \cdots \\ &\quad + (\$100{,}000 - \$59{,}000)^2(.00) \\ &= \$249{,}000{,}000\end{aligned}$$

We refer to the positive square root of the variance as the *standard deviation.* It summarizes the same dispersion tendency, but has the same measurement units as the variable itself. Thus, we might summarize the two distributions in Exhibit 5.2 by observing that the first has a mean of μ_1 = \$60,000 and a standard deviation of σ_1 = \$21,213, whereas the second has a mean of μ_2 = \$59,000 and a standard deviation of σ_2 = \$15,780. That is, although the second has a lower mean and its possible outcomes are more tightly distributed about that mean.

(e) USE OF PROBABILITY THEORY. One could make numerous extensions of the cost measurement example in Exhibit 5.2. In particular, by representing the uncertainty with a probability measure, we gain access to the many results of probability theory. We might, for example, elect to represent the uncertainty with one of the standard probability distribution functions that analysts commonly use. By adopting the normal distribution, for example, we would admit to extremely large (indeed unbounded) negative and positive cost outcomes, though with extremely small—likely negligible—probability. But we would also gain use of all known results concerning the normal distribution, such as the probability that the cost lies within one standard deviation of the mean equals .68.[21]

Similarly, we might consider conducting experiments to better identify the nature of the cost distributions. By invoking appropriate assumptions as to the underlying process and the manner in which analysts perform the experiments, we gain access to the rich results of sampling theory and classical hypothesis testing.[22]

Finally, by observing events that correlate with the process in question, we may also systematically revise the probability assignments that we originally assigned to the outcomes.[23]

---

21. Anderson et al., *Essentials of Statistics for Business and Economics*; J. McClave et al., *Statistics for Business and Economics.*

22. Anderson et al., *Essentials of Statistics for Business and Economics*; J. McClave et al., *Statistics for Business and Economics.*

23. R. Schlaifer, *Analysis of Decisions Under Uncertainty* (New York: McGraw-Hill Book Company, 1969); Demski and Feltham, *Cost Determination.*

5.4 DECISION THEORY AS A MODEL OF CHOICE BEHAVIOR

A mathematical model, recall, is a symbolic representation of some system or process. In turn, probability is a particular type of model that, by specifying conditions the posited relation must satisfy, provides a rich set of theoretical results. Decision theory makes extensive use of probability theory and also provides a representation of choice behavior in terms of maximizing the value of a particular function. This, in turn, allows us to use the theory of optimization to study choice behavior.

(a) A MODEL OF A CHOICE PROBLEM. One can understand many of the central features of decision theory by focusing on a setting in which one must select some act from a set of available acts. (Presumably, at least two alternatives exist; otherwise, no choice presents itself.) For illustration purposes, we specifically construct the type of setting that we will explore.

We focus on a model relating dependent to controllable and uncontrollable independent variables. We need to specify or select the controllable independent variable that, in conjunction with the uncontrollable independent variables, results in the "best" or "most desirable" dependent variable value. (Decision theory literature offers a more specialized language for this cumbersome description.)

The controllable variables are termed *acts*. The basic problem is to select the best act from a specified set of available acts. The uncontrollable variables are termed *states*. If more than one state could exist, but one does not know which one is or will be present at the time of act selection, the problem becomes one of *choice under uncertainty*. (Otherwise, it is choice under subjective certainty.) The dependent variable of interest, in turn, is termed an *outcome*. Thus, a decision problem consists of a set of acts, set of states, and set of outcomes, and a relation specifying the outcome that will obtain for each possible act and state combination. Exhibit 5.3 provides a symbolic representation of the assumed structure: m acts are available (denoted $a_1, \ldots, a_m$), n possible states are conceivable (denoted $s_1, \ldots, s_n$), and outcome x_{ij} will obtain if act a_i is selected and state s_j is present.

We face, then, a task of selecting from among the set of possible acts, $A = \{a_1, \ldots, a_m\}$. If, in turn, we have a well-defined preference measure, say $F(a)$, that well measures

		Possible States						
		s_1	s_2	. . .	s_j	. . .	s_n
Possible Acts	a_1	x_{11}	x_{12}	. . .	x_{1j}	. . .	x_{1n}
	a_2	x_{21}	x_{22}	. . .	x_{2j}	. . .	x_{2n}
	⋮	⋮	⋮		⋮		⋮
	a_i	x_{i1}	x_{i2}	. . .	x_{ij}	. . .	x_{in}
	⋮	⋮	⋮		⋮		⋮
	a_m	x_{m1}	x_{m2}	. . .	x_{mj}	. . .	x_{mn}

EXHIBIT 5.3 MODEL OF CHOICE PROBLEM

our preference for each possible act, we could structure the task in terms of selecting the act with the highest preference measure:

$$\max_{a \varepsilon A} F(a)$$

(b) EXAMPLE OF A CHOICE PROBLEM. An example illustrates the nature of this structure. Consider a manager who must decide whether to accept an offer to produce a variant of one of the firm's major products. Accepting or rejecting the offer will have no effect on the firm's normal activities (excess capacity exists, no demand effects will materialize if the firm accepts the offer, and so on). The question therefore reduces to one of whether the offered revenue exceeds the incremental cost of production. If the firm accepts the offer, the firm will incur the following incremental revenue, labor cost, and material cost:

Incremental revenue		800,000
Incremental labor	300,000	
Incremental material	200,000	500,000
Contribution to other costs and profit		300,000

Incremental overhead remains the only other cost in question. All the manager knows is that incremental overhead might total \$100,000 or \$400,000. Thus, accepting the offer will result in either an incremental profit of \$200,000 or an incremental loss of \$100,000. Rejection, on the other hand, will result in neither gain nor loss. Exhibit 5.4 summarizes these data.

(c) REPRESENTATION OF CHOICE BEHAVIOR. In this fashion we use the state-act-outcome model to represent the manager's decision problem. To continue, we must now introduce the concept of preference in order to specify which act is best. Two classes of assumptions support preference: consistency and expected value representation. We discuss them in turn.

Consistency essentially requires that choice be a meaningful concept. We require that, when confronted with a pair of choices, individuals be able to identify whether one is better than the other or whether they are indifferent. Otherwise we have no concept of preference and cannot meaningfully engage in systematic analysis of the decision problem posed in Exhibit 5.3.

Consistency also requires that these expressions of preference be *transitive*. If confronted with three alternatives, with the first valued at least as good as the second and the second valued at least as good as the third, the individual must also rank the first as good

		Possible States	
		Low Overhead: s_1	High Overhead: s_2
Possible	a_1: accept	\$200,000	–\$100,000
Acts	a_2: reject	0	0

EXHIBIT 5.4 SPECIAL ORDER CHOICE PROBLEMS

as the third. Otherwise, the choice process may whirl about in circles, needlessly consuming resources in the process.[24] (Imagine attempting to select a tree in a large Christmas tree lot without transitive preferences.)

Consistency, then, refers to the desire or ability to rank all choices in a transitive manner. Of course, if this consistency requirement could be readily met for all problem representations, the choice problem would be easily resolved. The individual would simply know, after looking at the choices available, which act or set of acts is best. However, additional assumptions allow us to represent these consistent preferences in an expected value manner. And this, in turn, allows us systematically to analyze the question of which act or set of acts is best. Thus, by moving to the expected value representation, we are able to use analysis to support this oblique and demanding concept of consistent preference among acts.

Basically, these additional assumptions require that the individual assign probabilities to the various outcomes and then choose among the acts in a manner consistent with these probability assignments.[25] To illustrate, return to the example in Exhibit 5.4 and suppose that the manager assigns a probability of .6 to the low incremental overhead event, $\phi(s_1) = .6$, and .4 to the high incremental overhead event, $\phi(s_2) = .4$. (This implies a mean incremental gain of μ_1 = \$80,000 with a standard deviation of σ_1= \$146,969.) Further suppose that the manager's preferences for acts leading to incremental gains and losses are such that the manager always selects the act with the maximum *expected value of incremental gain.* With the assigned probabilities we then have:

$$F(a_1) = \text{Expected gain with } a_1 = \mu_1 = \$80{,}000$$

$$F(a_2) = \text{Expected gain with } a_2 = \mu_2 = \$0$$

And given the preference for acts that maximize expected value of incremental gain, the manager accepts the offer.

Once we properly specify a choice problem, then, we introduce a concept of preference to identify which act is best (relative to the specified preferences). With an expected value representation of these preferences, however, we have *decomposed* the analysis to assess beliefs and risk-taking preferences separately. In turn, we use arithmetic operations to evaluate each possible act; this, in its turn, allows us to use optimization theory in locating the best act. In particular, we can satisfy the consistency requirement, because we express our preferences in terms of the maximum expected value measure.

Theorists do not, however, confine expected value representation to reliance on the expected value of the outcomes. Such behavior is, in fact, an extreme form in which only the outcome's expected value has relevance when assessing the respective act's desirability. This assumption ignores the dispersion of the possible outcomes about their respective means. For example, in this case, one would prefer a_1 to a_2 as long as it had a positive expected outcome value, regardless of the variance of the outcome distribution. Such behavior demonstrates indifference toward risk (where we define risk in terms of

---

24. More specifically, suppose that a_1 is better than a_2, a_2 is better than a_3, but (violating transitivity) a_3 is better than a_1. It is now conceivable that the individual could be in possession of a_3, pay \$100 to switch to a_2, then pay \$100 to switch to a_1 and finally pay another \$100 to switch to a_3, thereby winding up at the initial position minus \$300!
25. See Demski and Feltham, *Cost Determination;* S. Kassouf, *Normative Decision Making* (Englewood Cliffs, N.J.: Prentice-Hall, 1970); and Schlaifer, *Analysis of Decisions Under Uncertainty.*

the variability or dispersion of the possible outcomes about their expected value). More technically, theorists refer to such behavior as risk-neutral behavior.

Therefore, one may want to account for the riskiness of the alternatives in selecting among them. Act a_2, guarantees a zero outcome here and therefore has no risk. Act a_1, however, guarantees an outcome of either \$200,000 or –\$100,000 and carries risk. The question is whether its riskiness exceeds an acceptable threshold.

We account for risk-taking attitudes in the analysis by introducing a utility function. This function represents the individual's outcome preferences. If the marginal utility of the outcome in question decreases as more of the outcome is provided (that is the utility of more increases at a decreasing rate), we have risk-avoiding or *risk-averse* behavior. For example, the following utility function might represent the manager's risk-taking behavior:

$$U(x) = (100{,}000 + x)^{1/4}$$

This particular function represents risk-taking behavior that demands a payment of at least \$375 to accept a 50–50 gamble on winning or losing \$10,000. That is, if the individual is paid \$375 to accept such a gamble and wins, the outcome will be $x = \$375 + \$10{,}000 = \$10{,}375$. And if the individual loses, the outcome will be $x = \$375 - \$10{,}000 = -\$9{,}625$. The expected value of the utility of these outcomes is

$$.50(100{,}000 + 10{,}375)^{1/4} + .50(100{,}000 - 9{,}625)^{1/4} = 17.78$$

which is precisely equal to the utility of not participating in the gamble,

$$(100{,}000)^{1/4} = 17.78$$

Now analyze the choices in Exhibit 5.4 with this particular attitude toward incremental gain and its risk. We see that the manager would deem the offer too risky:

$$F(a_1) = \text{Expected utility with } a_1 = .60(100{,}000 + 200{,}000)^{1/4}$$
$$+ .40(100{,}000 - 100{,}000)^{1/4} = 14.04$$
$$F(a_2) = \text{Expected utility with } a_2 = (100{,}000)^{1/4} = 17.78$$

With less risk aversion, the manager would not deem the offer as too risky. For example, with $U(x) = (100{,}000 + x)^{1/2}$, the manager would accept it:[26]

$$F(a_1) = \text{Expected utility with } a_1 = .60(100{,}000 + 200{,}000)^{1/2}$$
$$+ .40(100{,}000 - 100{,}000)^{1/2} = 328.63$$
$$F(a_2) = \text{Expected utility with } a_2 = (100{,}000)^{1/2} = 316.23$$

In sum, expected value representation allows for separate encoding of beliefs (in the probability function) and risk attitudes (in the utility function) in such a manner that the best act results in the maximum expected value of the utility function.[27] With uncertainty represented by the probability measure, we also have access to probability theory and, in

26. This utility function requires a payment of \$250 to accept a 50–50 gamble on winning or losing \$10,000.
27. Further note that procedures exist for assessing utility functions and there is no inherent reason to use a standard function such as a square root, logarithmic, or exponential.

particular, well-defined procedures for analyzing information-gathering options, discussed next.

(d) INFORMATION. In analyzing the choice problem in Exhibit 5.4, the manager compared the *accept* and *reject* acts in terms of the risks and returns each promised. In some circumstances, however, one can find out more about the uncertain outcomes associated with the various acts before committing to a particular act.

An extreme form of this question arises when we entertain the possibility of a clairvoyant revealing—with absolute certainty—which state will obtain before the manager must select an act. Quite obviously, if the clairvoyant revealed that the new project would have low overhead (s_1), the manager would accept the offer (select a_1). If the clairvoyant revealed that the project would have high overhead (s_2), the manager would reject the offer (select a_2). Of course, before the clairvoyant's revealing, the manager would not know what message (s_1 or s_2) the clairvoyant would provide. Hence, before the clairvoyant's revealing, the manager faces an outcome structure of $200,000 incremental gain if the clairvoyant reveals s_1 and 0 if the clairvoyant reveals s_2. Using the risk-neutral case, the manager would then perceive an expected outcome of

$$.60(\$200,000) + .40(\$0) = \$120,000$$

Conversely, because the manager would select a_1 (with an expected outcome of $80,000) without a clairvoyant, the manager would pay a maximum of

$$\$120,000 - \$80,000 = \$40,000$$

for a clairvoyant's services. Theorists refer to this amount as *the expected value of perfect information*. It is the maximum amount the manager would pay to learn more about the cost structure in this particular setting.[28]

We consider the clairvoyant's message as information because it causes the manager to revise the state occurrence probability assignments. Moreover, it derives its value from the fact that the manager's act choice depends on which message the clairvoyant conveys. That is, the manager selects a_1 if the message is s_1 and selects a_2 if the message is s_2. Compare this with the case where a_1 results in only a $100 incremental gain if s_2 obtains; all other data remain as before. In this case, the manager will select a_1 regardless of what the clairvoyant reveals. Without any information, the manager selects a_1 with an expected outcome of

$$.60(\$200,000) + .40(\$100) = \$120,040$$

The manager will not use the information or outcome to alter behavior:

$$.60(\$200,000) + .40(\$100) = \$120,040$$

Thus, the information has no value in this particular case. Information will surely alter the manager's beliefs, but it does not affect the act selected and we have therefore no reason to commit resources to altering the beliefs.

Finally, one can extend this type of analysis to questions of gathering less than perfect information. The information is again modeled in terms of probability revision. The only difference is that we do not alter the state probability assignments to the 0 or 1 extremes.

---

28. In the $U(x) = (100{,}000 + x)^{1/4}$ risk-averse case, we have an expected value of perfect information of $80,000 because $(100{,}000)^{1/4} = .60(300{,}000 - z)^{1/4} + .40(100{,}000 - z)^{1/4}$ when $z \cong 80{,}000$.

To illustrate, consider a situation in which the manager in the previous example may, before selecting between the two options, commission a special accounting study to analyze some similar products in the firm. Such a study will result in one of two conclusions. Either the previous cost experience was above expectations (High Cost) or below expectations (Low Cost). Moreover, the recent experience relates to current production possibilities in such a manner that observing the High Cost event will convince the manager that s_2 will obtain for certain, whereas observing the Low Cost event will convince the manager that s_1 will obtain with probability .75 (and s_2 with probability .25).

Evaluating this information option requires that the manager decide what to do upon receipt of either message and then, in conjunction with the message probabilities, evaluate the various possible outcomes. Given that the manager uses probability as a model of uncertainty, however, the message probabilities must show consistency with the other probability assignments. In particular, the manager must assign ϕ(High Cost) = .20 and ϕ(Low Cost) = .80.[29] Exhibit 5.5, where we display the joint probability of state and cost study conclusion, summarizes these assignments. For example, the joint probability that state s_1 and a Low Cost conclusion obtain is $\phi(s_1, \text{Low Cost}) = .6$. Further notice we continue to have $\phi(s_1) = 0 + .6 = .6$, and so on.

Continuing, the Low Cost conclusion will obtain with probability

$$\phi(\text{Low Cost}) = \phi(s_1, \text{Low Cost}) + \phi(s_2, \text{Low Cost})$$
$$= .60 + .20 = .80.$$

And, again insisting on consistency among the probabilities, from Bayes' Rule we have the probability that s_1 obtains, given we have observed a Low Cost report, is[30]

$$\phi(s_1 | \text{Low Cost}) = \phi(s_1, \text{Low Cost})/\phi(\text{Low Cost})$$
$$= .60/.80 = .75.$$

Observe, now, that if the study reports High Cost, the manager knows for certain that s_2 will obtain. (After all, from Exhibit 5.5 we see High Cost guarantees a high cost, or s_2

	s_1	s_2
High Cost	0	.20
Low Cost	.60	.20

EXHIBIT 5.5 JOINT PROBABILITY ASSIGNMENTS FOR SPECIAL ORDER EXAMPLE

29. Recall that $\phi(s_1) = .6$ and $\phi(s_1, \text{given Low Cost}) = \phi(s_1 | \text{Low Cost}) = .75$. Also, the High Cost event cannot—by assumption—occur in conjunction with s_1. Consistency in the probability assignments then requires that ϕ (Low Cost) = .60/.75 = .80. Moreover, we now encounter use of probability theory to revise probability assignments consistently. By Bayes' theorem, we have

$$\phi(s_1 \text{ given Low Cost}) = \frac{\phi(\text{Low Cost}|s_1)\phi(s_1)}{\phi(\text{Low Cost})} = \frac{\phi(s_1 \text{ Low Cost} | s_1)}{\phi(\text{Low Cost})}$$
$$= \frac{1 \times .6}{.8} = .75$$

and similarly, $\phi(s_2 | \text{Low Cost}) = .25$.

30. Let $\phi(W, Y)$ be the joint probability of events W and Y. Then conditional on event Y being present, Bayes' Rule provides the (conditional) probability of event W is $\phi(W|Y) = \phi(W, Y)/\phi(Y)$.

will obtain.) And in that event, the manager will reject the offer (select a_2). Conversely, if the study reports Low Cost, the manager assesses $\phi(s_1|$ Low Cost$) = .75$, and now will accept the offer:

$$\text{Expected outcome if Low Cost reported and } a_1$$
$$= .75(\$200{,}000) + .25(-\$100{,}000) = \$125{,}000$$
$$\text{Expected outcome if Low Cost reported and } a_2 = 0$$

If the High Cost event obtains, the manager faces an outcome of \$0; and if the Low Cost event obtains, the expected outcome equals \$125,000. Hence, prior to receiving the message (recalling that ϕ(Low Cost) = .80), the manager faces the following expected outcome:

$$.80(\$125{,}000) + .20(\$0) = \$100{,}000$$

Thus, recalling an expected outcome of \$80,000 without any additional information, the manager will pay a maximum of \$100,000 – \$80,000 = \$20,000 for this special cost study. See Exhibit 5.6. The information clearly improves the quality of the decision.

We see, in other words, that by employing probability as a model of uncertainty, one can systematically address questions of additional information by consistent revision of probability assessments.

5.5 GAME THEORY AS A MODEL OF STRATEGIC CHOICE BEHAVIOR

To this point, our excursion into choice behavior has viewed the controllable variable in the simple model in equation (1) of Section 5.2 as an act, or choice, and the uncontrollable variable as pure chance or nature's choice. In a strategic setting, at least two individuals or players make choices, and the outcome to any one depends on the others' act choices.

To illustrate, we revisit the special order example, but now interpret the special order as an additional product, and further assume that a competitor, a potential producer and seller of the additional product, exists. So we have two players, and each faces the choice between accepting or rejecting a new product proposal. Either one's incremental profit depends on the act choice of both players. Exhibit 5.7 displays the assumed incremental profit for each player; in each cell, the first number is the first player's incremental profit and the second is that of the second player. For example, if the second player selects *no*, the first player gains \$80,000 by selecting *yes* (just as in the earlier example of Section 5.4(c)).

Both players understand Exhibit 5.7, and choose their respective acts simultaneously.

Now suppose the second player selects *yes*. The first player is now confronted with a loss of \$10,000 (*yes*) or of \$20,000 (*no*), and will clearly select the lesser of two evils. That is, #1's best response to #2's *yes* is to play *yes*. Similarly, if the first player selects *yes*, the second player's best response is to play *yes*. Thus, *yes* by each player is equilibrium behavior, as each is a best response to the other.

To add a little structure, suppose #1 must select some act, $a \varepsilon A$, while #2 must select some act, $b \varepsilon B$. Player #1's preference measure, which now depends on both acts, is given by $F_1(a,b)$, while the counterpart for player #2 is given by $F_2(a,b)$. The act pair (a^*, b^*)

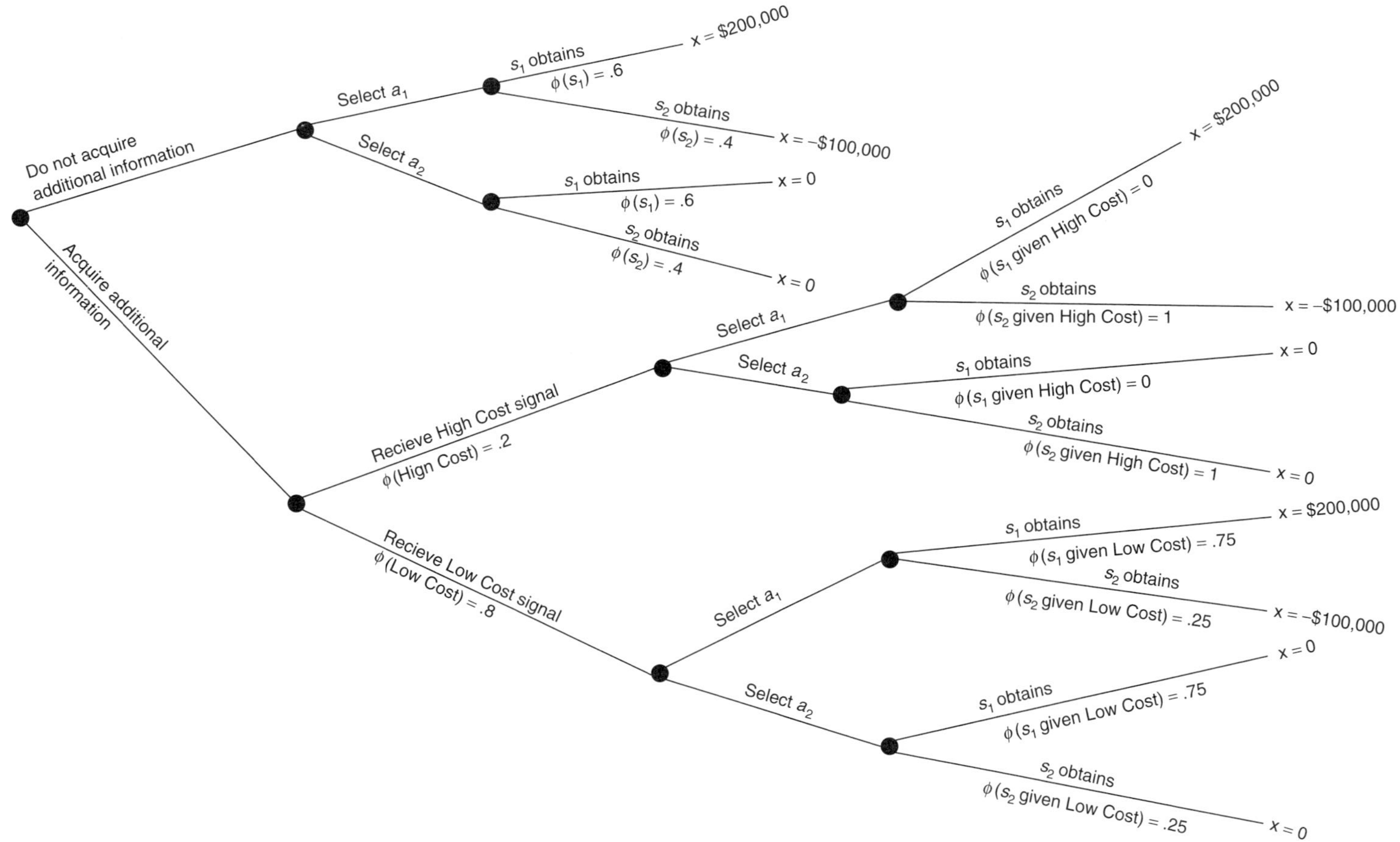

EXHIBIT 5.6 DIAGRAMMATIC STRUCTURE OF SPECIAL ORDER EXAMPLE

		Player #2	
		yes (b_1)	no (b_2)
Player #1	yes (a_1)	–10,000; –10,000	80,000; –20,000
	no (a_2)	–20,000; 80,000	0; 0

EXHIBIT 5.7 INCREMENTAL PROFIT FOR EACH PLAYER

is an *equilibrium* if a^* is best for #1 in the presence of b^* and simultaneously b^* is best for #2 in the presence of a^*:

$$\max_{a \varepsilon A} F_1(a,b^*) = F_1(a^*,b^*)$$

and

$$\max_{b \varepsilon B} F_2(a^*,b) = F_2(a^*,b^*)$$

This idea of mutual best response, or equilibrium behavior, attributable to Nash, provides the centerpiece of competitive analysis (e.g., how to best exploit a cost advantage), of auction theory (e.g., bidding on a construction contract), and of incentive compensation (e.g., use of employee stock options and other pay-for-performance arrangements).[31]

Questions of how to measure costs are, in fact, information questions and often have a strategic twist. The example in Section 5.4(d) of whether to perform a special cost study illustrates that cost measurement is a question of information. A firm deciding whether to charge a departmental overhead rate or a firm-wide rate provides another example. Yet another is whether a well-developed ABC system justifies its cost. In all cases, we analyze the cost measurement alternatives in terms of whether the firm will desire the outcomes they produce, by facilitating and influencing various decisions. Of course, this extends to concern about strategic issues. For example, will a sophisticated costing system—perhaps even within the framework of an enterprise resource planning (ERP) system—provide a strategic advantage? It also extends to concern for the cost of feeding appropriate and useful information to critical decision points in an organization, as well as providing on-point evaluation measures. Regardless, mathematics allows us to structure these issues and, with appropriate assumptions, to characterize them in terms of (strategically attuned) costs and benefits.[32]

31. R. Gibbons, *Game Theory for Applied Economists* (Princeton, N.J.: Princeton, 1992); R. Mayerson, *Game Theory: Analysis of Conflict* (Cambridge, Mass.: Harvard University Press, 1997); E. Rasmusen, *Games and Information: An Introduction to Game Theory* Blackwell Publishers, 2000); and Demski, *Managerial Uses of Accounting Information.* The structure of the setting in Table 6 illustrates the famous Prisoner's Dilemma game. Two thiefs, who work in consort, have been caught. If neither confesses, they go free; if one confesses, the other is dealt with harshly.

32. This approach to the resolution of cost accounting issues is described in Demski and Feltham, *Cost Determination,* and more broadly in Christensen and Demski, *Accounting Theory* and W. Scott, *Financial Accounting Theory* (Englewood Cliffs, N.J.: Prentice-Hall, 2003).

5.6 SUMMARY

We have concentrated on the use of models in exploring mathematical concepts in cost accounting. Companies have used models to analyze their cost measurement procedures, how they use data, and how they select among alternative methods of cost measurement. Ultimately, however, we must recognize that a model represents reality, and that the mathematical analysis tells us something about the model, not necessarily about reality. By endowing the model with sufficient mathematical properties, we can bring the results of mathematical development to bear on *the model.* But what such analyses tell us about *the problem at hand* depends on how faithfully the constructed model represents that problem. Models are not perfect; and in using them we must seek a proper balance between our ability to analyze them and our ability to learn from what that analysis produces.[33]

BIBLIOGRAPHY

Beckmann, P. *A History of π (Pi).* New York: Barnes & Noble Books, 1971.

Christensen, P., and G. Feltham. *Economics of Accounting*, Volumes I and II. Norwell, Mass.: Kluwer Academic Publishers, 2003 and 2005.

Dixit, A., and R. Pindyck. *Investment Under Uncertainty.* Cambridge, Mass.: Princeton University Press, 1994.

Kaplan, R., and A. Atkinson. *Advanced Management Accounting.* Englewood Cliffs, N.J.: Prentice-Hall, 1998.

Kreps, D. *A Course in Microeconomic Theory.* Cambridge, Mass.: Princeton University Press, 1990.

Suzuki, J. *A History of Mathematics.* Upper Saddle River, N.J.: Pearson Education, 2001.

33. Interestingly, the problem of model construction can itself be analyzed as a decision problem. That is, model selection is subject to cost-benefit tests.

CHAPTER 6

ACTIVITY-BASED COSTING AND MANAGEMENT

MICHAEL W. MAHER, PHD, EDITOR
University of California, Davis

CONTENTS

6.1 INTRODUCTION 217

6.2 OVERVIEW OF COST ALLOCATION METHODS 219

6.3 ALLOCATING FOR ENTIRE PLANT OR EACH DEPARTMENT 219
- (a) Using One Allocation Rate for the Entire Plant 219
- (b) Using a Different Allocation Rate for Each Department in the Plant 221
- (c) Choice Of Cost Allocation Methods: A Cost-Benefit Decision 221

6.4 ACTIVITY-BASED COSTING 221
- (a) Methods 222
- (b) Identifying Activities that Use Resources 222
- (c) Choosing Cost Drivers 224
- (d) Computing a Cost Rate Per Cost Driver 224
- (e) Assigning Costs to Products 226

6.5 ACTIVITY-BASED COSTING ILLUSTRATED 226
- (a) Department Allocation 226
- (b) Assigning Costs Using Activity-Based Costing 227
- (c) Unit Costs Compared 228

6.6 COST FLOWS THROUGH ACCOUNTS 229

6.7 CHOOSING ACTIVITY BASES IN MODERN PRODUCTION SETTINGS 229

6.8 ACTIVITY-BASED COSTING IN MARKETING AND ADMINISTRATION 231

6.9 ADDING VALUE WITH ACTIVITY-BASED COSTING 232

6.10 STRATEGIC USE OF ACTIVITY-BASED COSTING 233

6.11 ACTIVITY-BASED MANAGEMENT AND THE VALUE CHAIN 233

6.12 USING ACTIVITY-BASED COST INFORMATION TO MANAGE CUSTOMER RESPONSE TIME 235

6.13 COST HIERARCHIES 236

6.14 DISTINGUISHING BETWEEN RESOURCES USED AND RESOURCES SUPPLIED 237

6.15 ACTIVITY-BASED REPORTING OF UNUSED RESOURCES 238

6.16 IMPLEMENTING ADVANCED COST MANAGEMENT SYSTEMS 240

6.17 SUMMARY 241

6.1 INTRODUCTION

Imagine the following discussion at a meeting of senior executives in a company that has grown and added numerous new product lines over the past 10 years:

Barbara (chief operating officer): Ten years ago, we produced only a few products, but the company earned high profits. We have added popular new products. Each of these products appears to be profitable, but our profits for the company as a whole have shrunk to unacceptable levels. I want some ideas, people.

Lynn (vice president of marketing): Our prices barely exceed costs now. I think the problem is in production, where the costs are too high.

Maria (vice president of production): I think we could reduce costs if we had a better cost system to tell us where to direct our efforts. To be frank, I don't trust the cost numbers we're getting now; I think they are way out of line with reality. The accountants allocate overhead costs arbitrarily to our products. Overhead costs exceed 50 percent of the total costs of making the product. If you want me to reduce costs, then I want a better cost system than the one we have now!

Sam (controller): Our cost system has not kept up with the complexity of our production processes as we have added new products. I would like to study our cost and production problems and get back to you all in a week.

Barbara: Fine. We'll meet at this time one week from today.

Similar discussions have occurred in many companies over the past few decades. In particular, companies find substantial advantages from improving the sophistication of their costing systems if they have complex production or marketing processes (e.g., multiple products), have high levels of overhead, and face competitive product markets. Most large companies in economically developed countries have substantially improved their costing systems in recent years, mostly by implementing activity-based costing (ABC).

Activity-based costing assigns costs first to an organization's activities and then to the products based on each product's use of activities. An activity is any discrete task that an organization undertakes to make or deliver a product (e.g., placing a purchase order). Activity-based costing relies on the concept that products consume activities and activities consume resources.

Cost accountants generally agree that ABC became popular in the mid-1980s. One might reasonably ask why then and not before (or after). To answer that, I provide a bit of context to explain the popularization of ABC. After World War II, the United States dominated the Western world's economy. If U.S. companies could get the product out the door, then they would likely reap profits. In the 1970s, steel companies had slogans on their walls exhorting workers to get the product out and to meet output targets. These slogans did not encourage product quality or cost management, mostly because output dominated quality and cost control as a means of growth and profitability. In general, managers of U.S. companies did not focus on cost and quality management during the 1950s through the 1970s.

By 1980, the quality movement had hit full stride in Japan. Japanese companies did not have sophisticated costing systems, but they kept costs low by producing relatively fewer products, and producing them well. In response, U.S. companies needed to both reduce costs and increase quality to compete. Managers implemented ABC to help identify cost-reduction opportunities.

As this chapter will explain, ABC provides more detailed cost information about activities. This helps managers decide how to reconfigure production processes to reduce costs, how to reprice products to be competitive, and whether to drop unprofitable ones.

In keeping with most writing that examines this topic, this chapter will separate the discussion into *activity-based costing* and *activity-based management*, which deal with assigning costs to products and using the information for decision-making, respectively. The first half of this chapter deals with costing and the second half with using the cost information. If you wish to skip the details of product costing, proceed to Section 6.9, Adding Value with Activity-Based Costing.

6.2 OVERVIEW OF COST ALLOCATION METHODS

This chapter deals with allocating indirect costs to products. In this chapter, the cost object is a product. The product can be a good, such as an automobile, or a service, such as an X-ray examination in a hospital. Recall that indirect costs cannot be traced directly to a product.

Examples of indirect costs include the overhead costs incurred in manufacturing a good or providing a service, the costs incurred in marketing the product, and administration-related costs. Unlike direct costs, which one can trace directly to a product, accountants must *allocate* indirect costs to products.

The appendix of Chapter 16 explains how to allocate costs from one cost pool to another (e.g., service or support departments to production departments). *Cost pools* are simply groups of individual costs. This chapter describes how companies allocate costs from cost pools to products. This chapter defines cost pools as (1) plants, which are entire factories or stores; (2) departments within plants; or (3) activities.

6.3 ALLOCATING FOR ENTIRE PLANT OR EACH DEPARTMENT

(a) USING ONE ALLOCATION RATE FOR THE ENTIRE PLANT. We start with the simplest allocation method, known as *plant-wide allocation*. The *plant-wide allocation method* considers the entire plant as the cost pool. This method uses one overhead allocation rate, or one set of rates, to allocate overhead to products for *all* departments in a particular plant. We use the term *plant* to refer to an entire factory, store, hospital, or other multidepartment segment of a company. The key word in the definition is *all;* that is, every department uses a single rate or set of rates. Note that if a company has multiple plants, it might use a different rate at each plant.

Although we call this *plant-wide* allocation, both manufacturing and nonmanufacturing organizations can use this allocation concept. For example, a bank could apply overhead to different customer accounts, to different types of loans, and to other products using just one overhead rate for the entire bank. Although we refer to the allocated costs as *overhead* costs, the concepts apply to *any* indirect cost allocation.

The top portion of Exhibit 6.1 shows overhead allocation using plant-wide allocation. One can easily understand the mechanics of accounting for overhead: accountants record all overhead costs in one cost pool in the Manufacturing Overhead account for the plant without regard to the department or activity that caused them. Accountants use a single overhead rate to apply overhead to products, crediting Manufacturing Overhead. For example, to apply overhead using a rate per machine-hour, the amount of the credit to the Manufacturing Overhead account and the debit to Work in Process for overhead costs equals the rate per machine-hour times the total number of machine-hours worked.

Companies using a single plant-wide rate generally use a volume-based allocation base, such as direct labor-hours, machine-hours, volume of activity, or materials costs. This chapter discusses other types of allocation bases.

Simple organizations with only a few departments and not much variety in products could justify a single plant-wide rate. At Domino's Pizza, for example, using multiple overhead rates, as opposed to only one overhead rate, for all of the products probably

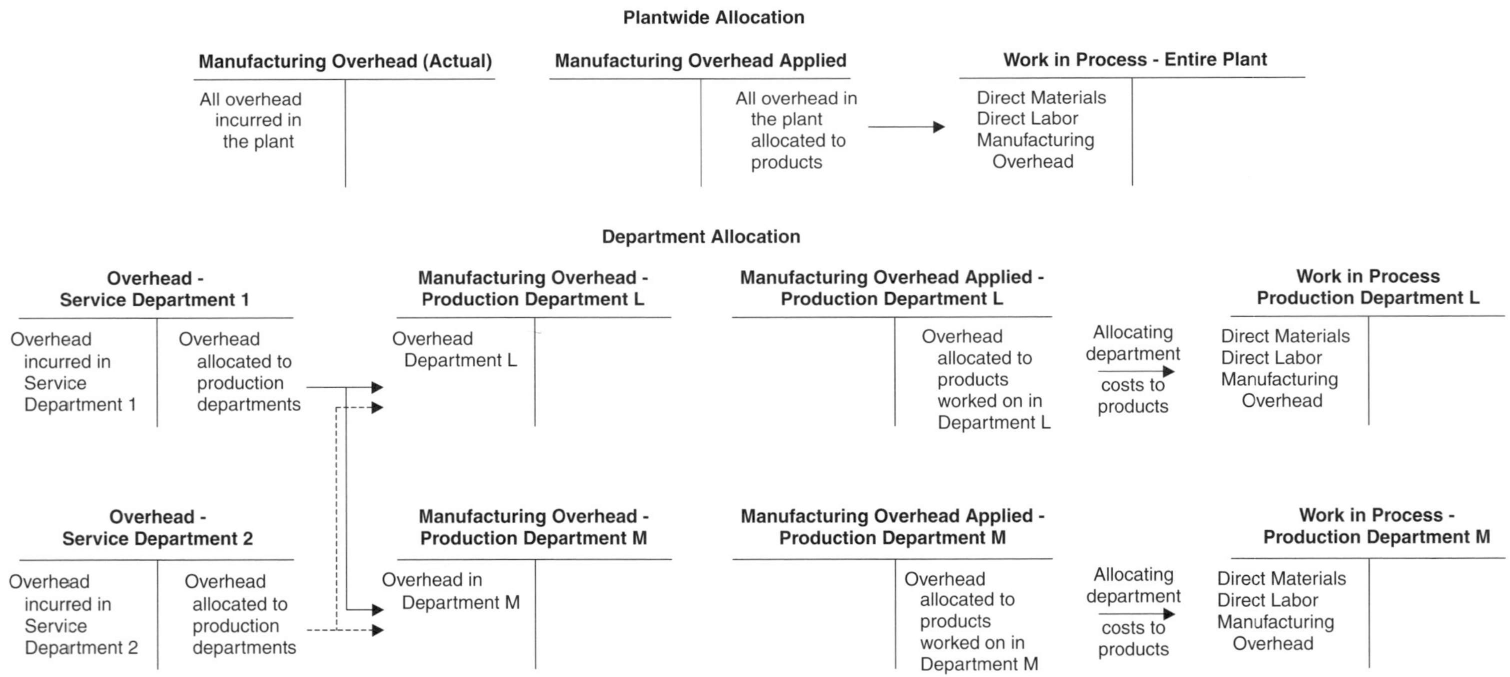

Note: Cost flows for direct materials and direct labor are omitted to simplify the presentation.

EXHIBIT 6.1 PLANT-WIDE VERSUS DEPARTMENT ALLOCATION

would not make much difference in the estimated costs of the regular or large pizzas. Suppose that Domino's becomes a more complex operation that includes extensive restaurant facilities as well as home delivery and food service for schools and hospitals. In this case, the company should use different overhead rates for different departments because different activities in different departments will likely drive overhead costs.

(b) USING A DIFFERENT ALLOCATION RATE FOR EACH DEPARTMENT IN THE PLANT. With the *department allocation method,* companies have a separate cost pool for each department. The company establishes a separate overhead allocation rate for each department and each production department is a separate cost pool. In contrast, the plantwide allocation method considers the entire plant as one cost pool.

The middle and bottom rows of Exhibit 6.1 show department allocation. Each department is a cost pool and has an allocation rate. The exhibit has four overhead cost pools, one each for Service Departments 1 and 2, and one each for Production Departments L and M. As each production department works on a product, it applies overhead based on the allocation rate for that department. The more departments the company has, the more overhead cost pools it has, and the more allocation rates the accounting department must compute.

(c) CHOICE OF COST ALLOCATION METHODS: A COST-BENEFIT DECISION. The choice of a plantwide rate versus the more complex department rate versus the even more complex activity-based costing, discussed in Section 6.4, requires managers to make a cost–benefit decision. Selecting more complex allocation methods requires more time and skill to collect and process accounting information. The firm needs to justify such incremental costs of additional information by an increase in benefits from improved decisions.

Note that companies using plantwide allocation, as shown in the top portion of Exhibit 6.1, do not allocate service department costs to production departments. Although it simplifies the calculations, omitting the allocation of service department costs to production departments could have negative behavioral effects for the company. Allocating service department costs to production departments enables management to assign responsibility for service costs to the people in the production department who wanted the services.

A departmental rate provides more detailed cost measures and more accurate product cost numbers than a plant-wide rate does, particularly if the departments perform different activities. For example, if one department is labor-intensive and another is machine-intensive, it makes little sense to use a rate based on either machine-hours or labor-hours for both departments. Companies can estimate product costs more accurately if they use labor-hours for the labor-intensive department and machine-hours for the machine-intensive department.

6.4 ACTIVITY-BASED COSTING

If managers want competitive products, they must know (1) the activities that go into making the good or providing the service and (2) the cost of those activities. To reduce a product's costs, managers will likely have to change the activities consumed by the product. Rarely will a manager's announcement that everyone is to reduce costs by ten percent prove sufficient to effect such a cost decrease. More likely, significant cost reduction requires managers, production and marketing people, accountants, engineers, and others to thoroughly examine the activities that a product consumes to identify how to rework those activities to make the product more efficiently.

When discussing activity-based costing, one should remember the following points:

- Different cost allocation methods result in different estimates of a product's costs.
- Activity-based costing provides more detailed measures of costs than do plant-wide and departmental allocation methods.
- Activity-based costing can help marketing people select and price products by providing more accurate product cost numbers.
- Activity-based costing also benefits production because it provides better information about how much each activity costs. In fact, it helps identify cost drivers (that is, the activities that cause costs) that managers did not previously recognize. To manage costs, production managers learn to manage the cost drivers.
- Activity-based costing provides more information about product costs but requires more recordkeeping. Managers must decide whether the benefits of improved decisions justify the additional cost of activity-based costing compared to departmental or plant-wide allocation.
- Installing activity-based costing requires teamwork among accounting, production, marketing, management, and others.

We next discuss the methods used for activity-based costing and then present an example.

(a) METHODS. Activity-based costing involves the following four steps:

Step 1. Identify the activities that consume resources and assign costs to them. These activities could include purchasing materials or setting up machines, for example.

Step 2. Identify the cost driver(s) associated with each activity. A *cost driver* causes, or drives, an activity's costs. For the purchasing materials activity, the cost driver could be number of orders.

Step 3. Compute a cost rate per cost driver unit or transaction. The cost driver rate could be the cost per purchase order, for example. Each activity could have multiple cost drivers.

Step 4. Assign costs to products by multiplying the cost driver rate times the volume of cost driver units consumed by the product. For example, the cost per purchase order times the number of orders required for product A for the month of December measures the cost of the purchasing activity for product A for December.

(b) IDENTIFYING ACTIVITIES THAT USE RESOURCES. Often the most interesting and challenging part of the exercise lies in identifying activities that use resources because it requires people to understand all of the activities required to make the product. Imagine the activities involved in making a simple product like a pizza—ordering, receiving, and inspecting materials; making the dough; putting on the ingredients; cooking; and so forth. Now imagine the number of activities involved in making a complex product like an automobile or computer.

Using common sense and the principle that the benefits of more detailed cost information should exceed the costs of getting the information, companies identify only the most important activities. For example, a Deere & Company plant identified six major activities required to produce its products and used one cost driver for each activity. Then it developed two cost rates for each cost driver, one for variable costs and one for fixed costs.

(i) Complexity as a Resource-Consuming Activity. One lesson of activity-based costing has been that costs are a function of both volume and complexity. One would expect that a higher volume of production consumes more resources, but assuming that the company has at least some variable costs, why does complexity consume resources?

To understand the answer to that question, imagine that you produce 100,000 gallons of vanilla ice cream per month and your friend produces 100,000 gallons of 39 different flavors of ice cream per month. Assume, further, that you sell your ice cream in only one-liter containers, but your friend sells ice cream in various container sizes. Although both of you produce the same total volume of ice cream, one would expect your friend's overhead costs to exceed yours. Your friend has more complicated ordering, storage, product testing (one of the more desirable jobs, nevertheless), and packing activities. Your friend has more machine setups, too. Presumably, you can set the machinery to one setting to obtain the desired product quality and taste; your friend has to set the machines each time he or she produces a new flavor.

In general, the number of activities that consumes resources is a function of the company's complexity. The number of cost drivers increases as companies become more highly automated and more complex. Cost systems based on a simple direct labor base generally prove inadequate in all but the simplest production or selling enterprise.

(ii) Volume and Overhead Allocation Rates. When accountants use allocation rates based on volume, such as direct labor-hours or machine-hours, they naturally allocate costs to products proportional to volume, if they hold the rate constant across levels of volume. The accountants allocate a high proportion of overhead costs to high-volume products, and allocate a low proportion of overhead costs to low-volume products. After installing activity-based costing, managers have frequently found that they should increase the allocated overhead for low-volume products. Low-volume products may be more specialized, requiring, for example, more drawings, specifications, and inspections.

Low-volume products often require more machine setups for a given level of production output because they are produced in smaller batches. In the ice cream example, one batch of 1,000 gallons of the low-volume 39th flavor might require as much overhead cost for machine setups, quality inspection, and purchase orders as one batch of 100,000 gallons of the highest-volume flavor. In addition, the low-volume product adds complexity to the operation by disrupting the production flow of the high-volume items. You appreciate this fact every time you stand in line when someone ahead of you has a special and complex transaction.

When accountants apply overhead based on the volume of output, they allocate high-volume products relatively more overhead than that allocated to low-volume products. High-volume products subsidize low-volume products in this case. Volume-based allocation methods hide the cost effects of keeping a large number of low-volume products. This has led many companies to continue producing or selling products without knowing their high costs.

Machine-hours	Computer time
Labor-hours or labor cost	Items produced or sold
Pounds of materials handled	Customers served
Pages typed	Flight hours
Machine setups	Number of surgeries
Purchase orders	Scrap/reword orders
Quality inspections	Hours of testing time
Number of parts in a product	Number of different customers
Miles driven	

EXHIBIT 6.2 EXAMPLES OF COST DRIVERS

(c) CHOOSING COST DRIVERS. Exhibit 6.2 presents several examples of the types of cost drivers that companies use. Most related either to the volume of production or to the complexity of the production or marketing process.

How do managers decide which cost driver to use? Consider three criteria for selecting cost drivers:

1. *Causal relation.* Choose a cost driver that causes the cost. This is ideal.
2. *Benefits received.* Choose a cost driver to assign costs in proportion to benefits received. For example, if the research and development (R&D) Department benefits more from the company's lab space than does the Marketing Research Department, the company should select a cost driver that recognizes such differences in benefits.
3. *Reasonableness.* Accountants cannot link some costs to products based on causality or benefits received, so they assign them on the basis of fairness or reasonableness. We noted earlier that Deere & Company selected six cost drivers for a certain product. Accountants allocated the costs of a seventh activity, general and administrative (G&A) overhead, to the product using the reasonableness approach. That is, they allocated G&A as a simple percentage of the costs of labor plus the other six activities that had been allocated to the product.

(d) COMPUTING A COST RATE PER COST DRIVER. In general, we compute predetermined rates for allocating indirect costs to products as follows:

$$\text{Predetermined rate} = \frac{\text{Estimated indirect cost}}{\text{Estimated volume of allocation base}}$$

This formula applies to any indirect cost, whether manufacturing overhead or administrative, distribution, selling, or any other indirect costs.

Companies using department rates compute the predetermined rate for each department. First we must consider the *activity center,* which is a unit of the organization that performs some activity. For example, accountants assign the costs of setting up machines to the activity center that sets up machines. Instead of a department rate, we use activity-based costing to compute a cost driver rate for each activity center. This means that each activity has an associated cost pool, as Exhibit 6.3 shows. If the cost driver is the number of inspections, for example, the company must estimate the inspection costs before the period and, ideally, track the actual cost of inspections as it is incurred during the period.

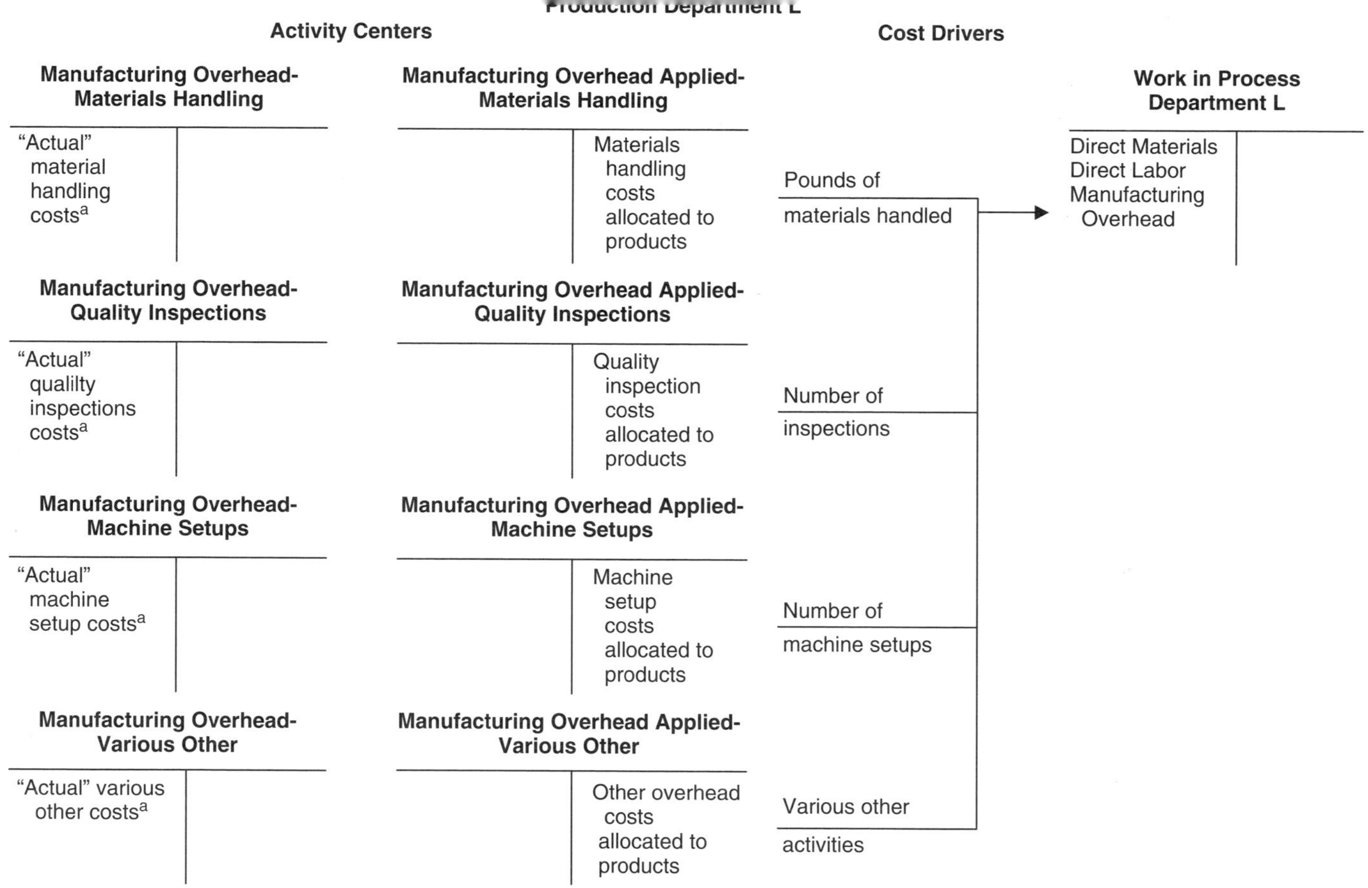

[a] "Actual" costs refer both to overhead costs directly traceable to the activity and to service department costs allocated to the activity.

EXHIBIT 6.3 COST POOLS AND ACTIVITIES

(e) ASSIGNING COSTS TO PRODUCTS. Workers and machines perform activities on each product as it moves through production. Companies allocate costs to a product by multiplying each activity's predetermined rate by the volume of activity used in making it.

Assume in Exhibit 6.3 that accounting has already allocated service department overhead costs to the production department's overhead accounts. Assume further that the exhibit applies to only one production department, Department L. This follows the convention of identifying numerous activities, or cost drivers, for each department.

As a product progresses through Department L, the operation moves materials to the work area. Accountants allocate materials handling overhead, such as the wages paid to the materials movers, to the product by multiplying the overhead allocation rate for materials handling times the number of pounds of materials moved. For quality inspections, the company allocates the overhead based on the rate for inspections times the number of inspections made on the product. All other activities progress through the same procedure, which repeats for each product worked on in Department L.

6.5 ACTIVITY-BASED COSTING ILLUSTRATED

The following example illustrates how companies compute unit costs when they use activity-based costing. We contrast the results using activity-based costing to those using a department-based rate.

Assume that SU Company makes two products, Standard and Unique. The Standard product line is a high-volume line, and the Unique line is a low-volume, specialized product. Assume that the overhead costs from service departments have already been allocated to Department A's Manufacturing Overhead account.

(a) DEPARTMENT ALLOCATION. Using department allocation, SU Company used the following procedure to allocate manufacturing overhead costs to the two products for January, Year 2.

- Late in Year 1, managers and accountants developed a predetermined overhead rate based on the following estimates for Year 2:

Estimated annual overhead for Department A for Year 2.	$2,000,000
Estimated machine-hours to be worked during Year 2 in Department A.	20,000 hours
Department A overhead rate ($2,000,000/20,000 hours)	$100 per machine-hour

- At the end of January, Year 2, the company had the following information for the month of January:

Actual machine-hours used in January, Year 2	
Standard products.	1,500
Unique products	500
Total actual machine-hours in January.	2,000

- Accountants then allocated overhead to the products worked on in January using the predetermined rate of $100 per hour times the actual machine-hours worked on each product in Department A:

Overhead allocated to products worked on in January	
Standard products ($100 × 1,500 hours)	$150,000
Unique products ($100 × 500 hours)...........	$ 50,000
Total overhead allocated to products	$200,000

(b) ASSIGNING COSTS USING ACTIVITY-BASED COSTING. When SU Company began to use activity-based costing, it first identified four activities that were important cost drivers used to allocate overhead: (1) purchasing materials, (2) setting up machines when starting a new product, (3) inspecting products, and (4) operating machines.

Management then estimated the amount of overhead and the volume of activity for each activity. For example, management estimated that the company would purchase 100,000 pounds of materials requiring overhead costs of $200,000 for the year. These overhead costs include the salaries of people who purchase, inspect, and store materials. Consequently, accountants assign each pound of materials used to make a product an overhead cost of $2 ($200,000/100,000 pounds).

The company made these estimates near the end of Year 1 and will use them during all of Year 2. (In practice, companies frequently set rates for the entire year; sometimes they set rates for shorter periods, such as a quarter.) Exhibit 6.4 shows the predetermined annual rates computed for the four activities. To calculate the rate in column (5), one divides the estimated overhead cost in column (3) by the cost driver volume in column (4).

The total overhead estimated for Year 2 using activity-based costing equals $2,000,000, as it was using department allocation. One should derive equal estimates of total overhead whether one uses plant-wide allocation, department allocation, or activity-based costing. The primary difference between activity-based costing and department allocation lies in the number of cost pools and activities used to allocate

1 Activity	2 Cost Driver Used to Allocate Overhead	3 Estimated Overhead Cost for the Activity	4 Estimated Cost Driver Volume for Year 2	5 Rate Col 3 / Col 4
1. Purchasing materials	Number of pounds of materials in each unit of product	$ 200,000	100,000 pounds	$2 per pound
2. Machine setups	Number of machine setups	800,000	400 setups	$2,000 per setup
3. Inspections	Hours of inspections	400,000	4,000 hours	$100 per hour
4. Running machines	Machine-hours	600,000	20,000 hours	$30 per hour
Total estimated overhead		$2,000,000		

EXHIBIT 6.4 PREDETERMINED ANNUAL OVERHEAD RATES FOR ACTIVITY-BASED COSTING

	Standard Product	Unique Product
1. Purchasing materials	6,000 pounds	4,000 pounds
2. Machine setups	10 setups	30 setups
3. Inspections	200 hours	200 hours
4. Running machines	1,500 hours	500 hours

EXHIBIT 6.5 VOLUME FOR FOUR COST DRIVER ACTIVITIES FOR SU COMPANY

		Standard Product		Unique Product	
Activity	Rate	Actual Cost Driver Units in January	Cost Allocated to Standard Product	Actual Cost Driver Units in January	Cost Allocated to Unique Product
1. Purchasing materials	$2 per pound	6,000 pounds	$12,000	4,000 pounds	$ 8,000
2. Machine setups	$2,000 per setup	10 setups	20,000	30 setups	60,000
3. Inspections	$100 per inspection hour	200 hours	20,000	200 hours	20,000
4. Running machines	$30 per hour	1,500 hours	45,000	500 hours	15,000
Total cost allocated to each product			$97,000		$103,000

EXHIBIT 6.6 OVERHEAD COSTS ASSIGNED TO PRODUCTS USING ACTIVITY-BASED COSTING

overhead costs. Department allocation uses only one cost pool per department; activity-based costing uses four in this case. In practice, companies generally use more than four cost pools because more than four activities are important; we use four to simplify the illustration.

By the end of January, Year 2, SU Company has collected the information about the actual cost driver volume for each of the two products for January, shown in Exhibit 6.5.

Multiplying the actual activity events for each product times the predetermined rates computed resulted in the overhead allocated to the two products shown in Exhibit 6.6.

(c) UNIT COSTS COMPARED. Assume that SU Company produced 1,000 units of Standard and 200 units of Unique in January. In addition, the direct materials cost is $100 per unit for Standard and $200 per unit for Unique. Direct labor cost is $20 per unit for Standard and $30 per unit for Unique. Comparing the overhead allocations of the department allocation and the activity-based costing allocation methods reveals the differences in unit costs shown in Exhibit 6.7.

Using activity-based costing, the company allocates more overhead per unit to the more specialized, lower-volume Unique product. This occurs primarily because activity-based costing recognizes the need for more setups and for as many inspection hours of Unique as for the higher-volume Standard. Because the company failed to assign costs to all of the activities, Standard was subsidizing Unique.

Many companies have found their situation to resemble this example. For example, a Hewlett-Packard division in Boise, Idaho found that conventional costing had excessively

	Department Allocation		Activity-Based Costing	
	Standard	Unique	Standard	Unique
Direct materials	$100	$200	$100	$200
Direct labor	20	30	20	30
Overhead	150[a]	250[b]	97[c]	515[d]
Total unit cost	$270	$480	$217	$745

[a] $150 = Overhead cost allocation to products using department allocation from the table on the top of page 227 ÷ Units produced (= $150,000/1,000 units).

[b] $250 = Overhead cost allocation to products using department allocation from the table on the top of page 227 ÷ Units produced (= $50,000/200 units).

[c] $97 = Overhead cost allocation to products using activity-based costing from Exhibit 6.6 ÷ Units produced (= $97,000/1,000 units).

[d] $515 = Overhead cost allocation to products using activity-based costing from Exhibit 6.6 ÷ Units produced (= $103,000/200 units).

EXHIBIT 6.7 COMPARISON OF PRODUCT COSTS USING DEPARTMENT ALLOCATION AND ACTIVITY-BASED COSTING

allocated costs to many of its high-volume products when compared to activity-based costing because conventional costing allocated costs proportional to volume. Activity-based costing revealed that low-volume, specialized products increased costs more than managers had realized.

6.6 COST FLOWS THROUGH ACCOUNTS

Exhibit 6.8 shows the flow of costs through accounts using activity-based costing. The amounts for direct labor and direct materials come from Exhibit 6.5. The manufacturing overhead applied appeared in Exhibit 6.6. We assume that the accounting department transferred all costs out of WIP Inventory–Department A to subsequent WIP departments.

6.7 CHOOSING ACTIVITY BASES IN MODERN PRODUCTION SETTINGS

When industries first began developing cost systems, companies were more labor-intensive than today. Much of the overhead cost related to the support of labor, so it made sense to allocate overhead to products based on the amount of labor in the products. Labor still ranks as a major product cost in many companies, especially service organizations like public accounting firms. Such companies often allocate overhead to products (which are called *jobs*) on the basis of the amount of labor in the product.

As companies have become more automated, including companies in the service sector such as banks, direct labor has become less appropriate as a basis for allocating overhead. As direct labor has dropped to less than 5 percent of product costs in many companies and overhead has increased, companies that stubbornly continue to allocate overhead to products based on direct labor have rate increases as high as 500 percent or more. (We have seen cases in which overhead rates exceed 1,000 percent of direct labor costs.)

When labor contributes so little to product costs, little or no relation exists between labor and overhead. In addition, small errors in assigning labor to products are magnified

Materials Inventory

	100,000[a]
	40,000[b]

Wages Payable

	20,000[c]
	6,000[e]

Work in Process—Department A

Standard:			
Direct Materials	100,000[a]	217,000 →	
Direct Labor	20,000[c]		
Manufacturing Overhead	97,000[d]		Costs transferred to subsequent departments
Unique:			
Direct Materials	40,000[b]		
Direct Labor	6,000[e]	149,000 →	
Manufacturing Overhead	103,000[d]		

Purchasing Materials

Manufacturing Overhead[f]		Manufacturing Overhead Applied[d]	
Actual costs			12,000 to Standard 8,000 to Unique

Machine Setups

Manufacturing Overhead[f]		Manufacturing Overhead Applied[d]	
Actual costs			20,000 to Standard 60,000 to Unique

Inspections

Manufacturing Overhead[f]		Manufacturing Overhead Applied[d]	
Actual costs			20,000 to Standard 20,000 to Unique

Running Machines

Manufacturing Overhead[f]		Manufacturing Overhead Applied[d]	
Actual costs			45,000 to Standard 15,000 to Unique

[a] $100,000 = 1,000 units x $100
[b] $40,000 = 200 units x $200
[c] $20,000 = 1,000 units x $20
[d] Given as the overhead applied in Exhibit 6.6
[e] $6,000 = 200 units x $30
[f] Actual manufacturing overhead for each activity center, or cost pool, in Department A is recorded here, including costs allocated to Department A.

Exhibit 6.8 Flow of Costs Through Accounts Using Activity-Based Costing

many times with overhead rates of several hundred percent or more of labor costs. Finally, allocating overhead on the basis of direct labor sends signals that direct labor costs more than it really does. This also creates tremendous incentives to reduce the labor content of products. Companies may desire this in particular circumstances, but they should base such decisions on accurate cost numbers, not those that are heavily biased because of an arbitrary cost allocation method.

6.8 ACTIVITY-BASED COSTING IN MARKETING AND ADMINISTRATION

One can also apply activity-based costing to marketing or administrative activities using the same principles and methods discussed in Section 6.4 and reiterated here:

- Identify activities that consume resources.
- Identify cost drivers associated with each activity.
- Compute a cost rate for each cost driver.
- Assign costs to products by multiplying the cost driver rate by the volume of cost driver units consumed for the marketing or administration activity.

Instead of computing the cost of a product, however, accountants compute a cost of performing an administrative or marketing service, as the following example illustrates.

Suppose that SU Company has an order-filling service. Customers can call an 800 number and order either the Standard or Unique product. Management has concerns about the cost for this service and might outsource it to another company. SU accepts bids from outside companies to perform the order-filling service, the lowest of which was $30 per unit. Managers want to know how much this service costs SU so they can decide whether to continue filling orders internally, and, if so, to identify ways to improve efficiency. The team appointed to the task proceeds as follows:

1. Identify the activities that cause costs. The team identified order taking, order filling, shipping, and customer returns, listed in column (1) in Exhibit 6.9.
2. Identify cost drivers, listed in column (2) for each activity in Exhibit 6.9.
3. Compute cost driver rates. Column (3) in Exhibit 6.9 presents the estimated monthly cost for each activity. Column (4) shows the estimated monthly cost driver volume, and column (5) shows the cost driver rate for each cost driver.

1	2	3	4	5
Activities	Cost Drivers	Estimated Monthly Cost	Estimated Monthly Cost Driver Volume	Cost Driver Rate
Order taking	Number of orders	$5,000	1,000	$ 5
Order filling	Number of orders	3,000	1,000	3
Shipping	1. Number of orders	1,000	1,000	1
	2. Number of units shipped	6,000	3,000	2
Customer returns	Number of units shipped	10,000	1,000	10
Total order filling costs				$21

EXHIBIT 6.9 ACTIVITY-BASED COSTING FOR SELLING-SU COMPANY

This analysis shows that order-filling costs total $21 per unit, much lower than the best outside bid of $30 per unit. Management decides to reject the idea of outsourcing this activity and takes action to improve the efficiency of its order-filling service. Recognizing that customer returns were expensive ($10 per unit), management looks for ways to reduce them. Management found that by improving its descriptions of the products in advertisements, the company could reduce the number of customer returns by nearly 50 percent.

6.9 ADDING VALUE WITH ACTIVITY-BASED COSTING

Activity-based costing offers many opportunities to add value to organizations. Many consulting firms have opened in the last decade to advise companies on activity-based costing systems, and many organizations have their own internal groups implementing activity-based costing. Surveys have indicated that hundreds and perhaps thousands of companies—including service, merchandising, and manufacturing companies—have implemented activity-based costing.

Experience over the past 10 to 15 years indicates two key ways to add value to companies using activity-based costing:

1. *Better information about product costs.* Activity-based costing uses more data than conventional costing and provides more informed estimates of product costs. Better product cost information helps managers make decisions about pricing and whether to keep or drop products. Although managers must respond to the market, they also consider their product costs in setting prices. Marketing managers, in particular, often strategically price these products below the market price to capture a larger share of the market. Or they may want to offer special prices to certain customers, such as the special discount fares offered by airlines or to open new markets in third world countries in which they must charge lower prices. Good product cost information can help them decide how far to drop these prices.

   Managers also use this information to decide whether to continue selling certain products. If a product's profit margins are too low, or if it loses money, managers will probably decide to stop selling it. Deciding to discontinue selling goods or services is difficult, and managers need the best possible information to make such decisions.
2. *Better information about the cost of activities and processes.* As noted in the order filling example of Section 6.8(a), activity-based costing helped managers realize the high cost of one of the activities (customer returns) and took steps to reduce its costs. By identifying the cost of various activities, managers gain useful information that the accounting system previously buried. The idea is analogous to lowering the water in a river to expose the rocks: Before lowering the water, you probably suspected or knew that the rocks were there. Until you lowered the water, however, you didn't know the location or size of the big ones. Sometimes managers find all sorts of interesting and helpful information about the cost of activities. Other times, implementing activity-based costing doesn't reveal anything new but confirms what managers already knew. Until you lower the water or implement activity-based costing, however, you don't know about the size of the rocks or the cost of the activities.

So far, the discussion has implied that implementing activity-based costing will add value to the organization. That will likely prove true in varying degrees. Companies with complex production processes that make many different products and that operate in highly competitive markets probably stand to benefit the most. That's why companies such as Hewlett-Packard, Chrysler, and IBM have implemented activity-based costing. Companies such as Starbucks and Nike would probably benefit also but less than more complex companies.

In considering how much value activity-based costing adds to a company, remember that implementing activity-based costing can be expensive. These costs include those of the accountants and other people who develop and implement activity-based costing, additional recordkeeping costs, software costs, and, possibly, consulting costs. It also shakes up the organization by changing the accounting rules. This can reap benefits, but many companies also have found it painful.

6.10 STRATEGIC USE OF ACTIVITY-BASED COSTING

Many experts think that activity-based costing offers strategic opportunities to companies. In the cost arena, companies develop competitive advantage by becoming a low-cost producer or seller. Companies such as Wal-Mart in retailing, United Parcel Service in delivery services, and Southwest Airlines in the airline industry have created a competitive advantage by reducing costs. Some companies have learned to use the information gained from their cost systems to cut prices substantially to increase market share.

Activity-based costing plays an important role in companies' strategies and long-range plans to develop a competitive cost advantage. While activity-based *costing* focuses attention on activities in allocating overhead costs to products, activity-based *management* focuses on managing activities to reduce costs. Cost reduction generally requires a change in activities. Top management can send notices to company employees to reduce costs, but the implementation requires a change in activities. If you have lived in a city that has had to reduce costs, you know that achieving the reduction required a change in activities such as fewer police patrols, a cut in library hours, and reduced social services. An entity cannot know the effect of a change in activities on costs without the type of cost information provided by activity-based costing.

6.11 ACTIVITY-BASED MANAGEMENT AND THE VALUE CHAIN

Activity analysis is an approach to operations control. As noted in Section 6.1, an *activity* is any discrete task that an organization undertakes to make or deliver a product or service. Specifically, activity analysis has four steps:

1. Identify the process objectives defined by what the customer wants or expects from the process.
2. Record by charting, from start to finish, the activities used to complete the product or service.
3. Classify all activities as value-added or nonvalue-added.
4. Continuously improve the efficiency of all value-added activities and develop plans to eliminate or reduce nonvalue-added activities.

Value-added activities make up the value chain. As Exhibit 6.10 illustrates, the value chain is a linked set of value-creating activities leading from research and development to the end use of goods and services produced.

EXHIBIT 6.10 THE VALUE CHAIN

Managers should constantly ask whether activities add value. As Exhibit 6.11 shows, managers should analyze activities and classify them as value added or nonvalue added. If they do not add value, management should try to eliminate or at least reduce them. If they add value, management should re-evaluate them regularly to ensure that they continue to add value.

Activity analysis represents a systematic way for organizations to think about the processes that they use to provide products to their customers. Companies can use activity-based management to identify and eliminate activities that add costs but not value to the product. Nonvalue-added costs are costs of activities that a company could eliminate without reducing product quality, performance, or value. For example, storing bicycle frames until needed for production does not add to the finished bike's value. Suppose that management can find ways to eliminate storing the frames by using just-in-time purchasing. If so, the company could save money without reducing the finished product's quality.

Firms should consider eliminating the following types of activities because they do not add value to the product:

- *Storage.* Storage of materials, WIP, and finished goods inventories present obvious nonvalue-added activities. Many companies have applied the just-in-time philosophy to purchasing and production to reduce or even eliminate storage.
- *Moving items.* Moving parts, materials, and other items around the factory floor does not add value to the finished product. A steel mill in Michigan once had hundreds of miles of railroad tracks to move materials and partially finished products from one part of the factory to another. Eliminating 100 miles or so of track reduced both labor and overhead costs, and even eliminated some spoilage because train accidents sometimes damaged products.

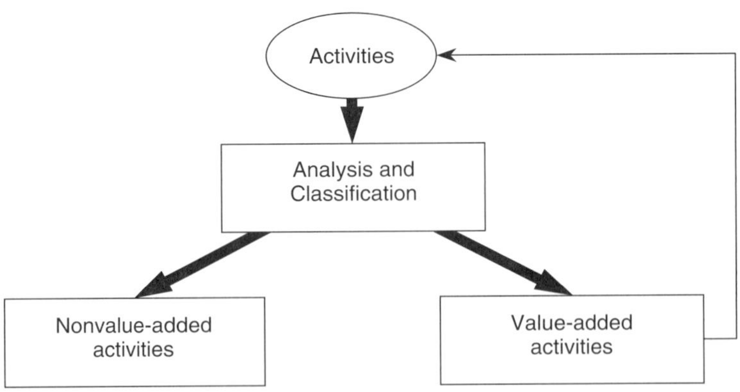

EXHIBIT 6.11 ARE ACTIVITIES VALUE-ADDED?

- *Waiting for work.* Idle time does not add value to products. Reducing the amount of time people wait to work on something reduces the cost of idle time.
- *Production process.* Managers should investigate the entire production process, from purchasing, to production, to inspection, to shipping; they should identify activities that do not add value to the finished product. Managers should ascertain whether the company needs as many setups, whether a reduction in inspection time could justify the cost of higher-quality materials and labor, whether the firm could reduce the cost of ordering, and so forth.

This list mentions only a few examples of nonvalue-added costs. If you observe activities at health care organizations, fast-food restaurants, construction sites, government agencies, and many other organizations, you will see numerous examples of nonvalue-added activities.

Activity-based costing helps measure the costs of nonvalue-added activities. For example, Deere & Company measured the variable cost of moving materials at $293 per load (defined as a movement of materials around the factory). If the company could have eliminated 1,000 loads per year, it would have saved $293,000, all things being equal, without reducing the value of the finished product.

6.12 USING ACTIVITY-BASED COST INFORMATION TO MANAGE CUSTOMER RESPONSE TIME

Exhibit 6.12 shows the chain of events from the placement of a customer order to customer delivery. Reducing that time can increase output, customer satisfaction, and profits. For example, suppose that a loan officer at a mortgage company can process 30 loan applications per month. If the company can improve the process so that the loan officer can process 30 loan applications in one-half month, several good things happen. Customer satisfaction increases with the shorter processing time, the cost per application goes down, and the company processes more applications per month.

Activity-based management helps to reduce customer response time by identifying activities that consume the most resources, both in dollars and time. For example, verification of required credit, bank, employment, and other information often delays mortgage loan applications. Use of computer networks could substantially reduce that verification time. Moreover, a mortgage company could easily reject or approve many loan applicants using limited financial information. In short, much of the paperwork that organizations require does not add value to transactions. Waiting, storing, moving, and

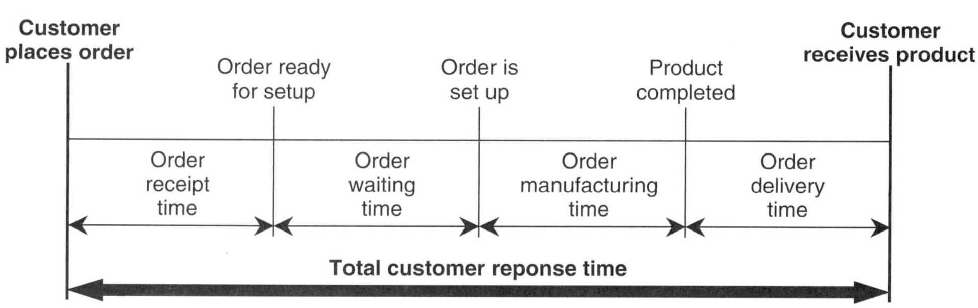

EXHIBIT 6.12 ELEMENTS OF CUSTOMER RESPONSE TIME

inspecting products are other examples that do not add value to customers. Activity-based management can help spot such nonvalue-added activities.

As we improve the efficiency of value-added activities or eliminate nonvalue-added activities, both customer response time and costs will fall. Of course, customers also value a quick response to their orders, another important benefit of short customer response time.

6.13 COST HIERARCHIES

Companies can associate some—but not all—costs with units of input or output. Consequently, allocating all costs (such as building leases) to units can mislead management if some costs do not vary with the volume of units. As a result, management cannot effectively control these costs by focusing on the volume of units. For example, the costs of machine setups generally relate to the number of batches. Each new batch of products requires a machine setup, whether the batch contains 1 unit or 1,000 units. The number of batches, not the number of units, affects the setup cost.

Management can establish a hierarchy of costs like that shown in Exhibit 6.13. The volume of units produced affect strictly variable costs, such as energy costs to run machines. These appear at the bottom of the exhibit as unit-level costs. Naturally, any variable costs such as direct materials costs are unit-level costs.

Capacity-related costs fall at the other extreme (the top of the exhibit). Management's decisions to have a particular size of store, factory, hospital, or other facility fix these costs. Although these costs are fixed with respect to volume, do not think that management has no control over them. Managers can make decisions that affect capacity costs. Such decisions, however, require a longer time horizon to implement than do decisions to reduce unit-level costs.

The way the company manages its activities affects the two middle categories of costs shown in Exhibit 6.13. A company that makes custom products will have more product/customer-level costs than a company that provides limited choices. A company that schedules its work to make one product on Monday, a second product on Tuesday, and so on through Friday has lower batch-related costs than if it produced all five products on

Cost Category	Cost-Generating Activities
1. Capacity-related costs	Plant management Building depreciation and rent Heating and lighting
2. Product- and customer-level costs	Customer records and files Product specifications Customer service
3. Batch-related costs	Machine setups Quality inspections
4. Unit-level costs	Energy to run machines Direct materials

Adapted from and permission granted by *Harvard Business Review* From "Profit Priorities from Activity-Based costing" by R. Cooper and R.S. Kaplan, (May–June 1991).

EXHIBIT 6.13 HIERARCHY OF PRODUCT COSTS

Monday, all five again on Tuesday, and so on through the week. In practice, many of the greatest opportunities for reducing costs through activity-based management exist in these middle categories of product/customer-level and batch-related costs.

Using a hierarchy similar to this, if management makes decisions that affect units, but not batches, products, customers, or capacity, it would analyze category 4 costs of unit-level activities. Management decisions that affect capacity, however, would probably affect all activities in categories 1 through 4, and managers would analyze costs in all four categories.

6.14 DISTINGUISHING BETWEEN RESOURCES USED AND RESOURCES SUPPLIED

In some situations, costs go up and down proportionately with the cost driver. Materials, energy, and piecework labor are excellent examples. Suppose that workers are paid $1.50 per crate to pick strawberries from a field. The cost driver is obviously crates of strawberries, and the cost driver rate is $1.50 per crate.

Now suppose that the farm hires strawberry workers for a month for $8 per hour. The cost driver might still be crates of strawberries. We calculate the cost driver rate as follows: estimated wages of strawberry workers for the month divided by estimated number of crates of strawberries that workers can pick during the month. Assume that this calculation gives a rate of $2 per crate. In general, this cost driver rate could be higher, lower, or the same as the piecework rate. We assume that the rate is $2, just to help you recognize that a difference exists between the piecework rate and the cost driver rate when the farm paid workers by the hour.

The grower employs five workers who each work eight-hour days. These workers each have the capacity to pick four crates per hour, or a total of 160 crates per day. Assume, however, that on Tuesday, the workers picked 140 crates. The grower had 20 crates, or $40 ($2 cost driver rate × 20 crates), of unused capacity on Tuesday. The grower has costs of $320 computed either of two ways:

- $320 = 5 Workers × $8 per hour × 8-hour day
- $320 = $2 per Crate × 160 Crate capacity

The grower supplied resources of $320 to the strawberry-picking activity. The operations used only $280 of strawberry-picking resources, however, leaving $40 of unused capacity ($280 = $2 × 140 crates actually picked). The grower knows that the five workers could have picked more strawberries without increasing the resources supplied to the activity.

The *resources supplied* to an activity are the expenditures or the amounts spent on the activity. In the strawberry example, resources supplied were the $320 paid to the strawberry pickers. Financial statements reflect expenditures for resources supplied. The difference between resources used and resources supplied represents *unused resource capacity.*

Activity-based management strives to reduce unused resource capacity. For example, the strawberry grower may look for ways to reduce the $40 (or 20 crates) of unused resource capacity. Suppose that the grower had not sufficiently trained the people to efficiently check each case for quantity and quality. Consequently, the checkers were slowing the picking process. The activity-based management information (provided by the activity-based costing system) signaled the existence of unused resource capacity, which helped the grower and workers improve the production flow.

Differences between resource usage and resource supply generally occur because managers commit to supply a certain level of resources before they are used. In the strawberry example, the grower committed to the $8 per hour in advance of the actual picking of the strawberries.

When management can arrange to supply resources as operations uses them, the resource supply generally equals the resource used, eliminating the unused capacity. Materials costs and piecework labor are good examples. If the grower had paid the piecework labor rate of $1.50 per crate, the resources supplied *and* the resources used would have been $1.50 per crate of strawberries picked. Thus, the farmer would eliminate unused resource capacity. The next section expands these ideas by suggesting a new reporting format that presents to managers important information about resources used, resources supplied, and unused resource capacity.

6.15 ACTIVITY-BASED REPORTING OF UNUSED RESOURCES

We now discuss an important way to add value to managers and their companies. Sections 6.13 and 6.14 demonstrated the importance of two key concepts, the cost hierarchy and the difference between resources used and resources supplied. Conventional management reports do not make those distinctions. Typical reports show costs as line items as shown for Cooper Company in Exhibit 6.14. Managers cannot distinguish resources used from resources supplied in such reports.

This section presents a new type of report that shows managers a comparison of resources used with resources supplied and classifies costs into cost hierarchies. This type of reporting will prove valuable to managers who want to manage resources wisely.

COOPER CO. JANUARY		
Sales		$180,000
Costs		
Materials	$30,000	
Energy	10,000	
Short-term labor	4,000	
Outside contracts	6,000	
Setups	20,000	
Quality inspection	10,000	
Parts management	7,000	
Marketing	15,000	
Customer service	4,000	
Engineering changes	6,000	
Long-term labor	7,000	
Depreciation (buildings)	20,000	
Administrative	13,000	
Total Costs		152,000
Operating Profit		$ 28,000

EXHIBIT 6.14 TRADITIONAL (DETAILED) INCOME STATEMENT

Exhibit 6.15 provides an example of this new type of report. Note first that it categorizes costs into the cost hierarchies discussed in Section 6.13. Managers can look at the amount of costs in each hierarchy and find ways to manage those resources. For example, managers see that the company spends $30,000 of resources on batch-related activities such as setups. They investigate how much they can save of that $30,000 by changing the production process, for example, to reduce the number of setups by half.

Perhaps of more interest, the report shows managers how much of the resources remain unused for each type of cost. Here's how it works: Assume that the cost driver for setup costs is hours of setup at a rate of $100 per hour. Based on the information in the

COOPER CO.
JANUARY

	Resources Used	Unused Resource Capacity	Resources Supplied	
Sales				$180,000
Sales				
Unit				
Materials	$ 30,000	$ -	$ 30,000	
Energy	10,000	-	10,000	
Short-term labor	3,500	500	4,000	
Outside contracts	6,000	-	6,000	
	$ 49,500	$ 500	$ 50,000	
Batch				
Setups	$ 14,000	$ 6,000	$ 20,000	
Quality inspection	8,500	1,500	10,000	
	$ 22,500	$ 7,500	$ 30,000	
Product and customer sustaining				
Parts management	$ 6,000	$ 1,000	$ 7,000	
Marketing	14,000	1,000	15,000	
Customer service	2,000	2,000	4,000	
Engineering changes	5,000	1,000	6,000	
	$ 27,000	$ 5,000	$ 32,000	
Capacity sustaining				
Long-term labor	$ 5,000	$ 2,000	$ 7,000	
Depreciation (buildings)	12,000	8,000	20,000	
Administrative	10,000	3,000	13,000	
	$ 27,000	$ 13,000	$ 40,000	
Total Costs	$126,000	$ 26,000	$152,000	
Operating Profit				$28,000

[a] This income statement was inspired by R. Cooper and R.S. Kaplan, "Activity-Based Systems: Measuring the Costs of Resource Usage," *Accounting Horizons* 6, no. 3 (1992), pp. 1–13.

EXHIBIT 6.15 ACTIVITY-BASED MANAGEMENT INCOME STATEMENT

income statement, Cooper spent $20,000 on setups. That represents 200 hours of setup capacity ($20,000/$100 per setup hour = 200 setup hours of available resource). However, operations used only 140 hours during the month ($14,000 resources used ÷ $100 cost driver rate = 140 hours of setup used). The report shows managers that $6,000 (or 60 hours) of unused setup resources are available.

All other things being equal, perhaps as much as 60 additional hours of setup could have been done in January without increasing expenditures. In reality, managers recognize the benefits of some unused resources. Having some unstructured time for ad hoc training, leisure, and thinking about ways to improve the work and work environment can prove useful for morale and productivity.

Note that some costs have more unused resources than others. The items listed under unit-related costs at the top of the report show little or no unused resources. These costs vary proportionately with output and often have little or no unused resources. Short-term labor, for example, is the cost of piecework labor or temporary help that is employed on an as-needed basis. Many of us have worked as short-term laborers during the summer in resorts, on farms, in forests fighting fires, or in retail stores or providing delivery services during the holidays.

Capacity-related costs have unused resources unless the company operates at full capacity. Long-term labor resources are the costs of employing people whom the firm does not lay off during temporary fluctuations in production.

6.16 IMPLEMENTING ADVANCED COST MANAGEMENT SYSTEMS

Accountants cannot implement activity-based management without becoming familiar with a company's operations. In identifying activities, accountants become part of a team with management and people from production, engineering, marketing, and other parts of the company who work to identify the activities that drive the company's costs. This often creates discomfort at first as accountants deal with unfamiliar areas, but in the long run, their familiarity with the company's operating activities can improve their contribution to it. Nonaccounting personnel also feel a greater sense of ownership of the numbers that the accounting system reports as accounting improves its credibility among nonaccountants.

To ensure success when implementing activity-based management, influential people in the organization must support the process. Accounting methods in companies resemble rules in sports; people become accustomed to playing by them and oppose change to something unknown. Employee resistance is the largest obstacle to implementing activity-based management.

For example, two analysts at one company spent several months and hundreds of hours of computer time developing an activity-based costing system. Their analysis revealed several hundred unprofitable products that the company should eliminate. However, the key managers who made product elimination decisions agreed to eliminate only about 20 products. Why? The analysts had failed to talk to these managers early in the process. When presented with the final results, the managers raised numerous objections that the analysts had not anticipated. The moral of this example: Anyone trying to make a change in a company or system should involve all of the people who are important to that change early in the process.

6.17 SUMMARY

This chapter discusses the allocation of indirect costs to products. Activity-based costing, one such method, assigns costs first to activities (discrete tasks that an organization undertakes to make or deliver a product) and then to the products based on each product's use of activities. Activity-based costing is based on the premise that products consume activities and activities consume resources. Activity-based costing involves four steps (discussed in Section 6.4).

Activity-based costing can help marketing and production personnel by providing detailed product cost information; it also helps management identify the processes that add value to the company. Implementing such a system can prove costly, however, and requires commitment from key decision makers.

Companies can use activity-based costing management to help manage activities that affect costs. One can group these activities and related costs into four categories: capacity related, product and customer related, batch related, and unit related. Companies can use such analyses to identify costly activities and manage them, identify nonvalue-added activities and eliminate them, and manage customer response time.

Companies can also use activity-based costing management to measure and minimize the difference between resources used and resources supplied. Management must try to match activities supplied to activities used to maximize efficiency.

CHAPTER 7

TARGET COSTING FOR NEW PRODUCT DEVELOPMENT*

ROBIN COOPER, DBA
Emory University

REGINE SLAGMULDER, PHD
INSEAD

CONTENTS

7.1 INTRODUCTION 243

7.2 MARKET-DRIVEN COSTING 245
- (a) Setting Long-Term Sales and Profit Objectives 246
- (b) Structuring the Product Mix 248
- (c) Setting the Target Selling Price 248
- (d) Establishing the Target Profit Margin 250
- (e) Computing the Allowable Cost 252

7.3 PRODUCT-LEVEL TARGET COSTING 253
- (a) Setting the Product-Level Target Cost 254
- (b) Designing the Product 256
- (c) Application of Disciplining Mechanisms of Product-Level Target Costing 257

7.4 COMPONENT-LEVEL TARGET COSTING 259
- (a) Selecting and Rewarding Suppliers 260
- (b) Setting the Target Costs of Major Functions 261
- (c) Setting the Target Costs of Components 265

7.5 SUMMARY 267

APPENDIX 7A TARGET COSTING EQUATIONS AND GLOSSARY 269

7.1 INTRODUCTION

Target costing is a structured approach to establish the cost at which a firm must manufacture a proposed product with specified functionality and quality to generate the desired profitability over its life-cycle at its anticipated selling price.[1] It is a tool of profit

---

* This chapter is based on material contained in *Target Costing and Value Engineering,* Robin Cooper and Regine Slagmulder, Portland, Ore.: Productivity Press; 1997.

1. Target costs should include any costs that are driven by the number of units sold. For example, if the firm accepts responsibility for disposing a product at the end of its useful life, the target cost would include these costs.

management as well as cost management. In Japan, where the lean enterprise[2] evolved, firms view target costing not as a stand-alone program, but as an integral part of their product development process. These firms have developed target costing to bring the competitive challenge of the marketplace to both the product designers and the firm's suppliers. When applied effectively, target costing creates a discipline that harmonizes the labor of disparate participants in the product development effort, from designers and manufacturing engineers to market researchers and suppliers.

At the heart of target costing lies a deceptively simple equation:

$$\text{Target cost} = \text{Target selling price} - \text{Target profit margin} \quad (1)$$

According to this equation, the firm need only select the price at which its future products will sell, subtract the required profit margin, and then design products so that it can manufacture them at their target costs. In fact, the process is more complicated than the equation suggests. First, before a firm can establish the target selling price, it must define the proposed product's quality and functionality. These product characteristics establish the value that the customers associate with the new product. Second, the firm must set the target profit margin so that the product will generate an adequate return on the up-front investment throughout its life. Before the firm can establish the target profit margin, however, it must estimate the product's sales volume. Thus, embedded into the target costing equation is an assumption about the proposed product's sales volume.

Target costing is the critical first step in managing product costs because once a firm locks in a product's design, many of the costs become immutable. For example, a product's design determines the number of components, the different materials used and the time required for assembly. Some authorities estimate that design drives as much as 90 to 95 percent of a product's costs–costs the firm cannot avoid without redesigning the product. Exhibit 7.1 shows that the level of committed costs increases as the design process advances with approximately 66 percent of costs committed at the end of the product planning stage, approximately 85 percent by the end of the preliminary design stage and approximately 95 percent by the end of the detailed design stage. Once a firm has

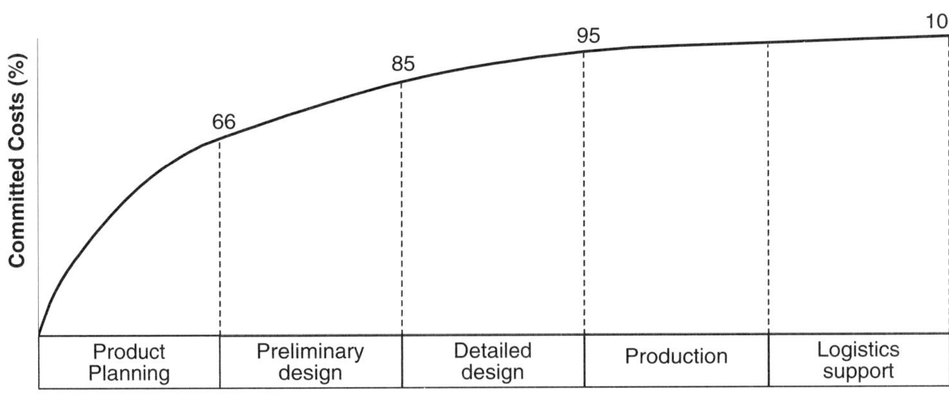

Source: Adapted from B.S. Blanchard, *Design and Manage to Life-Cycle Cost* (Portland, Ore.: Dilithium Press, 1978)

EXHIBIT 7.1 COMMITTED COSTS

2. Lean manufacturing is characterized by manufacturing a single part just-in-time for its incorporation into the product.

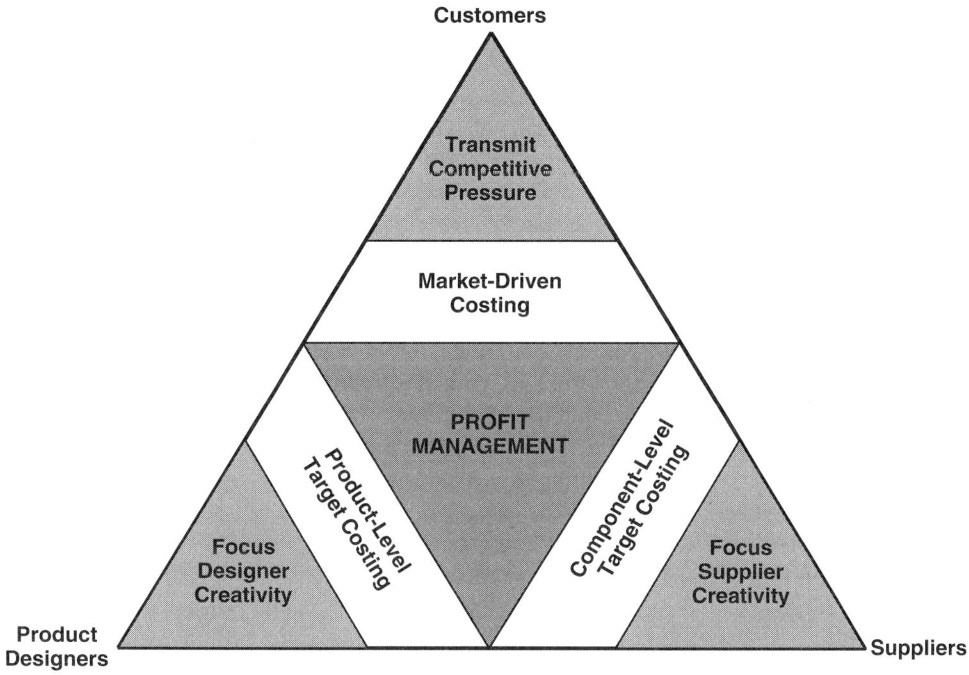

EXHIBIT 7.2 THE TARGET COSTING TRIANGLE

designed a product, it has little freedom to manage costs. Consequently, effective cost management programs must begin at the design and continue into the manufacturing phase of a product's life cycle.

Target costing's simple equation also masks the sophistication required to effectively use it. At many firms, the target costing process contains three major segments (see Exhibit 7.2).

- *Market-driven costing* identifies the allowable cost of the proposed products. It reflects the target selling price (driven by market conditions) and the firm's desired target profit margin, but ignores the cost management capabilities of the firm and its suppliers.
- *Product-level target costing* establishes the product's target cost that reflects more practical considerations (i.e., the firm and its suppliers' capabilities to affect cost) than does market-driven costing.
- *Component-level target costing* establishes the component-level target costs derived from product-level target costing.

We next discuss the elements of these three target costing segments and how they drive profit management.

7.2 MARKET-DRIVEN COSTING

The market-driven costing portion of target costing focuses on customers and their requirements and uses this information to transmit the competitive pressure to the product designers and suppliers (Exhibit 7.3).

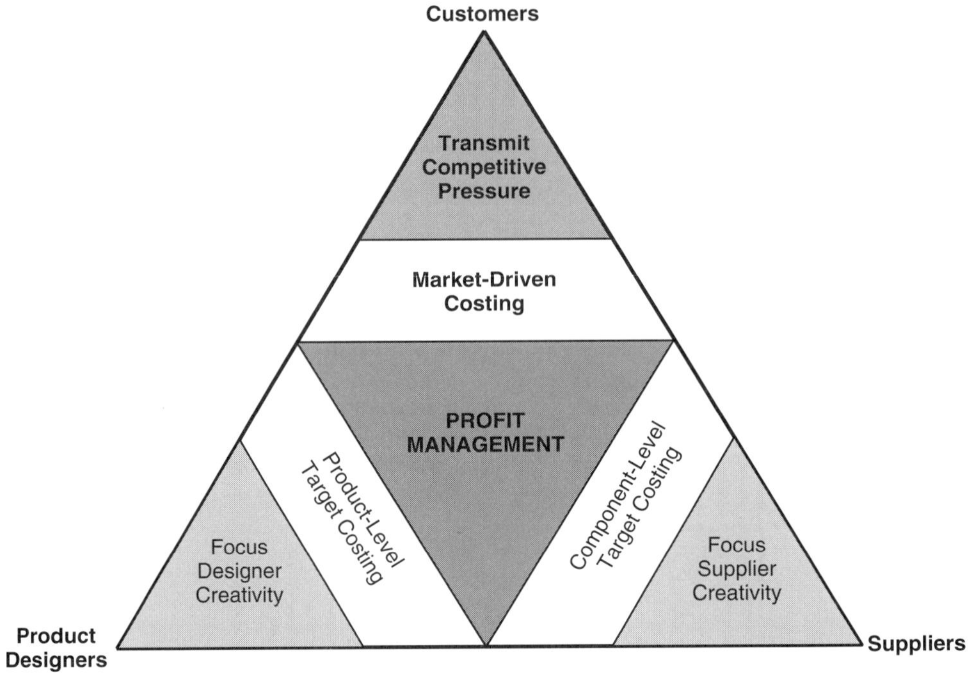

EXHIBIT 7.3 THE TARGET COSTING TRIANGLE: THE MARKET-DRIVEN COSTING STAGE

Market-driven costing consists of five major steps, illustrated in Exhibit 7.4. We list them here and offer an expanded explanation in the subsequent sections.

1. *Set long-term sales and profit objectives.* This step highlights the primary role of target costing as a technique for profit management.
2. *Structure the product mix to achieve maximum profitability.* This step highlights the importance of broad market analysis to effective target costing.
3. *Set the target selling price of the proposed product.* This step relies heavily on analysis of both customer and competitor behavior.
4. *Establish the target profit margin.* This step requires a life-cycle analysis of the product's profitability. This analysis should include the magnitude of the up-front investment, as well as estimates of the product's sales price, production costs and sales volumes over the product's life.
5. *Compute the allowable cost.* This step simply subtracts the target profit margin from the target selling price (Exhibit 7.5). The allowable cost is the product's theoretical target cost; the firm must manufacture the product at this cost to generate its target profit margin. As mentioned previously, it may not reflect a practical target cost, which is the function of product-level target costing, discussed in Section 7.3.

(a) SETTING LONG-TERM SALES AND PROFIT OBJECTIVES. Target costing begins with the firm's long-term sales and profit objectives. Target costing's primary objective is to ensure that, over its life, each product contributes its share of profits to the firm's

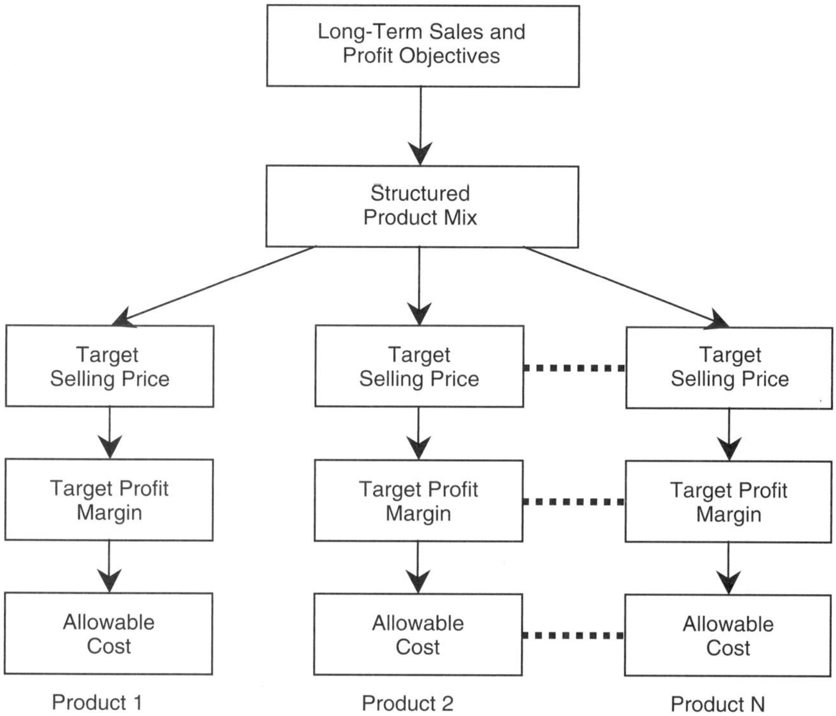

EXHIBIT 7.4 MAJOR STEPS OF MARKET-DRIVEN COSTING

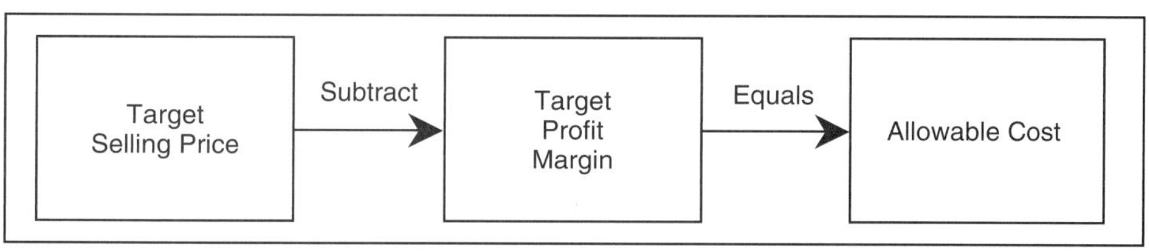

EXHIBIT 7.5 MARKET-DRIVEN COSTING

long-term profit objective. The credibility of the long-term plan becomes paramount in establishing the target costing discipline. The plan achieves credibility in three ways:

1. *It results from analysis of all relevant information that the firm collects.* The credibility of the analysis influences the degree of reliance that individuals in the firm place on the target costing process.
2. *The firm approves only realistic plans.* Whereas analysts may have a natural temptation to set optimistic sales and profit objectives, an effective target costing system must constrain optimism so that the firm approves only achievable long-term plans. If the firm approves unrealistic plans, the target sales volumes and profit margins will in turn reflect undue optimism. Experience has shown, however, that target costing proves effective only when the firm establishes realistic and achievable target costs.

3. *The firm should test the plan's robustness.* Plans that rely heavily on the success of a single product prove less robust than plans that rely on more moderate success of multiple products.

(b) STRUCTURING THE PRODUCT MIX. Products typically exist within the context of a product line. Any product's success comes from both its individual quality and functionality, and its relation to other products in the line. To ensure successful product lines, firms must first design them to satisfy diverse customer tastes without an unprofitably large number of different products. Too many products may confuse the firm's customers by giving them too many choices. Second, the product development costs become too high and the product line fails to achieve its profitability objectives.

Conversely, having too few products in the line can make customers dissatisfied with the firm's product offering, and they may purchase competitors' products. Consequently, structuring product lines reflects a cost–benefit trade-off. Only with well-designed product lines will every product sell sufficient volume to ensure that it remains profitable over its life cycle.[3]

Target costing helps discipline the structuring of product lines in two ways. First, it evaluates each product according to its ability to earn an adequate profit. If a proposed product cannot earn an adequate return, the target costing process includes an analysis of whether to launch the product. Second, it evaluates the proposed products' levels of quality and functionality to ensure that the firm can justify the costs of manufacturing at such levels. Target costing thus helps control undue increases in product functionality that product engineers may propose.

(c) SETTING THE TARGET SELLING PRICE. The target costing process requires that the firm establish a specific target selling price (Exhibit 7.6). A number of factors come into play when establishing the target selling price. These factors include the relative functionality and selling price of any competitive offerings that the firm anticipates will be available when it launches its new product. If the firm expects that the competitive offerings will have differing functionality and price than the proposed product, then its target selling price will have to take these differences into account. The target selling price should also reflect the firm's strategic objectives for the new product. The firm also needs to consider other factors, such as the desired market share for the new product and impact that the new product might have on corporate image. If the firm wants to aggressively pursue target market share, then the firm might have to lower the target selling price to make the new product more attractive on launching. Similarly, if the product plays an important role in establishing a corporate image (such as the Coca-Cola score boards in high school gyms), the firm might lower the price to make the new product more attractive. Finally, the selling price needs to reflect the perceived value that the customers associate with the product and their loyalty to the firm. The higher the perceived value or the higher the loyalty to the firm, the higher the potential selling price.

Since the target costing formula (equation 1 in Section 7.1) uses a single target selling price, when firms sell the same product at different prices—for example, in different countries—they must use a weighted average selling price.[4] Similarly, if the firm anticipates changing the selling price across the product's life, then it adopts the anticipated

3. The only exceptions should be strategic products designed to create a corporate image.

4. The weighted average would be computed by summing the product of each selling price and its associated volume, and then dividing by the total volume expected to be sold.

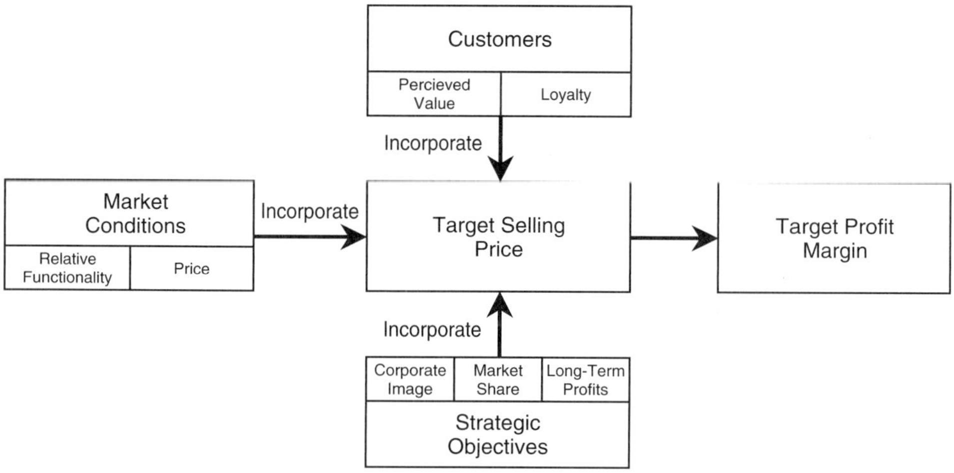

EXHIBIT 7.6 SETTING THE TARGET SELLING PRICE

selling price at launch. The firm uses the launch selling price rather than an estimated average price across the life of the product because of the high degree of uncertainty about that average and the ability to reduce costs through *kaizen* costing and other activities.[5]

Most firms work hard to set a realistic target selling price. Target selling prices reflect the market conditions that the firms anticipate at the product's launch date. Internal market factors include the position of the model in the firm's product line and management's strategic and profitability objectives for that model. External market factors include the corporation's image and level of customer loyalty, the product's expected quality level and functionality compared to competitive offerings, the product's expected market share, and, finally, the expected price of competitive products.

(i) Customers: Perceived Value and Loyalty. Perceived value lies at the heart of the price setting process. Customers will pay more for a product than they did for its predecessor only if they perceive an increase in value. Rather than undertake the analysis *de novo*, many firms take an incremental approach. They start with the predecessor product's actual selling price and adjust it accordingly, based on incremental perceived value. They then calculate the selling price of a new model as the selling price of the equivalent existing model plus any incremental value attributable to improved functionality. For example, adding air conditioning to an automobile's standard version will increase its price by the perceived value of air conditioning. To assess this incremental value of a new model, the firm must analyze market conditions. In a mature industry, such as the automobile industry, most new features already exist in some form on other models. For example, if the standard version will include air conditioning, the firm can evaluate its added value using the list price of optional air conditioners for other models. If no equivalent option existed—a rare event—then the firm's design engineers and market specialists estimate how much customers will pay for the added feature.

(ii) Competitive Offerings: Functionality/Price Tradeoff. The firm examines the interaction between functionality and price during the market-driven costing process. It considers

5. See Chapter 8, "Kaizen Costing for Existing Products."

perceived value when setting the product's functionality, and the product's functionality when setting prices. The firm aims to design a product that will sell at its target price and achieve the desired sales volume while generating its target profit margin. Thus, the availability of competitive products and their perceived value temper the price increases associated with incremental perceived value. Selling prices can increase only if the new product's perceived value not only exceeds that of the product's predecessor but also that of competing products.

The complexity of the task that the firm faces in setting target selling prices depends primarily on the similarity or difference between product generations. This becomes particularly difficult for a product that has no direct predecessor. In contrast, the task becomes relatively simple when the new products resemble those they will replace.

Some industries have little latitude for setting prices because the industry competes at defined price points. For example, a relatively simple point-and-shoot camera might sell in retail stores for $49.99, and the next model might sell for $59.99. Essentially, no cameras sell between these two prices in retail camera stores. Therefore, the firm must simply identify at which price the product will sell. Sometimes the product's specific or distinctive functionality establishes the price. For example, a camera's distinctive feature (e.g., the magnification capability of the zoom lens or the camera's small size) establishes its price. The competitive analysis and technology review used in developing the product plan drives the relation between distinctive features and prices. The product plan thus describes cameras only in terms of their distinctive feature. Product designers may add other features as the camera design nears completion.

In some markets, such as that for cameras, the price/functionality trade-off changes over time and the price for a given level of functionality falls. The reduced cost of camera technology allows the functionality of the camera sold at a given price to improve over time. Therefore, the functionality that previously defined the $59.99 price is now available at the $49.99 price. Such firms face the challenge of introducing new levels of functionality to maintain the high prices, while simultaneously decreasing the costs of existing levels of functionality sufficiently to generate adequate profits as prices fall. For example, the price at which a camera with given functionality sells tends to decrease over time with improvements in technology. Manufacturers typically hold prices constant for as long as possible by adding functionality to the cameras offered—for example, by adding a quartz date/day feature. Typically, a manufacturer introduces a given camera model at one price. The camera stays at that price for several years but with increasing functionality. Eventually, there is no incremental functionality that the firm can add so it simplifies the next generation of that distinctive functionality and issues it at the next lower price point. This process generates new price points at the low end. For example, the price point for the simplest compact camera was $150 in 1987 and $100 in 1990. The lowest price point by 2004 was down to $60.

Setting target selling prices requires analysis of how the customer perceives value and how competitive offerings deliver value. Given the importance of the target selling price to the target costing process, most firms aim to maximize the realism of their assumptions regarding target selling prices.

(d) ESTABLISHING THE TARGET PROFIT MARGIN. Firms set target profit margins at levels that will ensure that they can achieve their long-term profit plan, as Exhibit 7.7 illustrates. Responsibility for achieving the overall profit target typically rests with the division responsible for the product line. The division needs to set realistic target profit margins that will also prove sufficient to offset the product's life-cycle costs.

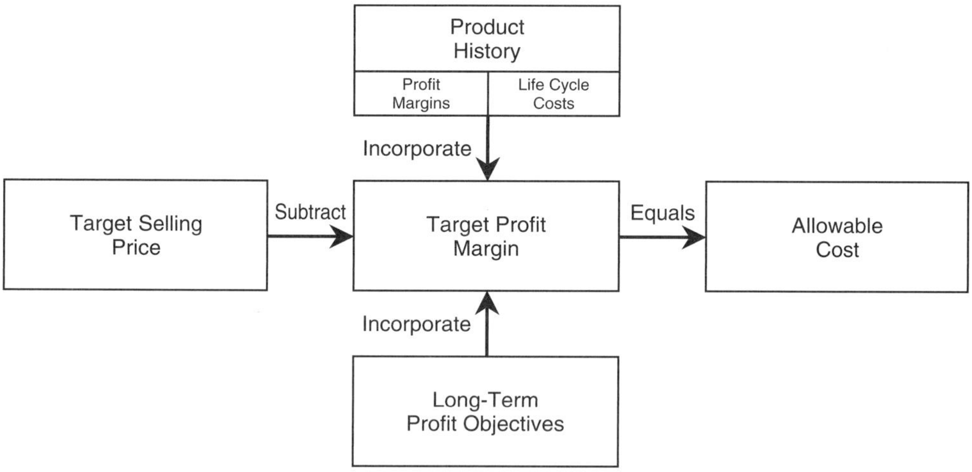

EXHIBIT 7.7 SETTING THE TARGET PROFIT MARGIN

(i) Setting Realistic Target Profit Margins. Firms can use one of two methods to set target profit margins. The first method starts with the actual profit margin of the predecessor product and then adjusts it for changes in market conditions. The other method starts with the target profit margin of the product line (or other grouping of products) and adjusts the target profit margin for each product based on the realities of the market place. The choice between the two approaches depends on several factors, including the diversity in the products. Firms often apply the second approach when the product line has similar products. As product diversity increases, the first approach typically dominates because the profit level of one product less well predicts the profitability of other products in the line.

The firm bases the target profit margin on historical profit levels (either of the individual product or its product line), the relative strength of competitive offerings, and its long-term profit objective. If the firm perceives the profit objective as unrealistic, it should reduce the target profit margin and thus increase the allowable cost. Setting target profit margins in this manner causes the allowable costs to reflect the firm's competitive position. An efficient firm will set target profit margins that exceed those of less efficient firms and hence have lower allowable costs for products selling at the same price. Similarly, a firm that has products with higher functionality than its competitors will typically have higher profit margins because it can sell its products at a premium price.

(ii) Adjusting the Target Profit Margin for Life Cycle Costs. To make target costing operational, the firm sets the target cost of a new product at the cost level that the firm expects the product to reach some time after product launch (this time period is often three months). It does not set it at the time of product launch because the production process needs time to settle down and the higher costs encountered directly after launch do not indicate the product's long-term manufacturing cost. The firm has to adjust target profit margins when products require high investments to launch, when the firm discontinues products, or when it expects selling prices and costs to change significantly during the products' lives. A firm would expect a product that requires higher up-front investment to generate higher margins than one that does not, *ceteris paribus.* These adjustments ensure that the product's expected profitability across its life will prove adequate.

If the firm decides that the product will make a satisfactory contribution throughout its life cycle, the conceptual design process will continue. An evaluation of unsatisfactory profit margins will induce the firm to redesign the product. When the product has a long development cycle, the firm may use multiple life-cycle analyses. Typically, the firm performs such life-cycle analyses at each major design step to ensure that the product will support the firm's profit objectives. Toward the end of the conceptual design stage, the firm often conducts a major review of the new product. This review includes an updated profitability study and an analysis of the model's performance characteristics. In the profitability study, the firm compares the product's expected profitability (i.e., target price minus target cost) to the latest estimates of the capital investment and remaining research and development expenditures required to complete the product's design and begin production.

Firms that can substantially reduce the cost of their products during the manufacturing stage use a different life cycle analysis. This analysis reflects any anticipated savings in production costs during the manufacturing phase in the target costing profitability analysis. Consequently, a firm will use a lower initial target profit margin for a product whose costs it expects to fall more rapidly than the selling price, and a higher initial margin for a product whose costs it does not expect to fall as fast as the selling price, *ceteris paribus*. Thus, the life-cycle adjustment ensures that the analysis considers all costs and savings when setting the target profit margin. Without such adjustments, the firm risks either launching products that do not earn an adequate return or not launching products that, over their lives, will earn an adequate return.

(e) COMPUTING THE ALLOWABLE COST. Once the firm has established the target selling price and profit margin, it can calculate the allowable cost using the following formula:

$$\text{Allowable cost} = \text{Target selling price} - \text{Target profit margin} \quad (2)$$

The allowable cost reflects the firm's competitive position. In competitive environments, efficient firms will have higher target profit margins and, hence, lower allowable costs than their less-efficient competitors. Consequently, to use allowable costs as a benchmark, the firm must set target profit margins that reflect the capabilities of the most efficient competitor. Such margins give benchmark profits, not the firm's lower, realistic long-term profit objectives. Firms at a significant competitive disadvantage will benefit most from estimating benchmark costs and calculating the difference between them and allowable costs. If the firm faces a significant disadvantage, it might not be possible to reach the benchmark costs in a single generation of product design. Such firms will have to adopt a multigenerational strategy of product design, setting ever more aggressive targets for each generation. The narrowing gap between the benchmark and allowable costs would monitor the achievement of competitive parity.

Thus, the allowable cost represents the cost at which, according to top management, the firm must manufacture the product to achieve the target profit margin when it sells the product at its target price. To all involved in the target costing process, the allowable cost signals the magnitude of the cost-reduction objective that the firm must eventually achieve. The allowable cost, however, reflects only the market's demands and the firm's profit requirements. It does not reflect the actual capabilities of the firm and its suppliers. Product-level target costing will incorporate those capabilities into the target cost, as explained next.

7.3 PRODUCT-LEVEL TARGET COSTING

Once the firm has calculated the allowable cost—the cost level that matches the firm's prices with its desired profit margin—it needs to decide whether or how it will achieve the allowable cost level. Product-level target costing provides such a method. Firms use product-level target costing to establish aggressive but achievable product-level target costs. These target costs should press the firm's product engineers to find ways to reduce the manufacturing costs of the products they design. Target costs differ from allowable costs because they incorporate the capabilities of the firm and its suppliers into the target costing process. In practice, the designers cannot always find ways to achieve the allowable cost and still satisfy the firm's customers; consequently, product-level target costing increases the product's allowable cost to a level that the firm can reasonably expect to achieve, given its capabilities and those of its suppliers (see Exhibit 7.8).

Product-level target costing consists of three major steps (see Exhibit 7.9). We list them here and provide an expanded explanation in the subsequent sections.

1. *Set the product-level target cost.* This step incorporates the capability of the firm and its suppliers into the allowable cost to establish an achievable product-level target cost.
2. *Design the product* so that the firm can manufacture it at its target cost. Achieving the target costs in most competitive settings requires considerable engineering. This engineering needs to take customer expectations into account, as well as cost.
3. *Apply the disciplining mechanisms of target costing* to ensure that the firm achieves the product-level target cost. These mechanisms include progress monitoring and validation and application of the cardinal rule of target costing.

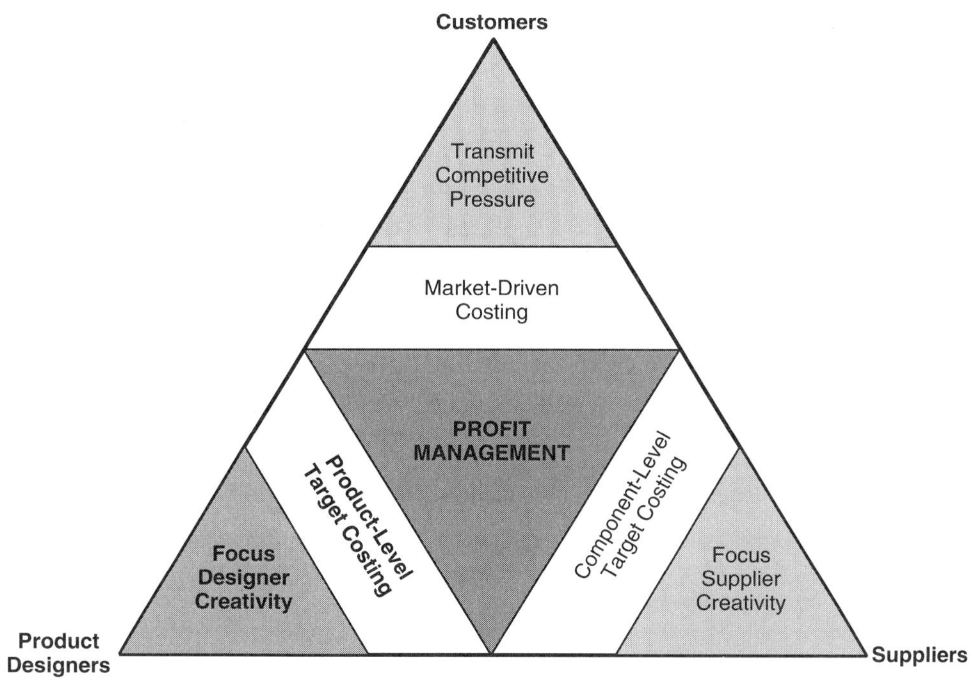

EXHIBIT 7.8 THE TARGET COSTING TRIANGLE: THE PRODUCT-LEVEL TARGET COSTING STAGE

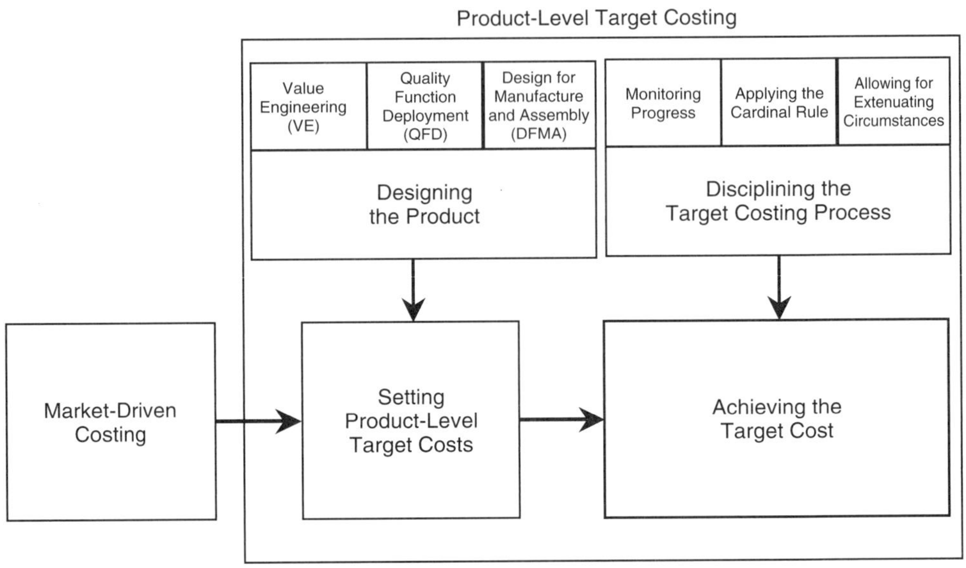

EXHIBIT 7.9 PRODUCT-LEVEL TARGET COSTING

The monitoring and validation process helps ensure that the firm achieves savings identified through value engineering. Application of the cardinal rule of target costing—namely, "Do not launch a product above its target cost"—maintains the discipline of target costing. If the designers know that violating the target cost does not lead to serious consequences, they feel less pressure to achieve the target costs.

(a) SETTING THE PRODUCT-LEVEL TARGET COST. In competitive markets, customers expect each generation of products to provide more value per dollar of price than do its predecessors. The firm can increase value by improving the quality or functionality of the products, or by reducing its prices, or by a combination of both actions. Any of these improvements or some combination thereof requires that the firm reduce costs to maintain its profitability. The cost reduction required to achieve the allowable cost is called the *cost-reduction objective,* calculated by the following formula:

$$\text{Cost-reduction objective} = \text{Current cost} - \text{Allowable cost} \quad (3)$$

Current cost is the cost of a proposed product if it were manufactured today using existing components or variants thereof. When computing the product's current cost, firms do not assume any future cost-reduction activities. To calculate a meaningful current cost, the components used in its estimation have to closely resemble those that the firm will eventually use in the proposed product. For example, if the existing model uses a 1.8 liter engine and the proposed model uses a 2.0 liter engine, the current cost should reflect the cost of the most similar 2.0 liter engine the firm produces or purchases.

Since the allowable cost reflects the market's demand rather than the firm's design and production capabilities, the firm runs the risk of not achieving the allowable cost. To maintain the discipline of target costing, the firm has to identify the achievable and the unachievable part of the cost-reduction objective. Analyzing the ability of the product designers and suppliers to remove costs from the product drives the achievable or target

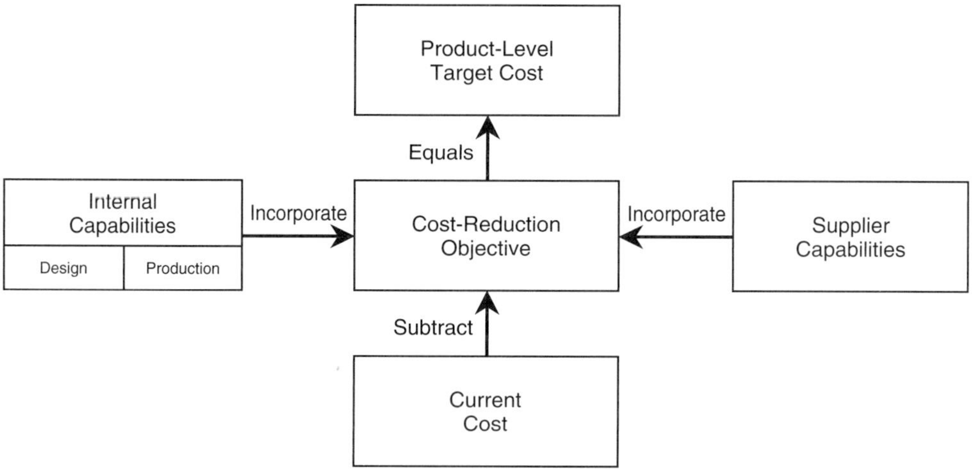

EXHIBIT 7.10 SETTING THE TARGET COST REDUCTION OBJECTIVE

cost-reduction objective. Thus, the target cost reduction objective reflects the internal capabilities of the firm's engineers to design and produce the internally manufactured items in the new product at a lower cost and of its suppliers to provide externally sourced items at a lower cost (see Exhibit 7.10).

The unachievable part of the cost-reduction objective is the *strategic cost-reduction challenge*. That is:

$$\text{Strategic cost-reduction challenge} = \text{Cost-reduction objective} - \text{Target cost reduction objective} \quad (4)$$

It identifies the profit shortfall that will occur because the designers cannot achieve the allowable cost, and it signals that the firm falls short of the efficiency demanded by competitive conditions. A firm with a well-established target costing system will achieve all or almost all of its cost reduction objective and will pressure its design team to ensure that the strategic cost-reduction challenge reaches or remains at zero.

For the most efficient firms, the achievable cost reduction for a product might exceed the cost-reduction objective. Such firms do not face a strategic cost-reduction challenge. They can take advantage of their superior efficiency either to increase market share by reducing the product's selling price or increasing its functionality while keeping the price constant or to increase profits by keeping both the price and functionality at their targeted levels.

To maintain the discipline of target costing, the firm must manage the size of the strategic cost-reduction challenge so that it reflects the firm's inability to match its competitors' efficiency. To ensure that the strategic cost-reduction challenge meets this requirement, management must set the target cost-reduction objective so that the firm can achieve the objective only if the entire organization makes a significant effort to reach it. If management consistently sets the target cost-reduction objective too high, the workforce will face excessive cost-reduction objectives, risking burn-out, and the firm will lose the discipline of target costing as it frequently exceeds target costs. If management sets the target cost-reduction objective too low, the firm will lose competitiveness because new products will have excessively high target costs.

The firm calculates the product-level target cost by subtracting the proposed product's target cost-reduction objective from its current cost:

$$\text{Product-level target cost} = \text{Current cost} - \text{Target cost-reduction objective} \quad (5)$$

The firm measures the strategic cost-reduction challenge by subtracting the allowable cost from the target cost

$$\text{Strategic cost-reduction challenge} = \text{Target cost} - \text{Allowable cost} \quad (6)$$

Note that this means that the firm can calculate the product-level target cost by adding back the strategic cost reduction challenge to the allowable cost

$$\text{Product-level target cost} = \text{Allowable cost} + \text{Strategic cost-reduction challenge} \quad (7)$$

Differentiating between the allowable cost and the target cost creates discipline in cost-control efforts. Most firms will—at some time—face an allowable cost too low to achieve, given the capabilities of the firm and its suppliers. Target costing systems derive their strength from the cardinal rule: Never allow manufacturing costs to exceed target costs.

The distinction between allowable and product-level target costs thus plays two roles. First, it identifies the strategic cost-reduction challenge, which pressures the design team of the product's next generation to become even more aggressive about cost reduction. In this way, the failure to achieve the allowable cost for the current product becomes a challenge for the future, not a current defeat. Second, it avoids weakening the cardinal rule, which applies only to target costs (which management can set), not allowable costs (which management cannot set). The firm must have a disciplined process to establish the strategic cost-reduction challenge. Otherwise, target costs will be too easy to achieve, thereby reducing the effectiveness of target costing. In most firms, top management approves the strategic cost-reduction challenge before the chief engineer sets the product-level target cost.

Technically, a product's target cost equals the target selling price, less the target profit margin, plus the strategic cost-reduction challenge. Many firms blur the distinction between the allowable cost and the target cost by stating that the target cost equals the target profit margin minus the target selling price, as we did in equation 1 in Section 7.1. This simplification helps people understand the price-driven nature of target costing. Obviously, if the strategic cost-reduction challenge equals zero, the allowable and target costs are identical.

(b) DESIGNING THE PRODUCT. Once planners have identified the target cost-reduction objective, product designers work toward achieving it. In this second stage of product-level target costing, several engineering techniques can help product designers reduce product costs (Exhibit 7.9). They include value engineering (VE),[6] design for manufacture and assembly (DFMA),[7] and quality function deployment

6. Value engineering can be defined as an organized methodology that identifies and selects the lowest life-cycle cost options in design, materials and processes that achieves the desired level of performance, reliability and customer satisfaction. It seeks to eliminate unnecessary costs in the above areas and is often a joint effort with cross-functional internal teams and relevant suppliers.

7. DFMA includes activities such as product simplification, should costing (should costing establishes a benchmark for what the product "should cost." Central to the should costing approach is accumulating real information about manufacturing costs), and supplier bid verification.

(QFD).[8] Value engineering, the most important of the three techniques, has the primary objective of maximizing customer value—it focuses on increasing functionality and quality while reducing cost. In contrast, DFMA focuses on reducing costs by making products easier to assemble or manufacture, while holding functionality at specified levels. Finally, QFD provides a structured approach to ensure that the design process does not compromise customer requirements.

Value engineering begins with the product's conceptualization and continues through the design process until the product advances to manufacturing. Even then the process continues, but under the name *value analysis (VA)*. VA and VE differ not in the approach taken or the tools used but the point at which they occur in the product's life cycle. In particular, the functionality of the product is considered a variable under VE, but is a constant under VA. The firm uses VE during the product design and development stages, and VA during the manufacturing stage and when purchasing parts. For this reason, target costing and value engineering become concurrent activities, as do *kaizen*[9] costing and value analysis.

One should not view VE as just another cost-reduction program. VE focuses primarily on product functions and only secondarily on cost. Firms use VE to ensure that the product achieves its basic function in a way that satisfies the customer at an acceptable cost. Consequently, VE programs occur in the product engineer's domain, not that of the accountant.

(c) APPLICATION OF DISCIPLINING MECHANISMS OF PRODUCT-LEVEL TARGET COSTING. Disciplining the product-level target costing process begins with monitoring and validating the progress of the design engineers toward reaching the cost-reduction objective. It continues to apply the cardinal rule of target costing: Never launch a product above its target cost. Sometimes the firm has to apply the rule in a more sophisticated way than the conventional, single-product perspective. When one product leads to increased sales of other products, the firm must adopt a multiproduct perspective; when it will lead to sales of future generations of products, the analysis requires a multigenerational perspective. The firm can violate the target cost rule only when getting the product to market becomes so imperative that cost merits secondary consideration. Finally, when the firm releases the product for mass production and can measure the actual cost of manufacturing, it may need to reduce those costs to the target level.

Once the firm has established the target cost-reduction objective, it can begin designing the product so that manufacturing will meet the target cost. The discipline of target costing requires that the chief engineer and his superiors continuously monitor and validate the progress the design engineers make toward this objective. This monitoring ensures that the designers can take corrective actions and that manufacturing costs will not violate the target cost rule.

Some firms specify an *as-if cost* at this point in the development process. The as-if cost reflects cost-reduction opportunities identified when the firm was designing or

8. QFD is a structured method that employs matrix analysis to link the market requirements with the development efforts that they dictate. This method is most valuable during the stage of development when a multifunctional team agrees on how customer needs relate to product specifications and features which deliver those. By explicitly linking these aspects of product design, QFD limits the chance of omitting important design characteristics or interactions across design characteristics. QFD is also an important mechanism in promoting multifunctional teamwork.
9. *Kaizen* is the Japanese term for continuous improvement. We refer the reader to Chapter 8, "Kaizen Costing for Existing Products."

manufacturing the product's previous generation. It is the cost at which the firm could manufacture the product if it did so today. The as-if cost usually exceeds the target cost of the new product. Therefore, the additional cost reduction that the firm must achieve equals the difference between the target cost and the as-if cost.

As the design process reduces costs of the major functions,[10] the estimated manufacturing cost gradually falls toward the target cost. Many firms call the updated estimate the *drifting cost.* Exhibit 7.11 shows the relation among current cost, as-if cost, drifting cost, target cost, and target cost reduction objective. Thus, the product design process starts with a current cost higher than the target cost, and across the design process reduces the expected or drifting cost until it reaches the target cost. At most firms, once the drifting cost equals the target cost, cost-reduction activities cease. The firm will reap no reward for achieving greater savings than those required to achieve the target cost. The engineers should instead devote efforts toward decreasing the drifting cost of other products to equal their target costs.

The firm will continue to compare the drifting cost to the target cost throughout the design process. For example, product designers often make a final review of the target cost's feasibility just before releasing the product to production. If the estimated production cost exceeds the target cost, designers will need to undertake additional analyses. Frequently, they need to make only relatively minor changes in the product's design to reduce the cost estimate to the target cost level. As long as these changes do not alter the product's selling price, then the design engineers decide to reduce the product's functionality (thereby reducing cost) and submit the product for approval. If the design changes will reduce the selling price, the research and development group typically redesigns the product.

For products that feature various options, the firm makes small adjustments to the target cost by specifying the features that the standard product will contain. For example, faced with excessive manufacturing cost, design engineers might convert one or more standard features to options for which the customer now has to pay. Converting features

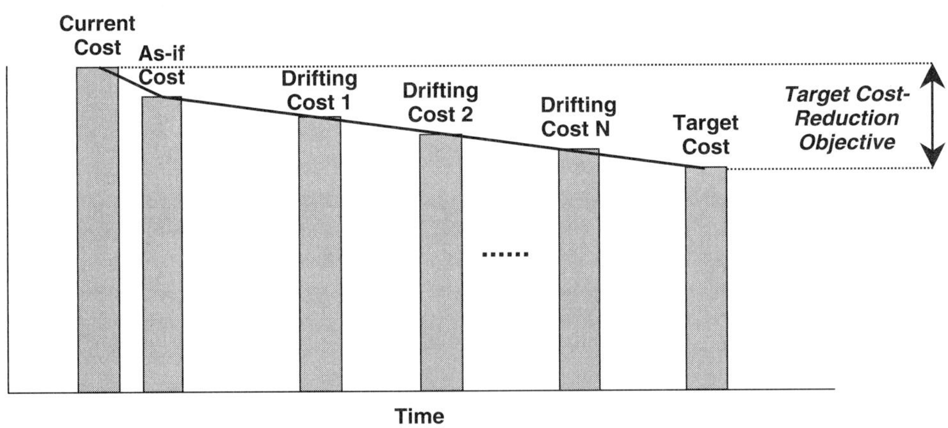

EXHIBIT 7.11 ACHIEVING THE TARGET COST

10. Major functions are the subassemblies that perform a critical function that supports the product in its ability to perform its primary function. For example, an engine cooling system is a major function of an automobile. The engine cooling system performs a major function, keeping the engine cool and hence running so the automobile can achieve its primary function—transporting people.

to options both reduces the cost of manufacturing the standard product, allowing the firm to achieve target cost, and increases the selling price of the originally specified product, allowing the firm to achieve target profit.

The firm should use market analysis to ensure that the customers will accept the reduction in the standard model's functionality. For example, the firm might convert the side-impact air bags from a standard feature to an optional one. Customers will accept this reduction in functionality as long as competitive offerings treat the side-impact air bags in the same way. This fine-tuning process allows firms more leeway to achieve target costs set several years in advance. Similarly, the firm does not fix actual selling price until just before it launches the product. Delaying these two critical decisions significantly reduces the uncertainty that a firm faces in a multiyear product development process.

The cardinal rule (abandon a product if manufacturing costs exceed target costs) plays an important role in maintaining the discipline of target costing. Engineers ensure that the sum of the component target costs does not exceed the product's target cost. Often, an increase in the cost of one component causes the engineers to explore ways to reduce the costs of other components by an equivalent amount. In addition, to help ensure enforcement of the cardinal rule, most firms have a policy against launching unprofitable products. After completing the design phase, the product moves to manufacturing. As part of this transition phase, the firm compares the target cost to the standard cost of production. If the analysis shows excessive standard cost, the firm usually takes steps to reduce manufacturing costs to the target level. If the standard cost lies at or below the target cost, the design engineers freeze the product's design for the rest of its life and the firm takes no further actions, other than general *kaizen* costing (see Chapter 8), to reduce the cost of the new product.

As with any rule, firms occasionally violate the cardinal rule. This occurs when a broader analysis indicates that doing so will benefit the firm. Target costing, by its nature, takes a single-product orientation. Sometimes this view proves too restrictive because the product may generate revenues beyond that attributed directly to sales of that product. Such products include flagship products that create high visibility for the firm, products that introduce the next generation of technology, or products that fill a critical gap in the product line. For such products, the firm often relaxes the target cost rule to allow for the hidden revenues. Typically, however, the firm continues to apply cost-reduction pressures during the early stages of manufacturing until it achieves the target cost.

7.4 COMPONENT-LEVEL TARGET COSTING

We now come to the third and final stage of the target costing process, component-level target costing (see Exhibit 7.12). This stage decomposes the product-level target cost to the component level. The component-level target costs identify the firm's acceptable cost for the components that it purchases. Thus, component-level target costing sets the selling prices of the components manufactured by the firm's suppliers and forces suppliers to design components at low cost. It uses interorganizational costing to achieve this objective by opening new communication channels among suppliers, customers, and product designers. (Chapter 9 discusses interorganizational costing.)

Component-level target costing consists of three major steps, illustrated in Exhibit 7.13. We list them here and offer an expanded explanation in the subsequent sections.

1. Select and reward suppliers.
2. Set the target costs of major functions.
3. Set the target costs of components.

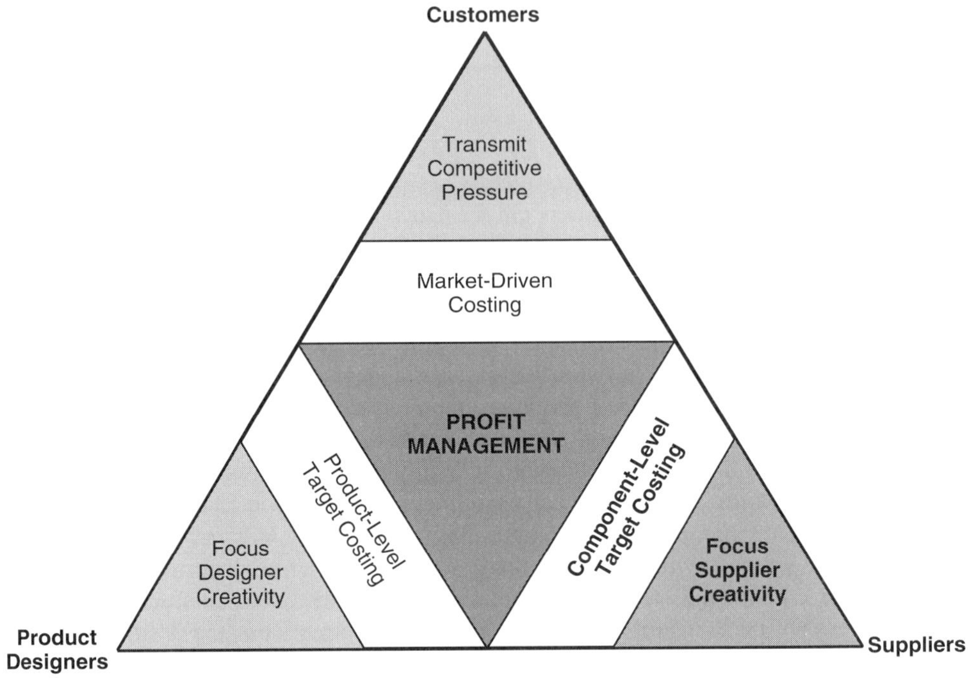

EXHIBIT 7.12 THE TARGET COSTING TRIANGLE: THE COMPONENT-LEVEL TARGET COSTING STAGE

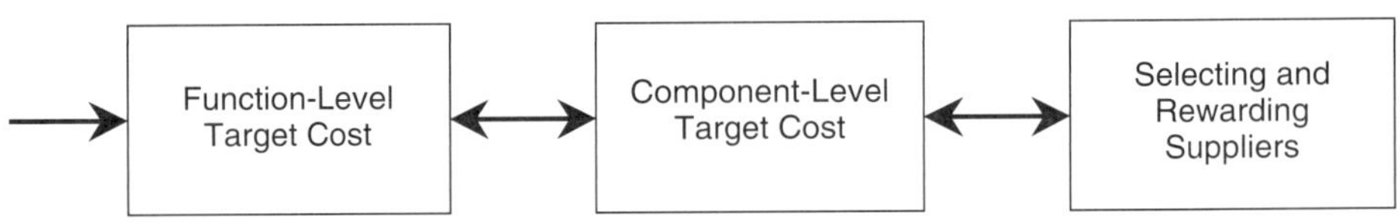

EXHIBIT 7.13 COMPONENT-LEVEL TARGET COSTING

(a) SELECTING AND REWARDING SUPPLIERS. The firm uses two sets of criteria to select suppliers. The first set of criteria deals with selecting the suppliers that will make up the firm's supplier base and the second set deals with rewarding individual suppliers for superior performance (see Exhibit 7.14).

The supplier-base objectives include maintaining supplier relations, extending the supplier base, and inducing supplier creativity. When a long-term supplier fails to make the lowest bid or develop the most innovative solution, the firm may still award it part of the contract. In this situation, the firm wants to create a stable buyer-supplier relation. (See also Chapter 9.) To increase the rate of innovation and enable the firm to adopt new technologies and production processes, the firm must continuously look for new suppliers. The firm needs to identify creative and innovative suppliers or suppliers that have developed considerable expertise in technologies that the firm wants to incorporate in its products. Finally, the firm uses contracts to reward suppliers for their innovations.

The firm rewards suppliers based on three major criteria: the competitiveness of their bids, their reputation, and the degree of innovation they have brought to the component.

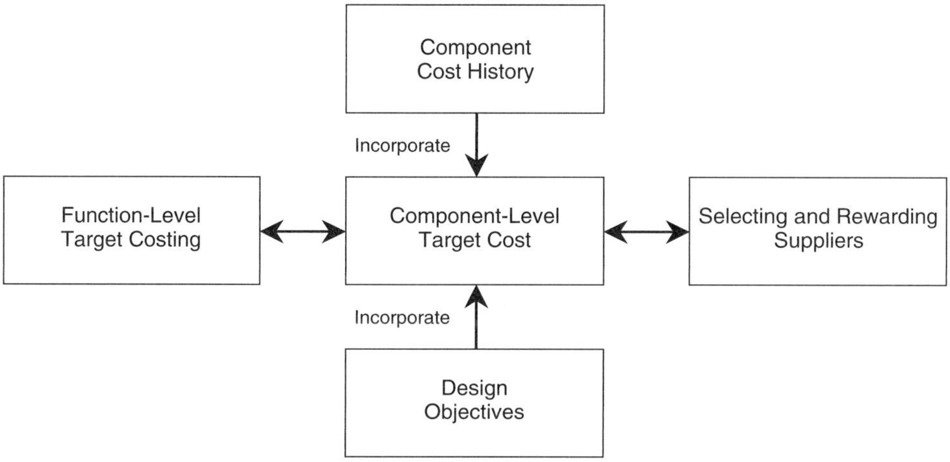

EXHIBIT 7.14 SETTING THE TARGET COSTS OF COMPONENTS

The firm collects the bids as early as possible in the target costing process and incorporates them through an iterative process into the component-level target costs. This process ensures that the firm can achieve individual component-level target costs that sum to the product's component-level target cost.

Supplier reputation for innovation influences the firm's willingness to accept slightly higher prices or lower levels of innovation for a particular order and still grant some of the business. The firm should retain innovative suppliers in the supplier base. For example, although the supplier rated with the highest value generally will win an order, firms will award at least part of that order to reputed good suppliers even if the suppliers' products do not have the highest value.

For a given component, the degree of innovation that the supplier introduces influences the value that the firm associates with the component. The higher the degree of innovation, the higher the value, all else being equal. Since the firm wants to reward innovation, it will typically select the most innovative design.

(b) SETTING THE TARGET COSTS OF MAJOR FUNCTIONS. Once the firm has established a product's target cost, it begins to disaggregate it to identify the target costs of the components that it contains. This process begins with developing target costs for the product's major functions and continues with developing component-level target costs. These steps enable the firm to achieve the second objective of target costing: transmitting the competitive cost pressure that the firm faces to its suppliers. This objective becomes critical in lean enterprises,[11] which have horizontal rather than vertical integration. Such firms purchase a significant portion of the parts and materials required to manufacture their products from external instead of internal suppliers. Thus, the horizontal integration that gives lean enterprises their flexibility and responsiveness creates a heavy reliance on suppliers. Target costing provides a powerful mechanism to discipline suppliers by allowing the firm to set the selling prices of the suppliers' products. With

11. Lean manufacturing is characterized by manufacturing a single part at a time just-in-time for its incorporation into the product (see Chapter 9.)

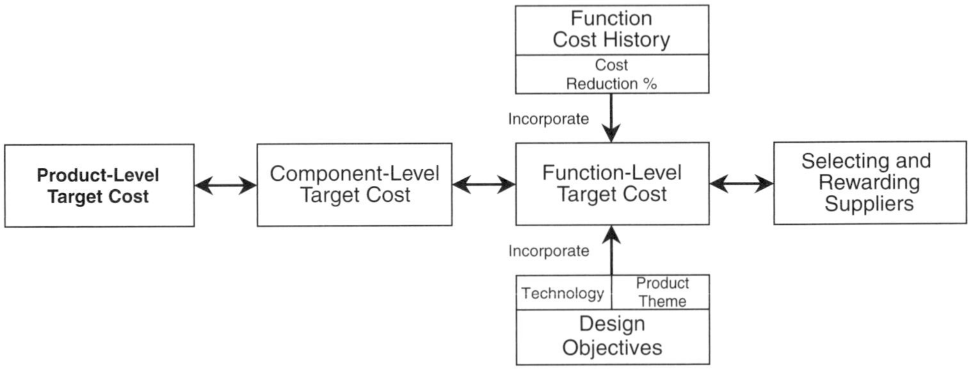

EXHIBIT 7.15 SETTING THE TARGET COSTS OF MAJOR FUNCTIONS

complex products,[12] the firm often sets target costs for externally acquired components by first establishing the target costs of the major functions and then, in a separate step, of the components they contain. Major functions are the subassemblies that provide the functionality that enables the product to achieve its purpose.

The process of establishing function-level target costs takes into account two major factors: the cost history of the major function and the design objectives for the product (Exhibit 7.15). The cost history of the function captures the historical rate at which the firm has reduced the cost of the major function. The firm uses this historical rate as the basis for estimating the likely cost reduction that it will achieve for the next generation. It adjusts the historical rate for the design objectives of the new product. For example, the new product might require a higher capacity engine cooling system (because the product theme was "A more powerful driving experience"), and, hence, the function-level target cost should increase compared with the previous generation (after allowing for the historical cost reduction rate). Alternatively, the firm might adopt a new technology, such as the shift from copper/brass radiators to aluminum, which would invalidate all historical cost information. Consequently, the firm should use the rate for aluminum radiators instead of the function cost history of copper/brass radiators.

Identifying major functions allows the engineers to organize the design process in multiple, somewhat independent tasks. Typically, a dedicated team has responsibility for the design of each major function. Design teams usually include representatives from a number of disciplines such as product design, engineering, purchasing, production engineering, manufacturing, and parts supply.

(i) Matrix Structure. Most firms using target costing organize product design around a matrix structure with a design team (responsible for each major function) reporting to the chief engineer (responsible for the entire product) and the head of the appropriate design division. The matrix structure balances each product's unique requirements with the desire to maintain common design philosophies across products. Exhibit 7.16 shows such a matrix. Assume the firm is Toyota and Major Function 1 (top row of vertical axis) is the engine cooling system. Products A through M represent different models (Avalon, Camry, Corolla, Highlander, Sequoia, etc.). The head of the design division for engine

12. A complex product is one that contains numerous components and has a multi-level bill of materials.

	Design Team Product A	Design Team Product B	Design Team Product C	....	Design Team Product M
Major Function 1 Division	Design Team A1	Design Team B1	Design Team C1		Design Team M1
Major Function 2 Division	Design Team A2	Design Team B2	Design Team C2		Design Team M2
Major Function 3 Division	Design Team A3	Design Team B3	Design Team C3		Design Team M3
				⋮	
Major Function *n* Division	Design Team A*n*	Design Team B*n*	Design Team C*n*		Design Team M*n*

EXHIBIT 7.16 MAJOR FUNCTION DESIGN TEAMS

cooling systems will control the relative functionality and quality of the engine cooling systems across the different models. Each model will have a dedicated design team for each of its major functions and a chief engineer. The chief engineer or product manager has overall responsibility for selecting the distinctive theme of the new product and coordinating the integration of all of the major functions into the vehicle so that it achieves it desired functionality and quality at its target cost. A relatively small team of design engineers usually supports the chief engineer.

This matrix approach has several advantages. First, the chief engineers have responsibility for coordinating the design process at the design divisions. The relatively autonomous design divisions need the chief engineers to develop a concept for the new vehicle that spans multiple design divisions. Keeping the design divisions autonomous is considered important as it allows expertise sharing across all design projects. For example, the firm quickly incorporates design advances in engine cooling systems for the Camry into future generations of other models. If the Camry design teams reported only to the chief engineer of that vehicle, they would possibly not share their innovations with the design teams of other models.

(ii) Setting the Cost-Reduction Rate. Most firms set different cost-reduction objectives for each major function. As Exhibit 7.17 shows, these different objectives acknowledge that the firm can reduce costs for some major functions (for example, Major Function 5 in the exhibit) more easily than it can for others (such as Major Function 6). For example, major functions that rely on new technologies and new designs often provide more opportunities for cost reduction than major functions that rely on mature technologies and designs.

The chief engineer has responsibility for setting the target cost of each major function, usually through an extended negotiation process with the design teams. The target costs typically reflect historical cost-reduction rates. If the cost of a major function historically has decreased by 5 percent a year, then the target cost will usually use that rate.

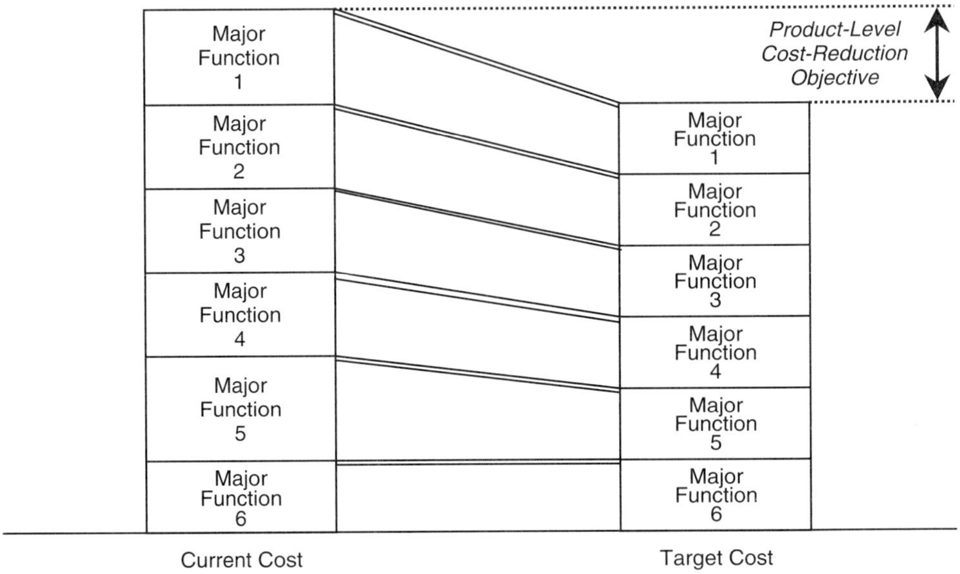

EXHIBIT 7.17 DECOMPOSING THE TARGET COST TO THE MAJOR FUNCTION LEVEL

Not all firms rely solely on historical cost-reduction rates. Some use market analyses to help set the target costs of new products. These market-based approaches apply particularly when the firm introduces new forms of product functionality. For example, Isuzu uses monetary values or ratios to help set the target costs of major functions, and asks customers to estimate how much they would pay for a given function. These market-based estimates, tempered by other factors such as technical, safety, and legal considerations, often lead to adjustments to the prorated target costs. For example, if the prorated target cost for a component is too low to allow the firm to produce a safe version, the firm increases the component's target cost, and decreases the target cost of the other components to compensate.

The chief engineer will modify the target costs derived either from historical rates or market analysis for three major reasons. First, if the sum of all the historical rates doesn't give the desired cost-reduction objective, the chief engineer will negotiate with the head of the design teams of the major functions for higher rates of cost reduction. These negotiations continue until the sum of the target costs of the major components equals the product's target cost.

Second, if the relative importance of the major function changes from one generation to the next, the chief engineer will modify the target costs accordingly. For example, if the product theme for the new vehicle is "quieter and sportier," the engineer might increase the target cost of the major functions responsible for achieving those objectives to make it easier for the design team to achieve both their functionality objective and target cost (see Exhibit 7.18). However, if the firm does not want to violate the cardinal rule of target costing, then the firm will have to reduce the costs of other major functions so the firm can achieve the overall target costing reduction objective.

Third, when the technology used by the major function changes, the historical cost-reduction rate of the old technology loses relevance. Instead, the firm should use the

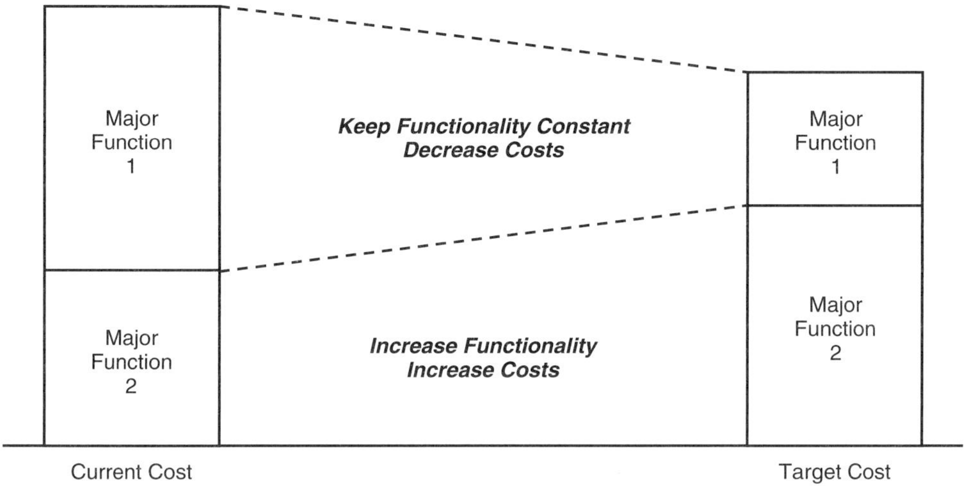

EXHIBIT 7.18 DISTRIBUTING THE TARGET COST ACROSS MAJOR FUNCTIONS

historical rate for the new technology, if available. Entirely new technologies complicate the cost estimation problem because no historical data on cost-reduction trends exist.

Once the firm has established target costs of the major functions, it decomposes the target costs to the group component and parts level as appropriate. The firm needs to set a purchase price for every externally acquired item—whether they are major functions, group components, or individual components.

(c) SETTING THE TARGET COSTS OF COMPONENTS. The process of setting component-level target costs (see Exhibit 7.19) resembles that used to establish function-level target costs (see Exhibit 7.15). The component cost history becomes the basis for estimating the target cost of each component, modified by the design objectives for the product.

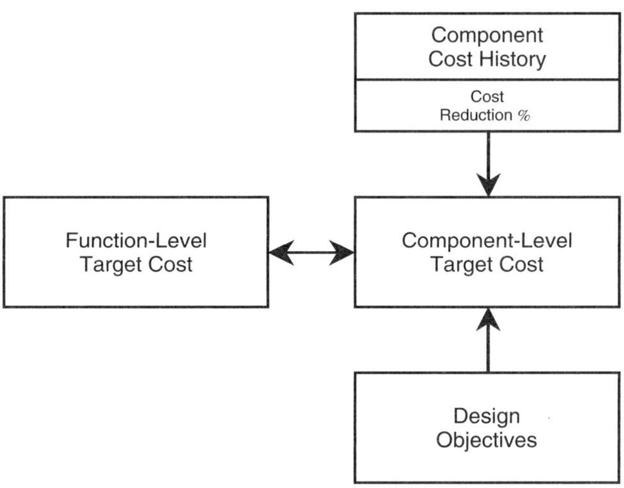

EXHIBIT 7.19 SETTING THE TARGET COSTS OF COMPONENTS

The firm can establish target costs for group and individual components only when the product design has reached the stage at which the design team can identify specific components. For example, many car manufacturers initiate value engineering after they have completed the engineering drawings for trial production to estimate allowable costs for each of the components in every major function of the automobile. The firms derive these estimates by identifying a cost-reduction objective for each outsourced item.

Typically, the major function design teams must decompose the target cost of the major function to the component level, as illustrated in Exhibit 7.20. Sometimes, however, the chief engineer also participates to ensure that the process meets the objectives for the product. If the proposed design requires a higher functionality for the outsourced item, its target costs might increase. In contrast, the firm might ask another supplier to reduce costs because the new part will be smaller or lighter than the old one. The firm might ask a third supplier to maintain the same cost, despite a change in materials, because the firm anticipates no change in performance.

For products with a large number of components, firms have to develop techniques to reduce the cost of developing target costs at the component level. Firms may estimate target costs for similar families of components from a base case. For example, an automobile company may calculate the target cost for the most popular variant of one of its products and then extrapolate the target costs of all of the other variants.

The completion of the target cost setting process for components signals the achievement of a major step in the product design process. The firm can now calculate the anticipated cost of the product by summing the costs of all the components, group components, and major functions either produced internally or acquired externally. The sum of these costs cannot exceed the product's target cost; otherwise, the firm must redesign the product.

Thus, the cardinal rule continues to operate throughout the design process. Even at this late stage, the firm will redesign the product if possible. The interaction between design and manufacturing ensures that the new product's manufacturing cost equals its target cost. Without such interaction, the target cost could significantly differ from the manufacturing cost, rendering the target costing system ineffective.

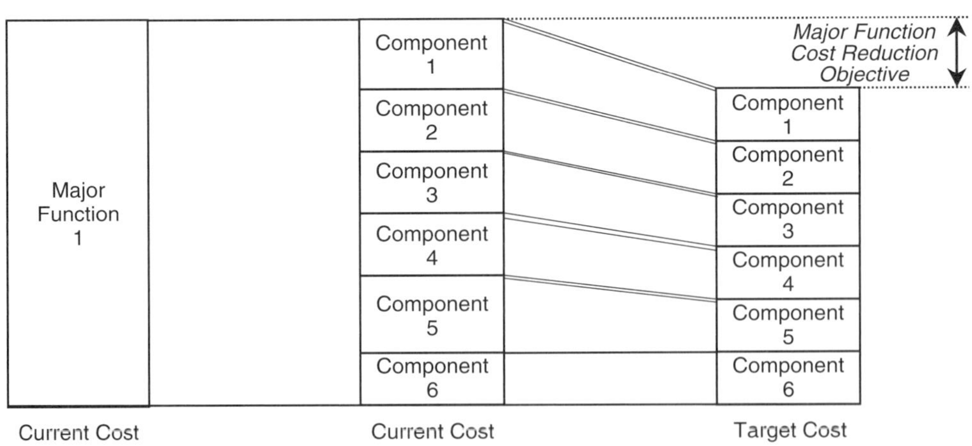

EXHIBIT 7.20 DECOMPOSING TARGET COSTS OF MAJOR FUNCTION TO THE COMPONENT LEVEL

7.5 SUMMARY

Target costing serves as a technique for profit management as much as it does for cost management. The process consists of three major segments: market-driven costing, product-level target costing, and component-level target costing. Exhibit 7.21 shows how these segments fit together. The market-driven costing stage leads to the allowable cost, which analysis converts into a product level target cost during the product-level target costing stage. Finally, the analysis decomposes the product level target costs into costs for the components in the component-level target costing stage.

Market-driven costing captures the external pressure placed on the firm by its customers and competitors and transmits this pressure to the product designers. Market-driven costing takes the anticipated selling price of a product under development and subtracts the desired margin to compute the allowable cost. The firm must manufacture the product at this allowable cost so the product will achieve its profitability objectives when sold at its target volume.

The allowable cost does not reflect the capabilities of the firm's product designers and manufacturing engineers. To develop achievable target costs, the second segment of target costing—product-level target costing—establishes a realistic but stretch (i.e., difficult to achieve) product-level target cost. The firm calculates the target cost by comparing the current cost of the product to its allowable cost. The resulting gap has two elements. The first, the cost reduction objective, captures the level of cost reduction that the firm's engineers believe the firm can achieve. The second element, the strategic cost reduction challenge, represents the unobtainable portion of the overall cost gap. It captures the firm's inability to achieve cost competitiveness. The chief engineer negotiates the split between the cost reduction objective and the strategic cost reduction challenge with senior management. These negotiations aim to keep the strategic cost reduction challenge as small as possible—preferably zero—while setting achievable cost reduction objectives.

Product-level target costing develops the product-level target cost. The firm expects to manufacture the product at this cost in the early days of the manufacturing stage of a

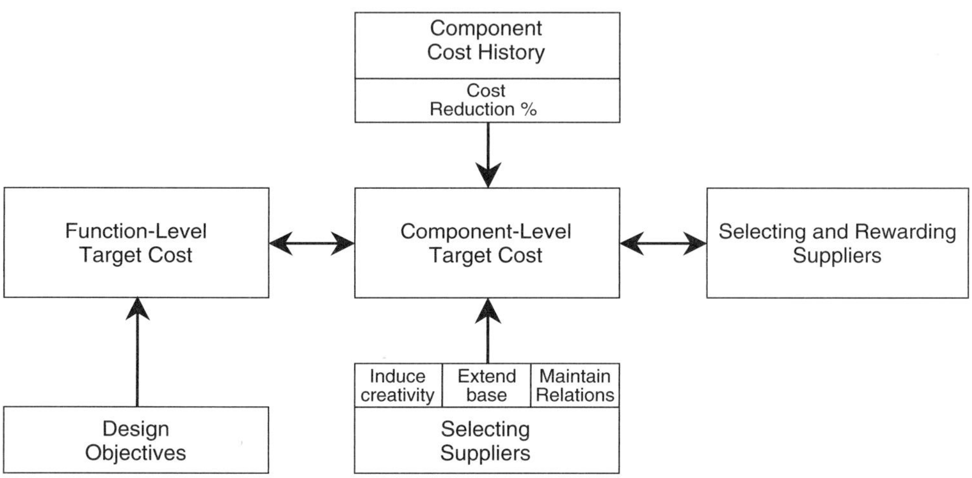

EXHIBIT 7.21 SETTING THE TARGET COSTS OF COMPONENTS

product's life cycle. Product designers can use various engineering techniques—including value engineering, design for manufacture and assembly, and quality-function-deployment—to try to ensure that the product achieves its target cost.

The firm should use the cardinal rule of target costing to maintain the discipline of target costing by canceling new product development projects that the firm does not expect to meet the product-level target cost.

The product-level target cost implicitly reflects anticipated supplier savings. The third phase of the target costing process—component-level target costing—explicitly addresses these savings. Component-level target costs define the suppliers' selling prices and thus, the level of savings the suppliers must achieve to meet their own target costs. Thus, target costing begins the interorganizational cost management process by extending the umbrella of cost management beyond the firm's boundaries.

APPENDIX 7A

TARGET COSTING EQUATIONS AND GLOSSARY

The fundamental equation of target costing identifies the *target cost*—the cost at which the firm must manufacture the product to generate a specified return if sold at its target selling price:

Target cost = Target selling price – Target profit margin

This equation appears in almost all of the discussions of target costing. Unfortunately, this fundamental equation is too simplistic to apply in practice because the market sets the target selling price and the realities of the economics of the product set the target profit margin. Consequently, one cannot guarantee that the firm can achieve the target cost defined in this way. Because we want the firm to rarely modify the target cost once it is set, we define a new term, *allowable cost*:

Allowable cost = Target selling price – Target profit margin

The allowable cost is the same as the conventional definition of the target cost. We can now define a new target cost that has the added property of being achievable about 80 percent of the time. To calculate this target cost, we identify the current cost--the cost at which the firm could build the new product today if it were already designed and the manufacturing facilities were ready. The current cost exceeds the allowable cost, because the firm has not yet pursued a low cost design of the new product or ways to reduce the costs of the manufacturing processes required to produce it.

The level of cost reduction required to achieve the allowable cost is called the *cost-reduction objective:*

Cost-reduction objective = Current cost – Allowable cost

Some firms set overly aggressive cost reduction objectives. They must then split the cost-reduction objective into two parts, one achievable and the other unachievable.

Cost-reduction objective =

Target cost-reduction objective + Strategic cost-reduction objective

The firm can achieve the *target cost-reduction objective* portion, but cannot achieve the *strategic cost-reduction challenge* portion.

The firm calculates the target cost by subtracting the proposed product's target cost-reduction objective from its current cost:

Target cost = Current cost – Target cost-reduction objective

One can also calculate the product-level target cost by adding the strategic cost reduction challenge to the allowable cost:

Target cost = Allowable cost + Strategic cost-reduction challenge

Simple algebra leads to the following observations. First, one can estimate the strategic cost-reduction challenge by subtracting the target cost-reduction objective from the cost reduction objective, as follows:

Strategic cost-reduction objective =

Cost-reduction objective – Target cost-reduction objective

Second, the firm can also estimate the strategic cost-reduction challenge by subtracting the allowable cost from the target cost

Strategic cost-reduction challenge = Target cost – Allowable cost

CHAPTER 8

KAIZEN COSTING FOR EXISTING PRODUCTS

ROBIN COOPER, DBA
Emory University

REGINE SLAGMULDER, PHD
INSEAD

CONTENTS

8.1 INTRODUCTION 271
(a) Achievability 272
(b) Controllability 273
8.2 GENERAL KAIZEN COSTING 273
(a) Kaizen Costing for Direct Costs 273
(b) Kaizen Costing for Indirect Costs 280
8.3 ITEM-SPECIFIC KAIZEN COSTING 283
(a) Product-Specific Kaizen Costing 283
(b) Component-Specific Kaizen Costing 286
8.4 SUMMARY 287

8.1 INTRODUCTION

Kaizen is the Japanese term for continuous improvement. It connotes a continuous process, in which the entire firm participates, of finding ways to become more efficient. Successful kaizen programs can do more than reduce costs; they also increase the quality of products and the safety of production processes. Kaizen costing is the application of continuous improvement principles to reduce costs in the manufacturing stage of a product's life. Kaizen costing should seamlessly integrate with the firm's target costing system.[1] Target costing applies to the design stage and kaizen costing to the manufacturing stage of the product life cycle. Two types of kaizen costing interventions occur, general and item-specific. Each of these has two additional categories.

1. *General kaizen costing* reduces the costs of the products that the firm produces. General kaizen costing consists of period-by-period programs that reduce direct costs and multiperiod programs that reduce overhead or indirect costs, as shown in Exhibit 8.1. Firms use *kaizen costing for direct costs* to continuously reduce the material and labor content of the products in their manufacturing phase. For this type of program, the firm sets cost reduction objectives for each period. Each

1. See Chapter 7, Target Costing for New Product Development.

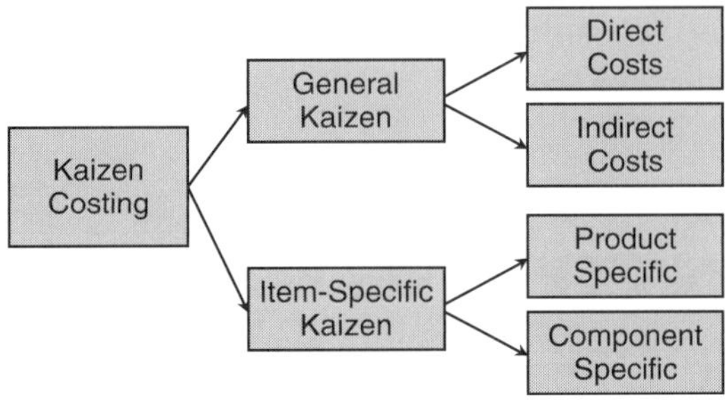

EXHIBIT 8.1 THE VARIOUS KAIZEN COSTING APPROACHES

budgetary period has modest savings objectives, but the savings accumulate over time. *Kaizen costing for indirect costs* reduces the demand for production support activities. The firm typically achieves these savings across multiple budgetary periods.

2. *Item-specific kaizen costing* reduces the costs of individual products and the components that they contain. *Product-specific kaizen costing* increases the rate of cost reduction for individual products that face particularly intense price competition in the marketplace. The firm uses the technique to ensure that the product will earn its life-cycle profit objectives. Firms apply *component-specific kaizen costing* to significantly and rapidly reduce the costs of components that have excessive costs. Savings from these interventions add to those achieved by the general kaizen costing programs.

Two principles govern the setting of effective cost-reduction objectives for any form of kaizen. The achievability principle deals with the commitment to the cost reduction objectives. The controllability principle deals with the individual or group's ability to influence the costs included in their cost-reduction objectives.

(a) ACHIEVABILITY. The achievability principle states that a firm should set challenging and realistic cost reduction objectives. Firms with successful kaizen costing programs typically expect about 80 percent achievement of goals. High achievement percentages ensure a high level of commitment to achieving the cost-reduction objectives. If the individual or group failed to achieve the last 10 objectives, they will have little motivation to achieve the next objective. Furthermore, a high failure rate means that failure has little or no stigma, even if success enjoys prestige. In contrast, high achievement will engender a strong stigma associated with failure while retaining significant prestige related to success. Achievable cost-reduction objectives must also ensure that the firm remains cost competitive. Consequently, a natural tension arises between setting achievable and adequate cost-reduction objectives. A firm can use two mechanisms to resolve this tension. First, it can translate the cost-reduction pressure imposed by the marketplace into the corporate cost-reduction objective. The decomposition process should maintain this pressure as the firm sets its cost-reduction objective at the material and labor level.[2] Second, it can ensure that knowledgeable individuals establish each level of cost-reduction objectives. If the higher-level negotiator has detailed knowledge about the lower-level negotiator's production processes and cost-reduction capabilities,

2. See Chapter 7, "Target Costing for New Product Development."

the lower-level negotiator will have less temptation to introduce slack into the process. The higher-level negotiator must set cost-reduction objectives that, while achievable, will also challenge. Some firms refer to these as *tiptoe objectives*, signifying that the firm can realize them only if everybody stretches to achieve them.

(b) CONTROLLABILITY. The controllability principle also governs the cost-reduction objective setting process. This principle states that cost-reduction objectives should include costs only if the group or individual can control them. For example, a kaizen program for blue-collar workers might exclude the costs of utilities, purchased parts for maintenance, office supplies, and white- and blue-collar wages. In contrast, a white-collar program might include these costs. Furthermore, the controllability principle governs the range of activities that the kaizen program considers. For example, it might expect white-collar workers to change the production processes to make them more efficient. In contrast, it wouldn't expect blue-collar workers to change the production processes, but rather, to accept them as given and make them more efficient. Given the different constraints on the two groups, the white-collar cost-reduction objectives often exceed the blue-collar objectives.

8.2 GENERAL KAIZEN COSTING

General kaizen costing has two categories. The first deals with direct costs, such materials, direct labor, and equipment maintenance. The second deals with the indirect costs. These costs include interactions with vendors, parts administration, and other costs that relate to the acquisition of externally sourced items.

(a) KAIZEN COSTING FOR DIRECT COSTS. Kaizen costing for direct costs aims to remove unnecessary inefficiencies from existing product designs and production processes. As the firm removes these inefficiencies, the overall direct costs of production—and hence, product costs—decline. In most settings, kaizen costing for direct costs is the responsibility of small groups of individuals who have responsibility for a distinct part of the production process. It creates a continuous pressure on these groups to reduce direct costs by a specified amount in the current period.

The process of setting direct cost-reduction objectives typically starts with the corporate profit plan. These plans incorporate assumptions about the level of cost-reduction objectives that the firm will achieve each period. The level of cost reduction demanded over time reflects the long-term cost-reduction pressure that the firm faces in the marketplace and top management's belief in the firm's improvement potential. The corporate cost-reduction objective incorporated into the profit plan identifies the level of cost reduction that the entire firm must achieve in the period. The plan typically does not, however, specify how the firm will achieve those savings. The process of establishing detailed cost-reduction objectives begins with identifying and then decomposing the corporate-level objective to the material and labor level. This is accomplished in four steps:

Step 1. Identify a corporate level objective.

Step 2. Decompose the corporate-level objectives to the divisional and then plant level. A predominately top-down negotiation process between corporate and plant management will identify these plant-level objectives.

Step 3. Decompose the plant-level objectives to the production group level. Typically, a more balanced negotiation process between plant management and group leaders establishes these objectives.

Step 4. Distribute the group-level objectives to the material and labor level.

(i) Corporate-Level Cost-Reduction Objective. Management develops the annual plan based on the corporation's long-term and/or medium-term plans, adjusted for current market conditions. The plan identifies the firm's sales and profit objectives for the coming year. These profit objectives reflect assumptions regarding the level of cost reduction that the firm will achieve during the year. Management then quantifies these assumptions into a specific cost-reduction objective for the corporation for the year.

Firms can use two approaches to setting plant-level cost-reduction objectives: the market-driven approach and the engineering-driven approach. In the market-driven approach, the cost-reduction objectives predominantly reflect the price pressures that the firm encounters in the marketplace. In the engineering-driven approach, the firm establishes cost-reduction objectives based on the savings that it can achieve. The most appropriate approach depends on how consistently the firm can remove direct costs from its products. The more consistent its history, the more effective the engineering-driven approach.

The market-driven approach starts with estimating the cost-reduction pressure that the firm faces in the marketplace and uses that estimate to set a corporatewide cost-reduction objective. Management then decomposes this objective to the plant level as shown in Exhibit 8.2. As denoted in Exhibit 8.2, the primary communication route is top-down, with the bottom-up communication more a reaction to the top-down communication than initiated in its own right. The magnitude of the corporate-level cost-reduction objective reflects the competitive pressure that the firm faces. As the competitive pressure grows, the firm must increase the cost-reduction objective accordingly to maintain its planned

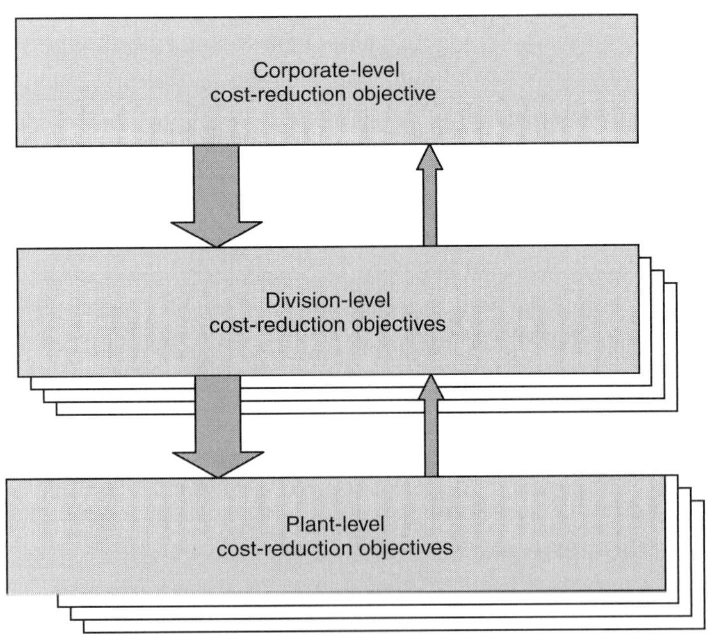

EXHIBIT 8.2 PERIOD-SPECIFIC KAIZEN SUBTRACTION APPROACH: TOP-DOWN PROCESS

profit levels. Typically, the cost-reduction objective reflects long-term anticipated competitive pressures adjusted for current conditions. The corporate planning process, particularly the firm's annual plan, communicates the desired magnitude of the cost-reduction objective.

The engineering-driven approach starts by establishing corporate-wide cost-reduction rates for each major cost element (see Exhibit 8.3). Cost elements include items such as direct material, indirect material, labor, and maintenance. These rates reflect historical experience and provide the basis for computing the plant and corporate-level cost-reduction objective. Management then compares the resulting overall level of cost reduction to the cost-reduction pressure encountered in the market. As Exhibit 8.3 shows, if management decides that the cumulative cost reduction lies below what the market dictates, it will pressure the plant to increase the individual plant-level objectives. These revised objectives begin again at the cost-element level and flow bottom-up. As denoted in Exhibit 8.3, the primary communication route is bottom-up, with the top-down communication more a reaction to the bottom-up communication than initiated in its own right.

The engineering-driven approach calculates the corporate-level cost-reduction objective using corporatewide or plantwide cost-reduction factors for all of the major cost elements of the firm's production processes. While practice varies, corporate planners identify cost-reduction factors for relatively few cost elements—perhaps 10 to 15. The factors reflect historical achievement levels. For example, if the firm has reduced the costs of a class of direct material by 3 percent a year, the planners will begin at 3 percent to estimate the current factor level.

Once the planners have established the cost-reduction factor for each element, they calculate the corporatewide cost-reduction objective for each cost element by multiplying the total quantity of each cost element expected to be consumed in the coming period by the corresponding factor. They then calculate the cost-reduction objective for the corporation by summing all the corporate-level cost-reduction objectives for each cost element. If the firm uses plantwide factors, the planners make the calculations at the plant level and cumulate them to the corporate level. The advantage of plantwide as opposed to corporatewide factors lies in the increased accuracy of the calculations. Plants that

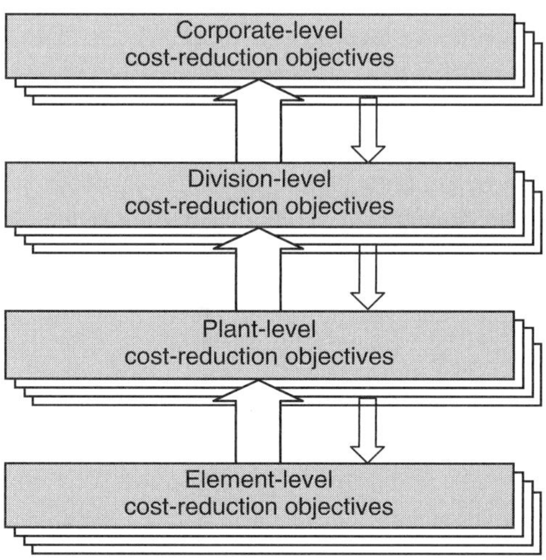

EXHIBIT 8.3 PERIOD-SPECIFIC KAIZEN ADD BOTTOM-UP PROCESS

manufacture new products typically can reduce costs faster than those that manufacture mature products.

In an engineering-driven approach that uses corporatewide factors, management decomposes the corporate-level cost-reduction objective to the plant level—usually by using one of two approaches. The first approach multiplies the corporatewide objective by the ratio of the plants' manageable costs—that is, those subjected to kaizen costing—to calculate the plant-level cost-reduction objective. The second approach multiplies the corporatewide objective by the ratio of the plants' actual costs for the previous periods.

Finally, in the last stage of the process, the planners modify these simplistic estimates to reflect each plant's idiosyncrasies. For example, they will typically increase the cost-reduction objective for plants manufacturing new products and decrease the objective for plants manufacturing mature products.

(ii) Plant-Level Cost-Reduction Objectives. Corporate and divisional management decompose the corporate cost-reduction objective to the plant level. Each plant-level planning group uses its long-term and/or medium-term plans as the basis for developing the plant-level annual plan under the umbrella of the corporate plan. This plan identifies a number of plant-level annual objectives, including sales, operating profits, inventory levels, investments, personnel levels, and quality targets. These objectives must reflect the plant's cost-reduction objective.

When setting plant-level cost-reduction objectives, the firm wants to maximize those objectives while ensuring that the workforce will commit to them. A pure top-down approach risks setting excessively aggressive cost-reduction objectives that violate the achievability principle. In addition, the individuals involved will likely have a low commitment to the mandated cost-reduction objectives, even with achievable objectives. Thus, a pure top-down process will usually prove ineffective. Alternatively, a pure bottom-up approach risks setting cost-reduction objectives too low to generate the desired level of corporate profits. Plant management will have no insights into the competitive pressures faced by the firm. Therefore, they have no way to benchmark their performance against that of the market. In addition, they will likely develop cost-reduction objectives that they know they can easily achieve. Thus, a pure bottom-up process may also prove ineffective.

A firm might best decide to take advantage of the strengths of the two approaches to reduce the risks. By having a formal top-down process and an informal bottom-up process, the firm ensures that the top-down process dominates and that the cost-reduction objectives reflect the market pressures. The bottom-up process moderates the top-down process to ensure achievable cost-reduction objectives to which the groups will commit.

Although the process functions in a predominantly top-down manner, the corporate and divisional plans incorporate input from the plants. Consequently, annual planning becomes an iterative process that mixes top-down and bottom-up interactions. Although the firm sets corporate, divisional, plant, and group-level objectives in a top-down manner, the process used to establish these objectives relies on a bottom-up information-collection process.

The divisional planning groups typically have daily contact with the individuals in each plant within the division and should develop a detailed understanding of the prevailing conditions. As the planning cycle approaches, the divisional planning groups discuss the magnitude of cost-reduction that each department can achieve. They combine these departmental estimates to develop a divisional estimate of achievable cost reduction. Management will then combine these divisional estimates to give a rough guide to the cost reduction that the firm can achieve for the year.

The information collected from the departments becomes the starting point for the top-down process that culminates in setting the annual cost-reduction objective for each plant. The objectives reflect the information collected, anticipated market conditions, and the firm's long-term profit objectives. Corporate planning typically requires cost-reduction objectives higher than those identified by the informal bottom-up process. Corporate planners increase the informal cost-reduction objectives so that the corporation will achieve its profit objective. Management then communicates the corporate objectives to the divisions and the plants.

(iii) Group-Level Cost-Reduction Objectives. Most production processes contain multiple steps, each performed by a different group. Typically, in lean enterprises[3] these groups have responsibility for producing a family of products or components in a production cell. The production cells start with raw material and end with finished goods using just-in-time (JIT) production methods.[4] The firm usually considers each of these groups as a cost center, but depending on the production process, sometimes the firm has several groups in a cost center. The groups have responsibility for period-specific kaizen costing.

Many firms expect group leaders to negotiate their group's cost-reduction targets. These negotiations occur within a hierarchical negotiation process which mixes top-down and bottom-up communications. Given the informality of some of the process at most firms, one cannot easily describe its exact sequence. The plant manager frequently becomes the critical player in the top-down negotiations of the group-level targets because this individual is the most senior manager who has access to detailed information about the performance on the factory floor. The plant manager acts as the conduit between the factory floor and the divisional manager, helping him or her identify realistic stretch targets for each group. Once the groups identify tentative targets, they enter formal negotiations to fine-tune the targets and commit to them.

Because the work groups set their own cost-reduction targets and then negotiate with senior management, one may not notice the top-down pressure. The negotiations, a mix of top-down and bottom up philosophies, usually result in cost-reduction targets that are more aggressive than those originally planned but still achievable. The power of these negotiations lies in the commitment they create to the cost-reduction targets at every level of the firm, even when senior management strongly influences those targets.

Most kaizen programs base the cost-reduction objective for each group on the anticipated savings potential. The level of savings depends on factors such as how long the group has been making the items, their historical achievements, and the maturity of the technology used. Kaizen programs aim to create the same level of pressure for each group. At some firms, when the cost-reduction objective for a group lies below the average required for the plant, the group must still achieve the average savings for the plant. If the group achieves the average level of cost reduction, then overall savings will exceed the plant-level objectives set by senior management (assuming all of the other groups

---

3. Lean manufacturing is characterized by manufacturing a single part just in time for its incorporation into the product.
4. Under a JIT philosophy, parts are manufactured and delivered just in time to be used in the manufacturing process. No significant inventories of work-in-process are maintained. One can contrast JIT to batch and queue philosophies where firms typically maintain large parts inventories.

also achieve their specified savings levels). Management still holds the group to the average, so that the firm reaps the extra savings if the group achieves the average. However, the plant-level profit plans do not anticipate these extra savings because they will not likely achieve them.

(iv) Selecting Cost-Reduction Objectives. Most firms use different methods to establish cost-reduction objectives for material and labor. As Exhibit 8.4 illustrates, management typically establishes the objectives for material at the product level; for example, a given product might have an objective of removing *X* percent of material from its cost. Management typically sets the objectives for labor at the production line level; for example, a given production process might have an objective of reducing labor costs by *Y* percent. Finally, management sets the objectives for purchased parts for each item purchased; for example, a given purchased part might have an objective of reducing its costs by *Z* percent. As explained next, these differences reflect how the firm consumes resources as it manufactures products. The nature of the kaizen process and the way it achieves cost reduction therefore differs for the three types of costs.

(v) Material Cost-Reduction Objectives. Period-specific kaizen costing establishes cost-reduction objectives for material at the product level because a one-to-one relation exists between the product and the material it consumes.[5] We state this relation as follows:

Product *X* consumes *Y* kilograms[6] (kg) of Material *A*.

The firm can change the amount (and hence cost) of material consumed by a product only by changing that underlying relation in one of three ways:

1. Changing the amount of Material *A* that it consumes (change *Y* kg to *Z* kg).
2. Changing the type of material used (change Material *A* to Material *B*). This may also affect the kilogram variable.
3. Changing the material's purchase price. Since the cost of material equals the price per kilogram times the number of kilograms consumed, any reduction in the purchase price will automatically lead to an equivalent cost reduction.

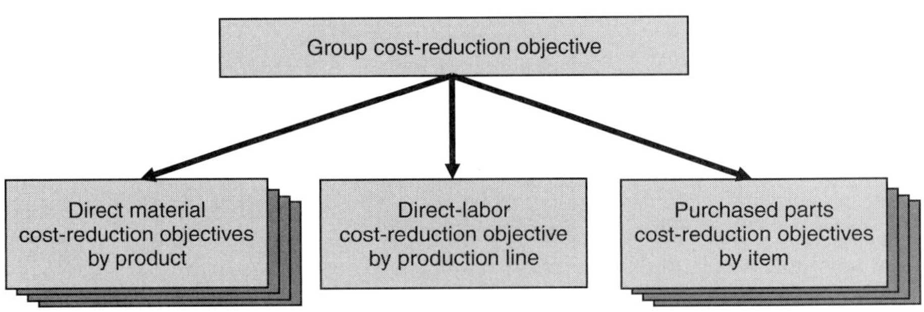

EXHIBIT 8.4 DECOMPOSING THE GROUP-LEVEL COST-REDUCTION OBJECTIVES

5. If the firm uses the material to create a common component (i.e., one that is used in multiple products), then the material cost of all of the products that use that component will be reduced.
6. We use kilogram in this explanation, but the material's appropriate unit or weight measure would apply here.

Most kaizen costing programs establish cost-reduction objectives at the overall—not individual—material level, leaving it up to the kaizen team to find ways to achieve the objective. This approach leaves the kaizen team with more freedom to identify cost-saving opportunities. Therefore, the firm simply states the material-specific kaizen cost-reduction objective for Product *X* in Period *Y* as, "Reduce material costs by *A* percent." Only as the kaizen intervention identifies individual savings opportunities will the process begin to measure savings at the individual material level. That is, the firm can state savings as follows:

- We can save *M* percent of Material *A* (by reducing the quantity consumed)
- We can save *N* percent of Material *B* (by substituting Material *D*)
- We can save *P* percent of Material *C* (by reducing the price of the Material *C*)
- Any combination of the above

To ensure a successful kaizen costing intervention, these savings taken together must equal the product's overall cost-reduction target (in this case, *A* percent).

Two aspects of material costs make it easy to ensure that resources supplied reflect reductions in the quantity or price of material consumed by a product—that is, in the overall cost of material for the period. First, the reduction occurs at the unit level. Each unit of the product subjected to a kaizen costing intervention consumes less material. Second, as the amount of material consumed drops, the amount supplied automatically drops as well. Therefore, the firm achieves real savings.

(vi) Labor Cost-Reduction Objectives. Firms establish period-specific kaizen cost-reduction objectives at the production line, not the product level. They cannot set meaningful cost-reduction objectives at the product level because the just-in-time production line is balanced for multiple products. A production line is balanced when every model in the product family that goes through the line takes approximately the same time to manufacture. Consequently, reducing the time it takes to manufacture a single product of the family has no effect. Likewise, the firm will not increase the speed of production because, under single-piece flow, the firm manufactures the products one at a time in random order. Therefore, speeding up the production time of one product simply means that it will have to wait until the preceding product has completed production.

To reduce the number of workers or to increase the speed of the line requires that production achieve a new balance. Such a balance requires that the firm reduce processing times for most, if not all, of the products that the line produces. Consequently, the firm should focus the kaizen intervention on improving the performance of the line as a whole rather than on improving a single product. In such environments, firms set the labor cost-reduction objectives at the product family level.

A firm should not set kaizen cost-reduction objectives at either the individual worker or production step level. Lean manufacturing environments have multiskilled workers who continually change places[7]; therefore, focusing on the individual will focus on the line by default. Focusing on the production step leads to excessively detailed cost-reduction objectives. Such micromanagement will decrease the kaizen team's motivation to identify ways to improve the production process.

---

7. The conditions inside a manufacturing cell make job specialization virtually impossible. One of the ways to balance the line is by giving individuals multiple tasks to perform. These tasks often vary with the product being produced.

A firm should manage direct labor costs at both the production line and the facility level. At the production line level, the kaizen process manages demands for labor; at the facility level the process manages supply of labor. Stable employment contracts between the firm and the workforce[8] drive the necessity to manage demand and supply separately. For material, a reduction in demand leads to an immediate reduction in supply (the firm simply orders less material); however, matching the supply of labor to the demand requires managerial action. Thus, labor kaizen costing has two elements: one program to reduce demand for labor and another program to bring supply in line with demand.

The kaizen program focuses on reducing the number of workers required to manufacture products. Since most firms with kaizen programs have agreed to no-layoff policies, however, the firms do not lay off these individuals. The firms have four primary ways to offset the resulting excess labor.

1. *Use natural attrition.* When workers retire, the firm does not automatically replace them.
2. *Move displaced workers.* The demand for products varies, and as a line becomes busy because of increased demand, the firm can use displaced workers to increase the number of operators.
3. *Insource products.* The firm could insource products from suppliers to create new jobs.
4. *Expand.* The firm can try to expand into new lines of business to create additional jobs.

(b) KAIZEN COSTING FOR INDIRECT COSTS. Period-specific and item-specific kaizen costing primarily focus on the direct costs, not the indirect ones. Kaizen costing programs aimed at reducing indirect costs achieve their objectives by reducing any unnecessary complexity in the production support functions. For example, having many unique parts to manage can lead to excessive parts administration costs. The firm can most effectively reduce these costs by decreasing the number of unique parts in its parts list—thus reducing the number of different parts that it has to design, order and process—while removing the need to interact with as many suppliers. If the firm can achieve such simplifications for a number of products, then the indirect costs of production will decrease. Thus, even if the direct costs of products do not change, total product costs will decrease.

Firms that lack a sophisticated cost system will have difficulty quantifying the benefits from an indirect kaizen cost initiative. Traditional cost systems do a poor job of identifying the underlying causes of indirect costs. If they cannot identify the drivers for these indirect costs, these systems cannot predict the savings that will result from a kaizen costing program to reduce complexity. To achieve that objective requires more sophisticated cost systems, such as activity-based costing.[9] Firms that do not have such

8. For kaizen programs to be successful, the workforce must believe that the reward for becoming more efficient will not be lay-offs. Therefore, most successive kaizen programs are associated with employment security programs. The same does not hold true of the part time labor force. The supply of part-time workers can be adjusted every time a contract comes up for renewal.
9. Activity-based costing (ABC), discussed in Chapter 6 of this Handbook, is a cost-assignment approach where cost pools represent the major activities performed in the production of products. These activities are hierarchical in nature.

systems must either justify their kaizen programs for indirect costs on faith alone or undertake special studies to try to estimate the likely savings.

The savings in indirect costs become visible only if the reduction in complexity proves sufficient to redeploy the freed-up resources. As Exhibit 8.5 illustrates, the kaizen costing program must typically affect numerous products and extend over several years to have a detectable impact.

The initiative needs to focus on multiple products, because decreasing the number of unique parts required by a single product will lead to a reduced demand for parts administration that is too small to detect. Only when the initiative has reduced the number of parts required by numerous products will the firm convert the decreased consumption of indirect costs into savings.

Similarly, the kaizen costing initiative needs to extend over several years, because the firm can rarely reduce complexity quickly. It may require the redesign of a significant percentage of the firm's products before the number of unique components falls enough for the cost savings to become apparent. Consequently, these programs often contain several phases, with each subsequent phase taking a more aggressive and fundamental approach to complexity reduction until the firm has achieved the objective. At that point, the firm initiates a maintenance program to ensure that the complexity does not return.

Many kaizen programs to reduce indirect costs focus on reducing the number of parts that go into the firms' products. Firms can benefit from such programs because of the high costs associated with parts administration. An aggressive parts reduction program consists of four consecutive stages that focus on both existing and new models:

1. *Increase parts commonality.* Reducing the number of parts through parts commonality requires a careful analysis of all existing parts to assess whether other existing parts can replace them. Such parts commonality programs prove effective in firms that have encouraged design originality and innovation and have low levels of current parts commonality. For example, Olympus Optical designed a new mother camera for the Stylus line that contained components that they expected to become common both across a number of different models and a number of generations of those models.
2. *Eliminate low-volume variants.* This stage focuses on the discontinuance of low-volume models and parts. As stage 1 achieved parts commonality, the remaining low volume items typically relate to low volume end products. Activity-based costing has shown that such products typically cost many times their reported cost and exceed their perceived value. Often, firms should decide to discontinue them.

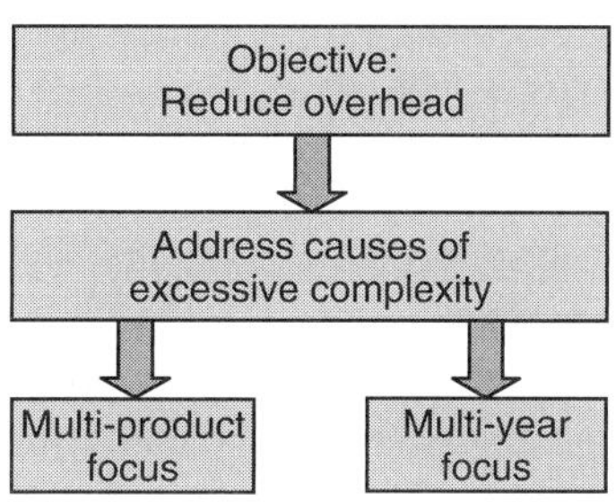

EXHIBIT 8.5 OVERHEAD-SPECIFIC KAIZEN

3. *Reduce the number of parts.* Reducing the number of parts by means of modular design and the purging-of-parts system helps limit the annual increase in the number of new parts. Modular design considers a major portion of a product as a single item, as opposed to a number of distinct components. The parts list no longer contains the components that the modules now subsume. Thus, the product designers have access only to the modules, not the components they contain. The firm then uses these modular designs as widely as possible in all new products. Thus, it amounts to a more sophisticated parts commonality program. A firm can also reduce the number of parts by changing its marketing and sales strategy to introduce fewer new products—particularly, the variants with low sales volume. This reduction can occur at either the product level (no longer support low-volume products) or at the variant level (no longer produce customized components but work from a limited number of standard components to produce effectively equivalent customized products.)
4. *Perform follow-up activities.* This stage includes finishing the stage 3 tasks and setting up some new activities to reinforce the cost-reduction efforts. For example, the emergence of global sourcing might initially increase the number of new parts introduced. A firm can retain reasonable numbers of components by managing the procurement process and aggressively replacing local components that cost more than those obtained globally.

Kaizen costing programs for indirect costs focus on simplifying the complexity of the tasks performed in the production support functions. In addition to parts commonality programs (explained in number 3 above), they include the following:

- *Universal tooling.* The firm designs products and production processes so that the tooling required to make them becomes common across families of products. Such commonality reduces the need to design new tools for each new product.
- *Product line simplification.* The firm uses simplification to eliminate redundant products, especially low volume ones.
- *Matrix tear-down.* The firm removes low-volume components from products. The firm creates a matrix of parts and products. The cell entries are the volume of parts used by that product for the period. The total of all of these volumes equals the total volume for the period of that part. The firm has identified low total volume parts to remove from the product designs, although if it cannot remove a part from all products, this initiative has no payoff.

For all of these projects, the firm will have difficulty assessing how aggressively to set the complexity reduction objectives. Unlike period-specific or item-specific kaizen costing, where the market helps identify the necessary level of cost reduction, kaizen costing for indirect costs offers no obvious guideline regarding optimal cost reduction. Given the lack of activity-based cost systems, the firms typically set the kaizen costing objectives for these programs in nonfinancial terms. These objectives imply an optimal level of complexity. Once the firm has reached this level, the program focuses on maintaining a constant level of simplification. For example, if Isuzu tried to reduce parts count much further, it believes it would lose the ability to increase the functionality of its products at a competitive rate.

8.3 ITEM-SPECIFIC KAIZEN COSTING

Firms initiate kaizen costing interventions to ensure that products in the manufacturing phase of their life cycles achieve their profit objectives. Item-specific kaizen costing initiatives focus on specific products or major functions or group components that the firm has identified as candidates for cost reduction. Firms initiate product-specific programs when the cost problem occurs at the product level and a specific product has a risk of becoming unprofitable or has become unprofitable.

When the firm has an effective target costing system, most product-specific kaizen costing interventions will involve mature products.[10] Although these products earned adequate returns when the firm launched them, changing conditions have reduced those returns to inadequate or at risk of becoming inadequate. Although a steady decrease in profitability over time will trigger aggressive and ongoing general kaizen activity, an unexpected and significant decrease in profitability (current or future) will push the firm to evoke a product-specific kaizen intervention. Consequently, such programs are episodic.

In contrast, component-specific kaizen costing programs have an ongoing time line as the firm's engineers continually look for ways to reduce costs at the component level. Two conditions often lead to component-specific interventions. The first occurs when design engineers identify more cost efficient ways to provide the same functionality. The second occurs when a profitability analysis of the products indicates that the component costs too much.

(a) PRODUCT-SPECIFIC KAIZEN COSTING. Product-specific kaizen costing initiatives focus on individual products. Typically, the firm has established a cost-reduction objective for the product and uses kaizen costing intervention to find ways to achieve it. Product-specific kaizen costing functions as a natural extension of target costing. The primary difference between target costing (which is, by definition, product specific) and product-specific kaizen costing lies in the ability to change product functionality. In target costing, the product's functionality becomes a variable in the costing process. If the firm cannot manufacture the specified product at its target cost, then it can sometimes decrease the product's functionality to reduce its costs. If this results in sufficient cost reduction, then the firm can manufacture the product for its target cost.[11] In contrast, kaizen costing focuses on products with fixed functionality. The functionality of the production line's first unit must be identical to the last unit's functionality. This constraint does not require that the material content and the way the firm manufactures the product cannot change, only that any changes must become invisible to the customer.

A firm initiates a product-specific kaizen costing intervention when a current product has or will have unacceptable profitability unless the firm takes specific actions to reduce the product's cost. Three conditions typically trigger product specific kaizen costing:

1. A product fails to achieve its target cost.
2. The firm has imputed aggressive kaizen cost savings into the target cost and must ensure that it achieves these savings.
3. The relation between a mature product's selling price and its cost deteriorates unexpectedly, and the firm must take steps to bring its costs into line with its revenues. For example, the firm might expect a product's profitability to fall by

10. Chapter 7 discusses target costing systems.

11. See Chapter 7, "Target Costing for New Product Development."

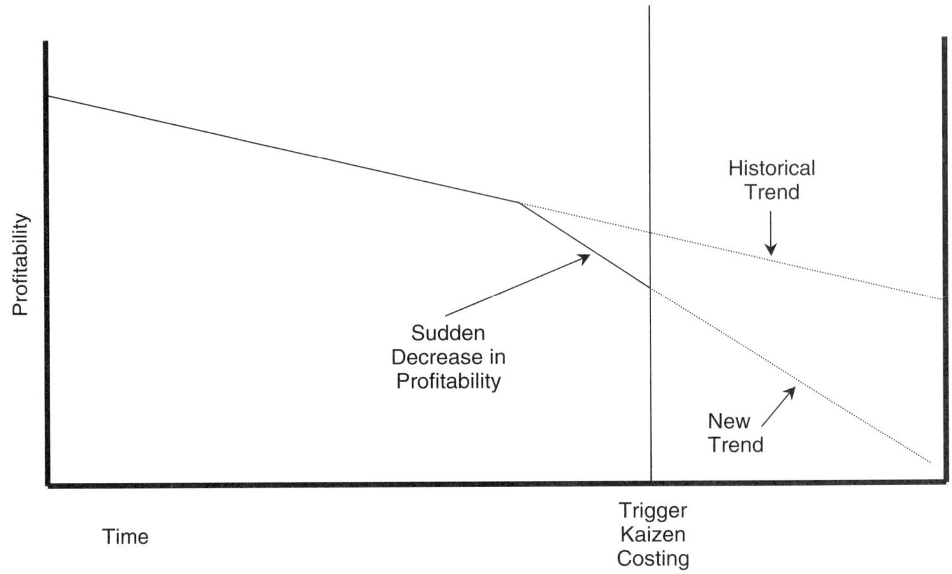

EXHIBIT 8.6 UNEXPECTED CHANGES IN PRODUCT PROFITABILITY AS TRIGGER OF PRODUCT-SPECIFIC KAIZEN COSTING

> ten percent per year. In year three, however, it falls unexpectedly to 50 percent of the previous year's level, as illustrated in Exhibit 8.6. The kaizen costing intervention will need to increase the profitability back to the anticipated levels.

No significant difference exists between product-specific kaizen costing interventions for new products and mature ones. For both classes of products, the critical issue becomes whether the firm has enough time to undertake a successful intervention and recoup the cost of that intervention. It takes time to identify a cost problem, identify a solution, and incorporate it into manufacturing. If the new product has a short life, the firm might not have adequate time to incorporate the change and recoup the investment in cost reduction. The same holds true for mature products as they approach the end of their lives. If the firm doesn't have sufficient time, it should expend the cost-reduction effort on the next generation of product. If the firm has sufficient time, then it can justify the cost-reduction effort if a positive cost/benefit trade-off exists. Two factors play a dominant role in this cost/benefit trade-off: (1) the magnitude of the expected volume of product sales and (2) the anticipated magnitude of the investment required to reduce the costs. The higher the expected sales volume and the lower the anticipated magnitude of the investment, the easier it is to justify the program.

If the firm has failed to achieve the target cost for a new product at the time of launch, it might for strategic reasons decide to launch the product anyway. For example, Olympus Optical made a strategic decision to design its first camera to act as a mother camera, to introduce parts commonality. Senior management estimated that the company could derive considerable savings from the parts commonality program and decided to launch the product even though the firm would manufacture it above its target cost. Typically, firms will immediately initiate an item-specific kaizen costing intervention to try to reduce their manufacturing costs back to the level established by their target costing process. The item-specific kaizen intervention must reduce the cost of the new product to its

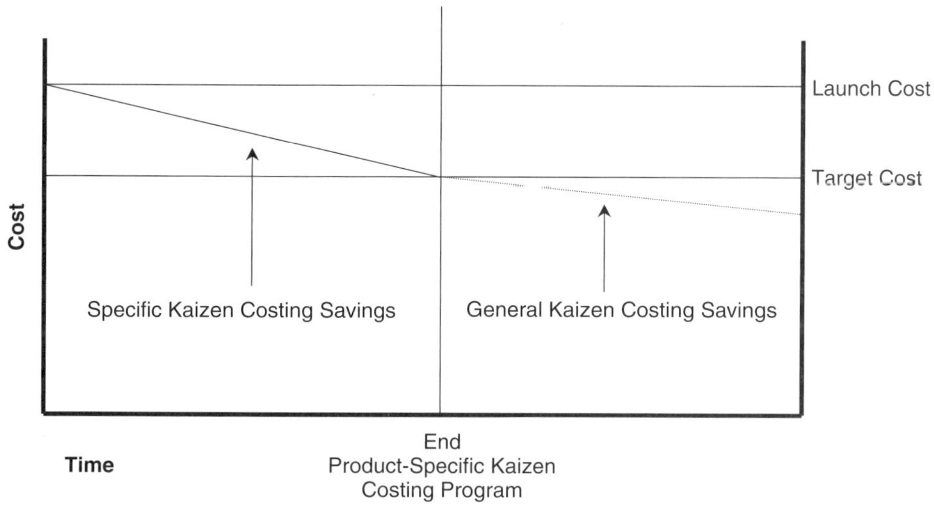

EXHIBIT 8.7 ACHIEVING TARGET COST POST LAUNCH

target cost level, as illustrated in Exhibit 8.7. To maintain the discipline of target costing, management must view such kaizen costing interventions as the exception rather than the rule. Following the cardinal rule of target costing—never launch a product above its target cost—helps maintain the discipline, but the firm may decide to launch some strategic products regardless.

Two primary conditions lead to a firm's failure to achieve target costs: underestimation of the product's costs and overestimation of its revenues.[12] Underestimation of costs typically occurs when the engineers fail to anticipate either technological or engineering difficulties inherent to the new product's design. Cost overruns can occur for many reasons. For example, if an innovative technology fails to work reliably, the firm may need to substitute it with a more expensive solution based on existing technology. Similarly, cost savings that appeared reasonable during the target cost setting process may become impossible to fully realize. Overestimation of revenues occurs when the target selling price or the target volume exceeds actual amounts. If the firm identifies these overestimations before it completes the product development process, it can reduce the product-level target cost, making it more difficult for the engineers to achieve their new higher cost-reduction objectives.

Firms that can significantly reduce the costs of their products through kaizen costing during the manufacturing phase often impute these savings into their target cost calculations. Such imputation makes sense because target costing adopts a life-cycle perspective with respect to adequate profits. Ignoring kaizen savings (or other cost reductions during the manufacturing phase) would lead to unnecessarily aggressive product-level target costs. Including the savings, however, increases the need to achieve them. The firm's long-term profit plan would incorporate a level of kaizen costing savings.

Two conditions lead to the loss of profitability of existing products: (1) the selling price drops faster than the costs and (2) costs increase faster than selling prices. The product-specific kaizen costing intervention aims to return the product to adequate levels

12. We have ignored cost overruns that occur due to poor implementation of target costing.

of profitability. To avoid lost profitability, the firm initiates these product-specific kaizen costing interventions as soon as it detects the decay in profitability. For example, some firms monitor the rate at which selling prices fall for all their products. When the firm expects a product's selling price to fall below its cost in the near future, it subjects the product to an intense product-specific cost-reduction analysis. This analysis consists of identifying the product's major cost components to assess whether the firm can produce them at a lower cost. For example, if the largest costs relate to machining, then design engineers explore ways to replace the machined parts with stamped or plastic components.

For most product-specific programs, the firm can easily establish cost-reduction objectives. For a new product that has exceeded its target cost, the obvious cost-reduction objective becomes that of reducing costs back to target levels. If the problem is imputed kaizen savings, the objective becomes that of achieving those savings. Finally, if a mature product experiences reduced profitability, the usual objective becomes that of returning the product to historical or desired profitability levels or, with a serious cost overrun, assessing whether to eliminate the product. For component-specific kaizen costing programs, the firm should set cost-reduction objectives so that the products that contain the components achieve their profitability objectives.

If the achievable cost reductions identified prove insufficient to reduce costs so that the product will remain profitable, then the firm needs to explore whether to completely redesign the product without changing its functionality. If complete redesign fails to make the product profitable, the firm usually discontinues the product. Thus, kaizen costing carries it own rule similar to that of target costing—namely, that the product mix should maintain only products that can generate an adequate return during manufacturing.

(b) COMPONENT-SPECIFIC KAIZEN COSTING. When it becomes apparent that a major function[13] or group component[14] has a poor design that leads to excessive costs, the firm should subject that component to a specific kaizen costing intervention designed to reduce its costs. The firm can identify such kaizen costing opportunities in several ways:

- All products that contain the item report low profitability. This will hold true if the item represents a significant fraction of the product's total value added.
- Tear-down of a competitive product might indicate a considerable cost-savings opportunity if the firm redesigns the item.
- Cost reductions achieved in previous periods might not suffice, and the intervention might aim to bring the item's cost in line with expectations.
- Finally, increases in material or other input costs might cause the item to exceed its original target cost and hence become a candidate for redesign.

The firm achieves kaizen cost savings by applying value analysis principles and can reduce costs in five ways: reduce parts count, use less expensive materials, increase supplier performance, shift production overseas, and reduce labor content.

---

13. A major function is a subassembly that supports a major part of the functionality of the end product. Examples include the gearbox and the engine cooling system of an automobile.
14. A group component is a subassembly that makes up a signify portion of a major function. Examples include the starter motor and radiator of an automobile.

(i) Reduce Parts Count. A firm can use several methods to reduce parts count. Two such ways include performing functions electronically, as opposed to mechanically, and creating more sophisticated molds to reduce the number of molded components. For example, the front lighting system of an automobile might originally have consisted of four molded components: two headlight panels and two side and indicator panels. A more sophisticated mold might allow a single panel to contain the headlight and side and indicator lights, thus reducing the number of parts from four to two.

(ii) Use Less Expensive Materials. Substituting high priced materials for lower priced ones has been a major source of cost-reduction opportunities for many firms since the 1970s and 1980s. For example, many firms now use plastic instead of glass or metal. Many firms, however, find it difficult to identify even cheaper materials.

(iii) Increase Supplier Performance. Given the high percentage of components that many firms source externally, they can reduce costs by educating suppliers (both independent and subsidiaries) in ways to reduce their costs.[15]

(iv) Shift Production Overseas. Firms can shift their manufacturing activities to lower cost production locations, such as some Asian countries.

(v) Reduce Labor Content. Firms can reduce the labor content of their products by increasing the level of automation or speeding up the production process. They can increase the level of automation by using more flexible machines such as robots. They can increase the speed of production by reducing the time it takes to perform a step in the production process for all product family members.

8.4 SUMMARY

Kaizen costing applies the philosophy of kaizen to specifically reduce the costs of products. Kaizen costing comprises two major programs: general and item specific. General kaizen costing programs reduce the costs of all products through focusing on either their direct or indirect costs. Kaizen costing for direct costs creates a steady cost-reduction pressure; the firm measures the program's objectives by time period. The firm might state the objective as "reduce overall production costs by N percent this year." Kaizen costing for indirect costs reduces indirect manufacturing costs by reducing overall complexity. Firms typically achieve this objective by significantly reducing parts complexity over a number of periods.

The item-specific programs operate at the individual product or component level. Events that indicate excessively expensive individual products or components trigger these programs. The programs reduce the costs of specific items by a preset amount. For new products, this amount typically equals the difference between their launch costs and target costs. The product-specific kaizen costing program takes over from the target costing program to ensure that the product quickly achieves its target cost. For mature products, the program focuses on maintaining its anticipated level of profitability so that the product achieves its life-cycle profitability objectives.

---

15. See Chapter 9.

A firm initiates component-specific kaizen costing when evidence suggests that an individual component is too expensive and that the firm needs to implement specific cost reduction. A firm can use several methods to identify the need for component-level kaizen costing. These include tear down of competitive products, overall low profitability of products that contain common components, and finally, a general belief that a particular component is too expensive.

CHAPTER 9

INTERORGANIZATIONAL COSTING*

ROBIN COOPER, DBA
Emory University

REGINE SLAGMULDER, PHD
INSEAD

CONTENTS

9.1 INTRODUCTION 289
9.2 COORDINATING TRANSACTION-RELATED ACTIVITIES 291
(a) Coordinating Network Activities 291
(b) Coordinating Buyer–Supplier Interface Activities 292
9.3 COORDINATING PRODUCT-RELATED ACTIVITIES 300
(a) Coordinating Product Development Activities 300
(b) Coordinating Manufacturing Activities 309
9.4 SUMMARY 311

9.1 INTRODUCTION

Interorganizational cost management (hereafter IOCM) offers a disciplined approach to managing costs through the cooperative actions of firms in a supplier network. The firms can achieve this objective by recognizing that all entities within the chain will benefit through cooperation; the firms must then focus on increasing the efficiency of the entire supplier network and not just of themselves. A more efficient network will generate higher profits for the firms to share. IOCM seeks to increase profitability of supplier networks and the firms in them.[1]

Interorganizational cost management is a structured approach to coordinating the activities of firms in a supplier network in order to reduce total network costs. Through coordinated actions between buyers and suppliers, IOCM programs aim to identify lower-cost solutions than would be possible if the firms tried to reduce costs independently. This

* This chapter is based on material contained in *Interorganizational Cost Management*, Robin Cooper and Regine Slagmulder, (Portland, Ore.: Productivity Press, 1999).

1. Authors' note: The sort of cooperation required by supplier/buyer coordination does not appear to present antitrust issues, where the focus tends to be on price collusion in selling to others. Although we are not expert in legal matters, we know of no companies that have run afoul of antitrust laws from such coordination as this chapter describes.

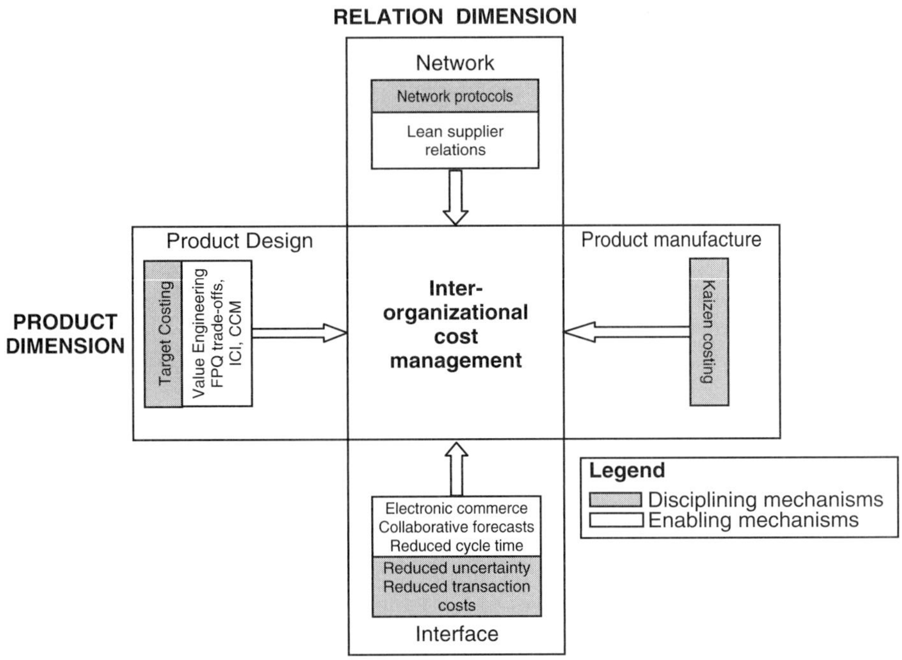

EXHIBIT 9.1 THE INTERORGANIZATIONAL COST MANAGEMENT PROCESS

heavy reliance on cooperation means that only supplier networks—characterized by interdependence, trust, and extensive information sharing—can successfully implement IOCM. Such relations are common among supply chains that have adopted lean manufacturing philosophies.[2] In contrast, a network where buyers and suppliers have an adversarial regard for each other is not conducive to IOCM. Such relations are more common among supply chains that still rely on a batch and queue manufacturing philosophy.[3]

For IOCM to succeed, all the firms must share the additional profits from any improvements among all the firms involved. This sharing creates an incentive for everyone to cooperate, irrespective of each firm's relative strength. The weaker firms will not cooperate unless they receive some of the benefits. The powerful firms will share additional profits only if they anticipate a benefit from sustaining the network's ability to undertake IOCM.

Interorganizational cost management motivates independent, external suppliers to become more efficient in ways that benefit the entire supplier network. It can also motivate internal divisions and subsidiaries acting as suppliers. Internal suppliers frequently lack competitive drive and the related vigilance in cost management. Experience shows, however, that firms can apply IOCM, albeit with some modification, to internal suppliers. In that case, IOCM centers on establishing transfer prices that create realistic pressure on the division or subsidiary to reduce costs at about the same rate as that of external suppliers.

---

2. Lean manufacturing is characterized by manufacturing a single part just in time for its incorporation into the product.
3. Here products are manufactured in batches and there are queues of batches waiting to be processed.

Using IOCM to coordinate the cost-reduction programs at the firms in a supplier network can help reduce costs across two dimensions (Exhibit 9.1). The transaction dimension (shown vertically) deals with the buyer-supplier interactions. This dimension contains two elements: the network, which deals with the environment of IOCM, and the buyer/supplier interface, which together capture the costs incurred by the network members when transacting with each other. The product dimension (shown horizontally) has two elements: product design (including design coordination across buyer and supplier through IOCM) and product manufacture (including coordination of manufacturing processes across buyer and supplier).

9.2 COORDINATING TRANSACTION-RELATED ACTIVITIES

This section explores ways in which firms in a supplier network can reduce transaction costs by coordinating their activities. Firms have two major ways to reduce transactions costs: by coordinating network activities and by coordinating buyer-supplier interface activities. Firms coordinate network activities by adopting lean supplier relations and developing network protocols that foster cooperation. Buyers and suppliers can coordinate their interface by initiating improvement efforts either jointly or separately.

(a) COORDINATING NETWORK ACTIVITIES

(i) Lean Supplier Relations. A lean supplier network typically provides the most conducive environment for IOCM. Such a network has two aspects: (1) Most of the firms that constitute the network have to be lean, and (2) they have to practice lean supply, which tightly coordinates the buyers' and sellers' production activities.

At the heart of lean supply lies the concept of single-piece flow, with the supplier acting as an extended just-in-time (JIT)[4] factory for the buyer. The tight connections between each production step that characterize lean production bring the entire production process to a halt when failure occurs at any step. Likewise for the supply chain: If one supplier delivers defective parts, the buyer's production process will have to stop until the supplier delivers new, nondefective parts. This reliance on suppliers forces the lean producer to develop relations with its suppliers because the firms become tightly connected through their production processes.

Four major characteristics define lean buyer–supplier relations. The first characteristic deals with the reduced supplier base compared to that of mass producers, which typically rely on many suppliers. The second deals with the level of the relation, which depends on the extent to which the buyer relies on the supplier for innovation in product design. The third characteristic captures the nature of the lean buyer–supplier relation: stability over time, cooperation, and mutual benefit. The final characteristic looks at how the buyer and supplier firms blur organizational boundaries as they begin to share resources. Once the two firms have developed the right types of relations, they can realize the related benefits; in particular, they can begin to implement IOCM.

To achieve the full advantages of lean supply, all the firms in the supply chain must adopt lean buyer–supplier relations. Lean supplier networks function in many respects as a single entity dedicated to producing low-cost products that have the high functionality and quality that the end customers demand. The primary advantages of these networks lie in their flexibility and responsiveness compared to that of vertically integrated mass producers.

---

4. Under a JIT philosophy, parts are manufactured and delivered just in time to be used in the manufacturing process. No significant inventories of work-in-process are maintained. JIT can be contrasted to batch and queue philosophies where large inventories of parts are maintained.

(ii) Network Protocols. Three types of supplier networks exist. Each type reflects where the core, or dominating, firm exists within the network. The first type of network, a *kingdom*, emerges when a single firm adopts the core position. Typically, this is the firm that sells the end product to the consumer. These networks operate to support the central firm that dominates the entire network. The second type of network, a *barony*, emerges when several firms populate the core position. The barons dominate the other firms, but they have less power than the core firm in a kingdom. Finally, the third type of network, a *republic,* emerges when no core firm exists. Here, no firm has any significant power over the others and complex coordinated interactions such as IOCM rarely develop.[5]

To maximize its advantages, the network must create and enforce protocols that govern individual firm behavior. Network protocols or rules of conduct extend the behavior patterns developed between individual buyers and suppliers to the level of the network as a whole. They represent common values and shared behaviors. These protocols aim to mitigate negative repercussions from excessive competition and to encourage the necessary cooperation where a situation requires coordination of activities across the boundaries of firms. This coordination can be horizontal or vertical. For example, the adoption of standards such as ISO 9000[6] provides horizontal coordination, while the adoption of cost-management techniques such as target costing (explained in Section 9.3(a)(i) and Chapter 7) provides vertical coordination.

Different kingdoms and baronies will use different methods to establish and enforce these protocols. In a kingdom, the core firm enforces the network protocols in a top-down fashion. Such protocols might include not taking unfair advantage of information learned about member firms during information sharing sessions and guaranteeing a minimum level of business in the near future, or agreeing to provide design support. In a barony, the barons negotiate the protocols and dominate the process. These barony specific protocols might include none of the barons placing excessive pressure on the member firms to support them at the expense of the other barons and the suppliers agreeing not to share proprietary information gained about one of the barons with the other barons. Network protocols help maintain stable patterns of inter-firm collaboration without sacrificing the benefits from competition between firms in the network.

The bargaining power of the dominant firms in lean kingdom and barony networks enables IOCM to spread beyond the single buyer-supplier interface to all buyer-supplier interfaces in the supply chain of each outsourced item. Such networks effectively practice IOCM with dominant buyers initiating the process, which then cascades down to the lowest levels of the supply chains. Such a process does not occur in a republic. In that type of network, the short-term nature of the relations makes formal IOCM almost impossible to practice.

(b) COORDINATING BUYER–SUPPLIER INTERFACE ACTIVITIES

(i) Buyer–Supplier Interface Improvements. A lean supply system tightly coordinates the buyer's and the supplier's production processes. Lean production and supply allows the buyer to adopt a kanban (pull) approach to ordering parts. In this approach, the supplier

---

5. Since IOCM rarely occurs in republic type networks, we will not discuss them in this chapter.
6. The International Organization for Standardization (ISO) published the ISO 9000 series of quality management and quality assurance standards in 1987 as a means to rationalize the many various national approaches to the subject of product quality. The ISO 9000 series has been widely recognized as an aid in developing manufacturing and service organizations' quality management as an additional assurance to product purchasers that the products and services they buy will consistently meet quality objectives.

delivers a small quantity of parts at frequent intervals to the buyer, thereby minimizing inventories and extending JIT production to the supplier base.

The buyer-supplier interface includes all activities and processes associated with the transfer of goods or services from one firm to another. It includes order placement, billing and payment, inventory management of finished goods at the supplier and purchased parts at the supplier, and transportation and external logistics. The network can increase the efficiency of the buyer-supplier interface by reducing the costs associated with these activities and processes, primarily that of transaction processing. As discussed in Sections 9.2 (b)(iii) and (iv), reducing uncertainty with respect to a supplier's ability to deliver on time and a buyer's demands for goods also increases efficiency.

Activity-related improvements lead to reduced transaction processing costs. The network can reduce these costs by first eliminating activities, primarily targeting those that locations duplicate. Second, the network can simplify some processes to consume fewer resources. Processes that trigger common activities at both firms—such as outgoing inspection at the supplier firm and incoming inspection at the buyer firm—become prime candidates for simplification. Third, the firms can standardize activities and processes, particularly when the activities and processes are high-volume, routine, and common to all buyer-supplier interfaces. Finally, the firms can automate activities, particularly standardized, repetitive, and high volume activities.

The improvements aimed at reducing uncertainty lead to lower inventory levels at both firms. The buyer uses inventory to buffer against the supplier's failure to deliver goods to the line on time, and the supplier uses inventory to buffer against unexpected demands from the buyer. If the firms can eliminate these two sources of uncertainty, then buyer and supplier can reduce buffer inventories, thus reducing investments in inventory and increasing the buyer's asset turnover. To reduce these uncertainties, the two firms can increase the amount of information they share and reduce the time required to process transactions that bridge the interface.

Efficient buyer-supplier interfaces can lead to other benefits. Customer and supplier relations may improve as more accurate transactions result in fewer disagreements. More efficient processing of invoices can expedite the cash flow between firms. Finally, the cost of administering the procurement function may decrease as the number of persons involved in the function decreases.

To improve the efficiency of the interface, both firms need to change how they interact. Some of these changes relate to joint projects that require close cooperation and coordination between supplier and buyer, while others originate with initiatives from one of them. The following discussion examines these three types of efficiency improvements.

(ii) Jointly Initiated Improvements. Joint improvements require both the buyer and supplier to take cooperative and coordinated actions to increase the efficiency of their interface. Typically, networks make such improvements by using information technology (IT) to automate information transfer between the two firms—referred to as electronic commerce (EC). The networks may also decide to standardize the order-delivery process to reduce its cycle time. Finally, collaborative forecasting can help reduce uncertainties across the buyer–supplier interface and hence further reduce inefficiencies.

USING ELECTRONIC COMMERCE

Several related developments make EC possible: the rapid development of the Internet, the spread of corporate intranets, and the recent introduction of commercially viable electronic commerce software. These three technologies support inter firm electronic communication. Electronic commerce systems offer the promise of considerably reducing the cost of buyer-supplier interactions while significantly increasing their effectiveness. Firms can develop EC through customized solutions or the Internet. Customized solutions offer the advantage of faster communication between the firms, relative to that of the Internet. However, they suffer from high cost, making them attractive primarily to suppliers responsible for a high percentage of the outsourced value-added. Low value-added suppliers (e.g., common suppliers and subcontractors) typically adopt the Internet approach.

The Internet's easy accessibility offers another advantage. Individuals who want to obtain information about the firm and its products can use the Internet to access the firm's Web pages. The firm doesn't need to expend resources identifying and contacting the individual. Thus, if the firm wants to make any information (e.g., catalogs, price lists, product availability) readily available to anyone 24 hours a day, seven days a week, it can publish it on the Web.

Many firms use electronic data interchange (EDI) to improve the efficiency of the buyer/supplier interface. EDI is the electronic transmission of standard business documents in a predefined format from one company's business computer application to that of another. EDI increases efficiency through improved transaction handling and increased information sharing. EDI can reduce the costs of processing transactions between the two firms by reducing the need to create, handle, and store paper documents. Also, it eliminates the need to reenter data supplied by one firm into the IT systems of the other firm. Third, it reduces clerical errors introduced by reentering data. Finally, it reduces the cycle time needed for one firm to initiate a transaction and the other firm to respond.

EDI also increases the flow of useful information between the firms. With paper transactions, the recipient firm typically enters only a fraction of the information into its computer system. The high cost of data entry causes firms to electronically store only the information that they anticipate they will definitely need. Firms frequently ignore information that they have not stored electronically or access it only if they encounter a problem. With EDI, all the information is electronically available, usually in a uniform format. These two characteristics enable firms to use the data to support better decisions and perhaps automate the decision process.

Order processing, billing, and advanced shipment notices present the three primary applications of EDI. For these high-volume, routine transactions, different firms will perform activities that rely on the same information. To be effective, EDI requires standardization of the order and billing processes of all the participating firms. This standardization allows the firms to communicate easily. A less common, more sophisticated application of EDI automates the release of inventory from the supplier to the buyer. Such applications require both sophisticated computerized inventory management capabilities and translation software and hardware that enable the various computer systems to communicate with each other.

The network can use an EC program in numerous ways to increase the efficiency of the buyer-supplier interface. Potential applications for both EDI and the Internet include the following:

- Purchasing
- Order entry
- Inventory management
- Accounts payable

- Accounts receivable
- Invoicing
- Payment
- Transportation/logistics

The cost–benefit trade-off governs whether to adopt any techniques to increase efficiency. As the cost of implementing and operating the technique increases, the benefits must increase. The larger the supplier and the more business transacted, the more justification for sophisticated techniques. The interface of a core firm with its first-tier suppliers who are family members and major suppliers represents most of the value of outsourced items. Consequently, these firms become prime candidates for electronic commerce.

Even though family members and other major suppliers may supply a high value (i.e., the major components) of the items the lean firm produces, the firm will conduct many transactions with subcontractors and common suppliers which supply a low value (e.g., nuts, bolts, and screws) toward the firm's product. The supplier base of the firm resembles a pyramid with four levels. The family members appear at the apex, followed by the major suppliers, then the subcontractors, and ending with the common suppliers (see Exhibit 9.2).[7] If only one firm sits above this supplier base, then it is a kingdom. In contrast, if several firms sit above this supplier base, then it is a barony (see Exhibit 9.3). The potential aggregate savings but small individual savings in a barony makes automating the subcontractor and common supplier interfaces challenging.

Increasing the efficiency of buyer–supplier interfaces across an entire supply chain provides additional benefits, as the savings at each step are cumulative. Member firms realize benefit from increasing the efficiency of the interfaces across the entire supplier

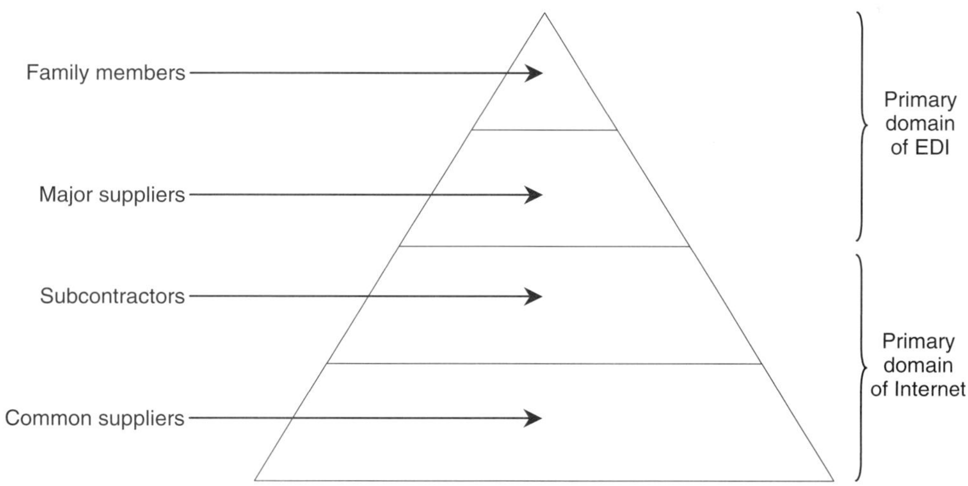

EXHIBIT 9.2 THE SUPPLIER BASE STRUCTURE OF A LEAN ENTERPRISE AND ELECTRONIC COMMERCE

7. Note that this exhibit reflects the number of suppliers, not the dollar value of the supplies from each level. Such a figure would be an inverted pyramid with the relatively few family members or major suppliers providing the highest dollar value of the product's components.

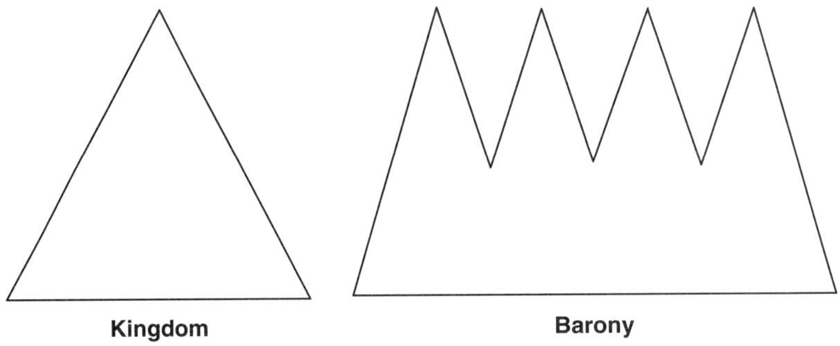

EXHIBIT 9.3 STRUCTURE OF A KINGDOM AND BARONY

network. The firms in a typical supply chain, however, decrease in size and increase in number as one moves down the pyramid. Only the larger firms in the chain usually can support the more expensive techniques to increase the efficiency of the interface. The firms at the bottom of the chain are often too small to justify the more sophisticated approaches (see Exhibit 9.4). Since these firms typically produce the largest number of items, which lower tiers assemble into fewer, more complex, items, they also generate many transactions in the network. The automation of these interfaces represents both a major way to reduce costs and a major challenge.

As EC systems mature, they move away from capturing only instructional or action documents (such as orders and bills) and expand to include status information (such as shipment or payment status). These status applications reduce uncertainty by ensuring that both parties remain current regarding changing business conditions of mutual interest. For example, if the firms transmit price lists via EDI, they minimize the risk of using out-of-date prices. Automated access to status information is available 24 hours a day, seven days a week. For firms that compete in a global marketplace, this availability can provide a competitive advantage.

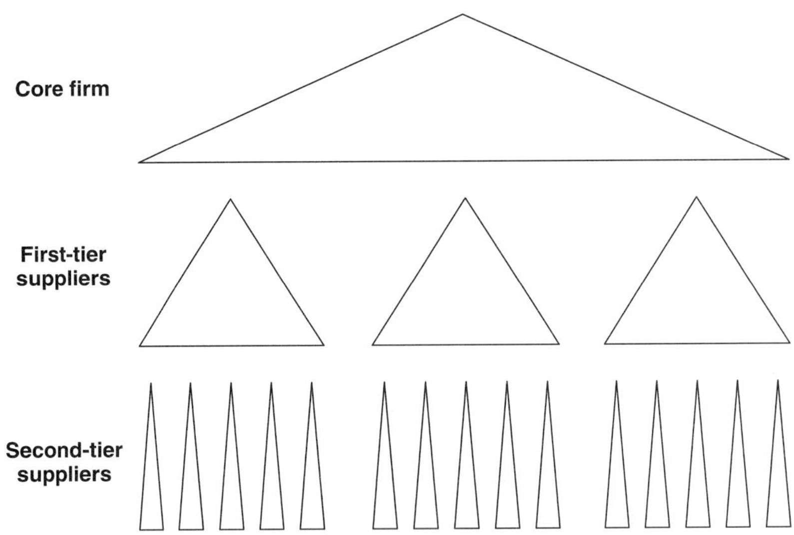

EXHIBIT 9.4 THE SUPPLIER NETWORK FOR A LEAN ENTERPRISE

A network can also use information technology to automate the collection of information about physical transfers using, for example, bar coding. In this situation, the buyer and supplier have to invest in the equipment to prepare and read bar codes. They have to develop a common set of codes that they can use to identify each of the items exchanged between the two firms.

Some special applications of EC link the buyer with specified suppliers. For example, the buyer can identify a list of standard items that departments or individuals can purchase electronically without formal approval. The supplier has to develop the capability to process such orders and ensure that it ships only authorized items. The buyer can also use the Internet to communicate an open order to a number of pre-specified suppliers. The buyer prepares a standardized e-mail that includes the order form that the supplier has to complete and sends it to all the approved suppliers for that item. The suppliers complete the order if they can have the items available by the specified date and e-mail it back to the buyer. The buyer selects the supplier (or suppliers) that will fill the order and sends back confirming e-mails to all suppliers. Thus, the firm can complete the entire process electronically. In a similar process, the buyer can initiate e-mail bidding among nonspecified suppliers when they purchase commodities.

Standardizing the Order-Delivery Process

The second major joint initiative to make the buyer-supplier interface more efficient improves the order-delivery process between the two firms. First, all participating firms standardize their order-delivery process. Second, improved integration of order processing systems reduces the cycle time to process and deliver orders at each firm. Finally, the firms develop collaborative forecasts.

The major firms in the supplier network should standardize the order process before automating it, to simplify the process and make it as common as possible to all the firms. As part of this standardization, the firms should reduce to a minimum the time required to process orders. The shorter the order-delivery cycle, the lower the buffer inventories required by the buyer.

Developing Collaborative Forecasts

The participating firms develop collaborative forecasts by sharing forecasts with each other and coordinating them across the network. The development of common forecasts across multiple supply chains has several advantages. Firms can identify shortages earlier in the planning process and can take corrective actions sooner. For example, if a third-tier supplier's factory suffers heavy damage, the firms in the second tier can either find or create new sources for the outsourced item. Collaborative forecasts prevent firms from introducing slack, with attendant inventory carrying costs, in the forecasts at each interface. For example, if each firm adds 10 percent to the anticipated volume to ensure available capacity, the forecasts will contain 30 percent excess volume at the fourth-tier firms. Finally, the joint involvement will expedite forecasting for each supply chain and will increase efficiency of the forecasts because firms will not need to rework the forecasts as new information arrives from the lower-tier firms.

(iii) Buyer-Initiated Improvements. Buyer-initiated improvements require that the buyer change its behavior in ways that benefit the supplier, although sometimes the supplier may also need to make minor changes. The buyer can adopt seven major initiatives to improve the efficiency of the buyer-supplier interface. Four of these—managing demand, providing adequate order lead time, reducing special ordering, and sharing forecasts—primarily reduce uncertainty. The other three—the use of purchase contracts, payment on receipt, and improved accuracy of communications with the supplier—reduce transaction processing costs.

Improvements that Reduce Uncertainty

- *Manage demand.* The reduction of inventories that characterizes lean supply reduces the supplier's ability to handle unexpected surges in demand. To reduce the supplier's uncertainty, the buyer must manage demand to minimize unanticipated changes. When these changes do occur, the buyer must promptly inform the supplier and indicate whether the change is temporary or permanent.
- *Provide adequate order lead time.* Furthermore, the buyer should have reasonable order lead times and give the supplier sufficient notice so that the supplier can manufacture the order without expediting material or production. The buyer must also minimize changes to orders already placed. Changes that can disrupt the supplier's normal production flow include altering the volume and specifications of items ordered and their delivery dates.
- *Reduce special orders.* The buyer can also reduce the number of special orders it places. Although lean enterprises can economically produce a broader range of products than their mass producer counterparts, the network can support only a limited diversity of products. Consequently, the buyer can reduce the supplier's costs (and hence its own) by ordering standardized parts.
- *Share forecasts.* In addition, the buyer can share its forecasts with its suppliers, thereby reducing the suppliers' uncertainty. As a result, the supplier can better anticipate demand and identify possible capacity constraints. Thus, shared forecasts, including forecasted sales plans and production schedules, help reduce buffer stocks of finished inventory. Sharing forecasts is the first step in developing collaborative forecasts.

Improvements that Reduce Transaction Costs

- *Adopt extended purchase contracts.* The buyer can reduce transaction costs by adopting extended purchase contracts, as opposed to individual purchase orders, for critical items. The extended purchase contract has two purposes. First, it locks in the supplier to help guarantee availability. Second, it allows the buyer to accumulate individual requests for products and make a single payment each period. In contrast, when the buyer uses purchase orders, the firms must process each order as a separate economic transaction. Typically, firms prepare purchase contracts for either a specified quantity of items or for a specified price. The process requires renegotiations only when the parties have completed the contract.
- *Use payment on receipt.* For the noncritical items, the buyer can shift to spot purchases and adopt pay-on-receipt. In this situation, the receipt of the packing slip automatically triggers payment. The supplier does not have to generate an invoice and wait another 30 to 60 days for payment. Bar coding facilitates pay-on-receipt because of the greater accuracy, ease of data entry into the buyer's system, and standardized format.
- *Ensure accuracy of communications.* Finally, the buyer can work to increase the accuracy of its communications with its suppliers. For example, it can increase the accuracy of its orders and its payments. Removing these defects means that both entities have to perform fewer reconciliation and error-correction activities.

(iv) Supplier-Initiated Improvements. Supplier-initiated improvements require that the supplier change its behavior in ways that benefit the buyer, although sometimes the buyer must also make minor changes. The supplier can adopt eight major initiatives to improve the efficiency of the buyer-supplier interface. Five of them—increasing on-schedule deliveries, reducing delivery time, reducing production cycle time, sharing performance metrics, and giving the buyer access to order status information—primarily reduce uncertainty. The other two—improved quality control/extended supplier control over inventories and improved accuracy of its communications with the buyer—reduce transaction processing costs.

IMPROVEMENTS THAT REDUCE UNCERTAINTY

- *Increase on-schedule deliveries.* The supplier can improve the efficiency of the interface by increasing its on-schedule deliveries. A more reliable supplier allows the buyer to reduce buffer inventories.
- *Reduce delivery time.* Reducing delivery times reduces the buyer's uncertainty because it helps contract the overall order-delivery time. This reduction allows the buyer to place orders later without increasing the supplier's uncertainty. The primary advantage of this reduction is that the buyer has more timely information when it places the order.
- *Reduce production cycle time.* Reducing the production cycle time increases the supplier's ability to produce the items ordered by the buyer in the interval between order receipt and scheduled delivery. Decreased production times also enable the supplier to more rapidly observe and correct defects in the production process, thus reducing the risk of late delivery.
- *Share performance metrics.* Suppliers can reduce the buyer's uncertainty by sharing their performance metrics, including defect levels, cycle times, and on-time delivery statistics. This information sharing enables the buyer to identify the suppliers that perform the best and to source accordingly.
- *Give buyer access to order status information.* The supplier can also share shipping status, inventory, and order status information. This information helps the buyer plan its production schedule because it can avoid launching products into manufacturing that will not have all the outsourced parts available. In addition, the buyer can manage its customers' expectations better if it has earlier notice of when it will fail to deliver on time because of parts shortages.

IMPROVEMENTS THAT REDUCE TRANSACTION PROCESSING COSTS

- *Improve quality control to extend supplier control over inventories.* The supplier can adopt total quality management and reduce defects to as near zero as possible. High supplier quality enables the buyer to eliminate inspections when it receives the outsourced items. The elimination of buyer-based inspection allows the supplier to adopt new approaches to the management of the interface inventory. Some of these approaches all but eliminate the concept of separate buyer and supplier inventories. Instead, the supplier has control of the inventory until the buyer can incorporate the items into its products.
- The supplier can improve inventory handling through automated replenishment, vendor-managed inventory, and JIT delivery to the line. In automated replenishment, the buyer sends the supplier a signal that it needs to replenish inventory. The supplier then takes all further actions, including filling the inventory bins at

the buyer. Having the supplier take all responsibility for inventory, including managing the levels at the buyer and making the replenishment decisions without buyer involvement, can extend this process further. Finally, the supplier delivers the order exactly when the buyer's production process requires them. The supplier then becomes fully integrated into the buyer's JIT production process.

- *Improve accuracy of communications.* Finally, the supplier can increase the accuracy of its interactions with the buyer. For example, it can increase the accuracy of its advance shipment notices and of its invoices. Removing these defects means that both sides can reduce the number of reconciliation and error-correction activities.
- Suppliers—particularly small firms—may find some of these techniques too costly to implement. The buyer, however, can realize significant benefits, especially if it has already automated its interactions with larger suppliers. The buyer can reward the supplier, for instance, by giving it access to its advanced technology. For example, the buyer can let the supplier have access to its enterprise resource planning system. The supplier can use this system to gain access to the buyer's EC capabilities.

9.3 COORDINATING PRODUCT-RELATED ACTIVITIES

This section explores ways in which firms in a supplier network reduce manufacturing costs by coordinating product related activities (the horizontal axis of Exhibit 9.1). Firms have two major ways to reduce manufacturing costs: coordinating product development and coordinating manufacturing activities. Firms achieve the first objective by adopting chained target costing (discussed in Chapter 7), functionality-price-quality-trade-offs, interorganizational cost investigations, and concurrent cost management. They achieve the second objective by initiating interorganizational kaizen costing (see Chapter 8) and individual buyer-led and supplier-led initiatives.

(a) COORDINATING PRODUCT DEVELOPMENT ACTIVITIES

(i) Chained Target Costing. Target costing is a structured approach to identify the cost at which a firm must produce a product to generate the desired level of profitability over its life-cycle at its anticipated selling price.[8] Target costing systems consist of three major steps. In the first step, market-driven costing, the firm establishes the proposed product's selling price. In the second, product-level target costing, the firm establishes the product design. In the final step, component-level target costing, the firm establishes the purchase prices of outsourced components.

Target costing systems become especially effective when they form a chain. A chained target costing system emerges when the output of a buyer's target costing system becomes an input to a supplier's target costing system. Component-level target costing at the buyer establishes the target selling prices used by the market-driven costing section of the supplier's target costing system to set the allowable costs of the components. These allowable costs become the basis for setting the product-level target costs and hence the component-level target costs for the supplier. The component-level target costs then establish the selling prices of the next firm in the supply chain. Thus, the primary benefit of chained target costing systems lies in their ability to transmit the competitive pressure faced by the firm at the top of the chain to the other firms in the chain (see Exhibit 9.5).

8. See Chapter 7 for a detailed discussion on target costing.

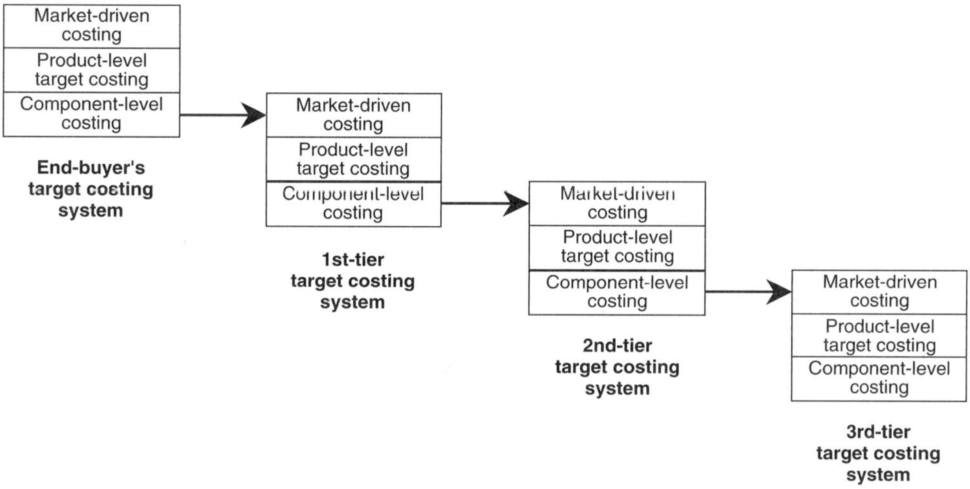

EXHIBIT 9.5 CHAINED TARGET COSTING: MULTIPLE FIRMS

The buyers can transmit this pressure through their demands for the components' quality, functionality, and target costs. This pressure makes chained target costing systems valuable by creating a powerful incentive for the entire supply chain to become more efficient. In particular, the marketplace dictates the rate at which the firms become more efficient. Chained target costing systems force each firm in the chain to reduce costs at a rate that will enable all the firms in the chain to maintain adequate levels of profitability.

A target costing chain can consist of all or part of a supply chain. The buyer's ability to dictate selling prices to its suppliers identifies both the beginning and end of a target costing chain (see Exhibit 9.6). A firm exists at the top of the chain when its customers lack the power to dictate its selling prices and the firm has the power to use its target costing system to dictate selling prices to its suppliers. Firms are in the middle of a chain when (1) their customers' target costing systems set their selling prices, and (2) they have the ability to use their own target costing system to dictate their suppliers' selling prices. A firm exists at the end of the chain when (1) its customers' target costing systems determine its selling prices and (2) the firm purchases its inputs from suppliers that have more power that it does. With more powerful suppliers, the firm at the end of the chain cannot use target costing to set the prices of the components and raw materials that it purchases.

Although a target costing chain can have only one firm at the top and one firm at the end, theoretically, it can have any number of firms in the middle. Since in practice, however, a supply chain typically has two to six levels of firms, most target costing chains contain only two to four firms.

Interorganizational cost management occurs at the interface between the buyer and supplier. The relative power of the two firms that constitute the interface shapes the nature of the interface and the target costing process at the interface. Chained target costing acts at two levels. First, it helps define the nature of the buyer-supplier interface and second, it helps establish some of the codes of behavior that create the supplier network's overall stability. Chained target costing becomes particularly effective when the design teams of the buyer and supplier can interact to change the specifications for the component in ways that make it easier to manufacture at its target cost but that do not alter the

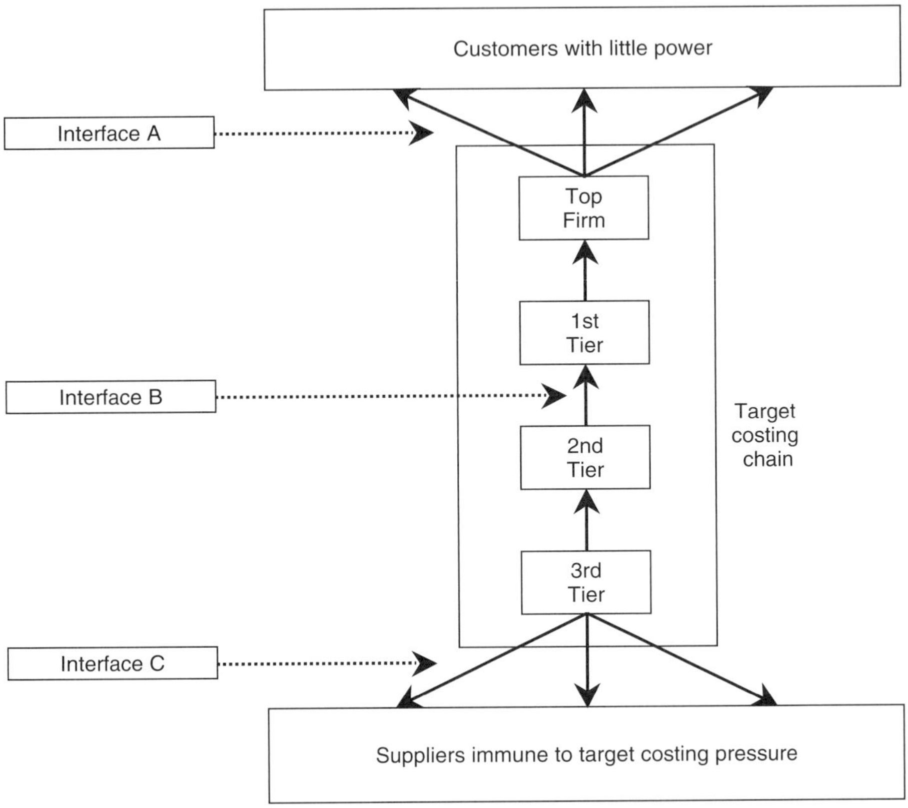

EXHIBIT 9.6 THE THREE TYPES OF INTERFACES IN A TARGET COSTING CHAIN

final product's specifications. Such trade-offs (discussed below in section 9.3(a)(ii) play an important role in ensuring that all firms in the chain remain profitable.

The nature of the interface between the buyer and supplier and the associated target costing process depends on the position of the firms in the target costing chain (see Exhibit 9.6). A unique interface exists between the top firm and the individuals or firms that buy its products (interface A in Exhibit 9.6). Here, the buyer has little or no individual power over the supplier; however, the market gives buyers considerable collective power. Toyota, and other automobile manufacturers, have this type of interface with most customers. In the middle of the chain, the firm's buyers exercise power over it, and the firm, in turn, exercises power over its suppliers (Interface B in Exhibit 9.6). Firms in the middle have two interfaces, one as a supplier (interface B1 in Exhibit 9.7) and one as a buyer (interface B2 in Exhibit 9.7). The B1 interface links the market-driven costing portion of the middle firm's target costing system with the component-level target costing portion of the firm that buys from the middle firm. An example is the interface between an automobile manufacturer and a supplier of cooling systems. The B2 interface is between the component-level target costing portion of the middle firm's target costing system and the market-driven costing portion of the target costing system of the firm that supplies the middle firm. An example of this second type of interface would be between the cooling system manufacturer and a firm that supplies it with radiators. At the end of the chain, the buyers exercise power over the firm, but the firm exercises little or no power over its suppliers (interface C in Exhibit 9.6). This lack of power means that the

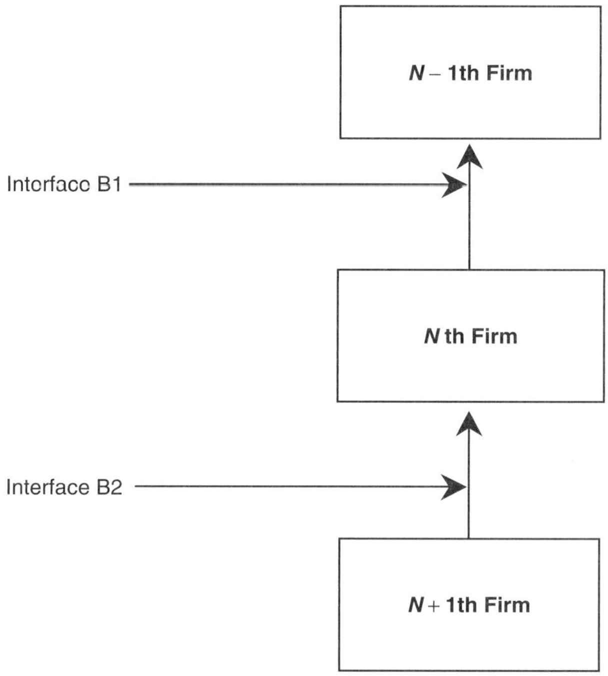

EXHIBIT 9.7 THE TWO DIFFERENT INTERFACES FOR THE *N*TH FIRM IN THE MIDDLE OF A TARGET COSTING CHAIN

firm at the end of the chain faces intense cost-reduction pressure that it cannot transmit to its suppliers. For this reason, we do not consider the interface between the firm at the end of the chain and its suppliers as part of the target costing chain. An example of this type of interface would be that between the radiator manufacturer and the suppliers of aluminum.

As one moves along the target costing chain, the shifting nature of the various buyer-supplier interfaces influences how firms structure their target costing processes. In particular, it shapes the nature of the market-driven costing and component-level target costing processes. All firms in the chain have the same product-level target costing process. Product-level target costing is primarily an internally driven process and thus relatively unaffected by the firm's position in the chain. The only significant difference occurs when the product engineers look for cost-reduction opportunities. For firms at the top or in the middle of the chain, heavy interaction with suppliers provides a major way to reduce costs. In contrast, the firm at the end of the chain has almost no ability to influence supplier costs. This lack of power over its suppliers makes it difficult for the end firm to transmit cost-reduction pressures to its suppliers. Like the customers of the firm at the top of the chain, the end firm must, along with the other customers of its suppliers, try to create collective pressure on its suppliers to reduce costs.

The market-driven costing process decreases in sophistication from top to bottom of the target costing chain. This lower degree of sophistication reflects the reduced need to identify target selling prices through market analysis. The buyer's target costing system most often sets the target selling price. The component-level target costing process is least sophisticated at the end of the chain because that firm has little ability to influence its suppliers' selling prices. Thus, firms tailor certain aspects of their target costing systems to the type of interface they have with their buyers and suppliers.

(ii) Functionality-Price-Quality (FPQ) Trade-Offs. Firms in the middle of the target costing chain have a simplified market-driven costing process because their buyers' target costing systems set their selling prices. Therefore, these firms typically do not have extensive market analysis subsystems designed to identify the target selling prices of their products. Even though these firms have little influence over the selling prices because of the buying power of their customers, they can modify the functionality and quality of their products. For firms in the middle of the target costing chain, survival depends on their ability to manage the functionality and quality of their products by negotiating reductions in functionality and quality with their customers. Such negotiations will have success only if the reductions do not lead to a significant decrease in the final product's functionality or quality.

In an FPQ trade-off, firms explore ways to provide their customers with products whose reduced functionality and quality the customers will still accept. Successfully achieving this trade-off allows these firms to find solutions to a customer's product requirements that generate adequate returns. Lowering the functionality and quality of a component without decreasing the functionality or quality of the end product allows these firms to reduce manufacturing costs. Since the selling price remains unchanged, the firms hope to increase their profits to acceptable levels. Thus, balancing functionality, price, and quality becomes key to survival in the middle or end of the chain.

Buyer and supplier firms can successfully negotiate reductions in functionality and quality only when the buyer has over-specified some aspect of the component. Over-specification occurs when the buyer demands too much of the FPQ components, lacks knowledge of, or ignores the supplier's cost-benefit trade-offs, or uses component specifications to create negotiating space for the supplier.

The intense competitive pressure that the buyer faces often requires the firm to improve all three primary characteristics of the product: price, functionality, and quality. Overreacting to this pressure, the buyer might demand improvements from its suppliers along all three characteristics. Such improvements in the components need not provide benefits to the final consumers. If the supplier can identify such over-specifications and get the buyer to relax them, then its costs will decrease.

Alternatively, the improvements may provide benefits to the final consumers, but the consumers place insufficient value on these improvements to justify the higher costs (of improved quality and functionality) imposed on the supplier. In such cases, the buyer's target cost for the component is too low, and the supplier will not realize an adequate return. This condition may emerge because the buyer has insufficient knowledge of its suppliers' cost functions.

Finally, the buyer might over-specify the component to create some negotiating space with the supplier. Buyer and supplier firms need to maintain a cooperative relation so the buyer may plan for this negotiating space to allow the supplier some success in the negotiations. By gaining some concessions, the supplier might view the contract as more acceptable than it would have if the buyer had forced the supplier to accept specifications.

Occasionally, the supplier can use FPQ trade-offs to get the buyer to increase component-level target costs by adding value to the components. The supplier can add value in two ways. First, the increased functionality or quality translates into higher selling prices for the buyer. These higher prices lead to increased product-level target costs and hence increased component-level target costs. Alternatively, the supplier can add value by decreasing the buyer's costs, for example, by rendering a subsequent production step unnecessary. In such a case, the buyer's manufacturing costs will fall so the component-level target costs can increase without violating the overall target cost.

(iii) Interorganizational Cost Investigations. A limitation of chained target costing emerges when the buyer designs a component that leads to unnecessarily high manufacturing costs for the supplier. The poor design usually results from the buyer's limited knowledge of the production economics of the firms in the supply chain. Since the buyer cannot design components that benefit from the supplier's manufacturing skills, the supplier must manufacture components that do not make optimal use of its production processes. This limitation becomes a problem when the buyer's component specifications make it impossible for the supplier to generate an adequate return on the component. Under chained target costing, the supplier has only two choices: either say no, thus obeying the *no loss* rule of target costing[9]; or try to negotiate a higher selling price, a difficult objective given the buyer's reliance on target costing. A third option is to initiate an interorganizational cost investigation (ICI). Under an ICI, the firms can make more fundamental changes to the product and component specifications than they would achieve using an FPQ trade-off.

The more pervasive nature of the design changes possible under ICI requires greater levels of interaction among the design teams. These interactions involve the application of value engineering techniques.[10] To justify the time invested toward the redesign, the part being redesigned must be both significant in value and amenable to redesign.

The power of ICIs derives from the increased scope of the design changes that the network can make to both the end product and the components it contains. Chained target costing fixes the specifications of the end product. Although FPQ trade-offs allow some relaxation of the quality and functionality specifications of components, the functionality and quality of the buyer's product must remain unchanged in the eyes of its customers. However, more fundamental changes, such as redesigning a component in a way that requires the buyer to modify other aspects of the end product, call for an interorganizational cost investigation.

The increased scope of the design changes and the interaction between product designers from both buyers and suppliers allow the network to design the parts to increase cost efficiency at all stages from raw material to finished product. In other words, the network can design products and components so that they reflect global, not local, production economics. Networks can use ICI to reduce costs in two ways. First, they can change the location of activities to increase efficiency (see Exhibit 9.8). Second, they can reduce or avoid some activities by redesigning the product and the components it contains to take full advantage of the manufacturing skills throughout the target costing chain (see Exhibit 9.9).

The decision to shift the location of an activity requires knowledge about the production processes and economics of the entire chain. Several questions require answers before one decides to move an activity (see Exhibit 9.10).

- Can other firms in the chain perform the activity?
- Can any of those firms perform that activity more efficiently?
- Do synergies exist between that activity and those already performed at any of those firms that would allow overall cost reduction by undertaking them in the same location? For example, moving machining operations to the same location may enable the firms to perform the operation only once. Even if the relocated

9. The no loss rule of target costing is designed to stop member firms selling products at a loss (or insufficient profits). The only exceptions are strategic products (see Chapter 7).
10. For a detailed description of value engineering, see Chapter 7.

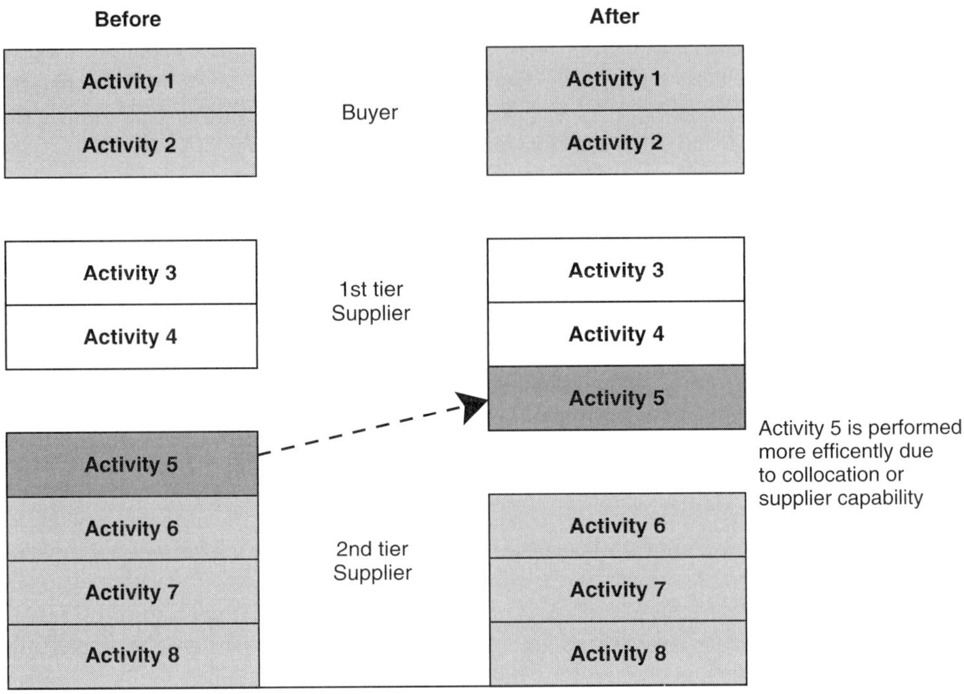

EXHIBIT 9.8 MOVING ACTIVITIES

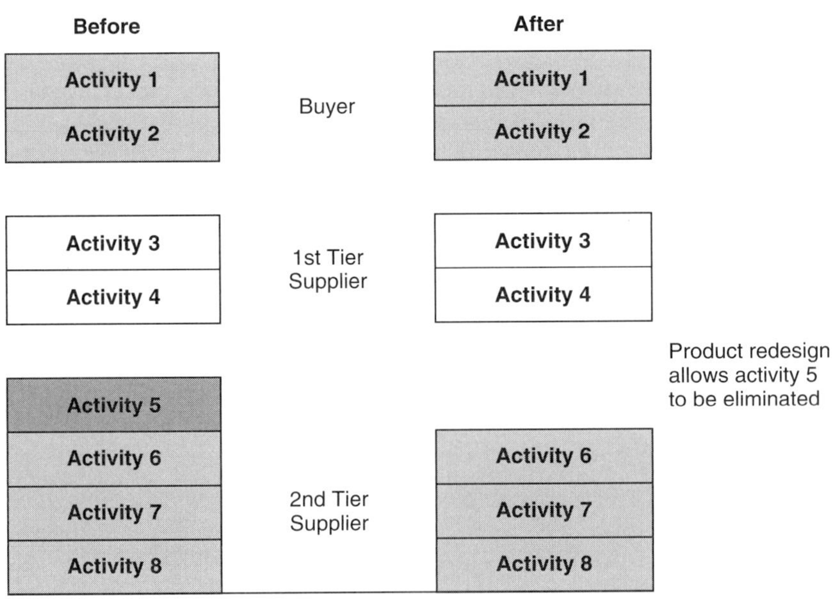

EXHIBIT 9.9 AVOIDING ACTIVITIES

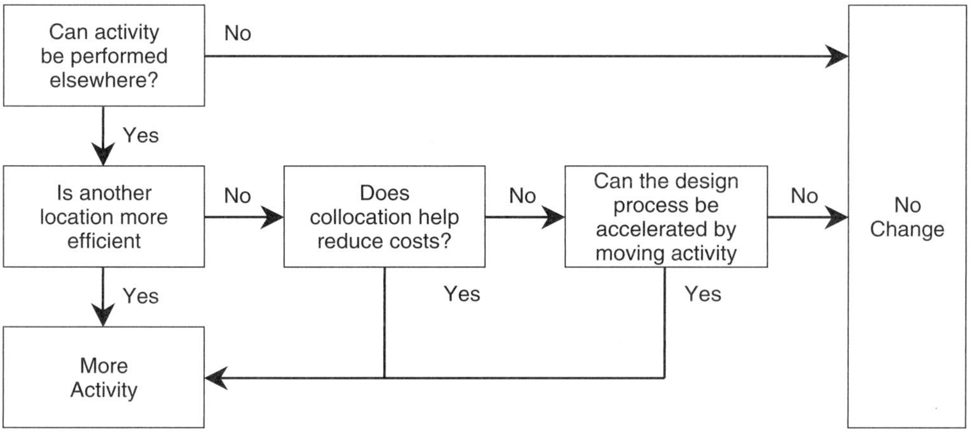

EXHIBIT 9.10 THE DECISION TO MOVE ACTIVITIES AMONG FIRMS IN THE TARGET COSTING CHAIN

activity performs less efficiently at the new location, overall costs will decrease if the savings due to collocation dominate.

- Can the network accelerate the design process by moving activities at a reasonable cost?

A network can also use an ICI to redesign the product or the components it contains to take better advantage of the entire supply chain's production capabilities.

The inability of at least one firm in the network to achieve the target costs set by its buyer usually triggers the cost investigation. Under the *no loss* rule, this firm should reject the order. Interorganizational cost investigations, however, can help firms avoid such occurrences. If the firms do not use chained target costing, then presumably the supplier's inability to negotiate a price that enables it to make adequate profit on the component will trigger the ICI.

The ability to initiate an ICI resembles the ability of any worker in a JIT production setting to stop the line when he encounters a defect. The inability of one of the firms in a network to achieve its target costs demonstrates that a defect has occurred in the target costing process. The usual source of the problem lies in the component design. As in the production setting, once a person or entity identifies the defect, all surrounding workers (in this case, the design teams at the other firms) get together to resolve the problem.

(iv) Concurrent Cost Management. The addition of ICIs to chained target costing increases the scope of the design changes that the network can make to the end product and its components. These two techniques, however, still limit the extent to which the suppliers can influence the design of the buyer's product. This limitation occurs because suppliers become involved in the buyer's product development process at a relatively late stage, typically when the buyer is well into the design stage of the product development process. This late involvement often makes it impossible for suppliers to get approval for cost-reduction ideas that require fundamental modifications to the end product because implementing them would delay the launching of the product. The network can eliminate this limitation by involving suppliers much earlier in the design process, so they can suggest design changes when the buyer still has time to incorporate those changes into the end product's design.

When the buyer outsources research and development for a major function or group component, concurrent cost management (CCM) becomes a powerful approach to managing costs. Concurrent cost management comprises two major approaches: parallel and simultaneous engineering. In parallel engineering, the buyer provides the supplier with high-level specifications for the major function. These specifications allow the supplier to design the major function in isolation. The buyer's design team can make any alterations to the product as long as they do not lead to changes in the high-level specifications of the outsourced major functions. Similarly, the supplier's design teams can make changes in the design of the major function as long as they do not lead to changes in the high-level specifications. Parallel engineering's primary advantage is that the supplier can uncouple its product development cycle from that of the buyer. The buyer keeps the supplier informed about its new product plans, and the supplier uses this information to guide its product development process.

In the second approach to CCM—simultaneous engineering—the buyer's and supplier's design teams work together to identify mutually beneficial designs for both the end product and the outsourced major function.

To select which engineering approach to use, the firms should weigh the benefits from close interactions between the buyer's and supplier's design teams. If they anticipate little benefit from such interaction, they should use parallel engineering. If they anticipate a high benefit from close interactions, they should use simultaneous engineering.

Under both approaches, a fundamental shift in supplier relations occurs because the buyer now asks its suppliers to design a major function or group component as opposed to individual components. For example, instead of ordering the individual components of a cooling system—such as a radiator, fan, and electric motor—separately, the buyer now orders a complete engine cooling system (a major function) or starter motor (a group component). The suppliers thus take responsibility for some, if not all, of the research and development for the major function or group component.

The outsourcing of research and development increases the interdependence between the buyer and supplier. The buyer now depends on the supplier for its technical expertise, and the buyer represents a significant portion of the supplier's business. Under such conditions, stable, cooperative, and balanced buyer–supplier relations become critical. The higher level of interdependence means that the component-level target cost setting process depends more heavily on negotiation and less on the more powerful buyer dictating the selling price, functionality, and quality. To reflect the suppliers' importance, many buyers refer to such suppliers as partners or family members.

Concurrent cost management provides several benefits. First, it allows family members more time to design their products, and hence provides more opportunity to reduce costs. Second, with the greater sharing of strategic information, family members can develop new generations of their products independent of their customers' product design processes. For example, the family member that supplies cooling systems can develop the next generation of such systems independently of the buyer as long as the family member knows that it will get the future business and that the buyer will require cooling systems with additional capacity. Third, concurrent cost management allows faster introduction of products because the product development processes of the buyer and supplier occur at the same time. Finally, it reduces overall costs by allowing the two firms to jointly design the end product and the major function.

Concurrent cost management has some potential drawbacks. The two firms lose independence as they become critical to each other's success. For the buyer, this dependency can lead to technological obsolescence if the family member does not remain on the development frontier. For the family member, it can mean loss of volume if the buyer fails to remain competitive with its competitors. In addition, the buyer faces the disadvantage of losing much of its ability to differentiate products based on any proprietary technology used in the major function it sources through its family members. This loss of proprietary technology causes more difficulties in baronies because the suppliers also sell their products to the other, competitor, barons. Hence, the family needs to develop protocols against sharing proprietary technologies. In a kingdom, the problem is less serious, as the suppliers are captive to a single firm. If the buyer does not consider the technology a core competence, however, this drawback should have minimal effects.

(b) COORDINATING MANUFACTURING ACTIVITIES

(i) Initiating Interorganizational Kaizen Costing. Kaizen costing[11] has become the primary technique to coordinate manufacturing activities in a supplier network. Interorganizational kaizen costing starts when the buyer transmits the cost-reduction pressure it faces in the marketplace to its suppliers by telling them how rapidly it expects their selling prices to fall over time. Most kaizen costing programs set the same cost-reduction objectives for all external sourced items. For example, the buyer might tell all of the suppliers to achieve an annual cost-reduction target of 3 percent. In more sophisticated approaches, it might set different cost-reduction rates depending on the nature of the outsourced items. The flat cost-reduction objectives established for suppliers by the buyer's kaizen costing program differ significantly from the component-specific objectives set by the buyer's target costing program that are unique to each outsourced item.

The difference in the two approaches reflects two fundamental differences between the cost-reduction capabilities of target and kaizen costing. First, target costing can achieve larger savings than those of kaizen costing. These larger savings reflect the firm's greater ability to manage costs during the product design phase as opposed to the manufacturing phase. Therefore, expending more energy on setting item-specific target costing objectives than on kaizen costing ones will likely have higher payoff.

Second, if firms neglect cost savings measures in the design phase, they will lose them until they design the product's next generation because once a firm has designed a product, it typically will not change that design until the next generation.[12] In contrast, most cost savings during the manufacturing stage deal with improving production processes. Therefore, a firm can capture such cost savings for as long as it continues to use the manufacturing process. Reflecting this ability, many firms set their kaizen cost-reduction objectives based on current market conditions. If the market supports existing price levels, firms set relatively low cost-reduction objectives, whereas with decreasing prices, the firms adopt more aggressive objectives. Furthermore, production processes often remain the same across multiple generations of products. So while the firms realize smaller annual savings, these savings will accumulate over a longer period of time than those of target costing. These two properties of kaizen costing—smaller cost savings that firms can achieve over multiple years—make it less critical to achieve the savings in a given year. This justifies setting a single cost-reduction rate at the level demanded by the

---

11. *Kaizen* is the Japanese term for continuous improvement. For a detailed discussion on kaizen costing see Chapter 8.

12. This statement is especially true for products with a short life cycle. As the life cycle gets longer, the willingness of firms to consider product redesign if the cost overrun is significant increases,

market and fine tuning that overall rate from year to year rather than setting specific objectives for each outsourced item.

As with many IOCM techniques, either the buyer or the supplier[13] can initiate kaizen costing interventions. For buyer-led interventions, the buyer either augments the supplier's cost-reduction capabilities or gives the supplier access to cost-reduction opportunities that the supplier cannot access otherwise. In supplier-led initiatives, the supplier finds new ways to manufacture components that lead to lower overall costs in the supply chain.

The interactions between buyers and suppliers that lead to effective interorganizational kaizen costing during manufacturing rely heavily on the cooperative, stable, and balanced nature of lean buyer-supplier relations. The need for cooperation lies at the heart of interorganizational cost management. Only when buyers and suppliers actively cooperate can they identify real opportunities for interorganizational cost reduction. Stability becomes important because of the long-term nature of the savings, as kaizen savings accumulate over time. Each side will more willingly invest in the other if they both perceive that the relation will exist for an extended time. Finally, kaizen costing requires a balance of power to ensure that the buyer and its suppliers equitably share any savings. Otherwise, the suppliers may not participate in any processes initiated by the buyer or initiate their own interorganizational kaizen costing interventions.

(ii) Buyer-Led Initiatives. The buyer often has to take a proactive role in helping the supplier become more efficient. The buyer can use one of two approaches: educate the suppliers or give them access to cost savings they cannot achieve in isolation. The education route proves most effective when the buyer has more skill at outsourcing and engineering than do its suppliers. For example, if the supplier is a subcontractor and does not have any significant engineering skills, the buyer might provide some engineering help and train some of its workers in new techniques. Often, the buyer can achieve savings by designing the next generation of the part to make it easier for the suppliers to produce.

The buyer can also initiate such savings by giving the supplier access to cost savings that the supplier cannot achieve in isolation. Buyers achieve this objective in two ways, depending on whether they face a single supplier or multiple suppliers. In the single-supplier approach, the buyer identifies a less expensive source for items used by the supplier. The supplier then passes the savings on to the buyer through supplier price reductions.

The multiple supplier approach takes advantage of the combined buying power of the network. In this approach, the buyer identifies components used in its products by multiple suppliers and, often, itself, such as types of steel, nuts and bolts and other commonly used items. The buyer arranges with a single firm to source all of the supply chain's requirements for these components. The combined volume allows the buyer to negotiate greater discounts than the individual suppliers could. Again, the suppliers pass the savings on to the buyer through reduced supplier prices.

(iii) Supplier-Led Initiatives. Suppliers can also initiate interorganizational kaizen costing by identifying new ways to design a component to reduce its costs. In contrast with target costing, the component's functionality and quality will typically remain constant during the redesign process as the buyer will not want its customers to perceive its

13. As explained before, when the supplier shares in the benefit of the network's cost savings, it will have an incentive to initiate such an intervention.

product as having changed. If the design change has no implications for the buyer, it is an example of kaizen costing at the supplier. If the design change involves the buyer, however, it becomes an example of interorganizational kaizen costing.

The buyer's cooperation can take three forms. The most significant level of cooperation occurs when the buyer changes its product in some way to accommodate the new low-cost component. This level of cooperation will occur only for major components that have developed serious cost problems or for which the supplier's new design significantly reduces the buyer's costs through price reductions on the supplier's part.

The second level of cooperation occurs when the buyer agrees to change its production processes to accommodate changes in the component's design. The buyer will more likely agree to such changes if it views them as providing direct or indirect benefits. Potential direct benefits include elimination or simplification of the buyer's production activities, or supplier price reductions that offset any additional costs for the buyer. Potential indirect benefits include increasing the perceived value of the buyer's relation with the supplier. The buyer will value this strengthening relation with important suppliers that can be expected to reciprocate in the future.

The third level of cooperation occurs when the buyer provides the supplier with engineering support to help identify and approve changes in the design of the component or its production processes. By making such requests, the supplier demonstrates its willingness to work with the buyer to find new, low-cost solutions. In turn, the buyer demonstrates its willingness to expend resources on behalf of the supplier to help it achieve its cost-reduction objectives.

9.4 SUMMARY

Interorganizational cost management has two major dimensions: increased efficiency of the network between buyers and suppliers, and improved product design and efficiency in the manufacturing process. The network dimension captures the role of the supplier network and the network protocols in cultivating an environment for effective IOCM. It also captures the need to reduce transaction costs by making the buyer-supplier interface more efficient. The network can achieve these efficiency improvements through joint efforts that take advantage of electronic commerce or standardize joint processes. The buyers can reduce the uncertainty that their suppliers face by shortening the order cycle; the supplier can also take steps to reduce the buyer's uncertainty. These actions lower buffer inventories in the supply chain and create a more responsive supply chain.

The second dimension captures the IOCM processes associated with product design and product manufacture. Chained target costing systems occur when the output of the buyer's component-level target costing process feeds directly into the supplier's market-driving costing process. They enable the firm at the top of the chain to transmit the competitive pressure it faces to all the firms in the chain. Three major enabling mechanisms help the firms in the target costing chain achieve their cost-reduction objectives: FPQ trade-offs, interorganizational cost investigations, and concurrent cost management.

The buyer can use kaizen costing to transmit the cost pressure it faces to its suppliers. In this way it acts as a mechanism for IOCM during manufacturing. The interorganizational kaizen costing process focuses on the production processes the supplier uses to manufacture the items outsourced by the buyer. Unlike target costing, which sets individual cost-reduction objectives for each component, kaizen costing typically uses the same flat-rate objectives for all components. The exception occurs for high-priced components, which have specific cost-reduction objectives. The network adopts this simplified approach to setting cost-reduction objectives because kaizen costing generates lower annual savings that accumulate over a longer time period—missed savings one year can still be captured at a later period (though they will be lost for the intervening period).

Interorganizational kaizen costing aims to put relentless but attainable cost-reduction pressure on suppliers. For this reason, the buyer takes care to set realistic cost-reduction objectives that reflect the suppliers' capabilities. To set realistic objectives, the buyer must know details about both the suppliers' capabilities and the end market or markets in which it sells its products.

CHAPTER **10**

COSTS AND BENEFITS OF QUALITY IMPROVEMENT

CHRISTOPHER D. ITTNER, DBA
The Wharton School, University of Pennsylvania

DAVID F. LARCKER, PHD
The Wharton School, University of Pennsylvania

CONTENTS

10.1 INTRODUCTION 313

10.2 ASSOCIATIONS BETWEEN QUALITY INVESTMENTS, IMPROVEMENTS, AND FINANCIAL PERFORMANCE 313

(a) Quality-Related Costs 315

(b) Quality-Related Revenue Implications 318

10.3 MANAGING THE COSTS AND BENEFITS OF QUALITY IMPROVEMENT 320

(a) Analysis of Cost and Revenue Drivers 321

(b) Project Selection 321

(c) Monitoring and Measuring Progress 321

10.4 APPLYING THE FRAMEWORK 323

10.5 SUMMARY 327

BIBLIOGRAPHY 327

10.1 INTRODUCTION

Competitive requirements have forced nearly every firm to invest in quality improvement activities, ranging from standard product inspection and simple customer complaint processing to extensive efforts to transform the firm into a customer-focused organization. However, many companies experience difficulty identifying the quality improvement projects offering the highest returns, or quantifying the financial payback from these investments. These difficulties primarily result from the lack of adequate methods for estimating the costs and benefits of quality improvement. This chapter discusses some of the methods available to assess the financial implications of quality improvements, and provides a framework for integrating this information into the quality improvement process.

10.2 ASSOCIATIONS BETWEEN QUALITY INVESTMENTS, IMPROVEMENTS, AND FINANCIAL PERFORMANCE

The costs and benefits of quality improvement take a number of forms. Quality-related investments fall into three categories.

1. *Prevention expenditures* represent investments in employees, processes, and activities to avoid defects, errors, rework, or delay. Examples include expenditures on quality-related training and the development and operation of a quality control system, as well as the additional costs incurred when a firm purchases higher-quality materials and equipment to ensure that products and services meet customer requirements.
2. *Appraisal expenditures* go toward measuring or testing whether a product or service meets customer requirements. Typical appraisal activities include product inspection, proofreading documents, quality audits and reviews, and customer surveys.
3. *Product or service enhancement expenditures* improve customer satisfaction through the addition or improvement of features, functions, or service attributes valued by the customer.

Two potential benefits result from these investments. First, eliminating quality problems can reduce costs and improve productivity. Quality-related productivity losses can result from *internal failures*, which occur before delivery of the product or service to the customer, or from *external failures* occurring after delivery to the customer. The more tangible productivity benefits from higher quality arise through increased output of defect-free products and services and lower expenditures on scrap, corrections and revisions, inspection, and warranty costs. Other, less tangible, productivity benefits can also occur, such as fewer disruptions in operations due to defective purchases and production, elimination of buffer inventories and other assets held to compensate for poor quality, improved machine utilization, and reductions in quality-related schedule changes and downtime.

Second, quality improvements can increase revenues by lowering return rates and improving customer satisfaction. The delivery of defective products and services to customers not only causes revenue losses when customers return goods or the company grants price concessions, but it also generates *lost opportunities* when previous customers do not return or potential customers choose competitors based on others' unsatisfactory experience with the firm. A study by the U.S. Department of Commerce found that dissatisfied customers tell approximately 19 others about their bad experience with a product.[1] Similarly, marketing studies identify a number of benefits from higher customer satisfaction with the firm's goods or services, including increased loyalty of current customers, reduced price elasticities and higher profit margins, increased market share through positive word-of-mouth advertising, and enhanced firm reputation.

One can calculate the return on investment (ROI) from quality improvements using this formula:[2]

$$\text{ROI} = (\text{Revenue changes} + \text{Productivity changes})/\text{Investment}$$

The difficulties arise in measuring these costs and benefits. The following section discusses a variety of methods that analysts can use to assess the financial implications of quality improvement activities.

---

1. See Technical Assistance Research Programs (TARP), Consumer Complaint Handling in America: Final Report, Washington, D.C.: U.S. Department of Commerce, 1979.
2. Clearly, a net present value formulation is needed to calculate return-on-investment if the timing of cash inflows and outflows differ or if the revenue benefits from improved quality persist over multiple periods. We apply net present value approaches in later examples.

(a) QUALITY-RELATED COSTS. Quality improvement efforts can take various forms, including reducing or eliminating activities or features that provide little value to the customer, allocating additional resources to product or service characteristics that customers do value, or reducing costs arising from failure to meet customer requirements. Studies indicate that many manufacturers spend up to 25 percent of sales on the prevention, detection, and correction of quality problems, while service firms spend up to 40 percent of sales on these activities.[3] To identify profitable quality improvement opportunities, one must understand which of these expenditures add value to the customer and which have higher valued uses elsewhere. Firms have adopted a variety of techniques for assessing and classifying quality-related costs; we discuss four such techniques here: analysis of existing accounting records; activity analysis, statistical analysis, and simulation models.

(i) Analysis of Existing Accounting Records. Existing accounting records (especially those in manufacturing firms) may already track data on quality-related costs, such as scrap, rework, warranty claims, and quality department expenditures. Although existing accounting records provide a convenient source of information on the financial consequences of quality improvement, accounting systems designed without quality costing in mind typically identify only a fraction of quality-related expenditures.

A study sponsored by the Illinois Manufacturers Association found that the costs of quality-related activities and failures are four times higher than most manufacturers estimate, based on their existing accounting records. Most of these differences relate to quality activities in white-collar functions such as accounting, engineering, and marketing, costs that accounting systems rarely identify or highlight. Other studies estimate that quality-related costs can represent up to 50 percent of a white-collar function's budget, yet most companies have little or no capability to track these costs.[4] Because accounting systems generally do not provide information on the costs and benefits of quality improvement, firms need other sources to provide a more complete assessment of quality-related expenditures.

(ii) Activity Analysis. Activity analysis involves detailed studies of the activities performed by each department. This analysis first identifies the specific activities performed in each operation. Activity analysis then identifies activities related to the prevention and appraisal of quality problems or to the correction of quality failures. Often an activity contains both quality-related tasks and work required to deliver a product or service. The definitions in Exhibit 10.1 can be used to assign tasks to the appropriate categories.

Once analysts have identified and classified activities, they can estimate the cost incurred for each quality-related task. Techniques for assessing these costs include the following:

- *Time reporting.* In some job functions, time reports or work orders provide sufficient detail to identify employees' activities, which one can use to estimate quality-related costs. Job codes or titles may also indicate an employee's primary activities and responsibilities. Analysts must, however, avoid classifying activities on the basis of job titles that may have little relation to the work performed by the employee.

---

3. Danforth (1986).
4. Harrington (1987), p. 112.

Cost to be classified	Cost category
Cost is related to the prevention of poor-quality products or services.	Prevention
Cost is related to checking whether products or services conform to customer requirements.	Appraisal
Cost is due to a product or service not meeting customer requirements, identified before receipt by the customer.	Internal failure
Cost is due to a product or service not meeting customer requirements, identified after receipt by the customer.	External failure
Cost is not related to the tasks just described.	Not quality-related

EXHIBIT 10.1 CLASSIFYING QUALITY-RELATED COSTS

- *Time studies*. When time or cost data are unavailable or difficult to acquire, analysts can conduct special studies to monitor the amount of time devoted to quality-related tasks. Activity logs provide a practical means for tracking the time spent on various activities and the reason for each activity over a defined period of time. Exhibit 10.2 displays the activity worksheet used by a major telecommunications firm to determine the amount of time spent handling trouble reports.

	Trouble Report Handled/Time in Minutes							
Activities	#1	#2	#3	#4	#5	#6	Total	Avg.
1. Take customer trouble report call and type into system.	5	7	1	3	4	2	22	3.6
2. Review trouble report and system test.	1	1	2	1	3	1	9	1.5
3. Retest line manually.	1	120	15	35	10	1	182	30.3
4. Call customer to verify problem.	3	10	9	5	2	7	36	6.0
5. Assign dispatch status in system.	1	1	1	1	1	1	6	1.0
6. Monitor dispatch system for customer call-back requests.	0	0	5	8	0	10	23	3.8
7. System prioritizes trouble reports for dispatch.	5	120	240	360	50	480	1255	210.0
8. Technician retrieves trouble report information from access terminal.	1	1	1	1	1	1	6	1.0
9. Tech. reviews trouble report.	2	10	5	3	2	10	32	5.3
10. Tech. calls center for clarification.	0	5	0	10	0	15	30	5.0
11. Tech. isolates location of trouble.	40	120	30	180	20	120	510	85.0
12. Tech. fixes trouble.	10	15	10	30	10	20	95	15.8
13. Tech. post-tests to verify fix.	5	3	3	5	15	5	36	6.0
14. Customer contact to complete.	2	3	2	10	5	5	27	4.5
15. Complete trouble report is in system.	1	1	1	1	1	1	6	1.0
Total Process Time Minutes	77	417	325	653	124	679	2275	380.0
Hours	1.3	7	5.4	10.8	2	11.3	6.3 hrs./report (average)	

EXHIBIT 10.2 TIME STUDY RESULTS FOR SIX TROUBLE REPORTS RECEIVED IN A SINGLE DAY BY A TELECOMMUNICATIONS FIRM

The analysis found that 15 activities were required to handle each trouble report, with the six trouble reports received during the single day covered by the study requiring more than 37 hours to resolve.

- *Defect costing.* Most firms track a variety of operational quality measures, such as defect rates, down time, service errors, and customer complaints. Analysts can use standard or activity-based costing methods to translate these measures into dollar amounts. A major defense contractor uses defect costing to evaluate supplier performance and award contracts. The method assigns to each type of supplier quality problem a standard cost based on industrial engineering studies of the hours required to resolve the problem. For each type of problem, the number of occurrences during the previous quarter is multiplied by the associated standard cost to obtain total quality failure costs due to the supplier. A supplier rating index results from using the following formula:

  Supplier rating index = (Quality failure costs + purchase price)/total purchases

  The following example illustrates the method used to calculate the supplier rating index.

Total purchases during the rating period.	$250,000	
Quality failure costs during the rating period:		
Return to supplier (2 units @ $300 each).		$ 600
Under-shipment (5 shipments @ $350 each)		1,750
Late delivery (3 shipments @ $500 each).		1,500
Total quality failure costs.		$3,850
Supplier rating index = ($3,850 + $250,000)/$250,000 = 1.015		

  The output from the supplier rating system assists in identifying which suppliers require help in meeting quality and delivery standards. The index also serves as a bid multiplier during the supplier selection process to calculate the actual total cost of purchasing from a given supplier. A comparison of two potential suppliers for the same product illustrates the use of the bid multiplier.

	Supplier A	Supplier B
Quoted price per unit.	$100	$105
× supplier rating index.	1.1	1.0
Total cost per unit	$110	$105

  Based solely on quoted price, supplier A is the low-cost supplier. However, after factoring in past quality performance using the supplier rating index, supplier B represents the better value.[5]

- *Estimates.* Managers or workers can also estimate the number of employees or hours spent on a given activity. One can then multiply these figures by labor rates or compare them to total costs to estimate quality-related costs. Our experience indicates, however, that employees often inaccurately estimate the activities they perform each day and the duration of these activities, making this method the least reliable technique for identifying quality-related costs.

5. See Ittner (1999) for additional discussion of activity-based costing concepts for quality improvement.

(iii) Statistical Analysis. Although activity analysis can prove useful for identifying the more tangible costs of preventing, monitoring, and correcting quality problems, it often overlooks the less tangible productivity losses due to poor quality. These losses include factors such as the extra inventory and capacity held to accommodate quality problems, the congestion and confusion that arise when attempting to correct quality deficiencies, and the problems created in downstream operations.

If companies have sufficient data, *regression analysis* provides a powerful tool for assessing these less tangible costs. For example, a large appliance manufacturing plant reduced defect rates by 35 percent and increased productivity by 23 percent over a four-year period, but saw tangible quality-related costs such as inspection, scrap, and rework *increase* from $6.29 to $6.97 per equivalent unit. Analysts used regression analysis to estimate the association between the plant's productivity index and various quality measures to assess the extent to which the quality improvements yielded productivity gains. The statistical results indicated that the productivity gains from quality improvements produced *net* cost reductions of $800,000 annually.[6] Further analysis attributed these gains to reduced factory congestion, downtime, and schedule delays—less tangible benefits that analysts often find difficult to measure using other methods.

(iv) Simulation Models. Regression analysis requires historical data to estimate the models, a limitation when many quality improvement initiatives require dramatic changes in operations or activities, making historical data that reflect past practices uninformative. Simulation models provide one means for conducting what-if analyses comparing quality-related costs and benefits under current practices to various alternatives. Simulation involves developing a model of a process and then conducting experiments on the model to evaluate the process's behavior under different circumstances. Analysts have used simulation models to estimate quality-related costs and benefits in a variety of situations. These include reducing appraisal costs by improving the utilization of inspection personnel, addressing the timing of inspections to reduce internal failure costs, estimating indirect productivity losses from poor quality, assessing the effect of quality improvements on inventory levels and cycle time, and evaluating the revenue effects from defect reductions.[7]

(b) QUALITY-RELATED REVENUE IMPLICATIONS. The preceding techniques focus on quality-related costs, but in many cases the greatest improvement opportunities are the revenue gains achieved when higher-quality products or services increase customer satisfaction and loyalty. Most firms track some form of customer satisfaction measure, but few can link these measures to changes in revenues or profits. This limits firms' ability to identify the quality improvement projects offering the highest return on investment, or to evaluate the overall effectiveness of the quality program. Two methods have proven useful for estimating the revenue effects of product or service quality: lost sales models and statistical analysis.

(i) Lost Sales Models. Lost sales models provide a tool for assessing revenue losses due to quality problems. As with defect costing, most lost sales models use retention rates or

---

6. Additional details are provided in Ittner (1994).
7. See Flowers and Cole (1985); Freeman (1995); Schmahl, Dessouky, and Rucker (1997); and Sterman, Repenning, and Kofman (1997) for examples of simulation models for estimating quality-related costs and benefits.

standard losses per occurrence to estimate the revenue implications of quality problems. Xerox's approach evaluates the opportunity costs of lost sales using estimates based on historical data.[8] For example, a quality improvement team examining the customer support process for laser printers found that, due to preinstallation deadlines not being met, customers used an average of five loaner photocopy units each month. Sales personnel could not use these machines elsewhere to generate business. Based on historical data, the team estimated the opportunity cost for these five machines as follows:

$$5 \text{ potential orders} \times \$3{,}000 \times 12 \text{ months} = \$180{,}000$$

Another Xerox study found that 10 percent of customers canceled their leases because of quality problems. Assuming that 15 percent of these customers did not return, the estimated lost opportunity costs from these cancellations were:

$$\$60{,}000{,}000 \text{ revenue} \times 50\% \text{ margin} \times 10\% \text{ cancels} \times 15\% \text{ lost} = \$500{,}000$$

A leading camera manufacturer implemented a more sophisticated lost sales model for its products, basing the model on three criteria: the severity of the defect (cosmetic, product partially usable, product unusable); the net present value of expected *future* purchases of customers who experience a quality problem and of potential customers who observe the defect and choose not to buy the company's products; and the net present value of expected future purchase patterns of customers who do not experience a quality problem.

Based on market research, the company identified the level of severity that customers attached to each type of defect, and then categorized defects on a scale from minor to major. Analysts then assessed the probability that a customer would continue buying the company's product for each level of severity.[9] The lost sales model multiplied the estimated number of current and potential customers who experience or observe the defect multiplied by the probability of repurchase to estimate the number of lost customers. The model then multiplied the number of lost customers per defect category by the estimated net present value of future sales per customer to predict the amount of lost sales for each type of defect.

Prior to implementing the lost sales model, the camera manufacturer prioritized quality improvement projects based on the number of customer complaints for each type of problem. After developing the lost sales model, the company found that quality problems causing the most complaints do not necessarily translate into the greatest expected loss in future sales, leading the firm to shift the focus of its improvement projects and internal inspections to the elimination of defects with the greatest estimated effect on future sales.

(ii) Statistical Analysis. Companies can also use statistical analysis to assess the revenue benefits from improved quality. Exhibit 10.3 provides the hypothetical results from a regression model linking customers' perceptions of the quality of the firm's goods or services, customer satisfaction levels, and customer retention. The statistical results from this model provide the basis for assessing the retention benefits from improved quality. Assume that the firm increases perceived quality from 70 to 75 (where 0 = "did not meet expectations" and 100 = "exceeded expectations"). Given the estimated coefficients from the regression model, this change implies an increase in customer satisfaction from 80 to

---

8. The Xerox examples were developed by the Xerox United States Customer Organization cost of quality team (Xerox, 1987).
9. Market research by the firm indicated that a customer who experiences a major defect typically tells five others, one of whom will decide not to buy the company's products.

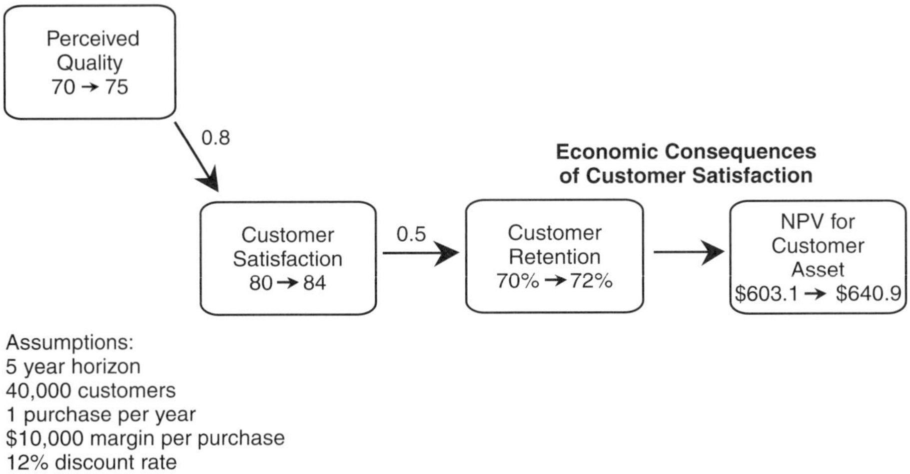

EXHIBIT 10.3 STATISTICAL ANALYSIS LINKING QUALITY IMPROVEMENTS TO REVENUE GAINS

84 and an increase in customer retention from 70 percent to 72.5 percent. Using the assumptions given in Exhibit 10.3, the net present value from the increase in perceived quality is $37.8 million (or $640.9 – $603.1 million).

10.3 MANAGING THE COSTS AND BENEFITS OF QUALITY IMPROVEMENT

The assessment of quality-related costs and revenue losses quantifies the financial effect of poor quality on the organization. The results from this assessment can help target specific areas for further investigation based on their potential return on investment. Before proceeding, however, one should ask whether customers value the quality attributes emphasized by the quality program. The ultimate test of any quality program is how well it helps the firm meet customer requirements or expectations. A firm should reduce or eliminate costs to provide any quality attribute (e.g., feature, function, service, and process) that provides little value to the customer. Alternatively, customers highly value an attribute, a firm might improve performance by increasing spending on that attribute. Unfortunately, many firms misallocate resources to quality improvement efforts because of poor knowledge of customer requirements. United Parcel Service, for example, assumed that its customers valued on-time delivery as the highest attribute. As a result, the firm's quality goals, action plans, and customer satisfaction surveys focused almost exclusively on time-related issues. When the firm modified its surveys to ask broader questions about how to improve customer service, it found that customers valued their interaction with delivery drivers more than they valued on-time delivery. The firm has since changed its quality plans and performance measures to focus more attention on customer contact.[10]

After confirming that the quality attributes emphasized by the firm are valued by customers, the framework in Exhibit 10.4 can be used to guide the quality program

10. Greising (1994).

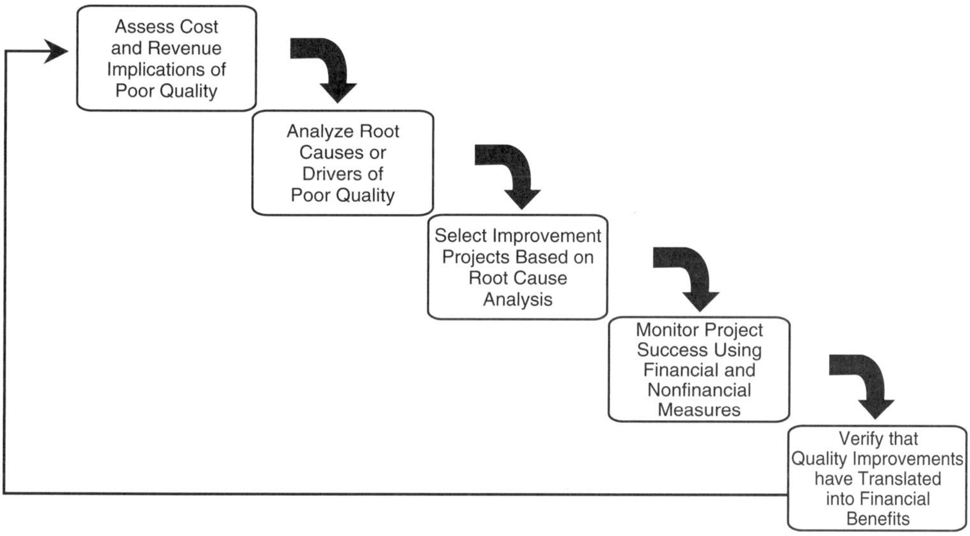

EXHIBIT 10.4 FRAMEWORK FOR LINKING QUALITY INITIATIVES TO FINANCIAL RESULTS

toward projects with the highest financial payback. The framework consists of a feedback loop from the initial assessment of costs and revenue losses to subsequent reassessments undertaken to ensure that quality improvement results have reached the bottom line. Three intermediate steps help to link improvement efforts to financial results: analysis of cost and revenue drivers, project selection, and monitoring and measuring progress.

(a) ANALYSIS OF COST AND REVENUE DRIVERS. Once the cost and revenue assessment has identified potential improvement opportunities, the firm needs a driver analysis to select the appropriate action. A driver analysis is a systematic method for linking a customer-perceived problem or opportunity to its underlying determinants. This information allows companies to estimate the net financial return from eliminating the cause of a quality problem or enhancing a driver of customer satisfaction.

(b) PROJECT SELECTION. Improvement projects are selected based on the potential return on investment estimated using data from the cost driver analysis and other considerations, such as strategic goals, competitive requirements, and so on. Xerox incorporates four factors in the project selection process using the worksheet in Exhibit 10.5. Instead of relying solely on quality failure costs and revenue losses for prioritizing improvement projects, the firm assesses three other factors: (1) the seriousness or urgency of the problem as the external customer perceives it, (2) the extent to which the quality improvement team controls the process and the required solution for the selected quality problem, and (3) the relative difficulty of solving the problem, considering both the time to resolve the problem and the amount of resources required.

(c) MONITORING AND MEASURING PROGRESS. Monitoring and measuring improvement project success is based on the financial and operational goals established in quality

Directions: In boxes across the top, write the outputs/problems your group is considering. Then rate them against the listed criteria by working across each row. The higher the total score, the greater the likelihood that the output/problem is appropriate for the group to work on.

Problem Statement →				
External Customer Impact 1 2 3 4 5 Little Great				
Ability to Control 1 2 3 4 5 Little Great				
Cost of Poor Quality 1 2 3 4 5 Little Great				
Degree of Difficulty 1 2 3 4 5 Little Great				

External customer impact: The seriousness or urgency of the problem as perceived by the customer.

Ability to control: The extent to which the group controls the problem or processes and can control the solution.

Cost of poor quality: The approximate, expected cost of poor quality from solving the problem, improving processes, or reducing the number of errors.

Degree of difficulty: A judgment about the relative difficulty of working through the problem to a solution considering both the time to resolve the problem and the amount of resources required.

Courtesy of Xerox Corporation, *Cost of Quality: A Guide to Applications,* prepared by the USCO Cost of Quality Team, Xerox Corporation (1987), p. 21.

EXHIBIT 10.5 THE XEROX UNITED STATES CUSTOMER ORGANIZATION QUALITY IMPROVEMENT PROJECT SELECTION WORKSHEET

improvement plans. In most cases, project-level operational quality measures, such as defect rates and customer complaints, provide more timely and focused indicators of implementation success. Management can then make periodic assessment of cost and revenue changes to decide whether the quality improvements have reached the bottom line.

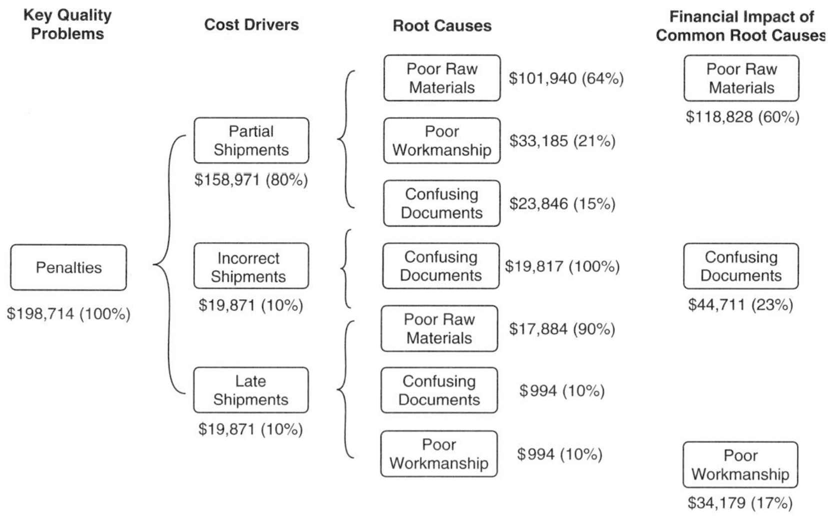

EXHIBIT 10.6 COMPLETED COST DRIVER ANALYSIS

10.4 APPLYING THE FRAMEWORK

An example from a manufacturer of high-alloy metal shafts illustrates the use of this framework for managing the costs and benefits of quality improvement.[11] Declining market share and eroding profit margins triggered the company's quality initiative. In response, the company assessed quality-related costs to quantify the effect of poor quality. Focusing only on appraisal and internal and external failure costs, the study found that these expenditures equaled 26 percent of sales. Following the assessment, the company selected the largest cost categories for the cost driver analysis.

Exhibit 10.6 depicts the completed cost driver analysis for delivery penalties, one of the categories targeted for further investigation. The investigation uncovered three primary drivers of delivery penalties: (1) partial shipments, (2) incorrect shipments, and (3) late shipments. Further analysis revealed a variety of underlying root causes, the largest of which was hard spots in the raw material. Moreover, cost driver analyses for other cost categories revealed widespread problems created by these hard spots. Based on this information, the company established a team to revise raw material specifications to eliminate the hard spots. A cost–benefit analysis for the project indicated the following financial benefit from improvements in material specification:

Cost to implement updated material specifications.	$ 145,000
Financial benefits from eliminating hard spots:	
Income statement effects	
Reduced penalties.	$ 119,830
Reduced uncontrolled material losses.	368,940
Reduced direct labor costs.	70,720

11. This example is taken from Atkinson et al. (1994) and is based on consulting work performed by a leading accounting firm.

Reduced inspection costs	518,470
Reduced returned goods	78,960
Total income statement effects	$1,156,920
Balance sheet effects	
Decreased inventory	$ 38,000
Decreased accounts receivable	168,560
Total balance sheet effects	$ 206,560
Estimated net financial benefits	$1,218,480

Exhibit 10.7 illustrates the monitoring system used to evaluate the performance of the materials specification improvement project. Management identified financial and operational performance measures for each affected department, based on the cost driver

Flow of Benefits	Cause-and-Effect Relations	Performance Measures	Participating Departments	Additional Considerations
Reduce hard spots in material ↓	Eliminate when new material specifications are implemented	Nonconforming material to total receipts	Purchasing monitors supplier performance	Reduce amount purchased as scrap and waste decline
Reduce tool breakage ↓	Reduce as hard spots are eliminated	Tool breaks per 10,000 cycles	Engineering monitors tool breaks	Shift personnel as need for setups and repair drop
Reduce excessive down time ↓	Reduce as tool breaks decline	Downtime to total hours	Operations monitors downtime	Work with production scheduling to update standards to reflect improved productivity
Reduce partial shipment ↓	Reduce as down-time decreases	Partial shipments to total shipments	Shipping monitors delivery performance	Redeploy personnel as returns decline
Reduce penalties ↓	Reduce due to fewer partial shipments	Penalties to operating costs	Accounting monitors penalties	Cash flow increases as inventory declines, and profit margins improve with lower penalties and labor costs, fewer setups, and improved machine productivity
Improve profitability and cash flow	Improve as penalties decrease	Profits, profit margins, cash flow	Accounting monitors financial performance for improvement	

EXHIBIT 10.7 IMPROVEMENT PROJECT PLAN FOR MONITORING THE ELIMINATION OF HARD SPOTS IN RAW MATERIAL

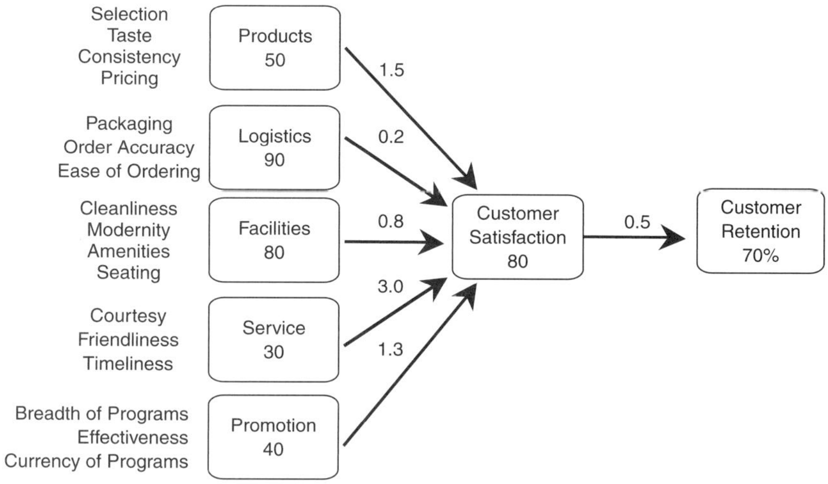

Note: Scores for customer satisfaction drivers and customer satisfaction levels range from 0 (lowest score) to 100 (highest score)

EXHIBIT 10.8 STATISTICAL ANALYSIS OF THE DRIVERS AND FINANCIAL CONSEQUENCES OF CUSTOMER SATISFACTION

analysis. Management then sequenced the expected performance changes based on expected cause-and-effect relations, with preliminary goals such as reductions in non-conforming materials and tool breakage leading to intermediate goals of down-time and partial shipment reductions, and, ultimately, to improved accounting performance. By sequencing performance measures in this way, management could receive early indication that benefits cascaded down to the income statement and balance sheet. If not, management could take corrective action to remove any organizational barriers or modify improvement plans.

The same framework can be applied to revenue-enhancing quality improvement initiatives. A hypothetical example using statistical analysis to identify the drivers and financial consequences of customer satisfaction is provided in Exhibit 10.8.[12] Based on market research, five firm-specific drivers of customer satisfaction are incorporated into the statistical model (products, logistics, facilities, service, and promotion). Each driver is also associated with actionable alternatives to guide the selection of quality initiatives offering the highest returns. The results from the model provide the basis for estimating the extent to which these drivers influence customer satisfaction and, ultimately, customer retention.

Exhibit 10.8 also provides the output from the statistical analysis. This output includes: (1) estimated scores for each of the drivers (on a scale from 0 [lowest performance] to 100 [highest performance]), (2) the relation between changes in driver scores and customer satisfaction, and (3) the relation between changes in customer satisfaction and customer retention.

Exhibit 10.9 plots the estimated driver score (i.e., how well the firm is currently doing with respect to that driver) versus the estimated impact of the driver on customer satisfaction. The exhibit indicates that drivers in the lower right-hand quadrant such as service have low performance rating scores, but high impact on customer satisfaction. These drivers provide the best opportunities for quality initiatives because they offer the

12. See Ittner and Larcker (1996) for additional details on the use of statistical methods to identify quality-related revenue drivers.

EXHIBIT 10.9 QUALITY IMPROVEMENT MATRIX FOR SELECTING PROJECTS

greatest room for improvement and have a substantial impact on customer satisfaction and loyalty. The lowest payback opportunities are the drivers in the upper left-hand quadrant such as logistics and facilities.

The estimated model provides the basis for assessing the financial consequences of quality initiatives. For example, assume that the firm undertakes a $1 million training program to improve service. As shown in Exhibit 10.10, the statistical analysis suggests that this expenditure will cause the service score to increase from 30 to 40, customer satisfaction to increase from 60 to 66, and customer retention to increase from 70 to 76 percent.

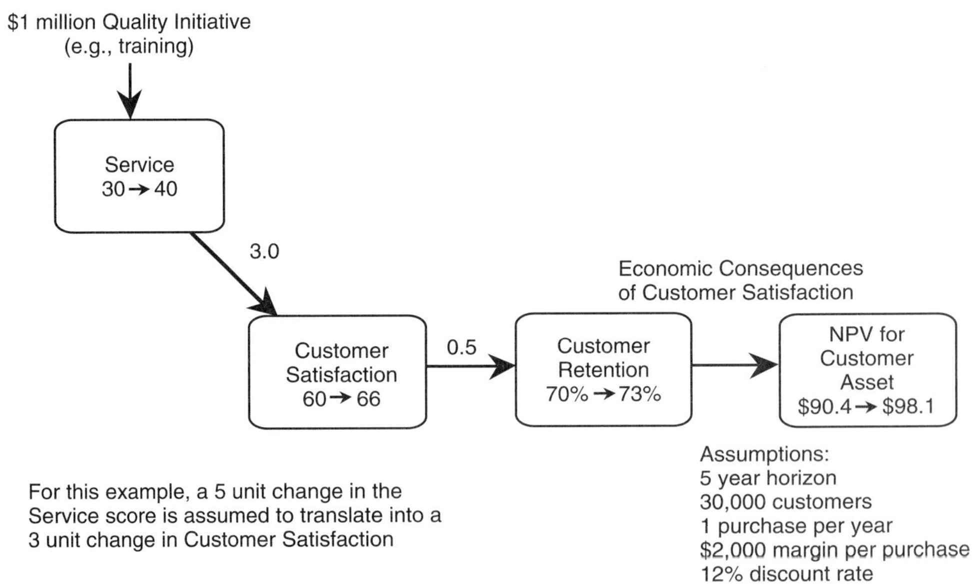

EXHIBIT 10.10 ESTIMATED FINANCIAL BENEFIT FROM QUALITY IMPROVEMENT PROJECT

Based on the assumptions in the figure, the \$1 million expenditure on training has a net present value of \$6 million (\$36.1 million – \$30.1 million). Subsequent measurement and analysis can assess whether the training program has been implemented successfully and calculate the actual returns from the investment.

10.5 SUMMARY

Accurately measuring the costs and benefits from quality improvements can become extremely difficult. Financial measures provide important inputs, however, for assessing the success of quality programs and allocating resources. The methods and framework presented in this chapter have proven useful for guiding quality initiatives in a wide variety of manufacturing and service firms. By performing comprehensive assessments of quality-related costs and benefits on a periodic basis, firms can target the improvement initiatives with the highest potential return on investment, monitor the progress of improvement projects, and more closely link the quality improvement program to the primary goal of the business—profitability.

BIBLIOGRAPHY

Atkinson, Hawley, John Hamburg, and Christopher Ittner. *Linking Quality to Profits: Quality-Based Cost Management*. Milwaukee, WI: ASQC Press, 1994.

Danforth, D.D., "A Common Commitment to Total Quality," *Quality Progress* 19, 1 (January 1986): 17.

Flowers, A.D., and J.R. Cole. An Application of Computer Simulation to Quality Control in Manufacturing, *IEE Transactions* 17 (1985): 277–283.

Freeman, J.M. Estimating Quality Costs. *Journal of the Operational Research Society* 46 (1995): 675–686.

Greising, David. Quality—How to Make It Pay. *Business Week* (August 8, 1994): 54–59.

Harrington, H. James. *Poor-Quality Costs*. Milwaukee, WI: ASQC Quality Press, 1987.

Ittner, Christopher D. An Examination of the Indirect Productivity Gains from Quality Improvement. *Production and Operations Management* 3, 3 (Summer 1994): 153–170.

Ittner, Christopher D. Activity-based Costing Concepts for Quality Improvement. *European Management Journal,* 17, 5 (October 1999): 492–500.

Ittner, Christopher D., and David F. Larcker. Measuring the Impact of Quality Initiatives on Firm Financial Performance. *Advances in the Management of Organizational Quality* 1 (1996): 1–37.

Schmahl, Karen E., Yasser Dessouky, and David Rucker. Measuring the Cost of Quality: A Case Study. *Production & Inventory Management Journal* 38, 4 (Fourth Quarter 1997): 58–64.

Sterman, John D., Nelson P. Repenning, and Fred Kofmann. Unanticipated Side Effects of Successful Quality Programs: Exploring a Paradox of Organizational Improvement. *Management Science* 43, 4 (April 1997): 503–521.

Technical Assistance Research Programs (TARP). Consumer Complaint Handling in America: Final Report. Washington, D.C.: U.S. Department of Commerce, 1979.

Xerox Corporation. *Cost of Quality: A Guide to Application*. Rochester, N.Y.: Xerox Corporation, 1987.

CHAPTER **11**

LOGISTICS AND MARKETING COSTS

JAMES M. REEVE, PHD, CPA
University of Tennessee

CONTENTS

11.1 INTRODUCTION 329

11.2 SUPPLY CHAIN ACTIVITIES 330
(a) Logistics Activities 330
(b) Marketing and Selling Activities 331

11.3 EXPENSE PLANNING AND CONTROL 332

11.4 TOTAL COST OF DELIVERY 336
(a) Total Cost of Ownership 339
(b) Relation Profitability Analysis 341

11.5 RELATION PROFITABILITY—EXAMPLE 345
(a) Direct Costs 345
(b) Activity Cost 346
(c) Post-Sale Activities 347
(d) Carrying Cost 347
(e) Margin Analysis 348

11.6 SUMMARY 349

11.1 INTRODUCTION

One day soon, you will sit down at a kiosk at an auto dealer and custom order your new car.[1] Within four days of order, the manufacturer will acquire and consume materials to assemble your car. In another three days, the car will arrive at the dealer's lot for you to drive away.

This illustration no longer confines the new automobile purchase to its product features, but also considers the underlying support systems for marketing and delivering the product. One-size-fits-all solutions no longer satisfy customers; this trend forces organizations to customize their marketing and distribution strategies into logical niches.[2] With this change, however, a fundamental question emerges. What tradeoffs exist between providing custom marketing and logistical solutions for increasingly narrow markets? What product and service functionality can a firm affordably provide to various segments? What asset commitments will allow a reasonable rate of return, and where can a firm maintain expense flexibility? This chapter will explore ways to answer these questions and examine case studies to illustrate the points.

The role of logistics is changing from one of warehousing and transportation to one of providing an integrated set of services that delivers the right product, in the right

1. See Ruderman, G., "The state of automotive make-to-order; Poor demand picture and legacy systems delay progress toward custom configurations" *MSI* Vol. 22, Issue 8, 2004.
2. Reeve, J. and Srinivasan, M., "How to Design Lean Supply Chains for Enhanced Flow," *Supply Chain Management Review*, forthcoming, 2005.

quantities, in the right quality, at the right time—all for the right cost. Consequently, organizations no longer consider logistics functions as only cost centers to squeeze for ever-increasing efficiency. Instead, logistics has a strategic role in the marketplace. Consider competing office furniture manufacturers. One offers furniture with a 30-day lead time and another with a seven-day lead time. Who wins? A seven-day lead time allows a building contractor to estimate the delivery and installation date better than does a 30-day lead time. Therefore, investments in short cycle logistical capabilities improve service functionality, resulting in enhanced revenue opportunities.[3]

Moreover, logistics integrate supplier and customer relations. As a result, we see increasing focus on managing logistical costs across organizational boundaries, rather than within a single organization.[4] When firms manage logistics across organizational boundaries, significant opportunities emerge to enhance the value of the total supply chain.[5] This creates, however, the new difficulty of apportioning the enhanced value to the individual value chain participants. This chapter shows how supply chain participants can establish the cost of supply chain activities in order to partition value among the participants.[6]

This chapter also addresses the cost management concerns associated with marketing expenditures. As with logistics costs, this discussion will show how to assess whether marketing expenditures return value to the firm. Such analyses often identify specific marketing costs with regions, customers, and channels. In addition, this chapter will show how to structure multidimensional contribution reports for evaluating several profit views simultaneously.

11.2 SUPPLY CHAIN ACTIVITIES

The supply chain consists of logistics and marketing activities that consume resources in the organization. This chapter will take an activity perspective in managing the costs and profit opportunities in the supply chain.

(a) LOGISTICS ACTIVITIES. Logistics consists of "the process of planning, implementing, and controlling the efficient, cost-effective flow and storage of raw materials, in-process inventory, finished goods, and related information from point of origin to point of consumption for the purpose of conforming to customer requirements."[7] Theorists have recently expanded this definition to include activities in the service sector, such as managing the physical flow of customers (e.g., patients in a hospital) or segmented service provisioning (e.g., customizing bank services to customer segments).

Exhibit 11.1 shows the typical activities that this term encompasses for a manufacturing firm.[8] The complete physical and informational activities form a closed loop linking

---

3. This is discussed in more detail in J. Reeve, "The Financial Advantages of the Lean Supply Chain," *Supply Chain Management Review* (March/April 2002):42-49.
4. As discussed in Statements on Management Accounting Number 4-P, *Cost Management for Logistics* (Montvale, N.J.: IMA, 1992).
5. For a discussion on the control mechanisms required to capture these values, see Dekker, H.C., "Control of inter-organizational relationships:evidence on appropriation concerns and coordination requirements," *Accounting, Organization, Society*, Vol. 29, 2004, pp. 27-49.
6. See a brief discussion of how this is accomplished within the context of target costing in R. Cooper and R. Slagmulder, "Interorganizational Costing, Part 2," *Journal of Cost Management* (November 2003).
7. Council of Logistics Management definition, 1986.
8. An excellent reference identifying activities with logistics processes and various channel configurations is in *Performance Measurement: Applying Vlaue Chain Analysis to the Grocery Industry* (Joint Industry Project on Efficient Consumer Response), 1994.

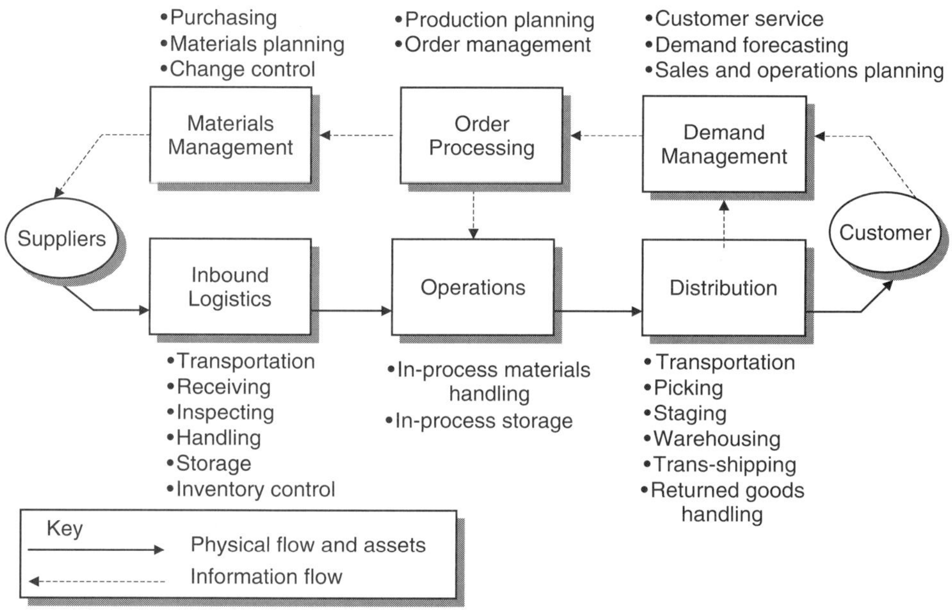

EXHIBIT 11.1 LOGISTICS ACTIVITIES

both upstream suppliers and downstream customers to the firm. The bottom of the exhibit identifies logistical activities required to physically move material from raw materials through distribution to the customer. These activities include the cost of people and assets required for moving and storing material through the various stages of transformation. The informational activities translate demand and inventory status information into production orders and materials requirements, as the top portion of the exhibit shows. These activities include the cost of transactions, planning, and change control typically considered a part of the support burden. Together, these activities form the backbone for managing logistics costs.

(b) MARKETING AND SELLING ACTIVITIES. In addition to logistics costs, firms incur marketing and sales costs in downstream, customer-directed activities. These activities include the costs of selling, order taking, merchandising, advertising, promoting, and customer development. These activities may have product-related drivers (as with brand advertising), distribution channel-related drivers (as with channel promotions), or customer-related drivers (as in the case of managing a customer relation). Exhibit 11.2 includes examples of selling and marketing activities by product, channel, and customer.

Firms can manage supply chain costs with expense planning and control, or with total cost of delivery. Exhibit 11.3 compares these two methods. Expense planning and control supports cost center managers, such as warehouse or transportation managers. In this approach, the firm uses an expense simulation to simulate resource requirements according to planned activity requirements. Product line, customer, or other commercial managers use total cost of delivery measures to support alignment of logistics and marketing resources with strategic and profit objectives. These objectives reflect the nature of the supplier and customer relations. In addition, supply chain analysis can identify opportunities to make complex interfirm cost tradeoffs. In both instances, the firm can use activity-based information to inform the analysis.

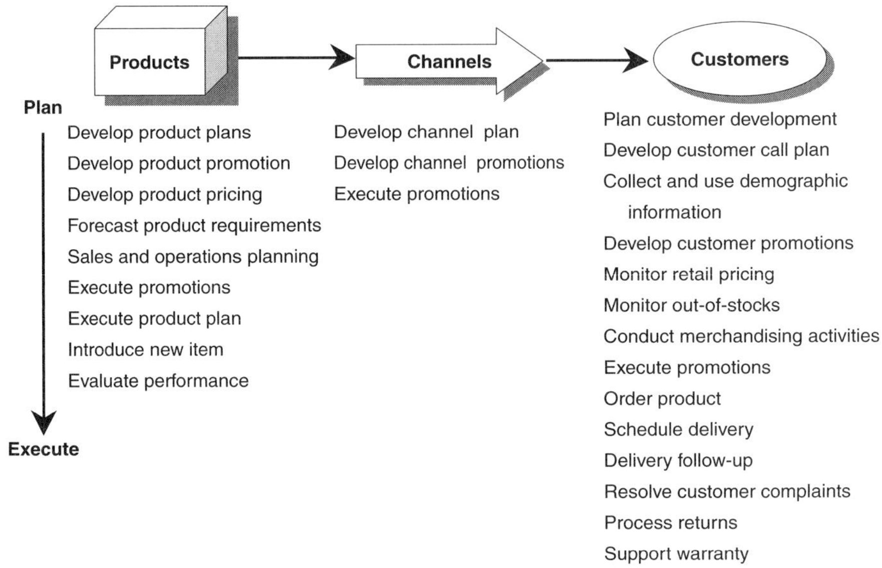

EXHIBIT 11.2 SELLING AND MARKETING ACTIVITIES

	Cost Management Methods	
	Expense Planning and Control	Total Cost of Delivery
Targeted User	Cost center manager (e.g., warehouse manager)	Product or customer manager
Scope	Intra-firm	Inter-firm supply chain
Objective	Plan resources (e.g., warehouse staffing levels) and identify actual variance from plan.	Manage profits in value chain relationships and identify complex inter-firm tradeoff opportunities.
Method	Expense simulation	Activity tracing to upstream or downstream value chain partners

EXHIBIT 11.3 EXPENSE PLANNING AND CONTROL AND TOTAL COST OF DELIVERY

11.3 EXPENSE PLANNING AND CONTROL

Organizations can plan and control logistics costs by relating activities to their underlying resources.[9] To illustrate, the Volunteer Juice Co. has six warehouse activities, as Exhibit 11.4 shows. Employees unload pallets of 12 oz., 16 oz., and 32 oz. glass bottles

9. Expense planning and control can be accomplished under a number of different design alternatives. My example is similar to an emerging design called the RCA (resource consumption accounting) model. See Anton Vand der Merwe, and David Keys, "The Case for RCA" (three part series) *Journal of Cost Management* (July/August-November/December) 2001 and Lynn Benjamin and Todd Simon, "A Planning and Control Model Based on RCA Principles," *Journal of Cost Management* (July/August 2003):. 20–27. See also T. Greenwood and J. Reeve, "Process Cost Management," *Journal of Cost Mangement* (Winter, 1994): 4–19.

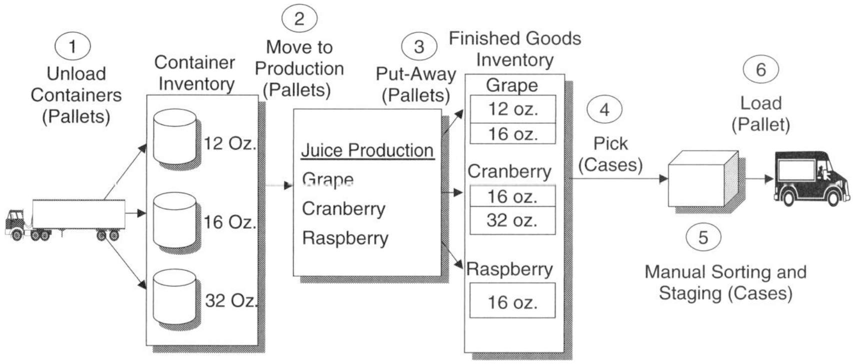

EXHIBIT 11.4 LOGISTICS ACTIVITIES: VOLUNTEER JUICE CO.

from trucks and put them into the container inventory (#1). Other employees then move the glass bottles to the production line to fill a production run of grape, or cranberry, or raspberry juice (#2). Workers place the completed production on pallets and put it into the finished goods inventory (#3). Customers purchase cases of juice product, which workers must select from the finished goods warehouse (#4).[10] Employees must sort, replace on pallets, and prepare these customized cases for delivery (#5). Workers then load the product on the truck (#6). Although an actual warehouse operation may have more products and activities, the basic concepts illustrated here will apply.

Expense planning begins by translating the anticipated demand into the six activities, which the firm then translates into resources. Exhibit 11.5 illustrates this relation. Reading from left to right, the firm plans and links the customer demand case volumes for the five juice SKUs (stock keeping units) to the six warehouse activities. The activity frequencies change in response to changes in the sales volume.[11] The process uses a physical measure of activity output, termed an activity base. For example, a *pallet move* measures the quantity effort, or service, associated with the *unload container* activity. Thus, in the first stage, the simulation must translate case volume from the demand information to activity bases, such as pallet moves.

Accountants must then link the physical activity base to their underlying resource requirements. Our example uses lift trucks and warehouse personnel as the two warehouse resources supporting the six activities. The cost simulation must model the unique cost behavior patterns of these resources. Resources may exhibit fully variable, fixed, stepped, or mixed cost behavior over a range of activity levels. In this example, the firm has a monthly cancelable lease for the lift trucks, so it incurs incremental step costs for the trucks. Thus, changes in lift truck demand results in incremental or avoidable costs. In contrast, the warehouse personnel have a union contract that prevents layoffs below 30 full-time equivalent (FTE) employees. Therefore, the firm faces fixed personnel cost

---

10. This simulation assumes that each order has multiple order lines, and that each order line is picked from the warehouse.
11. Sales volume is assumed equal to production volume. The simulation could be designed with unequal production and sales volumes and relating them separately to activities.

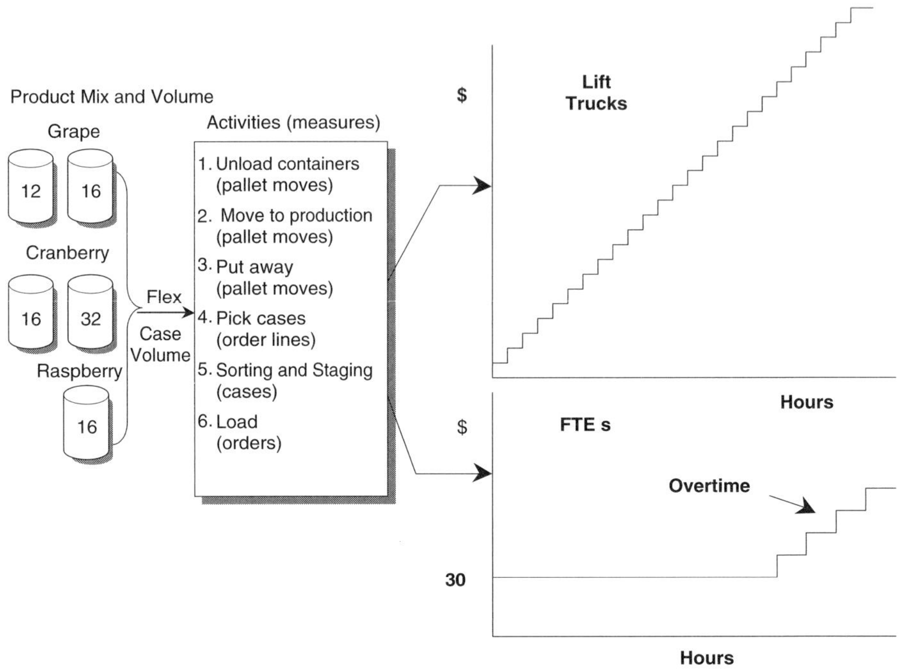

EXHIBIT 11.5 EXPENSE SIMULATION OVERVIEW

for all levels below 30 FTEs of effort. However, for requirements above 30 FTEs of effort, the firm must pay overtime.

The first stage of the simulation translates case demand information into activity base quantities. One can use a spreadsheet to model the necessary relations, as Exhibit 11.6 shows. Column two shows the monthly demand estimated for the five SKUs. Analysts need to develop a parameter that specifies the relation between demand and activity. This parameter translates the volume measure to a measure of activity base usage. For example, two activities in the spending simulation are "unload containers" and "pick cases." The

1	2	3	4	5	6
	Demand	Relation Parameters		Activity Base Frequency	
Products	Monthly Demand (cases)	Cases/ Full Pallet	Cases/ Order Line	Pallet Moves (Col.2 ÷ Col. 3)	Pick Moves, or Order Lines (Col.2 ÷ Col.4)
12 oz. Grape	12,000	32	10	375	1,200
16 oz. Grape	60,000	24	20	2,500	3,000
16 oz. Cranberry	24,000	24	12	1,000	2,000
32 oz. Cranberry	10,500	12	4	875	1,300
16 oz. Raspberry	46,800	24	18	1,950	2,600
Totals	153,300			6,700	10,100

EXHIBIT 11.6 DEMAND AND ACTIVITY

activity base measure for unload containers is *full pallet moves*, while for pick cases it is *pick moves*. Analysts can restate the demand information as full pallet moves by dividing the case demand by the number of cases per full pallet. Likewise, the pick moves, one for each order line, can be computed by dividing the demand by the cases per order line.

In the second stage, the simulation must translate the activity base into resource hours. The calculations in Exhibit 11.7 derive these relations. The first two columns of the table identify the six activities and their activity-base measures. The third column shows the total frequency for each activity base. This number comes from the first stage calculation. For example, the first three activities require 6,700 pallet moves to unload and put up the containers into the materials warehouse, move the containers to production, and put away the finished goods after filling. The number of pallet moves appears in Exhibit 6 as the fifth column sum. The first three activities have the same number of pallet moves because each activity moves full pallets. In addition, the empty containers have the same cubic size as full containers. Therefore, there is no difference in the activity frequency for moving empty or filled containers. This example also assumes that production runs result in output of exactly as many items as will fill an integer number of pallets, for any particular flavor, thus eliminating the need for any sorting during these activity phases.

Order lines drive the picking activity. An order line's size may not equal a full pallet size. Indeed, the average number of cases per order line is less than a full pallet for all five products (columns 3 and 4 in Exhibit 11.6). The total number of order lines shown in Exhibit 11.7 for the "pick case activity" is the sixth column total from Exhibit 11.6. Next, workers must sort the picked cases and stage them into full orders. The sorting and staging activity requires employees to handle individual cases, so the case volume drives this activity (sum of Exhibit 11.6 second column). Lastly, after staging, workers must load each order on an outbound truck. The average order has four order lines. Therefore, there are 2,525 orders (= 10,100 order lines for the month ÷ 4 average order lines per order) that drive the loading activity.

The analyst must then multiply the activity driver totals associated with each activity by a parameter. The parameter is the standard amount of time required to perform each

1	2	3	4	5	6	7
			Parameter	Resource	Resource Units	
Activities	Activity Unit of Measure	Activity Base Frequency	Hrs. per Activity Unit	Total Hours (Col. 3 × 4)	Number of FTEs (Col. 5 ÷ 160 hrs.)	Number of Trucks (Col. 5 ÷ 120 hrs.)
Unload containers	Pallet moves	6,700	0.07	469.00	2.93	3.91
Move to production	Pallet moves	6,700	0.05	335.00	2.09	2.79
Put away FG	Pallet moves	6,700	0.1	670.00	4.19	5.58
Pick cases	Order lines	10,100	0.1	1,010.00	6.31	8.42
Sorting and staging	Cases	153,300	0.02	3,066.00	19.16	
Load	Orders	2,525	0.08	202.00	1.26	1.68
Total					35.94	22.38

EXHIBIT 11.7 ACTIVITY AND RESOURCES

cycle of activity. This data input requires an engineering study. For example, it takes .10 hours (6.0 minutes), on average, to pick an order line from the finished goods warehouse and move it to the staging location. Multiplying the activity frequency by the standard cycle time yields the total amount of hours required to perform the work.

The last two columns of Exhibit 11.7 translate the total number of hours into the number of trucks and FTEs planned for the warehouse. One can calculate these numbers by dividing the total number of hours required to do the work by the monthly available hours per resource unit. We will assume that each employee has 160 hours available for productive work, while a truck has only 120 hours of available hours for productive work. The trucks have fewer available hours due to maintenance, congestion, and seasonal surge.

Calculations for resource units in columns 6 and 7 use the same total hours (column 5) calculation because every move activity requires both a driver and a truck. Therefore, the "hours per activity unit" parameter applies to both the truck and people resources simultaneously. More often, the resources will require unique parameters for the activities. Note the sorting and staging activity does not require a truck, and that the total hours do not include this resource.

Firms can plan resource requirements for alternative demand and operating scenarios. Inputting new demands in Exhibit 11.6 changes the scenario. A change in operations may require a change in activity or parameter relations. For example, if Volunteer Juice Co. improved their operations so that operations could load bottles from trucks directly to the line, then a new activity would replace two existing activities. One could then estimate the planned resource reduction from this change in operations.

Likewise, the simulation provides a tool for controlling of logistics operations. Assume the demand scenario in Exhibit 11.6 was the actual demand for the month. One could then compare the actual expenditures on people and capacities invested in trucks to the planned amount shown from the simulation in Exhibit 11.7. To illustrate, assume that Volunteer Juice Co. had 25 trucks for warehouse operations. The simulation suggests, however, that the warehouse needed only 23 to satisfy demand. The warehouse manager has spare capacity of two warehouse trucks. Depending on seasonal factors over the year, the company may have an opportunity to reduce the fleet. Assume further that the firm paid 30 employees straight time, and incurred another 1,200 hours of overtime. Was this overtime the right amount? The simulation indicates that the demand required 35.94 FTEs of work. Each FTE is worth 160 available hours. Therefore, the amount of overtime hours over 30 FTEs would equal 950 hours (= 5.94 FTEs × 160 hours per FTE), but the firm paid for 1,200 overtime hours. This difference would indicate inefficiencies in the warehouse operation. Furthermore, over time, the warehouse manager can estimate the tradeoff between hiring more employees and incurring overtime.

Although this illustration simplifies an actual scenario, it captures the essential elements of expense planning and control for logistics activities. The key element of this illustration lies in translating demand into activities, rather than translating demand directly into resources. This intermediate step provides greater precision in generating resource plans.

11.4 TOTAL COST OF DELIVERY

Exhibit 11.1 diagrammed supply chain activities. Exhibit 11.1 does not suggest that a single set of logistics activities will necessarily serve all customers for any single firm.

Rather than a single logistics system, organizations tailor their logistical systems to the unique requirements of the product, or channel, or customer.[12]

To illustrate, consider a firm that manufactures commercial aircraft components. The firm can manufacture components for the original equipment manufacturer (OEM), but must also make them available to airlines for after-market repairs. The components are the same, but each distribution channel has different logistics requirements, as shown in Exhibit 11.8.

The repair and overhaul distribution channel must respond quickly, especially if a damaged part grounds the aircraft (termed an *AOG*—aircraft on the ground). Consequently, the order is often unplanned, requiring a turnaround time within days. The firm must expedite the order and ship it by air to the point of need. In contrast, the firm can plan OEM orders and material requirements according to manufacturing lead-time offsets. The firm will process the orders in roughly first in, first out (FIFO) sequence; these orders represent demand for a period of time (a batch). The firm can plan for OEM requirements within the normal business systems of the organization, and must prepare for the unplanned high response events.

The firm must not only tailor the logistics systems to the various distribution channel/customer requirements, but also manage the cost and assets required to deliver unique customer values. This represents the *total cost of delivery.*

The total cost of delivery is the supply chain total cost, from supplier to end consumer. The firm can compare this cost to the customer's price preference to better align total delivery cost and service value. In the case of the aircraft component manufacturer, the customers of rapid response channel will be willing to pay a higher price than will the OEM customers. The airline customer values rapid response and will pay extra for this benefit, since an idled aircraft represents significant margin losses. Successful cost management in the supply chain provides such insight into the profit earned from alternative supply chain configurations. Armed with this type of information, managers can negotiate custom arrangements with suppliers and customers that reflect the total cost to deliver a product (or service).[13]

	Logistics Channels	
Characteristic	Rapid response channel	Planned response channel
Customer	Repair and overhaul (airlines)	OEM (aircraft manufacturer)
Span time	Inside manufacturing lead time	Outside manufacturing lead time
Transportation requirements	Immediate air freight	Over ground freight
Planning requirements	Unplanned	Planned
Handling	Expedite	FIFO
Storage	Strategic safety stock	Make to order (no inventory)
Volume	Singles	Batch

EXHIBIT 11.8 TAILORED LOGISTICS CHANNELS FOR AIRCRAFT COMPONENT MANUFACTURER

12. Joseph B, Fuller, James O. O'Conner, and R. Rawlinson, "Tailored Logistics: The Next Advantage," *Harvard Business Review* (May–June 1993): 87–98.

13. See Lisa M. Ellram and Ed Feitzinger, "Using Total Profit Analysis to Model Supply Chain Decisions," *Journal of Cost Management* (July/August 1997): 12–21.

Total cost of delivery shifts the customer/supplier relation away from negotiating only price. Using total delivered cost information, firms can negotiate price *and* behavior. For example, suppose a railroad provides transportation services for a company. A price based only on gross ton-miles does not distinguish between a customer providing predictable advance load requirements and one failing to do so. The customer providing load requirements in the morning of the train departure, for example, requires the railroad to incur significant additional costs. First, the railroad must maintain a sufficient railcar inventory on site to meet the customer's unknown and variable requirement, a significant investment by the railroad. In addition, the lack of prior notification makes it more difficult for the railroad to arrange back-haul opportunities (a full load for the return trip) on the rail cars, which again leads to poor use of assets. Lastly, the unknown load requirements can create system congestion and delays in blocking and classifying railcars.

How should the railroad respond to this situation? First, the railroad must identify the cost associated with the customer's behavior. With total cost of delivery, the railroad can identify the assets and expenses associated with non-notification. Then the railroad can begin to change its pricing to reflect the differences in customer requirements. The customer providing notification receives a low price, while the customer providing no notification must pay a higher price. This scenario resembles the airline industry's pricing of leisure versus business travel. Now the railroad customer has a price signal by which to evaluate the value of the service. The customer may discover that it can provide advance notification and prefer to take advantage of the price differential. Thus, these price signals can modify behavior and reduce total supply chain costs.

The tools to support supply chain profit analysis include *total cost of ownership* and *relation profitability analysis*.[14] Total cost of ownership focuses on upstream supplier relations, while relation profitability analysis focuses on downstream customer relations, as Exhibit 11.9 shows for the Towel and Tissue Paper Company.

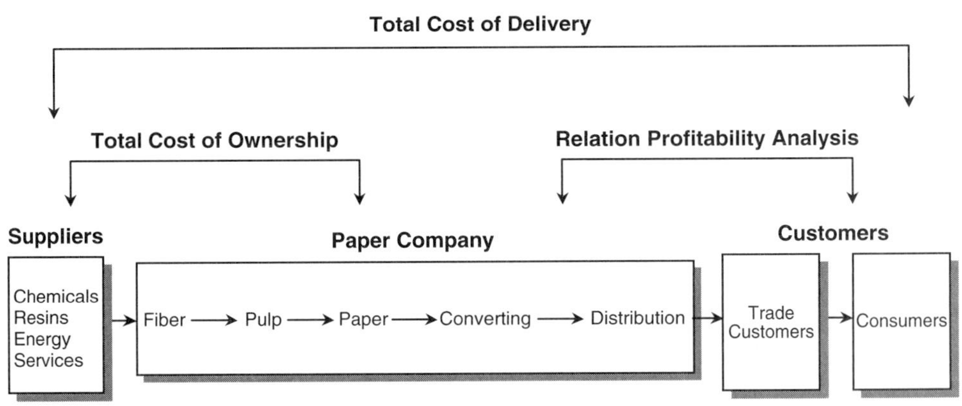

EXHIBIT 11.9 SUPPLY CHAIN PROFIT MANAGEMENT FOR A PAPER COMPANY

14. See also B.J. LaLonde and T.L. Pohlen,"Issues in Supply Chain Costing," *The International Journal of Logistics Management* 7, 1 (1996): 1–12.

(a) TOTAL COST OF OWNERSHIP. In the most limited sense, the total cost of ownership (TCO) is a method of calculating the total cost of acquiring goods and services from a supplier.[15] The total cost includes not only the purchase price, but also the costs of any additional activities associated with the supplier relation. Exhibit 11.10 lists examples of these additional activity costs.

For example, assume the Towel and Tissue Paper Company from Exhibit 11.9 uses TCO to calculate the cost of supplier relations. First, the company must identify the approximate cost of the various activities, such as those noted in Exhibit 11.10. For example, assume that an engineering study develops the following activity costs:

Receiving inspection	$ 40 per shipment
Short shipment	220 per shipment
Returned shipment................	600 per return
Late arrival	250 per shipment
Early arrival	140 per shipment

These activity costs reflect expenditure of resources (people, space, expenses) necessary to perform the activity. For example, the $140 for the early arrival includes the insurance and warehousing cost of holding the inventory for more days than required. Likewise, the returned shipment is the total cost of repackaging, loading, and administratively accounting for the return. In addition, the cost of the return should include an additional charge for the inventory held to accommodate the supplier's unreliability.

Assume two chemical suppliers each provide 4,000 gallons of the same chemical. The TCO performance of the two chemical suppliers appears in Exhibit 11.11.

Supplier A is not yet a qualified supplier; therefore, the firm must perform receiving inspections for all incoming shipments. In addition, of the 35 shipments, the firm rejected two and returned them to the supplier; another 18 shipments were either short or late. Supplier B is a qualified supplier: therefore, the firm need not perform any receiving inspection. Supplier B had only three shipments that deviated from plan. Therefore, although Supplier B's purchase cost per gallon exceeds that of Supplier A, Supplier B's total cost per gallon is less than Supplier A when considering TCO.

Purchasing Activity Costs	Receiving Activity Costs	Failure Activity Costs
Freight	Receiving inspection	Scrap disposition
Premium freight	Special handling	Rework
Purchase ordering	Receiving rejection and return	Lost yield
Problem resolutions	Short shipment	Warranty
Change due to nonavailability	Early arrival	
	Late arrival	

EXHIBIT 11.10 SUPPLIER-INDUCED TCO ACTIVITIES

15. See Lawrence P. Carr and Christopher, D. Ittner, "Measuring the Total Cost of Ownership: A Critical Linkage," *Journal of Cost Management* (Fall 1992): 42–51; and Lisa M. Ellram, "Activity-Based Costing and Total Cost of Ownership: A Critical Linkage," *Journal of Cost Management* (Winter 1985): 22–30; and Roodhooft, Filipt et al., "Optimized Sourcing Strategies Using Total Cost of Ownership," *Journal of Cost Management* (July/August 2003): 28–35.

	Supplier A		Supplier B	
	Frequency	TCO	Frequency	TCO
Purchase cost		$38,000		$42,000
Receiving inspections	35 × $ 40	1,400	None	-
Returned shipments	2 × $600	1,200	None	-
Short shipment	8 × $220	1,760	1 × $220	220
Late arrivals	10 × $250	2,500	2 × $250	500
Total		$44,860		$42,720

EXHIBIT 11.11 TCO COMPARISON OF CHEMICAL SUPPLIERS

Accountants can develop a TCO index used for evaluating supplier total cost performance. The index is the TCO per unit divided by the purchase price per unit. The index for Supplier A and B for 4,000 gallons would be:

$$\text{Supplier A: } \frac{\$11.215}{\$9.50} = 1.181 \qquad \text{Supplier B: } \frac{\$10.68}{\$10.50} = 1.017$$

Some firms use the index to adjust supplier price bids. Therefore, if Supplier A were to bid $10.00 per gallon, the firm would adjust the bid by a factor of 1.181, to $11.81 per gallon, for purposes of awarding the bid. A bid of $10.50 from Supplier B would be the low TCO bid ($10.50 × 1.017 = $10.68), even though the actual price bid exceeded that of Supplier A. TCO analysis rewards excellent supplier behavior and penalizes poor behaviors. This occurs when managing supply chain relations beyond price.

One must ask, however, if this emphasis on price and behavior reflects all criteria for selecting a supplier. If the firm views TCO as a method of managing supplier behaviors only, then it may neglect some important supplier integration issues. Given this concern, firms should expand TCO beyond its use as a tool for identifying supplier shortcomings. The supplier may add value to downstream elements (later functions) of the supply chain by providing additional service (earlier functions). For example, the chemical supplier could provide upstream engineering support to the downstream paper company, which reduces costs of manufacturing paper. The supplier may, for example, analyze the ways the chemical interacts with the paper-making process, and, thus, be able to improve yields, chemical input usage, or quality of the end product. The supplier provides a tangible benefit, at some cost. Without a method of valuing the costs and benefits, a rule for sharing the benefits will be difficult to establish.

Suppliers who adopt lean manufacturing principles can lead to significant downstream benefits. A lean supplier can respond faster to downstream requirements, while at the same time it can reduce inventory in the pipeline. These benefits can lead to significant savings to downstream customers. For example, the cost of markdowns represents the second largest cost of apparel retailing, after cost of goods. Markdowns occur when a retailer holds unsold goods that it purchased before the season began. Before the season begins, the firm must make the commitment. If the company orders too few goods, then it loses sales—if it orders too much, then markdowns result. What would happen if the apparel retailer could order and receive fashion goods weekly, rather than in quarterly programs? Would such a capability allow the retailer to catch most of the demand from a popular item and miss most of the markdowns from an unpopular item? Would the retailer be willing to pay more for such fast response capability? Transit time may require that domestic manufacturers (with higher labor costs) supply the goods, rather than more distant, perhaps Asian, operations that pay lower wages but have longer shipping times.[16] By evaluating the full total cost of ownership, one can answer these types of questions. Therefore, TCO should move beyond disciplining supplier shortcomings, but also reward behaviors that lead to tangible improvements.

(b) RELATION PROFITABILITY ANALYSIS. The flip side of TCO is the downstream, customer, side of the relation.[17] Unlike suppliers, the customer provides revenues, so one can expand the analysis to evaluate profitability of the distribution channel/customer relations. Partitioning profit among customer or channel participants, or both, provides insights regarding the following:

- The value provided by the firm to customers
- The maximizing sales effort for different customer/channels
- The drivers of underlying customer/channel costs
- The success or failure of customer strategies
- The pricing of various channel configurations
- The costs of horizontally linked functions

Relation profitability analysis combines logistics, marketing, and sales-related activities into a complete picture of the cost to serve the customer. A firm can examine the profitability of a relation for individual customers, region, distribution channel, and order size.

(i) Analysis by Individual Customers. One commonly sees the familiar Pareto principle in action: 20 percent of the customers yield 80 percent of the profitability. The other 80 percent are smaller customers whose business provides gross margins at break-even or below. One should also focus on the customer's potential in addition to its current profitability performance. A decision to invest in an unprofitable customer relation today may be justified upon its future potential. This suggests that a complete understanding of the profitability of a customer relation may require a longer, life-cycle, perspective. While few firms track this type of performance, a life-cycle perspective would provide insights about the financial returns on customer development activity.

Beyond analysis at the individual customer level, firms may classify individual customers along other attributes, such as region, distribution channel, and size. For example, Rigips, a German building supply company, stratifies its profit reporting as shown in Exhibit 11.12.

As Exhibit 11.12 shows, Rigips evaluates the profitability by individual retail outlets, by three different regional classifications of stores, by channel (e.g., local hardware, builder's wholesale, large retail), and by group (a chain of individual stores under a single corporate name).

(ii) Analysis by Region. Regional analysis groups customers within a geographical area under the responsibility of a manager. One can use regional profit information to evaluate regional managers and to support decisions such as the following:

- Changes in the intensity of sales coverage by adding or subtracting sales personnel.

16. T, Gilreath, J. Reeve, and C. Whalen, "Time Is Money," *Bobbin* (March 1995).
17. See also Foster, G., Gupta, M., and Sjoblom, L., "Customer Profitability Analysis: Challenges and New Directions," *Journal of Cost Management* (Spring 1996): 517.

Element	Dimension
Customer (store level)	Customer
Rural District	Customer
Sales District	Customer
Sales Region	Customer
Channel	Customer
Group	Customer

A customer aggregation hierarchy

Alternative customer aggregations

EXHIBIT 11.12 DIFFERENT CUSTOMER CLASSIFICATIONS

- Changes in the intensity of advertising and promotional activity.
- Changes in the sales region boundaries. The influences of population changes, population density, types of industry, traffic conditions, and factors that affect the mobility of salespersons on operating costs affect the boundary decision.
- Changes in the methods of covering a territory, such as telephone, personal visit, mail, local advertising, or Internet. The costs of each approach, effectiveness, and customer density of a geographic area will affect the optimal method of covering a territory.

The costs of a region include the direct costs, such as the occupancy costs of the district office, district salaries, sales force salaries, promotional costs and sales force support costs. In addition to the direct costs, firms can allocate corporate support costs—such as customer billing, collection, or personnel recruiting costs—to a sales region. Firms can usually allocate centralized credit, billing, customer accounting, and related costs to regions by using units of functional service, such as number of customers, number of invoices, number of sales order lines, and number of bills of lading.

Firms often incur significant freight costs. They can record costs of delivery by a common carrier through the accounts payable system and code them to the region. However, the firm may need to allocate the costs of a corporate fleet to the region. Trips that cross multiple regional boundaries may require ton-miles, or some other measure of service, allocated to the region.

Exhibit 11.13 shows an example of a regional profit report for a specialty chemicals company. This profit report assigns the additional direct costs of the region—such as sales compensation, sales expenses, and promotional cost—to each region manager's profit statement. The report also assigns to the region manager indirect costs, such as centralized support and hiring, that represent the cost of services consumed by the division. The firm can use a service charge rate to allocate these latter costs to the region. For example, the turnover charge could represent a charge associated with hiring a new salesperson. The actual charge rate may be a function of whether the firm moves a current employee from another division into the division (a low rate), places a new employee into the division (a medium rate), or uses an employment agency to find a new employee to place in the division (a high rate).

The regional profit report provides the regional manager incentives to manage the profitability of the sales effort, rather than just sales volume. This aligns costs associated with acquiring and maintaining volume. Therefore, the division manager can begin to evaluate the tradeoffs and associations between resource expenditure and sales volume.

Sales		$12,456,000
Cost of goods sold		6,645,000
Gross profit		$ 5,811,000
Sales compensation		3,267,000
Sales expenses		
Business travel	$ 243,000	
Automobile	153,600	
Communications	92,800	
Supplies	32,500	521,900
Centralized support		
Sales order administration	245,000	
Collections	71,000	
Quotation	94,500	410,500
Hiring		
Turnover charge	194,500	
Relocation costs	32,400	226,900
Promotional		
Samples	31,700	
Literature	46,700	
Meetings and conventions	167,000	245,400
Net Margin		$ 1,862,300
Net Margin % of Sales		14.95%

EXHIBIT 11.13 REGIONAL PROFIT REPORT

(iii) Analysis by Distribution Channels. Sellers often serve the same or different customers through different distribution channels. For example, the consumer of towel and tissue products may purchase the product from a club store, grocery store, or convenience store. All three of these represent different channels for selling the same product to the same customer. Alternatively, the seller may sell to some customers uniquely through different channels, such as wholesale, retail, consumer direct, or broker. The different channels have different costs for servicing and earn different margins. As a result, an organization can gain operational insight by evaluating channel profitability. For example, Exhibit 11.14 shows how a beverage company, such as Volunteer Juice Co., would evaluate the profitability of its major channels.

Exhibit 11.14 shows that the greatest net margins come from the airline distribution channel; however, this channel has small volume. Apparently, the airline channel has attractive pricing, and inexpensive distribution costs through the hub cities. At the other end of the spectrum, the university distribution channel has negative margins. The firm may decide to sacrifice margin to win exclusive distribution rights on campus, and, therefore, capture a new generation of consumers.

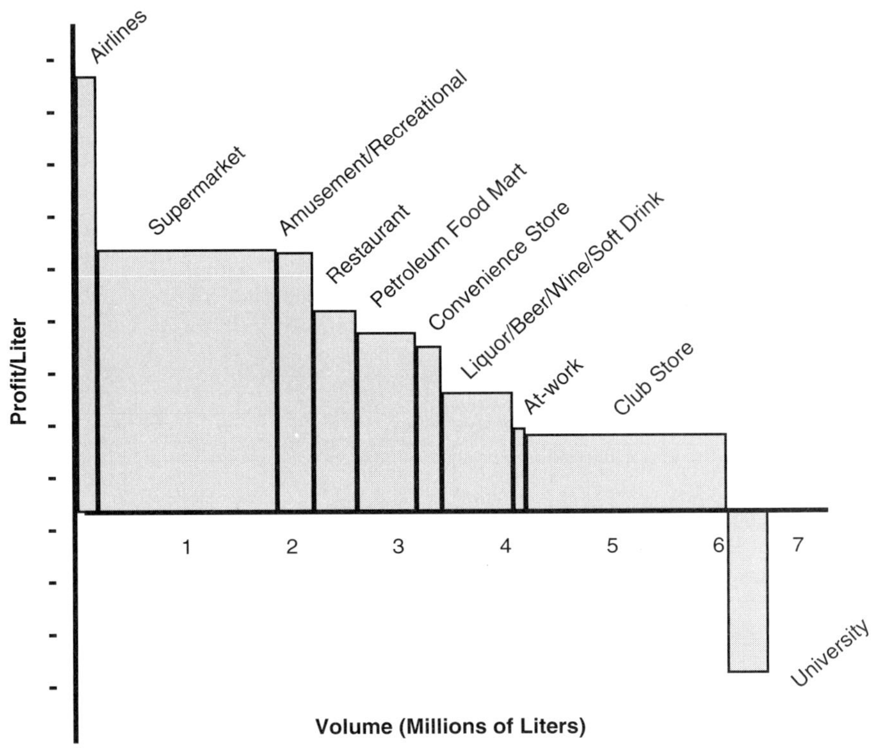

EXHIBIT 11.14 DISTRIBUTION CHANNEL PROFITABILITY ANALYSIS

(iv) Analysis by Order Size. The order size of a particular customer or distribution channel influences marketing and logistics activities. For example, getting and filling a smaller order may cost the same as that of a larger order. This occurs because many of these activities, such as sales visit, order taking, paperwork, shipping, picking, invoicing, and collecting, vary with the number of orders, not the number of units sold with an order. As a result, smaller orders can become a financial burden to an organization. A cost study of this problem can help the firm do the following:

- Identify differential pricing points as a function of order size.
- Identify minimum-order-size requirements.
- Identify cost-reduction opportunities.
- Identify the order characteristics of unprofitable customers.

New supply chain practices move away from large infrequent orders to more frequent smaller orders, because customers do not wish to purchase goods before using them. Many customers require that suppliers ship goods so that they arrive when the customer consumes them. For example, Toyota's Georgetown, Kentucky assembly plant receives many of its purchased parts three times per day. This allows the assembly plant to maintain a minimum materials inventory, while still meeting the requirements of the assembly line. Given the small order problem identified above, what can a vendor do? The answer lies in changing the order-getting and filling process so that it becomes more economical to execute order transactions for smaller quantities of product.[18] Examples of such strategies are the use of vendor management inventories, blanket purchase orders, electronic data interchange, ordering, lean manufacturing, distribution center cross-docking, advance shipping notices, and consumption/replenishment (Kanban) materials control. These lean supply chain concepts (discussed in other chapters in this *Handbook*) allow companies to profitably sell, produce, and ship in small order quantities.

11.5 RELATION PROFITABILITY—EXAMPLE

Here, we illustrate analysis of relation profitability using the Towel and Tissue Company (TTC) data in Exhibit 11.9.[19] We will assume TTC sells home-use towel and tissue products to a number of trade customers and distribution channels as follows:

- Wal-Mart
- Target
- Kroger
- Sam's Warehouse
- Broker Distribution Channel
- Convenience Store Distribution Channel

These customers do not require the same logistics and marketing activities. TTC will use the activity information to identify the relation profitability for these customers. We begin by developing an activity worksheet for each relation. Exhibit 11.15 has a sample activity worksheet for the assumed Wal-Mart relation.

Note that the net revenue of the relation includes gross revenues, less discounts and incentives. After calculating gross profit, the firm should subtract activity costs associated with the relation to calculate the customer margin. Exhibit 11.16 lists the activities used by TTC in evaluating its customer relations. The costs associated with the relation include direct costs of the relationship, such as freight costs; activity costs, such as loading; and carrying costs associated with inventory and receivables.

(a) DIRECT COSTS. The direct costs include the dollars spent on the customer relation for a particular activity. When possible, one should collect direct costs, rather than use allocated costs. For example, a firm can calculate the cost of advertising for the benefit of the customer (so-called *co-operative advertising*) by either tracking the direct costs of running ads from the accounts payable system or by assuming an activity rate for each ad. Under the latter approach, the firm must track the number of ads for each customer and multiply it by the advertising rate. While this tracks the frequency of advertising it does not capture differences in rates per ad. The analysis averages differences between a cooperative ad placed in a low circulation newspaper and a high circulation newspaper across all cooperative ads.

Our example tracks actual freight costs direct to each customer, thus avoiding averaging effects across all customers. The actual freight charge results from the interaction of the number of shipments, distance, size of shipment, weight, and cube. In this way, shipments of large quantities to close customers do not subsidize small quantities to distant ones. Moreover, this calculation captures additional movement and transshipment due to the customer's stock re-balancing demands.

18. A good illustration is provided in Harvard Business School case, *Pillsbury: Customer Driven Reengineering* (HBS 9-195-144).
19. This illustration is a stylized composite from a number of consulting experiences by the author.

Name	Units	Numbers
Revenue		
Gross Sales	dollars	75,400,000
Product returns	dollars	2,400,000
Volume Incentive	dollars	1,200,000
Net Sales	dollars	71,800,000
Product Costs		
Cost of goods	dollars	47,450,000
Plant Shipping and Handling Costs		
Freight Costs	dollars	940,000
Loading		
Bill of lading	shipments	450
Order loading	orders	700
Order sorting and consolidation	order lines	4.5
Material handling		
Number of warehouse moves	# of clamps	
Product Returns	# of returns	1,200
Inventory Carrying Costs		
Cycle inventory		
Order interval	months	1
Speculative inventory		
Cumulative forecast error	cases	30,000
Warranty costs	dollars	
Sales and Marketing Costs		
Customer planning and management	FTEs	1.5
Selling	orders	12
Collection administration		
Collection	invoices	
Adjustments	invoice adjustments	4
Cooperative advertising	dollars	
Order Entry Costs	order lines	
Receivable Carrying Costs		
Day's sales outstanding	Day's sales	58.1

EXHIBIT 11.15 RELATION ACTIVITY WORKSHEET: WAL-MART

(b) ACTIVITY COST. Often, the accounting system does not register activity costs directly from supporting payroll or accounts payable (AP) systems. Consequently, the firm must translate the resources into activities to facilitate assignment to the customer. For example, the loading activity is a function of three activity drivers, as follows:

Loading activity = [Order lines × Rate] + [Orders × Rate] + [Shipments × Rate]

Activity	Type
Freight costs	Direct cost
Loading activity	Activity cost
Material handling activity	Activity cost
Product return activity	Activity cost
Cycle inventory carrying costs	Carrying cost
Speculative inventory carrying costs	Carrying cost
Warranty costs	Direct cost
Customer planning and management	Activity cost
Selling	Activity cost
Collection administration	Activity cost
Cooperative advertising	Direct cost
Order entry costs	Activity cost
Receivable carrying costs	Carrying cost

EXHIBIT 11.16 ACTIVITIES RELATED TO CUSTOMER RELATIONS

The first term is the activity of sorting order lines into orders, the second term is the order loading activity, and the third term is the bill of lading paperwork. The analysis breaks down other activities in a similar manner. The rate represents the resource cost of performing an activity cycle, calculated by engineering analysis.

(c) POST-SALE ACTIVITIES. Beyond the current activities required to support a relation, additional relation activities occur after the point of sale. Obvious examples include longer-term servicing and warranty activities. These costs include the direct costs of the post-sale service, as captured by the accounting system, plus any additional administrative cost calculated by multiplying the activity rate by an activity driver, such as number of claims.

Post-sale activities also include costs that firms cannot easily estimate, such as environmental costs.[20] Under environmental costing, the firm must calculate the discounted present value of future environmental effects in order to estimate the profitability of a relation (or product). These future environmental effects include such events as *product take-back:* the disposition costs associated with a product at the end of its life. Accounting for the present value of product take-back can give companies incentive to design and sell products with end-of-life disposition in mind.

(d) CARRYING COST. In addition to the direct and activity costs of supporting a customer relation, one must also consider the imputed interest cost associated with assets invested in the relation. The analysis in Exhibit 11.15 includes both inventory and accounts receivable carrying costs. The accounting system registers accounts receivable directly to the customer in the accounting system, so its assignment is trivial. Inventory, however, will prove a more difficult asset to assign to the customer relation. One could address this by separating the inventory into the amount necessary to support the order

20. "Tools and Techniques of Environmental Accounting for Business Decisions" *Management Accounting Guideline #40*, IMA, 1996. See also work by Mark Epstein on this topic, e.g. M.J. Epstein, *Measuring Corporate Environmental Performance: Best Practices for Costing and Managing an Effective Environmental Strategy* (Montvale, N.J.: IMA, 1996).

cycle and the additional amount to support demand variation (or order uncertainty). The order cycle carrying cost is the imputed interest cost on the minimum inventory required to support the lead time. For example, if manufacturing lead time is one month from order, then to defend order fulfillment the firm must have an average safety stock of one month of inventory multiplied by the minimum daily demand rate. As lead time decreases, the amount of order cycle inventory required for the relation also decreases. Ultimately, a demand replenishment system may require only a few days of inventory in the system. Lead time reduction translates directly to inventory reduction and cost savings.

Firms may also need to hold speculative inventory in addition to order cycle inventory to cope with demand unpredictability. For example, if a customer has in the past ordered an average of 300 units per month with a standard deviation of 33 units, then the supplier must cope with this order variation by holding at least 400 units in inventory (a three-sigma defense—implying being able to satisfy demand 99 percent of the time; a two-sigma defense holds about 465 units, and guards against outages about 95 percent of the time.). The customer may also order fewer than 300 units, causing the supplier to hold inventory beyond that required by the demand. Firms can measure such variation over time and translate it into additional inventory that they must hold to cope with demand uncertainty. The sum of the mean absolute deviation from average provides an estimate of the amount of inventory required due to variation. A customer with variable demands places more extreme inventory pressures on the supplier than does one with lower variability. Likely, the noise in the estimates of statistical uncertainty (the standard deviation in the preceding example) will swamp the demand uncertainty, so that the results of the analysis are more likely guidelines than pinpoint control devices.

Some customers may require unique components for customer specific options. One can include these unique components in the customer specific inventory to calculate the carrying cost.

(e) MARGIN ANALYSIS. Exhibit 11.17 summarizes the assumed relation profitabilities of all the customers from the worksheet details in Exhibit 11.15.

The gross profit number indicates that the convenience store distribution channel offers the greatest gross profitability, and Sam's Warehouse offers the lowest gross profitability. The gross profit number, however, does not completely describe the profitability of the relations. The net relation profit as a percent of sales provides a different interpretation. The convenience store channel has the lowest net relation profit at 9 percent of sales, while Sam's Warehouse has the greatest net relationship profit at 19 percent of sales, the opposite of the gross profit order. Why? The activity and carrying cost percentages explain the net results. The convenience store channel has intensive shipping, ordering, and handling activities because the convenience store channel requires many smaller orders to each store. Thus, for a given volume of towel and tissue products, the convenience store channel requires the most logistical support. In contrast, Sam's Warehouse requires the least support for a given volume of sales because Sam's requires full pallets of a single product.

In addition, Sam's asset carrying cost is also the lowest as a percent of sales because it employs a vendor managed inventory (VMI) strategy. Vendors under VMI will replenish inventory based on the previous period's demand. Naturally, the goal is to match production to demand by keeping the replenishment period small. Thus, a replenishment approach minimizes order cycle inventory, the largest source of carrying cost.

An organization that understands the components of profitability by customer relation has a basis for negotiating prices that are consistent with the services provided. If a distribution channel or customer requires intensive logistical support, then the pricing

Customer	Gross Profit as % of Sales	Activity Cost as % of Sales	Carrying Cost as % of Sales	Relation Profit as % of Sales
Wal-Mart	34%	20%	2%	12%
Target.......................	30	15	4	11
Kroger	35	22	3	10
Sam's Warehouse..............	28	8	1	19
Broker channel...............	33	10	5	18
Convenience store channel	37	23	5	9

EXHIBIT 11.17 COMPARISON OF CUSTOMER RELATION PROFITABILITY

should reflect this bundle of additional services provided. Some companies unbundle and price the services separately from the product; this is termed *menu pricing.*

11.6 SUMMARY

This chapter explained how firms can manage logistics and marketing costs to support supply chain management. Firms can use total delivered cost to evaluate the supplier side of the supply chain, while they use relation profitability to support decisions for the customer side of the supply chain. In addition, they can use expense planning and control simulations to identify, plan, and control costs at any point in the supply chain.

CHAPTER 12

ESTIMATING COST BEHAVIOR

MICHAEL W. MAHER, PHD, EDITOR
University of California, Davis

M. LAURENTIUS MARAIS
William E. Wecker Associates, Inc.

CONTENTS

12.1 INTRODUCTION 351

12.2 DISTINCTION AMONG COSTS, EXPENSES, AND EXPENDITURES 352

12.3 FUNCTIONS OF COST ESTIMATION IN ORGANIZATIONS 352
- (a) Decision Making 353
- (b) Planning and Standard Setting 353
- (c) Cost Management 353

12.4 SIMPLE COST BEHAVIOR: VARIABLE COST ASSOCIATED WITH SINGLE COST DRIVER 353

12.5 MORE COMPLEX COST BEHAVIOR: SEVERAL COST DRIVERS 354
- (a) Cost–Benefit Test 354
- (b) Other Cost Patterns 354
- (c) Semi-Variable Costs 355

12.6 COST ESTIMATION METHODS 357
- (a) Statistical Cost Estimation Using Regression Analysis 357
- (b) Account Analysis Method 361
- (c) Data Problems 362
- (d) Engineering Method 362
- (e) Queuing Theory 363
- (f) Computer-Intensive Cost Modeling 365

12.7 CONCLUSION: CHOOSING AN ESTIMATION METHOD 366

12.1 INTRODUCTION

This chapter discusses the process of cost estimation: measurements, calculations, and projections of the resources sacrificed to acquire the factors consumed by specified activities, services or products. For example, consider the cost of automobile transportation. The problem of estimating this cost may arise in various circumstances for different purposes, leading to various approaches to informative, relevant cost estimation. Suppose, for example, that you want to estimate your personal automobile transportation costs related to commuting. You normally drive your car 15,000 miles per year, but if you used public transportation for commuting, you could reduce the annual mileage to 10,000 miles. How much would you save in automobile costs if you reduced your driving by 5,000 miles per year?

One cannot easily answer this question because some automobile costs vary as a direct result of the cost objective activity—the incremental miles driven—but others do not. Insurance and licensing costs probably will not directly relate to miles driven, but fuel costs will. Maintenance and repair costs depend on the number of miles driven, but not necessarily proportionately. The opportunity cost of ownership may depend on the number of miles driven, both through the decreased value of a more heavily used vehicle and, in the long run, through a more expensive choice of a larger, safer, more comfortable vehicle (in response to more driving).

Suppose that the automobile cost estimation problem arose in the context of buying equipment and setting prices for a limousine transportation business. For example, when analyzing the profitability of a proposed corporate contract for airport pickup and delivery, one might compare an offered flat fee per trip to the cost of providing the trip. Alternatively, the analysis might compare the total projected revenue from the customer to the total projected (opportunity) cost of providing the services. In either case, the comparison involves cost estimation.

Few analysts would find costs for a limousine business easy to estimate. For instance, the total cost of providing the limousine service would include the cost of unused capacity—in other words, the unused limousine time entailed by providing a fleet of limousines sufficient to ensure an acceptable trip refusal rate and response time.

12.2 DISTINCTION AMONG COSTS, EXPENSES, AND EXPENDITURES

Costs occur when an entity (or person) sacrifices resources to acquire factors. The acquired factors remain assets until the entity consumes them, at which time they become expenses. Because expenses represent the expiration of costs, people often use *cost* and *expense* as synonyms, particularly in the context of cost estimation. This chapter will also use *cost* and *expense* interchangeably.

The monetary denomination of costs usually parallels the associated expenditures of funds, but the timing and amounts of the actual expenditures often do not match those of specific cost items. You might expect the monetary value of costs to parallel the associated expenditures of funds in terms of timing and amount: You purchase a loaf of bread at a store and immediately pay for it with cash. Often, however, the timing and amounts of the expenditures do not match those of specific cost items. Consider, for example, an automobile's consumption of gasoline. Each trip consumes a portion of the gas in your automobile's tank. You incurred the expenditure of funds when you filled the tank. The cost of automobile tires is a similar but more extreme example. You could consider a new tire as a stock of tread to be consumed slowly as you drive the automobile. Each mile driven consumes a portion of the tire tread. Again, the expenditure on tires does not parallel the cost pattern.

This mismatch of costs and expenditures creates numerous practical complications for analysts who estimate costs, because current accounting information systems generally record expenditure transactions (e.g., the amount spent to purchase a tire) more effectively than costs (e.g., the wear on a tire).[1]

12.3 FUNCTIONS OF COST ESTIMATION IN ORGANIZATIONS

Organizations use cost estimates for three primary purposes: decision making, planning and standard setting, and cost management.

---

1. Depreciation based on usage is an attempt to impute cost data from expenditure data.

(a) DECISION MAKING. In deciding among alternative actions, managers must project the likely consequences of each alternative, including its effect on costs. The costs of alternative actions often become a major factor in decision making.

(b) PLANNING AND STANDARD SETTING. In planning the future of an organization, managers specify the activities that they expect people in the organization to perform. Cost estimation assigns costs to those activities. Based on the costs of component activities, managers forecast the likely costs of the organization, prepare financial forecasts, and estimate its cash flows. The projected costs of the component activities may also serve as standards or targets for monitoring the performance of departments and employees. (See Chapter 15 for a discussion of standards.)

(c) COST MANAGEMENT. Organizations must manage costs to be successful. Analysis of the costs of operations in terms of their component activities may identify reengineering opportunities for reducing costs and improving effectiveness. Thus, the process of cost estimation can help managers discover advantageous alternatives.

12.4 SIMPLE COST BEHAVIOR: VARIABLE COST ASSOCIATED WITH SINGLE COST DRIVER

Estimating the relation between costs and activities involves two key issues: (1) identifying the cost drivers and (2) estimating the cost behavior. In a simple world, analysts use only one cost driver and assume that costs linearly relate to cost drivers. Some organizations use multiple cost drivers. Analysts in a Hewlett-Packard plant in Germany, for example, used more than 100 cost drivers in their cost estimations.

At the current stage of technology, most organizations still assume a linear relation between costs and cost drivers.

The simplest cost behavior pattern separates costs into fixed and variable components. You probably understand the term *variable costs,* and know that total variable costs change proportionately with changes in total activity levels. In a simple world with one cost driver, costs divide simply into fixed and variable components; when costs increasing linearly with the cost driver, analysts estimate the following cost equation:

$$TC = F + VX$$

where

TC = total costs

F = fixed costs that do not vary with the cost driver

V = variable costs per unit for the cost driver (V is the cost driver rate)

X = the number of cost driver units.

Exhibit 12.1 contains a picture of this simple relation where the cost driver is number of miles driven for an automobile and the costs are hypothetical fixed (e.g., car payment, insurance, etc.) and variable costs (e.g., gasoline, wear on tires) related to the units (miles driven).

This simple cost breakdown into fixed and variable components misses important other types of cost behavior that we discuss in Section 12.5 of this chapter. Nevertheless, this simple model has value, and may satisfy a cost–benefit test better than a more complex, albeit more accurate, cost model.

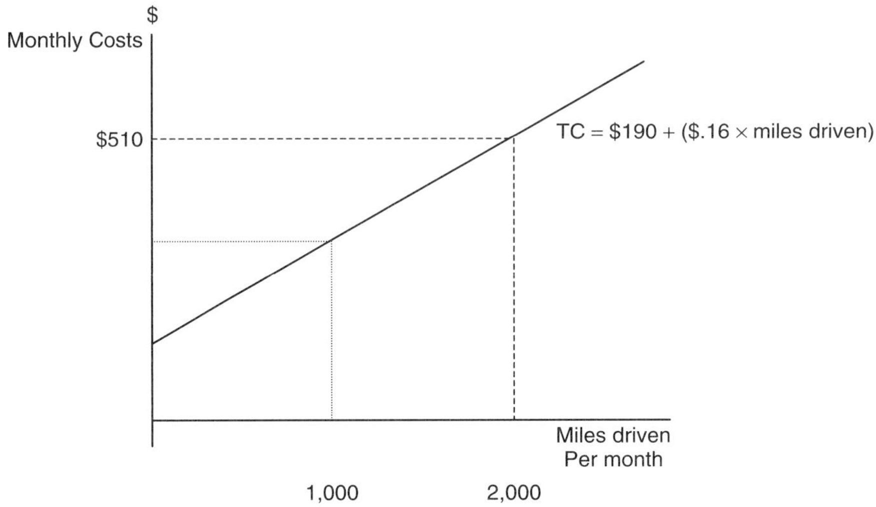

EXHIBIT 12.1 SIMPLE MODEL

For example, suppose you consider launching a new product and have not yet defined all the specifications. The simple model could help you decide whether to proceed with more detailed specification, given the simple estimate of costs. For companies with simple operations, the simple model may capture the relation between costs and activities rather well.

12.5 MORE COMPLEX COST BEHAVIOR: SEVERAL COST DRIVERS

(a) COST–BENEFIT TEST. A more complex world has multiple cost drivers and more complex cost behavior than indicated earlier. As a manager or analyst, you choose how complex to make the cost estimation model. Generally accepted rules do not exist for how simple or complex to make the model, but good business sense dictates that one should apply a cost–benefit test to the choice of model complexity. Because you probably will not know the costs and benefits of a particular model until you have estimated it (and perhaps not even then), you face the difficult task of attempting cost–benefit analysis before you have a good idea of either costs or the benefits. This commonly occurs in cost estimation. You will avoid serious cost–benefit errors if you avoid estimating complex models when they offer little over simple models. Cost–benefit tests will help you decide to estimate complex models only when they offer substantial advantages over estimating simple models.

(b) OTHER COST PATTERNS. Costs follow all sorts of patterns in the real world. Unlike the simple model presented in Section 12.4, many costs increase in steps or in curvilinear patterns as activity levels increase.

A diagram of step costs appears in Exhibit 12.2. A *step cost,* also called a *semi-fixed cost,* is any cost that increases in steps as cost driver volume increases. Many labor costs are step costs. In Exhibit 12.2, the costs are the costs per hour for quality control inspectors. One person can perform quality control inspections for 50 items per hour. The cost

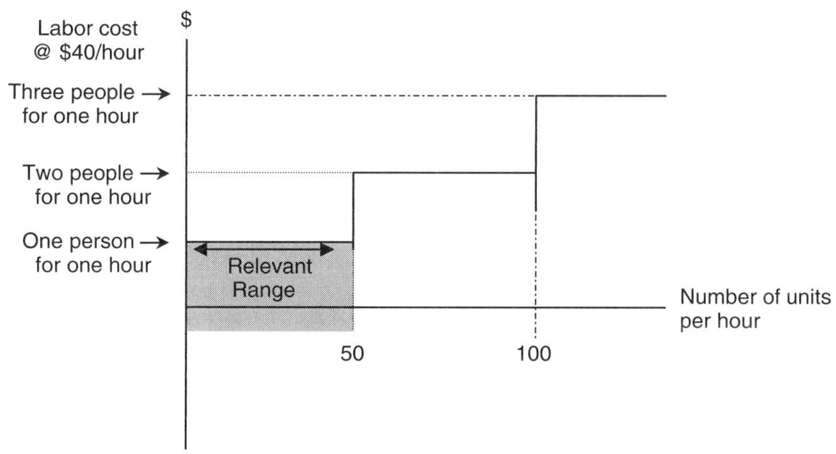

EXHIBIT 12.2 STEP COSTS: LABOR COSTS FOR QUALITY CONTROL

driver is the number of units to be inspected. If the company needs less than 50 units inspected per hour, the company hires one quality control person. If the number of units increases to the 51 to 100 units per hour range, then management increases the number of quality control people to two, and so forth, as shown in Exhibit 12.2.

Step costs occur when a firm hires people in time increments, such as hourly, daily, or monthly. Examples include nurses in a hospital, where the number of nurses increases in steps as the number of patients increase (but they won't be called in until the next shift); waiters and waitresses in restaurants (where the mid-afternoon hours will have fewer servers, but the dinner hour will have more servers); and teachers at a university (where the number of teachers changes with each term, as enrollment changes). In our experience, managers often ignore these steps, assuming the step costs are either purely fixed or variable. Yet research has shown that managers make erroneous decisions by treating step costs as variable costs.[2]

Managers may also rely on the concept of relevant range to deal with step costs. The *relevant range* is the range over which the company expects to operate. Within this range, managers assume particular cost-behavior patterns that are reasonably accurate. Such patterns would not hold true outside of the relevant range, however. For example, assume that a company does not produce more than 50 units per hour. Then management could assume that 1 to 50 units per hour is the relevant range, as shown in Exhibit 12.2. As long as management uses a quality control person, then it could consider quality control a fixed cost (within the relevant range of 1 to 50 units). If, however, the number of units per hour increased to 75—outside the relevant range—then management could no longer assume that quality control was a fixed cost.

(c) SEMI-VARIABLE COSTS. Semi-variable costs have both a fixed and variable component. Many utilities offer products (e.g., electricity, water) for a fixed cost up to a particular volume, after which they charge per unit. Exhibit 12.3 shows the semi-variable cost

2. See M. W. Maher and M. L Marais, "A Field Study on the Limitations of Activity-Based Costing When Resources Are Provided on a Joint and Indivisible Basis," *Journal of Accounting Research*, vol. 36, no. 1, pp. 129–142.

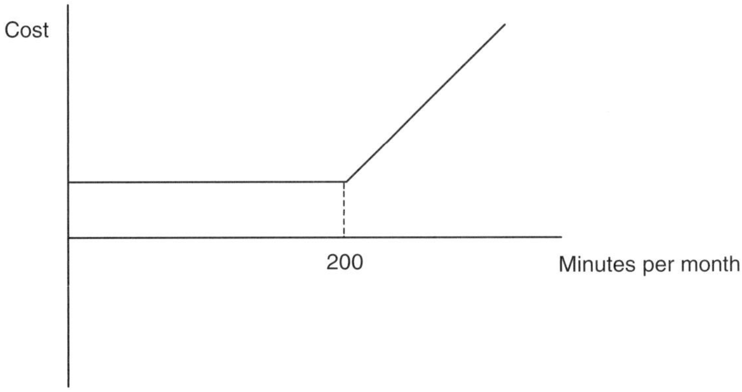

EXHIBIT 12.3 SEMI-VARIABLE COSTS: CELLULAR TELEPHONE

for a cellular telephone plan that charges a fixed amount per month for up to 200 minutes per month of usage then charges per minute for each minute used over 200 minutes.

Costs may also exhibit a curved behavior as number of units changes. Suppose a company gets a discount based on the volume of materials it buys, with the discount becoming increasingly larger as the volume purchased increases. Line A in Exhibit 12.4 represents this pattern, with variable costs decreasing per unit as volume per period increases. Line B represents variable costs that increase per unit as volume per period increases. For example, energy costs often increase per unit of production as total production per hour increases because managers bring on line machines that are less energy efficient.

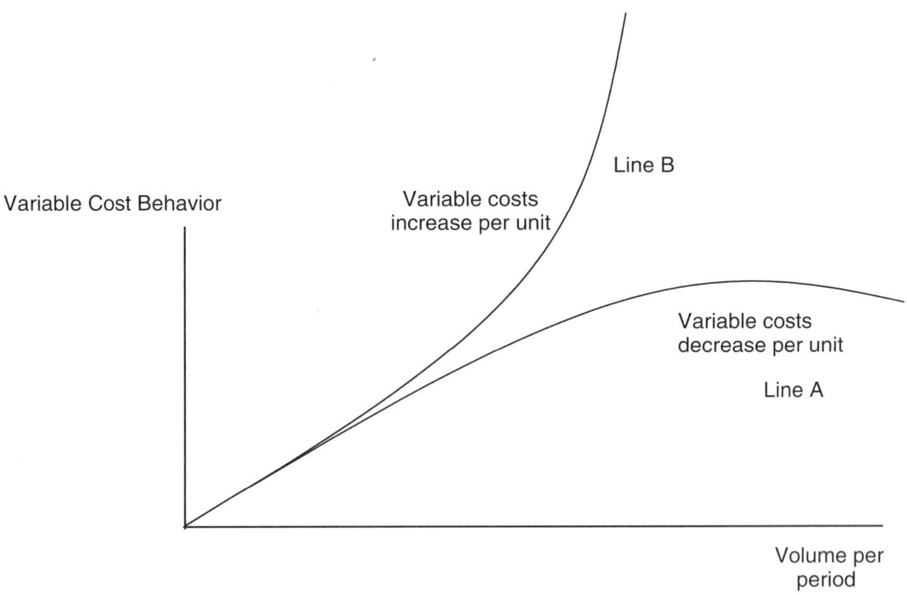

EXHIBIT 12.4 CURVED BEHAVIOR

12.6 COST ESTIMATION METHODS

We now discuss three cost estimation methods that practitioners commonly use:

1. Statistical methods (using regression analysis)
2. Account analysis
3. Engineering estimates

Results will likely differ across methods. Consequently, analysts often use more than one method to give them a sense of confidence (or lack of confidence) in the results. Managers and analysts who bear ultimate responsibility for all cost estimates frequently apply their own best judgment as a final step in the estimation process. You should view these methods, therefore, as ways to assist in arriving at the best cost estimates, but not as the final answer.

(a) STATISTICAL COST ESTIMATION USING REGRESSION ANALYSIS. This section discusses the use of regression analysis to estimate the relation between costs and activities. Regression analysis is a statistical method used to create an equation relating independent (or *X*) variables to dependent (or *Y*) variables. Regression analysis uses data from the past to estimate relations between costs (which are the dependent variable) and activities (which are the independent variables) that will have validity in the future.

When using regression analysis for cost estimation, one must first establish a logical relation between activities and the cost to be estimated. These activities are the *X* terms or *independent variables* of a regression equation. *Independent variables* are the activities that the analyst believes cause, or at least correlate with, the dependent variable, costs. The analysis aims to estimate the dependent variable, or the *Y* term, which represents cost. *Dependent variables* have a causal relation, or at least correlate with, independent variables. This distinction between dependent and independent variables should make sense because costs do not just happen, they *depend* on activities. We refer to the *Y* term as *TC* because the *Y* variable always provides some measure of total cost (*TC*) in our analyses. Depending on the context, *TC* may refer to the total costs of the organization, total overhead costs of the organization, or some other measure of total cost.

Regression analysis generates an equation (or visually, a line) that best fits a set of data points. In addition, regression techniques provide information that helps a manager measure how well the estimated regression equation describes the relation between costs and activities.

Popular computer spreadsheets such as Microsoft Excel®, as well as more powerful statistical packages such as SAS and SPSS, have the capacity to run regressions. We leave descriptions of the computational details to statistics books and documentation that comes with software packages. Instead, we deal with regression from the standpoint of accountants and managers who must interpret and use regression estimates.

Does a logical relation exist between costs and activities? One must first identify the activities that cause costs. If the relation between costs and activities have followed a particular pattern in the past and one expects that pattern to continue in the future, then one could reasonably use data from the past in estimating cost driver rates. If the past relation no longer has validity, however, then one must adjust the cost driver rates to reflect reality.

Over time, the cost-activity relation may change for several reasons. Technological innovation, change in product characteristics, and change in costs may make the past inappropriate for estimating the future. This particularly holds true for many high-tech companies and companies that have products with short life cycles.

The use of data about the past has value in companies that have stable production processes and products that do not change. Airlines, for example, use regression analysis to estimate the costs of various activities in flying airplanes. Because flight operations have not changed dramatically over the past several years, managers at these airlines think the use of past data is appropriate.

Although the use of past data for future cost estimation has limitations, in many cases it works quite well. Using past data is relatively inexpensive for analysts and managers because these firms have easy access to the data in their records. Past data do show the relations that held in prior periods and at least may provide a meaningful starting point for estimating costs as long as the analysts recognize their limitations.

(i) Relevant Range of Activity. As discussed in Section 12.6(b) of this chapter, the limits within which a cost projection may have validity form the *relevant range* for that estimate. Anything outside of the relevant range has the danger of walking on thin ice outside of known safety limits. Practitioners do it, but at a risk.

(ii) Simple Model: A Single Cost Driver. Section 12.4 of this chapter discussed the single cost driver model. This model presents a useful way to obtain a basic understanding about how to apply regression analysis to cost management. Section 12.6(a)(v) discusses a more complex and realistic model.

With one cost driver and costs divided simply into fixed and variable components, analysts estimate the following cost equation:

$$TC = F + VX$$

where

TC = total costs

F = fixed costs that do not vary with the cost driver

V = variable costs per unit for the cost driver (V is the cost driver rate)

X = the number of cost driver units (the independent variable).

In cost management, the independent variable is the cost driver. Although regression programs accept any data for the Y and X terms, entering numbers that have no logical relation will yield misleading estimates.

(iii) Application of the Simple Model. Assume we wish to estimate the variable cost per unit (V in the previous equation). From the company's records, we collect and input the data shown in Exhibit 12.5 into a regression program. Assume that we have 24 months of data. (We do not show every month to save space and avoid tedious reading.) Those data are the total costs of operating the company for each month and the total units sold each month.

When reading the output of a regression program for cost estimation purposes, many analysts treat the constant term ($16,086 in the results portion of Exhibit 12.5), or intercept, as an estimate of fixed costs. Of course, that interpretation may not prove reliable because the constant term at zero activity usually lies outside of the relevant range of observations. The coefficient of the X term (in this example, $423 per unit) provides an estimate of the variable cost per unit.

Month	Costs	Units
January, year 1	\$63,377	112
February, year 1	\$75,703	141
.	.	.
.	.	.
.	.	.
November, year 2	\$73,797	139
December, year 2	\$54,388	86

Results

The regression equation is

Total costs = \$16,086 + \$423 units

Predictor	Coefficient	Standard Error	*t* statistic
Constant	16,086	7,664	2.11
Units	423	81	5.22

$R^2 = 0.74$

EXHIBIT 12.5 SIMPLE REGRESSION INPUT DATA FROM THE COMPANY'S PAST RECORDS

The cost estimation equation based on this regression result is

$$\text{Total costs} = \text{Constant} + (b \times \text{units of activity})$$

$$\text{Total costs} = \$16{,}086 + (\$423 \times \text{units sold})$$

The *standard error* listed in the results section is a measure of uncertainty in the coefficients. The larger the standard error, the greater our uncertainty in the costs estimated by the coefficient. The *t statistic* is simply the coefficient divided by the standard error associated with the coefficient. For example, for units: 5.22 = 423/81. The *t* statistic provides us with information regarding whether the coefficient differs from zero. Analysts generally consider a *t* statistic greater than 2.0 sufficiently high to infer that the coefficient differs from zero. The *t* statistics in Exhibit 12.5 are certainly high enough to give such confidence. If you see *t* statistics less than 2.0, you should question whether the variable is an appropriate cost driver.

The *R-square* (R^2) is the proportion of the variation in the dependent variable (*TC* in our case) explained by the *X* or independent variables (the activities in our case). The *R*-square varies from 0 to 1.00, with 0 indicating no relation and 1.00 indicating a perfect linear relation between the independent variables and the dependent variable. The *R*-square indicates how much of the variation in the dependent variable that the independent variable explains. Exhibit 12.5 shows the *R*-square to be .74, meaning the variation in the activity—number of units sold—explains 74 percent of the variation in total costs.

(iv) Using Regression Results for the Simple Model. One could use the results for several purposes. First, you have an estimate of the variable cost per unit, \$423. You could use this estimate to set standards for performance evaluation, to plan, and to make various decisions. Assume you wish to estimate total costs for a month in which you expect the total volume of units sold to be 100 units. You would estimate the total costs for the month to equal \$16,086 + (\$423 × 100 units) = \$58,386.

(v) Using Regression Analysis to Estimate Cost Drivers for Activity-Based Management and Decision Making: Multiple Regression. Multiple regression is a regression equation with more than one independent variable. Using multiple regression analyses, company analysts learn much about cost behavior that simple regression does not reveal. Further, multiple regression has greater explanatory power: including more independent variables (cost drivers) will explain more of the variation in the dependent variable (total costs). Multiple regression requires more data. Consequently, one should consider the incremental costs and benefits of multiple regression over simple regression.

When performing multiple regression, one must first identify the activities that logically drive cost. Some organizations use many cost drivers—we know of organizations using more than 100 cost drivers. More cost drivers require more data but probably provide better information. The principle of diminishing marginal returns implies that at some point, the additional information from the additional cost driver is not worth the effort required to get the data. The use of numerous cost drivers can also lead to information overload. Decision makers generally have trouble processing the data if the analysis has too many cost drivers. In short, one must balance the benefits of more information against the costs of obtaining and using it.

For our purposes, assume we have identified the following four cost drivers:

1. *Units.* Units are the number of units sold.
2. *Batches.* Batches require setup costs for each batch of product. Further, stopping one batch, or job, and starting another may reduce production efficiency and increase quality costs.
3. *Products.* Each additional product requires specifications, blueprints, instructions, and other costly items.
4. *Customers.* Customer-related costs include the cost of customer files, billing costs, costs of obtaining additional customers, and the costs of dealing with irate customers.

These particular cost drivers correspond to the cost categories, called a *cost hierarchy* in activity-based costing jargon (see Chapter 6). The cost drivers that you choose in practice may or may not align with the cost hierarchy, depending on the nature of the organization. For example, a retail service company like Tower Records might not use a cost driver for number of customers because it cannot separate customer costs from unit costs. A utility company, however, would have substantial customer-related costs because it collects information about usage, prepares bills, collects and deposits payments received and maintains account records for each customer. Although organizations differ from each other, analysts can always begin identifying cost drivers by asking what drives the costs in four cost hierarchy levels: unit costs, batch costs, product costs, and customer costs.

(vi) Application of Multiple Regression. When estimating the costs for each of multiple cost drivers, companies must collect total cost and the number of units for each cost driver as Exhibit 12.6 shows.

The results for the multiple regression appear at the bottom of Exhibit 12.6. Note the adjusted R-square replaces the R-square that we showed for the simple regression. The adjusted R-square serves the same purpose as the R-square discussed in Section 12.6(a)(i) and (ii), but its calculation takes into account the number of independent variables in the regression. Analysts use the adjusted R-square, not the R-square, to judge the

Input Data from the Company's Records					
		Cost Driver Volume			
Month	Costs	Units	Batches	Products	Customers
January, year 0	$122,674	11,202	161	15	28
February, year 0	$145,703	14,106	183	11	39
.	.	.	.	.	.
.	.	.	.	.	.
.	.	.	.	.	.
November, year 3	$133,797	13,991	114	13	21
December, year 3	$123,797	11,114	125	12	33

Regression Results

The regression equation is

Total costs = $40,177 + $3.98 Units + $106 Batches + $986 Products + $406 Customers

Predictor	Coefficient	Standard Error	*t*-statistic
Constant	40177	8443	4.76
Units	3.98	1.16	3.43
Batches	106	45	2.36
Products	986	309	3.19
Customers	406	117	3.47

Adjusted $R^2 = 0.78$

EXHIBIT 12.6 MULTIPLE REGRESSION

quality of a multiple regression. At 0.78, the adjusted *R*-square is high, indicating the independent variables in the multiple regression do well in explaining the variation in total costs.

Assume we wish to estimate total costs for a month in which we estimate producing and selling 10,000 units, with 100 batches, 10 products, and 20 customers. Using the cost equation,

Total costs = $40,177 + $3.98 Units + $106 Batches + $986 Products + $406 Customers

we insert the number of planned cost driver units, as follows:

Total costs = $40,177 + ($3.98 × 10,000 units) + ($106 × 100 batches) + ($986 × 10 products) + ($406 × 20 customers)

= $108,577

(b) ACCOUNT ANALYSIS METHOD. *The account analysis* method is based on the past costs associated with each cost driver.

Account analysis requires more data because we must further separate total costs into categories that correspond to the cost drivers. For the example in Exhibit 12.6, one would analyze the cost accounts over the past 36 months to divide total monthly costs into four categories related to the four cost drivers, plus one category for fixed costs that we assumed the constant term estimated:

1. Unit costs
2. Batch costs

3. Product costs
4. Customer costs
5. Fixed costs

Analysts generally use account analysis in simple cases that have few observations and one or a few cost drivers.

(c) DATA PROBLEMS. Whether using regression or account analysis, the data's integrity will affect the results. The following problems complicate data collection:

- *Missing data.* Misplaced source documents or failure to record a transaction can result in missing data.
- *Outliers.* Extreme observations of cost-activity relations may unduly affect cost estimates. For example, a hurricane affected operations in a Florida company in August, resulting in high overhead due to one-time costs.
- *Allocated and discretionary costs.* Firms often allocate fixed costs on a volume basis, resulting in costs that may appear to be variable. Firms may also budget discretionary costs so that they appear variable (e.g., advertising expense budgeted as a percentage of revenue).
- *Inflation.* During periods of inflation, historical cost data do not accurately reflect future cost estimates.
- *Mismatched time periods.* The time period for the dependent and independent variables may not match (e.g., running a machine in February and receiving [recording] the energy bill in March).

Managers should be aware of problems in the data. No substitute exists for knowing how costs relate to activities, based on experience.

(d) ENGINEERING METHOD. Statistical methods and account analyses rely on data from the past. By contrast, the engineering method works with the present and future. Analysts make *engineering estimates* of costs by measuring the work involved in the activities that go into a product, then by assigning a cost to each of those activities. Analysts prepare a detailed step-by-step analysis of each activity required to make a product, together with the costs involved.

Analysts can usually obtain engineering estimates of the materials required for each unit of production from drawings and product specification records. People in the company's accounting and purchasing departments have data on the cost of materials that analysts can use to price the materials required to make a product. Analysts can perform time-and-motion studies or look at labor time records to ascertain the time required to perform each step. Labor records also provide typical wage rates for various jobs. Coupling those wage rates plus benefits with the time required to perform activities gives the estimated labor cost.

One can estimate other costs similarly. For example, analysts can estimate the size and cost of a building based on area construction costs and space requirements. They can estimate the necessary number of supervisors and support personnel based on a direct labor time estimate.

The engineering approach has an advantage over other cost-estimation methods because it details each step required to perform an operation. This permits benchmarking. Also, this approach does not require data from prior activities in the organization. Hence, analysts can use it to estimate costs for totally new activities.

The engineering approach can identify non-value-added activities. For example, if an engineering estimate indicates that an assembly process requires 80,000 square feet of floor area but the company has been using 125,000 square feet, managers may find it beneficial to rearrange the plant to make floor space available for other uses. Or if an engineering estimate indicates that the optimal production run is 1,000 units per setup but the company has been running only 100 units per setup, then the managers may change production scheduling to get the optimal production run length.

The engineering method has two disadvantages. Because the engineering approach analyzes each activity, it can become quite expensive. Furthermore, analysts often base engineering estimates on optimal conditions. Therefore, when evaluating performance, bidding on a contract, planning expected costs, or estimating costs for any other purpose, one should consider whether the actual work conditions will be less than optimal.

Using the engineering method for the four cost drivers plus fixed costs proceeds as follows.

(i) Unit Costs. To estimate unit costs, estimate the materials required from blueprints and product specification lists, and costs based on information from vendors. To estimate labor costs, figure the time required to perform the tasks required to produce a unit. Multiply the time by a wage cost that includes an allowance for payroll taxes and benefits.

(ii) Batch Costs. Batch costs are mostly labor costs, but may include some machine parts or even new machines. Preparing a batch includes taking the order, obtaining materials and workforce, providing instructions and training, setting up machines, obtaining parts for machines, moving the batch within the organization, delivering the product and following up with the customer. Analysts estimate the labor and materials required for each step from order taking to customer follow-up.

(iii) Product Costs. For each product added to the portfolio of products, companies incur costs of specifications, recordkeeping, training, quality testing methods, prototypes, machine dies, computer coding, marketing, and administrative activities.

(iv) Customer Costs. Customer costs are those that increase as the number of customers increases. Clearly, these costs include credit checking, billing, distribution, dealing with customer complaints, and marketing costs incurred to increase the customer base.

(v) Fixed (and Other) Costs. After estimating the costs related to cost drivers, analysts usually find that some unexplained costs remain. These may include administrative costs and fixed costs of operation that do not vary with any of the cost drivers.

(e) QUEUING THEORY. Many real-world processes and services must meet demands that have variable and uncertain timing. Often the resources committed to these activities have relatively long lead times. Thus, firms must commit the resources in advance of receiving and meeting the demands for outputs. This happens in various ways, for example, in the provision of emergency services, in telecommunications and transportation, and in hospitals. Under these conditions, firms cannot avoid the reality that committed resources that will sometimes be idle, and will at other times be insufficient to respond immediately to new demands for service. In principle, managers must find the optimum tradeoff between the cost of resources provided and the cost of delayed response and congestion.

Queueing theory, an area of study in operations research and probability theory, addresses probability models of such uncertain systems.[3] The exact mathematical results derived in queueing theory have limited scope, however. These results deal with the performance of relatively simple queueing systems under mathematically convenient assumptions, but do not capture many aspects of real-world processes and services that may, in particular cases, have important cost and performance consequences.

For those relatively simple queueing systems that lie within the scope of the mathematical theory, the theoretical results often reveal behaviors that would likely affect enterprise costs but will not likely be recognized by conventional, linear cost models. Exhibit 12.7 contains an example involving an activity *K*, such as a manufacturing cell or service center. The analysis assumes that units requiring the service of activity *K* will arrive at varying intervals, averaging one arrival every 12 minutes.[4] The average duration of activity *K* service is 10 minutes, and the firm has only one server. Under these conditions, the mathematical theory shows that the work in process backlog waiting for service at activity *K* will average 4.2 units and that the average time spent waiting will be 50 minutes.[5]

Suppose that the enterprise operates for 2,500 hours each year, and that the annual cost of operating and maintaining activity *K* equals $12.5 million. Adopting throughput as a linear cost driver for activity *K*, the cost of *K* per unit of activity would then appear to be $1,000 per unit (= $12.5 million ÷ [5 units per hour × 2,500 hours]). Suppose that managers are considering a proposal to expand the enterprise output by a factor of four. The cost of activity *K* is one input to this decision, and it might appear reasonable to summarize its cost impact solely in terms of the $1,000 unit cost estimate from the existing plant (albeit recognizing that the firm may have to acquire *K* in indivisible lumps).

Exhibit 12.7 shows the forecasted effect of two alternative expansion plans for activity *K:* (A) install three additional servers similar to the existing server in parallel with it;

Effect of Capacity Expansion Alternatives on Activity *K* Cycle Time and Congestion			
	Existing Facility	Alternative A	Alternative B
Average time between arrivals (minutes)	12	3	3
Average service duration (minutes)	10	10	2.5
Number of servers installed	1	4	1
Long-run average length of queue waiting for service	4.2	3.3	4.2
Long-run average waiting time in queue (minutes)	50.0	9.9	12.5
Calculated system performance assumes independent, exponentially distributed inter-arrival and service times (M/M/s queuing system).			

EXHIBIT 12.7 EXAMPLE OF QUEUEING PROBLEM

3. See, for example, F. S. Hillier and G. J. Lieberman, *Introduction to Operations Research,* 6th ed. (New York: McGraw-Hill, 1995), chapters 15–16.
4. Further assumptions underlying the mathematical theory are that the inter-arrival times are independently and exponentially distributed, as are the service times.
5. These averages are calculated using results from Hillier and Lieberman, chapter 15, for M/M/s queues.

or (B) replace the existing single server with a single server four times as fast. The exhibit shows that expansion has a potentially important side effect: a reduction of cycle time and, possibly, of congestion associated with work in process waiting for service. Specifically, under Alternative A (four servers), the average work in process drops to 3.3 units and the average waiting time to 9.9 minutes. Alternative B (one fast server) does not change the work in process, and the waiting time drops to 12.5 minutes. These two examples illustrate cost-relevant insights that may emerge from a more detailed process analysis than those of conventional linear cost models.

The most explicit and comprehensive results of the mathematical theory illustrated in Exhibit 12.7 are limited to the steady-state performance (as opposed to transient performance) of individual queueing systems (as opposed to networks of articulated queueing systems), with independent and exponentially distributed interarrival and service times. Real-world systems may experience mostly transient conditions, however, and may consist of networks of queueing systems where one system's output is the next system's input, and may experience interarrival and service times that do not conform to the exponential distribution and are not independent from one arrival to the next. Other real-world complications that add to the difficulty of a purely mathematical analysis of activity costs include the joint use of server resources by more than one activity.[6]

(f) COMPUTER-INTENSIVE COST MODELING. One can use computer simulation to analyze situations that lie beyond the reach of the current mathematical theory.[7] Such simulations exploit the relatively cheap, abundant, and powerful computer technology now available to construct virtual working models of the flow of transactions within the enterprise. These models cope relatively easily with real-world issues, such as the joint use of indivisible resources, congestion, and other complications arising from the interactions between service demands, processes, and personnel.[8] Using computer simulations, analysts can measure directly, within the virtual world of the simulation, the effects of alternative policies on enterprise costs and resource requirements, rather than rely on simple linear approximations.

Computer simulation is a powerful and flexible tool. As with other powerful tools (including other cost estimation tools), its effective use requires relevant expertise, in addition to appropriate computer equipment and software. Its data requirements differ from but overlap substantially with those of the other methods discussed in this chapter. For example, analysts need much of the same understanding of the articulation of enterprise activities to formulate effective multiple cost driver models that they need to formulate effective

6. See M. W. Maher and M. L Marais, "A Field Study on the Limitations of Activity-Based Costing When Resources Are Provided on a Joint and Indivisible Basis," *Journal of Accounting Research*, vol. 36, no. 1, pp. 129–142.
7. See, for example, Hillier and Lieberman, chapter 21.
8. See, in addition to Maher and Marais: A. Raviv, "Applications of Queuing Theory and Simulation to Staffing in the Semiconductor Clean Room Environment," Proceedings of the IEEE/UCS/SEMI International Symposium on Semiconductor Manufacturing, Austin, TX, 1995, pp., 252–256; M. Baudin, V. Mehrotra, B. Tullis, D. Yeaman, and R. A. Hughes, "From Spreadsheets to Simulations: A Comparison of Analysis Methods for IC Manufacturing Performance," Proceedings of the 4th Annual International Semiconductor Manufacturing Science Symposium, 1992; C. M. Huettner and H. J. Steudel, "Analysis of a Manufacturing System Via Spreadsheet Analysis, Rapid Modelling, and Manufacturing Simulation," *International Journal of Production Research*, 30, 12 (1992): 1699–1714; and P. Nag, W. Maly, and H. J. Jacobs, "Simulation of Yield/Cost Learning Curves with Y4," *IEEE Transactions of Semiconductor Manufacturing,* 10, 2 (1997): 256–266.

computer-intensive cost modeling. Information about the timing and duration of activity transactions that one does not usually need for conventional cost models may already have been collected for (or by) the enterprise's other information systems (including an Enterprise Resource Planning (ERP) system).

Whether the additional insights produced by computer-intensive cost modeling will likely justify the resources it requires will inevitably depend on the context. As holds true regarding the choice of using multiple cost drivers or a single cost driver in a linear cost model, a rational choice of whether to build a simulation model for cost analysis must depend on a cost–benefit test.

12.7 CONCLUSION: CHOOSING AN ESTIMATION METHOD

Each of the methods discussed has advantages and disadvantages. Probably the most informative estimate of cost behavior results from using more than one of the methods, because each has the potential to provide information that the others do not.

Each cost estimation method may yield a different estimate of the costs that will likely result from a particular management decision. This underscores the advantages from using two or more methods to arrive at a final estimate. By observing the range of cost estimates from different methods, management can better decide whether to gather more data. If different estimates yield similar cost estimates, management may conclude that additional information gathering is not warranted.

Management also must decide when to use a more sophisticated, and more costly, cost estimation method and when to accept a simpler approach. Like many managerial decisions, one must evaluate the costs and benefits of various cost estimation techniques.

CHAPTER 13

SPOILAGE, WASTE, AND SCRAP, INCLUDING GREEN ACCOUNTING*

WILLIAM N. LANEN
University of Michigan

CONTENTS

13.1 INTRODUCTION 367
(a) Definitions 368
(b) History 369

13.2 COST ACCOUNTING FOR SPOILAGE, WASTE, AND SCRAP 370
(a) General Issues 370
(b) Job Costing—Spoilage 370
(c) Process Costing—Spoilage 370
(d) A Comprehensive Example 373
(e) Standard Costs 373
(f) Scrap and Waste 374
(g) Green Cost Accounting 375

13.3 CONTROL AND EVALUATION SYSTEMS FOR SPOILAGE, WASTE, AND SCRAP 376
(a) General Issues 376
(b) Control of Generation 377
(c) Control of Handling 382
(d) Control of Disposal 383
(e) Green Accounting 383

13.4 PLANNING AND GREEN ACCOUNTING 384
(a) Life-Cycle Costing 384
(b) Full Cost Accounting 385
(c) Total Cost Assessment 385
(d) Other Planning Tools 386

13.5 SUMMARY 387

BIBLIOGRAPHY 388

13.1 INTRODUCTION

The cost accounting treatment of spoilage, waste, and scrap has changed little over the last 100 years. Interest in the topic depends on the relative magnitude of these items in manufacturing and the emphasis on conservation in industry. Traditionally, cost accounting separates waste into two components, normal and abnormal, and applies different costing treatments to each component. The distinction between normal and abnormal lies in whether the spoilage, waste, or scrap is an inherent part of the production process.

* Ronald J. Huefner wrote the original version of this chapter for the first edition of this reference, The *Handbook of Cost Accounting,* published by Prentice-Hall. I have preserved many of his ideas and words. I have adapted other material for use here and have developed ideas from still other material. Specific citations, where appropriate, appear in the body of this chapter. WNL

If so, we consider the waste a part of the product's manufacturing cost; if not, we expense the cost of the waste separately.

Recently, many cost accounting practitioners and commentators have expanded the definition of waste to include environmental pollutants,[1] and the inclusion of costs associated with these pollutants has become a matter of controversy. The treatment of environmental costs borne by the firm resembles that of more traditional costs associated with waste. Consequently, many methods suggested by advocates of environmental cost accounting simply apply traditional methods to new types of costs. Most cost accountants would agree that this treatment is appropriate.

The issue, however, is whether these approaches will prove cost-effective—that is, whether the benefits of these approaches justify the costs of implementation. For costs borne by parties external to the firm, the question of the proper treatment by the firm causing the waste is unclear. The appropriate treatment becomes more a question of firm strategy and view of societal cost than proper cost accounting.

(a) DEFINITIONS. The interchangeable terms *green accounting* and *environmental cost accounting* (ECA) have evolved recently. Authors and practitioners have yet to agree on their definition. As a result, they often appear to disagree over the treatment of costs associated with environmental impacts when in fact the disagreement relates to semantics. The disagreement occurs over how to record and report costs borne not by firms that emit the pollutants, but by those outside the organization.

Practitioners also use more traditional cost accounting terms—such as spoilage, waste, and scrap—interchangeably to refer to outputs from a production process that have little or no value. Some authors use these terms to refer to outputs with specific characteristics: undesirable, but resulting from either technological constraints in the production process or inefficient production processes. This chapter will use those definitions that appear most commonly in the literature. As with most cost accounting procedures, the approach aims to match the resource (cost) flow with the physical flow. This chapter uses the following terms throughout the discussion:

- *Internal costs.* Costs borne by the firm (the decision maker). The organization's financial system recognizes internal costs (although it might aggregate them with other costs) and includes them in its financial reports.
- *External costs/externalities.* Costs borne by individuals or organizations outside the decision-making firm. These costs include those associated with exposure to various effluents or noise. Because they occur outside the organization, the traditional financial reporting system does not capture or report these costs.
- *Environmental accounting/environmental cost accounting/green accounting.* The compiling and reporting of financial (cost) information that describes the effects of production processes on outputs commonly measured as part of environmental abatement programs such as air and water pollution and solid waste generation. Environmental accounting might or might not include externalities.
- *Spoilage/spoiled units.* Output that fails to meet the specifications for good output. The firm might identify spoiled (i.e., defective) units at any point in the production process. The disposition of the spoiled units varies, depending on the nature of the product and the extent of the defect. The firm can dispose of the

1. I use the term *environmental pollutants* or *pollution* to include any waste product (including air, water, and ground contamination of toxic or hazardous substances) that has an adverse effect on the environment.

units as waste (see Section 13.3), sell them for residual value, or use them as inputs in another process and sold after processing (referred to as *rework*).

- The resource flow associated with spoiled units is the same as for good units combining materials, labor, and overhead into the (defective) product. Spoiled units have two cost accounting issues: the assignment of the costs of producing the spoiled product and the treatment of any revenue (costs) associated with the sale (disposal) of the spoiled units. The treatment will depend on whether the accountant considers spoiled units an inherent part of the production process or the result of poor process controls.
- *Waste*. Traditionally, waste refers to the use of inputs without any resulting output. More recently, with the explicit consideration of environmental issues, practitioners and authors have defined waste to include the production of effluents (air and water pollution) and hazardous and toxic materials. The distinction between waste and spoiled units lies in waste being a byproduct of the production process whereas spoilage results from a failed production process. Recently, advocates of environmental accounting have considered environmental pollution a form of waste, often ignored in the calculation of costs.

  Because waste generally results in no measurable output of the firm's product, the production costs of the good output often include the costs of the inputs used in generating the waste. As with spoiled units, the primary issue lies in whether to include waste in the costs of the good product or record it separately.
- *Scrap*. Scrap refers to byproducts arising from the production process when that process wastes material inputs because of production process limitations. For example, unused wood and metal cuttings result from cutting and shaping processes. Rather than computing a cost directly for scrap, accountants generally treat it in terms of any sales value it can generate, as discussed in Section 13.2 and Chapter 16.

(b) HISTORY. The cost accounting treatment of spoilage, scrap, and waste has not changed markedly. A review of cost accounting texts from the 1920s through today shows a consistent treatment of the traditional costs associated with spoilage, waste, and scrap. Horngren et al. [2003] provide a thorough treatment of current cost accounting practices for spoilage, waste, and scrap.

Since the early 1970s, firms in the United States and many other countries have been subject to various environmental laws and regulations that hold the potential for substantial liabilities. For example, in 1976, Congress passed the Resource Conservation Recovery Act (RCRA), which requires companies to monitor materials potentially harmful to the environment. The Comprehensive Environmental Response, Compensation, and Liability Act (CERCLA or Superfund)—passed in 1980 and amended by the Superfund Amendments and Reauthorization Act (SARA) in 1986—imposes responsibility for toxic site cleanup on firms.

With this legislation, environmental impacts of operations became important not only for reasons of social concern but also because they came to represent real liabilities faced by corporations. Financial accountants have long been guided on dealing with contingent liabilities such as these by Financial Accounting Standards Board (FASB) Statement #5 (FAS #5), *Accounting for Contingencies*. FAS #5 requires firms to recognize a liability when a loss is both reasonably probable and estimable, and environmental liabilities often satisfy both of these conditions. The effect of this legislation on cost accounting has proven less clear.

A fundamental economic problem associated with incorporating environmental costs into a firm's accounting system, whether financial or managerial, is that the firm does not bear many of the costs. For example, the purchaser almost always has responsibility for disposal of products. Therefore, firms do not generally include in their cost calculations the environmental costs associated with disposal. (Presumably, purchasers included this cost in their decisions; the question remains whether they paid the full costs of disposal.) We discuss the inclusion of external costs in green accounting systems in Section 13.4.

13.2 COST ACCOUNTING FOR SPOILAGE, WASTE, AND SCRAP

(a) GENERAL ISSUES. The cost accounting for waste, spoilage, and scrap depends on the type of costing system used (job costing or process costing), the nature of the cost (spoilage, waste, or scrap), and whether the firm considers the spoilage, waste, and scrap normal or abnormal.

(b) JOB COSTING—SPOILAGE. When the firm considers spoilage abnormal, it will charge the cost of the spoiled units (net of sales value) in the period incurred. This treatment highlights the cost of producing spoiled units and the firm can use it as one of the performance measures of the responsible manager. The following entry records the spoiled units:

Inventory (at net realizable value)	xxx	
Loss	xxx	
Work in Process (Job #)		xxx

In job costing systems with normal spoilage, the issue is whether the spoilage relates to a particular job or with the production process in general. If the cost of the spoilage relates to a particular job, accountants typically credit the job with the net realizable value (if any) of the spoiled units. For example,

Inventory (at net realizable value)	xxx	
Work in Process (Job #)		xxx

This treatment charges the cost of the spoiled units to the particular job and is appropriate if one can attribute the normal spoilage to the particular job's characteristics.

If the firm attributes the cost of the normal spoilage to general production (all jobs), it will assign the cost of the normal spoilage (net of sales value) to overhead and allocate it to all jobs. In this case, the accountant records the entry as follows:

Inventory (at net realizable value)	xxx	
Overhead (residual)	xxx	
Work in Process (Job #)		xxx

(c) PROCESS COSTING—SPOILAGE. In process costing systems, the accountant can include the cost of spoiled units either implicitly or explicitly. If the accounting system does not count the spoiled units (excludes them from the computation of equivalent units), it implicitly spreads the cost of these units across all units of production for the period. This approach, while simple, fails to highlight the costs of spoiled units for control purposes and might result in misleading product costs across batches of output.

When the system explicitly counts spoiled units, it can assign the cost of the spoiled units to the different batches of production. The accountants can separately compute the cost of abnormal and normal spoilage, as with job systems.

The following example illustrates the effect of the two treatments. Assume the following data:

No beginning inventory

Units started: 12,000

Units completed: 9,000

Ending inventory: 2,400 units, fully complete with respect to materials, 75% complete with respect to labor and overhead

Inspection for spoiled units occurs when units are fully complete with respect to materials, 50% complete with respect to labor and overhead.

Costs incurred—material	$ 68,400
Costs incurred—labor and overhead	119,880
Total	$188,280

If the accounting system does not count the spoiled units (the implicit approach), it will assign costs to different batches as shown in Exhibit 13.1.

This approach implicitly includes the cost of the spoiled units in the cost per equivalent units for the two batches.

The second approach explicitly computes and reports the cost of the spoiled units, as shown in Exhibit 13.2.

If the firm considers the spoilage abnormal, it can record the cost as a loss for the period. If the firm considers the spoilage normal, it can allocate the costs between the two batches (completed units and work in process ending inventory) based on the number of

Equivalent Units	Physical Flow	Material	Labor and Overhead
Completed units	9,000	9,000	9,000
Ending work in process	2,400	2,400	1,800
	11,400	11,400	10,800
Total Costs		$68,400	$119,880
Cost per Equivalent Unit		$ 6.00	$ 11.10
Cost of Batches			
Completed goods			
9,000 × ($6.00 + $11.10)			$153,900
Ending inventory			
2,400 × $6.00		$14,400	
1,800 × $11.10		19,980	34,380
			$188,280

EXHIBIT 13.1 IMPLICIT APPROACH

Equivalent Units	Physical Flow	Material	Labor and Overhead
Completed units	9,000	9,000	9,000
Ending work in process	2,400	2,400	1,800
Spoiled units[a]	600	600	300
	12,000	12,000	11,100
Total Costs		$68,400	$119,880
Cost per Equivalent Unit		$ 5.70	$ 10.80
Cost of Batches			
Completed goods			
9,000 × ($5.70 + $10.80)			$148,500
Ending inventory			
2,400 × $5.70		$13,680	
1,800 × $10.80		19,440	33,120
Spoiled units			
600 × $5.70		$ 3,420	
300 × $10.80		3,240	6,660
			$188,280

[a] 600 = 12,000 – 9,000 – 2,400

EXHIBIT 13.2 EXPLICIT APPROACH

physical units in each batch. One can allocate the costs based on physical units because both batches are complete with respect to spoiled units, assuming that no additional inspections occur.

Although one can easily apply the implicit approach, the explicit approach has two advantages. First, from the perspective of product costing, it results in a better allocation of spoilage costs. If the accounting system uses the implicit method, then the units in work-in-process ending inventory will receive an additional allocation of spoilage costs in the next period, because the equivalent unit costs implicitly include the spoilage costs. Second, from a control perspective, the explicit approach highlights the cost of spoilage for the manager.

The previous example avoids the distinction between the weighted-average approach to process costing and the first-in, first-out (FIFO) approach by assuming no beginning work-in-process inventories.[2] The weighted average approach requires no modification from the example because if beginning inventory exists, the method combines the costs of the inventory with the current costs to develop a weighted average equivalent unit cost (including costs of spoilage). The FIFO approach requires additional consideration. To apply the FIFO approach consistently, one would have to distinguish the completed units from the beginning inventory from the completed units that were started and completed in the current period to compute the cost of normal spoilage. Costing systems often modify the FIFO approach, however, by using current normal spoilage cost and applying it to all goods completed in the period.

2. Most cost accounting texts discuss FIFO and weighted average methods used for process costing. We suggest that any reader unfamiliar with these methods consult such sources.

So far, we have ignored any value associated with the spoiled units. This assumes that the firm discards the spoiled units. Two additional possibilities exist, however. First, the spoiled units might have some recovery value. Second, the firm might be able to rework the spoiled units and sell them as regular units. In the first case, the accounting system needs value from the cost of normal spoilage before assigning the spoilage costs to the different batches. In the case of rework (which in most cases would occur outside the normal manufacturing process), the system transfers the cost of the spoiled units and adds the additional costs of reworking the units (material, labor, and overhead) to the units.

(d) A COMPREHENSIVE EXAMPLE. The following example best illustrates how an accounting system explicitly considers spoilage. Assume the following facts:

Beginning inventory: 2,500 units, fully complete with respect to materials, 40% complete with respect to labor and overhead

Units started: 17,500

Units completed: 15,000

Ending inventory: 2,000 units, fully complete with respect to materials, 75% complete with respect to labor and overhead

Inspection for spoiled units occurs when units are fully complete with respect to materials, labor and overhead

Costs incurred (current and inventory), material	$ 90,000
Costs incurred, (current and inventory) labor and overhead	107,250
Total	$197,250

Normal spoilage is considered to be 15% of production

Normal spoilage that can be reworked is 4% of the spoiled units

No abnormal spoilage can be reworked

Cost to complete reworked units: $2.00 per unit

Recovery value of spoiled units: $1.00 per unit

The approach computes the costs for the different batches, as Exhibit 13.3 shows.

Ending work-in-process inventory would equal $17,250. The accountant would not assign spoilage costs to this batch because it has not yet reached the inspection point (at the end of the production process). The accountant would, however, charge the abnormal spoilage cost of $7,500 less the recovery value of $750 (= 750 units × $1.00), or $6,750 as a loss in this period. The reworked units would go into inventory at a cost of $900 plus the cost to rework of $180 (= 90 units × $2.00), assuming the rework had been completed. The accountant would assign the remaining costs to the goods transferred to finished goods inventory. This cost would equal $169,440 (= $150,000 + $21,600 – $2,160). The sum of the costs charged, $194,340 (= $169,440 + $17,250 + $6,750 + $900) equals the total production costs, $197,250, less the recovery value of the spoiled units, $2,910.

(e) STANDARD COSTS. The discussion and examples used to illustrate the accounting for spoilage assume that the firm used actual costs. Most costing systems use some form of standard costing. (Chapter 15 discusses standard costing). The systems can develop

Equivalent Units	Physical Flow	Material	Labor and Overhead
Completed units	15,000	15,000	15,000
Normal spoilage[a]	2,160	2,160	2,160
Abnormal spoilage[b]	750	750	750
Reworked units[a]	90	90	90
Ending work in process	2,000	2,000	1,500
	20,000	20,000	19,500
Total Costs		$90,000	$107,250
Cost per Equivalent Unit		$ 4.50	$ 5.50

Cost of Batches		
Completed goods (before spoilage) 15,000 × ($4.50 + $5.50)		$150,000
Normal spoilage 2,160 × ($4.50 + $5.50)		21,600
Abnormal spoilage 750 × ($4.50 + $5.50)		7,500
Reworked units 90 × ($4.50 + $5.50)		900
Ending inventory		
2,000 × $4.50	$ 9,000	
1,500 × $5.50	8,250	17,250
		$197,250

[a] Normal spoilage, before rework: 15,000 × 15% = 2,250 units; Reworked normal spoilage: 2,250 × 4% = 90 units; Normal spoilage, not reworked: 2,250 – 90 = 2,160 units.

[b] Abnormal spoilage: 20,000 – 15,000 – 2,160 – 90 – 2,000 = 750 units.

EXHIBIT 13.3 ACCOUNTING FOR SPOILAGE

the standard costs to include an allowance for normal spoilage. The accountant computes actual spoilage at the end of the period, treating spoilage above normal as abnormal spoilage. The accountant does not include additional costs for normal spoilage. The standard cost approach aids control (see Section 13.3) by highlighting the difference between estimated and actual spoilage.

(f) SCRAP AND WASTE. Costing systems typically ignore the cost of scrap and waste and implicitly include these costs in the cost of the good output. The only accounting treatment of scrap is the recognition of any revenue realized from its sale. One can use this approach when the scrap has a small value. With a significant value of the scrap, one must address the cost more explicitly.

In job costing systems, the treatment of scrap depends on whether the scrap relates to a particular job or to production in general (similar to the treatment of spoilage costs). When the scrap relates to a particular job, the costing system deducts the net value of the scrap from the cost of the job and places it in inventory at this value.

Inventory (Spoiled units at net realizable value)	XXX	
Work in Process (Job #)		XXX

When the scrap relates to general production (e.g., if wood is cut for multiple jobs from a single board), the accountant credits the overhead control account:

Inventory (Spoiled units at net realizable value)	XXX	
Overhead control		XXX

(g) GREEN COST ACCOUNTING. New approaches to manufacturing have caused accountants to reconsider some of the methods of product costing as applied in practice. The accounting profession has become increasingly concerned that traditional methods of costing have distorted product costs that have misled managers making product mix, pricing, and sourcing decisions. Accounting organizations have had several discussions about the adequacy of traditional costing and the extent to which some of the new methods are really different from well-known and widely used methods or appropriate for certain situations.

Activity-based costing (ABC) is an example of a different approach to product costing (see Chapter 6). An ABC system first identifies manufacturing activities. The system then collects the costs associated with these activities along with a measure of activity. It then calculates overhead rates by activity and assigns the rates to the products (or product categories) based on the use of the various activities. This addresses accounting-related environmental issues because overhead costs include most environmentally related activities in manufacturing. Examples of these costs include depreciation on treatment equipment, environmental compliance staff, and tipping (landfill) fees. As overhead, traditional accounting systems often apply these costs to all products manufactured in the plant, although some products might use processes that require more treatment of air or water discharges or generate more waste sent to a landfill.

EXAMPLE 1.

A simple example illustrates the effect of using ABC when production involves environmental activities. Assume the following data:

Direct labor for the plant (annual)		40,000 hours @ $10
Emissions for the plant (annual)		40,000 pounds
Overhead costs (annual):		
Environmental compliance	$ 200,000	
Other overhead	800,000	
Total overhead	$1,000,000	

The firm can select between two feasible designs for a particular product, Design A and Design B. The two designs have the following characteristics:

	Design A	Design B
Direct labor/unit	4 hours	4 hours
Direct materials cost/unit.......	$60	$50
Emissions/unit.................	2 pounds	5 pounds

EXAMPLE 1. *(CONTINUED)*

In a traditional product costing system that applies overhead to products on a volume-based measure (e.g., direct labor hours), the firm would face the following reported costs for the two designs:

	Design A		Design B	
Direct material cost		$ 60		$ 50
Direct labor cost	(4 hours @ $10)	40	(4 hours @ $10)	$ 40
Overhead ($1,000,000/40,000)	(4 hours @ $25)	100	(4 hours @ $25)	100
Unit production cost		$200		$190

Based on these costs, design B emerges as the cost-effective design.

In contrast, an ABC system develops unit cost rates for the activities and uses them to apply overhead to the products. This example has two activities: environmental compliance and other overhead. Using emissions and direct labor as the two bases for overhead, this method computes the overhead rates as follows:

Activity	Activity Measure	Annual Activity	Overhead Rate
Environmental compliance	Emissions	40,000 pounds	$5/pound
Other overhead	Direct labor	40,000 hours	$20/hour

The firm will now compute the cost of the individual designs as follows:

	Design A		Design B	
Direct material cost		$ 60		$ 50
Direct labor cost	(4 hours @ $10)	40	(4 hours @ $10)	$ 40
Overhead:				
Compliance	(2 lbs. @ $5)	10	(5 lbs. @ $5)	25
Other	(4 hours @ $20)	80	(4 hours @ $20)	80
Unit production cost		$190		$195

The ABC method highlights the differential use of the environmental facilities by the two product designs. For additional discussion of the use of ABC for green accounting, see Kreuze and Newell [1994].

13.3 CONTROL AND EVALUATION SYSTEMS FOR SPOILAGE, WASTE, AND SCRAP

(a) GENERAL ISSUES. An effective control and evaluation system for spoilage, waste, and scrap requires: (1) a monitoring system to measure the extent of the generation; (2) a benchmark or standard against which to compare the performance; and (3) a set of control mechanisms to improve performance.

At each stage of the production process, the monitoring system must collect and report the levels of spoilage, scrap, and waste on a systematic, routine basis. As with all cost accounting processes, the costs and benefits of these reports dictate the detail and the frequency of these reports. As information technology (IT) improves and as regulatory requirements change, these collection and reporting requirements will likely become more detailed. The IT division must then disseminate the reports to managers who have responsibility for each stage in the process who will use them as the basis for implementing corrective actions.

Management uses the benchmark for performance evaluation to develop the measures of normal and abnormal spoilage, waste, and scrap discussed previously in Section 13.2. Management might base this benchmark on past performance at the unit (e.g., plant), performance at other units in the firm, competitor performance, or engineering and scientific principles. For example, the firm might generate some unavoidable scrap, given the shape of the final part and the shape of the incoming raw material. Similarly, some evaporation of chemicals might occur naturally given the production technology and process controls. An effective monitoring system, combined with a relevant benchmark, allows the firm to evaluate current processes for modifications that will improve spoilage, waste, and scrap performance. As with all standards, the benchmark for performance of spoilage, waste, and scrap will change over time as management applies technology and learning to a particular situation. The establishment of the benchmark requires a tradeoff between maintenance of a constant benchmark over time, for purposes of consistency, with the frequent updating of the benchmark for purposes of relevance.

Finally, a control system requires a basis for the evaluation of performance and the penalties and rewards, if any, that management will give to the responsible parties. The firm may use financial or nonfinancial performance measures and explicit or implicit rewards and penalties. For example, a traditional, financial measure of performance might include the variance between the benchmark (standard) and the actual spoilage. The reward might be explicit cash bonuses tied to performance. Alternatively, the nonfinancial measure of performance might be environmental violations and the implicit reward increased opportunities for promotion.

The process of accounting must address three stages of spoilage, scrap, and waste: generation, handling, and disposal. A firm generates waste when it uses inputs but produces no output, with the possible exception of emissions or trash that the firm must discard.

In the handling process, the firm must rework the spoiled units into units that meet specifications (rework), hold them as *seconds* for later sale, or hold them for disposal. Similarly, the firm must hold scrap to sell as a byproduct or hold it for disposal. The firm might not measure some waste streams (e.g., excess energy, which might not require handling by the firm). Other waste streams, however, such as pollutant-type wastes (e.g., toxic wastes) or trash, do require handling by the firm—often at considerable expense—until it disposes of the waste. In the disposal stage, the firm will either sell or otherwise remove the spoiled units, scrap, and waste.

(b) CONTROL OF GENERATION. A control system at the generation stage should ensure that the spoilage, scrap, and waste produced represent an optimum trade-off between the costs of handling and disposal against the cost of process improvements. As a result, the firm needs to design the control system subject to the production process, the strategy of the firm with respect to quality and environmental practices, technological limitations, and other factors. Furthermore, the firm should review the control system frequently to ensure that it achieves the optimum tradeoff and to implement modifications in the control system as needed.

As in other types of control systems, the control of spoilage, waste, and scrap requires a set of standards or benchmarks, a monitoring and reporting system (to indicate whether a problem might exist), and a set of potential sources of problems so that investigation of poor performance can focus on likely solutions.

(i) Sources of Spoilage, Waste, and Scrap. Spoilage, waste, and scrap result from either the inputs used (materials and labor), the production process itself, or other, miscellaneous, causes. Although the sources of spoilage, waste, and scrap vary by situation, the following general sources appear common to most processes:

- Defective material
- Improper materials (materials not meeting specifications)
- Evaporation
- Obsolete materials
- Failure of environmental controls
- Spills
- Lack of operator training
- Inadequate supervision
- Operator error
- Handling damage in material movement
- General carelessness
- Defective tooling and equipment
- Product design deficiencies
- Machine breakdowns

Although this list does not include all sources, it provides the basis for designing both standards and reports.

(ii) Standards. Performance standards serve as the basic device for controlling the generation of spoilage, waste, and scrap (see also Chapter 15). The standards depend on the source of the spoilage, waste, or scrap and might take different forms. For example, some of the causes of waste and scrap derive from the handling and usage of materials. One important control device in this area is the *standard bill of materials.* This document specifies, for each product, the description and quantity of materials required and perhaps also the manufacturing methods to be employed. Purchasing prepares material requisitions for production from the standard bill of materials. Thus, the store (direct materials inventory) should issue the proper types and quantities of materials, thereby reducing losses due to wrong materials, or excessive quantities. Specifying a standard bill of materials also fixes the responsibility of the production department. Production will have to separately requisition additional materials required due to losses in the production stage (operator error, machine malfunctions, etc.) and the cost system will therefore note the presence of an exception. This latter feature might well encourage production personnel to exercise better control over issued material, rather than have to make additional requisitions that the performance report will report as variances.

The firm must apply different types of standards to the generation of spoilage, waste, and scrap in the process of production. Here, the firm must design input and output standards that reflect the amount of spoilage, waste, or scrap that it will consider normal—that is, inherent in the process, or not economical to eliminate. Establishing the normal standard might involve considerations of engineering design, production methods, quality control, and so forth. However computed, management will then incorporate these normal allowances into the appropriate input-output standards. We illustrate such standards below.

(iii) Measurement and Reporting. A system of generation control should measure spoilage, waste, and scrap with reasonable accuracy, and the appropriate individual should receive regular reports. The reports should include sufficient information to identify problems for correction. Such information would include the following:

- The part or component produced
- Quantity
- Location in the production process (operation)
- Disposition
- Cost

If the cause of the defect relates to the material used, the cost accounting system should collect additional information to manage the cost of production. This information includes:

- Type of material
- Vendor
- Lot
- Quantity
- Manufacturing source

Management can then use this information to evaluate the cost of individual suppliers. The full cost of the supplier—including costs associated with defective material—provides a better source for purchasing decisions over simply the original cost of the material.

In general, any reporting system on the generation of spoilage, waste, or scrap should present data on quantities (subdivided between normal and abnormal, if standards exist), causes, responsibility, and costs. Frequent reports will enable the responsible people to take prompt action to reduce excessive losses.

The following example illustrates the use of standard variance analysis techniques to control spoilage, waste, and scrap. A firm uses a single material input, B, to manufacture a unit of product, A. The production process routinely results in spoilage, waste, and scrap. Waste consists of two types: loss of input for miscellaneous reasons (e.g., theft) and wastewater that the firm must treat before disposing into the local sewage treatment facility. If possible, the firm reworks spoiled units and sells them as new. Otherwise, the firm sells them as is. The firm sells scrap. Because of the nature of material B, the firm cannot store it and purchases it as needed.

EXAMPLE 2.

Assume the following data:

- Standards:
  - Standard cost sheet (materials only) Material B: 1.85 pounds @ $6.51
  - Normal spoilage: For every 90 good units, 10 are spoiled
  - Spoiled units that can be reworked: 50%
  - Material B required for rework: 1 pound
  - Disposal value of spoiled units not reworked: $0.76
  - Standard scrap allowance: 2% of standard inputs
  - Resale value of scrap: $1.90/pound
  - Wastewater generated: 0.1 gallons per unit of final output (good and spoiled)
  - Treatment cost for wastewater: $10.00/gallon
- Actual Results of Operations:
  - Purchases of material B: 920,000 pounds at a total cost of $5,989,200
  - Production of product A: 428,000 good units (before rework)
  - Spoilage: 50,000 units; 28,000 were reworked and 22,000 were sold for $0.76 per unit
  - Scrap: 18,200 pounds sold for $1.90 per pound
  - Wastewater treated: 50,000 gallons @ $10.00

The data quote all prices at standard to focus the analysis on the control of spoilage, waste, and scrap quantities.

To analyze the variances, first calculate the standard cost of materials for each unit of good output. This cost will incorporate three components: the cost of producing the good unit directly; an allowance for normal spoilage (net of rework and sales value); and an allowance for normal scrap (again, net of sales value). The system calculates cost by analyzing what happens in production. Assume the firm produces 100 total units. The following table shows the relation between inputs and outputs:

	Units of A	Pounds of B
For each 100 units of product A	100	185
Normal spoilage (10%)	(10)	
Units reworked (standard: 50%)	5	5
Totals.........................	95	190

The standard input of material B per finished unit of product A equals 2 pounds (190/95). This includes the allowance for normal spoilage that the firm

EXAMPLE 2. *(CONTINUED)*

can rework. To incorporate the scrap and the spoilage that production cannot rework, we compute the standard material cost for a unit of good output:

Standard material input.	2 pounds @ $6.51	$13.02
Sales value of spoiled units not reworked . .	0.05 units @ $0.76 × (100/95)	(0.04)
Sales value of scrap	2% × 2 pounds × $1.90 × (100/95)	(0.08)
Standard cost of material per good unit . . .		$12.90

Management can now use this standard cost ($12.90 per unit of finished output) as the basis for evaluating performance.

The actual expenditures (net of scrap and spoilage sales) for the period equal the following:

Material B purchases (and use).	$5,989,200
Wastewater treatment	500,000
Subtotal	$6,489,200
Sales of spoiled units (22,000 × $0.76) . . .	(16,720)
Sales of scrap (18,200 × $1.90)	(34,580)
Total	$6,437,900

The standard costs given the 456,000 good units (428,000 initially produced + 28,000 reworked) should have cost:

Material B purchases (and use) (=456,000 × $12.90)	$5,882,400
Wastewater treatment (=478,000 × 0.1 × $10)	478,000
Total	$6,360,400

The total variance due to abnormal spoilage, waste, and scrap equals $77,500 unfavorable (= $6,437,900 – $6,360,400). Management can decompose this variance to provide additional information to improve performance. Exhibit 13.4 lists the individual components of the variance.

1. Wastewater treatment	
Actual treatment costs	$500,000
Standard treatment costs for actual output	478,000
Wastewater treatment variance	$ 22,000 *U*
2. Rework variance	
Actual units reworked.	28,000
Standard rework (456,000 good units/.95) × 5%	24,000
Excess units reworked	4,000
Materials required (1 pound × 4,000)	4,000
Cost per pound	$ 6.51
Rework variance	$ 26,040 *U*

EXHIBIT 13.4 CALCULATING COMPONENTS OF SPOILAGE, WASTE, AND SCRAP

3. Spoilage variance

Actual units spoiled (net of rework)	22,000
Standard spoilage (456,000 good units/.95) × 5%	24,000
Excess units spoiled	(2,000)
Materials required (saved) (1.85 pound × 2,000)	(3,700)
Cost per pound	$ 6.51
Subtotal	$ 24,087
Loss of spoilage sales (2,000 × $0.76)	($1,520)
Net spoilage variance	$ 22,567 *F*

4. Scrap variance

Actual scrap recovered (net of rework)	18,200
Standard scrap (456,000/.95 × 2% x 2 pounds)	19,200
Shortage of scrap	1,000
Recovery value per pound	$ 1.90
Net scrap variance	$ 1,900 *U*

5. Other waste variance

Pounds of material purchased		920,000
Material accounted for:		
Production (478,000 × 1.85)	884,300	
Used for rework (28,000 × 1.00)	28,000	912,300
Material wasted		7,700
Cost per pound		$ 6.51
Waste variance		$ 50,127 *U*

Summary of Variances:

Variance	Amount
Wastewater treatment	$22,000 *U*
Rework	$26,040 *U*
Spoilage	$22,567 *F*
Scrap	$ 1,900 *U*
Other waste	$50,127 *U*
Total	$77,500 *U*

EXHIBIT 13.4 CALCULATING COMPONENTS OF SPOILAGE, WASTE, AND SCRAP *(CONTINUED)*

This example demonstrates that management can use standard variance analysis procedures to evaluate performance regarding the generation of spoilage, waste, and scrap. As in all variance analyses, the relative costs and benefits drive the level of detail that management uses to analyze the variances.

(c) CONTROL OF HANDLING. When the firm plans and manages handling procedures, it must ensure that it (1) receives maximum value for the spoiled units and scrap, (2) treats wastes (especially effluents) cost effectively, and (3) complies with current practices and regulatory requirements.

As with all control systems, the key to effective management of spoilage, waste, and scrap lies in the measurement and reporting of the material to ensure management awareness and attention. A system for recording quantities (and other data) concerning spoiled goods or scrap materials establishes an initial control point for recovery. One approach, similar to the control at the generation phase, focuses on developing standards for handling both quantities and prices or costs, and then computing and reporting variances from those standards.

In designing recovery and handling procedures, the firm should focus on achieving the maximum economic benefit from spoilage and scrap that has occurred. The control system should identify items that production can rework, recondition, reuse, or the firm can sell. As previously suggested, the system should separate material by type, grade, and so forth. If production mixes several kinds of scrap material together, for example, the sales price will likely approximate that of the least valuable material in the mix. Other handling procedures, such as cleaning, bundling, and the like, might also increase the recoverable value.

Control over storage involves the typical problems of protecting the goods from theft, damage by the elements, and so forth. The storage procedures should maintain the separation of materials, and prevent inclusion of good, reusable, or returnable materials with salable scrap.

(d) CONTROL OF DISPOSAL. During the disposal stage, the firm needs to maximize revenue from the sale of the spoiled units or scrap or minimize the treatment costs associated with effluents. For spoiled units and scrap, disposal procedures can use many of the same controls that ensure optimum performance for regular products, after accounting for the smaller value of spoiled or scrap items. For example, management can implement internal controls to prevent theft or other losses from shrinkage.

For industrial wastes and pollutants, disposal generally means treatment rather than sale. In measuring treatment costs, the firm should consider not only the direct costs, but also the indirect costs of treatment. These include costs associated with potential contingencies such as accidental spillages, the risks associated with future changes in legislation and best practices and other costs—difficult to identify and quantify, but very real—associated with the treatment of industrial pollutants.

(e) GREEN ACCOUNTING. Many firms have begun to include environmental performance measures in their control and evaluation systems. Examples include both 3M and Dow Chemical Company. These systems provide incentives for managers to consider the adverse environmental consequences of their decision making either by explicitly identifying the costs of adverse consequences (e.g., through transfer prices) or by including environmental effects as part of a general performance measurement program. Dow Chemical and other firms use a transfer price for their landfills. Bringer and Benforado [1994] discuss various performance measurement programs at 3M. These programs include both voluntary programs where employees submit suggestions on methods to reduce adverse environmental effects and corporatewide programs that consist of formal, periodic reporting of environmental performance at the plant and division level.

Control systems that become part of environmental cost accounting systems often use nonfinancial measures of performance—waste generated, environmental citations, environmental penalties—instead of or in addition to financial measures of performance, such as variances that we previously discussed. Nonfinancial measures have advantages over financial measures. Operating personnel find nonfinancial measures more timely, less aggregate, and often easier to understand. For example, 3M has measured the weight of the waste (emissions, pollutants, trash) as part of a program to reduce waste generated at the plant level. Epstein [1996] and Ditz et al. [1995] provide useful summaries of the type of control systems that firms use to manage adverse environmental consequences.

13.4 PLANNING AND GREEN ACCOUNTING

Traditionally, little emphasis has been placed on planning for spoilage, waste, and scrap beyond setting standards for identifying normal and abnormal levels. Budgeting consisted primarily of building in allowances to the bill of materials. The increased emphasis on environmental liabilities and costs that has resulted from environmental legislation as well as incorporating environmental positions in strategic planning has led many firms to consider the long-term consequences of design and production for environmental performance. This awareness has led to the development of planning tools to consider the environmental effect, measured in financial terms, of products and processes. Many of these tools are modifications of existing tools or the application of existing tools with an emphasis on environmental benefits and costs. Sections 28.6(c) and (d) of Chapter 28 also discuss some of these tools.

(a) LIFE-CYCLE COSTING. Recycling requirements have been enacted in Europe for certain products, and managers in many U.S. industries, such as automobile manufacturing, expect them here. Under this approach, the manufacturer has responsibility for the product after its useful life. This has increased the interest of firms potentially affected by these new regulations in *life-cycle costing* or *life-cycle analysis.* Originally a technique used primarily by the Department of Defense to analyze weapons systems, life-cycle costing attempts to measure the costs associated with a product through the various stages of its life cycle: development, raw materials acquisition, manufacturing, transportation, use, and disposal. Exhibit 13.5 illustrates these stages.

Life-cycle costing captures many costs incurred before or after manufacturing that conventional product costing systems do not charge to the product. For example, in Exhibit 13.5, a traditional accounting system would include the raw materials costs,

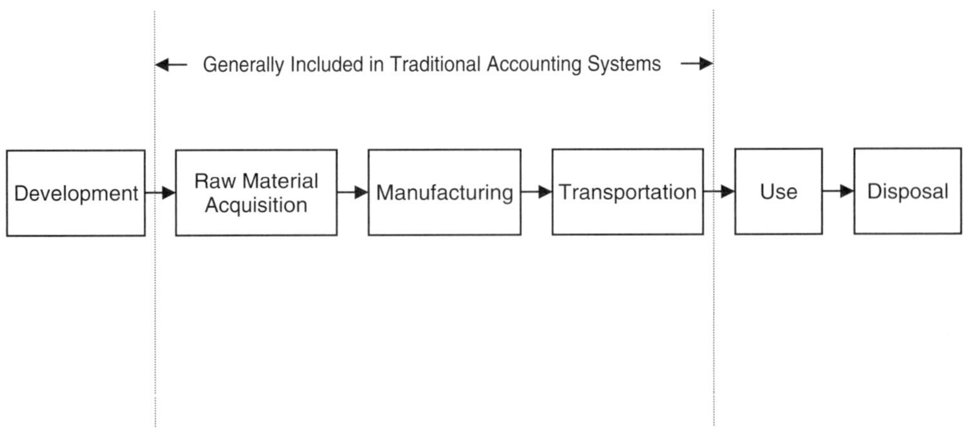

EXHIBIT 13.5 THE STAGES OF A PRODUCT'S LIFE CYCLE

manufacturing costs, and possibly transportation costs. Traditional accounting would not, however, include other costs in the product's life cycle, especially use and disposal costs. This occurs because the firm does not bear these costs—either the consumers bear these costs, or they become externalities (e.g., environmental pollution). Advocates of life-cycle costing argue that the analysis should include all costs associated with the product. Thus, in addition to the usual material and labor costs, a life-cycle analysis will also include costs associated with future liabilities and disposal. See the articles by Keoleian et al. (1993) and Krueze and Newell (1994) for more discussion. Section 28(d) of Chapter 28 also discusses life-cycle assessment.

(b) FULL COST ACCOUNTING. Full cost accounting (FCA) assigns the full costs to products; thus, it might relate as much to product costing as it does to planning. FCA extends traditional product costing in two ways. First, it assigns many overhead costs directly to products. In this sense, it resembles cost management systems—such as ABC—that analyze overhead for those costs that it can attribute to specific products and product families. FCA also differs by including a broader range of the costs (and benefits) considered.

Identifying overhead with products, especially overhead arising from environmental costs, serves a control purpose as well as a planning function by highlighting the hidden costs of adverse environmental consequences. Some of these costs include training, environmental audits, compliance costs, as so forth. The cost accounting system would normally capture these costs, but would not allocate them to individual products. FCA considers other financial consequences, including contingent liabilities associated with adverse environmental impacts (possibly considered in the planning stage in a conventional system but not routinely included in the computation of environmental costs) as well as benefits such as consumer goodwill.

(c) TOTAL COST ASSESSMENT. Total Cost Assessment (TCA) offers an approach to planning that considers the environmental effects of products, processes, and activities. TCA relates closely to capital budgeting (see Chapters 21 and 22) but includes a wider range of costs and benefits in the analysis. Its advocates argue that TCA also applies the use of a longer time horizon, the more comprehensive financial indicators, and a fuller allocation of costs to products and processes than does conventional firm capital budgeting analyses. Whereas, in theory, conventional capital budgeting approaches incorporate these factors, TCA advocates view typical applications of traditional capital budgeting methods as incomplete. For example, many applications of TCA (e.g., White et al., 1993) distinguish among four categories of costs and benefits to include in an analysis: direct costs, indirect costs, liability costs, and less tangible benefits. Many capital budgeting analyses focus on the direct costs of a project, but ignore, for example, the effect of a project on employee health. These advocates argue that the application of capital budgeting methods is deficient, not the methods themselves.

Direct costs include both capital expenditures (e.g., buildings and machinery) and operations costs (e.g., material and labor). Indirect costs include costs of compliance, waste management, and other environmental costs. Liability costs include penalties and fines associated with operations. Less tangible benefits include the effect of the project on firm image and employee relations. Exhibit 13.6 provides a list of possible costs in each category. Section 28(d) of Chapter 28 also discusses total cost assessment.

DIRECT COSTS

- capital expenditures
- buildings
- equipment
- utility connections
- equipment installation
- project engineering
- operation and maintenance expenses/revenues
- raw materials
- labor
- waste disposal
- utilities: energy, water, sewerage
- value of recovered material

INDIRECT OR HIDDEN COSTS

- compliance costs
- permitting
- reporting
- monitoring
- manifesting
- insurance
- on-site waste management
- operation of on-site pollution control equipment

LIABILITY COSTS

- penalties and fines
- personal injury and property damage

LESS TANGIBLE BENEFITS

- increased revenue from enhanced product quality
- increased revenue from enhanced company and product image
- reduced health maintenance costs from improved employee health
- increased productivity from improved employee relations

Source: White et al. (1993). Reprinted with permission of John Wiley & Sons, Inc.

EXHIBIT 13.6 COST CATEGORIES AND ELEMENTS FOR TCA

(d) OTHER PLANNING TOOLS. In many respects, the planning and control issues associated with spoilage, scrap, and waste resemble those of accounting and planning for quality improvements (see Chapter 10). Therefore, management can adapt many of the tools that it uses to measure and plan for quality costs to planning for improvements in environmental performance (including the reduction of spoilage, scrap, and waste). To

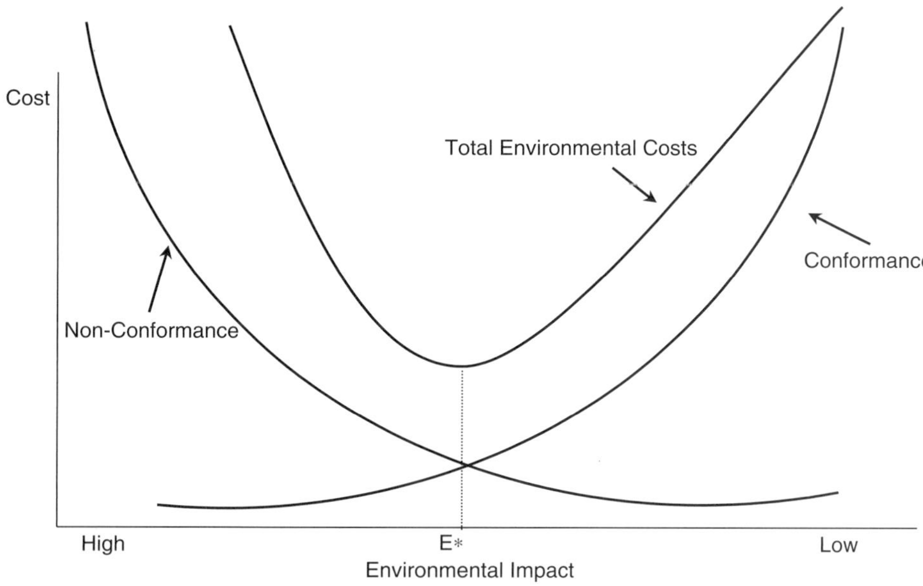

EXHIBIT 13.7 TRADE-OFF BETWEEN ENVIRONMENTAL COSTS

illustrate, consider the concept of the Cost of Quality (COQ) (see Simpson and Muthler, 1987). COQ classifies costs associated with quality as either conformance costs (i.e., cost incurred to assure high quality) or nonconformance costs (i.e., cost incurred output). The sum of conformance and nonconformance costs is the cost of quality and firms attempt to minimize it.

In a manner analogous to COQ, a firm can view the costs of environmental activities as consisting of four types grouped into two broader categories. The first category addresses costs associated with reducing any adverse environmental effects. The firm incurs these costs (similar to conformance costs in COQ) to either ensure that it uses process and product designs that lead to low negative impact or to acquire monitoring technology that enables the firm to ensure that its operations have low environmental impact. One could refer to these types of costs as design costs and monitoring costs, respectively.

The second cost category consists of those costs associated with higher negative environmental impacts (analogous to nonconformance costs in COQ). These costs include treatment costs for wastes generated by production but not released into the environment and the fines and penalties associated with releases of wastes into the environment. Analyzing these four costs (design, monitoring, treatment, and fines/penalties) allows the firm to make tradeoffs between improving environmental performance and the costs of generating higher levels of waste. Exhibit 13.7 illustrates the tradeoffs between conformance and nonconformance costs.

13.5 SUMMARY

Accounting for spoilage, waste, and scrap has received increasing attention in recent years because of a focus on cost management, improved quality, and concern over the adverse environmental consequences of manufacturing and other activities. As a result, leaders in the accounting profession have developed several approaches to measuring and reporting these costs, especially environmental costs. These approaches might have different names, but they have two common themes. First, to manage these costs, the cost control system must differentiate them from general overhead. This requirement to separately consider costs and not simply include them under a general overhead account is common to many other ideas associated with modern cost accounting systems. As information systems improve, this approach will likely become more common.

A second, more controversial, theme relates to the type of cost the firm should measure and report. The accounting literature contains two views on this question. The first proposes that the costing system assign to the product all the costs, tangible and intangible, borne by the firm and associated with the product. The firm can then use this full cost in all decisions concerning this product (e.g., pricing decisions). Advocates of this approach generally mention the hidden benefits to environmentally friendly products. They argue that with proper accounting and cost analysis, firms will find costs decreasing as they manufacture products with less adverse environmental impact. At this point, the only reservation firms might have with this approach relates to the cost of collecting better information.

A second view holds that the firm should consider *all* costs associated with a product, including those externalities where the existing structure of property rights does not assign responsibility for certain costs (e.g., health effects associated with poor air quality related to emitted pollutants) to the firm. Here, corporate strategy issues become paramount as managers and shareholders establish the position for the firm with respect to environmental issues.

BIBLIOGRAPHY

Bringer, R. P., and D. M. Benforado. "Pollution Prevention and Total Quality Environmental Management." In *Environmental Strategies Handbook: A Guide to Effective Policies and Practices*, ed. R. V. Kolluru. Englewood Cliffs, N.J.: Prentice-Hall, 1994.

Ditz, D., J. Ranganathan, and R. D. Banks. *Green Ledgers: Case Studies in Corporate Environmental Accounting*. Washington, D.C.: World Resources Institute, 1994.

Epstein, M. J. *Measuring Corporate Environmental Performance: Best Practices for Costing and Managing an Effective Environmental Strategy.* Chicago: Irwin, 1997.

Gartner, S. P. *Evolution of Cost Accounting to 1925.* Tuscaloosa, Al: University of Alabama Press, 1954.

Horngren, C. G. Foster, and S. Datar. *Cost Accounting: A Managerial Emphasis,* 11th ed., Englewood Cliffs, N.J.: Prentice-Hall, 2003.

Keoleian, G. A., D. Menerey, and M. A. Curran. "A Life Cycle Approach to Product System Design." *Pollution Prevention Review* (Summer 1993): 293–306.

Kreuze, J. G., and G. E. Newell. "ABC and Life-Cycle Costing for Environmental Expenditures." *Management Accounting* (February 1994): 38–42.

Simpson, J., and D. Muthler. "Quality Costs: Facilitating the Quality Initiative." *Journal of Cost Management* (Spring 1987): 25–34.

White, A. L., M. Becker, and D. E. Savage. "Environmentally Smart Accounting: Using Total Cost Assessment to Advance Pollution Prevention." *Pollution Prevention Review* (Summer 1993): 247–260.

CHAPTER 14

JOB, PROCESS, AND OPERATIONS COSTING

MICHAEL W. MAHER, EDITOR
University of California, Davis

CONTENTS

14.1 INTRODUCTION 389
14.2 OVERVIEW OF DIFFERENT PRODUCTION AND COSTING SYSTEMS 389
14.3 THE BASIC COST FLOW MODEL 391
(a) Application 391
(b) Application to Manufacturing and Service Organizations 391
(c) Perpetual versus Periodic Inventories 392
14.4 JUST-IN-TIME (JIT) PRODUCTION SYSTEMS AND BACKFLUSH COSTING 393
(a) Just in Time (JIT) 393
(b) Backflush Costing 394
14.5 JOB COSTING 396
(a) The Importance of Knowing the Cost of Jobs 397
(b) Tracking Costs 398
(c) Completing the Operating Cycle 404
(d) The Whole Picture: Summary of Job Cost Flows 406
14.6 PROCESS COSTING 410
(a) The Importance of Cost Information to Manage Processes 411
(b) Assigning Costs to Products 411
(c) Assigning Costs to Inventory 414
(d) Assigning Costs to Products Using First-In, First-Out (FIFO) Costing 418
14.7 OPERATION COSTING 420
(a) Product Costing in Operations 420
(b) Illustration of Operation Costing 422
14.8 DESIGNING COST SYSTEMS FOR MANAGERIAL PURPOSES 422
14.9 SUMMARY 423

14.1 INTRODUCTION

This chapter provides an overview of different cost systems: job costing, backflush costing (used with just-in-time production), process costing, and operation costing. Management's decision making needs should drive the selection and design of a cost system. Successfully designed cost systems reflect the needs of these decision makers (those who will use the information) and ensure that the system's benefits exceed its costs.

14.2 OVERVIEW OF DIFFERENT PRODUCTION AND COSTING SYSTEMS

A *job costing system* (discussed in Section 14.5) records costs and revenues for each job. Companies using job costing include construction companies such as Morrison-Knudsen, defense contractors such as Lockheed and Northrop-Grumman, hospitals such as the Mayo Clinic (where the jobs would be called *cases*), moviemakers such as Universal Studios, public accounting firms such as Deloitte & Touche and PricewaterhouseCoopers (where the jobs are often called *clients*), and John Wiley & Sons, the publisher of this book. These companies produce customized products.

By contrast, *process costing* (discussed in Section 14.6) is an accounting system used when identical units are produced through uniform production steps; this system does not separate and record costs for each unit. Firms that use process costing have *continuous flow processing* production methods, which lie at the opposite end of the spectrum from job shops. Process systems generally mass produce a single, homogeneous product in a continuing process. For instance, firms that make chemicals, grind flour, and refine oil use process systems. The next time you have a soft drink, consider whether the manufacturer kept track of the cost of the liquid you are drinking. Not likely!

Exhibit 14.1 shows a continuum of production methods ranging from those requiring job costing to those needing process costing. Many organizations use job systems for some projects and process systems for others. A home builder might use process costing for standardized homes with a particular floor plan. The same builder might use job costing when building a custom-designed home for a single customer. Honeywell, Inc., a high-tech company, uses process costing for most of its furnace thermostats but job costing for specialized defense and space contracting work.

Many companies use a hybrid of job and process costing, called *operation costing* (discussed in Section 14.7). An *operation* is a standardized method of making a product that is performed repeatedly in production. Companies that use operation costing produce goods using standardized production methods, like companies that use process costing, but materials can be different for each product or batch of products, as indicated in Exhibit 14.1.

Accounting System	**Job Costing**	**Operation Costing**[a]	**Process Costing**
Type of Production	Job shops • Construction • Movie studios • Hospitals	Batch production • Clothing • Automobiles • Computer terminals	Continuous flow processing • Oil Refinery • Paper • Paint
Type of Product	Customized product	Different batches of products but standardized within a batch	Standardized product

[a] Operating costing is a hybrid of job and process costing

EXHIBIT 14.1 PRODUCTION METHODS AND ACCOUNTING SYSTEMS

For example, Nissan manufactures a variety of models of cars and trucks on one assembly line in its manufacturing plant near Nashville, Tennessee. Each car or truck goes through the same work stations, such as the same painting station. Each vehicle type has a different set of materials, however. For example, trucks have a different body from cars.

14.3 THE BASIC COST FLOW MODEL

The basic cost flow model provides the fundamental framework for recording costs. Managers use this model to assign costs to jobs. The model is as follows:

Beginning balance (BB) + Transfers-in (TI) – Transfers-out (TO) = Ending balance (EB)

(a) APPLICATION. Accountants and managers frequently do not have key accounting information and use this model to solve for unknown amounts in accounts. For example, suppose that Hurricane Josie has just wiped out the inventory of fine clothes in your store. The insurance company will pay for the cost of the destroyed inventory, but you have to prove the cost of the inventory, which no longer exists. Unfortunately, nobody counted the inventory before the storm hit.

The basic accounting model comes to your rescue. Last year's financial statements show that the ending inventory at the end of the year was $500,000, which was also the beginning inventory this year. Your suppliers indicate that you purchased $1,200,000 of clothes so far this year, and sales records show that you have sold clothes that cost $1,400,000. You know, therefore, that the beginning balance equals $500,000, the amount transferred in to inventory equals $1,200,000, and the amount transferred out of inventory equals $1,400,000. Using the basic cost flow model,

$$BB + TI - TO = EB$$

$$\$500{,}000 + \$1{,}200{,}000 - \$1{,}400{,}000 = EB$$

$$\$300{,}000 = EB$$

You can report lost inventory costing $300,000.

In practice, auditors use the cost flow models frequently to perform reasonableness checks on the data they receive from clients. For example, a client may report that ending inventory equals $500,000 based on a count of the inventory. If you know from the basic cost flow model that the inventory should equal $400,000 (i.e., BB + TI – TO = $400,000), you know something is wrong.

Auditors discover many financial frauds when they find that the amounts based on the basic cost flow model differ from those the client reported. An instance of using the model to expose fraud occurred at a food distribution company in which a senior official became curious about the high inventory levels reported on the divisional financial statements of a particular division. Based on the division's purchases (transfers in) and cost of goods sold (transfers out), the amount of ending inventory seemed high compared to that of other divisions in the company. When asked about the high inventory levels, the division manager confessed that he had overstated the inventory numbers to make his divisional profits look better than they really were. (Overstating the ending balance in inventory understates cost of goods sold, which overstates gross margin and profits.)

(b) APPLICATION TO MANUFACTURING AND SERVICE ORGANIZATIONS. Service and manufacturing organizations have both Work in Process and Finished Goods Inventory accounts. The basic cost flow model ties these accounts together as shown in

Exhibit 14.2. Note that the *transfer-out (TO)* of work in process (WIP) inventory is the *transfer-in (TI)* to finished goods inventory. The TO of finished goods inventory is the cost of goods sold.

(c) PERPETUAL VERSUS PERIODIC INVENTORIES. *The perpetual inventory method* requires an ongoing record of transfers in and transfers out of inventory accounts. Using the perpetual inventory method requires that the firm update inventory levels continuously. For example, using the perpetual inventory method, Macy's Department Store records the reduction in inventory for each item of merchandise it sells. Management knows the level of inventory for each item without taking a physical inventory count.

In contrast to the perpetual inventory method, the *periodic inventory method* does not continuously update inventory levels. Instead of maintaining continuous records of transfers in or out of inventory accounts, people must take a physical inventory. Then they derive the amount sold or transferred from one inventory account to another using the basic cost flow model.

For example, consider the sale of Super Sweet tennis rackets at Martha's Sport Shop in March. Beginning inventory was 10 rackets. Management counted the ending inventory on March 31 and found 15 rackets. Based on records of purchases, management knew that 40 rackets had been purchased during March. All rackets cost \$10 each, so the company records the cost amounts as follows:

Beginning inventory (10 rackets at \$10)	\$100
Ending inventory (15 rackets at \$10)	150
Purchases (40 rackets at \$10).	400

Using the basic cost flow model,

$$BB + TI - TO = EB$$

management solves for the unknown cost of goods sold (also referred to as Transfer Outs, or *TO*), as follows:

$$TO = BB + TI - EB$$

$$TO = \$100 + \$400 - \$150$$

$$TO = \$350$$

A perpetual inventory provides more data than a periodic inventory does. For example, with a perpetual system, up-to-date inventory balances and cost of goods sold are

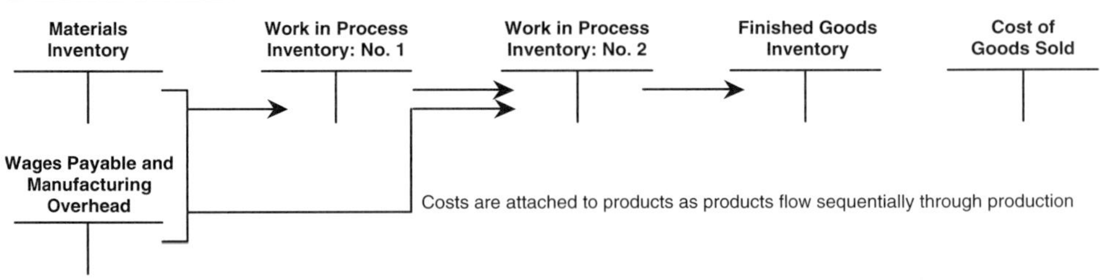

EXHIBIT 14.2 FLOW OF PRODUCTS

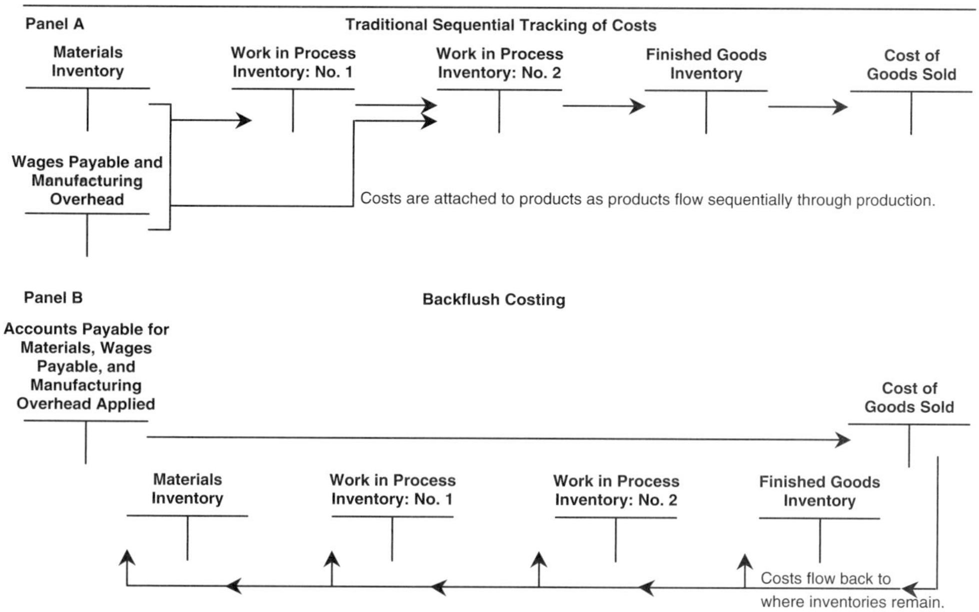

EXHIBIT 14.3 COMPARISON OF TRADITIONAL SEQUENTIAL TRACKING OF COSTS WITH BACKFLUSH COSTING

always available. But with a periodic system, these data are available only after taking a physical inventory count. Perpetual inventory is also useful for control purposes because management and auditors can compare the clerical record of transfers out with a physical count to check for theft, spoilage, and other problems. However, the perpetual method requires more expensive data maintenance systems.

With the expanded use of bar codes and other computerized inventory systems, nearly all large organizations use perpetual inventories. Periodically—say, every six months—they may take a physical inventory to check for shortages, theft, and clerical accuracy and to satisfy internal or external auditors. They often use the periodic method for office supplies and small merchandise.

Traditional costing systems use sequential tracking to record product costs. That is, as a product goes through its production steps, the costing system tracks it and attaches costs at each step. Panel A of Exhibit 14.3 shows the flow of costs through T-accounts using a traditional costing system. This sequential tracking required for traditional costing systems becomes time-consuming and expensive, not only for accountants but also for workers and managers who must keep records of labor time and other costs incurred at each step.

14.4 JUST-IN-TIME (JIT) PRODUCTION SYSTEMS AND BACKFLUSH COSTING

(a) JUST IN TIME (JIT). The preceding section assumed that accountants record product costs as the product flows from one work station to another. Accountants in many companies that use just-in-time (JIT) production methods employ an alternative approach to recording costs, known as backflush costing. Before discussing backflush costing, we list the advantages of JIT:

- *Reduces inventory on hand* because the manufacturer obtains materials just in time for production rather than stockpiling them in a warehouse. Chapter 26 discusses a value chain, wherein firms identify and promote activities that increase the value of its goods or services and reduce or eliminate any non-value-added activities. Storing inventory is a non-value-added activity. Implementing a JIT system will help a company substantially reduce inventory levels.
- *Refines the production process* as the focus shifts to improving quality and reducing non-value-added activities. A JIT production system forces the company to immediately correct processes resulting in defective units because no warehouse exists where the firm can send defective units to await reworking or scrapping.
- *Reduces the time required to manufacture a product*, giving users of a JIT system more flexibility in meeting customer demands and reducing the amount of work in process at any point in time.

Each element of the process results in several financial benefits. By decreasing inventory levels, companies no longer need to tie up cash in inventory or in warehouse space to store inventory. The emphasis on eliminating non-value-added activities and improving the production process results in reduced production costs. JIT also eliminates the risk of producing inventory that becomes obsolete—especially important in high-tech industries.

In theory, a JIT system eliminates the need for inventories because production doesn't occur until the firm knows that it will sell the item. Consequently, JIT requires reliable suppliers who deliver a quality product on time.

Companies using JIT also normally have a backlog of orders for their finished product so they can keep their production operations going continuously. A company loses the benefits of the JIT system if it has to shut down its operations for lengthy periods of time while awaiting receipt of a new order.

Implementing a JIT system requires the highly efficient coordination of purchasing, production, and marketing functions. Companies that have consistent problems with any of these functions should not implement JIT until it has resolved the problems.

(b) BACKFLUSH COSTING. Companies that implement a JIT production system need not focus on *tracking costs* for inventory valuation because inventory levels are generally insignificant. Instead, accountants record all manufacturing costs directly in the Cost of Goods Sold account. This saves considerable time and effort and reduces computational errors. At the end of the accounting period, if the accountants learn that the company has some inventory, they can use backflush costing to record inventory values.

The *backflush costing method* works backward from the cost of goods sold to assign manufacturing costs to work in process inventories. The term *backflush* probably arose because costs are "flushed back" through the production process to the points at which inventories remain. Exhibit 14.3 compares the traditional method of sequential costing (panel A) with the backflush approach (panel B). Backflush costing initially records costs at the *end* of the production process in Cost of Goods Sold on the grounds that little or no inventories exist at the end of the period.

If no inventories exist at the end of the period, the company does not need to record the backflow of costs. (The diagram indicates the backflow of costs by the arrows pointing to the left and up in Panel B of Exhibit 14.3.) If inventories exist, the company must backflush costs from the end of the production process (e.g., from Cost of Goods Sold) to the inventories, as the following example demonstrates.

Example 1. Example of JIT and Backflush

Denton Biotechnics Corp., which uses the JIT system, sells diagnostic kits for medical use. Direct materials cost $5 per kit. The company received an order for 10,000 kits in January, which was its only business in January. It had no beginning inventory that month. Materials costs of $50,000 were incurred, as were conversion costs of $94,000. Materials costs were credited to Accounts Payable as they were purchased. Of the conversion costs, $54,000 was credited to Manufacturing Overhead and $40,000 to Wages Payable, as incurred. Using backflush costing and charging the costs directly to Cost of Goods Sold, the journal entries for January are

Cost of Goods Sold	50,000	
Accounts Payable		50,000
To record the purchase and use of materials.		
Cost of Goods Sold	94,000	
Wages Payable		40,000
Manufacturing Overhead		54,000
To record conversion costs.		

This example presents the extreme version of JIT production by charging all manufacturing costs to Cost of Goods Sold as they were incurred. Other versions charge labor and overhead costs to the account Conversion Costs and then assign these conversion costs to Finished Goods Inventory or Cost of Goods Sold. Whatever peculiarity you encounter in practice, remember that accountants normally do not need to track costs in work in process inventories for external reporting if the company has no work in process at the end of the accounting period.

If Denton Biotechnics Corp. had sold all 10,000 kits and had no inventories at the end of January, the company would not need additional entries. If the company had inventories at the end of January, however, it must assign costs to those inventories. To demonstrate, we assume that the company had the following inventories at the end of January:

- *Work in process inventory.* 1,000 units complete as to materials costs and 40 percent complete as to conversion costs.
- *Finished goods inventory.* 1,000 units completed but not yet shipped.

The company further computes its conversion costs to be $10 for each completed kit. In addition, the company incurs direct materials costs of $5 per kit at the beginning of work in process. Based on this information, we compute the cost of each ending inventory as follows:

- *Work in process inventory.* (1,000 units × $5 for materials) + (40% stage of completion × 1,000 units × $10 per unit for conversion costs) = $5,000 + $4,000 = $9,000
- *Finished goods inventory.* 1,000 units × ($5 for materials + $10 for conversion costs) = $15,000.

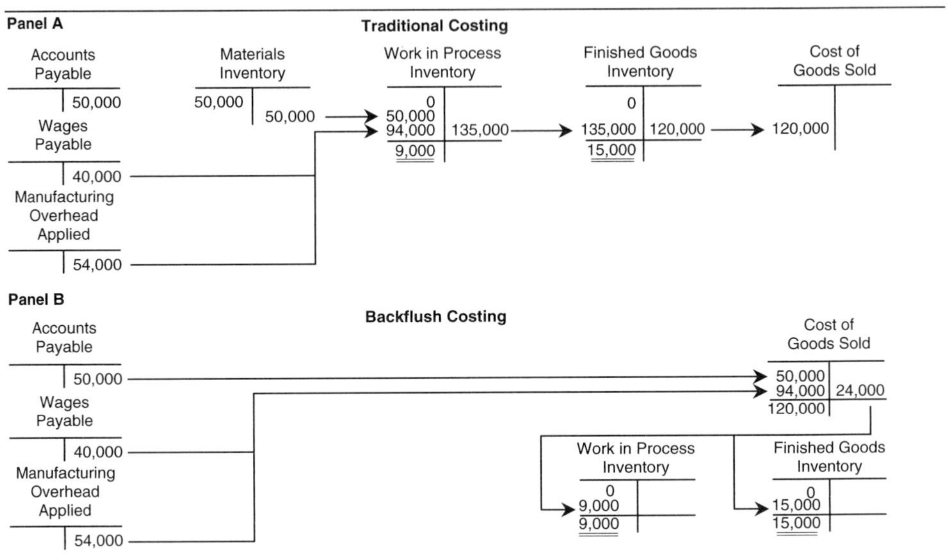

EXHIBIT 14.4 COMPARISON OF TRADITIONAL COST FLOWS TO BACKFLUSH COSTING

The entries to backflush the costs of inventories out of Cost of Goods Sold follow:

Work in Process Inventory.	9,000	
Finished Goods Inventory.	15,000	
Cost of Goods Sold		24,000
To record inventories.		

If the costs of these kits had been charged to the accounts using traditional sequential costing, we would have recorded materials in Materials Inventory when they were purchased. As the company used materials and incurred conversion costs, these costs would have been recorded in Work in Process and Finished Goods and, finally, in Cost of Goods Sold. Exhibit 14.4 compares diagrams of the cost flows, first using the traditional method (Panel A) and then using backflush costing (Panel B).

What happens to the beginning inventory next period? The company can either use traditional sequential costing to record the movement of costs and products out of the inventory accounts, or it can reverse the backflush entry. By reversing the backflush entry, the company credits the inventory accounts and debits Cost of Goods Sold, thus recreating the situation that appeared before making the backflush entry. (If you recall how adjusting and reversing entries work, the backflush entry can be treated as an adjusting entry at the end of a period that is reversed at the beginning of the next period.)

14.5 JOB COSTING

The previous sections of this chapter have provided an overview of alternative production methods and costing systems. They have also discussed the basic cost flow model and several methods used to derive costs of the inventory component of the basic model: perpetual, periodic, and backflush (used with JIT production systems). We now move to a closer examination of job costing, and discuss how to account for overhead in such a system.

(a) THE IMPORTANCE OF KNOWING THE COST OF JOBS. When you see construction sites for new homes, repaired highways, remodeled office buildings, or rapid transit systems, you see job costing at work. *Jobs* are units of a product that one can easily distinguish from other units. If you or your family remodel or build a home, the construction work is called a *job* because it can be easily distinguished from other construction jobs.

Companies need to track the cost of each job, for three reasons:

1. *Managers use their knowledge of the cost of jobs to estimate the costs of prospective jobs.* Good cost estimates on future jobs help them prepare good bids. Construction contractors, for example, know that if they bid too high, they will not win the job. However, if they bid too low, they will lose money. Construction contractors and other people who bid on jobs need to have a good estimate of the costs of prospective jobs so they can prepare bids that are low enough to win but high enough to make money.
2. *Managers compare actual job costs to the estimated (sometimes called budgeted) job costs to control costs.* A contractor once pointed out that if she did not have job cost information, she could be experiencing huge cost overruns without knowing it. For example, on one job she estimated the cost of lumber at a certain level. Then a hurricane hit the southeastern United States, causing lumber prices to double. She did not realize that the lumber shipped to the job was at the higher post-hurricane price until she received the job cost information. Based on the revised prices, she redesigned the job to use less lumber in places where it was not essential.
3. *Managers can use job cost information to renegotiate contracts with customers.* The original specifications of a job often go through many revisions. Sometimes these changes are inexpensive, and the contractor does the extra work as part of good customer service. Other times the changes become expensive and the customer and contractor need to negotiate who will pay for them. Good cost information helps the contractor know (1) whether the changes are expensive or inexpensive and (2) what the changes cost so the parties can renegotiate the bid or the specifications.

Movies and television shows are jobs. Some are successful; some are not. Studios must decide what to do with the cost of unsuccessful ones, the flops. Some studios have been criticized for assigning the cost of flops to successful shows, which in turn reduced profits available under profit-sharing agreements with actors, actresses, directors, and others associated with the successful show. One studio carried the cost of flops in inventory, thereby overstating assets and understating expenses. When investors learned about this practice, the company's stock price plummeted.

Job costing becomes important for pricing and cost control. Prospective customers always ask for estimates, and they frequently award jobs on a competitive cost basis. Consequently, suppliers must be able to estimate costs accurately to be competitive and profitable.

To illustrate such a bidding situation, assume that Public Consultants, a firm that customizes accounting systems for government agencies, recently completed jobs for two municipalities. The job for Gotham City, a large metropolis, required 7,000 hours of staff time and several sophisticated computer applications. The job for Smallville, a modest farming community, required 70 hours of staff time and one very simple computer application. When bidding for the two jobs, Public Consultants could have averaged the estimated total costs for the two jobs to bid the same amount for both cities. Clearly, the company would have overbid Smallville (and lost the contract) and underbid Gotham City (and lost money). Instead, Public Consultants used job costing to accurately estimate the costs for each job separately. Thus, they could submit a competitive bid and still make a reasonable profit on each job.

(b) TRACKING COSTS. In job operations, managers estimate and control costs by keeping separate records of costs for each job. *Source documents* are basic records that accountants use to initiate an accounting entry. The source document for a job is a *job cost record,* sometimes referred to as a *job cost sheet, card,* or *file*. We now discuss how managers use job cost records to assign costs in a job cost system.

Exhibit 14.5 presents a printout of a job cost record for Job 102 for New Abilities Manufacturing Company, which makes customized health care equipment for people with physical limitations. Note that this record shows detailed calculations for the direct materials, direct labor, and manufacturing overhead charged to the job.

NEW ABILITIES MANUFACTURING

Job Number:	102	Customer:	D. Bell
Date Started:	Jan 8	Date Finished:	Jan 26
Description:	Manufacture custom equipment according to specifications		

Assembly Department

Direct Materials			Direct Labor			Manufacturing Overhead	
Date	**Requisition Number**	**Cost**	**Date**	**Employee Number**	**Cost**	**Date**	**Cost**
Jan 8	102-A1	$20,000	Jan 8–14	88	$980	Jan 31	$48,000
Jan 13	102-A2	4,000	Jan 12–18	87	720		
			(Many more employees were added to this list. In total, $40,000 direct labor cost was incurred.)				

Total Costs

Direct materials	$24,000	
Direct labor	40,000	
Manufacturing overhead	48,000	$112,000

Transferred to Finished Goods Inventory on Jan 26

Total job costs:	
Direct materials	$ 24,000
Direct labor	40,000
Manufacturing overhead	48,000
Total	$112,000

Explain any unusual items below:

None

EXHIBIT 14.5 JOB COST RECORD

Managers compare the actual costs reported on the job cost record to the job costs estimated before the job was started to evaluate employee performance in controlling costs, to provide information for negotiating price increases with the customer, and to provide feedback on the accuracy of the job cost estimation process, which is important for pricing.

(i) Recording Job Costs in the Accounts. Most companies with jobs follow the basic steps presented in this section. We show the journal entries to record cost flows using New Abilities Manufacturing Company as an example. Work in Process Inventory is a control account because it is supported by records in the subsidiary ledger. Each job cost record (as shown in Exhibit 14.5) records costs associated with a specific job. Thus, job cost records serve as *subsidiary ledgers* to the Work in Process Inventory (WIP) account. This enables management to identify the costs for a single job by reviewing its job cost record.

New Abilities had one job in process on January 1, Job 101. After some minor work, it was completed and shipped to a customer in January. The job cost record in Exhibit 14.15 showed the costs for New Abilities' second job, Job 102. Manufacturing started the job in January and moved it to finished goods inventory on January 26. At January 31, it awaited shipment to a customer. Manufacturing began a third job in January, Job 103, which was still in process on January 31.

(ii) Beginning Inventories. Exhibit 14.6 shows the flow of costs through accounts. Materials Inventory on hand on January 1 was $10,000. Beginning Work in Process Inventory on January 1 was Job 101, which had incurred the following costs:

Direct Materials	$14,000
Direct Labor	22,000
Manufacturing Overhead	25,000
Total	$61,000

Hence, the Work in Process Inventory account balance on January 1 was $61,000.

Note the difference between Materials Inventory, $10,000, that has not yet been sent to production departments, and the materials component of beginning Work in Process Inventory, $14,000. The latter has already been sent to production.

Exhibit 14.6 shows these beginning balances. There was no beginning Finished Goods Inventory.

(iii) Accounting for Materials. Assume that in January, New Abilities purchased $60,000 of direct and indirect materials and accumulated the costs in one account. This purchase was recorded as follows:

(1) Materials Inventory	60,000	
Accounts Payable		60,000

When the supplier sends an invoice or bill for the shipment, New Abilities records the payable as shown in entry (1). The company records subsequent payment with a debit to Accounts Payable and a credit to Cash.

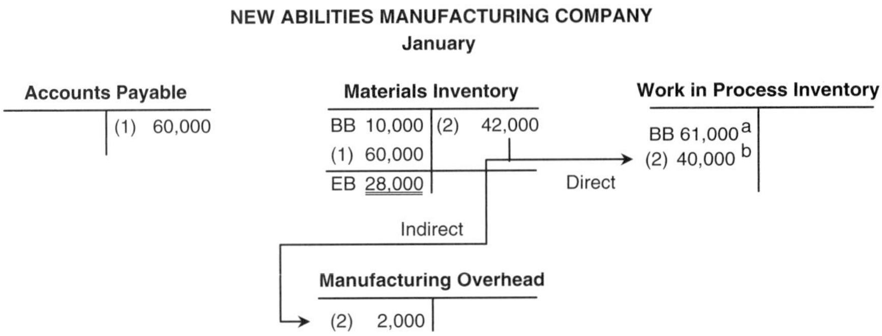

Note: BB = Beginning balance; EB = Ending Balance. Numbers in parentheses correspond to journal entries presented in text.

[a] Beginning work in Process Inventory is composed of

Direct Material	$14,000
Direct Labor	22,000
Manufacturing Overhead	25,000
Total	$61,000

[b] $40,000 = $24,000 for Job No. 102 + $16,000 for Job No. 103.

EXHIBIT 14.6 COST FLOWS THROUGH T-ACCOUNTS—MATERIALS

A job supervisor or other authority requisitions the materials needed for a job using a *materials requisition* form. It is the source document for the entry transferring materials from Materials Inventory to the job.

No materials were requisitioned for Job 101 in January. Job 102 had requisitions for materials totaling $24,000 (see Exhibit 4.1). The entry to record this transfer of direct materials follows:

(2a) Work in Process Inventory	24,000	
Materials Inventory		24,000
To record the requisition of materials.		

Direct materials of $16,000 were requisitioned for Job 103 and recorded in entry (2b). Materials inventory is also used for indirect materials and supplies that the firm does not assign to specific jobs but charges to the Manufacturing Overhead account. For New Abilities, the $2,000 of indirect materials requisitioned in January were recorded in the following entry.

(2b) Work in Process Inventory.	16,000	
Manufacturing Overhead	2,000	
Materials Inventory.		18,000
To record direct materials costs of $16,000 assigned to Job 103 and indirect materials costs of $2,000 charged to Manufacturing Overhead.		

Note that journal entry (2) in Exhibit 14.2 combines entries (2a) and (2b) into one journal entry.

Exhibit 4.2 also presents the ending materials inventory balance, which one can calculate by using the basic cost flow equation:

$$\text{Beginning balance } (BB) + \text{Transfers in } (TI) - \text{Transfers out } (TO) = \text{Ending balance } (EB)$$

$$\$10{,}000 + \$60{,}000 - \$42{,}000 = EB$$

$$\$28{,}000 = EB$$

(iv) Accounting for Labor. Companies usually pay an hourly rate to production workers, who account for their time each day on time cards, time sheets, or other records. The time record provides space for them to account for the hours spent on the job during the day and becomes the basis for the company's payroll.

The total cost to the company includes gross pay plus the employer's share of social security and employment taxes, employer's contribution to pension and insurance plans, and any other benefits that the company pays for the employee. In general, these costs range from about 15 percent to about 70 percent of the wage rate, depending on a company's fringe benefit plans. Companies commonly add their fringe benefit costs to the wage rate to assign costs to jobs, although fringe benefits also may be part of overhead.

New Abilities' payroll department recorded accumulated costs of $110,000 for manufacturing employees. Of the $110,000 total, $80,000 was attributed to direct labor costs, including employee benefits and taxes. The $80,000 is charged (debited) to Work in Process Inventory and assigned to the specific jobs worked on during the period. Based on time cards, Job 101 was charged with $10,000 in January, Job 102 was charged with $40,000 as in the job cost record in Exhibit 14.1, and Job 103 with $30,000.

The remaining $30,000 is indirect labor and charged to Manufacturing Overhead. This indirect labor includes the costs of supervisory, janitorial, maintenance, security, and timekeeping personnel, as well as idle time and overtime premiums paid to direct laborers.

The following entry records labor costs in January.

(3) Work in Process Inventory	80,000	
Manufacturing Overhead	30,000	
Wages Payable (or Accrued Factory Payroll) . . .		110,000
To record direct labor costs of $80,000 assigned to jobs and indirect labor costs of $30,000 charged to Manufacturing Overhead.		

Exhibit 14.7 shows the flow of labor costs through the T-accounts.

(v) Accounting for Manufacturing Overhead. Accounting for manufacturing overhead tends to be more difficult than accounting for direct labor and direct materials. Companies typically pool manufacturing overhead costs together into one account and allocate them to individual jobs based on a relatively arbitrary overhead base (for example, machine-hours or direct labor-hours). We discuss the process of creating predetermined overhead rates in Section 14.5(b)(vi).

The Manufacturing Overhead account usually accumulates indirect manufacturing costs, including indirect materials and indirect labor. Each department typically has its own Manufacturing Overhead Summary account, so top management can hold department managers accountable for departmental overhead costs and evaluate how well they control costs. This stage of cost allocation is to allocate costs from the accounts in which they were initially entered to responsibility centers. In this case, the responsibility centers are departments.

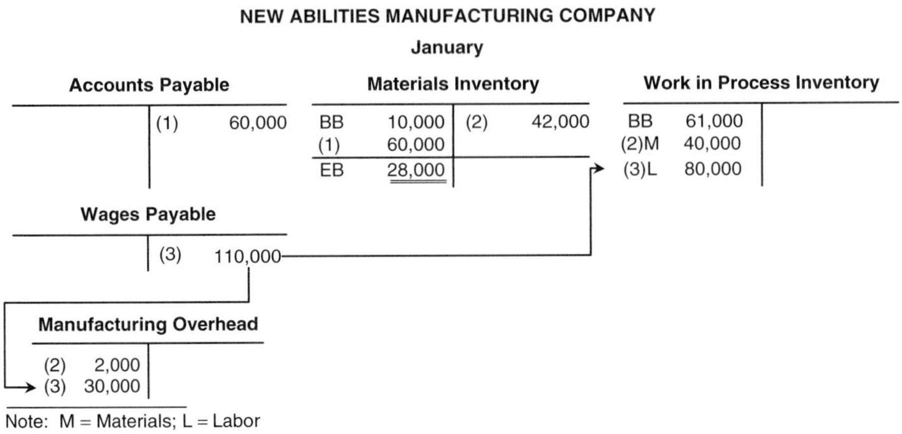

EXHIBIT **14.7** COST FLOWS THROUGH T-ACCOUNTS—LABOR COSTS

For example, in January, New Abilities charges indirect materials costs of $2,000 and indirect labor costs of $30,000 to the Manufacturing Overhead account as described in entries (2) and (3) above. Utilities and other overhead costs credited to Accounts Payable were $46,000. Actual overhead includes the portion of prepaid taxes and insurance applicable to the period, $7,000, and depreciation of $19,000. These items total $72,000 and represent the actual overhead incurred during the period.

The journal entry to record manufacturing overhead follows:

(4) Manufacturing Overhead.	72,000	
Accounts Payable.		46,000
Prepaid Expenses		7,000
Accumulated Depreciation.		19,000
To record actual manufacturing overhead costs other than indirect labor and indirect materials.		

We label this entry as (4) in the T-account diagram in Exhibit 14.8.

(vi) Predetermined Overhead Rates. We have discussed why accounting for manufacturing overhead can prove difficult. Companies generally use a predetermined overhead rate, which equals the total estimated overhead for the coming period divided by the total estimated overhead allocation base for the coming period. Companies usually establish the rate before the year in which it is to be used and use it for the entire year.

By using a predetermined overhead rate, a company normalizes overhead applied to jobs. Over time, manufacturing overhead costs can prove erratic. Preventive maintenance costs often increase in months with low activity. In cold climates, utility costs in the winter exceed those of the summer; the opposite holds true in warm climates. A job may require more actual overhead costs in some months than in others. In addition, a company might not know its actual overhead costs until the close of an accounting period. All of these factors can send monthly overhead rates on a roller coaster ride that management can smooth out by using predetermined overhead rates. This will help management prepare understandable financial statements and provide more accurate estimates of product costs.

Predetermined overhead rates normalize the application of manufacturing overhead to jobs; hence, the resulting product costs are called *normal costs*. *Normal costing* is an accounting system that charges direct materials and direct labor to objects at actual costs and applies manufacturing overhead using predetermined rates. Managers can use the following five-step approach to establish predetermined overhead rates.

EXAMPLE 2. NORMAL COSTING FOR NEW ABILITIES MANUFACTURING

Step 1. Identify the costs to include as indirect costs. New Abilities has developed a detailed list of cost items included as manufacturing overhead. The total of these costs represents its total manufacturing overhead.

Step 2. Estimate the totals for each cost item identified in Step 1. If the budget period is one year, budgeted (i.e., estimated) manufacturing overhead costs for New Abilities total $1,200,000, based on last year's actual manufacturing overhead adjusted for anticipated changes this year.

Step 3. Select the cost allocation base(s). Operating personnel at New Abilities have identified the number of machine-hours as the major driver of manufacturing overhead costs. That is, manufacturing overhead costs are primarily a function of the number of machine-hours incurred. Machine-hours become the cost allocation base because of this cause-and-effect relation.

Step 4. Estimate the amount of the cost allocation base identified in Step 3. New Abilities anticipates using 10,000 machine-hours during the year based on expected customer demand for its products.

Step 5. Compute the predetermined overhead rate (as follows).

$$\text{Predetermined rate} = \frac{\text{Estimated manufacturing overhead cost for the year}}{\text{Estimated machine hours for the year}}$$
$$= \frac{\$1,200,000}{10,000 \text{ machine-hours}}$$
$$= \$120 \text{ per machine-hour}$$

New Abilities used its predetermined rate to charge manufacturing overhead to individual jobs as follows.

	Actual Machine-Hours Used		Predetermined Overhead Rate		Manufacturing Overhead Applied
Job 101	100	×	$120 per mh	=	$12,000
Job 102	400	×	120	=	48,000
Job 103	300	×	120	=	36,000
Total	800	×	120	=	$96,000

We refer to the overhead applied to a cost object in this manner (i.e., using a predetermined overhead rate) as *applied overhead.* The entry to record the allocation of manufacturing overhead to jobs using a predetermined overhead rate is

(5) Work in Process Inventory.	96,000	
Manufacturing Overhead Applied		96,000
To record application of manufacturing overhead to jobs.		

Exhibit 14.8 shows a separate account for Manufacturing Overhead Applied. Two overhead accounts may be used to separate actual and *applied overhead.* We title the account that records actual overhead *Manufacturing Overhead* and call the new account that records applied overhead *Manufacturing Overhead Applied.*[1] These accounts are closed at the end of the period, as described later in this chapter.

Exhibit 14.8 illustrates the flow of these costs through T-accounts.

(c) COMPLETING THE OPERATING CYCLE

(i) Transfers to Finished Goods Inventory. When the company transfers jobs out of production to the finished goods storage area, an entry is made transferring the costs of the jobs from the Work in Process Inventory account to the Finished Goods Inventory

NEW ABILITIES MANUFACTURING COMPANY
January

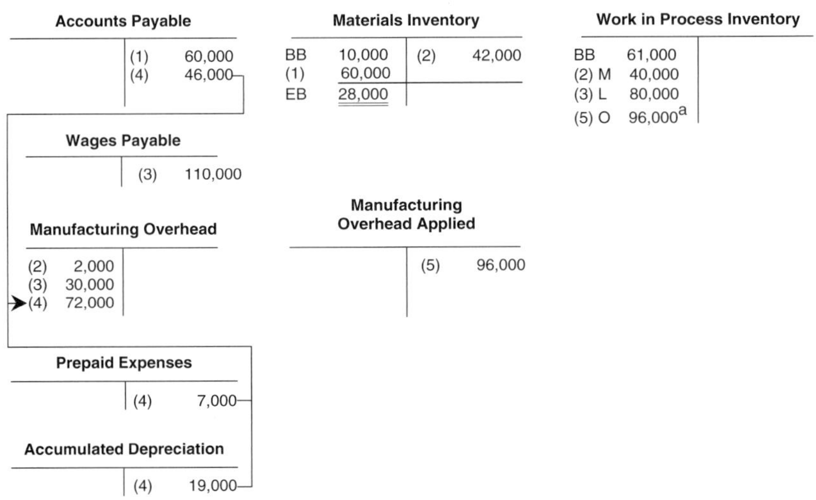

Note: M = Direct materials; L = Direct labor; O = Manufacturing overhead

[a] Overhead application rate = \$120 per machine-hour = $\frac{\text{Estimated manufacturing overhead for year}}{\text{Estimated machine-hours for year}} = \frac{\$1{,}200{,}000}{10{,}000 \text{ machine-hours}}$

EXHIBIT 14.8 COST FLOWS THROUGH T-ACCOUNTS—MANUFACTURING OVERHEAD COSTS

1. Companies can combine the overhead into one account. In such a setting, the left side of the account is basically overhead "incurred" and the right side is overhead "applied."

account. For example, New Abilities completed Jobs 101 and 102 in January and transferred them to the Finished Goods Inventory account. The journal entry is

(6) Finished Goods Inventory	195,000	
Work in Process Inventory		195,000
To transfer completed jobs to the finished goods storage area.		

Note that the amount transferred includes costs incurred in both the current period and previous periods. For example, the transfer for Job 101 includes $61,000 from beginning work in process inventory and $22,000 of costs incurred in January to complete the job.

(ii) Transfers to Cost of Goods Sold. When the goods are sold, they are transferred from the Finished Goods Inventory account to the Cost of Goods Sold account. For example, New Abilities sold Job 101 in January for $120,000 on account. When it was sold, the journal entry to record the cost of goods sold was

(7) Cost of Goods Sold	83,000	
Finished Goods Inventory		83,000
Accounts Receivable	120,000	
Sales Revenue		120,000
To transfer finished goods inventory to cost of goods sold and to record corresponding sales revenue.		

Manufacturing overhead accounts are temporary accounts. At the end of an accounting period, the actual and applied overhead accounts are closed. Usually this is not done until the end of the year when the books are closed. For illustrative purposes, however, we assume that New Abilities closes its books for January.

Under normal costing, the amount debited to the Manufacturing Overhead account (the actual manufacturing overhead) is unlikely to equal the amount applied (based on budgeted overhead). The difference between the actual and the applied manufacturing overhead is the *overhead variance*. We use a Manufacturing Overhead Variance account to record the variance as follows.

Assume that $96,000 was credited to Manufacturing Overhead Applied (based on budgeted overhead) and $104,000 was debited to Manufacturing Overhead (actual overhead) during January, as shown in Exhibit 14.9. In that case, the entry to close the actual against applied overhead for New Abilities is

(8) Manufacturing Overhead Applied.........	96,000	
Manufacturing Overhead Variance	8,000	
Manufacturing Overhead................		104,000
To close actual and applied overhead accounts.		

Exhibit 14.9 shows this entry. The following section discusses methods to dispose of the manufacturing overhead variance.

Overhead: Normal Costing

Manufacturing Overhead		Manufacturing Overhead Applied		Work in Process Inventory	
104,000	(8) *104,000*[a]	(8) *96,000*[a]	96,000	→ 96,000	

Manufacturing Overhead Variance

Debit	Credit
(8) *8,000*[a]	

[a] Refers to closing entry.

EXHIBIT 14.9 CLOSING ENTRIES FOR MANUFACTURING OVERHEAD

(d) THE WHOLE PICTURE: SUMMARY OF JOB COST FLOWS

(iii) Marketing and Administrative Costs. The flow of all manufacturing costs from buying materials to sale of product appears in Exhibit 14.10. Note that the cost of goods sold statement in Exhibit 14.11 presents the data from T-accounts in Exhibit 14.10. You should cross-reference each item in the statement in Exhibit 14.11 to the T-accounts in Exhibit 14.10.

Marketing and administrative costs do not flow through inventory accounts. These expenses are recorded in accounts to be closed at the end of the accounting period. For example, New Abilities' marketing and administrative costs (all on account) were $10,000 in January. The entry to record these costs is

Marketing and Administrative Costs	10,000	
Accounts Payable		10,000
To record marketing and administrative costs incurred in January.		

We do not show T-accounts for this entry but note that the costs appear on the income statement in Exhibit 14.11.

(iv) Understanding the Overhead Variance. The $8,000 amount in the Manufacturing Overhead Variance account in Exhibit 14.10 appears in the income statement in Exhibit 14.11 as Underapplied Manufacturing Overhead. *Underapplied overhead* occurs when actual overhead exceeds applied overhead. New Abilities' *underapplied* overhead is shown as a debit to the Manufacturing Overhead Variance account. *Overapplied overhead* occurs when actual overhead is less than applied overhead. Overapplied overhead is shown as a credit to the Manufacturing Overhead Variance account.

Why does actual overhead typically differ from applied overhead? Remember that applied overhead is based on a predetermined overhead rate (i.e., estimates). Managers use the five-step approach (as outlined in Section 14.5(b)(vi) of this chapter) to establish the predetermined rate. New Abilities *estimated* total overhead manufacturing costs of $1,200,000 and machine-hours of 10,000. Thus, for every machine-hour incurred, the firm applies $120 in manufacturing overhead to WIP. Because we base this application of overhead on budgeted amounts, total applied overhead will not equal actual overhead at the end of the accounting period (unless, of course, budgeted amounts equal actual amounts).

NEW ABILITIES MANUFACTURING COMPANY

January

Accounts Payable

Debit		Credit	
		(1)	60,000
		(4)	46,000

Materials Inventory

Debit		Credit	
BB	10,000	(2)	42,000
(1)	60,000		
EB	28,000		

Work in Process Inventory

Debit		Credit	
BB	61,000	(6)	195,000
(2) M	40,000		
(3) L	80,000		
(5) O	96,000		
EB	82,000		

Finished Goods Inventory

Debit		Credit	
BB	-0-	(7)	83,000
(6)	195,000		
EB	112,000		

Cost of Goods Sold

Debit		Credit	
(7)	83,000		

Wages Payable

Debit		Credit	
		(3)	110,000

Manufacturing Overhead

Debit		Credit	
(2)	2,000		
(3)	30,000		
(4)	72,000	(8)	104,000

Manufacturing Overhead Applied

Debit		Credit	
		(5)	96,000
(8)	96,000		

Manufacturing Overhead Variance

Debit		Credit	
(8)	8,000		

Prepaid Expenses

Debit		Credit	
		(4)	7,000

Accumulated Depreciation

Debit		Credit	
		(4)	19,000

EXHIBIT 14.10 SUMMARY OF JOB COSTING

New Abilities Manufacturing Company
Income Statement
For the Month Ended January 31

Sales Revenue	$120,000
Cost of goods sold (see statement below)	83,000
Underapplied manufacturing overhead	8,000[a]
Gross Margin	29,000
Less marketing and administrative costs	10,000
Operating profit	$ 19,000

Cost of Goods Sold Statement
For the Month Ended January 31

Beginning work in process inventory, January 1	$ 61,000		
Manufacturing costs during the month			
Direct materials			
Beginning inventory, January 1	$ 10,000		
Add purchases	60,000		
Materials Available	70,000		
Less ending inventory, January 31	28,000		
Total materials used	42,000		
Less: Indirect materials used	2,000		
Direct materials put into process		$40,000	
Direct labor		80,000	
Manufacturing overhead		96,000	
Total manufacturing costs incurred during the month			216,000[b]
Total costs of work in process during the month			277,000
Less work in process inventory, January 31			82,000
Cost of goods manufactured during the period			195,000[c]
Beginning finished goods inventory, January 1			-0-
Less ending finished goods inventory, January 31			112,000
Cost of goods sold			$ 83,000[d]

[a] This is the amount of manufacturing overhead underapplied during the month.

[b] This amount equals the total debits made to Work in Process Inventory during January (not counting the beginning balance.)

[c] This amount equals the total debits to Finished Goods Inventory during January.

[d] This amount equals the total credits to Finish Goods inventory during January.

Exhibit 14.11 Income Statement

For example, budgeted overhead manufacturing costs (the numerator in calculating a predetermined overhead rate) of $1,200,000 may have been based on prior year costs and, thus, not adjusted for increases in utility rates, rent, or other overhead costs.

(v) Reporting This Information to Management. At year-end, the manufacturing overhead variance is either (1) prorated to Work in Process Inventory, Finished Goods Inventory, and Costs of Goods Sold or (2) assigned in total to Cost of Goods Sold. Exhibit 14.12 recaps the costs of jobs before proration at New Abilities Manufacturing.

METHOD 1: PRORATE THE OVERHEAD VARIANCE

If the firm prorates the variance to Work in Process Inventory, Finished Goods Inventory, and Cost of Goods Sold, it will adjust the cost of each job to approximate actual cost. For New Abilities, Exhibit 14.12 shows the status and cost of each job before prorating the overhead variance. We prorate the variance so that each account and job bears a share of the $8,000 manufacturing overhead variance. For our example, this share is proportional to the overhead applied to the account during the month, as shown in Exhibit 14.13. Firms can use other methods for allocating the overhead variance, including the total cost of jobs before the allocation.

We make the following entry to prorate the variance:

Cost of Goods Sold.	1,000	
Finished Goods Inventory.	4,000	
Work in Process Inventory.	3,000	
Manufacturing Overhead Variance		8,000

METHOD 2: ASSIGN THE VARIANCE TO COST OF GOODS SOLD

Many companies do not prorate the manufacturing overhead variance to inventories and Cost of Goods Sold; instead they transfer the entire variance to Cost of Goods Sold for both internal and external reporting using the following journal entry:

Cost of Goods Sold	8,000	
Manufacturing Overhead Variance		8,000

In a company with many kinds of products and inventories, proration can become complicated. If the amounts to prorate are immaterial relative to net income for external reporting or do not affect managerial decisions, the firm may not need to prorate (note, however, that laws generally require proration for financial reporting and tax purposes). The difference in net income between prorating the variance and assigning it to Cost of Goods Sold depends on timing. A company will eventually expense (or credit to expense) any difference between actual and applied overhead, even if the company prorates. Prorating the overhead variance merely defers expensing the portion allocated to

NEW ABILITIES MANUFACTURING COMPANY

Job No.	Beginning Inventory	Direct Materials	Direct Labor	Manufacturing Overhead Applied in January	Total Costs Charged to Jobs	Status of Job at End of Month
101.	$61,000	-0-	$10,000	$12,000	$ 83,000	Cost of Goods Sold
102.	-0-	$24,000	40,000	48,000	112,000	Finished Goods Inventory
103.	-0-	16,000	30,000	36,000	82,000	Work in Process Inventory
	$61,000	$40,000	$80,000	$96,000	$277,000	

EXHIBIT 14.12 COSTS OF JOBS BEFORE PRORATING THE MANUFACTURING OVERHEAD VARIANCE

		New Abilities Manufacturing Company			
	(1)	(2)	(3)	(4)	(5)
Job	Account	Manufacturing Overhead Applied in January[a]	Percentage of Total Overhead Applied in January[b]	Overhead to Be Prorated	Prorated Variance
101.	Cost of Good Sold	$12,000	12.5 ×	$8,000 =	$1,000
102.	Finished Goods Inventory	48,000	50.0 ×	8,000 =	4,000
103.	Work in Process Inventory	36,000	37.5 ×	8,000 =	3,000
		$96,000	100.0		$8,000

[a] $120 per machine-hour

[b] 12.5% = $12,000 ÷ $96,000; 50.0% = $48,000 ÷ $96,000; 37.5% = $36,000 ÷ 96,000.

Exhibit 14.13 Prorating Variances

inventories until they are sold. For managerial purposes, one must asses the merit of revaluing work in process and finished goods inventories to actual cost. A large overhead variance may affect some cost control, performance evaluation, pricing, and other decisions, but proration probably will not prove worthwhile with a small variance.

Regardless of how the company disposes of the variance, managers need to understand why actual and applied overhead differ. Management may need to revise overhead rates, impose new cost control procedures, or take other action.

(vi) Interim Reporting. When companies use normal costing and do not close overhead accounts monthly, they have two ways to report the balance in the Manufacturing Overhead Variance account on financial statements. They can report the balance on the income statement (as a line item below cost of goods sold, for example), or carry it on the balance sheet as an adjustment to inventory. The first option treats the adjustment as a period cost, the second as a product cost.

Managers generally do not want to address this variance unless they believe that it indicates a problem. Regardless of managers' interest in this number (or lack thereof), we recommend reporting it as a separate line item on the income statement so they will notice it and take appropriate action (if any).

14.6 PROCESS COSTING

We now focus on *process costing*, which assigns costs equally to homogeneous units within a particular time period. Companies that have continuous flow production, such as BP (petroleum) and Dow Chemical (chemicals), use process costing.

Unlike job shops that record costs for specific jobs, companies with continuous flow production first assign costs to departments and then assign costs to the units (for example, barrels of petroleum) passing through the department. Exhibit 14.14 shows this distinction.

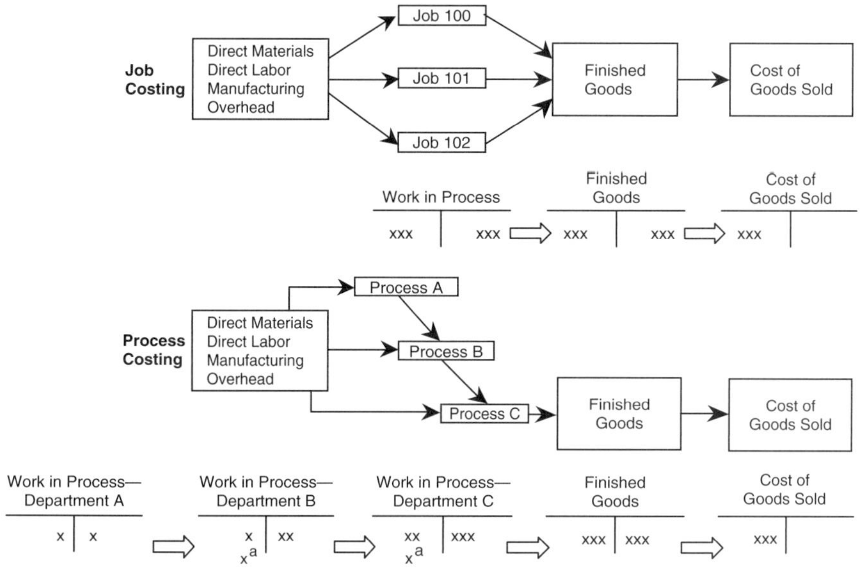

a Direct materials, labor, and manufacturing overhead added in production in the department

EXHIBIT 14.14 COMPARISON OF JOB AND PROCESS COSTING

(a) THE IMPORTANCE OF COST INFORMATION TO MANAGE PROCESSES. Imagine that you work for a consulting firm that sends you to help the manager of a Kellogg's cereal division. This expresses concern that competitors that produce generic cereals are pricing their products substantially below Kellogg's prices. (In this case, the producers sell the generic cereals under a store's name, such as Safeway or IGA, or as generic cereal without a brand name.) Kellogg's expects to charge a premium because of its well-known brand name, but it knows it will lose market share if the generic cereals are much cheaper.

The manager of the Kellogg's division wants to cut prices to compete with generic cereals. He does not want, however, to drop prices below costs. You first should help the division improve its cost system so it will know how much each cereal product costs. This section addresses this problem of learning the costs of products in a process (for items such as cereal).

Management commonly uses the costs assigned to products to help set prices, particularly in periods of severe competition or economic downturn. Companies also use these product costs to identify which products appear to be too costly and should be redesigned or dropped.

Firms also use costs assigned to products to assess inventory value for financial reporting purposes and to evaluate the efficiency of production operations.

(b) ASSIGNING COSTS TO PRODUCTS

(i) All Units Fully Completed (No Beginning or Ending WIP Inventory). This section explains how to assign costs to products using a five-step process, given two simple scenarios. The first scenario has no beginning or ending work in process (WIP) inventory. This commonly occurs in companies with successful just-in-time production. Some companies schedule production so that they will have no inventory at the end of a day because work in process could deteriorate or spoil.

Both scenarios involve a company named Color Enterprises that produces paint. During October, the blending department, which had no beginning inventory, started 8,000 units (measured in gallons). The plant incurred the following manufacturing costs in October:

Direct materials	$16,000
Conversion costs	5,600
Total costs to be assigned	$21,600

Color Enterprise's process costing system has two cost categories: direct materials and conversion costs. Conversion costs are direct labor and manufacturing overhead.

By the end of October, the company had completed all units placed into production in during the month. The unit cost of goods completed equals $2.70 (= $21,600/8,000). Broken into components, manufacturing unit costs are as follows:

Direct materials ($16,000/8,000)	$2.00
Conversion costs ($5,600/8,000)	0.70
Manufacturing unit cost of a completed unit	$2.70

Managers at Color Enterprises do not know that a particular gallon of paint cost $2.70—only that the average cost per gallon equaled $2.70.

(ii) Some Units Not Fully Completed (Ending WIP Inventory Exists). Assume the same facts as for the above scenario, except that, by the end of October, the firm had completed and transferred out of production only 6,000 of the 8,000 units started during the month. These 6,000 units were either sold or still in the finished goods warehouse at the end of October. The firm had added direct materials to the production process for all 8,000 units. It had incurred sufficient conversion costs to complete 6,000 units. Only 20 percent of the conversion costs had been incurred for the 2,000 units in ending WIP inventory.

Accountants assign these costs to ending WIP inventory and to units completed (transferred out of WIP inventory) by using the concept of equivalent unit (E.U.). An equivalent unit is the amount of work partially done translated into the work required to complete an equal number of whole units. If a company starts four units at the beginning of a month, and completes 25 percent of each unit at the end of the month, the cumulative work done on these units would be one equivalent unit. Exhibit 14.15 demonstrates the equivalent unit concept: two glasses of water one-half full are equivalent to one full glass.

For Color Enterprises:

- For direct materials, E.U. = 8,000.
- For conversion costs, E.U. = 6,400 units, or 6,000 completed and transferred out + 400 E.U. remaining in work in process. (400 E.U. = 2,000 × 20% complete for conversion costs)

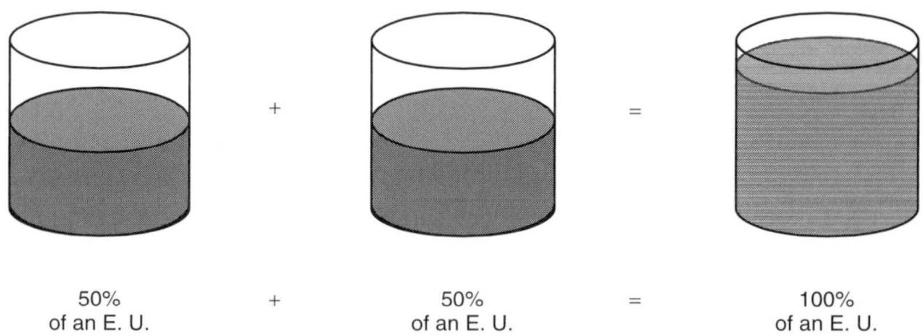

EXHIBIT 14.15 EQUIVALENT UNITS (E.U.) CONCEPT

Exhibits 14.16 and 14.17 report this information and the costs of units produced, transferred out, and in ending inventory.

Note that overstating equivalent units could lead to overstating ending inventory and understating losses. This occurred with Rynco Scientific Corporation, a contact lens manufacturer. After investigating Rynco's method for computing equivalent units of production, the Securities and Exchange Commission (SEC) alleged that Rynco committed financial fraud by erroneously calculating the equivalent units of production. This calculation allegedly overstated ending inventory and understated losses. As a result of the SEC's investigation, Rynco agreed to hire an accounting firm to conduct a thorough study of its financial statements for a five-year period, and agreed to restate its financial statements.

Next we discuss the more complex task of accounting for costs when companies have beginning *and* ending work in process inventory exists.

		(Step 2) Equivalent Units	
	(Step 1) Physical Units	Direct Materials	Conversion Costs
Flow of Units			
Units to be accounted for			
Beginning work in process inventory	-0-		
Units started this period	8,000		
Total units to account for	8,000		
Units accounted for			
Completed and transferred out	6,000	6,000	6,000
In ending work in process inventory	2,000	2,000	400[a]
Total units accounted for	8,000	8,000	6,400

[a] 2,000 units x 20% complete

EXHIBIT 14.16 EQUIVALENT UNITS

	Total	Direct Materials	Conversion Costs
Flow of Costs			
Costs to be accounted for (Step 3)			
Costs in beginning of work in process inventory.	-0-	-0-	-0-
Current period costs.	$21,600	$16,000	$5,600
Total costs to be accounted for	$21,600	16,000	5,600
Costs per equivalent unit (Step 4)		$ 2[a]	$0.875[b]
Costs accounted for (step 5)			
Costs assigned to units transferred out.	$17,250	$12,000[c]	$5,250[d]
Costs of ending inventory	4,350	4,000[e]	350[f]
Total costs accounted for.	$21,600	$16,000	$5,600

[a] $2 = $16,000 ÷ $8,000 E.U. from Exhibit 14.16

[b] $0.875 = $5,600 ÷ 6,400 E.U. from Exhibit 14.16

[c] $12,000 = $2 x 6,000 E.U. from Exhibit 14.16

[d] $5,250 = $0.875 x 6,000 E.U. from Exhibit 14.16

[e] $4,000 = $2 x 2,000 E.U. from Exhibit 14.16

[f] $350 = $0.875 x 400 E.U. from Exhibit 14.16

EXHIBIT 14.17 PRODUCTION COSTS

(c) ASSIGNING COSTS TO INVENTORY

(i) Weighted-Average Costing. Companies generally use either first-in, first-out (FIFO) or weighted average costing methods. *Weighted-average costing*, which we discuss first, combines the costs in beginning inventory with costs incurred during the period to compute unit costs. Panel A of Exhibit 14.18 shows a diagram of unit flows for Color Enterprises's blending department for the month of December. We assume the following:

- The department had 2,000 units in beginning WIP inventory, which it finished during December.
- Of the 12,000 units that the firm started in December, the blending department completed 8,000, and had the remaining 4,000 partially completed units in ending WIP inventory.

Weighted-average costing does not require separating units or costs in beginning inventory from those started in the current period. Panel B of Exhibit 14.18 shows the costs to be as follows:

Beginning inventory	$ 3,000
Costs incurred during December	$27,000

The manager of the blending department must account for $30,000 in costs for the month of December.

The question marks in Panel B of Exhibit 14.18 indicate the numbers we need to calculate; namely, how much of the $30,000 should the firm assign to the 10,000 units transferred out? How much of the $30,000 should the firm assign to the partially completed 4,000 units in ending WIP inventory?

SPIRIT BEVERAGES
Blending Department
Month Ending December 31

Panel A

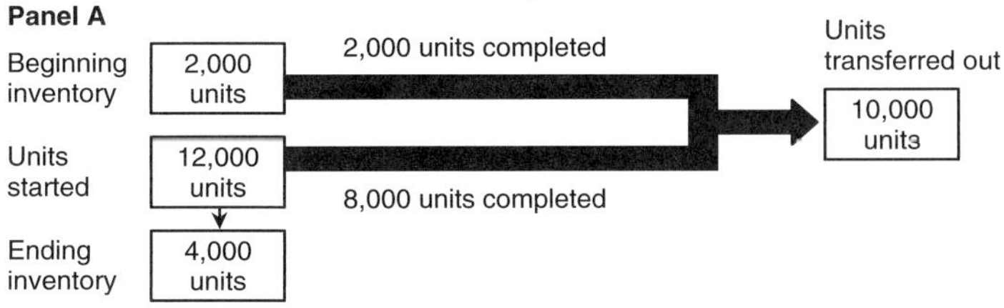

Panel B

Cost and Unit Data	**Units**	**Percent Complete: Direct Materials**	**Percent Complete: Conversion Costs**	**Total Costs**
Beginning work in process, Inventory, December 1	2,000	40%	80%	$ 3,000
Costs incurred in December				27,000
Transfers out of blending	10,000	100	100	?
Ending work in process, Inventory, December 31	4,000	25	60	?

EXHIBIT **14.18** DATA FOR BLENDING OPERATION

(ii) Equivalent units. We calculate equivalent units separately for direct materials and for conversion costs because Color Enterprise's WIP inventory is at different stages of completion for these two cost categories. Units transferred out are 100 percent completed. Panel B of Ending WIP inventory is 25 percent complete for direct materials and 60 percent complete for conversion costs.

So we compute equivalent units of work completed in December as follows:

	Direct Materials	Conversion Costs
Units transferred out	10,000	10,000
Units in ending WIP inventory		
Materials: 4,000 × 25%	1,000	
Conversion: 4,000 × 60%		2,400
Total equivalent units	11,000	12,400

Assume that total costs are separated into direct materials and conversion costs as follows:

	Total Costs	Direct Materials	Conversion Costs
Costs to be accounted for			
Costs in beginning WIP inventory	$ 3,000	$ 2,000	$1,000
Current period costs	27,000	20,000	7,000
Total costs to be accounted for	$30,000	$22,000	$8,000

We compute costs per equivalent unit with a straightforward calculation, simply dividing costs by equivalent units, as follows:

	Direct Materials	Conversion Costs
Total costs to be accounted for	$22,000	$ 8,000
Divided by equivalent units.	$11,000	$12,400
Equals cost per equivalent unit.	$ 2.00	$ 0.645

Finally, we multiply the cost per equivalent unit by the number of equivalent units in ending WIP inventory and transferred out for the period. This computation accounts for the $30,000 costs, as follows:

Transferred out		
Direct materials (10,000 units × $2)	$20,000	
Conversion costs (10,000 units × $0.645) . . .	6,450	
Total transferred out		$26,450
Ending work in process, December 31		
Direct materials (1,000 E.U. × $2)	$ 2,000	
Conversion costs (2,400 E.U. × $0.645).	1,550 (rounded)	
Total work in process.		3,550
Total costs accounted for		$30,000

(iii) Presentation in T-Accounts. Exhibit 14.19 shows the flow of costs through WIP for the blending department, with the top panel showing only the costs to be accounted for, and the bottom panel showing the costs after accounting for costs as transferred out or in ending inventory.

(iv) Reporting this Information to Managers: The Production Cost Report. Exhibit 14.20 presents a production cost report for the blending department of Spirit Beverages for

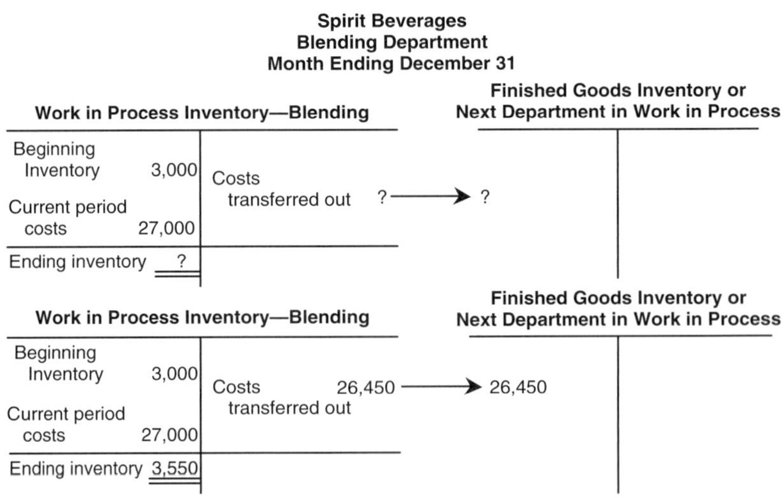

EXHIBIT 14.19 COST FLOWS—WEIGHTED AVERAGE

SPIRIT BEVERAGES
BLENDING DEPARTMENT
MONTH ENDING DECEMBER 31

		(Section 2) Equivalent Units	
	(Section 1) Physical Units	Direct Materials	Conversion Costs
Flow of Units			
Units to be accounted for			
Beginning WIP inventory	2,000		
Units started this period	12,000		
Total Units to Account For	14,000		
Units accounted for			
Completed and transferred out	10,000	10,000	10,000
In ending WIP inventory	4,000	1,000[a]	2400[b]
Total Units Accounted For	14,000	11,000	12,400

	Costs (Sections 3 through 5)		
	Total	Direct Materials	Conversion Costs
Flow of Costs			
Costs to be accounted for (Section 3)			
Costs in beginning WIP inventory	$ 3,000	$ 2,000	$1,000
Current period costs	27,000	20,000	7,000
Total Costs to Be Accounted For	$30,000	$22,000	$8,000
Costs per equivalent unit (Section 4)		$ 2.00[c]	$0.645[d]
Costs accounted for (Section 5)			
Costs assigned to units transferred out	$26,450	$ 20,000[e]	$6,450[f]
Costs of ending WIP inventory	3,550	2,000[g]	1,550[h]
Total Costs Accounted For	$30,000	$22,000	$8,000

[a] Ending inventory is 25 percent complete. 1,000 E.U. = 25% x 4,000 units
[b] Ending inventory is 60 percent complete. 2,400 E.U. = 60% x 4,000 units
[c] $2.00 = $22,000 ÷ 11,000 E.U.
[d] $0.645 = $8,000 ÷ 12,400 E.U.
[e] $20,000 = 10,000 E.U. x $2 per E.U.
[f] $6,450 = 10,000 E.U. x $0.645 per E.U.
[g] $2,000 = 1,000 E.U. x $2 per E.U.
[h] $1,550 (rounded) = 2,400 E.U. x $0.645 per E.U. + $2 rounding error

EXHIBIT 14.20 PRODUCTION COST REPORT—WEIGHTED AVERAGE

December. This report summarizes the production and cost results for a period. Managers use this information to monitor the flow of production and costs, to evaluate whether inventory levels are getting too high, whether costs are sufficiently low, or whether the number of units produced is too low.

(d) ASSIGNING COSTS TO PRODUCTS USING FIRST-IN, FIRST-OUT (FIFO) COSTING

(i) Differences between FIFO and Weighted-Average Costing. Weighted-average costing mixes current period costs with the costs from prior periods that are in beginning inventory. This mixing makes it impossible for managers to know the *current period* cost of manufacturing the product. *First-in, first-out (FIFO) costing addresses this problem by assuming* that the first units worked on are the first units transferred out of a production department. FIFO separates current period costs from those in beginning inventory. In FIFO costing, the costs in beginning inventory are transferred out in a lump sum. FIFO costing does not mix costs from prior periods (that are in beginning inventory) with current period costs.

To illustrate accounting for process costing using FIFO, we use the data from the Color Enterprises example. This enables you to compare FIFO and weighted-average costing and to see how the results differ. Recall the following facts:

		Costs	
	Units	Direct Materials	Conversion Costs
Beginning WIP inventory....	2,000	$2,000	$1,000
Current period............	12,000	20,000	7,000
Transferred out...........	10,000	?	?
Ending WIP inventory	4,000	?	?

Recall that *beginning* WIP inventory is 40 percent complete for direct materials and 80 percent complete for conversion costs; *ending* WIP inventory is 25 percent complete for direct labor and 60 percent complete for conversion costs.

Under FIFO, we compute equivalent units as follows:

1. *Equivalent units to complete beginning WIP inventory.* For Color Enterprises, 2,000 units in beginning inventory were 40 percent complete for direct materials and 80 percent complete for conversion costs at the beginning of the period. Completing the beginning inventory required 1,200 equivalent units for direct materials [= (100% × 40%) × 2,000 units], and 400 equivalent units for conversion costs [= (100% × 80%) × 2,000 units].
2. *Equivalent units of goods started and completed during the current period.* We can derive the units started and completed from our knowledge about the physical flow of units. Because manufacturing started 12,000 units in December and 4,000 units remained in ending inventory, manufacturing must have completed the remaining 8,000 units. Thus, 8,000 units were started and completed. We also get that result by observing that, of the 10,000 units completed during December, 2,000 came from beginning inventory, so the remaining 8,000 units completed must have been started during December. Either way, manufacturing started and

completed 8,000 units. These 8,000 units started and completed represent 8,000 equivalent units produced during the current period for both direct materials and conversion costs.

3. *Equivalent units of goods still in ending WIP inventory.* Ending inventory of 4,000 units is 25 percent complete with respect to direct materials and 60 percent complete for conversion costs. Thus, there are 1,000 equivalent units (= 25% × 4,000) for direct materials and 2,400 equivalent units (= 60% × 4,000) for conversion costs in ending WIP inventory.

(ii) Compute Costs per Equivalent Unit. FIFO bases the costs per E.U. on the costs incurred this period, $27,000, and the equivalent units produced this period, the sum of those computed in Steps 1 through 3, above (10,200 for direct materials and 10,800 for conversion costs). In formula form,

Cost per equivalent unit = Current period costs/ E.U. of production this period

Note that the numerator includes only current period costs. The FIFO method excludes the beginning WIP costs from the cost per equivalent unit calculation. We show calculations for direct materials and conversion costs next.

- *Direct materials*

Cost per equivalent unit = $20,000/10,200 equivalent units
= $1.96078 per E.U.

- *Conversion costs*

Cost per equivalent unit = $7,000/10,800 equivalent units
= $0.64815 per E.U.

(iii) Assign Costs to Goods Transferred Out and to Ending WIP Inventory. The cost of goods transferred out includes costs from beginning inventory and current period costs.

Costs in beginning WIP inventory	$ 3,000
Costs to complete beginning inventory	2,612 (1)
Cost of the 8,000 units started and completed this period	20,872 (2)
Cost of ending WIP inventory	3,516 (3)
Total costs accounted for	$30,000

Computations follow:

(1) Costs in December to complete beginning inventory = (1,200 E.U. × $1.96078 for direct materials) + (400 E.U. × $0.64815 for conversion costs).

(2) Costs of 8,000 units started and completed = (8,000 E.U. × $1.96078 for direct materials) + (8,000 E.U. × $0.64815 for conversion costs).

(3) Costs of ending WIP inventory = (1,000 E.U. × $1.96078 for direct materials) + (2,400 E.U. × $0.64815 for conversion costs).

(iv) Important Comparisons of FIFO and Weighted-Average Costing. Note that the costs to be accounted for in December, $30,000, equal the costs accounted for, $30,000, whether accountants use FIFO or weighted-average costing. The following lists comparative unit costs:

	Direct Materials	Conv. Costs	Total
Weighted-average cost per unit....	$2.00	$0.65	$2.65
FIFO..............................	$1.96	$0.65	$2.61

In this case, the unit costs are nearly equal. Recall that the unit costs for FIFO include only current period (i.e., December) costs, whereas the unit costs for weighted-average costing include costs from the previous period that were in December's beginning WIP inventory. The results for Color Enterprises indicate that direct materials costs were lower in December than in previous months.

14.7 OPERATION COSTING

This chapter has discussed job costing and process costing systems. Companies use job costing systems for customized products, such as construction jobs, movies, and consulting services. Companies use process costing for continuous flow processes that produce identical units, such as soft drinks, cereal, or bricks. We now examine *operation costing systems*, which are hybrids of job and process costing systems, as shown in Exhibit 14.21. A company using operation costing typically uses a variety of different materials for products that pass through the same operation. Such products would include shoes, shirts, and cars.

An *operation* is a standardized method of making a product. For example, a motorcycle assembly plant makes several models on the same assembly line. Each model has handlebars. The common operation is installing handlebars, but different models could have different styles of handlebars. Companies use operation costing in manufacturing goods that have some common characteristics plus some individual characteristics.

(a) PRODUCT COSTING IN OPERATIONS. In *product costing operations*, each product passing through a particular operation typically has identical conversion costs but different direct materials costs. Accountants treat the conversion costs like process costing and the materials costs like job costing.

For example, assume that Spota Motorcycle Company is a subsidiary of a major automobile manufacturer. Spota, which operates in a developing country, makes two models of cars: Jets and Sports. The Sport has a larger engine and generally more costly direct materials. Exhibit 14.22 shows the flow of products through departments (assume that

Job Costing	**Operation Costing**	**Process Costing**
Job shops making customized products	Operations: Separate materials for each batch; common operations	Mass production in continuous processes

EXHIBIT 14.21 COMPARISON OF THREE COSTING METHODS

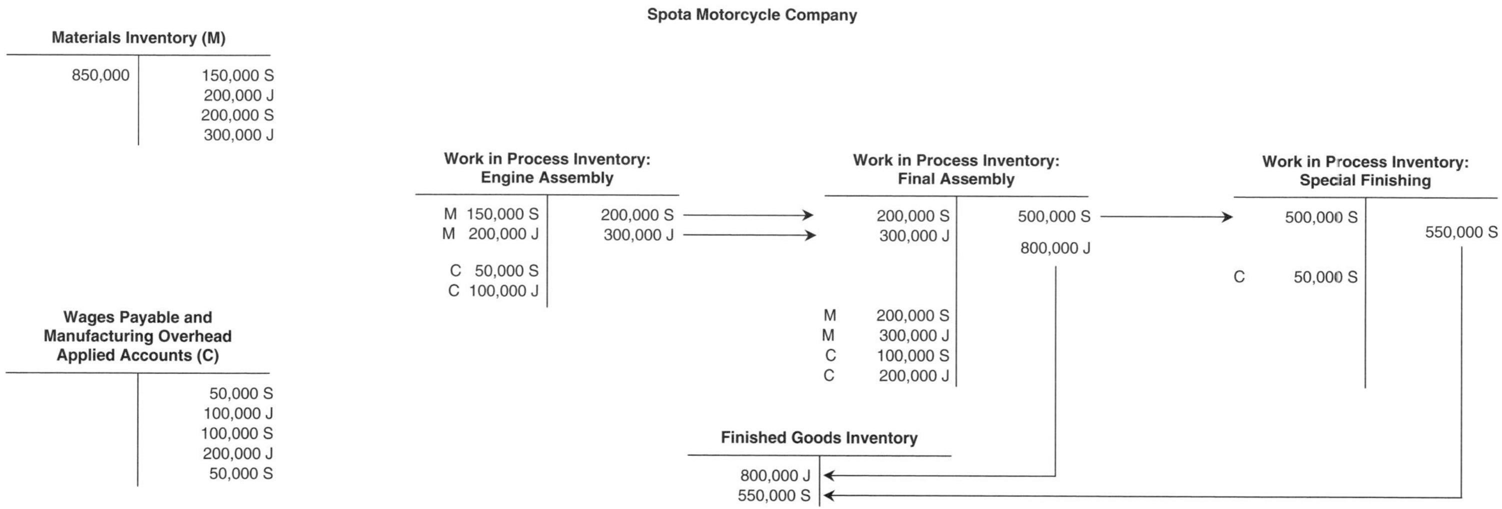

S = Sports
J = Jets
M = Direct materials, credit to Materials Inventory
C = Conversion costs, credit to Wages Payable and Manufacturing Overhead Applied Accounts

EXHIBIT 14.22 COST FLOWS THROUGH T-ACCOUNTS FOR OPERATION COSTING

each department has one operation). Jets pass through only the first two departments, where both types of cars have identical operations, but Sports pass through all three departments. The Spota Motorcycle Company adds direct materials costs to both models in Engine Assembly and Final Assembly. The company incurs conversion costs for Jets in the first two departments and for Sports in all three departments.

(b) ILLUSTRATION OF OPERATION COSTING. Assume that Spota Motorcycle Company management gave the following production work order for the month.

SPOTA MOTORCYCLE COMPANY

	Work Order 101		Work Order 102	
Number and model of motorcycles	100	Sports	200	Jets
Work order costs				
Direct materials				
Engine parts	$150,000		$200,000	
Other parts	200,000		300,000	
Conversion costs				
(direct labor and manufacturing overhead)				
Engine assembly	50,000		100,000	
Final assembly	100,000		200,000	
Special finishing	50,000		0	
Total costs	$550,000		$800,000	

Note that the materials costs per unit for Sports exceed those for Jets, but the conversion costs per unit are equal for the two operations that both models pass through. For example, engine assembly conversion costs are \$500 per unit for both models (\$500 = \$50,000/100 units for Sports and \$500 = \$100,000/200 units for Jets). Exhibit 14.22 shows the flow of these costs through T-accounts to Finished Goods Inventory.

14.8 DESIGNING COST SYSTEMS FOR MANAGERIAL PURPOSES

This chapter and all others in this book rely on several key themes that have proven critical to successfully designing a cost system for managerial purposes. Before designing a new cost system, we must ask several important questions: How will managers use the information that the system provides? What types of decisions will managers make using the cost information? Will benefits of improved decision making outweigh the costs of implementing the new cost system? These are valid and important questions to ask. When designing a new cost system for managers, firms should follow three guidelines:

1. **Cost systems should have a decision focus.** Cost systems must meet the needs of the decision makers. Remember that the decision makers are the customers (or users) of cost accounting. If, for example, the president of a company wants a customer profitability analysis, the decision focus is the most profitable customers. If the cost system does not provide these data, it will not meet the president's needs. Clearly, one must design the cost system to facilitate the user's decision making.
2. **Managers use different cost information for different purposes.** What works for one purpose might not work for another purpose. For example, financial

reporting requires the use of cost information from the past. Managerial decision-makers, however, require information about the future. They often use cost information to assess departmental profitability; they use other information to review customer profitability. Clearly, the cost information must provide the appropriate data for its intended purpose.

3. **Cost information for managerial purposes must meet the cost-benefit test.** One can always improve cost information. However, the benefits of improvements (i.e., better decision making) must outweigh the costs to make the improvements. For example, if customer profitability analyses do not provide the president with additional information needed to make better decisions, the costs of preparing this information may outweigh the benefits. If the president, however, uses this information to decide where to focus marketing efforts—and the information did not exist previously—the benefits *may* outweigh the costs. Cost information systems can become costly to implement, so management should ask one basic question before establishing a new system: Will the benefits outweigh the costs?

14.9 SUMMARY

This chapter compares job costing systems (which record costs for individual jobs, such as construction work), process costing systems (which average costs across identical units, such as soft drink syrup) and operations costing (a hybrid of the two, such as automobile manufacturing). Most companies have elements of all three production methods. The chapter introduces the basic cost flow model ($BB + TI - TO = EB$) and shows how one can use it to solve for unknown amounts in accounts and to detect fraud. The chapter also discusses just-in-time (JIT) production methods and the backflush costing system that JIT companies use to calculate work in process inventory. The chapter closes by discussing the important themes that underlie the design of successful cost systems: (a) cost systems should have a decision focus, (b) companies use different cost information for different purposes, and (c) cost information systems should meet the cost-benefit test.

CHAPTER 15

STANDARD COST SYSTEMS

JAMES A. LARGAY III, PHD, CPA
Lehigh University

CONTENTS

15.1 INTRODUCTION 425

15.2 REVIEW OF STANDARD COSTS 426
- (a) Effect of Standards on Behavior 426
- (b) Importance of Learning and the Learning Curve 427
- (c) Illustration of Standard Cost Calculations 428

15.3 DEVIATIONS FROM STANDARD COST: VARIANCE ANALYSIS 428
- (a) Two-Factor Variances in General 428
- (b) Raw Material Variances 432
- (c) Direct Labor Variances 434
- (d) Flexible Budget Preparation 435
- (e) Variable Overhead Variances 435
- (f) Fixed Overhead Variances 436
- (g) Three-Way Analysis of Overhead Variances 439
- (h) Three-Factor Variances in General 439
- (i) Production Mix and Yield Variances 440
- (j) Sales and Profit Variances 441

15.4 ACCOUNTING ENTRIES IN A STANDARD COST SYSTEM 444
- (a) Accounting Disposition of Variances 445
- (b) Proration of Production Cost Variances 446

15.5 INTEGRATED FORMAT FOR SALES AND PRODUCTION COST VARIANCE 446

15.6 VARIANCE ANALYSIS IN ACTIVITY-BASED COSTING 449
- (a) Secondary Cost Driver Considerations 452
- (b) Setup and Batch Considerations 452
- (c) Numerical Illustrations 453

15.7 *EX POST* VARIANCE ANALYSIS 454
- (a) Introduction to *Ex Post* Analysis. 454
- (b) *Ex Post* Analysis in a Simple Marginal Analysis Model 455

15.8 THE DECISION TO INVESTIGATE COST VARIANCES 457
- (a) The In-Control/Out-of-Control Dichotomy 457
- (b) Costs and Benefits from Investigating Variances 457
- (c) The Control Chart Approach 459
- (d) The Decision-Theoretic Approach 461

15.9 SUMMARY 464

BIBLIOGRAPHY 464

15.1 INTRODUCTION

Cost accounting systems have two principal functions. The first measures *product costs to calculate income and value inventory.* The second aids in *cost and production control* to help management better identify problem areas and formulate corrective actions. Systems that accumulate only actual production costs generally suffice for product costing but tend to fall short for control purposes. Firms usually compare a *standard* or *yardstick* against actual results to facilitate cost control. Favorable or unfavorable deviations from reasonable standards provide important data to management. For example, when such a comparison indicates that actual costs exceed the standard, management can investigate and take corrective action. When actual costs are below the standard, investigation may reveal increased efficiency that can lead to significant cost savings.

Standards appear in the form of production costs, budgets, and sales targets; broadly speaking, they represent management's plans. Firms that quickly know when actual results differ from planned results may have better control of costs. This chapter describes the role of standards in an accounting system, with particular emphasis on the cost accounting system. The chapter also examines the use of standards as control devices in areas outside the cost accounting system.

15.2 REVIEW OF STANDARD COSTS

Standard costs are estimates of what *should* occur under given operating conditions. They reflect assumptions about the level of production, prices of input resources, specifications of materials, competence of the labor force, production technology, and, perhaps, the state of the economy. These predetermined targets reflect acceptable levels of effectiveness and efficiency. Moreover, standards provide a means for communicating goals for satisfactory performance so that employees and their supervisors know what the firm expects of them.

The most useful standards are those considered *currently attainable,* given input prices, the production process, normal efficiency, and so forth. Companies should revise standards periodically so that they reflect current conditions. They should reflect the firm's goals in the production area and should be achievable. Other concepts of standards include *basic standards* and *theoretical standards.* Companies rarely change *basic standards,* which they can use to highlight trends over a long period of time. *Theoretical standards* reflect ideal conditions, such as maximum capacity, no downtime, no absenteeism, and so forth. Firms use theoretical standards as ideal benchmarks, even though they will never attain such measures. Basic standards may soon become obsolete in a world of rapidly changing prices and technology.

Currently attainable standards, then, appear to have the greatest potential for motivating employees and for effectively controlling operations. This chapter focuses on such standards.

(a) EFFECT OF STANDARDS ON BEHAVIOR. Effective standards must have employees' acceptance and motivate the desired behavior. The following lists some of the factors that firms should consider when setting standards, keeping in mind that idiosyncracies in people and firms affect the generality of these factors.

- Do the standards *validly measure* important aspects of performance and do equitable rewards follow from achieving the standards? People seek to look good on those dimensions of their performance that the company measures and rewards.
- Are the standards *both achievable and sufficiently challenging* to be taken seriously? Evidence associates feelings of accomplishment, competence, and growth with achievement of performance in the 50 percent likelihood range of occurring.
- Do the standards result from a *participative process* with mutual communication of information that fosters trust, self-esteem, and the buy-in that stimulates intrinsic motivation?

- Does the standards system provide *feedback on performance* during or soon after task completion? Timely receipt of knowledge that one has met or exceeded goals soon after one completes the specific task motivates future performance.

(b) IMPORTANCE OF LEARNING AND THE LEARNING CURVE. New or unfamiliar operations usually require progressively less time with repetition. *The reduction of cost due to a process being learned through repetition is the learning effect.* Early applications of learning occurred in airframe and weapons manufacture—the number of direct labor-hours required to build an aircraft body declined at a constant rate as the number of units built increased. A commonly observed constant rate of decline gave rise to the so-called 80-percent learning curve, where 80 percent represents the reduced cumulative average labor cost per unit as production doubles. Exhibit 15.1 illustrates an example of an 80-percent learning curve.

The learning curve is a well-established, practical phenomenon, applicable to setting labor time standards and labor-generated overhead cost standards. Because the learning effect tends to level out as the process transitions from the startup (i.e., learning phase of production) to the steady-state phase, standards will change only during the learning phase. Standards formulated during the learning phase should progressively reflect the learning changes. Applying standards during the startup phase that erroneously reflect steady-state production and prove too difficult to attain will not motivate good performance.

Theorists and practitioners often express learning curves in terms of logarithms to restate the curve as a straight line, linear in the logarithms. The learning curve expression is

$$T_N = KN^s$$

where

T_N = effort, such as labor-hours, required to produce the Nth unit

N = unit number

K = a constant, the effort such as labor-hours required to produce the first unit

s = learning rate; a negative constant = –.80 for an 80 percent learning curve

then

$\log T_N$ = log K – $s \log N$, a log-linear expression.

Managers should compare standards based on a projected learning curve with actual experience at frequent intervals, and adjust them if necessary. One can accomplish this by plotting actual observations against the projected learning curve on log-log graph

Quantity		Time in Minutes	
Per lot	Cumulative	Cumulative	Cumulative Average per unit
10	10	300	30.0
10	20	480	(30.0 × 80%) = 24.0
20	40	768	(24.0 × 80%) = 19.2
40	80	1,232	(19.2 × 80%) = 15.4
80	160	1,968	(15.4 × 80%) = 12.3

EXHIBIT 15.1 AN 80 PERCENT LEARNING CURVE

paper. Or, with sufficient observations, one can use regression analysis to estimate the learning rate *s*. For more on this subject, see Ostwald's book listed in the Bibliography.

(c) ILLUSTRATION OF STANDARD COST CALCULATIONS. The most relevant standards are those formulated for relatively stable operations or processes. Many manufacturing operations have large numbers of identical, repetitive operations and inflexible specifications for the use of materials and parts. Jobs on an assembly line, steel sheets used in stamping appliance cabinets, and sorting operations in a clearinghouse all provide sound bases for establishing standards.

To develop standards, one usually starts at the most detailed level possible to estimate the cost of a direct labor-hour and a unit of material, when these are cost drivers. One can establish the *standard direct cost* by calculating the number of direct labor-hours and units of material required to fabricate a unit of final product. Cost accountants add an appropriate share of variable and fixed manufacturing overhead to develop the standard cost of a unit (or batch) of product. To prepare a production budget, one then multiplies standard unit costs by planned production levels.

Exhibit 15.2 shows how the Argosy Corporation calculates the inputs (time and material) and the price of the inputs for two different product lines, a regular and a super model. The regular model requires less time and materials, both at less expensive rates than those of the super model. The exhibit also shows how the company calculates and allocates variable and fixed overhead on a per-unit basis. Thus, the total per-unit standard costs for the regular model equals $16.50 and for the super model equals $24.00.

If Argosy expects to produce 10,000 of both the Regular and Super models next period, the production budget is $405,000 [= (10,000 × $16.50) + (10,000 × $24.00)].

15.3 DEVIATIONS FROM STANDARD COST: VARIANCE ANALYSIS

Evaluating deviations between actual results and the existing standards uses the techniques of *cost variance analysis*. One can categorize cost variances into two groups:

1. Price, rate or spending variances
2. Quantity, efficiency or volume variances

These variances measure the differences between an actual cost and a standard cost. The price/quantity differentiation highlights the portions of the total variance attributable to (1) deviations from standard input prices and (2) deviations from standard input quantities. This is known as *the two-factor variance model.*

(a) TWO-FACTOR VARIANCES IN GENERAL. Let P_a = actual price, Q_a = actual quantity, P_s = standard price, and Q_s = standard quantity. Then

$$\begin{aligned} \text{Actual Cost} &= P_a Q_a \\ \text{Standard Cost} &= P_s Q_s \\ \text{Total Variance} &= \text{Actual Cost} - \text{Standard Cost} \\ &= P_a Q_a - P_s Q_s \end{aligned}$$

Exhibit 15.3 graphically represents the total variance.

Input Resource	Units required (how determined)	Price	(source)	Extensions
	Regular Model			
Direct labor	1.5 hours (time and motion studies)	\$4.00/hour	(union contract)	\$ 6.00
Direct materials:				
A.	2 lb (engineering specifications and	\$2.00/lb	(current replacement cost	4.00
B.	2 lb material usage studies)	1.00/lb	from suppliers)	2.00
Variable overhead ...	—	\$1.75/DLH	(flexible budget)[1]	2.625
Fixed overhead......	—	\$1.25/DLH	(flexible budget and normal activity estimate)[2]	1.875
Total				\$16.50
	Super Model			
Direct labor	2 hours (time and motion studies)	\$4.00/hour	(union contract)	\$ 8.00
Direct materials:	(engineering specifications and		(current replacement cost	
A.	5 lb material usage studies)	\$2.00/lb	from suppliers)	10.00
Variable overhead ...	—	\$1.75/DLH	(flexible budget)[1]	3.50
Fixed overhead......	—	\$1.25/DLH	(flexible budget and normal activity estimate)[2]	2.50
Total				\$24.00

NOTES:

[1] The company determined that variable overhead is closely related to the number of direct labor hours (DLH) worked. The flexible overhead budget formula is: Overhead Cost = \$43,750 + \$1.75 × DLH, where \$43,750 is the estimated fixed overhead for the period and variable overhead is estimated to increase by \$1.75 for each direct labor hour worked.

[2] Normal activity is estimated at 35,000 DLH. Therefore, the fixed overhead rate per DLH is \$1.25 (= \$43,750/35,000 DLH)

EXHIBIT 15.2 PER-UNIT STANDARD COSTS

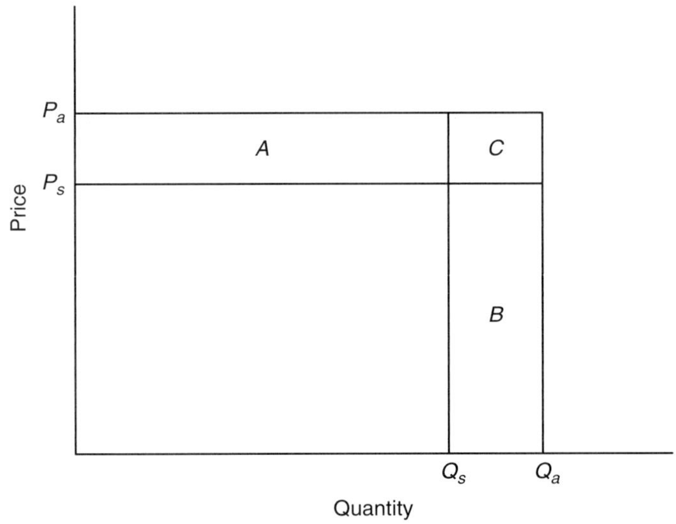

EXHIBIT 15.3 GRAPHIC REPRESENTATION OF TWO-FACTOR VARIANCES: THREE-WAY ANALYSIS

(i) Three-Way Analysis. Exhibit 15.3 shows the total variance as $P_aQ_a - P_sQ_s = A + B + C$. The following equations express the three variance components:

Pure Price Variance A = (Actual price – Standard price) × Standard quantity
$= (P_a - P_s)Q_s$

Pure Quantity Variance B = (Actual quantity – Standard quantity) × Standard price
$= (Q_a - Q_s)P_s$

Joint or Mixed Variance C = (Actual price – Standard price) × (Actual quantity – Standard quantity)
$= (P_a - P_s)(Q_a - Q_s)$

Thus, three-way analysis identifies three components of variance:

1. *Pure price variance* that isolates the deviation resulting from the difference between actual price and standard price at standard quantity.
2. *Pure quantity variance* that isolates the deviation due to the difference between actual quantity and standard quantity at standard price.
3. *Joint variance* that isolates the deviation attributable to both the difference between actual price and standard price and the difference between actual quantity and standard quantity.

This breakdown suggests that the purchasing department should have responsibility for the pure price variance and that the production supervisor should have responsibility for the pure quantity variance. Because the joint variance results from deviations in both prices *and* quantities, some managements prefer to keep it separate and not attempt to arbitrarily assign responsibility for it.

These variances are *favorable* or *unfavorable*, depending on their sign:

- A *positive* variance indicates that actual quantities and/or prices exceeded their standard amounts and is *unfavorable*, denoted by *U*.
- Conversely, a *negative* variance is *favorable* (denoted by *F*) because it indicates that actual prices and/or quantities were less than their standard amounts.

(ii) Two-Way Analysis. Most practical applications assign the joint variance arising in the three-way analysis to either the price or the quantity factor. The advantages of doing so include (1) the desire to do away with the troublesome and sometimes confusing joint variance and (2) the belief that clearly defined areas of responsibility contribute to more effective control. Assigning the joint variance to one of the two factors establishes the rules of the game and removes the joint variance that could serve as a point of contention or friction.

By convention, analysts most often assign the joint variance to the price factor, although no compelling reason exists for doing so in all cases. Assigning the joint variance to one of the other factors results in an analysis of cost variances that is two-way, rather than three-way. Exhibit 15.4 portrays this graphically, using the A, B, C symbols from Exhibit 15.3 in the three-way analysis. Exhibit 15.4 represents total variance as $P_aQ_a - P_sQ_s = A' + B$, and $A' = A + C$. The total variance now has two rather than three components.

Price Variance A' = (Actual Price – Standard Price) × Actual Quantity
$= (P_a - P_s)Q_a$

Quantity Variance B = (Actual Quantity – Standard Quantity) × Standard Price
$= (Q_a - Q_s)P_s$

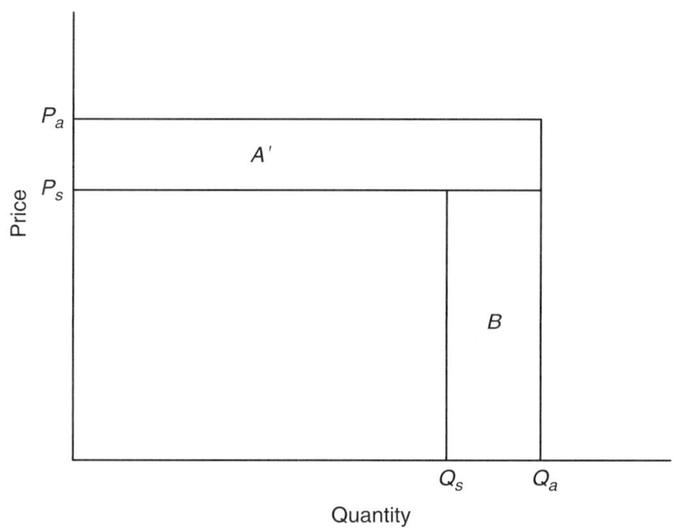

EXHIBIT 15.4 GRAPHIC REPRESENTAION OF TWO-FACTOR VARIANCES: TWO-WAY ANALYSIS

(iii) Offsetting Variances. Variances that offset one another often arise when a process uses an input resource having different quality and price than called for by the standards. For example, using a higher-priced, higher-quality resource may result in an unfavorable price variance and a favorable quantity variance, leading perhaps to a small total variance. Similarly, the use of a lower priced, lower-quality resource tends to generate favorable price variances and unfavorable quantity variances. Exhibit 15.5 depicts the offsetting variances arising when a manufacturer uses the higher-priced, higher-quality resource.

The three-way analysis in Exhibit 15.5 leads to an unfavorable pure price variance (A + C), a favorable quantity variance (B), and a favorable joint variance (C). Two-way analysis yields an unfavorable price variance (A = the pure price variance less the joint variance) and a favorable quantity variance (B).

This exhibit shows that analysts should not consider price and quantity variances independently. If the substitution of a better-quality, higher-priced resource caused the offsetting variance, the firm should not penalize the purchasing manager and reward the production manager solely on the basis of the reported variances. Indeed, if the substitution resulted in an overall favorable variance, the firm should revise standards accordingly.

The remainder of this chapter adopts the convention that assigns the joint variance to the price factor, as in the two-way analysis. Now we turn to some specific applications.

(b) RAW MATERIAL VARIANCES. Raw material variances have two components: (1) the dollar effect of deviations in actual prices paid for raw materials from the predetermined standard prices and (2) the dollar effect of deviations in actual quantities of raw materials used in production from the predetermined standard quantities.

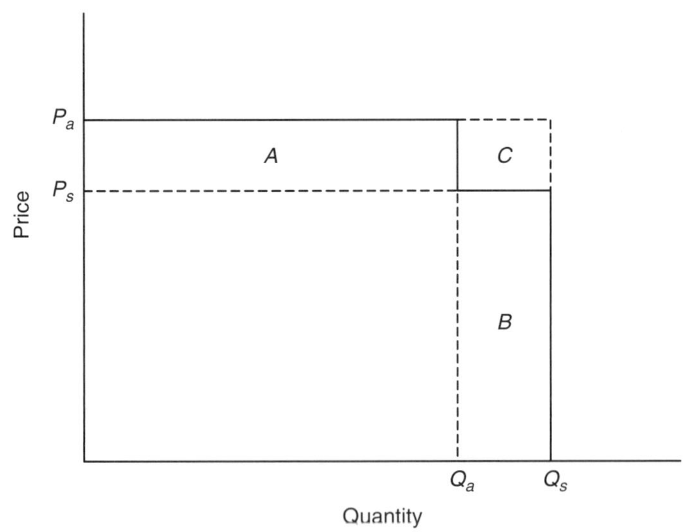

EXHIBIT 15.5 PARTIALLY OFFSETTING TWO-FACTOR VARIANCES

(i) Raw Material Price Variance. Analysts use two ways to calculate the raw material price variance. The method selected depends on how quickly management wants price variance information.

1. Compute and record the price variance when the firm purchases material, not later when it uses the material.
2. Compute and record the price variance when the material goes into production.

Method 1 generates material price variance information more quickly than method 2 does. Moreover, the choice of method affects the actual computation. Method 1 uses the actual quantity *purchased* as the actual quantity measure. Method 2 uses the actual quantity *used in production* as the actual quantity measure. Because these amounts are not necessarily identical, the choice of method affects the magnitude of the raw material price variance. The formula is

$$\text{Raw material price variance} = (\text{Actual price} - \text{Standard price}) \times \text{Actual quantity purchased (or used)}$$

The examples that follow demonstrate the raw material price variance calculation under both methods, using the Argosy Corporation information in Exhibit 15.1. Assume that Argosy purchased 100,000 pounds of material A for $205,000 and used 76,232 pounds in production. Argosy also purchased 25,000 pounds of material B for $27,500 and used 19,800 pounds in production. Under method 1, which uses the quantity purchased, the analyst calculates the total raw material price variance as $7,500 *U.*

METHOD 1

Price variance (material A) = ($2.05 – $2.00) × 100,000 =	$5,000 *U*
Price variance (material B) = ($1.10 – $1.00) × 25,000 =	2,500 *U*
Total raw material price variance (method 1)	$7,500 *U*

With method 2, however, the analyst calculated total raw material price variance as $5,792.

METHOD 2

Price variance (material A) = ($2.05 – $2.00) × 76,232 =	$3,812 *U*
Price variance (material B) = ($1.10 – $1.00) × 19,800 =	1,980 *U*
Total raw material price variance (method 2)	$5,792 *U*

(ii) Raw Material Quantity Variance. Calculations of the quantity variance include only the actual quantities used, compared with the standard quantities that production should have used. Therefore, analysts need consider only one formula, expressed by the following:

$$\text{Raw material quantity variance} = (\text{Actual quantity} - \text{Standard quantity}) \times \text{Standard price}$$

The calculations for the Argosy Corporation follow. Assume production of 11,000 Regular models and 9,600 Super models. The standard quantity of material A was 70,000 pounds [= (11,000 × 2) + (9,600 × 5)] and 22,000 pounds (= 11,000 × 2) of material B.

Quantity variance (material A) = (76,232 – 70,000) × $2.00 =	$12,464 *U*
Quantity variance (material B) = (19,800 – 22,000) × $1.00 =	–2,200 *F*
Total raw material quantity variance	$10,264 *U*

Observe that analysis of the individual variances, as opposed to an aggregation, can provide useful information. The total raw material quantity variance is \$10,264 *U*. This amount results from partially offsetting quantity variances for the two materials. In particular, the total quantity variance alone conceals the unfavorable quantity variance for material A and the favorable quantity variance for material B. In other situations, reporting a single total raw material variance might conceal large offsetting price and quantity variances.

(c) DIRECT LABOR VARIANCES. One can analyze deviations between actual and standard direct labor cost with direct labor variances. The total direct labor variance—actual direct labor cost minus standard direct labor cost for the actual production—has two dimensions, analogous to the raw material case:

1. A price dimension represented in calculating a *wage rate variance*
2. A quantity or efficiency dimension indicated by a *labor efficiency variance*

Where

W_a = the actual wage rate

W_s = the standard wage rate

H_a = the actual direct labor-hours worked

and

H_s = the standard direct labor-hours.

Using the two-way analysis, the formulas for the two variances follow.

$$\text{Wage rate variance} = (\text{Actual wage rate} - \text{Standard wage rate}) \times \text{Actual hours}$$
$$= (W_a - W_s)H_a$$
$$\text{Labor efficiency variance} = (\text{Actual hours} - \text{Standard hours}) \times \text{Standard wage rate}$$
$$= (H_a - H_s)W_s$$

Return to the Argosy Corporation for a numerical example. Actual direct labor cost incurred on the total of 20,600 units produced equals 34,408 hours worked at an average wage rate of \$4.50, or \$154,836. The standard number or direct labor-hours for the assumed output of 11,000 regular models and 9,600 super model equals 35,700 [= (1,000 × 1½) + (9,600 × 2)]. The following calculations show the variances.

Wage rate variance = (\$4.50 – \$4.00) × 34,408	= \$17,204 *U*
Labor efficiency variance = (34,408 – 35,700) × \$4.00	= –5,168 *F*
Total direct labor variance	\$12,036 *U*

Analysts may need to investigate or speculate about the causes of these variances. A wage rate in excess of standard obviously causes the unfavorable wage rate variance. This, in turn, might imply that Argosy employed better-qualified workers. Indeed, the highly favorable labor efficiency variance lends credence to the suggestion that the firm employed better-qualified workers. If operations has a favorable total variance, Argosy should consider resetting standards to call for fewer hours of higher-paid labor.

(d) FLEXIBLE BUDGET PREPARATION. Setting standards for overhead usually relates to preparation of a *flexible budget* for overhead. The flexible budget expresses the relation between total cost and levels of activity:

$$TC = a + bX$$

where

TC = estimated total cost

a = estimated fixed portion of total cost

b = estimated variable cost per unit of activity

X = units of activity, such as direct labor-hours (DLH) or machine-hours.

To prepare a flexible budget for overhead, collect the level of total overhead cost at various levels of activity. A scatter diagram prepared from these observations appears in Exhibit 15.6. After collecting the data, the analyst uses regression analysis, visual curve fitting, or a similar method to fit a straight line to the data points. The line through the data points in Exhibit 15.6 illustrates the relation between total overhead cost and level of activity. The interpretation of this line is that for activity levels between X_1 and X_2, the fixed portion of overhead cost is a, the intercept, and the variable overhead cost per unit of activity is b, the slope of the estimated budget line. Because one can now readily calculate the total budgeted overhead for any amount of production between levels X_1 and X_2, the *flexible budget* title fits.

For the Argosy Corporation, the flexible budget equation for overhead is $TC =$ \$43,750 + (\$1.75 × DLH). Normal capacity is given as 35,000 DLH. With budgeted fixed overhead of \$43,750, the standard fixed overhead rate equals \$1.25 (= \$43,750/35,000) per DLH, and the standard variable overhead rate equals \$1.75 per DLH.

Thus, the flexible budget for overhead provides standard cost data for variable and fixed overhead. A firm must next develop and compute the overhead variances arising in a standard cost system.

(e) VARIABLE OVERHEAD VARIANCES. Variable overhead includes all those indirect manufacturing costs that vary with the level of manufacturing activity. Because variable

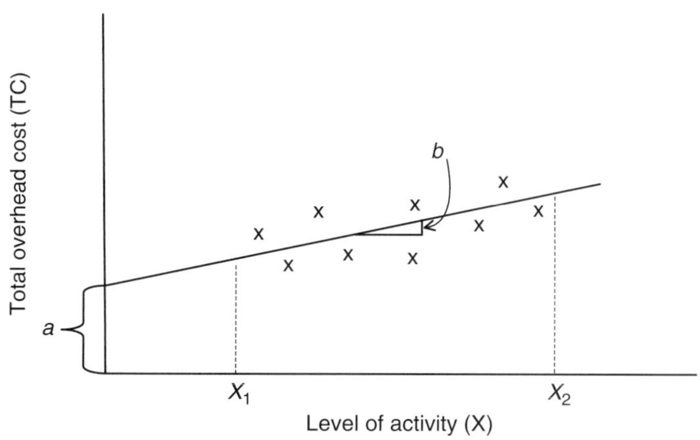

EXHIBIT 15.6 ILLUSTRATION OF SCATTER DIAGRAM AND ESTIMATED FLEXIBLE BUDGET LINE

overhead is a production cost, one must allocate it to units produced on one or more reasonable bases. To do so requires analyzing the historical relation between overhead cost and various measures of activity. Analysts use the measure(s) of activity that bear the closest relation to movements in overhead costs. Typical bases are direct labor-hours worked, machine-hours used, and number of setups. This chapter illustrates preparation of a flexible budget based on the estimated variable overhead rate per unit of a single activity measure.

The total variable overhead variance has two dimensions. One results from a difference between the actual and standard overhead rates. This difference is called the *variable overhead budget variance* or, alternatively, the *variable overhead rate variance.* The second dimension results from a deviation between the actual and standard measures of production activity on which the firm allocates overhead, such as direct labor-hours. It is known as the *variable overhead efficiency variance. Let* V_a = the actual variable overhead rate and V_s = the standard variable overhead rate derived from the flexible budget. H_a and H_s are actual and standard direct labor-hours, respectively. The formulas for the variable overhead variances follow.

Total variable overhead variance = Actual variable overhead − Standard variable overhead applied to production

$$= V_aH_a - V_sH_s$$

Variable overhead budget variance = (Actual variable overhead rate − Standard variable overhead rate) × Actual direct labor-hours

$$= (V_a - V_s)H_a$$

Variable overhead efficiency variance = (Actual direct labor-hours − Standard direct labor-hours) × Standard variable overhead rate

$$= (H_a - H_s)V_s$$

Observe that the variable overhead budget variance reduces to the difference between *actual* variable overhead, V_aH_a, and *budgeted* variable overhead, V_sH_a. Similarly, the variable overhead efficiency variance equals the difference between budgeted variable overhead, V_sH_a, and variable overhead applied to production, V_sH_s.

For the Argosy Corporation, actual variable overhead equals $61,246; V_a equals $1.78 (= $61,246/34,408). Calculation of these variances yields the following.

Total variable overhead variance	= ($1.78 × 34,408) − ($1.75 × 35,700)	=	$−1,229 *F*
Variable overhead budget variance	= (1.78 − $1.75) × 34,408	=	$ 1,032 *U*
Variable overhead efficiency variance	= (34,408 − 35,700) × $1.75	=	−2,261 *F*
			$−1,229 *F*

(f) FIXED OVERHEAD VARIANCES. Fixed manufacturing overhead consists of indirect manufacturing costs that remain invariant over the relevant range of production. Examples include depreciation allocated on the basis of time (rather than units of production), rent on factory plant and equipment, and supervisors' salaries. Generally accepted accounting principles (GAAP) require that firms base product costs on *full absorption costing*, which charges fixed manufacturing costs to production. GAAP does not accept an alternative product costing method, known as *direct costing* or *variable costing.* Because direct costing considers fixed manufacturing overhead a *period* rather than a *product* cost, the setting of fixed overhead standards and the calculation of fixed overhead variances become unnecessary. Given current accounting principles, however, this discussion examines the fixed overhead variances that arise when firms use absorption costing.

(i) Two-Way Analysis. This approach has two major fixed overhead variances.

1. A *fixed overhead budget variance* shows the difference between actual and budgeted fixed overhead.
2. The *fixed overhead volume variance,* sometimes referred to as the *idle capacity variance,* indicates the extent to which fixed overhead charged to production differs from budgeted fixed overhead.

Companies allocate fixed overhead to production based on the activity measure(s) employed in constructing the flexible budget. Because the flexible budget provides an estimate of *total* fixed manufacturing overhead, one must calculate the standard fixed overhead rate *per unit* of activity. Letting F_s = the standard fixed overhead rate, the formula is

$$F_s = \frac{\text{Budgeted fixed overhead}}{\text{X, an activity level}}$$

Because the analysis needs to allocate fixed overhead to production, the denominator should represent some measure of capacity use. Further, the level of capacity use chosen affects the size of F_s and hence, the standard cost of production. One can select from the following measures of capacity to choose X, the activity level in the denominator of the formula for computing the standard fixed overhead rate.

- *Expected capacity* is the expected activity level for next period's production.
- *Theoretical capacity* represents the activity level that would occur under the ideal conditions of full capacity use and no down time.
- *Normal capacity* is an annual measure of the average production required to meet consumer demand over an intermediate time horizon, usually three to five years, assuming efficient operation of the plant and the usual amount of down time.

Firms typically prefer normal capacity over the alternative activity measures just suggested. Because theoretical capacity represents an ideal that a firm rarely attains, its use seems to lead to consistent underabsorption of fixed overhead to production. Expected capacity also usually does not suit this purpose. If fixed overhead remains relatively constant while production varies, the use of expected capacity causes the standard fixed overhead rate to vary as well. Therefore, the use of a fixed overhead rate based on expected capacity could lead to variations in product cost at the same time as general cost conditions remained the same. Normal capacity, then, provides the best basis for standard fixed overhead rates. It should lead to more consistent product costs by not consistently underabsorbing fixed overhead.

The Financial Accounting Standards Board (FASB) affirmed the use of normal capacity in FASB *Statement No. 151,* "Inventory Costs" (2004). Paragraph 2 states that "the allocation of fixed production overheads to the costs of conversion is based on the normal capacity of the production facilities" and goes on to discuss the considerations involved in measuring normal capacity.

We now present the fixed overhead variances using the following notations and assuming that the basis for allocation is normal capacity, measured in direct labor-hours.

H_a = actual direct labor-hours worked

H_s = standard direct labor-hours for the actual production

H_n = normal capacity in direct labor-hours

F_a = actual fixed overhead rate

F_s = standard fixed overhead rate

$$= \frac{\text{Budgeted Fixed Overhead}}{H_n}$$

In two-way analysis, the *total fixed overhead variance* (actual fixed overhead less standard fixed overhead applied to production = $F_aH_a - F_aH_s$) has two dimensions.

- One results from the difference between actual and budgeted fixed overhead and leads to the *fixed overhead budget variance.*
- The second, known as the *fixed overhead volume variance,* arises from the difference between normal capacity in direct labor-hours and standard direct labor-hours for the actual production.

The *fixed overhead budget variance,* (*or idle capacity variance*), measures the extent to which the *actual* fixed manufacturing overhead for a period differs from the amount *budgeted.*

$$\text{Fixed overhead budget variance} = \text{Actual fixed overhead} - \text{Budgeted fixed overhead}$$
$$= F_aH_a - F_sH_n$$

The *fixed overhead volume variance,* by contrast, measures the over- or underabsorption of fixed overhead.

$$\text{Fixed overhead volume variance} = \text{Budgeted fixed overhead} - \text{Fixed overhead applied to production}$$
$$= F_sH_n - F_sH_s = (H_n - H_s)F_s$$

The Argosy Corporation reported actual fixed overhead of \$45,763; with 34,408 direct labor-hours worked, F_a equals \$1.33 (= \$45,763/34,408), and the fixed overhead variances equal the following.

Total fixed overhead variance	= (\$1.33 × 34,408) – (\$1.25 × 35,700)	=	\$1,138 *U*
Fixed overhead budget variance	= (\$1.33 × 34,408) – \$43,750	=	\$2,013 *U*
Fixed overhead volume variance	= (35,000 – 35,700) × \$1.25	=	–875 *F*
			\$1,138 *U*

These variances arose because (1) actual fixed overhead exceeded the budgeted amount and (2) standard DLH for the actual activity of the period exceeded normal activity. Some analysts argue that an unfavorable volume variance measures the cost of idle capacity. This would occur only by coincidence; the actual cost of the idle capacity should equal the capacity's *opportunity cost*—the net profit that the firm could derive from the capacity's best alternative use, if any.

(ii) Three-Way Analysis. An alternative approach factors the total fixed overhead variance into *three* dimensions:

1. The fixed overhead budget variance just described

2. A fixed overhead efficency variance = $F_sH_a - F_sH_s = F_s(H_a - H_s)$

3. A different fixed overhead volume variance = $F_sH_n - F_sH_a = F_s(H_n - H_a)$

Note that this approach divides the fixed overhead volume variance into two components to attribute the over- or underabsorption of fixed overhead to (1) direct labor performance reflected in off-standard hours—$F_s(H_a - H_s)$—and (2) the over- or underuse of capacity—$F_s(H_n - H_a)$.

(g) THREE-WAY ANALYSIS OF OVERHEAD VARIANCES. Analysts often find it convenient to combine variable and fixed overhead variances into a single analysis for purposes of management review. One can accomplish this by combining the variable and fixed overhead budget variances and presenting them along with the variable overhead efficiency variance and the fixed overhead volume variance. Observe that the total overhead variance equals the sum of the variable and fixed overhead budget variances, the variable overhead efficiency variance, and the fixed overhead volume variance.

$$\begin{aligned}\text{Total overhead variance} &= (V_a + F_a)H_a - (V_s + F_s)H_s \\ &= [(V_a - V_s)H_a + F_aH_a - F_sH_n] \\ &\quad + (H_a - H_s)V_s + (H_n - H_s)F_s \\ &= \text{Total overhead budget variance} \\ &\quad + \text{Variable overhead efficiency variance} \\ &\quad + \text{Fixed overhead volume variance}\end{aligned}$$

One can explain these variances effectively with an exhibit similar to the one that follows.

$$\frac{\text{Actual overhead}}{[(V_a + F_a) \times H_a]} (-) \frac{\text{Budgeted overhead at actual output}}{(V_sH_a + F_sH_n)} (-) \frac{\text{Budgeted overhead at standard output}}{(V_sH_s + F_sH_n)} (-) \frac{\text{Overhead applied to product}}{[(V_s + F_s) \times H_s]}$$

Total overhead budget variance	Variable overhead efficiency variance	Fixed overhead volume variance
$(V_a - V_s)H_a + F_aH_a - F_sH_n$	$(H_a - H_s)V_s$	$(H_n - H_s)F_s$

Substituting the numbers in the formulas, we see that

$$\begin{aligned}\text{Total Overhead Variance} &= 34{,}408 \times (\$1.78 + \$1.33) - 35{,}700 \times (\$1.75 + \$1.25) \\ &= \$107{,}009 - \$107{,}100 \\ &= \$\text{–}91\ F \\ &= \$1{,}032\ U + \$2{,}013\ U - \$2{,}261\ F - \$875\ F \\ &= \$\text{–}91\ F\end{aligned}$$

(h) THREE-FACTOR VARIANCES IN GENERAL. Two-factor variances have the restriction of analyzing the price and quantity dimensions of a single resource input. Even though analysts can individually compute two-factor variances for any number of, say, raw materials, such variances cannot recognize the interaction between input resources, especially when operations can *substitute* these resources for each other. Therefore, analysts may partially attribute a given variance to a difference between the actual and standard mix of input resources as well as to deviations between actual and standard prices and quantities. We must therefore consider *mix* as a third factor.

To illustrate the general three-factor approach to cost variances, consider the following notation. Suppose that two substitutable input resources are used to produce an output product.

$$P_{xa}, P_{xs} = \text{Actual and standard unit prices of resource X}$$

$$P_{ya}, P_{ys} = \text{Actual and standard unit prices of resource Y}$$

$$Q_{xa}, Q_{xs} = \text{Actual and standard quantities of resource X}$$

$$Q_{ya}, Q_{ys} = \text{Actual and standard quantities of resource Y}$$

$$M_{xs}, M_{ys} = \text{Standard mix percentages for the resources X, Y}$$

$$= \left(\frac{Q_{xs}}{Q_{xs} + Q_{ys}}, \frac{Q_{ys}}{Q_{xs} + Q_{ys}} \right)$$

$$\text{Actual cost} = P_{xa}Q_{xa} + P_{ya}Q_{ya}$$

$$\text{Standard cost} = P_{xs}Q_{xs} + P_{ys}Q_{ys}$$

$$\text{Total variance} = (P_{xa}Q_{xa} + P_{ya}Q_{ya}) - (P_{xs}Q_{xs} + P_{ys}Q_{ys})$$

One can subdivide this total variance into three variances, assuming that the price variances include the joint variances for the two resources, as in the two-way analysis of the two-factor model. The two-factor model quantity variances include the quantity and mix components in the three-factor model.

$$\text{Price variance} = (P_{xa} - P_{xs})Q_{xa} + (P_{ya} - P_{ys})Q_{ya}$$

$$\text{Quantity variance} = [M_{xs}(Q_{xa} + Q_{ya}) - Q_{xs}]P_{xs} + [M_{ys}(Q_{xa} + Q_{ya}) - Q_{ys}]P_{ys}$$

$$\text{Mix variance} = [Q_{xa} - M_{xs}(Q_{xa} + Q_{ya})]P_{xs} + [Q_{ya} - M_{ys}(Q_{xa} + Q_{ya})]P_{ys}$$

The first term in each of the variances is for resource X, and the second is for resource Y. The quantity variance holds price and mix percentages constant to highlight the deviation between actual quantity given the standard mix and standard quantity. The mix variance holds price and quantity constant to measure the difference between actual quantity, and actual quantity given the standard mix.

The three-factor variance model has two principal applications:

1. Production price, mix and yield variances
2. Sales (or profit) price, mix, and quantity variances

The next two sections discuss these applications. Note that one can compute three-factor variances in several different ways; the method presented here illustrates the general formulation.

(i) PRODUCTION MIX AND YIELD VARIANCES. When production combines various raw materials or types of labor, a firm can vary the proportions of these input resources by substituting plastic for wood, highly skilled for less-skilled labor, and so forth. These substitutions affect the quantities of resources used and may affect the quantities of outputs produced. In the two-factor variance model, the quantity variance reports resource usage that deviates from standard but does not explain this deviation in terms of changes between the budgeted and actual mix of input resources. Nor does it focus on changes in quantities of finished product yielded by given amounts of input resources. The three-factor variance model permits disaggregation of the quantity variance into mix and yield components that, in conjunction with the price variance, explain the total cost variance. The formulas are the same as those presented in the discussion of the three-factor variance model.

EXAMPLE 1. THREE-FACTOR PRODUCTION VARIANCES EXAMPLE

A paint company blends several liquid materials in base paint to which retail outlets may later add pigment to custom mix for various colors on the color chart. The company has the following standards:

Per 9-gallon batch of paint:	
5 gallons of material X @ $ .70 =	$3.50
3 gallons of material Y @ 1.00 =	3.00
2 gallons of material Z @ .80 =	1.60
Total (10 gallons of input for 9 gallons of output; $.90 per gallon of output)	$8.10

During a recent production period, the company purchased and used the following materials:

45,000 gallons of X at actual cost of $.72 =	$32,400
33,000 gallons of Y at actual cost of .99 =	32,670
22,000 gallons of Z at actual cost of .80 =	17,600
100,000	$82,670
Good output was 92,070 gallons at a standard cost of $.90 per gallon	82,863
Total material variance	$ –193 *F*

A complete analysis of the total material variance in terms of its price, mix, and yield components appears in Exhibit 15.7.

What can we say about mix and yield variances? They provide more detailed information for decision making—information that two-factor quantity variances might conceal. Where materials and other factors of production have different qualities or specifications and the production process permits some substitution, management can measure the effects of changes in the mix of inputs and whether such changes affect the finished-product yield of input resources. The example in Exhibit 15.7 indicates that the actual mix of inputs deviated from the standard mix and generated an unfavorable mix variance of $1,100; the favorable yield variance of –$1,863 *F* more than offsets the unfavorable mix variance.

(j) SALES AND PROFIT VARIANCES. To this point, the chapter has concentrated on the measurement, treatment, and evaluation of standard production cost variances. Firms use such variances to identify potential problem areas as well as opportunities for cost savings. Variance analysis techniques have proven sufficiently general to have value in analyzing the components of deviations from other types of standards or plans. For example,

Material Price Variances

Material	$(P_a - P_s)Q_a$	
X	($.72 – $ .70) × 45,000	= $900 *U*
Y	(.99 – 1.00) × 33,000	= –330 *F*
Z	(.80 – .80) × 22,000	= 0
	Total material price variance	$570 *U*

Material Yield Variances

Material	$[M_s(Q_{xa} + Q_{ya} + Q_{za}) - Q_s]P_s$	
X	[(.5 × 100,000) – *51,150] × $ .70 =	$ –805 *F*
Y	[(.3 × 100,000) – *30,690] × 1.00 =	–690 *F*
Z	[(.2 × 100,000) – *20,460] × .80 =	–368 *F*
	Total material yield variance	$–1,863 *F*

*51,150 = 50,000 × (92,070/90,000)
30,690 = 30,000 × (92,070/90,000)
20,460 = 20,000 × (92,070/90,000)

Material Mix Variances

Material	$[Q_a - M_s(Q_{xa} + Q_{ya} + Q_{za})]P_s$	
X	[45,000 – (.5 × 100,000)] × $ .70 =	$–3,500 *F*
Y	[33,000 – (.3 × 100,000)] × 1.00 =	3,000 *U*
Z	[22,000 – (.2 × 100,000)] × .80 =	1,600 *U*
	Total material mix variance	$ 1,100 *U*

Total material variance = $570 – $1,863 + $1,100 = –$193 *F*

Note that the mix and yield variances sum to –$763 F. This agrees with the material quantity variances shown below, computed using the two-factor model.

Material Quantity Variances (Two-Factor Model)

Material	$(Q_a - Q_s)P_s$	
X	(45,000 – 51,150) × $.70 =	$–4,305 *F*
Y	(33,000 – 30,690) × 1.00 =	2,310 *U*
Z	(22,000 – 20,460) × .80 =	1,232 *U*
	Total Material Quantity Variance	$ –763 *F*

EXHIBIT 15.7 COMPUTATION OF MATERIAL PRICE, MIX, AND YIELD VARIANCES

one can apply variance analysis to comparisons between actual and planned sales, this year's and last year's net income, and so forth. Unlike production cost variances in a standard cost accounting system, sales and profit variances offer supplementary analytic devices only and do not enter the accounts. This section illustrates the use and computation of sales variances.

Sales variances present another application of the three-factor variance model. Total sales variance equals the difference between actual and planned sales revenue. It has three subvariances: sales mix variance, sales price variance, and sales quantity variance.

The formulas follow those discussed in the general application of three-factor variances (see Section 15.3(h)). These equations, however, reverse the order of the terms and the sign in each variance. This change enables us to continue the unfavorable interpretation of positive variances and the favorable interpretation of negative variances. For example, actual sales that exceed budgeted (or standard) sales will have a *favorable* variance and should have a negative sign. The discussion of these variances for a two-product firm will usc thc following notation:

P_{xs}, P_{ys} = standard unit price for products X, Y

P_{xa}, P_{ya} = actual unit price for products X, Y

Q_{xs}, Q_{ys} = budgeted sales quantity for products X, Y

Q_{xa}, Q_{ya} = actual sales quantity for products X, Y

M_{xs}, M_{ys} = budgeted mix percentages for products X, Y

$$= \left(\frac{Q_{xs}}{Q_{xs} + Q_{ys}}, \frac{Q_{ys}}{Q_{xs} + Q_{ys}} \right)$$

Sales mix variances identify the portion of the total sales variance attributable to the actual product mix differing from the budgeted mix. The formula follows:

$$\text{Sales mix variance} = [M_{xs}(Q_{xa} + Q_{ya}) - Q_{xa}]P_{xs} + [M_{ys}(Q_{xa} + Q_{ya}) - Q_{ya}]P_{ys}$$

The two expressions in the formula are the sales mix variances for products X and Y, respectively. For example, $M_{xs}(Q_{xa} + Q_{ya})$ is the quantity of product X that should have been sold based on the budgeted mix. Thus, one can attribute the difference between that quantity and the actual quantity of X that was sold, Q_{xa}, to a change in the mix.

Sales price variances quantify how much of the total sales variance is due solely to actual prices differing from their budgeted amounts. The formula follows:

$$\text{Sales price variance} = (P_{xs} - P_{xa})Q_{xa} + (P_{ys} - P_{ya})Q_{ya}$$

The two parts of the formula are the sales price variances for products X and Y, respectively.

Sales quantity variances highlight the portion of the total sales variance arising because actual quantities sold differed from those budgeted. The formula follows:

$$\text{Sales quantity variance} = [Q_{xs} - M_{xs}(Q_{xa} + Q_{ya})]P_{xs} + [Q_{ys} - M_{ys}(Q_{xa} + Q_{ya})]P_{ys}$$

For the Argosy Corporation, assume that product X is the regular model and product Y is the super model. Sales data appear in Exhibit 15.8. The variance calculations follow.

These three variances in Exhibit 15.8 sum to –$1,800 *F*, which agrees with the total sales variance of –$1,800 *F:*

$$-\$1{,}800\ F = [(10{,}000 \times \$20) + (10{,}000 \times \$30)] - [(11{,}000 \times \$19) + (9{,}600 \times \$30.50)]$$

Sales variances can prove especially useful when compared over time, because of the changing relation between selling prices and quantities sold. One could analyze the difference between this year's and last year's sales revenue by using last year's *actual* data as this year's *standards*. The firm may gain some insight into the nature of the demand curve it faces, in terms of general price/quantity tradeoffs as well as the *sensitivity* of sales volume to small or large price changes.

	Price		Quantity		Budgeted Mix
	Budget	Actual	Budget	Actual	Percentage
Regular model	$20.00	$19.00	10,000	11,000	50%
Super model	30.00	30.50	10,000	9,600	50%

Sales Mix Variance $= (.5 \times 20{,}600 - 11{,}000) \times \$20 + (.5 \times 20{,}600 - 9{,}600) \times \$30$

$= \$7{,}000\ U$

Sales Price Variance $= (\$20 - \$19) \times 11{,}000 + (\$30 - \$30.50) \times 9{,}600$

$= \$6{,}200\ U$

Sales Quantity Variance $= (10{,}000 - .5 \times 20{,}600) \times \$20 + (10{,}000 - .5 \times 20{,}600) \times \$30$

$= \$\text{–}15{,}000\ F$

EXHIBIT 15.8 SALES DATA AND SALES VARIANCE FOR THE ARGOSY CORPORATION

15.4 ACCOUNTING ENTRIES IN A STANDARD COST SYSTEM

Because standard cost systems usually carry inventories at standard cost, firms record amounts charged and credited to raw materials, work in process, and finished goods inventories at standard. Companies record variances when actual amounts differ from their standard amounts. Exhibit 15.9 presents the journal entries that record the production-related transactions of the Argosy Corporation. The exhibit records only the production cost variances based on the two-factor model. Sales variances do not enter the accounts.

	Debit	Credit	
Raw material inventory	225,000		(1)
Raw material price variance	7,500		
Accounts Payable		232,500	
To record purchase of raw materials, charging inventory for their standard cost [$225,000 = (100,000 × $2) + (25,000 × $1)], crediting accounts payable for their actual cost ($232,500 = $205,000 + $27,500), and charging raw material price variance (using method 1) for the amount previously calculated.			
Work in process	162,000		(2)
Raw material quantity variance	10,264		
Raw material inventory		172,264	
To record usage of raw material in production, charging work in process for the standard cost of the standard quantity [$162,000 = (70,000 × $2) + (22,000 × $1)], crediting raw material inventory for the standard cost of the actual quantity [$172,264 = (76,232 × $2) + (19,800 × $ 1)], and charging raw material quantity variance for the amount previously calculated.			

EXHIBIT 15.9 ACCOUNTING ENTRIES IN THE ARGOSY CORPORATION'S STANDARD COST SYSTEM

Account	Debit	Credit	Entry
Work in process	142,800		(3)
Wage rate variance	17,204		
Labor efficiency variance		5,168	
Wages payable		154,836	
To record direct labor production cost, charging work in process for the standard cost of the standard number of direct labor hours ($142,800 = 35,700 × $4), crediting wages payable for the actual direct labor cost ($154,836 = 34,408 × $4.50), and entering the variances as previously calculated.			
Factory overhead control	107,009		(4)
Various credits (supplies, payables, etc.)		107,009	
To record the period's actual factory overhead, charging the overhead control account, and crediting asset and liability accounts.			
Work in process	107,100		(5)
Factory overhead applied		107,100	
To record the factory overhead applied to production, based on standard rates and standard direct labor hours [$107,100 = 35,700 × ($1.75 + $1.25)].			
Factory overhead applied	107,100		(6)
Total overhead budget variance	3,045		
Variable overhead efficiency variance		2,261	
Fixed overhead volume variance		875	
Factory overhead control		107,009	
To close out the factory overhead *control* and *applied* accounts. The difference of $91 is the total overhead variance which is composed of the three overhead variances previously calculated in the three-way analysis.			
Finished goods inventory	411,900		(7)
Work in process		411,900	
To transfer completed production at standard cost [$411,900 = (11,000 × $16.50) + (9,600 × $24)].			

EXHIBIT 15.9 ACCOUNTING ENTRIES IN THE ARGOSY CORPORATION'S STANDARD COST SYSTEM *(CONTINUED)*

(a) ACCOUNTING DISPOSITION OF VARIANCES. At the end of the accounting period, firms employing standard cost systems must decide how to treat the variances that arise during the year. Materiality aside, the firm must decide whether to include the variances in inventory or enter them directly into income calculations for the period. Some argue that a firm should not capitalize the cost of inefficient operations on the balance sheet as part of inventory. This view holds that quantity and efficiency variances are not legitimate inventoriable product costs and should go directly to the income statement. In contrast, price variances are typically a function of the external market and not of the firm's internal organization. Because the firm normally does not control the external market, it appears that price variances affect this period's product costs and the system should charge them to inventories by prorating them across the appropriate inventory accounts.

These arguments seem reasonable in a hypothetical world characterized by accurate, currently attainable standards and no measurement errors in the accounting process. In practice, however, the causes and subsequent treatment of variances can become arbitrary. Thus, one could argue for closing all variances directly to income, normally through cost of goods sold. When *material* variances occur, however, management will probably conclude that the standard cost of product does not adequately measure production cost; the analyst then uses the variances to adjust standard production cost to actual by a proration process, which the chapter discusses in the next section.

FASB *Statement No. 151,* "Inventory Costs" (2004), mentioned in section 15.3 (f), also addresses the proration issue. In paragraph 2 it requires that "Unallocated overheads are recognized as an expense in the period in which they are incurred" and that "amounts of wasted materials (spoilage) require treatment as current period charges . . ." This ruling likely modifies any comprehensive proration of all production cost variances by limiting the variances that can be allocated to inventory accounts.

(b) PRORATION OF PRODUCTION COST VARIANCES. Once the analyst decides to prorate standard cost variances across the inventory accounts, the mechanics become straightforward. The analyst allocates each variance to the various inventory accounts in accordance with the proportion of total cost in each account. For example, suppose an unfavorable raw material price variance of $10,000 *U* results from $800,000 of standard raw material purchases, of which $100,000 resides in raw material inventory, $60,000 in work in process, $150,000 in finished goods inventory, and $490,000 in cost of goods sold. The journal entry to prorate the price variance follows:

Raw Material Inventory	1,250	
Work in Process.	750	
Finished Goods Inventory	1,875	
Cost of Goods Sold	6,125	
Raw Material Price Variance.		10,000
To allocate the $10,000 unfavorable raw material price variance to the appropriate inventory accounts.		

The accountant will similarly prorate other variances.

15.5 INTEGRATED FORMAT FOR SALES AND PRODUCTION COST VARIANCE

This section illustrates a form of reporting to management for a standard cost system that enables accountants to understand and reconcile budgeted, standard, and actual results of operations; such analyses then become valuable tools for evaluation and control purposes. The illustration uses the Argosy Corporation's data. For simplification, the analysis assumes no beginning or ending inventories and charges all standard cost variances to cost of goods sold. Furthermore, the illustration applies this comprehensive analysis to both a conventional absorption costing system and a variable costing system.

Shortly after the close of the reporting period, the analyst develops the following summary data for management.

	Budget	Actual	Variance
Sales.	$500,000	$501,800	$ –1,800 *F*
Cost of goods sold	$405,000	$441,609	$36,609 *U*
Selling, general, and administrative expenses	50,000	48,540	– 1,460 *F*
Total expenses	$455,000	$490,149	$35,149 *U*
Net income.	$ 45,000	$ 11,651	$33,349 *U*

The analysis uses data based on the detailed information appearing in Exhibit 15.10. Exhibit 15.11 presents the calculation of all relevant variances described in the preceding sections of the chapter. Exhibits 15.11 and 15.12 disaggregate the summary data and variances into their respective components for the absorption and variable costing systems, respectively.

	Budget Forecast		Actual	
Product	X	Y	X	Y
Sales (physical units)	10,000	10,000	11,000	9,600
Average unit selling price.	$20.00	$30.00	$19.00	$30.50
Production (physical units).	10,000	10,000	11,000	9,600
Unit production cost	$16.50	$24.00	$17.144	$26.1788

Unit Production Cost of X

	Standard	Actual
Pounds of material A	2.0	2.2
Cost per pound of material A	$ 2.00	$ 2.05
Pounds of material B	2.0	1.8
Cost per pound of material B	$ 1.00	$ 1.10
Materials cost	$ 6.00	$ 6.49
Hours of direct labor (DLH).	1.5	1.4
Wage rate per hour	$ 4.00	$ 4.50
Labor cost.	$ 6.00	$ 6.30
Variable overhead per DLH	$ 1.75	$ 1.78
Fixed overhead per DLH	$ 1.25	$ 1.33
Variable overhead cost	$ 2.625	$ 2.492
Fixed overhead cost	$ 1.875	$ 1.862
Total unit production cost.	$16.50	$17.144

EXHIBIT 15.10 ARGOSY CORPORATION: SALES AND PRODUCTION DATA

Unit Production Cost of Y

Pounds of material A	5.00	5.42
Cost per pound of material A	$ 2.00	$ 2.05
Material cost	$10.00	$11.111
Hours of direct labor (DLH)	2.00	1.98
Wage rate per hour	$ 4.00	$ 4.50
Labor cost	$ 8.00	$ 8.91
Variable overhead/DLH	$ 1.75	$ 1.78
Fixed overhead/DLH	$ 1.25	$ 1.33
Variable overhead cost	$ 3.50	$ 3.5244
Fixed overhead cost	$ 2.50	$ 2.6334
Total unit production cost	$24.00	$26.1788

Other Data

1. Fixed overhead is estimated at $43,750. The standard fixed overhead application rate is based on normal capacity of 35,000 DLH.
2. Selling, general, and administrative expenses have estimated fixed and variable components of $30,000 and $1 per unit sold, respectively.

EXHIBIT 15.10 ARGOSY CORPORATION: SALES AND PRODUCTION DATA *(CONTINUED)*

Sales Variances

Sales price variance			
Product X: ($20.00 – $19.00) × 11,000	=	$ 11,000 *U*	
Product Y: ($30.00 – $30.50) × 9,600	=	–4,800 *F*	
		$ 6,200 *U*	(1)
Sales mix variance			
Product X: [(.5 × 20,600) – 11,000] × $20	=	$ –14,000 *F*	
Product Y: [(.5 × 20,600) – 9,600] × $30	=	21,000 *U*	
		$ 7,000 *U*	
Sales quantity variance			
Product X: (10,000 – .5 × 20,600) × $20	=	$ –6,000 *F*	
Product Y: (10,000 – .5 × 20,600) × $30	=	–9,000 *F*	
		$–15,000 *F*	
Total sales operating volume variance		$ –8,000 *F*	(2)
Total sales variance = $6,200 U – $8,000 F		$ –1,800 *F*	(3)

Cost Variances

Material price variance:		
Material A: ($2.05 – $2.00) × 100,000	=	$ 5,000 *U*
Material B: ($1.10 – $ 1.00) × 25,000	=	2,500 *U*
		$ 7,500 *U*

EXHIBIT 15.11 ARGOSY CORPORATION: CALCULATION OF VARIANCES

Material quantity variance:			
Material A: (76,232 – 70,000) × $2.00	=	$ 12,464 *U*	
Material B: (19,800 – 22,000) × $ 1.00	=	–2,200 *F*	
		$ 10,264 *U*	
Total material cost variance		$ 17,764 *U*	(4)
Wage rate variance: ($4.50 – $4.00) × 34,408	=	$ 17,204 *U*	
Labor efficiency variance:			
(34,408 – 35,700) × $4.00	=	–5,168 *F*	
Total labor cost variance	=	$ 12,036 *U*	(5)
Overhead budget variance:			
Variable overhead: ($1.78 – $1.75) × 34,408	=	$ 1,032 *U*	
Fixed overhead: ($1.33 × 34,408) – $43,750	=	2,013 *U*	(8)
Total overhead budget variance		$ 3,045 *U*	
Variable overhead efficiency variance:			
(34,408 – 35,700) × $1.75	=	$ –2,261 *F*	
Fixed overhead volume variance:			
(35,000 – 35,700) × $1.25	=	$ –875 *F*	
Total variable overhead variance = $1,032 *U* – $2,261 *F*	=	$ –1,229 *F*	(7)
Total fixed overhead variance = –$2,013 *U* – $875 *F*	=	1,138 *U*	
Total overhead variance		$ –91 *F*	(6)

EXHIBIT 15.11 ARGOSY CORPORATION: CALCULATION OF VARIANCES *(CONTINUED)*

Examination of Exhibits 15.12 and 15.13 reveals that overall variance analysis should include both budget data at the forecast level of operations (column A) and budget data at the actual level of operations (flexible budget—column B). This approach isolates variances due solely to the difference between the planned and actual level of operations (column D—these could be called operating volume variances) from the conventional cost and sales price variances (column E). Notice that there is no fixed overhead volume variance in the variable costing system; the totals in column E differ by the amount of the fixed overhead volume variance, –$875 *F*.

15.6 VARIANCE ANALYSIS IN ACTIVITY-BASED COSTING

The foregoing demonstrates the general usefulness of standard costing to provide consistently reasonable product costs and variances that facilitate management by exception. The emergence of activity-based costing (ABC), however, and its focus on multiple activities/multiple cost drivers, led to alternative overhead variances. These alternatives can provide improved information for controlling the overhead costs that are increasingly significant components of total manufacturing cost in many industries. The ABC approach addresses these two concerns about conventional standard cost overhead variances:

- Focus on a single cost driver, such as direct labor.
- Use of that cost driver to generate overhead variances despite the influence on overhead levels of other factors, such as number and type of setups.

	A Forecast Budget X: 10,000 units Y: 10,000 units	B Flexible Budget X: 9,000 units Y: 11,000 units	C Actual X: 9,600 units Y: 11,000 units	D Operating Volume (A - B)	E Variances Sales Price - cost (B - C)	F Total (A - C)
Sales	$500,000	$508,000	$501,800	$8,000 *F* (2)	$ 6,200 *U* (1)	$ 1,800 *F* (3)
Less:						
Cost of Sales						
Materials	$160,000	$162,000	$179,764	$2,000 *U*	$17,764 *U* (4)	$19,764 *U*
Labor	140,000	142,800	154,836	2,800 *U*	12,036 *U* (4)	14,836 *U*
Overhead	105,000	107,100	107,009	2,100 *U*	91 *F* (6)	2,009 *U*
Total	$405,000	$411,900	$441,609	$6,900 *U*	$29,709 *U*	$36,609 *U*
Less:						
Selling, general, and administrative expenses	$ 50,000	$ 50,600	$ 48,540	$ 600 *U*	$ 2,060 *F*	$ 1,460 *F*
Net Income	$ 45,000	$ 45,500	$ 11,651	$ 500 *F*	$33,849 *U*	$33,349 *U*

NOTE: Numerical references to the right of the variances are related to the detailed variance calculations in Exhibit 15-11.

EXHIBIT 15.12 ARGOSY CORPORATION COMPREHENSIVE VARIANCE ANALYSIS—ABSORPTION COSTING

	A	B	C	D	E	F
	Forecast Budget X: 10,000 units Y: 10,000 units	Flexible Budget X: 9,600 units Y: 11,000 units	Actual X: 9,600 units Y: 11,000 units	Operating Volume (A – B)	Variances Sales price – cost (B – C)	Total (A – C)
Sales	$500,000	$508,000	$501,800	$8,000 *U* (2)	$ 6,200 *U* (1)	$ 1,800 *F* (3)
Less:						
Variable cost of sales						
Materials	$160,000	$162,000	$179,764	$2,000 *U*	$17,764 *U* (4)	$19,764 *U*
Labor	140,000	142,800	154,836	2,800 *U*	12,036 *U* (5)	14,836 *U*
Overhead	61,250	62,475	61,246	1,225 *U*	1,229 *F* (7)	4 *F*
Less:						
Variable selling general, and administrative expenses	20,000	20,600	19,800	600 *U*	800 *F*	200 *F*
Total variable costs	$381,250	$387,875	$415,646	$6,625 *U*	$27,771 *U*	$34,396 *U*
Contribution margin	$118,750	$120,125	$ 86,154	$1,375 *F*	$33,971 *U*	$32,596 *U*
Less:						
Fixed overhead	$ 43,750	$ 43,750	$ 45,763	—	$ 2,013 *U* (8)	$ 2,013 *U*
Fixed selling, general, and administrative expenses	30,000	30,000	28,740	—	1,260 *F*	1,260 *F*
Total fixed costs	$ 73,750	$ 73,750	$ 74,503		$7 53 *U*	$ 753 *U*
Net Income	$ 45,000	$ 46,375	$ 11,651	$1,375 *F*	$34,724 *U*	$33,349 *U*

Note: Numerical references to the right of the variances are related to the detailed variance calculations in Exhibit 15.11.

EXHIBIT 15.13 ARGOSY CORPORATION COMPREHENSIVE VARIANCE ANALYSIS—VARIABLE COSTING

ABC overhead variances disaggregate total variance amounts, attributing pieces thereof to more than one *basic* and *secondary* cost driver and, in batch processing, to off-budget setups or other lumpy cost components. The costs driven by a basic cost driver (BCD) produce ABC spending and efficiency variances identical to their traditional counterparts. But the secondary cost driver (SCD) allows a third variance attributable to the impact of deviations in BCD usage on SCD usage.

(a) SECONDARY COST DRIVER CONSIDERATIONS. Suppose electricity (e) is the secondary cost driver in a production process that has direct labor-hours (h) as the basic cost driver. The analysis measures electricity as kilowatt (KW) hour cost per labor-hour. Using notation similar to that used previously, these definitions apply:

P_{ae} = actual KW hour cost per labor-hour

P_{se} = standard KW cost per labor-hour

Q_{ae} = actual KW used per labor-hour

Q_{se} = standard KW hour used per labor-hour

Q_{ah} = actual labor-hours worked

Q_{sh} = standard hours worked for actual production

Here are the ABC variances:

$$\text{ABC variable overhead spending variance} = P_{ae}Q_{ae}Q_{ah} - P_{se}Q_{ae}Q_{ah} = (P_{ae} - P_{se})Q_{ae}Q_{ah}$$

$$\text{ABC variable overhead SCD efficiency variance} = P_{se}Q_{ae}Q_{ah} - P_{se}Q_{se}Q_{ah} = (Q_{ae} - Q_{se})P_{se}Q_{ah}$$

$$\text{ABC variable overhead BCD efficiency variance} = P_{se}Q_{se}Q_{ah} - P_{se}Q_{se}Q_{sh} = (Q_{ah} - Q_{sh})P_{se}Q_{se}$$

Summing these three variances and collecting terms gives the total overhead variance attributable to the secondary cost driver, electricity: $P_{ae}Q_{ae}Q_{ah} - P_{se}Q_{se}Q_{sh}$. The term $P_{se}Q_{se}Q_{ah}$ is the standard cost of electricity given the actual BCD hours worked. Bottom line, this analysis reveals how much of the total electricity cost variance is due to price deviations, usage per hour deviations, and labor-hour deviations—information concealed in conventional variance analysis.

(b) SETUP AND BATCH CONSIDERATIONS. When setup costs become important in batch processing, ABC helps us understand the variances in costs related to the setup process. Number of setups, hours per setup, and lubricants and similar materials used in each setup affect these costs. Because traditional analysis usually treated setups as part of fixed overhead, ABC emphasizes that setups are lumpy costs that can vary and offers a refined variance analysis of the setup process that can pinpoint problems that were previously subsumed in a black hole. An examination of setup hours illustrates the approach and uses this notation:

S_a = Actual number of setups

S_s = Standard setups for actual production

H_a = Actual hours per setup

H_s = Standard hours per setup

W_a = Actual hourly wage rate

W_s = Standard hourly wage rate

The ABC setup variances follow:

$$\text{ABC setup spending variance} = S_aH_aW_a - S_aH_aW_s = (W_a - W_s)S_aH_a$$

$$\text{ABC setup labor efficiency variance} = S_aH_aW_s - S_aH_sW_s = (H_a - H_s)S_aW_s$$

$$\text{ABC setup efficiency variance} = S_aH_sW_s - S_sH_sW_s = (S_a - S_s)H_sW_s$$

Thus, one can attribute the difference between the total actual setup labor cost and the setup labor cost budgeted for the actual production ($S_aH_aW_a - S_sH_sW_s$) to three factors:

1. Wage rate deviating from standard
2. Hours per setup differing from standard
3. Number of setups differing from those budgeted for the actual production

Although the wage rate may lie beyond the control of the production team, management can now address problems with inefficient setups and excessive number of setups (or batch size).

(c) NUMERICAL ILLUSTRATIONS. Data for the secondary cost driver and setup variance illustrations, followed by the variance calculations, appear in Exhibits 15.14 and 15.15, respectively.

Exhibit 15.14's analysis attributes the overall \$178.4 *U* electricity cost variance largely to the actual KWH price exceeding the standard. The –\$42 *F* BCD variance offsets the cost of excessive electricity use given actual hours, measured in the \$40.6 *U* SCD variance, because the budgeted amount for hours exceeds actual hours. Traditional variance analysis does not focus on a secondary cost driver. Therefore, an overall variable overhead rate driven by labor-hours hides the cost of electricity and its inefficient use, which the traditional two-way spending/efficiency analysis will not detect.

According to the analysis in Exhibit 15.15, the small –\$15 *F* total setup variance that traditional cost variances do not address includes two larger partially offsetting variances that indicate cost-saving opportunities that the firm likely could realize. The \$32 *F* setup labor efficiency variance suggests that the firm can achieve savings by reducing the standard number of hours per setup whereas the \$84 *U* setup efficiency variance indicates that actual production utilized too many setups.

Data for Illustration

P_{ae} = actual KW hour cost/labor-hour = \$.08	P_{se} = standard KW cost/labor-hour = \$.07
Q_{ae} = actual KW used/labor-hour = 124	Q_{se} = standard KW hour used/labor-hour = 120
Q_{ah} = actual labor-hours = 145	Q_{sh} = standard hours for actual production = 150

Variance Calculations

$$\begin{aligned}
\text{ABC Variable Overhead Spending Variance} &= (P_{ae} - P_{se})Q_{ae}Q_{ah} \\
&= (\$.08 - \$.07) \times 124 \times 145 \\
&= \$.01 \times 17980 \\
&= 179.80\ U \\
\text{ABC Variable Overhead SCD Efficiency Variance} &= (Q_{ae} - Q_{se})P_{se}Q_{ah} \\
&= (124 - 120) \times \$.07 \times 145 \\
&= 40.6\ U \\
\text{ABC Variable Overhead BCD Efficiency Variance} &= (Q_{ah} - Q_{sh})P_{se}Q_{se} \\
&= (145 - 150) \times \$.07 \times 120 \\
&= -42\ F \\
\text{The total variable overhead variance} &= 179.8 + 40.6 - 42 \\
&= (\$.08 \times 124 \times 145) - (\$.07 \times 120 \times 150) \\
&= 178.4\ U
\end{aligned}$$

EXHIBIT 15.14 ACTIVITY-BASED COSTING SECONDARY COST DRIVER VARIANCE ILLUSTRATION

Data for Illustration

S_a = actual number of setups = 11	S_s = standard setups for actual production	= 10
H_a = actual hours per setup = 6	H_s = standard hours per setup	= 7
W_a = actual hourly wage rate = \$12.50	W_s = standard hourly wage rate	= \$12.00

Variance Calculations

$$\begin{aligned}
\text{ABC Setup Spending Variance} &= (W_a - W_s)S_aH_a \\
&= (\$12.50 - \$12.00) \times 11 \times 6 \\
&= 33\ U \\
\text{ABC Setup Labor Efficiency Variance} &= (H_a - H_s)S_aW_s \\
&= (6 - 7) \times 11 \times \$12.00 \\
&= -132\ F \\
\text{ABC Setup Efficiency Variance} &= (S_a - S_s)H_sW_s \\
&= (11 - 10) \times 7 \times \$12.00 \\
&= 84\ U \\
\text{Total ABC setup variance} &= 33 - 132 + 84 \\
&= (11 \times 6 \times \$12.50) - (10 \times 7 \times \$12.00) \\
&= -15\ F
\end{aligned}$$

EXHIBIT 15.15 ACTIVITY-BASED COSTING SETUP VARIANCE ILLUSTRATION

15.7 *EX POST* VARIANCE ANALYSIS

(a) INTRODUCTION TO *EX POST* ANALYSIS. Standard cost and profit variances derived from comparisons between actual and standard costs and prices have proven useful for monitoring and controlling operations. In many situations, however, traditional cost variance analysis has limited value. Although it will disclose deviations between planned and actual results, it does not incorporate the *revision of plans* to fit the actual circumstances as they unfold. In other words, traditional variance analysis does not disclose the difference between actual results and *what should have been done* had the planning process incorporated all facts known at the end of the period.

In two early papers, Joel Demski developed a framework for a variance system distinguished by its ability to encompass *ex post* analysis.[1] *Ex post* analysis refers to a variance analysis that incorporates results based on what should have been done. To be a valid tool of analysis in a given firm, the following basic conditions should exist:

- The firm employs a relatively formal and explicit decision-making process.
- Management can ascertain whether observed variations are controllable and avoidable.
- Management and employees consider feedback information useful.
- The decision-making process structures the search for alternative decisions.

1. Joel S. Demski, "Analyzing the Effectiveness of the Traditional Standard Cost Variance Model," *Management Accounting* (October 1967), and Joel S. Demski, "An Accounting System Structured on a Linear Programming Model," *The Accounting Review* (October 1967).

The following discussion introduces the technique and motivates its use in practice. Interested readers should consult Demski's original papers for further details.

(b) *EX POST* ANALYSIS IN A SIMPLE MARGINAL ANALYSIS MODEL. Basic economic theory of the firm concludes that a firm earns maximum profit when it sets production at the point where marginal cost (*MC*) = marginal revenue (*MR*) and sets price at the point where a vertical line from the optimum production point (X^*) intersects the demand curve (*D*). Exhibit 15.16 depicts these relations, assuming constant marginal cost.

Suppose that $P^* = \$7$, $MC = \$4$ (assumed not to vary over the range of production possibilities), and $X^* = 100{,}000$. If the firm sets selling price at \$7, then it can sell 100,000 units and earn the highest profit. If fixed costs are \$120,000, profit equals \$180,000 [= (\$7 – \$4) × 100,000 – \$120,000]. Thus, the firm's budget projects a standard selling price of \$7, a standard variable cost of \$4, and net profit of \$180,000.

Now suppose that management receives the final accounting reports shortly after the end of the period. The firm realized all projected plans, except that actual cost during the period was less than the standard by \$.20 and actual profit equaled \$200,000. Thus, the firm had a favorable profit variance of \$–20,000 (= \$180,000 – \$200,000), caused by a favorable cost variance of \$–20,000 [= (\$3.80 – \$4.00) × 100,000].

Had the firm known about and reacted to its cost declining to \$3.80, it would have projected the different price/quantity policy shown in Exhibit 15.17 and set the price at \$6.90. Profit under this new policy would have been \$221,000 [= (\$6.90 – \$3.80) × 110,000) – \$120,000]. But traditional variance analysis reports only the favorable profit variance of \$–20,000 (i.e., \$180,000 – \$200,000) and attributes it to the favorable cost variance of \$–20,000 [= (\$3.80 – \$4.00) × 100,000].

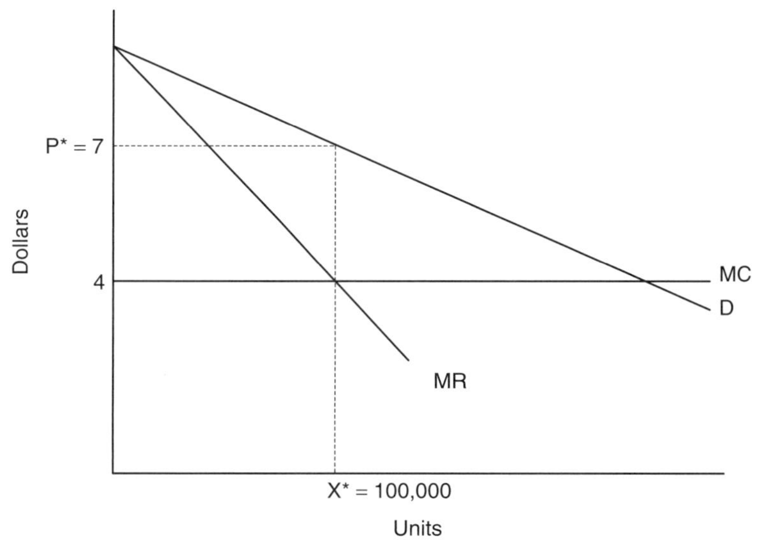

EXHIBIT 15.16 ILLUSTRATION OF *EX ANTE* OPTIMAL PRICE/QUANTITY POLICY

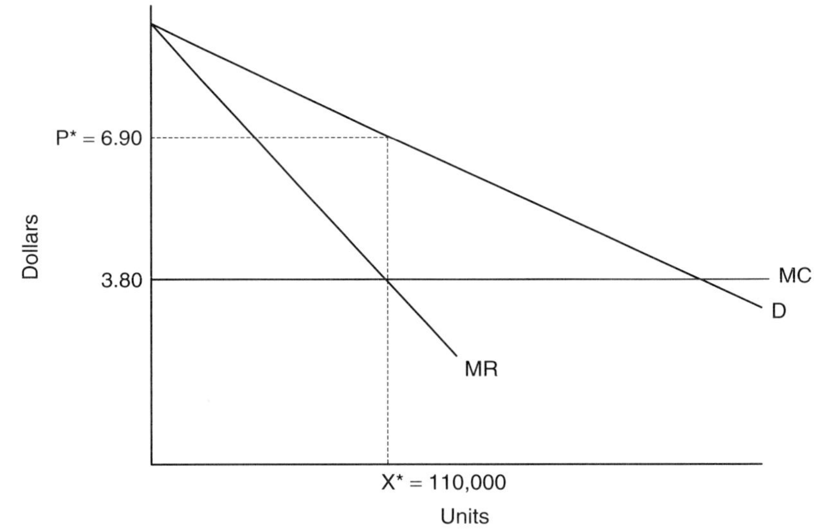

EXHIBIT 15.17 ILLUSTRATION OF *EX POST* OPTIMAL PRICE/QUANTITY POLICY

Ex post analysis explicitly recognizes the existence of the revised optimal policy given the actual data for the period. Symbolically, let

$$NI_a = \textit{ex ante} \text{ or planned profit} = \$180{,}000$$

$$NI_o = \text{actual or observed profit} = 200{,}000$$

$$NI_p = \textit{ex post} \text{ or revised profit} = 221{,}000$$

Therefore,

$$\begin{aligned}(NI_a - NI_o) &= (NI_a - NI_p) + (NI_p - NI_o)\\ \$180{,}000 - \$200{,}000 &= (\$180{,}000 - \$221{,}000)\\ &\quad + (\$221{,}000 - \$200{,}000)\\ \$-20{,}000 &= \$-41{,}000 + \$21{,}000\end{aligned}$$

The term on the left-hand side, $(NI_a - NI_o)$, is the traditional profit variance equal to the difference between planned and actual profit. The first term on the right-hand side, $(NI_a - NI_p)$, the difference between *ex ante* and *ex post* optimum profit, provides a rough indicator of the accuracy of the planning or *forecasting process.* It should highlight the need for additional forecasting and estimation effort. The second term on the right-hand side, $(NI_p - NI_o)$, is the difference between what the firm could have accomplished with the additional information—in this case, the lower production cost—and what the firm did accomplish. It measures the *opportunity cost,* or the cost of following a nonoptimal policy. The *forecasting variance,* $(NI_a - NI_p)$, although favorable, suggests considerable room for improvement. The firm has an unfavorable opportunity cost variance, $(NI_p - NI_o)$.

Before attempting to use these variances to evaluate performance, distinguish between controllable (and avoidable) factors and noncontrollable (and not avoidable) factors. For example, concluding that the decline in cost was random and, therefore, not controllable or predictable, may relieve forecasting personnel of responsibility for the forecasting variance. Similarly, if institutional arrangements limit the flexibility to revise selling prices, personnel involved in pricing decisions need not be responsible for the opportunity cost variance.

One might object that *ex post* analysis is second-guessing and many discourage this method as unfair. However, regular and continuing use of *ex post* analysis may aid in identifying functions evidencing systematic and recurring problems that management can correct.

15.8 THE DECISION TO INVESTIGATE COST VARIANCES

Cost variances provide signals to management that the firm typically uses in a *management by exception* context. Significant variances suggest areas where management needs to reduce excessive costs and tighten standards to achieve cost savings. Because reaction to reported variances for one of these purposes involves a commitment of time, effort, and financial resources, each manager faces a decision: *when is a variance significant enough to justify the cost of an investigative and perhaps corrective undertaking?*

Management rarely knows with certainty whether a given variance is due to a random fluctuation or to an underlying systematic problem, a situation that further complicates the decision making.

Many firms develop rules of thumb to assist them in assessing the significance of variances. Such rules may dictate investigations when the absolute size of the variance exceeds a specific amount or if the ratio of the variance to the total standard cost exceeds some predetermined percentage. These rules result from applying a heuristic approach to coping with the *significance and uncertainty* aspects of evaluating the signals provided by cost variances.

This section develops two more formal methods for dealing with this problem. One can learn from studying these methods, even if their practical application seems limited. The methods prove most helpful in suggesting ways to think about structuring the problem that may not initially appear self-evident.

(a) THE IN-CONTROL/OUT-OF-CONTROL DICHOTOMY. Before deciding to investigate the causal factors behind a cost variance, management should believe that the process generating the variance is, in some sense, *out of control.* Because both favorable and unfavorable variances can signal an out-of-control process, both become candidates for investigation.

A cost variance can have many different values, some of which are more likely to occur than others. Indeed, one can visualize the outcomes of a process generating cost variances as *a frequency or probability* distribution. Exhibit 15.18 illustrates graphically the in-control/out-of-control dichotomy with probability distributions.

Variances with values lying with the *in-control* (middle) distribution arise as a result of normal random fluctuations in a well-behaved process. Values lying within either the favorable or unfavorable *out-of-control* (outer) distributions do not represent random outcomes of a well-behaved process. Rather, they represent the outcomes from a process different from that specified by the standards. Thus, management may decide to revise the standards or correct an underlying problem so that the process once again is well behaved. Uncertainty exists with respect to values lying within either crosshatched area. The process may be *either* in control *or* out of control when such values occur.

(b) COSTS AND BENEFITS FROM INVESTIGATING VARIANCES. The decision to investigate a process reporting a cost variance should follow from a consideration of the

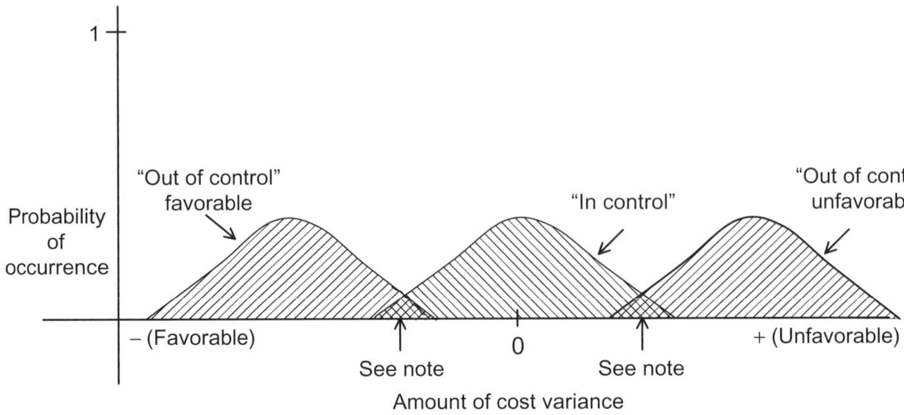

Note: Observed variances lying in these ranges can result from either an in-control or out-of-control process. The uncertainty stems from whether such observations are random and in control or systematic and out of control.

EXHIBIT 15.18 IN CONTROL/OUT-OF-CONTROL DISTRIBUTION OF COST VARIANCES

potential costs and benefits likely to flow from an investigation. The analyst must estimate these costs and benefits as accurately as possible.

(i) Cost of an Investigation. Firms must usually incur further costs to obtain additional information. The firm may need to hire additional personnel or pay overtime. The process may require expensive engineering studies and disassembly of equipment or manufacturing configurations. If the investigation discovers a problem, correcting the problem may require further outlays. Once management establishes the extent of the physical resources required of the investigation, management must compute the additional or incremental *out-of-pocket* costs associated with the investigative effort. Management should consider only incremental outlays, which do not include allocated costs or any other nonavoidable costs. A correct analysis balances the incremental cost of the investigative effort against the incremental benefits from correcting an out-of-control process (or the incremental cost of permitting an out-of-control process to continue).

(ii) Benefits from an Investigation. What will management gain if it discovers and corrects an out-of-control process? Management has two principal considerations: (1) the amount the firm will save each period and (2) the number of periods that the firm expects the savings to continue.

Reducing an unfavorable variance means decreasing the gap between actual and standard cost, either by reducing actual cost each period, by increasing standard cost, or a combination of the two. Correcting a favorable variance narrows the gap between actual and standard cost by reducing standard cost and holding actual cost in subsequent periods at its low level. The reduced standard cost then sets a new lower-cost benchmark. As before, only reductions in *out-of-pocket* costs represent true savings—changes in rates of nonavoidable and allocated costs generally have no economic benefit. Therefore, management needs some analysis to quantify the savings unless a trivial corrective action brings an obviously out-of-control process back into control.

After estimating the expected benefit per period, the accountant must estimate the number of periods over which the benefit will continue, a crucial consideration. With frequent variance reports (i.e., monthly or quarterly), correcting an out-of-control process should produce savings in several of these periods. Although the single-period saving may appear unimpressive, the *present value* of a series of periodic savings may be substantial. When the firm expects the savings to occur over more than three to six months, the analysis should discount the stream of expected periodic savings. Because the cost of an investigation requires an immediate outlay, the firm must balance it against the present value of the expected savings.

(c) THE CONTROL CHART APPROACH. The techniques of *statistical quality control* provide a useful tool for management, the *control chart,* when attempting to evaluate cost variances. Management often uses this chart to monitor physical processes by comparing critical output specifications with predetermined acceptable tolerances. So long as periodic measurements of these specifications lie between the chart's *upper and lower control limits,* management assumes that the process is in control.

The control chart can become a useful device for checking whether reported cost variances indicate that the underlying physical process is in or out of control. If one can assume that the distribution of observed variances follows the normal or bell-shaped probability distribution—such as those displayed in Exhibit 15.18—analysts can use the mean and standard deviation of a group of observations to set upper and lower central limits for the variance. In a normal distribution, about 68.3 percent of the observations lie within one standard deviation (σ) on either side of the mean ($\bar{X}$), about 95.5 percent lie within $\bar{X} \pm 2\sigma$, and about 99.7 percent lie within $\bar{X} \pm 3\sigma$. The control limits will be set at $\bar{X} \pm k\sigma$, where k reflects management's beliefs about the relative costs and benefits from an investigation. When costs are high relative to benefits, k will be large, perhaps 3, ensuring relatively few investigations and that some out-of-control situations may remain uncorrected (Type I errors). When benefits are high relative to costs, k will be lower, perhaps 1.5 to 2, ensuring more investigations, some of which will be of in-control situations (Type II errors).

EXAMPLE 2. CONTROL CHART: LABOR EFFICIENCY VARIANCES OVER THE PAST 12 MONTHS

Month	Labor Efficiency Variance
1	$ 400 *U*
2	700 *U*
3	1,000 *U*
4	−500 *F*
5	−100 *F*
6	1,000 *U*
7	−1,100 *F*
8	−1,000 *F*
9	600 *U*
10	800 *U*
11	−900 *F*
12	−900 *F*
	$ 0

The mean of these outcomes equals \$0 and the estimated standard deviation equals \$838.[2] If these outcomes follow a normal distribution with $\bar{X} = 0$ and $\sigma = 838$, then, for example, 2σ control limits are \$1,676 (upper) and –\$1,676 (lower). So long as the periodic labor efficiency variances remain inside these limits, the probability that the process is in control is .95; according to chance, 95 percent of the in-control periodic variances fall within these limits.

The control chart becomes most useful when it reflects a large sample of observations.[3] If accountants report weekly variances, one can easily obtain a large sample. Otherwise, monitoring the underlying physical process with a control chart may help simply draw attention to unusually large variances when they occur. When management uses control charts to monitor physical processes and each observation provides a sample of physical measurements, the following statistics apply:

$\bar{X}_i$ = Arithmetic mean of the ith sample

$\bar{\bar{X}}$ = Arithmetic mean of the sample means (the $\bar{X}_i$'s)

R_i = Range of the ith sample (high value minus low value)

$\bar{R}$ = Arithmetic mean of the sample ranges (the $\bar{R}_i$'s).

One need not compute the standard deviations, as conversion tables are available for various σ limits based on the normal probability distribution.[4] The formulas for the upper and lower control limits (UCL and LCL) of $\bar{X}$ and R follow.

$$UCL_{\bar{X}} = \bar{X} + A_2\bar{R} \qquad UCL_R = D_4\bar{R}$$

$$LCL_{\bar{X}} = \bar{\bar{X}} - A_2\bar{R} \qquad LCL_R = D_3\bar{R}$$

The A and D factors are taken from the appropriate table on the row corresponding to the number of items in each sample.

---

2. The estimated standard deviation, s, is calculated as follows:

$$s = \sqrt{\sum_{i=1}^{12} \frac{(X_i - \bar{X})^2}{n-1}} \approx 838$$

3. The assumption that the observations follow a normal probability distribution may not be justified with a small sample. When normality cannot be assumed, *Chebyshev's inequality* may be used to calculate control limits where the underlying distribution is unknown. This inequality states that $1 - (1/k^2)$ of the distribution lies between $\bar{X} \pm k\sigma$ for $k > 1$. If, in the numerical example, we desired 95 percent control limits, then

$$.95 = 1 - 1/k^2$$

$$.05 = 1/k^2$$

$$k^2 = 20$$

$$k \approx 4.5$$

Using Chebyshev's inequality, the upper control limit is \$3,771, and the lower control limit is –\$3,771. These limits are 225 percent as wide as those computed under the assumption of normality!

(d) THE DECISION-THEORETIC APPROACH. The control chart approach to assessing the significance of cost variances fails to dictate a course of action, the main weakness of this approach. By remaining silent on the cost–benefit aspects of a variance investigation, the chart does not disclose when the economics of the situation justify an investigation. The chart can suggest that a process is out of control, but it cannot suggest whether an investigation is warranted.

Analysts can address this shortcoming by applying statistical decision theory to cost variance investigation decisions. A *payoff table* or *matrix* that explicitly considers costs and benefits forms the basis for this approach. Such a table appears in Exhibit 15.19, providing for two possible states of nature (the process is *in control* or *out of control*) and two possible actions (*investigate* or *do not investigate*). This formulation rests on several simplifying assumptions:

- The costs, C, M, and L, remain constant.
- An investigation always detects and corrects an out-of-control process.
- Once the process goes out of control, it remains out of control until corrected.

The decision maker then computes the expected cost associated with each action and selects that action having the lowest expected cost. These calculations call for estimates of the probabilities that the process is in control, P, and out of control $(1 - P)$. The probabilities can be based on the decision maker's experience that the process is in control, say 90 percent of the time, such that $P = .9$ and $(1 - P) = .1$.

$$\begin{aligned}\text{Expected Cost (Investigation)} &= PC + (1 - P)(C + M)\\ &= C + (1 - P)M\\ \text{Expected Cost (No Investigation)} &= 0 + (1 - P)L\\ &= (1 - P)L\end{aligned}$$

Actions	States: In Control	States: Out of Control
Investigate	C	$C + M$
Do not investigate	0	L

C = cost of investigation
M = cost of correcting an out-of-control process
L = cost of permitting an out-of-control process to continue (or benefits foregone by not investigating and correcting an out-of-control process)

EXHIBIT 15.19 COST PAYOFF TABLE FOR VARIANCE INVESTIGATION DECISION

4. See Eugene L. Grant and Richard S. Leavenworth, *Statistical Quality* Control, 7th ed. (New York: McGraw-Hill, 1996), for a complete treatment of statistical quality control and as a source of the conversion tables.

If $C + (1 - P)M$ is less than $(1 - P)L$, management should investigate; otherwise, do not investigate. Note that by setting the expected costs of' the two actions equal to each other, we can solve for the value of P for which the decision maker shows indifference between the two actions. Calculation of this breakeven probability, P^*, follows.

$$
\begin{aligned}
C + (1 - P)M &= (1 - P)L \\
C &= (1 - P)(L - M) \\
C/(L - M) &= 1 - P \\
P^* &= 1 - C/(L - M)
\end{aligned}
$$

Given the costs C, M, and L, the decision maker who believes that P^* exceeds the in-control probability knows that investigating has the lowest expected cost and may proceed accordingly.

EXAMPLE 3. INVESTIGATION DECISION

The accounting system reports a \$10,000 unfavorable raw material quantity variance. If analysts can find and correct the cause of the variance, the firm will realize estimated cost savings of \$4,000 (L). Out-of-pocket investigation costs (C) equal \$600 and for correction (M) equal \$1,500. Management believes that the process is in control 80 percent of the time. What action should the firm take?

$$
\begin{aligned}
\text{Expected cost (Investigation)} &= C + (1 - P)M \\
&= \$600 + (1 - .8) \times \$1{,}500 \\
&= \$900 \\
\text{Expected cost (No investigation)} &= (1 - P)L \\
&= (1 - .8) \times \$4{,}000 \\
&= \$800
\end{aligned}
$$

Therefore, the model suggests that management should not investigate the variance.

Knowledge of the breakeven probability, P^*, can have value here.

$$
\begin{aligned}
P^* &= -C/(L - M) \\
&= 1 - [\$600/(\$4{,}000 - \$1{,}500)] \\
&= 1 - .24 \\
&= .76
\end{aligned}
$$

Suppose that the manager feels that the estimate of $P = .8$ is too high given recent material usage trends. If the manager's current estimate lies closer to .7 than .8, and less than P^*, the manager may decide to investigate anyway.

If C and M are fairly constant over time and for various types of investigations, one can prepare a decision chart using values of P^* computed at various amounts of L to identify combinations of P^* and L for which investigation leads to the lowest expected cost.

Example 4. Decision Chart

Suppose that L is typically 40 percent of a reported variance when the underlying process is out of control. Then for variances of \$8,000, \$10,000, \$12,000, and \$14,000, L becomes \$3,200, \$4,000, \$4,800, and \$5,600. The chart computes the values of P^* for C – \$600, M – \$1,500, and the above amounts of L. These coordinates of these P^* values create the indifference curve shown in the decision chart in Exhibit 15.20.

$$P^*_{3,200} = 1 - [\$600/(\$3,200 - \$1,500)] = .647$$

$$P^*_{4,000} = 1 - [\$600/(\$4,000 - \$1,500)] = .76$$

$$P^*_{4,800} = 1 - [\$600/(\$4,800 - \$1,500)] = .818$$

$$P^*_{5,600} = 1 - [\$600/(\$5,600 - \$1,500)] = .854$$

Exhibit 15.20 shows that for combinations of P and L to the left of the indifference curve, either P is too large or L is too small to trigger an investigation. The opposite holds true for the area to the right of the indifference curve.

(iii) Extensions of the Basic Decision-Theoretic Approach. The following lists some extensions to this simplified decision approach:

- Periodic revision of the in-control and out-of-control state probabilities, using Bayes' theorem
- Consideration of both exploratory and complete investigations
- The use of transition probabilities to allow for the chance that an out-of-control process will correct itself
- Expansion from a one-period to a multiperiod framework

These extensions lie beyond the scope of this chapter.

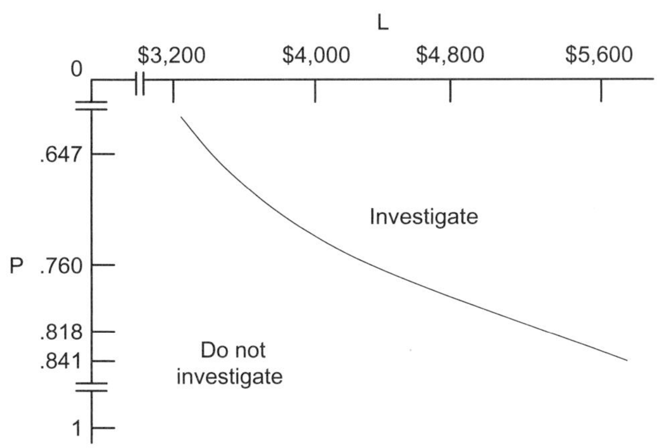

Exhibit 15.20 Cost Variance Investigation Decision Chart

15.9 SUMMARY

A properly functioning standard cost system provides both consistent product costs and signals to management regarding potential trouble spots in the firm's operations. Management can use traditional production cost variances, augmented by sales variances, to analyze the difference between budgeted and actual net income by disaggregating the total variance into several components. An activity-based costing framework aids in framing variances that reveal information not evident in the traditional cost variance model. Formal consideration of the costs and benefits likely to flow from an investigative and corrective action can help management employ its investigative resources effectively. Finally, the use of *ex post* analytical techniques can further assist in measuring opportunity costs and the general accuracy of the firm's forecasting activity.

BIBLIOGRAPHY

Demski, Joel S. "An Accounting System Structured on a Linear Programming Model" *The Accounting Review* (October 1967).

_________ "Analyzing the Effectiveness of the Traditional Standard Cost Variance Model." *Management Accounting* (October 1967).

_________*Information Analysis*. Reading, Mass.: Addison-Wesley Publishing Company, 1972.

Financial Accounting Standards Board, "Inventory Costs, an amendment of ARB No. 43, Chapter 4" *Statement of Financial Accounting Standards No. 151,* (Norwalk, CT: FASB, 2004).

Grant, Eugene L., and Richard S. Leavenworth. *Statistical Quality Control,* 7th ed. New York: McGraw-Hill Co., Inc., 1996.

Ostwald, Phillip F. *Cost Estimating for Engineering and Management.* Englewood Cliffs, N.J.: Prentice-Hall, 1974.

Stammerjohan, William W. "Better Information through the Marriage of ABC and Traditional Standard Costing Techniques." *Management Accounting Quarterly* (Fall 2001).

CHAPTER 16

ALLOCATIONS OF COST AND REVENUE*

ROMAN L. WEIL, CPA, CMA, PHD, EDITOR
University of Chicago

CONTENTS

16.1 INTRODUCTION 465

16.2 PURPOSES OF COST ALLOCATION 466

16.3 DEFINITIONS 466

16.4 THE FUNDAMENTAL PROBLEMS 467

16.5 COMMON, OTHER THAN JOINT, COST ALLOCATION 468
- (a) Stand-Alone Method 468
- (b) Incremental-Cost Method 468
- (c) Shapley Value Method 468
- (d) Theory Provides No Right Answer 469

16.6 JOINT COST ALLOCATION 469
- (a) Relative Sales Value (at Splitoff) Method 470
- (b) Net Realizable Value (at Splitoff) Method 470
- (c) Constant Gross Margin Percentage Method 472
- (d) Physical Quantities Methods 472
- (e) Benefits Received Methods 472
- (f) Ability to Bear Method 473
- (g) Do Not Allocate Joint Costs without Compulsion 473

16.7 BYPRODUCTS 474

16.8 ALLOCATION OF REVENUE 475
- (a) Theory Provides No Right Answer 475
- (b) Bundled Lease Allocations 476

16.9 FURTHER READING 477

APPENDIX 16A STEP-DOWN AND RECIPROCAL METHODS FOR ALLOCATING SERVICE DEPARTMENT COSTS 478

BIBLIOGRAPHY 481

16.1 INTRODUCTION

Allocation issues arise in accounting to the extent historical costs provide the basis for valuation. If all balance sheet amounts reported fair values, few allocation issues would

* Thanks to George Foster of Stanford University, some of whose unpublished writings I used in preparing this chapter. I have relied on Hugo Nurnberg's "Joint Products and By-Products," which appeared as Chapter 18 in the original *Handbook of Cost Accounting* and on M.W. Maher, C.P. Stickney, and R.L. Weil, *Managerial Accounting: An Introduction to Concepts, Methods, and Uses,* (Mason, Ohio: Thomson South-Western, 2006). The authors of the appendix to this chapter (Leslie Eldenburg and Naomi Soderstrom) originally wrote that material for Chapter 28. Because of its general applicability, the editors have moved it here.

arise.[1] This chapter discusses primarily cost allocations, but also discusses revenue allocations.

16.2 PURPOSES OF COST ALLOCATION

Accounting allocates costs to time periods (think amortization) and to products (think cost accounting). Why? Accountants allocate costs (and to a lesser degree, revenues) to do the following:

- Provide data to managers making decisions
- Aid in implementing decisions
- Evaluate how well implementations progress
- Motivate and evaluate employees
- Satisfy requirements of financial reporting
- Satisfy income tax regulations
- Provide the basis for reimbursement in cost-based contracts

Accountants tend to use the terms *cost assignment* and *cost allocation* interchangeably. Much of cost management focuses on the assignment of costs to cost objects, such as products, processes, and segments. Several other chapters in this book treat cost assignments. The easy issues in cost assignment involve direct costs and other costs where analysis can establish a cause-and-effect relation. If an activity or cost object causes a cost, the accountants assign that cost to the causing activity or cost object.

This chapter focuses on the more difficult issues where analysis cannot establish a cause and effect relation—situations involving joint products, joint costs, and common costs. The appendix to the chapter treats the allocation of service department costs to production departments. Although there is a cause-and-effect relation, no other chapter in this book addresses this issue, so the editors have put the material at the end of this chapter.

16.3 DEFINITIONS

Common costs. Common costs occur when a process produces multiple products. An automobile production line that produces sedans and SUVs incurs common costs. Costs can be common to periods of time, classes of customers, and sales territories.

Joint costs, joint-process costs, and *joint products. Joint costs* occur when a process inevitably produces multiple products (called joint products), not necessarily in fixed proportions, from a single process or resource. Here are some classic examples:

- A steer, whose total costs jointly enable production of the joint products meat and hides
- Petroleum lifted from underground, whose costs jointly enable production of the joint products gasoline and natural gas liquids

All joint costs are common costs, but not all common costs are joint. Management chooses to produce both sedans and SUVs on the same assembly line, causing the line's costs to be common. The commonality does not result from a fact of nature, but

1. I'm tempted to write *no,* but we learn never to say *never* in accounting—well, almost never.

from conscious choice. Some writers use the term *joint-process costs* to refer to the joint costs of a manufacturing process, in contrast to the joint costs of the raw materials input to the process.

Byproducts. When a joint product has small value relative to other joint products, accountants call that joint product a *byproduct* and use simplified allocation methods for it. The example in Section 16.6 considers saw dust and wood chips produced as the inevitable output of converting logs into lumber.

Separable costs, the splitoff point, and *depth-of-processing decisions.* In producing joint products, the process typically reaches a stage, called the *splitoff point,* where further costs, called *separable costs,* are direct and caused by decisions to process further. The slaughter of a steer causes simultaneously production of meat and hides. The dressing of meat and the tanning of hides occur after the splitoff point. Management now has discretion as to cost incurrence: dispose of the entrails or process them further. We refer to the decision of whether to process further as a *depth-of-processing decision.* The decision to process further causes *separable costs.*

16.4 THE FUNDAMENTAL PROBLEMS

All methods of allocating joint costs are arbitrary. We require that the methods be systematic and rational, but nevertheless they are arbitrary.[2] No causal relation identifies a portion of the joint cost resulting from an individual joint product. To get one product inevitably requires getting the other and incurring the costs for both.

Allocating joint costs poses issues for accountants because the needs of allocated joint costs for financial reporting differ from those for decision making. Cost accounting systems serve multiple purposes, including product pricing, product emphasis, cost control, and reporting to internal and external constituents. The same set of computations rarely satisfies every purpose, as discussed in Chapter 3. Rather, analysts adjust the information contained in a cost accounting system to tailor the resulting cost figures and cost reports to the specific purpose at issue. The purpose at issue guides the set of costing methods.

Common costs, other than joint costs, result from management discretion. That discretion leads to methods for allocating common costs based on cause-and-effect relations. The difficulties arise because, typically, no unique answer results from these methods.

Consider the assembly line that produces both sedans and SUVs. Assume the total, common, cost of the line is \$10 million. Assume further that an assembly line for sedans alone costs \$6 million and that an assembly line for SUVs alone costs \$9 million. If management says, "We started with sedans, the decision to add SUVs is incremental," then the accountant can say the decision to produce SUVs *causes* costs of \$4 million (= \$10 – \$6). Cause-and-effect analysis allocates \$6 million of common assembly line costs to sedans and \$4 million to SUVs. If, however, management says, "We started with SUVs; the decision to add sedans is incremental," cause-and-effect analysis allocates \$9 million of common costs to SUVs and \$1 (= \$10– \$9) million to sedans.

2. The word *arbitrary* in this context often causes difficulties in courtroom proceedings. Accountants use the word *arbitrary* to use terms in the *Oxford English Dictionary,* to imply discretion, that is, methods not based on the nature of things. Accountants do not mean whimsy nor random nor capricious, all of which to one degree or another associate with the word *arbitrary* in common usage.

In many situations, one cannot uniquely identify the base product and the incremental product, so these methods do not give unique answers. Because one can more easily understand the issues of allocating common—other than joint—costs, I address those first.

16.5 COMMON, OTHER THAN JOINT, COST ALLOCATION

Refer to the data in the previous example for the common $10 million cost of an assembly line for sedans and SUVs. Accountants have used the following methods to allocate these common costs.

(a) STAND-ALONE METHOD. Assume that if the manufacturer built separate, stand-alone assembly lines, one for sedans and one for SUVs, the total costs would equal $15 (= $6 + $9) million. The sedan line would cost 40 percent (6/15) of the total two-assembly line costs and the SUV line costs 60 percent (9/15). The stand-alone method uses these percentages to allocate the common costs: 40 percent, or $4 million, to sedans and 60 percent, or $6 million, to SUVs.

The stand-alone method allocates common costs in proportion to the costs the firm would incur if it undertook the common activities as separate activities. Some accountants think the stand-alone method is fair, but no one that I know of has an operational definition of *fair* to justify this label.

(b) INCREMENTAL-COST METHOD. The SUV and sedan example in Section 16.4 illustrates the incremental-cost method. This method assumes a base configuration of facilities and product, with a base cost. Then it hypothetically adds facilities and products, with incremental cost. The total of base cost and incremental cost equals the total common cost. The incremental-cost method allocates first to the base product all base costs and the incremental costs to the added product

The incremental-cost method generalizes to more than two common products. The assembly line could conceivably produce a third product, convertibles, a fourth, pick-up trucks, and so on. If one specifies the base product, and the order of incremental additions, a common cost allocation based on incremental costs results. If there are several, say n, products, each potentially incremental to the others, then there are $n \times (n - 1) \times (n - 2)\cdots 2 \times 1$ (often called "n factorial" and denoted $n!$) different allocations. For $n = 3$, there are potentially six different allocations ($3 \times 2 \times 1$).

In a negotiation context, whether allocating costs to cost objects within a company or in setting reimbursement rates in cost-plus contracts, every party wants to represent the incremental product or process, as incremental costs typically decline as the process adds products.

(c) SHAPLEY VALUE METHOD. Modern accounting theorists, following the lead of Joel Demski, have adopted the mathematical, game-theoretic construct of the Shapley Value to the incremental-cost method. (See Chapter 5 in this book, authored by Demski.) The Shapley Value method assigns to each of the common elements the average of the costs that the incremental-cost method would assign to each as primary and as incremental.

Consider Section 16.4's example: If sedans are the primary product, the allocation to them is $6 million; if they are the incremental product, their allocation is $1 million, an average of $3.5 [= (6 + 1)/2)] million. If SUVs are the primary product, the allocation to them is $9 million; if they are the incremental product, their allocation is $4 million, an average of \$6.5 [= (9 + 4)/2] million. The Shapley Value method assigns \$3.5 million to sedans and \$6.5 million to SUVs.

(d) THEORY PROVIDES NO RIGHT ANSWER. Which of these methods—stand-alone, incremental, traditional, or Shapley—is right in theory? That question has no answer. No allocation will, better than the other, enable management to make wealth-enhancing decisions.

If management can show that one of the common costs was, indeed, incremental to the other, then cause-and-effect allocations emerge and a unique answer emerges. The facts of the case matter.

If management needs such an allocation, that need likely results from some contractual provision, such as the need to pay license fees to inventors of processes used on the assembly lines. If the license holders of the rights to the processes for the two sets of intellectual property have the same interests in both lines, then the allocation between the two lines does not matter, as amounts paid to each owner will be the same, no matter the allocation. If the owners have different interests, then the allocation matters to the owners. Still, theory provides no uniquely right answer. To get a uniquely right answer, one needs to look to the contract that the licensees have with the manufacturer. Most likely, the contract will not specify a method; in this case, economic theory does not provide an answer.

When the difference matters because the situation involves large dollar amounts, and when the contract does not address the allocation method, the issue likely ends up in litigation. We advise the court to do what seems equitable under the circumstances; neither economics nor accounting has one, correct, answer. A right answer might emerge from the specific facts.

16.6 JOINT COST ALLOCATION

Why should cost managers deal with allocating joint-process costs when joint-cost allocations are arbitrary? Organizations allocate joint costs to measure performance, to calculate rate-regulated prices, to estimate casualty losses (such as from fire or flood), to satisfy contractual obligations, and to resolve contractual disputes. Manufacturing companies must allocate joint costs to value inventories and cost of goods sold for financial and tax reporting. Although no cause-and-effect method can trace joint costs to joint products as ABC costing seeks to do in other production processes (see Chapter 6), the results of allocating joint costs in different ways in practice often affect managerial decisions in planning, performance evaluation, and decision making. Joint cost allocations should not affect managerial decisions aimed at maximizing net present value of cash flows, but in practice they often do.

This section discusses the following methods of joint cost allocation and ends with a suggestion to avoid them all.

- Relative sales value (at splitoff) method
- Net realizable value (at splitoff) method
- Constant gross margin method
- Physical quantities methods
- Benefits received method
- Ability to bear method

Many companies, particularly those in forest products, oil and gas, and chemicals and mining, produce multiple joint products from a joint process. For example, a forest products company can process timber (logs) into lumber of various grades and sizes. The company can convert resulting sawdust and wood chips into paper pulp. One input (timber) can yield several different products.

Exhibit 16.1 presents data for the costs that Humboldt Lumber Company incurs to process logs into lumber for a month.[3] Raw materials (rough logs) cost $250,000 and processing costs $110,000, resulting in total costs of $360,000. As Humboldt processes the logs, two joint products emerge at the splitoff point—standard lumber and specialty lumber.

(a) RELATIVE SALES VALUE (AT SPLITOFF) METHOD. First, assume that a ready market for the two grades of lumber exists as they emerge from the splitoff point, enabling Humboldt to sell the two grades of lumber as is. Exhibit 16.1 shows these sales amounts as $504,000 for specialty lumber and $756,000 for standard lumber, $1,260,000 in total. Specialty lumber represents 40 percent (= $504,000/$1,260,000) of that total and standard lumber represents 60 percent. The relative sales value method allocates the joint costs in proportion to the relative sales values (see Panel A of Exhibit 16.1).

Some writers refer to this method as the Net Realizable Value Method, described next, because it represents a special case of that method, in that the firm need not incur additional processing costs necessary past splitoff to ready either joint product for immediate sale.

This method measures the value of the joint products immediately at the end of the joint process, and it is based on objectively measurable market prices. This method has no difficult calculations and requires no projections of management intent with respect to further processing and sales strategies. For these reasons, many accountants prefer this method when the company can sell the joint products immediately after splitoff.

(b) NET REALIZABLE VALUE (AT SPLITOFF) METHOD. Now, assume that at least one of the joint products, in this example specialty lumber, requires further processing before the firm can sell it. Panel B of Exhibit 16.1 shows the additional processing costs as $97,000, so the net realizable value of specialty lumber at splitoff no longer equals $504,000, as before, but is $407,000 (= $504,000 – $97,000). This method, sometimes called the *NRV method,* allocates the joint costs in proportion to the net realizable values of the joint products.

The relative sales value method, discussed above, is a special case of the NRV method, because the two methods give the same results when the firm does not incur additional processing costs.

The basis underlying the NRV method is that revenue dollars from each joint product earns the same percentage contribution at the splitoff point as the revenue dollars from any other joint product. The net realizable value approach matches the input costs with revenues generated by the total of all joint products.

The NRV method does not give unique cost allocations, as it results in a different allocation for each combination of additional processing procedures and costs. For example, assume Humboldt has the option to make specialty lumber ready for immediate sale

3. I have constructed this example from a simpler version of it in M.W. Maher, C.P. Stickney, and R.L. Weil, *Managerial Accounting: An Introduction to Concepts, Methods, and Uses,* (Mason, Ohio: Thomson South-Western, 2006), Chapter 15.

Joint Costs

	Total
Raw materials (Logs)	$ 250,000
Conversion costs	110,000
Total Joint Costs Requiring Allocation	$ 360,000

Allocation of Joint Costs

A. Sales Value at Splitoffs
(No Additional Processing Costs)

	Specialty Lumber	Standard Lumber	Total
Sales value at splitoff	$ 504,000	$ 756,000	$1,260,000
Less: Additional processing costs	-	-	-
Net Realizable Value at Splitoff Point	$ 504,000	$ 756,000	$1,260,000
Proportionate Share			
$504,000/$1,260,000	40%		
$756,000/$1,260,000		60%	
Allocated Joint-Process Costs			
$360,000 x 40%	$ 144,000		
$360,000 x 60%		$ 216,000	

B. Net Realizable Value at Splitoff
(With Additional Processing Costs)

	Specialty Lumber	Standard Lumber	Total
Final Sales Value	$ 504,000	$ 756,000	$126,000
Less: Additional processing costs	(97,000)	-	(97,000)
Net Realizable Value at Splitoff Point	$ 407,000	$ 756,000	$1,163,000
Proportionate Share			
$504,000/$1,260,000	35%		
$756,000/$1,260,000		65%	
Allocated Joint-Process Costs			
$360,000 x 35%	$ 126,000		
$360,000 x 65%		$ 234,000	

C. Constant Gross Margin Percentage Method

	Specialty Lumber	Standard Lumber	Total
Final Sales Value	$ 504,000	$ 756,000	$1,260,000
Less: Additional processing costs	(97,000)	-	(97,000)
Net Realizable Value at Splitoff Point	$ 407,000	$ 756,000	$1,163,000
Less: Joint costs			(360,000)
Gross Margin on All Joint Products			$ 803,000
Gross Margin Percentage All Products (= $803,000/$1,260,000)			63.7%
Gross Margin on Individual Products			
= 63.7% x $504,000	$ 321,200		
= 63.7% x $756,000		$ 481,800	
Allocated Joint-Process Costs			
$407,000 – $321,200	$ 85,800		
$756,000 – $481,800		$ 274,200	

D. Physical Units Method

	Specialty Lumber	Standard Lumber	Total
Board Feet of Lumber Produced	2,800	3,920	6,720
Proportionate Share			
2,800/6,720	42%		
3,920/6,720		58%	
Allocated Joint-Process Costs			
$360,000 x 42%	$ 150,000		
$360,000 x 68%		$ 210,000	

EXHIBIT 16.1 HUMBOLDT LUMBER COMPANY DATA FOR JOINT COST ALLOCATION EXAMPLES

using a different process, which takes more time and costs $100,000, but results in an immediate market price of $520,000. Exhibit 16.1 does not show this computation, but the allocations would change from 35:65 to 36:64. The supporters of the NRV method do not provide guidance on how to choose between alternative results.

(c) CONSTANT GROSS MARGIN PERCENTAGE METHOD. Whereas the NRV method assumes all joint products earn the same percentage gross margin at the splitoff point, the constant gross margin percentage method assumes all joint products earn the same percentage gross margin on final selling price, after additional processing costs. The NRV method does not use data on profits, as does the constant gross margin percentage method. In addition, in some circumstances, this constant gross margin percentage can result in negative allocations of joint costs to some products and allocations to other products larger than the total of joint costs. Exhibit 16.1, Panel C, demonstrates this method.

Although this chapter includes this method for the sake of completeness, no reason exists for preferring it to the NRV method.

(d) PHYSICAL QUANTITIES METHODS. The physical quantities method allocates joint-process costs based on a physical measure of volume, or weight, or other measure of physical characteristics. Consider the effect of this method on allocating the costs of a steer to bones and to steak based on weight. The resulting allocations bear no resemblance to economic amounts, so this method has little theoretical support.

Accountants sometimes use this method when volatile output product prices create uncertain market value after processing, or when significant additional processing of uncertain amounts must occur between the splitoff point and the first point of marketability. This approach may also be appropriate when the market does not set product prices—for example, regulated companies. In regulated industries, where market prices depend on allocated costs, allocating costs based on the regulated market prices would involve circularity.

Return to the Humboldt Company example. Assume that the company does not know market values at the splitoff point, but that it does know that for every $360,000 of joint costs in processing logs, it gets 2,800 board feet of specialty lumber and 3,920 board feet of standard lumber, a total of 6,720 board feet. This method allocates the joint costs, as in Panel D of Exhibit 16.1, in proportions 2,800/6,720 and 3,920/6,720.

(e) BENEFITS RECEIVED METHODS. Imagine an advertising campaign for a company with two products—one well known, with substantial sales, and one brand new in the market with few sales—for example, Starbucks coffee and Starbucks cola or Coca-Cola and Coca-Cola Coffee. Management wishes to allocate to the two products the common cost of the advertising program that promotes the general image of the company, rather than either specific product. Few companies can effectively accomplish this, but managements attempt it anyway.

Firms often use the benefits received criterion in situations that require a cost assignment, but no technically feasible way exists to relate specific causes and specific effects. Consider our advertising program example that promotes the corporation's general image. The firm can allocate the costs of such a program on the basis of product revenue. One could reason that products with higher revenues benefit more from the advertising than products with lower revenues and therefore ought to bear more of the advertising costs.

The benefits received method often arises in government contract accounting. Federal acquisitions regulations cite the benefits received criterion when discussing the costs allocable to a government contract:

> A cost (is) allocable if it is assignable or chargeable to one or more cost objectives in accordance with the relative benefits received or other equitable relationship.
>
> Subject to the foregoing a cost is allocable to a government contract if it:
>
> - is incurred specifically for the contract;
> - benefits both the contract and other work–and can be distributed to them in reasonable proportion to the benefits received; or it is necessary to the overall operation of the business, although a direct relationship to any particular cost objective cannot be shown.[4]

(f) ABILITY TO BEAR METHOD. The *ability to bear* method operates just as the benefits received method operates, but has a different rationale. Consider the allocation of central corporate overhead to divisions, one profitable and the other not. Some would allocate costs to the divisions in proportion to their profitability before the allocation, with profitability measured in any one of several ways. Allocations based on preallocation profitability are ability to bear methods.

If the only method that seems reasonable for allocating a joint cost is this ability to bear method, one should not allocate those costs at all. This method penalizes a profitable division with more allocated burden and subsidizes less-profitable divisions with fewer allocated costs. This can result in poor business decisions based on meaningless profitability numbers. Likely, nothing useful will result from such an allocation.

(g) DO NOT ALLOCATE JOINT COSTS WITHOUT COMPULSION. Accountants have long known that analysts will never make superior managerial decisions based on data resulting from joint cost allocations than when they base them solely on cause-and-effect or on incremental cost data. That is, if a cost does not result from some cause or incremental effort, then ignore it for decision making. Some managerial decisions require accounting data about joint processes and joint products but never do they require allocations of joint costs, unless regulations or contracts impose the requirement. Consider the following questions that require decisions about joint processes and joint products.

- Should management increase or decrease production of joint products?
- Given that management can change the mix of joint products (consider that the lumber mill might produce more standard lumber at the margin, by producing less specialty lumber), should it?
- Should we sell the joint product just after splitoff, or process it further (the depth-of-processing decision)?
- Has the purchasing department, which acquires raw materials for a variety of functions, been efficient?

None of these decisions requires joint cost allocations, nor will better decisions result from using allocated data.

Many managers believe they need joint cost allocations to derive prices. Economics teaches that markets determine selling prices based on industry-wide costs, not on specific

4. F. Alston, M. Worthington, and L. Goldsman, *Contracting With the Federal Government*, 3rd ed. (New York: Wiley), 1993, p. 136.

costs of specific firms. Some behavioral economists think a firm will generate more customer goodwill if customers believe sellers have based selling prices on costs. At that level, however, the difference in retail prices caused by differences in cost allocation methods likely has no impact on customer morale.

Legislative and administrative regulations of prices do, indeed, require cost allocations, but laws compel these. Net present value of cash flows does not increase from voluntarily allocated joint costs.

Some theorists advocate never giving decision makers data containing joint cost allocations. Others advocate *sterilized allocations,* by which they mean an allocation designed so as not to affect the decision.[5] Sterilized allocations pose problems because no one allocation sterilizes allocations for all decisions—each decision might need a different allocation. This means no single allocation method guarantees to sterilize for all decisions.

16.7 BYPRODUCTS

A byproduct results from a joint process but with small value relative to the joint products. The distinction is one of degree, not a bright line definition. The accountant can apply to byproducts the same accounting methods used for joint products, but because these methods were cumbersome before electronic data processing, accountants devised short-cut methods to deal with byproducts, by definition of low value.

The need to have separate accounting methods for byproducts has declined as electronic data processing has become widespread, so modern textbooks give little detail on methods specific to byproducts. Nurnberg provided the following summary:[6]

> There are two basic approaches to the accounting for by-products. In one, no accounting recognition is given to by-products at the time of production. Rather, accounting recognition is given at the time of sale, when either revenues or revenues less separable costs are recognized as a separate item in the income statement or as a reduction in the cost of the major products. In the other approach, accounting recognition is given to by-products at the time of production by assigning a portion of the joint costs to them at the splitoff point, thereby reducing the costs assigned to the major products.

Nurnberg illustrated eight methods of dealing with byproducts; these methods propose possible combinations of the following two revenue treatments and four reporting treatments. The two revenue treatments are

- Revenue from byproducts sold
- Revenue from products sold, less separable costs of processing and disposal

These revenue treatments can be reported in any of four ways:

- Additional revenue
- Other income
- A deduction from cost of the major products sold
- A deduction from cost of the major products produced

5. This notion originated with Arthur L. Thomas; see his *The Allocation Problem: Part Two,* Studies in Accounting Research No. 9, American Accounting Association, 1974.
6. Hugo Nurnberg, "Joint Products and By-Products," Chapter 18 in S. Davidson and R.L. Weil, *Handbook of Cost Accounting,* New York: McGraw-Hill, 1978, pp.18–18.

Nurnberg illustrated two additional methods that report either the net realizable value (or net realizable value reduced by a normal profit margin) as a deduction in the cost of the major products produced.

None of these has any theoretical superiority over any of the others, nor to treating byproducts as joint products. To repeat: All the methods produce arbitrary allocations and provide no aid to effective managerial decisions.

16.8 ALLOCATION OF REVENUE

Companies often bundle into a single sale items that they also sell separately. An example pertinent for this writer is the bundling of students' textbooks with accompanying study guides: the publisher sells each separately, or shrink-wraps the two together to sell at a discount. Because companies voluntarily bundle these items, the issues in dealing with the single revenue for a bundle of products resemble the issues of common cost, other than joint cost, allocation.

When all the components of the bundled product have separate selling prices, the allocation of revenue to the individual products can follow the stand-alone methods or the incremental product method.

In the textbook example, assume that the textbook sells for $100, the study guide sells for $40, and the joint, shrink-wrapped package for $112. How should the publisher allocate the $112 revenue to the two separate books? The publisher will need such allocations for royalty purposes, if the authors of the two books have different ownership percentages of the two books.

The stand-alone methods would allocate the $112 revenues in the proportions 100/140 to the text, resulting in $80 (= 100/140 × $112) and 40/140 to the study guide; $32 (= 40/140 × $112). The incremental methods would allocate $100 to the text and $12 (= $112 – $100) to the study guide if, as is likely, it viewed the textbook as the primary product and the study guide as incremental.

(a) THEORY PROVIDES NO RIGHT ANSWER. Which of these methods—stand-alone or incremental—enjoys the strongest theoretical support? That question has no answer. Neither allocation will, better than the other, enable management to make wealth-enhancing decisions. The logic here parallels that for choosing between common cost allocations. If the facts show that one product offers incremental value to the package, then the analysis will result in a unique, cause-and-effect allocation.

If management needs an allocation, and facts do not provide guidance, that need likely results from some contractual provision, such as the need to pay royalties to the authors of the two books. If the authors of the two books have the same interests in both books, then the allocation between the two books does not matter, as amounts paid to each author will be the same, no matter the allocation. If the authors have different interests, then the allocation matters to the authors. Still, theory provides no uniquely right answer. To get a uniquely right answer, one needs to look to the contract that the authors have with the publisher, which will likely not specify a method. In that case, economic theory also does not provide a unique answer.

When the difference matters because the situation involves large dollar amounts, and when the contract does not address the allocation method, the issue likely ends up in litigation. I advise the courts to do what seems equitable to them because neither economics nor accounting offers a single, correct, answer.

(b) BUNDLED LEASE ALLOCATIONS. Difficulties arise when no readily identifiable, separate market exists for each of the products in the bundle. The Financial Accounting Standards Board (FASB) and the Securities and Exchange Commission (SEC) have required firms to allocate the total revenue to the components.[7]

Consider the modern lease, such as occurs when Xerox leases copying equipment to Motor Company (MC). Assume that Xerox enters into a seven-year lease with MC for a constellation of copying equipment. The lease requires MC to pay to Xerox $14,816.20 at the end of each of the seven years following the date of Xerox's delivering and installing the equipment on MC's premises. The copying equipment cost Xerox $23,000 to manufacture.

- The lease requires that Xerox will provide MC with on-site service and maintenance at no cost additional to the annual payment. Such service contracts ordinarily cost $2,000 per year.
- The lease requires that Xerox will provide MC with all toner and other supplies at no cost additional to the annual payment. Such supply contracts ordinary cost the user $1,200 per year.
- MC ordinarily must pay 15 percent per year, compounded annually to finance, over seven years, borrowings equivalent to that implicit in the lease.

Generally accepted accounting principles require Xerox to unbundle the monthly payment and allocate the amounts to four components: the machine, interest on the lease, supplies, and service/maintenance. Xerox transacts a substantial amount of its business through bundled leases, which because of the bundling, obscures the fair value of the equipment. Furthermore, Xerox's outright (i.e., unbundled) sales of equipment do not provide a practicable basis for making a direct estimate of fair value. Outright sales reflect many combinations of terms and prices, because of the variety of equipment configurations available. Furthermore, these outright sales take place within a wide range of possible prices negotiated between the salesperson and the customer. In addition, Xerox designs its outright sales prices to encourage customers to lease rather than buy, and therefore the prices for unbundled equipment sales do not directly relate to the fair value of the equipment as part of a bundled lease.

Thus, Xerox finds impracticable using outright sales of equipment as a basis for direct estimates of fair value. Because Xerox has difficulty making direct estimates of the equipment element of its bundled leases, the company instead makes direct estimates of the financing element. Xerox estimates the lessee's borrowing rate, then applies this rate to the known cash flow data for its leases for the period to measure the dollar amount of the leases' financing element and the equipment's implied selling price. Exhibit 16.2 illustrates this allocation.

Chapter 31 discusses how the SEC alleged that Xerox manipulated income by manipulating the interest rate, 15 percent in the example, used in the allocation.

---

7. As this book goes to press, the FASB has this item on its agenda and the operative rules appear in EITF Consensus 00-21, *Revenue Arrangements with Multiple Deliverables*, issued January 2003. *EITF* means the Emerging Issues Task Force, a joint effort of the FASB, AICPA, and SEC. The FASB publishes these pronouncements.

Annual payment = $14,816.12; servicing and supplies total $3,200 per year
Amount allocated to equipment and financing = $14,816.12 - $3,200.00 = $11,616.12
Discount rate = Lessee's borrowing rate = 15 percent per year
Present value of seven annual payments discounted at 15 percent = $48,328
(See Table 4 at end of the book, seven-period row; 15 percent column where factor is 4.16042; $11,616 x 4.16042 = $48,328)

End of Year	Gross Margin on Equipment		Revenue from Servicing		Revenue from Sales of Supplies		Interest Revenue[b]		Book Value of Lease Receivable	
									$48,328	
1	$25,328	[a]	$ 2,000		$1,200		$ 7,249		43,961	
2			2,000		1,200		6,594		38,939	
3			2,000		1,200		5,841		33,164	
4			2,000		1,200		4,975		26,522	
5			2,000		1,200		3,978		18,884	
6			2,000		1,200		2,833		10,101	
7			2,000		1,200		1,515		(0)	
	$25,328	+	$14,000	+	$8,400	+	$32,985	=	$80,713	[c]
Annual Payment =	$14,816.12		$11,616.12	=	for machine and interest					

$48,327.93 = Present value of payments for equipment
23,000.00 = cost of equipment
[a] $25,327.93 = Gross margin on equipment

[b] Amount for year is .15 x book value of lease receivable from end of preceding year
[c] $ 80,713 = Gross margin, service and suppplies
23,000 = Cost of machine
$ 103,713 = Total cash in
= 7 × $14,816.12

EXHIBIT 16.2 ALLOCATION OF BUNDLED REVENUE TO FAIR VALUE OF EQUIPMENT AND FINANCING

16.9 FURTHER READING

This chapter has purposefully focused on the underpinnings of allocations and has given only a few examples, none of them detailed. For comprehensive illustrations of some of these methods, refer to cost accounting and managerial accounting textbooks. None, including those by the editors of this book, provides more thorough coverage than those by Horngren, Datar, and Foster.[8]

8. Charles T. Horngren, Srikant M. Datar, and George Foster, *Cost Accounting: A Managerial Emphasis,* (Upper Saddle River, N.J.: Prentice-Hall, 2003), with new editions every three years. Any edition of this text will likely provide useful examples.

APPENDIX 16A

STEP-DOWN AND RECIPROCAL METHODS FOR ALLOCATING SERVICE DEPARTMENT COSTS[9]

LESLIE ELDENBURG, PHD
University of Arizona

NAOMI SODERSTROM, PHD
University of Colorado, Boulder

Organizations have departments whose sole function is to service other departments within the organization, providing no products or services to customers. Examples include the employee cafeteria, the payroll department, the cleaning staff, and the information technology or computing services department. As part of their cost reporting requirements or preferences, organizations frequently allocate the costs of service departments to final products or processes. This allocation, which is a full cost allocation, ensures that all costs appear somewhere in the costs of goods and services provided to customers.[10] The preferred methods for allocating service department costs to producing departments are the step-down and reciprocal methods. Some regulators require that organizations use one of these.

STEP-DOWN METHOD

The step-down method parallels other cost allocation methods. All methods, one way or another, do the following:

1. Trace all costs as far as practicable.
2. Allocate to all departments (both service and revenue generating) any unallocated costs that apply to all departments—for example, building lease costs.
3. Allocate service department costs to revenue-producing departments.
4. Allocate revenue-producing department costs to products.

---

9. The authors of this material originally included it in Chapter 28 of this book. The material generalizes to so many cost management contexts, that the editors have moved it from the original chapter and put it here, with other material on allocations.
10. Other chapters in this book discuss the merits of full costing, and its alternatives. Here we show how to derive full costs, including service department costs; we do not argue that organizations should prefer full costing.

The following provides a simple example of calculations for each of the four steps. This example pertains to a health care setting, but the step-down method could apply to all organizations with service and production departments.

Step 1. Trace all costs as far as practicable.

COSTS BEFORE ALLOCATION (IN THOUSANDS)					
	Maint.	Admin.	Adult Clinic	Children's Clinic	Total
Building lease.....					$ 60
Salaries..........	$5	$10	$50	$45	$110
Supplies.........	$4	$ 6	$30	$35	$ 75
SOME POSSIBLE ALLOCATION BASES					
Square feet......	400	100	4,500	5,000	10,000
Hours spent......	350	650	1,000	3,000	5,000

The accounting system usually traces salary and supply information to each department. Most organizations have recordkeeping systems that gather this information internally. The system cannot trace some costs, such as the building lease, to particular departments but must allocate them to all departments.

Step 2. Allocate to departments any costs not already traced to departments. This step allocates the building lease costs based on each department's square footage.

ALLOCATION OF BUILDING LEASE COST					
	Maint.	Food Admin.	Adult Clinic	Children's Clinic	Total
Square feet......	400	100	4,500	5,000	10,000
	4%	1%	45%	50%	100%
Building lease....	$ 2.4	$ .6	$ 27.0	$ 30.0	$ 60.0
Salaries.........	$ 5.0	$10.0	$ 50.0	$ 45.0	$110.0
Supplies.........	$ 4.0	$ 6.0	$ 30.0	$ 35.0	$ 75.0
Total...........	$11.4	$16.6	$107.0	$110.0	$245.0

After accountants have traced direct costs to each department and allocated common costs to all departments, they allocate service department costs (administration and maintenance in this example) to the revenue-generating departments, adult and children's clinics. A measure of service usage serves as the allocation base. This example uses the number of hours spent in each department to assign administration costs to the clinic, and uses the number of square feet per department to assign maintenance cost.

The step-down method reflects half of the interactions among service departments because each department drops out of the allocation scheme after the procedure has allocated its costs to other departments. The method allocates service department costs in a fixed sequence. Accountants allocate costs of the first service department to *all* other departments. They then allocate the costs of the second service department to all other departments (except the first service department). Once the analysis allocates a service department's costs to other departments, it does not allocate any further costs back to it. The process continues until accountants have allocated all service department costs to revenue-producing departments. Accountants often decide the order in which to allocate service departments by ranking the departments by their direct costs (largest to smallest) or by the amount of service provided to other departments. The analysis begins by allocating costs from the largest department (or the one that services the most other departments), followed by the next largest, and so on until all of the service departments' costs have been allocated.

Step 3. Allocate the service department costs to revenue-generating departments using the step-down method. In this example, administration is the largest department; accountants will allocate its costs first. Once the accountant has allocated the administration's costs, they omit the department from further allocation, so administration does not receive allocated costs from the maintenance department, even though maintenance provides service to the administration department.

	Maint.	Admin.	Adult Clinic	Children's Clinic	Total
Total	$ 11.4	$ 16.6	$107.0	$110.0	$245.0
Hours spent	400		4,500	5,000	9,900
	4%		45%	51%	
Admin.	$ 0.7	$(16.6)	$ 7.4	$ 8.5	
Square feet			4,500	5,000	9,500
			47%	53%	
Maint.	$(12.1)		$ 5.7	$ 6.4	
Full cost	$ 0.0	$ 0.0	$120.1	$124.9	$245.0

Step 4. To calculate a cost per service, or per patient, the accountant divides the fully allocated cost of each department by the number of services provided, or by the number of patients seen in the clinic over the time period that the organization incurred the costs. In this example, if the adult clinic recorded 5,000 patient visits, then the cost per patient for the adult clinic would equal $120,100/5,000—or $24.02 per patient.

RECIPROCAL METHOD

While the step-down method ignores interactions of the service departments, the *reciprocal* method of allocating costs takes them into consideration. For example, maintenance workers clean the administration area and administration personnel issue payroll checks and provide other services for maintenance workers. In our example, using the step-down method, we allocated administration costs to maintenance, but not vice versa. The reciprocal method recognizes the interactions through use of simultaneous linear equations of the sort taught in high school algebra.

The first two steps are identical to those in the step-down method. The analysis then takes the following steps.

Step 3. Set up simultaneous equations for the interactions among the service departments and solve them.

Admin. = (100/9,600)Maint. + $16.6

Maint. = (350/4,350)Admin. + $11.4

Solve these equations using the substitution method (and with rounding).

Admin. = .01(.08Maint. + $11.4) + $16.6

Admin. = .0008Maint. + $.1 + $16.6

.999Admin. = 16.7

Admin. = 16.7/.999 = 16.7

Substitute this into the Food Service equation.

Maint. = (.08)(16.7) + 11.4

Maint. = 12.7

Step 4. Allocate the costs from each service department to all other departments.

	Maint	Admin.	Adult Clinic	Children's Clinic	Total
Total	$ 11.4	$ 16.6	$107.0	$110.0	$245.0
Hours spent	350		1,000	3,000	4,350
	8%		23%	69%	
Admin.	$ 1.3	$(16.7)	$ 3.9	$ 11.5	
Square feet		100	4,500	5,000	9,600
		1%	47%	52%	
Maint.	$(12.7)	$ 0.1	$ 6.0	$ 6.6	
Full cost	$ 0.0	$ 0.0	$116.9	$128.1	$245.0

In this example, the reciprocal method's allocations are quite similar to the step-down method's allocation. As the number of service departments grows, allocated costs will vary more across the revenue-generating departments. The reciprocal method more accurately reflects cause-and-effect of service department costs because it reflects interactions of the service departments. Most spreadsheet programs have functions that will calculate solutions for simultaneous equations. Linear programming software will also perform these calculations.

BIBLIOGRAPHY

Alston, F., Worthington, M., and Goldsman, L. *Contracting With the Federal Government*, 3rd ed. (New York: Wiley), 1993, p. 136.

EITF Consensus 00-21. *Revenue Arrangements with Multiple Deliverables*. Issued January 2003.

Horngren, Charles T., Datar, Srikant M., and Foster, George. *Cost Accounting: A Managerial Emphasis* (Upper Saddle River, N.J.: Prentice-Hall, 2003).

Maher, M.W., Stickney, C.P., and Weil, R.L. *Managerial Accounting: An Introduction to Concepts, Methods, and Uses* (Mason, Ohio: Thomson South-Western, 2006), Chapter 15.

Nurnberg, Hugo. "Joint Products and By-Products." Chapter 18 in S. Davidson and R.L. Weil, *Handbook of Cost Accounting* (New York: McGraw-Hill Publishing Co., 1978), pp.18-18.

Thomas, L. *The Allocation Problem: Part Two.* Studies in Accounting Research No. 9, American Accounting Association, 1974.

CHAPTER 17

COST-VOLUME-PROFIT ANALYSES*

NICHOLAS DOPUCH, PHD, CPA
Washington University

UPDATED BY

MICHAEL W. MAHER, PHD, EDITOR
University of California, Davis

CONTENTS

17.1 INTRODUCTION 483

17.2 SHORT-RUN ECONOMIC MODEL 484
- (a) Using Linear Functions for Revenues and Costs 486
- (b) The Accountant's Breakeven Chart 487
- (c) Profit-Volume Analyses 487
- (d) Assessing the Effect on Profit of Changes in Prices, Variable Costs, Fixed Costs, and Units of Output 488
- (e) The Use of Breakeven Charts and Profit-Volume Graphs in Control 489
- (f) Breakeven and Profit-Volume Analyses for Multiproduct Firms 489
- (g) Other Sources 494

17.3 ABC'S MULTIPLE COST DRIVERS AND COST HIERARCHIES 494

17.4 ANALOGOUS CVP DECISION SITUATIONS 495
- (a) Add or Drop a Product 495
- (b) Make or Buy a Unit 496
- (c) Sell Now or Process Further 496
- (d) Summary 496

17.5 SHORT-RUN MULTIPRODUCT MODELS—LINEAR PROGRAMMING EXTENSIONS OF COST-VOLUME-PROFIT 497
- (a) A Graphic Solution to a Linear Programming Problem 497
- (b) Sensitivity of Solution to Accounting Estimation Errors 498

17.6 UNCERTAINTY AND CVP ANALYSIS 500

BIBLIOGRAPHY 501

17.1 INTRODUCTION

Cost-volume-profit (CVP) analysis examines the relation between changes in volume (output) and changes in profit. CVP analyses commonly assume that the firm (department, division, or the relevant decision unit) commits itself to holding various forms of capacity for at least another operating period. Analysts define capacity as plants, buildings, equipment,

* Nicholas Dopuch wrote the original version of this chapter for the first edition of *The Handbook of Cost Accounting*. I have preserved most of his ideas and words. MWM.

and managerial and other skilled labor (both manufacturing and nonmanufacturing). Practitioners may also classify inventories that will be carried over from one period to another as capacity.

The commitment to hold capacities results in the incurrence of fixed capacity costs—that is, the firm will incur costs whether it utilizes the capacities or allows them to remain idle. The costs incurred may be current cash outlays or allocations of prior period outlays. The cash outlays include salaries for managerial and other skilled personnel, taxes, and insurance on properties owned (plant, buildings, equipment, inventories), rentals or lease payments on fixed contracts, and interest and principal payments on existing debt, assuming that the latter will be kept outstanding to finance asset acquisitions of the decision unit. Fixed costs that are allocations of prior period outlays include depreciation on fixed tangible assets, allocations of patent costs, and of other intangible assets (advertising, research, etc.). Very often, fixed costs represented by cash outlays are quite significant in comparison with the noncash fixed costs, an important factor in CVP analyses under uncertainty.

Of course, firms acquire and hold capacities primarily because the services they provide are necessary in the production of some commercial output, either tangible products or services. Presumably, the incremental value of the output produced during an operating period will exceed the incremental costs of producing and selling the output. One can measure the incremental costs of production and distribution as the total incremental cash outlays incurred during the operating period, fixed and variable, plus any opportunity costs incurred in holding and using various forms of capacities. Many CVP analyses assume that the opportunity cost of using capacities equals zero, because the next best alternative to using the capacities is to allow them to remain idle. But analysts often make this assumption for convenience rather than its reflection of actual situations, as Section 17.4 demonstrates.

This chapter explores the relation among fixed and variable costs, profit, volume, and activity. We first discuss the short-run economic model that should be familiar to readers who have studied basic microeconomics. We then show how analysts use linear approximations of these economic models, and we illustrate some of the more basic breakeven calculations. The basic CVP model divides costs into fixed and variable components, where variable costs increase (decrease) in total as the volume of output increases (decreases). Activity-based costing (ABC) analyses have taught us that cost behavior can be more complex than a simple fixed/variable cost structure, so we examine that complexity.

Next, we consider other types of decision situations that extend breakeven analysis. In each of these situations, the analyst also assumes that the firm will hold certain forms of capacity for another operating period.

We then discuss formal programming models for allocating capacities to alternative mixes of outputs. Except where otherwise noted, the typical breakeven models assume a single output (or constant output mix).

17.2 SHORT-RUN ECONOMIC MODEL

Exhibit 17.1 shows the nonlinear revenue and nonlinear cost curves typically assumed in the economist's model of a short-run output problem. The exhibit includes the specific revenue and cost functions, listed above the graph. The figure's nonlinear revenue curve reflects the assumption that the decision unit sells its output in an imperfect market wherein the firm can sell additional units of output only as the output's price decreases.

Revenue Function: TR = 200x – 10 x²

Cost Function: TC = 2x³ – 20x² + 100x + 200

x	TR(x)	TC(x)
0	$ 0	$ 200
1	190	282
2	360	336
3	490	374
4	640	408
5	750	450
6	840	512
7	910	605
8	960	744
9	990	938
10	1,000	1,200

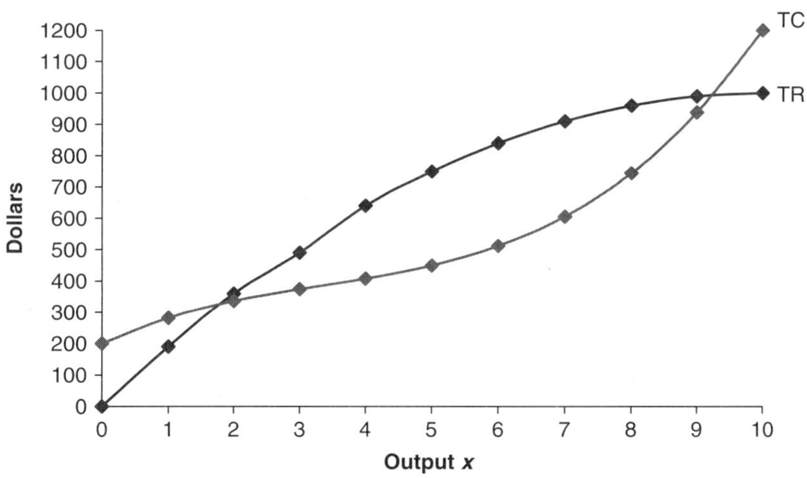

EXHIBIT 17.1 NONLINEAR REVENUE AND COST CURVES

The nonlinear cost function reflects increased economies of scale, up to a point, followed by diseconomies.

To maximize a decision unit's profits in the short run, the firm should increase output as long as the marginal revenue from additional units of output exceeds the marginal cost of producing and selling these additional units. One can calculate the optimal output level by differentiating the firm's profit function, $\pi = TR - TC$, with respect to output x, and setting this derivative equal to zero. In this case, we would differentiate:

$$\pi = TR - TC = (200x - 10x^2) - (2x^3 - 20x^2 + 100x + 200)$$

Taking the derivative, $d\pi/dx$, and setting this equal to zero, we have

$$\frac{d\pi}{dx} = (200 - 20x) - (6x^2 - 40x + 100) = 0$$

Solving for x (subject to $x \geq 0$ and assuming that the second-order condition is met) yields an optimal output, denoted by x^*, of 6.0 (closer to 6.1).

At an output of 6.0, the decision unit will receive total revenues of $840 and incur total costs of $512, yielding a profit, π, of $328. Note that total revenue of $840 at an output of 6.0 implies an average selling price of $140 per unit.

This model for the short-run decision problem is deterministic in the sense that it assumes the decision maker has certain knowledge of the revenue and cost functions over the entire range of feasible outputs. Unfortunately, the decision maker often cannot generate the type of detailed information about the unit's revenues and costs needed to arrive at an optimal solution to the output problem. One could reasonably assume, however, that the decision maker possesses at least an intuitive idea about the general behavior of the revenue and cost functions for ranges of output encompassing typical operations. This assumption provides the basis for simplifying the economist's model to obtain the accountant's breakeven model, which relies on linear functions.

(a) USING LINEAR FUNCTIONS FOR REVENUES AND COSTS. Suppose that we restrict our attention to a range between 4 and 8 units. Using the information shown in Exhibit 17.1, we note that total revenues will be $640 for an output of 4 units, implying an average price of $160 per unit; at 5 units, total revenues will be $750, implying a price of $150 per unit. For outputs of 7 and 8 units the relevant figures are $910 (average price of $130) and $960 (average price of $120), respectively. Assume that on the basis of other supporting data, the decision maker selects the combination of an output price of $140 and expected output of 6 units, by coincidence the optimal output obtained earlier. This will produce an expected total revenue of $840.

Consider now the cost curve for this decision unit. The cost figures for outputs of 4 to 8 units represent the optimal costs for each of these outputs. That is, we assume that the decision maker adjusts the fixed and variable inputs in such a way that the cost of $408 for 4 units, $450 for 5, $512 for 6 units, and so on, is the minimum cost for each of these outputs consistent with the fixed capacities and available technology. Suppose that we draw a line, then, connecting the vertical intercept of the nonlinear cost curve, that is, $200, with the point on the curve for $x = 6$, or $512. This will yield a linear estimate of the total cost curve, as shown in Exhibit 17.2.

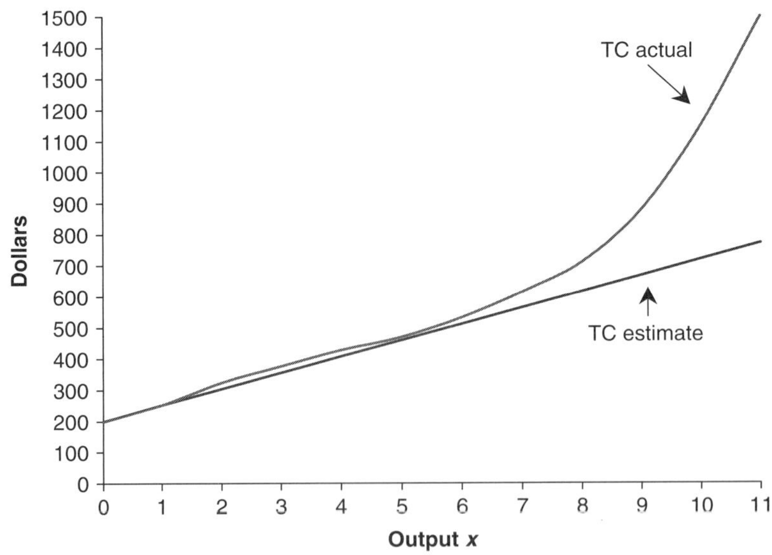

EXHIBIT 17.2 RELATION BETWEEN ACTUAL AND ESTIMATED COSTS

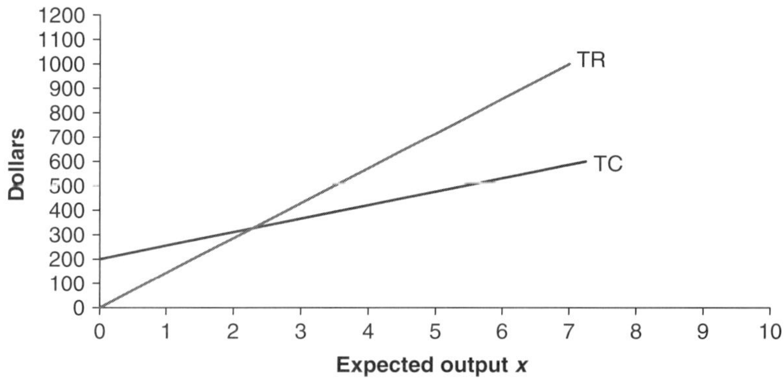

EXHIBIT 17.3 RELATION BETWEEN TOTAL REVENUES AND TOTAL COSTS AS A FUNCTION OF OUTPUT

The slope of the linear line is \$52, which represents an average of the changes in the total cost per unit from an output of $x = 0$ to $x = 6$. Note that if we take the derivative of the total cost curve at $x = 6$, the estimate of the marginal cost is \$76, which indicates that our linear estimate would lose its accuracy if we went much beyond $x = 6$ units of output. Exhibit 17.2 shows this graphically.

(b) THE ACCOUNTANT'S BREAKEVEN CHART. The typical breakeven chart merely brings together the linear estimates of a decision unit's revenue and cost curves. Exhibit 17.3 shows a breakeven chart that conforms to the data given above. It shows fixed costs of \$200, a revenue line that has a slope of \$140 (the average price), and a cost line with a slope of \$52. The point at which total revenues equal total costs is $x = 2.27$ (approximately).

The breakeven chart is merely a simplification of a commitment to produce and sell at \$140 per unit an output of 6 units, incurring an average variable cost of \$52. At no point was any suggestion made that this particular decision unit could produce up to 10 units of output and sell all of these at the same average price of \$140 and incur the same average variable costs of \$52. If the firm contemplates an output of 10 units, the analyst would need to prepare a new breakeven chart based on an average selling price of \$100 and a linear estimate of the total costs based on that output. The decision maker might not be committed to an output of 6 units, an expected breakeven point of 2.27 units, and an expected profit, π, of \$328. The decision maker may adopt new decisions that change the revenue and cost curves of the unit, thereby providing different possible outputs with different expected profits and breakeven points. We consider examples of these changes next.

(c) PROFIT-VOLUME ANALYSES. Most profit-volume analyses use the following simple equation:

$$\pi = px - bx - a$$

where

π = profit

p = average selling price per unit

x = number of units of output

b = average rate of change in total costs as output increases; for simplicity, this is assumed to measure the average variable costs of production, distribution, and administration per unit of product produced and sold

a = an estimate of total fixed costs (for production, distribution, and administration)

Of course, a decision unit breaks even when total revenues equal total costs, or $px - bx - a = 0$. By rearranging this simple breakeven equation, the breakeven output is $x_{be} = a/(p - b)$. The denominator, $(p - b)$, is called the *contribution margin*, and measures the average change in profit per unit of x.

Breakeven in sales dollars (revenues) can be calculated by multiplying both sides of the breakeven equation by p, the selling price per unit. If we then simplify the right-hand side of the result, we observe that breakeven in sales dollars is equal to fixed costs, a, divided by the contribution margin ratio, or $(p - b)/p$. That is,

$$p(x_{be}) = p\frac{a}{(p-b)} = \frac{a}{(p-b)/p}$$

Using the previous figures as the basis for illustrations, we have

$$x_{be} = \frac{\$200}{(\$140 - \$52)} = \frac{\$200}{\$88} = 2.27 \tag{1}$$

$$p(x_{be}) = \frac{\$200}{(\$140 - \$52)/\$140} = \frac{\$200}{\$88/\$140} = \frac{\$200}{.63} = \$317.5 \tag{2}$$

One could more conveniently display this relation by using the profit-volume graph. Such a graph shows the difference between the selling price and the variable cost per unit—the contribution margin—along units of output, thereby indicating the dollar amount of profit for various levels of output. Exhibit 17.4 shows a profit-volume graph defining the relevant concepts of cost-volume-profit analysis; Exhibit 17.5 shows the same graph using the previous figures.

(d) ASSESSING THE EFFECT ON PROFIT OF CHANGES IN PRICES, VARIABLE COSTS, FIXED COSTS, AND UNITS OF OUTPUT. Analysts can use breakeven charts and profit-volume graphs to assess proposed changes contemplated by management. These changes might include an increase or decrease in the selling price per unit, a substitution of fixed

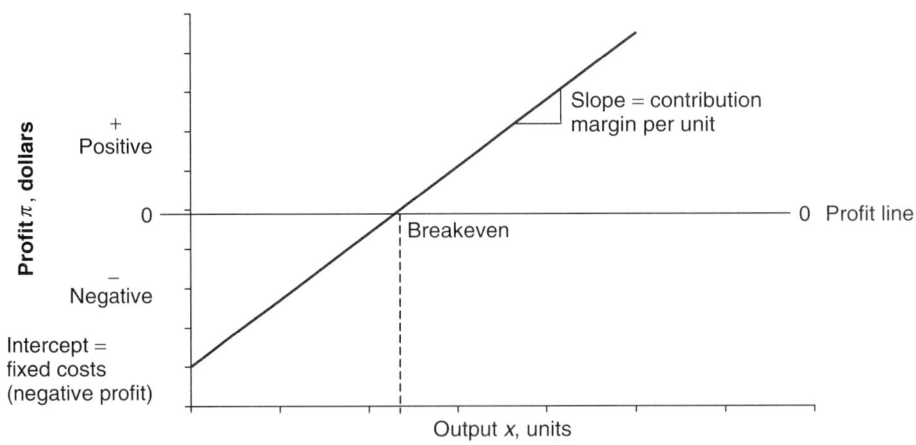

EXHIBIT 17.4 PROFIT-VOLUME GRAPH

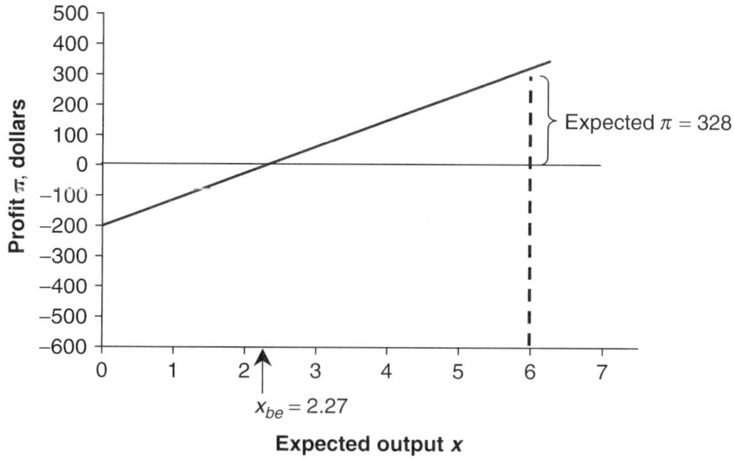

EXHIBIT 17.5 PROFIT-VOLUME GRAPH USING DATA OF EXHIBIT 17.4

for variable factors, or an increase (decrease) in fixed expenditures. In addition to changing the dollar figures of the variables involved, changes in prices and fixed expenditures can affect expected units of output and sales. To illustrate, management might contemplate increasing advertising expenditures to increase the number of units sold at a particular selling price. Exhibit 17.6a graphs one possible effect on expected profit, where the dashed line reflects the effect of the contemplated action. Similarly, management might wish to assess the effect of adding more labor (another shift) and cutting back on leased capacities, which would lower the fixed cash costs but increase the average variable cost of production. One would graph this as a decrease in the contribution margin per unit, because $(p - b)$, the original contribution margin, would exceed $(p - b')$, the new contribution margin. Figure 17.6b illustrates the combined effect of this change. Finally, Exhibit 17.6c graphs the effect of an increase in selling prices with the corresponding change in expected output. This graph assumes an increase in selling price that will raise the contribution margin per unit from $(p - b)$ to $(p' - b)$, but decrease expected units of output to x'.

(e) THE USE OF BREAKEVEN CHARTS AND PROFIT-VOLUME GRAPHS IN CONTROL. The discussion so far has implied that firms mainly use breakeven charts and profit-volume graphs during the planning stage, where management wants to assess various strategies regarding prices, cost functions, production levels, and so on. Firms can also use the techniques illustrated in Exhibit 17.6 in an after-the-fact or *ex post* manner by labeling one line the *planned line* and the other, the dashed line, as the *actual line.* Exhibit 17.7 includes such a graph, where we assume that actual profit exceeded expected or planned profit because the average contribution margin per unit was higher than planned because (1) average variable costs were less than anticipated, (2) fixed costs slightly exceeded planned amounts, and (3) actual output exceeded planned output, allowing the increased contribution margin per unit to absorb this increased fixed cost. Exhibit 17.7 also lists the actual and planned financial data used in the graph.

(f) BREAKEVEN AND PROFIT-VOLUME ANALYSES FOR MULTIPRODUCT FIRMS. The preceding discussion assumes that the decision unit in question either produced a single

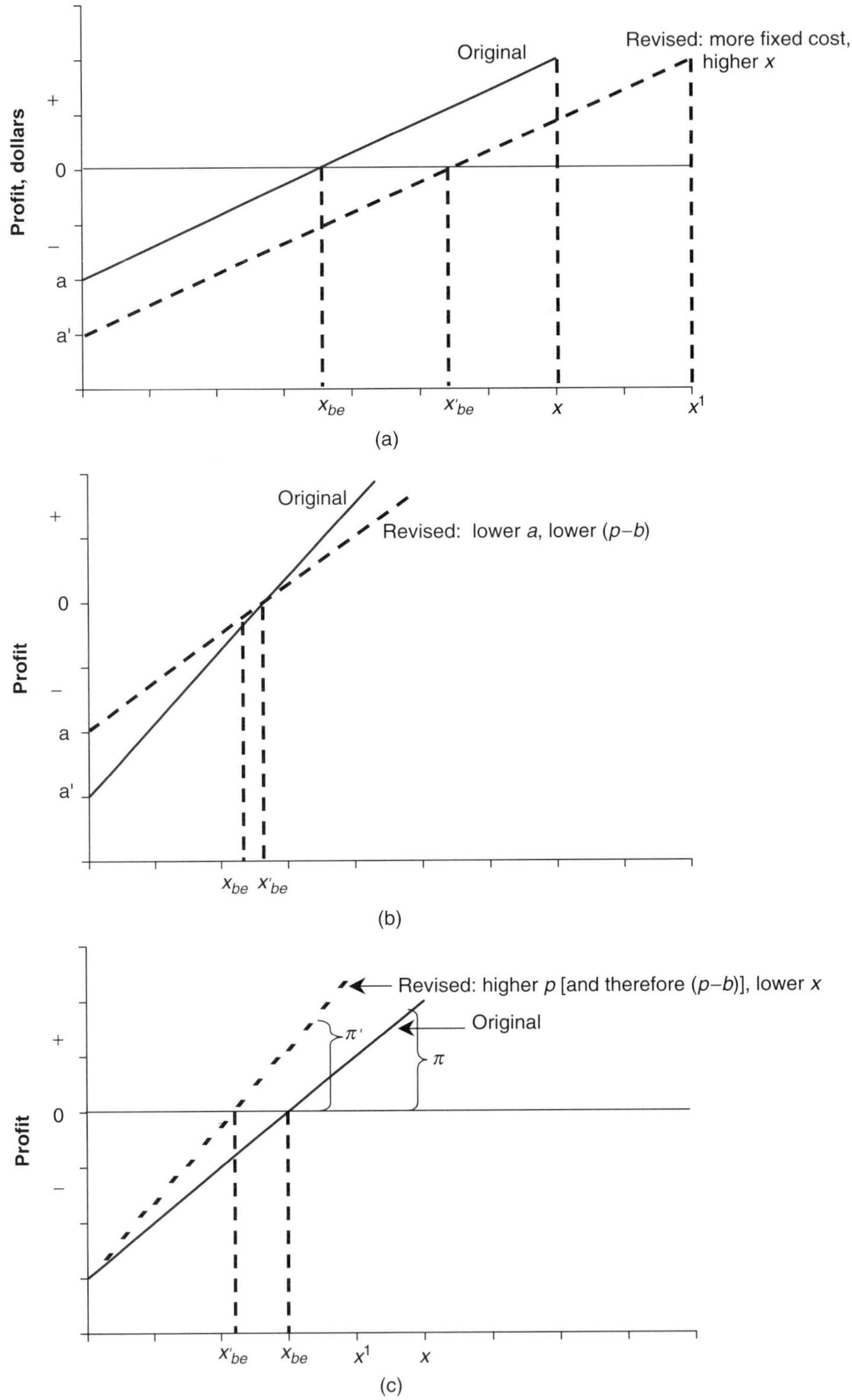

EXHIBIT 17.6 EFFECT ON BREAKEVEN POINT OF VARIOUS CHANGES IN THE COST STRUCTURE

	Planned	Actual
Average selling price P	$ 2.00	$ 2.00
Average variable cost	1.00	.80
Average contribution margin	$ 1.00	$ 1.20
Fixed costs a	$5,000	$6,000
Output x_i	10,000	12,000
Profit	$5,000	$8,400

Difference in π Due to

(a) Change in x: C.M. (Δx)	= $1 (2,000)	= + $2,000
(b) Change in C.M./unit:	$\simeq$ 10,000(ΔC.M.)	
	= 10,000($.20)	= + 2,000
(c) Change in a	= a – a'	= – 1,000
(d) Joint effect		
(Δx) (ΔC.M.)	= 2,000($.20)	= + 400
	Net $\Delta\pi$	= + 3,400

C.M. = contribution margin

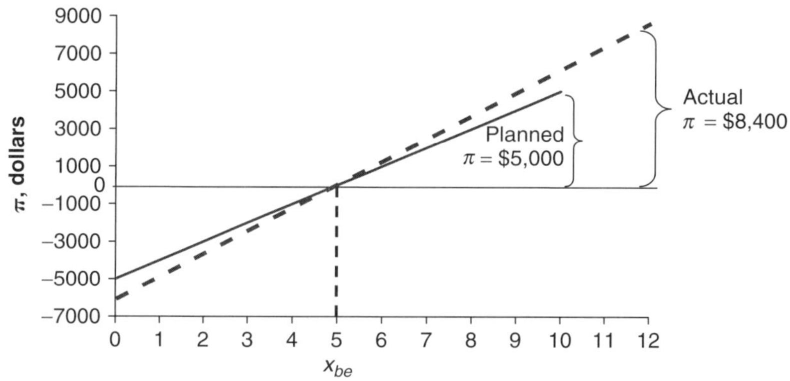

EXHIBIT 17.7 ACTUAL AND PLANNED FINANCIAL OUTCOMES

product or had committed itself to a certain sales mix of products. In the latter case, the revenue and cost lines shown in Exhibit 17.3 would reflect a combination of the individual revenue and cost functions; the slopes of each aggregate line reflect a weighted average of the slopes of the individual revenue and cost lines. To illustrate, suppose that a decision unit produces three products, A, B, and C, with average selling prices of $200, $120, and $60, respectively. The average variable cost per unit for each product is $60, $50, and $40, respectively, resulting in contribution margins of $140 for A, $70 for B, and $20 for C. Suppose that the contemplated outputs are 24,000 units of A, 24,000 units of B, and 12,000 units of C, giving a total output of 60,000 units. Note that the output of A represents 40 percent of total output, as does the output of B. The output of C, then, represents 20 percent of total output.

If we use these percentages to weight the respective figures given earlier, we shall have a weighted average price used in constructing Exhibit 17.3. Similarly, the weighted average variable cost per unit will equal .40($60) + .40($50) + .20($40) = $24 + $20 + $8 = $52, as before. This results in a weighted average contribution margin of $88, the same contribution margin used in the previous illustrations. Assume that the firm estimates total fixed costs at $2 million. Using these figures, we can develop a breakeven chart (Exhibit 17.8a) and profit-volume graph (Exhibit 17.8b) that are multiples of our earlier ones, but interpreted now to reflect the decisions of a multiproduct decision unit. Exhibit 17.8b also shows the individual contribution margins, to indicate the total contribution to profit of each of the three products. Note that the breakeven point, where the weighted average contribution line crosses the zero profit line, is more a contrived calculation because the firm will not break even with an output of approximately 22,700 units unless these units break down into 40 percent (22,700 units) of A, 40 percent (22,700 units) of B, and 20 percent (22,700 units) of C. This is unlikely, and the assumption of a constant sales mix typically makes breakeven analysis highly questionable in multiproduct situations.

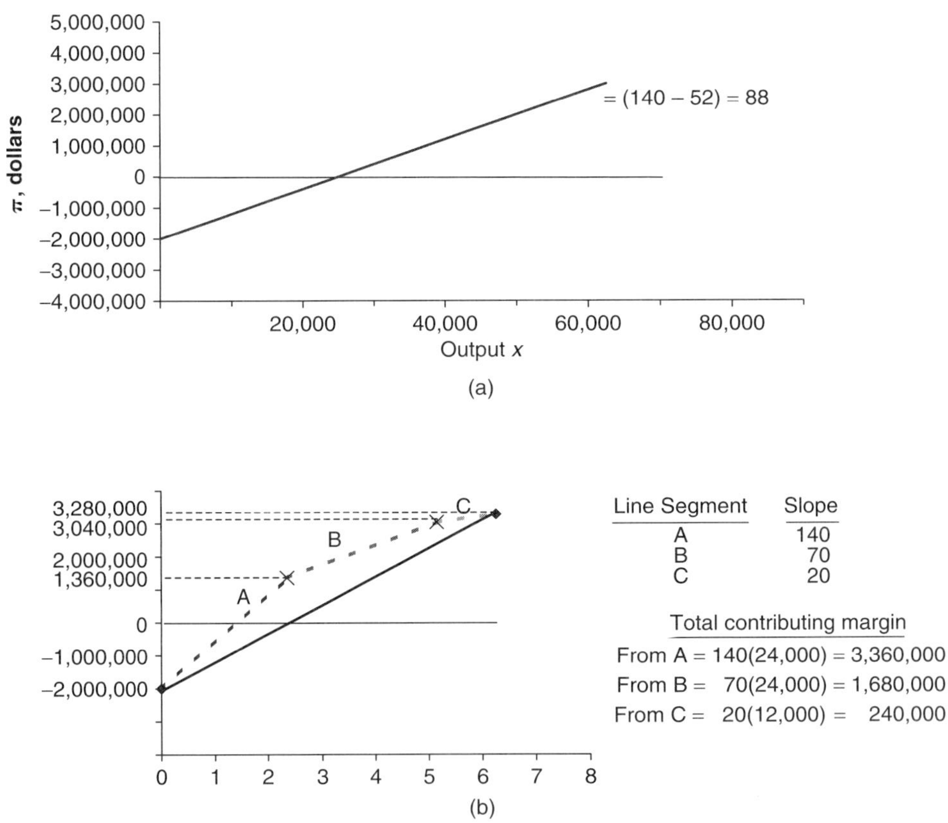

EXHIBIT 17.8 MULTIPRODUCT BREAKEVEN CHART (a) AND PROFIT-VOLUME GRAPH (b).

A multiproduct setting poses the problem of choosing the output that leads to an optimal profit. Section 17.5 discusses programming models developed for this purpose.

When using linear estimates of revenue and cost curves, one can resolve cost-volume-profit decisions in terms of a fundamental notion: as output increases, revenue will increase at a faster rate than costs (the contribution margin is positive), or costs under one alternative will increase at a slower rate than under another alternative. As a result, increases in output contribute to the absorption of fixed costs and ultimatcly to positive amounts of profit.

Note, then, that the critical decision variables are units of output, x, the selling price or revenue per unit of output, p, the estimate of the variable cost per unit, b, and an estimate of the total fixed costs, a, that the firm will incur because of the decision to hold certain capacities. Short-run output decisions must address the degree of accuracy in the estimates for these main decision variables. Of course, the optimal degree of accuracy for the estimate of the decision variables becomes a decision problem in itself, because one can always increase accuracy by investing additional resources in the estimation process. Firms must balance the additional costs from this type of investment against the incremental benefits from increased accuracy.

A complete analysis of the value of information under conditions of uncertainty lies beyond the scope of this chapter; see Chapter 6 (Activity-Based Costing and Management) for more discussion of this topic. We note here, however, that benefits from increased accuracy can occur only if a better estimate leads to a better decision. In some cases, the better estimate will not affect the short-run decision. For example, if we assume that the fixed costs in Exhibit 17.1 will be \$250 instead of \$200, this does not change the optimal output of 6 units. If we know that fixed costs will increase, then we can calculate a reduction in expected profit from \$388 to \$338. This new information, however, does not affect the optimal short-term decision of the decision unit to produce 6 units. The same might hold true for small revisions in selling price and the average variable cost per unit. Section 17.5, which discusses multiproduct modeling, illustrates how to assess the sensitivity of decisions to revised estimates.

Analysts use several methods to estimate the average variable cost, b, and the fixed costs, a. In developing our linear estimate of the cost curve, we used only two points on the curve, the intercept (at $x = 0$) and the total cost at $x = 6$. This method of estimating the cost curve is known as the *account classification method of cost estimation.* Suppose that we observe total cost equal to \$512 at $x = 6$ units. In general, the \$512 is made up of fixed and variable costs. If we could classify the cost accounts (which sum to \$512) into fixed costs and variable costs, we would have the basis for calculating the two parameter values of the linear cost equation, $TC = a + bx$. Hence, assuming that the fixed cost accounts sum to \$200, then $bx = \$312$, and $b = \$312/x = \$312/6 = \$52$.

Alternatively, we could obtain linear estimates of the cost curve by using all of the observations, and then fit a line to these observations according to some criterion. For example, we could fit the line to minimize the sum of the squared deviations of the observation from the estimated line. The least square regression method achieves this minimum. We could also fit the line to minimize the sum of the absolute deviations. Chapter 12 (Estimating Cost Behavior) discusses these and other methods of cost estimation.

Estimating total costs using the account classification method assumes that all individual cost items are either fixed or entirely variable. Many cost items, however, are mixed items in the sense that they possess both fixed and variable components. The two classes of mixed costs are semifixed costs (those that rise in discrete steps) and semivariable costs (those that have a fixed component and then rise continuously thereafter). Of these, the semifixed, or step, costs present the main problems in cost-volume-profit analyses. For example, to increase output significantly, a firm may need a second shift of workers, leading to an increase in supervision and other setup costs. Analysts find it difficult to graph these and other step costs along the output axis because doing so presupposes knowledge of the optimal production and sales plans as output increases. A linear estimate of the total cost curve assumes that management will make the proper decisions regarding how to acquire inputs to produce different levels of outputs and that an observed cost, say \$512 at $x = 6$ units, represents the results of these input decisions.

Note also that breakeven charts and profit-volume graphs do not provide sufficient information to calculate either an optimal output level or output mix. The use of linear estimates of revenue and cost curves suggest that the firm should expand output up to the maximum capacity available. But an expansion of output beyond the immediate *relevant* range requires different linear estimates of the revenue and cost curves.

(g) OTHER SOURCES. Most texts that focus on cost-volume-profit analyses include the topics that this chapter has addressed thus far. You will find references to Hilton, Maher, and Selto (2006); Maher, Stickney, and Weil (2006); and Horngren, Datar, and Foster (2003) in the bibliography at the end of this chapter.

17.3 ABC'S MULTIPLE COST DRIVERS AND COST HIERARCHIES

In some situations, the use of a single cost driver does not reflect the firm's cost structure. Costs can have multiple drivers. Chapter 6 discusses activity-based costing (ABC), which accommodates multiple-cost drivers. ABC can provide a more complete picture of cost-volume-profit relations and more data to managers.

Activity-based costing analysts often use the following cost driver categories, which they call *cost hierarchies*.

- *Unit-level activities* are performed for each individual unit of product (e.g., adding materials to product, performing tasks on a piecework basis).
- *Batch-level activities* are performed to benefit multiple units of output in batches (e.g., change a machine to produce a different size of product).
- *Product-level activities* are needed to support a specific product—that is, an entire product line (e.g., designing products, advertising products, and maintaining product specifications).
- *Customer-level activities* are performed when meeting the needs of specific customers (e.g., unique packaging, shipping, handling specific customer accounts).
- *Facility-level activities* are required for an organization to have the capacity to produce goods and services (e.g., managing the company, renting space for production activities).

These activity categories will change the nature of the CVP model, resulting in the following total cost expression:

$$\begin{aligned}\text{Total cost} = {} & (\text{Unit-level cost} \times \text{Number of units}) + (\text{Batch-level cost} \times \text{Batch CDA}) \\ & + (\text{Product-level cost} \times \text{Product CDA}) + (\text{Customer-level Cost} \\ & \times \text{Customer CDA}) + (\text{Facility-level cost} \times \text{Facility CDA})\end{aligned}$$

where CDA = cost driver activity (e.g., number of batches, number of customers, number or size of facilities, and so on).

Some costs that analysts view as fixed under the traditional CVP analysis are now considered variable with respect to the appropriate cost drivers under the ABC approach.

17.4 ANALOGOUS CVP DECISION SITUATIONS

(a) ADD OR DROP A PRODUCT. A decision unit will add (drop) a product if the incremental revenues from the product are greater (less) than the incremental costs of producing and distributing the product. In general, the incremental costs consist of the incremental cash outlay costs plus the opportunity costs of using the capacities to produce the product. The firm will have positive opportunity costs if it has the option of diverting the capacities from the current product and use them to produce another product.

The question of whether to add a product generally arises in job-shop operations, where a decision to bid on a new order constitutes a decision to add a new product (the order). The capacity needed to work on the new order is available to the decision unit, and the firm must decide whether to devote the capacity to the new order, to other products (other orders), or let it remain idle.

The decision of whether to add a new product in a continuous processing type of operation is less common, because the firm may need to acquire the capacity needed to produce the new product through additional investments. When this occurs, the analysis must rely on capital budgeting techniques, such as a discounting model, to resolve the decision (see Chapters 21 and 22). The same rule would hold if the decision to drop a product would result in the liquidation of long-lived capacities, such as the sale of fixed assets. The liquidation of long-lived capacities will reduce cash flows—revenues and cash costs—of future time periods beyond the immediate operating period.

In short, firms can treat the decision to add or drop a product as a short-run, cost-volume-profit decision only if the level of capacities held does not vary with the decisions. For continuous processing firms this would usually take place only for incidental items. For example, the decision to further process a by-product, given available capacities, is effectively a decision of whether to add the product (process further). Similarly, the decision to make a subunit rather than to purchase it is a decision of whether to add the product (make the unit) in order to obtain the subunit at a lower incremental cost than its purchase price from an outside supplier.

Generally, the critical estimates in decisions to add or drop a product are the estimates of the incremental costs of producing and distributing the product. If the product is a new order, decision makers will face uncertainty about the required outlays for materials, labor, and incremental overhead, as well as the opportunity costs of devoting the capacities to the new order. Even though the order calls for an output that the decision unit has previously produced, there will still be uncertainty about the incremental overhead costs associated with the order and the opportunity costs of the capacities. The uncertainty about the incremental overhead remains because many overhead items rise in discrete steps (semifixed costs), making it difficult to estimate their new level should the firm accept a specific order.

Analysts have difficulty estimating the opportunity cost of using capacity to manufacture a particular product because the estimation requires knowledge of future opportunities. If a decision unit currently has idle capacity, adding a product that uses only an incidental amount of this capacity does not incur an opportunity cost. (If the firm will not have to reject future opportunities because of a new project, then the new project has zero opportunity cost.) If the product will use a significant amount of capacity, however, then its acceptance will more likely require the decision unit to reject future profitable opportunities. The difficulty lies in predicting which, if any, future opportunities will have to be rejected at the time that the firm is deciding whether to add a product.[1]

If a firm doesn't know the incremental costs for adding a product, it also doesn't know the reduction in costs if the firm drops a current product (e.g., the order is refused, the byproduct is not processed further, the subunit will be purchased, etc.). To simplify the analysis, practitioners often approximate the incremental outlay costs by the variable costs of production and distribution, with some adjustment for changes in significant step costs, such as supervision or setup costs. A relatively large spread between the revenue per unit and the total variable cost per unit—the contribution margin—creates a margin of safety to absorb underestimates of changes in semifixed costs and the opportunity costs of devoting capacities to the product. Once analysts have classified the incremental outlay costs into variable and relatively fixed items, decision-makers can use the same types of breakeven and profit analyses explained in Section 17.2(e) to assess the effect of different volume levels on profit.

(b) MAKE OR BUY A UNIT. A firm may have capacities available that it can use to manufacture a subunit rather than to purchase the subunit from an outside supplier. Firms can make this decision each operating period, opting to make the unit in some periods and purchase it in others. The firm will manufacture the unit if the incremental costs of purchasing exceed the incremental costs of manufacturing. The incremental costs of manufacturing are the incremental outlay costs plus the opportunity costs of devoting the capacities to the subunit. The latter will be zero if the capacities would otherwise stand idle. These costs will be positive if the firm could use the capacities devoted to the subunit to manufacture another profitable product, such as a main product or another type of subunit.

As with a product addition, analysts can estimate the incremental outlay costs of manufacturing as the total variable costs of production, b', plus any change in semifixed costs. The total variable costs will equal the variable cost per unit times the number of units to be acquired. Thus, one can view the difference between the outside purchase price per unit, p', and the variable cost per unit, b', as the contribution per unit from manufacturing, CM'_m. That is, the savings per unit are analogous to the difference between revenue per unit and variable costs per unit in a typical breakeven problem. The firm will break even on the decision to manufacture rather than to purchase at an output x'_{be}, where x'_{be} equals incremental fixed costs divided by CM'_m. Note also that all of the problems encountered in estimating incremental costs for adding a product discussed in Section 17.4(a) apply here, as well.

(c) SELL NOW OR PROCESS FURTHER. In general, a decision unit will process a product further rather than sell it immediately if the incremental revenues from processing exceed the incremental costs of processing. The incremental revenues are measured by the difference between the selling price of the unit after processing and the selling price if sold immediately times the number of units to be processed — that is, $(p_{\text{later}} - p_{\text{now}})$ total units. The incremental costs are the incremental outlay costs of processing and the opportunity costs of using the capacities to process the product. As already noted, this decision situation is simply a variation of the decision to add a product. Consequently, analysts use the same method, except for the measure of incremental revenues, which is based on the increase in selling price after the product has been processed further.

(d) SUMMARY. The three situations described in this section rely on the basic assumption of cost-volume-profit analyses—that is, a decision unit intends to hold a set of capacities during the subsequent operating period that will result in the incurrence of fixed costs, whether or not the unit uses the capacities in some productive effort. Generally, if the firm uses the capacities, revenues increase at a faster rate than costs. As a result, the firm will decide for utilization, for example, by adding a product. Discussion in the three situations assumed that only a single other alternative existed for the capacities. When the decision problem involves more than one alternative, the simple rules outlined above no longer hold. Wc discuss this problcm situation next.

17.5 SHORT-RUN MULTIPRODUCT MODELS—LINEAR PROGRAMMING EXTENSIONS OF COST-VOLUME-PROFIT

In a direct sense, one can consider linear programming as the multiproduct analogue of the cost-volume-profit analysis (or breakeven model). A linear programming problem develops whenever a firm uses common facilities to produce two or more different types of output. As a rule, the common facilities constrain the maximum amounts of each output that the firm can produce. A single-product firm usually finds it profitable to expand output as long as revenues exceed variable costs. In a multiproduct firm, however, an increase of the output of one product usually introduces an additional cost—the opportunity cost of not being able to produce an alternative product or products.

(a) A GRAPHIC SOLUTION TO A LINEAR PROGRAMMING PROBLEM. To illustrate, suppose that a firm may produce products X_1 and X_2. Product X_1 has a contribution margin (i.e., revenue minus variable costs) of $3; product X_2's contribution margin is $2. The firm has an available capacity of 500 hours. Each unit of output of X_1 requires 2 hours of capacity and each unit of output of X_2 requires 1 hour of this capacity. Thus, the firm can produce 250 units of X_1, 500 units of X_2, or various linear combinations of X_1 and X_2, provided that $2X_1 + 1X_2 \leq 500$ hours.

One can solve this simple problem by comparing relative contribution margins. We note that a unit of X_1 uses 2 hours of the scarce resource and returns $3 in contribution margin. Stated alternatively, X_1 returns $1.50 per hour of capacity used. However, X_2 returns $2 per hour of capacity used; therefore, X_2 is relatively more profitable than X_1. Because all the relations in the problem are linear, it follows that the firm should produce 500 units of X_2 and no units of X_1 (i.e., every unit of X_1 produced forces the firm to forgo two units of X_2; the net effect is a loss of $1 of contribution margin). Five hundred units of X_2 yield a total contribution margin of $1,000. This is the maximum contribution margin possible, given the statement of the problem.

One could also solve this problem using graphic techniques. Letting the horizontal axis in the graph in Exhibit 17.9 represent output of X_1 and the vertical the output of X_2, one can graph the constraint $2X_1 + X_2 \leq 500$ as a straight line joining the X_1 and X_2 coordinates of (250, 0) and (0, 500). Any point on this line represents a feasible combination of X_1 and X_2 that does not does not violate the constraint of $2X_1 + X_2 \leq 500$. The dashed lines shown in Exhibit 17.9 represent equal amounts of total contribution margin resulting from combinations of outputs of X_1 and X_2. For example, 300 units of X_2 yield the same total contribution margin ($600) as 200 units of X_1. Similarly, 500 units of X_2 yield the same total contribution margin ($1,000) as 333 units of X_1. However, 333 units of X_1 is not feasible, because this output would require 666 hours of capacity. Hence, the maximum contribution margin possible is $1,000, achieved by producing 500 units of X_2.

Note that the optimal solution occurs at a point where the total contribution margin line (in this case, cm = $1,000) touches an extreme point of the feasible region. The

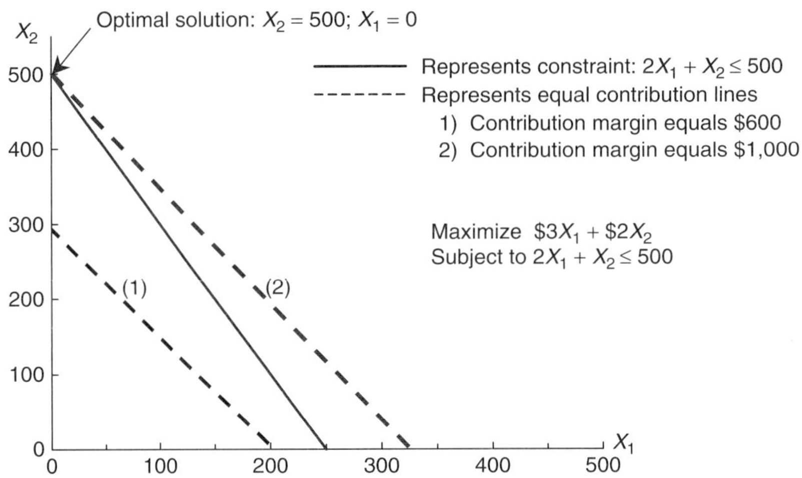

EXHIBIT 17.9 CONTRIBUTION MARGINS AND FEASIBILITY CONSTRAINTS

feasible region is formed by the triangle with the points moving counterclockwise, (0, 0), (250, 0), (0, 500).

Suppose, now, that the problem has a second constraint. For example, assume that the outputs of X_1 and X_2 must pass through a second production department with the following constraint: $1.5\ X_1 + 2X_2 \leq 480$ hours. This constraint implies that the second department can produce the two extremes of either 320 units of X_1 or 240 units of X_2. Imposing this constraint with the previous one shown in Exhibit17.9 will modify the feasible region as shown in Exhibit 17.10. The first constraint still restricts the output of X_1 to a maximum output of 250 units of X_1. The second constraint primarily reduces the maximum output of X_2 from 500 to 240 units. This constraint remains binding as we move down it to the right, substituting the output of X_1 for X_2 until we reach the intersection of the two constraints ($X_1 = 208$, $X_2 = 84$), after which the first constraint again becomes binding, as shown in Exhibit 17.10.

The solution, $X_1 = 208$ and $X_2 = 84$, again occurs where the dashed line representing equal contribution margin touches an extreme point of the feasible region. A contribution margin of \$792 is the maximum contribution margin possible with the constraints of $2X_1 + X_2 \leq 500$ and $1.5X_1 + 2X_2 \leq 480$.

(b) SENSITIVITY OF SOLUTION TO ACCOUNTING ESTIMATION ERRORS. The linear programming solution obtained in Section 17.5(a) relies on estimates of the contribution margins of X_1 and X_2 and their technical coefficients of production. The latter are basically engineering data. However, firms measure contribution margins using accounting estimates of product variable costs, along with estimates of the revenue per unit of output. These accounting measurements are subject to error, and we now discuss how to assess the significance of these errors.

One can assess the significance of measurement errors in contribution margins in part by analyzing the sensitivity of the solution of the linear programming model to changes in contribution margins. If the solution proves sensitive to small changes, it may be profitable to obtain more reliable estimates of variable costs and revenue. To illustrate, suppose that past data indicate that the actual variable costs of product X_2 fluctuate in such a manner that its

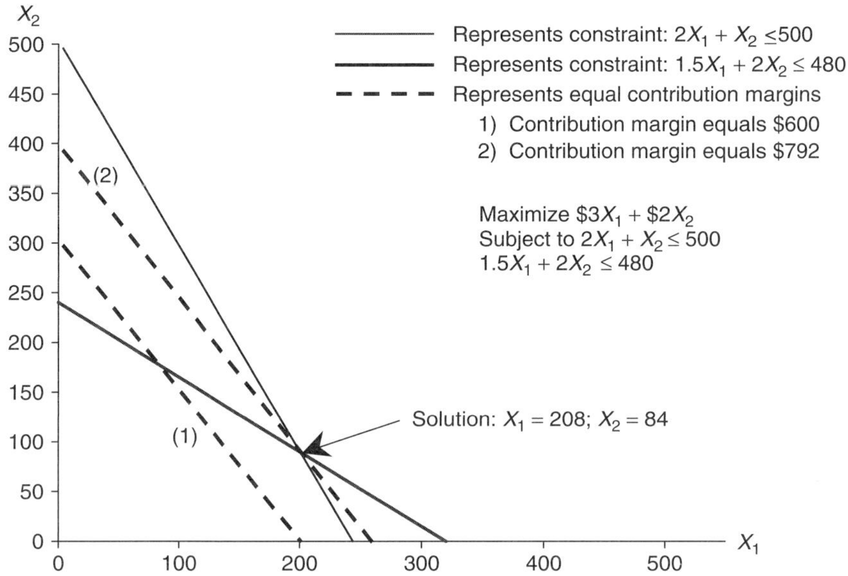

EXHIBIT 17.10 CONTRIBUTION MARGIN AND FEASIBILITY CONSTRAINTS

contribution margin may fall anywhere in the range \$1.00 to \$3.00 (unlikely, perhaps, but useful for illustrative purposes).

Exhibit 17.4 shows that if X_2's contribution margin were \$1.00, while X_1's remains at \$3.00, the new optimal solution will become $X_1 = 250$, $X_2 = 0$. Total contribution margin would be \$3(250) + \$2(0) = \$750. However, if X_2's contribution margin were \$3.00, the new optimal solution would be the same as the original one—that is, $X_1 = 208$, $X_2 = 84$, but with a revised total contribution margin of \$3(208) + \$3(84) = \$876.

One can interpret these sensitivity results as follows: If the estimator knew with certainty that X_2's contribution margin would be \$1.00 during the next operating period, the decision unit would revise its production plan and produce 250 units of X_1 and 0 units of X_2. In contrast, no revision would be necessary were the actual contribution margin of X_2 to increase to \$3.00.

Note, however, that the estimator does not know for sure the contribution margin of X_2 for the next operating period. Instead, the estimator relies on a best estimate, which we assume is \$2.00. Suppose, then, that the decision unit implements the original production plan and actual output is $X_1 = 208$, $X_2 = 84$. Unfortunately, the actual contribution margin of X_2 drops to \$1.00, so that the decision unit obtains only \$3(208) + \$1(84) = \$708. Recall that if X_2's contribution margin dropped to \$1.00, the optimal solution was $X_1 = 250$, $X_2 = 0$, yielding a total contribution margin of \$3(250) = \$750.

Hence, the opportunity cost of not knowing in advance the actual contribution margin of X_2 is simply \$750 – \$708 = \$42 (i.e., the optimal value of the objective function minus the actual value).

We now expand the example to consider other possible outcomes for contribution margins along with the prior probabilities of their occurrence. This would permit us to calculate the *expected value of perfect information* by weighting the opportunity cost of each estimation error by the probability of its occurrence. For example, suppose that the probabilities for the contribution margin of X_2 were as follows:

Estimate of CM_2	Probability	Opportunity Cost of Error	Weighted Opportunity Cost
1.00	.25	$42	.25 ($42) = $10.50
2.00	.50	0	
3.00	.25	0	0
			Total $10.50

In words, this indicates that the estimator can expect to gain only $10.50 on average per operating run with perfect knowledge of CM_2 prior to making the decision. More accurately, the estimator will save $42 once out of every four runs if a perfect estimate of CM_2 were available. This represents the upper limit on the value of a perfect estimate of X_2's contribution margin. If the cost of obtaining better estimates of CM_2 exceeds an expected value of $10.50 per operating run, the business unit shouldn't invest in the estimation process. If the cost is less than $10.50, the problem becomes a little more complicated because the business unit will not likely obtain a perfect estimate. Instead, it is more realistic to assess the value of, say, reducing the range of the estimate from $1.00 to $3.00 to perhaps $1.75 to $2.25.

The difficulty with this example, and with sensitivity analysis in general, is that *ad hoc* procedures usually dictate the selection of the estimate(s) to vary and the ranges in which their observed values might vary. For example, the estimator will have to decide whether to perform the sensitivity analyses on the contribution margins, the contribution margin components separately (i.e., the individual revenue and cost estimates), the disaggregated costs, the technological constraints, or various combinations of these.

See Hillier and Lieberman (2001) for more extensive discussions about linear programming.

17.6 UNCERTAINTY AND CVP ANALYSIS

The previous sections assumed either that parameter values (e.g., prices, variable costs, quantities of outputs, etc.) were known with certainty or that an estimator could use certainty equivalent estimates to obtain the same results. The latter type of analysis would use a summary measure, say the mean, of the probability distributions of possible values for decision parameters as certainty equivalent estimates and the decision rule would be to *maximize the expected level of profits*. A choice of the best summary measure might pose a problem in itself, depending on the shape of the probability distribution, among other things, but that is not important at this point. The crucial issue lies in whether decision makers are willing to maximize the expected level of profit and, in the process, to ignore other aspects of the probability distributions of random variables such as the variance around the mean.

A rule to maximize the expected level of profit under conditions of uncertainty will be optimal for a decision maker who has a neutral attitude toward risk. That is, the utility function for increasing levels of profit would be linear, so that two times the level of profit, 2π, would be worth twice the utility of π, and three times the level, 3π, would be worth three times the utility of π, and so on. The disutility for losses would also be linear, so that the disutility of -2π would be twice the disutility of $-\pi$, and so on.

Many economic models under uncertainty, however, assume that decision makers are *risk-averse*—in mathematical terms, the utility function is concave, continuous, and differentiable, with the first derivative greater than zero and the second less than zero.

Although merely assuming risk aversion is insufficient for generating specifically how uncertainty will affect output and pricing policies, the general rule is that risk-averse decision makers require higher expected returns for higher-risk investments. This suggests that knowledge of the degree of riskiness of individual investments or of portfolios of investments would prove useful information to a decision maker. Although practitioners still disagree on how best to represent riskiness in uncertainty models, most models use the variance (or standard deviation) around the mean as a surrogate measure of riskiness.

BIBLIOGRAPHY

Hillier, F.S. and G.J. Lieberman. *Introduction to Operations Research*, 7th ed. Burr Ridge, Ill.: McGraw-Hill/Irwin, 2006.

Hilton, R. W., M.W. Maher and F.H. Selto. *Cost Management: Strategies for Business Decisions*, 3rd ed. Burr Ridge, Ill.: McGraw-Hill/Irwin, 2006.

Horngren, C. T., S.M. Datar, and G. Foster. *Cost Accounting: A Managerial Emphasis,* 11th ed. Upper Saddle River, N.J.: Prentice-Hall, 2003.

Maher, M.W., C. Stickney and R.L. Weil. *Managerial Accounting: Concepts, Methods and Uses*, 9th ed. Mason, Ohio: Thomson International/South-Western Publishing, 2006.

CHAPTER 18

FORECASTING PRO FORMA FINANCIAL STATEMENTS*

JAMES M. WAHLEN, PHD
Indiana University

CONTENTS

18.1 INTRODUCTION TO FORECASTING 504

18.2 PREPARING PRO FORMA FINANCIAL STATEMENTS 505
- (a) General Forecasting Principles 505
- (b) Six-Step Forecasting Plan 506
- (c) Practical Tips for Implementing the Six-Step Plan 509
- (d) Introduction to Starbucks: A Comprehensive Example 510

18.3 STEP 1: PROJECTING SALES AND OTHER REVENUES 514
- (a) Projecting Sales 514
- (b) Projecting Other Revenues 517

18.4 STEP 2: PROJECTING OPERATING EXPENSES 518
- (a) Projecting Cost of Sales 518
- (b) Projecting Store Operating Expenses 518
- (c) Projecting Other Operating Expenses 519

18.5 STEP 3: PROJECTING THE ASSETS ON THE BALANCE SHEET 519
- (a) Projecting Individual Assets 521
- (b) Projecting Assets that Vary as a Percent of Total Assets 526

18.6 STEP 4: PROJECTING LIABILITIES AND SHAREHOLDERS' EQUITY 527
- (a) Projecting Liabilities 527
- (b) Projecting Shareholders' Equity 528

18.7 STEP 5: PROJECTING INTEREST EXPENSE, INTEREST INCOME, INCOME TAX EXPENSE, AND THE CHANGE IN RETAINED EARNINGS 529
- (a) Interest Expense 529
- (b) Interest Income 530
- (c) Income Taxes 530
- (d) Net Income 530
- (e) Retained Earnings 530

18.8 BALANCING THE BALANCE SHEET 531

18.9 CLOSING THE LOOP: SOLVING FOR CO-DETERMINED VARIABLES 533

18.10 STEP 6: DERIVING THE STATEMENT OF CASH FLOWS 534

18.11 SHORTCUT APPROACHES TO FORECASTING 536

18.12 ANALYZING PRO FORMA FINANCIAL STATEMENTS 536

18.13 SENSITIVITY ANALYSIS AND STRATEGIC PLANNING 537

18.14 SUMMARY 537

* This chapter reflects many of the ideas developed in Chapter 10 of *Financial Reporting and Statement Analysis: A Strategic Perspective*, by Clyde Stickney, Paul Brown, and James Wahlen, Thomson International Southwestern Publishing, 5th edition. The interested reader should refer to that text for more complete discussion of pro forma financial statement forecasting in the context of financial statement analysis and equity valuation.

18.1 INTRODUCTION TO FORECASTING

This chapter discusses accounting for the future. Analysts use forecasting to develop a set of realistic expectations for the outcomes of future business activities. To capture these expectations, analysts use a set of forecasts referred to as *pro forma financial statements*.[1] Pro forma forecasts of financial statements–expected future income statements, balance sheets, and cash flow statements–present an integrated, articulated portrayal of the results of the firm's future operating, investing, and financing activities. These activities will determine the firm's future growth, profitability, cash flows, financial position, and risk. Using a forecasted set of financial statements, management aims to capture expectations for *all* of the factors that will determine the firm's future value-relevant payoffs to stakeholders.

Pro forma financial statements provide important analytic tools for managers and analysts because forecasts of future payoffs play a central role in valuation and other financial decision contexts. A firm's share value depends on its expected future payoffs to equity stakeholders, discounted for time and risk. Using a set of financial statement forecasts, the analyst can derive the future value-relevant payoffs to equity shareholders–earnings, cash flows, and dividends–which provide the fundamental bases for equity share value. Credit decisions require expectations for future cash flows available to make required future interest and principal payments. Managers' decisions about firm strategy, potential customer or supplier relations, potential mergers or acquisitions, potential carve-outs of divisions or subsidiaries, and even whether a firm presents a good employment opportunity, depend on their expected future payoffs and the risks of those payoffs.

Developing forecasts of future payoffs poses difficulties because one must estimate the effects of the activities that one expects to occur in the future, an analysis that involves uncertainty. Forecast errors can prove costly. Optimistic forecasts of future earnings and cash flows can lead the manager to overestimate a firm's value, and therefore make poor decisions based on an inflated value of the firm. On the other hand, conservative forecasts can lead the manager to understate a firm's future earnings and cash flows, missing valuable investment opportunities. Forecasters need to develop *realistic* (unbiased and objective–not optimistic nor conservative) expectations of future earnings and cash flows that lead to informed decisions.

To develop reliable forecasts that form the bases for sound decision-making, managers and analysts should draw upon all of their knowledge of the business to project the future. Developing forecasts draws upon the disciplines of accounting, finance, economics, and strategy. The analyst should base pro forma financial statements on expectations that reflect the economics of the industry, the competitive advantages and risks of the firm's strategy, the quality of the firm's accounting, and the drivers of the firm's profitability, growth, and risk. These elements provide the necessary foundations for forecasting, and they inform the analyst about the firm's critical risk and success factors. The same critical factors that serve as the focal points for the firm's strategy, growth, profitability, and risk become the focal points for forecasting pro forma financial statements.

This chapter first outlines a set of six steps for forecasting pro forma financial statements. The chapter then illustrates each of the steps by applying them to Starbucks, developing detailed pro forma financial statements for each of the three primary financial

1. Throughout this chapter, we use the term *pro forma financial statements* to denote the expected future income statements, balance sheets, and statements of cash flows that capture the analyst's forecasts of the firm's future operating, investing, and financing activities.

statements. The chapter also describes a set of techniques to enhance the reliability of forecasts, including sensitivity analysis, iteration, and validity checks. The chapter also discusses some simplifying steps for shortcut forecasts based on time-series projections of sales, future earnings, and cash flows, and the conditions under which such shortcuts will not create forecast errors.

18.2 PREPARING PRO FORMA FINANCIAL STATEMENTS

Preparing a set of pro forma financial statements requires that an analyst consider numerous assumptions and relations. We suggest that one establish at the outset a flow, or a sequence of steps, to project the three principal financial statements (cash flow statement, balance sheet and income statement). One should implement these steps while following several general but important principles. This section offers a set of such principles, describes a six-step forecasting plan, and then concludes with several practical coaching tips on implementing the six-step sequence.

(a) GENERAL FORECASTING PRINCIPLES. Several key principles of forecasting deserve mention.

First, the objective of forecasting is to produce objective and realistic expectations of the future business activities. To maximize forecast reliability and minimize costly forecast errors, pro forma financial statements should provide unbiased predictions of the firm's future operating, investing, and financing activities, and should be neither conservative nor optimistic.

Second, pro forma financial statements should be comprehensive. The pro forma financial statements should include *all* expected future operating, investing, and financing activities to ensure complete forecasts. For example, suppose an analyst forecasts expected future sales growth and then simply projects expected future earnings assuming a constant profit margin on sales. This approach fails to consider all of the elements that determine profitability from sales, and leads to incomplete earnings forecasts. By assuming a constant profit margin on sales, one would ignore whether selling, general, and administrative (SG&A) expenses will increase more slowly than sales growth because of economies of scale or scope.

Third, pro forma financial statements must have internally consistent assumptions and relations. Pro forma financial statements should rely on the *additivity* within financial statements and the *articulation* across financial statements to avoid internal inconsistencies in forecasts. The analyst can rely on the internal discipline of accounting across the three primary financial statements to reduce the possibility of errors from internally inconsistent assumptions. For example, sales growth forecasts will likely drive forecasts of growth in related elements of the financial statements, including future costs of sales, inventory, accounts receivable, and property, plant, and equipment. In turn, forecasts of future growth in inventory, receivables, and property, plant, and equipment will likely affect growth in related elements, including accounts payable, depreciation, short-term and long-term borrowing, interest expense, and owners' equity issues. Each of these elements will, in turn, have implications for the firm's cash flows. To capture the complex relations among operating, investing, and financing activities, pro forma financial statements should add up and should articulate with each other. The balance sheet should reflect all of the elements of financial position and should balance; the income statement should reflect all of the revenues, expenses, gains, and losses each period; the statement of cash flows should reflect all of the cash inflows and outflows implied by the income statement and the changes in the firm's balance sheet.

Fourth, pro forma financial statements must have externally valid assumptions. Forecast assumptions should pass the tests of common sense and reality checks. For example, do the sales growth forecast assumptions reflect the competitive conditions in the industry, including market demand and price elasticity for the firm's products? Analysts should ensure that the assumptions in the pro forma financial statements reflect the past as well as plans and capabilities for the future. In addition, analysts should avoid building forecasts based on wishful thinking. That is, analysts should not create forecasts based on what they hope the firm will do, nor on what they think the firm should do, but instead the forecasts should capture what the analyst believes the firm actually can and will do in the future.

(b) SIX-STEP FORECASTING PLAN. To prepare a set of pro forma financial statements, analysts should organize the numerous assumptions and relations that they will use into operating, investing, and financing activities. This *activity-based forecasting* perspective enables analysts to identify the necessary sequence of steps to project the three principal financial statements. The particular sequence of steps may vary, depending on the reason for preparing the pro forma financial statements. For most forecasts, this six-step sequence works well:

Step 1. Project revenues from sales and other revenue-generating activities.

Step 2. Project operating expenses (for example, cost of goods sold and SG&A expenses) and derive projected operating income (income before interest expense, interest income, and income taxes).

Step 3. Project the operating assets and liabilities (for example, cash, inventory, receivables, property, plant, and equipment, accounts payable, accrued expenses) necessary to support the level of operations projected in steps 1 and 2.

Step 4. Project the funding structure (for example, short-term and long-term borrowing, short-term and long-term investments in financial assets, and shareholders' equity except for retained earnings) necessary to support the level of operations projected in step 3.

Step 5. Calculate the cost of financing the funding structure projected in step 4.

- **a.** From projected operating income from step 2, subtract interest expense on short-term and long-term borrowing and add interest income on short-term and long-term financial asset investments to derive projected income before tax.
- **b.** Subtract projected income tax to derive projected net income.
- **c.** Subtract expected dividends from net income to obtain the projected change in retained earnings.
- **d.** At this point, check to ensure that the projected balance sheets are in balance. If they do not balance, the projected financial structure may need adjustments (for example, the firm may need additional financing), and analysts will need to repeat steps 4 and 5 until the balance sheet balances.

Step 6. Derive the statement of cash flows from the projected income statements and balance sheets.

Exhibit 18.1 summarizes this six-step procedure.

Statement of Income and Retained Earnings				Balance Sheet	
				Assets	**Liabilities and Shareholder's Equity**
Revenues + Sales Revenue + Other Operating Revenues	⇦	**STEP 1: Project Operating Revenues**		Cash Accounts Receivable Inventories Other Current Assets Property, Plant and Equipment	Accounts Payable Accrued Expenses
Operating Expenses: – Cost of Goods Sold – Selling, General and Administrative Expenses **Operating Income**	⇦	**STEP 2: Project Operating Expenses**			
		STEP 3: Project Operating Assets and Liabilities	⇨		
		STEP 4: Project Financial Capital Structure	⇨	Short-term and Long-term Investment Securities	Short-term and Long-term Borrowing Contributed Equity Capital
– Interest Expense + Interest Income – Income Taxes **Net Income** – Dividends *Change in Retained Earnings*	⇦	**STEP 5: Project Interest Expense, Interest Income, Income Taxes, Net Income, Dividends, and the Change in Retained Earnings**	⇨		Retained Earnings
				Total Assets =	**Total Liabilities and Shareholders' Equity**

EXHIBIT 18.1 PREPARING PRO FORMA FINANCIAL STATEMENTS

STEP 6: Project Cash Flows from Operating, Investing and Financing Activities					
		⇩			
		Statement of Cash Flows			
Operations				*Investing Activities*	*Financing Activities*
Net Income				Net Capital Expenditures on	Change in Short-term and
Depreciation Expense				Property, Plant and	Long-term Borrowing
Other Adjustments				Equipment	Issue or Repurchase of
Change in Receivables				Purchase or Sale of Short-	Common Equity
Change in Inventories				term and Long-term	Dividends
Change in Other Current				Investment Securities	Other Financing
Assets				Other Investing Transactions	Transactions
Change in Accounts Payable				***CASH FLOW FROM***	***CASH FLOW FROM***
Change in Accrued Expenses				***INVESTING***	***FINANCING***
CASH FLOW FROM OPERATIONS					

EXHIBIT 18.1 PREPARING PRO FORMA FINANCIAL STATEMENTS *(CONTINUED)*

(c) PRACTICAL TIPS FOR IMPLEMENTING THE SIX-STEP PLAN. We suggest several practical tips on implementing the six-step sequence. *Analysts should consider these six steps as integrated and interdependent tasks, not necessarily sequential or linear.* The order in which an analyst implements these six steps and the amount of emphasis placed on each step will depend on the integration of the firm's operating, investing, and financing activities. For example, forecasts of revenues for a retail chain or restaurant chain may first require forecasts of the number of new stores that will open. The sales forecasts for a manufacturer may depend on building a new productive plant, which may depend on obtaining additional long-term debt financing.

The amounts on the three pro forma financial statements must articulate. For example, the change in retained earnings should include net income minus dividends. The change in accumulated depreciation on the balance sheet should reflect depreciation expense on the income statement. The change in the property, plant, and equipment amounts on the balance sheet should incorporate the effects of any capital expenditures, and the statement of cash flows should add the amount of depreciation expense (a non-cash expense) back to net income, and subtract capital expenditures. The net cash flow on the statement of cash flows must agree with the change in the cash balance on the balance sheet.

Preparing pro forma statements requires at least one flexible financial account, and an iterative and circular process. Firms rely on flexible accounts–usually financial assets and liabilities–to expand and contract with the firm's need for capital. For example, a firm that needs to finance growth in assets may need to increase short-term or long-term borrowing, or reduce investments in short-term or long-term financial assets, or issue equity shares. A firm that generates excess cash may deploy that cash by paying down debt, or investing in financial assets, or paying dividends, or repurchasing its own shares. Therefore, the analyst should adjust flexible financial accounts as necessary to appropriately match the firm's future financial structure with the firm's future operations. Thus, the process of producing a set of pro forma financial statements will require several iterations and a degree of circularity. For example, the first pass through a set of pro forma financial statements may reveal to the analyst a need to increase borrowing to finance future expenditures and to make the balance sheet balance. Increased borrowing, however, will require the analyst to increase interest expense to reflect the cost of the additional debt capital, which in turn means that income taxes will fall and net income will fall. As a consequence, retained earnings will fall, which means the analyst may have to increase borrowing a bit more. The analyst will repeat the process until the balance sheet balances and it articulates with the income statement and the statement of cash flows.[2]

The quality of the pro forma financial statements, and therefore the quality of the decisions based on those statements, will not exceed the quality of the forecast assumptions. Less technically: garbage-in, garbage-out. The analyst should justify each assumption, especially the most important assumptions that reflect the critical risk and success factors of the firm's strategy. In addition, the analyst can impose reality checks on the assumptions by analyzing ratios and common-size financial statements (which express income statement amounts as a percent of revenues and balance sheet amounts as a percent of total assets) using the pro forma financial statements. These analytical tools may identify certain assumptions as unrealistic or inconsistent with one another.

---

2. Most computer spreadsheet software packages facilitate iterative and circular processes. For example, in *Excel*, under the Tools/Options/Calculation menu, one can check the Iteration box to set the spreadsheet to automatically compute iteratively (for example, 100 times) until the iterated computations converge to a specified maximum change.

Analysts should conduct sensitivity analyses on the pro forma financial statements. The analyst should assess, for example, the extent to which earnings will vary across different sales growth scenarios (for example, comparing across different growth rate assumptions that reflect most likely, optimistic, and pessimistic forecasts). Some of the assumptions will have bigger consequences than others, and sensitivity analyses will help the analyst assess the extent to which pro forma forecast results depend on key assumptions.

(d) INTRODUCTION TO STARBUCKS: A COMPREHENSIVE EXAMPLE. The subsequent sections of this chapter illustrate the six-step procedure described above by using the analysis of Starbucks' financial statements through 2003, referred to in the exhibits as "Year 13." Starbucks is the leading U.S. retail chain of premium coffee shops. Starbucks successfully developed and expanded a European idea–enjoying a coffee-based beverage, and sharing that experience with others in a comfortable, friendly environment. The Starbucks 2003 Annual Report refers to this as the *Starbucks Experience*.

Starbucks has grown from just a single store near Pike's Place Market in Seattle to a global company with 7,225 locations worldwide at the end of 2003. In 2003 alone, Starbucks opened 1,201 new retail locations; Starbucks owns and operates 602 of these locations, and licenses the remaining 599 to others.[3] Most of Starbucks' retail stores (5,201 stores) at the end of 2003 are in the United States, amounting to one Starbucks retail location for approximately every 50,000 U.S. residents.[4] Starbucks does not want to focus only on the U.S. market, however, and has plans to expand globally, with already more than 2,000 stores outside of the United States.

To further expand the business model, Starbucks also has a licensing agreement with Kraft Foods to market and distribute Starbucks' whole bean and ground coffee throughout the United States in approximately 19,500 grocery and warehouse club stores. Furthermore, Starbucks sells whole bean and ground coffee through institutional foodservice companies (such as SYSCO Corporation) that service business, education, office, hotel, restaurant, airline and other foodservice accounts.

Exhibit 18.2 presents the financial statements for Starbucks for Years 11 to 13. Exhibit 18.2 also presents Starbucks' financial statement data in common-size format and in rate of change format.[5] This chapter analyzes these financial statement data to develop forecast assumptions and to compute pro forma financial statements for Starbucks for Year 14 to Year 18, which we label Year +1 to Year +5 to denote that they are forecasts, rather than actual statements.[6]

---

3. In addition, in 2003 Starbucks acquired 64 company-owned stores and 74 licensed stores in an acquisition of Seattle's Best Coffee Co.
4. By comparison, in year 13 there is one Subway sandwich shop for approximately every 19,000 U.S. residents, and one McDonalds restaurant for approximately every 21,000 U.S. residents.
5. Common size income statements present all income statement items scaled as a percent of sales, while common size balance sheets present all balance sheet items scaled as a percent of total assets. Rate of change financial statements present all items on the financial statements expressed as a percent of growth relative to the prior year. The compound rate of change is the compound growth rate in each financial statement item over the relevant period.
6. A spreadsheet program (like Microsoft *Excel*) is a useful computational tool for preparing pro forma financial statements. The proper design and the preparation of a spreadsheet for pro forma financial statements provide an excellent learning process to enhance and solidify understanding of the relationships between various financial statement items. Once you become comfortable with pro forma financial statements and spreadsheets, then using the forecast spreadsheets will save considerable time when preparing forecasts in the future.

STARBUCKS: CONSOLIDATED STATEMENTS OF INCOME:
FISCAL YEARS 11–13

	Amounts in Millions			Common-Sized			Rates of Change		
	11	12	13	11	12	13	12	13	Compound
Retail	$2,229.6	$2,792.9	$3,449.6	84.2%	84.9%	84.6%	25.3%	23.5%	24.4%
Specialty	419.4	496.0	625.9	15.8	15.1	15.4	18.3	26.2	22.2
Net Revenues	$2,649.0	$3,288.9	$4,075.5	100.0%	100.0%	100.0%	24.2%	23.9%	24.0%
Cost of Sales (including occupancy)	1,112.8	1,350.0	1,685.9	42.0	41.0	41.4	21.3	24.9	23.1
Gross Profit	$1,536.2	$1,938.9	$2,389.6	58.0%	59.0%	58.6%	26.2%	23.2%	24.7%
Store Operating Expenses	868.0	1,109.8	1,379.6	32.8	33.7	33.9	27.9	24.3	26.1
Other Operating Expenses	72.4	106.1	141.3	2.7	3.2	3.5	46.5	33.2	39.7
Depreciation and Amortization	163.5	205.6	237.8	6.2	6.3	5.8	25.7	15.7	20.6
General and Administrative Expenses	179.9	234.6	244.6	6.8	7.1	6.0	30.4	4.2	16.6
Income from Equity Investees	27.7	33.4	38.4	1.0	1.0	0.9	20.6	14.8	17.6
Operating Income	$ 280.2	$ 316.3	$ 424.7	10.6%	9.6%	10.4%	12.9%	34.3%	23.1%
Interest and Other Income, Net	10.8	9.3	11.6	0.4	0.3	0.3	–13.6	25.0	3.9
Other Gains (Losses)	(2.9)	13.4	–	(0.1)	0.4	0.0	(554.5)	na	(100.0)
Income Before Income Taxes	288.0	339.0	436.3	10.9	10.3	10.7	17.7	28.7	23.1
Provision for Income Taxes	107.7	126.3	168.0	4.1	3.8	4.1	17.3	33.0	24.9
Net Income	$ 180.3	$ 212.7	$ 268.3	6.8%	6.5%	6.6%	17.9%	26.2%	22.0%

EXHIBIT 18.2 STARBUCKS FINANCIAL STATEMENTS FROM YEAR 11 TO 13

Starbucks: Consolidated Balance Sheets:
Fiscal Years 11–13

	Amounts in Millions			Common-Sized			Rates of Change		
	11	12	13	11	12	13	12	13	Compound
Current Assets									
Cash and Equivalents	$ 113.2	$ 99.7	$ 200.9	6.1%	4.5%	7.4%	(12.0)%	101.6%	33.2%
Short-Term Investments	107.3	227.7	149.1	5.8	10.3	5.5	112.1	(34.5)	17.9
Receivables	90.4	97.6	114.4	4.9	4.4	4.2	7.9	17.3	12.5
Inventories	221.3	263.2	342.9	12.0	11.9	12.6	18.9	30.3	24.5
Prepaid Expenses and Other Assets	29.8	42.4	55.2	1.6	1.9	2.0	42.0	30.3	36.0
Deferred Income Taxes, net	31.9	42.2	61.5	1.7	1.9	2.3	32.4	45.6	38.9
Total Current Assets	$ 593.9	772.6	924.0	32.2%	34.9%	33.9%	30.1%	19.6%	11.7%
Long-term Investments	–	–	$ 136.2	0.0%	0.0%	5.0%	na	na	na
Equity and Other Investments	$ 63.1	$ 102.5	144.3	3.4	4.6%	5.3%	62.5%	40.7%	51.2%
Property and Equipment, Gross	1,741.0	2,080.2	2,434.7	94.3	93.9	89.2	19.5	17.0	18.3
Accumulated Depreciation	(605.2)	(814.4)	(1,049.8)	(32.8)	(36.8)	(38.5)	34.6	28.9	31.7
Property and Equipment, Net	$1,135.8	$1,265.8	$1,384.9	61.5%	57.2%	50.7%	11.4%	9.4%	10.4%
Other Assets and Goodwill	53.7	73.5	140.4	2.9	3.3	5.1	36.8	91.1	61.7
Total Assets	$1,846.5	$2,214.4	$2,729.7	100.0%	100.0%	100.0%	19.9%	23.3%	21.6%

Exhibit 18.2 Starbucks Financial Statements from Year 11 to 13 *(Continued)*

FISCAL YEARS 11–13

	Amounts in Millions			Common-Sized			Rates of Change		
	11	12	13	11	12	13	12	13	Compound
Current Liabilities									
Accounts Payable	$ 127.9	$ 136.0	$ 169.0	6.9%	6.1%	6.2%	6.3%	24.3%	14.9%
Accrued Expenses	157.4	229.4	310.6	8.5	10.4	11.4	45.7	35.4	40.5
Accrued Taxes	70.3	54.2	54.9	3.8	2.4	2.0	(22.9)	1.3	(11.6)
Deferred Revenue	26.9	42.3	73.5	1.5	1.9	2.7	57.0	73.9	65.2
Current Portion of Long-Term Debt	62.7	0.7	0.7	3.4	0.0	0.0	(98.9)	1.7	(89.3)
Total Current Liabilities	$ 445.3	$ 462.6	608.7	24.1%	20.9%	22.3%	3.9%	31.6%	16.9%
Deferred Income Taxes, net	19.5	23.5	34.2	1.1	1.1	1.3	20.4	45.6	32.4
Long-Term Debt	5.8	5.1	4.4	0.3	0.2	0.2	(12.3)	(14.2)	(13.3)
Total Liabilities	$ 470.6	$ 491.2	647.3	25.5%	22.2%	23.7%	4.4%	31.8%	17.3%
Shareholders' Equity									
Common Stock	791.6	930.4	998.5	42.9%	42.0%	36.6%	17.5%	7.3%	12.3%
Retained Earnings	589.7	801.3	1,069.7	31.9	36.2	39.2	35.9	33.5	34.7
Accumulated Other Comp. Income/(Loss)	(5.4)	(8.6)	14.2	(0.3)	(0.4)	0.5	58.7	(266.0)	na
Total Shareholders' Equity	$1,375.9	1,723.2	2,082.4	74.5%	77.8%	76.3%	25.2%	20.8%	23.0%
Total Liabilities and Shareholders' Equity	$1,846.5	2,214.4	2,729.7	100.0%	100.0%	100.0%	19.9%	23.3%	21.6%

EXHIBIT 18.2 STARBUCKS FINANCIAL STATEMENTS FROM YEAR 11 TO 13 *(CONTINUED)*

All financial statement amounts throughout this chapter appear in millions. The spreadsheets make all computations to multiple decimal places. Because we report all dollar amounts in this chapter in millions, some minor rounding differences will occasionally arise and make it appear that various subtotals and totals disagree with the sum of the individual items that comprise the subtotal or total.

18.3 STEP 1: PROJECTING SALES AND OTHER REVENUES

(a) PROJECTING SALES. One must first project revenues from the principal business activities of the firm, which often involve sales of products or services. The expected level of revenues can serve as a basis for deriving many of the other amounts in the pro forma financial statements.

Sales volumes and prices determine sales numbers. In the case of sales *volume*, some firms (e.g., automobile manufacturing and beverages firms) report sales volume figures, enabling the analyst to assess separately volume and price as drivers of historical sales growth, and to use them as a framework for predicting future sales. Other firms report volume-related measures of operating activities that the analyst can use to forecast sales, such as new stores for retailers and restaurant chains, and passengers and passenger-seat-miles for airlines. A firm in a mature industry (for example, consumer foods) with little expected change in its market share might anticipate volume increases equal to the growth rate in the population within its geographic markets. A firm that has increased its operating capacity consistent with the high growth rate anticipated in a particular industry (for example, biotechnology or computer software) might use this expected growth rate when projecting volume increases.

When projecting *prices,* one must consider the expected rate of general price inflation in the economy, and the effects of changes in foreign currency exchange rates on sales denominated in foreign currencies. One must also consider factors specific to the firm and its industry that might affect demand and price elasticity, such as excess capacity, shortages of raw materials, substitute products, technological changes in products or production methods, and similar factors. Capital-intensive firms, such as paper manufacturers, may require several years to add new capacity. If a firm competes in a capital-intensive industry that analysts expect to operate near capacity for the next few years, then price increases will likely occur. On the other hand, if a firm competes in an industry in which excess capacity already exists or new capacity will become available soon, then price increases seem less likely. A firm in transition from the high growth to the maturity phase of its life cycle, or a firm that plans technological improvements in its production processes (e.g., some portions of the computer industry) might expect increases in sales volume but decreases in sales prices per unit. If a firm has established a competitive position for its brand name in its markets, or has successfully differentiated unique characteristics for its products, then that firm may have a greater potential to increase prices, or to avoid price declines, than another firm with generic products.

If sales have grown at a reasonably steady rate in prior periods and nothing indicates that economic, industry, or firm-specific factors will change significantly, then the analyst can project this growth rate into the future. If a major acquisition or divestiture affected the historical growth rate, then the analyst should remove the effect of this event when making projections (unless the firm's strategy includes additional future acquisitions). Projecting sales for firms with cyclical sales patterns (for example, heavy machinery, property-casualty insurance, investment banking) can prove difficult. Their historical growth rates for sales might reflect wide variations in both direction and amount from year to year. The analyst can project a varying growth rate that maintains this cyclical sales pattern in these cases.

(i) Starbucks Sales Growth. Starbucks competes in the fast food chain industry through its chain of coffee shops, and in the consumer foods industry through its sales of coffee beans and ground coffee in grocery stores and foodservice accounts. One would characterize both of these industries in the United States as mature and competitive. In consumer foods, for example, industry sales have grown recently at the growth rate for the general population, approximately 2 percent per year.

Starbucks has defied the characteristics of firms in mature industries, generating an average compounded sales growth rate of 24.0 percent between 1999 and 2003 (Year 9 and Year 13 in the exhibits). Total sales and sales growth rates for Starbucks appear in Exhibit 18.3.

Starbucks discloses information about sales and operating profits for its two major operating segments, Retail and Specialty. The Retail segment includes retail sales of coffee beverages and related products through Starbucks' U.S. and international company owned and operated stores. The Specialty segment includes revenues from licenses of Starbucks stores and related sales of product to store licensees, as well as revenues from product sales through its distributorship arrangements, such as with Kraft (grocery stores and warehouse clubs) and SYSCO (foodservice accounts). Starbucks discloses information about new store openings and comparable store sales, two key drivers of their sales growth in both the Retail and Specialty segments. Net sales amounts, growth rates, new store openings, and growth rates by segment for Starbucks appear in Exhibit 18.4. By analyzing these sales growth data, an analyst can develop more detailed and accurate sales forecasts for each segment.

(ii) Retail Sales Forecasts. The Retail segment, Starbucks' largest segment generating roughly 85 percent of total sales, experienced a compound sales growth rate of 24.2 percent between Years 11 and 13, driven largely by increases in new company-operated stores each year (roughly 600 new stores per year) coupled with modest increases in sales per average store-year (averaging roughly 4.0 percent). The modest increase in average sales per store-year likely reflects the relatively mature price-competitive coffee market, and the fact that Starbucks already charges premium prices for its coffee beverages. An analyst might expect that sales growth per average store-year will continue at 4.0 percent per year into the future, and that Starbucks will continue to open roughly 600 company-operated stores per year. If these projections hold, then Exhibit 18.5 shows the Retail segment sales forecasts for Years +1 to +5 (in millions).

(iii) Specialty Sales Forecast. Starbucks' Specialty segment accounted for roughly 15 percent of total sales, and experienced a compound sales growth rate of 22.2 percent

	Year 11	Year 12	Year 13
Total Sales	$2,649.0	$3,288.9	$4,075.5
Growth rates		+24.2%	+23.9%
Compound growth rate			+24.0%

EXHIBIT 18.3 TOTAL SALES AND GROWTH RATES (IN MILLIONS)

	Year 11	Year 12	Year 13
Retail Segment Sales (millions)	$2,229.6	$2,792.9	$3,449.6
Percent of total sales	84.2%	84.9%	84.6%
Growth rates		+25.3%	+23.5%
Compound growth rate			+24.4%
Total company-operated stores	3,266	3,880	4,546
Net new stores opened during year	647	614	666
Growth rate in company-operated stores	+24.7%	+18.8%	+17.2%
Sales per average store-year (in thousands)	$ 757.8	781.7	818.8
Sales growth rates per average store-year		+3.2%	+4.7%
Specialty Segment	$ 419.4	$ 496.0	$ 625.9
Percent of total sales	15.8%	15.1%	15.4%
Growth rates		+18.3%	+26.2%
Compound growth rate			+22.2%
Specialty revenue components:			
Other revenue.	$ 272.6	$ 313.8	$ 369.1
Growth rate in other revenues		+15.1%	+17.6%
License revenue	$ 146.8	$ 182.2	$ 256.8
Growth rate in license revenues		+24.1%	+40.9%
Total licensed stores	1,443	2,006	2,679
Net new licensed stores opened during year	561	563	599
Growth rate in licensed stores	+63.6%	+39.0%	+33.5%
Revenue per average store-year (in thousands)	$ 126.3	$ 105.7	$ 109.6
Revenue growth rates per average licensed store-year		−16.5%	+3.7%

EXHIBIT 18.4 STARBUCKS SALES GROWTH ANALYSIS BY SEGMENT (IN MILLIONS)

Year	New Stores	Total Stores at Year End	Average Store-Years (a)	Sales per Average Store-Year (b)	Total Retail Sales (c = a × b)	Expected Growth Rate
13 (actual)		4,546	4,213	$0.8188	$3,449.6	
+1 (forecast)	+600	5,146	4,846	0.8516	4,126.9	+19.6%
+2 (forecast)	+600	5,746	5,446	0.8856	4,823.0	+16.9%
+3 (forecast)	+600	6,346	6,046	0.9210	5,568.4	+15.5%
+4 (forecast)	+600	6,946	6,646	0.9579	6,366.2	+14.3%
+5 (forecast)	+600	7,546	7,246	0.9962	7,218.5	+13.4%

EXHIBIT 18.5 RETAIL SALES FORECASTS (IN MILLIONS)

between Years 11 and 13. Starbucks discloses that the largest share of Specialty sales arises from sales of Starbucks products through distributorships. These sales have grown at a compounded rate of roughly 16 percent per year over Years 11 to 13. An analyst might expect that these sales will continue to grow at double-digit rates (assume 12 percent growth on average) for the next five years. The other main contributor to

Starbucks' Specialty sales comes from license revenues. License revenues grow, in part, with Starbucks licensing new stores in the United States and around the world. Over Years 11 to 13, Starbucks licensed between 560 and 600 new stores a year. An analyst might expect Starbucks' to license roughly 600 new stores a year over the next five years, and that average revenues from license stores will grow at 3.0 percent per year, based on worldwide inflation and population growth. Exhibit 18.6 shows sales forecasts for the Specialty segment over the next five years (in millions).

(iv) Combined Sales Growth. Combining both sets of sales forecasts for these segments, we assume that Starbucks will generate sales growth of 19.7 percent in Year +1, and continue to generate double-digit sales growth through Year +5 (see Exhibit 18.7).

(b) PROJECTING OTHER REVENUES. Other revenues for Starbucks primarily include earnings from unconsolidated equity-method affiliates (reported as Income from Equity Investees on Starbucks' 2003 [Year 13] income statement). This source of income has grown steadily for Starbucks in recent year:14.8 percent growth in year 13. For simplicity, we project Income from Equity Investees will continue to grow at 14.0 percent per year in the future. To be consistent, when we forecast the balance sheet we will forecast that Starbucks' investments in equity affiliates will also grow at a 14.0 percent annual rate. Together, these assumptions imply Starbucks will earn a constant average rate of return from its unconsolidated equity method subsidiaries.

	Other Revenues		License Revenues						
Year	Growth Rates	Amount (a)	New Stores	Stores at Year End	Avg. Store-Years (b)	Revenue per Avg. Store-Year (c)	Amount (d = b × c)	Total Specialty Revenue (e = a + d)	Growth Rate
13 actual		$369.1		2,679	2,343	$0.1096	$256.8	$625.9	
+1 forecast	+12%	413.4	+600	3,279	2,979	0.1129	336.3	749.7	+19.8%
+2 forecast	+12%	463.0	+600	3,879	3,579	0.1163	416.3	879.3	+17.3%
+3 forecast	+12%	518.6	+600	4,479	4,179	0.1198	500.7	1,019.3	+15.9%
+4 forecast	+12%	580.9	+600	5,079	4,779	0.1234	589.7	1,170.6	+14.8%
+5 forecast	+12%	650.5	+600	5,679	5,379	0.1271	683.7	1,334.2	+14.0%

EXHIBIT 18.6 SPECIALTY SALES FORECASTS (IN MILLIONS)

Year	Total Retail Sales	Total Specialty Revenues	Total Revenues	Expected Growth Rate
13 (actual)......	$3,449.6	$ 625.9	$4,075.5	
+1 (forecast)....	4,126.9	749.7	4,876.6	+19.7%
+2 (forecast)....	4,823.0	879.3	5,702.3	+16.9%
+3 (forecast)....	5,568.4	1,019.3	6,587.7	+15.5%
+4 (forecast)....	6,366.2	1,170.6	7,536.8	+14.4%
+5 (forecast)....	7,218.5	1,334.2	8,552.7	+13.5%

EXHIBIT 18.7 COMBINED SALES GROWTH (IN MILLIONS)

18.4 STEP 2: PROJECTING OPERATING EXPENSES

The procedure for projecting operating expenses depends on the degree to which the various operating expense items have fixed or variable components. If certain operating expenses behave as variable costs and the analyst anticipates no changes in their behavior relative to sales, then the analyst can project those future operating expenses by multiplying the sales forecast by the appropriate common-size income statement percentages, as from Exhibit 18.2. Equivalently, we can project those operating expenses to grow at the same rate as sales.

Alternatively, if the cost structure contains certain expenses with fixed-cost components that will not change (or will change relatively slowly) as sales increase (that is, the firm experiences economies of scale), then using the common size income statement approach described above can result in excessive expense projections. In this case, the analyst should estimate the firm's variable and fixed cost structure. Capital-intensive firms often have high proportions of fixed costs in their cost structures. When the percentage change in cost of goods sold or selling and administrative expenses in prior years is significantly less than the percentage change in sales, one can assume the presence of fixed costs. Using the historical growth rates for individual cost items presents one way of reflecting the effects of different mixes of variable and fixed costs.

When projecting operating expenses using projections as a percent of sales, the analyst should remember that an expense as a percent of sales can change over time as: (a) expenses change, holding sales constant, or (b) sales change, holding expenses constant, or (c) both types of changes occur simultaneously. As an example of case (a), the analyst may expect an expense to become a smaller fraction of sales over time if the firm will reduce the expense per dollar of sales through economies of scale or operating efficiencies. As an example of case (b), the analyst may expect the firm will hold expenses constant, but will face increased competition for sales and therefore may have to lower sales prices, causing the expected expense-to-sales ratio to increase. In scenario (c), if the analyst expects both effects will occur simultaneously, the net result on the projected expense-to-sales percentage will depend on which of the two the analyst expects to have a proportionally greater effect.

(a) PROJECTING COST OF SALES. Starbucks' cost of sales amounts include costs of coffee beverages and other products sold, as well as expenses for store rent. The cost of sales percentage declined from 42.0 percent of sales in Year 11 to 41.4 percent in Year 13. This pattern suggests that Starbucks has some proportion of the cost of sales that behaves like a fixed cost; a likely candidate is the rent component, because store rent remains relatively fixed as sales grow. Based on this pattern and a proportion of fixed costs, an analyst might assume that Starbucks will achieve additional reductions in the cost of sales percentage over time, gradually reducing this cost to roughly 40.0 percent of sales by Year +5. Our costs of sales forecasts through Year +5 appear in Exhibit 18.8.

(b) PROJECTING STORE OPERATING EXPENSES. Starbucks' store operating expenses include labor and payroll related expenses. This expense item increased from 32.8 percent to 33.9 percent of sales during Years 11 through 13. In part, these increases reflect rising salary and benefits costs for Starbucks employees. Given that Starbucks' strategy includes providing high quality service as part of the *Starbucks Experience*, one might project store operating costs to continue to rise slowly as a percent of sales in the future. Assuming marginal increases in store operating costs as a percent of sales in future years, Exhibit 18.9 shows our forecasts for store operating costs.

Year	Total Revenues	Percentage of Revenues	Costs of Sales
13 actual	$4,075.5	41.4%	$1,685.9
+1 forecast ...	4,876.6	41.0%	1,999.4
+2 forecast ...	5,702.3	40.8%	2,326.5
+3 forecast ...	6,587.7	40.5%	2,668.0
+4 forecast ...	7,536.8	40.2%	3,029.8
+5 forecast ...	8,552.7	40.0%	3,421.1

EXHIBIT 18.8 COSTS OF SALES FORECASTS (IN MILLIONS)

Year	Total Revenues	Percentage of Revenues	Costs of Sales
13 actual	$4,075.5	33.9%	$1,379.6
+1 forecast....	4,876.6	34.1%	1,662.9
+2 forecast....	5,702.3	34.3%	1,955.9
+3 forecast....	6,587.7	34.5%	2,272.7
+4 forecast....	7,536.8	34.7%	2,615.3
+5 forecast....	8,552.7	34.9%	2,984.9

EXHIBIT 18.9 FORECASTS FOR STORE OPERATING COSTS (IN MILLIONS)

(c) PROJECTING OTHER OPERATING EXPENSES. Starbucks recognized various recurring operating expenses, labeled on the income statement as other operating expenses (3.5 percent of total revenues in year 13), and general and administrative expenses (6.0 percent of total revenues in year 13). For simplicity, we assume that these expenses will remain the same proportions of total revenues in the future. Depreciation expense (5.8 percent of total revenues in year 13) will grow with capital expenditures on property, plant, and equipment. Section 18.5(a)(vi) describes the forecasts of depreciation expense together with property, plant, and equipment.

Exhibit 18.10 presents pro forma statements of income and retained earnings for Years +1 through +5. We discuss the projections of interest income, interest expense, income tax expense, net income, and the change in retained earnings after projecting Starbucks' balance sheet.

18.5 STEP 3: PROJECTING THE ASSETS ON THE BALANCE SHEET

We prepare the asset side of the pro forma balance sheet next. We project individual assets and then sum individual asset amounts to obtain total assets. We take this approach first to illustrate how to develop forecasts that capture different drivers of growth in different types of assets, allowing the mix of the firm's assets to change over time. Section 18.11 briefly describes short-cut approaches for projecting total assets, such as using sales and total asset turnover rates to forecast total assets and then using the common-size balance sheet percentages, as from Exhibit 18.2, to allocate this total among individual asset items.

Starbucks: Forecasts of Pro Forma Consolidated Income Statements								
	Actual			Forecasts				
(Amounts in millions)	11	12	13	Year +1	Year +2	Year +3	Year +4	Year +5
Retail	$2,229.6	$2,792.9	$3,449.6	$4,126.9	$4,823.0	$5,568.4	$6,366.2	$7,218.5
Specialty	419.4	496.0	625.9	749.7	879.3	1,019.3	1,170.6	1,334.2
Net Revenues	$2,649.0	$3,288.9	$4,075.5	$4,876.6	$5,702.3	$6,587.6	$7,536.8	$8,552.7
Cost of Sales (including occupancy)	1,112.8	1,350.0	1,685.9	1,999.4	2,326.5	2,668.0	3,029.8	3,421.1
Gross Profit	$1,536.2	$1,938.9	$2,389.6	$2,877.2	$3,375.7	$3,919.6	$4,507.0	$5,131.6
Store Operating Expenses	868.0	1,109.8	1,379.6	1,662.9	1,955.9	2,272.2	2,615.3	2,984.9
Other Operating Expenses	72.4	106.1	141.3	170.7	199.6	230.6	263.8	299.3
Depreciation and Amortization	163.5	205.6	237.8	289.5	335.5	381.5	427.5	473.5
General and Administrative Expenses	179.9	234.6	244.6	292.6	342.1	395.3	452.2	513.2
Income from Equity Investees	27.7	33.4	38.4	43.8	49.9	56.9	64.8	73.9
Operating Income	$ 280.2	$ 316.3	$ 424.7	$ 505.3	$ 592.6	$ 696.5	$ 813.1	$ 934.7
Interest and Other Income, Net	10.8	9.3	11.6	14.4	15.7	17.6	19.4	21.2
Other Gains (Losses)	(2.9)	13.4	–	–	–	–	–	–
Income Before Income Taxes	$ 288.0	$ 339.0	$ 436.3	$ 519.7	$ 608.2	$ 714.1	$ 832.5	$ 955.9
Provision for Income Taxes	107.7	126.3	168.0	197.5	231.1	271.3	316.4	363.2
Net Income	$ 180.3	$ 212.7	$ 268.3	$ 322.2	$ 377.1	$ 442.7	$ 516.2	$ 592.6

Exhibit 18.10 Forecasts of Starbucks' Pro Forma Financial Statements from Year +1 to +5

(a) PROJECTING INDIVIDUAL ASSETS. To develop forecasts of individual assets, the analyst must first link historical growth rates for individual assets to historical growth rates in sales or other activity-based drivers of assets. The analyst can then use those links to develop forecasts of individual assets based on sales growth forecasts, particularly for assets integrally related to sales (accounts receivable, inventories, and fixed assets). By using turnover rates to develop forecasts for individual assets, the analyst can capture the projected level of operating activity and permit changes in the expected relation between individual assets and operating activities such as sales. Our projections of individual assets for Starbucks illustrate the use of a combination of drivers, including common-size percentages, growth rates, and asset turnovers. Exhibit 18.11 presents the projected balance sheets through Year +5. The following discussion explains the projections of individual assets.

(i) Cash and Investment Securities. Starbucks' cash holdings varied between Years 11 to 13, while it has increased its holdings of short-term and long-term investment securities. At the end of Year 13, Starbucks had an unusually large cash balance roughly equivalent to 18 days of sales (computed as 365 days divided by the ratio of total revenues to ending cash, or 365 / [$26,935 /$683]), but its average cash balances were closer to 14 days' sales in Years 11 and 12. Starbucks needs a certain amount of cash on hand to maintain sufficient liquidity for day-to-day operations. We assume Starbucks will maintain year-end cash balances equivalent to roughly 14 days of sales, leading to the projections in Exhibit 18.12.

To make the three primary pro forma financial statements articulate, the change in cash balance on the balance sheet each year should agree with the net change in cash on the projected statement of cash flows. Section 18.8 of this chapter shows how to compute the implied statement of cash flows.

Short-term and long-term investments on Starbucks' Year 13 balance sheet have grown to represent 5.5 percent and 5.0 percent of total assets, respectively. We assume that these investment securities balances will continue to grow but remain in the same proportion to total assets. We therefore project the dollar amount of short-term and long-term investment securities each year as a function of all of the other asset amounts. We also include on the pro forma income statements any interest income that we expect the cash and investment securities to earn.

(ii) Accounts Receivable. Starbucks' retail sales are primarily cash-based sales of coffee beverages to retail consumers, but the Specialty revenues are primarily sales to commercial enterprises that will involve credit terms and accounts receivable. Starbucks' accounts receivable collection period has declined steadily from an average of 79 days in Year 11 to an average of 67 days in Year 13 (computed as 365 days divided by the ratio of specialty revenues to ending accounts receivable, or 365/[$625.9/$114.4]). We project accounts receivable by assuming Starbucks will maintain an average 67-day collection period in the future. The projected amounts appear in Exhibit 18.13.

Because we rely on ending accounts receivable balances to compute turnover rates and collection periods, the above approach produces estimates of the *ending* accounts receivable balance for the year. Forecasts based on asset turnover rates using year-end account balances assume a degree of stationarity in the relation between sales and ending balances. This approach can, however, introduce artificial volatility in ending balances. For example, if Starbucks experienced an unusually small increase in receivables relative to sales in Year 13 (just prior to our forecast period), then the Year +1 projected increase in receivables could become quite large. The large increase in Year +1 then triggers

	Actual			Forecasts				
	11	12	13	Year+1	Year +2	Year +3	Year +4	Year +5
Current Assets								
Cash and Equivalents	$ 113.2	$ 99.7	$ 200.9	$ 187.0	$ 218.7	$ 262.7	$ 289.1	$ 328.0
Short-Term Investments	107.3	227.7	149.1	167.4	185.8	201.8	215.4	227.0
Receivables	90.4	97.6	114.4	137.6	161.4	187.1	214.9	244.9
Inventories	221.3	263.2	342.9	405.4	471.7	540.9	614.3	693.6
Prepaid Expenses and Other Assets	29.8	42.4	55.2	60.9	67.6	73.4	78.3	82.5
Deferred Income Taxes, net	31.9	42.2	61.5	60.9	67.6	73.4	78.3	82.5
Total Current Assets	$ 593.9	$ 772.6	$ 924.0	$1,019.1	$1,172.7	$1,329.2	$1,490.3	$1,658.6
Long-Term Investments	–	–	136.2	152.2	168.9	183.4	195.8	206.3
Equity and Other Investments	63.1	102.5	144.3	164.5	187.5	213.7	243.6	277.8
Property and Equipment, Gross	1,741.0	2,080.2	2,434.7	2,894.7	3,354.7	3,814.7	4,274.7	4,734.7
Accumulated Depreciation	(605.2)	(814.4)	(1,049.8)	(1,339.3)	(1,674.8)	(2,056.2)	(2,483.7)	(2,957.2)
Property and Equipment, Net	1,135.8	1,265.8	1,384.9	1,555.4	1,680.0	1,758.5	1,791.0	1,777.5
Other Assets and Goodwill	53.7	73.5	140.4	152.2	168.9	183.4	195.8	206.3
Total Assets	$1,846.5	$2,214.4	$2,729.7	$3,043.4	$3,377.9	$3,668.2	$3,916.6	$4,126.5

EXHIBIT 18.11 STARBUCKS: FORECASTS OF PRO FORMA CONSOLIDATED BALANCE SHEETS (IN MILLIONS)

	Actual			Forecasts				
	11	12	13	Year+1	Year +2	Year +3	Year +4	Year +5
Current Liabilities								
Accounts Payable	127.9	136.0	169.0	180.9	209.9	240.1	272.2	307.1
Accrued Expenses	157.4	229.4	310.6	371.6	434.6	502.0	574.4	651.8
Accrued Taxes	70.3	54.2	54.9	65.7	76.9	88.8	101.6	115.3
Deferred Revenue	26.9	42.3	73.5	87.9	102.8	118.8	135.9	154.2
Current Portion of Long-Term Debt	62.7	0.7	0.7	0.7	0.7	0.7	0.7	0.7
Total Current Liabilities	$ 445.3	$ 462.6	$ 608.7	$ 706.8	$ 824.8	$ 950.4	$1,084.7	$1,229.0
Deferred Income Taxes, net	19.5	23.5	34.2	40.9	47.9	55.3	63.3	71.8
Long-Term Debt	5.8	5.1	4.4	3.7	3.0	2.3	1.6	0.9
Total Liabilities	$ 470.6	$ 491.2	$ 647.3	$ 751.4	$ 875.6	$1,008.0	$1,149.6	$1,301.7
Shareholders' Equity								
Common Stock	791.6	930.4	998.5	1,113.2	1,235.6	1,341.8	1,432.6	1,509.4
Retained Earnings	589.7	801.3	1,069.7	1,164.5	1,252.4	1,304.2	1,320.2	1,301.2
Accumulated Other Comp. Income/(Loss)	(5.4)	(8.6)	14.2	14.2	14.2	14.2	14.2	14.2
Total Shareholders' Equity	$1,375.9	$1,723.2	$2,082.4	$2,291.9	$2,502.3	$2,660.2	$2,767.0	$2,824.8
Total Liabilities and Shareholders' Equity	$1,846.5	$2,214.4	$2,729.7	$3,043.4	$3,377.9	$3,668.2	$3,916.6	$4,126.5

EXHIBIT 18.11 STARBUCKS: FORECASTS OF PRO FORMA CONSOLIDATED BALANCE SHEETS (IN MILLIONS) *(CONTINUED)*

	Annual Sales	Average Sales per Day	Days Sales in Cash	Year-End Cash Balances
Year +1 Projected	13.4	$ 4,876.6	14 days	$187
Year +2 Projected	15.6	5,702.3	14 days	219
Year +3 Projected	18.0	6,587.7	14 days	253
Year +4 Projected	20.6	7,536.8	14 days	289
Year +5 Projected	23.4	8,552.7	14 days	328

EXHIBIT 18.12 PROJECTED YEAR-END CASH BALANCES

	Specialty Revenues	Accounts Receivable Collection	Ending Accounts Receivable
Year +1 Projected	$ 749.7	67 days	$138
Year +2 Projected	879.3	67 days	161
Year +3 Projected	1,019.3	67 days	187
Year +4 Projected	1,170.6	67 days	215
Year +5 Projected	1,334.2	67 days	245

EXHIBIT 18.13 PROJECTION OF ENDING ACCOUNTS RECEIVABLE

an unusually small increase in Year +2 to compensate, and so on, creating an artificial volatility in ending receivables. The analyst can mitigate the variability in this pattern by estimating the average rate of growth in receivables expected over several periods and use this growth rate. One could also use average asset turnover rates to forecast average balances and then compute the ending balance implied by the beginning balance and the average (that is, the implied ending balance should equal two times the average balance minus the beginning balance). For our purposes, we will rely on turnover rates based on year-end balances because it introduces only slight measurement error in the case of Starbucks.

(iii) Inventories. Based on the ending balance in inventory in Year 13, Starbucks took an average of roughly 74 days to sell inventory (computed as 365 days divided by cost of sales divided by ending inventory). We project inventories using an average inventory turnover period of 74 days, or equivalently, an average turnover rate of roughly 4.9 times per year. The projected amounts appear in Exhibit 18.14.

	Cost of Sales	Inventory Turnover	Ending Inventories
Year +1 Projected	$1,999.4	4.9	$405
Year +2 Projected	2,326.5	4.9	472
Year +3 Projected	2,668.0	4.9	541
Year +4 Projected	3,029.8	4.9	614
Year +5 Projected	3,421.1	4.9	694

EXHIBIT 18.14 PROJECTED ENDING INVENTORIES (IN MILLIONS)

(iv) Other Current Assets. Starbucks' balance sheet includes other current assets, such as prepaid expenses and deferred income taxes, net. These two other current asset accounts have remained at roughly 2.0 percent of total assets over Years 11 through 13, so we assume that they will each remain at 2.0 percent of total assets in the future.

(v) Equity and Other Investments. Starbucks' equity and other investments primarily represent its equity interests in unconsolidated affiliates. As mentioned in the discussion of Income from Equity Investees in Section 18.3(b), we assume that these investments will grow at an annual rate of 14.0 percent during the next five years.

(vi) Property, Plant, and Equipment (PP&E). Starbucks' capital expenditures involve acquiring fixed assets for new stores, refurbishing old stores, and expanding infrastructure such as roasting plants, information systems, and administrative offices. Starbucks' recent past capital expenditures data (from the statement of cash flows) implies that each new store requires an average of roughly $600,000 in new PP&E. Assuming they will add 600 new company-owned stores a year amounts to $360 million in store-based capital spending. In addition, we assume that Starbucks will spend roughly $100 million per year on other capital expenditures, totaling $460 million per year in capital expenditures.[7] Each year of additional capital spending will trigger additional depreciation. In Year 13, Starbucks recognized $238 million in depreciation expense. Depreciation expense forecasts assume a ten-year useful life, straight-line depreciation, and zero salvage value. Growth in net property, plant, and equipment will therefore reflect the gross capital expenditures minus depreciation expense each year. The projected amounts appear in Exhibit 18.15.

When forecasting fixed assets for capital-intensive firms or firms for which fixed asset growth is a critical driver of future sales growth and earnings, analysts should invest time and effort in developing detailed forecasts of capital expenditures and depreciation expense schedules. For such firms, these capital expenditures can comprise a large part of the balance sheet and can have a material effect on the analysts' forecasts of earnings, cash flows, and firm value.

	Property, Plant, and Equipment				
Year	Capital Expenditures	Ending Balance at Cost	Depreciation Expense	Accumulated Depreciation	Ending Balance Net
13 actual		$2,435		$(1,050)	$1,385
+1 Forecast	$460	2,895	$(289)	(1,339)	1,555
+2 Forecast	460	3,355	(335)	(1,675)	1,680
+3 Forecast	460	3,815	(381)	(2,056)	1,759
+4 Forecast	460	4,275	(427)	(2,484)	1,791
+5 Forecast	460	4,735	(473)	(2,957)	1,778

EXHIBIT 18.15 PROJECTED PROPERTY, PLANT AND EQUIPMENT (IN MILLIONS)

7. In the management and discussion section of Starbucks' Year 13 annual report, management noted it expected capital expenditures of $450 to $475 million in our forecast Year +1, so our estimate is in the ballpark.

Cash	$ 187
Accounts Receivable	138
Inventories	405
Property, Plant and Equipment (net)	1,555
Equity and Other Investments	165
Subtotal of assets	$2,450

EXHIBIT 18.16 PROJECTION OF ASSETS FOR YEAR +1

(vii) Other Assets and Goodwill. Other assets for Starbucks include goodwill and other identifiable intangible assets from acquisitions. U.S. GAAP no longer requires amortization of goodwill or other intangible assets with indefinite lives. These assets, however, will undergo periodic impairment tests, which could trigger significant write-downs of goodwill if the test results deem them impaired. These intangible assets can increase dramatically in a given year as a result of an acquisition of another firm with significant intangible assets (as Starbucks did in Year 13).

In the case of Starbucks, Other Assets and Goodwill amount to 5.1 percent of assets in Year 13. Analysts find it difficult to project with confidence substantial increases or decreases in other intangible assets from corporate events such as acquisitions, sales of subsidiaries, or impairment test write-downs. We can project, however, that Starbucks will likely continue to invest in other intangible assets as it acquires companies with new products and brands in order to drive future sales growth. Therefore, we forecast that other assets and goodwill grow in proportion to total assets, remaining roughly 5.0 percent of total assets in the future.

(b) PROJECTING ASSETS THAT VARY AS A PERCENT OF TOTAL ASSETS. We can now project asset amounts that we expect will vary as a percentage of total assets, including short-term investment securities (5.5 percent), long-term investment securities (5.0 percent), prepaid expenses (2.0 percent), deferred tax assets (2.0 percent), and other assets and goodwill (5.0 percent), for a total of 19.5 percent. Exhibit 18.16 shows the projected amounts for Year +1 for all of the individual assets other than these assets.

The $2,450 subtotal represents 80.5 percent (= 100 percent – 19.5 percent) of total assets. Projected total assets therefore equal $3,043 (= $2,450/0.805). Short-term investment securities equal $167 million (= 0.055 × $3,043), long-term investment securities equal $152 million (= 0.050 × $3,043), prepaid expenses equal $61 million (= 0.020 ×$3,043), deferred tax assets equal $61 million (= 0.020 × $3,043), and other assets and goodwill equal $152 million (= 0.050 × $3,043). Exhibit 18.17 shows the

Year	Total Assets	Short-Term Investments (5.5%)	Long-Term Investments (5.0%)	Prepaid Expenses (2.0%)	Deferred Tax Assets (2.0%)	Other Assets and Goodwill (5.0%)
+1	$ 3,043	$ 167	$ 152	$ 61	$ 61	$ 152
+2	3,378	186	169	68	68	169
+3	3,668	202	183	73	73	183
+4	3,917	215	196	78	78	196
+5	4,127	227	206	83	83	206

EXHIBIT 18.17 PROJECTED TOTAL ASSETS FOR YEARS +1 TO +5

projected amounts for total assets, short-term investment securities, long-term investment securities, prepaid expenses, deferred tax assets, and other assets and goodwill in Years +1 to +5.

18.6 STEP 4: PROJECTING LIABILITIES AND SHAREHOLDERS' EQUITY

Once analysts forecast the asset side of the pro forma balance sheet, they must next project liabilities and shareholders' equity. For firms that target and maintain a particular capital structure over time, the analyst can use the common-size balance sheet percentages to project amounts of individual liabilities and shareholders' equities. The common-size balance sheet for Starbucks in Exhibit 18.2 shows that the balance sheet percentages for total liabilities fluctuated from 25.5 percent of total assets in Year 11, down to 23.7 percent in Year 13. Complementarily, shareholders' equity fluctuated from 74.5 percent of total assets in Year 11, up to 76.3 percent in Year 13. If the analyst believes that Starbucks' funding will consist of roughly 25.0 percent liabilities and 75.0 percent equities in the future, then one could use these common-size percentages to project individual liabilities and equities. Alternatively, the analyst can project individual liabilities and shareholders' equity accounts using historical growth rates or turnover ratios. This section illustrates how to forecast Starbucks' individual liabilities and equities using a combination of common-size percentages, growth rates, and turnover ratios, in order to develop forecasts that incorporate the projected levels of operating activities and permit changes in the expected behavior of individual liability and equity amounts over time. We consider each account next.

(a) PROJECTING LIABILITIES

(i) Accounts Payable. Future credit purchases of inventory and Starbucks' payment policy to its suppliers will likely drive accounts payable. During the last three years, the average payables period has averaged roughly 32 days. We assume Starbucks will maintain an accounts payable period of 32 days in the future. To forecast future accounts payable balances, we begin by calculating forecasts of purchases on account, and then divide an accounts payable turnover ratio of 11.4 [= 365 days/32 days] to compute the ending balance in accounts payable, as Exhibit 18.18 shows.

(ii) Accrued Expenses, Accrued Taxes, Deferred Revenues, and Deferred Income Taxes, net. Starbucks' accrued expenses liability amounts to $311 million at the end of Year 13 and it reflects expenses related to store operating activities (payroll, utilities, etc.), other operating activities, general and administrative activities. In addition, Starbucks

	Year +1	Year +2	Year +3	Year +4	Year +5
Cost of Sales	$1,999	$2,327	$2,668	$3,030	$3,421
Plus Ending Inventory	405	472	541	614	694
Less Beginning Inventory	(343)	(405)	(472)	(541)	(614)
Purchases	$2,061	$2,394	$2,737	$3,103	$3,501
Payables Turnover Ratio	11.4	11.4	11.4	11.4	11.4
Accounts Payable	$ 181	$ 210	$ 240	$ 272	$ 307

EXHIBIT 18.18 PROJECTING ACCOUNTS PAYABLE

also recognizes a current accrued liability for income taxes payable amounting to $55 million at the end of Year 13. Also, Starbucks recognizes a current liability for deferred revenue in the amount of $74 million, which comprises advances that Starbucks' customers have made for gift and debit cards, redeemable for Starbucks' beverages and products. Starbucks also recognizes a small liability for deferred income taxes, which amounts to $34 million at the end of Year 13. Because these accrued liability amounts vary with sales and taxable income, we forecast that they will grow proportionately with total revenues, as Exhibit 18.19 shows. The analyst interested in greater forecast precision could forecast the amounts more specifically based on underlying drivers directly related to each liability (such as growth in store openings for accrued expenses, growth in taxable income for accrued taxes and deferred taxes, etc.)

(iii) Short-term Borrowing, Long-term Debt and Current Portion of Long-term Debt. Starbucks does not rely on a significant amount of short-term or long-term debt to finance its operations, but it uses 5- to 10-year operating leases for their stores, which, under U.S. GAAP in Year 13, do not appear on the balance sheet. Long-term debt on the balance sheet at the end of Year 13 amounts to only $4.4 million, with an additional $0.7 million recognized as a current portion of long-term debt. Starbucks' annual report footnotes provide a schedule for when the remaining payments to retire long-term debt come due. Each year over the 5-year forecast horizon, an incremental $0.7 million payment is due, and the outstanding balance in long-term debt falls accordingly. We use these amounts for the forecasts of future long-term debt and current portions of long-term debt. Note that if the analyst expects Starbucks will find it necessary or desirable to borrow substantial amounts in the future to finance growth, then the forecasts of long-term debt should reflect these future borrowings. Given that Starbucks has not had significant amounts of long-term debt in the past, and given that our forecasts of future cash flows will ultimately show a healthy cash flow from operations to finance future growth, it does not appear Starbucks will need (or will likely choose) to begin long-term borrowing.

(b) PROJECTING SHAREHOLDERS' EQUITY

(i) Common Stock. This equity capital account increases as the firm raises capital by selling shares to investors. Common stock has steadily grown for Starbucks from $792 million at the end of Year 11 to $999 million at the end of Year 13, in part due to Starbucks using stock for acquisitions of other companies and in part due to issues of stock to employees for compensation and bonuses. We assume that common stock issues will

Year	Total Revenue Growth Rates	Accrued Expenses	Accrued Taxes	Deferred Revenues	Deferred Taxes
13....		$ 311	$ 55	$ 74	$ 34
+1....	+19.7%	372	66	88	41
+2....	+16.9%	435	77	103	48
+3....	+15.5%	502	89	119	55
+4....	+14.4%	574	102	136	63
+5....	+13.5%	652	115	154	72

EXHIBIT 18.19 PROJECTION OF ACCRUED LIABILITIES THAT VARY WITH REVENUE (IN MILLIONS)

Year	Total Assets Growth Rates	Common Stock
13.		$ 999
+1.	+11.5%	1,113
+2.	+11.0%	1,236
+3.	+8.6%	1,342
+4.	+6.8%	1,433
+5.	+5.4%	1,509

EXHIBIT 18.20 FORECAST OF COMMON STOCK (IN MILLIONS)

occur in the future, and that common stock will grow in proportion to total assets. Exhibit 18.20 shows our forecasts of Starbucks common stock.

(ii) Accumulated Other Comprehensive Loss. According the Starbucks' Statement of Common Shareholders' Equity at the end of Year 13, Accumulated Other Comprehensive Loss primarily includes the cumulative effects of gains and losses from foreign currency translation adjustments, and to a lesser extent some unrealized fair value gains and losses on investments securities deemed available for sale. The foreign currency translation adjustments relate to Starbucks' international operations in countries whose currencies have changed in value relative to the U.S. dollar. We assume Starbucks will continue to hold and possibly expand these international operations. It is difficult to forecast, however, whether the U.S. dollar will increase or decrease in value relative to the foreign currencies of Starbucks' international operations, or whether Starbucks will either hedge or limit their exposure to foreign currency movements. Thus, we project that Starbucks will experience gains/losses on foreign currency translation adjustments (and fair value gains and losses) that are on average zero (equally likely to be positive or negative in any given year), and so Accumulated Other Comprehensive Loss will remain at its current level.

(iii) Treasury Stock. If a firm repurchases some of its outstanding shares, then the firm recognizes the cost of the repurchases in a treasury stock account (a contra-equity account). The treasury stock account decreases (that is, becomes more negative) when the firm repurchases some of its shares. The treasury stock account increases (becomes less negative) when the firm's treasury shares are reissued on the open market, are used to meet stock option exercises, are exchanged in merger or acquisition transactions, or are retired. Starbucks does not have a treasury stock account in Year 13, so we forecast that this will remain the case in future years.

18.7 STEP 5: PROJECTING INTEREST EXPENSE, INTEREST INCOME, INCOME TAX EXPENSE, AND THE CHANGE IN RETAINED EARNINGS

(a) INTEREST EXPENSE. We can now project our first-iteration estimate of interest expense, based on our projected balances in interest-bearing capital, including Short-term Borrowing, Current Maturities of Long-term Debt, and Long-term Debt, and the

Year	Cash, Short-Term, and Long-Term Investments			Rate of Return	Interest Income
	Beginning	Ending	Average		
+1	$ 486.2	$ 506.6	$ 496.4	2.9%	$ 14.4
+2	506.6	573.4	540.0	2.9%	15.7
+3	573.4	637.8	605.6	2.9%	17.6
+4	637.8	700.3	669.1	2.9%	19.4
+5	700.3	761.3	730.8	2.9%	21.2

EXHIBIT 18.21 PROJECTING INTEREST INCOME (IN MILLIONS)

interest applicable to each of those types of debt. The terms, interest rates and maturity dates of outstanding debt usually appear in a firm's long-term debt footnote to the financial statements. As discussed above, Starbucks has an immaterial amount of interest-bearing debt and therefore an immaterial amount of interest expense. We did project that Starbucks will not borrow additional interest-bearing debt in the future, so it is safe to forecast that interest expense will be immaterial.

(b) INTEREST INCOME. We can also project our first-iteration estimates of Starbucks' interest income on financial assets, such as cash and cash equivalents as well as short-term and long-term investments in securities. In Year 13, Starbucks recognized $11.6 million in income on an average balances in cash, short-term, and long-term investments of $406.8 (= [$99.7+$200.9+$227.7+$149.1+$0+$136.2]/2) million during Year 13, for an average return of 2.9 percent. This rate of return is probably reasonable because it reflects the low interest rate environment in the economy in Year 13, and it is likely that Starbucks holds cash, short-term, and long-term investments in low-risk but liquid instruments. Assuming interest rates remain at low levels, the projected amounts for Interest Income appear in Exhibit 18.21.

(c) INCOME TAXES. Starbucks' income tax note shows the reconciliation between the statutory tax rate and the average, or effective, tax rate. Starbucks experienced an effective tax rate of 38.5 percent during Year 13. Starbucks discloses that it expects to face an effective tax rate of approximately 38.0 percent in the future. Following this disclosure, we assume that the effective tax rate for Year +1 and beyond will be 38 percent.

(d) NET INCOME. We have now projected all of the elements of the income statement, including first-iteration assumptions about interest expense and interest income. Recall that Exhibit 18.10 contains the complete pro forma income statement forecasts. Exhibit 18.22 shows our projected net income amounts and the implied growth rates in net income.

(e) RETAINED EARNINGS. The Retained Earnings account typically increases by the amount of net income (or decreases for net loss) and decreases for dividends. Starbucks' dividend payout policy for common shareholders has been zero (no dividends paid) during Years 11 to 13. For our first pass assumptions, we project that Starbucks will maintain a zero dividend payout policy in the future, as Exhibit 18.23 shows.

	Net Income	Percentage Increase
Year 13 Actual.	$268	
Year +1 Projected	322	20.1%
Year +2 Projected	377	17.0
Year +3 Projected	443	17.4
Year +4 Projected	516	16.6
Year +5 Projected	593	14.8

EXHIBIT 18.22 PROJECTING NET INCOME AND GROWTH RATES (IN MILLIONS)

	Year +1	Year +2	Year +3	Year +4	Year +5
Beginning of Year	$ 1,070	$ 1,392	$ 1,769	$ 2,212	$ 2,728
Plus Net Income.	322	377	443	516	593
Less Dividends to.					
Common Shareholders	(0)	(0)	(0)	(0)	(0)
End of Year	$ 1,392	$ 1,769	$ 2,212	$ 2,728	$ 3,321

EXHIBIT 18.23 PROJECTING RETAINED EARNINGS (IN MILLIONS)

18.8 BALANCING THE BALANCE SHEET

Even though we have completed first-iteration forecasts of all of the amounts on the income statement and balance sheet, our balance sheet will not balance, because we have forecast individual asset and liability accounts to capture their individual operating activities, which do not vary together perfectly. Currently, our projections of total assets minus our projections of liabilities and common shareholders' equity (other than retained earnings), and retained earnings indicate the amounts by which our balance sheets do not balance. (See Exhibit 18.24).

The difference between the projected totals of assets and the projected totals of liabilities and shareholders' equity each year represents the amounts by which we must adjust a flexible financial account to balance the balance sheet. The change in the difference

Projections:	Year +1	Year +2	Year +3	Year +4	Year +5
Total Assets	$3,043	$3,378	$3,668	$ 3,917	$ 4,127
Liabilities.	751	876	1,008	1,150	1,302
Shareholders' Equity (other than Retained Earnings	1,127	1,250	1,356	1,447	1,524
Retained Earnings	1,392	1,769	2,212	2,728	3,321
Total Liabilities and Shareholders' Equity . .	3,270	3,895	4,576	5,325	6,147
Difference	(227)	(517)	(908)	(1,408)	(2,020)
Change in the difference	(227)	(290)	(391)	(500)	(612)

EXHIBIT 18.24 OUT-OF-BALANCE BALANCE SHEET

	Year +1	Year +2	Year +3	Year +4	Year +5
Beginning of Year	$ 1,070	$ 1,165	$ 1,252	$ 1,304	$ 1,320
Plus Net Income	322	377	443	516	593
Less Dividends to Common Shareholders	(227)	(290)	(391)	(500)	(612)
End of Year	$ 1,165	$ 1,252	$ 1,304	$ 1,320	$ 1,301

EXHIBIT 18.25 RECALCULATION OF RETAINED EARNINGS (IN MILLIONS)

represents the new increment by which we must adjust the flexible financial account each year. Thus, in Year +1, our first-iteration forecasts project that liabilities and equities will exceed assets by $227 million. We need to adjust a flexible financial account by $227 million (either increase a financial asset account or decrease a financial liability or shareholders' equity account) to balance the balance sheet. In Year +2, our first-iteration projections indicate liabilities and equities will exceed assets by $517 million, so we will need an additional adjustment of $290 million in Year +2, and so on.

We could use a number of Starbucks' flexible financial accounts for this adjustment, depending on Starbucks' strategy for investments and capital structure. We could consider the following options:

- Increase cash or short-term securities if we expect Starbucks will reinvest this capital in liquid securities;
- Increase long-term investment securities if we expect Starbucks will reinvest this capital in long-term investments;
- Initiate dividends or treasury stock repurchases if we expect Starbucks will distribute this capital to shareholders.

Our forecasts imply that Starbucks will continue to generate substantial amounts of positive cash flow, so we assume that Starbucks will initiate dividend payments in the future. We therefore adjust upwards our dividends forecasts each year by the amount of the necessary adjustment to balance the balance sheet. We refer to this amount as an *implied dividend.* Note that we could have assumed that Starbucks will distribute the excess capital to shareholders through treasury stock repurchases rather than dividends *per se*. In either case, the assumption that Starbucks will return the cash to shareholders through increased dividends or treasury stock repurchases will have equivalent effects on total assets, total liabilities, total shareholders' equity, and net income. After adjusting our dividends projections to include the implied dividends necessary to balance the balance sheet, we recalculate retained earnings as shown in Exhibit 18.26.

Projections:	Year +1	Year +2	Year +3	Year +4	Year +5
Total Assets	$3,043	$3,378	$3,668	$3,917	$4,127
Liabilities	751	876	1,008	1,150	1,302
Shareholders' Equity other than Retained Earnings	1,127	1,250	1,356	1,447	1,524
Retained Earnings	1,165	1,253	1,304	1,320	1,301
Total Liabilities and Shareholders' Equity	$3,043	$3,378	$3,668	$3,917	$4,127
Difference	$ 0	$ 0	$ 0	$ 0	$ 0

EXHIBIT 18.26 SUMMARY OF PRO FORMA BALANCE SHEET (IN MILLIONS)

Implied Cash Flows:	Forecasts Year +1	Year +2	Year +3	Year +4	Year +5
Operating Activities:					
1. Net income	$ 322.2	$ 377.1	$ 442.7	$ 516.2	$ 592.6
2. Depreciation and amortization	289.5	335.5	381.5	427.5	473.5
3. Deferred income taxes, net	7.3	0.2	1.6	3.0	4.3
4. Accounts receivable	(23.2)	(23.8)	(25.7)	(27.8)	(30.0)
5. Inventories	(62.4)	(66.3)	(69.2)	(73.4)	(79.3)
6. Prepaid expenses	(5.7)	(6.7)	(5.8)	(5.0)	(4.2)
7. Accounts payable	11.9	29.0	30.2	32.1	34.8
8. Accrued compensation	61.0	62.9	67.5	72.3	77.4
9. Accrued taxes	10.8	11.1	11.9	12.8	13.7
10. Deferred revenue	14.4	14.9	16.0	17.1	18.3
Cash flows from operations	$ 625.9	$ 734.0	$ 850.7	$ 974.9	$1,101.2
Investing Activities:					
11. Short-term investments	(18.3)	(18.4)	(16.0)	(13.7)	(11.5)
12. Long-term investments	(16.0)	(16.7)	(14.5)	(12.4)	(10.5)
13. Equity and other investments	(20.2)	(23.0)	(26.2)	(29.9)	(34.1)
14. Changes in PP&E	(460.0)	(460.0)	(460.0)	(460.0)	(460.0)
15. Changes in other assets and goodwill	(11.8)	(16.7)	(14.5)	(12.4)	(10.5)
Cash flows from investing activities	$(526.3)	$(534.9)	$(531.2)	$(528.4)	$ (526.6)
Financing Activities:					
16. Changes in long-term debt	(0.7)	(0.7)	(0.7)	(0.7)	(0.7)
17. Changes in common stock	114.7	122.4	106.2	90.9	76.8
18. Implied dividends paid	(227.4)	(289.1)	(390.9)	(500.2)	(611.6)
Cash flows from financing activities	$(113.4)	$ (167.5)	$(285.5)	$(410.0)	$ (535.5)
19. *Net cash flow*	$ (13.8)	$31.7	$34.0	$36.4	$39.0
Beginning balance	200.9	187.0	218.7	252.7	289.1
Ending balance	$ 187.0	$ 218.7	$ 252.7	$ 289.1	$ 328.0

EXHIBIT 18.27 FORECASTS OF STARBUCKS' PRO FORMA STATEMENTS OF CASH FLOWS FOR YEAR +1 TO +5 (IN MILLIONS)

Exhibit 18.27 summarizes the final pro forma balance sheet amounts (shown in detail in Exhibit 18.11).

18.9 CLOSING THE LOOP: SOLVING FOR CO-DETERMINED VARIABLES

Instead of balancing the balance sheet by adjusting implied dividends, we can plug the excess funds to interest-earning accounts (for example, investment securities). For firms with significant amounts of debt, we can assume the firm uses the excess funds to pay down interest-bearing debt. In either case, we would need to adjust accordingly the projected amounts for interest income or interest expense on the income statement. This would create an additional set of co-determined variables within our pro forma financial statements forecasts. For example, assume we use Long-term Investments as our flexible financial account and adjust it upward by the amount Starbucks will require to balance assets with liabilities and shareholders' equity. To calculate the necessary plug to Long-term Investments, we need to know all of the other asset, liability, and shareholders' equity amounts, including retained earnings. To forecast retained earnings, we must know net income, which depends on interest income on Long-term Investments. To calculate Retained Earnings, we also need to know dividends, which might vary with Net Income. Thus, we need to solve for at least five unknown variables simultaneously.

This problem is not as intractable as it might seem, thanks to computational capabilities of computer spreadsheet programs such as *Excel*. To solve for variables simultaneously in *Excel*, for example, first click on the Tools menu, and then click on the Calculations menu, and then click on the Iterations box, so that *Excel* will solve and resolve circular references 100 times until all the calculations fall within the specified tolerance for precision. Then we can program each cell to calculate the variables we need, even if they are simultaneously computed.

18.10 STEP 6: DERIVING THE STATEMENT OF CASH FLOWS

The final step involves deriving projected statements of cash flows directly from the projected income statements (Exhibit 18.10) and balance sheets (Exhibit 18.11). We capture all of the changes in the pro forma balance sheets each year and express these changes in terms of their implied effects on cash. Increases in assets imply uses of cash; decreases in assets imply sources of cash. Increases in liabilities and shareholders' equity imply sources of cash; decreases in liabilities and shareholders' equity imply uses of cash. Exhibit 18.27 presents the pro forma statement of cash flows for Starbucks for Years +1 through +5. The derivation of each line item appears below.

Line 1, Net Income: We use the amounts in the pro forma income statement.

Line 2, Depreciation and Amortization Expense: We assume that the addback for depreciation expense equals the change in accumulated depreciation on the pro forma balance sheets. The addback for amortization expense is zero because we forecast that under U.S. GAAP in Year +1, Starbucks will not amortize goodwill or other intangible assets with indefinite lives on the pro forma balance sheets. If Starbucks recognizes certain types of intangible assets with definite lives that it amortizes, then adding back zero amortization expense is an error but the error is not material. This error primarily understates cash flow from operations (by the amount of the omitted amortization addback) and overstates cash flow from investing (where the change in Other Assets appears), but does not affect net cash flows.

Lines 3–10, Changes in Operating Asset and Liability Accounts: Changes in current and noncurrent accounts that reflect operating activities (other than cash), including inventories, receivables, accounts payable, accrued expenses, and deferred revenue, appearing on the pro forma balance sheets.

Lines 11–13, Short- and Long-Term Investment Securities and Equity Investments (net): The statement of cash flows classifies purchases and sales of investment securities as investing transactions. We use the changes in these accounts on the pro forma balance sheet to derive the amounts for these items on the statement of cash flows.

There is likely to be some error in the implied cash flow amount from investment securities. This change should be increased (become less negative) for the excess (if any) of equity earnings over dividends received from unconsolidated affiliates (which is a non-cash increase in this asset amount). Similarly, the excess of equity earnings over dividends received should also be subtracted from net income in the operating section of the statement of cash flows. Rather than making assumptions about this relatively immaterial item (the effects of which completely offset each other), we chose to simply treat the changes in investments fully as investing transaction. This choice will slightly overstate cash flows from operating activities, and slightly understate cash flows from investing activities by an equivalent amount, but it will not affect the net change in cash each year.

Line 14, Property, Plant and Equipment: The amount on this line equals the projected capital expenditures included in the change in property, plant, and equipment on the pro forma balance sheet in Exhibit 18.11. We assume that Starbucks did not sell or retire depreciable assets each year. As a check, the analyst should be sure that the statement of cash flows captures the net cash flow implications of property, plant, and equipment (for example, the addback for depreciation expense minus capital expenditures, net of any asset sales is equal to the change in net property, plant, and equipment on the pro forma balance sheet).

Line 15, Other Assets: We enter the change in Other Assets and Goodwill on this line. The change in Other Assets on the pro forma balance sheet is the net of acquisitions. As discussed above, we assume that the amount of amortization of goodwill is zero, and the amortization of other intangible assets is sufficiently immaterial that we treat the change in Other Assets fully as an investing transaction.

Line 16, Debt Capital: Changes in debt capital (current portions of long-term debt and long-term debt) on the pro forma balance sheet are financing activities.

Line 17, Changes in Common Stock: The amounts represent the changes in the Common Stock account on the pro forma balance sheet.

Line 18, Dividends: The amount for common dividends equals the projected amount each year (discussed in Section 18.7(e)).

Line 19, Net Change in Cash: The aggregate of the amounts on lines (1) to (18), which should equal the change in cash on the pro forma balance sheet.

The analyst should note that the statement of cash flows will not reconcile with the pro forma income statement and balance sheets if the balance sheets do not balance and if the income statement does not articulate with the balance sheets (that is, the change in retained earnings should include net income).

Unlike historical balance sheets and income statements, historical statements of cash flows commonly do not provide good bases for projecting the future because many of the line items on the statement are difficult to reconcile with historical changes in balance sheets. This occurs because the statement of cash flows can aggregate numerous cash flows on each line item and the analyst may not be able to identify what amounts have been aggregated. For example, the statement may report separately the aggregate cost of a business acquisition on one line, but the business acquisition could cause changes in many asset and liability accounts, recognizing the acquisition of various assets and liabilities. In addition, the analyst may not be able to verify the details of the reported cash flows. For example, the statement might disclose separately the amount of marketable securities purchased and sold, and the analyst cannot verify those amounts because the analyst can observe only the net change in the marketable securities balance during the year. Thus, we recommend simply computing the implied statement of cash flows from the pro forma income statements and balance sheets, which the analyst can observe and verify.

18.11 SHORTCUT APPROACHES TO FORECASTING

Thus far, the chapter has emphasized a methodical, detailed approach to forecasting individual accounts on the pro forma income statement and balance sheet, allowing the analyst to incorporate expected changes in operating activities related to each account. In some circumstances, however, it may be necessary to forecast income statement and balance sheet totals directly without carefully considering each account. Shortcuts have the potential to introduce forecasting error if the shortcut assumptions do not fit each account very well. On the other hand, if the firm is stable and mature in an industry in steady-state equilibrium, then it may be efficient and reliable to use shortcut forecasting techniques that project current steady-state conditions to the future.

One shortcut approach projects total sales and net income using the firm's recent sales growth rates to project sales, and common size income statement percentages to project individual expenses and net income. This shortcut approach assumes existing relations between sales and expenses will persist into the future.

In a similar vein, we can take a shortcut approach to forecast the balance sheet by projecting total assets using the recent historical growth rate in total assets. An alternate shortcut approach to projecting total assets uses the total asset turnover ratio, which explicitly links sales growth and asset growth. Once the analyst projects total assets, common-size balance sheet percentages provide the basis for allocating this total to individual assets, as well as to liabilities and shareholders' equity. In using these common-size percentages, the analyst assumes that the firm maintains a constant mix of assets, liabilities, and equities, regardless of the level of total assets. Equivalently, the analyst assumes that each asset, liability, and equity account grows at the same growth rate as that of total assets. Using common-size balance sheet percentages to project individual assets, liabilities and shareholders' equity encounters (at least) two potential shortcomings. First, the common-size percentages for individual assets, liabilities, and shareholders' equity are not independent of each other. Second, using the common-size percentages does not permit the analyst to easily change the assumptions about the future behavior of an individual asset.

18.12 ANALYZING PRO FORMA FINANCIAL STATEMENTS

As a reality check on the reasonableness of our forecast assumptions and their internal consistency with one another, one can analyze the pro forma financial statements using financial statement analysis ratios and other analytical tools. For example, the analyst can compare projected growth rates in sales with projected growth rates in net income, to assess whether the income statement assumptions imply reasonable profit margins in light of sales growth projections.

The analyst can also check the implications of forecast assumptions on the projected rate of return on assets and the projected rate of return on common equity (and its components—profit margin, asset turnover, and capital structure leverage). If the results show increases in the rates of return on common equity, for example, the analyst can assess whether the profitability, efficiency, and leverage assumptions driving the increase are reasonable.

The analyst can also assess whether the forecast assumptions imply changes in liquidity ratios, solvency ratios, and interest coverage ratios over time. Analyzing such ratios can help the analyst assess whether the projections are likely to alter the firm's credit risk.

Financial statement ratios can confirm whether our forecast assumptions are reasonable and whether we have implemented them correctly (that is, we have done the computations correctly). Unfortunately, such ratios cannot confirm whether our assumptions are correct. These ratios do not tell us whether we have accurately and realistically captured Starbucks' sales growth and profitability in the future. For this confirmation, only time will tell.

18.13 SENSITIVITY ANALYSIS AND STRATEGIC PLANNING

Pro forma financial statement forecasts can serve as the base case from which the analyst assesses the impact of various critical forecast assumptions for the firm, and from which the analyst can test strategic planning ideas for the firm. For example, with these pro forma financial statements, the analyst can assess the sensitivity of projected net income and cash flows to key assumptions about the firm's sales growth rates, gross profit margins, selling, general and administrative expenses, and other assumptions. For example, using the pro forma financial statements as the base case, the analyst can assess the impact on Starbucks' profitability from a one-point increase or decrease in sales growth, or from a one-point increase or decrease in the gross profit margin.

The analyst can also use the pro forma financial statements to assess the sensitivity of the firm's liquidity and leverage to changes in key balance sheet assumptions. For example, the analyst can assess the impact on Starbucks' liquidity and solvency ratios from varying the long-term debt to assets ratios and the interest expense assumptions. Lenders and credit analysts can use the pro forma financial statements to assess the conditions under which the firm's debt covenants may become binding. For example, suppose Starbucks' long-term debt and revolving line of credit agreements require that Starbucks maintain certain minimum liquidity and interest coverage ratios. The pro forma financial statements provide the analyst a structured approach to assess how far net income and cash flows would need to decrease, and how much long-term debt and interest expense would need to increase before the minimum interest coverage ratio becomes binding.

Pro forma financial statements also enable the analyst to test the potential impact of strategic planning ideas. Suppose Starbucks is considering at the beginning of Year +1 a new contract with a distribution channel that should enable Starbucks to increase revenues by $1 billion by Year +3, and that it should be able to sustain this new level of sales into the future. The analyst can adapt the pro forma financial statements to incorporate the projected effects of these potential future sales, as well as related incremental expenses, receivables, inventory, property, plant and equipment, and capital relatively efficiently into expectations for Starbucks' future earnings, balance sheets, and cash flows.

18.14 SUMMARY

The preparation of pro forma financial statements requires numerous assumptions about the growth rate in sales, cost behavior of various expenses, levels of investment in working capital and fixed assets, mix of debt and equity financing, and others. The analyst should develop realistic expectations for these activities, and capture those expectations in pro forma financial statements that provide an objective and realistic portrait of the firm in the future. The analyst should study the sensitivity of the pro forma financial statements to the assumptions made and to the impact of different assumptions. After developing realistic expectations for future earnings, cash flows, and dividends using pro forma financial statement projections, the analyst can then begin to make decisions with these data, including decisions about the firm as a potential equity investment, or a potential credit risk, or a strategic plan.

CHAPTER 19

OPERATING BUDGETS AND BUDGETING—BENEFITS AND COSTS*

MICHAEL D. SHIELDS, PHD
Michigan State University

CONTENTS

19.1 INTRODUCTION 539
19.2 BUDGETING 541
19.3 BENEFITS AND COSTS OF BUDGETING 543
(a) Benefits 543
(b) Costs Related to Gaming Behavior 543
19.4 TEN COMPONENTS OF BUDGETING 545
(a) Multiple Uses of Budgeting 545
(b) Participation in Budgeting 547
(c) Negotiating Budgets: Top-Down and Bottom-Up 548
(d) Budget Goals 551
(e) Budget-Based Performance Evaluations 554
(f) Budget-Related Performance Measures 556
(g) Budget-Based Incentives 561
(h) Static and Flexible Budgets 563
(i) Activity-Based and Subunit Budgets 564
(j) Annual and Rolling Budgets 565
19.5 REALIZING THE BENEFITS OF BUDGETING 566
(a) Contingent Design of Budgeting 566
(b) Complementarity Design of Budgeting 568
(c) Integrative Design of Budgeting 569
19.6 SUMMARY 572
BIBLIOGRAPHY 572

19.1 INTRODUCTION

This chapter does not explain how to construct a budget. It reviews the benefits and costs to the organization of designing and implementing budgets. Many organizations and books on budgeting minimize their emphasis on organizational and environmental factors that affect the success of the budgeting, but instead focus on technical aspects of budgeting.[1] They focus on the mathematical correctness of calculations; adherence to policies concerning the timing, form, aggregation, and documentation of budgets; and the numerical consistency of budgets across organizational subunits in achieving organizational

* The author thanks Annie Farrell, Joan Luft, Michael Maher, Jeff Shields, Geoff Sprinkle, and Alex Woods for their valuable feedback on drafts of this chapter.

1. For detailed discussions of the technical aspects of budgeting, see Charles Horngren, Srikant Datar, and George Foster, *Cost Accounting: A Managerial Emphasis,* 11th ed. (Upper Saddle River, NJ: Prentice Hall, 2003), Robert Rachlin and H. W. Allen Sweeny, *Handbook of Budgeting,* 3rd edition (New York: John Wiley & Sons, 1993).

goals. Most large organizations have technically elegant and efficient operating budgeting systems. Such technical correctness, however, does not suffice for budgeting to increase organizational success because "the real ... [budgeting]... issues are not process related or systems related; they're individuals related."[2]

The existence of operating budgets and budgeting[3] in organizations provide indications of good management. Surveys consistently indicate that almost all but the smallest established business organizations have operating budgets, and a large survey indicates that 78 percent of business organizations rate the effectiveness of their budgets as "good" or "extremely effective."[4] Many business organizations report that they obtain significant benefits from their budgets, including improved planning, coordinating, communicating, and evaluating.[5]

Many other business organizations, however, have problems with their operating budgets and budgeting. Specifically, they cite the following potential problems:[6]

- Budgets limit the development and implementation of new ideas and projects after budget approval because the budget does not include such costs.
- Budgets control the wrong things, like headcount, but not the right ones, like quality and customer service.
- Budgets create barriers between parts of an organization and between an organization and its customers. This results in lack of coordination and customer satisfaction because managers of organizational subunits focus on achieving their own budgets instead of the success of their entire organization.
- Budgets become an end, not a means (e.g., organizations distort plans to fit the budgeting process, and budget line items—not current circumstance—dictates spending).
- Budgets can cause unproductive top management attention and action, especially when achieving them leads to significant rewards, in which case managers' response to these budget-based rewards is incompatible with organizational goals, such as spending on nonessential resources because authorization for spending the funds will soon expire.
- Budgets can induce gaming behavior at the cost of more productive behavior congruent with organizational goals, such as developing new products, improving existing products, and acquiring new customers. Budgets focus measurement on expenditures, not outcomes such as customer service.
- Budgets focus measurement on results, not on the processes used to produce the results.

---

2. Cathy Lazere, "All Together Now," *CFO* 14 (February 1998), 28–36.
3. Organizations prepare many types of budgets—capital budgets, cash flow budgets, flexible budgets, manufacturing budgets, and so on. This chapter will discuss only operating budgets and the related budgeting process. To help the flow of the text, therefore, the chapter will use only the words "budgeting" or "budgets" when referring to operating budgeting and budgets.
4. Horngren, Datar, and Foster, *Cost Accounting;* Srinivasan Umapathy, *Current Budgeting Practices in U.S. Industry: The State of the Art* (New York: Quorum Books, 1987).
5. Ibid.
6. Thomas Stewart, "Why Budgets Are Bad for Business," *Fortune* (June 4, 1990), 179–86. For similar lists of costs, see Stephen Hansen, David Otley, and Wim Van der Stede, "Practice Developments in Budgeting: An Overview and Research Perspective," *Journal of Management Accounting Research* 15 (2003), 95–116; Kenneth Merchant and Wim Van der Stede, *Management Control Systems* (Harlow, England: FT Prentice Hall, 2003).

A recent study documented CFOs' dissatisfaction with their current approaches to budgeting, which arises because managers base budgets on operating plans that do not clearly relate to well-defined strategies, budget results lack individual accountability, and organizations do not use meaningful performance measures by which to evaluate and reward budget-related performance.[7] Other organizations have reduced or ceased using budgets, preferring to search for alternative planning and control mechanisms.[8]

Why do so many organizations benefit from budgets, while so many others are dissatisfied? This chapter will discuss why and how organizations realize both benefits and costs from operating budgeting, as well as how to increase the net benefit. This chapter has two underlying assumptions:

1. When properly designed, budgeting positively affects individuals' attitudes, beliefs, judgments, decisions, and motivation as well as their actions, which then affects individual and organizational learning, efficiency, quality, and profits.
2. Obtaining net benefits from budgeting depends on whether the organization has designed the 10 components of budgeting to be complementary (positive synergy) and contingent on factors related to organizations and their environments. Exhibit 19.1 lists these 10 budgeting components and environmental and organizational factors.

This chapter has four sections. Section 19.2 defines budgets, the budgeting process and their components. Sections 9.3 and 9.4 identify potential benefits and costs of budgeting, and how these potential benefits and costs vary, depending on both the relation between their design and specific organizational and environmental factors, and relations between ten components of budgeting. Section 19.5 discusses three approaches to designing budgets that will increase their net benefits.

19.2 BUDGETING

Organizations use budgets to plan, coordinate, and communicate intended performance, then to evaluate and reward actual performance. An operating budget is a quantitative statement of the approved goal and plan of management's actions for an organizational unit or activity for a particular time period. The following list expands on salient features of this definition:[9]

- *Quantitative statement.* Budgets contain quantitative information, stated in financial metrics.
- *Approved goal and plan.* Managers propose and approve budgets.
- *Management's actions.* Managers have responsibility for implementing the plans that budgets establish to achieve specific goals. This chapter usually refers to managers as superiors or subordinates, depending on their relative position in the management hierarchy.
- *Organizational unit or activity.* Budgets apply to organizational units (or groups of units) or to activities. While operating budgets exist in almost all large business

7. Lazere, "All Together Now."
8. Hansen, Otley, and Van der Stede, "Practice Developments in Budgeting."
9. Horngren, Datar, and Foster, *Cost Accounting*; Umapathy, *Current Budgeting Practices.*

Panel A: Components of Budgeting

- Multiple uses of budgeting
- Participation in budgeting
- Negotiating budgets: top-down and bottom-up
- Budget goals (clarity, specificity, difficulty)
- Budget-based performance evaluations
- Budget-related performance measures
- Budget-based incentives
- Static and flexible budgets
- Activity and subunit budgets
- Annual and rolling budgets

Panel B: Nonbudgeting Factors that Influence the Net Benefits of Budgeting

Organizational

- Task uncertainty
- Information asymmetry between managers
- Strategic mission
- Competitive strategy
- Decentralization
- Subunit interdependence
- Size
- Diversity of products, technologies, markets, and operating locations

Environmental Factors that Influence Budgeting

- Environmental uncertainty
- Competition
- National culture

Exhibit 19.1 Components of Budgeting and Factors that Influence the Net Benefits of Budgeting

organizations, other types of organizations, such as government and nonprofit organizations, increasingly use them.

- *Time period.* Organizations specify their budgets for a particular time period (usually one year, frequently partitioned into quarters).

Budgeting is the managerial process used to develop and approve budgets. Budgeting is a part of planning, an important management activity along with organizing, staffing, coordinating, implementing, evaluating, and rewarding. Planning has three components.[10] First, in strategic planning, top management develops an organization's missions and goals and the competitive strategies to achieve them. Second, programming

10. Merchant and Van der Stede, *Management Control Systems*.

identifies action programs such as new product development and customer management that the organization will implement during a specific time horizon to achieve the strategic plans. Third, budgeting is the process of developing financial plans to implement the programs. A survey indicates that 97 percent of large business organizations have formal budgeting (e.g., meetings, manuals, forms, approvals, reviews), and of these, 91 percent have budgets that cover a one-year period.[11] Budgeting includes both the technical (arithmetic) process by which organizations construct budgets and meet ings in which managers and other employees develop plans that drive the budgets.

Budgeting is a management process and budgets are the output of the process.[12] Together, they constitute a system that managers can use to ensure that the organization uses resources effectively and efficiently to achieve intended operating goals and strategies. As with other systems, budgeting has a set of components (listed in Exhibit 19.1 and discussed in Section 19.4) that work together to achieve intended goals.

Two forces determine the function and success of budgeting—how the components work together, and how they relate to organizational and environmental factors (listed in Exhibit 19.1)—which in turn affect the managerial processes of planning, coordinating, evaluating, and rewarding. The remainder of this chapter focuses on how the interrelations between budgeting and these organizational and environmental factors influence the benefits and costs of budgeting.

19.3 BENEFITS AND COSTS OF BUDGETING

(a) BENEFITS. When appropriately designed, budgeting can provide many benefits, which include better plans, resource allocation, coordination, communication, performance evaluation, and rewards. Successful budgeting also leads to better individual attitudes, beliefs, judgments, decisions, motivation, and actions, which lead to improved organizational performance.

(b) COSTS RELATED TO GAMING BEHAVIOR

(i) Budgeting Process Games. Poorly designed budgeting can lead to reduced and biased learning, motivation, trust, and communication; myopic decisions; increased gaming behavior during and after budgeting, which leads to lower individual and organizational performance. One study measured the cost of budgeting gaming behavior at about 1.5 percent of sales (with a range of 0 percent to 5 percent)[13] and a range of 20 percent to 40 percent of operating costs.[14] In budget gaming, subordinate managers provide their superiors with no, or inaccurate, information during budgeting to manipulate the final budget. The inaccurate information includes understating expected future volumes, sales prices, efficiencies, excess/idle capacity or cost reductions, as well as overstating expected future costs or expenses. Providing no, or inaccurate, information typically biases budgets to be easier to achieve than senior management intended. These budgets reduce performance

11. Umapathy, *Current Budgeting Practices.*
12. For parsimony, hereafter, *budgeting* is used to refer to both budgets and budgeting. When referring only to budgeting as a process, the term *budgeting process* will be used. *Budget* will be used only when referring to a budget.
13. Christopher Bart, "Budgeting Gamesmanship," *The Academy of Management Executive* 11 (1988), 285–94.
14. Alan Dunk and Hossein Nouri, "Antecedents of Budgetary Slack: A Literature Review and Synthesis," *Journal of Accounting Literature* 17 (1998), 72–96.

through suboptimal resource allocations, suboptimal budget-related incentives, and faulty performance evaluations, rewards, and promotions.

Budgeting games distort evaluation of management goals, such as the introduction of new programs, increases to existing programs, and budget cuts in existing programs. Writers have given names to these various games and described them: foot in the door, hidden ball, shell game, razzle-dazzle, make a study, witches and goblins, gardening, duck hunting, entrepreneurer, gambling, surgery, good soldier, drowning man, savior, and honest guy.[15]

Such games create budgetary slack[16]—an intentional bias created by subordinate managers but unknown to their superiors—that makes a budget easier to achieve. Slack requires both the opportunity and motive. Individuals can create slack when information asymmetry and participative budgeting exist: the former occurs when subordinate managers have better information regarding their productivity and revenue opportunities than do their superiors, and the latter provides an opportunity for subordinates to bias their better information during budgeting to their advantage.

(ii) Post-Budget-Approval Games. Budget gaming behavior also occurs after budget approval, when employees can play four types of games, described next, intended to improve measured performance relative to the budgets. Information asymmetry and superiors' inability to directly monitor all aspects of their subordinates' behavior and performance provide the opportunity to engage in post-budgeting gaming behavior. A rigid performance evaluation style and significant budget-based rewards provide the motive to play these games. These post-budgeting games include accounting games, operating games, investment games, and financing games:

- Accounting games (Chapter 31 discusses these games):
  - Revising accounting policies and decisions, such as for depreciation and write-offs of receivables
  - Making favorable decisions about the timing of revenue or expense recognition, such as increasing expenses in periods where the organizational unit will miss the budget target, to increase the likelihood that the unit can achieve the targets in later periods
  - Capitalizing expenditures where expensing is more appropriate, such as treating maintenance as a betterment or improvement
  - Manipulating reported income with biased changes in reserves such as for product returns, warranty costs, and uncollectible accounts
  - Producing excess inventory, which, under absorption costing, will defer to future periods costs that should be expenses in the current period
- Operating games:
  - Altering the timing of sales with price reductions or channel stuffing

15. Robert Anthony and David Young, *Management Control in Nonprofit Organizations,* 5th ed. (Burr Ridge, IL: Irwin, 1994), 500–08; Sigmund Ginsburg, "Negotiating Budgets: Games Individuals Play," *INC.*, (September, 1981), 89–91. See also Frank Collins, Paul Munter, and Don Finn, "The Budget Games Individuals Play," *The Accounting Review* 62 (January 1987), 29–49.
16. Dunk and Nouri, "Antecedents of Budgetary Slack."

  - Decreasing expenditures on discretionary items critical for long-term success, such as quality, employee training, innovation, maintenance, R&D, environmental issues, and advertising
  - Local myopia so that, for example, the purchasing department buys cheaper, low-quality materials because its performance evaluation depends on price, not quality, and the manufacturing department, responsible for costs, not profits, refuses to expedite rush orders from key customers

- Investment games:
  - Selling assets with a market value in excess of book value to generate reported income
  - Keeping old assets instead of buying new ones when the organization makes a capital charge for assets based on gross book values

- Financing games:
  - Engaging in financial transactions to improve financial performance measures, such as off-balance sheet financing through sale-leasebacks

19.4 TEN COMPONENTS OF BUDGETING

How an organization deals with the ten components of budgeting identified in Exhibit 19.1 affects the benefits and costs of budgeting. This section discusses each of these ten components and how their potential benefits and costs relate to various organizational and environmental factors introduced earlier.

(a) MULTIPLE USES OF BUDGETING. Many organizations use budgets for several management purposes, including planning, motivating, evaluating, and rewarding performance. In contrast, other organizations primarily use budgets for one purpose, usually either planning or evaluating performance. The benefits and costs of budgeting depend on the purposes of the budget, and how management has designed it to serve these various purposes.

(i) Benefits. Several potential benefits arise from the purpose, role, or use of budgeting in organizations, including the following:[17]

- Planning the actions to take and the desired economic effects of those actions
- Allocating resources to their most effective uses to help accomplish the goals and strategies embedded in plans
- Coordinating decisions and actions across parts of an organization
- Communicating intended goals, strategies, assumptions, plans, actions, and organizational culture to employees
- Motivating managers to be committed to implementing the actions and achieving the goals contained in the budget
- Evaluating managers, organizational units, products, and so on, relative to the budget
- Rewarding managers for their performances relative to their budgets

---

17. Umapathy, *Current Budgeting Practices*; M. Edgar Barrett and LeRoy Fraser, "Conflicting Roles in Budgeting for Operations," *Harvard Business Review* (July–August, 1977), 137–46; Neil Churchill, "Budget Choice: Planning vs. Control," *Harvard Business Review* (July–August, 1984), 4–11.

Most large business organizations use budgeting for more than one purpose. Multiple uses of budgeting increase budget-related performance arising from consistency in the management process. For example, using one budget for planning and allocating resources can help evaluate and reward performance because it identifies the actions and performance that management expects subordinates to implement and achieve. Such consistency can also positively motivate subordinates when they know that the goals developed during planning and used for allocating resources will be the goals they are subsequently accountable for in performance evaluation and rewards.

(ii) Costs. Using budgets for multiple purposes generates extra costs, as one budget often cannot effectively serve several purposes. For example, organizations frequently set budgets for planning purposes at the expected level of performance to develop accurate plans, which then improves resource allocation. In contrast, organizations frequently set budget targets used for controlling performance at higher levels to motivate higher performance. Since most organizations use one budget for both planning and controlling purposes, they must decide whether to set budgeted performance to facilitate planning (the expected level of performance) or controlling (a higher level of performance).

Superior and subordinate managers often have divergent preferences for the budgeted numbers. Superiors prefer to set budgets for planning at their expected values. In contrast, subordinates prefer to set such budgets at higher performance levels to increase the resources allocated to them so that they can operate at less efficient levels and still achieve the budgets, consume perquisites not identified in the budgets, and have extra resources with the flexibility that these provide. Regarding budgets used to control performance, superiors prefer such budgets to have goals that challenge subordinates to perform beyond the expected level of performance, thereby increasing their motivation. In contrast, subordinates would prefer less challenging budgets to increase the probability that actual performance will exceed budgeted performance to maximize performance evaluations and rewards.

Even though conflicts can exist when using budgets for multiple purposes, organizations can also see benefits in terms of improving subordinates' behavior. Budgets used only for evaluating would give subordinates incentive to intentionally *understate* their expected performance to increase the probability that actual performance will exceed budgeted performance. Alternatively, budgets used only for planning would give subordinates incentive to intentionally *overstate* their expected performance to result in more resources being allocated to them. If, however, organizations used budgets for planning and evaluating, then subordinates' incentives to intentionally under- or overstate their expected performance would largely cancel out.[18] Using budgets for both planning and evaluating, as most organizations do, can balance and greatly reduce subordinates' motivation to over- or understate their expected performance during budgeting. In addition, evidence indicates that using budgets for both planning and evaluating, as opposed to using budgets for evaluating only, results in subordinates providing their superiors with higher initial budget proposals, lower slack in approved budgets, and higher performance relative to the approved budget.[19]

---

18. Barrett and Fraser, "Conflicting Roles in Budgeting"; Churchill, "Budget Choice"; Joseph Fisher, Laureen Maines, Sean Peffer, and Geoffrey Sprinkle, "Using Budgets for Performance Evaluation: Effects of Resource Allocation and Horizontal Information Asymmetry, Budget Slack, and Performance," *The Accounting Review* 77 (2002), 847–865.
19. Fisher, Maines, Peffer, and Sprinkle, "Using Budgets for Performance Evaluation."

(iii) Revising Budgets. Organizations revise budgets used for planning more often than they revise budgets used for evaluating.[20] Revising the planning-type budget will maintain the budget's accuracy. Revising budgets used for evaluating provides for more accurate *(ex post)* benchmarks by which to evaluate performance. Changing budget goals, however, can adversely affect managers' motivation and commitment to achieving budgets. If subordinate managers expect budget goals to be revised to become less challenging, their motivation might decrease.

Revisions to budgets should relate to changes in either the assumptions on which budgets are based or the resources available to achieve them so that subordinates do not believe that the organization uses budgets to manipulate them. Motivation can decline when management mechanically tightens budgets over time when such changes do not relate to changes in the operating assumptions.

(b) PARTICIPATION IN BUDGETING. Participative budgeting is the degree of subordinates' involvement with and influence on establishing their own budgets. The question arises: How much involvement and influence should subordinates have in setting their own budgets? This critical budgeting decision affects subordinates' and superiors' communication and trust, which then influence the content of the budget that arises from budgeting. The type and degree of involvement and influence in budgeting is usually considered to have two archetypes, with most organizations' budgeting located between these two extremes.

(i) Authoritative. At one extreme is *authoritative* budgeting, which occurs when superiors alone decide subordinates' budgets. Authoritative budgeting is efficient, without haggling and repeated meetings, and offers centralized coordination across subunit budgets. However, these budgets incorporate only the superiors' information, which can result in inaccurate budgets and a reduction of subordinates' motivation and commitment to achieving budgets. Subordinates often view authoritative budgeting as unfair because of their lack of influence on their approved budget; this attitude can then reduce their motivation and organizational commitment as well as trust in their superiors and budgeting.

(ii) Self-Selection. At the other extreme is *self-selection*, which occurs when subordinates alone decide their own budgets.[21] Self-selection budgets incorporate subordinates' information, but might be inaccurate because of faulty subordinate information or biased by the incentives facing subordinates.

(iii) Participative. Most organizations' budgeting process does not lie at either extreme of authoritative or self-selection, but instead, both superiors *and* subordinates have *involvement* and *influence* on subordinates' approved budget. When both parties have involvement and influence, budgeting is *participative;* it becomes a social process in which superiors and subordinates engage in persuasive communication and negotiation to obtain the budget they desire for the subordinate. Participative budgeting involves

---

20. Umapathy, *Current Budgeting Practices.*

21. Little evidence exists that organizations use pure self-selection budgeting. However, in concept it exists as one extreme form of budgeting, and economics research investigates it to understand various resource allocation mechanisms. For a summary of research on self-selection budgeting, see S. Mark Young and Barry Lewis, "Experimental Incentive-Contracting Research in Management Accounting," in Robert Ashton and Alison Ashton (editors), *Judgment and Decision-Making Research in Accounting and Auditing* (Cambridge, MA: Cambridge University Press, 1995), 53–75.

negotiation between superiors and subordinates as they share information to converge on a mutually agreeable budget. Several factors affect the participation process, including the two parties' mutual trust and relation, the degree of information asymmetry, and the performance evaluation and reward system. Superiors use participative budgeting to learn about the subordinates' information, to develop budgets that they expect will achieve the organizations' goals and strategies, and to increase subordinates' motivation and commitment to achieving the budgets.

Participative budgeting leads to improved budget accuracy and less biased budgets due to information sharing, which reduces information asymmetry. Participative budgets increase subordinate motivation and commitment to achieving the budget, increase subordinate performance, and improve subordinate attitude about and satisfaction with the budget and budgeting.[22]

Participative budgeting can reduce process efficiency arising from time spent exchanging information and negotiating budgets. This process also has the risk that subordinates might not share all of their information, resulting in inaccurate or slack budgets. Another problem arises when superiors and subordinates use persuasion tactics, which might bias the budgets.

The performance effects of participative budgeting depend on environmental uncertainty.[23] As environmental uncertainty increases, an increase in participative budgeting will increase performance. In contrast, when an organization has low environmental uncertainty, participative budgeting does not increase performance and can actually decrease performance. In situations with stable, and, hence, predictable environments, organizations gain little informational benefit from participation because superiors have sufficient information to develop budgets. As subordinates' environmental uncertainty increases, however, superiors increasingly do not have sufficient information to make effective budget decisions. In such situations, participation allows superiors to learn about these changes in subordinates' strengths, weaknesses, opportunities and threats (called *SWOT analysis*).

(iv) Pseudo-Participation. Budgeting should avoid *pseudo-participation.* This occurs when employees believe their involvement in budgeting will influence the budget, but the superior does not intend, or allow for, their involvement to have any influence. Pseudo-participation is dangerous because it deceives employees: if employees believe that pseudo-participation exists, it will damage superior-subordinate trust and communication, subordinates' motivation and commitment to achieving the budget, and their attitude toward, and satisfaction with, budgeting. If an organization doesn't want subordinate input into the budgeting process, it should make that clear to subordinates from the beginning of the process. In the long run, the organization will probably have better relations with subordinates than it would if it used pseudo-participation.

(c) NEGOTIATING BUDGETS: TOP-DOWN AND BOTTOM-UP

(i) Observations on Negotiations. Most organizations' budgeting is participatory, involving negotiation between superior and subordinate managers. The budgeting negotiation

22. Jeffrey Shields and Michael Shields, "Antecedents of Participative Budgeting," *Accounting, Organizations and Society* 23 (1998), 49–76.
23. Vijay Govindarajan, "Impact of Participation in the Budgetary Process on Managerial Attitudes and Performance: Universalistic and Contingency Perspectives," *Decision Sciences* 17 (1986), 496–516.

is most commonly structured as follows:[24]

1. Budgeting negotiations begin with the superior manager top-down setting the general goals and constraints of budgeting and the resultant budgets.
2. Consistent with a bottom-up process, the subordinate makes the initial budget proposal, which the superior then counters.
3. After this first round of negotiations, if the parties do not reach sufficient agreement, then a second and frequently a third round of offers and counteroffers are made.
4. At this point, if the parties still fail to agree, then the superior imposes a budget, resolving the impasse.

Evidence indicates that this typical negotiation process affects the budgeting process, and the resulting budget and performance in the following ways:[25]

- Subordinates initially offer lower levels of performance than what they expect their performance to be
- Both parties make concessions after their initial offers and counteroffers such that approved budgets lie between their initial positions
- Likelihood of superiors and subordinates reaching agreement increases when their initial positions are close
- Failure to negotiate to an agreement is common, and then superiors impose budgets
- Budgets set by negotiation imply lower levels of performance than do the budgets superiors would have imposed if subordinates had not participated
- When the parties agree on a budget, budgets have more slack than when superiors impose budgets either after impasses or without any negotiations
- When negotiations do not reach agreement and the superior sets the budget, subordinates believe they have less power in the negotiations, they are less satisfied with the budgeting process, have less commitment to achieving the budget, and lower performance relative to the budget
- Subordinates perform better when the parties agree on a budget compared to how they perform when superiors impose budgets after negotiation impasses

The effects of the negotiation process on budgeting depend on information asymmetry—the degree to which subordinates have better information about their SWOT than do their superiors. For example,[26]

- The difference between the initial negotiating positions of superiors and subordinates increases as information asymmetry increases.
- The difference in budget slack between negotiations ending and not ending in agreement increases as information asymmetry increases.

---

24. Govindarajan, "Impact of Participation in the Budgetary Process on Managerial Attitudes and Performance"; Robert Anthony and Vijay Govindararajan, *Management Control Systems,* 10th Edition (New York: McGraw-Hill Irwin, 2001).
25. Joseph Fisher, James Frederickson, and Sean Peffer, "Budgeting: An Experimental Investigation of the Effects of Negotiation," *The Accounting Review* 75 (2000), 93–114.
26. Joseph Fisher, James Frederickson, and Sean Peffer, "The Effects of Information Asymmetry on Negotiated Budgets: An Empirical Investigation," *Accounting, Organizations and Society* 27 (2002), 27–43.

(ii) Deciding Between Top-Down and Bottom-Up Budgeting. Organizations use bottom-up budgeting more frequently and extensively as information asymmetry between superiors and subordinates increases.[27] In many organizations, subordinates have better information about their SWOT than do superiors. This information difference tends to increase as organizations become more diverse, decentralized, and larger, because top management typically knows less than lower-level managers do about the numerous and varied operating units' current and possible inputs, processes, outputs, and customers' preferences and behavior. Thus, as information asymmetry increases, a more bottom-up budgeting process can produce more accurate budgets arising from the use of subordinates' better information and opportunities for superiors to learn more about their subordinates' operating environment.

When information asymmetry exists, bottom-up budgeting can result in inaccurate budgets if subordinates use their better information to bias budgets. Alternatively, if an organization uses top-down budgeting and superiors do not possess the necessary information to develop accurate budgets, not only will budgeting produce inaccurate plans, resource allocations and coordination, but subordinates may reject the budget because it lacks consistency with their information about their operating situation. Such a budget will fail to motivate them, or will motive them incorrectly, or it will induce them to play budget games (explained in Section 19.3(b)).

The balance of these benefits and costs creates a more favorable climate for bottom-up budgeting in decentralized and large organizations. In other contexts, such as the following, top-down budgeting can provide more benefits:[28]

- Superiors have the knowledge necessary to develop accurate budgets, which can occur for programmable or engineered activities (i.e., input-output relations are known).
- History provides an effective guide for developing future plans.
- Superiors have had experience managing the activities being budgeted.
- Subordinates lack budgeting skills and experience.
- Subordinates have a history of developing biased budgets.

(iii) Budgeting and Organizations' Life Cycles. Budgeting typically changes over organizations' life cycles.[29] New (and small) organizations typically are centralized and lack budgeting. As organizations grow and become more diverse and complex, demands arise for increased coordination of resource allocation and use, and centralization gives way to decentralization. At this point, budgeting is mostly top-down because subordinates lack experience with or knowledge about budgets, and top management provides organizational subunits with budgets intended to direct growth and to increase efficiency and coordination among subunits.

Many organizations hire consultants to develop their first budgets. Over time, as organizations become more diverse, decentralized and larger, information asymmetry increases, as superiors increasingly lack the information required to develop subunit budgets and subordinates increasingly have better information. At this point, budgeting

27. Michael Shields and S. Mark Young, "Antecedents and Consequences of Participative Budgeting: Evidence on the Effects of Asymmetric Information," *Journal of Management Accounting Research* 5 (1993), 265–280.
28. Merchant and Van der Stede, *Management Control Systems.*
29. Merchant and Van der Stede, *Management Control Systems*; Robert Simons, *Performance Measurement and Control Systems for Implementing Strategy* (Upper Saddle River, NJ: Prentice Hall, 2000).

incorporates a bottom-up process in which subunit managers negotiate with top management in developing, approving, and revising subunit budgets. This top-down and bottom-up combined process[30] has a sequential pattern in which top management identifies organizational goals and environmental assumptions (e.g., inflation), and then subunits propose plans and budgets that are consistent with these goals and assumptions. Top management, with the help of a budget staff, analyzes and consolidates these budgets to assess whether they collectively achieve organizationwide goals. When the budgets do not achieve these goals, top management provides guidance to the subunit managers about needed changes to the budgets and goals. This cycle repeats itself until the organization creates a consolidated budget that satisfies both top management's goals and subunit managers' capabilities.

(d) BUDGET GOALS

(i) Clarity and Specificity. Budget goals (also called targets) have particular levels of *clarity, specificity,* and *difficulty.* Budgets with clear and specific goals have several benefits. Clear and specific goals, such as "increase profit by 10 percent" can motivate subordinates more than do general goals, such as "improve performance."[31] They can increase subordinates' motivation because they provide an unambiguous statement about the behavior and performance that the organization expects. This effect on performance of stating goals is separate from the effect of rewards. Thus, independent of how an organization evaluates and rewards performance or how difficult to achieve a budget is, an organization can increase performance by stating clear and specific budget goals.

Organizations more commonly use financial budget goals than they use nonfinancial budget goals. The most important financial budget goal is return on investment, followed by operating income, sales revenue, and production costs.[32, 33] The most commonly used nonfinancial budget goals are (in order) productivity, quality of product/service, human resource development, and new product/service development.

(ii) Difficulty. Organizations can affect motivation to achieve budget goals not only by stating them clearly and specifically, but also by setting their difficulty. How difficult should budgets be to achieve? When used for planning purposes, assuming risk neutrality, organizations should set budgets at the expected value of performance (a 50 percent probability of achievement) to improve planning, resource allocation, and coordination. When organizations use budgets to motivate people, however, setting goals higher or lower than the expected value of performance can result in higher performance.

The appropriate level of budget difficulty will likely depend on several factors.[34] Setting budget difficulty above the expected value of performance can produce higher subordinate performance when subordinates are committed to achieving the budget, subordinates' ability does not largely determine their performance, subordinates' tasks have short duration and low uncertainty and complexity, and exogenous (uncontrollable)

30. Rachlin and Sweeny, *Handbook of Budgeting.*
31. Edwin Locke and Gary Latham, *A Theory of Goal Setting & Task Performance* (Englewood Cliffs, NJ: Prentice Hall, 1990).
32. Horngern, Datar, and Foster, *Cost Accounting.*
33. While many organizations regard return on investment as their most important budgetary goal, economic value added is increasingly being recommended as better than return on investment. See the EVA discussion in Chapter 26.
34. Kenneth Merchant and Jean-Francois Manzoni, "The Achievability of Budget Targets in Profit Centers: A Field Study," *The Accounting Review* 64 (1989), 539–58.

factors do not influence subordinates' performance. But how much above expected performance should the budget be set? Analysis and evidence from psychology indicate that as goal difficulty increases, individuals' levels of aspiration increase, and hence, their motivation and performance increase, up to the point of their performance capability, which results both from their own knowledge and effort as well as from external factors such as pay, technology, other employees, and materials.[35] When goal difficulty increases to the level at which individuals believe the goal is unattainable or unfair, their levels of aspiration, motivation and performance decrease. Actual performance relative to performance capability is high when the probability of goal achievement equals .50 and increases as the probability of achievement decreases, to as low as somewhere around .40 to .25.

When these conditions are not present—that is, when subordinates have no commitment to achieving the budget; their ability largely explains performance; tasks have long duration, uncertainty, and complexity; and exogenous factors influence performance—then organizations should have less difficult budget targets. For example, profit-center managers typically achieve their budgets 80 to 90 percent of the time. Profit-center managers, however, consider their budgets challenging (*ex ante*) because of uncertainty, competition, and interdependencies among subunits; they achieve their budgets because they work hard, long, and smart. The highly achievable budgets for profit-center managers have several benefits:[36]

- They increase motivation and commitment to achieve budgets, including creating or sustaining winner's confidence.
- They reduce budget-gaming behavior.
- They provide extra resources either as buffers against the adverse affects of uncertainty or to enable employees to experiment to learn how to improve performance.
- They reduce the costs of unnecessary interventions, which occur when superiors investigate subordinates' performance that falls short of goals, but in fact results from excessively challenging budget goals.

Realizing these potential benefits from challenging-but-highly-achievable budgets depends on how the organization uses them. These budgets can lead to higher performance when the following conditions exist:[37]

- The organization uses participative budgeting.
- The organization sets clear and specific budget goals.
- The organization has sufficient resources to achieve the budget goals.
- Subordinates accept the budget goals as attainable and then expect or intend to achieve them.
- The organization provides feedback regarding performance.
- The organization provides incentives to meet and exceed the budget goal, but does not penalize employees for performance shortfalls (see Section 19.4(e)).

---

35. Merchant and Manzoni, "The Achievability of Budget Targets in Profit Centers"; Merchant and Van der Stede, *Management Control Systems*.
36. Ibid.
37. Merchant and Manzoni, "The Achievability of Budget Targets in Profit Centers"; Mark Hirst and Philip Yetton, "The Effects of Budget Goals and Task Interdependence on the Level and Variance in Performance: A Research Note," *Accounting, Organizations and Society* 24 (1999), 205–16.

(iii) Ratchet Budgets. When actual performance does not equal budgeted performance, the organization must decide whether to revise future budget goals. Some organizations use ratchet budgets that automatically increase (decrease) budget targets by a certain percentage of the amount by which performance is greater (lesser) than the existing budget goal. Organizations design ratchets so that when performance exceeds (is lower than) the budget, the next period's budget target is higher (lower) than the prior budget target. Two issues arise in setting ratchet budgets:

1. Should the organization use the same absolute percentage change in a new budget target, whether the current performance is above or below the current budget target?
2. What percentage of the difference between budgeted and actual performance should be used?

The scant formal evidence on these issues does not exhibit a consensus among organizations. Some organizations use the same percentages to ratchet up and down the budget, whereas others use a larger percentage to increase than to decrease their budgets. For example, one business organization uses a 90 percent ratchet when performance exceeds the budget and a 40 percent ratchet to reduce the budget when performance falls short of the budget. In contrast, H.J. Heinz Company ratchets its budgets by 115 percent of the difference between performance and budget by which performance exceeds or falls short of the current budget.[38]

Organizations must carefully manage ratchets because if subordinates believe that budgets will automatically increase by the amount that performance exceeds the budget, they may lose incentive to exceed the budget, unless they believe the rewards for having more difficult budgets will warrant expending the extra effort required to achieve the more difficult goals. Ratchet budgets assume that employees can work either harder (increase effort duration or intensity), which may require providing more budget-based rewards, or smarter, which requires that they can and want to learn how to improve performance. Learning how to improve performance requires the necessary resources and motivation. Many organizations use ratchet budgets as part of their kaizen (continuous-improvement) programs (Chapter 8 discusses kaizen costing).

(iv) Stretch Budgets. Organizations have increased their use of stretch budgets (frequently called *stretch targets*), which contrast with ratchet budgets by requiring discontinuous improvement in performance.[39] With stretch budgets, organizations might ask managers to double or triple performance from the prior time period, which organizations can usually accomplish only by major changes in the operating process. Imposing stretch budgets, however, can prove costly because they can reduce managers' motivation and trust and increase conflict, which might reduce performance. Organizations considering the use of stretch budgets should design them appropriately. Organizations have successfully implemented stretch budgets under the following conditions:[40]

---

38. Andrew Leone and Steve Rock, "Empirical Tests of Budget Ratcheting and Its Effect on Managers' Discretionary Accrual Choices," *Journal of Accounting and Economics* 33 (2002), 43–67; Robert Holthausen, David Larcker, and Richard Sloan, "Annual Bonus Schemes and the Manipulation of Earnings," *Journal of Accounting and Economics* 19 (1995), 29–74.
39. Shawn Tully, "Why Go for Stretch Targets," *Fortune* (November 14, 1994), 145–58; Strat Sherman, "Stretch Goals: The Dark Side of Asking for Miracles," *Fortune* (November 13, 1995), 231.
40. Tully, "Why Go For Stretch Targets" and Sherman, "Stretch Goals."

- They base the stretch on organizational goals.
- They empower employees to change the operating process and provide them with appropriate resources and incentives to do so.
- They motivate employees to find smarter ways of working, not merely to work harder or longer.
- They use benchmarking to provide employees with evidence that the performance improvement has been achieved by others and to explain how they achieved it.
- They consider the effects of stretch budgets on other parts of an organization to ensure coordination.
- They do not give stretch targets to employees who already feel stress.
- Employees believe they can attain the stretch without enduring too much stress.
- They share gains from performance improvements with employees.
- They do not punish failure to achieve stretch targets.

(e) BUDGET-BASED PERFORMANCE EVALUATIONS. Organizations frequently evaluate managers' performance in comparison with their operating budget. Organizations should consider two key issues in designing effective budget-based performance evaluations:

1. The style the superior will use in comparing the budget and the performance measures.
2. The measures that will be used to evaluate performance relative to the budget.

These two issues are not independent: different styles of evaluating performance will use different performance measures. Section 19.4(f) discusses issues related to performance measures.

Organizations can use either a *flexible* or a *rigid* style of evaluating the budget-based performance of a subordinate.[41]

(i) Flexible Evaluation Style. A flexible style has several characteristics:

- The organization considers the effects of managers' behavior on long-term organizational success, in contrast to limiting the evaluation of performance to that period's budget (e.g., spending more than budgeted to reduce future-period spending by a larger amount, such as extra maintenance that eliminates the need for a major overhaul or replacement).
- The organization allows tradeoffs among budget-line items (e.g., looking favorably on spending more on repairs or training than the budget allots if such spending provides larger gains in reducing waste and improving quality).
- The organization doesn't limit the evaluation to financial performance measures that directly relate to budget line items (e.g., nonfinancial measure of customer satisfaction).

---

41. Kim Langfield-Smith, "Management Control Systems and Strategy: A Critical Review," *Accounting, Organizations and Society* 22 (February 1997), 207–32; Michael Briers and Mark Hirst, "The Role of Budgetary Information in Performance Evaluation," *Accounting, Organizations and Society* 15 (1990), 373–98; Frank Hartmann, "The Appropriateness of RAPM: Toward the Further Development of Theory," *Accounting, Organizations and Society* 25 (2000), 451–82.

- The organization subjectively evaluates performance in contrast to reliance on a prespecified formula.
- Subordinates participate in the evaluation of their own performance.

A flexible style of evaluating budget performance focuses on whether the managers are on track to achieving long-run profit success even though their current-period performance may not meet the current budget measures.

A flexible style of evaluating performance usually relies on an approach in which superiors subjectively consider and weigh the benefits and costs of subordinates' behavior in terms of its effects on long-run organization success. Subjective evaluations can prove beneficial when the superior possesses the necessary information and subordinates have trust in, and good communications with, their superiors. Subjective performance evaluations have the benefits of using valuable qualitative information and of subjectively adjusting quantitative information when doing so objectively would prove costly.[42] Subjective performance evaluations can have bias for the following reasons:

- Imperfect adjustments to quantitative information (i.e., incorrectly valuing, weighting, and combining information into an overall evaluation)
- Favoritism
- Biased attributions (e.g., the tendency of evaluators to overstate (understate) the influence on performance of factors external (internal) to the evaluatees)
- Outcome and hindsight effects, wherein the outcome performance unduly influences performance valuation judgments (e.g., a manager makes a good decision based on *ex ante* information, but a bad outcome occurs, due to the adverse effects of subsequent uncontrollable and unpredictable events).[43]

(ii) Rigid Evaluation Style. A *rigid* style of evaluating performance has the opposite characteristics of a flexible style:

- The organization limits the evaluation of performance to that budget period.
- The organization does not allow for tradeoffs among budget line items.
- The organization limits the evaluation only to budget-related performance measures.
- The organization uses a predetermined formula to evaluate performance.
- The organization does not permit subordinates to participate in their own performance evaluation.

(iii) Comparing the Two Styles. Several factors influence the effectiveness of these two styles of evaluating performance.[44] Using a flexible (rigid) style of evaluating performance generally results in higher subordinate or organizational performance when the following are true:

---

42. Christopher Ittner and David Larcker, "Innovations in Performance Measurement: Trends and Research Implications," *Journal of Management Accounting Research* 10 (1998), 205–38.
43. Ittner and Larcker, "Innovations in Performance Measurement"; Merchant and Van der Stede, *Management Control Systems*.
44. Langfield-Smith, "Management Control Systems and Strategy"; Hartmann, "The Appropriateness of RAPM."

- Environmental or task uncertaintys high (low).
- The strategic mission is build (harvest).[45]
- The competitive business-unit strategy is differentiation (low-cost) or prospector (defender).[46]
- A high (low) level of interdependence between organizational subunits exits.
- Managers participate (do not participate) in developing their own budget.
- Financial performance measures are incomplete (complete) representations of managers' actions. (A measure or set of measures is incomplete when it does not capture all of the effects of managers' actions.) For example, consider a situation where a manager purchases training for employees. The performance measures capture the current-period cost of the training but not the full benefit of this training that the organization realizes in the current and future periods, thus understating the net benefit of the manager's behavior.

Managers tend to use the same style—flexible or rigid—to evaluate their subordinates as their superior uses to evaluate them—a *contagion* effect.[47] Consequently, performance evaluation styles should be part of management systems that top management designs and uses so that the intended styles systematically cascade down the organizational hierarchy.

(f) BUDGET-RELATED PERFORMANCE MEASURES

(i) Two criteria. Related to choosing a style of evaluating subordinates, organizations have to decide how to measure performance so they can compare budgets to performance. Organizations should use two criteria to guide the selection and design of performance measures: goal congruence and informativeness.[48] Performance measures (as well as the other budgeting components) should *motivate* managers to have *goal-congruent* behavior, which means that their goals are aligned with the goals of the owner. Performance measures should also be *informative*, which means that they provide information

---

45. Strategic mission indicates the organization's intended trade-off between market share growth and maximizing short-term profits. A *build mission* intends to increase future market share even though this may decrease short-term profits whereas a *harvest mission* aims to maximize short-term profits and cash rather than increase market share. Langfield-Smith, "Management Control Systems and Strategy."

46. Competitive strategy concerns how a business unit such as a division intends to compete in the market. A *differentiation strategy* focuses on providing products with unique attributes that are highly valued by customers, which allows charging higher product prices, whereas a low-cost strategy aims to provide products at the lowest market prices. A *prospector strategy* involves continually searching for market opportunities such as by new product innovation and intensive and extensive marketing, whereas a *defender strategy* results in having stable products that are sold at low prices by emphasizing operating efficiency. Langfield-Smith, "Management Control Systems and Strategy."

47. Anthony Hopwood, "Leadership Climate and the Use of Accounting Data in Performance Evaluation." *The Accounting Review* 49 (1974), 485–95.

48. Rick Antle and Joel Demski, "The Controllability Principle in Responsibility Accounting," *The Accounting Review* (October 1988), 700–18; Merchant, *Modern Management Control Systems*. See also Rajiv Banker and Srikant Datar, "Sensitivity, Precision, and Linear Aggregation of Signals for Performance Evaluation," *Journal of Accounting Research* 27 (Spring 1989), 21–39; Gerald Feltham and Jim Xie, "Performance Measure Congruity and Diversity in Multi-Task Principal/Agent Relations," *The Accounting Review* 69 (July 1994), 429–53; Kenneth Merchant, *Rewarding Results* (Boston: Harvard Business School Press, 1989).

about managers' behavior beyond the information provided by other measures. A performance measure's informativeness increases with its *sensitivity* and *precision.* A measure is more sensitive when the managers' behavior has a larger expected effect on it. A measure is more precise when a larger portion of the variation in the measure is caused by the managers' behavior. A precise measure is *controllable,* meaning that the managers can *influence* it; in the extreme, a completely precise (controllable) measure is influenced only by the managers' behavior. In contrast, an *uncontrollable* measure is not precise because not all of its variation is influenced by the managers; in the extreme, a completely uncontrollable measure is completely imprecise and insensitive because the managers' behavior has no influence on the measure. As managers have more influence on performance measures, the measures are more controllable and hence more precise to their behavior.

(ii) Benefits of Using Uncontrollable Performance Measures. Some performance measures can seem *ex ante* uncontrollable, but organizations still hold managers accountable for them. The managers will react in one of two ways: either they will become frustrated, resentful and unmotivated, or they will find a way to gain more knowledge, plan differently, or experiment to influence what initially seemed uncontrollable. Many organizations use partially or totally uncontrollable performance measures to evaluate managers for several reasons:

- They provide information about the managers' behavior.
- They provide managers with information about the total costs of their behavior.
- They motivate managers to learn how to make them controllable.

The following examples illustrate these reasons.

EXAMPLE 1.
Consider the case of purchasing managers: The organization measures their performances using raw materials purchases. Although the purchase of raw materials causes raw materials expenditures to increase, other (at least partially) uncontrollable factors—such as the economywide supply, demand for products, and inflation—will also influence the timing and amount of the increase. Using raw materials purchases as a performance measure encourages purchasing managers to consider the effects of these uncontrollable factors when making purchasing decisions, thus reducing the expected amount of raw material purchases since they may have the best information to predict and explain these prices and to make the best purchase decisions. In contrast, when uncontrollable factors do not affect their performance measure, then they will pay less attention to uncontrollable factors and hence the expected expenditures on raw materials would increase. In this case, using a performance measure that is not completely controllable provides the benefits of motivating managers to make more goal-congruent decisions (minimizing purchasing expenditures) and providing information about the managers' behavior.

EXAMPLE 2.
Purchasing, product-design, and manufacturing managers have varying but not complete control of direct material costs, which are affected by the price, quantity, quality, delivery timeliness, and efficiency-in-use of raw materials. In such situations, the critical issue is not the degree of control that the managers have over material costs. Instead, one should ask whether including these costs in performance measures motivates the managers to have goal-congruent behavior and whether the measures are informative about managers' behavior. Using direct material costs as a performance measure for each manager might provide the best way to motivate managers to minimize those costs and to provide performance information about their decisions and behavior.

EXAMPLE 3.
Consider manufacturing organizations that measure managers' performance by reference to profit, and not just cost. The organization would expect these managers to react differently to rush orders from key customers. If measured only on cost performance, this customer demand might not motivate them because processing a rush order can increase managers' costs. If the organization also includes revenues in their performance measure, then they would weigh the expected incremental costs and revenues to decide how best to deal with this rush order. Thus, using this partially controllable performance measure can motivate manufacturing managers to have goal-congruent behavior.

EXAMPLE 4.
Many organizations allocate corporate overhead to departmental managers, even though they can't completely control this cost because the allocation motivates managers to reduce their consumption of corporate services, as well as that of other managers. Allocating overhead also informs department managers on the full cost of operations and products, which can influence their decisions about product pricing, mix, and quantity. Such allocations also present a more informative representation of the organizational resources needed or used to support local managers' operations even though the department managers cannot completely control either the cost of corporate overhead or its allocations.

(iii) Costs of Uncontrollable Performance Measures. The foregoing examples show that an organization can benefit from using performance measures that employees cannot completely control. Uncontrollable performance measures can also have costs. When uncontrollable factors affect performance measures, managers might view the performance measurement system as unfair because of a low correlation between their behavior and changes in the performance measure. Feelings of unfairness can lead to stress for the managers as well as a lack of trust in the measures, the management system and their superiors, which can lead to biased decisions, reduced motivation, gaming behavior, and poor interpersonal relations.[49] This situation will more likely occur and have more negative consequences when partially controllable performance measures indicate poor performance. For example, managers could work hard, smart, and long, but still miss their budgets because (partially) uncontrollable events negatively affect performance measures. Such a situation could decrease managers' motivation since they might believe that they can justify their actual performance shortfalls by these events. In the extreme, managers could conclude that their ability to influence key decisions and behavior that affect these performance measures is so low that attempts to influence them are futile and, as a result, they may experience job-related stress, believe the performance-measurement system is unfair and, thus, play games (Section 19.3(b) explains gaming behavior).

(iv) Adjusting Uncontrollable Performance Measures. To reduce the costs of using uncontrollable measures, many organizations attempt to limit managers' exposure to the adverse effects of uncontrollable factors. Organizations have different policies for different types of uncontrollable factors:[50]

- Economic and competitive factors such as inflation and environmental regulations. Organizations rarely exclude the effects of these events from managers' measured performance.
- Acts of nature, such as fires and earthquakes. Organizations frequently exclude their effects from managers' performance measures if they are large and uncontrollable and the manager previously implemented preventive and pre-recovery actions, such as insurance and multiple sourcing of inputs.
- Interdependence, which occurs when a manager's unit is not self-contained. This occurs when, for example, goods flow from purchasing to manufacturing to marketing. Manufacturing managers depend on purchasing for their inputs and marketing to dispose of their outputs, or a superior forces a subordinate to take certain actions. Many organizations protect managers from uncontrollables by using standard costs and transfer prices so that, for example, if purchasing pays more than the budget for goods, manufacturing is charged only the budgeted amount. Thus, the manufacturing manager's cost measure is not affected.

When organizations do not want to expose managers to the effects of these types of uncontrollable factors, organizations can use several objective and subjective methods to adjust for or eliminate the effects of uncontrollable factors from performance measures:

- Exclusion of uncontrollable factors from the definition of a performance measure (e.g., defining profits as profits before financing activities for managers who do not control financing)
- Flexible budgets and variance analysis to remove the effects of uncontrollable factors

49. Briers and Hirst, "The Role of Budgetary Information in Performance Evaluation"; Hartmann, "The Appropriateness of RAPM."
50. Merchant and Van der Stede, *Management Control Systems*; Merchant, *Rewarding Results*.

- Use of relative performance evaluation that compares managers' measured performance to the measured performance of other managers who face similar uncontrollable factors but work independently from these managers, as in a chain of retail stores
- Subjective adjustments to budgets and measured performance
- Lenient performance evaluations
- Easier future goals to balance the effects of the current period's uncontrollable factors

Subjective methods can prove effective if superiors possess the requisite information to adjust budgets and performance measures and if subordinates trust superiors. See also Section 19.4(g), which discusses how budget-based bonuses can insulate managers from uncertainty and Section 19.4(h)(i), which discusses how flexible budgets can adjust for uncontrollable factors.

(v) Incomplete Financial Performance Measures. Most organizations use financial performance measures that are incomplete in that they are not sensitive to all of the effects of managers' behavior. For example, a manager invests in product innovation and the measurement system captures the current-period innovation costs but not (all of) the reduced future-period costs or increased revenue due to the innovation that results from the expenditures. When managers believe the performance measures used to evaluate and reward their performance are incomplete, this can motivate goal-incongruent behavior and cause job-related stress and a loss of trust in the performance-measurement system.

Financial performance measures might not capture the full effects of managers' behavior, for example, with regard to improving customer relations or product quality, which can lead managers to game them or not to focus as much on them as they should. Financial performance measures can incompletely represent managers' budget-related behavior for the following reasons:[51]

- The organization might find a complete financial measure too costly, so it uses incomplete financial measures.
- Organizations usually do not completely know their cost and revenue functions, so predictions in financial metrics imperfectly measure how the organization transforms inputs into outputs.
- Financial performance measures usually focus internally on a particular department and exclude the effect on the measures of factors outside that department.
- Financial performance measures focus on outputs, and not on managerial and technical processes.
- Organizations usually limit financial performance measures to ones that capture short-term effects but not long-term effects.

(vi) Nonfinancial Performance Measures. Despite these potential limitations, organizations frequently use financial performance measures because they can increase goal-congruent motivation and are informative. Organizations can increase the goal

51. Anthony Hopwood, "An Empirical Study of the Role of Accounting Data in Performance Evaluation," *Journal of Accounting Research* Supplement 10 (1972), 156–82.

congruence and informativeness of performance measures by supplementing financial measures with nonfinancial measures. Nonfinancial performance measures can have the following benefits:

- They can be informative about managers' behavior, capturing information about the behavior that financial measures do not capture. For example, nonfinancial measures of product quality, such as percentage defects and on-time deliveries, provide information that can explain managers' behavior and help predict how the managers' current behavior will influence future product quality and sales beyond the predictive ability of financial measure of product quality.[52]
- Subordinates have more control over them (e.g., purchasing manager has more control over purchase quantities than prices).
- They provide more information to employees about goal-congruent behavior because they indicate cause-effect relations more transparently.
- They motivate subordinates toward more goal-congruent behavior. For example, supplementing cost and revenue measures with nonfinancial measures of quality such as percentage defects and mean-time-between-failure or customer relations can influence managers' future behavior to improve quality and customer relations.[53]

(g) BUDGET-BASED INCENTIVES. Many organizations financially reward managers for their performance, compared to budget targets. They typically give these rewards annually in the form of immediate cash payment (called *budget-based bonuses* or *compensation*). Organizations frequently use budget-based bonuses to motivate managers to meet or exceed the budget.

Organizations can decide on a budget-based bonus subjectively or by formula, and either approach can affect performance. For example, one study observed higher performance in organizations that used a subjective approach to deciding budget based bonuses when they have a build strategic mission, and observed higher performance in organizations that used a formula approach when they have a harvest strategic mission (i.e., maximizing current-period profits even at the expense of market share).[54] A build mission has the goal of increasing future market share, which frequently requires increasing new product innovation, marketing, and production expenses, thus potentially decreasing current-period profits. A subjective approach to determining bonuses can provide a more flexible basis for evaluating how well an organization is doing at increasing its market share, including not reducing a manager's bonus when market share increases but current profits do not meet budget targets. In contrast, consider a harvest strategic mission, which focuses on maximizing current profits. To motivate short-term profit maximization, use of a formula provides clear and specific information to managers that their goal is to maximize short-term profits and how the organization expects them to maximize those profits.

---

52. Venky Nagar and Madhav Rajan, "The Revenue Implications of Financial and Operational Measures of Product Quality," *The Accounting Review* 76 (2001), 495–513.
53. Ittner and Larcker, "Innovations in Performance Measurement."
54. Vijay Govindarajan and John Shank, "Strategic Cost Management: Tailor Controls to Strategies," *Journal of Cost Management* 6 (Fall 1992), 14–24.

When organizations use a formula approach to calculate a budget-based bonus, they should design formulas to motivate managers to maximize their performance relative to the budget. A frequently used bonus formula that provides this motivation follows:[55]

$$B = \begin{cases} u \times (a - b), \ if\ a > b \\ 0, \text{ if } a < b \end{cases}$$

where

B = total bonus

u = unit bonus

a = actual profit performance

b = budgeted profit.

Compared to other forms of financial incentives, such as piece-rate and flat-rate, budget-based incentives have the largest positive effects on performance.[56] This occurs because budget-based rewards include two powerful motivating forces, while these other financial incentives do not. These motivators are a goal per se and pay for performance (respectively, b and $u \times (a - b)$ in the formula above). In contrast, piece-rate incentives motivate effort by paying for performance but lack goals, and flat-rate incentives have less positive performance effects because they lack both goals and pay-for-performance.

Although budget-based rewards can increase managers' motivation to achieve budget goals, they also introduce uncertainty about whether managers' behavior will result in achieving the goals because of the effects of uncontrollables. For example, a manager might work hard, smart, and long but not achieve budget goals because of the adverse effects of uncontrollable events like changes in inflation and consumer preferences. Risk-averse managers do not like being exposed to compensation risk. This risk can be eliminated or reduced in several ways:

- The organization can adjust the budget goal (b) for the effects of uncontrollables by having easier budget goals and/or by having budgets that adjust for the realized values of uncontrollables (discussed in Section 19.4(h)).
- The organization can exclude those effects from or adjust for them in performance measures (discussed in Section 19.4(f)(iv)).
- The organization can increase the fixed salary to compensate (risk-averse) managers for exposure to those risks.

When firms use budget-based incentives, whether they adopt a subjective or formula approach, they must decide on the weights to put on the performance measures (or the differences between measured performance and budget as in u in the formula above).

55. Richard Henderson, *Compensation Management: Rewarding Performance* (Englewood Cliffs, NJ: Prentice Hall, 1989).

56. Sarah Bonner et. al, "A Review of the Effects of Financial Incentives on Performance in Laboratory Tasks: Implications for Management Accounting," *Journal of Management Accounting Research* 13 (2000); Sarah Bonner and Geoffrey Sprinkle, "The Effects of Monetary Incentives on Effort and Task Performance: Theories, Evidence, and a Framework for Research", *Accounting, Organizations and Society* 27 (2002), 303–45.

The weights should increase as the informativeness of the measures increase, where informativeness is defined as sensitivity × precision.[57] Thus, the weights on measures should increase as the sensitivity of the measures to the managers' behavior increases and as the measures are more precise with respect to the managers' behavior. When the precision of measures decrease—they are less controllable by the managers—the weights on the measures should decrease, which then exposes the (risk-averse) managers to less compensation risk arising from uncontrollable events and actions affecting the measures.

(h) STATIC AND FLEXIBLE BUDGETS. *Static* budgets are based on the planned activities and outputs at the time that the organization develops the budge; the budgeted amounts do not change for actual operating activities and volumes that differ from the original plans. In contrast, *flexible* budgets are adjusted for the actual levels of key factors that are not completely controllable by the manager responsible for the budget. The most common factor that flexible budgets adjust for is output (sales). Other factors that flexible budgets can adjust for include raw material prices, weather, interest rates, and technology efficiency. Large business organizations more often use static than flexible budgets.[58] Section 19.4(j) discusses other methods for revising budgets—the use of annual and rolling budgets.

(i) Static Budgets. Static budgets do not adjust for changes in assumptions that were made when organizations develop budgets. Thus, even though static budgets have the benefits of simplicity and low cost to develop, they do not reflect changing situations, which can reduce their accuracy for planning, coordinating, communicating, evaluating, and rewarding.

(ii) Flexible Budgets. Flexible budgets can adjust for the effects of uncontrollable factors (see Section 19.4(f) for a discussion of uncontrollable factors). For example, when output volume is at least partially uncontrollable, the typical flexible budget adjusts for the effects of this uncontrollable factor by adjusting the budget so that the budget line-item amounts are based on the realized volume. In addition to changes in output volume, organizations can design flexible budgets to adjust for other uncontrollable factors, including inflation, degree of competition, machine efficiency or breakdown rate, and employee skill.

Flexible budgets also provide more accuracy in planning, coordinating, and communicating, as well as in evaluating and rewarding, because the organization bases budget adjustments on the expected (for planning, coordinating, communicating) or actual (for evaluating and rewarding) levels of the pertinent uncontrollable factors. Flexible budgets can also increase motivation: the adjustments for uncontrollable factors can increase commitment to achieving the budget because subordinates will believe that the budget provides an accurate benchmark by which to assess their performance.

Potential disadvantages of a flexible budget include inaccurate budget adjustments and lack of motivation to influence seemingly uncontrollable events that the budget adjusts for. When several factors affect operations, adjusting budgets only for volume can result in biased budgets. This implies that organizations shouldn't limit adjustments to flexible

57. Banker and Datar, "Sensitivity, Precision, and Linear Aggregation of Signals for Performance Evaluation"; Feltham and Xie, "Performance Measure Congruity and Diversity in Multi-Task Principal/Agent Relations."

58. Umapathy, *Current Budgeting Practices* and Merchant; Van der Stede, *Management Control Systems.*

budgets to operating volume; instead, they should adjust flexible budgets for all sources of uncontrollable variation in costs that can affect planning, coordinating, evaluating, rewarding, and motivating. If organizations make such comprehensive adjustments, however, this could reduce subordinates' motivation to learn how to influence those apparently uncontrollable events, which do not affect their measured performance.

(i) ACTIVITY-BASED AND SUBUNIT BUDGETS. Most organizations develop *subunit* budgets in which the scope of each budget follows the organization's hierarchical structure into subunits. Organizations develop static or flexible budgets for each subunit, which they then aggregate up the organization's hierarchy. The subunits typically have been functional departments like marketing and production.

Many organizations, however, have begun shifting the basis of their design from functional hierarchies to cross-functional teams based on value-chain processes and activities that comprise processes.[59] These organizations increasingly focus less on functional hierarchies and more on horizontal processes from suppliers to customers. As the management of organizations shifts from vertical (hierarchy) to horizontal (process), designing budgets not based on subunits but on the activities that constitute processes will become more effective. Organizations have increased their use of *activity-based* budgets (ABB) based on the activities used to design, produce, market, and distribute products and services to customers.[60]

ABB facilitates planning, coordinating, and communicating across subunits, which helps to reduce departmental myopia. That is, ABB can reduce managers' preoccupation with limiting their attention only to their own subunits to the neglect of other parts of the entire organization, a form of functional-silo mentality. Since many processes and activities span across departments, ABB reduces the barriers between subunits and increases the focus on the customer by promoting cross-functional communication and coordination. ABB might complicate evaluation of subunits when activities cross subunit boundaries. Organizations could remedy this by shifting the focus of management and evaluations from subunits to horizontal processes and activities and how they satisfy customers.

ABB has potential to refocus budgeting to reflect the increasing use of flatter organizations that focus on cross-functional teams that manage value-creating processes. As organizations redesign themselves based on horizontal—not vertical—structures and processes, ABB can result in budgeting that supports, if not leads, managements' competitive strategies. ABB can also help managers reframe their scope of influence and responsibility from subunits to activities, processes, and value chains. Moreover, ABB has more accuracy than a subunit flexible budget does because it can include many cost drivers, including important non-volume drivers, rather than just operating volume, as most flexible budgets do.[61] Incorporating more drivers allows ABB to provide more accurate estimates of costs for planning and coordinating and also for motivating and evaluating by adjusting for a wide range of uncontrollable factors.

Organizations can construct an ABB from an activity-based costing (ABC) model by reversing the analysis used for the ABC model. (See Chapter 6 for a discussion of ABC.)

---

59. Value chain is a set of activities—such as inbound logistics, operations, outbound logistics, marketing, sales, and post-sale service—that create and maintain competitive advantage. John Shank and Vijay Govindarajan, "Strategic Cost Management and the Value Chain," in Barry Brinker (ed.) *Handbook of Cost Management* (New York: Warren Gorham and Lamont, 1993).

60. For a detailed example of activity-based budgeting, see Robert Kaplan and Robin Cooper, *Cost & Effect* (Boston: Harvard Business School Press, 1998).

61. Ibid.

That is, while ABC models usually use the following sequence to measure the cost of products and customers:

resources → activities → products → customers

ABB analysis has the reverse sequence of analysis:

customers → products → activities → resources

ABB can provide accurate budgets based on analysis of expected product sales to customers, which can then be worked back to develop estimates of the resources needed for those products and customers. Thus, ABB has the promise of eliminating much of the guessing and negotiating, and hence politics and games, from budgeting.[62]

(j) ANNUAL AND ROLLING BUDGETS. Many organizations have traditionally developed *annual* budgets, which they sometimes revise periodically or revise when certain contingencies occur, such as a designated change in prices or when a new competitor enters the market.[63] Annual budgets maintain a low cost of budgeting and managers have a constant target throughout each 12-month period. For most organizations, however, budgets become more inaccurate as time passes. For example, if budgeting occurs during the final quarter of the preceding annual period, then the budget is being developed for the next 15 months, a long time for many sectors of the economy because of change and uncertainty. Some organizations try to keep their annual budgets more current and hence accurate by having periodic revisions or contingency budgets. Some organizations periodically revise their budgets during the year,[64] with quarterly reviews the most common, followed by monthly reviews. One way to periodically revise annual budgets is to use a flexible budget. Contingency budgets are predetermined budgets that will be automatically implemented when specific events occur such as when a competitor changes strategy or the price of raw materials changes by greater than a certain percentage. Organizations must take caution that revising annual budgets or implementing budget contingencies might transform the budget into a rubber yardstick that doesn't provide a good basis for performance evaluation because subordinates are confused about the budget goals that will become their performance measures.

In response to the desire for more accurate budgets, many organizations adopt *rolling budgets*, which they typically revise and extend monthly or quarterly so that budgets always cover the upcoming 12 months. This design helps focus managers' attention beyond the remainder of the current annual time period. Unlike revisions to annual budgets or contingency budgets, rolling budgets result in budgeting every month or quarter, independent of the existing budget's accuracy. Rolling budgets require continuous planning, which results in more accurate budgets because of the increased amount of planning that occurs closer to the events. Again, more accurate budgets facilitate planning, coordinating, motivating, and evaluating managers' behavior. Relative to annual budgets, rolling budgets can increase or decrease motivation to achieve the budget. Rolling budgets have the potential to increase motivation from the increased participation in budgeting (i.e., participating monthly or quarterly rather than just annually): the repeated estimating and interacting tend to increase the accuracy of budgets and to build commitment

---

62. Ibid.
63. Anthony and Govindarajan, *Management Control Systems*, Merchant and Van der Stede, *Management Control Systems* and Umapathy, *Current Budget Practices.*
64. Anthony and Govindarajan, *Management Control Systems*; Merchant and Van der Stede, *Management Control Systems* and Umapathy, *Current Budget Practices*; Churchill, "Budget Choice."

to and ownership of the budget, all of which increase motivation to achieving the budget. However, if the organization uses the frequent budgeting as a ratchet so that each revised budget becomes more difficult when the task itself does not become easier, then employees may overstate costs to counter the ratchet. Organizations that use rolling budgets as ratchets and base significant rewards on achieving budget will have ineffective budgeting that can create conflict in organizations.

19.5 REALIZING THE BENEFITS OF BUDGETING

This chapter has examined the cost and benefits of the ten controllable components of budgeting, listed in Exhibit 19.1 and described in Section 19.4. This section considers how these components can fit together to form a successful budgeting system that will increase the performance of individuals and their organizations. This final section discusses three connections that organizations need to make regarding those components to ensure such a system:

1. Relations between the ten controllable components and the organizational and environmental factors in Exhibit 19.1, also known as *contingent* factors
2. The complementary relations among the ten budget components
3. The integration of contingent factors with the complementarities among the 10 components

Managers have two ways to think about how these budget components can fit together to create this system. One is contingencies and the other is complementarities.

(a) CONTINGENT DESIGN OF BUDGETING. More than 25 years of theoretical analysis and empirical evidence indicates that success of budgeting depends on specific non-budgeting factors.[65] When budgeting design is based on these factors, positive effects occur. The theory of contingent design postulates that the design of controllable factors (in this case, the ten budgeting components listed in Section 19.4 and in Exhibit 19.1 and discussed throughout the chapter) should be contingent on non-budgeting factors.

Two groups of contingent factors affect the design of budgeting and budgeting performance: environmental and organizational factors, as shown in Exhibit 19.1. The interaction between these factors and budgeting characteristics affects managers' behavior and performance as well as the success of the budgeting process. This section provides examples of how an organization should design the 10 components of budgeting, contingent on these non-budgeting factors.

The design and effects of budgeting depend on *environmental and task uncertainty* and *information asymmetry* across managers.[66] Environmental uncertainty refers to uncertainty outside an organization such as uncertainty about purchase prices or customer preferences, whereas task uncertainty relates to tasks (activities) performed in organizations, such as designing and manufacturing products. Both types of uncertainty stem from lack

65. Christopher Chapman, "Reflections on a Contingent View of Accounting," *Accounting, Organizations and Society* 22 (1997), 189–205; Robert Chenhall, "Management Accounting Within Its Organizational Context: Findings from Contingency Modeling and Directions for Future Research," *Accounting, Organizations and Society* 28 (2003), 127–168.

66. Chapman, "Reflections on a Contingent View of Accounting"; Chenhall, "Management Accounting Within Its Organizational Context"; Shields and Young, "Antecedents and Consequences of Participative Budgeting."

of information about environments or tasks, or changes in them. Uncertainty increases when organizations operate in environments in which input and output prices and quantities vary unpredictably and when organizations have more *subunit interdependence* and *diversity* of products, technologies, markets, and operating locations. Many organizations that experience significant environmental or task uncertainty divide themselves into subunits, with each subunit intended to specialize in managing a particular type of uncertainty (e.g., marketing, distribution, R&D, production, legal services, and accounting). The typical organizational structure *decentralizes* responsibility for decision making, budget achievement, and performance. Consequently, environmental and task uncertainty are not evenly dispersed across managers: different managers know more or less about various aspects of an organization and its environment.

This difference in knowledge between subordinate and superior managers (or between two subordinate managers) in an organization is called an *information asymmetry*,[67] discussed in Section 19.3(b)(i). For example, one would expect decentralized managers of profit centers in large, geographically and functionally diverse organizations to have more and better information than that of central management about the status of their current and possible inputs, processes, outputs, and customers' preferences and behavior. This information asymmetry is an important basis for the demand for budgeting.

When decentralized managers have better information about their local operations, central management can use budgeting to learn about these local conditions. For example, they can use participative budgeting (discussed in Section 19.4(c)) to monitor or scrutinize local managers' plans and decisions without appearing to violate a decentralization policy. Organizations with information asymmetries—larger, more diverse, functionally differentiated, or decentralized organizations—use budgeting more frequently, because it is more important to managerial success. Such organizations typically prepare more detailed and sophisticated budgets that use many of the budgeting components discussed in this chapter. It follows that these organizations' budgeting processes involve budgeting staff, meetings, reviews, policies, and procedures.[68] These organizations usually have extensive subordinate participation in budgeting and budget-based evaluations, and place more emphasis on achieving budgeted performance.

Organizations also design their budgeting process contingent on *competition, strategic mission,* and *competitive strategy.* For example, organizations use flexible budgets more frequently as competition increases, particularly in response to increases in competition related to product quality and variety.[69] Competitive business-unit strategies can also affect the design of budgeting and the use of budgets for performance evaluation.[70] For example, business units with a defender strategy focus on maximizing operating efficiency in order to have low costs for their products, thus headquarters accountants typically have budgeting responsibility to ensure cost efficiency. In contrast, business units with a prospector strategy use new product development and marketing to introduce new

---

67. Shields and Young, "Antecedents and Consequences of Participative Budgeting."
68. Merchant and Van der Stede, *Management Control Systems,* Umapathy, *Current Budgeting Practices.*
69. Pradip Khandwalla, "The Effect of Different Types of Competition on the Use of Management Controls," *Journal of Accounting Research* 10 (Autumn 1972), 275–85.
70. Langfield-Smith, "Management Control Systems and Strategy," and Govindarajan and Shank, "Strategic Cost Management."

products to change markets and thus give budgeting responsibility to line managers who use budgeting to learn about new opportunities.[71]

Organizations that operate in different *national cultures* must decide whether to design their budgeting contingent on the national culture of its managers.[72] Since national cultures vary on characteristics such as individualism/collectivism and equality of individuals in decision-making processes, they can bear on individuals' budgeting interactions and preferences. Thus, national cultural differences have implications for the design of budgeting, such as the degree of subordinate participation in budgeting and whether budgets are for individuals or teams of managers. Adverse effects on individual behavior as well as individual and organizational performance can occur when budgeting designs do not reflect managers' national culture.

When organizations base the design of budgets and budgeting on these organizational and environmental contingencies, expected organizational performance increases. For example, performance is higher in larger or more functionally differentiated organizations that have more detailed and formal budgets and budgeting.[73] The effectiveness of budget-based performance-evaluations and bonuses also depends on a business unit's strategic mission and competitive strategy.[74] For example, when an organization uses a low-cost strategy, performance increases when the evaluation emphasizes budget information because focusing the evaluation on the budget motivates managers to minimize costs. In contrast, when an organization uses a differentiation strategy that focuses on providing products with unique attributes that customers highly value, performance increases when an organization deemphasizes current-period budget information as the basis for evaluations because the key to strategic success is not short-term financial maximization but development of long-term programs such as new product innovation and customer service that find and create products and product features that customers highly value.

(b) COMPLEMENTARITY DESIGN OF BUDGETING. Organizations should design the budgeting components to accommodate not only organizational and environmental factors, but also to maximize complementary relations among the components. Complementarities occur when the net benefits of one budget component increase due to an increase in the presence of another budget component, and vice versa.[75] Unlike contingent design, which focuses on designing a budget component in response to non-budgeting

71. Robert Simons, "The Role of Management Control Systems in Creating Competitive Advantage: New Perspectives," *Accounting, Organizations and Society* 15 (February 1990), 127–43. *See also,* note 45 of this chapter.
72. Chee Chow, Michael Shields, and Anne Wu, "The Importance of National Culture in the Design of and Preference for Management Controls for Multi-National Operations," *Accounting, Organizations and Society* 24 (July/August 1999), 441–62 and Graeme Harrison and Jill McKinnon, "Cross-Cultural Research in Management Control System Design: A Review of the Current State," *Accounting, Organizations and Society* 24 (July/August 1999), 483–506.
73. Kenneth Merchant, "The Design of the Corporate Budgeting System: Influences on Managerial Behavior," *The Accounting Review* 56 (October 1981), 813–29; Kenneth Merchant, "Influences on Departmental Budgeting: An Empirical Examination of a Contingency Model," *Accounting, Organizations and Society* 9 (June 1984), 291–307.
74. Langfield-Smith, "Management Control Systems and Strategy"; Govindarajan and Shank, "Strategic Cost Management."
75. Paul Milgrom and John Roberts, *Economics, Organization & Management* (Englewood Cliffs, NJ: Prentice Hall, 1992); Paul Milgrom and John Roberts, "Complementarities and Fit: Strategy, Structure, and Organizational Change in Manufacturing," *Journal of Accounting and Economics* 19 (1995), 179–208.

factors, complementarity design is the simultaneous design of two or more budgeting components. Evidence indicates that budgeting complementarities exist.[76]

(c) INTEGRATIVE DESIGN OF BUDGETING. The preceding sections of this chapter have described budgeting as having ten components and illustrated how organizations design these components contingent on nonbudgeting factors and as complementarities with each other. (Exhibit 19.1 lists the components and factors.) This section will bring together the contingent and complementarity design of budgeting components to identify integrative designs of these components that result in effective and efficient budgeting. Integrative designs are based on designing more than one budget component (and preferably all 10 components) simultaneously based on contingencies and complementarities. These integrative designs have passed the market test: CFOs recommend them as common practices and interpret them as prevailing best practices.

Integrative design, based on contingencies and complementarities, assumes that organizations should design budgeting components by considering the components as packages in which the design of each component depends on the design of the other components, and the design of components is contingent on non-budgeting factors. Organizations should not design budgeting by considering only one budgeting component at a time, such as, "Budgets should be very difficult to achieve" or "Managers should not be evaluated on uncontrollable budget line items." Instead, designs should be based on complementarities among these components: "More difficult budgets should be related to larger bonuses for achieving those budgets," and "Managers evaluated on uncontrollable budget items should receive compensation to offset that risk exposure."

The following examples illustrate three integrative designs for budgeting based on contingencies and complementarities. These independent design proposals share many similarities.

(i) Sophisticated Budgeting. Many organizations use *sophisticated budgeting,*[77] in which contingent design responds to large information asymmetries arising from large size, diversity, decentralization, interdependent subunits, high rates of change, or growth strategies. To ensure budgeting's effectiveness in these organizations, they will more likely use sophisticated budgeting, which has the following components:

- Budgets for multiple purposes such as planning, allocating resources, coordinating, communicating, motivating, evaluating, and rewarding
- More formalized and extensive budgeting processes, along with bottom-up and participative budgeting that result in clear, specific and less-difficult budget goals
- Budgets based on long-term plans
- Flexible budgets, contingency budgets, rolling budgets, budget reviews and revisions, and budgets partitioned by subunits, products, geographical areas, and technologies, and that separate controllable from uncontrollable factors

---

76. David Cherrington and J. Owen Cherrington, "Appropriate Reinforcement Contingencies in the Budgeting Process," *Journal of Accounting Research*, Supplement 11 (1973), 25–253; Mikel Tiller, "The Dissonance Model of Participative Budgeting: An Empirical Exploration," *Journal of Accounting Research*, 21 (1983), 581–595; Howard Rockness, "Expectancy Theory in a Budgeting Setting: An Experimental Investigation," *The Accounting Review*, 52 (1977), 893–903.
77. Umapathy, *Current Budgeting Practices*.

A survey found that CFOs believe that two types of sophisticated budgets—activity-based budgets and rolling budgets—are "significantly to extremely valuable."[78] They also believe that organizations can realize more benefits from budgeting only by a massive reengineering program that standardizes data used in budgeting, shares information across entire organizations, and links budgeting to strategic planning, balanced scorecards, and compensation.[79]

(ii) Tight and Loose Budgeting System. Budgeting comprises combinations of the budgeting components that vary, overall, in how tight or loose the budgeting as a system is.[80] The tightness of a budgeting system depends on more than just the budget's difficulty. A tight budgeting system has the following integrative package of components:[81]

- Clear, specific, and difficult budget goals
- Performance measures for every important budget line item
- Frequent, detailed, nonparticipative, budget line-item analysis of performance by superiors, which does not allow for tradeoffs among the budget line items
- Budget-based performance evaluations that include the effects of uncontrollable events on performance measures
- A formula to calculate the bonus to be given for performance relative to the budget
- A significant expected bonus, according to the subordinate's perspective
- No or infrequent budget revisions

In a loose budgeting system, the various components have the opposite characteristics.

Organizations benefit from tight budgeting systems because their components result in high probabilities that actual behavior and performance conform to top managements' intended behavior and performance. Loose budgeting systems provide less assurance that actual will equal intended performance. Achieving the benefits of a tight budgeting system becomes more difficult as information asymmetries increase. Top management prefers tight budgeting systems when information asymmetries exist, but such situations make tight budgeting systems unlikely or expensive because organizations need to gather and process information about SWOT and arrange for extensive monitoring, measuring, and auditing of behavior and performance. Conversely, organizations can realize the benefits of tight budgeting systems when information asymmetries do not exist, but in such situations, tight budgeting has less potential benefit.

Tight budgeting systems affect subordinates' behavior, which can be a cost or a benefit. It provides subordinates with little opportunity to deviate from the behaviors and results intended in budgets, which can hinder quick reaction to unexpected threats and opportunities and discourage spontaneous experimenting intended to improve performance. Tight budgeting can also provide pressure (sometimes too much) to conform to budgets, which can induce behaviors that do not support the budget targets. Alternatively, when an organization can integrate the tightness of budgeting with appropriate organizational and environmental factors, or subordinates have good interpersonal and

78. Lazere, "All Together Now."
79. Lester, "Cutting the Ties That Bind."
80. Merchant and Van der Stede, *Management Control Systems.*
81. *Ibid.*

organizational relations, tight budgeting can provide benefits by inducing subordinates to behave in ways consistent with those implied by the budget.

(iii) Elements of Successful Budgeting Design. An article in *Fortune* provides examples of many organizations that consider budgets as "bad for business" because (using the terminology of this chapter) organizations do not design them contingent on non-budgeting factors, nor to increase complementarities among budgeting components.[82] The article suggested that the key to successful budgeting lies in basing its design not on financial budgets, but rather on an organization's strategic goals, critical success factors, and related performance measures. More specifically, the article provides five recommendations for the design of budgeting that is *good for business,* that is, ones that maximize the realized benefits from budgeting:

1. Measure output, not input:
   - A focus on inputs induces behavior that is myopic, inwardly directed, cost minimizing, and blaming.
   - Outputs include financial performance, quality, market share, customer satisfaction, and innovation.
   - Measure outputs in financial or nonfinancial metrics as appropriate.
2. Plan first, budget later:
   - Avoid extending last year's budget (e.g., next budget = last budget +/– X).
   - Sequentially develop a long-term plan, a long-term budget, a short-term plan, and finally a short-term—operating—budget.
   - Set discretionary program expenses during the long-term planning process and don't change them during the short-term planning and budgeting process. For example, don't reduce them in tough times or when the aggregated total of subbudgets is not consistent with desired organizationwide future performance.
   - Exclude some strategic resources from subunit budgets if there is pressure to reduce operating budgets or budgeted spending.
3. Budgeting is for managers, not accountants:
   - Don't base budgeting designs on financial accounting or tax regulations and practices.
   - Tie budgeting to strategic and operating planning, not financial and tax accounting.
4. Design against turf wars:
   - Budgets designed around functional departments such as marketing and manufacturing that link vertically with similar functional units leads to myopic behavior intended to protect the functional departments at the expense of the organization and its customers.
   - Organize budgets by customers, geography, products, technology, and business processes, to focus employees and budgets on customers.

---

82. Stewart, "Why Budgets Are Bad for Business." See the Introduction for the features of budgeting that make them bad for business.

5. Build budget busting into the system:

- Develop contingency plans during budgeting to promote planning and fast reaction to changes in SWOT.
- Allow budget revisions to include new products and processes after a budget is approved.

19.6 SUMMARY

This chapter explains how organizations can increase the net benefits of budgeting by designing their budgeting components contingent on the specific organizational and environmental factors listed in Exhibit 19.1, and by designing the components of budgeting (also listed in Exhibit 19.1) to increase complementarities among them.

BIBLIOGRAPHY

Merchant, Kenneth. *Rewarding Results: Motivating Profit Center Managers.* Boston: Harvard Business School Press, 1989.

Merchant, Kenneth, and Wim Van der Stede. *Management Control Systems.* Harlow, England: FT Prentice-Hall, 2003.

Rachlin, Robert, and H. W. Allen Sweeny. *Handbook of Budgeting, 3rd ed.* New York: John Wiley & Sons, 1993.

Simons, Robert. *Levers of Control.* Boston: Harvard Business School Press, 1995.

Umapathy, Srinivasan. *Current Budgeting Practices in U.S. Industry: The State of the Art.* New York: Quorum Books, 1987.

CHAPTER 20

THEORY OF CONSTRAINTS*

ERIC NOREEN, PHD, CPA, CMA
University of Washington

CONTENTS

20.1 INTRODUCTION 573

20.2 CONSTRAINTS IN A JOB SHOP 574

20.3 THE GOAL 574

20.4 THROUGHPUT ACCOUNTING 575

20.5 CREATING WEALTH AS MEASURED BY PRESENT VALUE OF CASH FLOW 575

20.6 THE PROCESS OF ONGOING IMPROVEMENT 576

(a) Step 1: Identify the System's Constraint(s) 576
(b) Step 2: Exploit the System's Constraint(s) 576
(c) Step 3: Subordinate All Else to Exploiting the System's Constraint(s) 577
(d) Step 4: Relax the Constraint(s) 578
(e) Step 5: If the Constraint Has Been Broken, Go Back to Step 1 578

20.7 IMPLICATIONS OF TOC FOR COST AND MANAGEMENT ACCOUNTANTS 579

(a) Total Quality Management (TQM) and Business Process Reengineering 579
(b) Efficient Production Scheduling 580
(c) Implications for Efficiency Measures 580
(d) Controlling Fixed Costs in TOC 582
(e) Measuring the Profitability of Products 582
(f) Constraint Pricing 583
(g) Strategic Pricing in TOC 584

20.8 SUMMARY 585

BIBLIOGRAPHY 585

20.1 INTRODUCTION

The Theory of Constraints (TOC) can affect all aspects of management—decision making, planning, day-to-day operations, and performance evaluation. Any organization can use it. Most organizations will find TOC revolutionary because it fundamentally changes the way an organization functions. Similarities exist among portions of TOC and popular management movements such as just in time (JIT, discussed in other chapters of this *Handbook*), time quality management (TQM), and the balanced scorecard (discussed in Chapter 25).

---

* Some of the material in this chapter has been taken, with permission, from *The Theory of Constraints and Its Implications for Management Accounting,* by Eric Noreen, Debra Smith, and James T. Mackey (Great Barrington, Mass.: The North River Press, 1995). The book was the result of a project sponsored by the Institute of Management Accountants' Foundation for Applied Research and Price Waterhouse-Europe.

One chapter cannot examine the full breadth and range of TOC. This chapter will discuss TOC solutions to the problem of managing a job shop. Note, however, that TOC focuses on *deriving* solutions to problems; it does not offer a collection of solutions to specific problems. This chapter provides only an example of the kinds of solutions that one can derive using TOC techniques. Nevertheless, the solutions to the problem of managing a job shop prove interesting and important in their own right and have direct and obvious implications for cost and management accountants.

20.2 CONSTRAINTS IN A JOB SHOP

A job shop consists of multiple work centers, each performing various tasks. The work centers typically work at various rates. Different products (or services) can take different routes through these work centers and can place different demands on the work centers. Also, different products (or services) have different due dates and the job shop produces them in different volumes. This diversity presents a challenge to anyone managing a job shop.

Every job shop is in one of two situations: Either capacity equals or exceeds demand for the company's products, or demand exceeds capacity. If demand exceeds capacity, the company has a production constraint. We will discuss this situation first.

Managing a job shop becomes much more difficult when demand exceeds capacity than when capacity exceeds demand. If capacity exceeds demand, management can exploit slack to take on more work and to expedite jobs that are behind schedule. If demand exceeds capacity, any changes or disruptions in the schedule can have ripple effects that negatively affect many jobs.

What determines the capacity of a job shop? To keep the discussion simple, assume all products and services go through the same work centers in the same sequence, and they all require roughly the same amount of processing at each work center. Further assume that the rate of output does not vary at any work center. In this simple case, the work center with the lowest rate of output will determine the entire system's capacity. This work center is the *bottleneck* in the system.

The TOC literature makes a useful analogy between a system and a chain. Just as the weakest link determines the strength of a chain, the rate of output of the slowest work center determines the system's output (i.e., capacity).

If different products go through different routing sequences and place different demands on work centers and if the rate of output of each work center varies, then the bottleneck may not be the work center with the lowest *average* rate of output. Any one system, however, will still have only one bottleneck. (A system consists of all the steps required to make one product or service.) A system with more than one bottleneck will prove inherently unstable, and a single bottleneck will shortly emerge.

In summary, each system has only one bottleneck, and the average rate of output of the bottleneck determines the entire system's capacity. This insight has several implications for managing job shops. Before discussing those details, we need to establish what management should try to accomplish.

20.3 THE GOAL

An organization can specify any goals it desires, but in most cases, a company's primary goal is to increase owners' wealth—to earn income. This requires a focus on the net present value of cash flows. Consequently, management should evaluate every decision based on its effect on cash flows, both now and in the future. This line of reasoning places the Theory of Constraints solidly in the relevant costs school of thinking pioneered by Ronald Coase in Britain in the 1930s and adopted by all mainstream management accounting textbooks since the 1950s.

Note that if a company focuses on maximizing its cash flows, both now and in the future, we cannot speak of *attaining the goal.* The desire for more is insatiable.

20.4 THROUGHPUT ACCOUNTING

The distinction between fixed and variable costs becomes important when decisions involve choices between different levels of activity. For small changes in activity, only the variable costs are relevant because, by definition, changes in activity (up to some quantity) do not affect fixed costs. Accounting theorists have advocated variable costing for decades as a way to structure accounting reports to highlight the difference between variable and fixed costs. Variable costing includes only variable production costs in inventory valuations and treats fixed production costs as period expenses. The income statement deducts the variable costs from sales to arrive at the total contribution margin. Net profit equals the contribution margin less fixed cost.

The Theory of Constraints uses a version of variable costing called *throughput accounting*. In throughput accounting, the contribution margin is called *throughput* and fixed costs are called *operating expenses*. To avoid confusion, this chapter uses the more conventional terms *contribution margin* and *fixed costs*. Also, this chapter uses the term *throughput* to mean the rate at which the company produces output. In the Theory of Constraints, the unit contribution margin equals the selling price minus the costs of direct materials and other totally variable costs. Labor is not a totally variable cost.

Throughput accounting takes a more conservative approach than conventional financial accounting to revenue recognition. Throughput accounting delays revenue recognition until a consumer makes an irrevocable purchase. For example, sales to wholesalers or retailers who can return the product do not count as revenue in throughput accounting.

When placed in the context of the history of management accounting thought, TOC updates variable costing to recognize the fixed nature of much of direct labor and to delay revenue recognition. TOC recognizes that management can use variable costing statements to estimate relevant costs and benefits much more easily than absorption costing statements. TOC, like variable costing, contains no incentives to boost income by building inventories.

20.5 CREATING WEALTH AS MEASURED BY PRESENT VALUE OF CASH FLOW

Companies have only two ways to increase the net present value (NPV) of cash flows: either reduce spending on fixed cost items or increase the company's total contribution margin. A company will realize limited savings from reduced spending on fixed items. Reduced spending will, at some point, cut into productive capacity. Moreover, if reduced spending involves involuntary changes in personnel, morale will likely suffer. If morale suffers, the quality and quantity of goods and services produced for sale will likely drop. Even if management could reduce spending on fixed items to zero without any loss of productive capacity and without any effect on the company's total contribution margin, the goal of increasing NPV of cash flows requires increasing the total contribution margin. Sooner or later, managers must focus on increasing the total contribution margin.

A company can increase the total contribution margin in four different ways: (1) changing selling prices (discussed in Section 20.7(g)), (2) changing the product mix (discussed in Section 20.7(e)), (3) reducing variable costs, and (4) increasing the quantity of goods that it produces and sells. The third method, reducing variable costs, may not be feasible. But even if the company can reduce variable costs, it can increase the NPV of cash flows only a limited amount by taking this approach. A production constraint would seem to rule out the fourth method—that of increasing the quantity of goods produced and sold. By effectively managing the constraint, however, the company can uncover additional hidden capacity. Moreover, this can usually be done without incurring any significant additional fixed costs. The next section provides an overview of how an organization can accomplish this.

20.6 THE PROCESS OF ONGOING IMPROVEMENT

Exhibit 20.1 summarizes the process of managing constraints to obtain more throughput. TOC refers to this as the *process of ongoing improvement* because a company that follows these five steps can continually increase its throughput and hence its profits.

(a) STEP 1: IDENTIFY THE SYSTEM'S CONSTRAINT(S). If you want to increase the system's throughput (i.e., the rate of output) and the average rate of output of the system's bottleneck determines the system's throughput, then clearly the company has to increase the average rate of output of the bottleneck. The first step is to identify the system's bottleneck (i.e., constraint). For now, suppose management has identified the constraint as a specific work center.

(b) STEP 2: EXPLOIT THE SYSTEM'S CONSTRAINT(S). If demand exceeds capacity, the company can't satisfy all of its potential customers. Management has to decide what to do and *what not to do.* It must prioritize. How should management prioritize jobs? The answer to this question lies in nearly every introductory management accounting textbook. The company should prioritize the use of a constrained resource using the contribution margin per unit of the constrained resource. The following example illustrates this principle.

A workshop in Indonesia makes brass gongs and brass bells using a simple process. Workers pour molten brass into a mold, allow it to cool, and then file and polish the brass. The workshop produces molten brass from brass ingots that it heats in a kiln. With a capacity of 10 kilograms of molten brass per hour, the kiln is the constraint in the system. Data concerning the gongs and bells appear in Exhibit 20.2. (The currency in Indonesia is the rupiah, denoted here by Rup.)

Step 1. Identify the system's constraint(s).
Step 2. Exploit the system's constraint(s).
Step 3. Subordinate everything else to exploiting the constraint(s).
Step 4. Elevate the constraint(s).
Step 5. If a constraint has been broken, go back to Step 1.

EXHIBIT 20.1 THE PROCESS OF ONGOING IMPROVEMENT

The constraint is the amount of molten brass that the kiln can produce. The capacity of the kiln is 10 kilograms of brass per hour.

	Gongs	Bells
Selling price per unit	Rup 10,000	Rup 5,000
Variable cost per unit	6,000	2,000
Contribution margin per unit (a)	Rup 4,000	Rup 3,000
Molten brass per unit (b)	0.50 kg	0.25 kg
Contribution margin per kg of molten brass (a) ÷ (b)	Rup 8,000 per kg	Rup 10,000 per kg

Contribution margin per unit of the constrained resource

EXHIBIT 20.2 AN EXAMPLE OF PRIORITIZING THE USE OF A CONSTRAINED RESOURCE

If demand exceeds capacity, which of the two products—gongs or bells—should receive higher priority? We can see from Exhibit 20.2 that the gongs have a higher contribution margin per unit than the bells. A gong, however, requires twice as much molten brass (0.50 kg) as does a bell (0.25 kg). To maximize the amount of money the company makes, it should maximize the contribution margin generated from the limited supply of molten brass. (Any fixed costs are irrelevant because the company will be operating at capacity and incurring the same fixed costs whether it produces gongs or bells.) If one kilogram of molten brass is available, the workshop can use it to make two gongs or four bells. The contribution margin from two gongs is Rup 8,000 (= 2 gongs × Rup 4,000 per gong) and from four bells is Rup 12,000 (= 4 bells × Rup 3,000 per bell). Therefore, even though the bells have a lower contribution margin per unit than the gongs, they make more efficient use of the constrained resource and should have higher priority. Note that one can obtain the same answers—Rup 8,000 for gongs and Rup 12,000 for bells—by dividing the contribution margin per unit by the amount of the constrained resource each unit requires as in Exhibit 20.2.

To summarize, if a bottleneck exists, an organization cannot fully satisfy demand. To decide which work to do and which to omit, management should compute the contribution margin per unit of the constrained resource for each job or product. In the absence of overriding factors—such as maintaining good relations with a key customer—the company should first drop the job or product with the lowest contribution margin per unit of the constrained resource.

(c) STEP 3: SUBORDINATE ALL ELSE TO EXPLOITING THE SYSTEM'S CONSTRAINT(S). Recall the chain analogy in Section 20.2. If management wants to increase the chain's strength, it doesn't make sense to waste time increasing the strength of links that are already stronger than the weakest link. Instead, improvement efforts should focus on strengthening the weakest link.

In a job shop, management should focus on increasing the bottleneck's rate of output and ensuring that the bottleneck never has downtime waiting for work. The bottleneck sets the pace for the entire system.

(d) STEP 4: RELAX THE CONSTRAINT(S). Relaxing the constraint means increasing the constraint's effective capacity. Management can do this in various ways, including the following:

- *Don't waste any of the constrained resource.* For example, inspect units before they go through the constraint, not after. A defective unit rejected after it passes through the constraint reduces the total output and sales of the company by one unit. A defective unit rejected before it passes through the constraint has no effect on total output and total sales.
- *Keep the bottleneck operating all of the time.* Arrange for relief workers when bottleneck workers take breaks. Schedule maintenance during holidays, weekends, and after normal working hours.
- *Reduce setup time on the bottleneck.* Setups that take a work center off-line reduce total output and total sales. Assign otherwise idle workers to the bottleneck to help with setups or to do setups off-line.
- *Focus reengineering efforts on the bottleneck.* Eliminate unnecessary steps. Use the creative energies of workers to find new ways of doing things better and faster. Reengineer products so that they require less of the bottleneck resource.
- *Add capacity to the bottleneck.* Add another machine or another worker to the bottleneck. Subcontract bottleneck work.

Some of these examples of relaxing the constraint cost little, while others involve some expenditures. How does a manager know when the cost of relaxing the constraint exceeds the benefit? How does one measure the benefit of relaxing the constraint? The benefit of relaxing the constraint equals the additional contribution margin that the company would realize. Returning to the example of the Indonesian company that makes gongs and bells, suppose that the workshop could fabricate additional molten brass by paying overtime wages to the foundryman at the rate of Rup 7,000 per hour. Does the benefit of paying overtime wages exceed this cost? To answer this question, we need to know what the company would do with the additional molten brass if it were available. From the earlier discussion, the company would probably have shifted production from gongs to bells because of the bells' higher contribution margin per kg of molten brass. (Recall that the gongs' contribution margin per kg of molten brass was Rup 8,000, whereas the bells' was Rup 12,000.) Assuming that the workshop already satisfies all of the existing demand for bells without working overtime, the company would use the additional molten brass from working overtime to produce gongs. The benefit to the company from producing more gongs would equal Rup 8,000 per kg of molten brass. Since the kiln generates 10 kg of molten brass per hour, the value of adding another hour of capacity in the foundry equals Rep 80,000 (= 10 kg × Rup 8,000 per kg). Since this exceeds the cost of Rup 7,000 per hour for the foundry worker, the benefit of overtime exceeds the cost.

In general, the value of relaxing the constraint (i.e., increasing its capacity) is the contribution margin per unit of the constrained resource for the marginal job, the one management would next add to the schedule if the workshop had additional capacity.

(e) STEP 5: IF THE CONSTRAINT HAS BEEN BROKEN, GO BACK TO STEP 1. A company may increase the constraint's capacity so much that it is no longer the bottleneck. If that happens, the whole cycle begins again. Management identifies the new constraint, exploits it, relaxes it, and, perhaps, eliminates it. Through this process, the organization continues to increase the NPV of cash flows.

Note that this process never ends. If the goal is to increase cash flow, which has no limit, the organization will always face at least one constraint.

This concludes the brief overview of the five steps for ongoing improvement. This overview provides the basis for the next section, which examines some implications of TOC for cost and management accountants.

20.7 IMPLICATIONS OF TOC FOR COST AND MANAGEMENT ACCOUNTANTS

(a) TOTAL QUALITY MANAGEMENT (TQM) AND BUSINESS PROCESS REENGINEERING. Interest in TQM and business process reengineering has waned, partly because companies have tried to embrace too many business movements (including TOC) in rapid succession. Perhaps even more important, operating improvements that resulted from TQM and business process reengineering frequently failed to increase profits. When viewed through a TOC lens, this failure seems almost inevitable unless companies can focus TQM and business process reengineering on constraints.

Suppose that a company uses TQM, or business process reengineering, or some other technique to improve a process that is not a bottleneck. Improvement usually means redesigning the process to increase its rate of output while consuming fewer resources—perhaps by omitting non-value-added steps. How can such an improvement at a *non-bottleneck* increase profits? If the process is not a bottleneck, speeding it up just creates more excess capacity. Excess capacity has some value, since it provides additional protection from random disruptions, but the benefits may be small and seldom realized.

Business process improvements can also lead to more profits by eliminating spending on no-longer-needed resources or redeploying them to better uses. Note that reducing the use of a resource or even eliminating the resource entirely doesn't increase profits unless the company also reduces spending. For example, writing off obsolete machines does nothing to improve future cash flows or current profits. To benefit from the reduction in the use of a resource, the company must reduce spending or redeploy the resource to a better use. When people are the excess resource, reducing spending can become a delicate problem. If a TQM or reengineering exercise identifies positions that the company no longer needs, future improvement efforts will face resistance and will likely fail. The alternative to laying off people is to reassign them. But where should the company reassign the excess people? On the one hand, reassigning them to a nonbottleneck work center will simply increase the excess capacity in that work center. Transferring excess personnel to the bottleneck, on the other hand, can have an immediate and dramatic effect on profits by increasing the amount of finished output that the company can produce and sell.

Note what happens if the business improvement program focuses on the bottleneck constraint. Speeding up the bottleneck yields immediate and substantial improvements in the bottom line. If the company can process one more unit per hour at the bottleneck, the contribution margin from that unit will drop directly to the bottom line.

In sum, to significantly affect profits, *business process improvement efforts should focus on the bottleneck constraint.* Moreover, if improvements in a work center that is not a bottleneck create excess resources, the company should ordinarily redeploy excess resources to the bottleneck.

(b) EFFICIENT PRODUCTION SCHEDULING. The problem of scheduling a job shop to ensure that diverse jobs are completed on time has bedeviled managers for decades. TOC solves this problem by focusing on the bottleneck.

Ordinarily, the work centers that lie downstream from the bottleneck, where work follows the bottleneck in time, are not critical. These downstream work centers can process units at a faster pace than the bottleneck, so anything that the bottleneck finishes will pass through the remaining work centers with only minimal delays.

However, work centers that lie upstream from the bottleneck in the production process should be closely monitored. The upstream work centers must ensure that the bottleneck is not idle. Any time lost on the bottleneck is lost forever and results in lower profits. The upstream work centers should also be monitored to ensure that work in process inventories do not pile up in front of the bottleneck. As we will discuss below, some inventories are necessary in front of the bottleneck. However, without sufficient monitoring, these inventories can pile up and become a real problem. The bottleneck should dictate the pace of all other upstream work centers. In particular, managers must resist the temptation to increase the rate of output of the upstream work centers beyond the bottleneck's capacity. If the bottleneck can process only 10 units per hour, but the upstream work centers process 12 units per hour, work-in-process inventory will grow at the rate of two units per hour. As long as the upstream work centers continue producing at a faster pace than the bottleneck can process units, the work-in-process inventory will increase.

The just-in-time (JIT) movement has taught us that excessive work in process inventories create operating problems, such as long cycle times, high defect rates, obsolescence, poor on-time delivery performance, and high holding and storage costs. Indeed, JIT strives to eliminate work in process inventories entirely.

TOC takes a slightly less radical approach than does JIT, striving to eliminate work in process inventories everywhere except at one location—just before the bottleneck. This strategically located buffer inventory protects the bottleneck from upstream disruptions. If the work centers upstream of the bottleneck experience problems that disrupt the flow of throughput, the buffer inventory should allow the bottleneck to continue processing units until the disruption ends. In the absence of this buffer inventory, any upstream disruption shuts down the bottleneck. This wastes productive capacity and results in the permanent loss of contribution margin and of profit.

TOC refers to this efficient production scheduling as *drum-buffer-rope.* The *drum* is the bottleneck. The *buffer* is the inventory maintained in front of the bottleneck to ensure that it is not idle. The *rope* pulls jobs through the manufacturing system.

(c) IMPLICATIONS FOR EFFICIENCY MEASURES. Almost all job shops rely on some measure of work center efficiency to help control operations and to evaluate the performance of direct labor workers and their supervisors. TOC shows that this reliance is misplaced.

Labor efficiency measures take several forms, but almost all compare hours earned (or charged to product) to hours actually worked or hours actually paid. Hours earned is the standard hours allowed for the actual output of the period. For example, if center Z has processed 100 units of Product X this month, and if the standard for Product X is 0.2 hour per unit in work center Z, then work center Z would earn 20 hours (= 0.2 hour per unit × 100 units). In some organizations, the efficiency measure equals the ratio of hours earned to actual hours. In other organizations, the efficiency measure is a standard cost variance that equals the difference between the actual hours and the hours earned multiplied by the standard hourly wage rate. If the actual hours exceed the actual hours earned, the variance is unfavorable. If the actual hours earned exceed the actual hours, the variance is favorable.

The actual hours in the efficiency measure may be the actual hours worked during the month or it may be the actual hours paid during the month, the difference between the two consisting of idle time, training time, break time, and so on. Suppose the actual hours in the efficiency measure refer to the actual hours paid. In many companies, direct labor workers are permanent employees who work at least a specified number of hours a week—in the United States, commonly 40 hours a week. Employees receive payment for the entire 40 hours, even if the organization does not have enough work to keep them fully occupied.

How can work center supervisors avoid unfavorable labor efficiency variances if the company guarantees direct-labor workers payment for a 40-hour week? Supervisors can accomplish this by ensuring that everyone in the work center produces a rate of output at least as high as the standard specifies for every hour they receive payment. If the workers receive payment for 40 hours a week and the standard equals five units per hour, then the work center must process 200 units (= 40 hours/week × 5 units per hour) per week per worker to avoid an unfavorable variance.

Companies vary in how they set standards, but let us suppose that a company bases its standard on how much time a reasonably competent worker should require to complete a task when working efficiently, with some allowances for required personal breaks. By setting the standard in this way, the work center will avoid an unfavorable variance only if it operates at capacity all of the time.

What happens if every work center attempts to operate at capacity so as to avoid unfavorable efficiency variances? If work centers upstream of the bottleneck process units at a faster pace than the bottleneck can handle, work in process inventories will pile up in front of the bottleneck, with no increase in completed units. This will increase costs and create operational problems, with no increase in revenues.

Furthermore, if the organization holds work center supervisors responsible for direct labor efficiency variances, supervisors will tend to run large batches of the products with the most generous standards rather than produce small batches of products that customers may prefer. This will lead to large inventories of products that the work center can easily make (but the customers may not want) and insufficient production of items that customers demand.

Nonbottleneck work centers *should* be idle part of the time. If they are not, the result is excessive work-in-process inventories with no increase in revenue. Therefore, assuming that the standards have been set to encourage operating each work center at capacity, *the nonbottleneck work centers ordinarily should have unfavorable labor efficiency variances.*

Should the labor efficiency variance at the *bottleneck* be favorable or unfavorable? At least initially, the bottleneck should have an unfavorable labor efficiency variance. After management has initially identified a constraint, supervisors should temporarily assign to the bottleneck people who would otherwise be idle. By doing mundane housekeeping chores, they can free the time of more experienced workers and thereby increase the total amount that the workshop produces at the bottleneck. The output per worker (including the temporarily assigned workers) at the bottleneck work center may decline, but the total output will increase. When business process improvement efforts focus on the bottleneck, the output per worker should increase and the labor efficiency variance should improve.

In summary, all of the work centers—except for the bottleneck—should have *unfavorable* labor efficiency variances. Moreover, it is not clear whether the bottleneck should have a favorable or unfavorable labor efficiency variance. This suggests that management should abandon the use of labor efficiency measures to evaluate performance.

Management could fix the labor efficiency variance reporting system by recalibrating the labor standards to indicate a favorable variance if a nonbottleneck work center meets the plan and an unfavorable variance otherwise. This would require recalibrating the labor standard each period because the amount of work that a nonbottleneck work center should do depends on the precise product mix. Companies can use other, simpler, and more direct ways to monitor how well the nonbottleneck work centers follow the plan. For example, managers can generally spot problems quickly by checking the buffer inventory that immediately precedes the bottleneck. A decreasing buffer inventory signals that the company may have problems upstream from the bottleneck that it should immediately address.

TOC requires many managers to change their basic approach—particularly those who manage nonbottlenecks. Those managers should *not* focus on whether everyone works hard and maximizes efficiency. Instead, their basic task is to feed the bottleneck on schedule.

This section has discussed labor efficiency. The same issues occur with measures of machine efficiency and with overhead efficiency variances. If the company holds work center supervisors responsible for these variances, excess work in process inventories will almost inevitably result.

(d) CONTROLLING FIXED COSTS IN TOC. TOC pays little attention to fixed costs, but leads to insights for controlling fixed costs. Fixed costs are the costs of providing capacity. Ordinarily, additional resources should be provided only at the bottleneck. Additional resources to expand capacity in nonbottleneck work centers should be questioned. Of course, resources may expand capabilities as well as capacity, and additional capacity may be required even in a nonbottleneck work center if it occasionally becomes the bottleneck. Nevertheless, managers in TOC tend to take a hard line on increases in fixed costs, ignoring pleas for additional resources in nonbottleneck work centers. This approach contrasts with the presumption in some non-TOC organizations that entitles every department to last year's budget plus some percentage. To a large extent, TOC organizations control fixed costs by just saying no to increases.

(e) MEASURING THE PROFITABILITY OF PRODUCTS. Managers often want to know the relative profitability of segments of the business. The segments could be products, customers, regional sales offices, or any other way of looking at a part of the overall organization. For discussion purposes, we will focus on products, but the analysis would apply to any other segment.

Relative profitability differs from absolute profitability. A product is absolutely profitable if the company makes higher profits with the product than without the product. Managers need to know absolute profitability, but they also should rank the profitability of all the absolutely profitable products. Why? If a situation forces the company to choose between producing and selling product A or product B, for example, management will want a measure of relative profitability.

What would force a company to choose among products? A constraint of some sort must exist. If no constraint exists, management need not make a tradeoff. If a constraint exists, the company cannot satisfy the demand for all products and must rank the products.

(*Note:* The constraint does not necessarily have to be a production constraint. It could be a policy constraint. This extremely important issue is discussed in the TOC literature.)

How should one measure the relative profitability of products in the presence of a constraint? This question was discussed in Section 20.6(b) as step 2 of the process of ongoing improvement. To correctly rank products, customers, projects, or any other segment, management should measure relative profitability as the contribution margin per unit of the constrained resource.[1] Unfortunately, common practices such as measuring relative profitability in terms of gross margin as a percentage of sales are incorrect.

(f) CONSTRAINT PRICING. According to surveys, managers in most companies try to set prices by marking up some version of full cost. This common practice differs considerably from the price-setting mechanism described in microeconomics. The apparent contradiction between theory and practice has puzzled economists for decades and has provided grist for many articles in economics and accounting that have tried to rationalize full cost pricing. Interestingly, pricing in TOC follows microeconomic theory more closely than does the common practice of marking up full cost. TOC organizations set prices according to what managers believe customers will pay, with an eye to competitive conditions. The organization considers cost only when setting a lower boundary on the price.

Suppose a company already operating at capacity is considering accepting a new order. Clearly, the company should not accept the order if it provides less profit than other potential orders. For illustration, assume that the constraint is labor in process X. Clearly, the company should not accept an order that generates \$10 of contribution margin per labor-hour in process X if it means giving up another order that would generate \$12 per labor-hour. Stated in terms of a formula, the new order is acceptable only if the following holds:

$$\frac{\text{Price - Variable cost}}{\text{Amount of constrained resource required}} \geq \begin{array}{c}\text{Contribution margin per unit of the}\\ \text{constrained resource for the marginal job}\end{array}$$

The marginal job in this formula refers to the job that the new order would displace. Recall the earlier example of the brass foundry, where the marginal job is gongs. Bells provide more profit per kilogram of molten brass than gongs. Therefore, the workshop would produce bells as long as demand exists and would use the remaining capacity to produce gongs. Since any new order would displace production of gongs, the contribution margin per unit of the constraint for the new order should at least equal the contribution margin per unit of the constraint for the gongs, which is Rup 8,000 per kilogram of molten brass.

Note that fixed costs play no role in the pricing formula. This occurs because the company would be operating at capacity (with presumably the same total fixed costs) whether or not it accepts a new order. The fixed costs should not affect a decision of whether to accept the new order, or what price to charge, since the decision does not affect fixed costs.

---

1. When ranking discrete segments, management should interpret the contribution margin as the difference between the segment's incremental cash inflows and the incremental cash outflows. For example, when the constraint is investment funds, management can rank investment projects by dividing their net present values by the amounts of investment funds they require. The net present value of a project is a way to summarize its incremental cash inflows and outflows.

One can use the preceding inequality to solve for the minimum acceptable price for the new order as follows:

$$\text{Price} \geq \text{Variable cost} + \left(\begin{array}{c}\text{Amount of constrained resource required} \times \\ \text{Contribution margin per unit of the} \\ \text{constrained resource for the marginal job}\end{array}\right)$$

For example, suppose a customer has requested a bid on a set of chimes that would require 100 kilograms of molten brass and that would have a variable cost of Rup 70,000. The minimum acceptable price for the chimes would be Rup 870,000, established as follows:

$$\text{Price} \geq \text{Rup } 70{,}000 + (100 \text{ kilograms} \times \text{Rup } 8{,}000 \text{ per kilogram}) = \text{Rup } 870{,}000$$

The minimum acceptable price for the new order equals Rup 870,000 and consists of two parts: the variable cost of Rup 70,000 and the opportunity cost of Rup 800,000. The opportunity cost is the contribution margin from the gongs that the company would have to give up to accept the new order.

Opportunity cost plays an important role in such decisions. Accepting the new order means that 100 kilograms of molten brass would not be available for making gongs. Since each gong requires 0.5 kilogram of molten brass, accepting the new order for chimes would require reducing the production of gongs by 200 units. Each gong generates contribution margin of Rup 4,000. Therefore, accepting the new order for chimes would require giving up a total contribution margin of Rup 800,000 (= 200 gongs × Rup 4,000 per gong). This reflects the opportunity cost of accepting the new order for chimes. One can also calculate the opportunity cost by multiplying the amount of constrained resource required for the new order (100 kilograms of molten brass) by the contribution margin per unit of the constrained resource for the marginal job (Rup 8,000 per kilogram of molten brass).

When pricing calculations include opportunity costs, the costs often exceed even fully allocated costs. A company that prices its products by applying a markup above its fully absorbed product costs might actually be losing money on some products.

Note that cost does not determine price in TOC; it simply sets a lower bound on price. The market or the value of the product or service to the customer determines the price.

(g) STRATEGIC PRICING IN TOC. Even in markets that one would consider competitive, companies often have some discretion in setting prices. How can a company use pricing to increase its profits?

Taking a variable costing perspective, profit equals the difference between total contribution margin and fixed costs:

$$\text{Profit} = \text{Total contribution margin} - \text{Fixed costs}$$

By dividing and multiplying the total contribution margin by the total amount of the constrained resource used, we get the following equation:

$$\text{Profit} = \left[\left(\frac{\text{Total contribution margin}}{\text{Total amount of constrained resource used}}\right) \times \begin{array}{c}\text{Total amount of constrained} \\ \text{resource used}\end{array}\right] - \text{Fixed costs}$$

We can restate the equation as follows:

$$\text{Profit} = \left[\begin{array}{c}\text{Average contribution margin per} \\ \text{unit of the constrained resource}\end{array} \times \begin{array}{c}\text{Total amount of constrained} \\ \text{resource used}\end{array}\right] - \text{Fixed costs}$$

At this point, we need to ask how the company can use pricing to increase profits. Assuming that capacity is not altered, the company's pricing practices should not affect fixed costs. However, prices can directly affect the average contribution margin per unit of the constrained resource and the total amount of the constrained resource used. For example, a company could increase the prices of all of its products. This would increase the average contribution margin per unit of the constrained resource, but would probably result in a decrease in the total amount of the constrained resource used. This may lead to a decrease in overall profits. The trick in pricing is to somehow increase the average contribution margin per unit of the constrained resource while keeping the company operating at full capacity. How can a company do this?

Assuming that the company operates in competitive markets, with known prices, it can compute the contribution margin per unit of the constrained resource for every product. Some products will prove more profitable than others, according to this profitability index. A company can increase the average contribution margin per unit of the constrained resource by shifting the product mix toward the more profitable products. It can do this by slightly discounting the prices of the more profitable products and charging a premium for any products whose prices otherwise would not cover variable plus opportunity costs. Through the pricing mechanism, the product mix will naturally shift, resulting in a higher average contribution margin per unit of the scarce resource. Of course, this strategy will work only as long as competitors do not retaliate. Competitive conditions in the industry become important in assessing the delicacy with which one should proceed when changing prices.

20.8 SUMMARY

Fundamentally, the Theory of Constraints focuses on the process of solving problems; it is not a collection of solutions to specific problems. Nevertheless, this chapter discusses some generic TOC solutions to common problems encountered in job shops. When the company's constraint is a physical process, management should follow the five steps for ongoing improvement. The five steps work by focusing on the constraint, elevating it through process improvements and other means, and eventually eliminating it. Once the company eliminates one constraint, another will appear and the cycle begins again.

The contribution margin per unit of the constrained resource plays a pivotal role in TOC. This measure is used to prioritize the use of the constraint, to estimate the benefits of elevating the constraint, to assess profitability, and to set prices. TOC regards many cost accounting and management accounting practices—such as absorption costing and standard cost variance reporting—as counterproductive.

BIBLIOGRAPHY

Goldratt, Eliyahu M. *The Haystack Syndrome.* Great Barrington, Mass.: North River Press, 1990.

Goldratt, Eliyahu M., and Jeff Cox. *The Goal: A Process of Ongoing Improvement, Second Revised Edition.* Great Barrington, Mass.: North River Press, 1992.

Goldratt, Eliyahu M. *It's Not Luck.* Great Barrington, Mass.: North River Press, 1995.

Noreen, Eric, Debra Smith, and James T. Mackey. *The Theory of Constraints and Its Implications for Management Accounting.* Great Barrington, Mass.: North River Press, 1995.

CHAPTER 21

CAPITAL BUDGETING: CONCEPTS AND METHODS

ROMAN WEIL, CPA, CMA, PHD, EDITOR
University of Chicago

CONTENTS

21.1 INTRODUCTION 587

21.2 INDEPENDENCE OF INVESTMENT AND FINANCING DECISIONS 588

21.3 CASE STUDIES FOR INVESTMENT DECISIONS 588
- (a) Cash Flows versus Income Flows 588
- (b) The Net Present Value Graph 590

21.4 THE COST OF CAPITAL 591

21.5 SENSITIVITY OF PROFITS TO ESTIMATES 592

21.6 INCOME TAX CONSIDERATIONS 593

21.7 ALTERNATIVE METHODS FOR EVALUATING PROJECTS 595
- (a) Excess Present Value Index 595
- (b) The Internal Rate of Return 595
- (c) Shortcomings of the Internal Rate of Return Rule for Choosing Between Investment Projects 596
- (d) Payback Period 598
- (e) Discounted Payback Period 599
- (f) Bailout and Discounted Bailout Periods 599
- (g) Accounting Rate of Return 600

21.8 SUMMARY OF EVALUATION RULES 600

21.9 SPECIAL PROBLEMS IN EVALUATING AND CHOOSING BETWEEN INVESTMENT PROJECTS 601
- (a) Capital Rationing 601
- (b) Ranking Projects 602

21.10 SEPARATING THE INVESTMENT AND FINANCING DECISIONS 602
- (a) Managerial Evaluation of Noncancelable Leases 603
- (b) Why Do Leasing and Borrow-Purchase Appear More Attractive than Outright Purchase? 604

21.11 ANALYSES WITH UNCERTAIN FUTURE CASH FLOWS 608

BIBLIOGRAPHY 609

21.1 INTRODUCTION

Management must often decide whether to add a product to a line, whether to buy a new machine, or, in general, whether to make investments of funds today in return for benefits that will flow in later. Ideally, management makes a decision to accept, or reject, based on incremental analysis of future cash receipts and expenditures caused if it accepts. This chapter discusses the theory and the mechanism for making investment decisions when cash outlays today create future cash inflows. The proper mode of analyzing investment decisions is one of the most controversial topics in accounting. We first present the most desirable method for making capital expenditure decisions, and then discuss some alternative methods that are less desirable, indicating their shortcomings. Chapter 22 discusses implementation issues.

21.2 INDEPENDENCE OF INVESTMENT AND FINANCING DECISIONS

A firm faced with a decision, such as adding a new product line or buying plant assets, must decide both whether to undertake the new project and how to raise the funds required by the new activity. Once the firm decides to undertake a project, the firm can raise the necessary funds in a combination of ways. For example, the firm can raise funds through borrowing, or by retaining assets generated by earnings rather than distributing dividends, or by issuing additional capital stock.

The theory of financial economics instructs that the firm should make the investment decision independently of the financing decision.[1] That is, the firm should first make the investment decision—go or no go—and only after a project gets the go-ahead should management begin to consider how to finance it. All of the equities of the firm finance all of its assets, without earmarking of specific sources of funds to specific assets. This fact underlies the conclusion that the firm should make the investment decision independently of the financing decision for new undertakings. A new project will involve investing funds, but once the firm adds the project to its portfolio of activities, that project becomes one of the pool of activities that all the firm's equities finance.

Raising funds and managing cash are important for a firm; however, this chapter does not consider those issues. It discusses only the investment decision—the ranking of investment projects.

21.3 CASE STUDIES FOR INVESTMENT DECISIONS

Rational investment decisions require analysis of cash or fund flows over the life of the investment, not periodic income flows. To illustrate why, and to introduce the investment decision, we examine a typical project.

(a) CASH FLOWS VERSUS INCOME FLOWS. Consider the decision facing the Garden Winery Company, which is contemplating acquiring equipment that will allow it to bring to market a new variety of wine. The equipment costs $10,000 and is expected to last four years. Exhibit 21.1 shows information about the new equipment, the cash outlays (required for labor, grapes, and bottles), as well as the revenues expected from the sales of the new variety of wine. The decreasing pattern of revenues over the four years of the machine results in part from the equipment becoming less productive over time and in part by the expected reaction of other wine sellers, who will copy the new wine variety and force down the selling price in the market. For simplicity, assume that Garden Winery Company uses straight-line depreciation, that the equipment has an estimated salvage value of zero, that the company pays income taxes at the rate of 40 percent of taxable income, and that all cash flows occur at the end of each year.

---

1. An exception arises for nonrecourse loans. If a lender will finance a project while expecting debt service payments only from the project itself, without recourse to other assets of the firm, then proper analysis requires the simultaneous consideration of both the investing and financing decisions.

GARDEN WINERY COMPANY
REVENUES, EXPENSES, INCOME, AND CASH FLOWS FROM NEW WINE PROJECT

End of Year	Revenues	Cash Outlays	Pretax Cash Inflow (outflow)	Deprecia-tion Charge	Pretax Income	Income Tax	Net Income	Net Cash Inflows (Outflows)
(1)	(2)	(3)	(4)	(5)	(6)	(7)	(8)	(9)
0	-	$ 10,000	$(10,000)	-	-	-	-	$(10,000)
1	$ 6,000	1,000	5,000	$ 2,500	$ 2,500	$ 1,000	$ 1,500	4,000
2	5,000	1,000	4,000	2,500	1,500	600	900	3,400
3	4,500	1,000	3,500	2,500	1,000	400	(600)	3,100
4	4,000	1,000	3,000	2,500	500	200	300	2,800
Total	$ 9,500	$(14,000)	$ 5,500	$ 10,000	$ 5,500	$ 2,200	$ 3,300	$ 3,300

(2), (3): Given
(4) = (2) – (3)
(5) = $10,000/4
(6) = (4) – (5)
(7) = .40 × (6)
(8) = (6) – (7)
(9) = (4) – (7)
= (8) + (5) in years 1–4

EXHIBIT 21.1 PROJECTED FINANCIAL INFORMATION FOR PROPOSED INVESTMENT

At the end of year zero—that is to say, at the start of the project—the firm purchases the equipment for $10,000, as column (9) of Exhibit 21.1 shows. In each of the next four years, the firm earns revenues as in column (2), and makes current cash outlays for materials (grapes, bottles, and so on) and labor, as in column (3). Inflows of funds or cash, as forecast, from operations appear in column (4). Column (5) shows depreciation charges of $2,500 per year and column (6) shows pretax income [columns (2) – (3) – (5) = (6)]. Column (7) shows income taxes as 40 percent of pretax income. Column (8) shows net income [= column (6) – column (7)]. Column (9) shows the net cash flows for each of the years from either of two computations:

1. Column (9) = cash inflows, column (2), less cash outflows [=column (3) + column (7)]
2. Column (9) = net income, column (8), plus expenses (depreciation) not using cash, column (5). Note that the only effective use of the depreciation amounts in the decision making process is in the computation of the income taxes payable for a year.

Over the life of the project, the sum of the net income amounts is $3,300, which equals the sum of net cash flows. Although the two data series have the same totals over the four years, the timing of the amounts differs. The accounting income figures shown in column (8) for the Garden Winery project result from an assumed asset expiration of $2,500 each year (for depreciation). The asset requires, however, a cash outlay of $10,000 at the beginning of the first year. Making investment decisions on the basis of accounting income figures, such as those in column (8), ignores the time value of cash flows. The cash flows shown in column (9) accurately depict the time dimension of the economic costs and benefits to the firm.

Once the analyst compiles the data on projected cash flows for a project (not necessarily an easy task), the capital budgeting problem requires evaluating those data to decide whether to undertake the project. Throughout, this chapter assumes that all projected cash flows have equal probabilities of occuring, so no problem of relative uncertainty of cash flows arises.

(b) THE NET PRESENT VALUE GRAPH. Given the cash flow data for a project, a *net present value graph,* such as the one in Exhibit 21.2 for the Garden Winery project, provides a convenient way to assess the profitability of a project. The horizontal axis shows the discount rate, and the vertical axis shows the net present value of the cash flows computed for each discount rate. The *net present value* of a series of cash flows equals the sum of the discounted present values of each individual cash flow. For example, at a discount rate of zero, the net present value of the project equals the sum of the net cash flows, or \$3,300. Thus, the net present value curve shown in Exhibit 21.2 intersects the vertical axis at \$3,300. Next, plot points on the curve for positive discount rates, such as for a discount rate of 10 percent per year, derived in Exhibit 21.3.

For each cash flow, for example the \$3,400 that flows in at the end of the second year, the present value (at the start of year 1) of that flow equals \$2,810 (calculated as \$3,400 × .82645, from the present value of \$1 numbers shown in Table 2 of Appendix A). The initial outlay of \$10,000 has present value of \$10,000, regardless of the discount rate. Next, compute the present values of each of the years' cash flows and sum those numbers. That sum, \$687, equals the net present value of the cash flows from the project with a discount rate of 10 percent per year. Exhibit 21.2 shows this net present value of \$687 for a 10 percent discount rate. For any other discount rate, compute a net present value and plot a point on the curve. (The net present value curve, never a straight line, shown in Exhibit 21.2 connects net present value amounts plotted for discounts rates $r = 0, 1, 2, \ldots, 15$ percent.)

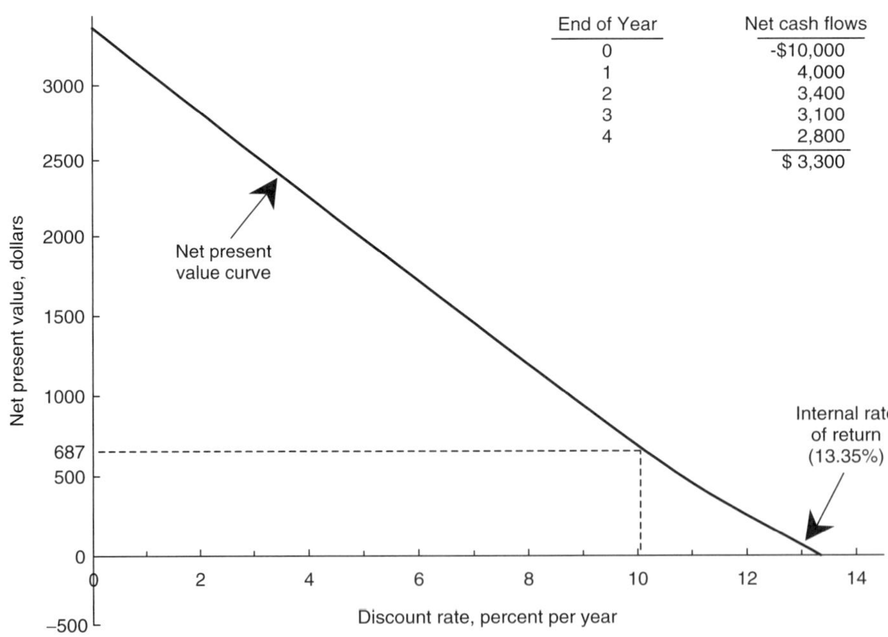

EXHIBIT 21.2 GARDEN WINERY COMPANY – NET PRESENT VALUE GRAPH

GARDEN WINERY COMPANY PROJECT EVALUATION
PRESENT VALUES OF CASH FLOWS DISCOUNTED AT 10 PERCENT A YEAR

End of Year	Net Cash Flows		Present Value (Discounted at 10%) of $1		Present Value (Discounted at 10%) of Cash Flows from Project
0	$(10,000)	×	1.00000	=	$(10,000)
1	4,000	×	.90909	=	3,636
2	3,400	×	.82645	=	2,810
3	3,100	×	.75131	=	2,323
4	2,800	×	.68301	=	1,912
Totals	$ 3,300				$ 687

EXHIBIT 21.3 PRESENT VALUE OF CASH FLOWS FOR PROPOSED INVESTMENT

The internal rate of return is the discount rate, 13.35 percent in the example, where the net present value curve crosses the horizontal axis. It plays a special role in capital budgeting analysis. The *internal rate of return* of a series of payments is the discount rate that equates the net present value of those payments to zero. One method for evaluating investment projects chooses among alternatives with the largest internal rate of return.

The net present value graph shows, then, for various discount rates, the net present value of the cash flows from a project. This investment decision rule will result in maximizing the firm's wealth: If, for the appropriate discount rate, the cash flows from a proposal have a positive net present value, then the firm should undertake the project. What is that appropriate discount rate? Use the firm's cost of capital.

21.4 THE COST OF CAPITAL

To make optimal investment decisions, use the firm's cost of capital: a concept easy to define, but hard to measure. The *cost of capital* equals the *opportunity cost* of funds invested in a business–the rate of return that rational owners require an asset to earn before they will devote that asset to a particular purpose. Often, analysts measure the cost of capital as the average annual rate that a company must pay for its funding—its liabilities and owners' equities. In efficient capital markets, the expected present value of all future cash flows discounted at the cost of capital equals the market value of common stock at a given time. Analysts often measure the cost of capital by taking a weighted average of the firm's debt and various equity securities and refer to the measurement so derived as the "composite cost of capital." Many analysts confuse this measurement of the cost of capital with the cost of capital itself. For example, if the right side of the balance sheet includes substantial amounts for the deferred income tax liability, the composite cost of capital will underestimate the cost of capital—the required rate of return on a firm's assets—because the deferred income tax liability has no explicit cost.

The modern theory of financial economics can demonstrate the equivalence of the following definitions of the *cost of capital:*

- The average rate that the firm must pay for funds invested in the firm
- The average rate the firm would earn if it reacquired its own equity securities and paid off its liabilities in the proportions those liabilities are outstanding

- The rate of return for new investment projects such that, if all projects undertaken by the firm yield that rate, then the market value of the firm's shares will remain unchanged
- The rate of return the firm earns on its marginal investments in assets, which have risk equal to the average risk of all assets of the firm

The cost of capital for most firms usually lies between 10 and 20 percent, after taxes. One could also think of the cost of capital by asking what the firm could do with new funds without changing the firm's basic nature. The firm can purchase marketable securities or additional inventories and can retire some of its debt. The earnings rate from the average investment (with risk and return equal to that from the average project in the firm), regardless of the actual financing method, equals the firm's cost of capital.

The discount rate appropriate for capital budgeting decisions—the cost of capital—has three separate elements:

1. *A pure rate of interest that reflects the productive capability of capital assets.* You can think of this as the rate a riskless borrower, such as the U.S. government, must pay to borrow for a period when the marketplace expects no inflation to occur over the term of the loan. (Economists debate the results of empirical research, but most would agree that the pure rate of interest generally lies between 0 and 4 percent.)
2. *A risk factor that adds a premium to the pure rate and reflects the project's riskiness.* The greater a project's risk, the higher the discount rate. (Investing a company's funds in a high-risk R&D project, rather than low-risk bonds, requires such a risk factor. The federal government has the lowest probability of default, so U.S. government bonds usually have the lowest risk premiums.)
3. *A further increase that reflects inflation the market expects will occur over the life of the project.* Higher expected inflation implies a higher discount rate.

The *risk-free rate* includes the pure interest rate increased to reflect expected inflation. Many financial economists would say that, by definition, the U.S. government rate has no default risk, and they call it the *risk-free rate.*

The *real interest rate* includes the pure interest rate and a premium for the risk of the investment, but no increase for expected inflation. The *nominal interest rate* includes all three factors—pure interest, risk premium, and expected inflation.

Analysts typically forecast project cash flows in nominal dollars—the actual dollar amounts they expect the project will generate in the future. Analysts generally expect that the larger the rate of inflation, the larger will be the nominal dollar receipts from the project. Analysts who forecast a project's cash flow in nominal dollars should use a nominal discount rate. The examples and analysis in this chapter use cash flow forecasts in nominal dollars and nominal discount rates.

A firm should undertake an investment project if the cash flows have positive net present value when the discounting process uses the cost of capital rate.

21.5 SENSITIVITY OF PROFITS TO ESTIMATES

A computation of the net present value of a project using an estimate of the cost of capital as the discount rate will usually give an unequivocal signal: the proposal clearly has merit, or clearly does not. Only when the net present value approaches zero would one worry about the accuracy of the cost of capital estimate. Investments with large positive or negative net present value would have minimal sensitivity regarding the cost of capital estimate: the net present value may be more or less positive (or negative) with changes in cost of capital, but will remain positive (or negative). But when the net present value approaches zero, the firm becomes indifferent to accepting or rejecting the project: It will make or lose little net present value with the investment. Consequently, the firm will make nearly optimal decisions by approximating the cost of capital, as opposed to incurring costs to develop an accurate measure. The firm will likely suffer only small losses from errors caused by an incorrect estimate of the cost of capital, almost surely smaller than the cost of errors made in estimating cash flows.

The decision rule for evaluating investment projects: accept a project that has a positive net present value with cash flows discounted at the cost of capital rate and reject it otherwise. In the Garden Winery example, the cash flows have positive net present value for all discount rates less than 13.35 percent. Consequently, if management estimated its cost of capital at about 10 percent, then it should undertake the project, because the net cash flows from the project have present value of flows of \$687. For any cost of capital less than 13.35 percent, the stockholders will be better off if management accepts, rather than rejects, the project.

What loss does the firm suffer if it incorrectly calculates its cost of capital? Suppose that Garden Winery's cost of capital is 15 percent, while management acts as though it is 10 percent. Management miscalculates the cost of capital by 500 basis points—a 50 percent error, so large one would not expect to see in practice. That large error still has a small effect on the firm. Management believes that the firm will be \$687 better off by accepting the project. When the firm accepts the project and the cost of capital is 15 percent, the firm will find itself \$312 worse off, because the net present value at 15 percent is –\$312. The total error of the estimate in present value dollars equals \$999 [= \$687 – (\$312) = \$687 + \$312], about 10 percent of the initial investment, \$10,000. Thus, a 50 percent error in the calculation of the cost of capital rate used to make the decision implies only a 10 percent error in terms of the amount of the initial investment. In general, a marginally profitable project for a given cost of capital will ordinarily not result in significant losses at slightly higher rates.

Conversely, projects that have large positive net present value when discounted at 10 percent will likely remain worthwhile at higher discount rates.

21.6 INCOME TAX CONSIDERATIONS

Income tax regulations affect both the *amounts* of cash flows and the timing of cash flows, so they affect investment decisions. The tax laws affect investment decisions through the accelerated depreciation deductions from otherwise taxable income that they allow. Accelerating depreciation charges on the tax returns shifts taxable income to later years from earlier years. Although accelerated depreciation does not change the total tax liability generated by a project over its life, it does influence profitability measured in present-value terms because of the effect on the timing of cash flows.

Suppose, for example, that the Garden Winery Company decides to use the double-declining-balance method (not allowed by tax regulations as this book goes to press) to depreciate the machine required by the new wine variety. Exhibit 21.4 shows the net cash flows for the project.

GARDEN WINERY COMPANY
CASH FLOWS ASSUMING DOUBLE-DECLINING-BALANCE DEPRECIATION

End of Year	Revenue Less Cash Expenses	Depreciation Charge	Pretax Income	Income Tax	Net Cash Inflows (Outflows)
	(1)	(2)	(3)	(4)	(5)
0 . . .	-	-	-	-	$(10,000)
1 . . .	$ 5,000	$ 5,000	$ 0	$ 0	5,000
2 . . .	4,000	2,500	1,500	600	3,400
3 . . .	3,500	1,250	2,250	900	2,600
4 . . .	3,000	1,250	1,750	700	2,300
Total	$15,500	$10,000	$5,500	$2,200	$ 3,300

(1), (2) Given (3) = (1) – (2) (4) =.40 × (3) (5) = (1) – (4)

EXHIBIT 21.4 NET CASH FLOWS FOR PROPOSED INVESTMENT 3

Compare Exhibit 21.4 with Exhibit 21.1. Note that in both cases the net cash flows total $3,300 and the income taxes payable total $2,200. The accelerated method, however, shifts $1,000 of taxes payable from the first year to the third year ($500) and to the fourth ($500). Exhibit 21.5 compares the net present values from the project at various discount rates. With straight-line depreciation, the project has barely positive net present value (so, accept) at 13 percent and negative net present value (so, reject) at 14 percent, but with double-declining-balance depreciation, the net present value remains positive for cost of capital rates almost as high as 15 percent. Nothing has changed except the depreciation method the taxpayer uses for tax purposes.

Other tax-delaying and tax-saving aspects of the income tax regulations include the treatment of long- and short-term capital gains, effects of offsetting losses from one project against gains from another, and the off-again, on-again tax-saving device known as the *investment tax credit* used as an instrument of fiscal policy during the 1960s and 1970s.

GARDEN WINERY COMPANY
NET PRESENT VALUES USING DIFFERENT DEPRECIATION METHODS

Discount Rate in Percent per Year	Depreciation Method	
	Straight-line	Double-declining-balance
10	$687	$880
11	474	680
12	268	487
13	68	300
14	(125)	(119)
15	(312)	(57)

EXHIBIT 21.5 COMPARISON OF NET PRESENT VALUE AT VARIOUS DISCOUNT RATES AND DEPRECIATION METHODS

21.7 ALTERNATIVE METHODS FOR EVALUATING PROJECTS

Analysts use many methods for evaluating projects, most conceptually inferior to using the net present value method with a discount rate equal to the cost of capital. Some alternatives take the time value of cash flows into account and often give the same decision results as the net present value rule so, in practice, prove to be satisfactory. The alternative methods that do not take the time value of money into account have little merit, except that managers have found them easy to use.

(a) EXCESS PRESENT VALUE INDEX. The excess present value index equals the number of present value dollars of cash inflows per dollar of initial outlay. See the example calculations in column (5) of Exhibit 21.6. For example, project A returns $1.42 (= $17,000/$12,000) in present value of cash inflows for every $1 invested in the project. The excess present value index rule calculates the excess present value index for each project and ranks projects according to their score, or index. The rule rejects projects that result in less than $1 of present value cash inflows per $1 of initial outlay. The excess present value index rule will give the same results as the net present value rule so long as projects are not mutually exclusive.

Consider projects A, B, C, and D shown in Exhibit 21.6 and assume a cost of capital of 12 percent. If the firm can undertake only one of these projects, then it should prefer project A, as indicated by the net present value rule, because it has the greatest net present value of cash inflows and will increase firm wealth the most. The excess present value index rule prefers Project D, which has the smallest net present value. The excess present value index rule pays no attention to the amount of cash that the firm can invest in a project. Ignoring the amount of the investment will lead to wrong decisions, as discussed below in connection with the internal rate of return.

(b) THE INTERNAL RATE OF RETURN. The *internal rate of return,* sometimes called the *time-adjusted rate of return,* of a stream of cash flows is the discount rate that equates the net present value of that stream to zero. Exhibit 21.2 illustrates that the internal rate of return is the point on the net present value graph where the net present value line crosses the horizontal axis. The decision rule for using the internal rate of return specifies a *cutoff rate* (such as 10 percent for the Garden Winery Company) and says this: Accept projects when the internal rate of return on the project exceeds, or equals, the cutoff rate and reject them otherwise.

		At Cost of Capital of 12 Percent		
Project Name (1)	Initial Cash Outlay Required (2)	Present Value of Cash Inflows (3)	Net Present Value of Cash Flows (4)	Excess Present Value Index (5)
A	$12,000	$17,000	$5,000	1.42
B	11,000	15,000	4,000	1.36
C	7,000	10,000	3,000	1.43
D	3,000	5,500	2,500	1.83

(4) = (3) – (2) (5) = (3)/(2)

EXHIBIT 21.6 DATA FOR CAPITAL RATIONING ILLUSTRATION

Advocates of the internal rate of return argue that using the method does not require knowing the firm's cost of capital, so they prefer it to the net present value method, which does. For the internal rate of return rule to give the correct answers, however, the cutoff rate must equal the cost of capital. Otherwise, the analysis will reject some projects that will increase the value of the firm to its owners or accept some that will not.

A technical shortcoming of the internal rate of return rule results from the fact that a project can have more than one internal rate of return. This mathematical quirk can occur when the pattern of yearly net cash flows contains an intermixing of net cash inflows and outflows. For example, if a project requires an initial cash outlay and then, at the end of its life, further cash expenditures to return the plant site to its original condition, then individual cash flows can be negative both at the beginning and at the end of a project's life, but positive in between. Projects with intermixing of cash inflows and outflows likely will have multiple internal rates of return.[2]

The internal rate of return rule ranks projects in the same order as the net present value rule only when the project and implementation satisfy all of the following four conditions:

1. The cutoff rate used for the internal rate of return rule equals the cost of capital.
2. The projects are not mutually exclusive.
3. The projects have the same life.
4. The cash flows yield only one internal rate of return.

Otherwise, the internal rate of return rule may lead to a wrong decision, which the following examples illustrate.

(c) SHORTCOMINGS OF THE INTERNAL RATE OF RETURN RULE FOR CHOOSING BETWEEN INVESTMENT PROJECTS

(i) Mutually Exclusive Projects. Assume an after-tax cost of capital of 10 percent per year and that the firm can choose only one of the two projects, E or F, as shown in Exhibit 21.7. Mutually exclusive projects result when the firm can use a given resource for only one of several alternatives or can implement a new strategy with only one of several alternatives.

Project E provides a simple illustration for calculating the internal rate of return. The internal rate of return on project E is the rate r such that

$$-\$100 + \frac{\$120}{1 + r} = 0$$

2. Solving for the internal rate of return involves finding the roots of a polynomial. Descartes's rule of signs tells how to calculate the limit to the number of roots of such a polynomial. It says that a series of cash flows will have a nonnegative number of *internal rates of return*. The number is equal to the number of variations in the sign of the cash flows, the first occurring now and the others at subsequent yearly intervals: –100, –100, +50, +175, –50, +100. The internal rates of return are the numbers for r that satisfy the equation

$$-100 - \frac{100}{(1+r)} + \frac{50}{(1+r)^2} + \frac{175}{(1+r)^3} - \frac{50}{(1+r)^4} - \frac{100}{(1+r)^5} = 0$$

The series of cash flows has three variations in sign: a change from minus to plus, a change from plus to minus, and a change from minus to plus. The rule says that this series must have either three or one internal rates of return; in fact, it has only one, about 12 percent. Note, however, that if the analysis assumes a reinvestment rate, multiple internal rates of return will never occur. The *reinvestment rate* is a rate of earnings assumed for cash inflows that occur before the project's completion.

Project Name	Cash Flows by Year End of Year 0	1	Internal Rate of Return	Net Present Value at 10%
E	$(100)	$120	.20	$ 9.09
F	(300)	345	.15	13.64

EXHIBIT 21.7 DATA FOR PROJECTS E AND F

Solving for r gives $r = .20$. The internal rate of return in project F equals 15 percent. The internal rate of return rule would rank project E superior to F, whereas the net present value rule prefers project F. To see that the firm should prefer project F, consider what the firm must do with the idle $200 it will have to invest if it choses project E. It will invest that $200, by definition, at the cost of capital of 10 percent, which will result in a cash outflow of $220 at the end of the first year. So if the firm chooses Project E, it will realize total flows at the end of the first year of $340 (= $120 + $220), less than the $345 available from project F. The firm will prefer the results from choosing project F, as the net present value rule signals.

Exhibit 21.8 shows the net present value graphs for projects E and F. Note that E crosses the horizontal axis farther to the right than does F; but at 10 percent, the firm's cost of capital, the net present value of F exceeds E's.

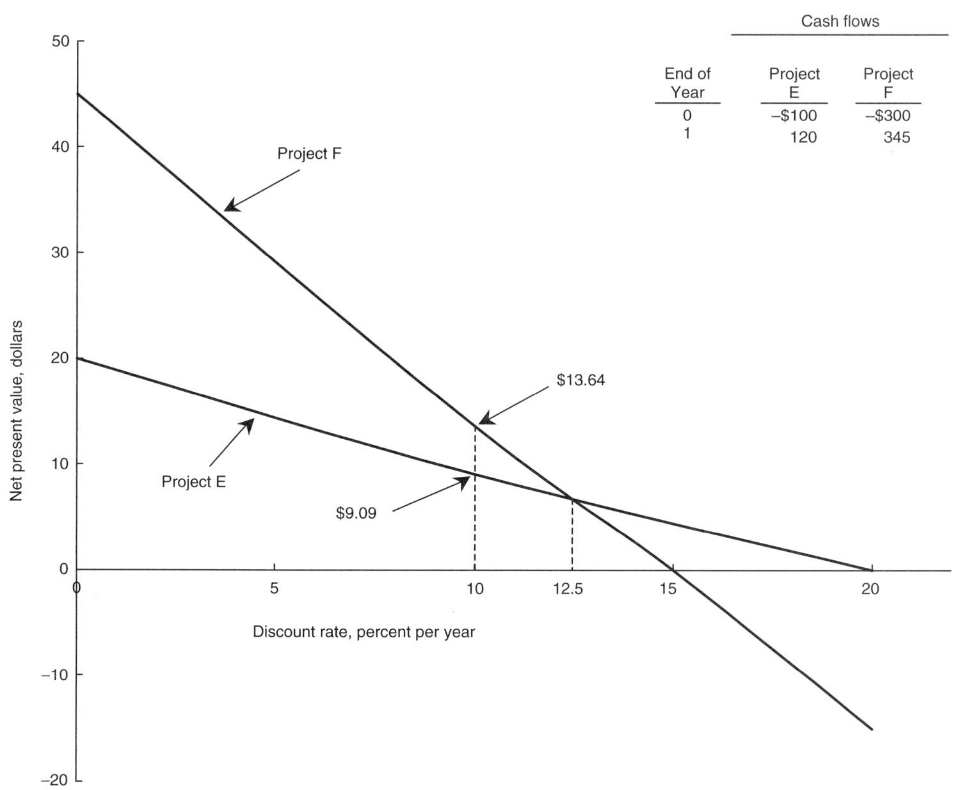

EXHIBIT 21.8 NET PRESENT VALUE GRAPHS FOR PROJECTS E AND F

The net present value graph makes the rankings of the two projects clear. The two net present value curves cross at 12.5 percent, the rate r that satisfies the equation

$$-\$100 + \frac{\$120}{1 + r} = -\$300 + \frac{\$345}{1 + r}$$

For costs of capital less than 12.5 percent, the firm will prefer project F to project E, and for costs of capital greater than 12.5 percent, it will prefer project E to project F.

Consider whether you would rather invest \$.10 today to get \$2 a year from now or invest \$1,000 today to get \$2,500 a year from now. You may not do both. Likely, you prefer the second alternative, even though the internal rate of return on the first exceeds that on the second by a factor of eight. The internal rate of return rule, applied to mutually exclusive projects, ignores the amount of funds that the firm can invest at that rate. This shortcoming, sometimes called the *scale effect,* applies to the excess present value index rule as well.

(ii) Projects with Different Lifetimes. Refer to the data for projects G and H in Exhibit 21.9. You can verify that project H's internal rate of return equals 20 percent by using the 20 percent column of Table 2 in Appendix A, found in the back of this *Handbook*. The internal rate of return rule prefers project G to H, whereas the net present value rule prefers project H to G. To see why the firm should prefer project H, consider what the firm must do during year 2 with the funds it receives at the end of year 1 from project G. It will invest the cash inflow of \$125 at the firm's cost of capital in the average investment project available to the firm, 10 percent. At the end of year 2, the firm will have \$137.50 (= \$125 × 1.10). If the firm accepts project H, the \$50 cash inflow at the end of the first year will also earn 10 percent and will grow to \$55 (= \$50 × 1.10) by the end of year 2. Thus, the total funds available at the end of the second year are \$139 (= \$55 + \$84), which exceed the \$137.50 from project G. The internal rate of return rule ignores the fact that the firm must invest idle funds at the cost of capital.

(d) PAYBACK PERIOD. Lazy analysts often use the payback period criterion in evaluating investment projects. The *payback period* is the length of time that elapses before total cumulative after-tax cash inflows from the project equal the initial cash outlay for the project. Refer to Exhibit 21.1 and 21.4 for data on the Garden Winery Company's project. The Garden Winery Company project has a payback period of about three years for both methods of depreciation, although if the cash flows occur uniformly during each year, then the payback period for straight-line exceeds that for the accelerated depreciation method. The payback-period decision rule states that the firm accept projects when the payback period ends before or at a designated cutoff time period, such as two years, and reject them otherwise.

Project Name	Cash Flows by Year, End of Year 0	1	2	Internal Rate of Return	Net Present Value at 10 Percent
G . . .	\$(100)	\$125	-	.25	\$13.64
H . . .	(100)	50	\$84	.20	14.87

EXHIBIT 21.9 DATA FOR PROJECTS G AND H

The payback-period rule ignores both the time value of money and all cash flows subsequent to the payback date. One project can have a shorter payback period than another but smaller net present value. The payback-period rule emphasizes concern with the firm's liquidity. The net present value rule, however, also takes liquidity into account because the cost of capital used for discounting cash flows, by definition, accurately measures the costs of securing additional funds should the firm need to.

If a project has constant net cash inflows per year that occur for a number of years at least twice as long as the payback period and if the firm's cost of capital exceeds 10 percent per year, then the reciprocal of the payback period approximately equals the internal rate of return on the project. Thus, under the conditions in the preceding sentence, the payback period will rank projects in the same way that the internal rate of return analysis will.

(e) DISCOUNTED PAYBACK PERIOD. Given the widespread use of the payback-period rule and its inability to yield good decisions for the most general case, some accountants have suggested that firms that want a payback rule should use the discounted payback period. The *discounted payback period* is the length of time that elapses before the *present value* of the cumulative cash inflows first exceed initial cash outlay. The discounted payback period gives some recognition to the time value of funds that flow before payback occurs. Projects J and K in Exhibit 21.10 have the same ordinary payback periods, three years, but the discounted payback criteria will properly rank K as better than J.

Either payback rule would improperly prefer both J and K to project L. Analysts sometimes recommend the discounted payback rule to firms that are wary of applying the net present value rule to projects like project L. The manager who made the original forecast for $50,000 cash inflow for year 5 may have left the firm before top management learns of the optimism embodied in the original and can hold him responsible.

(f) BAILOUT AND DISCOUNTED BAILOUT PERIODS. The payback period criteria ignore the cash flows after payback has been achieved and the possible residual value of equipment of a project that, for whatever reason, does not last its estimated life. The *bailout period* is the shortest elapsed time from the start of the project until the cumulative cash inflows from a project, plus the residual value of the equipment at the end of the period equal the cash outflows for the project.

(i) Example of Bailout Period. Assume that a project involving acquisition of equipment requires an initial cash outflow of $100 and yields cash inflows of $25 at the end of each year for seven years. Also assume that the firm could sell the equipment for $60 at the end of the first year, $50 at the end of the second year, $40 at the end of the third year, $30 at the end of the fourth year, and so on until salvage is zero at the end of the

Project Name	Cash Flow at End of Year 0	1	2	3	4	5
J	($10,000)	$2,000	$3,000	$5,000	$3,000	–
K . . .	(10,000)	5,000	3,000	2,000	3,000	–
L	(10,000)	–	–	–	–	$50,000

EXHIBIT 21.10 ILLUSTRATIVE DATA FOR PAYBACK RULES, PROJECTS J, K, AND L

seventh year. The payback period is four years, but by the end of the second year, cumulative cash inflows have totaled \$50 and the firm can salvage equipment for \$50, so the bailout occurs after only two periods.

(ii) Example of Discounted Bailout Period. The discounted bailout period uses the present value of estimated cash flows and the present value of the residual values. In the preceding example, assuming a discount rate of 10 percent per period, the discounted bailout period is five years. The present value of the cash inflows of \$25 per year discounted at 10 percent per year for five years equals \$95 and the present value of the \$20 salvage at the end of the fifth year equals \$12. Only by the end of the fifth year does the sum of these two present values for the first time exceed the initial investment of \$100. Thus, the discounted bailout period equals five years.

The payback period (or the discounted payback period) will always exceed the bailout period (or the discounted bailout period) if the equipment has any residual value at the end of the payback period. Bailout criteria dominate payback criteria because bailout takes into account the residual value subsequent to the considered termination date. Because the estimated residual value at any date incorporates an estimate of the present value of the cash flows from the equipment after that date, the bailout criteria use more of the relevant information available than do the payback criteria.

(g) ACCOUNTING RATE OF RETURN. The *accounting rate of return,* sometimes called the *return on investment (ROI)* or the *rate of return on book value* for a project is

$$\frac{\text{Average Yearly Income from the Project}}{\text{Average Investment in the Project}}$$

In the Garden Winery Company example, the total income from the project is \$3,300 over four years, or an average of \$825 per year. The average investment in the project, assuming straight-line depreciation, is \$5,000. Hence, the accounting rate of return is \$825/\$5,000, or 16.5 percent. The accounting rate of return pays no attention to the time value of money because it uses income, rather than cash flow, data.

The accounting rate of return suffers another shortcoming. Decreasing the denominator of a fraction increases its amount. Managers evaluated with ROI often fail to undertake profitable projects because undertaking them reduces ROI when the proposed project, although worthwhile for the firm, reduces the manager's current ROI. Residual income and economic value added (EVA) measures, discussed in Chapter 26, deal with this shortcoming of accounting rates of return.

One can easily compute the accounting rate of return and sometimes, by coincidence, it provides good answers for decision makers.

21.8 SUMMARY OF EVALUATION RULES

All modern firms should use methods for evaluating investment projects that take into account the time value of cash flows. All the methods that consider the time value of money require a cutoff rate or discount rate. To ensure optimal economic decisions, set the cutoff or discount rate equal to the cost of capital. If the firm uses its cost of capital rate to make decisions, then the net present value rule requires no more data nor computations than do the others. Moreover, using it will lead to decisions that will make present value of the firm's wealth equal to or larger than that from using any of the other rules.

21.9 SPECIAL PROBLEMS IN EVALUATING AND CHOOSING BETWEEN INVESTMENT PROJECTS

The preceding sections teach that the best decision rule for evaluating capital expenditures has the firm use the net present value of the project's cash flows and accept only when that number exceeds zero. This section discusses the use of that rule when several projects have positive net present values.

(a) CAPITAL RATIONING. A special problem arises in the context of capital rationing. Suppose that a manager faces a set of investment alternatives, each of which requires current cash outlays and has a positive net present value; the total capital outlay for all investments, however, requires more funds this year than higher management has authorized. For example, assume that senior management tells a manager to invest no more than $20,000 in projects and to use a 12 percent cost of capital. The manager has four projects, not mutually exclusive, to decide on, and may undertake any combination of these four, shown in Exhibit 21.6. The four projects do not interact with each other, aside from their demands on a common pool of available cash.

All four projects represent worthwhile investments, but the manager, given a $20,000 constraint on first-year cash outlays, may not undertake all of them. Juggling the possibilities, we can see from Exhibit 21.11 that the manager must choose one from several combinations of projects.

What is the manager to do? To maximize the net present values of the cash flows to the firm, the manager must choose the combination of projects A and C and reject the others. (Senior management will invest any funds not used for these four projects elsewhere in the firm and those funds will, presumably, earn the cost of capital.) The manager must reject the most profitable project per dollar of investment, project D, if the manager acts rationally within the capital constraints.

The problem arises from the inherent contradiction in telling a manager to use a cost of capital of, say, 12 percent while simultaneously limiting the capital budget. A limited capital budget implies a high, if not infinite, cost of capital for funds beyond the budget. With a budget constraint, senior management signals to the manager that funds in excess of $20,000 per year have such high cost that the manager should not consider spending more. But because all the firm's capital finances all its projects, then the higher cost of capital is the rate the manager (and the firm) should use for evaluating all potential investment projects. For these purposes, the cost of capital does not necessarily increase as the firm uses more capital. Using the cost of capital to calculate net present values of

Project Combinations (1)	Initial Cash Outlays (2)	Sum of Present Value of Cash Inflows (3)	Sum of Net Present Values (4)	Excess Present Value Index (5)
A, C	$19,000	$27,000	$8,000	1.42
A, D	15,000	22,500	7,500	1.50
B, C	18,000	25,000	7,000	1.39
B, D	14,000	20,500	6,500	1.46
C, D	10,000	15,500	5,500	1.55

EXHIBIT 21.11 DILEMMA CAUSED BY CAPITAL RATIONING

cash flows contains the only needed budgeting device: managers will not invest funds in projects returning less than the cost of capital because the net present values of such projects will be negative. Capital rationing has no place in a profit-seeking firm that chooses between investment alternatives by taking the time value of money into account. If management perceives a constraint on funds available for investment, then senior management should have all managers use a higher cost of capital than they had used before. If, when managers use the higher discount rate in evaluating projects, the total funds required still exceed the perceived constraints, then senior management should increase the discount rate to a still higher level. If, at the higher discount rate, managers would not use all of the available funds, senior management should reduce the rate.[3]

(b) RANKING PROJECTS. Some analysts classify capital budgeting decisions into one of three kinds:

1. Deciding whether to accept or reject investment projects–ones whose future cash flows are independent of each other
2. Choosing the best of a set of mutually exclusive projects
3. Ranking investments in order of desirability

The preceding discussion has dealt with all three of these kinds of decisions. The third kind of decision, ranking investments, does not, at least with current knowledge, have a general solution. A firm will find an investment project either acceptable or not: For a given discount rate, the project will have either a nonnegative net present value (so the firm accepts the project), or a negative net present value (so the firm doesn't accept the project). As between independent projects, all with nonnegative net present values computed for a given discount rate, we know no general rule for constructing a ranking. One can, however, vary the discount rate to learn which of the projects acceptable at a given discount rate will first become unacceptable as the rate increases.

21.10 SEPARATING THE INVESTMENT AND FINANCING DECISIONS

Sections 21.2 and 21.3 of this chapter pointed out that (1) a firm should undertake an investment project only if the project has a net present value greater than zero with cash flows discounted at the cost of capital and (2) the analyst should separate the investment decision from the financing decision. The preceding sections have analyzed the desirability of the net present value rule. This section illustrates the required separation of the purchase and financing decisions, by analyzing the factors in a decision of whether to lease or buy an asset.

Firms can acquire rights to use assets through long-term noncancelable leases. Leasing transactions pose two separate problems for managers: (1) whether to enter into the lease and (2) how to report the effects of leasing transactions in the financial statements. Readers will more easily understand the issues if we first discuss the financial accounting aspects of leases.

---

3. See H. Martin Weingartner, *Mathematical Programming and the Analysis of Capital Budgeting Problems* (Englewood Cliffs, NJ.: Prentice-Hall, 1963), for a discussion of the use of mathematical programming to deal with capital, and other, constraints in capital budgeting analyses. See also Fama and Miller, *The Theory of Finance,* pp. 134–137, for a criticism and discussion of Weingartner's suggestions. Asymmetric information sets can induce capital rationing. For a discussion of modern agency theory in this context, see Antonio E. Bernardo, et al., "Capital Budeting in Multidivisional Firms: Information, Agency and Incentives," *The Review of Financial Studies,* 17, 3 (2004).

We examine the accounting for leases in the context of the Garden Winery Company example introduced in Section 21.3. The Garden Winery Company project requires equipment that costs $10,000, that will last for four years, and that has zero expected salvage value at the end of the four-year period.

Assume that the Garden Winery Company can borrow for four years at 8 percent per year. The manufacturer is willing to sell the equipment for $10,000 or to lease it for four years on a noncancelable basis. That is, Garden Winery Company must make payments for four years no matter what. Garden Winery Company must pay for property taxes, maintenance, and repairs of the equipment under either the purchase or leasing plans.

Assume that Garden Winery, as lessee, signs the lease on December 31, 20X0, and commits to make lease payments on December 31, 20X1, 20X2, 20X3, and 20X4. In practice, leases usually specify payments made in advance, but assuming payments in arrears makes the computations simpler. Compound interest computations show that each of the lease payments, rounded to the nearest dollar, must be $3,019. The present value at December 31, 20X0, of $1 paid at the end of 20X1 and each of the next three years, is $3.31213 when the interest rate is 8 percent per year. (See Table 4 of the Appendix A to this Handbook.) Because the lease payments must have a present value of $10,000, each payment must be $3,018 (= $10,000/3.31213).

Analysts often mistakenly confuse the investment and the financing decisions in the context of making the lease-versus-purchase decision. A long-term noncancelable lease is a form of borrowing which is, in turn, a form of financing. Evaluating an asset acquisition, whether with explicit debt or with a lease, requires that one understand how to treat the financing cash flows. Under a noncancelable lease, the firm commits itself to payments over the term of the lease whether it continues to use the leased asset, or does not.

(a) MANAGERIAL EVALUATION OF NONCANCELABLE LEASES. Return to the example of the Garden Winery Company. The company has decided to acquire an asset with a four-year life, which costs $10,000 and which it will use to help bring a new variety of wine to the market. Assume that the manufacturer of the asset agrees to lease it to Garden Winery for four years with annual lease payments, in arrears, based on an 8 percent interest rate. If the interest rate implicit in the lease contract is 8 percent per year, then the annual lease payments, in arrears, are $3,019. Exhibit 21.12 shows the schedules of cash flows that will result from buying the asset outright and from leasing it for four years from the manufacturer.

(i) Case I: Purchase. *Case I* reproduces the information from Exhibits 21.1 and 21.3 that apply when the firm purchases the asset outright and discounts annual cash flows at 10 percent per year. The net present value of the investment project equals $687. Because the net present value exceeds zero, Garden Winery Company finds the project worth undertaking. The initial cash outflow is $10,000. In each of the following years, the cash flows consist of sales less cash operating expenses and income taxes.

(ii) Case II: Lease for Four Years. The *Case II* schedule in Exhibit 21.12 shows the net cash flows each year if the firm leases the asset and makes annual payments of $3,019, implying an interest rate of 8 percent per year. Column (2) shows the cash revenues less other cash expenses, just as with the purchased asset. Column (4) shows the annual lease payments, assumed to occur at the end of each year. Column (8) shows the pretax income, revenues minus lease payments. A taxpayer may deduct lease payments for tax purposes. Column (9) shows income tax expense, 40 percent of pretax income. Column (10) shows net income (for accounting purposes), and column (11) shows net cash inflows and outflows. With a leased asset, the firm has no depreciation so accounting income each year equals net cash flow each year. Finally, column (12) shows the present value of each of the cash flows discounted at 10 percent, the discount rate used by Garden Winery Company in making investment decisions. Notice that the net present value of the leasing plan equals $1,775, about 2.5 times larger than the net present value derived in case I for purchasing the asset.

Some managers would note the much larger net present value for the leasing plan and conclude that leasing surely dominates buying outright. *Comparing the net present values of the results in cases I and II, buying outright versus leasing, is invalid.* Doing so confounds the investment decision with the financing decision. A noncancelable lease is a form of borrowing. In case I, the firm does not borrow; in case II it borrows. To evaluate the leasing plan, the manager should construct a series of cash flows in which the firm borrows equivalent amounts of funds for the equivalent interest rates implicit in the lease contract and then compare a borrow-purchase alternative with the leasing alternative. Correct managerial decisions require comparable financing plans. Because the leasing contract effectively combines the financing and investment decisions, the valid alternative to leasing is a borrow-purchase alternative equivalent to leasing in terms of financing such as the alternative illustrated in case III.

(iii) Case III: Borrow for Four Years and Purchase. If the leasing company is willing to lend to Garden Winery Company at 8 percent per year, then the company can presumably borrow from a bank at 8 percent per year. The borrower can repay a loan of $10,000 by making four annual payments of $3,019 each.

Part of each payment to the bank applies toward interest and part applies toward principal prepayment. These amounts appear in columns (6) and (7) of Exhibit 21.12. To compute the deductible interest amounts for tax reporting requires separating the annual payment into interest and principal repayment, because the taxpayer can deduct interest expense, but not repayment of loan principal.

If the company borrows and purchases the asset, it will report depreciation each year identical with that if it purchases without borrowing. Column (3) shows the depreciation charges. In the case of borrow-purchase, pretax income is revenues less other cash expenses, column (2), less interest expense, column (5). Column (9) shows income taxes, which are 40 percent of pretax income. Net cash flow for the period shown in column (11) equals revenues less other cash expenses, column (2), less payments to the bank to service the debt, column (5), less income taxes, column (9). Column (12) shows the present values of each of the net cash flows discounted at 10 percent per year.

The net present value of the borrow-purchase alternative equals $1,806, which exceeds the net present value of the lease alternative because of the timing of income tax payments. In this illustration, borrowing turns out to be slightly superior to leasing as a form of financing.

(b) WHY DO LEASING AND BORROW-PURCHASE APPEAR MORE ATTRACTIVE THAN OUTRIGHT PURCHASE? Both leasing and borrow-purchase have net present values more than 2.5 times as large as the net present value of the outright purchase. Why? We can rephrase this issue to make the managerial implications clearer. Suppose that the analysis in case I, outright purchase, showed a negative net present value because the cash flow at the end of Year 1 is $4,000, $1,000 less than in the base example of Exhibit 21.12. Under this assumption, the project has a negative net present value in Case I, but

Garden Winery Company

Annual Net Cash Flows and Net Present Values of Alternatives Available for Acquiring Asset
(Discount Rate is 10 Percent per Year; Income Taxes are 40 Percent of Pretax Income)

End of Year (1)	Revenues Less Other Operating Cash Expenses[a] (2)	Depreciation[b] (3)	Lease Payments (4)	Payments to Service Debt: Total = (5)	Interest Expense[c] + (6)	Principal Repayment[d] (7)	Pretax Income[e] (8)	Income Tax Expense[f] (9)	Net Income[g] (10)	Net Cash Inflows (Outflows)[h] (11)	Present Value of Net Cash Flows at 10%[i] (12)
Case I: Purchase Assets; No Borrowing (See Exhibits 21.1 and 21.2)											
20X0 . . .	-	-	-	-	-	-	-	-	-	$(10,000)	$(10,000)
20X1 . . .	$ 5,000	$ 2,500	-	-	-	-	$2,500	$1,000	$1,500	4,000	3,636
20X2 . . .	4,000	2,500	-	-	-	-	1,500	600	900	3,400	2,810
20X3 . . .	3,500	2,500	-	-	-	-	1,000	400	600	3,100	2,329
20X4 . . .	3,000	2,500	-	-	-	-	500	200	300	2,800	1,912
	$15,500	$10,000					$5,500	$2,200	$3,300	$ 3,300	$ 687
Case II: Lease Asset; Lease Payments Imputed at 8 Percent Interest Rate; Four Payments in Arrears											
20X0 . . .	-	-	-	-	-	-	-	-	-	-	-
20X1 . . .	$ 5,000	-	$ 3,019	-	-		$1,981	$ 792	$1,189	$1,189	$1,081
20X2 . . .	4,000	-	3,019	-	-	-	981	392	589	589	486
20X3 . . .	3,500	-	3,019	-	-		481	193	288	288	216
20X4 . . .	3,000	-	3,019	-	-	-	(19)	(8)	(11)	(11)	(8)
	$15,500		$12,076				$3,424	$1,369	$2,055	$2,055	$1,775

Exhibit 21.12 Annual Net Cash Flows and Net Present Values of Alternatives Available for Acquiring Asset

End of Year (1)	Revenues Less Other Operating Cash Expenses[a] (2)	Deprecia-tion[a] (3)	Lease Payments (4)	Payments to Service Debt: Total = (5)	Interest Expense[a] + (6)	Principal Repay-ment[a] (7)	Pretax Income[e] (8)	Income Tax Expense[f] (9)	Net Income[g] (10)	Net Cash Inflows (Outflows)[h] (11)	Present Value of Net Cash Flows at 10%[i] (12)
Case III: Purchase Asset; Borrow $10,000 at 8 Percent to Be Repaid in Four Annual Installments											
20X0 . . .	-	-	-	-	-	-	-	-	-	$ 0[k]	$ 0[k]
20X1 . . .	$5,000	$ 2,500	-	$ 3,019	$ 800	$ 2,219	$1,700	$ 680	$1,020	1,301	1,183
20X2 . . .	4,000	2,500	-	3,019	622	2,397	878	351	527	630	521
20X3 . . .	3,500	2,500	-	3,019	431	2,588	569	228	341	253	190
20X4 . . .	3,000	2,500	-	3,019	223	2,796	277	110	167	(129)	(88)
	$15,500	$10,000		$12,076	$2,076	$10,000	$3,424	$1,369	$2,055	$2,055	$1,806

[a] Refer to Exhibit 21.1; the amounts shown here are the amounts in column (2) less the amounts shown in column (3) of Exhibit 21.1.

[b] Straight-line method; $10,000 cost/4-year life.

[c] Eight percent of outstanding loan. Outstanding loan is $10,000 less cumulative principal repayments shown in column (7).

[d] Lease payment ($3,019) less portion allocated to interest expense from column (6).

[e] Amount in column (2) less amounts in columns (3), (4), and (6).

[f] Forty percent of amount in column (8).

[g] Amount in column (8) less amount in column (9); or 60 percent of amount in column (8).

[h] Amount in column (2) less amounts in columns (4), (5), and (9).

[i] Amount in column (11) multiplied by present value factor for 10-percent discount rate: 1,000 for cash flow at end of 20X0, .90909 for cash flows at end of 20XI,.82644 for cash flows at end of 20X2,.75131 for cash flows at end of 20X3, and .68301 for cash flows at end of year 20X4. See Table 2 of the Appendix and Exhibit 21.3.

[j] By actual multiplication, this number is $192; rounding to the nearest dollar has caused the sum of numbers in this column to be in error by $1. This number has been changed to undo the rounding effects.

[k] At the end of 20X0, $10,000 is borrowed and used immediately to acquire asset; this number is +$10,000 – $10,000 = $0.

Exhibit 21.12 Annual Net Cash Flows and Net Present Values of Alternatives Available for Acquiring Asset *(Continued)*

will still show positive net present values in cases II and III. Both of the borrowing plans show a positive net present value that suggests the firm should undertake the project if it can finance with debt. What should the manager conclude?

The answers to both questions involve an understanding of the difference between the interest cost of debt and the cost of capital used in making investment decisions. In the illustration for Garden Winery Company, the after-tax cost of capital equals 10 percent, whereas the borrowing rate is 8 percent. (In general, the difference between these two rates is even larger than in this illustration. A difference of two percentage points is about as small as we would expect to see.)

In the analysis of both the leasing and borrow-purchase alternatives, the Company pays interest on borrowings at 8 percent, but discounts the cash flows at 10 percent. *Any time one discounts a series of interest payments with a rate larger than the borrowing rate, the present value of the loan payments will have a lower net present value than the face amount of the borrowing.* The excess represents the apparent benefits of financial leverage—borrowing at one rate (8 percent in the examples here) and investing the funds at a larger rate (10 percent in the examples here). Leverage appears to produce income effortlessly, but modern financial economics shows that the increase in risk that the borrowing imposes on the firm offsets the apparent benefit. Theorists argue whether increase in risk fully offsets the benefit.

The difference between the net present values of borrowing and outright purchase results from showing the expected returns to financial leverage as a part of the return to the specific project. But, of course, the firm always has the option to borrow at the current market rate of interest. The returns and risks of leverage accrue to the firm's financing policy as a whole, and the decision maker should not attribute that benefit to any one investment project.

Thus, we reach the conclusion that if the net present value for outright purchase is negative even though the net present value for one of the borrowing alternatives is positive, then the firm should not undertake the project. Lease contracts by their very nature involve a simultaneous consideration of investment and financing. Because the financial analysts cannot easily separate the two aspects, the analyst should first evaluate the project assuming outright purchase. Only after outright purchase appears worthwhile, because the project has a positive net present value, should the financial manager decide how to finance it. An analyst who knows the lease terms can ascertain the payment schedule for a conventional loan that is similar in terms of amounts borrowed and timing of repayments to that implied in the lease. Then the analyst can choose between the borrowing and leasing alternatives.[4]

---

4. The nature of leasing contracts can be somewhat more complicated than indicated here. For example, lease payments can be made in advance, with the initial lease payment being immediately deductible for tax purposes. It is not usually possible to arrange a straight loan with interest payable in advance that is deductible for tax purposes. (In theory, there is no such thing as interest paid in advance.) If payments are made before interest has accrued, then theory says that those payments must be a reduction in the principal amount of the loan, not interest. Another complication arises when the manufacturer offers a package deal where the combined interest payments and asset cost are together smaller than they would be separately. (Automobile dealers often are willing to sell at a lower price when the buyer borrows from the dealer than when the buyer makes an outright purchase.) The questions raised by some leasing contracts are beyond the scope of this discussion. The reader interested in a fuller discussion is referred to Chapter 8 of the *Handbook of Modern Accounting*, 2nd ed., edited by Sidney Davidson and Roman L. Weil (New York: McGraw-Hill Book Company, 1977).

Warning: The borrowing plan must be analogous to leasing. Take care in constructing the borrowing alternative to compare with the leasing alternative. Make the periodic payments under the assumed borrowing roughly equal to (or at least proportional to) the amounts of the assumed lease payments. If they are not, then the method illustrated will likely give the wrong answer. For example, if the proposed lease requires equal annual payments at the end of the year, then the assumed borrowing should resemble a mortgage (with equal annual payments) rather than a bond (with small periodic interest payments until maturity, when the entire principal comes due). If one compares bond-type borrowing to leasing, then borrowing would almost always appear preferable to leasing in the kind of analysis illustrated here. In a bond-type borrowing, the firm borrows for a longer period of time on average than in lease-type (or mortgage-type) borrowing. That is, in any period after the first, bond-type borrowing implies borrowing larger amounts than does lease-type borrowing. We have seen earlier that when one borrows at one rate and discounts the cash flows at a higher (cost of capital) rate, then a positive net present value—the benefits of leverage—will exist. Do not confound the benefits of leverage with the benefits of a specific project where the firm borrows no (or less) money.[5]

21.11 ANALYSES WITH UNCERTAIN FUTURE CASH FLOWS

Throughout, this chapter has assumed that projected cash flows are equally likely to occur. For example, the analysis in Exhibit 21.1 assumes that the $4,000 inflow at the end of year 1 is as likely to occur as the $2,800 inflow at the end of year 4. Equally likely projected cash flows also assume that the contemplated investment projects have equal risk, and that the risk for any one proposal equals the average risk in all activities of the firm. In practice, of course, such assumptions about the nature of investment projects will prove flawed. Theorists have proposed at least three solutions for dealing with the question of how to treat nonconstant risk in investment projects:

1. Change the discount rate used in computing net present values. As the cash flows from a project become more risky, use a higher discount rate.
2. Use a risk-free discount rate, rather than the cost of capital, in computing a net present value, and from it subtract a risk premium expressed in dollars.
3. Use the capital asset pricing model developed by Sharpe and others[6] to treat the portfolio of the investment projects as a portfolio of equity securities in modern portfolio theory.

Both of the first two methods have drawbacks in that no one has yet specified an analytical method for quantifying the risk in terms of increased discount rates on the one hand or in terms of the dollar risk premium on the other. The third method has stringent

5. Earlier, we pointed out that an exception arises for non-recourse loans. If a lender will finance a project while expecting debt service payments only from the project itself, without recourse to other assets of the firm, then proper analysis requires the simultaneous consideration of both the investing and financing decisions.
6. J. Lintner, "The Valuation of Risk Assets and the Selection of Risky Investments in Stock Portfolios and Capital Budgets," *Review of Economics and Statistics,* 47 (February 1965): 13–37; J. Mossin, "Equilibrium in a Capital Asset Market," *Econometrica* (October 1966): 768–775; W. F. Sharpe, "Capital Asset Prices: A Theory of Market Equilibrium Under Conditions of Risk," *Journal of Finance* (September 1964): 425–442.

data requirements and, so far as we know, has not withstood practical testing. For a description, see Chapters 10 through 12 of Bierman and Smidt.[7]

One could best summarize the current state of the art by saying that firms make capital budgeting decisions under the three assumptions listed above in this section; the decision makers will then modify the results as they choose, on the basis of intuition, experience, and judgment. Chapter 22 discusses some of the implementation issues of capital budgeting.

BIBLIOGRAPHY

Bierman, H., and S. Smidt. *The Capital Budgeting Decision,* 4th ed. New York: Macmillan Company, 1975.

Dean, Joel. *Capital Budgeting.* New York: Columbia University, 1951.

Fama, Eugene F. "Risk, Return and Equilibrium: Some Clarifying Comments." *Journal of Finance,* 23 (March 1968): 29–40.

______ and Merton H. Miller. *The Theory of Finance.* New York: Holt, Rinehart and Winston, 1972.

Fisher, Irving. *The Theory of Interest.* New York: Macmillan Company, 1930.

Hamada, R. S. "Portfolio Analysis, Market Equilibrium, and Corporation Finance." *Journal of Finance,* 24 (March 1969): 13–31.

Hirshleifer, Jack. "On the Theory of Optimal Investment Decision." *Journal of Political Economy* (August 1958): 329–352.

Klammer, Thomas. "Empirical Evidence of the Adoption of Sophisticated Capital Budgeting Techniques." *Journal of Business,* 45 (July 1972): 393.

Lintner, J. "The Valuation of Risk Assets and the Selection of Risky Investments in Stock Portfolios and Capital Budgets." *Review of Economics and Statistics,* 47 (February 1965): 13–37.

Lorie, J. H., and L. J. Savage:. "Three Problems in Capital Rationing." *Journal of Business* (October 1955): 229–239.

Lutz, Friedrich, and Vera Lutz. *The Theory of Investment of the Firm,* Princeton, N.J.: Princeton University Press, 1951.

Mossin, J. "Equilibrium in a Capital Asset Market." *Econometrica* (October 1966): 768–775.

Sharpe, W. F. "Capital Asset Prices: A Theory of Market Equilibrium Under Conditions of Risk." *Journal of Finance* (September 1964): 425–442.

Solomon, Ezra, ed. *The Management of Corporate Capital.* New York: Free Press, 1959.

Weingartner, H. Martin. *Mathematical Programming and the Analysis of Capital Budgeting Problems.* Englewood Cliffs, N.J.: Prentice-Hall, 1963.

---

7. H. Bierman and S. Smidt, *The Capital Budgeting Decision,* 4th ed. (New York: Macmillan Company, 1975), chaps. 10–12.

CHAPTER 22

CAPITAL BUDGETING: IMPLEMENTATION*

ROMAN L. WEIL, PHD, CPA, CMA, EDITOR
University of Chicago

CONTENTS

22.1 INTRODUCTION 611

22.2 PITFALLS OF TRADITIONAL CAPITAL BUDGETING 612
(a) Poor Capital Acquisition Planning 612
(b) Inadequate Justification Analysis 614
(c) Negligible Post-Implementation Evaluation 618
(d) Inadequate Capital Budgeting Infrastructure 618

22.3 INVESTMENT MANAGEMENT 619

22.4 INVESTMENT MANAGEMENT GUIDING PRINCIPLES 619
(a) Principle #1: Relate Investment Decisions to Strategic Plans and Operational Goals 620
(b) Principle #2: Invest in Integrated Technology 620
(c) Principle #3: Evaluate Investment Alternatives Consistently 620
(d) Principle #4: Evaluate Investments by Financial and Nonfinancial Criteria 620
(e) Principle #5: Assess Risk 620
(f) Principle #6: Use Cost and Performance Data 621

22.5 INVESTMENT MANAGEMENT FRAMEWORK 621
(a) Strategic Planning 621
(b) Investment Portfolio Development 622
(c) Decision Analysis 623
(d) Execution and Tracking 625

22.6 SUMMARY 625

22.1 INTRODUCTION

A company's long-term survival and prosperity requires capital budgeting. For some managers, this practice has often involved striking a balance between logical reasoning and blind faith. This results from managers' erroneous belief that the future will resemble the present.[1]

---

* Brad Anderson, formerly of Ernst & Young, Irvine TX, wrote the original version of this chapter. Weil joined the effort several years ago, so that the chapter that appears here is a joint product. We have made several unsuccessful attempts to locate Brad Anderson. If he will come forward, we can put his name in its rightful place as top-listed author of this chapter.

1. Robert H. Hayes and David A. Garvin, "Managing As If Tomorrow Mattered," *Harvard Business Review* (May–June 1982), p.70.

This chapter addresses the pitfalls that can prevent traditional capital budgeting programs from achieving their goals and proposes a framework for a broader process of investment management. The chapter serves as an implementation guide for the methods discussed in Chapter 21, Capital Budgeting: Concepts and Methods.

22.2 PITFALLS OF TRADITIONAL CAPITAL BUDGETING

To have success with capital budgeting programs, companies must plan, justify, and, after implementing, evaluate them. In addition, companies need an adequate capital budgeting infrastructure to manage the process and to ensure that they realize the value sought from acquiring capital assets. Companies fall victim to four primary pitfalls when they approach capital budgeting in the traditional manner (see Exhibit 22.1):

- Poor capital acquisition planning
- Inadequate justification analysis
- Negligible post-implementation evaluation
- Inadequate capital budgeting infrastructure

(a) POOR CAPITAL ACQUISITION PLANNING. At the beginning of the capital budgeting process, companies sometimes do not properly plan their capital acquisitions. Sometimes the failure stems from a myopic focus on quickly realizing the potential value of the acquired capital assets. Focusing on the value of asset acquisition in isolation can disrupt a company's long-term health, especially if the acquisition does not align with the company's strategic direction or management cannot effectively integrate it with other assets.

(i) Nonalignment of Investment Decision with Company Strategy. One might suppose that a company acquiring a new capital asset would decide to do so based on the company's

Poor Capital Acquisition Planning	Inadequate Justification Analysis	Negligible Post-Implementation Evaluation	Inadequate Capital Budgeting Infrastructure
• Non-alignment of investment decision with company strategy • Failure to integrate capital budget with expense budget • Lack of portfolio approach • Limited vision of future technology advancements • Failure to establish performance targets • Failure to identify all capital requirements	• Evaluation against wrong baseline • Poorly understood cost behavior patterns • Excessively high hurdle rates • Inadequate treatment of risk	• Inadequate post-implementation audits • Failure to monitor performance targets	• Cumbersome policies and procedures • Decision authority that limits investment vision • Lack of understanding by finance of the drivers of cost • Mismatch of finance and technical knowledge

EXHIBIT 22.1 PITFALLS OF TRADITIONAL CAPITAL BUDGETING

strategic requirements. Companies often choose between investment options solely according to the net present value derived from discounted cash flows (DCF), ignoring value-generating projects with hard-to-estimate future cash flows but with strategic directional considerations for the firm.[2] Because net present value calculations require estimates of future cash flows, companies with this mindset gravitate toward asset acquisitions where they can project cash flow streams.

This approach often fails for two types of companies:

1. High-tech companies that need significant capital infrastructure to support new product development
2. Manufacturing companies that might want to employ flexible manufacturing systems to improve their flexibility and ability to respond quickly to market changes

(ii) Failure to Integrate Capital Budget with Expense Budget. A company's capital budget and its expense budgets typically result from separate decision-making processes. Yet, most capital acquisition decisions depend on reducing operating expenses to generate positive cash flows. For example, in deciding whether to acquire a new machine, the manager will often make assumptions about its ability to reduce the cost of supplies and materials for manufacturing operations. The production line manager, however, manages the budget for these expenses. If that manager does not make the annual budget for the production line reflect this reduction, then the firm will not realize all the benefits of acquiring the new machine. If top management undertakes companywide cost reduction efforts, the capital budgeter will overestimate the asset's beneficial impact.[3]

(iii) Lack of Portfolio Approach. Decisions to invest in a project require consideration of all alternative projects. (See Chapter 21's discussion of mutually exclusive projects in the context of the internal rate of return.) Some companies err by comparing a proposal against the status quo. The decision maker, to make sound decisions, must also analyze the opportunity costs of not investing. Consider, for example, a company contemplating the installation of a flexible manufacturing system in one of its manufacturing plants. It has three mutually exclusive courses of action:

- Invest in the project
- Retain the status quo
- Liquidate the plant's assets to use the harvested funds in other areas of the company

If the firm decides to invest, then the company must decide when to invest in the new project. Once it actually invests in the project, it has effectively killed its options (mutually exclusive alternatives) to invest at other times. A company must weigh the decision to invest now against the possibility of waiting for new information that could affect the desirability of investing at all or the timing of the investment, or both.[4]

2. John P. Van Blois, "Economic Models: The Future of Robotic Justification," Thirteenth ISIR/Robots 7 Conference, April 17–21, 1983
3. John A. Boquist, Todd T. Milbourn, and Anjan V. Thakor, "How Do You Win The Capital Allocation Game?" *Sloan Management Review* (Winter 1998), p. 59.
4. Avinash K. Dixit and Robert S. Pindyck, "The Options Approach to Capital Investment," *Harvard Business Review* (May–June 1995).

(iv) Limited Vision of Future Technology Advancements. Companies face global competition, deregulation, and rising customer demands. To survive in this climate, most firms must foresee and then use some of the new technologies that will emerge as time passes. Realizing such benefits can take years. Companies that choose investments solely using DCF techniques may implicitly reject, because they ignored, projects that would ensure their competitive position within the marketplace in the years to come. Companies should make current assumptions about future technologies and should consider the infrastructure capital requirements needed today to employ such advanced technologies in the future.

(v) Failure to Establish Performance Targets. During an investment's planning phase, a company should set performance targets so it can measure the success or failure of the project against the strategic objectives that management expected it to achieve. Typical performance target criteria include the following:

- Improved customer satisfaction
- Reduced operating cost
- Improved quality or production yields
- Reduced operational cycle time
- Improved economic value added (EVA) measures

If management fails to establish targets during the planning phase, management cannot easily, later, decide whether the project, once undertaken, meets planned objectives. Major undertakings, such as installing a flexible manufacturing system, may take years for general payback on investment. The firm needs a memory to evaluate such long-ago decisions.

(vi) Failure to Identify All Capital Requirements. A successful capital budgeting decision requires the manager to account for all input variables, including funds needed to generate information (e.g., for market research, prototype development, and testing).[5] Further, the company must assess the cash needed to provide sufficient staff and to teach them how to work with the new asset. For example, a company seeking to implement a new Spanish- and English-speaking customer-service call center would need to ensure that the local job market offers sufficient bilingual workers with appropriate technical skills or the capacity to learn them, within the cash budgets planned for those workers.

(b) INADEQUATE JUSTIFICATION ANALYSIS. A successful capital budgeting program requires that a company choose between investment alternatives. The analysts must understand the cost drivers to project cash flows for a potential investment. Additionally, the analysts must project cash flows of the no-investment option. Some companies set hurdle rates too high or ignore the varying aspects of risk inherent in each investment decision, or both.

(i) Evaluation Against Wrong Baseline. To assess the cash flows for a potential investment, a firm typically considers the projected incremental cash flows from investing in the project against the option of not investing at all. The firm may err in assuming that

5. John A. Boquist, Todd T. Milbourn, and Anjan V. Thakor, "How Do You Win The Capital Allocation Game?" *Sloan Management Review* (Winter 1998), p.59.

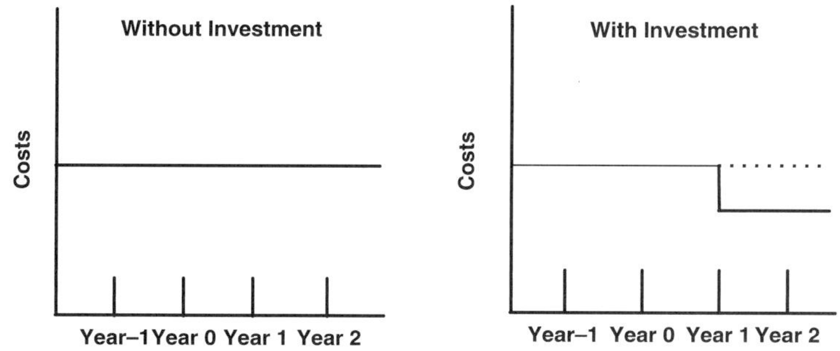

EXHIBIT 22.2 TRADITIONAL ASSUMPTIONS OF COST REDUCTION SAVINGS

the status quo of the industry and of the firm will remain constant throughout the investment's projected life. (see Exhibit 22.2). Industry conditions and machine performance degradation and maintenance costs will likely change. If the company does not initiate the project, competitors could initiate similar ventures that can alter the nature of the industry.[6] Thus, the firm should employ a moving baseline approach in which it compares the cash flows of the investment alternative to those of the status quo, taking into account projections of industry and machine performance. Exhibit 22.3 shows the effects of moving baselines, discussed next.

(ii) Poorly Understood Cost-Behavior Patterns. Any capital budgeting decision embodies assumptions about changes in cost. Making realistic assumptions becomes more difficult as

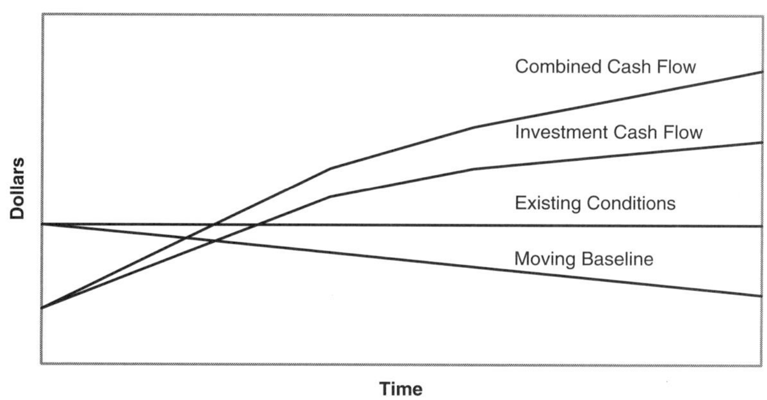

EXHIBIT 22.3 THE EFFECT THE MOVING BASELINE HAS ON INVESTMENT DECISIONS

6. David H. Sinason, "A Dynamic Model For Present Value Capital Expenditure Analysis," Emerging Practices in Cost Management, 1992.

overhead and research and development (R&D) costs become a larger portion of total operating expenditures.[7]

Traditional cost accounting systems have the following shortcomings for supporting the capital budgeting process:

- The systems fail to reflect development or selling, general and administrative (SG&A) costs in product-line profitability.
- They distort product line costs as a result of arbitrary allocation of overhead.
- Lack of focus on cause and effect causes inability to identify cost drivers.
- Nonfinancial measures (e.g., cycle time, quality, customer satisfaction, flexibility) are not quantified.
- The systems fail to support the justification of new investments and to monitor the benefits obtained
- They make it difficult to integrate analysis of business processes that vary across divisions of a given firm.

To make effective capital budgeting decisions, firms must develop cost information that will enable quantification of cash flows associated with large-scale investments, including the indirect benefits on cash flow from improved quality and better customer service. To this end, many companies employ activity-based costing systems that assign overhead expenditures to product lines (the specific cost objects in this application of ABC) by looking at the resource consumed by various activities, as shown in Exhibit 22.4. With this cause-and-effect method, a company can assess the changes in cost cash flows expected from a new capital investment.

(iii) Excessively High Hurdle Rates. Companies that employ DCF techniques to rank investment alternatives will erroneously reject projects by setting hurdle rates too high.

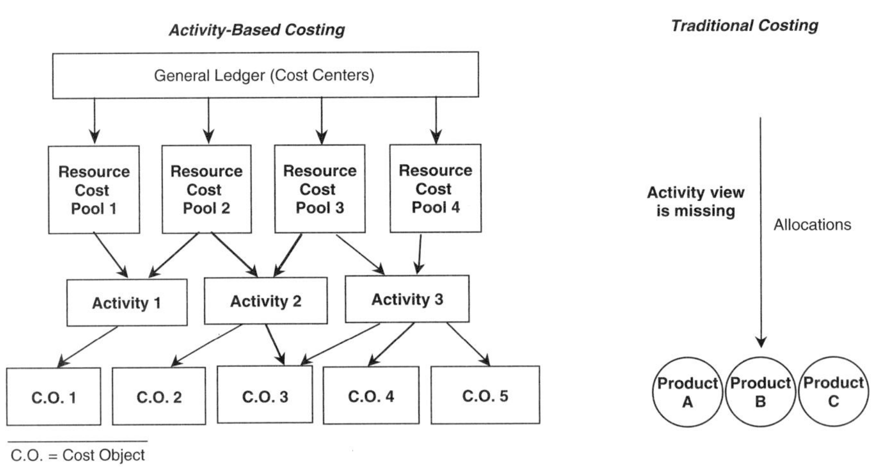

EXHIBIT 22.4 ACTIVITY-BASED COSTING MORE ACCURATELY ASSIGNS COSTS

7. Suresh Kalagnananam and Suzanne K. Schmidt, "Analyzing Capital Investment in New Products," *Management Accounting* (January 1996).

Setting high rates will ensure that it will select only high-value projects, but also that the company will narrow the range of projects that can meet the acceptance criteria. By choosing projects only when they have high returns, companies risk foregoing investing in advanced technologies that could enhance their position in the marketplace.[8]

(iv) Inadequate Treatment of Risk. In financial markets, an investment has an expected return that reflects its inherent risk. For example, government bonds provide only a small return on investment because of the low probability that the government will default on making debt service payments. Bonds offering a higher return, such as the so-called *junk bonds,* have a greater potential of default. Companies making investment decisions should weigh the risk and expected returns from each alternative. For example, two projects may present similar net present value calculations. But the first requires development of a new technology, while the second uses technology currently available. The evaluation of the first project should include some assessment of the risk of not successfully developing the new technology. In evaluating risks, companies may fall into one or more of the following traps:[9]

- *Evaluating all business units' strategies and acquisitions against a single hurdle rate.* Using a single hurdle rate overstates the riskiness of low-risk business units and understates the riskiness of high-risk business units.
- *Adding extra points to the hurdle rate for safety.* Uniformly padding the hurdle rate for all proposals eliminates investments with lower returns on investment. It does not guard against differential project risk.
- *Using a cost of capital that reflects total risk rather than systematic risk.* To minimize the risk of owning any one stock, investors diversify their investment portfolios with several stocks. Although this strategy reduces exposure to the *specific* risk of the individual stock, it still leaves the investor exposed to the risk *systematic* to the market. Because investors can diversify away from specific risk, they receive compensation only for the systematic risk that they cannot diversify away. Companies face a similar dilemma. By investing in several projects, a company may diversify its exposure to the risk of one investment. In making an investment decision, a company should use a cost of capital that reflects the systematic risk.
- *Deeming the cost of investment-specific financing as the cost of capital.* Debt costs less than equity. A company may err in using a specific debt financing's interest cost, a rate less than the overall firm's cost of capital, in selecting a project. All of a firm's equities finance all of its assets, so the firm should use the overall average cost of capital when it seeks such a rate for discounting. Only when the lenders for a specific debt financing have no recourse to the borrowing firm's assets, but can claim cash flows for debt service only from the specific project's cash flows, should the firm use the specific debt financing's rate in its calculations. Chapter 21 illustrates the pitfalls in intermixing investment and financing decisions.
- *Adopting identical target capital structures for every business unit.* Because business units have different risks and strategies, the capital structure differs among

8. Callie B. Henkel and James A. Brimson, "Cost Management for Today's Advanced Manufacturing," *Harvard Business School Press* (1998), p.17.
9. Philip J. Eynon, "Avoiding the Seven Sins of Strategic Risk Analysis," *Emerging Practices in Cost Management* (1992).

them. The hurdle rate established for each business unit should reflect its individual capital structure, not the capital structure of the company as a whole.

(c) NEGLIGIBLE POST-IMPLEMENTATION EVALUATION. The size and irreversible nature of many projects make post-implementation evaluation difficult, especially for enterprisewide initiatives such as an implementation of a material resources planning system, where the costs and benefits become entangled in the operations of the business. Companies add to their burden by not appropriately conducting post-implementation audits and by not establishing performance measures for monitoring project performance.

(i) Inadequate Post-Implementation Audits. Firms often ignore, or inadequately perform, the post-implementation evaluation. Project auditors may make the mistake of comparing only the costs and benefits projected from the original project justification, ignoring the unanticipated costs and benefits that have occurred since the inception of the project.[10]

(ii) Neglect to Monitor Performance Targets. Some managers ignore performance targets established during the planning phase of the project by the time the project goes forward. This typically occurs because the company's cost management and performance measurement system cannot monitor performance adequately. For example, a recently installed production line aims to reduce total operating expenditures by 20 percent. If the company employs a standard direct costing system, then assessing the cost reduction of *direct* expenditures such as direct labor presents no difficulty. But it loses track of the additional *indirect* costs of items such as human resource department-provided employee training and expensive facility space within the overhead allocation rates.

(d) INADEQUATE CAPITAL BUDGETING INFRASTRUCTURE. The responsibility for capital budgeting traditionally falls to a firm's finance department. In many companies, the finance function cannot excel at this service because it lacks both cost management and operational business knowledge. In addition to the finance function's shortcomings, cumbersome policies and procedures may cause delays in the capital budgeting process.

(i) Cumbersome Policies and Procedures. Policies and procedures for governing the capital budgeting process should ensure two things: first, that someone has responsibility for due diligence as part of the analysis of the investment option and, second, that the appropriate authorities sign off on the decision. However, these policies and procedures may cause the organization to fall into a state of *analysis paralysis* whereby the investment analysis gets bogged down in a tangle of red tape. Not only can bureaucratic requirements delay the start of the project, but it can also consume resources that reduce the benefits projected. Companies should design their policies and procedures to ensure that they support investment analysis in a timely fashion.

(ii) Decision Authority that Limits Investment Vision. To expedite the capital budgeting process, a company may specify ever-higher levels of decision authority related to ever-higher amounts of capital outlays. For example, a product line manager might have authorization to implement capital projects that do not exceed $25,000, while the plant manager may implement capital projects up to $100,000. This decision authority structure

10. Ed Heard, "The Cost Justification Charade," *Journal of Cost Management* (Spring 1996).

can cause managers to limit their focus to just those projects that fall within their authorization level.

(iii) Lack of Understanding by Finance Department of the Drivers of Cost. Traditionally, the finance function provides monthly financial reporting and budget analysis but often ignores the responsibility for, or inadequately staffs, cost management. Without an understanding of the business drivers of cost, the finance function cannot adequately support analysis of projected investment cash flows. For example, in the insurance industry, cost management emphasizes the actuarial function's ability to forecast expected losses from claims. Since losses from claims typically account for 70 percent of total expenditures, managers view the remaining 30 percent of operating expenditures as less significant. For this reason many insurance companies do not have an adequate cost management infrastructure that focuses on identifying and minimizing the drivers of cost. For example, Caterpillar has 200 accountants who work full time to help the manufacturing units solve problems.[11]

(iv) Mismatch of Finance and Technical Knowledge. Sound financial analysis must integrate with operational business knowledge. A company's technical specialists (i.e., marketers, engineers, and information technology specialists) who conceive project ideas lack the financial experience to adequately assess project requirements. Conversely, finance personnel sophisticated in capital budgeting techniques lack operational knowledge.[12] This mismatch may lead to delays in the capital budgeting process or provide insufficient justification analysis. It can also lead to a mistrust between the operational units and finance department: the operational units may contend that the finance department arbitrarily sets roadblocks, while finance personnel may believe that the operational functions carelessly select their projects.[13]

22.3 INVESTMENT MANAGEMENT

Investment management provides a holistic approach for capital budgeting. This process-driven approach focuses on identifying, evaluating, and implementing both new activities and alternative ways to perform existing activities to improve the future performance of the firm.[14] Investment management rests on the premise that companies achieve strategic success by making sound investment decisions. Thus, companies should align investment decisions with strategic goals and operational objectives, and managers must ensure that investments perform to expectations.

22.4 INVESTMENT MANAGEMENT GUIDING PRINCIPLES

In their book *Cost Management for Today's Advanced Manufacturing,* Callie B. Henkel and James A. Brimson offer some general principles that companies should consider

11. L. Jones, "Justifying and Monitoring a $1.5 Billion Manufacturing Revolution at Caterpillar," *Corporate Controller* (July–August 1990), p.21.
12. Ed Heard, "The Cost Justification Charad," *Journal of Cost Management* (Spring 1996).
13. David Dugdale and Colwyn Jones, "Finance, Strategy, and Trust in Investment Decision-Making," *Emerging Practices in Cost Management* (1996).
14. Callie B. Henkel and James A. Brimson, "Cost Management for Today's Advanced Manufacturing," *Harvard Business School Press* (1998), p.17.

when developing an investment portfolio. Although they originally geared these principles toward manufacturing companies, the principles apply to all industries. They hold true especially for information technology investments, such as a payroll processing systems or data warehouses.

(a) PRINCIPLE #1: RELATE INVESTMENT DECISIONS TO STRATEGIC PLANS AND OPERATIONAL GOALS. Management theory suggests that success requires that a company have a sound strategic plan. To meet strategic initiatives, firms must make the right decisions on capital deployment. Thus, the investment portfolio should grow directly out of the strategic planning process. Additionally, since the firm targets operational goals with its strategic analysis, management should link investment selection, implementation, and measurement closely to operations. In this way, a firm can verify that the investment decisions made align with its short-term operating goals and long-term strategic vision.

(b) PRINCIPLE #2: INVEST IN INTEGRATED TECHNOLOGY. Consider technology investments as interrelated elements rather than as individual projects. In analyzing a technology investment, firms must ascertain the technology's synergistic impact on other currently deployed capital. For example, a company that invests in a flexible manufacturing system must assess its effects on legacy technology systems that handle procurement and production planning information.

(c) PRINCIPLE #3: EVALUATE INVESTMENT ALTERNATIVES CONSISTENTLY. Use a consistent method to evaluate investment alternatives. Chapter 21 attempts to persuade readers that the net present value (NPV) rule dominates, in the sense that it gives results never worse and often better, than does the internal rate of return (IRR) rule. Even so, some firms still use IRR. The policy should set the acceptance criteria (i.e., NPV, IRR) for companywide use and the extent to which management will evaluate the decision makers with nonfinancial performance measures (such as quality yields and customer satisfaction). The policy aims to ensure that investments meet the firm's strategic goals.

(d) PRINCIPLE #4: EVALUATE INVESTMENTS BY FINANCIAL AND NONFINANCIAL CRITERIA. Firms should evaluate investments with qualitative and nonfinancial quantitative criteria, as well as with traditional financial criteria, such as return on investment. Because these measures rate only one aspect of an investment's potential performance, a firm should incorporate other measurement criteria to align the chosen investment alternative with the designated strategic direction. For example, a strategic objective of high-quality products may dictate the purchase of a piece of production equipment that does not clear the firm's preset hurdle rate, but that raises the production yield percentage from 80 percent to 95 percent.

(e) PRINCIPLE #5: ASSESS RISK. Any investment decision carries a risk of project failure. Companies should develop their investment portfolios with assumptions about risk for the investment strategy overall and for individual project alternatives. Assess risk for the following three categories:

1. *Economic risk.* The risk of not achieving projected economic benefits.
2. *Technological risk.* The risk of depending on technology that the company cannot procure from an outside vendor or through internal development.
3. *Implementation risk.* The risk of not effectively implementing an investment because of barriers caused by human behavior or organizational factors.

(f) PRINCIPLE #6: USE COST AND PERFORMANCE DATA. The typical investment decision aims to achieve cost savings and operational improvements. To ensure that an investment meets these objectives, firms must develop and implement effective cost management and performance measurement systems. Such systems will provide management the feedback to verify that the investment performs as expected.

22.5 INVESTMENT MANAGEMENT FRAMEWORK

The investment management framework should attempt to achieve the following:

- Select an investment portfolio that aligns with the firm's strategic objectives.
- Evaluate the inherent risk of each investment alternative and the impact on future technology options.
- Provide a cost management and performance measurement infrastructure that supports the comparison, evaluation, selection, and measurement of capital investments.
- Supply management with a complete set of tools for managing the investment portfolio.
- Improve future strategic initiatives and investment planning by learning from previous experience.

This investment management framework comprises four main phases, discussed in the following sections: strategic planning, investment portfolio development, decision analysis, and execution and tracking (see Exhibit 22.5).[15]

(a) STRATEGIC PLANNING. Before the investment selection and evaluation process can begin, a firm must set its competitive strategy. Management at both the corporate and business-unit level should understand the strategic vision so they can make appropriate decisions about capital investments. Management should make capital investments only

Phase	Steps
Strategic Planning	• Perform strategy position assessment • Define strategic goals • Set operational business objectives • Establish performance targets
Investment Portfolio Development	• Identify costs and cost drivers affected • Identify alternative approaches • Identify resource constraints • Identify candidate technologies
Decision Analysis	• Assess risks • Evaluate investment alternatives
Execution and Tracking	• Integrate investment management into cost management system • Establish performance tracking system

EXHIBIT 22.5 INVESTMENT MANAGEMENT FRAMEWORK

15. Thomas Klammer, *Managing Strategic and Capital Investment Decisions,* (Burr Ridge, IL: Irwin Professional Publishing, 1993).

when they link with the strategic goals and operational business objectives that the company pursues. For example, a company has a strategic goal of being recognized as being a low-cost producer within its industry. To accomplish this, the company establishes operational objectives that support this strategic goal. Examples include "reduce cost per product by 10 percent" and "increase production throughput by 20 percent." The company might decline an investment that would allow it to provide customized products, which sell at a higher price, but which conflict with strategy. Any investments that affect the manufacture of products should in some way support the achievement of these operational objectives and the overriding strategic goal. In addition, management must establish both financial and nonfinancial performance targets to adequately measure project implementation success, as shown in Exhibit 22.6.

(i) Perform Strategy Position Assessment. To define strategic direction, firms must first assess their competitive position in the marketplace. This analysis should cover the business environment, core competencies and capabilities, and competitive advantages.

(ii) Define Strategic Goals. After assessing its position within the marketplace, a firm must identify the strategic goals that will chart its future direction. Typical strategic goals relate to a company's desired competitive performance in the areas of cost, quality, and customer satisfaction. In selecting investment portfolios, companies should align investments with the strategic goals pursued.

(iii) Set Operational Business Objectives. Operational business objectives provide the short-term milestones that help a company achieve its long-term strategic goals. Managers typically derive operational objectives at the business-unit level. Sample objectives include reducing operating overhead, improving quality yields, and increasing production and sales volumes.

(iv) Establish Performance Targets. Often, only those things that get measured, get done. To ascertain if the firm achieves its strategic goals, a firm must establish detailed performance targets that reflect its operational business objectives. Performance targets include specific reductions in cost per product, percentage increases in production quality yields, volume increases in production throughput, and decreases in the cycle time required to deliver goods or services to the customer.

(b) INVESTMENT PORTFOLIO DEVELOPMENT. Developing successful investment portfolios parallels an effective strategic planning process. Firms can develop investment

Strategic Goals:	Cost competitiveness	Market leadership in customer satisfaction
Business Objectives:	Reduce operating overhead	Increase customer satisfaction
Performance Targets:	• Reduce product cost by 10% • Increase production throughput by 20%	• Decrease cycle time to delivery by 15% • Decrease product defects by 5%

EXHIBIT 22.6 STRATEGIC PLANNING PROCESS

portfolios in two ways. In the first, a top-down approach, the firm selects investment portfolios at the corporate level during the development of the strategic plan. The second, bottom-up approach, develops investment portfolios by consolidating the investment requirements supplied by the various business units.

(i) Identify Costs and Cost Drivers Affected. Typically, an investment project aims to reduce costs. To target accurately the costs that an investment will affect, a firm must first understand its cost drivers and resulting costs. In defining the investment portfolio, the firm should examine non-value-added costs, such as product rework, and cost drivers, such as equipment down time, to find costs that it can eliminate or reduce.

(ii) Identify Alternative Approaches. To meet the strategic plan, a company should ascertain the alternative investment approaches that it can pursue. These may include developing the capital asset internally or purchasing from an outside vendor. The company should also include an analysis of not investing at all. However, to measure cash flows accurately for the "do nothing" scenario, it should include assumptions about declining productive output and the maintenance costs of currently employed assets. A company cannot make the false assumption that current operations will continue, as is, indefinitely.

(iii) Identify Resource Constraints. The ideal investment portfolio implements projects using current resources. Sometimes, they cannot. For instance, a company weighing different information technology systems must ascertain whether its current technical personnel can implement the plans or whether it will require new technical expertise. The company must include assumptions about resource constraints and costs of expanding beyond them for each investment alternative.

(iv) Identify Candidate Technologies. Decision makers must assess technologies and their impact on currently employed capital assets. Many industries, for example, now use enterprise resource planning (ERP) information system implementations, such as SAP, Oracle, and PeopleSoft. Companies must evaluate these technologies for their projected benefits and their ability to interface with existing systems. Employing these technologies may require additional capital investments in information technology infrastructure. Additionally, a company must make assumptions about future technological advances. Without this kind of planning, a company risks losing its position in the market to competitors able to implement and operate new technology.

(c) DECISION ANALYSIS. Successful management of investment processes requires decision analysis. A company may successfully select its strategic direction but then erroneously choose and implement a capital asset that fails to accomplish its purpose. In recent years, failed ERP implementations by companies that inadequately assessed the risks and costs of moving to an enterprisewide information system platform have resulted from poor investment decision analysis. Too often the proposed benefits of a project blinds management to the inherent risks and costs involved. A company may also analyze investment alternatives improperly by not using consistent evaluation criteria and techniques.

(i) Assess Risks. For each investment alternative, the company should assess the impact of the economic, technological, and human resource risks on project success.

The company bears the economic risk that a project will not produce its anticipated economic benefits. Technological risk refers to the possibility that the firm cannot develop or purchase or implement the required technology. Human resource risk relates to a company's potential inability to implement an investment because of barriers, such as a lack of technical knowledge or employees' resistance to change. The company should establish a risk management plan to reduce each risk identified. For example, some firms successfully use a change-management program, which supports employee acceptance of new assets, to reduce human resource risks.

(ii) Evaluate Investment Alternatives. To ensure a consistent evaluation process that will result in work products comparable to one another, companies should follow three steps:

1. *Establish investment critical success factors (CSFs).* Information on strategies, performance criteria, markets, competitors, and so on help analysts derive potential measures of success. As an example of a CSF, consider a new machine for a production line that the firm must have operational within, say, six months to take advantage of projected market conditions. The decision makers would drop from the analysis any machines that cannot meet this CSF.
2. *Use consistent evaluation criteria and analysis tools.* Compare investment alternatives on a consistent basis. For example, if the firm uses the NPV selection criterion, then analysts should use it to analyze all investment alternatives. Use consistent tools such as the NPV distribution-strategy grid, which shows the range of NPV values of projects for varying levels of risk (see Exhibit 22.7).
3. *Assess impact on processes and activities.* Companies that employ activity-based costing systems can identify activities and processes that implementation of the new asset will affect. Without activity-based costing, a company trying to decide if it should implement a new production line may analyze the cash flows associated only with the new line. Implementing the new line will drive up the human resource department's activity cost of staffing and training. The analysis should include these increases in cash outflows.

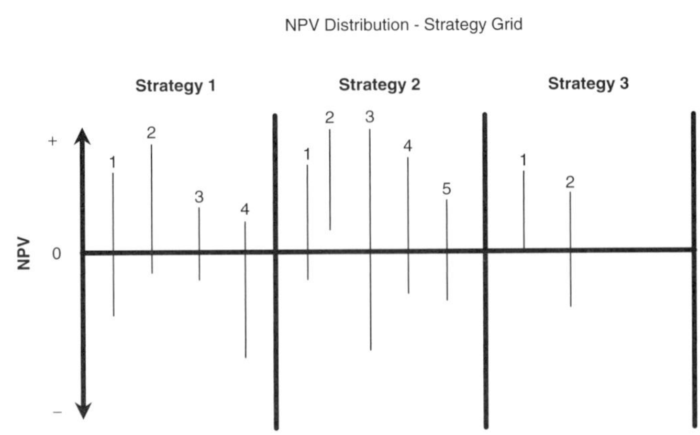

EXHIBIT 22.7 NET PRESENT VALUE DISTRIBUTION OF INVESTMENTS FOR VARIOUS LEVELS OF RISK

(d) EXECUTION AND TRACKING. The last phase includes execution and tracking, which provides managers the opportunity to learn from outcomes of the company's current investments in order to make better investment decisions in the future. But to invest more wisely, companies must go beyond the traditional post-capital budgeting audit by integrating the investment management process directly into their cost management system. Further, they should employ performance-tracking systems that enable managers to monitor the benefits achieved by each investment.

(i) Integrate Investment Management into the Cost Management System. Do not conduct the investment management process in isolation. Integrating the investment management process into the cost management system provides the bridge between the capital and expense budget. Cost center managers who understand the projected benefits of an investment can manage their cost structure accordingly or identify problems that require resolution.

(ii) Establish Performance Tracking System. To monitor a project's progress, companies should employ continuous tracking systems that go beyond periodic post-implementation audits. In addition, managers should have ready access to information from the performance tracking system, which allows them to respond to variances in a timely manner. Activity-based costing provides an excellent tracking system in that it enables management to monitor the activities affected by investments. The following lists the steps in developing a performance tracking system:

- Identify the tracked data elements.
- Assess the availability of cost-benefit data.
- Develop a cost-benefit data validation method.
- Design a conceptual cost-benefit tracking system.
- Validate cost models, analyze actual costs to budget variances.
- Develop procedures for responding to variances.
- Design a cost-benefit reporting system.
- Install the system.
- React to feedback.

22.6 SUMMARY

In recent years, some companies have moved toward the investment management framework outlined in this chapter. The following list shows some of the leading practices identified by the authors in working with businesses across multiple industries for each major phase of the investment management process.

Strategic Planning

- Investment and infrastructure planning closely link to business and strategic planning.
- Cross-functional teams generate and refine strategic, investment, and infrastructure plans.
- Strategic efforts focus on identifying and maximizing drivers of success, which management reinforces by measuring results and assigning accountability.
- Management establishes yearly strategic milestones and monitors progress.

Investment Portfolio Development

- All projects must align with strategic initiatives, such as:
    - Improve customer satisfaction
    - Increase speed
    - Reduce cost
    - Plan for growth
    - Add value.
- Planners document investment proposals.
- If resource use does not meet strategic objectives, management rejects the investment.

Decision Analysis

- Comprehensive quantitative and qualitative support is provided for projects.
- The analysis defines standardized project preappraisal critical success factors.
- Different risk categories and discount rates are used for each type of project, based on strategic objectives.
- Cash flow assumptions and risks are documented.
- Sensitivity analysis is performed on key risks.
- The status quo ("Do nothing") scenario is analyzed.
- Alternatives are analyzed and considered.

Execution and Tracking

- Companies update their capital and expense budgets regularly.
- Managers track commitments and actual booked expenditures as they emerge from the purchase order system.
- Cost variances greater than 10 percent require additional approval.
- Scope changes require additional approval.
- Managers document post-implementation audit procedures.
- Managers establish the post-implementation audit schedule before the project starts, not at the time of the audit.
- Analysts bundle projects allowing simultaneous audit of multiple investments.
- Decision makers apply lessons learned to future investment decision making.
- Analysts conduct regular post-implementation audits, rather than one-time, post-completion reviews.
- Individuals involved in investment decisions play an integral role in the post-implementation audit.

CHAPTER 23

COMPOUND INTEREST: CONCEPTS AND APPLICATIONS

Roman L. Weil, PhD, CPA, CMA, Editor
University of Chicago

CONTENTS

23.1 INTRODUCTION: COMPOUND INTEREST CONCEPTS 627
(a) Simple Interest 628
(b) Power of Compound Interest 628

23.2 FUTURE VALUE 628
(a) Examples: Computing Future Value 629
(b) Present Value 629
(c) Present Value Terminology 630
(d) Examples: Computing Present Values 630

23.3 CHANGING THE COMPOUNDING PERIOD 630
(a) Nominal and Effective Rates 630
(b) Examples: Changing the Compounding Period 631

23.4 ANNUITIES 632
(a) Terminology for Annuities 632
(b) Ordinary Annuities (Annuities in Arrears) 633
(c) Examples: Ordinary Annuities 635

23.5 PERPETUITIES 640
(a) Examples: Perpetuities 640
(b) Perpetuity With Growth 641

23.6 IMPLICIT INTEREST RATES: FINDING INTERNAL RATES OF RETURN 642
(a) Example: Implicit Interest Rates 643
(b) Rules of Thumb 644

23.7 SUMMARY 644

23.1 INTRODUCTION: COMPOUND INTEREST CONCEPTS

Contracts typically state interest cost as a percentage of the amount borrowed per unit of time. Examples include "12 percent per year" and "1 percent per month," which differ from one another. When the statement of interest cost does not explicitly state a period, then the rate applies to a year, so that "interest at the rate of 12 percent" means 12 percent per year. Some inflation-ravaged countries, such as Brazil, quote interest rates for a month.The amount borrowed or lent is the *principal*. *Compound interest* means that the amount of interest earned during a period increases the principal, which thus becomes larger for the next interest period. For example, if you deposit $1,000 in a savings account that pays compound interest at the rate of 6 percent per year, you will earn $60 by the end of one year. If you do not withdraw the $60, then $1,060 will earn interest during the second year. During the second year, your principal of $1,060 will earn $63.60 in interest: $60 on the initial deposit of $1,000 and $3.60 on the $60 earned the first year. By the end of the second year, your principal will total $1,123.60. When only the original principal earns interest during the entire life of the loan, the interest due at the time the borrower repays the loan is called *simple interest*. Simple interest calculations ignore interest on previously earned interest. If the lender may withdraw interest earned, or the borrower must make periodic payments with further interest charges for late payments, then compound interest techniques will still apply.

(a) SIMPLE INTEREST. *Simple interest rarely applies to economic calculations, but accounting often uses it for convenience.* The use of simple interest calculations in accounting arises in the following way: If you borrow \$10,000 at a rate of 12 percent per year but compute interest for any month as \$100 (= \$10,000 × 0.12 × 1/12), you are using a simple interest calculation. Nearly all economic calculations, however, involve compound interest. When firms use simple interest to compute amounts for periods less than a year, some distortion of periodic numbers results, but no harm. Early periods get charged "too much" interest and later periods get charged "too little," but the distortions are minor.

(b) POWER OF COMPOUND INTEREST. The force, or effect, of compound interest exceeds the amount suggested by the intuition of some. For example, compounded annually at 8 percent, an invested amount doubles itself in nine years. Put another way, if you invest \$100 at 8 percent compounded annually, you will have \$200 in nine years. If you invested \$1 in the stock market at age 25 and left it there for 45 years and the market increased for the next 45 years the way it has for the last 20 years, you would have more than \$150 by the time you reached age 70.

Problems involving compound interest generally fall into two groups with respect to time.

- We may want to know the future value of cash invested or loaned today, as in the two examples in the preceding paragraph.
- We may want to know the present value, or today's value, of cash to be received or paid at later dates. (If I want to have \$1,000,000 available at retirement, how much must I invest today?)

In addition, the accountant must sometimes find the interest rate implicit in specified payment streams. For example, assume a bank will lend you \$1,000 in return for your promise to repay \$91.70 per month for one year or \$73.24 per month for 15 months. You might want to know that the implied rate of interest is 1.5 percent per month for the first offer and 1.2 percent per month for the second.

23.2 FUTURE VALUE

If you invest \$1 today at 12 percent compounded annually, it will grow to \$1.12000 at the end of one year, \$1.25440 at the end of two years, \$1.40493 at the end of three years, and so on, according to the following formula:

$$F_n = P(1 + r)^n,$$

where

F_n = accumulation or future value

P = one-time investment today

r = interest rate per period

n = number of periods from today.

The amount F_n is the *future value* of the present payment, P, compounded at r percent per period for n periods. Table 1 in Appendix A at the back of the book shows the future values of $P = \$1$ for various numbers of periods and for various interest rates. Extracts from that table appear here in Exhibit 23.1.

(a) EXAMPLES: COMPUTING FUTURE VALUE

(i) Example 1. How much will \$1,000 deposited today at 8 percent compounded annually grow to in 10 years?

Refer to Exhibit 23.1, in the10-period row, 8 percent column. One dollar deposited today at 8 percent will grow to \$2.15892; therefore, \$1,000 will grow to $\$1,000 \times (1.08)^{10} = \$1,000 \times 2.15892 = \$2,158.92$.

(ii) Example 2. Macaulay Corporation deposits \$10,000 in an expansion fund today. The fund will earn 12 percent per year. How much will the \$10,000 grow to in 20 years if Macaulay leaves the entire fund and all interest earned on it on deposit in the fund?

One dollar deposited today at 12 percent will grow to \$9.64629 in 20 years. Therefore, \$10,000 will grow to \$96,463 (= $\$10,000 \times 9.64629$) in 20 years.

(b) PRESENT VALUE. The preceding section developed the computation of the future value, F_N, of a sum of cash, P, deposited or invested today. You know P, and you calculate F_N. This section deals with the problems of calculating how much principal, P, you must invest today in order to have a specified amount, F_N, at the end of n periods. You know the future amount, F_N, the interest rate, r, and the number of periods, n; you want to find P. In order to have \$1 one year from today when deposits earn 8 percent, you must invest P of \$.92593 today. That is, $F_1 = P(1.08)^1$ or $\$1 = \$0.92593 \times 1.08$. Because $F_N = P(1 + r)^N$, dividing both sides of the equation by $(1 + r)^N$ yields

$$\frac{F_n}{(1 + r)^n} = P,$$

or

$$P = \frac{F_n}{(1 + r)^n} = F_n(1 + r)^{-n}.$$

$F_n = (1 + r)^n$

Number of Periods = n	Rate = r: 8 Percent	Rate = r: 12 Percent
1.	1.08000	1.12000
2.	1.16640	1.25440
3.	1.25971	1.40493
10.	2.15892	3.10585
20.	4.66096	9.64629

EXHIBIT 23.1 FUTURE VALUE OF \$1 AT 8 PERCENT AND 12 PERCENT (EXCERPT FROM TABLE 1)

(c) PRESENT VALUE TERMINOLOGY. The number $(1 + r)^{-n}$ equals the present value of \$1 to be received after n periods when interest accrues at r percent per period. Analysts often use the words *discount* and *discounted value* in this context as follows. The discounted present value of \$1 to be received n periods in the future is $(1 + r)^{-n}$ when the discount rate is r percent per period for n periods. The number r is the *discount rate,* and the number $(1 + r)^{-n}$ is the *discount factor* for n periods. A discount factor $(1 + r)^{-n}$ is the reciprocal, or inverse, of a number, $(1 + r)^{n}$, in Exhibit 23.1. Portions of Table 2 at the back of the book, which shows discount factors or, equivalently, present values of \$1 for various interest (or discount) rates for various numbers of periods, appear in Exhibit 23.2.

(d) EXAMPLES: COMPUTING PRESENT VALUES

(i) Example 3. What is the present value of \$1 due 10 years from now if the interest rate (equivalently, the discount rate) r is 8 percent per year?

From Exhibit 23.2, in the 8 percent column, 10-period row, the present value of \$1 to be received 10 periods hence, at 8 percent, equals \$0.46319.

(ii) Example 4. You issue a single-payment note that promises to pay \$160,000 three years from today in exchange for used equipment. How much is that promise worth today if the discount rate appropriate for such notes is 12 percent per period? (An accountant needs to know the answer to the question to record the acquisition cost of the used equipment just acquired.)

One dollar paid three years hence discounted at 12 percent has a present value of \$0.71178. Thus, the promise is worth \$113,885 (= \$160,000 × 0.71178). (Record the equipment at a cost of \$113,885.)

23.3 CHANGING THE COMPOUNDING PERIOD

(a) NOMINAL AND EFFECTIVE RATES. "Twelve percent, compounded annually" states the price for a loan; this means that interest increases, or converts to, principal once a year at the rate of 12 percent. Often, however, the price for a loan states that compounding will occur more than once a year. A savings bank may advertise that it pays 6 percent, compounded quarterly. This means that at the end of each quarter the bank credits savings accounts with interest calculated at the rate of 1.5 percent (= 6 percent/4). The investor can withdraw the interest payment or leave it on deposit to earn more interest.

$$P = F_n(1 + r)^{-n}$$

	Rate = r	
Number of Periods = n	8 Percent	12 Percent
1.	0.92593	0.89286
2.	0.85734	0.79719
3.	0.79383	0.71178
10.	0.46319	0.32197
20.	0.21455	0.10367

EXHIBIT 23.2 PRESENT VALUE OF \$1 AT 8 PERCENT AND 12 PERCENT PER PERIOD (EXCERPT FROM TABLE 2)

The sum of \$10,000 invested today at 12 percent, compounded annually, grows to a future value one year later of \$11,200. If the rate of interest is 12 percent compounded semiannually, the bank adds 6 percent interest to the principal every six months. At the end of the first six months, \$10,000 will have grown to \$10,600; that amount will grow to \$10,600 × 1.06 = \$11,236 by the end of the year. 12 percent compounded semiannually is equivalent to 12.36 percent compounded annually. Suppose that the bank quotes interest as 12 percent, compounded quarterly. It will add an additional 3 percent of the principal every three months. By the end of the year, \$10,000 will grow to \$10,000 × $(1.03)^4$ = \$10,000 × 1.12551 = \$11,255. At 12 percent compounded monthly, \$1 will grow to \$1 × $(1.01)^{12}$ = \$1.12683 and \$10,000 will grow to \$11,268. Thus, 12 percent compounded monthly provides the same ending amount as 12.68 percent compounded annually. Common terminology would say that *12 percent compounded monthly* has an "effective rate of 12.68 percent compounded annually" or is "equivalent to 12.68 percent compounded annually."

For a given nominal rate, such as the 12 percent in the previous examples, the more often interest compounds, the higher the effective rate of interest paid. If a nominal rate, r, compounds m times per year, the effective rate equals $(1 + r/m)^m - 1$.

In practice, to deal with situations that require computation of interest quoted at a nominal rate r percent per period compounded m times per period for n periods, use the tables for rate r/m and $m \times n$ periods. For example, 12 percent compounded quarterly for five years is equivalent to the rate found in the interest tables for $r = 12/4 = 3$ percent for $m \times n = 4 \times 5 = 20$ periods.

Some savings banks advertise that they compound interest daily or even continuously. The mathematics of calculus provides a mechanism for finding the effective rate when interest is compounded continuously. If interest compounds continuously at nominal rate r per year, the effective annual rate is $e^r - 1$, where e is the base of the natural logarithms. Six percent per year compounded continuously is equivalent to 6.1837 percent compounded annually. Twelve percent per year compounded continuously is equivalent to 12.75 percent compounded annually. Do not confuse the compounding period with the payment period. Some banks, for example, compound interest daily but pay interest quarterly. These banks do not employ computers to calculate interest every day. They derive an equivalent effective rate to apply at the end of each quarter.

(b) EXAMPLES: CHANGING THE COMPOUNDING PERIOD

(i) Example 5. What is the future value five years hence of \$600 invested at 16 percent compounded semiannually?

Sixteen percent compounded two times per year for five years is equivalent to 8 percent per period compounded for 10 periods. Exhibit 23.1 shows the value of $F_{10} = (1.08)^{10}$ to be 2.15892. Six hundred dollars, then, would grow to \$600 × 2.15892 = \$1,295.35.

(ii) Example 6. How much cash must you invest today at 16 percent compounded semiannually in order to yield \$10,000 in 10 years from today?

Sixteen percent compounded two times a year for 10 years is equivalent to 8 percent per period compounded for 20 periods. The present value, Exhibit 23.2, of \$1 received 20 periods hence at 8 percent per period is \$0.21455. That is, \$0.21455 invested today for 20 periods at an interest rate of 8 percent per period will grow to \$1. To have \$10,000 in 20 periods (10 years), you must invest \$2,146 (= \$10,000 × \$0.21455) today.

(iii) Example 7. A local department store offers its customers credit and advertises its interest rate at 18 percent per year, compounded monthly at the rate of 1.5 percent per month. What is the effective annual interest rate?

One and one-half percent per month for 12 months is equivalent to $(1.015)^{12} - 1 =$ 19.562 percent per year. See Table 1, Appendix A, 12-period row, 1.5-percent column, where the factor is 1.19562.

Under truth in lending legislation, lenders must disclose the effective annual interest rate, called the *APR* or *annual percentage rate,* to borrowers.

(iv) Example 8. If prices increased at the rate of 6 percent during each of two consecutive six-month periods, how much did prices increase during the entire year?

If a price index is 100.00 at the start of the year, it will be $100.00 \times (1.06)^2 = 112.36$ at the end of the year. The price change for the entire year is $(112.36/100.00) - 1 = 12.36$ percent.

23.4 ANNUITIES

An annuity is a series of equal payments, one per period for periods equally spaced through time. Examples of annuities include monthly rental payments, semiannual corporate bond coupon payments, and annual payments to a lessor under a lease contract. Armed with an understanding of the tables for future and present values, you can solve any annuity problem. Annuities arise so often, however, and their solution is so tedious without special tables or calculator functions, that annuity problems merit special study and the use of special tables or functions.

The common computer spreadsheet programs such as Microsoft *Excel* include functions for annuity and other compound interest functions. Knowing which function to use to solve a given problem and which values for the variables to insert into the formula requires the same clear understanding required to use the tables. Hence, if you want to use spreadsheet functions, you must master the use of the tables in this book or gain equivalent knowledge.

(a) TERMINOLOGY FOR ANNUITIES. *An annuity involves equally spaced payments of equal amounts.* If either the time between payments or the amounts of the payments vary, then the stream is not an annuity. An annuity with payments occurring at the end of each period is an *ordinary annuity (annuity in arrears).* Semiannual corporate bonds usually promise that debt service (coupon) payments will be paid in arrears or, equivalently, that the first payment will not occur until after the bond has been outstanding for six months. An annuity with payments occurring at the beginning of each period is an *annuity due* or an *annuity in advance.* Rent paid at the beginning of each month is an annuity due. In a *deferred annuity,* the first payment occurs sometime later than the end of the first period.

Annuity payments can go on forever. Such annuities are *perpetuities,* discussed in Section 23.5. Bonds that promise payments forever are *consols.* The British and the Canadian governments have issued consols from time to time. A perpetuity can be in arrears or in advance. The only difference between the two is the timing of the first payment.

$$F_A = \frac{[(1+r)^n - 1]}{r}$$

	Rate = r	
Number of Periods = n	8 Percent	12 Percent
1.	1.00000	1.00000
2.	2.08000	2.12000
3.	3.24640	3.37440
5.	5.86660	6.35285
10.	14.48656	17.54874
20.	45.76196	72.05244

EXHIBIT 23.3 FUTURE VALUE OF AN ORDINARY ANNUITY OF $1 PER PERIOD AT 8 PERCENT AND 12 PERCENT (EXCERPT FROM TABLE 3)

Many people find annuities confusing. A time line, such as the one shown here, can help one understand them.

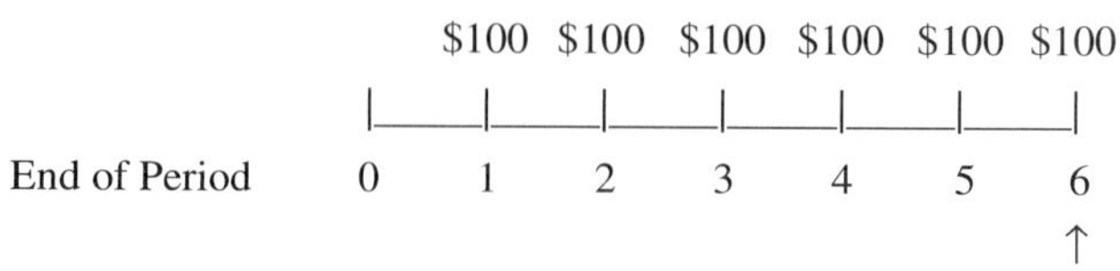

A time line marks the end of each period, numbers the period, shows the payments to be received or paid, and shows the time in which the accountant wants to value the annuity. The time line above represents an ordinary annuity (in arrears) for six periods of $100 to be valued at the end of period 6. The end of period 0 is *now.* The first payment occurs one period from now.

(b) ORDINARY ANNUITIES (ANNUITIES IN ARREARS). The future values of ordinary annuities appear in Table 3 at the back of the book, portions of which Exhibit 23.3 reproduces.

Consider an ordinary annuity for three periods at 12 percent. The time line for the future value of such an annuity is as follows:

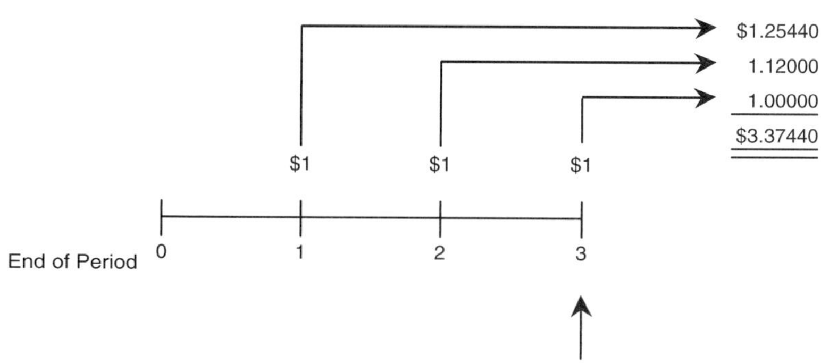

EXHIBIT 23.4 FUTURE VALUE OF ORDINARY ANNUITY

$$P_A = \frac{[1-(1-r)^{-n}]}{r}$$

Number of Periods = n	Rate = r 8 Percent	12 Percent
1.	0.92593	0.89286
2.	1.78326	1.69005
3.	2.57710	2.40183
5.	3.99271	3.60478
10.	6.71008	5.65022
20.	9.81815	7.46944

EXHIBIT 23.5 PRESENT VALUE OF AN ORDINARY ANNUITY OF $1 PER PERIOD AT 8 PERCENT AND 12 PERCENT (EXCERPT FROM TABLE 4)

The $1 received at the end of the first period earns interest for two periods, so it grows to $1.25440 at the end of period 3 (see Exhibit 23.1). The $1 received at the end of the second period grows to $1.12000 by the end of period 3, and the $1 received at the end of period 3 is, of course, worth $1.00000 at the end of period 3. The entire annuity is worth $3.37440 at the end of period 3. This amount appears in Exhibit 23.3 for the future value of an ordinary annuity for three periods at 12 percent. Factors for the future value of an annuity for a particular number of periods sum the factors for the future value of $1 for each of the periods. The future value of an ordinary annuity is as follows:

$$\text{Future value of ordinary annuity} = \text{Periodic payment} \times \text{Factor for the future value of an ordinary annuity}$$

Thus,

$$\$3.37440 = \$1 \times 3.37440$$

Table 4 in Appendix A shows the present value of ordinary annuities. Exhibit 23.5 reproduces excerpts from Table 4.

The time line for the present value of an ordinary annuity of $1 per period for three periods, discounted at 12 percent, is as shown in Exhibit 23.6.

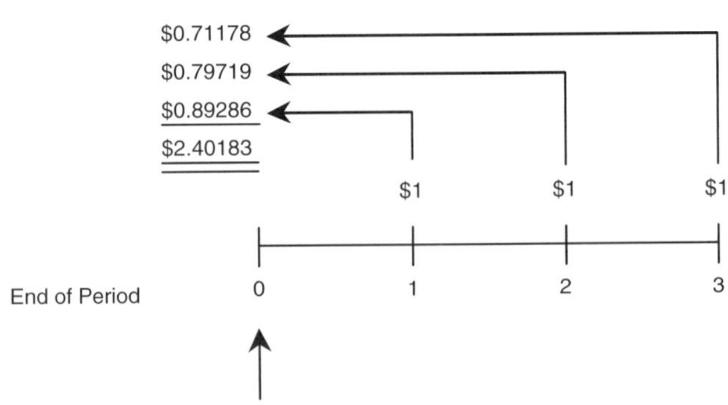

EXHIBIT 23.6 PRESENT VALUE OF ORDINARY ANNUITY

The $1 due at the end of period 1 has a present value of $0.89286, the $1 due at the end of period 2 has a present value of $0.79719, and the $1 due at the end of period 3 has a present value of $0.71178. Each of these numbers comes from Exhibit 23.2. The present value of the annuity sums these individual present values, $2.40183, shown in Exhibit 23.4.

The present value of an ordinary annuity for *n* periods is the sum of the present value of $1 received one period from now plus the present value of $1 received two periods from now, and so on until we add on the present value of $1 received *n* periods from now. The present value of an ordinary annuity is as follows:

$$\begin{array}{c}\text{Present value}\\ \text{of an}\\ \text{ordinary annuity}\end{array} = \begin{array}{c}\text{Periodic}\\ \text{payment}\end{array} \times \begin{array}{c}\text{Factor for}\\ \text{the present}\\ \text{value of an}\\ \text{ordinary annuity}\end{array}$$

Thus,

$$\$2.40183 = \$1 \times 2.40183$$

(c) EXAMPLES: ORDINARY ANNUITIES

(i) Example 9. You plan to invest $1,000 at the end of each of the next 10 years in a savings account. The savings account accumulates interest of 8 percent compounded annually. What will be the balance in the savings account at the end of 10 years?

The time line for this problem is as follows:

		$1,000	$1,000	$1,000	$1,000	···	$1,000
End of Period	0	1	2	3	4	···	10
							x ↑

The symbol x denotes the amount you must calculate. Exhibit 23.3 indicates that the factor for the future value of an annuity at 8 percent for 10 periods is 14.48656. Thus,

$$\begin{array}{c}\text{Future value}\\ \text{of an}\\ \text{ordinary annuity}\end{array} = \begin{array}{c}\text{Periodic}\\ \text{payment}\end{array} \times \begin{array}{c}\text{Factor for}\\ \text{the future}\\ \text{value of an}\\ \text{ordinary annuity}\end{array}$$

$$x = \$1{,}000 \times 14.48656$$

$$x = \$14{,}487$$

(ii) Example 10. You want to receive $600 every six months, starting six months hence, for the next five years. How much must you invest today if the funds accumulate at the rate of 8 percent compounded semiannually?

This example has the following time line:

		$600	$600	$600	$600	···	$600
End of Period	0	1	2	3	4	···	10
	x ↑						

The factor from Table 4 for the present value of an annuity at 4 percent (= 8 percent per year/2 semiannual periods per year) for 10 (= 2 periods per year × 5 years) periods is 8.11090. Thus,

$$\text{Present value of an ordinary annuity} = \text{Periodic payment} \times \text{Factor for the present value of an ordinary annuity}$$

$$x = \$600 \times 8.11090$$

$$x = \$4{,}866.54$$

If you invest $4,866.54 today, the principal plus interest compounded on the principal will provide sufficient funds that you can withdraw $600 every six months for the next five years.

(iii) Example 11. A company borrows $125,000 from a savings and loan association. The interest rate on the loan is 12 percent compounded semiannually. The company agrees to repay the loan in equal semiannual installments over the next five years, with the first payment six months from now. What is the required semiannual payment?

This example has the following time line:

						...	
		x	x	x	x	...	x
End of Period	0	1	2	3	4	...	10
	$125,000						

This problem resembles Example 10 because both involve periodic future payments discounted to today. Example 10 gives the periodic payments and asks for the present value. Example 11 gives the present value and asks for the periodic payment. Table 4 indicates that the present value of an annuity at 6 percent (= 12 percent per year/2 semi-annual periods per year) for 10 periods (= 2 periods per year × 5 years) is 7.36009. Thus,

$$\text{Present value of an ordinary annuity} = \text{Periodic payment} \times \text{Factor for the present value of an ordinary annuity}$$

$$\$125{,}000 = x \times 7.36009$$

$$x = \frac{\$125{,}000}{7.36009}$$

$$x = \$16{,}983$$

To find the periodic payment, divide the present value amount of $125,000 by the present value factor.

Exhibit 23.7 presents the amortization table for this loan. That exhibit shows the amount of each semiannual payment as $17,000, rather than $16,983, and the last payment as $16,781, less than $17,000, to compensate for the extra $17 paid in each of the preceding periods and the interest on those amounts. For each period it shows the balance at the beginning of the period, the interest expense for the period, the cash payment for the period, the reduction in principal for the period, and the balance at the end of the period. (The last payment, $16,781 in this case, often differs slightly from the others because of the cumulative effect of rounding payments to the nearest dollar or hundred

6-Month Period (1)	Loan Balance Start of Period (2)	Interest Expense for Period (3)	Payment (4)	Portion of Payment Reducing Principal (5)	Loan Balance End of Period (6)
0					$125,000
1	$125,000	$7,500	$17,000	$ 9,500	115,500
2	115,500	6,930	17,000	10,070	105,430
3	105,430	6,326	17,000	10,674	94,756
4	94,756	5,685	17,000	11,315	83,441
5	83,441	5,006	17,000	11,994	71,447
6	71,447	4,287	17,000	12,713	58,734
7	58,734	3,524	17,000	13,476	45,258
8	45,258	2,715	17,000	14,285	30,973
9	30,973	1,858	17,000	15,142	15,831
10	15,831	950	16,781	15,831	0

Note: In preparing this table, we rounded calculations to the nearest dollar.
Column (2) = column (6) from previous period.
Column (3) = .06 x column (2).
Column (4) is given, except row 10, where it is the amount such that column (4) = column (2) + column (3).
Column (5) = column (4) – column (3).
Column (6) = column (2) – column (5).

EXHIBIT 23.7 AMORTIZATION SCHEDULE FOR $125,000 MORTGAGE (OR NOTE), REPAID IN 10 SEMIANNUAL INSTALLMENTS OF $17,000, INTEREST RATE OF 12 PERCENT, COMPOUNDED SEMIANNUALLY (6 PERCENT COMPOUNDED EACH SIX MONTHS)

dollars.) All long-term liabilities have analogous amortization schedules, which aid in understanding the timing of payments to discharge the liability.

You can see that, in this example, part of each payment is interest and part is repayment of principal. Only when the lender issues a bond or note at par (i.e., the coupon rate equals the market rate at the time of issue), will the periodic payment equal interest for the period. In most practical applications, the periodic payment does not equal interest expense. Almost everyone in business refers to the periodic payments as *interest payments,* particularly for notes and bonds. This phrase causes confusion because the amount of interest expense for a period almost never equals the amount of these payments for that same period. The periodic payment will always include some amount to pay interest to the lender, but not necessarily all interest accrued since the last payment. If the payment exceeds all accrued interest, then the payment will discharge some of the principal amount. Both payment of interest and payment of principal serve to reduce the debt, so one all-purpose term used for the payments is *debt service payments.* Do not call them, or even think of them, as interest payments until you have understood why they do not equal interest expense. You will never be wrong to call them *debt service payments.*

(iv) Example 12. A company signs a lease acquiring the right to use property for three years. The company will make lease payments of $19,709 annually at the end of this and the next two years. The discount rate is 15 percent per year. What is the present value of the lease payments?

This example has the following time line:

		\$19,709	\$19,709	\$19,709
End of Period	0	1	2	3
	x ↑			

The factor from Table 4 for the present value of an annuity at 15 percent for three periods is 2.28323. Thus,

Present value of an ordinary annuity	=	Periodic payment	×	Factor for the present value of an ordinary annuity
x	=	\$19,709	×	2.28323
x	=	\$45,000		

(v) Example 13. A company promises to make annual payments to a pension fund at the end of each of the next 30 years. The payments must have a present value today of \$100,000. What must the annual payment be if the fund expects to earn interest at the rate of 8 percent per year?

This example has the following time line:

		x	x	x	x	...	x
End of Period	0	1	2	3	4	...	30
	\$100,000 ↑						

Table 4 indicates that the factor for the present value of \$1 paid at the end of the next 30 periods at 8 percent per period is 11.25778. Thus,

Present value of an ordinary annuity	=	Periodic payment	×	Factor for the present value of an ordinary annuity
\$100,000	=	x	×	11.25778
x	=	$\frac{\$100{,}000}{11.25778}$		
x	=	\$8,883		

(vi) Example 14. Mr. Mason is 62 years old. He wants to invest equal amounts on his 63rd, 64th, and 65th birthdays so that, starting on his 66th birthday, he can withdraw \$50,000 on each birthday for 10 years. His investments will earn 8 percent per year. How much should he invest on the 63rd through 65th birthdays?

This example has the following time line:

		x	x	x	–\$50,000	–\$50,000	···	–\$50,000
End of Year	62	63	64	65	66	67	···	75
					↑			

At 65, Mr. Mason needs to have accumulated a fund equal to the present value of an annuity of \$50,000 per period for 10 periods, discounted at 8 percent per period. The factor from Exhibit 23.4 for 8 percent and 10 periods is 6.71008. Thus,

Present value of an ordinary annuity	=	Periodic payment	×	Factor for the present value of an ordinary annuity
x	=	\$50,000	×	6.71008
x	=	\$335,500		

The time line now appears as follows:

				\$335,500				
		x	x	x	–\$50,000	–\$50,000	···	–\$50,000
End of Year	62	63	64	65	66	67	···	75
				↑				

The question now becomes one of how much Mr. Mason must invest on his 63rd, 64th, and 65th birthdays to accumulate to a fund of \$335,500 on his 65th birthday. The factor for the future value of an annuity for three periods at 8 percent is 3.24640. Thus,

Future value of an ordinary annuity	=	Periodic payment	×	Factor for the future value of an ordinary annuity
\$335,500	=	x	×	3.24640

$$x = \frac{\$335{,}500}{3.24640}$$

$$x = \$103{,}350$$

The solution above expresses all calculations in terms of equivalent amounts on Mr. Mason's 65th birthday. That is, the present value of an annuity of \$50,000 per period for 10 periods at 8 percent equals the future value of an annuity of \$103,350 per period for three periods at 8 percent, and both of these amounts equal \$335,500. You could work this problem by selecting any common time period between Mr. Mason's 62nd and 75th birthdays.

One alternative expresses all calculations in terms of equivalent amounts on Mr. Mason's 62nd birthday. To solve the problem in this way, first find the present value on Mr. Mason's 65th birthday of an annuity of \$50,000 per period for 10 periods (\$335,500 = \$50,000 × 6.71008). Discount \$335,500 back three periods using Table 2 for present value of single payments: \$266,330 = \$335,500 × .79383. The result is the present value of the payments to be made to Mr. Mason measured as of his 62nd birthday. Then, find the amounts that Mr. Mason would have to invest in the future, on his 63rd, 64th, and 65th birthdays, to provide a present value on his 62nd birthday equal to $266,330. The calculation is as follows:

Present value of an ordinary annuity	=	Periodic payment	×	Factor for the present value of an ordinary annuity
$266,330	=	x	×	2.57710
x	=	$103,350		

We computed the same amount, $103,350, previously.

23.5 PERPETUITIES

A periodic payment to be received forever is a *perpetuity*. Future values of perpetuities are undefined. One dollar to be received at the end of every period discounted at rate r percent has a present value of $\$1/r$. Observe what happens in the expression for the present value of an ordinary annuity of $A per payment as n, the number of payments, approaches infinity:

$$P_A = \frac{A[1 - (1 + r)^{-n}]}{r}$$

As n approaches infinity, $(1 + r)^{-n}$ approaches 0, so that P_A approaches $A(1/r)$. If the first payment of the perpetuity occurs now, the present value is $A[1 + 1/r]$.

(a) EXAMPLES: PERPETUITIES

(i) Example 15. The Canadian government offers to pay $30 every six months forever in the form of a perpetual bond. What is that bond worth if the discount rate is 10 percent compounded semiannually?

Ten percent compounded semiannually is equivalent to 5 percent per six-month period. If the first payment occurs six months from now, the present value is $30/0.05 = $600. If the first payment occurs today, the present value is $30 + $600 = $630.

(ii) Example 16. Every two years, the Bank of Tokyo gives ¥5 million (Japanese yen) to the university to provide a scholarship for an entering student in a two-year business administration course. If the university credits 6 percent per year to its investment accounts, how much must the bank give to the university to provide such a scholarship every two years forever, starting two years hence?

A perpetuity in arrears assumes one payment at the end of each period. Here, the period is two years. Six percent compounded once a year over two years is equivalent to a rate of $(1.06)^2 - 1 = 0.12360$, or 12.36 percent compounded once per two-year period. Consequently, the present value of the perpetuity paid in arrears every two years is ¥40.45 (= ¥5/0.1236). A gift of ¥40.45 million will provide a ¥5 million scholarship forever. If the university will award the first scholarship now, the gift must be ¥45.45 (= ¥40.45 + ¥5.00) million.

(iii) Example 17. This example illustrates the *relief from royalty method* for valuing trademarks. Burns, Philp & Company (B-P) wants to value its trademark for Fleischmann's Yeast using the relief from royalty method. B-P estimates that sales of the product will continue at the rate of \$100 million per year in perpetuity and that if it had to pay a royalty to another firm that owned the trademark, it would have to pay 4 percent of sales at the end of each year. It uses a discount rate of 10 percent per year in computing present values. What is the value of the trademark under these assumptions?

If B-P paid royalties of 4 percent of sales, these would total \$4 (= 0.04 × \$100) million per year, in perpetuity. The present value of a perpetual stream of payments of \$4 million per year, discounted at 10 percent per year, is \$40 (= \$4/0.10) million. Under these assumptions, the trademark has a value of \$40 million.

(b) PERPETUITY WITH GROWTH. B-P, more realistically, might estimate that sales will grow each year by, say, 2 percent more than the rate of inflation. When one assumes that a perpetuity's payments, which start at p per period, \$4 million in this example, will grow at a constant rate g, 2 percent in this example, then the value of the perpetuity is $p/(r - g)$ = \$4/(0.10 – 0.02) = \$50 million in this example.

The arithmetic of perpetuities with growth provides the foundation for a popular technique of valuation analysis. Often, analysts multiply an annual number, such as earnings (or cash flow from operations or earnings before depreciation, interest, income taxes, and amortization) by a price-earnings ratio, a multiple, to compute the value of the entity producing that annual income (see Exhibit 23.8). You can think of the multiple as the present value of a \$1 perpetuity. For example, if the discount rate is 8 percent, the perpetuity has value of \$12.50 (= \$1.00/.08) and the multiple is 12.50. If the analyst expects the earnings to grow, then the perpetuity-with-growth formula applies. The derived multiple, 12.50, assumes no growth in earnings. The analyst who expects earnings at 3 percent per year can compute the present value of the perpetuity as \$1.00/(0.08 – 0.03) = \$20.00 and the multiple is 20. These computations are easy to do but not sufficiently sensitive to realistic complications to provide more than guides.

Multiple = $1/(r - g)$					
	Discount Rate [r] =				
Growth Rate (g) =	8%	10%	12%	15%	20%
0.0%	12.5	10.0	8.3	6.7	5.0
0.5%	13.3	10.5	8.7	6.9	5.1
1.0%	14.3	11.1	9.1	7.1	5.3
1.5%	15.4	11.8	9.5	7.4	5.4
2.0%	16.7	12.5	10.0	7.7	5.6
2.5%	18.2	13.3	10.5	8.0	5.7
3.0%	20.0	14.3	11.1	8.3	5.9
3.5%	22.2	15.4	11.8	8.7	6.1
4.0%	25.0	16.7	12.5	9.1	6.3
5.0%	33.3	20.0	14.3	10.0	6.7

EXHIBIT 23.8 PERPETUITY-WITH-GROWTH MULTIPLES P/E MULTIPLES IMPLIED BY VARIOUS COMBINATIONS OF GROWTH AND DISCOUNT RATES

In valuation models, often the analyst will forecast cash flows for 5 to 10 years, then measure a terminal value based on the perpetuity-with-growth model. In many valuations we have seen, so much of the valuation resides in the terminal value—and so much of the terminal value depends on the growth rate assumed, and the time period for that growth rate starts so far in the future—that the analyst needs to use caution. Analysts will find the perpetuity-with-growth model easy to use, but they will be better served to make nonuniform estimates, such as 10 percent growth for five years, then 8 percent for the next five, and growth at some macro-economic rate after that.

23.6 IMPLICIT INTEREST RATES: FINDING INTERNAL RATES OF RETURN

The preceding examples computed a future value or a present value, given the interest rate and stated cash payment. Or, they computed the required payments given their known future value or their known present value. In other calculations, however, you know the present or the future value and the periodic payments; you must find the implicit interest rate. For example, consider a purchase of equipment with a cash price of \$10,500, which the buyer acquires in exchange for a single-payment note. The note has a face value of \$16,000 and matures in three years. To compute interest expense over the three-year period, you must know the implicit interest rate (internal rate of return). This example has the following time line:

	+\$10,500	0	0	–\$16,000
End of Year	0	1	2	3

The implicit interest rate is r, such that

$$0 = \$10{,}500 - \frac{\$16{,}000}{(1 + r)^3} \tag{1}$$

$$\$10{,}500 = \frac{\$16{,}000}{(1 + r)^3} \tag{2}$$

That is, the present value of \$16,000 discounted three periods at r percent per period equals \$10,500. The present value of all current and future cash flows discounted at r per period must be zero. In general, to find such an r requires trial and error. In cases where r appears only in one term, as here, you can find r analytically. Here

$$r = (\$16{,}000/\$10{,}500)^{1/3} - 1 = .1507 = 15.1 \text{ percent.}$$

The general procedure is *finding the internal rate of return of a series of cash flows.* The internal rate of return of a series of cash flows is the discount rate that makes the net present values of that series of cash flows equal to zero. The following steps will lead to the internal rate of return:

1. Make an educated guess, called the *trial rate,* at the internal rate of return. If you have no idea what to guess, try zero.
2. Calculate the present value of all the cash flows (including the one at the end of Year 0).

3. If the present value of the cash flows is zero, stop. The current trial rate is the internal rate of return.
4. If the amount found in step 2 is less than zero, try a larger interest rate as the trial rate and go back to step 2.
5. If the amount found in step 2 is greater than zero, try a smaller interest rate as the new trial rate and go back to step 2.

The iterations in Exhibit 23.9 illustrate the process for the example in equation (1). With a trial rate of 15.1 percent, the right-hand side is close enough to zero that you can use 15.1 percent as the implicit interest rate in making the adjusting entries for interest expense. Continued iterations would find trial rates even closer to the true rate, approximately 15.0739 percent.

Finding the internal rate of return for a series of cash flows can prove tedious; you should not attempt it unless you have at least a calculator. An exponential feature, which allows the computation of $(1 + r)$ raised to various powers, helps. Computer spreadsheets, such as Microsoft *Excel*, have a built-in function to find the internal rate of return.

(a) EXAMPLE: IMPLICIT INTEREST RATES

(i) Example 18. Alexis Company acquires a machine with a cash price of $10,500. It pays for the machine by giving a note for $12,000, promising to make payments equal to 7 percent of the face value, $840 (= 0.07 x $12,000), at the end of each of the next three years and a single payment of $12,000 in three years. What is the interest rate implicit in the loan?

This example has the following time line:

	$10,500	–$840	–$840	–$12,840
End of Year	0	1	2	3

The implicit interest rate is r, such that

$$\$10,500 = \frac{\$840}{(1 + r)} + \frac{\$840}{(1 + r)^2} + \frac{\$12,840}{(1 + r)^3} \tag{3}$$

Compare this formulation to that in equation (1). Note that the left-hand side equals 0 in equation (1), but not in equation (3). You may use any left-hand side that you find convenient for the particular context.

Iteration Number	Net Present Value: Trial Rate = r	Right-Hand Side of Equation 23.1
1.	0.0%	$(5,500)
2.	10.0	(1,521)
3.	15.0	220
4.	15.5	116
5.	15.2	34
6.	15.1	7

EXHIBIT 23.9 ITERATIVE CALCULATIONS FOR IMPLICIT INTEREST RATE

Iteration Number	Trial Rate	Right-Hand Side of Equation 23.3
1.	7.0%	$12,000
2.	15.0	9,808
3.	11.0	10,827
4.	13.0	10,300
5.	12.0	10,559
6.	12.5	10,428
7.	12.3	10,480
8.	12.2	10,506
9.	12.1	10,532

EXHIBIT 23.10 INTERNAL RATE OF RETURN CALCULATION WITH NON-ZERO ENDPOINT

The iteration process shown in Exhibit 23.10 finds an internal rate of return of 12.2 percent to the nearest tenth of 1 percent.

(b) RULES OF THUMB. Adept financial analysts can approximate many of the results of compound interest computations with mental arithmetic or simplified back-of-the-envelope computations. One useful shortcut lies in computing the doubling periods for a stated interest rate; that is, for how long must one leave an amount growing at a given rate for that amount to double.

The easiest such doubling rule is the *rule of 72*. This rule says: Divide the number 72 by the interest rate for a period—a period of any length, such as a month or a year—stated as a percentage; the result is the number of periods required for a sum to double when invested at that rate. For example, if the interest rate is 3 percent per period (think months or years), the rule of 72 says that amounts will double in 24 (= 72/3) periods (months or years). The right answer is 23.45 periods. The rule of 72 works well for interest rates between 2 and 10 percent per period

For interest rates outside that range, the *rule of 69* works better, giving results accurate to within one-tenth of a period for interest rates between one-quarter of one percent and 100 percent per period. This rule says: Divide the number 69 by the interest rate per period stated as a percentage and add .35; the result is the number of periods required for a sum to double when invested at that rate. For example, if the interest rate is .25 percent per month, the rule of 69 computes the doubling time is 276 (69/.25) + .35, or 276. The exact answer is 277 months. The rule of 72 gives the answer as (72/.25), or 288 periods.

In my experience, no matter how sophisticated the calculator or computer you use, you still need to be able to think about the arithmetic involved and have the capability to approximate the answers you expect to see. You need to know which functions to use and the inputs for that function.

23.7 SUMMARY

Accountants typically use one of four kinds of compound interest calculations: (1) the present value or (2) the future value of (3) a single payment or of (4) a series of payments. In working annuity problems, you may find a time line helpful in deciding the particular kind of annuity involved. Computer spreadsheet programs have a built-in function to perform the computations that this chapter describes.

CHAPTER 24

PERFORMANCE EVALUATION IN DECENTRALIZED ORGANIZATIONS

MICHAEL W. MAHER, PHD, EDITOR
University of California, Davis

CONTENTS

24.1 INTRODUCTION 645

24.2 DECENTRALIZED ORGANIZATIONS 646

(a) Goal Congruence and Performance Measurement 646
(b) The Two Fundamental Questions 647

24.3 WHY DECENTRALIZE THE ORGANIZATION? 647

(a) Advantages of Decentralization 647
(b) Disadvantages of Decentralization 648

24.4 TYPES OF RESPONSIBILITY CENTERS 648

(a) Cost Centers 648
(b) Discretionary Cost Centers 649
(c) Revenue Centers 649
(d) Profit Centers 649
(e) Investment Centers 649
(f) Responsibility Centers and Organization Structure 649

24.5 PERFORMANCE MEASUREMENT 650

(a) Discretionary Cost Centers 650
(b) Profit Centers 651
(c) Investment Centers 651

24.6 EVALUATING PERFORMANCE IN DECENTRALIZED ORGANIZATIONS 653

(a) Relative Performance versus Absolute Performance Standards 653
(b) Evaluating Managers' Performance versus Economic Performance of the Responsibility Center 654
(c) Relative Performance Evaluations in Organizations 654

24.7 SUMMARY 655

24.1 INTRODUCTION

This chapter identifies the advantages and disadvantages of decentralization, explains the relation between organization structure and responsibility centers, discusses advantages and disadvantages of both financial and nonfinancial performance measures, and discusses advantages of alternative incentive compensation plans. We focus on internal organizational performance measures that top managers use to evaluate upper-middle and middle managers.

Top management's task becomes increasingly difficult as an organization becomes large and complex. No one individual can manage more than 10 to 30 subordinates. All but small organizations delegate managerial duties. This chapter discusses some of the ways to evaluate employee and business unit performance in decentralized organizations.

Managers generally rely heavily on the accounting system to measure the performance of those to whom they have delegated responsibilities. Consequently, we call the use of accounting for performance evaluation *responsibility accounting*. Other chapters in this book also discuss responsibility accounting. Chapter 19 discusses behavioral issues in budgeting, Chapter 26 examines economic value added, which many organizations use for performance evaluation, and Chapter 25 considers the balanced scorecard.

24.2 DECENTRALIZED ORGANIZATIONS

When companies decentralize authority, a superior, whom we call a *principal,* delegates duties to a subordinate, whom we call an *agent.* We find principal–agent relations in many settings, including those in Exhibit 24.1.

In the principal–agent relation, the principal must find cost-effective ways to encourage agents to act in the principal's interest. Macy's store managers develop financial performance measures, such as daily sales compared to last year same-day sales, to evaluate department managers. Further, Macy's store managers set performance goals (e.g., this year's sales should exceed 105 percent of last year's sales).

(a) GOAL CONGRUENCE AND PERFORMANCE MEASUREMENT. Total *goal congruence* means that all members of an organization have incentives to perform in the common interest. This occurs when the group acts as a team in pursuit of a mutually agreed upon objective. Individual goal congruence occurs when an individual's personal goals concur with organizational goals. Many organizations work hard to create an *esprit de corps* to achieve goal congruence. In most business settings, however, personal goals and organization goals differ. These firms need to design performance evaluation and incentive systems to encourage employees to behave as if their goals coincided with organization goals. This results in *behavioral congruence*; that is, an individual behaves in the best interests of the organization, regardless of his or her own goals.

Managers constantly face choices between their self-interest and the interests of their organization. Consider the case of a plant manager who believes that she will receive a promotion and bonus if the plant has high operating profits. She must decide whether to close the production line for much-needed maintenance, which will reduce short-run profits but improve the company's long-term performance. The manager must decide between doing what makes her look good in the short run and doing what benefits the company in the long run.

To deal with this problem, some companies budget maintenance separately. Others encourage employees to take a long-run interest in the company through stock option and pension plans tied to long-run performance. Still others retain employees in a position long enough that any short-term counterproductive actions catch up with them.

The structure of decentralized organizations amplifies this problem. For example, how does a cost center ensure that the employees share the goals of the center, and how

Principals	Agents
General Motors (GM) stockholders	Top GM management
Corporate (top) GM managers	Divisional managers (Chevrolet Division, Saturn Division, etc.)
Yellow Cab company managers	Taxicab drivers
Macy's retail store managers	Department managers (women's clothing, men's wear, etc.)

EXHIBIT 24.1 EXAMPLES OF PRINCIPAL–AGENT RELATIONS

does the company ensure that the cost center manager's goals coincide with those of the company? We discuss these issues throughout this chapter.

(b) THE TWO FUNDAMENTAL QUESTIONS. Managers must address two basic questions when thinking about their performance evaluation systems:

1. What behavior *does* the system motivate?
2. What behavior *should* the system motivate?

In practice, we see many instances in which the performance evaluation system does not create the right incentives because managers have not satisfactorily addressed these two questions. We see many cases in which people work hard and make the right decisions despite the lack of explicit rewards provided by the company. At a minimum, organization managers should design performance evaluation systems to reward people when they do the right thing and never have systems that penalize people when they do the right thing.

24.3 WHY DECENTRALIZE THE ORGANIZATION?

In centralized organizations, such as the military, top management makes decisions that the organization passes down to subordinates who carry them out. In decentralized companies, divisional and departmental managers make decisions.

Most companies fall between these two extremes. For example, General Motors decentralizes operating units and centralizes the research and development (R&D) and finance functions. Many companies begin with a centralized structure but become more decentralized as they grow, for the reasons stated in Section 24.1.

I interviewed the owner of a small restaurant chain who described to me how his organization became more decentralized. His testimony shows that he learned the importance of decentralization from experience:

> At first, I did a little of everything–cooking, serving, bookkeeping, and advertising. I hired one full-time employee. There was little need for any formal management control system: I made all important decisions, and my employee or I carried them out. Soon we had eight outlets. I was still trying to manage everything personally. I could not make decisions until I had all of the information that I wanted, which slowed our response to all sorts of decisions. A particular outlet would receive food shipments, but I had not authorized anyone to accept delivery. If an outlet ran out of supplies or change, its employees had to wait until I arrived to authorize whatever needed to be done. With only one outlet, I was able to spend a reasonable amount of time on high-level decision making—planning for expansion, arranging financing, developing new marketing strategies, and so forth. But with eight outlets, all of my time was consumed with day-to-day operating decisions.
>
> Finally, I realized that the company had grown too big for me to manage alone. So I decentralized, setting up each outlet just like it was an independent operation. Now each outlet manager takes care of day-to-day operating decisions. This has not only freed my time for more high-level decision making but also provides a better opportunity for the managers to learn about management, and it gives me a chance to evaluate their performance for promotion to higher management positions, which I intend to create soon.[1]

(a) ADVANTAGES OF DECENTRALIZATION. The larger and more complex an organization, the more advantages decentralization offers, such as the following:

- *Faster response.* As the owner-manager of the fast-food chain described, local managers can react to a changing environment more quickly than top management can. With centralized decision making, delays occur while lower-level employees transmit information to decision makers, and further delays occur while decision makers communicate instructions to lower-level managers and employees.

- *Wiser use of management's time.* The owner-manager of the fast-food chain complained that he had too little time for high-level decision making. Top management usually has a comparative advantage over middle management in this area. When day-to-day operating decisions consume a high-level manager's attention, he or she neglects important strategic decisions. Moreover, local managers often make better operating decisions because of their technical expertise and knowledge about local conditions.
- *Reduction of problems to manageable size.* Humans have a limited capacity to solve complex problems. Decentralization reduces the complexity of problems by dividing large problems into smaller, more manageable parts.
- *Training, evaluation, and motivation of local managers.* Decentralization allows managers to receive on-the-job training in decision making. Top management can observe the outcome of lower-level managers' decisions and evaluate their potential for advancement. Moreover, ambitious managers will likely be frustrated if they implement only the decisions of others and never have the satisfaction of making their own decisions and carrying them out. This satisfaction can provide an important motivational reward for managers.

(b) DISADVANTAGES OF DECENTRALIZATION. Decentralization has many disadvantages as well. The major disadvantage is that local managers may make decisions that do not coincide with the preferences of top management and constituents of the organization (such as stockholders). Thus, decentralized companies incur the cost of monitoring and controlling the activities of local managers. They incur the costs that result when local managers make decisions and take actions that do not follow the best interest of the organization.

A company must weigh the costs and benefits of decentralization and decide on an economically optimal level. One can assume that the disadvantages of decentralization for highly centralized organizations outweigh the advantages, while the reverse holds true for decentralized companies.

24.4 TYPES OF RESPONSIBILITY CENTERS

Organizations have five basic types of decentralized units:

1. Cost centers
2. Discretionary cost centers
3. Responsibility unit in an organization, such as a department in a store or a division revenue center
4. Profit centers
5. Investment centers

A *center* is a business unit in a company, such as a department or a division.

(a) COST CENTERS. In *cost centers*, managers have responsibility for the cost of an activity for which a well-defined relation exists between inputs and outputs. One often finds cost centers in manufacturing operations where management can specify inputs, such as direct materials and direct labor, for each output. The production departments of manufacturing plants are examples of cost centers. Some nonmanufacturing organizations also use cost centers. For example, banks can establish standards for check processing, so banks might designate check-processing departments as cost centers. Hospitals often set up food-service departments, laundries, and laboratories as cost centers.

Managers of cost centers have responsibility for the costs and volumes of inputs used to produce an output. Often, someone other than the cost center manager–such as the marketplace, top management, or the marketing department–determines these costs and volumes. The company often gives a plant manager a production schedule to meet as efficiently as possible. If the firm operates the plant as a cost center, the firm will use manufacturing cost variances, such as those discussed in Chapter 15. (Exhibit 24.2 shows how the cost center typically appears on the organization chart.)

(b) DISCRETIONARY COST CENTERS. The cost centers described in Section 24.4(a) require a well-specified relation between inputs and outputs for performance evaluation. When companies hold managers responsible for costs, but do not specify the input-output relation, a *discretionary cost center* results. Firms usually consider legal, accounting, R&D, advertising, and many other administrative and marketing departments as discretionary cost centers (see Exhibit 24.2). Discretionary cost centers also are common in government and other nonprofit organizations that use budgets as a ceiling on expenditures. Nonprofit organizations usually evaluate managers on bases other than costs but impose penalties for exceeding the budget ceiling.

(c) REVENUE CENTERS. Managers of *revenue centers* typically have responsibility for marketing a product, evaluated by sales price or sales activity variances. An example of a revenue center is the sportswear department of a large department store in which the manager has responsibility for merchandise sales.

(d) PROFIT CENTERS. Managers of *profit centers* have responsibility for profits. They manage both revenues and costs (as shown in Exhibit 24.2). For example, a Burger King franchise may operate its warehouses as cost centers but its restaurants as profit centers. Managers of profit centers have more autonomy than do managers of cost or revenue centers.

(e) INVESTMENT CENTERS. Managers of investment centers have responsibility for profits and investment in assets. These managers have relatively large amounts of money with which to make capital budgeting decisions. For instance, in one company, the manager of a cost center cannot acquire assets that cost more than $5,000 without a superior's approval, but an investment center manager can make acquisitions costing up to $500,000 without higher approval. Companies evaluate investment centers using some measure of profits related to the invested assets in the center.

(f) RESPONSIBILITY CENTERS AND ORGANIZATION STRUCTURE. As Exhibit 24.2 shows, the type of responsibility center closely relates to its position in the organization structure. For the company shown, plant managers run cost centers, and district sales managers operate revenue centers. Moving up the organization chart, we find that division managers in charge of both plant managers and district sales managers have responsibility for profits.

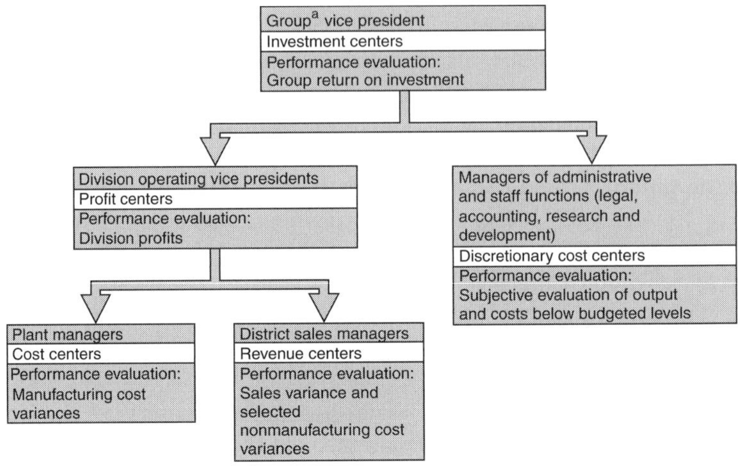

[a] *Group* refers to a group of divisions

EXHIBIT 24.2 ORGANIZATION STRUCTURE AND RESPONSIBILITY CENTERS

Of course, every company can choose from numerous decentralized organization structures (some decentralized companies establish manufacturing plants as profit centers, for example). Generally, however, higher levels in an organization have broader scope of authority and responsibility; hence, companies identify profit or investment centers at this level.

24.5 PERFORMANCE MEASUREMENT

We discuss the use of cost variances for evaluating performance in Chapter 15. This section considers additional performance measures in discretionary cost centers, profit centers, and investment centers.

(a) DISCRETIONARY COST CENTERS. Organizations often have difficulty managing discretionary costs, which may include those for R&D and accounting systems, because costs do not clearly relate to output. For the same reason, firms have difficulty evaluating the performance of a discretionary cost center manager. Companies have tried numerous methods of identifying appropriate relations between discretionary costs and activity levels and comparison with other firms. But relating costs to activity levels remains primarily a matter of management judgment or discretion. Consequently, companies typically give managers of discretionary cost centers a budget and instruct them not to exceed it without higher-level authorization. Most governmental units cannot legally exceed the budget without first obtaining authorization from a legislative body (e.g., Congress, the state legislature, the city council).

Such situations can invite suboptimal behavior. Managers have incentives to spend all of their budgets, even if they could achieve some savings, to support their request for the same or higher budgets in the following year. Furthermore, companies often lack a specified relation between the quality of services and their costs. (Would the quality of research and development decrease 10 percent with a 10 percent cut in funds? Would crime increase 10 percent if police department funds were cut 10 percent?)

Ideally, companies should measure performance in a specified way–for example, compare actual inputs to standard inputs in a cost center. But companies face difficulties and costs when measuring the performance of the manager and workers in a discretionary cost center. Thus, it also becomes difficult to provide incentives for employees to perform at the levels that best achieve organization goals.

(b) PROFIT CENTERS. Decentralized organizations depend heavily on profit measures to evaluate the performance of decentralized units and their managers. The difficulties of measuring profits have prompted many companies to use multiple performance measures. In the early 1950s, General Electric proposed an extensive and innovative performance measurement system that evaluated market position, productivity, product leadership, personnel development, employee attitudes, public responsibility, and balance between short-range and long-range goals in addition to profitability. But even when a company uses a broad range of performance measures, accounting results continue to play an important role in performance evaluation. One commonly hears that "hard" measures of performance tend to drive out "soft" measures. Nevertheless, no accounting measure can fully gauge the performance of an organizational unit or its manager.

In profit centers, we encounter the usual problems related to measuring profits for the company as a whole plus an important additional one: How does the company allocate revenues and costs to each profit center? A profit center that is totally separate from all other parts of the company operates like an autonomous company. The company can uniquely identify profits of that type of center.

One seldom finds a completely independent profit center, however. Most profit centers have costs (and perhaps revenues) in common with other units. The profit center may share facilities with other units or use headquarters' staff services, for example. If so, the company faces a cost allocation problem (see Chapter 16).

A related problem involves the transfer of goods between a profit center and other parts of the organization. The company must price such goods so that the profit center manager has incentives to trade with other units when the organization's best interests dictate such practices. Chapter 27 discusses this transfer pricing problem in more detail.

Most companies have difficulty deciding how to measure performance in a profit center and leave much to managerial judgment. No matter what process the firm chooses, it should have straightforward objectives: Measure employees' performance in ways that motivate them to work in the best interest of their employers and compare that performance to standards or budget plans.

(c) INVESTMENT CENTERS

(i) Return on Investment. Managers of investment centers have responsibility for profits and investment in assets. Companies evaluate them on their ability to generate a sufficiently high *return on investment (ROI)* to justify the investment in the division.[1]

One computes the ROI as follows:

$$\text{ROI} = \text{Operating profits/Investment center assets}$$

1. Readers should look to Chapters 21 and 22 for a full discussion of capital investments.

It often is divided into profit margin and asset turnover components, as follows:

ROI = Profit margin × Asset turnover
= Operating profit/Sales × Sales/Investment center assets
= Operating profit/Investment center assets

The profit margin measures the investment center's ability to control its costs for a given level of revenues. The lower the costs required to generate a dollar of revenue, the higher the profit margin.

The asset turnover ratio measures the investment center's ability to generate sales for each dollar of assets invested in the center.

Relating profits to capital investment has intuitive appeal. Capital is a scarce resource. If one unit of a company shows a low return, the firm may better employ the capital in another unit with a higher return, invest it elsewhere, or pay it to shareholders.

Relating profits to investment also provides a scale for measuring performance. Consider the example in Exhibit 24.3. For example, investment A generated $200,000 in operating profits, while investment B generated $2 million. But investment A required a capital investment of $500,000, while investment B required an investment of $20 million. As you can see from Exhibit 24.3, ROI provides a different picture from operating profits.

Although companies commonly use ROI, as a performance measure, it has limitations. The many difficulties of measuring profits affect the numerator, and problems in measuring the investment base affect the denominator. Consequently, one cannot easily make comparisons among investment centers. Chapters 21 and 22 discuss investment-related decisions.

(ii) ROI versus Residual Income. Many companies use ROI to evaluate their divisions' investment opportunities and management. However, the method has some drawbacks: If firms encourage division managers to maximize ROI, they may turn down investment opportunities that will perform above the minimum acceptable rate for the corporation but below the rate their center currently earns. For example, suppose that a corporation has a 15 percent cost of capital. A division has an opportunity to make an additional investment that will return $400,000 per year for a $2 million investment. The ROI for this project equals 20 percent ($400,000/$2,000,000), so the project qualifies at the corporate level in meeting ROI targets. Assuming that the project meets all other corporate requirements, the manager should accept it. However, the manager of the division in which the investment would occur may reject it if the division's ROI exceeds 20 percent. For example, suppose that the center currently earns the following:

ROI = $1,000,000/$4,000,000 = 25 percent

	A	B
1. Operating profits	$ 200,00	$ 2,000,000
2. Investment	500,000	20,000,000
3. Return on investment (1)/(2)	40%	10%

EXHIBIT 24.3 COMPARISON OF RETURN ON INVESTMENT (ROI)

With the new investment, ROI can be computed as follows:

$$\text{ROI} = \$1{,}000{,}000 + \$400{,}000/\$4{,}000{,}000 + \$2{,}000{,}000 = 23.3 \text{ percent}$$

Because a comparison of the old and new returns implies that performance had worsened, the center's manager might hesitate to make such an investment, even though the investment would have a positive benefit for the company as a whole.

Alternatively, companies could measure *residual income (RI),* currently known by its commercial name—economic value added (EVA). Chapter 26 discusses EVA in considerable detail, so we present just the basic idea here. If your organization uses or considers using EVA, then you should read Chapter 26.

We define residual income as follows:

$$\text{Investment center operating profits} - (\text{Capital charge} \times \text{Investment center assets})$$

where the capital charge is the minimum acceptable rate of return.

Using the numbers from the previous example, we can see the impact of the investment in additional capacity on residual income. Before the investment,

$$\begin{aligned} \text{RI} &= \$1{,}000{,}000 - (.15 \times \$4{,}000{,}000) \\ &= \$1{,}000{,}000 - \$600{,}000 \\ &= \$400{,}000 \end{aligned}$$

The residual income from the additional investment in plant capacity is

$$\begin{aligned} \text{RI} &= \$400{,}000 - (.15 \times \$2{,}000{,}000) \\ &= \$400{,}000 - \$300{,}000 \\ &= \$100{,}000 \end{aligned}$$

Hence, after the additional investment, the residual income of the division will increase to

$$\begin{aligned} \text{RI} &= (\$1{,}000{,}000 + \$400{,}000) - [.15 \times (\$4{,}000{,}000 + \$2{,}000{,}000)] \\ &= \$1{,}400{,}000 - (.15 \times \$6{,}000{,}000) \\ &= \$1{,}400{,}000 - \$900{,}000 \\ &= \$500{,}000 \end{aligned}$$

The additional investment in plant capacity increases residual income, appropriately improving the measure of performance.

24.6 EVALUATING PERFORMANCE IN DECENTRALIZED ORGANIZATIONS

(a) RELATIVE PERFORMANCE VERSUS ABSOLUTE PERFORMANCE STANDARDS. Companies often find themselves tempted to compare the performance of their decentralized centers and even to encourage competition among them. The problems inherent in some performance measures, particularly ROI, complicate such comparisons. In addition, the centers may be in very different businesses: one cannot fairly compare the performance of a manufacturing center with the performance of a center that provides consulting service and has a relatively small investment base. One should also consider differences in the riskiness of centers, particularly investment centers. Companies should consider these systematic differences when comparing the performance of investment centers.

When diverse centers exist, management frequently establishes target performance measures for the individual centers. For example, management might evaluate the investment center by comparing the actual ROI with the target ROI. Such a comparison procedure resembles the budget versus actual comparisons that firms make for cost centers, revenue centers, and profit centers. Companies may find more logic in comparing the performance of a center with that of a company in the same industry, rather than comparing it with that of other centers within a company.

(b) EVALUATING MANAGERS' PERFORMANCE VERSUS ECONOMIC PERFORMANCE OF THE RESPONSIBILITY CENTER. The evaluation of a manager is not necessarily identical to the evaluation of the cost, profit, or investment center. As a general rule, companies should evaluate managers based on a comparison of actual results to targets. For example, when a company asks a manager to take over a marginal operation and turn it around, the company may give the manager a minimal ROI target, consistent with the divisions' past performance. The firm would reward a manager who meets or exceeds that target. Even with the best management, however, some centers cannot improve performance. Thus, companies may decide to disband a center even though the manager received a highly positive evaluation. Senior management should reward the manager that performs well in an adverse situation but needs to recognize when it should bail out of a bad operation if it can make better use of company resources.

An interesting problem arises in implementing this concept in an ongoing division. How does one evaluate the performance of a manager who takes over an existing division whose assets, operating structure, and markets are established prior to the manager's arrival at the helm? New managers cannot control the assets they must work with or the markets in which the division operates at the time they take over.

As a general rule, evaluating the manager on the basis of performance targets, as suggested earlier in this chapter, overcomes this problem. The new manager establishes a plan for operating the division and works with top management to set targets for the future. The company compares those targets to actual results as the manager enacts the plan, and evaluates the manager based on those results. In short, the longer the manager leads the division, the more responsibility the manager takes for its success.

(c) RELATIVE PERFORMANCE EVALUATIONS IN ORGANIZATIONS. When evaluating center or divisional performance, companies must separate performance results that managers can control from the effect of factors outside of their control. (See Chapter 19.) As mentioned in Section 24.6(b), companies generally hold division managers accountable for meeting or exceeding targets established for that particular division. However, these targets are often independent of the manager's performance as compared to those of peers (e.g., other divisions operating in similar product markets). *Relative performance evaluations (RPE)* address this issue by comparing managers of one division to their peers. A division earning a 10 percent profit margin will receive more favorable evaluations if the peers averaged 5 percent rather than 20 percent.

RPE goes beyond setting internal targets (e.g., divisional return on investment) and compares managers or divisions to other comparable divisions. A division might meet or exceed its internal targets yet perform well below its peer group. Companies can identify such a problem only by comparing the division with its peers.

24.7 SUMMARY

The advantages of decentralization include faster response time; wiser use of management's time; reduction of problems to manageable size; and training, evaluation, and motivation of local managers. The disadvantage of such an organization is the potential for local managers to make wrong or bad decisions.

As with all organizations, managers must address two basic questions when developing performance evaluation systems for decentralized organizations: (1) What behavior does the system motivate? (2) What behavior should the system motivate? Managers should design performance evaluation systems to reward people for doing the right thing. Relative performance evaluation compares the performance of similar types of responsibility centers. Senior management often distinguishes between evaluating performance of the people from that of the responsibility center.

Companies usually evaluate cost centers, revenue centers, and profit centers based on a comparison of actual performance with budgeted goals. They evaluate investment centers on the basis of how efficiently the center uses the assets employed to generate profits. Companies usually use ROI to measure performance of investment centers; they also use residual income, also known as economic value added (EVA®).

CHAPTER 25

THE BALANCED SCORECARD AND NONFINANCIAL PERFORMANCE MEASURES

MICHAEL W. MAHER, PHD, EDITOR
University of California, Davis

CONTENTS

25.1 INTRODUCTION: BEYOND THE ACCOUNTING NUMBERS 657

25.2 RESPONSIBILITIES BY LEVEL OF ORGANIZATION 658

(a) Values of the Organization 659
(b) The Balanced Scorecard 659

25.3 FOUR BASIC BALANCED SCORECARD PERSPECTIVES 659

25.4 BUILDING THE INCENTIVE PLAN AROUND THE BALANCED SCORECARD 661

(a) The Learning and Growth Perspective 661
(b) The Internal Business and Production Process Perspective 661
(c) The Customer Perspective 662
(d) The Financial Perspective 663

25.5 IMPLEMENTING THE BALANCED SCORECARD 663

25.6 IMPROVING PERFORMANCE MEASUREMENT 664

(a) Continuous Improvement 664
(b) Benchmarking 664

25.7 PERFORMANCE MEASUREMENT: THE MEASURES 664

(a) Customer Satisfaction Performance Measures 665
(b) Functional Performance Measures 665
(c) Nonfinancial Performance and Activity-Based Management 666

25.8 SUMMARY 668

BIBLIOGRAPHY 668

25.1 INTRODUCTION: BEYOND THE ACCOUNTING NUMBERS

Companies have traditionally relied heavily on financial performance measures to evaluate employee performance because one can easily quantify them and they motivate employees to improve the company's accounting profits. In recent years, companies have begun using nonfinancial measures such as customer satisfaction and product quality measures. These companies discovered that nonfinancial performance measures direct employees' attention to those things that they can control. For example, consider the case of a food server in a restaurant. The food server can have a big effect on customer satisfaction. Measuring his or her performance in terms of customer satisfaction should have a meaningful effect on the server's performance. It would be difficult, however, to measure the effect of the food server's performance in pleasing customers on the restaurant's profits because many factors outside the server's control affect profits. Furthermore, the food server might not even understand how the restaurant earns or calculates profits. Therefore, it makes sense to reward the food server directly for creating customer satisfaction rather than for his or her effect on profits.

This chapter discusses innovative ways to evaluate performance beyond the numbers. Performance evaluation starts with an understanding of the organization's objectives and strategy. For example, does the firm want to position itself as a low-cost producer or an innovator? In what markets will it compete? The organization evaluates performance by first defining what it wants to accomplish. Then it develops measures that help it evaluate its performance in achieving those accomplishments.

25.2 RESPONSIBILITIES BY LEVEL OF ORGANIZATION

Performance measurement has two components. First, it focuses all organization members on the organization's objectives and reflects how individuals or units contribute to them. Second, it reflects the extent to which each organization level can affect results.

Performance measurement emphasizes different things at different levels of the organization. At the lower levels in the organization, such as the sportswear department at Macy's department store or the painting center at a Honda automobile assembly plant, nonfinancial performance measures focus on customer satisfaction and product quality and reflect what these employees control. The performance measures emphasize customer satisfaction if employees deal directly with customers as they do at Macy's, Burger King, and Citibank, for example. The performance measures for employees in production, such as those at the Honda assembly plant, or those at Upjohn, emphasize product quality.

At middle levels in organizations, nonfinancial performance measurement focuses on how well the operating systems work together and the effectiveness of these systems compared to those of competitors. At this organization level, coordination and improvement of ongoing activities take place in addition to redesigning products and processes. For example, middle managers have responsibility for inferior customer service at Macy's that one could attribute to poorly trained sales personnel. The following lists some of the nonfinancial performance measures that organizations use to evaluate middle managers' performance:

- Amount of unwanted employee turnover
- Frequency of meeting customer delivery requirements
- Employee development performance, such as quality and amount of training
- Performance in dealing with business partners, such as quality of supplier relations and the frequency of miscommunicated orders to suppliers

At the organization's top levels, performance measurement focuses on assessing whether the organization will meet its responsibilities from the perspectives of its stakeholders. An organization's *stakeholders* are groups or individuals who have a stake in what the organization does. Stakeholders include shareholders, customers, employees, the community in which the organization does business, and, in some cases, society as a whole. For example, employees depend on an organization for their employment. Shareholders depend on an organization to generate a return on their investment. Performance at this level requires delicately balancing tradeoffs.

People at different levels in the organization have different responsibilities. Consequently, the performance measurement system measures different things at different levels in the organization. In general, performance measures should relate to what people at different levels control.

(a) VALUES OF THE ORGANIZATION. An organization uses a *mission statement* to describe its values, define responsibilities to stakeholders, and identify the major *business-level strategies* the organization plans to use to meet its commitments.

Mission statements should answer the following questions:

- Who are the organization's stakeholders? Who matters to the organization?
- How will the organization add value to each stakeholder group? This identifies the *critical success factors,* the factors important for the organization's success.

(b) THE BALANCED SCORECARD. The balanced scorecard is a model of lead and lag indicators of performance that includes both financial and nonfinancial performance measures. Consider the following example. Rentz rental car company trains its employees in efficiency. Consequently, its satisfied customers remain loyal to Rentz. Rentz has created a link between employee training, business efficiency, customer satisfaction, and financial performance. The balanced scorecard would reward managers responsible for employee training because of their effect on future financial performance. Carrying the balanced scorecard concept to its logical conclusion, management should show each person in the organization how his or her job contributes to the organization's ultimate goals.

This chapter provides a basic introduction to the balanced scorecard. You will find many books and videos available that discuss the balanced scorecard in considerable detail. The bibliography lists a sample of them.

25.3 FOUR BASIC BALANCED SCORECARD PERSPECTIVES

Most organizations use four categories of performance measures, or perspectives, as Exhibit 25.1 shows. The financial perspective indicates whether the company's strategy and operations add value to shareholders. For organizations that do not have shareholders, the financial perspective indicates how well the strategy and operations contribute to improving the organization's financial health. The customer perspective indicates how the company's strategy and operations add value to customers. The internal business and production process perspective indicates the ability of the internal business processes to add value to customers and to improve shareholder wealth. Finally, the learning and growth perspective indicates the strength of the infrastructure for innovation and long-term growth. This important perspective presents the source of the organization's future value.[1]

---

1. Adapted from R. S. Kaplan and D. P. Norton, *The Balanced Scorecard: Translating Strategy Into Action* (Boston: Harvard Business School Publishing, 1996).

Reprinted by permission of *Harvard Business Review.* From "Using the Balanced Scorecard as a Strategic Management System," by R. S. Kaplan and D. P. Norton, Jan–Feb, 1996.

EXHIBIT 25.1 BALANCED SCOREBOARD

25.4 BUILDING THE INCENTIVE PLAN AROUND THE BALANCED SCORECARD

We next examine how to build an incentive plan around the four perspectives of the balanced scorecard.

(a) THE LEARNING AND GROWTH PERSPECTIVE. For incentive purposes, the learning and growth perspective focuses on the capabilities of people. Managers would be responsible for developing employee capabilities. Key measures for evaluating managers' performance would be employee satisfaction, employee retention, and employee productivity.

(i) Employee Satisfaction. Employee satisfaction recognizes the importance of employee morale for improving productivity, quality, customer satisfaction, and responsiveness to situations. Managers can measure employee satisfaction by sending surveys, interviewing employees, or observing employees at work.

(ii) Employee Retention. Firms committed to retaining employees recognize that employees develop organization-specific intellectual capital and provide a valuable nonfinancial asset to the company. Furthermore, firms incur costs when they must find and hire good talent to replace people who leave. Firms measure employee retention as the inverse of employee turnover—the percent of people who leave each year.

(iii) Employee Productivity. Employee productivity recognizes the importance of output per employee. Employees create physical output (i.e., miles driven, pages produced, or lawns mowed), or financial output (i.e., revenue per employee or profits per employee). The number of loans processed per loan officer per month would provide a simple measure of productivity for loan officers at a bank.

A good incentive system rewards managers who promote high employee satisfaction, low employee turnover, and high employee productivity. An environment that supports employees provides greater opportunities for improving internal business processes, as discussed next.

(b) THE INTERNAL BUSINESS AND PRODUCTION PROCESS PERSPECTIVE. A cause-and-effect relation exists between the learning and growth perspective and internal business and production process perspective. Employees who do the work provide the best source of new ideas for better business processes. For example, an autoworker demonstrated that increasing the height of an automobile assembly line made it easier for workers to screw on the lug nuts for wheels. Raising the height of the assembly line improved productivity and reduced back injuries.

(i) Supplier Relations. Supplier relations are critical for success, particularly in retail and manufacturing assembly. Companies depend on suppliers to receive goods and services on time, at a low price, and of a high quality. Supplier problems can shut down entire companies. Good supplier relations have become key to corporate success as companies increasingly outsource important parts of the supply chain.

To provide incentives for good supplier relations, companies develop supplier rating systems that indicate which suppliers have certification for delivery of product without inspection and which do not.

Company managers should have incentives to certify suppliers, working with them to reduce their costs and increase quality. Thus, evaluation of supplier performance plays an important part of any incentive plan.

(ii) Process Improvement Incentives. Customers value receiving goods and services reliably and on time. Suppliers can satisfy customers if they hold large amounts of inventory to ensure availability of goods. But holding lots of inventory leads to high inventory carrying and storage costs, inventory obsolescence, and a host of other problems. The supplier can avoid excessive inventory buildup by reducing throughput time, the total time between receipt of an order and delivery of the product. Reducing throughput time can help a customer who wants the goods or services as soon as possible.

(c) THE CUSTOMER PERSPECTIVE. The customer perspective focuses on the expectations of a firm's customers. Designing an incentive compensation system around customers' expectations requires, first, that the company define its customers and, second, that it know their expectations.

Federal Express developed successfully by knowing its customers and their expectations. It knew that its customers wanted the function of overnight delivery with defect-free quality. It also found that its customers would pay a premium for that function and quality, compared to what they could expect from the U.S. Postal Service. In addition to knowing its customers and their expectations, a firm must provide incentives to managers and employees to meet customers' expectations. FedEx's incentive compensation plan encourages employees to go out of their way to ensure that they deliver packages reliably on time.

Companies use the following performance measures, among others, when considering the customer perspective:

- Customer satisfaction
- Customer retention
- Market share
- Customer profitability

(i) Customer Satisfaction. Customer satisfaction measures indicate whether the company meets or exceeds customers' expectations. You have probably completed customer satisfaction forms for restaurants, hotels, or automobile repair shops.

(ii) Customer Retention. Customer retention or loyalty measures indicate a company's ability to keep its customers. A rule of thumb states that it costs five times as much to get a new customer as it does to keep an existing one. While we might quibble with the number five, the point has truth: Companies find it easier to retain current customers than to cultivate new ones.

(iii) Market Share. Market share measures a company's proportion of the total business in a particular market. Companies typically measure market share in terms of dollar sales, unit volume, or number of customers.

(iv) Customer Profitability. Customer profitability refers to how much profit your customers make for you. Loyal customers and a large market share do not always ensure profitability. For instance, firms will have happy, loyal customers by providing a quality product well below cost. But that action would not keep the company in business for long.

Consultants and researchers have found evidence that better customer satisfaction leads to increased customer profitability. The researchers discovered, however, that increasing customer satisfaction appears to pay off only up to a point. One could think of this result as the difference between happy and ecstatic customers—euphoria is nice for the customers but does little for the company's economic value.

(v) Customer Perspective in Nonprofit Organizations. The customer perspective rises to the top of the various perspectives in nonprofit organizations, because managers of nonprofits care more about servicing their students, patients, and clients than about generating profits. Financial goals have importance in nonprofits because organizations must be financially sound to sustain themselves, but nonprofit mission statements emphasize servicing their customers above all else.

(d) THE FINANCIAL PERSPECTIVE. The balanced scorecard uses financial performance measures, such as net income and return on investment, because all for-profit organizations use them. Financial performance measures provide a common language for analyzing and comparing companies. People who provide funds to companies, such as financial institutions and shareholders, rely heavily on financial performance measures in deciding whether to lend or invest funds. Properly designed financial measures can provide an aggregate view of an organization's success.

Financial measures by themselves do not provide incentives for success. Financial measures tell a story about the past, but not the future; they have importance, but will not guide performance in creating value.

The balanced scorecard, as the name implies, looks for a balance of multiple performance measures—both financial and nonfinancial—to guide organizational performance towards success.

25.5 IMPLEMENTING THE BALANCED SCORECARD

We have presented four perspectives for the balanced scorecard and discussed numerous performance measures. Managers should use the performance measures that provide the right incentives. They must remember that each performance measure has a cost for data collection and too many performance measures can confuse employees, particularly if some seem contradictory. Thus, a tradeoff exists between the costs and benefits of additional performance measures.

The method of weighting various performance measures presents a problem for designers of balanced scorecards. Assigning a particular weight to each performance measure (e.g., customer satisfaction will count 15 percent of the total performance score) does not allow for flexibility in assessing performance and for recognition of unforeseen problems arising during the performance period. For example, assume the designers assigned a weight of 15 percent to customer satisfaction, but a particular division did superb work in improving customer satisfaction. Senior management might want to reward such performance more than implied by the 15 percent weighting. Research has shown that the use of flexibility, such as assigning weights to performance measures after the performance period and incorporating subjective performance evaluations, resulted in complaints about favoritism.

Senior management has developed and used the balanced scorecard to support the organization's development of strategies. Implementing it at lower levels has proved problematic. Typically, implementing the balanced scorecard requires months or even years. Furthermore, this process becomes iterative because targets, performance measures, and even strategies change over time. People comfortable with only a single objective performance measure that never changes, such as return on investment, will probably find the balanced scorecard frustrating. However, using the balanced scorecard can provide a more realistic view about the complexities and tradeoffs that organizations face.

After considering the costs and benefits of balanced scorecard performance measures, I view it as a useful tool with good ideas. Use of nonfinancial performance measures that are lead indicators of an organization's financial performance should align employees' incentives with those of the organization.

25.6 IMPROVING PERFORMANCE MEASUREMENT

(a) CONTINUOUS IMPROVEMENT. Many organizations use the continuous improvement philosophy to meet responsibilities and evaluate performance. It means continuously reevaluating and improving the efficiency of activities. Such efforts aim to (1) improve the activities in which the organization engages through documentation and understanding, (2) eliminate non-value-added activities, and (3) improve the efficiency of value added activities. (Section 6.9 of Chapter 6 discusses value added and non-value-added activities.)

(b) BENCHMARKING. This involves the search for, and implementation of, the best way to do something as practiced in other organizations or in other parts of one's own organization. Using benchmarking, managers identify an activity that needs improvement, find the person most efficient at that activity (sometimes in one's own organization), study the process of the most efficient person, and then adopt (and adapt) that efficient process to their own organization.

Companies use benchmarks to measure the performance of an activity, operation, or organization relative to others. Some important guidelines follow:

- Don't benchmark everything at the best-in-the-business level. No company can dominate in everything.
- Only benchmark best-in-class processes and activities that have the most strategic importance.
- Look for internal, regional, or industry benchmarks for less important support activities.

Exhibit 25.2 presents some common questions raised in the benchmarking process.

25.7 PERFORMANCE MEASUREMENT: THE MEASURES

A company must base its performance measures on its responsibilities, goals, and strategies, which will differ across organizations. You will likely use or observe the following examples of performance measures in organizations. The examples use customer satisfaction measures, which have importance to the success of any organization, and functional

Product Performance. How well do our products perform compared to those of our competitors? (Many U.S. automobile, steel, camera, and television companies found that, much to their dismay, they were not performing well in the 1980s compared to their Japanese competitors.)

Employee Performance. How well do our employees perform compared to our competitors' employees? Are our employees as efficient as our competitors' employees? Are our employees as well trained as our competitors' employees?

New Product/Service Development. Are we as innovative as our competitors in developing new products and services?

Cost Performance. Are our costs as low as those of our competitors?

EXHIBIT 25.2 COMMON BENCHMARK QUESTIONS

measures, which test how well the organization's internal processes function. These examples should convey a sense of the types of nonfinancial measures that organizations use; they are not a comprehensive cookbook of the measures available.

(a) CUSTOMER SATISFACTION PERFORMANCE MEASURES. Customer satisfaction measures reflect the performance of the organization on several internal factors, including quality control and delivery performance.

(i) Quality Control. This factor focuses on increasing customer satisfaction with the product, reducing the costs of dealing with customer complaints, and reducing the costs of repairing products or providing a new service. (Measures may include number of customer complaints, number of service calls, and number of returns.)

(ii) Delivery Performance. This factor focuses on delivering goods and services when promised. (Measures may include the percentage of on-time deliveries and percentage of deliveries damaged.)

(b) FUNCTIONAL PERFORMANCE MEASURES. As well as an external customer focus, an organization must maintain internal functional performance evaluation. Companies perform many activities throughout the product life cycle. The efficiency level of processing activities affects the overall performance of the organization in meeting its responsibilities to other stakeholders, such as shareholders and employees. Exhibit 25.3 presents several internal functional performance measures that the organizations use.

As you can see, many internal performance measures also relate to customer performance. For instance, quality assurance relates *directly* to customer satisfaction performance while production control and product development relate *indirectly* to customer satisfaction.

(i) Manufacturing Cycle Time. Companies refer to the time required to produce a good or service as *manufacturing cycle time.* The cycle time includes processing, moving, storing, and inspecting. A product's service, quality, and cost all relate to cycle time. As cycle time increases, so do the costs of processing, inspecting, moving, and storing; service and quality, however, decrease with cycle time increases.

Accounting Quality
Percentage of late reports
Percentage of errors in reports
Percentage of errors in budget predictions
Manager satisfaction with accounting reports

Clerical Quality
Errors per typed page
Number of times messages are not delivered

Product/Development Engineering Quality Measurements
Percentage of errors in cost estimates
How well product meets customer expectations

Forecasting Quality
Percentage of error in sales forecasts
Number of forecasting assumption errors
Usefulness of forecasts to decision makers

Procurement/Purchasing Quality
Percentage of supplies delivered on schedule
Average time to fill emergency orders

Production Control Quality
Time required to incorporate engineering changes
Time that assembly line is down due to materials shortage

Quality Assurance Quality
Time to answer customer complaints

EXHIBIT 25.3 FUNCTIONAL MEASURES OF PERFORMANCE

(ii) Manufacturing Cycle Efficiency. Manufacturing cycle efficiency measures the efficiency of the total manufacturing cycle. We calculate manufacturing cycle efficiency for one unit as follows:

$$\text{Manufacturing cycle efficiency} = \frac{\text{Processing time}}{(\text{Processing time} + \text{Moving time} + \text{Storing time} + \text{Inspection time})}$$

This formula calculates a percentage representing the time spent processing the unit. The higher the percentage, the less the time (and costs) spent on non-value-added activities such as moving and storage. Higher-quality control of the process and inputs results in less time spent on inspections.

(c) NONFINANCIAL PERFORMANCE AND ACTIVITY-BASED MANAGEMENT. Many experts argue that organizations should manage by using activity data rather than cost data. Knowing the amount of time it takes to produce and deliver a product (e.g., materials handling, storage space used, and rework) could lead to improvement. Organizations could use the activity data to identify problems, suggest an approach to solve problems, and prioritize improvement efforts.

Organizations also may find value in knowing the amount of time required to complete a sequence of activities. Elimination of long cycle times might also reduce the costs of nonproduction personnel, equipment, and supplies. Customers also value a prompt response and a short order processing time.

As discussed in Section 25.7(b), many believe that a product's service, quality, and cost relate to cycle time: As cycle time increases, cost increases and service and quality decrease. So, as the organization improves the efficiency of value-added activities or eliminates non-value-added activities, the process cycle time and cost will decrease.

Many organizations involve workers in creating ideas for improving performance on critical success factors. Competent managers know that workers have good ideas for improving a company's operations. After all, the workers are much closer to those operations than are managers.

Worker involvement has importance for three reasons:

1. Many managers believe that when workers take on decision-making authority, their commitment to the organization and its objectives increases.
2. When decision-making responsibility lies with workers closer to the customer, workers become more responsive and make informed decisions.
3. Giving decision-making responsibility to workers uses their skills and knowledge and motivates them to further develop the skills and knowledge in an effort to improve the organization's performance.

How do companies evaluate their own performance in getting workers involved and committed? Exhibit 25.4 lists performance measures that organizations can use to assess how well they perform in terms of worker involvement and commitment. Increasing the percentages on these performance measures demonstrates the organization's attempt to increase worker involvement and commitment to the organization. For example, managers may attempt to increase worker commitment by providing mentors for them. (See the first item in Exhibit 25.4.) As the number of workers in mentor programs increase, so will their commitment to the organization.

Effective worker involvement presents three challenges for management. First, management must create a system that conveys the organization's objectives and critical success factors to all members. Information and training sessions and the performance indicators themselves determine the extent to which employees understand what behavior the organization desires of them.

Second, the measures the organization uses to judge individual performance determine the success of the system in promoting goal congruence. Management must analyze the performance measures chosen by each unit to ensure that they (1) promote the desired behavior, (2) address all desired behaviors, (3) support the achievement of organization objectives, and (4) reflect the unit's role in the organization.

Finally, management must apply the performance measures consistently and accurately. The measures used to evaluate performance reflect each unit's understanding of its contribution to the organization.

Worker Development: Percentage of workers in mentor programs
Worker Empowerment: Percentage of workers authorized to issue credit
Worker Recognition: Percentage of workers recognized by awards
Worker Recruitment: Percentage of employment offers accepted
Worker Promotion: Percentage of positions filled from within the company
Worker Succession Planning: Percentage of eligible positions filled through succession planning

EXHIBIT 25.4 WORKER INVOLVEMENT AND COMMITMENT MEASURES

25.8 SUMMARY

This chapter discusses innovative ways to evaluate performance beyond financial measurements. The organization's mission statement should drive the focus and implementation of its nonfinancial measures.

At lower levels in the organization, control and performance measurement focus on how people carry out the daily activities that create the organization's products. At the middle level, performance measurement focuses on the organization's ability to meet its responsibilities to various stakeholder groups, how well the operating systems work together to meet these needs, and the effectiveness of these systems. At the upper level of the organization, performance measurement focuses on whether the organization is on track with meeting its responsibilities and performance targets from the stakeholders' perspective.

The balanced scorecard is a set of performance targets and results that show the organization's performance in meeting its objectives relating to financial, customer, process, and innovation factors. Many firms use a method called *continuous improvement* to implement a balanced scorecard system. This method eliminates non-value-added activities and improves the efficiency of activities that add value.

The chapter discussed examples of nonfinancial performance measures for customer satisfaction (directed at service, quality, and cost) and efficiency in a manufacturing environment (measured by manufacturing cycle time and manufacturing cycle efficiency).

Employee involvement is important in an effective performance measurement system for three reasons: (1) it increases commitment to the organization and its goals, (2) it leads to more responsive and informed decision making, and (3) it utilizes worker skills and knowledge. Management must create a system that conveys the organization's goals and critical success factors to the workers.

BIBLIOGRAPHY

Brown, Mark Graham. *Keeping Score: Using the Right Metrics to Drive World-Class Performance*. Winnipeg: AMACOM Books, 1996.

Kaplan, Robert S. and Norton, David P. *The Strategy-Focused Organization: How Balanced Scorecard Companies Thrive in the New Business Environment*. Boston: Harvard Business School Press, 2000.

Niven, Paul R. *Balanced Scorecard Step by Step: Maximizing Performance and Maintaining Results*. New York: John Wiley & Sons, 2002.

Olve, Nils-Goran, Roy, Jan, and Petri, Carl-Johan. *Making Scorecards Actionable: Balancing Strategy and Control*. New York: John Wiley & Sons, 2003.

CHAPTER 26

ECONOMIC VALUE ADDED (EVA®)

JAMES J. WALLACE, PHD
Claremont Graduate University

CONTENTS

26.1 INTRODUCTION 669
26.2 THE EVA® CONCEPT 670
(a) Proprietary versus Entity 670
(b) Residual Income Calculation 670
(c) Residual Income and Shareholder Wealth 673
26.3 EVA® ADJUSTMENTS TO TRADITIONAL EARNINGS MEASURES 675
26.4 EVIDENCE OF EVA®'S SUCCESS AND PROBLEMS 676
(a) EVA® and Shareholder Returns 676
(b) Managerial Incentives 678
(c) Subsequent Firm Performance 679
26.5 IMPLEMENTATION ISSUES 679
26.6 CONCLUSION 680
BIBLIOGRAPHY 681

26.1 INTRODUCTION

More than 10 years have passed since Stern Stewart & Co. developed and introduced *economic value added* (EVA®), a shareholder value and management concept derived from residual income. Even though the concept underlying EVA® is easy to understand, people do not agree on its effectiveness. Advocates for and against EVA® use words that place them at polar ends of the spectrum. Eugene Vesell, managing director of Oppenheimer Capital, proclaims that the "EVA® mindset is at the root of how we measure ourselves and manage our portfolios." Richard Bernstein, director of Quantitative & Equity Derivatives Research for Merrill Lynch, counters that "Equity investors would probably be better served by incorporating into their stock selection process more traditional measures of corporate valuation and success that have historically contributed more to stock outperformance than has EVA®."

This chapter will explain the basics of EVA® and discuss the evidence regarding its effectiveness. Much of the evidence does not point to a clear verdict on the merits of EVA®, a situation that one could attribute to flawed EVA® implementation. Thus, this chapter will also discuss implementation issues.

26.2 THE EVA® CONCEPT

EVA® is one of several shareholder value metrics that consider shareholder wealth creation as a central premise.[1] Other stakeholders—such as employees, customers, and suppliers—also have importance in EVA® as drivers of shareholder wealth creation that a firm should neither exploit nor neglect.[2] EVA® makes two adjustments to traditional accounting earnings. The first adjustment recognizes a charge for equity capital, a computation that traditional earnings measures do not include. The second adjustment, or rather series of adjustments, corrects for what EVA® proponents refer to as accounting distortions.

(a) PROPRIETARY VERSUS ENTITY. Traditional earnings calculations assign debt a cost in the form of interest expense but do not assign such an expense to equity. One could attribute this omission of an equity charge to policy makers' *proprietary* view of the firm, which does not differentiate between the firm and the owners (shareholders). This proprietary view considers dividends a return of capital and not an expense, but expenses interest payments to debt holders. Proponents of the proprietary view consider it improper to charge an expense against oneself for equity interest. In contrast, proponents of the residual income concept (or EVA®) adopt the *entity* view of the firm that distinguishes between the firm and its shareholder owners. Proponents of the entity view argue that equity investors expect a return on their investment based on its risk, and therefore management should not consider the cost of these funds as free to the firm. Those who adopt the entity view further argue that omitting a charge for equity capital can lead to suboptimal management behavior if management incentives are tied to accounting earnings as defined under the proprietary view. Enron's risk manual stated the following:

> Reported earnings follow the rules and principles of accounting. The results do not always create measures consistent with underlying economics. However, corporate management's performance is generally measured by accounting income, not underlying economics. Risk management strategies are therefore directed at accounting rather than economic performance.[3]

(b) RESIDUAL INCOME CALCULATION. The recognition of a charge for equity capital transforms traditional accounting earnings into residual income. General Electric coined the term *residual income* in the 1950s and David Solomons (1965) later popularized it when he argued for the measure as a divisional performance measure. The concept, however, has been around much longer. Hamilton (1777) recognized as far back as the 1770s that one could calculate a merchant's gain only after deducting from his gross profits an interest charge on his stock. Alfred Sloan, the legendary leader of General Motors, implemented an EVA®-like system in the 1920s.

To compute residual income, one must first calculate an earnings number that is free of all financing charges. Normally this involves adding back the after tax cost of interest

---

1. Other popular shareholder value metrics include cash flow return on investment (CFROI) as developed by Holt Value Associates, total business return by Boston Consulting Group, shareholder value added by LEK/Alcar, discounted economic profits by Marakon Associates, and economic value management by KPMG, Economic Profit by McKinsey, and Economic Earnings by A.T Kearney.
2. For a more thorough discussion of the linkage between shareholder value creation and multiple stakeholders, see Wallace (2003).
3. G. Bennett Stewart III, "How to Fix Accounting—Measure and Report Economic Value," *Accenture Journal of Applied Corporate Finance*, 15, no. 3 (Spring 2003).

to net income. Accountants commonly refer to the resulting number as net operating profits after tax (NOPAT). Next, we subtract the total cost of capital from NOPAT to produce residual income (RI). We compute the total cost of capital by multiplying the weighted-average cost of capital (WACC)[4] times the total cost of all invested capital (CAPITAL), including both debt and equity capital. The following shows the calculation in equation form, where the subscript t refers to the time period:

$$RI_t = \text{NOPAT}_t - (\text{WACC}_t \times \text{CAPITAL}_{t-1}) \tag{1}$$

We can rewrite equation (1) in a form that separates the return on invested capital (e.g., return on assets [ROA]) from the cost of capital. Written in this way, equation (1) becomes:

$$RI_t = (\text{ROA}_t \times \text{CAPITAL}_{t-1}) - (\text{WACC}_t \times \text{CAPITAL}_{t-1}) \tag{2a}$$

By combining the CAPITAL terms, one can rewrite equation (2a) as follows:

$$RI_t = (\text{ROA}_t - \text{WACC}_t) \times \text{CAPITAL}_{t-1} \tag{2b}$$

Alternately, one can define residual income in terms of traditional net income (NI), the cost of equity capital (k), and the book value of equity capital (BV) as follows:

$$RI_t = NI_t - (k_t \times BV_{t-1}) \tag{2c}$$

We can now see that three primary methods exist to increase residual income, holding all else equal:

- Increase NOPAT (e.g., increase efficiency of operations).
- Decrease WACC (e.g., swap debt for equity).
- Increase the spread between ROA and WACC (e.g., shed capital that does not earn its cost of capital, and invest in new projects that earn more than their cost of capital).

This provides the foundation for the incentive structure of EVA® when the firm ties management's reward system to the measure.

The following numerical examples illustrate how a focus on residual income can help overcome deficiencies in traditional accounting measures, such as earnings and return on assets (ROA). The first two examples demonstrate that simply increasing earnings-based measures will not always serve the shareholders' best interest.

---

4. WACC is calculated by multiplying the cost of each capital component by its proportional weighting and then summing:

$$\text{WACC} = \frac{\text{E}}{\text{V}} \times \text{Re} + \frac{\text{D}}{\text{V}} \times \text{Rd} \times (1 - \text{Tc})$$

where

Re	=	Cost of equity
Rd	=	Cost of debt
E	=	The market value of the firm's equity
D	=	The market value of the firm's debt
V	=	$E + D$
E/V	=	Percentage of financing that is equity
D/V	=	Percentage of financing that is debt
Tc	=	The corporate tax rate.

EXAMPLE 1.

Suppose a manager has five separate one-year investment projects and adequate capital to finance all five. The risk of each of the five projects roughly equals the risk of the company's average project. The firm has a target capital structure that comprises 50 percent debt and 50 percent equity. The firm's after-tax cost of debt equals 10 percent and the firm's cost of equity equals 20 percent. Therefore, the firm's weighted average cost of capital (WACC) equals 15 percent. For simplicity, assume each project consists of an initial outlay of $1,000 and each project terminates after one year. Exhibit 26.1 shows the details for each project, along with four commonly used measures to evaluate each project.

According to capital budgeting theory, managers should evaluate projects based on a net present value (NPV) analysis. Given the previous choices, the manager should select projects 1 and 2, be indifferent to project 3, and reject projects 4 and 5. Suppose, however, that the manager receives compensation based on earnings. Further suppose that the manager knows that the firm will finance projects 1 through 4 with debt and project 5 with internal funds. The manager will now have an incentive to take all five projects because each will increase earnings. The firm's earnings will increase by 12 percent of the invested capital for project 4, but will only be charged with 10 percent (the after-tax cost of debt). The spread of 2 percent will show up as an increase in earnings. Similarly, project 5 will increase earnings by the entire 3 percent of invested capital because no charge will occur against earnings for the cost of capital.[5]

EXAMPLE 2.

Next, consider two managers who have compensation plans tied to their individual business unit ROA. ROA-based compensation plans can also provide incentives for the manager to make investment decisions that increase the manager's personal wealth while at the same time decreasing shareholder wealth.

Assume both managers A and B receive bonuses that equal some multiple of their business units' ROA. Manager A's unit, Star, currently has an ROA of 25 percent. Manager B's unit, Dog, currently has an ROA of only 5 percent. Further assume the two managers face the same five investment projects previously shown in Exhibit 26.1. Neither manager faces capital rationing. The firm's opportunity cost of funds remains at 15 percent.

5. ROA is computed as the sum of net profit plus after tax interest divided by the initial outlay. For project 1 this is (200 + (166.67 – 66.67))/1000 = 30%. NPV is computed as the sum of net cash inflow plus principal repayment plus after tax interest, discounted one period at 15 percent, less the initial outlay. For project 1 this is ((200 + 1000 + (166.67 – 66.67)) × (1/1.15)) – 1000 = 130.43. Residual income is computed as net cash flow plus after tax interest less a capital charge equal to the initial outlay times 15 percent. For project 1, this is (200 + (166.67 – 66.67)) – (1000 × .15) = 150

EXAMPLE 2. (CONTINUED)

Shareholders' wealth will increase if the managers select either projects 1 or 2, remain unchanged if they select project 3, and decrease if they select either project 4 or 5. Unfortunately, the compensation plan leads to incentives that starve the Stars (i.e., underinvest in projects for this group) and feed the Dogs (i.e., overinvest in projects for this group). Manager A's ROA, and hence compensation, will increase with project 1; however, project 2, which also increases shareholder wealth, will decrease manager A's ROA and related compensation. Manager A will likely choose to underinvest in good projects.

Manager B faces a different situation. Projects 1 through 4, if selected, will increase Dog unit's ROA, and manager B's related compensation. Unfortunately, project 4 does not even promise to cover the cost of capital needed to invest in it. Shareholders' wealth will decrease if the manager selects this investment. In this case, the ROA-based compensation leads manager B to overinvest in bad projects. Also note that residual income (EVA®) and NPV criteria lead to the same correct investment decisions.

(c) RESIDUAL INCOME AND SHAREHOLDER WEALTH. Another claimed advantage of residual income is its linkage to shareholder wealth. One can understand this connection by considering the common dividend discount model of equity valuation. Equation (3) equates the market value of equity (MVE_t) to the present value of all future net dividends.

$$MVE_t = \sum_{\tau=1}^{\tau=\infty} \frac{D_{t+\tau}}{(1+k)^{\tau}} \tag{3}$$

	Now	Project 1	Project 2	Project 3	Project 4	Project 5
Initial outlay	$(1,000)					
Increase revenue		$ 2,300	$ 2,150	$ 2,050	$ 2,000	$ 1,850
Increase expense		(800)	(800)	(800)	(800)	(800.00)
Interest expense		(167)	(167)	(167)	(167)	0
Pre-tax cash flow		1,333	1,183	1,083	1,033	1,050
Depreciation		(1,000)	(1,000)	(1,000)	(1,000)	(1,000)
Pre-tax profit		333	183	83	33	50
Tax @ 40%		(133)	(73)	(33)	(13)	(20)
Net profit		200	110	50	20.00	30
Principal repayment		(1,000)	(1,000)	(1,000)	(1,000)	(1,000)
Net cash flow		$ 200	$ 110	$ 50	$ 20	$ 30
Return on Assets		30%	21%	15%	12%	3%
Earnings		$ 200	$ 110	$ 50	$ 20	$ 30
NPV @ 15% discount rate		130	52	0.00	(26)	(104)
Residual income		150.00	60.00	0.00	(30)	(120)

EXHIBIT 26.1 DETAILS OF PROJECTS

Let us assume that the book value of equity changes only through earnings and dividends (also know as a *clean surplus relation*), expressed by the following:

$$BV_t = BV_{t-1} + NI_t - D_t \tag{4}$$

(where D_t represents dividends net of capital contributions). Then we can solve for NI_t from equation (2c), D_t from equation (4), and substitute into equation (3). This leaves us with equation (5), which computes the value of the firm's equity in terms of the book value of the firm's equity and its discounted residual income. Note that equation (4) is general enough to allow either a proprietary or an entity definition of net income. Under the proprietary view, BV_t equals the book value of equity. The entity view defines BV_t as the book value of equity and debt.

$$MVE_t = \sum_{\tau=1}^{\tau=\infty} \frac{RI_{t+\tau} + (1+k)BV_{t+\tau-1} - BV_{t+\tau}}{(1+k)^{\tau}} \tag{5}$$

Finally, if we make the reasonable assumption that $BV_{t+\tau} / (1+k)^{\tau}$ approaches 0 as τ approaches ∞, then we can express the MVE_t in a simplified form as equation (6).

$$MVE_t = BV_t + \sum_{\tau=1}^{\tau=\infty} \frac{RI_{t+\tau}}{(1+k)^{\tau}} \tag{6}$$

One should note that equation (6) holds for RI (EVA®) but not for traditional earnings because traditional earnings lack a charge for equity capital necessary for the equivalence. Another simple example illustrates this.

EXAMPLE 3.

Assume a firm is deciding whether to use internal funds to purchase a \$1,000 machine with a four-year life. At the end of the four years, the firm can sell the machine for its book value of \$200. Yearly net cash flows from the machine are expected to be \$300. The appropriate discount rate for this project is 15 percent. Exhibit 26.2 shows cash flows, depreciation, net income, and residual income.

Year 4 cash flow includes the \$200 salvage value proceeds from the sale of the equipment. Notice that although residual income is a one-period measure, the NPV of all the annual installments of residual income equal the NPV of the cash flows. This occurs because residual income, by subtracting the cost of capital, automatically sets aside a return sufficient to recover the value of the capital employed.

One should also note that discounting the annual installments of net income in this Example 3 results in a faulty investment decision. The net income installments generate a positive NPV, even though the scenario has a negative NPV of the cash flows after including the initial outlay. This occurs because net income does not explicitly consider the cost of equity capital. The results do not change with different depreciation methods. In fact, the same equivalence would occur if the firm chose to expense rather than capitalize the initial purchase.

This equivalence between NPV analysis and RI (EVA®) may lead some to assume that EVA® better explains current stock returns than traditional earnings does. This assumption poses a major problem, however, in that the market does not know with certainty what future realizations of EVA® will be. It only knows past and current realizations. Section 26.4(a) of this chapter discusses this issue.

26.3 EVA® ADJUSTMENTS TO TRADITIONAL EARNINGS MEASURES

Because EVA® places a strong emphasis on capital management through its equity charge, one might think EVA® offers nothing more than a repackaged residual income measure. EVA® proponents, however, claim that EVA® is much more than that. They recommend this single measure as the foundation of a complete financial management system. Firms can use the measure to make business decisions regarding new investment and divestiture; working capital management; and performance targets, measurement, and rewards. To shift residual income closer to economic value, EVA® proponents have identified more than 160 possible adjustments to traditional GAAP earnings. One need not consider all possible adjustments to fully realize EVA®'s value to any firm. Consultants rarely recommend more than about 5 to 15 adjustments for any particular client. The set of adjustments are uniquely designed for each firm based on such dimensions as organizational structure, firm strategy, and, of course, accounting policies. Research has shown that the proper choice of adjustments considers both the complexity of adding additional adjustments with the increased accuracy of measuring economic profit.

Although EVA® focuses on moving traditional earnings closer to economic value, a closer look at the adjustments reveals that many of them reduce suboptimal incentives linked to traditional earnings. One could not say, however, that these adjustments simply move measurements closer to that of cash earnings. Some adjustments do move closer to cash earnings by undoing accruals (e.g., eliminate deferred taxes and replace with actual cash taxes paid, reverse bad debt accrual to reflect cash basis). Other adjustments, however, create new accruals (e.g., capitalization and subsequent amortization of research

Initial Outlay	$1,000
Yearly Net Cash Flow	300
Annual Depreciation	Declining
Salvage Value	$ 200
Discount Rate	15%

Year	0	1	2	3	4	NPV
Cash flow	($1,000.00)	$ 300	$ 300	$ 300	$500	$(29)
Depreciation		(400)	(200)	(125)	(75)	
Net income		(100)	100	175	225	231
Capital charge		150	$ 90	60	41	
Residual income		$(250)	$ 10	$ 115	$183	$(29)

EXHIBIT 26.2 CASH FLOWS, DEPRECIATION, NET INCOME, AND RESIDUAL INCOME

and development expenditures). Finally, some adjustments simply switch from one type of accrual to another with the intent of increasing comparability (e.g., requiring FIFO accounting).

The EVA® adjustment to capitalize and subsequently amortize intangibles such as research and development (R&D) has prompted much discussion.[6] This adjustment provides an example of undoing accounting conservatism. The EVA® system uses this adjustment to discourage short-term behavior, such as reducing R&D, to enhance the firm's current net income. Note that this adjustment moves earnings further from cash earnings, but closer to economic value. It does not, however, completely move in the direction of economic value since EVA® records R&D at historical cost less accumulated amortization, not at current value.

Some adjustments attempt to discourage earnings management (e.g., manipulating earnings through accounting choices) by eliminating certain discretionary accruals. Examples include the provisions for bad debts or warranty work. Instead of allowing managers to estimate these accruals, the EVA® method recognizes these expenses on a cash basis.

The book value of an asset rarely equals the asset's economic value since depreciation rarely equals the change in economic value of an asset. This difference leads to accounting gains and losses on dispositions that may distort the manager's proper decision regarding retention and disposition. For example, consider the case where a firm owns an asset with a book value of $15 million but it has no productive value to the firm. The firm has the opportunity to sell the asset for $5 million. Since the asset does not generate any revenue, it makes economic sense to sell; however, under conventional accounting methods the firm will recognize a $10 million loss. A manager evaluated on such earnings may be reluctant to sell. EVA® proponents address this issue by advocating that no gain or loss be recorded when retiring this asset. Instead, the calculations subtract the proceeds from the disposition from the remaining assets' net book value. This adjustment revalues the disposed asset for accounting purposes at its disposal price. It also allows the manager to worry only about operational considerations instead of accounting treatment. Exhibit 26.3 provides a list of some of the common EVA® adjustments to traditional GAAP earnings.[7]

26.4 EVIDENCE OF EVA®'S SUCCESS AND PROBLEMS

(a) EVA® AND SHAREHOLDER RETURNS. We now consider EVA® and its explanatory power with regard to shareholder returns. In other words, does EVA® drive stock prices better than other traditional measures, such as earnings per share (EPS), return on equity (ROE), and ROI? Academic researchers independently conducted several large-scale studies. In one such study (Biddle et al., 1997), conducted jointly by myself, Gary Biddle, and Robert Bowen, we examined whether EVA® explains more of the variation in

6. Proponents also advocate the capitalization and subsequent amortization of other intangibles such as goodwill and advertising expenditures.

7. For a more complete discussion of this example, see Stewart (1994, p. 79). For more discussion of EVA® adjustments, also see Stewart (1991) and O'Hanlon and Peasnell (1998), Ehrbar (1998), and Young and O'Byrne (2001).

COMMON AREAS WHERE GAAP-BASED ACCOUNTING IS ADJUSTED*	GAAP TREATMENT	NATURE OF ADJUSTMENTS**
Marketing and R&D costs	Expense	Record as asset and amortize
Deferred taxes	Record as asset and/or liability	Reverse recording of asset and/or liability to reflect cash basis reporting
Purchased goodwill	Record as asset; amortize over up to 40 years	Reverse amortization to reflect original asset amount
Unrecorded goodwill	Not recorded under pooling of interests	Unrecorded goodwill is added to both goodwill and to equity capital
Successful efforts to full cost	Record to income nonrecurring gains and losses such as restructuring charges and asset dispositions	Cumulative unusual losses, less gains, after taxes are added back to capital
Operating leases	Expense	Record asset and amortize; record liability and related interest
Bad debts and warranty costs	Estimate accrual	Reverse accruals to reflect cash basis reporting
LIFO inventory costing	LIFO permitted	Convert to FIFO
Construction in progress	Record as asset	Remove from assets
Discontinued operations	Include in assets and earnings	Remove from assets and earnings

* For example, the effect of capitalizing R&D is to add to CAPITAL (assets) past R&D expenses, less accumulated amortization. The effect on NOPAT (earnings) is to add back current R&D expenses and subtract the period's amortization of capitalized R&D. For a firm experiencing growth (decline) in R&D, the adjustment increases (reduces) contemporaneous NOPAT. The effect on EVA® depends on the amount of capitalized R&D. For a firm in steady state, the adjustment has little net effect on NOPAT, but increases CAPITAL, thereby reducing EVA®.

** Rationales for these adjustments include (a) to better represent the underlying economics of the transactions; (b) to reduce incentives for dysfunctional or sub-optimal decision making; and (c) to improve comparability externally (across firms) and internally (e.g., across divisions) by putting the accounting on a similar basis. Not all rationales apply to each adjustment.

EXHIBIT 26.3 EXAMPLES OF TYPICAL EVA ADJUSTMENTS FOR ALLEGED ACCOUNTING DISTORTIONS

share price than does GAAP earnings. We concluded that net income dominated both EVA® and CFO (cash flow from operations) in explaining contemporaneous share returns. We also found that the EVA® components (e.g., accounting adjustments, such as capitalizing R&D) contribute only marginally to the information already available through net income and operating cash flow.

One might wonder why EVA® would not outperform traditional earnings measures in this and similar studies. After all, compelling theory links EVA and firm value, and the intuition behind the EVA® system appears sound. Several reasons may explain why

EVA® does not dominate earnings in association with stock returns and firm values,[8] but the most compelling reason may be that EVA® seems more relevant as an internal measure used to motivate certain value enhancing behavior and "encourage managers to behave like owners." Some of the EVA® adjustments, such as capitalizing the cost of R&D, interject a noisy measure of the component's value that GAAP avoids by expensing these expenditures in the period they occur. GAAP, therefore, provides a more reliable method to estimate the value of a firm. Whereas GAAP earnings may error toward reliability, EVA® may error toward relevance at the expense of reliability. Evidence suggests that the market values reliability, especially when more relevant surrogates exist for many of the accounting numbers.

(b) MANAGERIAL INCENTIVES. The focus on correlations with current share prices may cloud a more important question: Does the adoption of EVA® provide internal incentives that lead to a better performing firm? The empirical studies and theoretical papers discussed below address this question.

(i) Does EVA® Enhance Shareholder Value? Merrill Lynch performed a study of correlations between various performance metrics, including EVA® and share prices and concluded the following:

> EVA is indeed an important analytical tool for corporate managers as are all tools that focus on returns in excess of capital requirements. However, there is nothing in these results that supports the contention that earnings are irrelevant. This work suggests that EVA techniques by themselves will probably be no more effective in enhancing shareholder value than will other management techniques if the EVA process does not ultimately drive earnings and earnings growth. (Bernstein 1998b, p. 6)

(ii) Does EVA® Improve Asset Management? I studied (Wallace 1997) whether EVA® (and other EVA®-type incentives) promoted greater capital awareness, wherein managers become more selective in new investment and more willing to dispose of underperforming assets. My results indicate that the firms adopting economic profit measures are more willing to dispose of assets and, although they still increase new investment after the adoption, they do so at a significantly lower pace relative to the matched control sample of firms.

My study also considered how firms managed assets in place, and found that asset turnover, defined as sales divided by average total assets, increases significantly following adoption, relative to the control firms. I also reasoned that the capital charge will provide incentive to return capital to shareholders that under prior incentives may have been kept in low return form. My results confirmed that dividends and share repurchases for firms that adopt economic profit measures increase relative to control firms that did not adopt such measures. I also found that residual income for the adopting firms increased relative to that of the control firms.

---

8. First, consider that the firm's valuation model is specified in terms of discounted future EVA—not on past and current realizations. In this light, the evidence suggests that realized earnings are a better predictor of future EVA than realized EVA itself. (Realized earnings are similarly more predictive of future free cash flows than are cash flow themselves. This is not surprising since earnings smooth irregular cash flow realizations and accruals allow managers to convey to market participants inferences regarding their firms' future prospects.) Second, recall that the key differences between NI and EVA is the cost of equity capital and the accounting adjustments. Earnings could dominate EVA if market participants use cost of capital estimates different from those provided by EVA consultants.

(iii) Does EVA® Lead to Underinvestment? Critics of EVA® claim that the system's increased focus on the cost of capital causes a bias against growth and that it encourages managers to milk a business through underinvestment. EVA® proponents counter that the EVA® framework encourages investment as long as it yields positive net present value.

In independent papers, O'Byrne (1999) and Rogerson (1997) both theorized that the problem of underinvestment could be solved through negative depreciation, an EVA®-type adjustment that allows lesser charges in early years and more depreciation taken in the later years to match the cash flows of the asset. O'Byrne knows of only one firm that uses negative depreciation, making empirical research and comparisons impossible.

(c) SUBSEQUENT FIRM PERFORMANCE. Research indicates that managers alter behavior when adopting economic profit measures, and that these changes may enhance shareholder value. We now discuss studies that investigate whether this behavior affects future shareholder value.

(i) Stern Stewart Studies. Stern Stewart (1999 and 2002) studied the market returns of publicly traded Stern Stewart clients, which have all implemented EVA® systems. The study compared performance of these firms to peer firms, based on industry and firm size, and to the overall S&P index of firms; the studies covered overall up markets and overall down markets. Stern Stewart found that EVA® firms, on average, outperform their peer firms and the overall market by a wide margin in both studies.

One might criticize Stern Stewart's method for selecting matching control firms because it did not consider pre-event performance as a criterion. Firms that make major changes, such as the adoption of an economic profit metric, tend to be poor performers initially. Firms rarely make these changes if they find the current system successful. Thus, one might conclude that firms became Stern Stewart clients because they had been underperforming; they had a strong incentive to improve that other, successful, firms in their peer group lacked.

(ii) Hogan and Lewis Study. Hogan and Lewis (2003) used the improved matching method in their study and found mixed evidence on the long-term market performance of firms adopting economic profit plans, such as EVA®. They concluded that economic profit plans do not outperform traditional plans for creating shareholder wealth.

(iii) Conclusions from Studies. What can we learn from these two studies? Other than the difference in control group criteria, the degree and depth of adoption in firms that fall into the adopting firm category may differ. Different sample firms had implemented their performance metric to different degrees, from a full-blown EVA® system to a homegrown system that showed only a weak commitment to implementation. Since Stern Stewart has been on the cutting edge of developing and implementing EVA®, its clients may have had stronger commitment and a more thorough implementation of the system. The following section discusses issues related to implementation of EVA®.

26.5 IMPLEMENTATION ISSUES

My study (Wallace 1998) provides evidence that the degree of adoption may greatly affect the results garnered from the adopted measures. I studied 40 firms that had deeply integrated EVA® into their corporate culture—including their incentive compensation program—and 36 firms that were using EVA® in their decision making, but did not use it in incentive compensation. I developed the following conclusions:

- Firms with deeper implementation of EVA® report more awareness of their cost of capital, compared to those with less implementation.
- Managers of these firms with deeper EVA® implementation report more selectiveness when choosing new investment projects and more willingness to sell underperforming assets.
- In the deeper EVA® implementation firms, higher percentages of the managers report better working capital management, including reduced age of accounts receivable, increased account payable cycle, and increased inventory turnover.
- Full implementation of EVA® can prove very complex. Adopters should keep the concept as simple as possible.
- EVA® must have the full support of upper management to succeed. Training is crucial for the concept to be fully understood.

O'Byrne (2001) also studied differences between successful and unsuccessful EVA® implementations. The following lists his findings, which concur with those of the Wallace (1998) study:

- Firms with substantial shared resources tend to be less successful EVA® implementers because of the potential complexity of allocating capital as part of the EVA® measurement.[9]
- Firms with more autonomous business units benefit more than firms with more centralized structures. This occurs because an EVA® system provides strong incentives that can reach down multiple layers within the organization.
- Firms that provide substantial wealth incentives tied to the EVA® metric have more success. The incentive plans must be simple enough to understand and provide certainty in their payouts. Less successful implementations appear to rely more on incentives tied to stock options and exercise more discretion in compensation payouts.
- Managers must perceive that their superiors take the metric seriously. Successful implementations have a CEO who is a strong EVA® advocate.
- Firms with greater stability within the management ranks have greater success with EVA® implementation. Stability establishes accountability and controllability that situations with frequent transfers lack.

26.6 CONCLUSION

So what do we make of all this? First, how do we reconcile the evidence that EVA® might not correlate highly with contemporaneous shareholder returns, yet appears to drive value-enhancing behavior? Second, how do we interpret the mixed evidence concerning EVA® and subsequent firm performance?

---

9. An example of shared resources is a multidivision firm with one central purchasing department. Somehow the firm must devise an allocation method for this shared resource so that each division receives its share to the costs for central purchasing.

Biddle, Bowen, and Wallace (1999) address the first question. We argue that one can separate the issues of a measure's incentive effects and its information content to the market. In that article, we state:

> It is possible for a metric to be quite useful for internal incentive purposes even though it conveys little if any news to market participants regarding the firm's future prospects. Similarly, a measure that is useful to capital market participants for determining share price is not necessarily useful as a management incentive tool. Therefore, EVA and residual income could prove effective in motivating shareholder wealth creation without conveying new information to investors, and claims linking the two should be interpreted with care.

Two observations merit mention. First, as explained in Section 26.5, not all firms implement economic profit measures such as EVA® with equal commitment, and not all types of firms will have successful implementations. Second, many firms adopting EVA®-type measures subsequently perform better. We do not know yet whether we can fully or even partially attribute this improvement to EVA® adoption. Unfortunately, differences in sample selection methods and matching make it difficult to ferret out the answer, leaving us still wondering if EVA® is, as *Fortune* proclaimed, "The real key to creating wealth" (Tully 1993).

BIBLIOGRAPHY

Bernstein, R. *An Analysis of EVA—Part II*, Merrill Lynch & Co. Global Securities & Economics Group, Quantitative & Equity Derivative Research Department, 1998. pp. 1–8.

Bernstein, R. *Quantitative Viewpoint an Analysis of EVA—Part II*, Merrill Lynch & Co. Global Securities & Economics Group, Quantitative & Equity Derivative Research Department, 1998. pp. 1–7.

Biddle, G., R. Bowen, and J. Wallace. "Does EVA Beat Earnings? Evidence on Association with Stock Returns and Firm Values." *Journal of Accounting and Economics* 24 (1997): 301–336.

Biddle, G., R. Bowen, and J. Wallace. "Evidence on EVA." *Journal of Applied Corporate Finance* 12 (1999): 69–79.

Ehrbar, A. *Stern Stewart's EVA: The Real Key to Creating Wealth*. New York: John Wiley & Sons, 1998.

Hamilton, R., *An Introduction to Merchandize*. Edinburgh, 1777.

Hogan, C., and C. Lewis. "The Long-Run Performance of Firms Adopting Compensation Plans Based on Economic Profits." Working Paper, Vanderbilt University, 2003.

O'Byrne, S. "Does Value-based Management Discourage Investment in Intangibles?" Working paper, 1999.

O'Byrne, S., and S Young. *EVA and Value-Based Management: A Practical Guide To Implementation*. New York: McGraw-Hill, 2001.

Rogerson, W., "Intertemporal Cost Allocation and Managerial Investment Incentives: A Theory Explaining the Use of Economic Value Added as a Performance Measure." *Journal of Political Economy* 105 (1997): 770–795.

Solomons, D. *Divisional Performance: Measurement and Control*. Homewood, Ill.: Irwin, 1965.

Stern Stewart "EVA Works: The Superior Stock Market Performance of Stern Stewart Clients." *Stern Stewart web site*. http://www.eva.com, 1999.

Stern Stewart "Stern Stewart's EVA Clients Outperform the Market and Their Peers." *Stern Stewart web site,* 2002.

Stewart III, G. B. *The Quest for Value.* New York: Harper Business, 1991.

Tully, S. "The Real Key to Creating Wealth." *Fortune* 128 (1993): 38–44.

Wallace, J. "Adopting Residual Income-based Compensation Plans: Do You Get What You Pay For?" *Journal of Accounting and Economics* 24 (1997): 275–300.

Wallace, J. "EVA Financial Systems: Management Perspectives." *Advances in Management Accounting* 6 (1998): 1–15.

Wallace, J. "Value Maximization and Stakeholder Theory: Compatible or Not?" *Journal of Applied Corporate Finance* 15(3) (2003): 120–127.

CHAPTER 27

TRANSFER PRICING

MICHAEL W. MAHER, PHD, EDITOR
University of California, Davis

CONTENTS

27.1 INTRODUCTION 683

27.2 HOW TRANSFER PRICING AFFECTS PERFORMANCE MEASUREMENT 684

27.3 SETTING TRANSFER PRICES 684
- (a) Case I: No Outside Suppliers 684
- (b) Case II: Transfer Pricing When Outside Suppliers Are Available (Selling Division *below Capacity*) 684
- (c) Case III: Transfer Pricing When Outside Suppliers Are Available (Selling Division *at Capacity*) 685
- (d) Case IV: Transfer Pricing When Outside Suppliers Are Available (Selling Division *below* Capacity with Alternative Facility Utilization) 686

27.4 HOW TO HELP MANAGERS ACHIEVE THEIR GOALS WHILE ACHIEVING THE ORGANIZATION'S GOALS 687

27.5 TOP MANAGEMENT INTERVENTION IN TRANSFER PRICING 689

27.6 CENTRALLY ESTABLISHED TRANSFER PRICE POLICIES 689
- (a) Establishing a Market Price Policy 689
- (b) Establishing a Cost Basis Policy 690
- (c) Alternative Cost Measures 691
- (d) Remedying Motivational Problems of Transfer Pricing Policies 692
- (e) Dual Transfer Prices 692

27.7 NEGOTIATING THE TRANSFER PRICE 693

27.8 GLOBAL PRACTICES 693

27.9 MULTINATIONAL TRANSFER PRICING 693

27.10 SEGMENT REPORTING 695

27.11 SUMMARY 695

27.1 INTRODUCTION

Suppose a business unit of a particular organization produces a good or service for another business unit of that same organization. In effect, the transferring business unit has made a sale and the receiving unit has made a purchase. Accountants assign a value to this transaction, which credits the seller for the sale and charges the purchaser for the purchase. Accountants call the price assigned to that transfer of product from one business unit to another a *transfer price*. Accountants have considerable discretion in setting the transfer price because this exchange takes place inside the organization instead of in the market.

This chapter explains the basic incentive problems that transfer pricing addresses, demonstrates the general transfer pricing rules, and discusses the underlying basis for these rules. It also presents the behavioral issues and incentive effects of negotiated transfer prices, cost-based transfer prices, and market-based transfer prices. It discusses the economic consequences of multinational transfer prices and describes how transfer prices affect segment reporting.

27.2 HOW TRANSFER PRICING AFFECTS PERFORMANCE MEASUREMENT

Responsibility centers in decentralized organizations often exchange products with each other in addition to their exchanges with outsiders. At General Motors, for example, divisions buy direct materials from a number of suppliers, including other GM divisions.

If top management evaluates the divisions using a profitability measure, such as return on investment (ROI), then the transfer price can affect the performance of each division. For example, the higher the transfer price, the more profitable the selling division (from higher revenues) and the less profitable the buying division (from higher costs), all other things being equal.

27.3 SETTING TRANSFER PRICES

The company uses transfer prices to transfer goods and services between divisions while allowing them to retain their autonomy. The transfer price can motivate managers to act in the best interest of the company.

To help explain the issues involved with transfer pricing, we will discuss four transfer pricing scenarios:

1. No outside suppliers are available.
2. Outside suppliers are available, but the selling division is below capacity.
3. Outside suppliers are available, and the selling division is at capacity.
4. Outside suppliers are available, the selling division is below capacity, and alternative facility uses exist.

Each example requires a differential revenue/cost analysis.

(a) CASE I: NO OUTSIDE SUPPLIERS. If a company evaluates division managers on division profit measures, they will consider transfer price important. The company as a whole, however, will receive the same operating profit regardless of the transfer price, assuming that it cannot purchase the part from another company (externally).

For example, assume that Tech-Products has two decentralized divisions, Hardware and Computers. Computers division has always purchased certain units from Hardware division at $50 per unit, but Hardware might raise the price to $70 per unit (the current market price). Hardware has variable costs per unit of $50, and annual fixed costs of $10,000. The Computers division bundles the units with other products and sells them for $100 each. Computers incurs no additional variable costs, and annual fixed costs total $5,000. Computers produces 1,500 units per year. Given this information, which transfer price will provide Tech-Products with the highest operating profit? As Exhibit 27.1 shows, the transfer price will not affect overall company operating profit.

Clearly, a change in transfer price does not change the total company operating profit, but does affect division performance. Hardware division would likely prefer the higher transfer price because its operating profit increases from a loss of $10,000 to a profit of $20,000, especially if the company evaluates the division on its operating profit. Computers division, however, would prefer the lower transfer price.

(b) CASE II: TRANSFER PRICING WHEN OUTSIDE SUPPLIERS ARE AVAILABLE (SELLING DIVISION *BELOW CAPACITY*). Using the same data as in Case I for Tech-Products, let's add an additional option for Computers division: purchasing units from an outside supplier

Transfer Price of $50/Unit

	Hardware		Computers
Sales			
$50 × 1,500	$ 75,000		
$100 × 1,500			$150,000
Variable costs			
$50 × 1,500	75,000		
$50 × 1,500			75,000
Fixed Costs	10,000		5,000
Operating profit	$(10,000)		$ 70,000
Total company operating profit		$60,000	

Transfer Price of $70 per unit

	Hardware		Computers
Sales			
$70 × 1,500	$105,000		
$70 × 1,500			$150,000
Variable costs			
$50 × 1,500	75,000		
$70 × 1,500			105,000
Fixed Costs	10,000		5,000
Operating profit	$ 20,000		$ 40,000
Total company operating profit		$60,000	

EXHIBIT 27.1 PROFIT CALCULATION WITH NO OUTSIDE SUPPLIERS

for $60 (the outside supplier offers a good deal to get Computers' business). *If Computers buys from an outside supplier, the facilities that Hardware uses to manufacture these units would remain idle.* Which option yields the highest total company operating profit for Tech-Products (transfer from Hardware or purchase from outside supplier)?

As Exhibit 27.2 shows, purchasing units from an outside supplier will result in a loss in companywide operating profit of $15,000, the additional cost to the company of purchasing the units externally for $60 versus purchasing the units internally for $50 ($15,000 = [$60 – $50] × 1,500 units).

The general economic transfer pricing rule when the seller is operating below capacity (with idle capacity) states that the seller should set the transfer price at the variable cost per unit (or the differential cost of production). Thus, in this example, the seller should set the transfer price at its variable cost ($50 per unit) to maximize overall company operating profits and to send the correct signal from the Hardware Division to the Computers Division that the variable cost of producing the item is $50.

(c) CASE III: TRANSFER PRICING WHEN OUTSIDE SUPPLIERS ARE AVAILABLE (SELLING DIVISION *AT* CAPACITY). Using the data as in Case II for Tech-Products, we change one assumption. Assume that Hardware does not have idle capacity if Computers buys from an outside supplier. Instead, *if Computers buys from an outside supplier, Hardware can sell all of its units to the outside at the market price of $70 (i.e., Hardware is operating*

Transfer Price of $50/Unit from Case I, Exhibit 27.1

	Hardware		Computers
Sales			
$50 × 1,500	$ 75,000		
$100 × 1,500			$150,000
Variable costs			
$50 × 1,500	75,000		
$50 × 1,500			75,000
Fixed Costs	10,000		5,000
Operating profit	$(10,000)		$ 70,000
Total company operating profit		$60,000	

Purchase Externally for $60 per Unit

	Hardware		Computers
Sales			
$70 × 0	$ 0		
$70 × 1,500			$150,000
Variable costs			
$50 × 0	0		
$60 × 1,500			90,000
Fixed Costs	10,000		5,000
Operating profit	$ (20,000)		$ 55,000
Total company operating profit		$45,000	

EXHIBIT 27.2 PROFIT CALCULATION WITH OUTSIDE SUPPLIERS AVAILABLE, SELLING DIVISION *BELOW* CAPACITY

at capacity). Which option yields the highest total company operating profit for Tech-Products (transfer from Hardware or purchase from outside supplier)?

Exhibit 27.3 shows that purchasing units from an outside supplier results in a gain in companywide operating profit of $15,000, which is the savings for Computers of purchasing the units externally for $60, versus purchasing the units internally for $70 ([$70 – $60] × 1,500 units = $15,000).

The general economic transfer pricing rule *when the seller is operating at capacity* is that the seller should transfer at the market price. Thus, with this example, the seller should set the transfer price at its market price ($70 per unit) to maximize overall company operating profits.

(d) CASE IV: TRANSFER PRICING WHEN OUTSIDE SUPPLIERS ARE AVAILABLE (SELLING DIVISION *BELOW* CAPACITY WITH ALTERNATIVE FACILITY UTILIZATION). Using the same data as in Case I for Tech-Products, we make additional changes in our assumptions. Assume that Hardware has idle capacity if Computers buys from an outside supplier for $60 per unit. However, *if Computers buys from an outside supplier, the firm can use the Hardware idle capacity for other purposes, resulting in cash operating savings of $35,000.* Which option yields the highest total company operating profit for Tech-Products (transfer from Hardware or purchase from outside supplier)?

Transfer Price of $70/Unit

	Hardware		Computers
Sales			
$70 × 1,500	$ 105,000		
$100 × 1,500			$150,000
Variable costs			
$50 × 1,500	75,000		
$60 × 1,500			105,000
Fixed Costs	10,000		5,000
Operating profit	$ 20,000		$40,000
Total company operating profit		$60,000	

Purchase Externally for $60 per Unit

	Hardware		Computers
Sales			
$70 × 0	$105,000		
$70 × 1,500			$150,000
Variable costs			
$50 × 1,500	75,000		
$60 × 1,500			90,000
Fixed Costs	10,000		5,000
Operating profit	$ 20,000		$ 55,000
Total company operating profit		$75,000	

EXHIBIT 27.3 PROFIT CALCULATION WITH OUTSIDE SUPPLIERS AVAILABLE, SELLING DIVISION *AT* CAPACITY

As Exhibit 27.4 shows, purchasing units from an outside supplier results in a gain in companywide operating profit of $20,000: the operating savings ($35,000) less the additional cost of purchasing the units externally ([$60 – $50] × 1,500 units = $15,000).

The preceding examples demonstrate the two rules for establishing a transfer price:

1. If the selling division *is operating at capacity,* the transfer price should be the market price.
2. If the selling division *has idle capacity,* and the division cannot use the idle facilities for other purposes, the transfer price should be at least the variable costs incurred to produce the goods.

27.4 HOW TO HELP MANAGERS ACHIEVE THEIR GOALS WHILE ACHIEVING THE ORGANIZATION'S GOALS

As one might expect, a conflict can arise between the company's interests and an individual manager's interests when the firm uses transfer price-based performance measures. The following example demonstrates such a conflict.

Gamma Industries Company's Production Division was operating below capacity. Its Assembly division received a contract to assemble 10,000 units of a final product, XX-1. Each unit of XX-1 required one part, A-16, which Production Division made. Both divisions

Transfer Price of $50/Unit (from Case I and Exhibit 27.1)

	Hardware		Computers
Sales			
$50 × 1,500	$ 75,000		
$100 × 1,500			$150,000
Variable costs			
$50 × 1,500	75,000		
$50 × 1,500			75,000
Fixed Costs	10,000		5,000
Operating profit	$(10,000)		$ 70,000
Total company operating profit		$60,000	

Purchase Externally for $60 per Unit

	Hardware		Computers
Sales			
$70 × 0	$ 0		
$70 × 1,500			$150,000
Variable costs			
$50 × 0	0		
$60 × 1,500			90,000
Fixed Costs	10,000		5,000
Operating savings	35,000		0
Operating profit	$ 25,000		$ 55,000
Total company operating profit		$80,000	

EXHIBIT 27.4 OUTSIDE SUPPLIERS ARE AVAILABLE(SELLING DIVISION BELOW CAPACITY WITH ALTERNATIVE FACILITY UTILIZATION)

are decentralized, autonomous investment centers, and the company evaluates them based on operating profits and ROI.

The vice president of Assembly division called the vice president of Production division and made a proposal:

> *Assembly VP*: I know your department is running below capacity. I'd like to buy 10,000 units of A-16 at $30 per unit. That will enable you to keep your production lines busy.
>
> *Production VP*: Are you kidding? I happen to know that it would cost you a lot more if you had to buy A-16s from an outside supplier. We refuse to accept less than $40 per unit, which gives us our usual markup and covers our costs.
>
> *Assembly VP*: We both know that your variable costs per unit are only $22. I realize I'd be getting a good deal at $30, but so would you. You should treat this as a special order. Anything over your differential costs on the order is pure profit. If you can't charge less than $40, then I'll have to go elsewhere. I have to keep my costs down, too, you know.

The Production VP would not agree to charge less than $40, so the Assembly division subsequently sought bids on the part and obtained part A-16 from an outside supplier for $39 per unit, which was $17 above Ace Company's variable cost of $22. The Production Division continued to operate below capacity. The actions of the two divisions cost the company \$170,000: the difference between the price paid for the part from the outside supplier (\$39) and the variable costs of producing in the Assembly Division (\$22) times the 10,000 units in the order.

How can a decentralized organization avoid this type of problem? Companies use three approaches to address such an incentive problem:

1. Direct intervention by top management
2. Centrally established transfer price policies
3. Negotiated transfer prices

Each of these approaches has advantages and disadvantages and may be appropriate under different circumstances. We discuss these alternatives in the next sections.

27.5 TOP MANAGEMENT INTERVENTION IN TRANSFER PRICING

Gamma Industries' top management could have directly intervened in this pricing dispute and ordered Production division to produce the A-16s and transfer them to Assembly division at a management-specified transfer price. For extraordinarily large orders or rare internal product transfers, direct intervention might offer the best solution to the problem.

Direct intervention has some disadvantages: Top management may become swamped with pricing disputes, and individual division managers will lose the flexibility and other advantages of autonomous decision making. Thus, direct intervention promotes short-run profits by minimizing the type of uneconomic behavior demonstrated in the Gamma Industries case but reduces the benefits from decentralization.

As long as the transfer pricing problems occur infrequently, the benefits of direct intervention may outweigh the costs. However, if transfer transactions become common, direct intervention can prove costly by requiring substantial senior-management involvement in decisions that the divisions should make.

Moreover, when selling and buying divisions cannot sell and buy all they want in perfectly competitive markets, transfer pricing can become complex. Some divisions may not have an outside market. Companies often find that not all transactions between divisions occur as top management prefers. In extreme cases, the transfer pricing problem creates so many difficulties that top management reorganizes the company so that buying and selling divisions report to one manager who oversees the transfers.

27.6 CENTRALLY ESTABLISHED TRANSFER PRICE POLICIES

A transfer pricing policy should allow divisional autonomy yet encourage managers to pursue corporate goals consistent with their own personal goals. Additionally, the use of transfer prices to calculate the selling division's revenue and the buying division's cost should reinforce the company's performance evaluation system. Market prices and cost provide the two economic bases a firm can use to establish transfer price policies.

(a) ESTABLISHING A MARKET PRICE POLICY. Theorists and practitioners consider externally based market prices as the best basis for transfer pricing when a competitive market exists for the product and the divisions can buy and sell at market prices. When a firm uses market prices, the buying and selling divisions can buy and sell as many units as they want at that price. Managers of both buying and selling divisions are indifferent as to trading with each other or with outsiders. The company should agree with this arrangement as long as the supplying unit operates at capacity.

Such markets exist rarely, however. Usually, differences exist between products produced internally and those that the buyer division can purchase from outsiders, such as costs, quality, or product characteristics. The existence of two divisions that trade with each other in one company indicates that such an arrangement offers advantages over dealing with outside markets.

For example, when Chevrolet Division of General Motors buys parts from other General Motors divisions, quality control and reliable delivery become less problematic. Furthermore, dealing internally can reduce or eliminate costs of negotiating transactions.

When such advantages exist, the company should create incentives for internal transfer. Top management may establish policies that direct two responsibility centers to trade internally unless they can show advantages of trading externally. Some firms establish a policy that provides a discount to the buying division for items purchased internally. To encourage transfers that will increase companywide profits, management may set a transfer pricing policy based on market prices for the intermediate product, such as part A-16.

As a general rule, a *market price–based transfer pricing* policy contains the following guidelines:

- The policy sets the transfer price at a discount from the cost to acquire the item on the open market.
- The selling division may elect to transfer or to continue to sell to the outside.

(b) ESTABLISHING A COST BASIS POLICY. A cost-based transfer pricing policy should adopt the following rule:

> Transfer at the differential outlay cost to the selling division (typically variable costs) plus the opportunity cost to the company of making the internal transfers ($0 if the seller has idle capacity; selling price minus variable costs if the seller is operating at capacity).

Using the Gamma Industries example to demonstrate, recall that the seller (Production division) could sell in outside markets for $40 and had a variable cost of $22, which we shall assume is its differential cost.

Now consider two cases. In case 1, the seller (Production division) operates below capacity, in which case the internal transfer has no opportunity cost because it doesn't forgo any outside sale. In case 2, the seller operates at capacity and would have to give up one unit of outside sales for every unit transferred internally.

In case 2, the opportunity cost of transferring the product to a division inside the company reflects the forgone contribution of selling the unit in an outside market. Consequently, the optimal transfer price for Gamma Industries is $22 for the below-capacity case or $40 for the at-capacity case, as Exhibit 27.5 shows.

A seller operating at capacity is indifferent between selling in the outside market for $40 or transferring internally at $40. Note that this is the same solution as the market price rule for competitive markets (ignoring the wholesaler's markup) because sellers can sell everything they produce at the market price. Consequently, as a rule of thumb, firms can implement the economic transfer pricing rule as follows:

- A seller operating below capacity should transfer at the differential cost of production (variable cost).
- A seller operating at capacity should transfer at market price.

	Differential Outlay Cost	+	Opportunity Cost of Transferring Internally	=	Transfer Outlay Cost
If the seller (that is, Production Division), has idle capacity	$22	+	-0-	=	$22
If the seller has no idle capacity . . .	22	+	$18 ($40 Selling price –$22 Variable price)	=	40

EXHIBIT 27.5 APPLICATION OF GENERAL TRANSFER PRICING RULE—GAMMA INDUSTRIES

A seller operating below capacity is indifferent between providing the product and receiving a transfer price equal to the seller's differential outlay cost or not providing the product. For example, if the production division received $22 for the product, it would be indifferent between selling it or not. In both the below-capacity and at-capacity cases, the selling division is no worse off if it makes the internal transfer. The selling division does not earn a contribution on the transaction in the below-capacity case, however. It earns only the same contribution for the internal transfer as it would for a sale to the outside market in the at-capacity case. The general rule optimizes the company's profit, but does not benefit the selling division for an internal transfer. (For practical purposes, we assume that the selling division will transfer internally if it is indifferent between an internal transfer and an external sale.)

(c) ALTERNATIVE COST MEASURES

(i) Full-Absorption Cost-Based Transfers. Although the transfer rule (the transfer price should equal the differential outlay cost to the selling division plus the opportunity cost to the company of making the internal transfer) assumes that the company has a measure of differential or variable cost, this does not always hold true. Consequently, manufacturing firms sometimes use full absorption.

If the company does not have measures of market prices, it cannot compute the opportunity cost component of the general rule. Consequently, companies frequently use full-absorption costs, which exceed variable costs but are probably less than the market price.

The use of full-absorption costs does not lead to the profit-maximizing solution for the company; however, it has some advantages. First, the company already has the cost data. Second, full-absorption costs provide the selling division with a contribution equal to the excess of full-absorption costs over variable costs, which gives the selling division an incentive to transfer internally. Third, the full-absorption cost might provide a better measure of the differential costs of transferring internally than would variable costs. For example, the transferred product may require engineering and design work that hides buried in fixed overhead. In these cases, the full-absorption cost might reasonably measure the differential costs, including the unknown engineering and design costs.

(ii) Activity-Based Costing. Many companies implement activity-based costing to improve the accuracy of costs in cost-based transfer pricing. (Chapter 6 discusses activity-based costing.) Deere and Co. developed activity-based costing to improve the accuracy of cost numbers in its internal transfers of parts.

(iii) Cost-Plus Transfers. We also find companies using *cost-plus transfer pricing* based on either variable costs or full-absorption costs. These methods generally apply a normal markup to costs as a surrogate for market prices when the product does not have intermediate market prices.

(iv) Standard Costs or Actual Costs. A company that uses actual costs as a basis for the transfer passes on any variances or inefficiencies in the selling division to the buying division. However, isolating the variances that the transaction has transferred to subsequent buyer divisions becomes extremely complex. To promote responsibility in the selling division and to isolate variances within divisions, companies usually use standard costs as a basis for transfer pricing in cost-based systems.

For example, suppose that Gamma Industries makes transfers based on variable costs for part A-16. The standard variable cost of producing the part is $22, but the actual cost is $29 because of inefficiencies in the production division. Should the buying division absorb this inefficiency? The answer is usually no, to give production division incentives toward efficiency. In these cases, companies use standard costs for the transfer price. If standards do not reflect reasonable estimates of costs (e.g., outdated standard costs), the firm should use actual cost for the transfer price.

(d) REMEDYING MOTIVATIONAL PROBLEMS OF TRANSFER PRICING POLICIES. When the transfer pricing policy does not give the supplier a profit on the transaction, motivational problems can arise. For example, transfers made at differential cost deny the supplier contribution toward profits on the transferred goods. A company can remedy this situation in several ways.

The company can organize a supplier with almost all internal transfers as a cost center. The company holds the center manager responsible for costs, not for revenues; hence, the transfer price does not affect the manager's performance measures. Companies that designate such a supplier as a profit center should consider the artificial nature of the transfer price when evaluating the results of that center's operations.

When a supplying center does business with both internal and external customers, the company could set it up as a profit center for external business when the manager has price-setting power and as a cost center for internal transfers when the manager does not have such power. The company would measure performance on external business as if the center were a profit center; it would measure performance on internal business as if the center were a cost center.

(e) DUAL TRANSFER PRICES. A company could install a *dual transfer pricing* system to provide the selling division with a profit but charge the buying division with costs only. That is, the company could charge the buyer the cost of the unit (however the company calculates cost), and it could credit the selling division with cost plus some profit allowance. The company could account for the difference in a special centralized account. This system would preserve cost data for subsequent buyer divisions and would encourage internal transfers by providing a profit on such transfers for the selling divisions.

Some companies use dual transfer prices to encourage internal transfers; however, they can use other methods to encourage internal transfers. For example, many companies recognize internal transfers and incorporate them explicitly in their reward systems. Other companies base part of a supplying manager's bonus on the purchasing center's profits.

27.7 NEGOTIATING THE TRANSFER PRICE

Another alternative for setting transfer prices permits managers to negotiate the price for internally transferred goods and services. Under this system, the managers involved act in much the same way as the managers of independent companies. *Negotiated transfer pricing* preserves the autonomy of the division managers. This system has two disadvantages, however: the negotiating process might consume a great deal of management effort, and the final price and its implications for performance measurement may depend more on the manager's ability to negotiate than on the company's best interest.

In the Gamma Industries case, the two managers have room to negotiate the price between \$22 and \$40. They may choose to split the difference or develop some other negotiating strategy.

27.8 GLOBAL PRACTICES

The authors of surveys of corporate practices, summarized in Exhibit 27.6, reported that nearly half of the U.S. companies surveyed used a cost-based transfer pricing system; 33 percent used a market price–based system; and 22 percent used a negotiated system. Similar results have been found for companies in Canada and Japan.

Generally, we find that when companies negotiate prices, the results are between the market price at the upper limit and some measure of cost at the lower limit.

No optimal transfer pricing policy dominates all others. An established policy will not always work to induce the economically optimal outcome. As with other management decisions, however, the company must weigh the cost of any system against its benefits. Improving a transfer pricing policy beyond some point (for example, to obtain better measures of variable costs and market prices) will result in the costs of the system exceeding its benefits. Thus, management tends to settle for a system that seems to work reasonably well rather than devise a textbook-perfect system.

27.9 MULTINATIONAL TRANSFER PRICING

In international transactions, transfer prices may affect tax liabilities, royalties, and other payments because of different laws in different countries (or states). Because tax rates vary among countries, companies have incentives to set transfer prices that will increase revenues (and profits) in low-tax countries and increase costs (thereby reducing profits) in high-tax countries.

Methods	United States[a]	Canada[b]	Japan[c]
Cost based	45%	47%	47%
Market based	33	35	34
Negotiated transfer prices	22	18	19
Total	100%	100%	100%

Note: Companies using other methods were omitted from this illustration. These companies were 2 percent or less of the total.

[a] Source: S. Borkowski, "Environmental and Organizational Factors Affecting Transfer Pricing: A Survey," *Journal of Management Accounting Research* (Fall 1990).

[b] Source; R. Tang, "Canadian Transfer Pricing Practices," *CA Magazine* (March 1980).

[c] Source: R. Tang, C. Walter, and R. Raymond, "Transfer Pricing—Japanese vs. American Style," *Management Accounting* (January 1979).

EXHIBIT 27.6 TRANSFER PRICING PRACTICES

Tax avoidance by foreign companies using inflated transfer prices has been a major issue in recent U.S. presidential campaigns. Foreign companies that sell goods to their U.S. subsidiaries at inflated transfer prices artificially reduce the profit of the U.S. subsidiaries. Some presidential candidates claim that the United States could collect billions per year in additional taxes if transfer pricing was calculated according to U.S. tax laws. (Many foreign companies dispute this claim.)

To understand the effects of transfer pricing on taxes, consider the example of Nehru Jacket Corp. Its facility in Country N imports materials from the company's Country I facility. The tax rate in Country N is 70 percent, but in Country I it is 40 percent.

During the current year, Nehru incurred production costs of $2 million in Country I. Costs incurred in Country N, aside from the cost of the jackets, amounted to $6 million. (We call these "third-party" costs.) Sales revenues in Country N totaled $24 million. Similar goods imported by other companies in Country N would have cost an equivalent of $3 million. However, Nehru points out that because of its special control over its operations in Country I and the special approach it uses to manufacture its goods, the appropriate transfer price is $10 million. Exhibit 27.7 shows the tax liability in both countries with both the $3 million and the $10 million transfer prices.

Nehru Jacket Corp. can save $2,100,000 in taxes simply by changing its transfer price!

To say the least, international taxing authorities look closely at transfer prices when examining the tax returns of companies engaged in related-party transactions that cross national boundaries. Companies frequently must have adequate support for the use of the transfer price that they have chosen for such a situation. Transfer pricing disputes also occur at the state and province level because of different tax rates.

Assuming a $3 million transfer price

	Country I		Country N
Revenues	$ 3,000,000	→	$24,000,000
Third-party costs	2,000,000		6,000,000
Transferred goods costs	-		3,000,000
Taxable income	1,000,000		15,000,000
Tax rate	40%		70%
Tax liability	$ 400,000		$10,500,000
Total tax liability		$10,900,000	

Assuming a $10 million transfer price

	Country I		Country N
Revenues	$10,000,000	→	$24,000,000
Third-party costs	2,000,000		6,000,000
Transferred goods costs	-		10,000,000
Taxable income	8,000,000		8,000,000
Tax rate	40%		70%
Tax liability	$ 3,200,000		$ 5,600,000
Tpta; tax liability		$8,800,000	

EXHIBIT 27.7 OUTSIDE SUPPLIERS ARE AVAILABLE(SELLING DIVISION BELOW CAPACITY WITH ALTERNATIVE FACILITY UTILIZATION)

27.10 SEGMENT REPORTING

The FASB requires companies engaged in different lines of business to report certain information about segments[1] that meet the FASB's technical requirements. This reporting requirement measures the performance of the significant segments of a company.

The requirement includes the following items:

- Segment revenue
- Segment operating profits or loss
- Identifiable segment assets
- Depreciation and amortization
- Capital expenditures
- Certain specialized items

In addition, if a company has significant foreign operations, it must disclose revenues, operating profits or losses, and identifiable assets by geographic region.

Requirements for external segment reporting generally do not accept negotiated transfer prices, which the company may find useful for internal purposes. In general, the accounting profession has indicated a preference for market-based transfer prices. This preference arises because segment disclosure enables an investor to evaluate a company's divisions as though they were free-standing enterprises. Presumably, the divisions would be sales on market transactions, not on the ability of managers to negotiate prices.

Although market-based transfer prices have a sound conceptual basis in this setting, the practical application may prove difficult. Frequently, companies have interdependent segments, so market prices may not reflect the same risk in an intracompany sale that they do in third-party sales.

In addition, companies often lack readily available market prices for some or all products. When these problems arise, management usually attempts to estimate the market by obtaining market prices for similar goods and adjusting the price to reflect the characteristics of the goods transferred within the company. Alternatively, a company could begin with the cost of the item transferred and add an allowance to represent the normal profit for the item.

27.11 SUMMARY

When companies transfer goods or services between divisions, they assign a price to that transaction. The dollar value assigned to the transfer can have significant implications in measuring divisional performance. Establishing transfer prices can prove difficult. It depends on individual circumstances. The chapter outlined four common scenarios and two general rules that depend on whether the selling division is operating at capacity or has idle capacity.

Companies may base transfer pricing systems on direct intervention, market prices, costs, or negotiation among the division managers. The appropriate method depends on

1. As defined by *APB Opinion No. 30,* a segment of a business is "a component of an entity whose activities represent a separate major line of business or class of customer. . . . [It may be] a subsidiary, a division, or a department, . . . provided that its assets, results of operations and activities can be clearly distinguished, physically and operationally for financial reporting purposes, from the other assets, results of operation and activities of the entity." (taken from the glossary of chapter 1 of this *Handbook.*)

the markets in which the company operates and on management's goals. Top management usually tries to choose the appropriate method to promote corporate goals without destroying the autonomy of division managers. Different approaches to transfer pricing create different motivations for behavior.

The chapter also discussed transfer pricing practices for external reporting. Because tax rates vary in different countries and states, companies have incentives to set transfer prices to increase revenues (and profits) in low-tax countries and increase costs (thereby reducing profits) in high-tax countries. The SEC requires companies with significant segments to report on those segments separately in the financial statements. The accounting profession has indicated a preference for market-based transfer prices when reporting on a segment of a business.

CHAPTER 28

A MANAGERIAL ACCOUNTING GUIDE FOR NONPROFIT MANAGERS*

LESLIE ELDENBURG, PHD
University of Arizona

NAOMI SODERSTROM, PHD
University of Colorado, Boulder

CONTENTS

28.1 INTRODUCTION 697

28.2 COMPARING NONPROFIT AND FOR-PROFIT ORGANIZATIONS 698
(a) Compensation in Nonprofit Organizations 699
(b) Tax Status of Nonprofit Organizations 700
(c) Financial Reporting for Nonprofits 701

28.3 APPLICATION OF CURRENT COST ACCOUNTING PRACTICES IN NONPROFIT ORGANIZATIONS 702
(a) Activity-Based Costing 703
(b) Benchmarking 703
(c) The Balanced Scorecard 704
(d) Target and Kaizen Costing 704

28.4 ACCOUNTING PRACTICES AND COST ACCOUNTING ISSUES FOR SPECIFIC TYPES OF NONPROFIT ORGANIZATIONS 705
(a) Service Organizations 705
(b) Operating Leverage 706
(c) Step Down and Reciprocal Methods of Cost Allocation 707

28.5 HOSPITALS 707

28.6 GOVERNMENT ENTITIES AND ENVIRONMENTAL ACCOUNTING REPORTS 710
(a) Government Accounting—Fund Accounting 710
(b) Regulatory Reporting Requirements for Government Contracts—CASB Standards 712
(c) Environmental Accounting 713
(d) Regulatory Reporting Requirements for Environmental Accounting 714

BIBLIOGRAPHY 718

28.1 INTRODUCTION

This chapter provides a broad overview of accounting for nonprofit organizations. We have designed it for accountants (both for-profit and nonprofit) who wish to understand managerial incentives and cost behavior in nonprofit organizations and for nonprofit managers who want to analyze and reduce costs in their organizations. Section 28.2 discusses

* This chapter originally included a discussion of step-down and reciprical methods to allocate service department costs, which the editors moved to the Appendix of Chapter 16.

differences between for-profit and nonprofit organizations and presents managerial incentives and compensation considerations in the nonprofit setting. Section 28.3 applies current managerial accounting techniques to nonprofit organizations. Section 28.4 discusses issues specific to nonprofit organizations. Section 28.5 examines special issues facing hospitals. Section 28.6 presents accounting issues that pertain to government entities, requirements for firms contracting with the government, and information about required environmental accounting reports.

28.2 COMPARING NONPROFIT AND FOR-PROFIT ORGANIZATIONS

Nonprofit organizations differ from for-profit firms on a number of dimensions. To better understand the issues that arise in nonprofits, one should compare the operations within the two types of entities. Nonprofit organizations tend to dominate in areas such as education, religion, and research. Donations frequently support a portion of the operating costs in these types of organizations. Fama and Jensen[1] suggest that nonprofits survive as organizations supported by donors because this type of ownership offers an efficient solution to problems that would arise if private individuals owned the organization. These so-called *agency problems* result from conflicts of interest over efficient use of funds and use of surplus funds generated by organizations.

A for-profit firm with positive net cash flows either reinvests in the organization or distributes to its residual claimants. Residual claimants are those individuals who have contracted with the firm for rights to net cash flows. In privately held firms, these individuals own the firm. In publicly held firms, these individuals are shareholders. In nonprofit organizations, donors prefer that any net cash flows support the mission of the organization, and want more investment in program-related activities and less investment in non-program-related activities, such as perquisites for the managers. The nonprofit ownership structure, therefore, does not include a role for residual claimants such as shareholders. This is the primary difference between nonprofit and other ownership structures.

Over the years, the business environment of nonprofits has changed. Originally, donations provided the only source of funds. For example, prior to 1900, hospitals were charitable organizations founded to provide services for the poor. They did not charge for their services because wealthy donors completely funded hospital costs. Although a large group of nonprofit organizations still rely completely on donations (religious organizations, for example), many others—such as educational institutions and health care providers—receive operating funds from donors, government and other grants, and fees for services provided. As organizations receive increasingly larger proportions of their operating funds from fees, their need for donations diminishes.

Funding sources provide nonprofit organizations with two types of funds: (1) restricted funds that can be used only for purposes specified by the funding source; and (2) unrestricted funds that the organization may use at its discretion. Theoretically, nonprofit organizations use any net cash flows to support their nonprofit missions. Therefore, they use surplus (profit) to deliver products at lower prices, increase the amount of charitable services provided, or increase capacity. These uses of funds eliminate surplus available for distribution to residual claimants.

---

1. E. Fama and M. Jensen. "Agency Problems and Residual Claims" *Journal of Law and Economics* 26, (June 1983): 327–350.

The absence of residual claims in nonprofits does not mean that nonprofits make no profits or that seeking those profits is risk-free. The organization uses net cash flows to expand outputs or to lower the price of outputs. These organizations need some financial cushion to remain viable, and to the extent the cushion is inadequate, employees, consumers, and suppliers bear some risk. Although nonprofits use their residual cash flows, no one owns the right to share in them. For example, nonprofit hospitals require current medical technology and so may invest surplus funds in assets that provide updated diagnostic and treatment capabilities. Alternatively, nonprofit hospitals with surplus funds might provide more charity care, defer increases in rates, or increase the quality of their services.

Although nonprofit organizations do not have residual claimants, a variety of individuals—referred to as stakeholders—do have expectations for the organization, and these are usually of an implicit nature. These stakeholders include vendors with whom the organizations contract: donors, employees, and the communities served by nonprofits. In a hospital, for example, stakeholders include donors, physicians, employees, suppliers, patients, and the community served by the hospital. Although none of these stakeholders can lay claim to the organization's surplus cash flows, they all expect the hospital to honor some implicit contracts. For example, physicians expect hospitals to provide an adequate number of beds and an appropriate level of technology for patient treatment. Managers of nonprofit organizations may need incentives to align their goals with stakeholder expectations. Compensation packages can provide these types of incentives.

(a) COMPENSATION IN NONPROFIT ORGANIZATIONS. For-profit organizations often use residual claims (compensation in the form of stock or based on stock prices) to link managers' incentives to shareholders' wealth. As managers increase their share of the firm, their preferences become increasingly similar to shareholders' preferences. Because nonprofit organizations have no residual claimants, no comparable incentive schemes can exist. Therefore, to create appropriate incentives, the organization frequently ties a portion of the managers' compensation to performance measures.

Because the mission or objective of a nonprofit organization (by definition) is service rather than earnings, operating surplus (net income) may not appropriately measure success for managers or organizations. Accordingly, many nonprofit organizations use measures of expenses relative to budget. This incentive scheme, however, creates a tendency for managers to add slack to the budget to guarantee that expenses do not exceed budgeted amounts. Because most nonprofit organizations endeavor to deliver services in the most efficient manner possible, other performance measures may more appropriately drive bonus-based compensation. Benchmarks for productivity, or measures of quality of services and client satisfaction, or a combination of performance measures that reflect the organizations' objectives help to align the incentives of nonprofit managers with those of the overall organization.

As financial risk in the nonprofit business environment increases, the need for performance-based compensation increases. For example, hospitals that were relatively inefficient, hence, more adversely affected by Medicare's reimbursement change in 1983, tended to implement bonus contracts more often (see Lambert and Larcker, 1995) than those that were not as adversely affected.[2] This study also found that hospitals closely monitored by either the state or their boards of directors were less likely to use bonus-based compensation.

---

2. R. Lambert and D. Larcker, "The Prospective Payment System, Hospital Efficiency, and Compensation Contracts for Senior-Level Hospital Administrators," *Journal of Accounting and Public Policy* (14) (1995): 1–31.

Organizations with strong visions and clear missions can benefit from using bonus incentives based on measures of financial and nonfinancial performance, such as benchmarks or balanced scorecards, that reflect the organization's values. Chapter 25 discusses these types of performance measures. This chapter briefly discusses them later in Sections 28.3(b) and 28.3(c). When an organization ties the managers' incentives to performance measures that reflect its values, the firm is likely to perform better in those areas measured.

(b) TAX STATUS OF NONPROFIT ORGANIZATIONS. Nonprofit ownership confers the benefit of tax-exempt status. Although for-profits and nonprofits may operate similarly, nonprofits remain tax-exempt entities as long as no residual claimants exist. In the United States, the Supreme Court and the Internal Revenue Service (IRS) have affirmed a community-benefit standard as the most appropriate for deciding the tax-exempt status for health care providers and other service-oriented nonprofits.

To be tax exempt, organizations apply to the IRS for nonprofit status. Section 501(a) of the Internal Revenue Code explains the requirements for federal income tax exemption. To qualify under Section 501(a), an organization must conform to one of several descriptions listed in the code and must prove that it satisfies all of the requirements. Most organizations qualify under Section 501(c)(3) requirements, which include the following:

- The firm must forbid any form of private benefit or private inurement (laying claim to any surplus) by individuals within the organization.
- The firm must operate exclusively for charitable purposes or for the promotion of social welfare.
- The firm must serve public rather than private interests.
- The firm cannot engage in political or lobbying activities.
- The firm must operate in accordance with established public policy (Fahey and Murphey, 1990).

Nonprofits secure that status under Section 501(c) by filing Form 1023 with the IRS. Once a firm has applied for nonprofit status, the applicant organization may file an annual information return (usually Form 990) for tax-exempt organizations while the application for recognition of tax exemption is pending. Once the IRS has recognized an organization's tax-exempt status, the organization cannot voluntarily relinquish it. Health care organizations such as nonprofit hospitals and homes for the aged or handicapped must provide information to the IRS in addition to that required of charitable organizations in general. For more information, see Hyatt and Hopkins, 1995.[3]

In the United States, tax-exempt organizations may deduct donations from their income when calculating their federal income tax. A nonprofit firm that does not rely on donations, however, may elect to operate without formal recognition as a tax-exempt entity and still achieve the same basic objective—the nonpayment of tax. For example, an organization may operate so that its expenses equal or exceed recognizable income in any taxable year. Cooperatives, other than formally tax-exempt ones, function on this basis without having to pay income tax. Cooperatives issue patronage dividends to reduce any income and avoid paying federal income taxes.[4]

3. T. Hyatt and B. Hopkins, *The Law of Tax-Exempt Healthcare Organizations* (New York: John Wiley, 1995).
4. Cooperatives do not pay taxes on earnings that are reinvested or distributed as patronage dividends based on individuals' purchases during the fiscal year. However, patrons must declare patronage dividends as income in the year they are received.

Individual states also require that nonprofit organizations file for tax-exempt status. Requirements resemble those of the federal government, but may vary by state. States regulate the process of raising funds for charitable purposes. All but three states (Delaware, Montana, and Wyoming) have some form of statutory structure (termed *a charitable solicitation act*) that regulates fund-raising. Any nonprofit organization that raises funds within a state must abide by the comprehensive charitable solicitation acts established by that state. These regulations usually require annual reports regarding the fund-raising program, describe recordkeeping requirements, list prohibited acts, and detail the sanctions that the state can impose for failure to comply with the law.

Exemption from state and federal taxes may give nonprofits a competitive advantage (lower costs) over for-profit businesses in the same industry. For-profit organizations occasionally complain to government regulators that nonprofits have not provided community benefits in amounts that qualify for tax-exemption. If the tax forms that the organization files reveal, for example, that high-level managers receive excessive compensation, the IRS or state governments could decide that these managers are essentially residual claimants and revoke the nonprofit's tax-exempt status. The organization may also jeopardize its tax-exempt status by not providing adequate community benefit.

(c) FINANCIAL REPORTING FOR NONPROFITS. In addition to preparing information for tax purposes, nonprofit accountants prepare financial statements for various stakeholders. Accounting regulation has traditionally focused on financial reporting for external stakeholders. Financial accounting standards dictate the presentation of financial information for organizations. Over time, nonprofit firms have increasingly depended on the fees they charge for providing service, thereby diminishing the financial accounting differences between nonprofit and for-profit organizations.

Accordingly, during the late 1980s, the Financial Accounting Standards Board (FASB) began to pressure nonprofit organizations to use accounting methods that conformed more with generally accepted accounting principles used by for-profits. In December 1985, the FASB issued the Statement of Financial Accounting Concepts (SFAC) No. 6, Elements of Financial Statements, which replaced SFAC No. 3, Elements of Financial Statements of Business Enterprises (FASB 1994/1995).[5] With SFAC No. 6, FASB extended the concepts and definitions presented in SFAC No. 3 (originally applied only to for-profit entities) to nonprofit organizations. FASB stated that because all organizations have assets and liabilities, the definitions of equity (net assets), revenues, expenses, gains, and losses should fit both for-profit and nonprofit organizations. In response to SFAC No. 6, the AICPA substantially revised the 1987 Audit Guide for Hospitals and issued "Audits of Providers of Health Care Services" in 1990 and updated it in 1994 (AICPA, 1994).[6] The 1994 guide requires health care organizations' financial statements to conform to standards applied to for-profit organizations.

The standards for nonprofit and for-profit firms differ in a few areas, especially for nonprofit health care providers. Recognition of volunteers' time remains one difference. Because nonprofit firms have difficulty placing a monetary value on donated services, they do not usually record value for donated services. The Audit and Accounting Guide for Health Care Services states that if all of the following conditions exist, the firm must

---

5. Financial Accounting Standards Board. *Statements of Financial Accounting Concepts: Accounting Standards.* (New York: Irwin, 1994/1995).
6. AICPA. *Audit and Accounting Guide for Hospitals* (1994).

report the estimated value of donated services as an expense and report a corresponding amount as a contribution:

1. Services performed are significant and form an integral part of the efforts of the entity as it is currently constituted; the services would be performed by salaried personnel if donated services were not available to accomplish its purpose; and the entity would continue this program or activity.
2. The entity controls the employment and duties of the service donor and is able to influence their activities in a way comparable to the control it would exercise of employees with similar responsibilities. This includes control over time, location, and nature and performance of donated or contributed services.
3. The entity has a clearly measurable basis for the amount to be recorded.[7]

FASB Statement No. 116[8] states that a nonprofit firm should recognize contributions of services only if they (a) create or enhance nonfinancial assets; or (b) require specialized skills that are provided by individuals possessing those skills and would typically need to be purchased if not provided by donation. Volunteer participation in philanthropic activities generally does not meet these criteria, however, because no effective employer–employee relation exists (as required in #2, in the list above).

From a managerial accounting perspective, volunteer services may cause significant cost savings for the organization. Organizations with such cost savings should include an estimate of the benefit from volunteer services in cost estimates. Even though measuring these benefits can prove difficult, including rough estimates of their value more accurately reflects operations than ignoring such benefits altogether.

This concludes the general discussion of the difference between nonprofits and for-profits. Many of the accounting practices and innovations introduced in other chapters apply to both for-profits and nonprofits. Section 28.2 briefly introduces relevant information from other chapters and describes any special considerations for nonprofit organizations. From a cost accounting perspective, an important characteristic of nonprofit organizations is their tendency to have relatively high fixed costs. Many for-profit service organizations may have similar cost structures, and the following discussion will apply to them as well.

28.3 APPLICATION OF CURRENT COST ACCOUNTING PRACTICES IN NONPROFIT ORGANIZATIONS

Nonprofits must gather information for regulatory reports. Consequently, they often base their internal accounting systems on the information systems required to produce regulatory reports. Unfortunately, these reporting systems do not provide relevant information for the wide variety of decisions that managers must make. Managers need to consider the types of decisions that they make and develop accounting techniques and systems appropriate to support their decision-making processes.

Development of appropriate accounting techniques requires an understanding of the nature of the organization's costs. For example, many nonprofits have proportionately high fixed costs. These service-oriented firms must often devote a large proportion of their operating expenses to the fixed cost of salaries and benefits. To improve output, the

7. AICPA, *Audit and Accounting Guide for Hospitals* (1994), p. 8.
8. Financial Accounting Standards Board. *Statements of Financial Accounting Standards No. 116.*

organization needs to analyze these fixed costs, along with output efficiency. Managerial accounting techniques developed for and applied in the for-profit sector do not always directly apply to nonprofit organizations. The following discussion examines several cost accounting techniques developed in the for-profit sector and their relevance and flexibility within the nonprofit sector.

(a) ACTIVITY-BASED COSTING.[9] When firms use activity-based costing (ABC), they must first analyze production processes to identify a set of activities that drive production costs. ABC aggregates costs in cost pools for specific activities and then identifies cost drivers to measure the activities. For example, a firm could track the cost of purchasing all of its materials and supplies and then designate the number of purchase invoices as the cost driver. This results in a cost per invoice for the activity of purchasing. Once the firm identifies a set of cost pools and drivers, it can set standards and make cost allocations using the cost driver for that activity as an allocation base. (Chapters 6 and 11 discuss ABC).

Early versions of ABC included both fixed and variable costs in each activity cost pool. Information developed in this manner tended to overstate incremental cost, especially for firms with high fixed costs. For example, Noreen and Soderstrom[10] examined a sample of hospital overhead accounts for an average of 108 hospitals over a 15-year period. They found that, on average, 80 percent of costs were fixed and that an activity-based costing model overstated incremental costs by more than 40 percent.

More recent advances in ABC include the development of separate cost pools for flexible and committed costs, as well as categorization of costs into a cost hierarchy, with some categories that do not affect decision making. Implementing these more complex ABC systems, however, can prove time consuming and expensive.

When physicians become part of the team that develops an ABC system, they will more likely believe in the cost information's credibility and consider it in their decision making. In addition, the quality of the cost information improves because those who employ the resources participate in mapping resource usage to cost. Accounting research over the years provides mixed results on the effectiveness of ABC systems in for-profit organizations.

(b) BENCHMARKING. Analysts use the term benchmarking to refer to the process of measuring products, services and activities against the best levels of performance. One can find these best levels of performance within the organization through internal benchmarking information or through external benchmarking information gathered from competing organizations or from consulting firms that offer benchmarking services.

The hospital industry uses consulting firms that produce benchmark information for departments, service products, and activities undertaken by hospitals. These consultants analyze cost information submitted by hospitals to various U.S. regulatory bodies and generate reports that compare specific hospitals with other similar U.S. hospitals. Hospital administrators use these reports to direct attention to areas with above-average costs. The reliability of individual hospital cost data used in these benchmark reports varies. Hospitals with less refined cost accounting systems may produce unreliable data. In addition, the cost-allocation process affects benchmarking information. Additional factors that

---

9. See Chapter 6 for a more complete discussion of activity-based costing.

10. E. Noreen, and N. Soderstrom, "The Accuracy of Proportional Cost Models: Evidence from Hospital Service Departments, *Review of Accounting Studies* (2) (1997): 89–114.

warrant analysis for hospitals include perceived quality of service to patients, success rate of procedures and operations, and satisfaction of employees and physicians.[11]

Benchmarking information has become a valuable source for development of best practices throughout the for-profit and nonprofit sectors. The process of developing benchmarks can promote a dialog among administrators and encourage adoption of identified best practices. Nonprofit organizations that have no counterparts with which to share information can develop internal benchmarks and identify cost-effective practices. For example, nonprofit organizations with numerous branches across the country, such as the YWCA, could gather information from multiple branches and prepare benchmarking information applicable to their branches of similar size and clientele.

(c) THE BALANCED SCORECARD.[12] A balanced scorecard is a set of financial and nonfinancial performance measures and targets that reflect an organization's performance with respect to various stakeholders in the organization, such as its customers, employees, business partners, and the community. For many years, nonprofit firms focused primarily on cost-effective service delivery. During the late 1980s and early 1990s, this focus shifted from the financial perspective to quality or customer concerns. Nonprofits typically have multiple objectives, however, and therefore need to emphasize both financial and other relevant performance measures. Balanced scorecards with multiple financial and nonfinancial performance measures therefore prove especially useful. With a balanced scorecard, nonprofit organizations can balance the weights placed on performance measures associated with nonfinancial objectives against the weights placed on financial measures such as earnings or operating margin and productivity or cost effectiveness measures. Organizations promote multiple objectives by incorporating multiple performance measures into executives' bonus-based compensation plans. Use of performance measures in areas such as the following help organizations fulfill their goals:

- Client or customer expectations and satisfaction
- Cross-departmental teamwork toward a common goal
- Ability to identify waste, such as service delays and errors in decision making, that affect clients or patients
- Ability to identify surplus that the organization can use to increase efficiency
- Ability to accelerate the rate at which the organization learns[13]

As with other types of performance measures, organizations need to ensure that it reinforces only optimal behavior for the organization. For example, if the firm compensates employees for reducing hazardous waste when the organization does not have appropriate environmental policies and procedures in place, employees may pour hazardous chemicals down the drain rather than dispose of them properly, thus exposing the company to legal liability.

(d) TARGET AND KAIZEN COSTING. Japanese manufacturers developed target and kaizen costing. (Chapters 7 and 8 discuss these methods.) Although one usually sees target

11. For further examples of the use of benchmarking information, in general and within a hospital setting, see Horngren, Foster, and Datar (1997), pp. 235–236.
12. See also Chapter 25, a chapter focused on balanced scorecard issues.
13. R. Lynch and K. Cross, "Performance Measurement Systems." *Readings and Issues in Cost Management*, edited by James Reeve, (Mason, Ohio: South-Western College Publishing, 1995).

costing in the manufacturing sector, the nonprofit and service sectors can also apply target costing principles. Target costing is a cost control method that occurs at the design phase of new product development. After a market survey, the firm sets a target price and then calculates a target cost, based on its desired profit margin. The firm decides to manufacture the product only if it can meet the target cost. Thus, the method builds cost control into the production process in the development and design phase. As the organization develops a new product, the design team considers tradeoffs in price, functionality, and quality to meet the target cost.

Using techniques that analyze the relevant time and costs to provide a particular service, a nonprofit organization could develop a production plan for a specific service at a predetermined target cost. Because many service organizations have a large proportion of fixed costs, capacity levels affect the variability of their costs. Organizations with ample capacity would not include fixed costs in their estimated product costs. If, however, the firm faces capacity limits, the estimated product cost should include costs to increase capacity or efficiency of throughput. For example, suppose a nonprofit daycare program wanted to add after school care to its program. If the daycare were housed in a building large enough to accommodate increased volume, cost estimates would not include fixed costs related to the building. If the daycare must rent new space, however, the cost estimates should include rent.

Once an organization has established a specific product line, kaizen costing provides an effective method for reducing costs over time.[14] Under kaizen costing, organizations set specific goals for cost reduction (e.g., a 15 percent reduction in labor cost after the first six months of product introduction). These goals anticipate a reduction in market price due to increased competition. As the business environment for nonprofit service providers becomes more competitive, demand becomes more price-sensitive. Kaizen costing builds cost reduction into the product life-cycle plan. Nonprofit firms can use kaizen principles to develop specific cost-reduction goals over time. Because proportionately high fixed costs characterize service firms, if a firm has extra capacity and can reduce costs so that prices fall and volumes increase, increased volumes will likely lead to an increase in profits.

28.4 ACCOUNTING PRACTICES AND COST ACCOUNTING ISSUES FOR SPECIFIC TYPES OF NONPROFIT ORGANIZATIONS

We next examine accounting practices and cost accounting issues for service organizations in general, and for two specific types of service organizations: hospitals and governments.

(a) SERVICE ORGANIZATIONS. The environment of service organizations (which includes charitable organizations and social service providers) has changed in the past decades. Adequate revenue streams of the past have diminished, and donors and other funding organizations demand increasing accountability with respect to cost. Service organization revenues generally come in four forms:

- Unrestricted lump-sum grants and donations
- Grants or contracts (lump-sum) to develop a program for performance of specific services
- Contracts for performance of specific services priced per unit of service
- Contracts for performance of specific services on a *capitated* basis

14. See Chapter 8 for a more complete discussion of kaizen costing.

Under *capitation,* the organization receives a fixed fee to provide individuals with necessary services for a fixed period of time. In this setting, cost control becomes a critical issue, not only for development of appropriate and competitive bids, but also for the organization to remain viable, because it bears all of the financial risk associated with capitated programs.

As service organizations grapple with more competitive business environments, they face issues associated with managing costs. For example, both internal and external stakeholders request increasing amounts of information about the effectiveness of their donations and grants. Therefore, nonprofit organizations increasingly need to know the percentage of total costs spent on direct service versus administration and fundraising. Charitable donors, in particular, want to know that their funds support the work of the charity and not fund raisers or perquisites for administrators. Abuses of charitable donations abound. In May, 2003, the Supreme Court ruled that a telemarketer could be sued for keeping 85 percent of funds raised while falsely assuring donors that most of their money would go toward charitable activities, such as Thanksgiving food baskets.[15] Tracking the proportion of costs spent on administration not only controls abuses, but also increases the chances for success over time. Consider an organization such as United Way, which raises money through various corporate campaigns using different campaign strategies. Comparing the costs of administering the campaigns to the amount of money raised helps United Way identify effective fundraising methods. Lumping all fundraising activities into administrative costs would make such analysis impossible.

Service organizations also benefit from defining internal benchmarks and tracking performance against these benchmarks. In addition to focusing on cost, organizations need to emphasize service quality. Unfortunately, nonprofit firms frequently face tradeoffs between cost and quality of service, and evaluate performance based on both financial and nonfinancial metrics.

Benchmarking requires development of appropriate metrics. As Section 28.3(b) discussed, the firm should consider the behavioral implications of any performance measure and adjust these measures over time to align employees' incentives with the organization's objectives. Unique service organizations may not have appropriate benchmarks from outside the organization. In this situation, the firm could define areas of the organization—such as accounting and human resources—for which available external benchmarks exist. The firm could also develop internal organization-specific measures and track performance over time. Each organization must also establish the relative weights given to the financial and nonfinancial performance measures.

(b) OPERATING LEVERAGE. As discussed previously, most social service organizations have a large percentage of fixed costs, which leads to a high degree of operating leverage. The higher the proportion of fixed costs, the higher the operating leverage. Because operating leverage affects an organization's financial risk, social service managers and accountants need to understand it. Some organizations base their fees on cost. For example, a nursing home might charge residents a monthly fee based on their annual operating costs and increase these fees only as operating costs increase. If all of their residents pay based on the monthly fees, operating leverage is unimportant because payments will always exceed costs. If, however, some residents have insurance that pays based on a predetermined daily rate that the nursing home cannot increase, its revenues are based on

---

15. *Wall Street Journal* (May 6, 2003), D2.

volume rather than cost and its profits become more variable if operating leverage is high. To reduce earnings variability, the degree of operating leverage should be reduced.

Because service organizations increasingly rely on fees rather than donations for revenue, their income depends on volume. Operating leverage becomes important as volumes decrease because by definition, fixed costs do not decrease with decreasing volumes. Many social service organizations attempt to reduce the proportion of fixed cost in their cost structures, thereby reducing their operating leverage. Hospitals typically have a high degree of operating leverage and have suffered decreasing inpatient volumes in the past decade. Accordingly, managers have responded by increasing the proportion of variable costs in their cost structures.[16] Hospitals have several ways to reduce fixed costs: (1) increase the proportion of employees who are compensated on hourly wages instead of a salary; (2) lease equipment on an operating lease basis rather than purchase it; (3) use smaller, mobile equipment rather than large pieces that require a dedicated space; and (4) outsource activities that are not part of their core competencies, such as cafeteria services.

As revenue sources tighten, service organizations seek new funding opportunities. Organizations need to analyze each funding source, not only in terms of the types of available funds, but also for any requirements associated with funding. For example, some funding agencies may require detailed reporting and cost tracking. Such tracking can prove extremely costly to the organization receiving the funds and may actually outweigh the benefits of receiving funds from that source. Organizations also need to understand funding requirements and set up systems to track all expenditures that they can bill to available funding streams.

(c) STEP DOWN AND RECIPROCAL METHODS OF COST ALLOCATION. As part of their cost reporting requirements, funding agencies frequently require service organizations to submit cost reports that require the calculation of a cost per service or cost per client. The required cost is usually a fully allocated cost that reflects use of support services such as accounting, information systems and general administration. The organization therefore needs to assign all costs for these service departments to the departments that either receive revenue or provide charitable services. State and federal regulators often require nonprofits to use the step-down or reciprocal method of allocating costs for reporting purposes. The Appendix to Chapter 16 illustrates these methods.

28.5 HOSPITALS

Hospitals have prominence as social service organizations. Accordingly, we devote this section to special issues that affect hospitals, such as the proliferation of for-profit firms in the industry. The increasing presence of for-profit hospitals has changed the nature of the business environment by increasing competition, particularly for the more profitable services that hospitals provide. For-profit hospitals have no obligation to provide charity care, although to meet federal requirements for Medicare reimbursement, all hospitals—regardless of ownership type—must provide emergency room care for any patient, without consideration of the patient's ability to pay. For-profit hospitals can turn away other charity care patients. This system burdens some nonprofit hospitals with increasing amounts of charity care patients and they must trade off between providing services for

---

16. L. Eldenburg and S. Kallapur, "Changes in Hospital Cost Structure as a Risk Management Strategy," Working paper, The University of Arizona, 1998.

indigent patients and the hospital's bottom line. Moreover, to remain competitive with for-profit hospitals, nonprofits need to offer appropriate compensation packages to their top executives. Because for-profit organizations can provide compensation packages that include stock options and profit-sharing programs, nonprofits must be able to offer similar types of packages. Performance-based compensation has increasingly become a larger part of the entire compensation package for hospital executives.[17]

To ensure a steady supply of patients, hospitals must attract a large group of physicians with admitting privileges. Since reimbursement has increasingly become either fixed per episode or based on capitation, hospitals must also enlist physicians' cooperation in treating patients in a cost-effective manner. On one hand, hospitals must provide ample resources such as capital equipment, the latest technology and adequate capacity. On the other hand, hospitals must encourage physicians to use these resources in a cost effective manner. Before the era of managed health care, insurers paid patients' bills on the basis of cost, a system that aligned physician with hospital incentives, which did not include cost reduction. Hospitals readily provided whatever treatment physicians ordered for their patients and physicians had no incentive to include cost of treatment in their decisions. During this period, hospitals increased in size and in technological capability. This behavior led to increasing health costs.

These rapidly increasing costs led to changes in reimbursement practices. HMOs and large insurers controlled blocks of patients and began negotiating with hospitals for discounts or capitated services, which has resulted in several problems for hospitals. First, hospital incentives no longer coincide with physicians' incentives. Some physicians build labs and service centers to compete with hospitals. Some hospitals have purchased physicians' practices and put the physicians on a salary in a move to have more control over their practice patterns. When the hospital later sells these practices, the new firm may have completely different capital improvements and compensation for the physicians. Thus, hospitals and physicians have, in some instances, become rivals.[18]

In addition, billing practices have become complex and bill amounts are increasingly unrelated to cost. Large insurers have negotiated discounts, squeezing the industry's profits. Hospitals bill uninsured patients and those insurers without negotiating power at higher rates to compensate for losses on negotiated contracts. Because of these practices, a congressional probe began examining the issue in 2004, first examining the high rates that the nation's top 20 hospital chains charge uninsured patients.[19]

Because cost-based reimbursement was standard for so many years, hospitals tended to focus primarily on enhancing reimbursement. For example, hospitals have traditionally passed the cost of charity care onto paying patients by incorporating the cost of charity cases into hospital prices. When reimbursement schemes began to change, hospitals continued to focus on reimbursement and fine-tuned their ability to adjust their charges to their payor mix to ensure profits. As payors negotiated discounts, hospitals focused on increased efficiency. This focus has had two directions: (1) provision of cost-effective services; and (2) managing patient treatment.

Provision of cost-effective services became the first effort toward cost containment. As hospitals began to examine the cost of providing specific services, a demand for

---

17. R. Lambert and D. Larcker, "The Prospective Payment System, Hospital Efficiency, and Compensation Contracts for Senior-Level Hospital Administrators," *Journal of Accounting and Public Policy* (14) (1995): 1—31.
18. *Wall Street Journal* (October 25, 1997), A1 and A14.
19. *Wall Street Journal* (February 20, 2004), A1.

information about other hospitals' costs of service arose. Benchmarking has thus become well-developed in this industry, to the point of being featured in cost accounting text books.[20] Hospitals can compare the cost of providing specific services with the cost in similar hospitals.

Managing patient treatment poses more problems for hospitals, because physicians make treatment decisions, while the hospital bears the costs of treatment. Because of this dynamic, many hospitals have encouraged physicians to develop practice guidelines for specific diagnoses. The hospital then monitors patient treatment and attempts to hold physicians to the guidelines. A relatively easy and inexpensive alternative exists, however. Hospitals can provide physicians with three sets of information:

1. The cost of any treatment or procedure the physician may order
2. The accumulating costs of treatment per case
3. A benchmark—either hospital, state, or nationwide—of the cost to treat a similar patient

Hospitals that provide all three sets of information tend to have relatively lower average charges, after controlling for other factors.[21] When physicians have this cost information, they use their knowledge of the efficacy of treatment and the patient's response to treatment to make marginal decisions about the cost-effectiveness of additional care. Physicians have access to an increasing amount of information about the cost-effectiveness of different types of treatment, and consultants have established practices to help educate physicians in the most cost-effective ways to treat patients.

Hospitals face a regulatory environment that differs from that of other nonprofit organizations. Because a large percentage of patient revenues result from the treatment of Medicare patients, hospitals must conform to any requirements that the Centers for Medicare & Medicaid Services (CMMS)[22] stipulates as necessary for Medicare reimbursement. For example, CMMS requires hospitals to submit an annual Medicare Cost Report that calculates costs related to Medicare patients. The report first assigns all directly traceable costs for individual departments (e.g., salaries and wages) to those departments as direct costs. Second, it reclassifies costs among departments according to Medicare guidelines. For example, the hospital must reclassify drugs purchased directly by departments such as the operating room to the pharmacy department. The CMMS disallows some costs—such as bad debts and charity care—as not attributable to Medicare patients. The report subtracts these costs at the department level. Third, the report allocates the costs of service departments (such as laundry and linen, housekeeping, and administrative services) to the revenue-generating departments. The guidelines require such calculations to compute the full costs of providing service in the revenue-generating departments.

These allocation methods do not generate absolute per-unit costs. Use of a different allocation base (such as square feet of space instead of hours for housekeeping) changes amounts allocated to each of the departments. Because of this, regulations frequently specify both the allocation bases and the order of allocation for the step-down method. CMMS developed a set of allocation guidelines to prevent manipulation by hospitals. The CMMS

20. For example, C.T. Horngren, G. Foster, and S. Datar, *Cost Accounting—A Managerial Emphasis*, 9th ed. (Upper Saddle River, N.J.: Prentice-Hall, 1997).
21. L. Eldenburg, "The Use of Cost Information in Total Cost Management." *The Accounting Review*, 69(1) (1994): 96–121.
22. CMMS was formerly called the Health Care Financing Administration (HCFA).

awards contracts to private intermediaries (e.g., Blue Cross in Washington State) to audit the annual cost reports, as required, and to handle reimbursement for the CMMS.

In addition to Medicare cost reports, many states require that hospitals submit annual budgets as well as annual actual cost information. Reporting requirements for these budgets and cost reports resemble Medicare's requirements, but states want information about all patients, not just a specific group. Some states use this information to evaluate resource allocations, such as whether a hospital should increase its inpatient capacity or purchase new equipment. States also can use this information to monitor hospital prices under rate-setting regulation. In these states, hospitals must conform to profitability limits. The state department of health or the state hospital commission has information about hospital accounting requirements. Details about requirements for individual states lie beyond the scope of this chapter. Although federal and state governments require reports of hospitals and other social service agencies, governments (including municipal) must also provide accounting reports about their own services.

28.6 GOVERNMENT ENTITIES AND ENVIRONMENTAL ACCOUNTING REPORTS

(a) GOVERNMENT ACCOUNTING—FUND ACCOUNTING. Government entities need to demonstrate that they have carried out their functions effectively and efficiently. From an accounting perspective, governments have stewardship responsibilities to serve their constituencies as those who manage other's property or finances, acting as administrators and held accountable for appropriately using resources. To fulfill this stewardship responsibility, these entities use two types of financial controls: fund accounting and budgets. The Government Accounting Standards Board (GASB) Statement of Governmental Accounting Concepts No. 1, issued in 1987, emphasizes governments' accountability to their constituencies. Financial reports must compare actual results with a legally adopted budget, assess financial conditions and results of operations, assist in evaluating compliance with finance-related laws, rules, and regulations, and assist in measuring efficiency and effectiveness.

For internal reporting purposes, governmental entities use fund accounting, a type of accounting frequently used in the nonbusiness sector. Financial management in nonprofit and government organizations focuses on the acquisition and use of financial resources—that is, the flow of funds. In 1979, the National Council on Governmental Accounting issued 12 principles of fund accounting and reporting. In 1984, the GASB adopted these principles and required all government entities to produce financial statements that met these requirements.

Fund financial statements regard state and local governments as combinations of distinctly different fiscal and accounting entities. Each entity should have a separate set of accounts to reflect their independent operations. Whereas business managers use the term *fund* to reflect a portion of the firm's assets, such as a petty cash fund, in government accounting, a *fund* reflects a separate accounting entity. For example, the motor pool for a government entity would have its own fund. Fund accounting uses a modified accrual basis. This method generally recognizes revenues in the accounting period in which they become available and measurable. The method recognizes expenditures in the accounting period in which the entity incurs the fund liability, if measurable. *Available* means that the government entity recognizes revenue during the period of time that it expects collection. For example, property taxes are often due in installments. Revenue recognition occurs on the date the installments are available, that is, during the fiscal year in which the entity will collect them. *Measurable* means the entity knows the amount. The entity cannot predict the timing of payment of some taxes, such as licensing fees, so it recognizes this type of revenue on a cash basis. Government entities classify fund revenues by fund and by source.

Expenditures by government entities include outlays for expenses, retirement of debt, and capital outlays. Entities classify expenditures by fund, function (program), organization unit, activity, the period benefited, or by object (type of items purchased or services obtained). They classify interfund transfers and proceeds of long-term debt issues separately from fund revenues and expenditures.

Some government entities receive proprietary fund revenues and must use the same classifications that a similar business organization would use. For example, a county-owned hospital treats both paying and nonpaying patients and receives patient fees as well as subsidies from the county to cover all costs. Regulations require this hospital to use the same revenue and expense classifications as privately owned nonprofit hospitals would use, and adopt the same accrual accounting methods.

One major difference between fund accounting and business accounting relates to use of Appropriation and Encumbrance accounts. Certain governmental resources receive funds through appropriations laws. Through temporary legislation, governing bodies assign amounts that specific agencies will spend for specific purposes. The appropriation also confers the legal authority to make expenditures from the assigned resources. The governing body sets up an *Appropriation* account to record these resource assignments. Then, as government executives make current expenditures and commitments, the amount of money available in the Appropriations account for further expenditures decreases. To ensure that the agency sets aside cash for expenditures and commitments, it uses an *Encumbrances* account. Journal entries to this account transfer cash balances to restricted asset accounts to honor expenditures and commitments that the agency makes.

Budgets have become another important part of control and planning within government agencies. In addition to these functions, government agencies use budgets to obtain resources by establishing levels of taxation or fees imposed and identifying the level of services to provide. Because budgets are so important in government reporting, GASB has listed the attributes of a legally adopted annual budget in GASB Codification, Section 100.119.[23]

Accounting and business firms have pressured the federal government to provide fiscal information comparable to financial statements prepared according to Generally Accepted Accounting Principles (GAAP). In 1997, the federal government attempted to apply GAAP standards to its books for the first time, with the General Accounting Office acting as outside auditor.[24] The audit was required by the 1994 Government Management Reform Act, one of a series of laws passed to require the federal bureaucracy to more frequently follow private-sector practices. The audit revealed many areas where government agencies violated GAAP, particularly in terms of asset valuation. Individual agencies have since worked toward remedying the deficiencies uncovered by the audit. GASB Statement No. 34 requires state and local governments to issue government-wide financial statements using accrual accounting as well as fund financial statements using a modified accrual method of accounting.

23. For further information on these requirements and government fund accounting, see J. Norvelle, *Introduction to Fund Accounting*, 5th ed., 1994.

24. *Wall Street Journal* (March 31, 1998), A2.

Public interest has increased regarding the cost-effectiveness of services provided by government and nonprofit organizations. GAAP financial statements, fund accounting and budget reporting do not provide adequate information to calculate a cost per service because they usually include no information about units of service. Choosing an appropriate unit of service or alternative performance measure requires consideration of behavioral implications. For example, suppose a municipal government measures a police department's cost-effectiveness by cost per arrest. Arithmetic dictates that when the number of arrests increases, cost per arrest will decrease—but an increase in arrests may not translate to a safer environment. The change in homeowners' insurance and automobile insurance rates might present a better measure of performance.[25] A decrease in these rates would indicate that fewer thefts had occurred than in the previous period and that the environment has become safer. Hence, the choice of units of service influences both the cost per outcome and the behavioral response to the measure. Government agencies need to consider these effects when implementing self-evaluation programs.

(b) REGULATORY REPORTING REQUIREMENTS FOR GOVERNMENT CONTRACTS—CASB STANDARDS. Governments must also work toward the cost effective use of taxpayer revenues. Because the U.S. government has stewardship of these public funds, it has established a special set of rules for defense contractors who are sometimes reimbursed based on cost. Incentives arise to load expenses onto those contracts or products that the government reimburses based on cost. The government frequently enters into contracts in the defense industry based on cost. To mitigate these cost-increasing incentives, the U.S. Congress established a public-sector board, the Cost Accounting Standards Board (CASB), in 1970 to provide uniform cost accounting standards for defense contractors and federal agencies. Between 1970 and 1980, CASB produced 20 cost accounting standards. Congress terminated the board in 1980, but recreated it in 1988 as an independent board of the Office of Federal Procurement Policy that no longer reports to Congress. The current board's objectives include the following:

- Increase the degree of uniformity in cost accounting practices among government contractors in like circumstances.
- Establish consistency in cost accounting practices in like circumstances by each individual contractor over periods of time.
- Require contractors to disclose their cost accounting practices in writing.[26]

CASB standards are not a comprehensive set of rules. Nevertheless, any companies bidding on or pricing cost-related contracts for the federal government must comply with the standards. Systematic cost tracking and documentation has become important under CASB. Because judgment can alter interpretation of the standards, court records and case outcomes from litigation between the government and various firms has set legal precedence and a "standard interpretation." Firms that contract with the government therefore need to understand this legal history to comply with the rules.

---

25. R. Todd, and K. Ramanathan, "Perceived Social Needs, Outcomes Measurement, and Budgetary Responsiveness in a Not-for-Profit Setting: Some Empirical Evidence," *The Accounting Review* 69 (1) (1994): 122–137.
26. R. B. Hubbard, "Return of the Cost Accounting Standards Board," *Management Accounting* (October 1990): 56.

(c) ENVIRONMENTAL ACCOUNTING. The federal government established CASB as part of its stewardship responsibilities. For similar reasons, in 1993, President Clinton signed Executive Order 12856, *Federal Compliance with Right-to-Know Laws and Pollution Prevention Requirements.* This Executive Order requires that each federal agency apply two relatively new managerial accounting tools when evaluating opportunities for pollution prevention: (1) Life-cycle analysis (assessment), a technique designed to measure, at the product level, environmental costs and benefits associated with production and consumption, and (2) Total Cost Accounting, a methodology that the EPA, along with Tellus Institute, developed to facilitate inclusion of environmental costs in evaluation of pollution prevention investments.

We begin our discussion of these methods with a general introduction to environmental accounting. Pollution prevention has become an issue for both for-profit and nonprofit organizations. Most organizations have traditionally ignored or funneled environmental costs into general overhead. As a result, organizations have not included these costs in decision-making processes. Organizations that develop accounting systems to address environmental costs not only reduce environmental costs, but also improve their products and processes. In a two-year period, Dow Chemical realized more than $17 million in savings from its Waste Reduction Always Pays program. Baxter International designed an Environmental Financial Statement that estimates worldwide environmental costs and savings. In 1996, it reported a total benefit from their environmental programs of $104.6 million (in increased income, cost savings and cost avoidance). Using a simplified version of Life Cycle Assessments, Bristol-Myers Squibb identified $3.5 million in potential savings.

Governmental agencies have also realized cost savings. For example, Tinker Air Force Base replaced toxic solvents with high-pressure water blast robotic technology for aircraft component stripping. This single project resulted in numerous benefits, including a financial savings of $1.3 million per year and a 30 percent reduction of worker turnover rate. The base also experienced reductions in turnaround time per aircraft component, occupational illnesses, personal protective equipment requirements, and safety hazards. In addition, the base eliminated each year 140,000 pounds of methylene chloride (a chemical paint stripper), 100,000 pounds of solid waste, and 8.3 million gallons of wastewater.

Standard accounting systems do not accommodate environmental costs. Most systems focus on costs for capital equipment and raw materials and either include environmental costs in corporate overhead or ignore them. The U.S. Environmental Protection Agency (EPA) has identified the following categories of environmental costs that accounting systems should address:[27]

- *Potentially hidden costs,* which result from compliance with environmental laws and regulations (i.e., regulatory costs), or from exceeding regulatory requirements (i.e., voluntary costs)
- *Contingent costs*, which a firm might or might not incur in the future, such as the cost of clean-up following future accidental pollution or victim compensation[28]
- *Image and relation costs*, which a firm incurs either to affect stakeholder perceptions of the organization (such as for production of environmental performance

27. U.S. EPA, *An Introduction to Environmental Accounting as a Business Management Tool: Key Concepts and Terms* (Washington, D.C.: EPA, 1995).

28. The reduction in contingent costs resulting from pollution prevention benefits is one of the significant benefits that has frequently been ignored in cost/benefit analyses of pollution prevention projects.

information), or as a result of poor environmental management (such as the negative public relations effects of an accidental spill)

(d) REGULATORY REPORTING REQUIREMENTS FOR ENVIRONMENTAL ACCOUNTING. Organizations have new accounting tools to facilitate inclusion of environmental costs in managerial decision making. The nonprofit and governmental sectors most often use two such tools:

1. Life cycle assessment (LCA), a technique designed to measure, at the product level, environmental costs and benefits associated with production and consumption
2. Total cost assessment (TCA), a method developed by Tellus Institute for the EPA to facilitate inclusion of environmental costs in evaluation of pollution prevention investments (EPA 1992)[29]

Executive Order 12856 requires that federal agencies develop agencywide pollution prevention strategies. These strategies must deal with the following: pollution prevention, voluntary goals to reduce total releases and offsite transfers of toxic chemicals or toxic pollutants, facility-level pollution prevention plans, and application of LCA and TCA principles when evaluating pollution prevention opportunities. Even though LCA and TCA prove most useful to individuals involved in recommending and evaluating projects, they will benefit any employee involved in procurement. These tools apply outside of the government arena; managers in any organization that has opportunities for pollution prevention should understand them. Several state governments (e.g., Massachusetts, Oregon, and Washington) have implemented requirements for analysis of pollution prevention alternatives by for-profit organizations at the state level.

(i) Life-Cycle Assessment (LCA). LCA offers a *cradle to grave* approach, which allows analysts to identify areas of potential environmental improvement throughout a product's life cycle. Scientists and engineers originally applied the technique in the 1960s as a mechanism to assess the energy requirements and chemical inputs and outputs of various production systems.[30] In 1990, the Society of Environmental Toxicology and Chemistry (SETAC)[31] established an LCA Advisory Group to facilitate application of LCA to reduce environmental impacts resulting from production processes' product packaging. LCA has become an accepted environmental measurement tool to aid businesses in their decision-making processes. Many diverse organizations have implemented different versions of the technique.

International Standards Organization's (ISO) ISO14000 environmental management standards has incorporated LCA.[32] ISO standards define LCA as a "...compilation and evaluation according to a systematic set of procedures, of the inputs and outputs and the potential environmental impacts of a product system throughout its life cycle."[33] LCA has three stages:

---

29. U.S. EPA, *Facility Pollution Prevention Guide* (Washington, D.C.: EPA [EPA/600-R-92-008] 1992).
30. C. Henn and J. Fava, "Life Cycle Analysis and Resource Management," *Environmental Strategies Handbook* (New York: McGraw-Hill, 1994), pp. 541–641.
31. SETAC was founded in 1979 and comprises professionals from academic, business, and government organizations who are interested in promoting the uses of multidisciplinary approaches to examining the impacts of chemicals and technology on the environment.
32. Although ISO standards are voluntary, conformance with them is becoming a condition for doing business across international boundaries (M. Epstein, *Measuring Corporate Environmental Performance* (Montvale, N.J.: IMA Foundation for Applied Research, 1996).
33. M. J. Bradley, *Applying Life-Cycle Assessment for a Forest Products Company*. Canfor Pulp and Paper Company, March 1996.

1. *Stage one:* In the first stage of an LCA (Inventory), the analyst sets boundaries on the aspects of a product's life cycle that relate to the environment. The analyst decides which environmental aspects to include and omit in the product's evaluation. Even though environmental regulations may drive consideration of some aspects, the analyst has flexibility to limit the analysis according to the purpose of the LCA. For example, the LCA exercise frequently omits environmental impacts associated with transportation or raw material extraction, particularly when the focus is on improvements in the processes inside of a company.
2. *Stage two:* In the second stage (Impact Assessment), the analyst assesses the environmental impacts of the production inputs and outputs. Here the analyst must rely on scientific data or research, or both, to quantify the product's environmental impacts.
3. *Stage three:* In the final stage (Improvement Analysis), the analyst identifies opportunities to reduce the environmental impact (and frequently, associated costs) of the product.

Despite LCA's potential usefulness, it also has some limitations. LCA results heavily depend on the chosen scope and assumptions underlying the analysis. In addition, standardized LCA tools and data sets do not exist. For example, a life-cycle assessment of almost any process entails calculation of the environmental impact of energy usage. The impact will depend on how and where an entity generated that energy. Assessing the full environmental impact can, therefore, become difficult (and expensive), although several organizations are developing databases that provide standardized impacts of various materials.[34] Accordingly, some organizations have limited the scope of their analyses to processes that occur within their walls (including disposal) and have quantified some of the inputs and outputs (such as the amount of energy used) without attempting to definitively assess the environmental impact of those inputs and outputs. This results in a greater focus on LCA as a means of process improvement and cost reduction while continuing to reduce environmental impact.

Evaluating results of LCAs can prove difficult because the environmental impacts do not have common measures. To evaluate different opportunities for environmental improvements, the analysis may trade off reduction in solid waste (measured in pounds or kilograms) with reduction in energy usage (measured in British Thermal Units), and reduction in waterborne wastes (measured in gallons or liters).[35] Analysts can facilitate comparison across categories by assigning a monetary cost to each impact. We call this extension of LCA a *Life-Cycle Cost Analysis.* Some companies use this method to calculate the full environmental cost of their products.[36] Once they have derived the costs, assigning those costs to different life-cycle stages becomes relatively simple. Calculating usage rates, proper valuation of natural resources, and costs of impacts can prove difficult, however. One should view cost estimates derived from such analyses with caution.

34. For example, Environment Canada, in partnership with the Canadian Standards Association, has developed a database on environmental impacts of various raw materials to make it easier for Canadian businesses to perform LCAs. The National Renewable Energy Laboratory is also involved in a project to develop such a database.
35. This discussion understates the problem; the same difficulties arise within the environmental impact categories as well. For example, should a kilogram of sulfur dioxide be equivalent to a kilogram of carbon dioxide emissions?
36. See, for example, J. Walsh, and M. Brown. "Pricing Environmental Impacts: A Tale of Two T-Shirts," *Illahe*11 (3, 4) (1995):. pp. 175–182.

Such analyses not only require assumptions for the basic LCA, but impose additional assumptions to convert impacts into costs. As both LCAs and Life-Cycle Cost Analyses grow in frequency, however, the demand for better cost and impact information should result in better data availability and less subjective analyses.[37]

(ii) Total Cost Assessment. Total cost assessment (TCA) facilitates inclusion of environmental costs in evaluation of pollution prevention investments. An organization can use this method to evaluate any project involving potential environmental or health and safety impacts. TCA extends the capital budgeting model to include costs that may prove difficult to measure or that accounting systems do not traditionally track.

TCA uses a four-tier hierarchy of costs. The cost tiers follow from EPA's cost categories described in Section 28.6(c): potentially hidden costs, contingent costs, and image and relation costs. The hierarchy progresses from conventional (and certain) costs in Tier 0 to the most difficult to estimate (and least certain) costs in Tier 3.

Identifying costs from the various tiers may prove difficult and costly. Organizations can minimize the cost of a TCA by focusing on one tier at a time, starting with Tier 0 costs. If analysis of Tier 0 costs does not reveal an economic benefit, then the analyst should consider Tier 1 costs, and so on. In this way, organizations will not have to incur the cost and effort involved in analyzing costs in all of the tiers. The EPA suggests the following analysis in each of the tiers:

Tier 0—Usual Costs

- Components: Costs that directly link to the project, products, or process under study. These typically include capital expenditures/depreciation cash flows such as buildings and equipment, utility connections, and equipment installation and operating and maintenance expenses such as materials, labor, utilities, and waste management.
- Suggested analysis:
    - Identify pollution prevention alternatives or the project to be analyzed.
    - Estimate the usual costs of current practice and/or proposed project.

Tier 1—Hidden Costs

- Components: Regulatory compliance or other costs that general accounts typically hide. (Managerial decision making frequently ignores hidden costs because they lie obscured in overhead accounts.) Hidden costs include reporting for compliance, permitting, legal support, testing, monitoring, waste manifesting, and closure (decommissioning) costs.
- Suggested analysis:
    - Establish the facility's regulatory status.
    - Estimate hidden capital expenditures.
    - Estimate hidden expenses.

Tier 2—Liability Costs

- Components: Contingent costs that may result from waste and materials management. In most accounting systems, these costs tend to hide in overhead and general

37. There are numerous resources available concerning LCAs. The EPA has been especially proactive in encouraging organizations to perform LCAs and in providing resources. Examples of resources include, *Life-Cycle Assessment: Inventory Guidelines and Principles* (Washington, D.C.: EPA/600-R-92-245) and SETAC's *A Technical Framework for Life-Cycle Assessment.*

expense accounts. These costs include future compliance costs, penalties and fines, personal injury damage, and legal expenses.

- Suggested analysis:
  - Identify regulatory programs under which the firm could incur penalties and/or fines.
  - Estimate expected annual penalties and fines associated with current practice and/or the proposed project.
  - Identify waste-management issues with which liabilities can be associated.
  - Estimate total expected liabilities.
  - Estimate expected years of liability incurrence.
  - Estimate the firm's share of total future liabilities.

TIER 3—LESS TANGIBLE COSTS

- Components: Savings for organizations that pursue environmentally beneficial projects. Savings accrue from increases in stakeholder goodwill through increased revenues and decreased expenses. Although analysts may find it difficult to predict the extent of these benefits with certainty, these benefits may be significant for some projects. Benefits can come from improvements in customer relations, employee satisfaction (with corresponding reductions in turnover), relations with regulators, and relations with local communities.
- Suggested analysis:
  - Identify qualitatively less tangible benefits of the project.
  - Quantify the less tangible costs and benefits of the project.[38]

After managers identify the costs and benefits associated with the tiers, they must analyze them. Managers should give special consideration to evaluation of financial performance when environmental costs exist. For example, many nonprofit organizations and governmental agencies use payback period to evaluate investments. Payback period represents the length of time required before the firm recoups costs of a new project, calculated by the following equation:

$$\text{Payback period (in years)} = \text{Start-up costs}/(\text{Annual benefits} - \text{Annual costs})$$

Using this method, the organization funds those investments that recoup their costs within a preestablished period of time (e.g., three years). Although analysts can easily calculate and interpret payback period, it has drawbacks, particularly for projects with environmental costs. Many types of environmental costs occur far into the future (e.g., liability or disposal costs). Because payback analysis ignores any cash flows that occur after the end of the preestablished period, the analyst may not fully consider these costs in the payback calculation. In addition, payback period does not provide for discounting of future costs and benefits. Hence, the method does not properly represent the tradeoff between a dollar today and a dollar in the future. Finally, payback period does not allow consideration of intangible costs and benefits. For costs and benefits to enter into the calculation, the analyst must express them in monetary terms.

---

38. Adapted from U.S. EPA, *Pollution Prevention Benefits Manual* (Washington, D.C.: EPA, [EPA-230-R-89-100]1989).

An alternative metric, Net Present Value (NPV), recognizes that a dollar today is worth more than a dollar in the future. This method reduces (discounts) future cash flows to the sum that the firm would have to invest today to produce that future amount. For federal facilities, the federal Office of Management and Budget (OMB) provides a required discount rate.[39] The analyst sums the discounted annual cash flows (including initial cash outflows) to derive the investment's net present value, calculated by the following equation:

$$\text{NPV} = \text{Discounted annual net cash flows} - \text{Initial investment}$$

The higher the NPV, the more desirable the project. Since government and nonprofit projects may not have any revenues, the NPV of the most attractive option will frequently have the smallest negative value.

Although applicable for most types of projects, NPV becomes particularly useful for evaluating projects with associated environmental costs and benefits. Pollution prevention efforts result in annual reductions in costs such as hazardous waste disposal and hazardous materials handling. Although small on an annual basis, if these savings persist for the life of the project, they can become substantial over time.

An organization should consider several issues when applying NPV to projects with environmental aspects. Many environmental projects have long-term horizons, uncertainty, and risk. For example, a firm may enjoy many environmental benefits—such as avoidance of future liability from personal injury, property damage, regulatory fines, and decommissioning costs—long past the usual timeframe included in most capital budgeting exercises. The analyst should therefore choose an appropriate timeframe that fully captures environmental costs and benefits.

The NPV method also has some drawbacks. For example, analysis of environmental risk and intangible costs and benefits can prove difficult. The discount rate for environmental projects should accurately reflect associated risk (or risk reduction). Alternatively, a nonmonetary environmental risk rating in the analysis can reflect the level of risk without specifying monetary effects. The analysis can similarly treat intangible costs and benefits that one cannot quantify.[40]

BIBLIOGRAPHY

Aalbregtse, R. "Target Costing." In *Readings and Issues in Cost Management* edited by James M. Reeve. New York: Warren, Groham & Lamont, South-Western College Publishing, 1995.

American Institute of Certified Public Accountants (AICPA). 1990. Audit Guide.

AICPA. *Audit and Accounting Guide for Hospitals,* 1994.

CCH *Medicare and Medicaid Guide,* Vol. 2. Chicago: Provider Reimbursement Manual. Commerce Clearing House, 1994.

The Center for Environmental Research Information. *A Primer for Financial Analysis of Pollution Prevention Projects.* Washington, D.C.: EPA (EPA/600-R-93-059), 1993.

---

39. Current rates can be obtained from the OMB's Office of Economic Policy at (202) 395–5873.

40. Resources for more information on TCA include U.S. EPA, *Pollution Prevention Benefits Manual.* (Washington, D.C.: EPA, 1989); U.S. EPA,. *Facility Pollution Prevention Guide* (Washington, D.C.: EPA [EPA/600-R-92-008], 1992). The Center for Environmental Research Information. *A Primer for Financial Analysis of Pollution Prevention Projects* (Washington, D.C.: EPA (EPA/600-R-93-059), 1993).

Eldenburg, L. "The Use of Cost Information in Total Cost Management". *The Accounting Review*, 69(1) (1994): 96–121.

Eldenburg, L., and S. Kallapur. "Changes in Hospital Cost Structure as a Risk Management Strategy". Working paper, The University of Arizona, 1998.

Environmental Protection Agency (EPA). *Pollution Prevention Benefits Manual,* Washington, D.C.: EPA, 1989.

EPA. *Facility Pollution Prevention Guide.* Washington, D.C.: EPA (EPA/600-R-92-008), 1992.

Epstein, M. *Measuring Corporate Environmental Performance.* Montvale, N.J.: IMA Foundation for Applied Research, 1996.

Fahey, T., and A. Murphey. "Tax Exemption and Charity Care—What Can Hospitals Expect?" *Trustee* (November 1990): 6–8.

Fama, E., and M. Jensen. "Agency Problems and Residual Claims." *Journal of Law and Economics* 26 (June1983): 327–350.

Financial Accounting Standards Board. *Statements Of Financial Accounting Concepts: Accounting Standards.* New York: Irwin, 1994/1995.

Financial Accounting Standards Board. *Statements of Financial Accounting Standards No. 116.*

Henn, C., and J. Fava. "Life Cycle Analysis and Resource Management." *Environmental Strategies Handbook.* New York: McGraw-Hill, 1994., pp. 541–641.

Horngren, C.T., G. Foster, and S. Datar. *Cost Accounting—A Managerial Emphasis*, 9th ed. Upper Saddle River, N.J.: Prentice-Hall, 1997.

Hubbard, R. B. "Return of the Cost Accounting Standards Board." *Management Accounting* (October1990): 56.

Hyatt, T., and B. Hopkins. *The Law of Tax-Exempt Healthcare Organizations.* New York: John Wiley & Sons, 1995.

Lambert, R., and D. Larcker. "The Prospective Payment System, Hospital Efficiency, and Compensation Contracts for Senior-Level Hospital Administrators." *Journal of Accounting and Public Policy*, 14 (1995): 1–31.

Lynch, R., and K. Cross. "Performance Measurement Systems." *Readings and Issues in Cost Management.* Edited by James Reeve. Mason, Ohio: South-western College Publishing, 1995.

Monden, Y., and J. Lee. "How a Japanese Auto Maker Reduces Costs." *Management Accounting,* (August1993): 22–25.

Noreen, E., and N. Soderstrom. "The Accuracy of Proportional Cost Models: Evidence from Hospital Service Departments." *Review of Accounting Studies,* 2 (1997): 89–114.

Norvell, J. *Introduction to Fund Accounting,* 5th ed. Tucson, Ariz.:Thoth Books, 1994.

Seay, J. D. "Community Benefit Prevails." *Health Progress* (Jan.–Feb. 1992): 38–41, 64.

Society of Environmental Toxicology and Chemistry (SETAC). *A Technical Framework for Life-Cycle Assessment.* J. Fava, R. Denison, B. Jones, M. Curran, B. Vigon, S. Selke, and J. Barnum, Eds. SETAC Foundation for Environmental Education, Inc., 1991.

Todd, R., and K. Ramanathan. "Perceived Social Needs, Outcomes Measurement, and Budgetary Responsiveness in a Not-for-Profit Setting: Some Empirical Evidence." *The Accounting Review* 69 (1) (1994): 122–137.

Walsh, J., and M. Brown. "Pricing Environmental Impacts: A Tale of Two T-Shirts." *Illahee* 11 (3, 4) (1995): 175–182.

CHAPTER 29

INTRODUCTION TO COSTS IN LITIGATION

ELIZABETH A. EVANS, CPA, CMA, CFA, MBA, JD
Analysis Group, Inc.

CONTENTS

29.1 INTRODUCTION 721
29.2 CONCEPTS 721
29.3 APPLICATIONS 724
(a) Liability Aspects 724
(b) Damages Aspects 726
29.4 CONCLUSION 730

29.1 INTRODUCTION

Most readers of this book will have little interest in applying their skills in a litigation setting, where every decision and calculation falls under intense scrutiny and criticism, and may have large consequences. But sometimes trouble comes looking for you. Perhaps someone has asked you to assist attorneys as they prepare a case for your firm. Or perhaps you have to help evaluate whether your firm should file suit or whether your firm should accept a specific settlement offer. In these circumstances you will need to understand how to use your craft in litigation in order to create a defensible financial model of costs, help lawyers prepare a case, and provide a useful answer to the question of pursuing litigation.

This need not be an overwhelming task. This chapter defines seven concepts used in cost accounting: variable costs, fixed costs, incremental costs, standard costs, allocated costs, learning curve effects, and economies of scale. Next, it discusses the liability aspect of litigation (i.e., where the plaintiff attempts to show the defendant's responsibility for some calamity that has befallen the plaintiff). Finally, it discusses how one uses the cost concepts defined previously in two types of damages calculations (i.e., assuming that the defendant is liable, how great a loss the plaintiff has suffered).

This chapter does not provide a definitive checklist of things to look for or to do, but instead will make you think about how costs function and what might have value when answering a question related to litigation.

29.2 CONCEPTS

Other chapters in this book, such as Chapter 2, discuss these concepts. Hence, I will provide only a cursory definition.

Variable costs change as some activity (or production level) changes. Variable costs usually combine direct costs and variable overhead that change (more or less) proportionally, either with the units produced or with the revenue generated. For example, if a widget requires a pound of iron and a firm produces 10 widgets, then total variable costs will include the cost of 10 pounds of iron. By contrast, if a firm produces computer software, then the variable costs will be a smaller fraction of total costs and likely relate more closely to revenue. That is, a firm may find that to adapt computer software for sale to a particular buyer requires the labor of computer programmers, and the firm may price the software based on the amount of time needed for the typical adaptation. Hence, for every revenue dollar recognized by the firm, the firm will generally recognize a certain percentage of those revenue dollars as costs.

Fixed costs, in contrast, do not change as the activity (or production level) changes, at least for some time period. Consider the rent for the widget factory site or the rent for the offices of computer programmers. One may consider this rent fixed even if widget production increases or additional customers require more computer programming hours.

However, ascertaining fixed costs requires selecting both a relevant range of production and the relevant time period. If the widget factory has the ability to make 100 widgets a week and currently makes 75 a week, increasing production to 80 widgets a week requires no extra capacity, only additional material for 5 widgets. Similarly, if the software firm has the office space for enough programmers to customize one hundred applications per month, an increase in the number of customers from 75 to 80 will not result in additional rent. However, if the widget factory increases production beyond current plant capacity or if the software company adds additional customers beyond current capacity, some of the costs initially considered fixed become variable. That is, the widget factory and the computer software firm may both need to rent additional space to accommodate their customers' demand for product.

Moreover, over a long enough time period, one can consider nearly all costs variable because the firm has the ability to change them. Over a short enough time period, one could consider nearly all costs fixed because the firm cannot change them. That is, over a long enough period of time (years) the cost of rent may change even if the firm uses a constant amount of space. Over a short period (days), the cost of rent will stay the same.

Incremental costs refer to the costs of a specified number of additional units or of an additional activity (for example, an additional product line). This concept assumes ongoing activity, which the firm increases with an additional level of production or an additional type of activity. Incremental costs usually combine variable costs and fixed costs. For example, consider a widget factory that currently makes 50 widgets a week and now adds production of 30 more widgets. In addition to the materials and direct labor needed for the 30 additional widgets, the firm may need to buy an additional widget-making machine and may need to hire an additional supervisor. The firm should consider the additional costs of the machine and overhead as much a part of the incremental costs as are the material and direct labor; without the additional machine and supervisor, the firm cannot produce the additional thirty widgets. Similarly, the software firm may find that to add another software product, it may need–in addition to more computer programmers—more supervisors or more space in which to house the programmers or even more marketing personnel to assist in the sales of this additional software product. We consider all additional costs that onc attributcs to this new activity as incremental costs.

The concept of incremental costs is broader than that of variable/fixed cost dichotomy because it allows for some costs to increase with activity levels, but at a less than proportional rate. Like the definition of fixed and variable costs, the character of incremental costs changes over longer periods of time.

Standard cost is the cost incurrence a firm anticipates for the production of a unit and may include both variable and allocated fixed costs. (See Chapter 15.) Prior to the beginning of a firm's fiscal year, management may decide that making one widget during the next year should cost $10. Hence, for every widget produced during the year, the firm records $10 in standard costs. However, standard costs will likely differ from the actual cost to make the widget. The firm will likely have variances from the standard cost. Hence, if one desires to use standard cost as a proxy for variable cost, one must make sure to include the price and efficiency variances also in the variable cost measurement while stripping out any fixed costs.

Allocated costs are costs from one account that a firm spreads over several accounts. (See Chapter 16 and its appendix.) Suppose one supervisor oversees two software products. When the firm examines the cost of one of the software products, the firm may decide to attribute part of the supervisor's salary and benefits to one software product and part to the other software product. This allocation may occur in several ways—the preferred methods are based on cause-and-effect relations. When no causal relation exists, the firm will base the allocation on some systematic, but arbitrarily chosen, relation. The firm could simply divide the cost of the supervisor equally between the two products. Alternatively, the firm could divide the costs in proportion to either the time the supervisor spent on the product or the revenue produced by the product. Such an allocation does not result from a cause-and-effect relation, but is plausible and systematic. If the firm believed that a direct causation relates revenue generated by the product to the cost of the supervisor, the firm would spread the cost of the supervisor over the two products in relation to the amount of revenue generated by the products.

Also, one needs to understand how the allocated cost relates to the specific product or activity. In some cases, firms allocate costs to various product lines even though the cost in question might not vary with the activity of that production line. Consider the salary of a firm's CEO or the cost of corporate headquarters. Many firms will allocate a portion of these items to all product lines, no matter how small the product line in question. In that case, one needs to consider whether to include this allocation in the costs measured for litigation purposes. In the cases of the CEO's salary and the cost of corporate headquarters, one might find that the CEO's salary or the cost of corporate headquarters would not vary in relation to the activity examined for the purposes of litigation. By contrast, consider the cost of a repair shop that a firm might allocate over several product lines, one of which is our widget product line. In that case, one could argue for including some allocation of repair shop costs in the widget cost estimation if the widget-making machines required the repair shop's services.

Learning curve effects refer to the decreased costs a firm enjoys as it gains experience making a new product. As the firm begins making more units of the new product, it uses the knowledge it has gained in its initial production to make the additional units either without previous mistakes or simply more effectively. For example, a firm may measure learning curve effects as a function reflecting the need for fewer hours of labor as the firm produces more widgets. Put differently, the economic cost of the initial items is less than it appears because the incurrence of those costs results in the future benefit of reduced costs in addition to the immediate production of a widget.

Economies of scale reflect that as the production level increases over a certain range, a firm will have lower fully absorbed costs as the accounting spreads fixed costs over more units.

29.3 APPLICATIONS

Generally, litigation has two phases. In the first phase, the plaintiff attempts to show that the defendant has breached some duty to the plaintiff or that the defendant has taken some action for which the defendant has legal responsibility and that has made the plaintiff worse off. That is, the plaintiff seeks to show that the defendant is liable to the plaintiff because of some action. In the second phase, the plaintiff attempts to quantify the harm done by the defendant. That is, the plaintiff seeks to show how the defendant has damaged the plaintiff. In both phases, of course, the defendant attempts to show that no harm occurred or that the defendant had no responsibility for that harm and that, in any event, the amount asserted by the plaintiff exceeds the actual harm.

Customary terminology refers to the first phase as the *liability* phase and the second as the *damages* phase. In some cases, these two phases occur in separate hearings; sometimes they go together. Cost concepts can play a role in either phase.

(a) LIABILITY ASPECTS. The following example illustrates some of the ways in which costs can play a role in establishing (or refuting) the defendant's liability. Consider the case where one firm purchases another. The purchaser and seller sign a contract in which the seller represents that the asset being acquired has specified certain financial characteristics (e.g., the acquired firm generates a certain level of profit margins or is profitable) or in which the seller agrees to provide the purchaser with financial statements as of a certain date (e.g., the date of the transfer of the business) that conform to generally accepted accounting principles (GAAP).

(i) Reporting the Amount of Costs Incorrectly. The seller could breach its duty to the purchaser by incorrectly measuring costs. If the seller represents the firm in the contract as having achieved a certain level of profitability in the past and the seller uses as evidence income statements in which the seller reports a lower amount of costs than the income statement should reflect, then the seller likely has breached a representation in the contract. Similarly, the seller and purchaser might agree to relate the final purchase price to the financial performance of the acquisition as measured by a set of GAAP financial statements as of the date of the transfer of ownership. If those financial statements reflect incorrect costs as established by GAAP, again the seller likely has breached the contract.

Sale contracts usually contain a materiality clause to prevent a buyer from suing over a small amount of incorrect measurement. Such materiality clauses state that a breach (i.e., a violation) of the contract must involve some amount meaningful enough to make a difference to the purchaser. In some cases, the parties may define a threshold for materiality by specifying a dollar amount (for example, $10 million). Other contracts have vague definitions of materiality, or none at all—relying on the definition under GAAP.

Current definitions in the accounting literature indicate that (1) a fact is material if the purchaser would view that fact as having significantly altered the total mix of information available to that investor or (2) if the fact would have probably changed the decision of a reasonable person relying on it.[1] Note that materiality can have both qualitative and quantitative aspects. Nevertheless, these definitions emphasize information that

1. See SEC Staff Accounting Bulletin No. 99 *Materiality*, 17 CFR Part 211; FASB Statement of Financial Accounting Concepts No. 2, paragraph 132, AU Section 312.10, *Audit Risk and Materiality in Conducting an Audit.*

both was unknown and would have been important to the decision maker—in this case, the purchaser.

In addition to the direct effect of incorrect costs on profitability measures, incorrectly reported costs may also affect *revenues*. For example, if the acquisition involves contracts where the firm uses the percentage-of-completion method for financial reporting and the seller recognizes revenues based on an overstated amount of costs recognized or an overstated completion percentage, the seller may also report an overstatement of revenues resulting in an overstatement of gross and net profit. That is, assume the seller's firm had a contract in which the revenues are $1 million and the estimated costs at the beginning of the contract total $800,000. A misstatement of revenues might occur if the seller either reports the costs as $600,000 when in fact the incurred costs are only $400,000, or if the seller reports the incurred costs as meaning that the contract is 75 percent complete when in fact the seller knows that the contract is only 50 percent complete. In either case, the seller will have recognized more revenue than allowable and, hence, more of the profit margin on the contract than allowable. As a result, the acquisition might look more profitable to a purchaser than it actually was. By the end of the contract period, the overstatement of costs will self-correct in the sense that the firm will recognize smaller revenues and profits later in the contract period. This, however, will be little comfort to a purchaser who acquired these contracts during the course of their performance.

(ii) Reporting the Costs in an Incorrect Position in the Financial Statements. Continuing with the acquisition example, the seller could also breach his duty by correctly measuring the amount of costs, but then inserting those costs into the financial statements in a manner that violates GAAP.

Take the example of costs or expenses that properly belong in the cost of goods sold and that a firm must subtract from revenue to ascertain the gross margin. Now assume an acquisition involving a relatively new product where the seller places some costs belonging to the category Cost of Goods Sold into the category Research and Development (R&D) or Marketing expenses. Then the seller might represent to a purchaser that after the new product becomes stable, the amount of research and development or marketing expenses will decline and that size and percentage of gross profits more accurately reflects the ongoing value of the acquisition. In truth, the seller may be hiding the inferior manufacturing process for the new product or underestimating various product requirements. That is, the seller is not telling the purchaser that the widgets need, say, rework before the firm can sell them or that the computer software programs need more programmer hours for adapting the program for individual customer use than anticipated or than the misconstructed income statement can reveal, even to the careful reader. One could also report the correct amount of costs in an incorrect manner by reflecting costs as extraordinary items when they are not. Extraordinary items must be both unusual and infrequent. Again, if a seller reports some costs as extraordinary when they are not, the seller may be misrepresenting to a purchaser the past or likely future financial performance of the acquisition.

A seller could also misrepresent the financial performance of an acquisition by removing costs from the income statement entirely. Consider capitalized costs that should represent expenditures that may benefit a future period; firms should record these costs as an asset rather than an expense. For example, under *SFAS 86*, a firm should capitalize its software R&D costs only if the product is technologically feasible. By incorrectly asserting that a software program has become technologically feasible, a seller might justify removing costs from the income statement onto the balance sheet. However, the seller would then need to amortize these capitalized costs, the rate at which such costs reduce income through amortization understates expense, which should equal the current cost incurrences for research and development. Hence, the seller could represent the acquisition as more commercially attractive and more profitable than it actually is because the net income will be higher as a result of the income statement reflecting only the amortization of costs, rather than the full amount of the costs as an expense.

(b) DAMAGES ASPECTS. Now consider how one should measure the effects of liability in causing harm, focusing on the role of costs in so doing. Two examples illustrate how one might use costs to measure the harm that the defendant did to the plaintiff: (1) lost profits for breach of contract, and (2) typical damages measurements in patent infringement cases.

Nevertheless, whether the plaintiff identifies as a cause of action a breach of contract or a patent infringement, damages usually equal the difference between the plaintiff's actual position and the position in which the plaintiff would have achieved "but for" the defendant's actions. That is, the plaintiff is entitled to the profits that it lost as the result of the defendant's costs. Hence, damages calculations require more than estimating the amount of the plaintiff's revenues affected by the defendant's conduct. Cost estimation plays a vital role in damages calculations.

(i) Lost Profits for Breach of Contract. Consider a case where the plaintiff agrees to sell and the defendant to buy 1,000 widgets. Alternatively, the contract might involve adapting for 1,000 store locations a particular computer software program sold by the plaintiff. The defendant then refuses to buy the widgets or the computer software. Because this chapter focuses on costs, we will assume that the parties agree on the revenue for the contract and that the plaintiff had the ability to produce and sell 1,000 widgets or to adapt the computer program for the additional store locations in addition to whatever widgets the plaintiff produced and sold or software applications adapted and sold during the relevant time period. We will also assume that the plaintiff could not mitigate damages by producing the items and selling them to someone else, perhaps at a lower price, but a price higher than incremental cost.

In many cases, we can ascertain the amount of damages simply by subtracting the variable costs of the contract from the revenues. That is, the court wants to place the plaintiff in the same position the plaintiff would have achieved had the defendant not breached the contract. As noted previously, variable costs change as the activity level changes. In this case, the activity level is the production of the additional widgets or the adaptation of the software program for an individual store. In one scenario, the plaintiff would incur the same level of fixed costs whether the plaintiff produced the additional 1,000 widgets or adapted the 1,000 software programs. Hence, the analysis subtracts the variable costs from the revenues the plaintiff would have received. The variable costs may include only the variable cost of production and delivery of widgets or the variable cost of programmers' time since the plaintiff had already found a buyer (the defendant) and had incurred sales, marketing, and R&D costs related to the contract. However, the person performing the damages calculation should always ascertain whether any variable costs apply to the contract other than the relatively direct costs. In other scenarios, the firm will have incremental capacity costs to sell the breached goods.

How does one ascertain the incremental costs related to the contract? Experts can choose from several methods, but commonly use account analysis and regression analysis.

In account analysis, one views the company's chart of accounts and ascertains the function of that account. Based on this fundamental analysis, the analyst can ascertain whether that account would be variable or fixed with relation to the contract. For example, one might identify the accounts containing the standard costs of producing widgets and the accounts containing the variances associated with those standard costs. Or one might identify the account containing the costs related to the programmers' time, expenses, and benefits for those people performing the software adaptations. There are two potential problems with this method: (1) identifying which costs vary with the contract may require subjective judgment[2] and (2) whether the accounts contain semi-variable costs.

Nevertheless, because firms usually have the data needed to do this type of analysis and because in many cases the damages calculation requires little judgment on the part of the person making the calculation or the person analyzing the costs can make assumptions that benefit the other party (making the calculation conservative), account analysis remains popular. Allocated costs provide an example of possibly semi-variable costs. Depending on how the firm allocated the cost in question, part of the cost may vary with activity levels while part of the cost may remain fixed. Hence, one uses the term *semi-variable* for such a cost. Because the method of allocation may not relate to cost measurement for a damages calculation, an allocated cost account may contain a mixture of variable and fixed costs, and one should consider its inclusion in the lost profit calculation carefully.

Regression analysis provides a statistical method for estimating fixed and variable costs. One can choose from many computer programs to perform regression analysis. Regression analysis uses historical costs as one (dependent) variable and relates those costs to other (independent) variables such as volume or revenue. (See Chapter 12.) Often one can view the relation graphically as a straight line where the cost of production (on the y-axis) increases as the number of items produced increases (on the x-axis). Regression analysis also allows someone to estimate costs when the relation between variables does not exhibit a straight line, but rather a curve, for example. Regression analysis also allows for the costs to vary in relation to more than one other variable. A simple regression analysis might produce a result stating that costs increase by $10 as the firm produces one additional widget. Another form of regression analysis would allow an analyst to estimate that for every dollar of revenue the firm receives, a certain percentage of that revenue represents costs.

Regression analysis has the advantage of reliability. That is, two people performing the same regression analysis on the same data should reach the same results. The two analysts may disagree, however, over which factors to include in the regression analysis and the particular technique (i.e., functional form) used. Regression analysis may also prove useful for dealing with allocated costs where an analyst can more clearly ascertain whether such costs should relate to the lost profit calculation and, if so, measure them.

Regression analysis requires suitable data. The most important two requirements are as follows:

1. *There must be comparable data in order to conduct a time series analysis.* If a firm has cost data for only one period (or just a few periods), one cannot (or

---

2. By describing this analysis as possibly being subjective, I mean that Person A may say that 10 accounts are variable, Person B may say that 6 accounts are variable, and Person B's 6 accounts may not be a subset of Person A's 10 accounts.

should not) perform a regression analysis. A firm may have costs for only one period because it is new or because it changed how it accumulated or accounted for its costs. Regression analysis requires several periods of observation. There will often be tradeoffs between using more data from more time periods where production processes have not remained constant over the time periods.

2. *The dependent and independent variables must have a logical relation for the regression analysis to have meaning.* Because the regression analysis is mechanical, a computer program will produce an answer when someone enters numbers and runs the program. Without a meaningful relation between the dependent and independent variables, however, the answer has no validity. Data analysts understand GIGO: garbage in, garbage out.

When the analyst has available sufficient historical data and meaningful variables to relate to one another, the analyst can find regression analysis an informative and time-saving process.

When should the analysis calculate something other than variable costs to ascertain the lost profits related to the contract? Damages relating to, for example, a breached contract of less than one year will have a different variable/fixed mix than that of a 10-year contract; similarly, variable and fixed cost calculations that involve an additional 1,000 widgets will differ if the addition represents a 5 percent versus 50 percent increase in production. As noted previously, the variable/fixed cost analysis works best over a particular range of production and over a particular time period. The relevant range of production and time period related to a firm's current variable/fixed costs differs depending on the particular case. However, if the analysis of costs requires the analyst to go outside of that the range of production or the time period relevant for the firm's current level of variable/fixed costs, then incremental costs may provide a better cost measurement for lost profits calculations.

For example, assume that to produce the 1,000 additional widgets, one needs to purchase an additional widget-making machine and hire an additional supervisor. The room within the factory will accommodate an additional machine, so rent remains a fixed cost. However, the firm now has two additional costs required (the machine and the supervisor) for producing the 1,000 widgets that one must consider to estimate the amount of lost profits the plaintiff should have received on the breached contract. Or, to adapt the computer software programs for the 1,000 store locations, a firm might find that it needs to hire more programmers and to rent additional space for those programmers. Hence, we find a cost that was fixed at the previous activity level, but now that activity levels have changed, some costs have changed also. The changed fixed costs have not changed because they have become variable, they have changed because the activity level has changed; once they adapt to the new activity level, they again remain fixed.

Finally, one should consider whether learning curve effects or economies of scale should affect the costs used in a lost profits calculation. For example, if the widgets or the software application adaptations are relatively new products, using unadjusted historic costs to estimate the costs related to the breached contract often results in an overstatement of costs and an understatement of lost profits. That is, the historic costs may include costs related to mistakes as the firm learned how to produce this new product. The analysis should reflect the benefit of learning—future reduced costs–related to the items for the breached contract. Even if the breached contract does not involve a new product, when the increased activity level results in economies of scale, historic costs again overstate costs that one should relate to the breached contract. Of course, another possibility arises for a firm nearing capacity: the additional production will result in diseconomies of scale; using historic costs would underestimate the costs associated with the breached contract.

(ii) Patent Infringement Damages. Patent holders have the exclusive right to produce, use, and sell their inventions for a set period of time. Assume that the plaintiff firm has proven that the defendant firm has used or infringed the plaintiff's patent to produce competing products. How does one calculate the damages related to the defendant's infringement? Similar to the case of a breached contract, the courts want to place the patent holder in the same place that it would have achieved but for the infringer's actions. Hence, one must analyze what the patent holder would have done with the patent. Generally, the patent holder would choose to use the patent to manufacture products, would license the patent to others for a royalty payment, or a combination of the two. Each choice has implications for cost estimation.

If the patent holder would have exclusively used the patent to produce products itself, the patent holder would be entitled to the lost profits on the sales that the infringer took from the patent holder. Many patent holders could have made the infringer's sales as well as its own. Further, patent cases do not consider mitigation (i.e., the patent holder making the product anyway and selling it to someone else) because of the nature of infringement. Thus, such cases calculate damages as the profits that the patent holder would have achieved on the sales that the infringer actually made. (In some cases, the patent holder may have sold even more units than the infringer sold; however, because this book focuses on costs, I will ignore that possibility.)

Up to the point that the patent holder would need to add manufacturing, or administrative, or marketing capacity, the analyst can subtract variable costs associated with the increased production from the revenues the patent holder should have received. Once the activity level requires some additional type of capacity, the analyst should use incremental costs. This calculation might resemble the calculation for the breached contract discussed in the previous section.

For patent infringement cases, however, the patent holder may suffer harmful effects on its cost structure that one might consider consequential damages. Put differently, the patent holder may suffer damages in addition to the lost profits on the sales that the infringer made. For example, the reduced sales might have resulted in a loss of economies of scale or the competition from the infringer might have caused the patent holder to engage in increased advertising, or other marketing, or research and development costs to hold onto sales. In these cases, in addition to the lost profits on the infringer's sales, the patent holder had lower profits on the sales that it (the patent holder) made.

Alternatively, the patent holder might have chosen to license the patent to the infringer. Analysts generally use the 14 factors cited in *Georgia-Pacific v. United States Plywood Corp.*, 318 F. Supp. 1116 (1970), to estimate the amount of a reasonable royalty rate. While most of the factors do not involve costs, factors 8, 9, and 10 do involve costs indirectly. The eighth factor is "the established profitability of the product made under the patent; its commercial success; and its current popularity." In order to know the profitability, one must know the costs to associate with the revenues involved, either actual or estimated. The ninth factor is the "utility and advantages of the patented property over the old modes of devices," and the tenth factor is "the nature of the patented invention, the character of the commercial embodiment of it as owned and produced by the licensor, and the benefits to those who have used the invention." Both of these factors focus on the patent's advantages. In many cases, the advantage of the patent may involve lower costs of production or sale.

General case law entitles a patent owner to lost profits, but never less than a reasonable royalty. Hence, an analyst usually prepares both lost profit and reasonable royalty calculations for a litigation. If patent holder and infringer firms produce the patented product in a competitive industry (i.e., an industry where the price of the product did not decrease because of the increased competition from the defendant) with constant returns to scale and no significant sunk costs, both a lost profits and a reasonable royalty calculation should result in the same amount of damages.

Sometimes the amount of reasonable royalty that the patent holder should have received exceeds the amount of lost profits calculated as damages–a situation that the language of the general case law does not contemplate. For example, the situation of receiving more damages from a reasonable royalty might exist in cases where the infringer had a much lower cost structure than the patent owner or where the infringer sold in a distribution channel that the patent owner could not serve. In the case of the lower cost structure, the infringer might possibly have such high profits that it could pay the patent holder a royalty higher than the profit the patent holder would have made on the sale. In the case of the distribution channels the patent holder could not serve, there are no lost sales for the patent holder and there is a royalty payment.

29.4 CONCLUSION

This chapter discusses topics for financial managers unfamiliar with litigation. One could use countless variations on the themes introduced herein; however, the reader should have noticed several repeating patterns. If you know how costs behave and how firms measure them and you understand the relevant issues in a particular litigation, then you should have the tools to effectively participate in the case.

CHAPTER 30

THE HISTORICAL DEVELOPMENT OF MANAGEMENT ACCOUNTING

RICHARD VANGERMEERSCH, PHD, CMA, CPA
Professor Emeritus, University of Rhode Island

HENRY SCHWARZBACH, PHD, CPA
University of Rhode Island

CONTENTS

30.1 INTRODUCTION 731
30.2 PACIOLI AND THE RENAISSANCE 732
30.3 INDUSTRIAL REVOLUTION 734
30.4 ERA OF ENGINEERING AND SCIENTIFIC MANAGEMENT 736
30.5 ALEXANDER HAMILTON CHURCH 737
30.6 PROFESSIONAL INSTITUTIONS 738
30.7 STANDARD COSTS 740
30.8 UNIFORMITY AND WORLD WAR I 741
30.9 J. M. CLARK'S STUDIES IN THE ECONOMICS OF OVERHEAD COSTS 742
30.10 DISTRIBUTION COSTS AND SUPPLY CHAIN MANAGEMENT 743
30.11 DIRECT COSTING 744
30.12 CAPLAN'S MANAGEMENT ACCOUNTING AND BEHAVIORAL SCIENCE 745
30.13 SOLOMONS'S DIVISIONAL PERFORMANCE: MEASUREMENT AND CONTROL 746
30.14 JOHNSON AND KAPLAN'S *RELEVANCE LOST* 746
30.15 TIMETABLE 747
30.16 SUMMARY 756
BIBLIOGRAPHY 756

30.1 INTRODUCTION

A wealth of literature exists regarding the historical development of management accounting, and accountants have many reasons to study this literature:[1]

1. It leads to rediscovery of old ideas that have been lost. A reading of the rich literature of management accounting can lead to alternative ideas or solutions. The ages-old saying of "Don't reinvent the wheel" applies to management accounting.
2. It enables one to support proposals with past writings. Quoting from an important work in management accounting can help sell a proposal or give credence to an idea.

1. Richard Vangermeersch, "Renewing Our Heritage: Ten Reasons Why Management Accountants Should Study the Classic Cost Accounting Articles," *Management Accounting* (July 1987), pp. 47–49.

3. As with study of any literature, it provides accountants with opportunities to improve their verbal abilities, both written and oral.
4. It familiarizes accountants with the intellectuals and innovators who have shaped how accountants practice their profession. This chapter will bring some of these notables to light.
5. It illustrates the state of the professionalism of the field.
6. It leads to an awareness of the controversial topics in the field. Many of the issues discussed in this book have a timeless nature. Hence, much of this past literature will always prove valuable.

As one might expect from professionals who practice meticulous referencing, the historical development of management accounting has a well-indexed body of resources. *The Accountants' Index*, published by the American Institute of CPAs (AICPA) from 1920 through 1991, has become the best-known index. In 1992, UMI of Ann Arbor, Michigan, began publishing the index and renamed it the *Accounting & Tax Index*. The 1920 index has 1,565 pages and included all items in the extensive library of AICPA (then the American Institute of Accountants (AIA)). Since the AIA library included books and manuscripts from the fifteenth century, the 1920 index is inclusive.

In addition to *The Accountants' Index* and the *Accounting & Tax Index, The Accountants' Handbook* has a nine edition collection, starting in 1921 and last published in 1999. *The Cost and Production Handbook* appeared in 1934 and in 1944, renamed as *The Cost Accountants' Handbook.* It became *The Accountants' Cost Handbook* in 1960 and last appeared in 1983.

The previous edition of this handbook appeared in 1978. The Institute of Management Accountants (IMA) in 1995 published an annotated and indexed bibliography of its research publications, *IMA's Legacy: Creating Value through Research.* In 1954, S. Paul Garner published his book, *Evolution of Cost Accounting to 1925.* M.C. Wells published in 1978 *A Bibliography of Cost Accounting: Its Origins and Development to 1914.* In 1996, Michael Chatfield and Richard Vangermeersch edited another example of a well-indexed reference source, *The History of Accounting: An International Encyclopedia.* There is a rich base for historical research on specific topics in management accounting.

This chapter proceeds roughly chronologically. Even though one cannot find the first management accountant or the first signs of the field, there is a consensus regarding the monumental importance of the first printed treatise on accounting by Luca Pacioli in 1494.

30.2 PACIOLI AND THE RENAISSANCE

The first vestiges of double-entry accounting came from various Italian city-states at about the very end of the 1200s. Historians consider the Renaissance to have begun in about 1200. In business, the scope of commercial activity gradually increased, both in terms of varied special ventures and of increasingly greater distances of trade. The first printed text of accounting came out of this period.

1994 marked the 500th anniversary of the printing of Luca Pacioli's textbook on mathematics, *Summa de Arithmetica, Geometria, Proportioni et Proportionalita*. This text was the leading mathematics textbook in Italy for many years. Pacioli named Part 1, Section 9, Treatise 11 of the textbook "Particularis de Computis et Scripturis" ("Particulars of Reckonings and Their Recordings").[2] This treatise contains 38 chapters of various lengths.

Anniversary celebrations of Pacioli's *Summa* occurred in Edinburgh, sponsored by the Institute of Chartered Accountants of Scotland, and in Venice, sponsored by the European Accounting Association. In Sansepolcro, Italy—Pacioli's birthplace— the Pacioli Society sponsored two celebrations, and a consortium of Italian organizations sponsored a third.[3] The AICPA displayed Pacioli's work in its New York office and published two mock interviews with him.[4] In addition, a feature article on the planned celebration by the Pacioli Society appeared in the *Wall Street Journal* of January 29, 1993.[5]

Hence, Pacioli has become much more recognized not only by accountants but also by the general public as a key figure of the Italian Renaissance. With this increased recognition, both management accounting practitioners and researchers can use Pacioli's treatise on accounting as good background material.

Accounting had already developed before 1494. Pacioli's treatise on *Double Entry Accounting* or "The Method of Venice," as practitioners have nicknamed it, described a method of accounting that bankers and merchants had practiced in the Italian city-states for about 200 years. The double-entry method eventually displaced the charge-discharge method of accounting that governments, feudal landowners, and religious orders had used from ancient times.

The double-entry system, popularized by Pacioli and those who copied the ideas in his treatise to develop similar works throughout Europe, allowed a much better way to visualize immediately the results of operations. Separate accounts allowed a hands-on approach by top management, most likely the owner or owners of a somewhat diverse merchant-type business. Pacioli stressed in Chapter 1 of his treatise the importance of owner involvement in the recordkeeping activities of the organization. Pacioli wrote:

> However, as is well known, there are principally three things necessary for those who wish to trade with due diligence, of which the most important is money . . . . The third and final necessary thing is that all transactions are recorded in good order so that information may be had quickly concerning debits and credits, which are the basis of trade.[6]

Chapter 4 of the treatise includes two other examples of top management involvement in accounting:

> Therefore the merchant can be said to be like a cock which of all animals is the most vigilant, and in winter and summer keeps his nocturnal watch and never rests. . . and a merchant's head may be compared to one with a hundred eyes which nevertheless are not sufficient for him in word or in deed.[7]

---

2. Giuseppe Galassi, "Pacioli, Luca," *The History of Accounting: An International Encyclopedia,* edited by Michael Chatfield and Richard Vangermeersch. (New York: Garland Publishing, 1996), pp. 445–47.
3. Chatfield and Vangermeersch, *History of Accounting,* viii.
4. Rick Elam, "An Interview with Luca Pacioli," and "FYI Interviews Pacioli on Fraud," *Accounting Educators* (March, 1994), p. 4 and May 1994, p. 4.
5. "Father of Accounting Is a Bit of a Stranger to His Own Profession," *Wall Street Journal* (January 29, 1993), p. 1 and p. 9
6. Basil Yamey, *Expositon of Double Entry Bookkeeping* (Venice: Allbrizzi Editore, 1994), pp. 41–42. The writers of this chapter urge readers to view the video "Luca Pacioli: Unsung Hero of the Renaissance" (Cincinnati: South-Western, 1990). The three producers of the video are William L. Weis, David E. Tinius, and Chauncey Burke. Weis and Tinius are cofounders of the Pacioli Society.
7. Yamey, *Exposition of Double Entry Bookkeeping*, p. 46.

Perhaps the most critical advantage of The Method of Venice lies in the concept of profit or loss arising from various inventory items or various ventures, or both. Pacioli wrote about diversified and global organizations.

Pacioli did not recommend a detailed analysis of what we today call *common costs* (i.e., overhead) because he did not want to trouble the merchant with minor details of freight and of the wages of employees and apprentices in the shop.[8] Pacioli enjoyed proverbs, as with this excerpt from Chapter 23: "The proverb says of one who runs a business and does not know everything about it, that the money will go like flies." Another appeared in Chapter 34: "Otherwise, if he is not a good bookkeeper, he will conduct his affairs tentatively as a blind man and could suffer much loss."[9]

Over the next 300 years, others extended the system popularized by Pacioli to include more sample journal entries, but it remained merchant-oriented, not manufacturing, in its approach. The beginnings of the industrial revolution called for another extension of accounting into a manufacturing environment. The basic premises of Pacioli, however, still dominated.

30.3 INDUSTRIAL REVOLUTION

The Renaissance period led to a great increase in the *scope* of business, but the Industrial Revolution led to an increase of the *scale* of business. This marked the changeover from an agrarian and handicraft economy to a machine-based economy. The small, handcraft system of the 1300s to 1750s was replaced by a factory system, in which employees replaced the independent contractors of the past.

Recent interest in the history of management accounting has led to a number of studies of British and French firms between 1750 and 1850. These studies have indicated a mixed level of expertise in management accounting in these firms, whereas prior studies by economic historians tended to discount management accounting as a significant factor.[10] The Carron Company and the Boulton & Watt Company offer two examples of companies in which management accounting played an important role.

The Carron Company, founded in Scotland in 1759, became a pioneer iron foundry. Note the location, because in 1777, Robert Hamilton—a Scotsman—wrote the first textbook containing significant management accounting references to a manufacturing company. He most likely knew of the company and its management accounting practices.[11] Through 1850, the Carron Company used many management accounting techniques: expense control; responsibility management*; product costing; overhead allocation; cost comparisons*, costs for special decisions*; budgets, forecasts, standards*; and inventory control. (In those starred (*) techniques, the Carron Company showed superior management.)[12] It did not integrate its cost records with its general ledger, especially in its earlier years. Overhead allocation occurred after the end of the year. Over the years, the company increased the amount of overhead it allocated to product. [13]

---

8. Ibid., pp. 70–71.
9. Ibid., pp. 73 and 86.
10. Richard K. Fleischman and Lee D. Parker, *What Is Past Is Prologue: Cost Accounting in the British Industrial Revolution,* 1760–1850 (New York: Garland Publishing, 1997), pp. 9–10.
11. Michael J. Mepham, *Accounting in Eighteenth Century Scotland* (New York: Garland Publishing, 1988), pp. 305–65.
12. Fleischman and Parker, *What Is Past...,* pp. 27–28.
13. Ibid., pp 173, 177.

Boulton & Watt became notable both because the company manufactured the steam engine—a technological breakthrough—and because the founders, James Watt, Jr. and Matthew Robinson Boulton, became pioneers in cost management.[14] Boulton & Watt used all of the Carron techniques, except for overhead allocation, and their methods show superior cost management regarding expense control; responsibility management; product costing; cost comparisons; budgets, forecasts, and standards.[15] Although Boulton & Watt did not have a good handle on overhead or on integration of its cost records with the general ledger, it did articulate material and labor standards in an acceptable manner. The company used time studies and a piecework system.

Robert Hamilton's *An Introduction to Merchandise (1777, Volume 1) (1779, Volume 2)*, blazed the trail in coverage of management accounting issues.[16] Hamilton was the rector of Perth Academy and had replaced John Mair, another noted Scottish accounting textbook writer, in that post. In 1779, Hamilton was appointed to the chair of Natural Philosophy at the University of Aberdeen. In 1817, he transferred to the chair of Mathematics.[17] Note the impressive academic credentials of the early accounting textbook authors and that Pacioli and Hamilton were professors of mathematics.

Hamilton realized the necessity for complex manufacturing firms to break out of the mechanical accounting model. He suggested using more books, that is *ledgers,* such as a Book of Material, a Book of Wages, and a Book of Work for outsourced work. He used a textile mill as the manufacturing example. He included such topics as transfer pricing, joint costs, calculation of the rate of return, and residual income.[18]

The next notable writer was Jean-Baptiste Payen, who, in 1817, wrote *Essai sur la Tenue des Livres d'un Manufacturier* (*Essay on the Bookkeeping of a Manufacturer*).[19] Payen, a lawyer who entered the chemical industry, wrote this book from his own industrial experiences. Although one could not easily understand the text, it did attempt to integrate cost records with the general ledger. Payen had a good grasp of overhead, including wear and tear on tools and depreciation of furnaces.[20]

The French company Saint-Gobain adopted double-entry accounting in about 1820, after about 150 years of using the charge-discharge system. A principal objective appeared to have been the calculations of costs.[21]

Although neither Charles Babbage nor Dionysius Lardner were management accountants, they both contributed to the field. Charles Babbage, also the heralded father of the computer, published in 1835 the fourth edition of his book, *On the Economy of Machinery and Manufactures*. Babbage based his work on his visits to factories both in England and on the Continent. He noted the dangers of relying on timing a worker, who, under observation, would temporarily speed up the process to unsustainable rates as to impress the observer. Babbage favored measuring the results of a fair day's work, a precursor of

14. Lyndall F. Urwick and William B. Wolf, editors, *The Golden Book of Management,* 2nd ed. (New York: AMACOM, 1984), pp. 16–19.
15. Fleischman and Parker, *What Is Past...*, pp. 27–28.
16. Mepham, *Accounting in... Scotland,* pp. 151–154.
17. David A. R. Forrester and Richard Vangermeersch, "Scotland: Early Writers in Double Entry Accounting," *History of Accounting,* p. 521.
18. Mepham, *Accounting in ...Scotland,* pp. 305–365.
19. Trevor Boyns, John Richard Edwards, and Marc Nikitin, *The Birth of Industrial Accounting in France and Britain* (New York: Garland Publishing, 1997), p. 88.
20. Ibid., pp. 101 and 103.
21. Ibid., pp. 161–65.

standard costing.[22] Babbage urged manufacturers to have a good notion of what costs should be before measuring them.[23] Babbage recommended that the name of the workman be noted on his efforts.[24] Babbage espoused Adam Smith's notion of the superiority of specialization in the division of labor.[25] Babbage called for a measurement of the wear and tear on machinery, so that companies could make cost comparisons to discover lower cost methods of accomplishing a task.[26] Babbage noted the importance of operating machinery 24 hours a day, to maximize output from such expensive capital investments.[27] Babbage's book is an important work that still holds true today.

Lardner's 1855 book, *Railway Economy,* reflected the importance of railroads and the public nature of their funding.[28] Their operating results provided important data. Lardner thought that a company should know the cost of each class of object transported.[29] He argued that past data would prove useful for future predictions.[30] Lardner illustrated different calculations on many different bases.[31] These publications no doubt ensured a strong awareness of management accounting by the end of the first half of the nineteenth century.

30.4 ERA OF ENGINEERING AND SCIENTIFIC MANAGEMENT

From 1880 to 1920, engineers dominated the progression of management accounting because they were the prime movers of the Scientific Management Movement. The meetings of the American Society of Mechanical Engineers (ASME) and the publications *Engineering Magazine* and *American Machinist* all conveyed cost findings by engineers. Some who contributed were Frederick W. Taylor, F.A. Halsey, H.L. Gantt, Alexander Hamilton Church, Sterling Bunnell, Oberlin Smith, and H.R. Towne.[32]

In 1885, Captain Henry Metcalfe, an American Army ordnance officer, wrote the first modern book on management accounting, *The Cost of Manufacturers and the Administration of Workshops*. He proposed a separate shop order card for each job. The system required that the workman note the time he spent on each job on a separate labor card, filed by job number. A similar system applied to materials. Hence, Metcalfe had a well-developed system for material and labor costs, although he did not develop a successful system regarding overhead.[33]

---

22. Charles Babbage, *On the Economy of Machinery and Manufactures,* 4th ed. (London: Charles Knight, 1835), reprinted (New York: Augustus M. Kelley, 1963), p. 117.
23. Ibid., p. 118.
24. Ibid., p. 144.
25. Ibid., p. 173.
26. Ibid., p. 203.
27. Ibid., p. 214.
28. Dionysius Lardner, *Railway Economy: A Treatise on the New Art of Transport* (London: Taylor, Walton & Maberly, 1855), 2nd ed., reprinted (New York: Augustus M. Kelley, 1968).
29. Ibid., p. 195.
30. Ibid., p. 196.
31. Ibid., p. 231
32. M. C. Wells, "Engineering and Accounting," *History of Accounting,* pp. 227–228. Richard Vangermeersch has questioned the views of M. C. Wells and S. Paul Garner that 1910 marked the cutoff of engineering contributions. Vangermeersch noted 1919 as the cutoff point in "A Comment on Some Remarks by Historians of Cost Accounting on Engineering Contributions to the Subject," *Accounting Historians Journal* (Spring 1984), pp. 135–140.
33. Michael Chatfield, "Metcalfe, Henry (1847–1927)," *History of Accounting,* pp. 415–6.

In 1887, Emile Garcke, an English electrical engineer, and John Manger Fells, an accountant, published *Factory Accounts: Their Principles and Practice*. They presented a tightly integrated system for prime costs, which featured perpetual inventory and a job order system. They also did not develop a strong system for overhead.[34]

Many still recognize Frederick Winslow Taylor (1856–1915) as dominant in industrial engineering. He is called the Father of Scientific Management. He was active in ASME as early as the mid-1880s, but he gained sudden fame in 1910 from publicity on scientific management generated by Louis D. Brandeis—later a U.S. Supreme Court Justice—in a rate hearing by the Interstate Commerce Commission. In 1911, Taylor published his two classics, the *Principles of Scientific Management* and *Shop Management*. Taylor is best remembered for the use of a stopwatch to identify the best way to perform a function. Taylor and the engineers were striving for a product that was uniformly constructed with the same materials and with the same production process so that uniformity of output would occur. His emphasis on standardization influenced accounting and led to standard cost accounting.[35]

30.5 ALEXANDER HAMILTON CHURCH

Management accounting historians probably consider Alexander Hamilton Church (1866–1936) the most influential figure of the early twentieth century. He was born in England and came to the United States in 1909. He was first involved in the electrical industry as a works manager and then worked for several significant British companies, including the Renold Company in Manchester. Church then became an editor in the London office of the *Engineering Magazine*. He worked as an efficiency engineer for various U.S. public accounting firms and his own firm. He ended his career as an industrial engineering consultant in Massachusetts.[36]

Church first wrote on overhead in 1901 in a series of articles in the *Engineering Magazine,* which he later revised in 1908 into *The Proper Distribution of Expense Burden*. He stressed that a system of organization should be as finely honed as a high-class machine tool. Church, anticipating what we now call *activity-based costing* in his accounting for a bicycle chain making machine, believed that a firm should not casually charge manufacturing overhead to a job by a direct labor method. He developed the little shop analogy, in which each production center was treated as a separate factory, to illustrate how the firm should charge each production center for each of the many types of manufacturing overhead. He also included a charge to each job for General Establishment costs, which included otherwise unallocated manufacturing overhead.[37]

Church published in 1909 a six-article series in the *Engineering Magazine*, which became the 1910 book *Production Factors in Cost Accounting*. Church, if not the first, was most important in putting aside the notion of allocating overhead based solely on direct labor. Accountants, he felt, must realize that the complexities of manufacturing result in many cost drivers, although he did not use that modern term, so his work presaged activity-based costing.[38]

---

34. Michael Chatfield, "Garcke and Fells," *History of Accounting,* p. 269.
35. Marc J. Epstein, "Taylor, Frederick Winslow (1856–1915)," *History of Accounting,* pp. 579–580.
36. Richard Vangermeersch, *Alexander Hamilton Church: A Man of Ideas of All Seasons* (New York: Garland Publishing, 1988), pp. 7–10.
37. Ibid., pp. 19–29.
38. Ibid., pp. 29–36.

Between 1910 and 1917, when he published the more accounting-detailed book *Manufacturing Costs and Accounts,* Church devoted his energy to popularizing his ideas in various journals, especially the *American Machinist*, edited by his co-author, L.P. Alford. Church's classic exchanges with the noted efficiency engineer, H.L. Gantt, appeared in that journal in 1915. Gantt wanted to charge idle time costs separately in the income statement and not add it to jobs. He adopted, in effect, an ideal capacity viewpoint. Church wrote that Gantt should have noted the works done by Church. Gantt then retorted that Taylor had preceded Church on the subject of the machine-hour-rate method. Church responded that it was he, not Taylor, who had written on this matter. Gantt finally ended the series of exchanges with an attempt at moderating the differences.[39]

Church's 1917 book and its 1929 revision expanded his writings on accounting. In them, Church discussed accounting for waste, and he more fully developed the machine-hour-rate method. In 1930, Church published *Overhead Expenses: In Relation to Costs, Sales, and Profits*, in which he further explored the issues of his books of 1908 and 1910 and recanted his prior position on the supplementary charge for idle time.[40]

Church contributed to the field of management as well as accounting. For example, his 1912 classic article co-authored with Alford, "The Principles of Management," accused Taylor's followers of trying to impose a standard solution on organizations without first identifying the peculiarities of each one.[41]

Church authored innovative and successful ideas regarding many facets of management. He placed accounting into the dynamics of management. His works remain timely for researchers in both management accounting and management.

30.6 PROFESSIONAL INSTITUTIONS

The two most significant institutions that have provided research for management accountants began in 1919 as outgrowths of the cost experiences of World War I. The National Association of Cost Accountants (NACA), in the United States, and the Institute of Cost Accountants, in the United Kingdom, dominated research in the field. The NACA became the National Association of Accountants (NAA) in 1957 and then the Institute of Management Accountants (IMA) in 1991. The Institute of Cost Accountants was later renamed the Institute of Cost and Works Accountants and in 1972 became the Institute of Cost and Management Accountants. In 1986, it became the Chartered Institute of Management Accountants (CIMA).

J. Lee Nicholson chaired the founding meeting of the NACA in Buffalo on October 13, 1919. The NACA immediately started its journal, first named *Official Publications*, then, in 1925, becoming Section 1 of the *NACA Bulletin*, renamed the *NAA Bulletin* in 1957, and renamed, again, in 1965 as *Management Accounting*. In 1999, it was renamed *Strategic Finance*. From 1920 through 1951, the NACA published its yearly conference proceedings as the *NACA Yearbook*. From 1952 through 1960, these proceedings appeared in Section 3 of various *NACA Bulletins*.[42]

39. Ibid., pp. 36–43.
40. Ibid., pp. 41–59.
41. Ibid., pp. 55–74.
42. Richard Vangermeersch and Robert Jordan, "Institute of Management Accountants," *History of Accounting*, pp. 334–336.

The IMA had from its start a research staff director and also a volunteer National Chairman/Director of Research. In addition to its journal and proceedings, the IMA, by 1995, had published 232 research documents. The IMA formed its Foundation for Applied Research on July 1, 1994. Its 1995 publication, *IMA's Legacy: Creating Value Through Research*,[43] has proven useful for readers and researchers in management accounting. This publication involved an annotated and indexed bibliography of those 232 research documents. The IMA membership has easy access to all of these 232 and subsequent research reports. Many of them—including the following—remained quite significant through the years. The first number in the following list corresponds to the IMA research report number.

021 in 1938, Practice in Applying Overhead and Calculating Normal Capacity

029 in 1941, Accounting for Excess Labor Costs and Overhead Under Conditions of Increased Production

038 in 1946, The Uses and Classifications of Costs

048 in 1949, The Analysis of Cost-Volume-Profit Relationship

056 in 1952, How Standard Costs are Being Used Currently

063 in 1954, Cost Control for Marketing Operations

068 in 1956, Accounting for Intra-Company Transfers

083 in 1961, Current Application of Direct Costing

090 in 1963, Accounting for Costs of Capacity

097 in 1966, Concepts for Management Accounting

113 in 1974, Human Resource Accounting: Past, Present and Future

130 in 1977, Corporate Social Performance: The Measurement of Product and Service Contributions

134 in 1978, The Distribution Channels Decision

138 in 1978, Financial Reporting and Business Liquidity

145 in 1980, The Pricing Decision

162 in 1984, The New Product Decision

178 in 1985, The Use of Performance Measures

205 in 1989, Corporate Codes of Conduct: An Examination and Implementation Guide

222 in 1992, Implementing Activity-Based Cost Management: Moving from Analysis to Action

CIMA, in the United Kingdom, remains actively involved in research. The Society of Management Accountants of Canada has become active in recent years. The Financial Executives Research Foundation (FERF) has published an annotated bibliography of its research publications from 1947 to 1996.[44] R.K. Mautz authored two books for

43. Patrick L. Romano, *IMA's Legacy: Creating Value Through Research* (Montvale, N.J.: IMA Foundation for Applied Research, 1995).

44. Financial Executives Research Foundation, *Annotated Bibliography of Financial Publications, 1947–1996* (Morristown, N.J.: FERF, undated).

FERF: *Financial Reporting by Diversified Companies* (1968) and *Effect of Circumstances on the Application of Accounting Principles* (1972).

30.7 STANDARD COSTS

From the beginning, standard costing has meant a compilation of what things should cost, a means for reporting deviations (variances) from the normative amounts, and a mechanism for deciding when deviations require attention. As F.W. Taylor was developing the concept of standardization, Harrington Emerson was popularizing the notion of time standards as part of his 12 principles of efficiency.[45] Although Emerson regarded the accountant as secondary to the engineer, G. Charter Harrison—the Father of Standard Costing—felt the accountant should hold the dominant position. Harrison's 1921 book, *Cost Accounting to Aid Production: A Practical Study of Scientific Cost Accounting*, called for a proactive—not reactive—role for accountants. He used variance analyses to focus management's attention on exceptional areas. Harrison thought accountants should dominate the standard cost system, but he did not want them to set operating standards.[46]

By the early 1930s, experts such as Harrison, Eric A. Camman, and Cecil Gillespie had written explicit how-to textbooks. With the first edition of *Standard Cost for Manufacturing,* Stanley Henrici became the leading writer on this topic from 1947 to the mid-1960s. In 1965, he introduced the concept of a superstandard for management, rather than for supervision, use. The superstandard would judge top management in their creation of an environment for cost reduction.[47] As already noted, the NACA/NAA/IMA has also contributed to the research literature on standard costing.

Standard costing experts have struggled with several issues, listed below. Perhaps because these experts have yet to resolve these issues, some writers have discredited standard costing in recent years.

- What should be the appropriate level of the standard—ideal, attainable, average, or normal?
- When should a firm revise standard costs—once a year, or when a significant change occurs during the year?
- Should the firm use standard cost amounts to value ending inventory for financial reporting? For internal reporting?
- How much should the standard cost system integrate with the general ledger?
- How should standard costing and budgeting interrelate?
- How should standard costs and prices interrelate?
- How many overhead variances should a firm have?
- How does one ascertain and report the causes of variances?

A critique on standard costing in 1964 by Zenon S. Zannetos of Massachusetts Institute of Technology (MIT) stressed the need for a more advanced probabilistic approach. He proposed the use of mathematical techniques based on Chebyshev's inequality.[48] In

45. Harrington Emerson, *The Twelve Principles of Efficiency* (New York: Engineering Magazine, 1912), pp. 341–367.
46. Richard Vangermeersch, "Standard Costing," *History of Accounting*, pp. 550–52.
47. Stanley B. Henrici, "New Views on Standards," *NAA Bulletin* (July 1965), pp. 3–8.
48. Zenon S. Zannetos, "Standard Costs As a First Step to Probabilistic Control: A Theoretical Justification, an Extension and Implications," *Accounting Review* (April 1964), p. 297.

1975, Robert S. Kaplan at Carnegie-Mellon reviewed several academic studies to help accountants understand statistical procedures.[49]

In 1987, Peter Miller (University of Sheffield) and Ted O'Leary (University College, Cork) used a behaviorist approach to criticize standard costing, stressing that it reflected the imposition of the power of the firm on its workers. Their argument traced the key events on the issue of power over workers throughout the history of standard costing.[50] As the United States was recognizing that it lagged behind Japan in manufacturing efficiency, criticism of standard costing intensified. A study in 1989 by Michiharu Sakurai (Senshu University) and Philip Y. Huang (Virginia Polytechnic Institute) noted that Japan used standard costing for financial accounting purposes. In place of standard costing for managerial purposes, the Japanese developed the target costing technique, which controls costs at the design stage.[51] (See Chapter 7 of this book.)

Another 1989 study indicated dissatisfaction with standard costing from a Just-in-Time (JIT) viewpoint. (See Chapter 14 of this book for a discussion of JIT.) C.J. McNair (Babson College), William Mosconi, and Thomas Norris (both of the former Coopers & Lybrand) found that a firm could better attain the JIT goal of continuous improvement by using a rolling average of job costs than by an inflexible standard costing system.[52] JIT is a management philosophy, not just an inventory and production system. It focuses on removing waste by making just what is needed, when it is needed, in the most efficient manner, continuously working to improve quality and lower cost.

Critics of standard costing have forgotten why standard cost became an important accounting concept. Standardization remains a must. The standard cost card reflects this standardization—the continuous goal of consistently producing a product to get the same excellent quality and quantity as desired by users. Standards can reflect continuous improvements in quality and cost reduction. This may explain why most manufacturers continue to use standard costing, employing many of the tools developed by Emerson, Harrison, Camman, and Henrici.

30.8 UNIFORMITY AND WORLD WAR I

The huge wartime expenditures during World War I led national governments to attempt to exert cost controls over the many manufacturers producing goods for the war effort. One way to exert cost control was to establish uniform accounting systems by industry. This uniformity of types of accounts would be used in cost-plus pricing agreements. In the United States, future President Herbert Hoover (who also served as Secretary of Commerce, 1921–1928) became a leader of this movement.

In their 1997 book, *Trade Associations and Uniform Costing in the British Printing Industry 1900–1963,* Stephen Walker and Falconer Mitchell recounted the experience of

---

49. Robert S. Kaplan, "The Significance and Investigation of Cost Variances: Survey and Extensions," *Journal of Accounting Research* (Autumn 1975), pp. 311–312.
50. Peter Miller and Ted O'Leary, "Accounting and the Construction of the Governable Person," *Accounting, Organizations and Society*, Vol. 12, No. 3, (1987), pp. 235–265.
51. Michiharu Sakurai and Philip Y. Huang, "A Japanese Survey of Factory Automation and Its Impact on Management Control Systems," in *Japanese Management Accounting: A World Class Approach to Profit Management,* ed. Yasuhiro Monden and Michiharu Sakurai (Cambridge, Mass.: Productivity Press, 1989), pp. 261–279.
52. C. J. McNair, William Mosconi, and Thomas Norris, *Beyond the Bottom Line: Measuring World Class Performances* (Homewood, Ill.: Dow-Jones-Irwin, 1989), p. 84.

one such trade association, the British Federation of Master Printers (BFMP).[53] They found that trade associations could not easily control uniform cost systems, no more than they could control collusion in pricing. The latter has become illegal under antitrust laws, but the former still seems worth achieving.

The National Recovery Administration (NRA) tried, in the United States, to establish industry cost codes—uniform types and names for accounts along with rules saying which ones prices must cover—to enable policing of pricing below costs. Franklin Roosevelt established the NRA during the first 100 days of his administration in 1933 as part of the New Deal. Most of the NRA industry codes outlawed the practice of selling below costs. The agency, however, could not enforce these provisions. Charles F. Roos, an official of the NRA, quoted a staffer as saying, "If the NRA had only adopted price fixing through cost formula in all codes, all the unemployed would have been needed to check compliance."[54] The U.S. Supreme Court in *Schechter v. United States* effectively ended the NRA in 1935.

30.9 J. M. CLARK'S STUDIES IN THE ECONOMICS OF OVERHEAD COSTS

J. M. Clark (1884–1963) was the son of the economist, professor John Bates Clark. J. M. Clark received a doctorate in economics from Columbia University in 1910. In 1923, he wrote *Studies in the Economics of Overhead Costs* while teaching at the University of Chicago. Clark returned to Columbia in that year to take the professorship previously held by his father.[55] J. M. Clark used the book to teach a course at the University of Chicago to students from both the School of Commerce and from the economics department. Clark used the inductive approach based on actual studies and, unlike some academics, he wanted businessmen to understand his book.[56]

Clark's text remains the most sweeping book on overhead (common costs). One of his major contributions to accounting is the four logical bases on which to apportion overhead: (1) ability to pay; (2) causal responsibility; (3) benefit or use; and (4) stimulus to more cost effective use by charging the cost against a cost object where the responsible party has the opportunity to reduce costs.[57] Another lasting contribution has been his notion of different costs for different purposes, which is the title and subject of Chapter 3 in this *Handbook*.[58] Perhaps the most effective way to illustrate the scope of Clark's text is to show its table of contents:

i. The Gradual Discovery of Overhead Costs
ii. The Scope of the Problem
iii. The General Idea of Cost and Different Classes of Costs
iv. and **v.** The Laws of Return and Economy, or the Variables Governing Efficiency

53. Stephen P. Walker and Falconer Mitchell, *Trade Associations and Uniform Costing in the British Printing Industry, 1900–1963* (New York: Garland Publishing, 1997).
54. Charles F. Roos, *NRA Economic Planning* (Bloomington, Ind.: Principia Press, Inc., 1937) reprint (New York: Da Capo Press, 1971), p. 276.
55. Paul J. Miranti, Jr., "Clark, John Maurice (1884–1963)," *History of Accounting,* pp. 125–127.
56. J. M. Clark, *Studies in the Economics of Overhead Costs* (Chicago: University of Chicago, 1923), pp. ix-xii.
57. Ibid., p. 32.
58. Ibid., pp. 175–203.

- **vi.** How and Why Large Plants Bring Economy
- **vii.** Economies of Combination
- **viii.** Different Kinds of Business Rhythms
- **ix.** Different Costs for Different Purposes: An Illustrative Problem
- **x.** What Is a Unit of Business?
- **xi.** Three Methods of Allocating Costs
- **xii.** Functions and Chief Methods of Cost Accounting
- **xiii.** Overhead Costs and Railroad Rate Problems
- **xiv.** The Transportation System as a Whole
- **xv.** Public Utilities
- **xvi.** Overhead Costs in Other Industries
- **xvii.** Labor as an Overhead Cost
- **xviii.** Overhead Costs and the Business Cycle
- **xix.** Discrimination in the Modern Market
- **xx.** Cut-Throat Competition and the Public Interest
- **xxi.** Costs of Government as Overhead Outlays
- **xxii.** Overhead Costs and the Laws of Value and Distribution
- **xxiii.** Conclusion

30.10 DISTRIBUTION COSTS AND SUPPLY CHAIN MANAGEMENT

Financial accounting literature no longer discusses distribution costs; that subject lies within the area of *managerial* accounting literature, which currently refers to it as *logistics or "supply chain management."* Chapter 11 of this book discusses distribution costs.

Accountants may want to become familiar with a few classics from the literature of accounting for distribution costs. Excerpts from Herbert Hoover's 1925 address to the National Distribution Conference appeared in the *Chain Store Review* in 1928. Hoover listed 15 kinds of waste, three of which pertained to distribution cost issues on which accountants could help management:

> 5. Waste from unnecessary multiplication of terms, sizes, and varieties;
> 10. Waste due to many links in the distribution chain and too many chains in the system; and
> 13. Wastes due to enormous expenditure of effort and money in advertising and sales promotion effort, without adequate basic information on which to base sales promotion.[59]

Hoover based his speech on the efforts of the Department of Commerce and one of its staff members, Wroe Alderson.[60]

In 1930, Howard C. Greer, a writer for five decades, stressed that cost accountants must give the same attention to distribution costs that they give to production costs.

---

59. Herbert C. Hoover, "The Merchant's Responsibility in Cutting Costs of Distribution," *Chain Store Review* (December 1928), p. 10.

60. Paul F. Anderson, "Distribution Cost Analysis Methodologies, 1901–1941," *Accounting Historians Journal* (Fall 1979), p. 45.

According to Greer, allocating distribution costs by commodities, territories, customers, and so forth required imagination. The accountant must add distribution cost to manufacturing cost when measuring profitability by line of business.[61]

In 1936, the pollster A.C. Nielsen stressed the importance of consumer sales—which included distribution costs—rather than factory sales, in measuring an entity's performance. He cautioned against overestimating sales of new products to the consumer, based on factory sales.[62] Hence, companies might lessen the danger of overproduction based on overoptimistic ordering by their distributors, not matched with consumer demand.

In 1938, Charles Reitell suggested that distribution costs use standard costing techniques, thus exchanging precision for guesswork.[63] In 1953, Heckert and Miner's book contained a series of lists, including a list of 43 items of distribution data that a firm should collect.[64] In 1955, Longman and Schiff discussed 35 possible actions to reduce losses in processing small orders.[65]

30.11 DIRECT COSTING

The concept of assigning manufacturing overhead to inventory cost emerged early in the twentieth century. Prior to that time, manufacturing overhead did not account for a high portion of total cost, and accounting techniques had not yet become sophisticated. A. H. Church increased the sophistication, starting in 1901. Church tested the easier, and less sophisticated, solution that inventory valuation should include only prime costs—direct materials and direct labor. The development of standard costing and the need to use management accounting information for wartime pricing during World War I led to development of the concept of full (or absorption) costing. With the government paying negotiated prices, not based on competitive markets for goods theretofore not traded in large quantities, both parties needed sensible costing rules—the supplier needed to cover costs, including the costs of capital, while the government wanted not to overpay. The Depression of the 1930s led to a significantly reduced demand for goods and, hence, lower production. Under the full costing concept, firms spread the fixed manufacturing overhead over fewer units, pressuring management to increase prices to maintain profit margins. This led to a further fall in demand, which cycled into higher full costs, higher prices to cover those costs, and further fall in demand. In that climate, Jonathan N. Harris wrote his 1936 article "What Did We Earn Last Month?" Harris presented a sample case in which management didn't understand why an increase in inventory caused net income to rise. Harris argued that inventory should include only direct materials, direct labor, and variable manufacturing overhead, and that fixed manufacturing overhead should be a period cost, or expense.[66]

---

61. Howard C. Greer, "Distribution Cost Analysis—Methods and Examples," *NACA Bulletin* (June 1, 1930), pp. 1305–1320.
62. A. C. Nielsen, "Continuous Marketing Research—A Vital Factor in Controlling Distribution Costs," *NACA Yearbook* (1936), pp. 220–255.
63. Charles Reitell, "Standard Costs in the Field of Distribution," *NACA Bulletin* (October 1, 1938), pp. 159–164.
64. J. Brooks Heckert and Robert B. Miner, *Distribution Costs* (New York: Ronald Press, 1953), pp. 214–215.
65. Donald R. Longman and Michael Schiff, *Practical Distribution Cost Analysis* (Homewood, Ill.: Richard D. Irwin, Inc., 1955), pp. 321–325.
66. Jonathan N. Harris, "What Did We Earn Last Month?" reprinted in Raymond P. Marple's *National Association of Accountants on Direct Costing* (New York: Ronald Press, 1965), pp. 17–40.

From the mid-1930s to the mid-1940s, the economy and accounting discussion focused on the increased demand due to World War II and little discourse regarding direct costing occurred. The direct costing movement started anew in 1947, however, and then strengthened in the early 1950s, owing to the National Association of Cost Accountants. It published a research study "Direct Costing" in 1953 and aggressively pushed the direct costing issue.[67] Direct costing became a full-fledged competitor to full costing, for internal reporting, if not for public and tax reporting.

A continuing thorn in the side of the advocates of direct costing has been *Accounting Research Bulletin* (ARB) No. 29 issued in July 1947 by the Committee on Accounting Procedure of the AIA (now AICPA). ARB No. 29 stated, "It should also be recognized that the exclusion of all overheads from inventory costs does not constitute an accepted accounting procedure."[68] As this ARB has remained a part of generally accepted accounting principles (GAAP), accountants consider direct costing prohibited for external reporting purposes.

The topic of direct costing versus full costing remained an ongoing issue through the 1980s. By the end of the 1980s, however, the direct costing approach met a more sophisticated opponent, activity-based costing (ABC; see Chapter 6). As firms resumed using overhead bases other than direct labor, many felt that the full costing approach was superior to the direct costing approach because the assignment of overhead costs rested on a firmer causal basis.

30.12 CAPLAN'S MANAGEMENT ACCOUNTING AND BEHAVIORAL SCIENCE

Starting in the 1960s, a number of accounting researchers extended the traditional field of management accounting by introducing findings from the behavioral school of management. Edwin H. Caplan of the University of New Mexico was an innovator in this effort. His 1971 book, *Management Accounting and Behavioral Science,* summarized his earlier efforts of the mid- and late 1960s.[69] Caplan's classic remains timely.

Caplan tested the traditional view of motivation by economic rewards. He warned that a tight control system may prove counter-productive (or dysfunctional) because it could foster negative attitudes toward the company and a fear of innovation.[70] He developed the traditional management accounting model into four parts:

1. Assumptions about organizational goals
2. Assumptions about the behavior of participants
3. Assumptions about the behavior of management
4. Assumptions about the role of management accounting[71]

Caplan then presented a contrasting set of assumptions using the works of behavioral science researchers and writers such as Max Weber, Elton Mayo, Kurt Lewin, Chester J.

67. Ibid., pp. 10–14.
68. Committee on Accounting Procedure, "Inventory Pricing," ARB No. 29 (New York: AIA, 1947), p. 237.
69. Edwin H. Caplan, *Management Accounting and Behavioral Science* (Reading, Mass.: Addison-Wesley, 1971).
70. Ibid., pp. 2–3.
71. Ibid, pp. 17–18.

Barnard, and Herbert Simon.[72] He compared and contrasted the traditional and modern view. He thought that the simpler traditional view was more limiting than the modern view.[73]

Caplan briefly reviewed contributions made about motivation and perception by behavioral experts such as Abraham H. Maslow, Frederick Herzberg, D.C. McClellan, and D.C. Dearborn.[74] This review of the history of management theorists thus led to their inclusion into the field of management accounting. Caplan's book also included the results of a questionnaire on standard costs[75] and reviewed several behavioral studies on budgeting written by (1) Selwyn Becker and David Green, Jr.; (2) Michael Schiff and Arie Y. Lewin; (3) Chris Argyris; (4) Harold J. Leavitt and R.A.H. Mueller; (5) Doris M. Cook; and (6) Andrew C. Stedry.[76] This work remains current for those desiring a concise view of behavioral science and managerial accounting.

30.13 SOLOMONS'S DIVISIONAL PERFORMANCE: MEASUREMENT AND CONTROL

In 1961, David Solomons (University of Pennsylvania) received a research grant from the Financial Executive Research Foundation to study how to optimize the performance of divisions within large corporations. He studied 25 large U.S. companies, including DuPont, General Electric, Johnson and Johnson, Scott Paper, and Sperry Rand.[77] His book, *Divisional Performance: Measurement and Control*, explained the results of his research. For Solomons, GE's residual income, the excess of net earnings over the cost of capital, was favored over the other measures and anticipated the more modern Economic Value Added, EVA.[78] (Chapter 26 examines EVA.)

30.14 JOHNSON AND KAPLAN'S *RELEVANCE LOST*

Little discussion and innovation in management accounting occurred in the 20 years leading up to 1987, when H. Thomas Johnson (a business historian with strong accounting training) and Robert S. Kaplan (an academic well trained in management science and mathematics) published *Relevance Lost: The Rise and Fall of Management Accounting*. It provides the foremost example of using historical analysis to prepare management accountants for a more proactive role in organizations. The authors placed management accounting within a business/economic history setting. They gave an excellent review of U.S. business/economic history from about 1810 to about the late 1920s.

Primarily using Johnson's excellent archival research, the authors examined management accounting in early New England textile mills, specifically the Lyman Mills. They posited that employee wage systems replacing the contracting-out labor systems resulted in a need for internal accounting information in order to establish a cost justification for substituting employee wages for independent contractors costs.[79]

72. Ibid, pp. 23–32.
73. Ibid, pp. 33–46.
74. Ibid, pp. 47–55.
75. Ibid, pp. 71–81.
76. Ibid, pp. 83–95.
77. David Solomons, *Divisional Performance: Measurement and Control* (Homewood, Ill.: Richard D. Irwin, 1965).
78. Ibid, pp. 59–84.
79. H. Thomas Johnson and Robert S. Kaplan, *Relevance Lost: The Rise and Fall of Management Accounting* (Boston: Harvard Business School Press, 1987), pp. 19–31.

A review of the Carnegie Steel Company described Andrew Carnegie's great interest in controlling and lowering prime costs. The development of railroads in the second quarter of the 1800s gave management accountants an opportunity to participate in controlling a geographically divergent organization. The book discusses Albert Fink's system of controlling costs at the Louisville & Nashville Railroad.[80] The authors criticized the view that management accounting most importantly functions to provide a basis for inventory valuation for financial accounting purposes.[81]

Johnson and Kaplan proceeded to offer hope for the recovery of the once important field of management accounting. They reviewed the works of J.M. Clark; Professors R.S. Edwards and Ronald Coase; William Vatter; Eugene Grant; George Terborgh and Joel Dean (who studied capital budgeting); G.E.'s residual income as described by Solomons; Robert Anthony, John Dearden, and Richard Vancil; as well as scholars of the operations research movement and of information economics.[82]

They insisted on abandoning simplistic direct labor bases for allocating costs. They again emphasized the work of Church and, in effect, led to the emergence, or reemergence, of activity-based costing. Johnson and Kaplan encouraged firms to look beyond the short-run nature of financial accounting.[83]

30.15 TIMETABLE

This chapter cannot explore all of the writings and discussions related to the history of management accounting. Readers who want a broader scope than this chapter presents can use the following timetable of publications, which starts with Pacioli's in 1494. The authors have developed this timetable from materials already published in the aforementioned Chatfield and Vangermeersch's *The History of Accounting: An International Encyclopedia.* The designation *C+V* refers to pages in this encyclopedia. The timetable also notes other references to help readers with their research.

Timetable of Key Events

1494 Luca Pacioli published the first printed treatise on accounting.

1563 Christopher Plantin maintained in Antwerp a job order cost system with a separate ledger account for each book he published. C+V, "Plantin, Christopher (1514–1589)," p. 465.

1577 The Fugger family in Austria began to collect materials and labor costs in a "mine and factory" account. C+V, "Fugger Cost Accounts," pp. 264–265.

1582 Simon Stevin introduced the concept of the present value of money. C+V, "Discounted Cash Flow," pp. 208–209.

1610 Robert Loder maintained a set of farm accounts. C+V, "Agricultural Accounting," pp. 29–31.

1689 Governmental budgeting began in Britain with the enactment of the 1689 Bill of rights. C+V, "Budgeting," pp. 84–87.

80. Ibid, pp. 32–46.
81. Ibid, pp. 47–59.
82. Ibid, pp. 153–181.
83. Ibid, pp. 183–263.

1697 John Collins's *The Perfect Methods of Merchant Accompts* was perhaps the earliest text dealing with management accounting.

1714 Roger North's *Gentleman Accomptant* was an early text on factory accounting.

1777 Robert Hamilton published his textbook, *An Introduction to Merchandise,* containing management accounting references to a manufacturing company.

1817 Jean-Baptiste Payen published *Essai sur la tenue des Livres d'un Manufacturier.*

1818 Frederic William Cronhelm published *Double Entry by Single Entry.*

1832 Charles Babbage published the first edition of *On the Economy of Machinery and* Manufacturers.

1850 Dionysius Lardner published *Railway Economy.*

1880 M.M. Kirkman published *Railway Expenditures: Their Extent, Object and Economy.* C+V, "Engineering and Accounting," pp. 227–229.

1885 Henry Metcalfe published *Cost of Manufacturers and the Administration of Workshops.*

H.R. Towne presented "The Engineer as an Economist" at the annual meeting of the American Society of Mechanical Engineers. C+V, "Engineering and Accounting," pp. 227–229.

1887 A.M. Wellington, an American civil engineer, published the *Economic Theory of the Location of Railways,* in which he anticipated capital budgeting. C+V, "Discounted Cash Flow," pp. 208–209.

Garcke and Fells published *Factory Accounts.*

1889 G.P. Norton treated comprehensively the cost problems of a firm using the process cost method in *Textile Manufacturers' Bookkeeping for the Country House, Mill and Warehouse.*

1896 J. Slater Lewis drew attention to accounting for manufacturing burden in *Commercial Organization of Factories.*

1901 Alexander H. Church published a series of articles "The Proper Distribution of Expense Burden" in the *Engineering Magazine.* C+V, "Church, A.H.," pp 124–125.

1903 Henry Hess published "Manufacturing: Capital, Costs, Profits, and Dividends" in the *Engineering Magazine.* C+V "Break-even Chart," pp. 79–81.

1907 Irving Fisher's "The Rate of Interest" was the first reference to present value in American economic literature. C+V, "Discounted Cash Flow," pp. 208–209.

1908 John Whitmore published "Shoe Factory Costs" in the May issue of the *Journal of Accountancy.* C+V "Standard Costing," pp. 550–552.

Alexander H. Church published a series of articles entitled "Production Factors in Cost Accounting and Works Management" in the *Engineering Magazine.*

1909 Herbert Hoover published Principles of Mining Valuation, Organization and Administration, Copper, Gold, Lead, Silver, Tin and Zinc.

J. Lee Nicholson stressed the imputation of interest on invested capital as a cost in *Factory Organization and Costs.*

1911 F.W. Taylor published *The Principles of Scientific Management and Shop Management.* C+V, "Taylor, Frederick Winslow (1856–1915)," pp. 579–580.

Holden Evans, a Navy engineer, published a series of articles, which became a book entitled *Cost Keeping and Scientific Management.* C+V, "Engineering and Accounting," pp. 227–229.

1912 Harrington Emerson published *The Twelve Principles of Efficiency.*

F. Donaldson Brown at DuPont pioneered the concept of "Return on Investment." C+V, "Brown, F. Donaldson (1885–1965)," pp. 83–84.

1913 The April issue of the *Journal of Accountancy* contained a series of articles, both pro and con, on the inclusion of interest as a manufacturing cost. C+V, "Imputed Interest on Capital," pp. 309–311.

1915 H.L. Gantt presented "The Relation Between Production and Costs" at the 1915 annual meeting of the American Society of Mechanical Engineers. C+V, "Gantt, Henry Laurence (1861–1919)," p. 269.

1916 Edward N. Hurley, Chairman of the U.S. Federal Trade Commission, was a leading proponent of uniform management accounting systems. C+V, "Uniformity," pp. 596–598.

Clinton H. Scovell published Cost Accounting and Burden Application.

1917 Alexander Hamilton Church published *Manufacturing Costs and Accounts.*

1918 The membership of the American Institute of Accountants (now the AICPA) voted to oppose the inclusion of imputed interest on capital as a cost of manufacturing. C+V, "Imputed Interest," pp. 309–311.

1919 Both the National Association of Cost Accountants (NACA) in the United States and the Institute of Cost Accountants in the United Kingdom were formed.

1920 J.P. Jordan and G.L. Harris published *Cost Accounting.*

The NACA issued its first research publication, "Accounting for by-Products."

G. Charter Harrison published the first set of formulas for the analysis of cost variances in the March issue of *Industrial Management.* C+V, "Harrison, G. Charter," pp. 291–292.

1921 Another theme at the annual meeting of the NACA was the hotly debated "The Distribution of Overhead Under Abnormal Conditions."

Clinton H. Scovell debated to support and Elmer E. Staub debated against the idea of imputed interest as a cost of manufacturing at the NACA annual meeting. Its membership voted 455 to 112 against imputed interest as a cost of manufacturing. C+V, "Imputed Interest on Capital," pp. 309–311.

Herbert Hoover began his two-term service as U.S. Secretary of Commerce with a strong interest in strengthening trade associations.

The Budgeting and Accounting Act established both the General Accounting Office and the Bureau of the Budget.

G. Charter Harrison wrote Cost Accounting to Aid Production: A Practical Study of Scientific Cost Accounting.

1922 J.O. McKinsey published *Budgetary Control.*

1923 J.M. Clark published *Studies in the Economics of Overhead Costs.*

R.S. Kellogg presented "The Use of Cost Data by Trade Associations," at the 1923 annual meeting of the NACA.

1924 J.O. McKinsey published *Managerial Accounting.*

Clinton H. Scovell published *Interest as a Cost.* C+V, "Imputed Interest," pp. 309–311.

F. Donaldson Brown of General Motors published a two part series "Pricing Policy in Relation to Financial Control" in *Management and Administration,* February and March.

1926 Henry Ford published *Today and Tomorrow,* which many authorities consider to be the start of the Just-in-Time Movement. C+V, "Just-In-Time Manufacturing," pp. 358–359.

The Bureau of Business Research of the University of Illinois published The Natural Business Year. C+V, "Natural Business Year," pp. 429–431.

T.H. Sanders published "Overhead in Economics and Accounting," in the April 15 issue of *NACA Bulletin.*

1927 F. Donaldson Brown presented "Centralized Control with Decentralized Responsibilities" at the annual meeting of the American Management Association.

1928 M.B. Folsom of Eastman Kodak presented "The Use of a Thirteen Month Calendar" at the annual meeting of the NACA.

1930 A.H. Church published *Overhead Expense: In Relation to Costs, Sales and Profits.*

1932 Eric A. Camman published *Basic Standard Costs: Control Accounting for Manufacturing Industries.*

1933 The National Recovery Administration (NRA) was established as a key New Deal agency with a goal of stopping selling below cost. The NRA was declared unconstitutional in 1935.

1934 Herbert F. Taggart published "The Relation of the Cost Accountant to the NRA Codes" in the June issue of the *Accounting Review.*

T.H. Sanders of Harvard published the second edition of *Accounting for Control.*

1936 Jonathan Harris published "What Did We Earn Last Month?" in the January 15 issue of the *NACA Bulletin.*

1937 Willard L. Thorp presented "Accounting for the Robinson-Patman Act" at the annual meeting of the NACA.

1938 The NACA published "Practice in Applying Overhead and Calculating Normal Capacity" in the April 1 issue of the *NACA Bulletin.*

Eric L. Kohler developed "activity accounting" during his stint as Controller of the Tennessee Valley Authority (TVA). C+V, "Activity-Based Costing," pp. 24–26.

1940 J. Brooks Heckert published *Distribution Costs*. A second edition with R.B. Miner was published in 1953.

J.A. Livingston, Staff Economist of *Business Week*, published "Forecasting" in the December issue of the *NACA Bulletin*.

1942 Wyman P. Fiske published "The Nature of Cost and Its Uses," in March 15 issue of thc *NACA Bulletin*.

1945 Charles C. James and E.G. Nourse debated "Capacity, Costs and Prices," at the annual meeting of the National Association of Cost Accountants.

Eric L. Kohler and W.W. Cooper published "Cost, Prices, and Profits: Accounting in the War Program" in the April issue of the *Accounting Review*.

1946 R.G. Lochiel presented "Long-term Profit Planning" at the NACA annual meeting.

1947 The Joint Accounting Improvement Program (JAIP) was composed of representatives from the General Accounting Office, the Treasury Department, and the Bureau of the Budget.

Theodore Lang published "Concepts of Cost, Past and Present" in the July 15 *NACA Bulletin*.

Accounting Research Bulletin (ARB)#29, "Inventory Pricing," ruled that direct costing was not a generally accepted accounting principle.

Stanley Henrici published *Standard Costs for Manufacturing*.

Billy Goetz published *Management Planning and Control: A Managerial Approach to Industrial Accounting*.

1948 Joel Dean published "Cost Structures of Enterprise and Break-even Charts," in *The Journal of Political Economy*. C+V, "Break-Even Chart," pp. 79–81.

1950 Carl T. Devine published *Cost Accounting and Analysis*.

William J. Vatter published *Managerial Accounting*.

1951 Joel Dean published *Managerial Economics*.

1952 David Solomons published "The Historical Development of Costing" in the book he edited entitled *Studies in Costing*. A second edition was published in 1968.

Chris Argyris published *The Impact of Budgets on People*.

1954 H. Simon, G. Kometsky, H. Guetzkow, and G. Tyndall published *Centralization and Decentralization in Organizing the Controller's Department*.

S. Paul Garner published his study, *Evolution of Cost Accounting to 1925*.

Thomas H. Sanders was elected to the Accounting Hall of Fame.

1956 The Committee of Cost Concepts and Standards of the American Accounting Association published "Tentative Statement of Cost Concepts Underlying Reports for Management Purposes" in the April issue of the *Accounting Review*.

1957 R. Lee Brummet published *Overhead Costing: The Costing of Manufactured Products*.

The NACA became the National Association of Accountants.

Glenn A. Welsch published Budgeting: Profit Planning and Control.

1958 Neil Churchill published "Another Look at Accounting for Idle Time" in the January issue of the *NAA Bulletin.*

I. Wayne Keller published "Capacity Utilization Studies for Cost Control and Reduction" in the July issue of the *NAA Bulletin.*

The American Marketing Association published *Distribution Costs: A Key to Profits.*

1960 Andrew C. Stedry published *Budget Control and Cost Behavior.*

1961 Theodore W. Schultz, a 1980 Nobel Prize winner in Economics, published "Investment in Human Capital" in the March issue of the *American Economic Review.* C+V "Human Resource Accounting," pp. 303–305.

Gordon Shillinglaw published *Cost Accounting: Analysis and Control.*

The NAA published a study entitled "Current Application of Direct Costing."

1962 The Subcommittee on Economic Statistics of the Joint Economic Committee holds hearings on *Measures of Productive Capacity.*

C.T. Horngren published *Cost Accounting: A Managerial Emphasis.*

1963 The National Association of Accountants published *Accounting for Costs of Capacity.*

A. Charnes, W.W. Cooper, and Y. Ijiri published "Breakeven Budgeting and Programming to Goals" in the Spring issue of the *Journal of Accounting Research.*

1965 R.P. Marple edited National Association of Accountants on Direct Costing: Selected Papers.

David Solomons published *Divisional Performance: Measurement and Control.*

James L. Pierce, long-time controller with A.B. Dick company and a leader of the Financial Executive Institute, was elected to the Accounting Hall of Fame.

Robert Anthony published *Planning and Control Systems: A Framework for Analysis.*

Stanley Henrici introduced the concept of the superstandard in the July issue of the *NAA Bulletin.*

President L.B. Johnson called for the adoption of the Planning-Programming-Budget System (PPBS) throughout the federal government.

1966 B.F. Kiker published "The Historical Roots of the concept of Human Capital" in the October issue of the *Journal of Political Economy.*

1966 Walter B.McFarland published *Concepts for Management Accounting.*

1967 Rensis Likert published *The Human Organization: Its Management and Value.*

G. H. Hofstede published *The Game of Budget Control.*

A. Charnes and W.W. Cooper published "Some Network Characteristics for Mathematical Programming and Accounting Approaches to Planning and Control" in the January issue of the *Accounting Review.*

1968 Admiral Hyman G. Rickover testified to the U.S. Congress as to the inadequacies of enforcing the Defense Production Act of 1950, because of a lack of uniformity in management accounting.

1969 R.H. Parker published *Management Accounting: An Historical Perspective.*

1970 President R.M. Nixon signed the law establishing the Cost Accounting Standards Board, which terminated in 1980, but whose standards apply to government contracting as this book goes to press.

1971 Edwin H. Caplan published *Management Accounting and Behavioral Science.*

George J. Staubus published *Activity Costing and Input-Output Accounting.*

1972 The Institute of Cost Accountants (U.K.) was renamed the Institute of Cost and Management Accountants.

1973 E.M. Sowell published *The Evolution of the Theories and Techniques of Standard Costs.*

P.A. Pyhrr published *Zero-Based Budgeting.*

1974 E.G. Flamholtz published *Human Resource Accounting.*

H.M. Schoenfeld published Cost Terminology and Cost Theory: A Study of Its Development and Present State in Central Europe. C+V, "Microeconomics in Germany," pp. 416–420.

Anthony G. Hopwood published *Accounting and Human Behavior,* in which he tested the organizational basis of accounting." C+V, "Hopwood, Anthony G. (1944)," pp. 300–301.

1975 Robert Anthony published *Accounting for the Cost of Interest.* C+V, "Imputed Interest," pp. 309–311.

Robert S. Kaplan published "The Significance and Investigation of Cost Variances: Survey and Extensions" in the Autumn issue of the *Journal of Accounting Research.*

H. T. Johnson published "The Role of Accounting History in the Study of Modern Business Enterprise" in the July issue of the *Accounting Review.*

1976 Joel S. Demski and G.A. Feltham published *Cost Determination: A Conceptual Approach.* C+V "Demski, Joel S.," pp 196–197.

The Cost Accounting Standards Board's Standard No. 414 permitted an imputation of interest on invested capital, C+V, "Imputed Interest on Capital," pp. 309–311.

1978 M.C. Wells published *A Bibliography of Cost Accounting: Its Origins and Development to 1914* and *Accounting for Common Costs.*

1981 The NAA promulgated in *Statement of Management Accounting (SMA)* 1A, a widely accepted definition of management accounting.

1983 R. S. Kaplan published "Managerial Manufacturing Performance: A New Challenge for Managerial Accounting Research" in the *Accounting Review's* October issue.

Henry R. Schwarzbach and Richard Vangermeersch published "Why We Should Account for the Fourth Cost of Manufacturing," in the July issue of *Management Accounting.*

1984 R. S. Kaplan published "The Evolution of Management Accounting" in the July issue of the *Accounting Review.*

1985 R. G. Eccles published *The Transfer Pricing Problem.* C+V, "Transfer Pricing," pp. 581–583.

1986 E. Goldratt and J. Cox published *The Goal: a Process of Ongoing Improvement.* This book integrated management accounting with concepts from their "Theory of Constraints."

1987 G. Foster and C. Horngren published "JIT: Cost Accounting and Management Issues" in the June issue of *Management Accounting.*

G.J. Staubus published "The Dark Ages of Cost Accounting: The Role of Miscues in the Literature" in the *Accounting Historians Journal*, Fall issue.

P. Miller and T. O'Leary published "Accounting and the Construction of the Governable Person" in vol. 12, No. 3 issue of *Accounting, Organizations, and Society.*

T. Johnson and R.S. Kaplan published *Relevance Lost: The Rise and Fall of Management Accounting.*

1988 Eric Flamholtz, D.G. Searfoss, and R. Coff published "Developing Human Resource Accounting as a Human Resource Decision Support System" in the September issue of *Accounting Horizons.*

1990 Robin Cooper published "Cost Classification in Unit-Based and Activity-Based Manufacturing Cost Systems" in the Fall issue of the *Journal of Cost Management.*

1991 The NAA became the Institute of Management Accountants.

1992 D. Hermanson, D.M. Ivancevich, and R.H. Hermanson published "Human Resource Accounting in Recessionary Times" in July in *Management Accounting.*

H. T. Johnson published *Relevance Regained: From Top-Down Control to Bottom-up Empowerment.*

1994 T.A. Stewart wrote "Your Company's Most Valuable Asset: Intellectual Capital" in the October 3, 1994 issue of *Fortune.*

1995 E. Noreen, D. Smith, and J. Mackey published the *Theory of Constraints and Its Implications for Management Accounting.*

Patrick L. Romano published *IMA's Legacy: Creating Value through Research.*

1996 The Society of Management Accountants of Canada and the Institute of Management Accountants promulgated "Measuring the Cost of Capacity" as MAG #42 (SMAC) and as SMA4Y(IMA).

Gloria L. Vollmers published "Academic Cost Accounting from 1920–1950: Alive and Well," in the 8th volume of *Journal of Management Accounting Research.*

1997 Three articles pertaining to the past, current, and future of the field were published in the Perspectives on Research in Management Accounting section of the *Journal of Management Accounting Research*: "Research in Management Accounting by North Americans in the 1990s;" Frontiers of Management Accounting Research;" and "New Directions in Management Accounting Research."

1998 G.J. Previts and B.D. Merino published *A History of Accountancy in the United States: The Cultural Significance of Accounting*.

C.J. McNair and R. Vangermeersch published *Total Capacity Management,* which included a five-chapter section on "Historical Trends in Capacity Cost Management" and an annotated bibliography of literature on the topic.

1999 Gloria Vollmers published "Using Distribution Costs in Decision Making at the Dennison Manufacturing Company, 1909 to 1949" in the June issue of the *Accounting Historians Journal.*

Germain Boer and John Ettlie published "Target Costing Can Boost Your Bottom Line" in the July issue of *Strategic Finance.*

Leslie S. Oakes, Mark A. Covaleski and Mark W. Dirsmith published "Labor's Changing Reponses to Management Rhetorics: A study of Accounting – Based Incentive Plans during the First Half of the 20th Century" in the December issue of the *Accounting Historians Journal.*

2000 Noah P. Barsky and Garry Marchant published "The Most Valuable Resource—Measuring and Managing Intellectual Capital" in the February issue of *Strategic Finance*.

Gary Spraakman and Alison Wilkie published "The Development of Management Accounting at the Hudson's Bay Company" in the Vol. 5, No. 1, issue of *Accounting History.*

Michael J. Barnet published "Benchmarking at its Best" in the December issue of *Strategic Finance.*

2001 Joseph A. Ness, Michael J. Schroeck, Rick A. Letendre, and William J. Douglas published "The Role of ABM in Measuring Customer Value" in the March and April issues of *Strategic Finance*.

Robert S. Kaplan and David P. Norton published "Transforming the Balanced Scorecard from Performance Measurement to Strategic Management" in the March and June issues of *Accounting Horizons*.

2002 H. Thomas Johnson published "A Former Management Accountant Reflects on His Journey through the World of Cost Management in the Vol. 7, No. 1, issue of *Accounting History.*

2003 Trevor Boyns published "In Memoriam: Alexander Hamilton Church's System of "Scientific Machine Rates' at Hans Renold Ltd., c. 1901–1920" in the June issue of the *Accounting Historians Journal.*

Richard K. Fleischman and R. Penny Marquette published "The Impact of World War II on Cost Accounting at the Sperry Corporation" in the December issue of the *Accounting Historians Journal.*

Paul A. Sharman published "Bring on German Cost Accounting" in the December issue of *Strategic Finance.*

2004 Trevor Boyns, Mark Matthews, and John Richard Edwards published "The Development of Costing in the British Chemical Industry, c. 1870-c. 1940" in the Vol. 34, No. 1, issue of *Accounting and Business Research.*

30.16 SUMMARY

The history of management accounting has enjoyed a burgeoning interest in recent years. We urge that readers consider searching the management accounting literature on issues affecting their organizations. At the minimum, such a search will provide a deeper understanding of management accounting issues.

BIBLIOGRAPHY

Boyns, Trevor, John Richard Edwards, and Marc Nikitin. *The Birth of Industrial Accounting in France and Britain.* New York: Garland Publishing, 1997.

Brummet, R. Lee. *Overhead Costing: The Costing of Manufactured Products.* Ann Arbor, MI: University of Michigan, 1957.

Caplan, Edwin H. *Management Accounting and Behavioral Science.* Reading, MA: Addison-Wesley, 1971.

Chatfield, Michael and Richard Vangermeersch. *The History of Accounting: An International Encyclopedia.* New York: Garland Publishing, 1996.

Clark, J. M. *Studies in the Economics of Overhead Costs.* Chicago: University of Chicago, 1923.

Fleischman, Richard K., and Lee D. Parker. *What Is Past Is Prologue: Cost Accounting in the British Industrial Revolution, 1760–1850.* New York: Garland Publishing, 1997.

Garner, S. Paul, *Evolution of Cost Accounting to 1925.* University: University of Alabama Press, 1954.

Johnson, H. Thomas, and Robert S. Kaplan. *Relevance Lost: The Rise and Fall of Management Accounting.* Boston: Harvard Business School Press, 1987.

McNair, C. J., and Richard Vangermeersch. *Total Capacity Management.* Boca Raton, FL and Montvale, NJ: St. Lucie Press and the IMA Foundation for Applied Research, 1998.

Parker, Robert H. *Management Accounting: An Historical Perspective.* New York: A. M. Kelley, 1969.

Previts, G. J., and B. D. Merino. *A History of Accountancy in the United States*, 2nd ed. Columbus: Ohio State University Press, 1998.

Romano, Patrick L. *IMA's Legacy: Creating Value Through Research.* Montvale, N.J.: IMA Foundation for Applied Research, 1995.

Solomons, David, *Divisional Performance: Measurement and Control.* Homewood, Ill.: Richard D. Irwin, 1965.

Solomons, David, ed. *Studies in Costing*. 2nd ed. Homewood, Ill.: Richard D. Irwin. 1968.

Sowell, Ellis Mast. *The Evolution of the Theories and Techniques of Standard Costs.* University: University of Alabama Press. 1973.

Vangermeersch, Richard. "Renewing Our Heritage: Ten Reasons Why Management Accountants Should Study the Classic Cost Accounting Articles." *Management Accounting*. July (1987): 47–49.

Vangermeersch, Richard. *Alexander Hamilton Church: A Man of Ideas for All Seasons.* New York: Garland Publishing, 1988.

Walker, Stephen P., and Falconer Mitchell. *Trade Associations and Uniform Costing in the British Printing Industry, 1900–1963.* New York: Garland Publishing, 1997.

Wells, Murray Charles. *A Bibliography of Cost Accounting*. 2 Vol. Urbana, Ill.: Center for International Education and Research in Accounting, 1978.

Wells, Murray Charles. *Accounting for Common Costs*. Urbana, Ill.: Center for International Education and Research in Accounting, 1978.

Yamey, Basil, with English translation by Antonia von Gebsattel. *Exposition of Double Entry Bookkeeping: Luca-Pacioli. Venice 1494.* Venice: Albrizzi Editore, 1994.

CHAPTER 31

CORPORATE SCANDALS: THE ACCOUNTING UNDERPINNINGS

KATHLEEN FITZGERALD, MBA, CPA
University of Chicago

ROMAN L. WEIL, PHD, CPA, CMA, EDITOR
University of Chicago

CONTENTS

31.1 INTRODUCTION 760

31.2 CURRENT FINANCIAL REPORTING ENVIRONMENT 761

(a) Recent History 761
(b) Who Is Watching the Shop? 764
(c) Conflicts of Interest 764
(d) Ignorance 765
(e) Cronyism 765
(f) Insufficient Time 765

31.3 MANAGEMENT INCENTIVES TO REPORT FRAUDULENT EARNINGS 765

(a) Raising Funds for Investment through the Issue of Shares of Stock 765
(b) Raising Funds with Debt Financing or Obtaining More Favorable Terms on Existing Debt Financing 766
(c) Dispelling Negative Market Perceptions 766
(d) Demonstrating Compliance with Financing Covenants 766
(e) Meeting Company Goals and Objectives 766
(f) Meeting Bonus Targets 767
(g) Holding Significant Financial Interest in the Company 767
(h) Increasing Dividend or Partnership Distributions 767
(i) Executing Mergers and Acquisitions 767
(j) Other Incentives 767

31.4 SPECIFIC METHODS TO MANIPULATE FINANCIAL REPORTS 767

(a) SEC Cases of Accounting Restatements 768
(b) Revenue 769
(c) Commonly Used Methods for Misrepresenting Revenues 770
(d) Use and Modifications of These Practices 772
(e) Expense and Asset Recognition 777
(f) Commonly Used Methods for Misrepresenting the Amount of Expenses, Assets and Liabilities 778
(g) Liability Recognition 783
(h) Commonly Used Methods for Understating Liabilities 784
(i) Disclosures Recognition 787
(j) What Information Must Reporting Companies Disclose? 788
(k) Where Does This Information Appear? 789
(l) Misleading or Fraudulent Disclosure 789

31.5 AUDITOR RESPONSIBILITY FOR DETECTING FRAUD 791

31.6 SIGNS OF TROUBLE 792

(a) Incentive or Pressure 792
(b) Opportunity 793
(c) Attitude and Rationalization 793

31.7 ANALYTIC DIAGNOSTICS TO DISCOVER ACCOUNTING FRAUD 794

31.1 INTRODUCTION

CORPORATE ACCOUNTING SCANDALS ROCK PUBLIC CONFIDENCE

SEC CHARGES FORMER TYCO OFFICERS WITH FRAUD

WORLDCOM CONTROLLER PLEADS GUILTY

MYERS ADMITS TO FALSIFYING NUMBERS, SAYS HE ACTED AT HIS SUPERIORS' BEHEST

FRAUD SUIT NAMES KPMG AND PARTNERS

HOW EXECUTIVES PROSPERED AS GLOBAL CROSSING COLLAPSED

FUN-HOUSE ACCOUNTING: THE DISTORTED NUMBERS AT ENRON

'YOU WUZ ROBBED!'

Hardly a week goes by without the press commenting on the state of financial reporting. Accounting scandals have captured the attention of government enforcement agencies, such as the Securities and Exchange Commission (SEC); standard setters, such as the Financial Accounting Standards Board (FASB) and the International Accounting Standards Board (IASB); investment banking companies; venture capital companies; corporate boards; and family members concerned with their retirement funds and investment activities. The accounting issues discussed in the financial press can confuse the accounting novice. The details can overwhelm even accounting professionals.

Fraudulent accounting practices impose real costs on individuals and the economy as a whole. Companies that report that they are restating their financial statements to correct errors or irregularities in previously issued financial statements often experience a significant drop in their market capitalization within moments of such a disclosure. The U.S. General Accounting Office reported in October of 2002 that of the 689 cases it analyzed from January 1, 1997 to March 26, 2002, the stock price of a company making an initial restatement announcement fell by almost 10 percent, on average, from the trading day before to the day after the announcement (the immediate effect). Unadjusted losses in the market capitalization of companies issuing initial restatement announcements totaled more than $100 billion, ranging from about $4.6 billion in 1997 to about $28.7 billion in 2000. The report further documents that losses over 60 trading days before and after the restatement announcements appear to have had an even greater negative effect on stock prices.[1] For example, Cendant Corporation lost $14.7 billion or 47 percent of its market capitalization; Microstrategy lost $11 billion, Waste Management lost $4.76 billion, and Sunbeam lost $3.64 billion after their restatements. Investors bear these losses and the economy as a whole suffers as these revelations undermine investor confidence.

This chapter explains the earnings management fundamentals behind the current scandals. Earnings management occurs when managers use judgment in financial reporting and in structuring transactions to alter financial reports to either mislead some

1. United States General Accounting Office Report to the Chairman, Committee on Banking Housing, and Urban Affairs, U.S. Senate, "Financial Statement Restatements: Trends, Market Impacts, Regulatory Responses, and Remaining Challenges." October 2002.

stakeholders about the underlying economic performance of the company or to influence contractual outcomes that depend on reported accounting numbers.[2]

We discuss earnings management that results in fraudulently reported earnings by management, and discuss earnings management that results in *low quality,* but not technically fraudulent, earnings. We refer to *fraudulent financial reporting* as "intentional or reckless conduct, whether [by] act or omission, that results in materially misleading financial statements."[3] Fraudulent financial reporting occurs when individuals or companies use accounting not allowed by Generally Accepted Accounting Principles (GAAP). *Low quality earnings* do not reflect future earnings potential, which some people call *non-sustainable earnings.* When we use the term *low-quality reporting*, we mean using rules within GAAP.

The discussion proceeds as follows:

- Section 31.2 describes the current financial reporting environment, which includes the incentives that management has to engage in deceitful or misleading practices.
- Section 31.3 explains the main areas where management can focus efforts to achieve its desired results and the existing regulatory enforcement to restrain management in these areas. You will realize that some of these regulatory controls do not work well because of the subjectivity in management's financial reporting decisions.
- Section 31.4 analyzes the specific methods management uses to manipulate financial reports to deceive the public, illustrating these methods with recent accounting scandals.
- Finally, Sections 31.5 and 31.6 discuss the auditors' responsibilities, analyses used to detect fraud, and recent reforms to corporate America's financial reporting practices.

31.2 CURRENT FINANCIAL REPORTING ENVIRONMENT

Accounting scandals have become a regular part of the business landscape, and we expect them to continue. Accounting fraud is not new, but only recently have billions of dollars of market value disappeared as investigators have uncovered corporate malfeasance. In these instances, management, board members, and accountants spend millions of dollars to defend and settle shareholder lawsuits connected with misrepresentations. Some executives even serve time in prison for their activities, and many more have their professional lives ruined.

(a) RECENT HISTORY. Although many of the publicized scandals became public only recently, as early as September 1998, Chairman Arthur Levitt of the SEC Commission signaled his concerns and suspicions in his speech, "The Numbers Game."[4] By that time, evidence of erosion in the quality of financial reporting had begun to appear. In hindsight, we know that the SEC knew of fraud by Waste Management and Sunbeam, but had not completed its cases against these companies at the time. In this speech, Mr. Levitt called for an end to the practice of earnings management and a return to the practice of

2. P.M. Healy and J. M.Wahlen, "A Review of the Earnings Management Literature and Its Implications for Standard Setting," *Accounting Horizons* (December 1999): 365–383.
3. Report of the National Commission on Fraudulent Financial Reporting, October 1987.
4. *http://www.sec.gov/news/speech/speecharchive/1998/spch220.txt.*

providing transparent and comparable financial statements. In his speech, he discussed five common accounting practices that companies had been misusing:

1. Big bath charges
2. Creative acquisition accounting
3. Miscellaneous cookie-jar reserves
4. Materiality thresholds
5. Revenue recognitions

We look at each of these in the following discussion.

(i) Big Bath Charges. This term dates back at least to the 1930s, when Benjamin Graham used it in his classic book, *Security Analysis*. Companies that take a *big bath* overstate current expenses (e.g., restructuring charges), by recording expenses early to make the books look unfavorable now, resulting in better future earnings reports.[5] Management hopes that the market will not incrementally penalize the company's valuation for the extra bad news. Then later, management can artificially boost income in hopes that the market will incrementally reward the extra income. (See also *big bath* in Chapter 1's glossary.)

(ii) Creative Acquisition Accounting. Mr. Levitt pointed out that one company purchasing another can create an effect similar to the *big bath* by incorrectly overestimating the part of the acquisition cost it classifies as *in-process research and development*. This is the portion of the purchase price allocated to the cost of existing research and development (R&D) efforts not yet found to be worthless or valuable. GAAP require companies to write off to expense any amounts so classified immediately after its acquisition. Similar to the big bath charges, creative acquisition accounting makes future earnings artificially higher, enables the write-off to appear separately from ordinary income items, and artificially boosts the apparent earnings quality.

(iii) Miscellaneous Cookie-Jar Reserves. Mr. Levitt noted that companies overestimate liabilities for warranties, or loan losses or sales returns, or allowances for accounts receivable. By doing so, management can inflate expenses in good times and reduce them during bad times. This has the effect of smoothing earnings, and gives management the power to ensure that it achieves its accounting objectives. Analysts sometimes refer to this as *making its numbers,* another way of saying that management reports numbers it believes the marketplace expects to see.[6]

Management sometimes excuses all the first three accounting actions as being conservative, which accountants generally consider a good thing. Conservatism is, in fact, an

5. We shall repeat this thought again, as the reader of financial statements should never forget: Over long-enough time spans, income is cash flow in less cash flow out, other than transactions with owners. So, as long as cash flow does not change, income over the time span will be a constant, with manipulations affecting the timing of reporting to the periods within the span. Hence, recording excess expense today, wrongly reducing income, necessarily means reporting higher income later.
6. See the preceding footnote. Management, by making expenses artificially high (or low) today can, at its discretion, make future income appear low (or high).

underlying accounting principle.[7] The distinction becomes fuzzy when an accounting practice is fraudulent, outside GAAP, or merely low quality reporting but within GAAP guidelines. For example, management might argue that depreciation is part of GAAP and that its use of long lives for some assets was not fraudulent, but merely aggressively within GAAP. Those executives facing criminal charges for fraudulent financial reporting will care about the distinction and which side of the line between outside GAAP (fraud) and inside GAAP (low quality reporting) the practice falls.

We like to remind our readers that *conservative* means *biased,* biased in the particular direction of reporting lower cumulative income, lower assets totals, and lower retained earnings, but nevertheless biased. A conservative estimate is purposefully inaccurate—off the mark. Often, circumstances suggest making a conservative estimate, but in financial reporting it can lead to fraud.

(iv) Materiality Thresholds. Mr. Levitt reported that some companies have intentionally recorded errors within a limited range defined by materiality considerations. GAAP define materiality in terms of what influences a decision-maker. The FASB takes the position that "no general standards of materiality could be formulated to take into account all the considerations that enter into an experienced human judgment," but that the Board may give quantitative materiality criteria in specific standards, as appropriate.[8] The typical accounting standard specifies the materiality threshold and allows that, "the provisions of this Statement need not be applied to immaterial items." A manipulating manager intentionally commits an accounting error, but keeps the amount within traditional materiality ranges.[9] Although

---

7. No authoritative definition of conservatism exists. In its most extreme form, conservatism is interpreted as "anticipate no gains, but anticipate all losses." FASB Concepts Statement 2 (SFAC 2), *Qualitative Characteristics of Accounting Information*, rejects that form of conservatism: "Conservatism in financial reporting should no longer connote deliberate, consistent understatement of net assets and profits." SFAC 2 reads, "Conservatism is a prudent reaction to uncertainty to try to ensure that uncertainties and risks inherent in business situations are adequately considered. Thus, if two estimates of amounts to be received or paid in the future are about equally likely, conservatism dictates using the less optimistic estimate; however, if two amounts are not equally likely, conservatism does not necessarily dictate using the more pessimistic amount rather than the more likely one. Conservatism no longer requires deferring recognition of income beyond the time that adequate evidence of its existence becomes available or justifies recognizing losses before there is adequate evidence that they have been incurred."

   The pre-SFAC 2 interpretation of conservatism is admonished by the International Accounting Standards Committee (IASC) in International Accounting Standard No. 1, Disclosure of Accounting Policies: "Uncertainties inevitably surround many transactions. This should be recognized by exercising prudence in preparing financial statements. Prudence does not, however, justify the creation of secret or hidden reserves."
8. *FASB Concepts Statement No. 2,* Qualitative Characteristics of Accounting Information, paragraph 131. Concepts Statement No. 2 states that the omission or misstatement of an item in a financial report is material if, in the surrounding circumstances, a reasonable person, relying on the report, would probably have changed a judgment had the company included or corrected the item.
9. Why would management have an incentive to do this? Imagine, as was true for many years, that auditors considered an accounting adjustment immaterial if its effect on income was less than 10 percent of reported income. Imagine the CFO learns that reported earnings per share will be only \$1.90, but that analysts are expecting \$2.00, and that to report anything less will cause the stock price to drop. The CFO fudges income by \$0.15 per share, raising it to \$2.05. The auditor excuses the fudge on the grounds that it is immaterial. The SEC has since clarified its meaning of materiality to stop this practice. SAB 99 says that exclusive reliance on quantitative benchmarks to assess materiality in preparing financial statements is inappropriate; misstatements are not immaterial simply because they fall beneath a numerical threshold. The SEC says its interpretation merely clarifies longstanding law, but some critics say the SEC made new law when it defined materiality in this way. We do not think the SEC made new law with its clarifications.

these errors violate GAAP, management argues that the amount is immaterial, so it doesn't matter. Some auditors acquiesced in this manipulation, until the SEC expressly prohibited it.

(v) **Revenue Recognition.** In this manipulation, a company recognizes revenue before it completes the sale or before it delivers the product to the customer, or when the customer still has the option to cancel the sale. GAAP require that the seller wait to recognize revenue until it has delivered the goods to the customer and the customer has no right of return or, if the customer has right of return, the seller can estimate the amount of the expected return with reasonable precision.

(b) WHO IS WATCHING THE SHOP? In 1998, Chairman Levitt seemed more concerned with low-quality earnings than with actual fraud; he indicated that he believed management used these five tools to manipulate the accounting numbers so that the share prices would remain high or not decline as much as they otherwise would. As time passed, *earnings management* became *fraud* for many companies. The law does not draw a clear line between the two. The distinction often involves the *intent* of the wrongdoer, which prosecutors find more difficult to prove than that the wrong, itself, occurred.

But just *who is* the wrongdoer? Who bears the blame when companies commit accounting fraud? Why do companies have so much opportunity to manage earnings or commit fraud? Doesn't someone have responsibility for monitoring management and making sure that it fairly presents the financial statements? What role do the internal auditors play? External auditors? Audit committees? Boards of directors? Analysts? Regulators? If some of these participants had been alert and knew what to look for, they would likely have identified some frauds earlier. The next sections discuss how management used the five tools just listed, as well as others, to deceive internal and external auditors, directors, regulators, investors, analysts, creditors, suppliers, and employees. But first, we discuss four causes of the collective failures to identify fraud: conflicts of interest, ignorance, cronyism, and insufficient time.[10]

(c) CONFLICTS OF INTEREST. Most internal audit departments report to management; this gives the internal auditors incentive to satisfy management goals to keep their positions, bonuses, and promotion prospects.

External auditors receive payment from the companies they audit. In addition, they earn a significant percentage of their fees by procuring consulting engagements for the same company. They have an incentive to satisfy management.

Analysts also have an incentive to make management happy. They work for brokerages that seek banking business from the companies, business such as underwriting (that is, managing for a fee) stock or bond issuances. Analysts like to obtain timely information from these companies. Brokerages that have employed analysts who unfavorably reviewed companies might not receive profitable banking business from those companies, nor might they receive timely information.

---

10. Congress has addressed several of these failures in recent legislation.

(d) IGNORANCE. Many individuals on the boards of directors, even on audit committees, simply don't have the accounting literacy needed to monitor management.[11] Audit committee members have not, historically, been independent nor financially literate, so these committees failed to adequately represent shareholder interests. As a result of new legislation, they will likely be better educated and more vigilant in their approach.

(e) CRONYISM. Relations among management, the board of directors, and audit committees have previously reflected some cronyism. Many of the members have been mutual friends and served on each other's boards or committees. Strong friendships have reduced the incentive to thoroughly investigate each other's accounting practices, which may violate standards of independence and prohibitions on conflict of interest.

(f) INSUFFICIENT TIME. Board members often do not take sufficient time to understand financial reporting issues and audit committee members do not properly understand their roles, in relation to both the type of information they should understand and how well they should understand it.

This becomes a more important problem because the SEC does not have enough resources, including time, to review the accounting practices and financial statements of every company. For example, the SEC had not reviewed Enron Corporation for at least three years before it went bankrupt in 2001.

However, even with many gatekeepers to the final financial reports, a management team, determined to deceive, could do so. So the real question is: Why would management want to deceive?

31.3 MANAGEMENT INCENTIVES TO REPORT FRAUDULENT EARNINGS

This section discusses management's many incentives and opportunities to distort financial reports.

(a) RAISING FUNDS FOR INVESTMENT THROUGH THE ISSUE OF SHARES OF STOCK. Suppose that management wants to invest in a new project, but the company does not have enough cash on hand to finance the project. Companies can raise cash by issuing shares of stock on the market. All else equal, the higher the company's reported earnings, the more likely that investors will pay more to purchase shares. Companies preparing for an initial public offering (IPO) want to show high and growing earnings to capture a higher price per share issued. A documentary that aired on U.S. public television (PBS) in January 2002 claimed that venture capital firms and investment banks manipulated many of the IPOs in the 1990s to pocket billions of dollars at the expense of

11. These frauds occurred in spite of the existence of audit committees at the affected companies. According to a report issued by the National Commission on Fraudulent Financial Reporting (the "NCFFR Report") in 1987, 69 percent of the companies pursued by the SEC in enforcement cases for fraudulent reporting between 1981 and 1986 had audit committees. Some of our own research suggests that audit committee members do not, as individuals, understand the critical accounting judgments management must make to prepare the financial statements, so that they cannot recognize accounting manipulations. See R.L. Weil, "Audit Committee Financial Literacy: A Work Not Yet in Progress," working paper from the University of Chicago, Graduate School of Business, 2002, and "Audit Committees Can't Add," *Harvard Business Review* (May 2004), pp 21 ff.

smaller investors.[12] By disseminating false information about future expected earnings, companies created demand for their stocks at inflated prices. Although PBS did not provide evidence to support the claims, more rigorous research done by John M. Friedlan (1994) uncovered some evidence consistent with companies managing earnings upwards in the accounting period prior to an IPO.[13]

(b) RAISING FUNDS WITH DEBT FINANCING OR OBTAINING MORE FAVORABLE TERMS ON EXISTING DEBT FINANCING. If the company would rather borrow funds to finance a project, it must show the potential creditors (e.g., banks or other lenders) that the company can make its debt service payments. When a company borrows from the bank, the borrower usually must meet certain financial criteria before the lender will provide funds. These criteria often take the form of ratios, such as the debt-to-equity ratio or the interest-coverage ratio. Companies trying to refinance their debt have similar needs. Thus, if a company needs to borrow, management has an incentive to enhance the position reflected in its financial reports. Improving the balance sheet reduces the debt-equity ratio, while boosting income makes interest coverage ratios look better. Most actions designed to benefit one accomplish the other because of the articulation of the balance sheet and the income statement.

(c) DISPELLING NEGATIVE MARKET PERCEPTIONS. If the company has been doing so poorly that interested parties worry about its viability, management has an incentive to demonstrate the company's improving health. Interested parties include shareholders, employees, the board of directors, suppliers, other creditors, and potential lenders.

(d) DEMONSTRATING COMPLIANCE WITH FINANCING COVENANTS. A company must meet certain financial requirements, typically stated in terms of financial statement ratios, before a bank will lend to it. The company must keep its financial health sufficiently robust that it meets these requirements, known as *debt covenants*, throughout the term of the loan. If the company violates the covenants, the bank usually has the right to call the loan. Given that covenant violations can impose heavy costs on the company, management has an incentive to avoid them. Research in this area has found evidence consistent with management using income-increasing techniques when the company's financials approach covenant violations.[14]

(e) MEETING COMPANY GOALS AND OBJECTIVES. If the company has publicly stated goals or objectives, then management has an incentive to make sure the numbers reflect those projections. Falling short of a projection usually results in a negative reaction in the market. Research shows that missing earnings by a little can cause the stock price of a company to drop a lot. It has been found that the ratios of market price to reported earnings (the price-earnings multiples) decline significantly when earnings decrease after a previous pattern of increases.[15] This suggests an additional target of showing increasing earnings in every period that might be accomplished by smoothing or managing the reported income stream.

---

12. *http://www.pbs.org/wgbh/pages/frontline/shows/dotcon/*
13. John M. Friedlan, "Accounting Choices of Issuers of Initial Public Offerings," *Contemporary Accounting Research*, 17, 1–31.
14. M. DeFond and J. Jiambalvo, "Debt Covenant Violation and Manipulation of Accruals," *Journal of Accounting and Economics*, 17 (1994), 145–176.
15. M. W. Finn, J. A. Elliott, and M. E. Barth, "Market Rewards Associated with Patterns of Increasing Earnings," *Journal of Accounting Research*, 37 (2) (1999), pp. 387–413.

(f) MEETING BONUS TARGETS. Management has an incentive to manipulate earnings to maximize the compensation of its executives through salary and bonuses. One might expect management to try to manipulate earnings upward if the company is close to reaching target earnings levels that will result in a bonus to executives. Conversely, when the company will clearly miss its target, management has incentive to take a big bath during this period if the company will miss the target anyway. Taking a big bath in one period makes it easier to reach earnings targets in the future. Research by Paul Healy and Gaver, Gaver and Austin find evidence consistent with this theory.[16]

(g) HOLDING SIGNIFICANT FINANCIAL INTEREST IN THE COMPANY. In addition to incentives that arise from bonus plans, managers often have significant financial interests in the company, such as providing personal guarantees for the company's debt. Whenever managers have a personal financial stake dependent on the company's performance, they have an incentive to enhance the numbers.

(h) INCREASING DIVIDEND OR PARTNERSHIP DISTRIBUTIONS. Generally, earnings levels constrain dividend policies and partnership distributions. If a company wants to increase dividends or distributions, then it must usually report increased earnings. Meeting the financial thresholds required for increasing dividends or partnership distributions can tempt management to increase earnings.

(i) EXECUTING MERGERS AND ACQUISITIONS. Companies often finance mergers or acquisitions with their own shares. The market will likely value shares higher when the company reports higher earnings. If the market thinks that the company has done well, and will continue to do well, then the price of the shares will likely exceed levels that will occur if the company reports lower earnings. The higher the price of the shares, the fewer shares the company must give up to raise a given dollar sum. Therefore, manipulating the earnings, if it increases share price, lowers the cost of acquiring a company.

(j) OTHER INCENTIVES. Different companies will have different reasons for wanting to improve the appearance of the financial reports. Other incentives exist: for instance, lowering the value of the company just prior to a management buyout, reducing taxes by shifting income to lower-tax-rate years, and reducing (increasing) regulatory costs (benefits). The savvy financial statement analyst will recognize when the company has greater incentive to engage in manipulations or fraudulent activity (e.g., right before an IPO).

31.4 SPECIFIC METHODS TO MANIPULATE FINANCIAL REPORTS

Once we recognize *when* management has incentive to manipulate financial reports, it is easier to think about *how* management might engage in such activities. What line items in the statements might management manipulate? What GAAP and securities laws might management violate when it uses these tools? This section illustrates the methods management has used to commit fraud and the tools management has used to distort the financial results that it reports.

---

16. P. M. Healy, "The Effect of Bonus Schemes on Accounting Decisions," *Journal of Accounting and Economics* (April 1985), pp. 85–107. J. J. Gaver, K. M. Gaver, and J. Austin, "Additional Evidence on Bonus Plans and Income Measurement," *Journal of Accounting & Economics* (February 1995), pp. 3–28.

Given that management can choose accounting practices from a set of policies required by GAAP, one should expect it to choose approaches to maximize the company's market value. While management generally will try to achieve the goals suggested in Section 31.3 through transparent financial reporting (that is, reporting with full disclosure of techniques and the related judgments), management has the ability to achieve these goals either by committing fraud or by opportunistically choosing accounting policies. We consider instances in which management exceeded the acceptable limits for managing earnings, and instances in which management has approached the acceptable limit in choosing its accounting practices for the financial reports provided to the public.

Managers can manipulate four key items to achieve accounting goals:

1. Revenue
2. Expenses and assets
3. Liabilities
4. Disclosures

For each, we discuss the guidance governing their proper accounting, describe how management can break the rules to achieve its earnings goals, and provide examples of management manipulations.

(a) SEC CASES OF ACCOUNTING RESTATEMENTS. The SEC prepared a summary of accounting restatements over a five-year period from July 1998 through June 2002, as shown in Exhibit 31.1.[17]

Improper Accounting Practice	Number of Enforcement Matters Involving Each Practice
Improper revenue recognition	126
Improper expense recognition	101
Improper accounting in connection with business combinations	23
Inadequate Disclosures in MD&A and elsewhere	43
Failure to disclose related-party transactions	23
Inappropriate accounting for nonmonetary and roundtrip transactions	19
Improper accounting for foreign payments in violation of the FCPA	6
Improper use of off-balance-sheet arrangements	3
Improper use of Non-GAAP financial measures	2

EXHIBIT 31.1 SUMMARY OF ACCOUNTING RESTATEMENTS, JULY 1998 THROUGH JUNE 2002

17. To address concerns raised by these restatements, and to restore public trust in the U.S. financial markets, Congress passed the Sarbanes-Oxley Act of 2002, which the president signed into law on July 30, 2002. Section 704 of the Sarbanes-Oxley Act directs the SEC to study enforcement actions over the five years preceding its enactment in order to identify areas of issuer financial reporting that are most susceptible to fraud or inappropriate earnings management. Over the study period, the Commission filed 515 enforcement actions for financial reporting and disclosure violations. The study, issued in January 2003, included 164 corporations and 705 individuals. SEC Report Pursuant to Section 704 of the Sarbanes-Oxley Act of 2002.

(b) REVENUE. Revenue is usually the largest single amount in a financial statement, and revenue recognition accounts for the single largest cause of financial statement restatements. Consequently, one must understand the issues involving revenue recognition.

A study Commissioned by the Committee of Sponsoring Organizations (COSO) of the Treadway Commission analyzed instances of fraudulent financial reporting alleged by the SEC in the Accounting and Auditing Enforcement Releases (AAERs) issued during the 11-year period between January 1987 and December 1997. The researchers looked at 200 companies involved in fraudulent reporting and found that more than half the frauds involved overstating revenues by recording revenues prematurely or fictitiously, which typically results in overstated receivables. The other half of the frauds involved overstating assets by understating allowances for uncollectible receivables, overstating the value of inventory, property, plant and equipment, and other tangible assets, and recording assets that did not exist.

Before December 1999, GAAP's only conceptual requirements for revenue recognition appeared in the Financial Accounting Standards Board's (FASB) Statements of Financial Accounting Concepts. A disparity arose between the general concepts and the detailed guidance provided for specific transactions in the authoritative literature because no conceptual standard for revenue recognition existed. The literature comprises pronouncements with differing degrees of authority such as Accounting Principles Board (APB) Opinions, FASB Statements, American Institute of Certified Public Accountants (AICPA) Audit and Accounting Guides, AICPA Statement of Positions (SOPs), FASB Interpretations, Emerging Issues Task Force (EITF) Issues, and Securities and Exchange Commission (SEC) Staff Accounting Bulletins. Standard setters developed this literature on an *ad hoc* basis in response to needs of specific transactions or industries for detailed implementation guidance. Each pronouncement focuses on a specific practice problem. Consequently, the pronouncements do not provide consistent guidance.[18] In December 1999, the SEC issued SAB 101, *Revenue Recognition in Financial Statements* in an attempt to align conceptual guidance and practice. The FASB expects to issue, in 2005, pronouncements that will further define appropriate practices. Until then, GAAP require that revenue recognition principles follow, first, the guidance in SAB 101, and then the FASB Concept Statements.

FASB *Statement of Financial Accounting Concepts 5: Recognition and Measurement in Financial Statements of Business Enterprises* sets forth revenue recognition criteria and required disclosures, including timing of disclosure, for information incorporated into financial statements. It focuses on the statements of earnings and comprehensive income and addresses measurement issues related to recognition. It requires that management measure revenues by the exchange value of the assets or liabilities involved. It states that management should recognize the revenue only after the transaction has met both of the following criteria:

1. *Revenue is realized or realizable.* Revenue is considered *realized* only when the seller has exchanged goods or services, merchandise, or other assets for cash or claims to cash. Revenue is considered *realizable* only when the seller can readily convert related assets received or held (e.g., accounts receivable) to known amounts of cash or claims to cash.
2. *Revenue is earned.* The seller may recognize revenue only after it has delivered goods or produced goods or rendered services or performed other activities that constitute its ongoing major or central operations.

---

18. FASB Proposal for a New Agenda Project. Issues Related to the Recognition of Revenues and Liabilities.

SEC Staff Accounting Bulletin: No. 101—Revenue Recognition in Financial Statements summarizes the staff's views in applying GAAP to financial reporting and, once issued, become part of GAAP. The staff provided guidance on revenue recognition because, in part, of the revenue recognition issues that registrants encounter. The staff said that revenue generally is realized or realizable and earned only when a transaction meets all of the following four criteria:

1. Persuasive evidence of an arrangement with a buyer exists.
2. Delivery has occurred or services have been rendered to the buyer.
3. The seller's price to the buyer is fixed or determinable.
4. Collectibility is reasonably assured.

These four SEC criteria amplify the criteria for revenue recognition set forth in the FASB *Statement*. The second, third, and fourth criteria resemble the two FASB criteria—"realized" or "realizable and earned." What's new? The SEC staff focuses on the existence of an arrangement with the buyer. The arrangement may take the form of a contract, or prior business dealings with a particular customer, or customary business practices by a company and its industry. The arrangement sets forth the responsibilities of the company and its customers with respect to the nature and delivery of goods or services, the risks assumed by the buyer and seller, the timing of cash payments, and similar factors. Having an arrangement in place permits more informed observations and judgments as to the SEC's second, third, and fourth criteria.

(c) COMMONLY USED METHODS FOR MISREPRESENTING REVENUES. Management might misrepresent the actual revenues of the company for a given period with the following:

- Inflated revenues, including phantom sales and improper classification of revenues
- Misestimations of contra revenue accounts
- Reporting revenue gross as an agent rather than net as a principal
- Reporting revenue gross in advertising barter transactions rather than net
- Shifting revenues across reporting periods through either channel stuffing (explained in Section 31.4(d)(ii) or manipulating completion estimates in applying percentage of completion accounting

Overstating revenues increases net income. Management can overstate revenues in several ways. First, consider the fraud of complete fabrication—recognizing revenue when the company did not make the sale. Management can record false journal entries—either recording fictitious sales to existing customers or to fictitious customers.

Recording a fictitious sale results in recording a fictitious debit, typically to Accounts Receivable. Auditors must check the amounts of Accounts Receivable, so these frauds should not escape notice for long. Moreover, creating revenue requires creating Cost of Goods (or Services) Sold and the recordkeeping manipulations to fudge inventories require steps auditors can detect.

(i) Case Study: Cendant Corporation. Despite the difficulties in creating fictitious sales, some companies have been accused of committing this fraud. One example of allegations involves Cendant Corporation. Cendant Corporation resulted from a December 1997 merger between CUC International, Inc., and HFS Incorporated. The Securities and Exchange Commission alleged that CUC made top-side adjustments[19] beginning in the 1980s, which continued until its discovery and disclosure by Cendant in April 1998. The SEC filed a civil enforcement action for two top former officers of CUC, alleging that they directed a massive financial fraud while selling on personal account. The SEC made the following allegations:

- The top two former officers of CUC earned millions of dollars by selling personal shares at inflated prices while they perpetrated the fraud.
- The top two officers also reviewed and managed schedules listing fraudulent adjustments to be made to CUC's quarterly and annual financial statements.

  At the end of each of the company's first three fiscal quarters and fiscal year end, senior managers compared the company's actual results for the quarter to the quarterly analyst expectations. They then directed mid-level financial reporting managers at CUC corporate headquarters to add the amounts required to bring CUC's quarterly income up to analyst expectations.
- In conjunction with these income statement changes, the managers cosmetically altered certain CUC balance sheet items. For example, they increased the reported cash amount to one more consistent with the income statement line items.
- To conceal the scheme, at year-end they repeatedly used unsupported post-closing journal entries carrying effective dates spread retroactively over prior months.
- CUC made sure that each major expense category bore approximately the same percentage relation to revenues as in the quarter before.
- CUC senior management used the adjustments to artificially increase income and earnings, defrauding investors by creating the illusion of a company that had ever-improving earnings and making millions for themselves along the way. For the period 1995 to 1997, they inflated pre-tax operating income reported to the public by an aggregate amount of more than $500 million.[20]

(ii) Case Study: Equity Funding. More than 30 years ago, management of Equity Funding engaged in overstating revenues by fabricating insurance policy sales. It evaded the auditors' detection by fabricating fictitious insurance policy files, quickly on demand, as the auditors asked for proof that a given policy existed. This was a billion dollar fraud with thousands of fictitious transactions that outside auditors should have caught.

The deceit began when the company had computer problems at the close of the financial year in 1964. The president instructed his employees to make up the bottom line to show about $10 million in profits and calculate the other figures consistent with that result. The transactions to generate that amount never materialized, but management kept the falsified financial statements. This gave management the idea to maintain the inflated share price by manufacturing false insurance policies. In time, management became greedier, and began selling these fake policies to other insurance agencies. In

---

19. *Top-side adjusting entries* refer to those not done in the ordinary course of end-of-period adjustments, but at the end of the process. The word *top* sometimes means that top management recorded the entry and sometimes means that the auditor prepared the entry on its top file, the file of final adjustments, not in detailed working papers. Not all top-side changes result from management entries, but the fraudulent ones typically do.
20. Accounting and Auditing Enforcement Release ("A.A.E.R."), No. 1372 (February 28, 2001), and AAER 1272 (June 14, 2000).

1972, the head of data processing calculated that by the end of that decade, at current rates of fabrication, Equity Funding would have insured the entire population of the world. Its assets would surpass the gross national product. The scheme fell apart only when an angry employee, forced to work overtime, reported it to the authorities.[21]

(iii) Bill-and-Hold Sales and Side Letters. Because creating fictitious revenue requires creating the asset accounts (debits) to match the faked credits, most cases of overstated revenue do not result from management's creating the revenues with false customers or fake accounts receivable. A more sophisticated (and harder-to-detect) way to manipulate earnings shifts authentic revenues between time periods. Although the auditors may detect these schemes while performing their analytical and confirmation procedures, the manipulating management might be able to persuade its vendors and customers to go along with a scheme and provide misleading information to the auditors. These practices, known as *bill-and-hold sales,* use *side letters*.

Legitimate bill-and-hold sales require that the buyer request the transaction be on a bill-and-hold basis; that the buyer must have a substantial business purpose for ordering the goods on a bill-and-hold basis; and that the risks of ownership must pass to the buyer.[22] Fraudulent management might get permission from the customer to ship, promising not to bill the customer until next period and giving the customer its usual grace period to pay, starting from that later date, next period.

A sales staff eager to boost its own sales commissions might send a letter, called a *side letter,* to the customer stating that the customer will accept the shipment and, if asked, confirm that it ordered the goods, but that the seller will not send an invoice until later, and the customer need not pay until later or can return the goods for full credit. Even honest management has a hard time locating these letters issued by dishonest sales staff. Management must be alert for this practice and deal severely with employees it finds issuing them. Some managers have said they disapprove of side letters, but do not enforce the policy. A bill-and-hold sale may involve a side letter, but the usual terminology uses the term *side letter* only when the seller has shipped the goods.

(d) USE AND MODIFICATIONS OF THESE PRACTICES

(i) Bill-and-Hold Sales. The SEC settled with management at ElectroCatheter for alleged fraudulent financial reporting involving bill-and-hold sales in the mid 1980s. Management engaged in so many fake bill-and-hold sales, that by the end, it was marking goods in its warehouse that were allegedly sold to customers but were of a type of goods these customers never bought or would buy. For example, one customer, a hospital, purchased only catheters. To generate a given dollar volume selling low-priced catheters created work for the fraudsters, who had to physically tag the sold goods. So, to save time, management said that the customer had bought high-priced computers, which enabled it, in a given time interval, to generate fake sales in higher amounts than if it had generated fake sales of catheters.

(ii) Channel Stuffing. Channel stuffing (a form of bill-and-hold sales), is a fraudulent activity that accelerates sales revenue into earlier periods. If the customer decides later to

21. M. E. Kabay, "The Equity Funding Fraud," NetworkWorldFusion.com, January 21, 2002.
22. *In the Matter of Stewart Parness,* Exchange Act. Rel. No. 23507, Accounting and Auditing Enforcement Rel. No. 108 (August 5, 1986).

return the goods, this practice results in recording revenues that never occur. Channel stuffing artificially inflates sales and earnings figures.[23] Assume a company ordinarily waits to record revenue until it ships goods that the customer has previously ordered. A company engaging in channel stuffing will ship goods not yet ordered but record them as sales, as though a real customer had ordered them. The Sunbeam case illustrates an allegation of this practice:

> Two of the suits allege that the company failed to disclose an "early buyout" program that allowed retailers to purchase grills in November and December, keep them in Sunbeam warehouses and not pay for them until June. The allegation is that the program, sometimes called channel-stuffing, masked declining grill sales.
>
> -David Sedore, "Five More Class Actions Target Sunbeam," *Palm Beach Daily Business Review,* August 17, 1998

In its May 2001 Sunbeam filing, the SEC states, "The undisclosed or inadequately disclosed acceleration of sales through 'channel-stuffing' materially distorted the Company's reported results of operations and contributed to the inaccurate picture of a successful turnaround." More specifically, the Commission alleged that beginning with the first quarter of 1997, Sunbeam achieved its sales goals, in large part, by offering its customers discounts and other incentives to place their purchase orders before the period when they would otherwise have done so. Since many customers who wished to take advantage of these inducements could not burden their warehouses with out-of-season merchandise, Sunbeam offered to hold product for a customer until the customer requested delivery. Sunbeam typically paid the costs of storage, shipment, and insurance on the product. Moreover, the customers often retained the right, through explicit agreement or established practice, to return unsold product to Sunbeam for full refund or credit. In the second quarter of 1997, Sunbeam recognized $14 million in sales revenue and more than $6 million in income from bill-and-hold sales, with no disclosure of this practice in its quarterly filing on Form 10-Q.[24]

(iii) Holding Books Open after the Close of a Reporting Period. By holding the books open after the close of a reporting period, a company may inappropriately include revenues not realized and earned in the current period. The SEC prosecuted Sirena Apparel Group, a women's swimwear manufacturer located in Los Angeles County, for this. In its filing, the Commission alleged that the CEO and CFO instructed Sirena personnel to hold open the March 1999 fiscal quarter until Sirena had reached its sales target for that period. The perpetrators held the quarter open by periodically resetting the date on Sirena's computer clock to March 30 or March 31. The company held open the quarter ending March 1999 until April 12, 1999. The filing alleged that the two executives ordered Sirena personnel to create false shipping records to conceal their scheme. The CEO settled the action against him by consenting to a permanent injunction, without admitting or denying the allegations in the complaint, and he agreed to pay a civil penalty in the amount of $30,000.[25]

(iv) Overestimating Revenues When Using the Percentage of Completion Method. Companies may recognize as revenue in a given period a percentage of the total contract price when they use the percentage-of-completion method of recognizing revenue. The

---

23. Note that the company also inflates the balance sheet by increasing accounts receivable for the same amount.
24. A.A.E.R. No. 1393 (May 15, 2001).
25. A.A.E.R No. 1325 (September 27, 2000).

company can base the percentage on the ratio of actual costs incurred during the period to total estimated costs for the entire product or project (see *cost-to-cost* in Chapter 1's glossary). A company may use this method only when it can reliably estimate progress toward completion of a contract and the collection of cash is likely. Thus, management must be able to reliably estimate the total costs required to complete the contract for the contract to qualify for the percentage of completion practice. Management must be able to reliably estimate any additional contract revenue (above the original contract price) and costs to be incurred related to cost overruns and changes requested by the customer.

For example, a company agrees to pay a builder a long-term contract with a total price of $100,000. The builder incurs contract costs of $20,000 in one period out of an estimated total cost of $80,000. The company should record 25 percent (= $20,000/$80,000) of the contract price, or $25,000 (= .25 × $100,000).

If management would like to accelerate revenues, then it may either underestimate the total amount of costs it expects to incur for the project or overestimate the amount of revenues that it expects to receive. Suppose, in the previous example, that the builder expects total costs to complete the project to be $80,000, but wants to increase revenues for the period when he incurred the costs of $20,000. By underestimating the expected total cost of the project, the builder can increase revenues. For example, say that the builder declares that the estimated total costs will be $62,500 rather than the $80,000 he expects. The company will recognize 32 percent (i.e., $20,000/$62,500) of the contract price, or $32,000 (= .32 × $100,000) as revenue in the current period. Since expenses stay the same at $20,000, net earnings for this period are increased by $7,000 (= $32,000 – $25,000). Alternatively, the builder could predict that the contract price would increase to $110,000 because of change orders increasing costs during the current period, which he thinks he is sure to collect. Now the ratio is $30,000/$110,000, or 27 percent, which means he will recognize revenues of $30,000 (= $.27 × $110,000), and net earnings for this period increase by $5,000 (= $30,000 – $25,000).

Critics have alleged that Halliburton Corporation, one of the world's largest oil services, construction, and engineering firms, improperly applied the percentage of completion rules by overestimating the amount of total revenues (i.e., contract price) it expected to receive. Halliburton uses the percentage-of-completion method to account for long-term contracts. Starting in 1998, Halliburton changed its accounting methods to include a portion of costs generated by change orders in expected receipts, hence boosting the amount of revenue recognized for each increment of work done on the contract. The lawsuits against Halliburton claim that it should not have included these expected cost recoveries in expected receipts because management could not reliably estimate the probable amounts. Halliburton claims that *not* including these expected cost recoveries will mislead financial statement users. Management also argued that it did not include the total dollar amount of the cost recoveries; it included only the portion it expected to collect. Management estimated the portion of the costs it expected not to recover. Whatever the merits of the arguments about the legitimacy of Halliburton's change in accounting methods, we agree with those who found that the disclosures of the changes were not transparent.

(v) Misclassifying Revenue Streams. The accounting practices for multiple-element, or bundled arrangements, provide opportunity for fraudulent manipulations. Consider a single sale combining the two elements of software and technical support service. SOP 97-2 allows a seller to recognize revenue on the software part of the sale combining software and service elements only if the customer can purchase the software separately from the services and only after the seller deducts revenue attributable to the service element from the total.[26]

MicroStrategy, a software company, began deriving its revenues in 1996 from product licenses, fees for maintenance, technical support, training, consulting, and development services. The SEC investigated MicroStrategy for improperly accounting for its multiple-element arrangements. The Commission alleged that MicroStrategy improperly separated product license sales from service elements and characterized the revenue in multiple-element transactions as product or software revenue recognizing it at the time of the transaction. For example, in the fourth quarter of 1998, MicroStrategy negotiated a $4.5 million transaction with ShopKo Stores, Inc. to provide software licenses as well as consulting and development services and a warranty permitting ShopKo to purchase 50,000 shares of MicroStrategy common stock. Although the product and service development depended on each other, MicroStrategy accounted for the software product as though the sale did not depend on the service and warranty obligations. In addition, MicroStrategy recognized the entire $4.5 million as software product license revenue, allocating no revenue to the extensive service obligations or to the warranty.[27]

Xerox Corporation ran into similar trouble with its accounting for lease arrangements, which typically involve a single quoted price for maintenance and supplies as well as use of a copying machine. On April 11, 2002, the SEC filed a civil fraud injunctive action against Xerox Corporation, alleging that Xerox employed a variety of undisclosed accounting actions to meet or exceed Wall Street expectations and disguise its true operating performance.[28] The complaint alleged that several of the accounting actions related to Xerox's accounting for lease arrangements wrongly boosted income. Revenue from Xerox's customer leases typically has several components: equipment, servicing, supplies, and a finance charge implicit for spreading the payments over time. Under GAAP, Xerox should book the revenue from the amount allocated to the capital lease of the equipment at the beginning of the lease, but should spread the revenue for the other items over the life of the lease. According to the complaint, Xerox relied on accounting actions to justify shifting more of the receipts to the equipment, so that it could recognize a greater portion of that revenue immediately. The SEC alleged that Xerox wrongly accelerated recognition of equipment revenue by more than $3 billion and increased its pretax earnings by approximately $1.5 billion over the four-year period from 1997 through 2000.[29]

(vi) Gross versus Net Revenue Recorded in Transactions. Should companies recognize revenue at the gross invoice amount or the net amount retained? This issue arises for Internet companies and other new businesses where some analysts believe they should base share price valuations on revenues per share, not earnings nor cash flow per share, because these latter two are negative for many new companies. For example, suppose that Hotwire collects $200 from a customer who rents a car online, keeps $15 and remits $185 to Avis. Similarly, Priceline collects $280 from a customer who purchases a discounted airline ticket to fly on Delta, keeps $15 and remits $265 to Delta. Should companies like Hotwire

---

26. AICPA Statement of Position (SOP) 97–2, Software Revenue Recognition.
27. A.A.E.R. No. 1350 (December 14, 2000).
28. Securities and Exchange Commission v. Xerox Corporation, Civil Action No. 02-CV–2780 (DLC) (S.D.N.Y.) (April 11, 2002).
29. A.A.E.R. No. 1542 (April 11, 2002).

and Priceline recognize revenues based on the full price the customers pay for the products? Or, should they recognize only the portion they get to keep from these sales?[30] The accounting rules require that only if the company assumes the risks and rewards of owning the product can it report gross amounts as revenues. If it acts merely as agent or broker, it must report only the net collections as revenues.

This issue arises for start-up companies because investors have appeared to value these companies based on revenues, rather than earnings or cash flows. Although reported net earnings do not depend on whether the company reports revenues net or gross, some financial advisors believe that the presentation of the financial statement affects the stock price. Consequently, in order to increase revenues, companies try to qualify for gross reporting requirements. Priceline operates the ultimate in just-in-time inventory management by taking ownership of the ticket it sells for a fraction of a second. The company works out an agreement with the airline for specific flights and seats that it can sell at an agreed upon price. Only when the customer places an order does Priceline buy the ticket from the airline that Priceline then sells immediately to the customer who has been waiting online briefly for the transaction to complete. This arrangement qualifies the entire amount collected as revenue, not just Priceline's net revenue. It seems to us that it flaunts the ordinary rule that the seller must own the item it sells before it can report the gross, not the net, amount as revenue. The owner who reports the gross revenue ordinarily bears the risks and rewards of ownership. The Priceline model allows Priceline to avoid all the risk of ownership.

(vii) Round-tripping Transactions. A round-tripping transaction has the same effect as inflating revenue without changing net income. In this transaction, one company sells goods or services to the buyer that the buyer doesn't need while making arrangements to purchase the same or equivalent assets back for the same cost. This transaction allows both companies to book revenue from the deal. Some Internet companies in the late 1990s and early 2000s used this revenue increasing practice. Some of these schemes became complex as several companies were involved in the round-tripping transactions to hide the bogus activities more easily. Although this practice does not usually increase the net earnings amount, it does inflate revenues, which can lead to inflated stock prices if analysts use revenue-based pricing models to value share prices.

The SEC and Justice Department probed round-trip deals by America Online Inc. and two of its partners. AOL has said it will restate revenues of $190 million based on its round-trip deals and could restate an additional $400 million more that the SEC has called into question.[31] The SEC investigated round-trip transactions at Unify Corporation, a manufacturer and seller of database management software. In May 2002, the SEC filed a complaint against two former executives of Unify Corporation, alleging that, in several instances, the two executives engaged in round-tripping. The allegations claimed that Unify provided funds to its customers who, in turn, bought Unify products, with no reasonable expectation that the customers would repay the funds, other than through

30. Priceline and Amazon report gross revenues as they actually take possession of the tickets and books, while eBay reports net revenues, never actually taking possession of the goods sold. Priceline reported 1999 gross revenue of $482.4 million with a net revenue of $72.8 million. If it reported only on net revenues, it would have had margins similar to eBay's rather than Amazon's.

31. Carrie Johnson. "Culture of Loopholes Bred Corporate Abuse; Tricks of the 1990s Are Focus of Accounting Reform," by *The Washington Post* (April 18, 2003).

product purchases.[32] In some instances, Unify made an investment in other companies, which then used most or all of the invested funds to purchase Unify products. In others, Unify contracted for services from other companies, but these companies provided no services, and simply used funds from Unify to buy Unify product.[33]

(viii) Barter Transactions. Here's an old story:

Husband: We just had a great day; I sold the dog for $10,000.

Wife: Great; where's the money?

Husband: I didn't get any money; I swapped the dog for two $5,000 cats.

If you get the point of that story—that barter transactions can have arbitrary dollar amounts attached to them—you understand the accounting problem. Barter transactions exist when two or more companies enter into a noncash transaction to exchange goods or services with each other. They represent another method for inflating revenue without changing net income and were popular with Internet companies in the late 1990s and early 2000s. A typical transaction, often seen in the last decade, involves the swap of advertising among Internet companies: Company A sells Company B $10,000 of banner advertising (creating revenue for Company A), and, in turn, pays for it by purchasing two $5,000 links on Company B's Web site. No cash changes hands. Some companies inflate revenue by recognizing equal revenue and expense amounts to account for these transactions. This does not affect earnings, but inflates revenues when companies overestimate the value of the goods or services provided and received. Analysts, who estimate share values based on revenue streams, rather than earnings, will overvalue the company if the financial statements do not reflect the details of these transactions.

The SEC investigated Critical Path, Inc. for improperly recognizing revenue from barter transactions. The Commission alleged that, in order to meet consensus earnings estimates by analysts who followed the company, Critical Path's president engaged in, or oversaw, several fraudulent revenue transactions in the third quarter of 2000. The largest misstated transaction involved a barter transaction with a software company. Critical Path had made plans to purchase some software; then it increased the order by $3.6 million in return for the software vendor becoming a revenue-producing customer of Critical Path's. The SEC alleged that in violation of GAAP,[34] Critical Path did not appropriately establish the fair value of either the software it received or the software it sold to the other company. In the end, Critical Path permanently reversed the amount.[35]

(e) EXPENSE AND ASSET RECOGNITION. The opportunities that management has to manipulate expense and asset recognition provide another tool for fraudulent reporting. The Financial Accounting Standards Board (FASB) *Statement of Financial Accounting Concepts No. 5* sets forth the requirements for expense and asset recognition.

32. This transaction has the effect of causing the cash to make a round trip from Unify to the customers and back, while Unify gives the customer some product. Ordinarily, this would be an income-decreasing activity for a seller, because it has, effectively, given away some of its product. This product, however, is software and has no, or near-zero, incremental cost.

33. Litigation Release No. 17522 (May 20, 2002).

34. Accounting Practice Bulletin 29, Accounting for Non Monetary Transactions.

35. A.A.E.R. 1503 (February 5, 2002).

(i) Expense Recognition. In double-entry recordkeeping, the accounting model interlocks these two kinds of fraud—expenses that are too small require that net assets are too large (e.g., assets overstated, shareholders' equity overstated or liabilities understated). Sometimes management commits fraud by purposefully overstating expenses (and liabilities), resulting in taking a *big bath*, explained in Chapter 1's glossary, and Section 31.2(a)(i). Accounting income is cash-flow in less cash-flow out over long-enough time spans, other than transactions with owners. Suppose that a company knows it will report a poor financial result, sufficiently bad that the market will likely respond by punishing the company's share price. In the big bath scheme, the company will make the bad result appear even worse than it is because the penalty in reduced value is likely to be less than proportionate to the artificially depressed income. In the future, the company's earnings will appear artificially better than actual to the extent that it can make the current results artificially worse than they actually are.

A company generally recognizes expenses when it consumes an asset's economic benefits in delivering or producing goods, rendering services, or other activities that constitute its ongoing operations. It recognizes losses when it judges that previously recognized assets have lost future benefits, losses sufficiently large to pass the test for impairments.[36] A business sometimes recognizes expenses in the period when it incurs costs or in a later period when it matches them to revenues recognized during the later period. The following lists the general distinctions for costs:

- *Product costs.* Expenses, such as cost of goods sold, match with revenues. The company recognizes them when it recognizes the associated revenues.
- *Period costs.* The company recognizes many expenses, such as selling and administrative expenses, during the period when it spends cash or incurs liabilities.
- *Allocated costs.* The company allocates costs, such as plant assets and insurance, with systematic and rational procedures to the periods during which it expects the related assets to provide benefits. This allocation process is known as *amortization,* and is called *depreciation* for physical assets.[37]
- *Loss or lack of future benefit.* The company will recognize a loss when it decides that previously expected future economic benefits of an asset have declined enough to pass the impairment test.

(ii) Asset Recognition. Assets are probable future benefits controlled by the company as a result of a past transaction. On first recognizing an asset in the balance sheet, the company generally records the asset's cost, based on current exchange prices on the date of acquisition. Once the company recognizes the asset, it will continue to record the asset at its initial amount until an event occurs that meets the criteria to record a change, which includes sale or other disposal of the asset, and changes in the expected future benefits reflected in amortization and impairment charges.

(f) COMMONLY USED METHODS FOR MISREPRESENTING THE AMOUNT OF EXPENSES, ASSETS AND LIABILITIES. Fraudsters manipulate earnings by understating expenses, which overstates net assets. Lowering expenses increases net income. A fraudster can lower expenses in the current period by either capitalizing costs that the company should expense or lengthening the depreciable life of assets beyond their economic life.

36. See the Glossary for the contrast between *expense* and *loss* and for the details of the *impairment* test.
37. Amortization and depreciation are processes of cost allocation, not of asset valuation.

Increasing the estimated salvage value of a depreciable asset beyond its expected life results in reducing current depreciation charges and overstating the balance sheet amount for the depreciable asset.

Underestimating bad debt expense overstates the asset for net accounts receivable. Underestimating warranty expense understates liabilities. Capitalizing costs that the company should expense overstates assets and shareholders' equity. To capitalize a cost means to put it on the balance sheet as an asset and then amortize it over time. Alternatively, the firm can expense the cost in the period incurred.

In this section, we provide examples of the following:

- Improper capitalization of assets or deferral of expenses
- Overstating ending asset values
- Improper use of restructuring reserves or manipulating recorded liabilities
- Improper use of asset reserves
- Failure to record asset impairments

(i) Improper Capitalization of Assets or Deferral of Expense. WorldCom, a major global communications provider with operations in 65 countries, appears to have capitalized costs it should have expensed. In a civil action against WorldCom, the SEC alleged that by transferring certain costs to asset accounts, rather than expensing them in the period incurred, WorldCom violated GAAP and falsely portrayed itself as a profitable business during 2001 and the first quarter of 2002. The SEC alleges that senior management approved and directed this practice, which overstated income before income taxes and minority interests by approximately $3.055 billion in 2001 and $797 million during the first quarter of 2002.[38] In this fraud, WorldCom removed operating expenses by paying fees to lease the phone networks and computer services of other companies, removing these fees from WorldCom's income statement, and putting them on their balance sheet as computer and leasing assets.[39]

WorldCom's internal audit team discovered the fraud when it received tips from other employees. After investigating and finding numerous instances of wrongdoing, on June 14, 2002, the internal audit team contacted WorldCom's audit committee, who asked management for documentation supporting its accounting treatment. Management provided

38. SEC Litigation Release No. 17588 (June 27, 2002); A.A.E.R. No. 1585 (June 27, 2002)

39. Imagine the following transaction. A company wants to rent a warehouse for Year 3, but doesn't need it for Years 1 and 2. The company is willing to pay up to $40,000 today to lock in the warehouse for that one-year period starting two years from today. It finds a landlord who will rent a suitable warehouse for three years starting today at $1,000 per month, $36,000 in total. The landlord requires full payment for the three-year rent in advance. The company judges that renting the warehouse for three years is a bargain relative to what it expected to pay. It pays $36,000 today, setting up an asset for Advances to Owner of Warehouse. One year from today, the question becomes, what should the carrying amount of the Advance to Owner be? We think it should be $36,000 because the future benefits contemplated on acquisition of the original lease have not diminished; the cost to secure the services wanted were cheaper to acquire with a three-year lease. Many accountants would disagree with us and mechanically require that $12,000 of expense are recognized for the first year, and show the asset at $24,000. Some newspaper accounts suggest that the WorldCom situation parallels this example: WorldCom paid for multiple years of capacity in advance to secure capacity several years later. Should WorldCom have recorded the expense at the end of the first year for capacity it had rented for that year even though it didn't need or want that capacity at that time? We don't know enough about the facts to be able to answer that question, but we can easily conceive circumstances that suggest the continuing capitalization of the cost was proper.

none and on June 25, WorldCom representatives announced that it had inflated profits by \$3.8 billion over the previous five quarters. Within a day or two, trading in WorldCom shares had halted and plaintiffs' lawyers had filed civil suits alleging fraud. Less than six weeks later, on July 21, WorldCom filed for bankruptcy.[40]

In another case, the SEC accused Waste Management, Inc., a company specializing in waste collection, of massive earnings management fraud similar to WorldCom's alleged fraud. The Commission alleged that, beginning in 1992 and continuing into 1997, the most senior officers of Waste Management engaged in a scheme to falsify and misrepresent Waste Management's financial results to enrich themselves and keep their jobs.[41] They understated depreciation expense on their garbage trucks by extending their useful lives and assigning unsupported and inflated salvage values to those trucks; they assigned arbitrary and significant salvage values to other assets that previously had zero salvage value; and they improperly capitalized a variety of expenses. All of these practices have the concurrent effect of overstating asset values and retained earnings on the balance sheet.

The SEC alleged that the Waste Management's long-time auditor, Arthur Andersen LLP, which repeatedly issued unqualified reports on the company's materially false and misleading annual financial statements, aided the defendant in its fraud. According to the Commission, Andersen annually presented the company management with Proposed Adjusting Journal Entries that would correct errors, fixing the understated expenses and overstated earnings in the company's financial statements. The executives refused to make the adjustments, but entered into a secret agreement with Andersen to correct the accumulated errors over 10 years and to change the underlying accounting practices, but to do so only in future periods.[42] In May of 2001, Andersen agreed with the SEC that it would not support this practice in the future.

In the fall of 2001, Enron collapsed, with some evidence suggesting that Arthur Andersen's partners had connived with Enron management in the accounting for Enron's complex transactions. Following within half a year of the resolution of the Waste Management irregularities, the Enron practices led the Justice Department to file criminal charges against Andersen. Andersen ultimately went out of business as a result of these charges.

(ii) Overstating Ending Asset Values. In the preceding examples, management understated expenses, which inevitably led to overstated net assets. In following example, management overstated assets, which led to understated expenses. The SEC alleged that Rite Aid, one of the nation's largest drugstore chains, failed to record \$8.8 million in shrinkage (the general name for disappearance of inventory through shoplifting, embezzlement, theft, breakage, and evaporation) for stores in which it conducted physical inventories and failed to record \$5.0 million in shrinkage for stores in which it had not conducted physical inventories.[43] As a result, Rite Aid's balance sheet showed \$13.8 million of inventory that it did not possess. By increasing Ending Inventory, Rite Aid understated its cost of goods sold and overstated its income before tax by the same amount:

$$\text{Cost of goods sold} = \text{Beginning inventory} + \text{Purchases} - \text{Ending inventory}$$

40. Presentation: The WorldCom Fraud, 2003, AICPA, Inc., New York, New York.
41. A.A.E.R. No. 1532 (March 26, 2002).
42. According to the Commission, in the end, Waste Management did not even comply with the agreement because the agreement would have prevented it from meeting earnings targets; *ibid.*
43. A.A.E.R. No. 1579 (June 21, 2002).

(iii) Improper Use of Restructuring Reserves or Manipulating Recorded Liabilities. Many companies record restructuring reserves,[44] which estimate the costs of restructuring, for activities such as closing down plants or changing product lines. Such costs include items such as severance pay for laid-off employees and costs to cancel leases. GAAP require companies to recognize some losses of this sort, with attendant liabilities, when it can estimate that it will incur such costs. Although GAAP require companies to record the losses and liabilities (reserves), the process invites abuse. Some managements can't resist the opportunity to overestimate future costs, artificially increasing reserve requirements, so that they can either reverse the reserves into future earnings that are short of earnings targets or simply report fewer expenses in the future. Both practices make future earnings look better at the expense of current earnings. This practice embodies the ideas of *big bath* and *cookie-jar reserves* that Arthur Levitt identified in his speech that we discussed earlier.

The SEC investigated Xerox Corporation, Sunbeam Corporation, and W.R. Grace & Company for engaging in improper use of restructuring reserves. The SEC alleged that Xerox manipulated its reserves to meet market expectations by maintaining $396 million in cookie jar reserves, which it periodically released into earnings to artificially improve operating results.[45] The SEC alleged that Sunbeam created cookie jar reserves in 1996 to increase its reported loss, and then reversed these excess reserves into income during 1997.[46] The SEC alleged that W.R. Grace recorded liabilities through the deferral of income, in order to build cookie jar reserves that it later used to meet earnings estimates.

(iv) Improper Use of Asset Reserves. The matching principle in GAAP requires that a company expense costs incurred to earn revenue in the same period for which it recognizes the revenue. For example, companies that make sales on credit will not receive cash from all the customers. Accordingly, management must make an estimate of the amount of sales for which it will never receive cash and reduce the balance sheet amount of accounts receivable for that amount. To bring about this reduction, companies charge bad debt expense on the income statement and reduce the accounts receivable account by a corresponding amount in a contra asset account often called the *allowance for bad debts* or the *allowance for uncollectible receivables,* or, regrettably, *bad debt reserves.* The company estimates the appropriate balance in this account either by the percentage of sales or by the aging method, both of which use historical information obtained by management. Because management estimates this balance, it has the opportunity to manipulate the amount to achieve earnings targets or expectations.

The SEC investigated Allegheny Health Education and Research Foundation, healthcare provider in Pennsylvania, for inappropriately manipulating its bad debt allowances. The SEC alleged that Allegheny masked its deteriorating financial condition by failing to

---

44. See the Glossary for *reserves.* No other word in accounting causes so much confusion for financial statement readers. In accounting, a reserve always has a credit balance, but many people think of them as debits, often in the form of assets. Reserves can represent asset contra accounts (Reserve for Bad Debts, better called *Allowance for Bad Debts,* Reserve for Depreciation, better called *Accumulated Depreciation*) or liabilities (as here, Restructuring Reserves means Estimated Liabilities for Restructuring Costs to be Incurred) or, occasionally, owners' equity accounts. Sometimes, users mean credits, say for future income, not appearing on the financial statements at all, as in *hidden reserves.*

45. A.A.E.R., No. 1542 (April 11, 2002).

46. A.A.E.R., No. 1395 (May 15, 2001).

increase its bad debt allowances to account for uncollectible accounts receivable by approximately $100 million.[47]

Similarly, in early 2003, several analysts alleged that Sears understated the expected losses on its credit card receivables, overstating assets and income, even after the company increased its allowance for future uncollectible credit-card debts by $189 million in October of 2002 and increased its write-offs of uncollectible accounts by $33 million for the same period.

(v) Failure to Record Asset Impairments. A company must recognize an impairment loss if it cannot recover the carrying amount of a long-lived asset from its undiscounted cash flows under SFAS No. 144, *Accounting for Impairment or Disposal of Long-Lived Assets*. If management judges the asset to be impaired, then management must write down the carrying amount for the asset on the balance sheet by the amount of the difference between the carrying amount and fair value of the asset. The accounting matches that asset write down with a corresponding impairment loss recognized on the income statement in the period in which management recognizes the asset's impairment. Failure to do so overstates the assets and net income of the company.

Management must use judgment to answer the questions: Has an asset's expected cash flows diminished and, if so, by how much? Accordingly, management may manipulate its company's financial results in three ways:

1. *Ignore impairments of assets when the company is in danger of missing its earnings estimates.* This has a straightforward effect—overstate assets and income by the amount of the omitted impairment.
2. *Record false impairments of assets in times when the company will exceed its earnings estimates.* This practice has a subtle effect on the income statement. When a company records false impairments, current-year earnings are lower, but future-years' earnings are higher because of artificially lower depreciation on the assets. This effect resembles the cookie-jar reserves, the artificially large credit balance in the accumulated depreciation account. Although we've not seen the term applied to this fraud, the term could apply here as well. If the company recorded the impairment with a direct credit to the asset account, with the effect of reducing it, the reserve becomes *hidden.*
3. *Write down the assets as part of a business combination (e.g., merger or acquisition).* This practice also has a subtle effect on the income statement and requires an understanding of purchase accounting principles and goodwill impairments that lie beyond the scope of this chapter.

The SEC alleged that CUC (later, Cendant) participated in all three types of these deceptive practices for impairments. The SEC alleged that for years ended January 31, 1996, and January 31, 1997, management inflated CUC operating income by avoiding charges that it should have recognized as impairment losses. When the company merged with HFS to become Cendant in December 1997, management created fraudulent estimated liabilities for future merger costs, often called *merger reserves.* Merger reserves resemble reserves resulting from restructuring charges and serve many of the same purposes. Management creates liabilities based on its representations that the company will incur these costs in the future. The liabilities provide estimates of expenditures that

47. A.A.E.R. No, 1283 (June 30, 2000).

management expects to make as a result of a business combination.[48] Management makes an estimate of the amount of the expenditures, expensing the full amount and setting up the reserve at the time of the estimate. Often, management has no clear idea of which items will result in future charges or write downs since the activity generating the liability has not yet occurred. Some managements take the opportunity to inflate the estimate (like a big bath where they report too much expense or loss now to enable reporting too much profit later, hoping the future boost to market price exceeds the current reduction). If management has created merger reserves larger than necessary, it can later inappropriately charge items such as plant and equipment impairments, non-recoverable receivable amounts, and obsolete inventory costs against the reserve.

At the time of merger, CUC allegedly overestimated the amount of merger costs by the amount of assets that it wanted to write down as impaired. By offsetting the asset write-downs against the merger reserves,[49] the financial statements showed the write-downs as unusual charges—not as ordinary, or operating, expenses—on the income statement. Thus, for assets already impaired, CUC would permanently avoid classifying ultimate write-downs as operating expenses, and when it eventually took the asset write downs, it would overstate them, allowing Cendant to report smaller operating expenses in the future and larger future income.

(g) LIABILITY RECOGNITION. Liabilities are probable future sacrifices of economic benefits arising from present obligations of a particular entity to transfer assets or provide services to other entities in the future as a result of past transactions or events.[50] The initial amount recorded for a liability uses a measurement based on current exchange prices on the date of recognition. Most liabilities are monetary, requiring payments of specific amounts of cash, while some are nonmonetary, requiring the delivery of goods or services. Monetary liabilities due within one year or less appear at the amount of cash the company expects to pay to discharge the obligation. If the payment dates extend more than one year into the future, a monetary liability appears at the present value of the future cash outflows.

When the company receives cash in advance from a customer for the future delivery of a good or service, the nonmonetary liability to deliver the goods and services appears on the balance sheet at the amount of cash received. Sometimes the company has an obligation to delivery a good or service but has not received an explicit cash amount in return for taking on that performance obligation. Then, the related nonmonetary liability appears on the balance sheet at the estimated cost of providing the goods or services. An example of this type of liability is estimated costs for warranty services, where the

48. EITF 94–3 permits merger reserves for (a) the recognition as a liability today of future expenditures for involuntary termination benefits to be paid to employees and (b) the recognition of a liability today for future expenditures that are directly associated with a plan to exit an activity—provided those expenditures will have no future economic benefit and provided four conditions laid down by the EITF are met. EITF 95–3 expands on 94–3 to say that, in a business combination, expenditures to relocate employees may also be recognized as a liability at the time of the business combination, in addition to the employee termination benefits and exit costs covered by 94–3.

49. Rather than debit an expense or loss account, debit the liability for merger reserves.

50. This definition comes from *SFAC No. 6*. See the Glossary; we think one will understand better the distinctions between liabilities and obligations that are not liabilities by defining a liability to be an obligation for a definite (or reasonably definite) amount due at a definite (or reasonably definite) time arising from a transaction that is not an executory contract (a mere exchange of promises).

customer paid a single price for the goods and the related warranty. The seller cannot disentangle the cash receipts into the amounts received for the goods and the amounts received for the warranty. If the seller can allocate the single receipt into components, it will record the nonmonetary liability using that allocation. An example is the sale of a TV and warranty contract in a single price, where the seller also separately offers the two items for sale.

One troublesome question of liability recognition relates to *contingent obligations.* Contingent obligations require some future event to occur before accounting can establish the existence or amount, or both, of a liability. Examples of contingent liabilities include unsettled lawsuits and loan guarantees. In both cases, the company does not clearly have an obligation, and even if it does, the amount is not clear until either the case is settled or the loan goes into default. GAAP requires the recognition of a liability only when the payment is probable—that is, likely to occur. Because the bodies that govern the accounting profession do not agree on what *probable* means, the decision to recognize the liability is based on a very subjective measure.

A typical accounting entry to record a liability credits the liability and debits the expense. If a company understates liabilities, it typically understates expenses, overstates income, and understates the debt-equity ratio. Sometimes the recording of a liability matches the recording of an asset (as in recording a financing lease), where omitting the liability has no immediate effect on reported income, but does distort the debt-equity ratio, making it appear smaller than it should.

(h) COMMONLY USED METHODS FOR UNDERSTATING LIABILITIES. Many liabilities require a management estimate. For example, when a company sells products with a warranty attached, management must estimate the amount of future warranty costs the company will incur on these products, and record an expense and a liability in the period of the sale. Management bases the estimate on experience and expected changes in the business environment. Whenever accounting requires a management judgment, it provides opportunity for earnings management or fraud.

Management can also reduce stated liabilities by constructing transactions so that the obligations stay off the balance sheet. Raising funds without showing the resulting obligations on the balance sheet is referred to as *off-balance-sheet* (OBS) financing. The most common (nonfraudulent) OBS financings arise from some leasing activities and by raising funds with debt incurred by related entities that the reporting company does not have to consolidate. Instances of the latter involve joint ventures, partnerships, or less-than-majority-owned subsidiaries. From 1990 until recently, accounting jargon referred to these entities as *special purpose entities* (SPEs), but now the FASB calls them *variable interest entities* (VIEs).

This section provides examples of the following types of liability manipulation:

- Improper estimation of liabilities, sometimes called *reserves*
- Improper use of off-balance-sheet arrangements
- Improper estimation of pension liabilities
- Improper (non-) recognition of contingent liabilities

(i) Improper Estimation of Liabilities, Sometimes Called Reserves. Companies that sell products with attached warranties must recognize, at the time of sale, an estimated warranty liability that results in reducing income and increasing liabilities for the estimated cost of fulfilling the promises given in the warranty. Some call this a *warranty reserve,* but you will understand it better if you think of it as a liability for Estimated Costs of Future Warranty Repairs.

The amount of this estimated expense results from management's past experience and its expectations of future changes. If the amount is underestimated, the result is to decrease expenses and increase net income. The SEC has alleged that Signal Tech, a publicly traded defense contractor, improperly understated its estimated warranty expenses. The Commission alleged that, in March of 1998, an executive for one of Signal Tech's divisions prepared a handwritten list of improper adjustments and directed his accounting staff to enter them directly into the general ledger. These adjustments took the form of unsupported reductions to each of the following:

- Estimated expenses on the income statement
- Balance sheet liabilities for estimated contract losses ($210,000)
- Balance sheet liabilities for estimated warranty costs ($121,000)
- Balance sheet amounts estimated for excess and obsolete inventory ($100,000) [51]

By underestimating the anticipated expenses for these activities, Signal Tech allegedly reported higher income and shareholder equity for the period.

(ii) Improper Use of Off-Balance-Sheet Arrangements. Companies use off-balance-sheet arrangements to provide financing, liquidity, market or credit risk support, or to engage in leasing, hedging, or research and development. These arrangements may involve the use of special purpose entities, called VIEs (variable interest entities) by the FASB. The misuse of these types of structures has only recently come to the attention of the general public, mostly as a result of the collapse of Enron. Since then, the FASB has developed new financial accounting standards to deal with these structures.

Prior to the new standards being implemented, the main violation occurred when companies failed to consolidate the financial results of affiliates that they should have consolidated.[52] The accounting rules for when a parent must consolidate an affiliate involve considerations of ownership and control, but applying those rules in practice presented management with opportunities for manipulation and bending of the rules.

Even before the Enron collapse, the SEC had investigated The PNC Financial Services Group, Inc. (PNC) for this type of inappropriate use of off-balance-sheet arrangements.[53] A press release issued on July 18, 2002, regarding the Cease and Desist Order given by the SEC to PNC, stated:

> The SEC's administrative Order found that in 2001, PNC endeavored to remove approximately $762 million of volatile, troubled or underperforming loans and venture capital investments from its financial statements by transferring them to three special purpose entities that were specially created to receive these assets and in which PNC held a substantial interest. PNC failed to consolidate the special purpose entities on its second and third quarter financial statements filed with the Commission even though the entities failed to meet the requirements under generally accepted accounting principles (GAAP) for non-consolidation. In connection with its improper

51. SEC Civil Action No. CO 2 – 01467.
52. A consolidated balance sheet is, approximately, the sum of two separate balance sheets. If an entity borrows funds, it will record a liability. If a parent company can avoid consolidating the balance sheet of an affiliated company that does borrow funds, the liability will appear on the balance sheet of the borrowing affiliate, but not on the consolidated balance sheet of the parent.
53. SEC Report Pursant to Section 704 of the Sarbanes-Oxley Act of 2002.

> accounting for its interest in the three special purpose entities, PNC also made materially false and misleading disclosures in certain press releases and in quarterly reports filed with the Commission for the second and third quarters of 2001 about its financial condition, earnings and exposure to the risks of its commercial lending activities.

In that same press release, an SEC official stated, "Today's action demonstrates that the Commission will closely scrutinize transactions with special purpose entities. Public companies engaged in transactions with special purpose entities not only must rigorously comply with GAAP, but also must assure that they accurately portray the material elements of the economic risks and realities that they face as a result of these transactions."

Soon thereafter, the SEC investigated Adelphia Communications Corporation, a large cable television provider, for deceptive off-balance-sheet arrangements. The SEC alleged that senior management caused Adelphia to fraudulently exclude more than $2.3 billion in bank debt by deliberately shifting those liabilities onto the books of Adelphia's off-balance-sheet, unconsolidated affiliates. Similar to PNC, these affiliates did not qualify for nonconsolidation under GAAP. Adelphia went one step further, though, and created fictitious documents to give the false appearance that it had repaid the debts, rather than transfer them to unconsolidated entities controlled by the founder, CEO, and Chairman of Board of Directors, John J. Rigas.[54]

Following Adelphia, the SEC cited Dynegy, Incorporated and its use of its special purpose entity, Alpha. Internal Dynegy documents suggest that Alpha's principal purpose was to address the "disconnect . . . between book and cash earnings" and to improve "quality of earnings"—that is, to create the appearance that Dynegy's operations generated more cash than they did.[55] Dynegy reported a $300 million loan from Alpha (which had effectively borrowed these funds from a syndicate of lenders, through other entities), as operating cash flow on the statement of cash flows. Dynegy should have reported this transaction as financing cash flow. This case particularly worried analysts as they had considered cash from operations to be both a key indicator of the financial health of a company and difficult to manipulate. As a result, analysts began to understand that companies were using VIEs to manipulate the placement of items in the statement of cash flows.

(iii) Improper Estimation of Pension Liabilities. The amount of a company's pension expense can differ from the amount of cash it contributes to its pension fund. Recognizing pension expense requires a debit to expense with a credit to a liability account. Funding pension liabilities requires a debit to the liability account and a credit to cash transferred to the pension fund. This issue here is the amount of pension expense that a company recognizes—the amount by which it reduces income in the current period.

The amount a company recognizes as pension expense depends on factors such as employee demographics, the expected rate of return on existing pension assets, anticipated wage increases, assumptions made about the return on invested pension assets, and the rate the company uses to discount future liabilities.[56] Overestimating the discount rate will understate liabilities on the balance sheet. Increasing the assumed rate of return to be earned on invested pension assets decreases the amounts of expense the company will

---

54. A.A.E.R., No., 1599 (July 24, 2002).
55. A.A.E.R., No., 1631 (September 24, 2002).
56. The discounting of future cash outflows allows raising the rate for discounting future liabilities decreasing the present value of the associated liabilities. Management records long-term liabilities, such as pension obligations, at the present value of future cash outflows.

record for any given year. Thus, higher estimates of interest rates and rates of return reduce both the amounts of pension liabilities and the current pension expenses. In October 2002, Standard and Poors downgraded its credit rating for General Motors because of its increasing pension liabilities. Executives prefer to have high rather than low credit ratings, which allows a management interested in manipulating the result to adjust the assumptions related to pension expenses to its advantage. In 2002, Lockheed Martin announced that its pension plan would contribute losses—expenses of as much as $100 million—rather than increase the bottom line by millions of dollars as it did during an earlier period. The stock price dropped by 6 percent over two days.[57] Although no fraud occurred, this situation shows the effect of such information on the value of the company's shares. Executives are cognizant of this effect and may intentionally try to hide this information from the public.

(iv) Improper (Non-) Recognition of Contingent Liabilities.[58] Contingent obligations arise from lawsuits, loan guarantees, environmental exposures, and repurchase agreements. Management must record the potential obligation as a liability when it is probable that the company has incurred the liability and when management can reasonably estimate its amount. If it is only *reasonably possible* that the potential obligation will become a liability, management must disclose the contingency in the footnotes to the financial statements.

Almost all large corporations report contingencies for ongoing civil litigation. A complex example of a contingency arose when Enron's unconsolidated partnerships (special purpose entities) issued bonds, which required the parent entity Enron to issue shares of its common stock to the bondholders under certain conditions, such as a downgrade in the bonds' ratings. Because Enron did not consolidate the bond-issuing entity, it did not fully disclose the nature of the contingency. As Enron's share prices declined, the bond indentures potentially required Enron to issue shares to the bondholders, which potentially increased the number of shares outstanding, which caused further decline in the market value of the shares. This process continued until Enron shares became worthless. The evidence available to us suggests that Enron should have consolidated those SPEs and should have disclosed the nature of the contingencies. Such disclosure, alone, would not have made the collapse of Enron less likely, but would likely have caused Enron management to abandon this form of raising funds and not to have issued the bonds in the first place.

(i) DISCLOSURES RECOGNITION. *Disclosure* refers to any information the company provides to the public beyond the basic financial statements, including notes to the financial statements, other information in the annual report (e.g., the Management Discussion and Analysis), press releases, and conference calls. The GAAP and SEC rules regulating disclosures apply to the following:

- Accounting policies
- Related parties

57. "Johnson, Culture of Loopholes Bred Corporate Abuse.

58. Many financial statement preparers and users refer to *contingent liabilities*. We deplore this usage, because by its very nature a liability appears in the balance sheet, while a contingency, a potential obligation and liability, does not. We prefer to use the word *liability* only when the item appears on the balance sheet, so we use *contingency* when the potential obligation is not yet a liability. You should be aware that many financial statements use the term *contingent liability* for items not in the balance sheet.

- Commitments and contingencies
- Risks and uncertainties
- Nonmonetary transactions

We discuss the types of information that companies must disclose and the regulation governing this disclosure, including how companies must both prepare and report the information. Then we show how companies violate these requirements.

(j) WHAT INFORMATION MUST REPORTING COMPANIES DISCLOSE? Under *Accounting Principles Board Opinion No. 22* (APB 22), "Disclosure of Accounting Policies," companies must provide the financial statement user with a description of the significant accounting polices the company adopts. These policies affect the presentation of a company's financial position, changes in financial position, and results of operations. Accordingly, the usefulness to readers of financial statements for making economic decisions about the reporting entity depends on the reader's understanding of the entity's accounting policies.[59]

For example, one company may use straight-line depreciation for its depreciable assets, while another uses accelerated depreciation. One company may use a LIFO cost flow assumption for inventories while another uses a FIFO cost flow assumption. Without this information, financial statement users would find it difficult if not impossible to compare financial statements of different companies using different accounting policies to prepare their statements. Recently, the SEC has begun to require companies to describe the critical accounting judgments management has to make to prepare the financial statements. A financial institution will discuss its procedures for estimating the amounts of loan losses, while a commercial company will discuss how it estimates the amount of bad debts. A retail company will discuss methods of estimating ending inventory valuations, while a manufacturing company using plant assets will discuss methods of estimating depreciable lives and salvage values.

Companies must provide information about the significant risks and uncertainties they face. In December 1994, the AICPA's Accounting Standards Executive Committee issued Statement of Position (SOP) 94-6, "*Disclosure of Certain Significant Risks and Uncertainties.*" This pronouncement requires non-governmental entities that prepare financial statements in conformity with GAAP to disclose risks and uncertainties that could significantly affect the amounts reported in those financial statements. This pronouncement provides more detailed practical guidance than does the FASB's *Statement of Financial Accounting Concepts No. 1,* which states that the purpose of financial accounting is to "provide information that is useful to present and potential investors and creditors and other users in making rational investment, credit, and similar decisions." SOP 94-6 requires disclosures in the following areas:

- The nature of operations
- The use of estimates in the preparation of financial statements
- Certain significant estimates
- Current vulnerability due to certain concentrations, such as having a disproportionate amount of business with a single customer or with many customers in a single foreign country

59. Accounting Principles Board Opinion, No. 22. (April 1972).

Reporting the nature of operations is straightforward, but understanding the other three areas requires further discussion. Many fraudulent activities relate directly to management estimates for items such as allowance for bad debts, estimated warranty liabilities, contingencies, and estimated costs to complete mergers. The relevant disclosure for GE reads:

> Accounting policies discussed in this section are those that we consider to be critical to an understanding of our financial statements because their application places the most significant demands on our ability to judge the effect of inherently uncertain matters on our financial results. For all of these policies, we caution that future events rarely develop exactly as forecast, and the best estimates routinely require adjustment.

This disclosure communicates the uncertainties inherent in measuring assets, liabilities, revenues, and expenses while alerting the reader that future events may differ from those anticipated by management when it prepared the financial statements. Management accused of preparing fraudulent financial statements often point to this disclosure in defense of its actions.

(k) WHERE DOES THIS INFORMATION APPEAR? Although some of this disclosure appears in the required notes to the financial statements in SEC filings such as the 10-K or the annual report, much of it appears in the Management Discussion and Analysis (MD&A) and the Letter to Shareholders. Companies provide further disclosures through press releases and conference calls. Item 303 of Regulation S-K, issued by the SEC, "Management's Discussion and Analysis of Financial Condition and Results of Operations," requires the MD&A to provide investors with "information that the registrant believes to be necessary to an understanding of its financial condition, changes in financial condition and results of operations." The section of the MD&A discussing forward-looking information often leads to allegations of manipulation or fraud by management. Management must provide information regarding the possible future effects of the most important, *existing* currently known demands, risks, uncertainties, events, conditions and trends. It may include forward-looking information about the possible effects of *anticipated* future demands, events, conditions, and trends. This forward-looking information may take the form of pro-forma financial information (defined in Chapter 1's glossary).

(l) MISLEADING OR FRAUDULENT DISCLOSURE. Most alleged misleading or fraudulent disclosure involve:

- Inaccurate estimates by management of asset and liability amounts, amounts for contingencies, and pension discount rates or investment return amounts
- Failure by management to advise financial statement users of possible risks to the company
- Management dissemination of misleading financial information through the use of non-GAAP pro-forma information

An example of inaccurate estimations by management of asset amounts is the case of Waste Management, discussed in Section 31.2(a). Examples of the other two fraudulent disclosure practices follow.

(i) Nondisclosure of Possible Risks. The SEC entered an enforcement action for inadequate MD&A disclosure in 1992 *In the Matter of Caterpillar, Inc.* (SEC Release No. 34-30532). In that action, the SEC found that Caterpillar had failed to comply with the reporting requirements of the Securities Exchange Act of 1934 (the "Exchange Act").

Caterpillar failed to disclose the concerns of its board of directors that the dramatic increase in revenues experienced in the company's Brazilian unit in 1989, which significantly contributed to the company's earnings, resulted from the combined effects of Brazil's currency hyperinflation and international exchange rates, and would not likely recur. The Caterpillar case illustrates that when management knows of adverse trends and uncertainties, it must disclose its concerns.[60] The SEC stated that, by omitting this information from its MD&A, management "left investors with an incomplete picture of Caterpillar's financial condition and results of operations and denied them the opportunity to see the company 'through the eyes of management'."

(ii) Non-GAAP Pro Forma Information. Management uses *pro forma financial statements* to show how financial statements would appear had events not occurred or, less often, show the financial results of events occurring that hadn't actually happened. Pro forma statements have long had a valid use in business forecasting and budgeting. For example, management might forecast, "If sales grow at 10 percent next year and the cost of goods sold remains 65 percent of sales while administrative expense ratios remain the same as the previous year, the income statement for the year will show . . . ." This would be a pro forma income statement useful in internal budgeting and planning. As a result, the term *pro forma statements* has an honorable past. The term now has less benign uses.

In recent years, companies have issued pro forma statements showing how the statements would have looked had there been no asset impairments or had two companies, which have not yet merged, been operating together with projected efficiencies from the merger.

The use of non-GAAP pro forma information has prompted the SEC to issue a warning regarding the release of pro forma information to the public.[61] In its statement, the SEC cautioned against providing misleading pro forma information. Specifically, the Commission reminded the reader that the antifraud provisions of securities laws apply to a company issuing pro forma information, thus companies should be particularly mindful of their obligation not to mislead investors who use the information. It stated, "A presentation of financial results that is addressed to a limited feature of a company's overall financial results (e.g., earnings before interest, taxes, depreciation and amortization), or that sets forth calculations of financial results on a basis other than GAAP, raises particular concerns." Such statements mislead investors when the company does not clearly disclose the basis of presentation. Effective March 2003, the SEC adopted a new disclosure regulation, Regulation G, which required public companies that disclose or release non-GAAP financial measures to include a presentation of the most directly comparable GAAP financial measure or reconciliation of the non-GAAP financial measure to the GAAP counterpart.[62]

In its first enforcement action addressing the abuse of pro forma earnings figures, the SEC alleged in January 2002 that Trump Hotels & Casino Resorts, Inc. (Trump), made misleading statements in its third-quarter 1999 earnings release. The SEC found that the release cited pro forma figures that presented purportedly positive operations results without disclosing that an unusual, one-time gain had caused these results rather than profitable, ongoing operating activities. The error was further compounded when the company excluded one-time losses from the calculation. The results would have shown a

60. A. John Murphy, Jr., and Charles S. Kaufman, "SEC Presses for Expanded MD&A Disclosure," Sheppard, Mullin, Richter, and Hampton LLP, March 29, 2002.

61. *http://www.sec.gov/rules/other/33–8039.htm.*

62. *http://www.sec.gov/rules/final/33–8176.htm.*

decline in both revenues and net income had Trump excluded from the quarterly pro forma results both the unusual gain and the one-time charge, which would have failed to meet analysts' expectations.[63] An SEC official stated, "In this case, the method of presenting the pro forma numbers and the positive spin the Company put on them were materially misleading. The case starkly illustrates how pro forma numbers can be used deceptively and the mischief that they can cause." The SEC found that Trump Hotels violated Section 10(b) of the Exchange Act, Rule 10b-5 and ordered the company to cease and desist from violating those provisions.

31.5 AUDITOR RESPONSIBILITY FOR DETECTING FRAUD

Earlier, we asked, "Who is watching the shop?" The auditors have the responsibility for attesting that management has prepared the financial statements in accordance with GAAP.

Now we ask, "Are the auditors responsible for detecting fraud?" Management prepares the financial statements. The rules of the game could make the auditors responsible for checking every assertion implied by these statements. Auditors know how to do these checks—to search systematically for fraud—but these audits would cost more than 10 times as much as audits now done under Generally Accepted Auditing Standards, called *GAAS audits*. Accepted practice implies that auditors should have some skepticism when reviewing financial statements but not assume that management is dishonest, which keeps the auditing costs reasonable. The generally accepted practice is "trust, but verify." This approach implies that auditors will not be as likely to find fraud as when their retention specifies that they search for it or that, at the end of the audit, the auditor will be confident that fraud has not occurred. GAAS do not require, nor even suggest, that the auditors will question management on every item. GAAS state that due professional care requires that the auditor exercise professional skepticism. Professional skepticism is an attitude that includes a questioning mind and a critical assessment of audit evidence. The standards go on to state that an auditor should neither assume that management is dishonest nor assume unquestioned honesty. In exercising professional skepticism, the auditor should not be satisfied with less than persuasive evidence because of belief that management is honest.[64]

Professional guidance regarding the auditor's responsibility to detect errors and fraud includes the following paragraph,

> The auditor has a responsibility to plan and perform the audit to obtain reasonable assurance about whether the financial statements are *free of material misstatement, whether caused by error or fraud*. Because of the nature of audit evidence and the characteristics of fraud, the auditor is able to obtain reasonable, but not absolute, assurance that material misstatements are detected. The auditor has no responsibility to plan and perform the audit to obtain reasonable assurance that misstatements, whether caused by error or fraud, that are not material to the financial statements are detected.[65]

This guidance makes the auditors responsible for attaining *reasonable assurance* that the statements are free of material misstatements. In practice, after the world discovers

63. A.A.E.R., No. 1499 (January 16, 2002).
64. Kurt Pany and Ray Whittington, "Fraud in a Financial Statement Audit: What Every Auditing Student Should Know about SAS 99," A Student Educational Manual Provided by the American Institute of CPAs, December 2002.
65. AU sec. 110, par 2.

that management has committed fraud, the auditors cannot easily show that the evidence entitled them to be reasonably assured there was no fraud, but that in spite of their reasonable assurance, fraud did occur and escaped notice.

The professional guidance quoted above doesn't help us figure out how the auditors should design their tests or their decision rules for stopping further digging into the facts underlying the financial statements. For this, we have the Statement on Auditing Standards (SAS) No. 99, *Consideration of Fraud in a Financial Statement Audit.* SAS 99 provides the auditor with defining characteristics of fraud, discusses the meaning and importance of professional skepticism, and suggests procedures for obtaining the information needed to identify the risks of material misstatement. It provides guidance on how the auditor should identify these risks, respond to the results of the assessment, and evaluate the audit evidence.[66]

In practice, after the fact, one cannot easily decide whether material misstatements resulted from error or from fraud, because of the inherent flexibility in GAAP and the need for management estimation in many regards. Apart from the blatant misappropriation of assets, proving that management intended to deceive the public requires more evidence than most investigations can find. Still, over the years, practitioners have developed successful analytical procedures for detecting fraud.

31.6 SIGNS OF TROUBLE

Investors, regulators, management, and auditors all want to prevent fraud or detect it once it occurs. Section 31.4 discussed the actions that management can take to commit fraud and how these affect the financial statements. Section 31.5 discussed the responsibilities of auditors to detect fraud. In this section, we discuss how financial statement users might identify fraudulent activities.

The financial statement user should understand the environment conducive for fraud. We have discussed specific situations in which management might become aggressive and engage in fraudulent financial reporting. *SAS No. 99* documents three general conditions often present when fraud occurs:

1. Incentive or pressure
2. Opportunity
3. Attitude and rationalization

(a) INCENTIVE OR PRESSURE. Incentives and pressure provide powerful motivation. Management of a company operating in a declining industry may try to offset the decreased demand by misstating the financial statements. If management has special performance incentives—such as a CFO who is about to retire and whose retirement pay depends on reported income in the last year before retirement, or management whose bonuses depend on accounting income—management may modify the financial statement to enhance the results. When top management pressures lower-level executives to achieve the forecasted target, fraudulent reporting can result, especially when top management has a practice of publicly committing to aggressive or unreasonable forecasts.

66. You can find further discussion of the auditor's responsibility by visiting the AICPA Web site at *http://www.aicpa.org/members/div/auditstd/index.htm.* The Sarbanes-Oxley Act established the Public Company Accounting Oversight Board (PCAOB), which now regulates auditors and the auditor process. The PCAOB has only recently begun its operations and its standards appear at *http://www.pcaobus.org/pcaob_standards.asp.*

(b) OPPORTUNITY. Opportunity opens possibilities that executives might never have considered. When a company has effective controls but its accounting requires management judgments that are hard to document, such as the need to estimate future warranty costs or environmental contingencies, opportunity arises. For example, estimates of loan losses critically affect the income reported in the banking industry, but rarely in the magazine industry. Estimates of estimated liabilities for civil penalties will likely affect both the tobacco and chemical industries, but may have little effect on the computer industry.

(c) ATTITUDE AND RATIONALIZATION. Management may adopt an attitude of acceptance when it can rationalize or justify its fraudulent activities. For example, management might believe that future years will be more profitable and inflated results now will keep the company from bankruptcy.

The financial statement user must identify whether the business environment could nurture fraudulent activities and, then, where in the financial statements evidence of these activities might appear. When fraud seems possible, the financial statement user should execute more detailed financial statement diagnostics to assess whether management has presented accurate financial results.[67] These diagnostics usually come in the form of financial statement ratios which the user compares either to results for the same company in prior years (time-series analyses) or to the results of different companies or an industry average for the same year (cross-sectional analyses).[68] These ratios will not provide conclusive evidence for or against earnings manipulation, but the results provide a starting point from which the financial statement user may decide to focus extra effort.

Fraudulent activities affect income in one of two ways. The first increases net income by increasing current revenues or decreasing current expenses. The second decreases net income by decreasing current revenues or increasing current expenses. The diagnostic ratios we suggest below can detect both types of fraud. The financial statement user should look for inconsistencies across time or across companies in either direction.

Most of the ratios used to detect overstated and understated revenues have net sales in the denominator (numerator) and some other targeted measure in the numerator (denominator). Examples include

- Cash flow from operations (CFO)/Net sales
- Bad debt expense/Net sales
- Warranty expense/Net sales

Unexplained differences in these ratios across time or across companies in the same industry signal the need for further investigation. By *unexplained*, we mean differences that the user can't attribute to typical growth rates for the company or for the industry or to changes in the business environment such as a recession or some other macroeconomic condition or to a change in business strategy. Consider the first ratio, CFO/Net Sales. An unexplained decrease (increase) in this ratio may signify overstated (understated) revenue. Notice that the other two ratios have an expense in the numerator and revenue in the denominator. Unexplained changes in these ratios require more investigation to decide whether misstated expenses or revenues caused them.

---

67. Obviously, internal auditors will have much greater access to management and the internal financial documents of the company. We confine our discussion here to information available to users *outside* of the company.
68. Industry averages are available on the Internet at such addresses as *http://www.bizstats.com*.

The financial statement user can implement simple ratios, such as bad debt expense/net sales or warranty expense/net sales, to detect inconsistencies in expense recognition. Misstated expenses usually mean misstated assets or liabilities. Expenses that result mainly from management judgment, such as pension expense, depreciation expense, bad debt expense or warranty expense, merit special review. The carrying values of the assets need testing for impairment. The notes provide clues to ascertain the existence of off-balance sheet liabilities. Calculate turnover ratios, such as inventory and accounts receivable turnover. These ratios reveal combined balance sheet and income statement effects of financial statement preparation and provide an additional perspective on possible inconsistencies.

The process of detecting potential fraud by financial statement users outside a company can prove time consuming and frustrating because you may pursue blind alleys, situations where ratios or other signals suggest investigation but nonfraudulent reasons exist for the results. Comparisons with other industry indicators can mislead, because some legitimate companies have such unstable operating results that the time series of diagnostics provides no information. Alternatively, companies in new industries do not have time series over which to perform the desired diagnostics or may not have any comparison companies. Regardless, using these analytic diagnostics provides a useful start in understanding financial statements.

31.7 ANALYTIC DIAGNOSTICS TO DISCOVER ACCOUNTING FRAUD

We have discussed the sorts of actions management takes to commit fraud and how these affect the financial statements. One action shows two kinds of accounting fraud affecting income:

1. Make current periods look better than they should be by accelerating or inventing revenue or by delaying expenses with fraudulent debits to an asset account.
2. Make bad current periods look worse to make future periods look better by booking fraudulent expenses and special charges, which create fake liabilities. The fraudster can then reverse these amounts in the future with credits to income statement accounts.

Of course, no easy answers exist regarding how to detect fraud early. Successful financial analysts often use diagnostics similar to those that we discuss next. Our examples focus on the first sort of fraud just described, where the fraudster makes current income look better than it should, but will work as well for the second kind that makes current periods look worse. They will not help diagnose fraudulent consolidation policy that affects on-balance-sheet debt.

We recommend that a serious analyst develop several years of diagnostic ratios based on quarterly data and construct similar data series for comparable companies, typically companies in the same industry. The analyst should define benchmarks against which to compare the studied company's results with an intent to find signals that point to the need for investigation. The following exhibits illustrate the computations for three years. In practice, analysts prefer to use quarterly data over a five-year period to provide a more accurate data series. The exhibits show how the ordinary turnover ratios and the ratio of cash flow from operations to net income can help the analyst focus on potential fraud.

Exhibit 31.2 on page 796 shows three years of operations for a profitable, growing company built on the following assumptions used to generate the financial statements

- **a.** Sales growth of 10 percent per year
- **b.** Cost of goods sold is 65 percent of sales
- **c.** Receivables turnover of 6, implying that the company collects its receivables, on average, two months after the sale
- **d.** Payables turnover of 12, implying that the company pays its suppliers, on average, one month after purchase[69]
- **e.** General and administrative expense growth at 8 percent per year
- **f.** Property, plant, equipment and depreciation charges of 7 percent per year
- **g.** Interest rate on long-term borrowings of 8 percent per year
- **h.** Income taxes of 40 percent of taxable income
- **i.** Dividends declared each year of 55 percent of after-tax income
- **j.** Long-term debt is ⅔ of owner's equity

We show three years of operating and cash flow data for this company and show standard financial ratios at the bottom of the exhibit. This set of financial statements illustrates a normal, nonfraudulent base case.

Exhibit 31.3 on page 798 shows results when, in Year 3, the company has an unexpected bad event, increasing pretax expenses (and expenditures) by $100. For our purposes, the cause of the extra $100 expense is not important; we show it as an increase in administrative expenses. Look at the diagnostic ratios at the bottom of the exhibit. The profitability ratios show the expected declines, but the turnover ratios do not change.

Exhibit 31.4 on page 800 shows what happens when management attempts to cover up fraud by inflating revenues.[70] Management increases revenues by $100, but takes no other steps. This feeble manipulation shows itself immediately because the balance sheet doesn't balance. No competent fraudster would attempt such a blatant fraud because anyone financially minded will know that a balance sheet must have equal amounts of assets and sources of funds (plus liabilities plus owners' equities). The word *signal* appears in the appropriate place to call your attention to the fraud signal. This exhibit provides testimony to the elegance and power of double-entry recordkeeping.

Exhibit 31.5 on page 802 shows the results of a more sophisticated fraud. It invents fake sales and matches those credits with inflated receivables (debits). It records the increase in income taxes, as well. The diagnostics—receivables turnover ratio and ratio of cash flow from operations to income—signal something worth investigating. This fraud overstates accounts receivable, so that a thorough audit of that account might detect the fraud, as well. GAAS audits might easily overlook one such fake receivable because they do not pretend to examine them all in ordinary circumstances. Note the signals, which some call *red flags*.

---

69. In most growing, successful businesses, the company finds itself paying its suppliers faster than it receives cash from its customers, creating a chronic cash shortage. Most new business managers find themselves surprised and in a panic. A new business should anticipate this chronic shortage of cash and make arrangements for long-term financing to solve the problem. Short-term borrowings from a bank will cover the situation, because financing receivables is a permanent need, in spite of the fact that it looks short term. Many bankers do not like to provide long-term financing.

70. In this exhibit and the following ones, we show both the nonfraud financial statements and the fraudulent ones.

	Balance Sheets	End of Year Yr 0	Yr 1	Yr 2	Yr 3
Plug	Cash	$ 78.0	$ 83.6	$ 91.9	$ 104.5
Turnover x/yr 6	Accounts Receivable	152.0	166.7	183.3	201.7
Turnover x/yr 4	Inventory	150.0	162.5	178.8	196.6
Grow at 7%	Plant & Equipment [Net]	500.0	535.0	572.5	612.5
	Total Assets	$880.0	$947.7	$1,026.4	$1,115.3
Turnover x/yr 12	Accounts Payable	51.0	54.2	59.6	65.5
D/OE = 0.67	Long Term Debt	331.6	357.4	386.7	419.9
OE = 1.5 D	Owners' Equity	497.4	536.1	580.1	629.9
	Total Sources of Financing	$880.0	$947.7	$1,026.4	$1,115.3

	Income Statements	Yr 1	Yr 2	Yr 3
Grow at 10%	Sales	$1,000.0	$1,100.0	$1,210.0
.65 of Sales	Cost of Goods Sold	650.0	715.0	786.5
Grow at 8%	Administrative Expenses	100.0	108.0	116.6
Grow at 7%	Depreciation Expense	80.0	85.6	91.6
Interest rate 8%	Interest Expense	26.5	28.6	30.9
	Pretax Income	$ 143.5	$ 162.8	$ 184.3
Y Tax rate = 40%	Income Tax Expense	57.4	65.1	73.7
	Net Income [= Y]	$ 86.1	$ 97.7	$ 110.6
Dividend Payout Rate = 55%	Dividends	47.3	53.7	60.8
	Add to Retained Earnings	$ 38.7	$ 44.0	$ 49.8

EXHIBIT 31.2 BASE CASE WITH NORMAL RESULTS

Statements of Cash Flows		End of Year	
	Yr 1	Yr 2	Yr 3
Income [= Y]	$ 86.1	$ 97.7	$ 110.6
Plus Depreciation	80.0	85.6	91.6
Less Increase Receivables	(14.7)	(16.7)	(18.3)
Less Increase Inventories	(12.5)	(16.3)	(17.9)
Plus Increase Payables	3.2	5.4	6.0
Cash Flow from Operations	$ 142.1	$ 155.8	$ 171.9
New Equipment Purchases	(115.0)	(123.1)	(131.7)
New Borrowing	25.8	29.3	33.2
Dividends	(47.3)	(53.7)	(60.8)
Total Increase in Cash	$ 5.6	$ 8.3	$ 12.6
Diagnostic Ratios			
Inventory Turnover per Year	4.16	4.19	4.19
Receivables Turnover per Year	6.28	6.29	6.29
Cash Flow from Operations/Year	1.65	1.59	1.55
Quick Ratio	1.54	1.54	1.59
Return on Assets	11.60%	12.10%	12.60%
Return on Owners' Equity	17.30%	18.20%	19.10%

EXHIBIT 31.2 BASE CASE WITH NORMAL RESULTS *(CONTINUED)*

	Balance Sheets	End of Year			
		Yr 0	Yr 1	Yr 2	Yr 3
Plug	Cash	$ 8.0	$ 83.6	$ 91.9	$ 59.5
Turnover x/yr 6	Accounts Receivable	152.0	166.7	183.3	201.7
Turnover x/yr 4	Inventory	150.0	162.5	178.8	196.6
Grow at 7%	Plant & Equipment [Net]	500.0	535.0	572.5	612.5
	Total Assets	$880.0	$947.7	$1,026.4	$1,070.3
Turnover x/yr 12	Accounts Payable	51.0	54.2	59.6	65.5
D/OE = 0.67	Long Term Debt	331.6	357.4	386.7	401.9
OE = 1.5 D	Owners' Equity	497.4	536.1	580.1	602.9
	Total Sources of Financing	$880.0	$947.7	$1,026.4	$1,070.3

	Income Statements	Yr 1	Yr 2	Yr 3
Grow at 10%	Sales	$1,000.0	$1,100.0	$1,210.0
.65 of Sales	Cost of Goods Sold	650.0	715.0	786.5
Grow at 8%	Administrative Expenses	100.0	108.0	216.6
Grow at 7%	Depreciation Expense	80.0	85.6	91.6
Interest rate 8%	Interest Expense	26.5	28.6	30.9
	Pretax Income	$ 143.5	$ 162.8	$ 84.3
Y Tax rate = 40%	Income Tax Expense	57.4	65.1	33.7
	Net Income [= Y]	$ 86.1	97.7	50.6
Dividend Payout Rate = 55%	Dividends	47.3	53.7	27.8
	Add to Retained Earnings	$ 38.7	$ 44.0	$ 22.8

EXHIBIT 31.3 BAD RESULT IN YEAR 3: EXPENSES INCREASE UNEXPECTEDLY BY $100.00

Statements of Cash Flows		End of Year	
	Yr 1	Yr 2	Yr 3
Income [= Y]	$ 86.1	$ 97.7	$ 50.6
Plus Depreciation	80.0	85.6	91.6
Less Increase Receivables	(14.7)	(16.7)	(18.3)
Less Increase Inventories	(12.5)	(16.3)	(17.9)
Plus Increase Payables	3.2	5.4	6.0
Cash Flow from Operations	$142.1	$155.8	$111.9
New Equipment Purchases	(115.0)	(123.1)	(131.7)
New Borrowing	25.8	29.3	15.2
Dividends	(47.3)	(53.7)	(27.8)
Total Increase in Cash	$ 5.6	$ 8.3	$(32.4)
Diagnostic Ratios			
Inventory Turnover per Year	4.16	4.19	4.19
Receivables Turnover per Year	6.28	6.29	6.29
Cash Flow from Operations/Y	1.65	1.59	2.21
Quick Ratio	1.54	1.54	0.91
Return on Assets	11.60%	12.10%	6.70%
Return on Owners' Equity	17.30%	18.20%	8.70%

EXHIBIT 31.3 BAD RESULT IN YEAR 3: EXPENSES INCREASE UNEXPECTEDLY BY $100.00 *(CONTINUED)*

In Year 3, Expenses Increase Unexpectedly by $100.0

Feeble attempt to repair damage: Inflate revenues in Year 3 by $100.0

Observe Balance Sheet doesn't balance, so need to be more sophisticated.

	Balance Sheets	**End of Year**					
		Yr 0	**Yr 1**	**Yr 2**	**No Fraud in Year 3**	**Fraud in Year 3**	
Plug	Cash	$ 78.0	$ 83.6	$ 91.9	$ 59.5	$ 59.5	
Turnover x/yr 6%	Accounts Receivable	152.0	166.7	183.3	201.7	201.7	
Turnover x/yr 4	Inventory	150.0	162.5	178.8	196.6	196.6	
Grow at 7%	Plant & Equipment [Net]	500.0	535.0	572.5	612.5	612.5	
	Total Assets	$880.0	$947.7	$1,026.4	$1,070.3	$1,070.3	**Signal**
Turnover x/yr 12	Accounts Payable	51.0	54.2	59.6	65.5	65.5	
D/OE = 0.67	Long Term Debt	331.6	357.4	386.7	401.9	401.9	
OE = 1.5 D	Owners' Equity	497.4	536.1	580.1	602.9	662.9	
	Total Sources of Financing	$880.0	$947.7	$1,026.4	$1,070.3	$1,130.3	**Signal**

	Income Statements	**Yr 1**	**Yr 2**	**Yr 3 (No Fraud)**	**Yr 3 (Fraud)**
Grow at 10%	Sales	$1,000.0	$1,100.0	$1,210.0	$1,310.0
.65 of Sales	Cost of Goods Sold	650.0	715.0	786.5	786.5
Grow at 8%	Administrative Expenses	100.0	108.0	216.6	216.6
Grow at 7%	Depreciation Expense	80.0	85.6	91.6	91.6
Interest rate 8%	Interest Expense	26.5	28.6	30.9	30.9
	Pretax Income	$ 143.5	$ 162.8	$ 84.3	$ 184.3
Y Tax rate = 40%	Income Tax Expense	57.4	65.1	33.7	73.7
	Net Income [= Y]	$ 86.1	$ 97.7	$ 50.6	$ 110.6
Dividend Payout Rate = 55%	Dividends	47.3	53.7	27.8	27.8
	Add to Retained Earnings	$ 38.7	$ 44.0	$ 22.8	$ 82.8

EXHIBIT 31.4 BAD EXPENSES IN YEAR 3 AND MANAGEMENT ATTEMPTS COVER-UP BY INFLATING REVENUES ONLY

Statements of Cash Flows	End of Year			
	Yr 1	Yr 2	No Fraud in Yr 3	Fraud in Yr 3
Income [= Y]	$ 86.1	$ 97.7	$ 50.6	$ 110.6
Plus Depreciation	80.0	85.6	91.6	91.6
Less Increase Receivables	(14.7)	(16.7)	(18.3)	(18.3)
Less Increase Inventories	(12.5)	(16.3)	(17.9)	(17.9)
Plus Increase Payables	3.2	5.4	6.0	6.0
Cash Flow from Operations	$142.1	$ 155.8	$111.9	$ 171.9
New Equipment Purchases	(115.0)	(123.1)	(131.7)	(131.7)
New Borrowing	25.8	29.3	15.2	15.2
Dividends	(47.3)	(53.7)	(27.8)	(27.8)
Total Increase in Cash	$ 5.6	$ 8.3	$ (32.4)	$ 27.6
Diagnostic Ratios				
Inventory Turnover per Year	4.16	4.19	4.19	4.19
Receivables Turnover per Year	6.28	6.29	6.29	6.81
Cash Flow from Operations/Y	1.65	1.59	2.21	1.55
Quick Ratio	1.54	1.54	0.91	0.91
Return on Assets	11.60%	12.10%	6.70%	12.10%
Return on Owners' Equity	17.30%	18.20%	8.70%	18.30%

EXHIBIT 31.4 BAD EXPENSES IN YEAR 3 AND MANAGEMENT ATTEMPTS COVER-UP BY INFLATING REVENUES ONLY *(CONTINUED)*

In Year 3, Expenses Increase Unexpectedly by $100.0
Inflate revenues and receivables in Year 3 by $100.0
Management records income taxes on the bogus income.
Note that an auditor who confirms receivables will discover error.

Balance Sheets — End of Year

		Yr 0	Yr 1	Yr 2	No Fraud in Year 3	Fraud in Year 3	
Plug	Cash	$ 78.0	$ 83.6	$ 91.9	$ 59.5	$ 59.5	
Turnover x/yr 6	Accounts Receivable	152.0	166.7	183.3	201.7	301.7	**Signal**
Turnover x/yr 4	Inventory	150.0	162.5	178.8	196.6	131.6	**Signal**
Grow at 7%	Plant & Equipment [Net]	500.0	535.0	572.5	612.5	612.5	
	Total Assets	$880.0	$947.7	$1,026.4	$1,070.3	$1,105.3	
Turnover x/yr 12	Accounts Payable	51.0	54.2	59.6	65.5	79.5	
D/OE = 0.67	Long Term Debt	331.6	357.4	386.7	401.9	401.9	
OE = 1.5 D	Owners' Equity	497.4	536.1	580.1	602.9	623.9	
	Total Sources of Financing	$880.0	$947.7	$1,026.4	$1,070.3	$1,105.3	

Income Statements

		Yr 1	Yr 2	Yr 3 (No Fraud)	Yr 3 (Fraud)
Grow at 10%	Sales	$1,000.0	$1,100.0	$1,210.0	$1,310.0
.65 of Sales	Cost of Goods Sold	650.0	715.0	786.5	851.5
Grow at 8%	Administrative Expenses	100.0	108.0	216.6	216.6
Grow at 7%	Depreciation Expense	80.0	85.6	91.6	91.6
Interest rate 8%	Interest Expense	26.5	28.6	30.9	30.9
	Pretax Income	$ 143.5	$ 162.8	$ 84.3	$ 119.3
Y Tax rate = 40%	Income Tax Expense	57.4	65.1	33.7	47.7
	Net Income [= Y]	$ 86.1	$ 97.7	$ 50.6	$ 71.6
Dividend Payout Rate = 55%	Dividends	47.3	53.7	27.8	27.8
	Add to Retained Earnings	$ 38.7	$ 44.0	$ 22.8	$ 43.8

EXHIBIT 31.5 BAD EXPENSES IN YEAR 3 AND MANAGEMENT ATTEMPTS COVER-UP BY INFLATING REVENUES AND RECEIVABLES

Statements of Cash Flows			End of Year		
	Yr 1	Yr 2	No Fraud in Year 3	Fraud in Year 3	
Income [= Y]	$ 86.1	$ 97.7	$ 50.6	$ 71.6	
Plus Depreciation	80.0	85.6	91.6	91.6	
Less Increase Receivables	(14.7)	(16.7)	(18.3)	(118.3)	
Less Increase Inventories	(12.5)	(16.3)	(17.9)	47.1	
Plus Increase Payables	3.2	5.4	6.0	20.0	
Cash Flow from Operations	$ 142.1	$155.8	$111.9	$111.9	
New Equipment Purchases	(115.0)	(123.1)	(131.7)	(131.7)	
New Borrowing	25.8	29.3	15.2	15.2	
Dividends	(47.3)	(53.7)	(27.8)	(27.8)	
Total Increase in Cash	$ 5.6	$ 8.3	$ (32.4)	$ (32.4)	
Diagnostic Ratios					
Inventory Turnover per Year	4.16	4.19	4.19	5.49	
Receivables Turnover per Year	6.28	6.29	6.29	5.40	**Signal**
Cash Flow from Operations/Year	1.65	1.59	2.21	1.56	**Signal**
Quick Ratio	1.54	1.54	0.91	0.75	
Return on Assets	11.60%	12.10%	6.70%	8.40%	
Return on Owners' Equity	17.30%	18.20%	8.70%	11.90%	

Entries for Fabricated Transactions:

Dr. Accounts Receivable	100	
Cr. Sales		100
Dr. Cost of Goods Sold	65	
Cr. Inventory		65
Dr. Income Tax Expense	14	
Cr. Payables		14
Cr. Cash		—

EXHIBIT 31.5 BAD EXPENSES IN YEAR 3 AND MANAGEMENT ATTEMPTS COVER-UP BY INFLATING REVENUES AND RECEIVABLES *(CONTINUED)*

In Year 3, Expenses Increase Unexpectedly by $100.0
Inflate revenues and receivables in Year 3 by $100.0
Management records cost of goods sold and income taxes on the bogus income.
Note that an auditor who confirms receivables will *NOT* discover error.

	Balance Sheets	End of Year				
		Yr 0	Yr 1	Yr 2	No Fraud in Yr 3	Fraud in Year 3
Plug	Cash	$ 78.0	$ 83.6	$ 91.9	$ 59.5	$ 59.5
Turnover x/yr	Accounts Receivable	152.0	166.7	183.3	201.7	301.7
Turnover x/yr	Inventory	150.0	162.5	178.8	196.6	131.6
Grow at 7%	Plant & Equipment [Net]	500.0	535.0	572.5	612.5	612.5
	Total Assets	$880.0	$947.7	$1,026.4	$1,070.3	$1,105.3
Turnover x/yr 12%	Accounts Payable	51.0	54.2	59.6	65.5	79.5
D/OE = 0.67	Long Term Debt	331.6	357.4	386.7	401.9	401.9
OE = 1.5 D	Owners' Equity	497.4	536.1	580.1	602.9	623.9
	Total Sources of Financing	$880.0	$947.7	$1,026.4	$1,070.3	$1,105.3

	Income Statements	Yr 1	Yr 2	Yr 3 (No Fraud)	Yr 3 (Fraud)
Grow at 10%	Sales	$1,000.0	$1,100.0	$1,210.0	$1,310.0
.65 of Sales	Cost of Goods Sold	650.0	715.0	786.5	851.5
Grow at 8%	Administrative Expenses	100.0	108.0	216.6	216.6
Grow at 7%	Depreciation Expense	80.0	85.6	91.6	91.6
Interest rate8%	Interest Expense	26.5	28.6	30.9	30.9
	Pretax Income	$ 143.5	$ 162.8	$ 84.3	$ 119.3
Y Tax rate = 40%	Income Tax Expense	57.4	65.1	$ 33.7	47.7
	Net Income [= Y]	$ 86.1	$ 97.7	50.6	71.6
Dividend Payout Rate = 55%	Dividends	47.3	53.7	27.8	27.8
	Add to Retained Earnings	$ 38.7	$ 44.0	$ 22.8	$ 43.8

EXHIBIT 31.6 (SEE PAGE 808 FOR DISCUSSION) BAD EXPENSES IN YEAR 3 AND MANAGEMENT ATTEMPTS COVER-UP BY INFLATING REVENUES AND RECEIVABLES WITH

Statements of Cash Flows	End of Year				
	Yr 1	Yr 2	No Fraud in Year 3	Fraud in Year 3	
Income [= Y]	$ 86.1	$ 97.7	$ 50.6	$ 71.6	
Plus Depreciation	80.0	85.6	91.6	91.6	
Less Increase Receivables	(14.7)	(16.7)	(18.3)	(118.3)	
Less Increase Inventories	(12.5)	(16.3)	(17.9)	47.1	
Plus Increase Payables	3.2	5.4	6.0	20.0	
Cash Flow from Operations	$142.1	$155.8	$111.9	$111.9	
New Equipment Purchases	(115.0)	(123.1)	(131.7)	(131.7)	
New Borrowing	25.8	29.3	15.2	15.2	
Dividends	(47.3)	(53.7)	(27.8)	(27.8)	
Total Increase in Cash	$ 5.6	$ 8.3	$(32.4)	$(32.4)	
Diagnostic Ratios					
Inventory Turnover per Year	4.16	4.19	4.19	5.49	**Signal**
Receivables Turnover per Year	6.28	6.29	6.29	5.40	**Signal**
Cash Flow from Operations/Y	1.65	1.59	2.21	1.56	**Signal**
Quick Ratio	1.54	1.54	0.91	0.75	
Return on Assets	11.60%	12.10%	6.70%	8.40%	
Return on Owners' Equity	17.30%	18.20%	8.70%	11.90%	

Entries for Fabricated Transactions:

	Dr.	Cr.
Dr. Accounts Receivable	100	
Cr. Sales		100
Dr. Cost of Goods Sold	65	
Cr. Inventory		65
Dr. Income Tax Expense	14	
Cr. Payables		14
Cr. Cash		—

EXHIBIT 31.6 (SEE PAGE 808 FOR DISCUSSION) BAD EXPENSES IN YEAR 3 AND MANAGEMENT ATTEMPTS COVER-UP BY INFLATING REVENUES AND RECEIVABLES WITH SIDE LETTER *(CONTINUED)*

In Year 3, Expenses Increase Unexpectedly by $100.0

Overvalue ending inventory to cover up by $100.0

Management records cost of goods sold and income taxes on the bogus income.

Note that an auditor who tests inventory will discover error.

	Balance Sheets	End of Year				
		Yr 0	Yr 1	Yr 2	No Fraud in Year 3	Fraud in Year 3
Plug	Cash	$ 78.0	$ 83.6	$ 91.9	$ 59.5	$ 59.5
Turnover x/yr 6	Accounts Receivable	152.0	166.7	183.3	201.7	201.7
Turnover x/yr 4	Inventory	150.0	162.5	178.8	196.6	296.6
Grow at 7%	Plant & Equipment [Net]	500.0	535.0	572.5	612.5	612.5
	Total Assets	$880.0	$947.7	$1,026.4	$1,070.3	$1,170.3
Turnover x/yr 12	Accounts Payable	51.0	54.2	59.6	65.5	105.5
D/OE = 0.67	Long Term Debt	331.6	357.4	386.7	401.9	401.9
OE = 1.5 D	Owners' Equity	497.4	536.1	580.1	602.9	662.9
	Total Sources of Financing	$880.0	$947.7	$1,026.4	$1,070.3	$1,170.3

	Income Statements	Yr 1	Yr 2	Yr 3 (No Fraud)	Yr 3 (Fraud)
Grow at 10%	Sales	$1,000.0	$1,100.0	$1,210.0	$1,210.0
.65 of Sales	Cost of Goods Sold	650.0	715.0	786.5	686.5
Grow at 8%	Administrative Expenses	100.0	108.0	216.6	216.6
Grow at 7%	Depreciation Expense	80.0	85.6	91.6	91.6
Interest rate 8%	Interest Expense	26.5	28.6	30.9	30.9
	Pretax Income	$ 143.5	$ 162.8	$ 84.3	$ 184.3
Y Tax rate = 40%	Income Tax Expense	57.4	65.1	33.7	73.7
	Net Income [= Y]	$ 86.1	$ 97.7	$ 50.6	110.6
Dividend Payout Rate = 50%	Dividends	47.3	53.7	27.8	27.8
	Add to Retained Earnings	$ 38.7	$ 44.0	$ 22.8	$ 82.8

EXHIBIT 31.7 (SEE PAGE 808 FOR DISCUSSION) BAD EXPENSES IN YEAR 3 AND MANAGEMENT ATTEMPTS COVER-UP BY INFLATING ENDING INVENTORY

Statements of Cash Flows	Yr 1	Yr 2	No Fraud in Yr 3	Fraud in Yr 3	
		End of Year			
Income [= Y]	$ 86.1	$ 97.7	$ 50.6	$110.6	
Plus Depreciation	80.0	85.6	91.6	91.6	
Less Increase Receivables	(14.7)	(16.7)	(18.3)	(18.3)	
Less Increase Inventories	(12.5)	(16.3)	(17.9)	(117.9)	
Plus Increase Payables	3.2	5.4	6.0	46.0	
Cash Flow from Operations	$142.1	$155.8	$111.9	$111.9	
New Equipment Purchases	(115.0)	(123.1)	(131.7)	(131.7)	
New Borrowing	25.8	29.3	15.2	15.2	
Dividends	(47.3)	(53.7)	(27.8)	(27.8)	
Total Increase in Cash	$ 5.6	$ 8.3	$ (32.4)	$ (32.4)	
Diagnostic Ratios					
Inventory Turnover per Year	4.16	4.19	4.19	2.89	**Signal**
Receivables Turnover per Year	6.28	6.29	6.29	6.29	
Cash Flow from Operations/Y	1.65	1.59	2.21	1.01	**Signal**
Quick Ratio	1.54	1.54	0.91	0.56	
Return on Assets	11.60%	12.10%	6.70%	12.10%	
Return on Owners' Equity	17.30%	18.20%	8.7%0	18.30%	

We show this as a reduction in the expense for Cost of Goods sold as a negative debit although typically reductions in expenses are positive credits.

Entries for Fabricated Transactions:

Dr. Accounts Receivable	—	
Cr. Sales		—
Dr. Cost of Goods Sold	(100)	
Cr. Inventory		(100)
Dr. Income Tax Expense	40	
Cr. Payables		40
Cr. Cash		—

Exhibit 31.7 (See Page 808 for Discussion) Bad Expenses in Year 3 and Management Attempts Cover-Up by Inflating Ending Inventory *(Continued)*

Exhibit 31.6 on page 804 shows still more sophistication. The salesperson who generates the bogus sale sends a side letter to the customer and has the company ship goods not yet ordered. The salesperson gets permission from the customer to ship, saying the company will not bill the customer until the next period and that the customer will get its usual grace period to pay the bill starting from that later date in the next period. This letter is a *side letter*.[71] An auditor's confirmation of accounts receivable will no longer detect this fraud unless the auditor specifically asks, and the customer fully responds, about the conditions of side letters. Still, the turnover ratios—both inventory and receivables—and the ratio of operating cash flow to income signal something unusual, worth investigating.

Exhibit 31.7 on page 806 shows another common fraud—overvaluing ending inventory, which reduces cost of goods sold and boosts income. The inventory turnover ratio and ratio of operating cash flow to income signal something worth investigating.

These exhibits show that the turnover and cash-flow-to-income ratios for a company committing fraud will go awry. They do not show the false positives—ratios gone awry when a company does not commit fraud. Hence, the analyst can use the ratios to decide where to focus extra effort. These ratios provide a starting point but not conclusive evidence of fraud.

71. Even honest management has a hard time locating these. Management must be diligent and deal severely with employees found issuing side letters.

APPENDIX **A**

COMPOUND INTEREST, PRESENT VALUE, AND ANNUITY TABLES

CONTENTS

TABLE 1 FUTURE VALUE OF $1

TABLE 2 PRESENT VALUE OF $1

TABLE 3 FUTURE VALUE OF ANNUITY OF $1 IN ARREARS

TABLE 4 PRESENT VALUE OF ANNUITY OF $1 IN ARREARS

Periods $= n$	$\frac{1}{2}\%$	1%	$1\frac{1}{2}\%$	2%	3%	4%	5%	6%	7%	8%	10%	12%	15%	20%	25%
1	1.00500	1.01000	1.01500	1.02000	1.03000	1.04000	1.05000	1.06000	1.07000	1.08000	1.10000	1.12000	1.15000	1.20000	1.25000
2	1.01003	1.02010	1.03023	1.04040	1.06090	1.08160	1.10250	1.12360	1.14490	1.16640	1.21000	1.25440	1.32250	1.44000	1.56250
3	1.01508	1.03030	1.04568	1.06121	1.09273	1.12486	1.15763	1.19102	1.22504	1.25971	1.33100	1.40493	1.52088	1.72800	1.95313
4	1.02015	1.04060	1.06136	1.08243	1.12551	1.16986	1.21551	1.26248	1.31080	1.36049	1.46410	1.57352	1.74901	2.07360	2.44141
5	1.02525	1.05101	1.07728	1.10408	1.15927	1.21665	1.27628	1.33823	1.40255	1.46933	1.61051	1.76234	2.01136	2.48832	3.05176
6	1.03038	1.06152	1.09344	1.12616	1.19405	1.26532	1.34010	1.41852	1.50073	1.58687	1.77156	1.97382	2.31306	2.98598	3.81470
7	1.03553	1.07214	1.10984	1.14869	1.22987	1.31593	1.40710	1.50363	1.60578	1.71382	1.94872	2.21068	2.66002	3.58318	4.76837
8	1.04071	1.08286	1.12649	1.17166	1.26677	1.36857	1.47746	1.59385	1.71819	1.85093	2.14359	2.47596	3.05902	4.29982	5.96046
9	1.04591	1.09369	1.14339	1.19509	1.30477	1.42331	1.55133	1.68948	1.83846	1.99900	2.35795	2.77308	3.51788	5.15978	7.45058
10	1.05114	1.10462	1.16054	1.21899	1.34392	1.48024	1.62889	1.79085	1.96715	2.15892	2.59374	3.10585	4.04556	6.19174	9.31323
11	1.05640	1.11567	1.17795	1.24337	1.38423	1.53945	1.71034	1.89830	2.10485	2.33164	2.85312	3.47855	4.65239	7.43008	11.64153
12	1.06168	1.12683	1.19562	1.26824	1.42576	1.60103	1.79586	2.01220	2.25219	2.51817	3.13843	3.89598	5.35025	8.91610	14.55192
13	1.06699	1.13809	1.21355	1.29361	1.46853	1.66507	1.88565	2.13293	2.40985	2.71962	3.45227	4.36349	6.15279	10.69932	18.18989
14	1.07232	1.14947	1.23176	1.31948	1.51259	1.73168	1.97993	2.26090	2.57853	2.93719	3.79750	4.88711	7.07571	12.83918	22.73737
15	1.07768	1.16097	1.25023	1.34587	1.55797	1.80094	2.07893	2.39656	2.75903	3.17217	4.17725	5.47357	8.13706	15.40702	28.42171
16	1.08307	1.17258	1.26899	1.37279	1.60471	1.87298	2.18287	2.54035	2.95216	3.42594	4.59497	6.13039	9.35762	18.48843	35.52714
17	1.08849	1.18430	1.28802	1.40024	1.65285	1.94790	2.29202	2.69277	3.15882	3.70002	5.05447	6.86604	10.76126	22.18611	44.40892
18	1.09393	1.19615	1.30734	1.42825	1.70243	2.02582	2.40662	2.85434	3.37993	3.99602	5.55992	7.68997	12.37545	26.62333	56.51115
19	1.09940	1.20811	1.32695	1.45681	1.75351	2.10685	2.52695	3.02560	3.61653	4.31570	6.11591	8.61276	14.23177	31.94800	69.38894
20	1.10490	1.22019	1.34686	1.48595	1.80611	2.19112	2.65330	3.20714	3.86968	4.66096	6.72750	9.64629	16.36654	38.33760	86.73617

TABLE 1 FUTURE VALUE OF $1

$F_n = P(1 + r)^n$

r = INTEREST RATE; n = NUMBER OF PERIODS UNTIL VALUATION; P = $1

Periods $= n$	$\frac{1}{2}\%$	1%	$1\frac{1}{2}\%$	2%	3%	4%	5%	6%	7%	8%	10%	12%	15%	20%	25%
22	1.11597	1.24472	1.38756	1.54598	1.91610	2.36992	2.92526	3.60354	4.43040	5.43654	8.14027	12.10031	21.64475	55.20614	135.5253
24	1.12716	1.26973	1.42950	1.60844	2.03279	2.56330	3.22510	4.04893	5.07237	6.34118	9.84973	15.17863	28.62518	79.49685	211.7582
26	1.13846	1.29526	1.47271	1.67342	2.15659	2.77247	3.55567	4.54938	5.80735	7.39635	11.91818	19.04007	37.85680	114.4755	330.8722
28	1.14987	1.32129	1.51722	1.74102	2.28793	2.99870	3.92013	5.11169	6.64884	8.62711	14.42099	23.88387	50.06561	164.8447	516.9879
30	1.16140	1.34785	1.56308	1.81136	2.42726	3.24340	4.32194	5.74349	7.61226	10.06266	17.44940	29.95992	66.21177	237.3763	807.7936
32	1.17304	1.37494	1.61032	1.88454	2.57508	3.50806	4.76494	6.45339	8.71527	11.73708	21.11378	37.58173	87.56507	341.8219	1262.177
34	1.18480	1.40258	1.65900	1.96068	2.73191	3.79432	5.25335	7.25103	9.97811	13.69013	25.54767	47.14252	115.80480	492.2235	1972.152
36	1.19668	1.43077	1.70914	2.03989	2.89828	4.10393	5.79182	8.14725	11.42394	15.96817	30.91268	59.13557	153.15185	708.8019	3081.488
38	1.20868	1.45953	1.76080	2.12230	3.07478	4.43881	6.38548	9.15425	13.07927	18.62528	37.40434	74.17966	202.54332	1020.675	4814.825
40	1.22079	1.48886	1.81402	2.20804	3.26204	4.80102	7.03999	10.28572	14.97446	21.72452	45.25926	93.05097	267.86355	1469.772	7523.164
45	1.25162	1.56481	1.95421	2.43785	3.78160	5.84118	8.98501	13.76461	21.00245	31.92045	72.89048	163.9876	538.76927	3657.262	22958.87
50	1.28323	1.64463	2.10524	2.69159	4.38391	7.10668	11.46740	18.42015	29.45703	46.90161	117.3909	289.0022	1083.65744	9100.438	70064.92
100	1.64667	2.70481	4.43205	7.24465	19.21863	50.50495	131.5013	339.3021	867.7163	2199.761	13780.61	83522.27	117×10^4	828×10^5	491×10^7

TABLE 1 FUTURE VALUE OF $1
$F_n = P(1 + r)^n$
r = INTEREST RATE; n = NUMBER OF PERIODS UNTIL VALUATION; P = $1 *(Continued)*

Periods = n	$\frac{1}{2}$%	1%	$1\frac{1}{2}$%	2%	3%	4%	5%	6%	7%	8%	10%	12%	15%	20%	25%
1	.99502	.99010	.98522	.98039	.97087	.96154	.95238	.94340	.93458	.92593	.90909	.89286	.86957	.83333	.80000
2	.99007	.98030	.97066	.96117	.94260	.92456	.90703	.89000	.87344	.85734	.82645	.79719	.75614	.69444	.64000
3	.98515	.97059	.95632	.94232	.91514	.88900	.86384	.83962	.81630	.79383	.75131	.71178	.65752	.57870	.51200
4	.98025	.96098	.94218	.92385	.88849	.85480	.82270	.79209	.76290	.73503	.68301	.63552	.57175	.48225	.40960
5	.97537	.95147	.92826	.90573	.86261	.82193	.78353	.74726	.71299	.68058	.62092	.56743	.49718	.40188	.32768
6	.97052	.94205	.91454	.88797	.83748	.79031	.74622	.70496	.66634	.63017	.56447	.50663	.43233	.33490	.26214
7	.96569	.93272	.90103	.87056	.81309	.75992	.71068	.66506	.62275	.58349	.51316	.45235	.37594	.27908	.20972
8	.96089	.92348	.88771	.85349	.78941	.73069	.67684	.62741	.58201	.54027	.46651	.40388	.32690	.23257	.16777
9	.95610	.91434	.87459	.83676	.76642	.70259	.64461	.59193	.54393	.50025	.42410	.36061	.28426	.19381	.13422
10	.95135	.90529	.86167	.82035	.74409	.67556	.61391	.55839	.50835	.46319	.38554	.32197	.24718	.16151	.10737
11	.94661	.89632	.84893	.80426	.72242	.64958	.58468	.52679	.47509	.42888	.35049	.28748	.21494	.13459	.08590
12	.94191	.88745	.83639	.78849	.70138	.62460	.55684	.49697	.44401	.39711	.31863	.25668	.18691	.11216	.06872
13	.93722	.87866	.82403	.77303	.68095	.60057	.53032	.46884	.41496	.36770	.28966	.22917	.16253	.09346	.05498
14	.93256	.86996	.81185	.75788	.66112	.57748	.50507	.44230	.38782	.34046	.26333	.20462	.14133	.07789	.04398
15	.92792	.86135	.79985	.74301	.64186	.55526	.48102	.41727	.36245	.31524	.23939	.18270	.12289	.06491	.03518
16	.92330	.85282	.78803	.72845	.62317	.53391	.45811	.39365	.33873	.29189	.21763	.16312	.10686	.05409	.02815
17	.91871	.84438	.77639	.71416	.60502	.51337	.43630	.37136	.31657	.27027	.19784	.14564	.09293	.04507	.02252
18	.91414	.83602	.76491	.70016	.58739	.49363	.41552	.35034	.29586	.25025	.17986	.13004	.08081	.03756	.01801
19	.90959	.82774	.75361	.68643	.57029	.47464	.39573	.33051	.27651	.23171	.16351	.11611	.07027	.03130	.01441
20	.90506	.81954	.74247	.67297	.55368	.45639	.37689	.31180	.25842	.21455	.14864	.10367	.06110	.02608	.01153

Table 2 Present Value of $1

$P = F_n (1 + r)^{-n}$

r = Discount Rate; n = Number of Periods Until Payment; F_n = $1

Periods = n	$\frac{1}{2}$%	1%	$1\frac{1}{2}$%	2%	3%	4%	5%	6%	7%	8%	10%	12%	15%	20%	25%
22	.89608	.80340	.72069	.64684	.52189	.42196	.34185	.27751	.22571	.18394	.12285	.08264	.04620	.01811	.00738
24	.88719	.78757	.69954	.62172	.49193	.39012	.31007	.24698	.19715	.15770	.10153	.06588	.03493	.01258	.00472
26	.87838	.77205	.67902	.59758	.46369	.36069	.28124	.21981	.17220	.13520	.08391	.05252	.02642	.00874	.00302
28	.86966	.75684	.65910	.57437	.43708	.33348	.25509	.19563	.15040	.11591	.06934	.04187	.01997	.00607	.00193
30	.86103	.74192	.63976	.55207	.41199	.30832	.23138	.17411	.13137	.09938	.05731	.03338	.01510	.00421	.00124
32	.85248	.72730	.62099	.53063	.38834	.28506	.20987	.15496	.11474	.08520	.04736	.02661	.01142	.00293	.00079
34	.84402	.71297	.60277	.51003	.36604	.26355	.19035	.13791	.10022	.07305	.03914	.02121	.00864	.00203	.00051
36	.83564	.69892	.58509	.49022	.34503	.24367	.17266	.12274	.08754	.06262	.03235	.01691	.00653	.00141	.00032
38	.82735	.68515	.56792	.47119	.32523	.22529	.15661	.10924	.07646	.05369	.02673	.01348	.00494	.00098	.00021
40	.81914	.67165	.55126	.45289	.30656	.20829	.14205	.09722	.06678	.04603	.02209	.01075	.00373	.00068	.00013
45	.79896	.63905	.51171	.41020	.26444	.17120	.11130	.07265	.04761	.03133	.01372	.00610	.00186	.00027	.00004
50	.77929	.60804	.47500	.37153	.22811	.14071	.08720	.05429	.03395	.02132	.00852	.00346	.00092	.00011	.00001
100	.60729	.36971	.22563	.13803	.05203	.01980	.00760	.00295	.00115	.00045	.00007	.00001	.00000	.00000	.00000

TABLE 2 PRESENT VALUE OF $1
$P = F_n (1 + r)^{-n}$
r = DISCOUNT RATE; n = NUMBER OF PERIODS UNTIL PAYMENT; F_n = $1 *(CONTINUED)*

No. of Payments $= n$	$\frac{1}{2}\%$	1%	$1\frac{1}{2}\%$	2%	3%	4%	5%	6%	7%	8%	10%	12%	15%	20%	25%
1	1.00000	1.00000	1.00000	1.00000	1.00000	1.00000	1.00000	1.00000	1.00000	1.00000	1.00000	1.00000	1.00000	1.00000	1.00000
2	2.00500	2.01000	2.01500	2.02000	2.03000	2.04000	2.05000	2.06000	2.07000	2.08000	2.10000	2.12000	2.15000	2.20000	2.25000
3	3.01503	3.03010	3.04523	3.06040	3.09090	3.12160	3.15250	3.18360	3.21490	3.24640	3.31000	3.37440	3.47250	3.64000	3.81250
4	4.03010	4.06040	4.09090	4.12161	4.18363	4.24646	4.31013	4.37462	4.43994	4.50611	4.64100	4.77933	4.99338	5.36800	5.76563
5	5.05025	5.10101	5.15227	5.20404	5.30914	5.41632	5.52563	5.63709	5.75074	5.86660	6.10510	6.35285	6.74238	7.44160	8.20703
6	6.07550	6.15202	6.22955	6.30812	6.46841	6.63298	6.80191	6.97532	7.15329	7.33593	7.71561	8.11519	8.75374	9.92992	11.25879
7	7.10588	7.21354	7.32299	7.43428	7.66246	7.89829	8.14201	8.39384	8.65402	8.92280	9.48717	10.08901	11.06680	12.91590	15.07349
8	8.14141	8.28567	8.43284	8.58297	8.89234	9.21423	9.54911	9.89747	10.25980	10.63663	11.43589	12.29969	13.72682	16.49908	19.84186
9	9.18212	9.36853	9.55933	9.75463	10.15911	10.58280	11.02656	11.49132	11.97799	12.48756	13.57948	14.77566	16.78584	20.79890	25.80232
10	10.22803	10.46221	10.70272	10.94972	11.46388	12.00611	12.57789	13.18079	13.81645	14.48656	15.93742	17.54874	20.30372	25.95868	33.25290
11	11.27917	11.56683	11.86326	12.16872	12.80780	13.48635	14.20679	14.97164	15.78360	16.64549	18.53117	20.65458	24.34928	32.15042	42.56613
12	12.33556	12.68250	13.04121	13.41209	14.19203	15.02581	15.91713	16.86994	17.88845	18.97713	21.38428	24.13313	29.00167	39.58050	54.20766
13	13.39724	13.80933	14.23683	14.68033	15.61779	16.62684	17.71298	18.88214	20.14064	21.49530	24.52271	28.02911	34.35192	48.49660	68.75958
14	14.46423	14.94742	15.45038	15.97394	17.08632	18.29191	19.59863	21.01507	22.55049	24.21492	27.97498	32.39260	40.50471	59.19592	86.94947
15	15.53655	16.09690	16.68214	17.29342	18.59891	20.02359	21.57856	23.27597	25.12902	27.15211	31.77248	37.27971	47.58041	72.03511	109.6868
16	16.61423	17.25786	17.93237	18.63929	20.15688	21.82453	23.65749	25.67253	27.88805	30.32428	35.94973	42.75328	55.71747	87.44213	138.1085
17	17.69730	18.43044	19.20136	20.01207	21.76159	23.69751	25.84037	28.21288	30.84022	33.75023	40.54470	48.88367	66.07509	105.9306	173.6357
18	18.78579	19.61475	20.48938	21.41231	23.41444	25.64541	28.13238	30.90565	33.99903	37.45024	45.59917	55.74971	75.83636	128.1167	218.0446
19	19.87972	20.81090	21.79672	22.84056	25.11687	27.67123	30.53900	33.75999	37.37896	41.44626	51.15909	63.43968	88.21181	154.7400	273.5558
20	20.97912	22.01900	23.12367	24.29737	26.87037	29.77808	33.06595	36.78559	40.99549	45.76196	57.27500	72.05244	102.44358	186.6880	342.9447

FUTURE VALUE OF ANNUITY OF $1 IN ARREARS

TABLE 3 $P_f = \frac{(1+r)^n - 1}{r}$

r = INTEREST RATE; n = NUMBER OF PAYMENTS

No. of Payments $= n$	$\frac{1}{2}\%$	1%	$1\frac{1}{2}\%$	2%	3%	4%	5%	6%	7%	8%	10%	12%	15%	20%	25%
22	23.19443	24.47159	25.83758	27.29898	30.53678	34.24797	38.50521	43.39229	49.00574	55.45676	71.40275	92.50258	137.63164	271.0307	538.1011
24	25.43196	26.97346	28.63352	30.42186	34.42647	39.08260	44.50200	50.81558	58.17667	66.76476	88.49733	118.15524	184.16784	392.4842	843.0329
26	27.69191	29.52563	31.51397	33.67091	38.55304	44.31174	51.11345	59.15638	68.67647	79.95442	109.18177	150.33393	245.71197	567.3773	1319.489
28	29.97452	32.12910	34.48148	37.05121	42.93092	49.96758	58.40258	68.52811	80.69769	95.33883	134.20994	190.69889	327.10408	819.2233	2063.952
30	32.28002	34.78489	37.53868	40.56808	47.57542	56.08494	66.43885	79.05819	94.46079	113.28321	164.49402	241.33268	434.74515	1181.881	3227.174
32	34.60862	37.49407	40.68829	44.22703	52.50276	62.70147	75.29883	90.88978	110.21815	134.21354	201.13777	304.84772	577.10046	1704.109	5044.710
34	36.96058	40.25770	43.93309	48.03380	57.73018	69.85791	85.06696	104.18375	128.25876	158.62667	245.47670	384.52098	765.36535	2456.118	7884.609
36	39.33610	43.07688	47.27597	51.99437	63.27594	77.59831	95.83632	119.12087	148.91346	187.10215	299.12681	484.46312	1014.34568	3539.009	12321.95
38	41.73545	45.95272	50.71989	56.11494	69.15945	85.97034	107.70955	135.90421	172.56102	220.31595	364.04343	609.83053	1343.62216	5098.373	19255.30
40	41.15885	48.88637	54.26789	60.40198	75.40126	95.02552	120.79977	154.76197	199.63511	259.05652	442.59256	767.09142	1779.09031	7343.858	30088.66
45	50.32416	58.48107	63.61420	71.89271	92.71986	121.0294	159.7002	212.7435	285.7493	386.5056	718.9048	1358.230	3585.12846	18281.31	91831.50
50	56.64516	64.46318	73.68283	84.57940	112.7969	152.6671	209.3480	290.3359	405.5289	573.7702	1163.909	2400.018	7217.71628	45497.19	280255.7
100	129.33370	170.4814	228.8030	312.2323	607.2877	1237.624	2610.025	5638.368	12381.66	27484.52	137796.1	696010.5	763×10^4	414×10^6	196×10^8

Note: To convert from this table to values of an annuity in advance, determine the annuity in arrears above for one more period and subtract 1.00000.

FUTURE VALUE OF ANNUITY OF $1 IN ARREARS

TABLE 3 $P_f = \frac{(1+r)^n - 1}{r}$

r = INTEREST RATE; n = NUMBER OF PAYMENTS *(CONTINUED)*

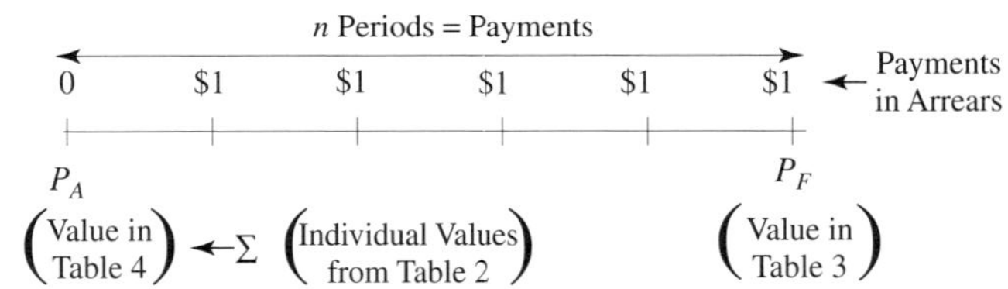

No. of Payments = n	$\frac{1}{2}\%$	1%	$1\frac{1}{2}\%$	2%	3%	4%	5%	6%	7%	8%	10%	12%	15%	20%	25%
1	.99502	.99010	.98522	.98039	.97087	.96154	.95238	.94340	.93458	.92593	.90909	.89286	.86957	.83333	.80000
2	1.98510	1.97040	1.95588	1.94156	1.91347	1.88609	1.85941	1.83339	1.80802	1.78326	1.73554	1.69005	1.62571	1.52778	1.44000
3	2.97025	2.94099	2.91220	2.88388	2.82861	2.77509	2.72325	2.67301	2.62432	2.57710	2.48685	2.40183	2.28323	2.10648	1.95200
4	3.95050	3.90197	3.85438	3.80773	3.71710	3.62990	3.54595	3.46511	3.38721	3.31213	3.16987	3.03735	2.85498	2.58873	2.36160
5	4.92587	4.85343	4.78264	4.71346	4.57971	4.45182	4.32948	4.21236	4.10020	3.99271	3.79079	3.60478	3.35216	2.99061	2.68928
6	5.89638	5.79548	5.69719	5.60143	5.41719	5.24214	5.07569	4.91732	4.76654	4.62288	4.35526	4.11141	3.78448	3.32551	2.95142
7	6.86207	6.72819	6.59821	6.47199	6.23028	6.00205	5.78637	5.58238	5.38929	5.20637	4.86842	4.56376	4.16042	3.60459	3.16114
8	7.82296	7.65168	7.48593	7.32548	7.01969	6.73274	6.46321	6.20979	5.97130	5.74664	5.33493	4.96764	4.48732	3.83716	3.32891
9	8.77906	8.56602	8.36052	8.16224	7.78611	7.43533	7.10782	6.80169	6.51523	6.24689	5.75902	5.32825	4.77158	4.03097	3.46313
10	9.73041	9.47130	9.22218	8.98259	8.53020	8.11090	7.72173	7.36009	7.02358	6.71008	6.14457	5.65022	5.01877	4.19247	3.57050

PRESENT VALUE OF ANNUITY OF $1 IN ARREARS

TABLE 4 $P_A = \frac{1-(1+r)^{-n}}{r} \times \$1.00$

r = DISCOUNT RATE; n = NUMBER OF PAYMENTS

No. of Payments $= n$	$\frac{1}{2}\%$	1%	$1\frac{1}{2}\%$	2%	3%	4%	5%	6%	7%	8%	10%	12%	15%	20%	25%
11	10.67703	10.36763	10.07112	9.78685	9.25262	8.76048	8.30641	7.88687	7.49867	7.13896	6.49506	5.93770	5.23371	4.32706	3.65640
12	11.61893	11.25508	10.90751	10.57534	9.95400	9.38507	8.86325	8.38384	7.94269	7.53608	6.81369	6.19437	5.42062	4.43922	3.72512
13	12.55615	12.13374	11.73153	11.34837	10.63496	9.98565	9.39357	8.85268	8.35765	7.90378	7.10336	6.42355	5.58315	4.53268	3.78010
14	13.48871	13.00370	12.54338	12.10625	11.29607	10.56312	9.89864	9.29498	8.74547	8.24424	7.36669	6.62817	5.72448	4.61057	3.82408
15	14.41662	13.86505	13.34323	12.84926	11.93794	11.11839	10.37966	9.71225	9.10791	8.55948	7.60608	6.81086	5.84737	4.67547	3.85925
16	15.33993	14.71787	14.13126	13.57771	12.56110	11.65230	10.83777	10.10590	9.44665	8.85137	7.82371	6.97399	5.95423	4.72956	3.88741
17	16.25863	15.56225	14.90765	14.29187	13.16612	12.16567	11.27407	10.47726	9.76322	9.12164	8.02155	7.11963	6.04716	4.77463	3.90993
18	17.17277	16.39827	15.67256	14.99203	13.75351	12.65930	11.68959	10.82760	10.05909	9.37189	8.20141	7.24967	6.12797	4.81219	3.92794
19	18.08236	17.22601	16.42617	15.67846	14.32380	13.13394	12.08532	11.15812	10.33560	9.60360	8.36492	7.36578	6.19823	4.84350	3.94235
20	18.98742	18.04555	17.16864	16.35143	14.87747	13.59033	12.46221	11.46992	10.59401	9.81815	8.51356	7.46944	6.25933	4.86958	3.95388
22	20.78406	19.66038	18.62082	17.65805	15.93692	14.45112	13.16300	12.04158	11.06124	10.20074	8.77154	7.64465	6.35866	4.90943	3.97049
24	22.56287	21.24339	20.03041	18.91393	16.93554	15.24696	13.79864	12.55036	11.46933	10.52876	8.98474	7.78432	6.43377	4.93710	3.98111
26	24.32402	22.79520	21.39863	20.12104	17.87684	15.98277	14.37519	13.00317	11.82578	10.80998	9.16095	7.89566	6.49056	4.95632	3.98791
28	26.06769	24.31644	22.72672	21.28127	18.76411	16.66306	14.89813	13.40616	12.13711	11.05108	9.30657	7.98442	6.53351	4.96967	3.99226
30	27.79405	25.80771	24.01584	22.39646	19.60044	17.29203	15.37245	13.76483	12.40904	11.25778	9.42691	8.05518	6.56598	4.97894	3.99505

PRESENT VALUE OF ANNUITY OF $1 IN ARREARS

TABLE 4 $P_A = \frac{1-(1+r)^{-n}}{r} \times \$1.00$

r = DISCOUNT RATE; n = NUMBER OF PAYMENTS *(CONTINUED)*

No. of Payments $= n$	$\frac{1}{2}\%$	1%	$1\frac{1}{2}\%$	2%	3%	4%	5%	6%	7%	8%	10%	12%	15%	20%	25%
32	29.50328	27.26959	25.26714	23.46833	20.38877	17.87355	15.80268	14.08404	12.64656	11.43500	9.52638	8.11159	6.59053	4.98537	3.99683
34	31.19555	28.70267	26.48173	24.49859	21.13184	18.41120	16.19290	14.36814	12.85401	11.58693	9.60857	8.15656	6.60910	4.98984	3.99797
36	32.87102	30.10751	27.66068	25.48884	21.83225	18.90828	16.54685	14.62099	13.03521	11.71719	9.67651	8.19241	6.62314	4.99295	3.99870
38	34.52985	31.48466	28.80505	26.44064	22.49246	19.36786	16.86789	14.84602	13.19347	11.82887	9.73265	8.22099	6.63375	4.99510	3.99917
40	36.17223	32.83469	29.91585	27.35548	23.11477	19.79277	17.15909	15.04630	13.33171	11.92461	9.77905	8.24378	6.64178	4.99660	3.99947
45	40.20720	36.09451	32.55234	29.49016	24.51871	20.72004	17.77407	15.45583	13.60552	12.10840	9.86281	8.28252	6.65429	4.99863	3.99983
50	44.14279	39.19612	34.99969	31.42361	25.72976	21.48218	18.25593	15.76186	13.80075	12.23348	9.91481	8.30450	6.66051	4.99945	3.99994
100	78.54264	63.02888	51.62470	43.09835	31.59891	24.50500	19.84791	16.61755	14.26925	12.49432	9.99927	8.33323	6.66666	5.00000	4.00000

Note: To convert from this table to values of an annuity in advance, determine the annuity in arrears above for one fewer period and add 1.00000.

PRESENT VALUE OF ANNUITY OF $1 IN ARREARS

TABLE 4 $P_A = \frac{1-(1+r)^{-n}}{r} \times \$1.00$

r = DISCOUNT RATE; n = NUMBER OF PAYMENTS *(CONTINUED)*

INDEX

A
Abacus, 1
Abatement, 1
Ability to bear method, 474
Abnormal spoilage, 1
Aboriginal cost, 1
Absolute performance standards, 653–654
Absolute profitability, 582
Absorbed overhead, 2
Accelerated cost recovery system (ACRS), 2
Accelerated depreciation, 2
Acceptance, 2
Account, 2
Accounts payable, 4, 527
Accounts receivable, 4, 8, 9, 13, 521, 524
Accounts receivable turnover, 4
Accountability center, 2
Account analysis method, 2, 361–362
Accountancy, 2
Accountant's comments, 2
Accountant's opinion, 2
Accountant's report, 2
Account classification method, 493–494
Account form, 2
Accounting, 2
Accounting adjustments, 2–3
Accounting and Tax Index, 3, 732
Accounting changes, 3, 193, 240
Accounting conventions, 3
Accounting cycle, 3
Accounting deficiency, 3
Accounting equation, 3
Accounting errors, 3
Accounting event, 3
Accounting games, 544
Accounting Horizons, 3
Accounting methods, 3
Accounting period, 3
Accounting policies, 3
Accounting principles, 3–4, 191–192
Accounting Principles Board of AICPA (APB), 11
Accounting procedures, 4
Accounting rate of return, 4, 600
Accounting Research Bulletin (ARB), 4, 745
Accounting Research Study (ARS), 4
Accounting Review, 4
Accounting standards, 4
Accounting Standards Executive Committee (AcSEC), 4
Accounting system, 4
Accounting Terminology Bulletin (ATB), 4
Accounting Trends and Techniques, 4
Accretion, 4
Accrual, 4
Accrual basis of accounting, 5
Accrued, 5
Accrued depreciation, 5
Accrued expenses, 527, 528
Accrued payables, 5
Accrued receivables, 5
Accrued taxes, 527, 528
Accumulated benefit obligation, 5
Accumulated depreciation, 5
Accumulated other comprehensive income, 5
Accumulated other comprehensive loss, 529
Accurate presentation, 5
Achievability principle, 272–273
Acid test ratio, 5
Acquisition cost, 5
Activities costs, 232, 346–347
Activity accounting, 5
Activity analysis, 315
Activity-based budgets (ABB), 564–565
Activity-based costing (ABC), 5, 217–233
  adding value with, 232–233
  assigning costs to products, 226
  choosing cost drivers, 224
  computing cost rate per cost driver, 224–225
  cost allocation methods, 219
  cost-benefit decision, 221
  cost drivers/cost hierarchies, 494–495
  cost flows through accounts, 229, 230
  department allocation, 221
  environmental issues in, 375–376
  identifying activities, 222–224
  illustration of, 226–229
  implementation of, 240
  in marketing and administration, 231–232
  in nonprofits, 703
  overhead allocation, 229, 231
  plant-wide allocation, 219–220
  standard cost systems vs., 449, 452–454
  steps in, 222
  strategic use of, 233

Activity-based costing (ABC) *(continued)*
and transfer pricing, 691
variance analysis in, 449, 452–454
Activity-based depreciation, 6
Activity-based forecasting, 506
Activity-based management (ABM), 6, 233–240
cost driver estimation for, 360
cost hierarchies in, 236–237
of customer response time, 235–236
implementation of, 240
nonfinancial data in, 666–667
reporting of unused resources, 238–240
resources used vs. supplied, 237–238
and value chain, 233–235
Activity basis, 6
Activity centers, 6, 224, 225
Activity variance, 6
Actual cost (basis), 6, 692
Actuarial, 6
Actuarial accrued liability, 6
Adding value:
with activity-based costing, 232–233
and functionality-price-quality tradoffs, 304
Additional paid-in capital, 6
Additional processing cost, 6
Additivity (in financial statements), 505
Adelphia Communications Corporation, 786
Adequate disclosure, 6
Adjunct account, 6
Adjusted acquisition (historical) cost, 6
Adjusted bank balance of cash, 6
Adjusted basis, 6
Adjusted book balance of cash, 6–7
Adjusted R-square, 359–360
Adjusted trial balance, 7
Adjusting entry, 7
Adjustments:
accounting, 2–3, 7
EVA, 675–677
for inflation, 169
Administration, activity-based costing in, 231–232
Administrative costs (expenses), 7
Admission of partner, 7
Ad valorem, 6
Advances:
to affiliates, 7
from (by) customers, 7
to suppliers, 7
Adverse opinion, 7
Affiliated company, 7
After closing, 7
After cost, 7
Agency cost, 7–8
Agency fund, 8
Agency problems, 698
Agency theory, 8
Agent, 8
Aging accounts receivable, 8
Aging schedule, 8
Alderson, Wroe, 743
Alford, L. P., 738
All-capital earnings rate, 8
All-current method, 8
Allegheny Health Education and Research Foundation, 781–782
All-inclusive (income) concept, 8
Allocate, 8
Allocated costs, 723
Allocation(s):
of income taxes, 8
of revenue, 476–478
sterilized, 475
Allocation base, 8
Allowable cost, 252, 254, 256, 269–270
Allowance, 8
for bad debts, 781
capital consumption, 22
for funds used during construction, 8–9
for uncollectibles (accounts receivable), 9, 781
Allowance method, 9–10
Alternative accounting, 187–195
comparison of cash flows, 191
depreciation, 188–189
income statements/income tax calculation, 189–191
inventory cost flow assumption, 188
managing earnings, 191–195
officers' bonuses, 189
American Accounting Association (AAA), 10
American Institute of Certified Public Accountants (AICPA), 8, 732
American Stock Exchange (AMEX) (ASE), 10
America Online Inc., 776
Amortization, 10
Amortization expense, 534
Amortized cost, 10
Annual budgets, 565–566
Annual percentage rate (APR), 632
Annual report, 10
Annuitant, 10
Annuities, 11, 632–640
Annuities due, 11, 632
Annuities in advance, 11, 632
Annuities in arrears (ordinary), 11, 102, 633–640
Annuity method of depreciation, 11
Antidilutive, 11

APB Opinion (APBs), 11, 769
APB Statement, 11
Applied cost, 11
Applied overhead, 11, 404
Appraisal, 11
Appraisal costs, 11
Appraisal expenditures, 314
Appraisal method of depreciation, 11
Appreciation, 11
Appropriation, 11
Appropriation account, 11, 711
Approximate net realizable value method, 11
Arbitrage, 12
Arbitrary, 12
Arm's length, 12
Arrears, 12
Arthur Andersen LLP, 780
Articles of incorporation, 12
Articulate/articulation, 12, 505, 509
As-if cost, 257–258
Assess, 12
Assessed valuation, 12
Assets, 12
  capital, 22
  misrepresenting, 778–783
  projecting, 519, 521–527
  shortcuts to forecasting, 536
  timing acquisition/disposition of, 192
Asset depreciation range (ADR), 12–13
Asset management, 678
Asset recognition, 777–778
Asset securitization, 13
Asset turnover, 13
Assignment of accounts receivable, 13
At par, 13
Attachment, 13
Attest, 13
Attestor, 13
Attribute measured, 13
Attribute(s) sampling, 13
Audit, 13
Audit committee, 13
Auditing Research Monograph, 14
Auditing standards, 14
Auditing Standards Board, 14
Auditors, 14, 791–792
Auditor's opinion, 14
Auditor's report, 14
Audit program, 13
Audit trail, 14
AudSEC, 14
Authoritative budgeting, 547
Authorized capital stock, 14
Available for sale, securities, 14
Available (term), 710–711
Average, 14
Average cost, 167–169
Average-cost flow assumption, 14
Average tax rate, 14
Average total cost (ATC), 167–168
Avis, 775
Avoidable cost, 14, 186

B

Babbage, Charles, 735–736
Backflush costing, 15, 394–396
Backlog, 15
Backlog depreciation, 15
Bad debt, 15
Bad debt expense, 15
Bad debt recovery, 15–16
Bad debt reserves, 781
Bailout period, 16, 599, 600
Balance, 16
Balanced scorecard, 16, 659–664
  building incentive plan around, 661–663
  implementation of, 663–664
  in nonprofits, 704
  perspectives in, 659–660
Balance sheet, 16
  balancing, 531–532
  projecting assets on, 519, 521–527
  shortcuts to forecasting, 536
Balance sheet account, 16
Balloon, 16
Bank balance, 16
Bank reconciliation schedule, 16
Bankrupt, 16
Bank statement, 16
Barony supplier networks, 292
Base stock method, 16–17
Basic accounting equation, 17
Basic accounting model, 391
Basic cost drivers (BCDs), 452
Basic cost-flow equation, 17
Basic earnings per share (BEPS), 17
Basic standards, 426
Basis, 17
Basis point, 17
Basket purchase, 17
Batch costs, 363
Batch-level activities, 17, 494
Batch-related costs, 236
Bear, 17
Bearer bond, 17
Beginning inventory, 17
Behavioral congruence, 17, 646
Benchmarking, 17, 664
  ex post, 547
  in nonprofits, 699, 703–704
  in spoilage, waste, and scrap accounting, 377

Benefits received methods, 473–474
Betterment, 17
Bias, 763
Bid, 17
Biddle, Gary, 676, 681
Big 4, 17
Big bath, 17, 762, 778, 781
Big N, 17–18
Bill, 18
Bill-and-hold sales, 772
Bill of materials, 18
Blocked currency, 18
Board of directors, 18
Bond, 18, 617
Bond conversion, 18
Bond discount, 18
Bond indenture, 18
Bond premium, 18
Bond ratings, 18
Bond redemption, 18
Bond refunding, 18
Bond sinking fund, 18
Bond table, 18
Bonuses, 18, 189, 194
  budget-based, 561–563, 568
  and manipulation of earnings, 767
Bonus method, 18–19
Book, 19
Book cost, 19
Book inventory, 19
Bookkeeping, 19
Book of original entry, 19
Book value, 19
Book value per share of common stock, 19
Boot, 19
Borrow-purchase, 604, 607–608
Bottleneck, 19, 576–580
Bottom-up approach:
  in budget negotiation, 549
  in cost reduction planning, 276
Boulton, Matthew Robinson, 735
Boulton & Watt, 735
Bowen, Robert, 676, 681
BP, 410
Branch, 19
Branch accounting, 19
Brandeis, Louis D., 737
Breach of contract, 726–729
Breakeven analysis, 19
Breakeven charts, 19–20, 487, 489
Breakeven point, 20
Break-even time, 20
Brimson, James A., 619
Bristol-Myers Squibb, 713
Budget, 20
Budgetary accounts, 20
Budgetary control, 20
Budget-based incentives, 561–563
Budget-based performance measurement, 556–561
Budgeted cost, 20
Budget goals, 551–554
Budgeting:
  flexible budget preparation, 435
  multiple uses of, 545–547
  negotiation in, 548–551
  participation in, 547–548
  process of, 542–543
Budget job costs, 397
Budget statements, 20
Bull, 20
Bundled lease allocations, 477–478
Bunnell, Sterling, 736
Burden, 180
Burn rate, 20
Business combination, 20–21
Business entity, 21
Business-level strategies, 659
Business process reengineering, 579
Buyer-supplier interfaces:
  improvements in, 292–300
  interorganizational kaizen costing, 309–311
Bylaws, 21
Byproducts, 21, 467, 475–476

C

Call, 21
Callable bond, 21
Called-up share capital, 21
Camman, Eric A., 740
Canadian Institute of Chartered Accountants, 21
Capacity, 21, 437, 483–484
Capacity costs, 21, 162, 182, 236, 240
Capacity variance, 21
Capital, 21–22
Capital acquisition planning, 612–614
Capital asset, 22
Capital budget and budgeting, 22, 587–609, 611–626
  accounting rate of return, 600
  bailout period, 590, 599
  and capital rationing, 601–602
  case studies for, 588–591
  cost of capital, 591–592
  discounted bailout period, 590, 599
  discounted payback period, 599
  excess present value index, 595
  income tax considerations, 593–594

internal rate of return, 595–598
investment management as holistic approach for, 619–625
and investment vs. financing decisions, 588, 602–608
net present value, 592–593
payback period, 598–599
pitfalls of, 612 619
and ranking of projects, 602
sensitivity of profits to estimates, 592–593
with uncertain future cash flows, 608–609
Capital carrying charges, 173
Capital consumption allowance, 22
Capital contributed in excess of par (or stated) value, 22
Capital expenditure (outlay), 22
Capital gain, 22
Capitalization:
of a corporation, 22
of earnings, 23
Capitalization rate, 23
Capitalize, 23
Capital lease, 22
Capital loss, 22
Capital markets, efficiency of, 193–194
Capital rationing, 22, 601–602
Capital stock, 22
Capital structure, 22
Capital surplus, 22
Capitation, 706
Caplan, Edwin H., 745–746
The Carron Company, 734
Carryback/carryforward/carryover, 23
Carrying cost, 23, 347–348
Carrying value (amount), 23
Cash, 23, 521
Cash basis of accounting, 23
Cash budget, 23
Cash change equation, 23
Cash collection basis, 23
Cash cycle, 23
Cash disbursements journal, 23
Cash discount, 23
Cash equivalent, 23–24
Cash equivalent value, 24
Cash flow(s), 24
comparison of, 191
income flows vs., 588–590
increasing NPV of, 669–670
from operations, 24
statement of, 137, 534–536
uncertain future, 608–609
Cash flow hedge, 24
Cashier's check, 24
Cash provided by operations, 24
Cash receipts journal, 24
Cash (surrender) value of life insurance, 24
Catch-up depreciation, 24
Caterpillar, 789–790
Cause-and-effect analysis, 24, 469
C corporation, 21
Cendant Corporation, 760, 770–771, 782, 783
Centers for Medicare & Medicaid Services (CMMS), 709
Central corporate expenses, 24–25
Central processing unit (CPU), 25
Certificate, 25
Certificate of deposit, 25
Certified check, 25
Certified financial statement, 25
Certified General Accountant (CGA), 25
Certified Internal Auditor (CIA), 26
Certified Management Accountant (CMA) certificate, 27
Certified public accountant (CPA), 25
Chain discount, 25
Chained target costing, 300–303
Change fund, 25
Channel stuffing, 25–26, 772–773
Charge, 26
Charge off, 26
Charitable solicitation act, 701
Charter, 26
Chartered accountants (CAs), 26
Chartered Financial Analyst (CFA), 26
Chartered Institute of Management Accountants (CIMA), 738, 739
Chart of accounts, 26
Chatfield, Michael, 732
Check, 26
Check register, 26
Chrysler, 233
Church, Alexander Hamilton, 736–738, 744–745
Circulating capital, 26
Clark, J. M., 176, 742–743
Clean surplus concept, 27, 674
Clearing account, 27
Clinton, Bill, 712
Close, 27
Closed account, 27
Closing entries, 27
Coase, Ronald, 575
Co-determined variables, 533–534
Coding of accounts, 27, 178–179
Coinsurance, 27
Collaborative forecasts, 297
Collateral, 27
Collectible, 27
Collusion, 27
Comfort letter, 27
Commercial paper, 27

Commission, 27
Committed costs, 27, 182, 244
Committee on Accounting Procedure (CAP), 27
Common costs, 27–28, 169–170, 466, 468–469
Common-dollar accounting, 28
Common monetary measuring unit, 28
Common shares, 28
Common-size statement, 28, 536
Common stock, 528–529, 535
Common-stock equivalent, 28
Comparative (financial) statements, 28
Compensating balance, 28
Compensation:
 budget-based, 561–563
 and manipulation of earnings, 767
 in nonprofits, 699–700
Competition (in budgeting process), 567–568
Competitive position:
 and allowable cost, 252
 and functionality-price-quality tradoffs, 304
Complementarity, 568–569
Completed contract method, 28
Complexity, cost as function of, 223
Compliance audit, 28
Compliance procedure, 28
Component-level target costing, 259–266
 for components, 265–266
 for major functions, 261–265
 supplier selection/rewards in, 260–261
Component-specific kaizen costing, 272, 286–287
Composite depreciation, 28
Composite life method, 28
Compound entry, 28
Compounding period, 29, 630–632
Compound interest, 29, 627–644
 with annuities, 632–640
 changing compounding period, 630–632
 continuous compounding, 32
 and future value, 628–630
 and implicit interest rate, 642–644
 with perpetuities, 640–642
 power of, 628
Compound interest depreciation, 29
Comprehensive budget, 29
Comprehensive Environmental Response, Compensation, and Liability Act (CERCLA), 369
Comprehensive income, 29–30
Comptroller, 30
Computer-intensive cost modeling, 365–366
Conceptual framework, 30
Concurrent cost management (CCM), 307–309
Confidence level, 30
Confirmation, 30–31
Conformance costs, 387
Conglomerate, 31
Conservatism, 31, 763
Consistency, 31
Consol, 31, 632
Consolidated financial statements, 31
Constant dollar, 31
Constant-dollar accounting, 31
Constant-dollar date, 31
Constant gross margin percentage method, 473
Constant returns to scale, 168
Constrained share company, 31
Constructive liability, 31
Constructive receipt, 31–32
Consumer Price Index (CPI), 32
Contagion effect, 556
Contingency, 32
Contingency budgets, 565–568
Contingent annuity, 32
Contingent issue (securities), 32
Contingent liabilities, 32, 787
Contingent obligations, 784
Continuing appropriation, 32
Continuity of operations, 32
Continuous budget, 32
Continuous compounding, 32
Continuous flow processing, 32, 390
Continuous improvement, 32, 664
Continuous inventory method, 32
Continuously Contemporary Accounting (CoCoA), 32
Contra account, 32
Contract costing, 172
Contributed capital, 32–33
Contributed surplus, 33
Contribution approach, 33
Contribution margin, 33, 171, 488, 498–499, 575
Contribution margin ratio, 33
Contribution per unit, 33
Contributory, 33
Control charts, 33, 459–460
Control (controlling) account, 33
Controllability principle, 273
Controllable costs, 33, 184–185
Controllable performance measures, 557
Controlled company, 33
Controller, 33
Control limits, 459
Control systems, 33
 charts and graphs in, 489
 for spoilage, waste, and scrap, 376–384

Conversion, 33
Conversion audit, 33
Conversion cost, 33, 181
Conversion period, 34
Convertible bond, 34
Convertible preferred stock, 34
Cookie-jar accounting, 34, 762–763, 781
Cooperatives, 34, 700
Cooperative advertising, 345
Coproduct, 34
Copyright, 34
Core deposit intangible, 34–35
Corner, 35
Corporate-level cost-reduction objectives, 274–276
Corporation, 35
Correcting entry, 35
Cost(s), 35, 175–186
  classifications of, 177–179
  controllable, 184–185
  cost-volume classification, 182–183
  for decision making, 185–186
  definitions of, 176–177
  direct, 184–185
  expenses vs., 352
  expense vs., 180–181
  interorganizational cost investigations, 305–307
  linear functions for, 486–487
  litigation concepts of, 721–730
  object of expenditures, classification by, 179–182
  purpose and concepts of, 176
  and responsibility accounting, 184
  uncontrollable, 184
  variable, 184
Cost, insurance, and freight (CIF), 26
Cost accounting, 35
  environmental (green), 368, 383–387
Cost Accounting Standards Board (CASB), 23, 712
Cost accumulation, 35
Cost-activity relationship, 357–358
Cost allocation, 35, 219–221, 466–476
  byproducts, 475–476
  choosing method for, 469
  cost-benefit decision in, 221
  definitions related to, 59–460
  department, 220, 221
  fundamental problems in, 467–468
  incremental-cost method, 468
  joint, 469–475
  plant-wide, 219–221
  reciprocal method, 481–482
  Shapley Value method, 468–469
  stand-alone method, 468
  step-down method, 479–481
Cost assignment, 170, 466
Cost-based transfer price, 35
Cost basis policy, 690–691
Cost behavior, 35, 615–616
Cost-benefit criterion, 35
Cost-benefit test/analysis:
  for assessing significance of variances, 457–459
  for budgeting, 543–547
  in cost allocation, 221
  for managerial information, 423
  with multiple cost drivers, 354
  in product-specific kaizen costing, 284
  for quality improvement, 313–314, 320–322
Cost centers, 35, 648–649
Cost drivers, 35, 224
  in activity-based costing, 494–495
  analysis of, 321, 323
  basic, 452
  computing cost rate per, 224–225
  identifying, 623
  multiple, cost estimation for, 354–356
  regression analysis of, 357–361
  secondary, 452
  single, cost estimation for, 353–354
  understanding of, 619
Cost driver rate, 35
Cost-effective, 35
Cost estimation, 35, 170, 351–366
  account analysis method, 361–362
  account classification method, 493–494
  computer-intensive cost modeling, 365–366
  data problems in, 362
  engineering method, 362–363
  for jobs, 397
  primary purpose of, 352–353
  and queuing theory, 363–365
  with several cost drivers, 354–356
  statistical method, 357–361
  using analysis, 357–361
  for variable cost with single cost driver, 353–354
Cost flow(s), 35
  basic model for, 391–393
  in job costing, 406–410
  in operation costing, 420–422
  through accounts, 229, 230
Cost flow assumption, 35
Cost-flow equation, 35
Cost hierarchies, 35, 236–237, 494–495, 716–717
Costing, 41

Cost management:
  concurrent, 307–309
  cost estimations in, 353
  interorganizational, 289–312
  and investment management, 625
Cost method:
  for investments, 35–36
  for treasury stock, 36
Cost object(ive), 36, 177, 178
Cost of capital, 36, 591–592, 617
Cost of goods manufactured, 36
Cost of goods purchased, 36
Cost of goods sold, 36, 394–396, 405
Cost-of-living adjustment (COLA), 27
Cost of Quality (COQ), 387
Cost of sales, 36, 518, 519
Cost percentage, 36
Cost-plus transfer pricing, 36, 692
Cost pools, 36, 219, 225
Cost principle, 36
Cost-recovery-first method, 36–37
Cost-reduction objectives:
  in kaizen costing, 273–278
  for major functions, 263–265
  strategic, 255, 269–270
  target, 254–256, 269–270
Cost savings, 167
Cost sheet, 37
Cost structure, 37
Cost systems, 389–423
  backflush costing, 394–396
  cost flow model, 391–393
  designing, 422–423
  job costing, 389–390, 396–410
  just-in-time, 393–394
  operation costing, 420–422
  process costing, 390, 410–420
  scrap and waste in, 374
  weighted average, 372, 414–415
Cost terminology, 37–41
Cost-to-cost, 41
Cost variance analysis, 428
Cost-volume-profit (CVP) analysis, 41, 483–501
  breakeven chart, 487
  and cost drivers/cost hierarchies in ABC, 494–495
  decision situations, 495–497
  effects of proposed changes, 488–490
  ex post use of charts/graphs, 489
  linear functions for revenues and costs, 486–487
  linear programming extensions of, 497–500
  for multiproduct firms, 489, 491–494
  profit-volume analyses, 487–488
  short-run economic model, 484–485
  short-run multiproduct models, 497–500
  and uncertainty, 500–501
Cost-volume-profit graph (chart), 41
Cost-volume relation, 183
Counterparty, 41
Coupon, 41
Coupon rate, 41
Covenant, 41, 766
Creative accounting, 41
Credit bureau, 42
Credit (Cr.), 41–42
Credit loss, 42
Credit memorandum, 42
Creditor, 42
Critical accounting judgments, 42
Critical Path, Inc., 777
Critical path method (CPM), 42
Critical success factors (CSFs), 42, 624, 659
Cross-reference (index), 42
Cross-section analysis, 42
Crown corporation, 42
CUC International, Inc., 770–771, 782–783
Cum div (dividend), 42
Cum rights, 42
Cumulative dividend, 42
Cumulative preferred shares, 42
Current assets, 42–43, 525, 534
Current cost, 43, 169, 173, 254, 258
Current cost accounting, 43
Current cost/nominal-dollar accounting, 43
Current exchange rate, 43
Current exit value, 43
Current funds, 43
Current liabilities, 43, 534
Currently attainable standard cost, 43
Current operating performance concept, 43
Current period cost, 418
Current purchasing power (CPP), 41
Current ratio, 43
Current realizable cost, 43
Current selling price, 43
Current service costs, 43
Current value accounting, 43
Current yield, 43
Curvilinear (variable) cost, 43
Customer costs, 363
Customer-level activities, 43, 494
Customer-level costs, 236
Customer loyalty, 249
Customer profitability analysis, 341, 342, 662–663
Customer response time, 44, 235–236
Customer retention, 662
Customer satisfaction, 662, 665
Customers' ledger, 44
Cutoff rate, 44, 595

D

Damages (litigation), 726–730
Data bank, 44
Database, 44
Database management system, 44
Data integrity, 362
Davidson, Signey, 176
Days of grace, 44
Debenture bond, 44
Debit and credit conventions, 44
Debit (Dr.), 44, 176
Debit memorandum, 45
Debt, 45
Debt capital, 45, 535
Debt covenants, 766
Debt-equity ratio, 45
Debt financing, 45, 766
Debtor, 45
Debt ratio, 45
Debt service fund, 45
Debt service payments, 45, 637
Debt service requirement, 45
Decentralized decision making, 45
Decentralized organizations, 566–567, 645–655
  advantages/disadvantages of, 647–648
  goal congruence in, 646–647
  performance evaluation in, 653–654
  performance measurement in, 646–647, 650–653
  reasons for, 647
  responsibility centers in, 648–650
Decision analysis, 623–624
Decision making:
  cost-benefit, 221
  cost driver estimation for, 360
  cost estimations in, 353
  costs for, 185
  cost-volume-profit analysis in, 495–497
  evaluating investment projects, 593
  for investigating cost variances, 457
  payoff table/matrix for, 461–463
Decision theory:
  and significance of variances, 461–463
Declaration date, 45
Declining-balance depreciation, 45
Decomposition, 266
Deep discount bonds, 45
Deere & Company, 223, 224, 235, 691
Defalcation, 45
Default, 45
Defeasance, 45–46
Defect costing, 317
Defensive interval, 46
Deferral, 46
Deferral method, 46
Deferred annuity, 46, 632
Deferred asset, 46
Deferred charge, 46
Deferred cost, 46
Deferred credit, 46
Deferred debit, 46
Deferred expense, 46
Deferred gross margin, 46
Deferred income, 46
Deferred income tax (liability), 46–47, 527–528
Deferred revenue, 47, 527, 528
Deferred tax, 47
Deficit, 47
Defined-benefit plan, 47
Defined-contribution plan, 47
Deflation, 47
Delivery, total cost of, 332, 336–338
Delivery performance, 665
Deloitte & Touche, 17, 390
Delphi technique, 47
Delta Airline, 775
Demand deposit, 47
Demand loan, 47
Demski, Joel, 454, 468
Denial of opinion, 47
Denominator volume, 47
Department(al) allocation, 47, 220, 221, 226–227, 229
Dependent variables, 47, 357
Depletion, 47
Depletion allowance, 47
Deposits:
  by customers, 48
  to sinking fund, 47
  in transit, 48
Deposit intangible, 47
Deposit method (of revenue recognition), 47–48
Depreciable cost, 48
Depreciable life, 48
Depreciation, 48, 188–189
  as cost vs. expense, 180–181
  income tax considerations with, 593–594
  on statement of cash flows, 534
Depreciation reserve, 48
Depth-of-processing decisions, 467
Derivative (financial instrument), 48
Descartes' rule of signs, 48–49
Design for manufacture and assembly (DF-MA), 256, 257
Detective controls, 49
Determine, 49
Development stage enterprise, 49
Differentiable cost, 49–50
Differential, 50

Differential analysis, 50
Differential cost, 166, 185
Dilution, 50
Dilutive, 50
Diminishing returns to scale, 168
Direct access, 50
Direct costs, 50, 184–185
 kaizen costing for, 271–280
 in relation profitability analysis, 345
 standard, 428, 429
 in Total Cost Assessment, 385, 386
Direct costing, 50, 436, 744–745
Direct-financing (capital) lease, 50
Direct labor cost, 50, 180, 229, 279–280
Direct labor variance, 50, 434
Direct material cost, 50, 179–180
Direct method, 50
Direct posting, 50
Direct write-off method, 50
Disbursement, 50
DISC (domestic international sales corporation), 50
Disclaimer of opinion, 50
Disclosure, 6, 50, 787–791
Discontinued operations, 50
Discount, 50
Discounted bailout period, 51, 599, 600
Discounted cash flow (DCF), 51
Discounted payback period, 51, 599
Discount factor, 51
Discount rate, 51, 591, 592
Discounts lapsed (lost), 51
Discovery sampling, 51
Discretionary costs, 51, 162, 182
Discretionary cost centers, 649, 650–651
Discussion Memorandum, 51
Dishonored note, 51
Disintermediation, 51
Distributable income, 52
Distributable surplus, 52
Distributed processing, 52
Distributions:
 on control charts, 459–460
 in-control/out-of-control, 457–458
Distribution channels, 343–344
Distribution costs, 743–744
Distribution expense, 52
Dividends, 52, 535, 767
Dividends in arrears, 52
Dividend yield, 52
Division, 52
Division return on investment (ROI), 52
Dollar sign rules, 52
Dollar-value LIFO method, 52
Domestic international sales corporation (DISC), 50
Donated capital, 52
Double declining-balance depreciation (DDB), 52–53, 593
Double entry, 53, 735, 778
Double taxation, 53
Doubtful accounts, 53
Dow Chemical Company, 383, 410, 713
Draft, 53
Drawings, 53
Drawing account, 53
Drifting cost, 258
Driver, cost driver, 53
Drop ship(ment), 53
Drum-buffer-rope, 580
Dry-hole accounting, 53
Duality, 54
Dual-transactions assumption (fiction), 53
Dual transfer prices, 53–54, 692
Dumping, 54
Dynegy, Incorporated, 786

E

e, 54
Earned surplus, 54
Earnings, 54
 EVA adjustments to, 675–677
 managing, 191–195
Earnings per share (EPS), 54
Earnings statement, 54
Earn-out, 54
Easement, 54
EBITDA (earnings before interest, taxes, depreciation, and amortization), 54–55
EBIT (earnings before interest and taxes), 54
Economic concepts of cost, 157–174
 applications, 170–173
 capacity costs, 162
 common cost, 169–170
 current cost, 169, 173
 fixed cost, 161–162, 170
 incremental cost, 166–167, 171
 joint cost, 170
 long-run average cost, 167–169, 172–173
 marginal contribution, 164–166, 171–172
 measurement concepts, 159–169
 negative increments, 167
 opportunity cost, 167
 present value, 169, 173
 programmed costs, 162
 short run and long run, 159–160
 short-run marginal cost, 162–164, 171
 situational concepts, 169–170
 sunk cost, 167
 variable cost, 160–161, 170
Economic consequences, 55
Economic depreciation, 55

Economic entity, 55
Economic life, 55
Economic order quantity (EOQ), 55
Economics, management accounting and, 158–159
Economic transfer pricing rule, 55
Economic value added (EVA®), 55, 669–681
  adjustments to traditional earnings measures, 675–677
  concept of, 670
  implementation issues with, 679–680
  managerial incentives, 678–679
  proprietary vs. entity, 670
  residual income and shareholder wealth, 673–675
  residual income calculation, 670–673
  and shareholder returns, 676–678
  and subsequent firm performance, 679
Economies of scale, 723, 728
EDGAR, 55
Effective interest method, 55
Effective interest rate, 55–56, 630–631
Efficiency measures, 580–582
Efficiency variance, 56
Efficient capital market, 56
Efficient market hypothesis, 56
ElectroCatheter, 772
Electronic commerce (EC), 293–297
Electronic data interchange (EDI), 294, 296
Electronic data processing (EDP), 56
Eligible, 56
Eliminations, 56
Emerging Issues Task Force (EITF), 56, 769
Emerson, Harrington, 740
Enabling costs, 56, 162
Encumbrance, 56, 711
Ending inventory, 56
Endorsement, 56
Endorser, 57
Engineered cost center, 57
Engineering-driven cost-reduction approach, 274–276
Engineering method (cost estimation), 57, 362–363
Enron Corporation, 670, 765, 780, 787
Enterprise, 57
Enterprise fund, 57
Enterprise resource planning (ERP), 623
Entity, 57
Entity theory, 57
Entity view, 670
Entry value, 57
Environmental cost accounting (ECA), 368–370, 713–718
Environmental costs, 713
Environmental uncertainty, 566–567
Equalization reserve, 57
Equities, 57
Equity, 57, 525
Equity Funding, 771–772
Equity method, 58
Equity ratio, 58
Equivalent production, 58
Equivalent units of work (E.U.), 58, 412, 415–416, 419
ERISA (Employee Retirement Income Security Act of 1974), 58
Ernst & Young, 17
Escalator clause, 58
Escapable cost, 58
ESOT (Employee Stock Ownership Trust), 58–59
Estate planning, 59
Estimates, 317
Estimated liability, 59
Estimated revenue, 59
Estimated salvage value, 59
Estimation sampling, 59
Evaluation:
  budgets for, 546–547
  performance, 546–547, 554–556, 568
  of projects, 595–600
  of spoilage, waste, and scrap, 376–377
Except for, 59
Excess present value, 59
Excess present value index (EPVI), 59, 595
Exchange, 59–60
Exchange gain or loss, 60
Exchange rate, 60
Excise tax, 60
Ex div (dividend), 59
Executory contract, 60
Exemption, 60
Exercise, 60
Exit value, 60
Expectancy theory, 60
Expected capacity, 437
Expected value, 60
Expected value of (perfect) information, 60, 499–500
Expendable fund, 60
Expenditures, 60, 314, 352
Expenses, 60, 176
  costs vs., 180–181, 352
  misrepresenting, 778–783
  recognition of, 777–778
Expense account, 60
Expense budget, 613
Expense planning and control, 331–336
Experience rating, 60
Expired cost, 60
Ex post variance analysis, 454–457

Exposure Draft (ED), 60–61
Ex rights, 59
External costs, 368
External failure costs, 61
Externalities, 368
External reporting, 61
Extraordinary item, 61
Extrinsic rewards, 61

F

Face amount (value), 61
Facility-level activities, 61, 494
Factoring, 61
Factory, 61
Factory burden, 61
Factory cost, 61
Factory expense, 61
Factory overhead, 61
Fair presentation (fairness), 61
Fair value, fair market price (value), 61
Fair-value hedge, 62
FASB Interpretation (FIN), 62, 769
Favorable variance, 62, 431, 443
Federal Express, 662
Federal income tax, 62
Feedback, 62
Fells, John Manger, 737
FICA (Federal Insurance Contributions Act), 62
Fiduciary, 62
Final 4, 17
Finance, 62
Financial accounting, 62
Financial Accounting Foundation, 62
Financial Accounting Standards Advisory Council (FASAC), 62–63
Financial Accounting Standards Board (FASB), 63, 695, 701, 763
Financial Executives Institute (FEI), 63
Financial Executives Research Foundation (FERF), 739–285
Financial expense, 63
Financial flexibility, 63
Financial instrument, 63
Financial literacy, 63
Financial model, 63
Financial position (condition), 63
Financial projection, 63
Financial reporting, 759–808
  analytic diagnostics for fraud detection, 794–808
  auditor responsibility for, 791–792
  current environment for, 761–765
  for disclosures, 787–791
  for expense and asset recognition, 777–778
  for expenses, assets, and liability misrepresentation, 778–783
  fraudulent, 760, 792–794
  for liabilities, 783–787
  management incentives for fraud in, 765–767
  manipulation of, 767–791
  for revenue, 769–777
  SEC cases of accounting restatements, 768
Financial reporting objectives, 63
Financial Reporting Release, 63
Financial statements, 63, 725–726
Financial structure, 64
Financial vice-president, 64
Financial year, 64
Financing activities, 64
Financing decisions, 588, 602–608
Financing games, 545
Financing lease, 64
Finished goods (inventory account), 64
Firm, 64
Firm commitment, 64
First-in, first-out (FIFO), 62, 188, 192, 372, 418–420
Fiscal year, 64
FISH (first-in, still-here), 64
Fixed assets, 64
Fixed assets turnover, 64
Fixed benefit plan, 64
Fixed budget, 64
Fixed charges earned (coverage) ratio, 64
Fixed cost (expense), 64, 161–162, 170, 171, 182, 183, 722
  cash vs. non-cash, 484
  in engineering method, 363
  profit and changes in, 488–490
  in Theory of Constraints, 582
  in throughput accounting, 575
Fixed cost price variance (spending variance), 64
Fixed interval sampling, 64
Fixed liability, 64
Fixed manufacturing overhead applied, 64
Fixed overhead budget variance, 437, 438
Fixed overhead variances, 65, 436–439
Fixed overhead volume variance, 437, 438
Flexible budgets, 65, 435, 563–564
Flexible budget allowance, 65
Flexible evaluation style, 554–556
Float, 65
Flow, 65
Flow assumption, 65
Flow of costs, 65–66
Flow-through method, 65
FOB (free on board), 66
Folio, 66
Footing, 66
Footnotes, 66

Forecast/forecasting, 66, 504–505
 collaborative, 297
 and *ex post* variance analysis, 456
 general principles for, 505–506
 queuing theory, 363–365
 shortcuts to, 536
Forecasting variance, 456
Foreclosure, 66
Foreign currency, 66
Foreign currency translation, 66
Foreign exchange gain or loss, 66
Foreign sales corporation (FSC), 66
Forfeited share, 66
Forward contract, 66
Forward-exchange contract, 66
Forward price, 66
Franchise, 66
Fraudulent conveyance, 66–67
Fraudulent financial reporting, 67, 761
Free cash flow, 67
Freight-in, 67
Freight-out, 67
Full-absorption cost-based transfers, 691
Full absorption costing, 67, 436
Full cost accounting (FCA), 385
Full costing, full costs, 67, 172
Full disclosure, 67
Fully diluted earnings per share, 67
Fully vested, 67
Function, 67
Functional classification, 68
Functional currency, 68
Functionality, 249–250, 283
Functionality-price-quality (FPQ) tradeoffs, 304
Functionality-price tradeoffs, 249–250
Fund (assets), 68, 710
Funds (working capital), 68
Funds provided by operations, 68
Funds statement, 68
Fund accounting, 68, 710–712
Fund balance, 68
Funded, 68
Funding, 68
Funny money, 68
FUTA (Federal Unemployment Tax Act), 68
Futures contract, 68
Future cash flows, 608–609
Future value, 68, 628–630

G

Gain, 69
Gaming behavior, 543–545
Gantt, H. L., 736, 738
Garcke, Emile, 737
Garner, S. Paul, 732
GDP Implicit Price Deflator (index), 69
Gearing, 69
Gearing adjustment, 69
General and administrative (G&A) overhead, 224
General debt, 69
General Electric, 651, 789
General expenses, 69
General fixed asset (group of accounts), 70
General fund, 70
General journal, 70
General kaizen costing, 271–273
General ledger, 70
Generally accepted accounting principles (GAAP), 70, 187, 193, 677–678, 711, 763, 768, 769
Generally accepted auditing standards (GAAS), 70–71, 791
Generally accepted rules, 354
General Motors, 647, 684, 690, 787
General partner, 70
General price index, 70
General price level-adjusted accounting (GPLA), 71
General price level-adjusted statements, 70
General price level (GPL), 71
General price-levels changes, 70
General purchasing-power accounting, 70
General purchasing power (GPP), 70
Geographic segment, 71
Gillespie, Cecil, 740
Goals:
 budget, 551–554
 organizational, 574–575
 strategic, 622
Goal congruence, 71, 556, 646–647
Going-concern assumption, 71
Going public, 71
Goods, 71
Goods available for sale (GAS), 71
Goods-in-process, 71
Goodwill, 71, 526
Goodwill method, 71
Governmental Accounting Standards Advisory Council, 71
Governmental Accounting Standards Board (GASB), 69, 71, 710, 711
Government entities, 710–718
 budgets, 711–712
 fund accounting, 710–712
 regulatory reporting for environmental accounting, 714–718
 regulatory reporting for government contracts, 712–714
Graded vesting, 72
Graham, Benjamin, 762

Grandfather clause, 72
Green accounting, 375, 383–387
Greer, Howard C., 743
Gross, 72
Gross domestic product (GDP), 72
Gross margin, 72
Gross margin percent, 72
Gross price method, 72
Gross profit, 72
Gross profit method, 72
Gross sales, 72
Group depreciation, 72
Group-level cost-reduction objectives, 277–278
Guarantee, 72

H

Half-year convention, 73
Halliburton Corporation, 774
Halsey, F. A., 736
Hamilton, Robert, 734, 735
Hardware, 73
Harris, Jonathan N., 744
Harrison, G. Charter, 740
Hash total, 73
Hasselback, 73
Health-care benefits obligation, 73
Hedge, 73
Hedge accounting, 73
Held-to-maturity securities, 73
Henkel, Callie B., 619
Henrici, Stanley, 740
Hewlett-Packard, 228, 229, 233, 353
HFS Incorporated, 770–771
Hidden costs, 716
Hidden reserve, 73–74
Hire-purchase agreement (contract), 74
Historical cost, 6, 74
Historical cost/constant-dollar accounting, 74
Historical exchange rate, 74
Historical summary, 74
History of management accounting, 731–756
  Caplan and behavioral school of management, 745–746
  Church's influence, 737–738
  Clark's studies of overhead costs, 742–743
  cost controls and expenditures during World War I, 741–742
  direct costing, 744–745
  distribution costs, 743–744
  engineering and scientific management era, 736–737
  Industrial Revolution, 734–736
  Pacioli and the Renaissance, 732–734
  professional institutions, 738–740
  Relevance Lost, 746–747
  Solomon's divisional performance, 746
  standard costing, 740–741
  timetable for, 747–756
H.J. Heinz Company, 553
Holdback, 74
Holding company, 74
Holding gain or loss, 74
Holding gain or loss net of inflation, 74
Hoover, Herbert, 741, 743
Horizontal analysis, 74
Horizontal integration, 74
Hospitals, 707–710
Hotwire, 775
House account, 74
Huang, Philip Y., 741
Human resource accounting, 74
Hurdle rates, 74, 616–617
Hybrid security, 74
Hypothecation, 74

I

IBM, 233
Ideal standard costs, 75
Idle capacity variance, 437, 438
Impairment, 75
Implicit interest, 75, 642–644
Implied dividend, 532
Imprest fund, 75
Improvement, 75
Improvement projects, 321–322
Imputed cost, 75
Incentives:
  budget-based, 561–563
  and fraud, 792
Incentive compatible compensation, 76
Incentive plan, 661–663
Income, 76
Income accounts, 76
Income before taxes, 76
Income determination, 76
Income distribution account, 76
Income flows, 588–590
Income from continuing operations, 76
Income from discontinued operations, 76
Income smoothing, 76
Income statements, 76, 189–191
Income summary, 76–77
Income tax, 77
  allocation of, 8, 77
  calculation of, 189–191
  and capital budgeting, 593–594
  on pro forma statements, 530
Incomplete performance measures, 560
In-control distributions, 457–458
Increasing returns to scale, 168
Incremental, 77

Incremental cost, 166–167, 171, 185, 722–723
Incremental-cost method, 468, 476
Incur, 77
Independence, 77
Independent accountant, 77
Independent variables, 77, 357
Indeterminate-term liability, 77
Indcxation, 77
Indirect costs, 77, 180
cost rates per cost driver for, 224
kaizen costing for, 272, 280–282
in Total Cost Assessment, 385, 386
Indirect cost pool, 77
Indirect labor (material) cost, 77
Individual proprietorship, 77
Industrial organization economists, 158, 159
Industrial Revolution, 734–736
Industry Audit Guides, 77
Inescapable cost, 77
Inflation, 77, 169
Inflation accounting, 77
Information asymmetry, 544, 566–568
Information circular, 78
Information system, 78
Information technology (IT), 293–297
Inherent interest rate, 78
Initial cash flows, 78
Initial public offerings (IPOs), 765–766
In-process R&D, 75–76, 762
Insolvent, 78
Installment, 78
Installment contracts receivable, 78
Installment sales, 78
Installment (sales) method, 78
Institute of Certified Management Accountants (ICMA), 78
Institute of Cost Accountants, 738
Institute of Cost and Management Accountants, 738
Institute of Internal Auditors (IIA), 78
Institute of Management Accountants (IMA), 78, 732, 738, 739
Insurance, 78
Intangible asset, 78–79
Integrative budget design, 569–572
Interamerican Accounting Association (IAA), 79
Intercompany profit, 79
Intercompany transaction, 79
Intercorporate investment, 79
Interdepartment monitoring, 79
Interest, 79, 181
Interest, imputed, 79
Interest expense, 529–530
Interest factor, 79
Interest income, 530
Interest method, 79
Interest rates, 79, 592
Interfund accounts, 79
Interim statements, 80
Internal audit, internal auditor, 80
Internal controls, 80
Internal costs, 368
Internal failure costs, 80
Internal rate of return (IRR), 80, 591, 595–598, 642–643
Internal reporting, 80
Internal Revenue Services (IRS), 80, 700
International Accounting Standards Board (IASB), 80
International Financial Reporting Standards (IFRS), 75
International Organization of Securities Commissions (IOSC), 80
Internet, 294
Interorganizational cost investigations (ICIs), 305–307
Interorganizational cost management (IOCM), 289–312
for product-related activities, 300–311
for transaction-related activities, 291–300
Interorganizational kaizen costing, 309–311
Interperiod tax allocation, 80
Interpolation, 80
In the black (red), 75
Intrastatement tax allocation, 80
Intrinsic rewards, 80–81
Inventoriable costs, 81
Inventory, 81
assigning costs to, 414–418
cost flow assumptions for, 188
in just-in-time system, 394
projecting, for balance sheet, 524
work in process, 411–414
Inventory equation, 81
Inventory profit, 81–82
Inventory turnover, 82
Invested capital, 82
Investee, 82
Investing activities, 82
Investment(s), 82
projecting, 525
quality-related, 313–314
Investment centers, 82, 649, 651–653
Investment credit, 82
Investment decisions, 82, 588, 602–608
Investment games, 545
Investment management, 619–625
Investment securities, 534–535
Investment tax credit, 82, 594
Investment turnover ratio, 82
Invoice, 82

I.O.U., 82–83
Isoprofit line, 83
Issue, 83
Issued shares, 83
Item-specific kaizen costing, 272, 283–287

J

Jobs, 83, 229, 397
Job costing, 83, 389–390, 396–410
  importance of, 397–398
  job cost flows summary, 406–410
  operating cycle completion, 404–406
  process costing vs., 411
  for scrap and waste, 370, 374–375
  for spoilage, 370
  tracking costs, 398–404
Job cost record (sheet/card/file), 83, 398
Job development credit, 83
Job shop, constraints in, 574
Johnson, H. Thomas, 746–747
John Wiley & Sons, 390
Joint cost, 83, 170, 466
Joint cost allocation, 83, 469–475
Joint process, 83
Joint-process costs, 466
Joint products, 83, 466
Joint variance, 430
Journal, 83
Journal entry, 83
Journalize, 84
Journal of Accountancy, 83
Journal of Accounting and Economics, 83
Journal of Accounting Research, 83–84
Journal voucher, 84
Judgment(al) sampling, 84
Junk bonds, 84, 617
Justification analysis, 614–618
Just-in-time (JIT), 84, 277, 291, 393–394, 580, 741

K

k, 84
Kaizen costing, 84, 271–288
  achievability principle in, 272–273
  component-specific, 272, 286–287
  controllability principle in, 273
  for direct costs, 271–280
  for indirect costs, 272, 280–282
  interorganizational, 309–311
  item-specific, 272, 283–287
  in nonprofits, 704–705
  product-specific, 272, 283–286
Kanban, 292–293, 345
Kaplan, Robert S., 741, 746–747
Kingdom supplier networks, 292
Kiting, 84
Korger, 349
KPMG Peat Marwick, 17

L

Labor costs, 180–182, 229, 279–280, 401
Labor efficiency variance, 85, 581–582
Labor price (or wage) variance, 85
Labor variances, 85
Laid-down cost, 85
Land, 85
Lapping (accounts receivable), 85
Lapse, 85
Lardner, Dionysius, 735, 736
Last-in, first-out (LIFO), 87, 188, 192
Lead time, 85
Lean supply system, 291–293, 340–341
Learning curve, 85, 723, 728
Learning effect, 427–428
Lease, 85
Leasehold, 85
Leasehold improvement, 85
Leasing, 604, 607–608
Least and latest rule, 85
Ledger, 86
Legal capital, 86
Less tangible benefits, 385, 386
Less tangible costs, 717
Letter stock, 86
Leverage, 86, 706–707
Leveraged lease, 86
Levitt, Arthur, 761–764
Liabilities, 86
  in litigation, 724–726
  misrepresenting, 778–783
  projecting, 527–528
  recognition of, 783–787
Liability costs, 385, 386, 716–717
Lien, 86
Life annuity, 87
Life cycle, organizational, 550–551
Life cycle assessment (LCA), 714–716
Life-Cycle Cost Analysis, 715, 716
Life cycle cost/costing, 251–252, 384–385
LIFO, dollar-value method, 87
LIFO conformity rule, 87
LIFO inventory layer, 87
LIFO reserve, 87
Limited, 89
Limited liability, 87
Limited partner, 87
Linear programming, 87, 497–500
Line-of-business reporting, 87
Line of credit, 87
Liquid, 87
Liquid assets, 87

Liquidating dividend, 87
Liquidation, 87
Liquidation value per share, 87–88
Liquidity, 88
LISH (last-in, still-here), 88
List price, 88
List price method, 88
Litigation, cost concepts in, 721–730
  damages aspects of, 726–730
  definitions of concepts, 722–723
  liability aspects of, 724–726
Loan, 88
Lockheed, 390
Logistics, 329–349
  changing role of, 329–330
  defined, 330
  expense planning and control, 332–336
  and relation profitability, 341–349
  supply chain activities, 330–332
  total cost of delivery, 336–338
  total cost of ownership, 339–341
Long-lived (term) asset, 88
Long run, long term, 88
  average cost, 167–169, 172–173
  construction contract accounting, 88
  cost concepts, 159–160
  debt ratio, 88
  liability (debt), 88, 528
  solvency risk, 88
Long-term investments, 534–535
Loophole, 88
Loose budgeting, 570
Loss, 88
Loss contingency, 88
Lost sales models, 318–319
Lower control limits, 459
Lower of cost or market (LOCOM), 88–89
Low quality earnings, 761
Ltd, 89
Lump-sum acquisition, 89

M

Macroeconomists, 158, 159
Macy's Department Store, 392, 646, 658
Maintenance, 89
Major functions, target costs for, 261–265
Make money, making money, 89
Make-or-buy decision, 89–90
Maker (of note) (of check), 90
Managed costs, 162
Management, 90
  activity-based, 6, 233–240
  by exception, 90, 457
  forms of cost data for, 176
  by objective, 90
Management accounting, 90, 158–159, 170–173
Management Accounting, 90
Management audit, 90
Management information system (MIS), 90
Management's discussion and analysis (MD&A), 90, 789–790
Managerial accounting, 90
Managerial economists, 158
Managing earnings, 191–195
Manufacturing, basic cost flow model for, 391–391
Manufacturing activities, 309–311
Manufacturing costs, 90, 180–181
Manufacturing cycle efficiency, 666
Manufacturing cycle time, 665
Manufacturing expense, 90, 180–181
Manufacturing overhead, 90, 180, 401–400, 406–410
Margin, 90
Marginal contribution, 164–166, 171–172
Marginal cost, 90, 162–164, 171, 185
Marginal costing, 90
Marginal revenue, 90
Marginal tax rate, 90
Margin analysis, 348–349
Margin of safety, 90
Markdown cancellation, 91
Marketable equity securities, 91
Marketable securities, 535–536
Market-based transfer price, 91
Market-driven costing, 245–252
  allowable cost, 252
  long-term sales and profit objectives, 246–248
  setting selling price, 248–250
  structuring product mix, 248
  in target costing chain, 303
  target profit margin, 250–252
Market-driven cost-reduction approach, 274–275
Marketing, activity-based costing in, 231–232
Marketing costs, 91, 331–332
Market price, 91, 689–690
Market price-based transfer pricing, 690
Market rate, 91
Market share, 662
Market value, 91
Mark to market, 91
Markup, 91
Markup percentage, 91
Master budget, 92
Master coding system, 178–179
Matching convention, 92
Material, 92
Materials price variance, 92

Materials requisition form, 400
Material costs, 179–182
  cost-reduction objectives for, 278–279
  raw material variances, 432–434
  tracking, 399–401
Material efficiency variance, 92
Materiality, 92, 763–764
Material variances, 92, 432–434, 442, 446
Mathematical concepts:
  queuing theory, 363–365
Matrix, 92
Matrix inverse, 92
Matrix product design structure, 262–263
Maturity, 92
Maturity value, 92
Mautz, R. K., 739–285
May Clinic, 390
McNair, C. J., 741
Measurable (term), 711
Measuring unit, 92
Menu pricing, 349
Merchandise, 92
Merchandise costs, 92
Merchandise turnover, 92
Merchandising business, 92
Merger, 92
Mergers and acquisitions, 767
Merger reserves, 782
Merrill Lynch, 678
Metcalfe, Henry, 736
The Method of Venice, 733–734
Microeconomists, 158
MicroStrategy, 760, 775
Miller, Peter, 741
Minority interest, 92
Minority investment, 92–93
Minutes book, 93
Mission statement, 659
Mitchell, Falconer, 741
Mixed cost, 93
Mix variance, 93
Models:
  computer-intensive, 365–366
  cost flow, 391–393
  lost sales, 318–319
  for short-run output problem, 484–485
  simulation, 318
  two-factor variance, 428
Modified Accelerated Cost Recovery System (MACRS), 93
Modified cash basis, 93
Monetary assets and liabilities, 93
Monetary gain or loss, 93
Monetary items, 93
Monetary-nonmonetary method, 93
Money, 93–94
Money purchase plan, 94
Morrison-Knudsen, 389
Mortality table, 94
Mortgage, 94
Mosconi, William, 741
Moving average, 94
Moving average method, 94
Multinational transfer pricing, 693–694
Multiple regression, 360–361
Multiple-step, 95
Municipal bond, 95
Mutual fund, 95
Mutually exclusive (investment) projects, 95, 596–598

N

NASDAQ (National Association of Securities Dealers Automated Quotation System), 95
National Association of Accountants (NAA), 95, 738
National Association of Cost Accountants (NACA), 738, 745
National Automated Accounting Research System (NAARS), 95
National Council on Governmental Accounting, 710
National Recovery Administration (NRA), 742
Natural business year, 95
Natural classification, 95
Natural resources, 95
Negative goodwill, 95–96
Negative increments, 167
Negative variance, 431
Negotiable, 96
Negotiated transfer price, 96, 693
Negotiating price, 693
Net, 96
Net assets, 96
Net bank position, 96
Net book value, 96
Net change in cash, 535
Net current assets, 96
Net current asset value (per share), 96
Net income, 96, 530, 531, 534, 536
Net loss, 96
Net markup, 96
Net of tax method, 96
Net of tax reporting, 97
Net operating profits, 97
Net operating profits after tax (NOPAT), 671
Net present value (NPV), 97
  of borrowing vs. purchase, 607
  in capital budgeting, 592–593
  of cash flows, 669–670

for government projects, 718
positive, choosing between projects with, 601–602
Net present value (NPV) graph, 590–591
Net price method (of recording purchase or sales discounts), 97
Net realizable (sales) value (NRV), 97, 470, 473
Net sales, 97
Network activities, IOCM for, 291–292
Network analysis, 97
Net working capital, 97
Net worth, 97
New product development time, 97
New York Stock Exchange (NYSE), 97
Nicholson, J. Lee, 738
Nielsen, A. C., 744
NIFO (next-in, first-out), 97
Nissan, 391
No loss rule of target costing, 305
Nominal accounts, 97
Nominal amount (value), 97
Nominal dollars, 98
Nominal interest rate, 98, 592, 630–631
Noncancelable leases, 603–606
Nonconformance costs, 387
Noncontributory, 98
Noncontrollable cost, 98
Noncurrent, 98
Noncurrent accrued expenses, 534
Nonexpendable fund, 98
Nonfinancial performance measures, 560–561
Noninterest-bearing note, 98
Nonmanufacturing costs, 98
Nonmonetary items, 98
Nonoperating, 98
Nonprofit accounting, 697–718
current cost accounting practices, 702–705
customer perspective in, 663
for-profit accounting vs., 698–702
government entities, 710–718
hospitals, 707–710
service organizations, 705–707
Nonprofit corporation, 98
Nonrecurring, 98
Non-sustainable earnings, 761
Non-value-added activity, 98
Nonvalue-added costs, 234–235
No par, 97
Normal capacity, 437
Normal cost, 98
Normal costing, 98
Normal costing system, 98–99
Normal spoilage, 99
Normal standard cost, normal standards, 99
Normal volume, 99
Norris, Thomas, 741
Northrop-Grumman, 390
Note (promise), 99
Notes (footnotes), 99
Note receivable discounted, 99
NOW (negotiable order of withdrawal) account, 99
Number of days sales in inventory (or receivables), 99
Nurnberg, Hugo, 475

O

Objective, 99, 622
Objective function, 99
Objectivity, 99
Object of expenditure, classification by, 177–182
Occupational Safety and Health Act (OSHA), 103
Off-balanced-sheet financing, 99–100, 784
Off-balance-sheet risk, 100
Offsetting variances, 432
Old Age, Survivors, Disability, and Health Insurance (OASDHI), 100
O'Leary, Ted, 741
Olympus Optical, 284
On consignment, 100–101
On-cost, 180
One-line consolidation, 101
One-write system, 101
Ongoing improvement, 576–579
On (open) account, 101
On-time performance, 101
Open account, 101
Operating, 101
Operating accounts, 101
Operating activities, 101
Operating budget and budgeting, 101, 539–571
activity-based and subunit budgets, 564–565
annual and rolling budgets, 565–566
benefits of, 543
budget-based incentives, 561–563
budget-based performance measures, 556–561
budget goals, 551–554
budgeting process, 542–543
complementary relations among components, 568–569
components of, 542, 545–566
contingent factors in, 566–569
costs related to gaming behavior, 543–545
defined, 541–542
integrative design of, 569–572
multiple uses of budgeting, 545–547
negotiating budgets, 548–551

Operating budget and budgeting *(continued)*
 nonbudgeting factors influencing, 542
 participation in budgeting, 547–548
 potential problems with, 540
 static and flexible budgets, 563–564
Operating cash flow, 101
Operating cycle, 101, 404–406
Operating expenses, 101, 518–520, 575
Operating games, 544–545
Operating goals, 620
Operating lease, 101
Operating leverage, 101–102, 706–707
Operating margin, 102
Operating margin based on current costs, 102
Operating ratio, 102
Operations, 102, 390
Operational measures of time, 102
Operation costing, 390–391, 420–422
Opinion, 102
Opinion paragraph, 102
Opportunity cost, 102, 167, 171, 186, 438, 456, 498–499, 591
Opportunity cost of capital, 102
Optimal output level, 485–486
Option, 102
Order costing, 83
Order-delivery process, standardizing, 297
Ordinary annuities (annuities in arrears), 102, 632, 633–640
Ordinary income, 102
Organization costs, 102–103
Organization goals, 103
Original cost, 103
Original entry, 103
OSHA (Occupational Safety and Health Act), 103
Other assets, 535
Other comprehensive income, 103
Outlay, 103
Outlier, 103
Out-of-control distributions, 457–458
Out-of-pocket cost, 103, 458
Out-of-stock cost, 103
Output, 103
Outside director, 103
Outstanding, 103
Over-and-short, 103
Overapplied (overabsorbed) overhead, 103, 406
Overdraft, 103
Overhead:
 allocation of, 229, 231
 based on volume of output, 223
 flexible budget for, 435
 general and administrative, 224
 predetermined rates for, 402–404
 tracking, 401–402
Overhead costs, 103
Overhead rate, 103
Overhead variance, 405–410, 435–439
Overspecification, 304
Over-the-counter, 103
Owners' equity, 104
Ownership, total cost of, 338–341

P

Pacioli, Luca, 732–734
Paid-in capital, 104
Paid-in surplus, 104
Paper profit, 104
Par, 104
Parallel engineering, 308
Parent company, 104
Pareto chart, 104
Pareto principle, 341
Partially executory contract, 104
Partially funded, 105
Partially vested, 105
Partial obsolescence, 104
Participating dividend, 105
Participating preferred stock, 105
Participative budgeting, 105, 547–548
Partner's drawing, 105
Partnership, 105
Par value, 104
Par value method, 104
Patent, 105
Patent infringement, 729–730
Payable, 105
Pay-as-you-go, 105
Payback period, 105, 598–599, 717
Payback reciprocal, 105
Payee, 105
Payen, Jean-Baptiste, 735
Payoff, future, 504
Payoff table/matrix, 461–463
Payout ratio, 105
Payroll taxes, 105–106
Pension Benefit Guarantee Corporation (PBGC), 106
Pension fund, 106
Pension liabilities, 786–787
Pension plan, 106
Per books, 106
Perceived value, 249
Percent, 106
Percentage depletion (allowance), 106
Percentage-of-completion method, 106
Percentage statement, 106
Performance evaluation:
 budget-based, 546–547, 554–556, 568
 in decentralized organizations, 653–654

flexible, 554–556
rigid, 555–556
Performance measures, 557–561
Performance measurement, 657–668
balanced scorecard, 659–664
benchmarking, 664
budget-based, 556–561
components of, 658
continuous improvement, 664
in decentralized organizations, 646–647, 650–653
improving, 664
measures used in, 664–667
and transfer pricing, 684
Performance targets, 614, 618, 622
Performance tracking, 625
Period, 106
Period cost, 106, 182, 436
Period expense (charge), 106
Periodic cash flows, 106
Periodic inventory, 106, 392–393
Periodic procedures, 106
Permanent account, 106
Permanent difference, 106–107
Permanent file, 107
Perpetual annuity, 107
Perpetual inventory, 107, 392–393
Perpetuities, 107, 632, 640–642
Perpetuity growth model, 107
Personal account, 107
PERT (Program Evaluation and Review Technique), 107
Petty cash fund, 107
Physical quantities method, 473
Physical units method, 107
Physical verification, 107
Planning and control process, 107
budgeting, 542–543, 546
cost estimations, 353
green accounting, 384–387
Plant, 107
Plant assets, 107–108
Plant asset turnover, 107
Plant-level cost-reduction objectives, 276–277
Plantwide allocation method, 108, 219–221
PLC (public limited company), 108
Pledging, 108
Pledging of receivables, 108
Plow back, 108
Plug, 108
PNC Financial Services Group, Inc., 785–786
Point of sale, 108
Pooling-of-interests method, 108
Population, 108
Portfolio approach, 613
Portfolio development, 622–623
Position assessment, 622
Positive confirmation, 108
Positive variance, 431
Post, 108
Post-closing trial balance, 109
Post-sale activities, 347
Post-statement events, 109
Potentially dilutive security, 109
Practical capacity, 109
Precision, 109, 557
Preclosing trial balance, 109
Predatory prices, 109
Predetermined (factory) overhead rate, 109, 402–404
Preemptive right, 109
Preference as to assets, 109
Preferred shares, 109
Preferred stock, convertible, 34
Premium, 109
Premium on capital stock, 109
Prepaid expense, 109
Prepaid income, 110
Prepayments, 110
Present value, 110, 169, 173, 459, 629–630
Prevention costs, 110
Prevention expenditures, 314
Price(s), 110
profit and changes in, 488–490
projecting, 514
tradeoff with functionality, 249–250
transfer, 684–687
Price earnings (P/E) ratio, 110
Price index, 110
Price level, 110
Price level-adjusted statements, 110
Priceline, 775, 776
Price variance, 110
PricewaterhouseCoopers, 17, 390
Pricing, 583–585
Primary earnings per share (PEPS), 110
Prime cost, 110, 182, 185
Prime rate, 110
Principal, 110, 627
Principle, 110
Prior-period adjustment, 110–111
Prior service cost, 111
Probable, 111
Proceeds, 111
Process costing, 111, 390, 410–420
ABC and information for, 232
assigning costs to inventory, 414–418
assigning costs to products, 411–414, 418–420
importance of, 411
job costing vs., 411
for spoilage, 370–373

Process improvement, 662
Process industries, costing in, 179
Products, 111
  assigning costs to, 226, 411–414, 418–420
  measuring profitability of, 582–583
Product cost, 111, 232, 244, 253–260, 363, 436
Product costing operations, 420–422
Product design, 256–257
Product development activities, 300–309
  chained target costing, 300–303
  concurrent cost management, 307–309
  cost investigations, 305–307
  functionality-price-quality tradeoffs, 304
Product enhancement expenditures, 314
Production cost, 111
Production cost account, 111
Production Cost Report, 416–418
Production cost variances, 446–451
Production cycle efficiency, 112
Production cycle time, 112
Production department, 111
Production method:
  accounting systems for, 390
  depreciation, 111
  revenue recognition, 112
Production mix variance, 440–442
Production process:
  in just-in-time system, 394
  scheduling, 580
Production volume variance, 112
Productive capacity, 112
Product-level activities, 112, 494
Product-level target costing, 253–259
  and costing chain position, 303
  designing product, 256–257
  disciplining mechanisms of, 257–259
  setting target cost, 254–256
Product life cycle, 111
Product mix, structuring, 248
Product-related activities, 300–311
  manufacturing activities, 309–311
  product development, 300–309
Product-related costs, 236
Product-specific kaizen costing, 272, 283–286
Product take-back, 347
Professional accounting institutions, 738–740
Profit, 112
  assessing effect of changes on, 488–490
  long-term objectives for, 246–248
  variances in, 441–444
Profitability:
  loss of, 285–286
  product, measurement of, 582–583
  relation profitability analysis, 338, 341–349
  relative vs. absolute, 582
Profitability accounting, 112
Profit-and-loss account, 112
Profit-and-loss (P&L) statement, 104, 112
Profit-and-loss sharing ratio, 112
Profit centers, 112, 649, 651
Profit margin, 112, 250–252
Profit margin percentage, 112
Profit maximization, 112
Profit plan, 112
Profit-sharing plan, 112
Profit variance analysis, 112
Profit-volume analysis, 112, 487–489, 491–494
Profit-volume ratio, 112
Pro forma financial statements, 111, 503–538
  analyzing, 536–537
  balance sheets, 531–532
  deriving statement of cash flows (step 6), 534–536
  general principles for, 505–506
  implementing, 509–510
  non-GAAP, 790–791
  preparation of, 505
  project assets on balance sheet (step 3), 519, 521–527
  project interest expense/interest income/income tax expense/change in retained earnings (step 5), 529–531
  project operating expenses (step 2), 518–520
  project sales and other revenues (step 1), 514–518
  for sensitivity analysis/strategic planning, 537
  shortcuts to forecasting, 536
  six-step plan for, 506–536
  solving for co-determined variables, 533–534
  Starbucks example of, 510–535
Pro forma income, 111
Program, cost classification by, 178
Program budgeting (PPB), 113
Programmed costs, 113, 162, 182
Programmed fixed costs, 171
Progressive tax, 113
Progress monitoring/measurement, 321–322
Projected benefit obligation, 113
Projected financial statement, 113
Project financing arrangement, 113
Projection, 113
Project liabilities, 527–528
Promissory note, 113
Proof of journal, 113
Property, plant, and equipment (PP&E), 525, 535
Property dividend, 113

Proportionate consolidation, 113
Proprietary accounts, 113
Proprietary view, 670
Proprietorship, 113
Proprietorship theory, 113
Prorate, 113
Proration of variances, 446
Prospectus, 114
Protest fee, 114
Provision, 114
Proxy, 114
Pseudo-participative budgeting, 548
Public accountant, 114
Public accounting, 114
Public Company Accounting Oversight Board, PCAOB, 114
PuPU, 114
Purchase allowance, 114
Purchase discount, 114
Purchase investigation, 114
Purchase method, 114
Purchase order, 114
Purchasing power gain or loss, 115
Pure price variance, 430
Pure quality variance, 430
Push-down accounting, 115
Put, 115

Q

Qualified report (opinion), 115
Quality, 115
  of earnings, 115–116
  of financial position, 116
Quality control, 665
Quality function deployment (QFD), 256–257
Quality improvement, 313–327
  costs and benefits of, 313–314
  framework for managing, 323–327
  managing costs/benefits of, 320–322
  quality-related costs, 315–318
  and revenue effects of quality, 318–320
Quantitative performance measure, 116
Quantity discount, 116
Quantity variance, 116
Quasi-reorganization, 116
Queuing theory, 363–365
Quick assets, 116
Quick ratio, 116

R

Railroad Accounting Principles Board (RAPB), 117
Random number sampling, 117
Random sampling, 117
Ratchet budgets, 553
Rate of return on assets, 117
Rate variance, 117
Ratios, 117–119, 536–537
Raw material, 119
Raw material variances, 432–434
Reacquired stock, 119
Real accounts, 119
Real amount (value), 119
Real interest rate, 119, 592
Realizable value, 119
Realization convention, 119
Realize, 119
Realized gain (or loss) on marketable equity securities, 119
Realized holding gain, 119
Real state, 119
Rearrangement costs, 119
Recapitalization, 119
Recapture, 119–120
Receipt, 120
Receivable, 120
Reciprocal cost allocation, 481–482, 707
Reciprocal holdings, 120
Recognize, 120
Reconciliation, 120
Record date, 120
Recourse, 120
Recovery of unrealized loss on trading securities, 120
Recurring, 120
Redemption, 120
Redemption premium, 120
Redemption value, 120
Refinancing, 120
Refunding bond issue, 120
Regional profitability analysis, 341–343
Register, 120
Registered bond, 120
Registrar, 120
Registration statement, 120
Regression analysis, 120–121, 318, 357–361, 727
Regressive tax, 121
Regulation G, 790
Regulation S-K, 121, 789
Regulation S-T, 121
Regulation S-X, 121
Rehabilitation, 121
Reinvestment rate, 121
Reitell, Charles, 744
Relation profitability analysis, 338, 341–349
  by distribution channels, 343–344
  by individual customers, 341, 342
  by order size, 344–345
  by region, 341–343
Relative performance evaluations (RPEs), 121, 654

Relative profitability, 582
Relative sales value method, 470–472
Relevant cost, 121
Relevant cost analysis, 121
Relevant range, 121, 355, 358
Relief from royalty method, 641
Remit earnings, 121
Remittance advice, 121
Renaissance, 732–734
Rent, 121
Reorganization, 122
Repair, 122
Replacement cost, 122
Replacement cost method of depreciation, 122
Report, 122
Report form, 122
Reporting objectives (policies), 122
Representative item sampling, 122
Reproduction cost, 122
Republic supplier networks, 292
Required rate of return (RRR), 122
Requisition, 122
Resale value, 122
Research and development (R&D), 122
Reserve, 122–123
Reserve recognition accounting (RRA), 123–124
Reset bond, 124
Residual income (RI), 124, 652–653, 670–675
Residual security, 124
Residual value, 124
Resources:
  constraints on, 623
  planning, 336
  for spoiled units, 369
  unused, 237–240
  used vs. supplied, 237–238
Resources supplied, 124, 237–238
Resources used, 124, 237–238
Resource Conservation Recovery Act (RCRA), 369
Responsibility accounting, 124, 184, 646
Responsibility centers, 124, 178, 648–650, 654
Restricted assets, 124
Restricted retained earnings, 124–125
Retail inventory method, 125
Retained earnings, 125, 529–531
Retained earnings statement, 125
Retirement method of depreciation, 125–126
Retirement plan, 126
Retroactive benefits, 126
Returns, 126
Returns to scale, 168
Return on assets (ROA), 126, 671–673
Return on capital, 126
Return on investment (ROI), 126, 314, 600, 651–652
Revenue, 126, 325
  drivers of, 321
  effects of quality on, 318–320
  linear functions for, 486–487
  projecting, 514–518
  received in advance, 126
  recognition of, 764, 769–777
Revenue allocation, 476–478
Revenue centers, 126, 649
Revenue expenditure, 126
Revenue (reversing) entry, 126–127
Reverse stock split, 127
Revolving fund, 128
Revolving loan, 128
Rework, 377
Right, 128
Rigid evaluation style, 555–556
Rigips, 341, 342
Risk, 128
  assessment of, 620, 623–624
  in capital budgeting, 617–618
  nondisclosure of, 789–790
Risk-adjusted discount rate, 128
Risk aversion, 501
Risk-free rate, 128, 592
Risk premium, 128
Rite Aid, 670
Rolling budgets, 565–566
Roos, Charles F., 742
Roosevelt, Franklin, 742
Round-tripping transactions, 776–777
Royalty, 128
R-square (R^2), 117, 359
Rule of 69, 128, 644
Rule of 72, 128–129, 644
Rule of 78, 129
Ruling (and balancing) an account, 129
Rutgers Accounting Web Site, 129
Rynco Scientific Corporation, 413

S

Safe-harbor lease, 130
Safety stock, 130
Saint-Gobain, 735
Sakurai, Michiharu, 741
Salary, 130
Sale(s), 130
  long-term objectives for, 246–248
  projecting, 514–518
  shortcuts to forecasting, 536
Sales activity variance, 130
Sales allowance, 130
Sale and leaseback, 130

Sales basis of revenue recognition, 130
Sales contra, estimated uncollectibles, 130
Sales costs, 331–332, 441–444
Sales discount, 130
Sales mix variances, 443
Sales price variances, 443
Sales quantity variances, 443
Sales return, 130
Sales-type (capital) lease, 130
Sales value method, 130
Sales volume variance, 130
Salvage value, 131
Sam's Warehouse, 348, 349
Sarbanes-Oxley Act, 131
SAS (Statement of Accounting Standards), 131
Scale effect, 598
Scatter diagram, 131
Schedule, 131
Schindler, James S., 176
Scientific Management Movement, 736–737
Scientific method, 131
S corporation, 130
Scrap, 369
Scrap value, 131
Sears, 782
Secondary cost drivers (SCDs), 452, 453
Seconds, 377
Secret reserve, 131
Securities and Exchange Commission (SEC), 131, 765, 768–773, 775, 777, 779–782, 785–786, 788–791
Securitization, 131
Security, 131
Security available for sale, 131
Security held to maturity, 131
Segment (of a business), 131–132
Segment reporting, 132, 695
Self-balancing, 132
Self-check(ing) digit, 132
Self-selection budgets, 547
Self-sustaining foreign operation, 132
Selling and administrative expenses, 132
Selling price, target, 248–249
Semifixed costs, 132, 354
Semivariable costs, 132, 355–356
Senior securities, 132
Sensitivity, 557, 592–593
Sensitivity analysis, 132, 510, 537
Separable costs, 170, 467
Sequential access, 132
Serial bonds, 132–133
Services, 133
Service basis of depreciation, 133
Service bureau, 133
Service cost, (current) service cost, 133
Service department, 133
Service department cost allocation, 133, 479–482
Service enhancement expenditures, 314
Service industries/organizations, 179, 184, 391–391, 705–707
Service life, 133
Service potential, 133
Setup, 133
Setup costs, 180, 452–453
Shadow price, 133
Shapley Value method, 468–469
Share, 133
Shareholder returns, 676–678
Shareholders' equity, 133, 527–529
Shareholder value, 678
Shareholder wealth, 673–675
Share premium, 133
ShopKo Stores, Inc., 775
Short run, 133
  cost concepts, 159–160
  marginal cost, 162–164, 171
  multiproduct models, 497–500
Short-run economic model, 484–485
  breakeven chart, 487
  ex post use of charts/graphs, 489
  linear functions for revenues and costs, 486–487
  for multiproduct firms, 489, 491–494
  profit-volume analyses, 487–488
  and uncertainty, 500–501
Short-term borrowing, 528
Short-term investments, 534–535
Short-term liquidity risk, 133
Short-term operating budget, 133
Shrinkage, 133–134
Shutdown cost, 134
Side letters, 772
Sight draft, 134
Signal Tech, 785
Simple interest, 134, 628
Simulation models, 318, 365–366
Simultaneous engineering, 308
Single-entry accounting, 134
Single proprietorship, 134
Single-step, 134
Sinking fund, 134
Sinking fund method of depreciation, 134
Sirena Apparel Group, 773
Skeleton account, 134
Slide, 134–135
Sloan, Alfred, 670
SMAC (Society of Management Accountants of Canada), 135
Smith, Oberlin, 736

Soak-up method, 135
Social Security taxes, 135
Software, 135
Sole proprietorship, 135
Solomons, David, 177, 670, 746
Solvent, 135
Sophisticated budgeting, 569–570
Sound value, 135
Sources and uses statement, 135
Source documents, 398
Source of funds, 135
Southwest Airlines, 233
Special assessment, 135
Special journal, 135
Special purpose entities (SPEs), 135, 784, 785
Special revenue debt, 135
Specific costs, 170
Specific identification method, 135–136
Specific item sampling, 136
Specific price changes, 136
Specific price index, 136
Spending variance, 136
Split, 136
Split-off point, 136, 467
Spoilage, defined, 136
Spoilage, waste, and scrap, 367–368
  control and evaluation systems for, 376–384
  cost accounting for, 370–376
  definitions related to, 368–369
  green accounting, 383–387
  history of accounting treatment for, 369–370
  use of terms, 368–369
Spot price, 136
Spreadsheet, 136
Squeeze, 136
Stabilized accounting, 136
Stable monetary unit assumption, 136
Staff Accounting Bulletin (SAB), 136, 769, 770
Stakeholders, 136, 658
Stand-alone method, 468, 476
Standards:
  accounting, 4
  auditing, 14
  for controlling spoilage, waste, and scrap generation, 378–379
  cost estimations in setting, 353
  efficiency, 581
  factors in setting, 426–427
Standard bill of materials, 378
Standard cost, 136–137, 373–374, 426, 692, 723
Standard costing, 137, 740–741
Standard cost(ing) system, 137, 425–478
  accounting entries in, 444–446
  activity-based costing vs., 449, 452–454
  assessing significance of variances, 457–463
  basic vs. theoretical, 426
  calculations, 428, 429
  direct labor variances, 434
  evaluating deviations from, 428, 430–444
  ex post variance analysis, 454–457
  factors in standard setting, 426–427
  fixed overhead variances, 436–439
  flexible budget preparation, 435
  integrated reporting for, 446–451
  and learning effect, 427–428
  production mix and yield variances, 440–442
  raw material variances, 432–434
  sales and profit variances, 441–444
  three-factor variances, 439–440
  two-factor variances, 428, 430–432
  variable overhead variances, 435, 436
Standard deviation, 460
Standard direct cost, 428
Standard error, 137, 359
Standard manufacturing overhead, 137
Standard price (rate), 137
Standard quantity allowed, 137
Standby costs, 137, 162, 182
Starbucks, 510–535
Stated capital, 137
Stated value, 137
Statement of Accounting Standards (SAS), 131
Statement of affairs, 137
Statement of cash flows, 137, 534–536
Statement of changes in financial position, 137
Statement of charge and discharge, 137
Statement of Financial Accounting Concepts (SFAC), 137, 701, 769, 788
Statement of Financial Accounting Standards (SFAS), 137
Statement of financial position, 138
Statement of Position (SOP), 138, 769, 788
Statement of retained earnings (income), 138
Statement of significant accounting policies (principles), 138
Statement on Auditing Standards (SAS), 138, 792
Statement on Standards for Accounting and Review Services (SSARS), 138
Static budgets, 138, 563
Statistical analysis:
  for cost estimation, 357–361
  of quality-related costs/revenues, 318–320
Status quo, 138

Statutory tax rate, 138
Step allocation method, 138
Step-down method, 138, 479–481, 707
Step method, 138
Step(ped) cost, 138, 354–355
Sterilized allocations, 138, 475
Stern Stewart & Co., 669, 679
Stewardship, 138–139
Stock, 139, 765–766
Stock appreciation rights, 139
Stock dividend, 139
Stock option, 139
Stockout, 139
Stockout costs, 139
Stock split(-up), 139
Stores, 139
Straight-debt value, 139
Straight-line depreciation, 139
Strategic cost-reduction objective, 255, 269–270
Strategic goals, 622
Strategic plan, 139, 620
Strategic planning:
  budgeting in, 542–543
  in investment management, 621, 622
  pro forma financial statements for, 537
Strategic pricing, 584–585
Stratified sampling, 139–140
Street security, 140
Stretch budgets, 553–554
Stretch targets, 553
Subchapter S corporation, 140
Subject to, 140
Subordinated, 140
Subscribed stock, 140
Subscription, 140
Subsequent events, 140
Subsidiary, 140
Subsidiary ledger, 140, 399
Subsidiary (ledger) accounts, 140
Subunit budgets, 564–565
Subunit interdependence, 567
Successful efforts costing, 140
Summary annual report (SAR), 140
Summary of significant accounting principles, 140
Sum-of-the-years'-digits depreciation (SYD, SOYD), 140
Sunbeam Corporation, 760, 761, 773, 781
Sunk cost, 140–141, 167, 185, 186
Superfund Amendments and Reauthorization Act (SARA), 369
Supplementary statements (schedules), 141
Suppliers:
  buyer-supplier interface improvements, 292–300
  and interorganization cost management, 290
  relations with, 661–662
  selecting/rewarding, 260–261
  total cost performance for, 340
Supplier networks, 291, 292, 305
Supplier rating index, 317
Supply chain:
  buyer-supplier interface in, 292–300
  interorganizational costing in, 290
  logistics activities in, 330–331
  logistics channels in, 337
  marketing and selling activities in, 331–332
  target costing chains in, 301
Supply chain management, 743
Supportive overheads, 162
Surplus, 141
Surplus reserves, 141
Suspense account, 141
Sustainable income, 141
Swap, 141
SWOT analysis, 548–550
System, 574

T

T-account, 141
Take-home pay, 141
Take-or-pay contract, 141
Taking a bath, 141
Tangible, 141–142
Target (company), 349
Target cost, 142, 269, 285
Target costing, 243–268
  chained, 300–303
  component-level, 259–266
  market-driven, 245–252
  no loss rule of, 305
  in nonprofits, 704–705
  and product launch decisions, 284–285
  product-level, 253–259
Target price, 142
Task uncertainty, 566–567
Tax, 142
Taxable income, 142–143
Tax allocation: interperiod, 142
Tax allocation: intrastatement, 142
Tax avoidance, 142
Tax basis of assets and liabilities, 142
Tax credit, 142
Tax deduction, 142
Tax evasion, 142
Tax shelter, 142
Tax shield, 142
Tax status, nonprofit, 700–701
Tax-transfer lease, 143
Taylor, Frederick W., 736, 737

Technical Bulletin (FASB), 143
Technology, 143
  assessing, 623
  information technology, 293–297
  integrated, 143
Temporary account, 143
Temporary difference, 143
Temporary investments, 143
10-K, 144, 789
Terms of sale, 144
Term bonds, 144
Terminal cash flows, 144
Term loan, 144
Term structure, 144
Theoretical capacity, 437
Theoretical standards, 426
Theory of Constraints (TOC), 144, 573–574
  for business process reengineering, 579
  controlling fixed costs in, 582
  and efficiency measures, 580–582
  for efficient production scheduling, 580
  and goals of organization, 574–575
  increasing NPV of cash flows, 669–670
  and measurement of product profitability, 582–583
  and pricing, 583–584
  process of ongoing improvement, 576–579
  strategic pricing in, 584–585
  throughput accounting in, 575
  for total quality management, 579
Thin capitalization, 144
Three-factor variances, 439–440
3M, 383
Three-way analysis, 438–439
Throughput accounting, 575
Throughput contract, 144
Throughput contribution, 144
Tickler file, 144
Tight budgeting, 570–571
Time-adjusted rate of return, 144, 595
Time cost, 144
Time deposit, 144
Time reporting, 315
Time-series analysis, 144
Times-interest (charges) earned, 144
Time studies, 316–317
Timing difference, 144
Tinker Air Force Base, 713
Tip-toe objectives, 273
Top-down approach, 276, 548–551
Toronto Stock Exchange (TSX), 144
Total assets, 536
Total assets turnover, 145, 536
Total cost:
  of delivery, 332, 336–338
  estimating, 493–494
  of labor, 401
  of ownership, 338–341
Total cost assessment (TCA), 385–386, 714, 716–718
Total fixed overhead variance, 438
Total quality management (TQM), 145, 579
Total sales, forecasting, 536
Towne, H. R., 736
Toyota, 344
Traceable cost, 145
Tracking costs, 394, 398–404
  beginning inventories, 399
  labor, 401
  manufacturing overhead, 401–402
  materials, 399–401
  predetermined overhead rates, 402–404
  recording job costs in accounts, 399
Trade acceptance, 145
Trade credit, 145
Trade discount, 145
Trade-in, 145
Trade-in transaction, 145–146
Trademark, 146, 641
Trademark right, 146
Trade payables (receivables), 146
Trade secret, 146
Trading on the equity, 147
Trading securities, 147
Transaction, 147
Transaction costs, 298, 299–300
Transaction-related activities, 291–300
  buyer-supplier interface activities, 292–300
  network activities, 291–292
Transfer, 147
Transfer agent, 147
Transfer price, 147, 683–687
Transfer pricing, 683–696
  centrally established policies for, 689–692
  global practices, 693
  and interests of company vs. individual managers, 687–689
  management intervention in, 689
  multinational, 693–694
  negotiating price, 693
  and performance measurement, 684
  and segment reporting, 695
  setting prices, 684–687
Transfer-pricing problem, 147
Translation adjustment, 147
Translation gain (or loss), 147
Transportation-in, 147
Transposition error, 147
Treasurer, 147
Treasury bond, 147

Treasury shares, 147–148
Treasury stock, 148, 529
Trend analysis, 148
Trial balance, 148
Trial rate, 642–643
Troubled debt restructuring, 148
Trump Hotels & Casino Resorts, Inc., 790–791
T-statistic, 148, 359
Turnover, 148
Turnover of plant and equipment, 148
T-value, 148
20-F, 148
Two-factor variances, 428, 430–432
Two-factor variance model, 428
Two T-account method, 148
2/10, n(et)/30, 148

U

UMI, 732
Unadjusted trial balance, 148
Unappropriated retained earnings, 148
Unavoidable cost, 148
Uncertainty:
  buyer-initiated reductions in, 298
  buyer-supplier reductions in, 293
  and cost-volume-profit analysis, 500–501
  environmental, 566–567
  supplier-initiated reductions in, 299
  task, 566–567
Uncollectible account, 148–149
Unconsolidated subsidiary, 149
Uncontrollable costs, 149, 184
Uncontrollable performance measures, 557–560
Underapplied (underabsorbed) overhead, 149, 406
Underinvestment, 679
Underlying document, 149
Underwriter, 149
Undistributed earnings, 149
Unearned income (revenue), 149
Unencumbered appropriation, 149
Unexpired cost, 149
Unfavorable variance, 149, 431
Unfunded, 149
Uniform Partnership Act, 149
Unify Corporation, 776–777
Unissued capital stock, 149
Units-of-production method, 149
Unit costs, 228, 363
United Parcel Service, 233
United Way, 706
Uniting-of-interests method, 149
Unit-level activities, 149, 494
Unit of output, 488–490
Unit-related costs, 236
Universal Studios, 390
Unlimited liability, 149
Unrealized appreciation, 149
Unrealized gain (loss) on marketable securities, 149
Unrealized gross margin (profit), 149–150
Unrealized holding gain, 150
Unrecovered cost, 150
Unused capacity, 150
Unused resources, 238–240
Unused resource capacity, 237–238
Upper control limits, 459
U.S. Environmental Protection Agency (EPA), 713
Usage variance, 150
Useful life, 150
Use of funds, 150
Usual costs, 716

V

Valuation, assessed, 12
Valuation account, 150
Value, 150
Value added, 150
Value-added activities, 150, 233–234
Value-added tax (VAT), 151
Value analysis (VA), 257
Value chain, 150, 233–235
Value engineering (VE), 150, 256, 257
Value variance, 150
Vangermeersch, Richard, 732
Variables sampling, 151
Variable annuity, 150
Variable budget, 150
Variable cost, 150, 160–161, 170, 182, 184, 353, 488–490, 722
Variable costing, 150, 436
Variable interest entity (VIE), 150–151, 784–786
Variable overhead budget (rate) variance, 436
Variable overhead efficiency variance, 151, 436
Variable overhead price variance, 151
Variable overhead variance, 151, 435, 436
Variable rate debt, 151
Variances, 151, 428, 430–444
  accounting disposition of, 445–446
  direct labor variances, 434
  ex post variance analysis, 454–457
  fixed overhead variances, 436–439
  flexible budget preparation, 435
  offsetting, 432
  production mix and yield variances, 440–442

Variances (*continued*)
proration of, 446
raw material variances, 432–434
sales and profit variances, 441–444
in standard cost systems, 457–463
three-factor variances, 439–440
two-factor variances, 428, 430–432
variable overhead variances, 435, 436
Variance analysis, 151
in activity-based costing, 449
ex post, 454–457
for spoilage, waste, and scrap control, 379–382
Variance analysis investigation, 151
Variation analysis, 151
VAT (value-added tax), 151
Vendor, 151
Vendor managed inventory (VMI), 348
Verifiable, 151
Verification, 151
Vertical analysis, 151
Vertical integration, 151
Vested, 151
Visual curve fitting method, 151–152
Volume:
allocation rates based on, 223
cost as function of, 223
on pro forma statements, 514
Volume variance, 152
Voucher, 152
Voucher system, 152
Vouching, 152

W

W. R. Grace & Company, 781
Wage, 152
Walker, Stephen, 741
Wallace, J., 676, 678–681
Wal-Mart, 233, 345, 346
Warning signal, 152
Warrant, 152
Warranty, 152
Warranty reserve, 784–785
Wash sale, 152
Waste, 152, 369
Waste Management, Inc., 760, 761, 780
Wasting asset, 152
Watered stock, 152
Watt, James, Jr., 735
Weighted average, 152–153, 372
Weighted-average costing, 414–415, 418–420
Weighted-average cost of capital, 153
Weighted-average inventory method, 153
Weil, Roman L., 176
Wells, M. C., 732
Where-got, where-gone statement, 153
Window dressing, 153
Wind up, 153
Withdrawals, 153
Withholding, 153
Without recourse, 153
With recourse, 153
Working capital, 153
Work(ing) papers, 153
Work-in-process (inventory account), 153, 411–414
Work sheet (program), 153
WorldCom, 779–780
Worth-debt ratio, 153
Write down, 153
Write off, 153
Write-off method, 154
Write up, 154

X

Xerox Corporation, 321, 322, 775, 781

Y

Yield, 154
Yield curve, 154
Yield to maturity, 154
Yield variance, 154, 440–442

Z

Zannetos, Zenon S., 740
Zero-base(d) budgeting (ZBB), 154–155